THE BRITISH ART & ANTIQUES DIRECTORY 1987

Published by

THE ANTIQUE COLLECTOR

How to Use This Book

After the editorial articles the book is divided into five main sections:

1. Directory (*begins on page 37*)
Dealers, auctioneers, packers, restorers, trade suppliers and related businesses are listed here, with address, telephone number, opening hours, and type of business or area of specialisation. Entries are listed in alphabetical order under town or village, within the relevant county and geographical area.

2. Gazetteer (*begins on page 265*)
This is an alphabetical list of the towns and villages mentioned in the Directory, showing the counties and geographical areas under which they are listed.

3. Index to Specialists (*begins on page 270*)
Directory entries are here listed under type of business or nature of stock.

4. Index to Business Names (*begins on page 363*)
All business names in the Directory are listed alphabetically with their town or village, county and geographical area.

5. Maps (*begin on page 391*)
Showing villages and towns listed in the Directory.

Note
Counties and geographical areas are listed with page references under 'Contents' on page 3.
Auctioneers are listed both in the main Directory under the relevant town or village, and in the Specialists index under 'Auctioneers'.
Abbreviations and names and addresses of useful organisations are listed on page 4.

ISBN 0 85223 539 9

ISSN 0140 8763

Typeset by SB Datagraphics, Colchester, Essex.
Printed by William Clowes, Beccles, Suffolk.

The British Art & Antiques Directory
National Magazine House, 72 Broadwick Street
London W1V 2BP. Tel: 01-439 7144

CONTENTS

ABBREVIATIONS AND USEFUL ADDRESSES

ABA **Antiquarian Booksellers Association,** Suite 2, 26 Charing Cross Road, London WC2 (Tel: 01-379 3041)

ADA **Antiquity Dealers Association,** The Secretary, 16 Goldstone Villas, Hove, Sussex

Art Sales Index, Pond House, Weybridge Park, Weybridge, Surrey (Tel: 0932 42678)

Arts Council of Great Britain, 105 Piccadilly, London, W1V 0AU (Tel: 01-629 9495)

ABPR **Association of British Picture Restorers,** Station Avenue, Kew TW9 3QA (Tel: 01-948 5644)

BADA **British Antique Dealers' Association Ltd,** 20 Rutland Gate, London SW7 1BD (Tel: 01-589 4128)

BAFRA **British Antique Furniture Restorers' Association,** 39 Blackmores Grove, Teddington, Middx. TW4 9AE (Tel: 01-223 9192)

BHI **British Horological Institute,** Upton Hall, Upton, Newark, Notts. (Tel: 0636 813795)

BIPP **British Institute of Professional Photographers,** 2 Amwell End, Ware, Herts. (Tel: 0920 4011)

BJA **British Jewellers Association,** 27 Frederick Street, Birmingham (Tel: 021 236 2657)

BNTA **British Numismatic Trade Association,** c/o Box 52c, Esher, Surrey, K10 8PW (Tel: 0372 625681)

BWCMG **British Watch and Clockmakers Guild,** West Wick, Marsh Road, Burnham-on-Crouch, Essex (Tel: 0621 783104)

CINOA **Confédération Internationale des Négociants en Oeuvres d'Art,** c/o BADA, 20 Rutland Gate, London SW7 1BD (Tel: 01-589 4128)

CADA **Cotswolds Antique Dealers' Association,** High Street, Blockley, Glos. (Tel: 0386 700280)

Crafts Council, 12 Waterloo Place, Lower Regent Street, London SW1 (Tel: 01-930 4811)

Federation of British Artists, 17 Carlton House Terrace, London SW1 (Tel: 01-930 6844)

FATG **Fine Art Trade Guild,** 192 Ebury Street, London SW1 (Tel: 01-730 3220)

GA **Gemmological Association of Great Britain,** 2 Carey Lane, London EC2 (Tel: 01-726 4374)

GMF **Glass Manufacturers Federation,** 19 Portland Place, London W1N 4BH (Tel: 01-580 6952)

GMC **Guild of Master Craftsmen,** 170 High Street, Lewes, E. Sussex BN7 1YE (Tel: 0273 477374)

GWW **Guild of Woodworkers,** PO Box 35, Hemel Hempstead, Herts. (Tel: 0442 41221)

GTA **Gun Trade Association,** St. Georges Square, Bishops Waltham, Southampton (Tel: 021 458 6171)

HADA **Highland Antique Dealers' Association,** Highland Antiques, 15 Tomnahurich Street, Inverness

ISVA **Incorporated Society of Valuers and Auctioneers,** 3 Cadogan Gate, London SW1 (Tel: 01-235 2282)

ICGA **Independent Craft Galleries Association,** 3 Barnes High Street, London SW13 (Tel: 01-878 1279)

IPG **Independent Publishers Guild,** 52 Chepstow Road, London W2 5BE (Tel: 01-727 0919)

IFF **Institute of Freight Forwarders,** Suffield House, 9 Paradise Road, Richmond, Surrey TW9 1SA (Tel: 01-948 3141)

IPC **Institute of Paper Conservation,** Leigh Lodge, Leigh, Worcester WR6 5LB

IDDA **Interior Designers and Decorators Association,** 45 Sheen Lane, London SW14 (Tel: 01-876 4415)

IAPN **International Association of Professional Numismatists,** 11 Adelphi Terrace, London WC2N 6YJ

ICOM **International Council of Museums,** Maison de l'Unesco, 1 rue Miollis, 75732 Paris, France

IIC **International Institute for Conservation,** 6 Buckingham Street, London WC2N 6BA (Tel: 01-839 5975)

IADA **Irish Antique Dealers' Association,** c/o Mr. J. O'Reilly, 17 Greygates, Stillorgan Road, Blackrock, Co. Dublin

IAVI **Irish Auctioneers and Valuers Institute,** 38 Merion Square, Dublin 2, (Tel: Dublin 762011)

JAC **Jewellery Advisory Centre,** c/o National Association of Goldsmiths, St. Dunstan's House, Carey Lane, London EC2 (Tel: 01-606 4936)

LAPADA **London and Provincial Antique Dealers' Association,** 3 Cheval Place, London SW7 1EW (Tel: 01-584 7911)

MCA **Master Carvers Association,** Stanhope Lodge, Arundel Road, Clapham, Worthing, Sussex, ND13 3UA

NADFAS **National Association of Decorative and Fine Arts Societies,** 38 Ebury Street, London SW1W 0LU (Tel: 01-730 3041)

NAG **National Association of Goldsmiths,** St. Dunstan's House, Carey Lane, London EC2 (Tel: 01-606 4936)

PADA **Perth Antique Dealers' Association,** Templeman Antiques, 28 Glasgow Road, Perth (Tel: 0738 29327)

PBFA **Provincial Booksellers' Fairs Association,** c/o Chandos Books, 111 Park Road, New Barnet, Herts. EN4 9QR (Tel: 01-449 9497)

PTS **Philatelic Traders Society,** 27 John Adam Street, London WC2 (Tel: 01-930 6465)

Royal Academy of Arts, Burlington House, Piccadilly, London W1 (Tel: 01-734 9052)

RICS **Royal Institute of Chartered Surveyors,** 12 George Street, London SW1 (Tel: 01-222 7000)

Royal Society of Painters in Water-Colours, and Royal Society of Painter-Etchers and Engravers, Bankside Gallery, 48 Hopton Street, London SE1 (Tel: 01-928 7251)

SOFAA **Society of Fine Art Auctioneers,** 7 Blenheim Street, New Bond Street, London W1Y 0AS (Tel: 01-629 2933)

SLAD **Society of London Art Dealers,** 80 Reading House, Leinster Gardens, London W2 (Tel: 01-262 9340)

UKIC **United Kingdom Institute for Conservation,** c/o Tate Gallery, Millbank, London SW1P 4RG (Tel: 01-821 1313)

Worshipful Company of Goldsmiths, Goldsmiths' Hall, Foster Lane, London EC2U 6BN (Tel: 01-606 8971)

Bobinet

102 Mount Street, London W1YD 5HF

TELEPHONE 01-408 0333/4

CLIFFORD WRIGHT
ANTIQUES LTD.

A rare *pair* of Queen Anne gesso mirrors retaining the original gilding and vauxhall bevelled glasses. English, Circa 1710.
Height 45½″ 116 cms
Width 24″ 61 cms

PERIOD MIRRORS

GILT FURNITURE

104 & 106 FULHAM ROAD, LONDON SW3   Telephone 01-589 0986

SMALL HOUSEHOLD TINS	COPPER & BRASS POLISH (Medium Size Bottles)	SADDLE SOAP
LARGE HOUSEHOLD TINS	FINE DUSTERS	INDUSTRIAL SIZES
BROWN WAX	LEATHER CREAM	ANTIQUAX FINE FURNITURE POLISH (1 litre tin)
EXTRA LARGE TINS	SIMULATED CHAMOIS LEATHER	ANTIQUAX DARK BROWN WAX (1 litre tin)
WAX POLISH AEROSOL	WOOD RESTORER	ANTIQUAX MEDIUM BROWN WAX (1 litre tin)
QUICK POLISH AEROSOL	PINE WAX (NATURAL)	LIQUID FLOOR WAX (1 litre tin)
ANTI-TARNISH LACQUER (Aerosol)	PINE WAX (BROWN)	PINE WAX (NATURAL) (2½ litre tin)
FURNITURE CLEANER (Tin)	PINE WAX (ANTIQUE BROWN)	PINE WAX (BROWN) (2½ litre tin)
FURNITURE CLEANER (Aerosol)	LIQUID PINE WAX	PINE WAX (ANTIQUE BROWN) (2½ litre tin)
FURNITURE CREAM (BEESWAX) (Jar)	TEAK OIL	ANTIQUAX FINE FURNITURE POLISH (5 litre tin)
GLASS CLEANER (Aerosol)	SILVER MITT	ANTIQUAX DARK BROWN WAX (5 litre tin)
CHANDELIER & GLASS CLEANER (Aerosol)	LIQUID FLOOR WAX	ANTIQUAX MEDIUM BROWN WAX (5 litre tin)
SILVER POLISH (Medium Size Bottles)	MARBLE WAX (WHITE)	LIQUID FLOOR WAX (5 litre tin)

Partridge (Fine Arts) Ltd.
Fine art dealers of New Bond Street, London.
Manufactured and distributed on their behalf by

James Briggs & Sons Ltd.
Established 1830

Lion Works, Old Market Street, Blackley, Manchester M9 3DU, England.
Telephone: 061-795 8410. Telex: 666259

H. W. KEIL LTD

Telephone
BROADWAY
0386 852408

TUDOR HOUSE
BROADWAY,
WORCESTERSHIRE

Member of the
British Antique
Dealers' Association

17th & 18th Century Furniture · Works of Art

Two of our many interesting rooms where we show an extensive stock of fine quality furniture from the Gothic times to the end of the 18th Century.

Including:
A set of late 17th century oak pierced high back single chairs

A late 17th century oak enclosed dresser with shelves, height 7ft, width 6ft 1in, depth 1ft 8½in

An attractive 17th century oak refectory table of medium size, length 9ft, width 2ft 8in, height 2ft 5½in

Including:
A fine early 18th century mahogany secretaire breakfront bookcase, height 8ft, width 7ft 10in, depth 1ft 9½in

An early 19th century mahogany two pillar table with two leaves supported on bars, height 2ft 5in, length 8ft 10in, width 3ft 10in

An unusual set of 10 + 2 walnut mid-18th century splat back chairs, with drop in seats

Originators of the well known Keil's dark and light Wax Polish available in ½ lb and 2 lb sizes

In association with H. W. Keil (Cheltenham) Ltd., 129-131 The Promenade, Cheltenham

BRITISH ART & ANTIQUES DIRECTORY 1987

EDITORIAL ARTICLES, GUIDE TO COURSES, GUIDE TO TOURS

How to Use This Book
After the editorial articles the book is divided into five main sections:
1 Directory (*begins on page 37*)
Dealers, auctioneers, packers, restorers, trade suppliers and so on are all listed here, with address, telephone number, opening hours, and type of business or area of specialisation. Entries are listed in alphabetical order under town or village, within the relevant county and geographical area.
2 Gazetteer (*begins on page 265*)
This is an alphabetical list of the towns and villages mentioned in the Directory, showing the counties and geographical areas under which they are listed.
3. Index to Specialists
(*begins on page 270*)
Directory entries are here listed under type of business or nature of stock.
4. Index to Business Names
(*begins on page 363*)
All business names in the Directory are listed alphabetically with their town or village, county and geographical area.
5 Maps (*begin on page 391*)
Showing villages and towns listed in the Directory.

Note
Counties and geographical areas are listed with page references under 'Contents' on page 3.
Auctioneers are listed both in the main Directory under the relevant town or village, and in the Specialists index under 'Auctioneers'.
Abbreviations and names and addresses of useful organisations are listed on page 4.

Eighteenth-Century English Furniture

by Christopher Claxton Stevens

The weaker dollar is bringing pieces back from the States to Britain, but the supply of really high-quality furniture is still dwindling. Certain areas, such as Regency furniture, continue to fetch high prices, and there is a growing interest in fine country woods, but oak and early walnut are more difficult to sell.

From as early as the 18th century fears have been expressed as to the increasing difficulty of finding the best quality pieces for collectors. There is certainly a constantly diminishing supply of finest furniture, but at the same time one of the effects of a quieter market is that fewer good pieces are put up for sale. After the heady days of 1984/5 the past year has generally been such a time. Dealers find it hard to replace stock once it is sold without lowering their standards, while the auction houses either have fewer specialist sales or include less important items.

Certain factors can help the situation, such as a weaker dollar encouraging the movement of pieces back from the States, and the reappearance of the same pieces on the market, sometimes after only a few years, with the expectation of profit. For example, in April 1986 Christie's New York sold a George II gilded side table dripping with carved cherubs, birds and masks for £150 000. This had come from the collection of the Earls of Shaftesbury whence it had been sold in 1980 for £38 000. Again, a pair of finely carved Rococo white and gilt oval mirrors, originally from Dyrham Park, which had fetched £12 000 at the sale of David Style's Wateringbury Place in 1978, re-emerged at Christie's in June 1985 to make £75 000.

The provenance or pedigree in both these cases had a considerable bearing on the prices. While quality, condition and function should always be the first priorities in assessing a piece of furniture, increasing importance is clearly being placed on provenance and attribution to known makers. With the *Dictionary of English Furniture Makers* due to appear in late 1986, this tendency can only increase. Extreme examples must be the pair of commodes sold by Christie's New York in October 1985 for £157 000 which, unlike so many close attributions (Figure 1), could be persuasively pinned down as having come from Chippendale's workshop in 1774, and the pair of silvered mirrors which, at £280 000, topped a number of pieces supplied by Chippendale to Harewood House, all making high prices in London in April 1986.

Discoveries like this are newsworthy and prestigious. Christie's had another success in June 1985 when they offered a painted wine cooler made after a design by Robert Adam for the Duke of Cumberland. This made £35 000 and was followed in November 1985 by the painted and gilded urns which may have come from the same sideboard ensemble (Figure 3). Besides their historic interest these illustrate another continuing trend in the market towards the painted and decorative world of Interior Design. A number of Continental dealers have established themselves in London, displaying their goods in a sumptuous and decorative manner. In September Christie's sold the contents of the late Geoffrey Bennison's home, recreating something of its atmosphere and layout, while Sotheby's, in an attempt to bring the private purchaser into greater contact with the London saleroom, which more than in New York has tended to be trade-orientated, began to offer monthly sales in room settings. The reception has been rather mixed. Many collectors see the advantage of buying from reputable dealers where, away from auction hysteria, they can often get a better deal and perhaps buy something which has not appeared on the open market and which has been properly restored.

Exceptional prices are not as unusual in provincial salerooms as they used to be. A number are improving their advertising and the quality of their catalogues, in both production and research. The year has not been one particularly noted for its contents sales, with the exception of Littlecote in Wiltshire, but the achievement of Woolley and Wallis at Barrington Court, Somerset in

Figure 1 (above left)
One of a pair of carved and gilded armchairs, attributed to Thomas Chippendale and very similar in its detail to his known work. About 1775.
Sold for £22 000
Sotheby's, 15 November 1985

Figure 2 (below)
George I walnut bureau cabinet of unusual small size and in superb condition, attributed to John Phillips, St. Paul's Churchyard, London. About 1720.
Norman Adams Ltd

October 1985 where £73 000 was paid for a stained maple and yew double-domed bureau bookcase of about 1695 is impressive. Besides the expectations of house sales in pushing up prices, this perhaps reflects the increasing interest in finely figured and coloured country woods. There can be no better example of this than the continually escalating prices of Windsor chairs and the outstanding £8000 paid for a pair of yew and elm armchairs by Prior of Uxbridge at Leominster in March 1986.

One of the effects of diminishing supply is that different areas become popular to satisfy demand. Regency furniture has made consistently high prices, especially among American collectors, with a burr yew and ormolu bookcase supplied by Marsh and Tatham for Carlton House in 1806 fetching £135 000 at Christie's in November 1985. As late 18th-century satinwood furniture becomes more expensive, so good late 19th-century copies rise in price for the decorative market. For example, a set of nine painted satinwood armchairs made as much as £45 000 at Christie's in June 1985, while a settee, almost en suite, managed only £2600. Settees are sometimes difficult to sell in the world of soft furnishings: even one supplied by Vile and Cobb for Croome Court went for well under the estimate at £8000 at Sotheby's in June 1985, while some exceptional ones did take off, like the George I walnut chairback example which caused a sensation in Clitheroe at £32 500, selling to the London trade.

Good dining tables and sets of chairs, the larger in number the better, have been in constant demand, the latter again forcing up the prices of good Victorian copies, although often still to hardly more than it would cost to reproduce them today. The twelve shield-back armchairs on a Gillow model of about 1790, sold to a private collector in New York for £137 000 at Sotheby's Herzog sale in April 1985, are obviously exceptional, but £20 000 at Phillips' for a good set of eight arched-back dining chairs with carved splats of perhaps ten years earlier, is less so.

Another form of seat furniture, finely carved library armchairs, especially with attractive needlework covers, have done very well with single ones sometimes into five figures and pairs rising as high as the £85 000 taken for the well-researched ones from Wentworth Castle at Christie's in November 1985. Their early 19th-century counterparts, the caned bergères, have also made new strides: £21 000 for a pair complete with their original adjustable reading slopes at Sotheby's in February 1986, following a more straightforward pair in June 1985 at £15 500. A single example might well not fetch more than a tenth of the price. Stools too, always scarce, have gone way over estimates and several into five figures: a Regency one based on a design by Thomas Hope went to £12 000 at Sotheby's in February 1986, and a rare George I gesso one to £21 000 at Christie's in November 1985, matching as it did three sold at Godmersham Park the previous year. This purchaser was content to pay at least £3500 more.

By no means in every field have things forged ahead. As with oak, early 18th-century walnut can be difficult. There are always collectors for unusual pieces of excellent colour and in top condition (Figure 3) but the second-rate, restored or dull have often been disappointing. In fact this seems to have been the general pattern at auction and even at the top London sales where very little was unsold, beneath the surface only cautious reserves saved a lot more failures. Having said which, 1985/6 has certainly seen some huge prices for 18th-century English furniture, increasing its standing in comparison with Continental furniture which seems on the whole more depressed. Yet the prices for provenanced American pieces seem to forge ahead still more. The Philadelphia carved mahogany tripod table which sold for a record £1 647 098 at Christie's New York is but the tip of the iceberg: a number of other examples, often closely resembling their English equivalents, have been selling for ten or even twenty times the price of similar English pieces.

In sum, the market has been very selective, and with a general consensus that 1986 began as the quietest year for dealers for quite some time, bearing in mind the level of the dollar and the world political situation, the pattern looks set to continue. □

Figure 3
Pair of painted and gilded urns, perhaps made for the Duke of Cumberland to a design by Robert Adam now in the Soane Museum. About 1780.
Sold for £20 000
Christie's, 21 November 1985

Christopher Claxton Stevens is a Director of Norman Adams Ltd.

Marklin Tinplate

by Hilary Kay

An unusual market which has suddenly come to the fore in recent years is that for tinplate toys, especially the finely-worked train sets produced by German manufacturers in the 19th century. The most sought-after of these are the products of the remarkable Marklin factory.

When a tinplate toy train realised £28 050 at a Sotheby's auction in 1984, those with half knowledge put index finger to nose and murmered, 'Ah, it must have been by Marklin'. And it is true that no other tinplate toy manufacturer's wares are as respected by collectors or as highly prized today.

The oldest manufacturer of toy trains in the world still in business today, the company's story begins in South Germany in 1859. Goppingham in the province of Wurttemberg saw a partnership then between Theodor Marklin, a one-time Master plumber turned Master sheet metal worker, and his second wife, Karoline. The company they founded with one apprentice began by producing miniature tinplate kitchens and utensils for dolls. The company grew steadily, adding dolls' house furniture and carriages to their early lines, and in 1888 the name of the company was altered to Gebrüder Marklin when Theodor and Karoline's two sons entered the business. The greatest expansion in the toy range, however, came in 1891 following the takeover of the sales and distribution of the Ludwig Lutz company from Ellwangen.

Ludwig Lutz, a qualified tinsmith, had set up in business in 1846 manufacturing lacquered tinplate wreaths, swiftly diversifying into the production of dolls' house furniture, tin soldiers and carriages. His portfolio of particularly delicate and finely lacquered toys later included ships, trains, forts, model castles and houses. The business was based in a small village and in time its isolated position, dependence on mechanisms purchased from abroad and lack of sufficient capital to mechanise forced the company in 1891 to accept Marklin's offer to purchase their toy inventory and production equipment.

Another takeover took place in 1904 with the assimilation of the Biberach company Rock & Graner, makers of lacquered tin ware since the 1830s. This company concentrated originally, as had Ludwig Lutz, on the production of doll's house furniture which was often painted to simulate the grain of wood; later horse-drawn carriages, forts, toy trains, station buildings, stations and layout accessories were added to the portfolio. Rock & Graner displayed a selection of their toys at the 1851 Great Exhibition in Hyde Park and an extract from the official programme informs the reader that '. . . The toys from Rock & Graner are not only offered in a wide variety, but they also display great taste . . .'; two juries duly awarded the company a medal at the exhibition. Eventually, towards the end of the 19th century, sales began to decline; manufacture had relied heavily on hand workers and the mechanisation which could have saved the company was not undertaken, owing in part to the apathy of the now sick owner. It is strongly believed that between 1904 and 1906 Marklin absorbed the portfolio of Rock & Graner designs. Certainly the 1905 Marklin catalogue uses plates very similar to those which had appeared originally in the Rock & Graner catalogue of 1902.

Figure 1 (above)
Marklin gauge one tinplate clockwork armoured train.
German, about 1902.
Sold for £9900
Sotheby's, 13 May 1982

Accurate identification of the early toys from Marklin, Lutz and Rock & Graner can be problematical since many were not stamped with any company trademark or monogram. The products of Ludwig Lutz can best be singled out as being of particularly delicate construction, intricately detailed and made from fairly thin gauge sheet tin. Lutz's carriages were pulled either by carved wooden horses, gesso covered and often painted as dapple greys, or by delicate moulded brass and tinplate horses finished as both greys and chestnuts. Early Marklin toys are constructed from much thicker gauge tinplate and tend to be of sturdier form; in addition some appear in their early trade catalogues, and a handful bear the Marklin trademark of a 'GM' monogram within a shield. Rock & Graner toys are of slightly thinner gauge tinplate but fortunately the 'R&GN' trademark (Rock & Graner's Nachfolger) found on some toys has helped in the correct classification of similar but unmarked examples.

The Marklin company faced strong competition from other prominent German toy manufacturers, particularly from the 1890s onwards — competitors such as Gebrüder Bing (established as retailers in 1863), Georges Carette (based in Nuremburg since 1886), Jean Schoenner (Nuremburg since 1886), and Ernst Plank (Nuremburg since 1866). All these manufacturers vied for a larger share of the market although the products they offered were similar in many ways. Something made Marklin's toy range particularly successful.

Unlike their contemporaries, the Marklin company was prepared to take risks in developing new types of toy. For instance, the Marklin stand at the 1891 Leipzig toy trade fair caused a sensation with its novel display of a train running on a sectional track (undoubtedly inspired by models and prototypes acquired in the Lutz takeover earlier in the year). The following year Marklin exhibited at the same Leipzig fair the first figure-of-eight track and clockwork locomotive. Over the next 30 years Marklin became particularly renowned for their comprehensive model railways, introducing the first electric train set to Europe in 1898, and creating the classification of the gauges from O Gauge (35mm wide) to III Gauge (75mm wide). Making train layouts of different sizes ensured that owners of smaller houses, who may have been unable to accommodate a large gauge layout, could still buy a suitable train set from Marklin to fit the restricted size of their rooms.

Marklin were unusual in swiftly translating the latest innovations into toy form without waiting to see whether a particular fad would be of lasting interest to the public. Their toys reflect all sides of human life,

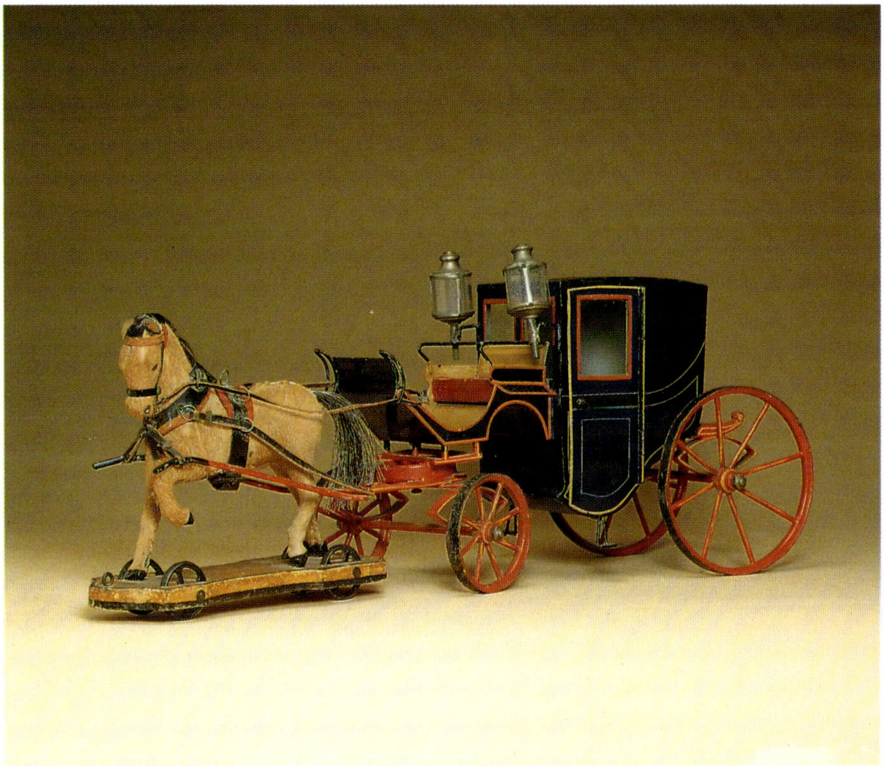

Figure 2 (left)
Marklin tinplate carriage and horses. German, about 1900. Private Collection.

covering both metropolitan and rural pursuits, and include a large group of toys depicting different types of transport. This latter group were particularly admired abroad and today provide the social historian with an accurate commentary on the important technical and design innovations to the full-size vehicles of the period. Marklin were, however, uncharacteristically slow to produce their first range of automobiles in 1900, 14 years after the invention of the motor car. Other innovations were swifter to be copied, and the 1908 catalogue illustrated airships, zeppelins and bi-planes based on those of the Wright brothers, who had first shown their successful flying machine in Europe earlier the same year. The design of passenger liners, river launches, battleships and torpedo boats were based on the full size vessels popular during the period and were often named accordingly 'Carmania', 'Lusitania', 'HMS Terrible' and so on.

The design qualities of all but the later railway locomotives and coaches are particularly appealing since the company tended to interpret the detail of the full size example rather than reproduce it exactly, thereby creating different emphases in the toy and giving it a whimsical quality which proved irresistible to children and adults alike.

Clever marketing techniques were used by Marklin, including the introduction of special liveries on transport toys, railway locomotives and accessories tailor-made for specific nationalities. America, France and England became the largest importers of Marklin toys; the biggest English toy retailers, A. W. Gamage of Holborn, often had Marklin place the Gamage lozenge-shaped metal label on the body or underside of a toy before it left their factory.

Marklin realised early on that adults would not balk at paying a little more for a toy of outstanding quality and their products tended to be fairly expensive at the time of purchase. Bought by middle and upper class families where play was usually supervised by nurses or governesses, many toys from the Marklin factory have survived in remarkably good condition. From these surviving examples it can be seen that the finish of most Marklin toys, prior to their widespread use of lithography in the 1920s, is outstanding. The hard enamelled paint baked onto the toy in several coats took on a jewel-like intensity of colour; details were hand stencilled or freely drawn beneath the final generous layer of varnish. The actual gauge of the tinplate used and the quality of the mechanisms, made within the Marklin factory whether steam, clockwork or electric, ensured that these toys stood apart from their mass-produced and mechanically finished rivals on toy shop shelves.

After the First World War the company began to reduce certain production lines such as the Gauge II model trains (1918) and Gauge I model trains (1935), whilst expanding into construction sets similar to Meccano, constructional vehicles and aeroplanes, and extending their portfolio of aeroplanes, boats and military toys. Marklin realised, eventually, that their quality, hand-finished production techniques could not compete profitably with competition in plastics from abroad and further reduced their lines after the Second World War until, today, they concentrate solely on the production of die-cast model vehicles and small Gauge HO trainsets. □

Hilary Kay is a Director and Head of the Collectors' Department at Sotheby's.

Figure 3 (below)
Marklin 'Fidelitas' tinplate clown car train. German, about 1909. Length 94 cm (37 in).
Sold for £9900
Sotheby's, 21 May 1985.

Watercolours

by Lowell Libson

The first 'Watercolours Fair', in January 1986, greatly boosted the already growing interest in this area, and prices are now escalating rapidly as supply diminishes. Fine Engish watercolours are particularly in demand, but the less well known names are still selling at affordable prices.

Figure 1
The Battle for Fort Seringapatum, by Joseph Mallord William Turner, about 1799. 42.2 × 65.4 cm ($16\frac{5}{8} \times 25\frac{3}{4}$ in).
Sold for £9180. Christie's.

It might be considered that as far as watercolours are concerned 1986 has been something of an '*annus mirabilis*'. Certainly, the year started off eventfully with the 'World of Watercolours' fair in January, which should now become an annual event at the Park Lane Hotel. This, the first of its kind, proved to be an immense success with some 10 000 visitors attending during its five-day duration. Other than its popular appeal, what was most remarkable was the fact that the 44 exhibitors included most of the best-known London dealers as well as many less well known names from London and the provinces. The fair provided a valuable opportunity for the novice to discover the wide range of pictures available in this versatile medium and also to assess the individual tastes and interests of the many exhibitors, who were showing watercolours priced between £50 and £200 000.

The 'World of Watercolours' seems almost, in retrospect, to have been a logical result of the magnificent and extremely popular watercolour exhibition held at the British Museum in 1985. The exhibition, perhaps the finest held on the subject since before the War, introduced many people to the pleasures of the English watercolour, and the fair was able to translate the experience into practical terms. Equally logical was the launch in January of *Watercolours*, a specialist magazine for collectors, the only publication of the sort to have appeared since the demise of *Walker's Quarterly* in the 1930s. Under the editorship of Huon Mallalieu, best known for his indispensible dictionary of watercolour painters, this new arrival at the bookstalls should provide a valuable forum for the latest research in the field.

In this article I have tried to concentrate on some of the trends which have been developing in the watercolour market over the last four or five years and which by 1986 seemed to have evolved into a definite pattern in collecting. Since the auction rooms are now such an important source for collectors as well as dealers, it seems sensible to regard 1986 as beginning at the start of the traditional auction season, in September 1985. I have also concentrated, for the most part, on English watercolours painted before 1850, since my particular interest lies there rather than with High Victorian, Continental, or Modern British watercolours — although most of the generalisations are equally applicable to these areas.

Over the last few years there has been a great awakening of academic interest in English art which has resulted in a considerable body of research being carried out, and certainly the collector and dealer of today have a far greater knowledge and repertoire of attributions than even 30 years ago. With this academic respectability has grown a commercial recognition of the quality and interest of English watercolours, which has in turn attracted the notice of Continental and American collectors to whom this particular market must seem remarkably reasonable when compared with other traditional fields of collecting. This, in conjunction with what seems to be a diminishing supply of fine pictures, has forced prices up to what even five years ago might have seemed outrageous levels. The high values now placed on the finest watercolours have resulted in benefits as well as the obvious problems, as it has created a vicious circle in which the field is taken more seriously by new buyers as the prices go up. Certainly, there is a case for being even more selective when buying than in the past. Anyone considering purchasing a watercolour should judge it on a few vital criteria: is it beautiful, is it in good condition and is it a good example of the artist's work? Once these have been satisfied, one should look at the other factors governing a picture's desirability, those of rarity and historical importance. The relevance of these individual elements will be different in the case of every picture, but they should all be considered.

It has now become almost automatic to expect some sort of dispersal of an important collection of watercolours in every season. Perhaps the highlight of 1984 was the sale, unusually by a dealer, Agnews, of Mrs Cecil Keith's collection. The most important group of watercolours and drawings to appear in the 1985-6 season was, at the time of writing, the quirky collection formed by Ray Livingston Murphy, an American who hastily assembled a large number of mainly 18th-century pictures in the early years of the 1950s. The sales of the collection at Christie's included works by Alexander Cozens, Turner, Fuseli and Hearne as well as many pictures by obscure artists. Of this particular collection perhaps the impressive group of watercolours by Edward Lear will be best remembered.

It is now not uncommon for many of the finest English watercolours to be worth over

Figure 2
Rouen from the Seine, by John Sell Cotman, 1823. 28.9 cm ×49.2 cm ($11\frac{7}{8}$ × $19\frac{3}{8}$ in).
Sold by the Leger Galleries, 1986.

£30 000, and among the artists whose works achieve these previously unthought of heights are John Robert Cozens, Thomas Gainsborough, Thomas Rowlandson, John Constable, Paul Sandby, Thomas Girtin, John Sell Cotman, Thomas Shotter Boys, Samuel Palmer and, of course, Joseph Mallord William Turner. Although it is usual to give prominence to the record-breakers at the top end of the market, it should be emphasised that in every dealer's stock or exhibition and at every important auction there are fine examples of the art to be had for a few hundred pounds. One can still purchase an excellent Rowlandson, for instance, for £2000 or £3000, although it is easily possible to spend ten or twenty times that amount on a great example, and this holds true for most of the major watercolourists. On the other hand, it is possible to form a fine collection of pictures by watercolourists who, though not household names, are important in the history of the development of the art. The watercolours of Edward Dayes, Hugh 'Grecian' Williams, Michael Angelo Rooker, Anthony Devis, William Payne, Joseph Farington, Samuel Atkins, John Varley, David Cox, George Fennel Robson and Paul Sandby Munn are a few of the many which should be in a comprehensive collection and which may still be owned without having thousands of pounds to spend.

Figure 3
Khanea, Crete, by Edward Lear, 1864.
28.3 × 48.9 cm ($11\frac{1}{8}$ × $19\frac{1}{4}$ in).
Sold for £15 120. Christie's.

It is also interesting to look at some of the purchases made by major English museums. The Print Room of the British Museum has acquired important works by Gainsborough, Rowlandson, Thomas Jones and Bonington, as well as many minor works which complement its already vast holdings. The Victoria and Albert Museum has also concentrated on buying works which fill out its existing collections, as well as a few major purchases such as the *Interior of a Cavern* by John Robert Cozens (happily from the Leger Galleries) as well as the important view of Walpole's 'Strawberry Hill' by William Pars. At the time of writing, the Tate Gallery has just purchased a fascinating early Turner of *The Battle of Seringapatum* (Figure 1), a study for which is in the Turner Bequest.

In addition to the usual dealers' exhibitions and watercolour auctions, we can look forward to the second 'World of Watercolours' fair in January 1987. Also, museum exhibitions will include the Victoria and Albert's 'Alexander Cozens' show at the end of 1986 and in 1987 exhibitions devoted to Sandby and Mulready, whilst at the Tate the opening of the Turner Wing will be a major event. □

Lowell Libson has worked at the Leger Galleries for several years; prior to that he ran the Watercolours and Drawings Department at Phillips the auctioneers.

GUIDE TO COURSES

Opportunities for education in the fine and decorative arts and restoration, summarised by Deborah Scott

Listed below are full-time, part-time and short or one-day courses in fine and decorative arts and restoration. There is a section on educational courses based abroad, and another on courses in arts administration, including museum studies. Please note that information given here is based on previous courses as well as projections for 1987, and details should be checked with the relevant establishment.

Further information about university courses is obtainable from the Universities Central Council for Admissions (UCCA), who publish a helpful handbook (Tel: Cheltenham (0242) 519091). There is also a book called *Which Degree?*, volume I of which advises on degrees available in arts subjects. It is published annually and is available from bookshops and from New Opportunity Press, 76 St. James's Lane, London N10 (Tel: 01-444 7281). For those in the Inner London area, a booklet called *Floodlight* is published in August every year (available from book-stores) and gives notice of the courses to be run from September onwards.

COURSES IN THE FINE AND DECORATIVE ARTS

Full-Time Courses

Christie's Fine Arts Course
63 Old Brompton Road, London SW7 3JS (01-581 3933).
Director: Robert Cumming.
Duration: 1 year, comprising 3 terms. Fees: £3500 + VAT (1987). 64 places.
The emphasis here is on the practical application of the knowledge acquired, with cataloguing projects being undertaken, and discussions on the workings of the art market and fashions in collecting. This is particularly sensible for those hoping to make a career in the art business, where practical application often carries more weight than academic prowess.

The syllabus is flexible, but concentrates on the arts of the western world over the past 350 years, since these are the most likely to be encountered. Tuition takes the form of lectures in the mornings, followed by seminars, tutorials and visits to galleries, museums and the saleroom. Field trips to historic houses and collections are made regularly. Since students come from different backgrounds, and no prior knowledge is required, they are split into tutorial groups according to their experience, and the tutors adjust their teaching accordingly. Continuous assessment – no exams. *Requirements:* fluent English, basic knowledge of art history. Students may attend mornings only. Fees for this part-time attendance: £2250 + VAT (1987).

Courtauld Institute of Art
(University of London)
20 Portman Square, London W1H 0BE (01-935 9292/5; 01-486 5913/4).
BA in Art History
Duration: 3 years. Fees: UK students £536 p.a.; overseas £3675 p.a. (1986/7). 28 places
This three-year course leads to an honours degree (BA) in the History of Art. It encourages depth of knowledge and increasing specialisation, and students are expected to look beyond established ideas found in text books. For this reason, those who are looking for a broad general course in art history will find this unsuitable. The first year does lay a general foundation of western art from antiquity to the present day, but thereafter attention is devoted to a 'Special Period' and then two 'Special Subjects'. The final examination at the end of the third year (consisting of eight three-hour papers) reflects this bias with only one paper on general art history, three on the Special Period, and two on each Special Subject. This is not a course for dilettantes, and should only be considered by those wishing to study the subject in depth. *Requirements:* Minimum three 'O' levels, two 'A' levels. Ability to read at least one foreign language, and an 'O' level in French, German or Italian. The Courtauld also offers further degrees which include an MA in the History of Art and an MA in the History of Dress (held biennially). These are both post-graduate degrees, although it is not essential that a first degree be held specificially in Art History.

Fine Art Tutors
85 Belsize Park Gardens, London NW3 (01-586 0312)
Principal: Candida Cochrane.
Diploma in Fine Arts
Duration: 1 year September-June, comprising 3 terms, or (preferably) part-time for 2 years.
Fees: £3135 + VAT p.a. (1986/7) (inc. study trip). 'Limited number' of places.
The course covers the history of European art from the 12th century to the present day. As its name suggests, this establishment teaches fine rather than decorative art, concentrating on painting, sculpture and architecture in depth. London's museums and galleries are visited, and there is a study trip to Europe (four or five days) guided by a tutor. Attention is paid to the commercial side of art, with visits to galleries and salerooms. Diplomas are awarded to successful students. *Requirements:* none.

Fine Art Tutors also offer Portfolio and Pre-Foundation courses, each lasting from one term to one year, in which a formal training in drawing and painting is given, as well as instruction in print making, sculpture, pottery, photography and history of art. They also prepare students for 'A' level History of Art and other arts 'A' levels.

Inchbald School of Design
7 Eaton Gate, Belgravia, London SW1 (01-730 5508).
Principal: Jacqueline Thwaites.
Fine and Decorative Arts Course
Duration: 1 year (Oct–July).
Fees: £3123.75 + VAT + travel (1986/7).
This gives students an education in the history of European style from 1500 to the present day. Architecture, painting and sculpture as well as the decorative arts are studied in depth. Emphasis is placed on a knowledge of techniques and conservation, as well as the commercial aspects such as art-dealing and auctions.

The course takes the form of lectures, visits and tutorials, backed up by independent study and research. A project is worked on, and this and the student's note book contribute to the final assessment. There is a final examination, and diplomas are awarded. *Requirements:* none.

It is possible to attend only one of the three terms of this course, if a student is interested in one period especially. The autumn term covers the period 1550–1660; spring 1660–1820; summer 1820–1985.
Interior Design Course
Duration: 1 year (Oct–July).
Fees: £5293.65 + VAT + extras (1986/87).
This should also be mentioned since it is interior design for which the school is best known. It aims to train students to devise and create interior schemes themselves, to a standard acceptable to professional design practices. It is not concerned only with the contemporary interior, but includes historical perspectives. Continuous assessments and a final examination lead to the school's Diploma.
Development of Interior Design 1700–1983
Duration: 4 weeks. Fees: £520 + VAT.
Concentrates on architecture, decorative techniques, textiles, upholstery, furniture, silver and other interior features.

Many other courses are available.

The New Academy for Art Studies
53 Albion Street, London W2 (01-262 5462).
Director: Roger Bevan.
Duration: 1 year (Oct–June, 3 terms).
Fees: £2100 + VAT. 30 places.
The course deals with the major movements in western art from the Middle Ages to the present day. The relationship between the fine and decorative arts is emphasised, as is the commercial side of these arts. The practices of auction houses and the trade are explained, and the policies of museums reviewed. Preservation and management of country houses, techniques of conservation and restoration, organisation of exhibitions, and the publication of art books are also featured. Visits are made to museums and galleries, historic buildings and collections. Foreign expeditions are arranged. Continuous assessment and examinations lead to a Diploma. *Requirements:* none, but students must be aged over 18.

Sotheby's
30 Oxford Street, London W1 (01-408 1100)
Works of Art Course
Course Principal: Derek Shrub.
Duration: 9 months (mid Sept–mid June, 3 terms). Fees: £3750 + VAT (1986/7).
Approximately 50 places.
The object of this course is 'to widen the visual experience of the students and to instil a broad knowledge of a variety of objects of many periods'. The course is formed around certain sales and temporary exhibitions, and students are encouraged to take an intelligent interest in the activities of the saleroom. There are also visits to museums and galleries, and to country houses containing important collections. The emphasis at Sotheby's is on practical preparation for a career in the art world, rather than solely academic study of the history of art. Continuous assessment but

no examination. *Requirements:* good knowledge of art history. Students should be aged approximately 20–23.

Three-Month Art Courses:

Course Principal: Barbara Morris

Duration: 12 weeks (3 times a year). Fees: £1200 + VAT (1986). 30 places on each course.

1. Styles in European Arts

The course aims to equip students with a sound knowledge of the stylistic development of European art from antiquity to the present day, and to provide them with the necessary critical skills to make informed judgements on works of art. This is achieved through lectures, seminars, and museum and gallery visits. Practical sessions are also included to provide first hand experience of a variety of techniques.

2. 17th–18th Century Decorative Arts Course

3. 19th–20th Century Decorative Arts Course

These courses aim to give the students a thorough grounding in the development of the decorative arts and to set the works in the wider context of their age, and also to develop the students' practical visual skills by working with actual objects. Students benefit from the knowledge of Sotheby's experts, who will preview relevant sales with them.

Islamic Works of Art Course

Duration: 12 weeks (March–June or Sept–December). Fees: £2000 + VAT. 12 places.

This course aims to establish familiarity with a wide range of Islamic objects and styles from the seventh century to the present day. Architecture, pottery, metalwork, glass, the art of the book (including miniature-painting, book-binding and calligraphy), textiles and rugs, numismatics and history are all included, and there are also lectures on conservation. In addition to lectures, students will visit private collections and museums, as well as the relevant sales held by Sotheby's. Applications should be made to the Islamic Works of Art Course, Sotheby's, 34–35 New Bond Street, London W1 (01-493 8080). *Requirements:* fluent English and a basic knowledge of Islamic history.

Study Centre for the History of the Fine and Decorative Arts

Correspondence only: 9 Westwood Gardens, Barnes, London SW13 (01-846 9224).

Director: Erica O'Donnell.

Diploma Course

Duration: 1 year (September–June, 5 terms).

Fees: £2000 + VAT (1986/7). 30 places.

An academic course covering the history of European architecture, decorative arts (furniture, ceramics, silver and glass) with some classes on the construction and repair of furniture, and European painting and sculpture from the 14th century to the present day. This is an intensive course, requiring some previous basic knowledge of history, and of the major European languages. The Study Centre has close links with the Victoria and Albert Museum, and makes full use of their facilities, as well as visiting other galleries. An examination comprising four papers ends the course, and is marked independently to University of London BA (Gen) standard. A Diploma is awarded to successful candidates. *Requirements:* applicants should preferably be post-graduates. Selection is by interview.

Decorative Arts Course

Duration: 10 weeks (3 courses per year). Fees: £550 + VAT (1986/7). 20 places.

Essentially the same course as the Diploma student's second term (concentrating on decorative arts), but with historical and architectural background filled in. Particularly suitable for those requiring background for a longer course, or for gaining a foothold in employment in the art world. *Requirements:* none.

The Study Centre is sponsored by Phillips Fine Art Auctioneers.

University of Leeds: Department of Fine Art

Leeds LS2 9JT (Leeds (0532) 431751 ext 6227).

Degree in History of the Fine and Decorative Arts

Duration: 4 years.

This is an unusual first degree course which examines various aspects of European decorative art and the history of style in post-Renaissance times, as well as referring to painting, sculpture and domestic architecture. There is also an option for students to take studio (practical) work as one of their subjects in the first year. One of the most interesting aspects of this course is its close association with Temple Newsam House, a fine country house museum specialising in furniture, water colours and the decorative arts in general. Full advantage is taken of this association, with study of the Temple Newsam collections throughout the course. *Requirements:* 3 'A' levels of grades C and D or above.

Victoria and Albert Museum and Royal College of Art

The Secretary, Department of Cultural History, Royal College of Art, Kensington Gore, London SW7 (01-584 5020).

MA in History of Design.

Duration: 2 years (full-time only).

Fee: £1680 p.a. (£4375 overseas) (1986/7).

This postgraduate course aims to take advantage of the unique facilities offered by the V & A and the Royal College of Art. Three related aspects of the history of design are investigated: Theories of Design (an intellectual and philosophical framework); Social and Economic Contexts; and Technology and Form of the Object (the effects of technological and material changes on the products of design). In the second year students devote their time entirely to research for a dissertation on a subject of their selection. Assessment is on the basis of three essays written in the first year, the dissertation (20–25 000 words), and a brief *viva voce* examination. *Requirements:* a good under-graduate degree in a relevant discipline. Applicants should be aged over 21.

Part-Time Courses

Birkbeck College (University of London)

Malet Street, London WC1E 7HX (01-580 6622)

BA in History of Art

Duration: 4 years (3 terms of 10 weeks each per year). Fees: £268 p.a. (1986/7).

This is a fully fledged degree course that is taken part time and is thus suitable for people with jobs or who are unable to attend a university full time for other reasons. The course involves attendance at the college on two nights every week of term, and lectures are given between 6 pm and 9 pm. Private study is also required, and visits to museums and galleries are an essential part of the course. At the end of the last year, eight final examinations are taken, and it is on these that the degree is awarded. *Requirements:* ideally, candidates for this course should have two 'A' levels, but mature students who can show evidence of ability are welcomed. Interviews are held with prospective candidates.

MA in History of Art

Duration: 2 years (3 terms of 10 weeks each per year).

Fees: £490 p.a. (1986/7).

This is also a part-time evening course. It is designed for graduates in need of an art-historical training – their first degree need not be in Art History, though they should have some background in the subject. They should also have a good reading knowledge of French, German or Italian. Attendance is two or three evenings a week for lectures, seminars and tutorials. The examination consists of one written paper, three 5–6000 word essays, and a dissertation.

Christie's Evening Courses

c/o Christie's Fine Arts Course,
63 Old Brompton Road, London SW7 3JS
(01-581 3933).

Fee: £149.50 (1986/7).

Each of these courses comprises a two-hour lecture/seminar (6.30–8.30 pm) one evening a week for ten weeks. Subjects for 1986/7 include The Age of Romanticism, Art Deco and Modernism, Japanese Art, 20th-Century British Art, and The Avant Garde 1900–1960. As well as a discussion of the development of styles in each field, mention is made of fakes, forgeries, values and restoration where appropriate. Each course is only given once a year, so check for details in good time.

Christie's Wine Course

63 Old Brompton Road, London SW7 3JS
(01-581 3933).

Fees: £100–£125 (1987) per session. 45 places.

This course is divided into two parts: Part I is an introduction to wine tasting based on the principal wines of France and Germany; Part II consists of specialist tastings of the major wines of Europe. Both parts consist of informal evening lectures by experts with the emphasis on the tasting of the wines under discussion. Part I involves five consecutive Tuesday evenings; the tastings in Part II can be booked individually or as a complete series of five evenings.

The City Lit

Stukely Street, Drury Lane, London WC2
(01-242 9872).

Fees: £18–£22 per course of 2–3 terms.

This educational establishment comes under the extensive wing of the Inner London Education Authority, and offers a wide range of courses in arts subjects. These tend to occupy 1½ to 3 hours weekly, and may extend for two or three terms. Recent courses have included History of European Art, The Twentieth Century and its Images, Major Paintings in the National Gallery and Great Figures of the Renaissance. There is also the opportunity to study for a Diploma in the History of Art, in association with the University of London (Extra Mural Studies) – this requires regular attendance and some extra work. One-day courses that include gallery visits are also available. Enrolment takes place at the above address, and priority is given to those who appear in person to enrol. Telephone first to find out precise office hours.

Grand Tours/Special Tours

Correspondence: 2 Chester Row, London SW1 9JH
(01-373 0333).

Fees: £35–£75 per course (1986)
Courses on various subjects are offered, taking the form of four or five weekly lectures, given in the mornings (i.e. only for those who are free or flexible). Courses given regularly include English furniture 1500–1837, porcelain, silver, glass and furniture restoration, as well as the English country house. Two others are of particular interest as they draw all the others together – these are on English interiors, 1660–1850, and 1850–1900. Courses are held mainly at the Victoria and Albert Museum. (See also p. 34.)

Modern Art Studies
Correspondence: 140 Sloane Street, London SW1X 9AY (01-730 5608).
History of Modern Art 1850–1986.
Duration: 1 year (diploma) of 3 terms, each of which may be taken separately.
Fees: £800, or £210 per term (1986/7).
This is the only course in London concentrating on the modern period, and is highly spoken of for the quality of its lectures, given by specialists and experts. The year's course is divided into three terms, during which lectures are given on three mornings a week, between 10 am and 12 am. The year starts in October with Courbet to Matisse, Impressionism and Fauvism. In the spring term, German Expressionism, Cubism and subsequent movements up to the Second World War are dealt with, finishing in the summer with Abstract Expressionism to the present day – Jackson Pollock, Pop Art and Carl Andre's notorious bricks. Diploma students have to write essays and take a final examination in June. *Requirements:* none, although some knowledge of art history, perhaps at 'A' level, is helpful for diploma students. Courses are held at the Institute of Contemporary Arts, London SW1. Weekend visits to Paris and Amsterdam are also arranged.

Morley College
61 Westminster Bridge Road, London SE1 7HT (01-928 8501).
Fees: £26 for a 1 year course, 2 hours per week (1986/7).
Morley College is a well established centre for educational activities of all types, although it is concerned predominantly with the arts and humanities. It offers a wide range of part-time courses, which may be taken either during the day or in the evening. Recent courses have included Classical Art and Architecture, Romanesque Art, Painting and Sculpture in Italy 1400–1600, The Architecture of Britain, and several others. Most of these courses take two hours, once a week, and tend to be spread over two terms, autumn and spring. (The University of London's Extra-Mural Department also holds classes at Morley; these include both Diploma and non-Diploma courses.) Enrolement takes place in September, although application may be made at any time during term-time, and avaiable places will be offered. Special concessions in price are offered to the young, the old and the unemployed.

Muir-London
32 Hestercombe Avenue, London SW6 5LG (01-736 0922).
Principal: Bonnie Muir.
Fees: £45–£100 (1986).
Bonnie Muir aims to 'fill the gap left by the excellent long courses' by offering short courses comprising three lectures on different aspects of a particular subject. These lectures are spread over three weeks, and are held at pleasant venues – the Capital or Hyde Park Hotels for example. They aim to give a taste of the subject, and to equip the student to visit exhibitions at museums and galleries. Lectures, lasting 1½ hours (10–11.30 am), are accompanied by slides, and students are encouraged to bring their own relevant objects to discuss. Good lecturers are chosen, and the overall atmosphere is one of cheerful enthusiasm. Subjects for courses in 1986 include Chinoiserie and Tuscan Hill Towns as well as English Furniture (4 days) and various porcelain subjects. In addition to study days and weeks, private views both of exhibitions and of stately homes not usually open to the public are arranged.

National Association of Decorative and Fine Arts Societies.
Correspondence: The Secretary, NADFAS, 38 Ebury Street, London SW1W 0LU (01-730 3041).
Membership fee: about £10, but varies from branch to branch.
NADFAS, formed in 1968, is a registered charity. It is made up of 185 societies throughout Great Britain and overseas, and is aimed at people of all types and ages. Each society organises its own programme of monthly lectures, and lecturers are of a high standard, 'vetted' by NADFAS. Societies meet in the morning or afternoon, but as more working people are now becoming interested, some societies are beginning to meet in the evenings. Contact the central office to find nearest branch.

The Open University
Associate Student Central Office, PO Box 76, Milton Keynes, MK6 6AN (Milton Keynes (0908) 74066).
The Open University is well known for its 'distance teaching' expertise and offers a range of courses from degree level to short personal interest study packs. The nature of the system is such that it is not possible to take a degree in art history alone. An Arts degree involves studying the arts in their broadest sense – literature, music, philosophy and even sociology. It is, however, possible, to be an associate student. This means that one can take only the individual course or courses that one wishes. Credits (course passes) gained as an associate student can always be transferred to the degree programme at a later date. Degree level courses likely to be of most interest to readers are 'Art in Italy 1480–1580' (ref A352) and 'Art in 15th Century Italy' (ref A353) (both half-credit courses; fees £199 each), and 'Modern Art and Modernism: Manet to Pollock' (ref A315) (full-credit course with summer school; fees £295 for the course, plus £99 for the summer school). Courses run from February to November, terminating in an exam. *Requirements:* students must be 18 and over and UK residents. Also likely to be of interest is the OU's study pack called 'Looking into Paintings'.

University of London: Department of Extra-Mural Studies.
26 Russell Square, London WC1B 5DQ (01-636 8000).
Fee: about £39 per full-length course (1986/7).
Many different classes are offered, mostly in the form of sessions which extend over autumn and spring terms, with 24 weekly two-hour meetings, either daytime or evening. Precise subjects change from year to year, but recent courses have been given on subjects ranging from Classical to Modern Art and the History of Silver to The Place of Photography in 19th- and 20th-Century Art. These courses take place in Adult Education Institutes and schools all over the London Area.

There is also a Diploma in History of Art, which involves three to four years of study, comprising four courses on broad topics of one's own choice from an extensive list.

The Victoria and Albert Museum: Education Department
South Kensington, London SW7 (01-589 6371).
On most weekdays and also at weekends there are lectures and gallery talks at the V & A. Subjects change from year to year, and have recently concentrated on the V & A's own collections in a new series of 'Highlight' gallery talks, and a series on 'Great Collections in the V & A' in which the Schreiber, the Jones and other recent collections were discussed. Study Days on a variety of subjects are also held regularly, in which students listen to illustrated talks, and are guided around the relevant collections. These are free, but tickets must be applied for as numbers are limited. Details available on application with s.a.e. There are also Saturday courses lasting between four and twelve weeks. The cost of these is based on a pro-rata figure of about £5 per half day. Weekday courses lasting from Monday to Thursday inclusive are also available. Details of all events are published regularly and may be obtained from the above address, either in person or by writing enclosing an s.a.e. Application in advance for Study Days and courses is essential.

Short/One-Day Courses

The British Library: Humanities and Social Sciences
Great Russell Street, London WC1B 3DG (01-636 1544 ext 333).
A variety of lectures is offered by the British Library in association with its collections. There are gallery talks which are held in the exhibition galleries, slide lectures in the seminar room, and lunchtime lectures in the British Museum Lecture Theatre. There are also short films on subjects related to the library. Subjects for lectures and talks have ranged from Manuscript Illumination to *Livres d'artiste* and Persian Miniatures. Admission to all lectures is free.

Burghley House Study Days
Burghley House, Stamford, Lincolnshire PE9 3JY (Stamford (0780) 52451).
Fee: £30.
Each study day is introduced by Lady Victoria Leatham who explains how the important Burghley House collections were formed, and gives a brief history of the House. Recent study days have included Silver by John Bly and English Porcelain by Gordon Lang. Further study days are planned for Spring 1987 when a variety of subjects will be covered including that of the special exhibition at Burghley for 1987, Portrait Miniatures.

Dilettanti
44 Paddenswick Road, London W6 0UB (01-749 7096).
Fee: £12.50–£25 per day, including transport and entry charges.
Dilettanti aims to promote interest in and enjoyment of the fine and decorative arts, together with their background social history. This is done through a programme of one-day events, usually

comprising two illustrated lectures in the morning, and a visit in the afternoon to a museum, exhibition, country house or other place of interest. Specialist courses on three consecutive days are also held twice a year (1986 fee £45), on such subjects as Techniques and Materials in Painting, Early English Porcelain, and London's 18th-Century Town House.

Dillington College for Adult Education
Dillington Park, Ilminster, Somerset TA19 9DT (Ilminster (04605) 2427/3875).
The college is set in rolling Somerset parkland and has a theatre and a public art gallery as well as facilities for short residential courses. Many of the courses offered are concerned with practical arts and crafts skills and with art appreciation topics such as English country houses, furniture and paintings. There are also courses in porcelain and furniture restoration. Fees range from about £46 (£28 for non-residents) for Friday evening to Sunday lunch, to about £145 (£80) for a week, Saturday evening to Saturday breakfast (1986).

Geoffrey Godden's Study Meetings
Geoffrey Godden, 17–19 Crescent Road, Worthing, Sussex (Worthing (0903) 35958).
Mr Godden is well known to porcelain collectors as a leading authority in the field, and he shares his knowledge at various meetings throughout the year, also inviting guest speakers to lecture on their own areas. His educational activities involve non-residential weekend study meetings on chosen subjects (e.g. 18th-century porcelains, Staffordshire etc), and residential weekends with a broader emphasis. Detailed information about subjects and dates for 1986/7 can be obtained from the address above.

Inchbald School of Design
37 Eaton Gate, London SW1W 9BA (01-730 5508).
The Inchbald school arranges short courses in many areas related to design and decorative art. One of particular interest to readers is the English Furniture Course, five days spent studying all aspects of furniture, including detection of fakes, and appreciation of conservation (1986 fee: £305 + VAT).

The Institute of Industrial Archaeology
Ironbridge Gorge Museum, The Wharfage, Ironbridge, Telford, Shropshire (Ironbridge (095245) 2751/3522).
This Institute, in association with the Ironbridge Gorge Museum and the University of Birmingham, organises research and course programmes which aim to advance the understanding of industrial history and archaeology, and provide the professional skills necessary for recording, conserving and managing industrial monuments and collections of artifacts. Many of its courses are thus specialised in areas not of immediate concern to readers, but the odd exception does occur. In 1985 courses were organised on the subjects of Decorative Paint Finishes, Coalport Ceramics and the Design of Decorative Glass. A programme listing all the courses organised by the Institute is produced annually and is available on request.

Looking at Art
18 Markham Square, London SW3 4UY (01-589 0037).
Director: Penelope Le Fanu Hughes.
One-day seminars and study days are offered which provide an introduction to a particular aspect of art, usually related to an important current exhibition. Morning lectures are followed by a visit to the exhibition, accompanied by guides, during the afternoon. The groups are informal and are led by graduate art historians who are also experienced lecturers. The fee for the day, usually about £15, includes transport and entrance to the exhibition, lunch and coffee. Short courses, and study tours outside London and on the Continent, are also arranged.

Sotheby's
30 Oxford Street, London W1 (01-408 1100).
Sotheby's Specialised Programmes
Duration: 5 days. Fees: £150–£180 (1986).
Programmes of lectures and visits exploring various areas of interest, some with a topical relevance to a current exhibition. Recent programmes included Homage to Barcelona, which sought to provide a context for the Hayward Gallery exhibition, and Treasures of Imperial China, which concentrated on later Chinese works of art.
Collector's Weeks
Fee: £150.
Series of talks by Sotheby's experts, illustrated with objects or slides, devised for collectors or would-be collectors with limited budgets.
Conservation Weeks
Fee: about £175, excluding accommodation.
Recognised experts from major museums and institutions advise owners and curators about the conservation of fine and decorative art, stressing when to leave well alone and seek professional advice. This programme was last held at Arundel Castle, the ancestral home of the Dukes of Norfolk, providing a unique opportunity to study the conservation of objects in their normal environment.
Buccleuch Studies
Duration: 5 days. Fee: about £300 (excluding accommodation).
Series of courses on patronage and the arts, based on the private collections of the Dukes of Buccleuch and Queensbury at two of the family's historic homes, Bowhill in the Scottish borders, and Boughton in Northamptonshire. The course may be booked either including or excluding accommodation.

University of London Department of Extra-Mural Studies: Summer Schools
26 Russell Square, London WC1 (01-636 8000 ext 3850).
Fees: £140–£145 per week inclusive (1985).
Apply by March 31.
Various residential courses are offered in a wide range of academic subjects, usually including some of interest to readers. The courses involve one or two weeks of the summer holidays, and in 1986 took place at Westonbirt School in Gloucestershire and Wye College, Kent.

West Dean College
West Dean, Nr Chichester, West Sussex (Singleton (024363) 301).
Set at the foot of the Sussex Downs in a fine Edwardian mansion, West Dean College is the home of the Edward James Foundation. In addition to its well-known restoration courses, it offers a variety of short courses for weekends or five or seven days in 100 art, craft and music subjects. A programme is issued three times a year. Although the emphasis is on crafts and restoration, past subjects have included weekends on The English Country House and Preservation and Conservation of Historic Landscapes, Decorative Arts, Art Appreciation and Music Appreciation. Fees range from £43 for non-resident weekend to £222 for seven days residential.

Courses Abroad

(See also 'Guide to Tours', pp. 31–33.)

Art History Abroad
5 Wetherby Place, South Kensington, London SW7 (01-244 8164).
Duration: 4 or 6 weeks. Fees: 4-week summer course £792 (1986); 6-week winter course £1170 (1986).
'A course run by young people for young people' with 'all connotations of stuffiness removed'. Art History Abroad offers a four-week summer course and a six-week winter course which give students the opportunity to study Italian art in Italy. The courses are designed for those taking 'A' levels, pre-university students, and undergraduates, and the study trip is described as 'intensive and yet informal and friendly'. The first week of each course is spent in London, and is devoted to lectures and seminars occupying about four hours a day. Thereafter the time is divided between Rome, Florence, Venice and Siena, visiting galleries and monuments, and examining styles in Italian art. Drawing classes are available for those who wish to pursue a practical interest. The Summer course takes place in August; the Winter course February/March. Fees include the return flight, accommodation, travel in Italy, museum entrance charges, and tuition.

The British Institute of Florence
Palazzo Lanfredini, Lungarno Guicciardini 9, 50125 Florence, Italy (Florence 28 40 31).
The British Institute in Florence offers short courses in History of Art subjects, as well as Italian language courses. History of Art may be studied as an 'A' level, and this requires attendance for a 20-week session with two hours of tuition per day. In addition to this, beginners must attend a ten-week session in advance. 1986 fees for these courses, which run from October to December and January to June, are £1250 for the whole year and £840 for January to June. Other courses available include four weeks on either Italian Renaissance or High Renaissance, Mannerism and Baroque. These comprise a series of lectures and conducted tours of museums, galleries and churches. They are offered regularly throughout the year, and cost £115 (1986). All are taught in English. These fees do not include accommodation, which may however be arranged through the Institute.

John Hall's Pre-University Interim Course
48 Beaufort Mansion, Beaufort Street, London SW3 (01-584 7335).
Director: John Hall.
Duration: October–March, 2 terms.
Fees: £3660 (1986/7).
This is the long established and widely renowned Venice-based course much favoured by incipient Oxbridge freshmen. Now that the 'seventh term entry' examination for Oxford has been abolished, the course has been extended to take advantage of the autumn term as well as the spring. The autumn term is divided into consecutive periods spent in Avignon, Paris and Bruges. The spring term is based in Venice with a 10-day visit to Florence and perhaps Rome. While the course is

planned as a comprehensive whole, students may enrol for a single term if they prefer (fees for one term: £1910 Autumn; £2040 Spring).

The formal aim of the course is 'to open the eyes, ears, intellect and imagination to various aspects of our European cultural tradition'. The course looks at French, Netherlandish and Italian art in the context of contemporary music and related topics such as artists' materials and techniques, restoration, the art market, and public and private galleries. Tuition takes the form of illustrated lectures given by various experienced lecturers who are well known in their fields. In addition there are talks on music, and opportunities for drawing, painting, photography, and various theatrical activities as well as language tuition. There is an optional test at the end of the course, and successful students receive a certificate. Fees include accommodation, which is arranged for all students, and all travel except return from Italy. *Requirements:* the course is for all school leavers with an interest in art history.

Istituto per L'Arte e il Restauro
Palazzo Spinelli, Borgo S. Croce 10, 50122 Florence, Italy (Florence (010 39 55) 24 48 08/09).
The institute organises academic courses 'on a professional-technical level' in subjects such as the Antiques Trade, Furnishing and Interior Design, and especially restoration of various kinds. There are two-year courses, one-year courses (October to June), and also summer courses of four weeks, which include History of Art among the more practical restoration courses. All classes are taught in Italian, but are open to Italian and foreign students. Language courses are available to assist those whose command of Italian is not up to scratch. Fees for 1986/7 range from L400.000–L800.000 per month for summer courses to L270.000 per month (9 months) for a 1-year course and L360.000 per month (18 months) for a 2-year course. There is an additional registration fee of L350.000 to pay in each case.

The Renaissance in Italy
Correspondence: 23 Georgian House, 10 Bury Street, St. James's, London SW1Y 6AB (01-930 5914).
Director: Charles McCorquodale.
Duration: 3 weeks. Fee: £2625 (1986).
This is a sophisticated and intelligent course for an international clientèle of all ages who require comfort and high academic standards. No academic qualifications are required. Through an intensive and varied programme of lectures in English, and visits to museums, palaces, churches and villas (sometimes when closed to the public), Renaissance art and architecture 1350–1600 is presented against a historical, musical and literary background. Demonstrations of art techniques fundamental to many of the works studied, such as fresco painting, marble cutting and bronze casting, are given by contemporary artists. Interior decoration, the decorative arts, gardens and even dance and costume are studied, and the course culminates in a spectacular performance of Renaissance court dance in costume. All lectures are held in the 16th-century Corsini Palace and its gardens, once home of Bonnie Prince Charlie. There are receptions in Florentine palaces, one weekend is usually spent in a country house in Tuscany, and there are other optional visits to notable Renaissance towns.

The course's price reflects its high standards and the inclusion of half-pension at a first-class hotel with swimming pool and roof restaurant, all transport, lectures, admission fees and many extras. Groups are limited to twenty participants, and the course normally runs in spring/summer and autumn.

In addition, Charles McCorquodale offers several shorter art programmes annually in Florence, Venice and Scotland.

COURSES IN ARTS ADMINISTRATION

The City University: Department of Arts Policy and Management
Level 12, Frobisher Crescent, Barbican, Silk Street, London EC2Y 8HB (01-628 5641/2).
MA in Arts Administration
Duration: 1 year (full-time); 2 years (part-time). Fee: £1775 full-time/£430 part-time (1986/7).
Students take four modules of study, then complete a long study on a chosen topic. Study of Government Framework is compulsory, and optional modules include European Arts, Popular Arts, Law, Policy Making in the Arts, Visual Arts, and several others.
Diploma in Arts Administration
Duration: 1 year (October–June). Fee: £1775 (1986/7).
Course includes Arts Management, Finance and Book-keeping, Law, Marketing and Publicity, and Policy Making in the Arts. It is designed for those with some experience of arts administration. This course is offered in conjunction with the Arts Council from whom bursaries may be available.

MA courses are also available in Librarianship and Art Administration (for qualified librarians), Arts Management in Education (for those involved in the promotion of arts in education), and Museum and Gallery Administration (for those with experience of management of museums or galleries in the public or private sector).

Requirements for all are a good first degree or equivalent with several years' experience. Intensive short professional courses are available, and there are also facilities for research.

University of Leicester: Department of Museum Studies.
105 Princess Road East, Leicester (Leicester (0533) 553560).
Graduate Certificate in Museum Studies
Duration: 1 year (Oct–June).
This is a vocational course for graduates who intend to make a career in the museum profession. The course combines the theoretical study of museums, their function, management and maintenance, with practical work including attachment to museums for short periods. *Requirements:* a degree in an approved subject, and clear evidence of vocational intention. There are also two-year MA and MSc courses in Museum Studies, which allow for some independent study. Closing date for applications: 1 February.

University of Manchester: Department of History of Art
Oxford Road, Manchester M13 (Manchester (061) 273 3333).
Diploma in Art Gallery and Museum Studies
Duration: 1 year (Oct–June). 20 places.
This is a postgraduate course which is vocational, training people for the museum profession and extending the skills of those already working in museums. The course links theoretical aspects of gallery and museum studies with practical experience, and includes an academic course in the applied arts. Students learn about the administration of galleries and museums – documentation, conservation, finance, planning, security, management – and the ways in which they relate to the public – educational services, exhibitions and displays, and so on. Practical work includes a project which may be the mounting of a travelling exhibition, or creation of some educational facility, and in the spring of every year a major public exhibition is mounted by the students at the Whitworth Art Gallery. Students spend four weeks working at a gallery or museum somewhere in the UK. There is also a dissertation (7–10 000 words) to be written. *Requirements:* applicants must be graduates of an approved university.

COURSES IN RESTORATION

Most full-time courses offer a 'Diploma' to successful students, but there is no standardisation of such qualifications – they are as good as the reputation of the establishment that provides them. BTEC (Business and Technicians Education Council, 01-388 3288) are attempting to provide standardisation for some of the courses, so some prospectuses may mention a BTEC General Diploma, or Higher Diploma.

As well as the courses mentioned here, many local education authorities offer evening classes in restoration and upholstery.

Full-Time Courses

Camberwell School of Art and Crafts
Peckham Road, London SE5 8UF (01-703 0987).
Diploma in Paper Conservation
Duration: 2 years.
Candidates must be aged 16 years or over, possess at least three suitably graded 'O' level passes including English language, and demonstrate evidence of craft ability.
Higher Diploma in Paper Conservation
Duration: 2 years
Opportunity to specialise in the conservation of either archival and library materials, or prints and drawings. Candidates must be aged 18 or over, and normally possess a Diploma in Paper Conservation. Applications from mature students with some conservation work experience will be considered.

Both the above courses are nationally recognised and validated by BTEC.

Cambridge University: Hamilton Kerr Institute
Whittlesford, Cambridge (Cambridge (0223) 832040).
Certificate in the Conservation of Easel Paintings
Duration: 3 years.
The course covers the conservation and restoration of easel paintings, art history with emphasis on European easel paintings, the history of painting techniques, related science, environmental causes of deterioration and their control, and technical examination using modern techniques. The practical side of the course predominates, and much of the theory is taught on the job, as well as through lectures and seminars. Successful stu-

dents may opt for a fourth-year attachment to the Institute's studio in London, or another conservation laboratory. *Requirements:* candidates normally need a first degree or equivalent qualification in Fine Arts, History of Art, Physics or Chemistry. Normal age of entrants 21–25.

City and Guilds of London Art School
124 Kennington Park Road, London SE11 4DJ (01-735 2306).
An unusual diploma course is offered in the Restoration of Wood, Stone and Allied Polychrome Finishes. This is a three-year course, but requires a foundation year as well, so is actually a four-year commitment. It is designed to prepare students for work in the conservation departments of museums and art galleries, and in the field of historic buildings and monuments. It includes ornament, life drawing, lettering, modelling, casting, carving, gesso, gilding, lacquer and related subjects. BTEC General and Higher Diploma courses (2 years) are also available in restoration, carving and polychrome.

Courtauld Institute of Art
20 Portman Square, London W1
(01-935 9292/5).
Diploma in Conservation of Paintings
Duration: 3 years. Fees: UK students £1680 p.a.; overseas students £4670 p.a. (1986/7). 3–5 places.
This respected course is open to graduates in art, art history or the natural sciences. In the first year, lectures complementary to previous educational experience are given, along with those on painting and conservation methods and materials. The rest of the course concentrates on practical conservation, and students are examined on all aspects of their work before diplomas are awarded.

Gateshead Technical College
Durham Road, Gateshead, Tyne and Wear NE9 5BN (Tyneside (091) 477 0524).
Higher Diploma in Conservation of Fine Art
Duration: 2 years. 12 places.
This is a well-established course with a good reputation. Students specialise in either the conservation of easel paintings, or the conservation of prints, drawings and watercolours. The course is designed to 'provide a thorough grounding in theory and practice of the examination and conservation of fine art, combined with a study of sciences related to conservation'. The scientific aspect of conservation is stressed, and students are examined in chemistry and physics at the end of their first year. Three-quarters of a student's time is spent on practical work. *Requirements:* minimum two 'A' levels or equivalent in art and a science, a good command of English and age over 18. Practical aptitude is essential.

London College of Furniture
41 Commercial Road, London E1 1LA (01-247 1953).
A variety of courses relating to furniture restoration are offered by this ILEA-backed college. Furniture Restoration, and Carving and Gilding with Turning, are two recent additions to the list. Both are advanced courses, and are intended for those who have completed at least two years in this field, and wish to specialise. The courses aim to develop specialist skills to the professional level necessary to manage a restoration or craft workshop.

Arthur Moore School of Restoration
3 Hove Park Villas, Brighton, Sussex (Brighton (0273) 25380).
Duration: 1 year. Fees: £3000 (1986/7).
A course is offered in the restoration of furniture with special interest in English clocks and barometers. Arthur Moore runs an antique restoration business in Hove, and takes on three students a year, teaching them on customers' goods. Each student keeps a full record of his work illustrated with photographs showing techniques. Apart from the practical work, the students also visit local fairs, auctions and shops to build up an idea of quality, authenticity and value. English clocks and barometers are studied, and their workings and practical repair explained. No academic qualifications are required. All previous students have found employment in good workshops.

Rycotewood College: Department of Fine Craftsmanship and Design
Thame, Oxfordshire, OX9 2AF (Thame (084421) 2501/2/3).
A two-year BTEC Diploma course is offered in fine craftsmanship and design, which aims 'to provide a thorough grounding in the technology, theory, practice and manipulation of wood, metal and plastics so that students can achieve a high degree of craftsmanship . . . and an understanding of design problems and their solution'. It is a broad course, but includes furniture restoration, and provides a good foundation for later specialisation in restoration. *Requirements:* four 'O' levels.

A one-year Higher Certificate course is also offered which enables its graduates to establish themselves as designer-makers of bespoke handmade furniture, many of whom will carry out restoration commissions. *Requirements:* BTEC Diploma or equivalent experience.

South East Conservation Centre
Old Brewery Yard, High Street, Hastings, East Sussex (Hastings (0424) 431157).
Duration: 3 years. Fees: £3400 p.a. (1986). 4 places.
Specialising in fine art restoration and conservation, gilding and lacquer work, the Centre offers a two year training programme in the restoration and conservation of easel paintings. The basic requirement is an art school foundation course but most students are graduates in art or history of art. A diploma is awarded to successful candidates based equally on their general progress, the final examination and a thesis.

The Tate Gallery
Millbank, London SW1P 4RG (01-821 1313 ext. 295).
The gallery runs four-year postgraduate courses in conservation in conjunction with the Courtauld Institute of Art (see above). They are traineeships and, as such, students receive a stipend for the duration of their training. Only British/Commonwealth subjects are eligible. The first year is spent at the Courtauld, attending full time; the second at the Tate Gallery with one day per week at the Courtauld during term time; and the third and fourth at the Tate Gallery. Students are assessed at the end of their third year for the Courtauld Diploma and successful candidates complete a further year at the Tate Gallery. Two students in painting are taken every other year and one in sculpture every fourth year. The next competition for both painting and sculpture will take place in 1988.

The Textile Conservation Centre
Apartment 22, Hampton Court Palace, East Molesey, Surrey KT8 9AU (01-977 4943).
Diploma Course in Textile Conservation
Duration: 3 years. 6 places (split 50:50 British: foreign students).
This highly regarded postgraduate course is held in conjunction with the Courtauld Institute of Art. Emphasis is laid on preventive conservation science and record-keeping (an essential part of conservation), and practical experience is gained by working on historic pieces of every kind. The Courtauld's facilities are available to students. The first year involves an intensive programme of lectures and seminars on all aspects of textiles. The second year provides for practical conservation experience. In the last year a research project is undertaken. This course is high powered and intensive, and not aimed at the dilettante. *Requirements:* applicants must have 'O' level Chemistry.

Victoria and Albert Museum
South Kensington, London SW7 (01-589 6371).
Duration: 4 years. 4 places.
A four-year diploma course in conservation is offered, and students may specialise in textiles, metalwork, sculpture, stained glass, furniture, etc. Only 'O' levels are essential, but because of demand most students have a degree in Art, Art History or a natural science and some experience in their specialism. The course begins again every four years; the next new intake will be in 1987.

West Dean College
West Dean, Nr Chichester, West Sussex (Singleton (024363) 301).
Duration: 1 year. Fees: £5100 (residents), £3576 (non-residents) (1986/7).
At West Dean one-year professional restoration courses are offered in three areas: antique furniture, clocks and ceramics. Established by the BADA in association with the Edward James Foundation at West Dean, they aim to pass on the skills of the finest restorers to a new generation of craftsmen. The best tutors are engaged, and the predominantly practical skills that are taught are balanced with lectures in science, history of furniture/clocks/ceramics, business practice and other related subjects. Only a small number of students are accepted each year, not only from Britain, and they are expected to do a further two years' apprenticeship before working independently. Students work on good pieces which are usually brought in by dealers. *Requirements:* There are no formal requirements for the courses, but proven manual dexterity and aptitude in relevant crafts are important, along with genuine interest. Also available: three-year Apprenticeship in the Making of Early Musical Instruments.

Short or Part-Time Courses

Caroline Barkes
The Garden Flat, 74 Harwood Road, London SW6 (01-731 1356).
Simple China Mending Course
Fees: £75 (1986).
Caroline Barkes offers a basic grounding in china mending. The idea is that in five consecutive half-day sessions beginners can learn how to do practical repairs rather than being rushed too

quickly into the complex techniques required for invisible restoration. A more advanced class is also available.

Touching Up Picture Frames
Fees: £45–£80 (1986).
An unusual idea, but again practical. Lasting one or two days, depending on experience of china mending techniques, students learn how to repair and touch up moulded gilt picture frames.

Peter and Frances Binnington
65 St. John's Hill, London SW11 (01-223 9192); 39 Blackmores Grove, Teddington, Middlesex (01-977 2570).
Water Gilding Courses
Duration: 5 days. Fees: £150 + VAT (1986). 8 places.
A practical course is offered, furnishing students with the basic skills in water gilding and its application to carved giltwood mirror frames, picture frames and decorated furniture. Anyone from museum conservators to interested laymen may attend. More advanced courses are offered to those who have completed the first.

Colin Campbell: International School of French Polishing and Wood Finishing
Sunnythwaite, Penton, Carlisle CA6 5RZ (Nicholforest (022877) 262).
Wood Finishing Course
Duration: 4 days. Fees: £125 (inc. materials).
Colin Campbell, a member of the Guild of Master Craftsmen, teaches antique polishing, French polishing, wax polishing, preparation and staining in a relaxed workshop environment. The courses run from March to November and are residential, accommodation (not included in fees) being offered at local hostelries. Students come from all walks of life and include not only people in the restoration business, but also (to quote Mr Campbell) 'doctors, bank managers and even housewives'. A video and accompanying workshop manual are also available for £35.

CoSIRA
141 Castle Street, Salisbury, Wiltshire SP1 3TP (Salisbury (0722) 336255) and at 32 county offices in England.
Duration: 2 days–1 week. Fees: (subsidised rate) £25–£120.
The Council for Small Industries in Rural Areas give assistance to small businesses. One form of this is the provision of short, intensive courses allowing busy craftsmen to acquire an additional skill. Most courses offered are therefore technical, but those concerning aspects of furniture restoration, such as woodturning, veneering, gilding and carving, may be of interest to readers. *Requirements:* these courses are intended for craftsmen with at least three years' experience or a City and Guilds Certificate, and for cabinet makers or upholsterers wishing to extend their skills.

Dillington College of Adult Education
Dillington Park, Ilminster, Somerset TA19 9DT (Ilminster (04605) 2427/3875).
Duration: 1 week. Fee: £148 (residents), £82 (non-residents).
Dillington is a residential college for adults, offering courses in a variety of arts and crafts. Relevant here are the one-week courses in China Restoration, Painting on Restored China, and Furniture Restoration. These are aimed at the keen amateur who wishes to be able to restore his or her porcelain or furniture at home, and teach basic skills. There is also a more advanced China Restoration course for whose who already have a basic training.

Missenden Summer School
Missenden Abbey, Great Missenden, Bucks (Great Missenden (02406) 4037).
Duration: 6 days. Fees: £180 (residents), £65 (non-residents).
Missenden Summer School offers study holidays in rural surroundings during the month of August. Amongst a wealth of craft workshops, language, music and drama courses are one or two on restoration. These include Ceramic Restoration, Antique Furniture Restoration, Practical Restoration of Antique and Modern Upholstered Furniture, and Craft Bookbinding.

The Roger Newton School of Decorative Finishes
27 Talina Centre, Bagley's Lane, London SW6 (01-736 1658)
Courses in Painting or Gilding Furniture
Duration: 1 week. Fees: Furniture Painting £175; Furniture Gilding £195 (non-residential). 10 places.
Roger Newton provides 'intensive training for anyone of a practical disposition' in either painting or gilding furniture. Trained at Colefax and Fowler, he ran a workshop in London for many years, and has now set up to teach his skills. The courses each extend from Monday to Friday throughout the year (except August), and provide a history of the art of gilding or painting, as well as knowledge of furniture preparation and restoration, and of the application of the decorative finishes themselves. Weekend courses may also be available in the future.

The Old Rectory, Fittleworth
Pulborough, W. Sussex
(Fittleworth (079882) 306).
Duration: 5–7 days. Fees: £68–£134 + VAT (residents); £42.50–£84 + VAT (non-residents) (1986).
The Old Rectory Adult Education College was started over 20 years ago 'to provide a meeting place to which young people could come'. The courses are, however, not restricted to any age group, and retired people are especially welcomed. The set-up is informal, and run on a family basis. Amongst the courses offered are those on China Restoration, Furniture Restoration and Upholstery and Chair Seating. Beginners and more advanced students are welcome.

Partridge Restorations
Peaton Lodge, Nr Craven Arms, Shropshire SY7 9DL
(Munslow (058476) 639)
Beginners and Advanced Porcelain Restoration
Duration: 4/5 days. Fees: £148 and £250.
All aspects of porcelain restoration taught.
Beginners Furniture Restoration: Polishing and Veneering
Duration: 3 days. Fees: £115.
Jane and Ian Way are professional restorers of porcelain and furniture. They also offer long weekend courses from March to November with small classes and expert individual tuition. Courses are non-residential, though comfortable local bed and breakfast accommodation can be arranged. Lunch, tea and coffee are included in the course fees.

Restorations Unlimited
Pinkney Park, Malmesbury, Wiltshire (Malmesbury (0666) 840888).
Fees: £80 (non-residential).
Regular weekend courses are offered in ceramic restoration and antique furniture restoration. A maximum of three people are accepted per course, and learn under the personal tuition of David Ellis, a professional restorer.

Sandra and Malcolm Rowney: 'Sitting Pretty'
Victoria Farmhouse, Private Road, Earsham, Norfolk NR35 2W (Bungay (0986) 4360).
Craft Weekends
Fees: £98–£196 (residential) (1986).
Courses are offered in various crafts including furniture restoration, porcelain restoration and upholstery (4-day upholstery courses also available) over weekends and bank holidays. Prices are inclusive of farmhouse or other local accommodation, 'good home cooking with local specialities', and use of tools and basic materials. Tutors are local professionals, and will teach beginners as well as those with some experience. Classes are held in a converted table block near the farmhouse. Students may also attend for one day only, and the fee for this (non-residential) is £25 (1986).

Jana Stuart Jones Antique Ceramic Restoration Courses
The Pound, Stawell, Bridgwater, Somerset (Chilton Polden (0278) 722023).
Jana Stuart Jones is a professional restorer, and has devised two courses for those wishing to study ceramic restoration seriously. The courses are intensive and should be supported by further practice at home. Only five people are taken on at a time, to give maximum individual tuition. There is a two-week course (10 days of tuition 9.30–5.30) on which students are taught the fundamental principles and practice of repair (£300 non-residents). A twelve-week course spread over a six-month period is also offered. This is for 'serious students wishing to make a career in restoration'; the course is arranged in three blocks of two weeks and two blocks of three weeks of intensive tuition, interspersed with practice at home on set work. Accommodation in the village can be arranged.

West Dean College
West Dean, Nr Chichester, West Sussex (Singleton (024363) 301).
Duration: one weekend or 5 or 7 days. Fees: £68–£158 (resident).
Many short courses in the arts and crafts and music are held at West Dean. These include topics such as Caring for Antique Furniture, and Restoration of Antique Books. Apply to the above address for full details and current programme of short courses.

Useful Addresses

The Victoria and Albert Museum (Conservation Department), South Kensington, London SW7 (01-589 3371).
The United Kingdom Institute for Conservation (UKIC), c/o the Conservation Department, Tate Gallery, Millbank, London SW1
Both of these publish lists of courses in conservation which are available on application.
See also addresses (such as BAFRA, IPC, Crafts Council) listed at the front of this book.

GUIDE TO TOURS

Elizabeth Pile

This guide is intended for those wishing to make cultural sightseeing the main objective of their holiday. It is divided into three sections: firstly those companies catering specifically for clients with a special interest in art, architecture or archaeology; secondly those companies specialising in travel to one particular area of the world; and finally a selection of escorted tours from the many large holiday companies which operate on a worldwide basis, without specialisation. Destinations covered include almost all parts of the world of cultural interest, and the tours range from a day in London to 3 or 4 weeks in China, India, Canada or Latin America.

NB Limitations of space make it impossible to include all relevant information, and readers should therefore treat this as a general guide, and refer to the individual brochures produced by each company for further details. In particular, please note the following:

1. Except where specifically indicated, all holidays and prices mentioned are taken from brochures for 1986. They are intended only to give some idea of the holidays offered and prices charged by each company, and there is no guarantee that the same holidays and prices will be available in subsequent years.

2. Prices given here are those quoted by each company as the minimum, i.e. per person in a twin-bedded room. There is great variation in what each price includes – generally, return transport from London, accommodation throughout the tour, and at least some meals are included, but other expenses (such as transfer costs, further meals, entrance fees and drinks) may or may not be. Quality of accommodation also varies widely, from tents to luxurious hotels. Readers should therefore be careful when comparing prices.

3. In a few cases tours may be taken at any time of the year, but usually only a limited number of possible commencement dates are offered, and occasionally the tour is a one-off arrangement. Since most tours mentioned here are for 1986, the dates available have only rarely been indicated.

SUBJECT SPECIALISTS

A. C. E. Study Tours
Association for Cultural Exchange, Babraham, Cambridge, CB2 4AP (0223 835 055)
Study Tours offers a huge range of study-holidays, catering for many different tastes and pockets, and including destinations as far apart as Iceland, Tibet and America. Each tour is accompanied by a lecturer, and the emphasis is on reaching interesting or unusual sights in relative comfort, rather than 'doing' the more conventional sights in luxury. As well as exotic destinations such as Bali, Java and Sumatra (22 days, from £1520), Sri Lanka (17 days, from £950), or Ottoman Turkey (11 days, from £590), there are many holidays in Europe, for example a journey along the ancient pilgrimage route to Compostela (15 days, from £650), an exploration of Minoan civilisation in Crete and Santorini (15 days, from £590), or a tour of the Loire Châteaux (9 days, from £285). There are also a number of fascinating day, weekend or week-long courses held within Britain — such as a tour of some of London's historic buildings (1 day, £5), or 10 days spent studying the art, architecture and civilisation of the Shetland Islands (from £250).

Detail from 'The Great Temple of Aboo Simble, Nubia', lithograph after David Roberts R.A. (1796-1864), from *Egypt & Nubia*, by David Roberts, 1846-49. Two copies of this book were sold at Christie's, 16 April 1986, for £4320 and £5400 respectively.

Cambridge Foreign Study Tours
University of Cambridge Board of Extra-Mural Studies, Madingley Hall, Madingley, Cambridge CB3 8AQ (0954 210 636)
As one would expect, these are fascinating but definitely educational tours, providing small groups led by expert tutors, with detailed study of the areas visited. The 1986 brochure offers 9 tours for those interested in art, architecture or archaeology. There is an unusual tour of Roman North Africa, crossing mountains and deserts from the Atlantic Ocean to Carthage (modern Tunis) and studying ancient Roman towns and forts (20 days, partly camping, from about £775). Another tour traverses Transylvania and Moldavia to study the ecclesiastical and military architecture of Romania (15 days, from £495). Other tours offer Renaissance art and architecture in Venice (9 days, from £430); the archaeology of Sardinia (15 days, from £495); Ancient Peru (20 days, from £1375); or Ancient China seen through the lives of its greatest artists (20 days, from £1659). The emphasis for all tours is on modest comfort, not luxury.

Christie's Tours
21–25 South Lambeth Road, London SW8 1SX (01-582 9990), or David B. Mitchell & Co, 200 Madison Avenue, New York, NY 10016, USA
Christie's arranges escorted tours enabling 'small, select groups' to visit some of Britain's country houses (including properties not normally open to the public), browse among London's best antique shops and markets and experience Christie's from behind the scenes. Each tour usually lasts 11 days, beginning and ending in London, and includes, in addition to 7 or so days travelling by private coach to visit country houses outside London, a guided sightseeing tour of London itself, visits to Osterley Park House, Covent Garden, and perhaps the Wallace Collection (all in London), and a cocktail reception at Christie's London headquarters to meet their experts. Costs are relatively high, but the tours do give participants a unique opportunity to see private houses and collections and to meet Christie's staff. Each tour takes a particular part of Britain or a specific subject area as its theme; those offered for late 1986 include the East Shires (October 8–18, from £2100), the 'Heart of England' (October 16–26, from £1975), Yorkshire (October 18–28, from £2100), and an Old Masters Study Tour (November 26–December 6, from £1950). Tours can also be arranged for private groups and individuals.

Contemporary Art Society
20 John Islip Street, London SW1P 4LL
(01-821 5323)
The Contemporary Art Society is a charity which fosters contemporary art and uses its funds to acquire works by living artists for gift or loan to public collections. It also organises tours abroad for its members, the profits from which are added to its purchasing funds. The tours offered vary each year; in 1986 there was a 10-day tour to Israel, including visits to important private collections as well as to sights both ancient and modern open to the public, a concert, and meetings with local artists and collectors (from £595). Another 1986 tour offered a weekend in Vienna to coincide with the British Festival there, including the Contemporary Art Society's own exhibition of contemporary British art, and museums, commercial galleries, architecture, private collections and the Vienna Boys' Choir (4 days, from £325). Previous destinations have included Russia, Mexico, Australia, Dublin and Stockholm. Although only three or four tours are organised each year, the advantage of the Society's special contacts make each one a unique experience.

Page & Moy
136–140 London Road, Leicester LE2 1EN
(0533 552521)
Page & Moy offers two types of holiday of interest to art-lovers: 'Castles, Country Houses and Stately Homes', and 'Ancient History Tours', the latter accompanied by a knowledgeable guest lecturer. All are very popular and quickly become fully booked up. The 'Castles, Country Houses and Stately Homes' tours are essentially short trips (5–7 nights) to Europe, each with a particular architectural theme, such as 'Palladian Villas of Northern Italy' (7 nights, from £349), 'Treasures of Burgundy' (6 nights, from £189), or 'Castles and Country Houses of Hungary' (7 nights, from £349). The Ancient History Tours, more archaeological in emphasis, include both European and more distant destinations — such as 'Ancient Egypt' (14 nights, including a Nile cruise, from £879), 'Ancient Turkey' (9 nights, from £549), 'Pompeii, Herculaneum and Rome' (7 nights, from £299), and the very popular 'Roman Provence' (7 nights, from £339). All tours are carefully scheduled to allow relaxation, wining and dining as well as sightseeing; accommodation is comfortable rather than luxurious; and all are ac-

companied by a courier. There are also occasional long weekends studying country houses in Britain (such as 'Lincolnshire Country Houses', 4 nights from £229).

Grand Tours/Specialtours
2 Chester Row, London SW1W 9JH
(01-730 2297/3138 and 373 0333)
Grand Tours and Specialtours are two well-known cultural tour organisers who have recently merged operations. Their combined knowledge and experience provide a wide range of luxurious and very imaginative holidays aimed specifically at those interested in art and architecture. Most of the tours are accompanied throughout by a lecturer with specialist knowledge of the area, and often the sights visited are not normally open to the public. The 1986 brochure includes, as well as the obligatory tour of 'Princely India' (17 nights, from £1995) and long weekend in Venice (5 nights, from £730), several more unusual themes and destinations — 10 nights in the Yemen Arab Republic (from £1735); 14 nights in Algeria (from £1255); an investigation of King Ludwig II's castles (5 nights, from £635); or a tour exploring not Renaissance but Etruscan Italy (9 nights, from £876 — there are tours for the Renaissance enthusiast too); or for the less adventurous, the Glasgow Collections (4 nights, from £315), or West Wales (4 nights, from £285). Some of the tours are open only to members of certain organisations, such as the Friends of the Royal Academy, or the National Art-Collections Fund, but all are so enticing that the membership fee seems a small price to pay.

Prospect Art Tours
10 Barley Mow Passage, Chiswick, London W4 4PH
(01-995 2163/4)
Prospect Art Tours is one of the best-known companies catering specifically for those interested in the visual arts. All of their tours are accompanied by an art historian or archaeologist; accommodation is comfortable rather than luxurious; and the schedules are carefully planned to allow participants to learn as much as possible about the area visited (the tour leader often gives evening lectures as well as guiding the group during the day) without becoming too exhausted to remember it all. Of the 100 or so tours offered in the 1986 brochure, almost half are to Italy; there are also tours in Great Britain, Western and Eastern Europe, and other areas of interest. The Italian tours are very varied — some concentrate on special topics, such as Byzantine Mosaics (6 nights, from £418), others on particular cities or regions (Western Sicily, 7 nights, from £448; The Veneto, 7 nights, from £421). Tours in Britain are 3 or 4 days long, each having a specific theme and forming part of a series, so that a particular interest can be followed over several years. Thus the 'English Romanesque' tour (3 days, from £99) forms part of a 'Medieval' series; the 'Gloucestershire Gardens' tour (4 days, from £156) is one of the 'Historic Gardens' series. The other European tours also follow particular cities, areas or themes, such as 'Impressionism and Beyond: Modern Art in Paris' (4 nights, from £245), or 'Prague at Christmas' (6 nights, from £378). A few tours outside Europe are also offered, with 1986 destinations including Turkey, China and Washington (the latter, 7 nights for £673, coinciding with the 'Treasure Houses of Britain' exhibition there).

Serenissima/Heritage/Voyages Jules Verne
Heritage Travel Ltd, 21 Dorset Square, London NW1 5PG (01-730 9841/01-723 6556)
Serenissima and Heritage both offer a wide selection of tours devised specifically for those interested in the arts. They differ in that Serenissima provides expert lecturers as well as tour managers, smaller groups (maximum 22 people), and very full programmes, while Heritage combines lecturer and tour guide in one person, and allows slightly larger groups and more free time on its tours. Between them in 1986 they offer about 50 tours, in Europe, the Middle East, Asia and Peru, ranging from 5 to 22 days in length, with prices starting at around £400. These tours are very carefully planned; accommodation is usually top-quality, and the guide-lecturers are experts in their subjects and experienced travellers in the countries concerned. Among the 1986 tours in Europe are 'The Painted Churches of Rumania' (Heritage, 11 days, from £490); Western Turkey (Serenissima, 16 days, from £1525), and Byzantine Venice and Ravenna (Serenissima, 8 days, from £1195). Further afield there are 'From the Tigris to the Euphrates', 12 days exploring ancient cities such as Baghdad, Babylon, Ninevah and Ur (Serenissima, from £1825); 'A Passage Through India' (Serenissima, 18 days, from £1995); Peru (Serenissima, 18 days, from £2495); 'The Silk Road: Kashgar to Kumbum' (Serenissima, 22 days, from £2935); Jerusalem (Heritage, 8 days from £850), and many more. There are also Heritage walking holidays, for example through Cévennes (10 days, from £765), or the Scottish Highlands (6 days, from £740). Heritage has traditionally concentrated on tours coinciding with music festivals: 12 of these were offered in 1986 including the Würzburg Mozart Festival, and the Madeira Bach Festival. Serenissima and Heritage have recently merged with Voyages Jules Verne, specialists in tours to China and 'Great Journeys of the World', which will allow them to extend their annual programme even further.

Sotheby's International Travel
38 New Bond Street, London W1Y 9HB
(01-409 2565)
Apart from their vineyard tours (see below), Sotheby's normally only arranges tours abroad for participants on its Works of Art courses (see p. 24). However, they do occasionally also have holidays open to the general public, such as their 10-day trip to Russia (Leningrad, Novgorod and Pskov) in September 1986, escorted by one of their own specialists (£1500).

Sotheby's Vineyard Tours
34–35 New Bond Street, London W1A 2AA
(01-493 8080)
In 1985 Sotheby's organised three 6-day vineyard tours to some of the major wine-producing areas of France and it is hoped that three further tours will be arranged for 1987. The emphasis for all tours is on small groups (12–15 people), first-class accommodation, exclusive properties and domaines, and maximum participation. Further information and prices (when available) from David Molyneux-Berry in the Wine Department.

Swan Hellenic
Canberra House, 47 Middlesex Street, London E1 7AL (01-247 0401)
Swan Hellenic, one of the great names in specialist cultural tours, offers a variety of meticulously planned holidays for those interested in the visual arts. Their Arts Treasures Tours — about 45 different tours were offered for 1986/7 — are all accompanied by a tour manager and specialist guest lecturer, and groups are limited to 34 persons or sometimes less. Destinations both near and far are included, from 'Bruges and Ghent' (6 days, from £388), to Peru (21 days, from £2450) or a 'Journey Across the Roof of the World', taking in India, Nepal, Tibet, China and Hong Kong (22 days, from £2840). Other interesting tours include Albania (17 days, from £891), Lombardy and the Italian Lakes (10 days, from £1029), India's 'Muslim Heritage' (21 days, from £1826), Pakistan (18 days, from £1651), and Korea and Taiwan (19 days, from £2250). Swan Hellenic also offers a selection of cruises in the Mediterranean, Egypt and Middle East, each accompanied by a guest lecturer, as well as various European tours coinciding with theatre and music festivals. There are also holidays arranged for Christmas or New Year — 1986/7 will include Christmas tours in Vienna (8 days, from £640) and Rome (8 days, from £745), and New Year in Scotland (5 days, from £540). Swan Hellenic also organises tours in association with societies such as the Friends of the Royal Academy or the Tate Gallery: for example, in April 1987 the Friends of the Tate will take a group of their members to S. W. China (22 days, from £2186).

Twickers World
22 Church Street, Twickenham, TW1 3NW (01-892 8164/7606), or 60 Marylebone Lane, London W1M 5FF (01-486 8371)
Twickers World is best known for its operations in the realm of wilderness, wildlife and adventure travel. However, it does also offer some unusual cultural tours, often with visits to game reserves or areas of great natural beauty combined. Although many of these expeditions (such as the trek to the North Pole) are physically demanding, the cultural tours tend to be less so. Examples from the 1986/7 catalogue include 'El Dorado Colombia Cultural and Amazon Tour' (24 days, from approximately £2943); 'The Inca Legacy', an expedition led by a Peruvian Cultural Anthropologist (24 days, from about £2470); 'A Touch of China', a more luxurious, hotel-based tour of the most notable sights of China (16 days, from about £1580); and 'India — Desert Castles and Lakes Tour', a lecturer-accompanied exploration of both famous landmarks and little-known desert castles, with overnight stays in some of the latter (16 days, from about £1435).

AREA SPECIALISTS

The Asia Experience
53 Bryanston Street, London W1H 7AR
(01-724 0271/0248)
Specialists in travel to India, Nepal and Thailand, Asia Experience offers various escorted tours to those countries, as well as itineraries tailor-made to suit the individual traveller. The tours combine some guided sightseeing with plenty of independent exploration and relaxation; one includes a 4-day trek to the Kolahai Glacier in the Himalayas and 2 days on a Kashmir houseboat (13 days in all, from £925). There is also the opportunity to travel through India on a luxurious steam train, such as the famous 'Palace on Wheels', made of carefully restored state carriages, which travels from Delhi through Jaipur, Udaipur, Bharatpur, Agra and back to Delhi (15 days, including return flight from London to Delhi and 8 days on the train, from £1395).

Coromandel
Andrew Brock Travel, 10 Barley Mow Passage, Chiswick, London W4 4PH (01-995 3642)
If you want the careful planning of a package tour, but prefer to travel alone, Coromandel may be the answer. They specialise in holidays to S. E. Asia, (especially India), which they divide into 'tours' (more or less luxurious sightseeing holidays), 'lotus-eating' (relaxation, for example in Bali, or on a Kashmir houseboat), 'brief encounters' (short visits to combine into longer holidays), and 'treks' (such as a week's journey on elephant back). For those mainly interested in art and culture, the tours will be of most interest: these include 'India by Private Car' (15 days or more, from £1172), 'Undiscovered India' (16 days, from £1698), and the 'Khyber Mail Tour' (16 days, from £1179). Participants travel alone, but local representatives and personal sightseeing guides are always on hand; Coromandel can also arrange tailor-made tours to suit individual needs. One advantage of Coromandel is that they offer their holidays all year round (though they advise against certain very hot or wet months), whereas many operators give only a limited set of dates.

Coromandel also offer some unusual 'Textile Study Tours'. Aimed at those interested in the history and techniques of textile production, the tours visit villages and workshops to see traditional methods in practice, and museums where textile history may be studied; more general sightseeing is also included. For 1986/7 there will be one tour to India (27 December 1986–11 January 1987; £1348) and one to Indonesia (6–22 April 1987).

Cox & Kings
46 Marshall Street, London W1V 2PA
(01-439 8292)
225 years' experience of organising travel to the Indian sub-continent, for the Duke of Wellington and his army among others, makes Cox & Kings one of the leaders in this area. Their holidays are at the luxurious end of the market, using the very best hotels, and with plenty of time for relaxation between the various sightseeing expeditions that the company organises. The more culturally-oriented tours include 'Indian Experience' (11 days, from £882, 'Indian Highlights' (9 days, from £659), with an optional 6 days extra in Kashmir, Goa or Nepal), and South India (17 days, from £1536); there are also holidays in Nepal and Sri Lanka.

Jasmin Tours
High Street, Cookham, Maidenhead, Berkshire SL6 9SQ (06285 31121)
Jasmin specialises in tours to two regions, 'The Near East', and 'The Himalayas and Beyond'. The escorted tours to the Near East — Egypt, Syria, Jordan and the Holy Land — offer a choice of hotels, and therefore of prices; all are accompanied by a lecturer and/or guide. They range from 5-day weekends, usually in one place, to 16-day tours which may take in two or three countries. One weekend destination is Petra, the ancient Jordanian city carved from rock (5 days, £577). The 'Pharaonic Weekend' takes in Cairo and Luxor (Thebes) and many of the Nile's most spectacular sights (5 days, from £630), while longer tours include a Nile Cruise accompanied by an Egyptologist (16 days, from £1236); Syria and Jordan (14 days, from £763); and Egypt, The Holy Land and Jordan (14 days, from £998). Jasmin's Asian holidays include, as well as the usual Indian tours, such as 'Highlights of India' (11 days, from £668), escorted tours of Pakistan (12 days, from £948 and Burma (10 days, from £998), and a trek through Nepal (15 days, from £1158). The company also arranges tours in Tibet or Bhutan, countries which are usually much less accessible.

NON-SPECIALIST

Bales Tours
Bales House, Barrington Road, Dorking, Surrey RH4 3EJ (9396 885991)
Bales, one of the best-known luxury tour operators, offers a selection of escorted tours to India, S. E. Asia, the Far East, Russia, Australia, New Zealand, North and South America, Egypt and the Middle East, all with the emphasis on first-class food and accommodation rather than academic content. Some of the more unusual tours include the 'Silk Route' through China (24 days, from £2096), Peking and Inner Mongolia (10 days, from £1179), India and Thailand (15 days, from £1142), and Bhutan with India, Nepal and Sikkim (19 days, from £1964). There are also coach tours of New England (10 days, from £1135) and the Canadian Rockies (9 days, from £995), as well as a round-the-world trip (Singapore, Australia, New Zealand, Fiji, Hawaii and the USA; 27 days, from £3180), and an archaeological tour of Mexico (15 days, from £1180). And for those demanding the very highest standards and personal service, Bales' 'Topmarket' tours include India and Nepal (Delhi, Kathmandu, Varanasi, Agra, Jaipur, Udaipur, Bombay; 21 days, from £2216), and China (Peking, Sian Nanking, Shanghai, Canton, Hong Kong; 20 days, from £2595) among their destinations.

Kuoni Travel
Kuoni House, Dorking, Surrey RH5 4AZ (0306 885044)
Kuoni Worldwide offers a huge selection of holidays to destinations all over the world, with prices starting at £300–£400 (£382 for a week touring Morocco's Imperial Cities, for example). Some of the most fascinating are those voted their 'Top Ten' holidays, all fully escorted by a tour manager and using first class accommodation. These include 'The Great American Adventure', 15 days touring cities and landscapes between Los Angeles, the Grand Canyon, Las Vegas and San Francisco (from £2085); Japan, Hong Kong and Thailand (16 days, from £1756); China, Hong Kong, Bali and Singapore (18 days, from £1798); 'Palaces of India' (17 days, from £1325); and a tour across Colombia, Peru, Bolivia and Brazil (22 days, from £1898).

Sovereign
Reservations 01-897 1336; other information from any ABTA Travel Agent.
If you don't feel strong enough to be dragged around 20 different towns in 3 days, but prefer to stay in one centre and explore it at your own pace, then the 'Cities Plus' holidays offered by Sovereign (British Airways) may be useful. Sovereign offers 3, 4, 7 or 14 nights, in any of 22 major cities, with a range of accommodation, from *pensiones* to deluxe hotels, and often a choice of method of travel as well. Most of the cities offered are in Western or Eastern Europe, but New York and Washington are also included. Prices vary enormously (3 nights in Lisbon from £187; 3 nights in New York, from £324). Tours in and around many of the cities are offered as an optional extra; there are also longer tours combined with the cities — for example, an 8-day coach tour of Paris (2 nights) and the Loire Valley (from £299) — and multi-centre holidays — such as 3 nights in Florence with 4 in Rome (from £344). Sovereign also offer summer cruises in the Mediterranean, all with opportunities for shore excursions (for example, a 7-day cruise to Ancient Greece, Istanbul and the Aegean Islands, from £880).

Thomas Cook Escorted Journeys
Thomas Cook Ltd, 45 Berkeley Street, London W1A 1EB (01-629 0999)
Thomas Cook offers fully-escorted tours to Canada, India, the Far East, Egypt and South America. These are holidays catering for a range of interests, and most provide both cultural sightseeing and magnificent scenery, with plenty of time for shopping and relaxation as well. All tours are accompanied by a tour manager to ensure smooth running of the tour; travel and accommodation are high-quality but, as with all operators, will not be luxurious in the more remote areas. There are two tours in Canada, one via the Trans-Canadian railway (17 days, from £995); both include Vancouver, Toronto, Ottawa and Montreal, as well as some breath-taking scenery. The Indian tours include one in Southern India (15 days, from £995), and a very comprehensive 'Indian Raj and Nepal' tour (20 days, from £1395). There are also two spectacular tours in China, one taking advantage of the ancient canals and waterways there (17 days, from £1590); and two in South America, of which one explores the relics of the ancient civilizations of Mexico and Peru (21 days, from £1865), while the other, in Peru, Bolivia, Paraguay and Brazil, reveals both the ancient culture and the later Spanish/Portuguese influences in the continent (24 days, from £1885). The holidays in Egypt include 'The Two Africas', a spectacular escorted tour of Egypt and Kenya (19 days, from £1275), and a Nile cruise (Cairo–Aswan) accompanied by a qualified Egyptologist (15 days, from £995).

Thomson Travel
Head Office: Greater London House, Hampstead Road, London NW1 7SD (01-387 9321)
For those looking for an economical and varied but not academic holiday, with a guaranteed standard of comfort, Thomson's huge range of 'Thomson Tours' may be ideal. Each year some 60 are offered, including destinations both in Europe and further afield, most of which are accompanied by a Thomson representative. 1986 offerings in Europe include a week exploring the cities of Andalucia (7 nights, from £175) or the wine routes of Portugal (7 nights, from £240); a 'Grand Tour of Europe' — 17 days taking in 7 countries with tours of Paris, Florence, Rome and Vienna (from £430); or a tour of Yugoslavia (7 nights, from £295). There are also more exotic destinations, such as 'Classical Turkey', including the site of ancient Troy (14 nights, from £536); Morocco; Israel; a selection of Nile cruises (for example 'Nile Odyssey', 14 nights, from £748); Russia (such as 'The Golden Road to Samarkand', 7 days, from £320); or Russia with India, Mongolia or Japan (Russia and Japan, for example, 14 nights, from £1283). In many cases there is also an opportunity to add an extra week in one place at the end of the tour. Thomson's 'Worldwide' holidays, including African safaris and some Far Eastern holidays — such as their wide-ranging tour of China (22 days, from £1925) — may also be of interest.

DIRECTORY TO LONDON, ENGLAND, ISLANDS, IRELAND, SCOTLAND, WALES

How to Use This Book
After the editorial articles the book is divided into five main sections:

1 Directory (*begins on page 37*)
Dealers, auctioneers, packers, restorers, trade suppliers and so on are all listed here, with address, telephone number, opening hours, and type of business or area of specialisation. Entries are listed in alphabetical order under town or village, within the relevant county and geographical area.

2 Gazetteer (*begins on page 265*)
This is an alphabetical list of the towns and villages mentioned in the Directory, showing the counties and geographical areas under which they are listed.

3 Index to Specialists
(*begins on page 270*)
Directory entries are here listed under type of business or nature of stock.

4 Index to Business Names
(*begins on page 363*)
All business names in the Directory are listed alphabetically with their town or village, county and geographical area.

5 Maps (*begin on page 391*)
Showing villages and towns listed in the Directory.

Note
Counties and geographical areas are listed with page references under 'Contents' on page 3.
Auctioneers are listed both in the main Directory under the relevant town or village, and in the Specialists index under 'Auctioneers'.
Abbreviations and names and addresses of useful organisations are listed on page 4.

Good late 18th century mahogany cylinder bureau, with well fitted interior.
Height: 40" (102 cm); Width: 33" (84 cm); Depth: 21½" (55 cm).

Anno Domini Antiques

66 Pimlico Road, London, SW1
01-730 5496

TABLE LINERS

GOOD · POSTAL

RELIABLE · SERVICE

Antique Leathers

The Recognised Specialists

We offer a superb selection of the finest quality loose leathers, with 23 carat gold tooling. Desks and table-tops relined on our own premises.
Tel: 01-435 8582 or 435 7799

4 PARK END, SOUTH HILL PARK, HAMPSTEAD, LONDON NW3 2SE

Samples on request

Trade only

LEATHER UPHOLSTERERS

Maurice Asprey Ltd.

41 DUKE STREET, ST. JAMES'S
LONDON SW1Y 6DF
Telephone 01-930 3921

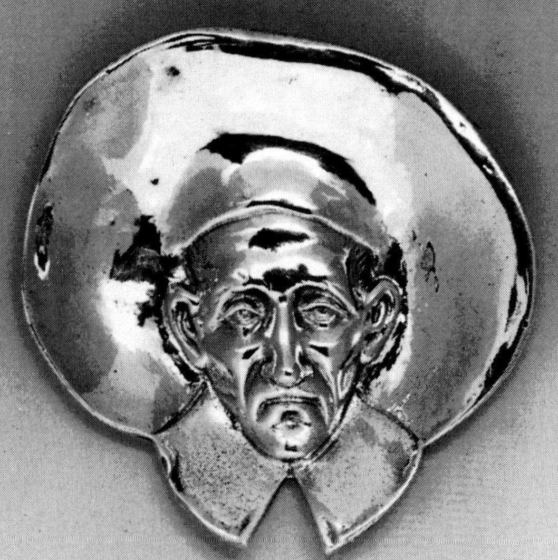

A Victorian Silver Dish in the form of a man's head, wearing a Puritan collar and hat by C.S. and F.S. London 1888.

BRITISH ART & ANTIQUES DIRECTORY 1987

LONDON

How to Use This Book
After the editorial articles the book is divided into five main sections:
1 Directory (*begins on page 37*)
Dealers, auctioneers, packers, restorers, trade suppliers and so on are all listed here, with address, telephone number, opening hours, and type of business or area of specialisation. Entries are listed in alphabetical order under town or village, within the relevant county and geographical area.
2 Gazetteer (*begins on page 265*)
This is an alphabetical list of the towns and villages mentioned in the Directory, showing the counties and geographical areas under which they are listed.
3 Index to Specialists
(*begins on page 270*)
Directory entries are here listed under type of business or nature of stock.
4 Index to Business Names
(*begins on page 363*)
All business names in the Directory are listed alphabetically with their town or village, county and geographical area.
5 Maps (*begin on page 391*)
Showing villages and towns listed in the Directory.

Note
Counties and geographical areas are listed with page references under 'Contents' on page 3.
Auctioneers are listed both in the main Directory under the relevant town or village, and in the Specialists index under 'Auctioneers'.
Abbreviations and names and addresses of useful organisations are listed on page 4.

London STD 01

A.D.C. Heritage Ltd
(F.M. Raeymaekers). 2 Old Bond St, W1X 3TD. Tel 493 5088. Open Mon-Sat 9.30-6; other times by appt. Antique silver, mainly 18thC. Sets of silver flatware. LAPADA

Aaron Galleries
(M. Aaron & D. Aaron). 34 Bruton St, W1X 7DD. Tel 499 9434. Open Mon-Fri 10-6; Sat by appt. Oriental carpets, Islamic and ancient art. LAPADA

Didier Aaron (London) Ltd
21 Ryder St, SW1Y 6PX. Tel 839 4716/7. Open Mon-Fri 10-6; other times by appt. 18thC French furniture, old masters, paintings and drawings.

Abbott & Holder
73 Castelnau, Barnes, SW13. Tel 748 2416. Open Sat 9-5; other times by appt. 18th to 20thC drawings, watercolours, paintings, prints.

Academy Framing
(J.T. Burns). Royal Academy of Arts, Burlington House, Piccadilly, W1V 0DS. Tel 734 9052 (priv 437 8472). Open Mon-Fri 10-5. Fine art picture framers & gilders.

Arthur Ackermann & Son Ltd
3 Old Bond St, W1X 3TD. Tel 493 3288. Open Mon-Fri 10-5.30, some Sats 10-1. Specialists in English sporting paintings and fine engravings of all subjects. SLAD

Acquisitions (Fireplaces) Ltd
269 Camden High St, NW1 7BX. Tel 485 4955. Open Mon-Sat 10-6. Fireplaces and architectural pieces, cast iron and stripped pine mantels and grates, Georgian, Victorian and Edwardian furniture.

Acrylic Design
697 Harrow Rd, NW10 4NY. Tel 969 0478. Open Mon-Sat; other times by appt. Manufacturers of clear acrylic stands for plates, cups and saucers etc.

Actino Antiques
(Ray Jones). 136 Lee High Rd, Lewisham, SE13. Tel 318 1273. Open 9.30-5.30; early closing Thurs; other times by appt. General and decorative items, including lamps and lighting. LAPADA

Adams Antiques
(Len & Yvonne Adams). The Royal Arcade, 28 Old Bond St, W1X 3HD. Tel 629 0717. Open Mon-Fri 10-6 (also Sat in spring); other times by appt. Fine 18th Meissen figures, 18th and 19thC European porcelain. BADA

Adams Antiques
(S.C. Copsey). 47 Chalk Farm Rd, NW1. Tel 267 9241. (Also at 53-55 Fulham High St, SW6 (Tel 736 9136.) Open every day 10-6; other times by appt. Trade warehouse at Houghton Rd, St Ives, Huntingdon. (Tel: 0480-300455). Antique Irish, English and Continental pine furniture.

Adams Room Ltd
(Mr. & Mrs. G. Seymour-Cole). 18-20 Ridgway, Wimbledon Village, SW19. Tel 946 7047 (priv 947 4784). Open Mon-Sat 9-5; other times by appt. Georgian, Regency furniture, mirrors, silver and old Sheffield plate. Large showrooms. French furniture. LAPADA

Norman Adams Ltd
8-10 Hans Rd, SW3 1RX. Tel 589 5266. Open Mon-Fri 9-5.30; other times by appt. Very fine 18thC English furniture, glass chandeliers and works of art. BADA

Addison-Ross Gallery
(D.A.A.Ross Esq and T.C.A.Ross Esq). 40 Eaton Tce, Belgravia, SW1. Tel 730 1536. (Also at 25 High St, Wooler, Northumberland.) Open normal shop hours; other times by appt. Paintings and prints, particularly sporting subjects. Also framing, restoration and interior design contracting.

Thos Agnew & Sons Ltd
43 Old Bond St, W1X 4BA. Tel 629 6176. Open Mon-Fri 9.30-5.30; Thurs 9.30-6.30. Important oil paintings, drawings, watercolours and engravings of all schools. Important special exhibitions. Sculpture and works of art. Also contemporary works of art. BADA

Ahuan UK Ltd
(Oliver Hoare). 17 Eccleston St, SW1W 9LX. Tel 730 9382. Open Mon-Fri 9.30-5.30. Islamic works of art.

AIR Gallery
(Fergus Muir). 6 & 8 Rosebery Ave, EC1. Tel 278 7751. Open Mon-Fri 11-6, Sat 11-2. Contemporary paintings, drawings, sculpture and printmaking.

Air Improvement Centre Ltd
(V.J. Taplin). 23 Denbigh St, SW1V 2HF. Tel 834 2834 (priv 821 8485). Open Mon-Fri 9-5; other times by appt. Specialists in humidifiers to prevent central heating damage. Free information pack and advisory service. London shop and nation wide despatch. Also dehumidifiers, air purifiers & mobile air conditioners. Trade terms available.

Al-Mashreq Galleries
(J.H.Mantoura). 110 Kensington Church St, W8 4BH. Tel 229 5453. Islamic art and antiques, including ceramics, metalwork, arms and armour, textiles, sculptures, and manuscripts. Also 19th and 20thC prints, watercolours and oils by European Orientalists.

Albany Gallery
(Bill Thomson). 1 Bury St, St James's, SW1Y 6AB. Tel 839 6119. Open Mon-Fri 9.30-5.30; other times by appt. Fine British school watercolours and small paintings of 17th to early 20thC. Not high Victorian or Edwardian.

Albert's of Kensington
(J.A. Wooster). 110 Campden Hill Rd, W8 7AR. Tel 221 4216. Open Mon-Fri 10-5; Sat 10-1. Cigarette card specialist. 40,000 sets in stock. Mail order & postal auction service. Album suppliers. Cigarette card framing service. Publishers of "The Guide to Cigarette Card Collecting" (Published annually).

Albion Fine Art
61 Ledbury Rd, W1. Tel 221 2977. Open Mon-Sat 9.30-6; other times by appt. English and Continental 18th and 19thC oil paintings; some modern paintings.

Patrick Aldridge Ltd
88-90 Hatton Garden, EC1. Tel 242 3209. Jewellery. BADA

Alex Antiques
5 Blenheim St, W1. Tel 629 0701. Open Mon-Fri 9-5. General antiques, mainly paintings, works of art and bullion.

Alexander & Berendt Ltd
1A Davies St, W1Y 1LL. Tel 499 4775. Open Mon-Fri 9.30-5.30. Fine 17th and 18thC French and Continental furniture and works of art.

David Alexander Antiques
102 Waterford Rd, SW6. Tel 731 4644. Open Mon-Fri 10-6; other times by appt. 16th-early 18thC English & Continental furniture.

Alfies Antique Market
13-25 Church St, NW8. Tel 723 6066. Open Tues-Sat 10-6. Large market of more than 100 dealers with a wide variety of stock.

Richard Allan Gallery
20 Park Walk, Chelsea, SW10. Tel 351 0410. Paintings.

Allegras Antiques
(Mrs E.Kingston). 22 Lower Richmond Rd, Putney, SW15. Tel 785 7755 (priv 789 7444). (Also Lighthouse Antiques in Wimbledon.) Open Mon-Fri 10-5.30; other times by appt. Antiques and collectors items including fine porcelain table lamps. Brass ceiling and wall lights and small fine furniture.

Peter Allen Antiques Ltd
17 & 17A Nunhead Green, Peckham, SE15 3QQ. Tel 732 1968. Open Mon-Fri 9-5; other times by appt. Large stock of good quality Victorian furniture, mahogany, walnut, rosewood etc.

Trevor Allen
Stand U4, Antiquarius, 139 King's Rd, SW3. Tel 352 7061. Antique jewellery and objets d'art.

Nicholas Alloway, Photographer of Antiques
(Nicholas Alloway). Basement studio, Chenil Galleries, 181 King's Rd, SW3. Tel 352 7217, 870 4677. Open 10-6; other times by appt. Specialising in photography of antiques for publicity, editorial, insurance, inventory or catalogue purposes, in or away from the studio.

John Allsopp Antiques
26 Pimlico Rd, SW1W 8LJ. Tel 730 9347. Open Mon-Fri 10-6, Sat 10-1; other times by appt. 18th and 19thC decorative furniture and objects.

Alton Gallery
72 Church Rd, Barnes, SW13. Tel 748 0606, 748 8244. 19th and 20thC British art. Framing service.

Alwin Gallery
9-10 Grafton St, Bond St, W1. Tel 499 0314. Open Mon-Fri 10-5.30; Sat 10-1. Contemporary art.

Amalgam
(T.A.M.Boon). 3 Barnes High St, SW13. Tel 878 1279. Open Tues-Sat 10-1, 2.15-6; other times by appt. Contemporary fine and applied arts, including studio pottery, original prints, watercolours, studio glass and paintings (exhibitions only). ICGA

Barling

OF MOUNT STREET LTD.

01-499 2858

Spanish 16th century
polychromed walnut papelera on table

Chinese Buddhist stele.
Tang Dynasty; dated 661 AD

EARLY ENGLISH AND CONTINENTAL
FURNITURE AND WORKS OF ART

ORIENTAL WORKS OF ART

112 MOUNT STREET, LONDON W1Y 5HE

Christopher Bangs

01 223 5676
By appointment only

LAPADA

Early metalware
and metalwork
and
works of art

Albert Amor Ltd
37 Bury St, St James's, SW1Y 6AU. Tel 930 2444. Open Mon-Fri 10-4.30. 18thC English pottery and porcelain, especially first period Worcester and 18thC English blue and white. Enamels.

George Amos & Sons (CB) Ltd
(A.J.Amos MD). 73 Leonard St, EC2. Tel 739 0448. Open Mon-Sat 10-5. Old panelled rooms and chimney pieces, architectural antiques. Restorers of furniture.

Anchor Antiques Ltd
(Mrs H Samne, Mr K.B.Embden). 26 Charing Cross Rd, (office 24A Charing Cross Rd), WC2H 0DG. Tel 836 5686. Open by appt. Trade only. European & Oriental ceramics. Some objects of vertu.

And So To Bed Ltd
638-640 King's Road, SW6. Tel 731 3593. Open Mon-Sat 10-6; other times by appt. (Also at 7 New Kings Rd, SW6; 96B Camden High St, NW1; 26 Castle St, Edinburgh; 5 Ridgefield, Manchester.) Brass, wooden, cane and fabric beds: antique, reproduction and contemporary. Bedroom accessories and bedlinens. Complete interior design service.

Maria Andipa Icon Gallery
162 Walton St, SW3. Tel 589 2371. Open Mon-Fri 11-6, Sat 11-2. Specialist in Greek, Byzantine, Russian, Ethiopian and Syrian icons. LAPADA BADA

Andreas Antiques
12 Church St, NW8. Tel 262 1370. General antiques and porcelain.

Anglebooks Ltd
2 Cecil Court, Charing Cross Rd, WC2. Tel 836 2922. Open Mon-Fri 10.30-6. Antiquarian books. ABA

Anglo-Persian Carpet Co Ltd
The Arcade, South Kensington Station, SW7 2NA. Tel 589 5457. Open Mon-Fri 9.30-6, Sat 9.30-2.30; other times by appt. Rare, old and antique Oriental carpets, rugs and kelims, antique Eastern textiles and European tapestries. Other rare and antique weavings and textiles. Also specialist cleaning, restoration and valuation services. BADA

Anno Domini
(F.Bartman). 66 Pimlico Rd, SW1. Tel 730 5496. Open Mon-Sat 10-1, 2.15-6; other times by appt. 17th-19thC furniture, mirrors, decorative items, glass and clocks of all periods. BADA

Stephen Anson
31a Matheson Rd, W14. Tel 602 5277 (24hr answering). Open by appt only. English oak and country furniture, 1600-1800.

Antichita
23 Molyneux St, W1H 5HU. Tel 262 2316 (priv 722 1907). Open Mon-Fri 10.30-5.30; other times by appt. Victoriana, silver, glass, copper, books and jewellery.

Antiquaria Ltd
10 Bury St, St James's, SW1. Tel 930 7793. Ancient, Medieval & Renaissance art.

Antiquarius
135-141 King's Rd, Chelsea, SW3. Tel 351 5353. (Correspondence to 15 Flood St, London SW3.) Open Mon-Sat 10-6. Over 200 standholders offering both specialised and general antiques of all periods from antiquities to fifties.

Antiquarius Camera Collectors Shop
(Nick Alloway). Stand L4, Antiquarius, 135 King's Rd, SW3. Tel 352 7217. Open Mon-Sat 10-5.30. Collectors' cameras. Equipment, daguerreotypes and photographs.

Antique & Modern Furniture Ltd
(J.G.E. & B.M. Stern). 160 Earls Court Rd, SW5 9QQ. Tel 373 2935. Open 9-1, 2.15-6; Thurs 9-1. Antique and general dealers.

Antique Connoisseur plc
(inc Pieces of Time. Director: J. Wachsmann). Grays Mews, 1-7 Davies Mews, W1. Tel 629 2422/3272. Open Mon-Fri 10-5.30. Clocks, watches, objects and Judaica.

The Antique Gallery
(John H.Yorfe). 40 Peckham Rye, SE15. Tel 732 7808 (priv 653 4279). Open Mon-Fri 9-5.30, Sat 9-1. Large stock of all types of furniture for export, especially Victorian and Edwardian furniture, also a wide range of oak furniture and shipping goods.

Antique Glass
(A Milford). 155 Portobello Rd, W11. Tel 485 6240. Open Sats only. 18thC glass & porcelain. LAPADA

The Antique Home
(Mrs M.Priestley & Mr B.T.Rolleston). 104A Kensington Church St, W8 4BU. Tel 229 5892. Open 10-1, 2.30-6; Sat 10-1. 18thC English furniture. BADA

Antique Leathers
(R. Holliday & Mrs. F. Crisp). 4 Park End, South Hill Park, NW3 2SE. Tel 435 8582/7799. Table liners and gilders of all types of leather, leather upholsterers and repairers of all leather goods such as backgammon and chessboards. LAPADA

The Antique Porcelain Company Ltd
(Mrs Rotraut Beiny). 149 New Bond St, W1Y 0HY. Tel 629 1254. (Also by appt New York Tel: 212-758 2363 U.S.A.) Open Mon-Thurs 9.30-6; Fri 9.30-5; other times by appt. Medium size showrooms of 18thC English and Continental porcelain and faience, French furniture and decorative arts.

The Antique Textile Company
(S.Franklyn, J.Wentworth). 100 Portland Rd, W11. Tel 221 7730. Open Mon-Fri, 10-6, closed Sat except by appt. Interesting textiles, mostly pre-1880, of all kinds (except kelims, tapestries, susannis and samplers). A large stock of paisley and Kashmir shawls. Toiles de jouy, chintz, ikats, kesas, kossu/kesi, ethnic textiles. LAPADA

The Antique Trader
(D.J.Rothera, B.Thompson). 357 Upper St, Camden Passage, N1. Tel 359 2019. (Also at 36 Upper Street, Islington, N1.) English country & period furniture, Biedermeier, arts and crafts, decorative items, art deco. LAPADA

The Antiques Exchange
(Robert Drasey). Number One, Bermondsey Sq, SE1. Tel 407 3635. Open Mon-Fri 10-4; Thurs until 6. Bric-a-brac and smalls. LAPADA

Antiquities
227 Ebury Street, SW1. Tel 730 5000. Open Mon-Fri 10-6; Sat 11-4. French furniture & objets d'art.

Antiquus
(E. Amati). 90-92 Pimlico Rd, SW1. Tel 730 8681. Open Mon-Fri 9.30-5.30; Sat 10-1; other times by appt. Gothic, Renaissance sculpture, glass, textiles.

Antiquus A G
(J.G. Fell-Clark). 17 Pembridge Sq, W2 4EH. Tel 229 0224. (Trade warehouse in Long Melford, Suffolk.) Open by appt only; res on prem. Oak and country furniture, some walnut, yew and mahogany. Tapestries, crewelwork and objects. LAPADA

Philip Antrobus
11 New Bond St, W1. Tel 493 4557. Jewellery.

Apollo Gallery
75A Ridgmount Gardens, WC1. Tel 580 6241. Open by appt. Archaeological items, Greek, Roman, Byzantine, Islamic and ancient art.

Appleby's
(B.J. Appleby, J.T. Carter). 8 Ryder St, St James's, SW1Y 6QB. Tel 930 6507. Open Mon-Fri 10-5.30; other times by appt. Fine paintings and watercolours of the 19thC. BADA

Apter-Fredericks Ltd
(Bernard S Apter, Carole C Apter). 265-267 Fulham Rd, SW3 6HY. Tel 352 2188. Open Mon-Fri 9-6; other times by appt. Fine 18th & early 19thC English furniture. BADA

Arbiter Antiques
Chenil Galleries, King's Rd, Chelsea, SW3. Tel 499 3361. Renaissance Italian Majolica and old master prints.

The Arcade Gallery
(Mr & Mrs Wengraf). 15 Royal Arcade, 28 Old Bond St, W1X3HD. Tel 493 1879 (priv 492 1706). Open Mon-Fri 9.30-5.30; Sat 10.30-2.30. Primitive art, antiquities and ethnographica.

Arcade Gallery
28 Old Bond St, W1. Tel 493 1879.

Architectural Antiques Ltd
(Peter Chapman, R.J.Henry). 133 Upper St, N1. Tel 226 5565. Open Mon-Sat 9.30-6. Fireplaces, stained glass, garden furniture, statuary, panelled rooms, wrought iron, larger furniture, decorative antiques.

Billi Arena
Stand E5, Antiquarius, 135 King's Rd, SW3. Tel 351 8734. Open Mon-Sat 10-6. General antiques.

Arenski
29-31 George St, W1H 5PE. Tel 486 0678. Glass, paintings, fine antique furniture, bronzes, objets d'art, clocks, papier mache and Faberge, with the emphasis on fine works of art of the 19thC.

Argenta
82 Fulham Rd, SW3. Tel 584 3119. Open Mon-Sat 9.30-5.30. Jewellery in contemporary and traditional materials. Export arranged for overseas buyers. ICGA

191/193/195 FULHAM ROAD
LONDON SW3 6JL
TELEPHONE: 01-352 9826/0807

H. C. Baxter & Sons

PARTNERS:
R. C. BAXTER · T. J. BAXTER · M. K. BAXTER · J. BAXTER · G. J. BAXTER

Specialists in 18th century Furniture

Susan Becker

Antiques

18 Lower Richmond Road, Putney,
London SW15 01-788-9082

LAPADA Registered Member

Selection of unusual Minton porcelain.

Exhibiting at Olympia and
London Ceramics Fair at The Cumberland Hotel.

Bernheimer

Founded 1864

Antique Furniture, Oriental Art and Porcelain, Sculpture and Textiles

BERNHEIMER
FINE ARTS LTD
32 ST GEORGE STREET
LONDON W1R 9FA
TEL: 01-499 0293
TELEX: 268091

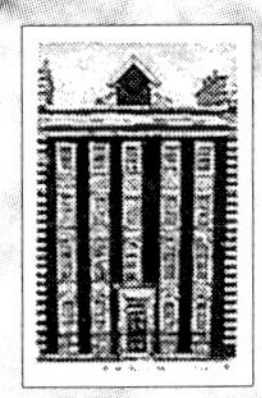

L. BERNHEIMER KG
LENBACHPLATZ 3
8000 MÜNCHEN 2
TEL: 089-59 66 43
TELEX: 5 212 724

Argyll Etkin Ltd
48 Conduit St, W1R 9FB. Tel 437 7800. Fine stamps and postal history.

Valerie Arieta
97B Kensington Church St, W8. English, Continental, and Oriental decorative arts and American Indian art.

The Ark Angel
14 Camden Passage, N1 8ED. Tel 226 1644. Open Tues-Sat 10.30-5.30. Early pine, primitive paintings, samplers, quilts, decorative objects.

Armada Antiques
Stand 122 Gray's Antiques Mkt, 58 Davies St, W1. Tel 499 1087. Open 10-6. Japanese, Oriental and European edged weapons and armour, antique firearms and medals. LAPADA

Karin Armelin Antiques
(Karin Armelin). 592 King's Rd, SW6. Tel 736 0375. Open Mon-Sat 10.30-5.30; other times by appt. 18th and 19thC furniture, decorative items, silver and silver plate.

Armitage
4 Davies St, W1Y 1LS. Tel 408 0675. Open Mon-Fri 10-5.30; Sat by appt. Fine silver. BADA

Armour-Winston Ltd
(C.A. Armour, A.J. Armour). 43 Burlington Arcade, Piccadilly, W1V 9AE. Tel 493 8937. Open Mon-Fri 9-4.30. Antique and secondhand jewellery.

Armoury Antiques
(C.C.Bowdell). Unit 123, Grays Antique Market, 58 Davies St, W1. Tel 408 0176. Open Mon-Fri 10-6. Arms & armour & Islamic works of art. LAPADA

Art Bronze Foundry (London) Ltd
(M.C.Gaskin). 1 Michael Rd, SW6. Tel 736 7292. Open Mon-Fri 8-4.30; other times by appt. Statuary foundry (lost wax process) for bronze and other non-ferrous metals.

Artemis Fine Arts (UK) Limited
15 Duke St, St. James's, SW1. Tel 930 1523. (Also David Carritt Ltd.) Prints and drawings.

Mario Ascione
53 Moreton St,(Basement), SW1. Old prints and watercolours, framing and gilding.

Ash Rare Books
(L.J.Worms). 25 Royal Exchange, Threadneedle St, EC3. Tel 626 2665. Open Mon-Fri 10-5.30. Antiquarian and rare books, antique maps and prints. ABA

Christopher Ashton & Anjula Daniel
114 Islington High St, Camden Passage, N1. Tel 359 9533. Open Wed & Sat; other times by appt. English and Continental antiques, decorative furniture and accessories.

Asprey PLC
165-169 New Bond St, W1Y 0AR. Tel 493 6767. Open Mon-Fri 9-5.30, Sat 9-1. Specialists in antique silver, jewellery, miniatures, fine period furniture, glass, watches, clocks, objets d'art, Faberge and Russian works of art. BADA

Maurice Asprey Ltd
(Maurice Asprey, Elizabeth Asprey). 41 Duke St, St James's, SW1. Tel 930 3921. Open Mon-Fri 9.30-5.30. Antique silver and jewellery, portrait miniatures, objects of vertu. BADA

Astleys Ltd
(Paul Bentley). 109 Jermyn St, SW1. Tel 930 1687. Open Mon-Fri 10-6, Sat 10-1. Antique pipes.

Astoria
(Joe Turner). 73A Kensington Church St, W8. Tel 937 0105. Open Mon-Sat 10.30-6; other times by appt. Decorative objects and furniture 1900-1960. Specialising in art deco & 1950s jewellery and art deco graphics.

Atmosphere
175 Muswell Hill Broadway, N10. Tel 883 1074. Open Mon-Wed, Fri & Sat 9.30-5, Thurs 9.30-1. Ceramics, jewellery, furnishing fabrics and wood. Contemporary prints and watercolours. Regular exhibitions of new work held six to eight times a year.

Audun Gallery
Chelsea Wharf, 15 Lots Rd, SW10. Tel 352 4080. Modern art and photography.

Ian Auld
1 Gateway Arcade, Camden Passage, N1. Tel 359 1440. Open Wed 9.30-4.30; Sat 11-5. Antiquities, mainly pottery. African, Oceanic and Pre-Columbian ethnographical items.

G.Austin & Sons Ltd
11-23 Peckham Rye, SE15. Tel 639 3163. (Also at 39-41 Brayards Rd, London, SE15 (Tel: 639 0480.) Open Mon-Sat 8.30-5.30; early closing Thurs. Large stock of old and secondhand furniture, china and silver.

Avakian Oriental Carpets Ltd
(Mr. M. Avakian, Mr. N. Avakian). 20 Davies St, W1Y 1LH. Tel 493 5758. Open Mon-Fri 9-6; Sat 10-2; other times by appt. Old rugs and carpets of Caucasian, Iranian and Turkish origin, mostly over 70 years old, but also much older pieces.

Axia
(Y. Petsopoulos). 43 Pembridge Villas, W11. Tel 727 9724. Open by appt only. Islamic and Byzantine works of art, icons, textiles, ceramics, metalwork, woodwork, glass, manuscripts and kilims.

B & T Antiques
(Mrs Bernadette Lewis). 79 Ledbury Rd, W11. Tel 229 7001. Wide selection of decorative objects, boxes, glass, silver, furniture and paintings.

B.P.Antiques
2A Ferdinand Place, Ferdinand St, Chalk Farm, NW1. Tel 482 4021 (24 hrs). Open 7 days 10-4, or by appt. Antique, Victorian and shipping furniture at trade prices.

The Badger
(Mr & Mrs Aalders). 12 St Mary's Rd, Ealing, W5 5ES. Tel 567 5601. Open Mon-Sat 9.30-6; closed Wed; other times by appt. Medium size stock of Georgian furniture and clocks, some Victorian furniture, pottery and porcelain.

Robert Bailey Oriental Carpets
51-53 Rivington St, EC2A 3DA. Tel 550 5435. Oriental rugs and carpets. LAPADA

Alexander Bailie (Antiques)
2 Lower Mall, 359 Upper St, Islington, N1 0PD. Tel 354 2839 (priv 354 1739). Open Wed, Fri, Sat 10-5; other times by appt. 18th and 19thC furniture, clocks etc.

Bainbridges Fine Art & General Chattel Auctioneers
(Mr P. Bainbridge). 2 Chapel Rd, Ealing, W13. Tel 579 2966. Open Mon-Fri 9-5; other times by appt. Auctioneers of fine art and general chattels. Valuations. House sales carried out on the premises.

A.H.Baldwin & Sons Ltd
11 Adelphi Tce, WC2N 6BJ. Open Mon-Fri 9-5. Appt advisable. Tel 930 6879 (coins and medals), 839 1310 (war medals and decorations). Important numismatists, coins of all periods and all countries, decorations, medals and tokens. Also new and antiquarian numismatic books. BADA, IAPN, BNTA

Christopher Bangs
Tel 223 5676. Open by appt only. Domestic metalwork & metalware, works of art and decorative objects. Early lighting & smoothing irons. LAPADA

The Bank House Gallery
(Robert S. James Ltd). 8-10 The Broadway, Mill Hill, NW7 3LL. Tel 906 3124. 19thC oil paintings. Restoration and framing service. Full colour catalogue available.

Bankside Gallery
(Michael Spender (Director)). 48 Hopton St, Blackfriars, SE1 9JH. Tel 928 7521. Open Tues-Sat 10-5; Sun 2-6; closed Mon. Fine paintings. Home of the Royal Society of Painters in Water-Colours and the Royal Society of Painter-Etchers and Engravers.

Barbican Art Gallery
Level 8, The Barbican, EC2.

Eddy Bardawil
(E.S. Bardawil). 106 Kensington Church St, W8. Tel 221 3967. Open Mon-Sat 9.30-6. 18th and early 19thC English furniture in mahogany & walnut, brass candlesticks, tea caddies, engravings, restorations, valuations. LAPADA

Barham Fine Arts
(M.J.Barham, R.Barham, A.Barham). 83 Portobello Rd, W11 2QB. Tel 727 3845. Open Mon-Fri 9.30-5.30, Sat 7.30-6; other times by appt. Victorian walnut and Continental furniture, clocks, bronzes, porcelain and paintings. Also large stock of Victorian writing boxes & tea caddies etc.

Celia Barker Mill
(Celia Barker Mill). 24 Iverna Gardens, Kensington, W8 6TN. Tel 937 9145. Open by appt only. Antique carpets, silks, velvets, needleworks. Ivory, tortoiseshell and all textile/carpet restorations.

David Barklem Ltd
(David N. Barklem). 3-5 Theberton St, Islington, N1. Tel 359 4997. Open Mon-Sat 9.30-5.30; Thurs 9.30-12; closed Sun. Country furniture, English & French farmhouse tables, dressers, unusual and decorative items. LAPADA

Robert Barley Antiques
48 Fulham High St, SW6. Tel 736 4429. Open Mon-Fri 9.30-5.30; other times by appt. Decorative furniture and objects 1500-1950.

Bond Street Silver Galleries

111/112 NEW BOND STREET, LONDON W1. Tel 01-493 6180

Directors: **A. & B. Bloomstein, G. Glass and E. Swonnell**

Above:
Charles II Porringer, London 1680
Left:
William & Mary Tankard, London 1694

The Bond Street Silver Galleries is a concentration of well-known antique silver dealers in the heart of London's West End. There are three floors of Individual showrooms offering an enormous selection of Silver and Sheffield Plate.

Britain's Internationally Best-selling Antiques Magazine

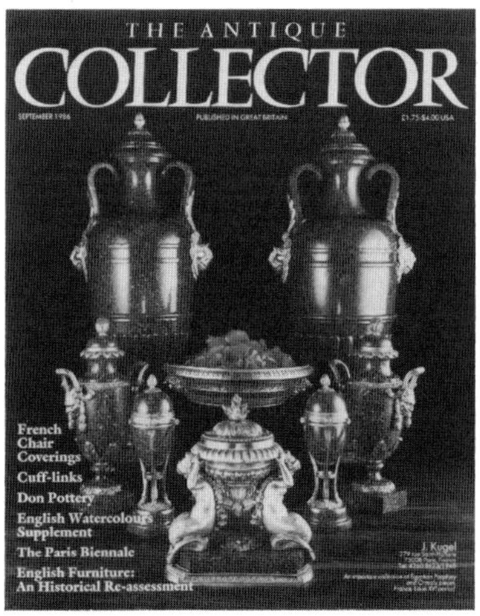

The beginning of a new era for The Antique Collector. A larger magazine, a more beautiful magazine, a better designed magazine and a more colourful magazine, but a magazine which is still as informed, as comprehensive, as authoritative, as well written and essential as it has always been.

For a complimentary copy and subscription details telephone or write to:
THE ANTIQUE COLLECTOR,
72 Broadwick Street, London W1V 2BP. Tel: 01-439 7144

A very fine Charles X ormolu and etched glass 16 branch chandelier.

RODNEY BROOKE

Tel: 01-870 7055

By Appointment only

Barling of Mount Street Ltd
112 Mount St, W1. Tel 499 2858. Open Mon-Fri 9.30-6; other times by appt. 15th to 17thC English and Continental furniture, medieval works of art and early Chinese, Japanese, Indian and S.E.Asian works of art. BADA

K.Barlow Ltd, Decorative Arts 1900-1950
27 Conduit St, W1R 9TA. Tel 629 1653. Open Mon-Fri 10-6, Sat 11-2. Decorative arts 1900-1950, specialising in unique designer pieces.

Barnes and Webster Limited
7a Hanson St, W1. Tel 631 0192. Open Mon-Fri 9-5. Fine art photographers.

R.A.Barnes Antiques
(R.A.Barnes & J.M.Langin). 26 Lower Richmond Rd, Putney, SW15 1JP. Tel 789 3371. Open Mon-Fri 10-5; other times by appt. Wedgwood, 19th and 20thC glass, English, Oriental and Chinese Export porcelain. Also Art Nouveau and Art Deco items, boxes and brass. Belleek, English and French cameo glass. LAPADA

Barnet Antiques and Fine Art
1180 High Rd, Whetstone, N20. Tel 445 9695. (Also at 236 High St, Barnet, Hertfordshire.) Open Mon-Sat 9-5; other times by appt. Good stock of 18th and 19thC English furniture and antiques.

H.Baron
136 Chatsworth Rd, NW2 5QU. Tel 459 2035. Open by appt only. Music, musical literature, periodicals, autograph music, letters, facsimile editions, portraits and prints. ABA

C.Barrett & Co
51 Burlington Arcade, Piccadilly, W1. Tel 493 2570. Open Mon-Fri 9.30-5.30; Sat 9.30-1. Ivories, netsukes, all kinds of objets d'art.

Nigel Bartlett
67 St.Thomas St, SE1. Tel 378-7895/6. Open Mon-Fri 9.30-5.30; other times by appt. Fine chimneypieces in marble, stone & wood. (24hr answer phone).

Basilisk Press
10 Adamson Rd, NW3 3HR. Tel 722 2142. Open by appt only. In print private press books. Detailed catalogue available.

Baskett & Day
(John Baskett Ltd, Richard Day Ltd). 173 New Bond St, W1. Tel 629 2991. Open 9.30-5.30 weekdays. Old Master & English drawings, prints. SLAD

Janet & Robert Bateman Antiques
92 Waterford Rd, SW6 2HA. Tel 736 4149. Open Mon-Sat 10-6. Early oak, country furniture, treen, metalwork and decorative items.

Baumkotter Gallery
63A Kensington Church St, W8. Tel 937 5171. Open Mon-Fri 9.30-6. Fine 17th to 19thC Continental paintings, especially Dutch oil paintings.

H.C.Baxter & Sons
191-193 Fulham Rd, SW3. Tel 352 9826. Open Mon-Fri 9-5; other times by appt. Good stock of English 18thC furniture and antiques generally. BADA

Stanley Beal Ltd
(Anthony S.Beal). 124 New Bond St, W1Y 9AE. Tel 499 2817. Open Mon-Fri 10-5.30; other times by appt. Antique and secondhand silver, old Sheffield plate and plated ware. LAPADA

Stanley Beal Ltd
(A.S.Beal). 41 Fairfax Rd, NW6. Tel 328 7525. Silver, plate. Repairs, replating and valuations.

J. & A. Beare Ltd
7 Broadwick St, W1V 1FJ. Tel 437 1449. Open Mon-Fri 9-12.15, 1.30-5. Appt advisable. Fine old and antique musical instruments of the violin family. Also bows and accessories. BADA

Beaver Coin Room
57 Philbeach Gardens, SW5 9ED. Tel 373 4553. Open Mon-Sat by appt only. European coins from Middle Ages to 1850. Commemorative medals of all periods. BNTA

Claudia Beck
(Claudia Beck). Bond Street Antique Centre, 124 New Bond St, W1. Tel 409 2854 (priv 359 4657). Open Mon-Fri 11-5.30; other times by appt. 19th & 20thC watercolours.

Susan Becker Antiques
(Susan Becker). 18 Lower Richmond Rd, Putney, SW15. Tel 788 9082. Open Mon-Fri 10-5.30; other times by appt. Fine quality English, Continental and Oriental porcelain, glass and objets d'art. LAPADA

Patricia Beckman Antiques
(Mrs P Beckman). 10A Heath Drive, NW3 7SN. Tel 435 5050. Open by appt only. 18th & 19thC furniture. LAPADA

William Bedford PLC
(J. Bedford, P. Hardy, R.Seelig, T. Wilkinson). The Merchants Hall, 46 Essex Rd, Islington, N1 8LN. Tel 226 9648. Open Mon-Sat 9.30-5.30. 15,000 sq.ft of fine period furniture, mirrors, accessories & decorative items, 17th to 19thC, including country furniture. Also fine quality reproduction furniture made to order. BADA, LAPADA

John Beer
191 Archway Road, N6. Tel 340 2183. Open Mon-Sat 9-1, 2-5; closed Thurs. 19th and 20thC British furniture.

Brian Beet
3b Burlington Gdns, Old Bond Street, W1X 1LE. Tel 437 4975. Open Mon-Fri 10-5.30, Sat by appt. Wine antiques, Colonial & Provincial silver, objets de vertu. LAPADA

Beetle & Poker
22 Crown Passage, St James's, SW1Y 6PP. Tel 930 6003. Open Mon-Fri 10-5.30. Two showrooms of 18thC to modern jewellery, antique pocket watches, silver, silver plate and porcelain.

Chris Beetles Ltd
(Chris Beetles). 5 Ryder St, St James's, SW1. Tel 930 8586. Open 10-5. 19th and 20thC watercolours and illustrators.

The Belgrave Gallery
(Irving Grose). 22 Masons Yard, Duke St, St James's, SW1. Tel 930 0294. British Post-Impressionist & modern paintings.

Anthony Belton
14 Holland Street, W8 4LT. Tel 937 1012. Open 10-1, 2-6; Sat 10-4.30; other times by appt. English & European pottery. Decorative and unusual furniture & objects. Primitive, topographical & marine watercolours & oil paintings. Mostly pre-1830. LAPADA

Benardout & Benardout
(Nissim Benardout). 7 Thurloe Place, SW7 2RX. Tel 584 7658. Open Mon-Sat 9-5, Sat 9-12.30; other times by appt. Oriental rugs, carpets, textiles and embroideries. Also cleaning and restoration service. BADA, LAPADA

Raymond Benardout Ltd
(Raymond Benardout and Linda Benardout). 4 William St, Knightsbridge, SW1X 9HL. Tel 235 3360 (priv 235 0504). (Also at 5 William St.) Open Mon-Fri 9-6; other times by appt. Antique furniture and works of art. BADA CINOA GMC

Raymond Benardout
(Raymond Benardout and Linda Benardout). 5 William St, Knightsbridge, SW1X 9HL. Tel 235 3360 (priv 235 0504). (Also at 4 William St.) Open Mon-Fri 9-6; other times by appt. Antique and decorative rugs, carpets and tapestries. Also cleaning, restoration and repairs of rugs, tapestries, embroideries and textiles. BADA CINOA

Ronald Benjamin Antiques
25B Hatton Garden, EC1N 8BQ. Tel 242 9105, 242 6188. Open Mon-Fri 10.30-5.30; other times by appt. (Entrance in Greville St.) Antique and secondhand jewellery, objets d'art, antique watches and silver. BJA

Paul Bennett
(M. Dubiner). 75 George St, W1. Tel 935 1555. Silver, plate, valuations. LAPADA

Bennison
91 Pimlico Rd, SW1. Tel 730 3370, 730 8076. Open Mon-Fri 10-6, Sat 10-4; other times by appt. Good stock of 17th to 19thC furniture, pictures and objets d'art. Also porcelain, needlework, rugs and the Bennison range of new printed fabrics.

Bentley & Co Ltd
65 New Bond St, W1Y 9DF. Tel 629 0651, 629 0325. Open Mon-Fri 10-5. Jewellers, goldsmiths and silversmiths. Antique and fine secondhand jewellery, silver, Faberge and objets d'art. Specialists in Russian works of art, antique watches and fine Victorian jewellery.

Peter Bentley
22 Connaught St, W2. Tel 723 9394. Open Mon-Fri 9.30-6, Sat 9.30-1. 18th and 19thC furniture, glass and paintings. LAPADA

Beresford Clark Antiques
558 King's Rd, SW6 2DZ. Tel 731 5079. Open Mon-Fri; Sats by appt. Antique furniture, paintings, objects both unusual and decorative.

Berkeley Galleries Ltd
(E.Ohly). 82 The Hall, Foxes Dale, SE3. Tel 852 0586. Open by appt only. Antiquities, tribal art and Far Eastern art.

Bermondsey Antique Market Ltd
251-255 Long Lane, SE1. Open Fri 5 am to at least 2pm. 150 stalls with silver, furniture, arms, carpets, toys, pictures, brass, copper, pewter and bric-a-brac.

Bernheimer Fine Arts Ltd
32 St George St, Mayfair, W1R 9FA. Tel 499 0293. (Also L.Bernheimer KG, Lenbachplatz 3, 8000 Munchen 2, W.Germany.) Open Mon-Fri 10-5.30. Antique furniture, sculpture and works of art, Chinese art, carpets, tapestries and textiles.

Bertram Rota Ltd
30-31 Long Acre, WC2E 9LT. Tel 836 0723. Open Mon-Fri 9.30-5.30; other times by appt. Autographs, first editions, private press books, general antiquarian stock. ABA

Peter Biddulph
35 St George St, Hanover Square, W1R 9DF. Tel 491 8621. Violin dealer and consultant.

Sue Biddulph
(Sue Biddulph). X10 Antiquarius, 135 King's Rd, SW3. Open Mon-Sat 11-6. Clothes and accessories from Victorian times to the 1940s, including beaded dresses, Victorian nighties, petticoats, bloomers, Chinese piano shawls.

Big Ben Clock Shop
(Roger Lascelles). 5 Broxholme House, New King's Rd, SW6. Tel 736 1770. Open Mon-Sat 10-5; other times by appt. Longcase clocks, wall clocks, bracket and mantle clocks and watches bought, sold and restored.

Tony Bingham
11 Pond St, NW3 2PN. Tel 794 1596. Open Mon-Fri 10-6.30. Specialists in musical instruments; also music books and 17th to 19thC oil paintings, watercolours and engravings of musicians. BADA

J.L.W.Bird
19 Grove Park Terrace, W4 3QE. Tel 995 9960. Fine art dealer.

Ian Birksted Gallery
(Ian Birksted, Dana Breen). 57 Wood Lane, Highgate, N6 5UD. Tel 348 7638. Open Mon-Fri by appt. Sat 11-1. 20thC and selected contemporary art.

Bizarre
(Aldo Taramasco). 24 Church St, NW8. Tel 724 1305. Art Deco pottery-Clarice Cliff, Grays, Shelley and Carlton ware. Decorative art 1900-1950. Specialising in French Art Deco furniture.

David Black Oriental Carpets
(David Black). 96 Portland Rd, W11 4LN. Tel 727 2566. Open Mon-Sat 11-6; other times by appt. Specialists in antique village and tribal rugs, rare kelims and embroideries. Restoration, cleaning and valuations. Also new rugs and kilims. BADA LAPADA

H.Blairman & Sons Ltd
(George J.Levy, Wendy Y.Levy, Martin P.Levy). 119 Mount St, W1. Tel 493 0444. Open Mon-Fri 9-6; other times by appt. 18thC English and French furniture, Regency furniture, Chinese mirror painting and 19thC designer furniture and metalwork. BADA

Blake Antiques
216 Westbourne Grove, W11 2RH. Tel 229 3232. Open Mon-Fri 10-5.30. General antiques, clocks and barometers.

Blond Fine Art
(Jonathan Blond). 22 Princes St, W1. Tel 437 1230. Open Mon-Fri 10-6, Sat 10-1; other times by appt. 20thC British and contemporary paintings, sculpture and prints. Specialist in modern British 1920-1960 paintings, wood engravings, woodcuts and linocuts from this period.

Anne Bloom Jewellers
10a New Bond St, W1. Tel 491 1213. Jewellery.

N.Bloom & Son (Antiques) Ltd
(Ian Harris). 40 Conduit St, W1R 9FB. Tel 629 5060. Open Mon-Fri 10-6. 19th and 20thC jewellery, antique English and Continental silver, animalier bronzes, carriage clocks, Russian enamels as well as unusual and interesting pieces. Also valuations and repairs. LAPADA

Bloomsbury Book Auctions
(Kerr, Herrmann and Stagg Ltd.). 3-4 Hardwick St, EC1R 4RY. Tel 636 1945, 833 2636/7. Open 9.30-5.30. London auction house specialising in books, manuscripts, atlases, maps and prints. About 20 sales per year.

A. & B. Bloomstein Ltd
Bond St Silver Galleries, 111-112 New Bond St, W1Y 0BQ. Tel 493 6180. Silver. BADA

Bluett & Sons Ltd
48 Davies St, W1Y 1LD. Tel 629 4018, 629 3397. Open Mon-Fri 9.30-5.30; other times by appt. Specialist in early Oriental ceramics, with a fine general stock of Chinese ceramics, jades and bronzes. Also South-East Asian works of art. BADA

Bobinet Ltd
(Andrew Crisford, Simon Bull & Sebastian Whitestone). 102 Mount St, W1YD 5HF. Tel 408 0333/4. Open Mon-Fri 9.30-5; other times by appt. Clocks, watches, scientific instruments and furniture. BADA

Bond Street Antique Centre
124 New Bond St, W1Y 9AE. Tel 351 5353. Open Mon-Fri 10-5.45; Sat 10-4. Twenty-five leading dealers in fine jewellery, silver, portrait miniatures and silhouettes, oriental porcelain and hardstone carvings, antique watches and rare collector's items. Also watercolours, oils, Art Nouveau & Deco, early majolica, antiquities.

Bond Street Silver Galleries
111-112 New Bond St, W1Y 0BQ. Tel 493 6180 (priv 935 2621). Open Mon-Fri 9-5. Important galleries with a large stock of silver, Sheffield plate and allied items on three floors.

Sue Bond
46 Greswell St, SW6 6PP. Tel 381 1324. Open Mon-Fri 9.30-5.30; other times by appt. Public relations consultant specialising in fine art and antiques.

L.W.Bondy
16 Little Russell St, WC1A 2HN. Tel 405 2733. Open Mon-Fri 10.30-6.30; Sat 10.30-5.15. Rare and old books of all periods, especially fine illustrated works. ABA

Bonhams
(W.&F.C.Bonham & Son Ltd). Montpelier Galleries, Montpelier St, Knightsbridge, SW7. Tel 584 9161. (Also at 65-69 Lots Rd, Chelsea (Tel 01-352 0466.) Open Mon-Fri 9-5.30; Tues till 7. Fine art auctioneers. SOFAA

Bonhams Chelsea
(W.& F.C.Bonham & Son Ltd). 65-69 Lots Rd, Chelsea, SW10. Tel 352 0466, 351 1380. (See Bonhams Montpelier Galleries for fine art auctions.) Auctioneers of antique and modern furniture, ceramics and pictures. Furniture sales weekly, ceramics, works of art and picture sales fortnightly.

R. Bonnett
582 Kings Rd, Fulham, SW6. Tel 736 4593 (priv 878 1695). Open Mon-Fri 9-5; Sat 9-1; other times by appt. Georgian and Victorian furniture. Victorian Staffordshire figures.

Bonrose Antiques
(K. Khazaei). 172 Kensington Church St, W8. Tel 229 5486, 221 3139. (Also Bonrose Gallery, 209-211 Kensington Church St.) Open Mon-Fri 10-6. 19thC French furniture, clock sets, porcelain. LAPADA

Bookham Galleries
(Janet & Jack Rowe). 164 Wandsworth Bridge Rd, Fulham, SW6. Tel 736 5125(priv 0372 52668). Open Tues-Sat 10-5.30; closed Sun and Mon; other times by appt. Good selection of 18th and 19thC furniture. A small stock of oriental rugs and carpets.

Joanna Booth
247 King's Rd, SW3. Tel 352 8998. Open Mon-Sat 10-6, other times by appt. European wood carvings, leather bound books and oak furniture; also Old Master drawings, tapestries and textiles. BADA

Claude Bornoff
(Claude Bornoff). 20 Chepstow Corner, Pembridge Villas, W2. Tel 229 8947. Open Mon-Fri 9.30-5.30; other times by appt. English and Continental porcelain and furniture; unusual items of any kind. BADA

Bourbon-Hanby
(L.E.Barrett, I.M.Towning). Stand 20, Chelsea Antiques Market, 245 King's Rd, SW3. Tel 352 2106 (Priv 751 0517). Open Mon-Sat 10-6. Antique jewellery, porcelain, glass and general antiquities.

J.H. Bourdon-Smith Ltd
(J.H. Bourdon-Smith). 24 Mason's Yard, Duke St, St James's, SW1Y 6BU. Tel 839 4714/5. Open Mon-Fri 9.30-6. Georgian and Victorian silver. Silver repairs and valuations, engraving, heraldic research. BADA

Bourne Fine Art Ltd
(P.S.Bourne). 14 Mason's Yard, Duke St, St James's, SW1. Tel 930 4215. Open Mon-Fri 10-6. Scottish paintings 1800-1950 and The Decorative Arts.

Box House Antiques
105 Pimlico Rd, SW1W 8PH. Tel 730 9257. Antique furniture and objets d'art etc. Valuations undertaken. BADA

The Box Shop
(Mrs.Coutinho). Chenil Galleries, King's Rd, Chelsea, SW3. Tel 352 2163. Antique boxes, chess sets and collectables.

Erika Brandl - Paintings
(Erika Brandl). 758 Fulham Rd, SW6 5SH. Tel 736 0497. Open Mon-Fri 10-6; Sat 10-1; other times by appt. Fine art dealers and restorers of oil paintings, specialising in British paintings (1900-1950).

Brandt Oriental Antiques
771 Fulham Rd, SW6. Tel 731 6835. Oriental furniture, ceramics and works of art. Also oriental embroideries.

Luigi Brian
(L. Brian). Vault 56, London Silver Vaults, 53 Chancery Lane, WC2 1QT. Tel 405 2484. Open Mon-Fri 10-5.30. Silver and objets d'art. LAPADA

Christine Bridge
K10-12 Grays in Davies Mews, 1-7 Davies Mews, W1Y 1AR. Tel 499 3562 (priv 741 5501). Open Mon-Fri 10-6. 18th and 19thC wine glasses, decanters and decorative glass, porcelain, bronzes, needlework and general decorative items.

F.E.A.Briggs Ltd
(F.E.A.Briggs). 73 Ledbury Rd, W11. Tel 727 0909 (priv 969 0297). Open Mon-Fri 8.30-1, 2-5.30; Sat 10-4. Victorian and Edwardian furniture, period oak, walnut, and mahogany.

Brisigotti Antiques Ltd
44 Duke St, St James's, SW1. Tel 839 4441. European works of art and Old Master paintings.

Britannia
Grays Antique Market, 58 Davies St, W1. Tel 629 6772. Commemoratives, Doulton and studio pottery.

British Crafts Centre
43 Earlham St, Covent Garden, WC2H 9LD. Tel 836 6993. Open Mon-Fri 10-5.30; Sat 11-5. Exhibitions, shop, bookstall, contemporary craft work, both traditional and progressive.

Aubrey Brocklehurst
124 Cromwell Rd, South Kensington, SW7 4ET. Tel 373 0319. Open Mon-Fri 9-6, Sat 10-1. Antique English clocks and barometers. Also the repair and restoration of furniture, clocks and barometers. BADA

Brod Gallery
(Thomas P.Brod, Brenda J.Auslander). 24 St James's St, SW1A 1HA. Tel 839 3871. Open Mon-Fri 9.30-5.30. Fine Old Masters, 19th & 20thC French and 18th & 19thC British paintings. BADA, SLAD

Rodney Brooke Antiques
(R.D. Brooke). 27A Elsynge Rd, SW18 2HR. Tel 870 7055. Open by appt only. English & Continental furniture, oriental art. LAPADA

Brotherton Gallery Ltd
(Mr Fleming). 77 Walton St, SW3. Tel 589 6848. Open Mon-Fri 10-1.30, 2.30-5.30; Wed 10-7; other times by appt. Natural history paintings and prints, English landscapes and Victorian and contemporary paintings.

David Brower Antiques
113 Kensington Church St, W8. Tel 221 4155. Open Mon-Fri 9.30-5.30. Large stock of Continental and Oriental porcelain, furniture, clocks and bronzes. LAPADA

I. & J.L. Brown
(Ian & Joyce Brown). 636 Kings Rd, Chelsea, SW6 2DU. Tel 736 4141. (Also 58 Commercial Rd, Hereford.) Open Mon-Sat 9-5.30; other times by appt. Matched sets of country chairs, also tables, dressers, desks and brassware. Specialising in English country & French provincial furniture.

Murray Brown
(G.M. Murray-Brown). 18 Halkin Arcade, Knightsbridge, SW1X 8JT. Tel 235 8385 (priv 0323 764298. Open Tues-Thurs 10.30-4; other times by appt. 18th & 19thC paintings,specialising in picture restoration & cleaning. Valuations. FATG

W.J.M.Brown
(W.J.M. Brown). Stand L6, Antiquarius, 135 Kings Rd, SW3. Tel 352 4690. Open Mon-Sat 10-6. Decorative antiquarian prints.

Browse & Darby Ltd
(William Darby & Paul Thomson). 19 Cork St, W1. Tel 734 7984. Open Mon-Fri 10-5.30, Sat 10.30-1. 19th and 20thC French & British paintings, sculpture and drawings.

Bruford & Heming Ltd
28 Conduit St, W1R 9TA. Tel 499 7644, 629 4289. Open 9-6. Antique and modern domestic silver, cutlery and jewellery. BADA

Buck & Payne Antiques
5 Camden Passage, N1. Tel 226 4326. Specialists in French country furniture; unusual and decorative accessories.

C.W.Buckingham
301-303 Munster Rd, Fulham, W6. Tel 385 2657. (Also in Cadnam, Hampshire.) Open Mon-Sat 9-6; early closing Thurs. Pine and Windsor chairs. LAPADA

Lorraine Buckland
186 Walton St, SW3 2HB. Tel 584 7268. Open by appt. Paintings, drawings, prints.

John Bull (Antiques) Ltd
(J.Bull, K.D. Bull). 111-112 New Bond St, W1. Tel 629 1251. Open 9-5. (Also at 163 Portobello Rd, London W11, Saturdays only 8-1.) Silver, silver plate and jewellery.

Tony Bunzl & Zal Davar
(Tony Bunzl & Zal Davar). 344 King's Rd, SW3. Tel 352 3697. Open Mon-Fri 10-5.30; other times by appt. Good stock of 17th and 18thC English oak, French provincial and other Continental furniture. Also pottery, brass and decorative items. LAPADA

Clive A.Burden Ltd
(Clive Burden, Pauline Burden). 13 Cecil Court, WC2N 4EZ. Tel 836 2177. (Also in Rickmansworth, Herts and Florida, U.S.A..) Open Mon-Fri 10-5.30; other times by appt. Antique maps and prints (topographical, natural history, caricatures, Vanity Fair) and antiquarian books. Specialising in Americana. ABA

The Burlington Gallery
10 Burlington Gdns, W1. Tel 734 9228. Open Mon-Fri 9.30-5.30; Sat 10-12. Sporting, topographical, decorative and marine prints. Caricatures.

Burlington Paintings
(Angus Lloyd, Michael Day). 12 Burlington Gdns, W1X 1LG. Tel 734 9984. Open Mon-Fri 9.30-5.30; Sat 10-5.

W.G.T.Burne (Antique Glass) Ltd
11 Elystan St, SW3. Tel 589 6074. Open Mon-Fri 9.30-5.30, Sat 9.30-1. Old English and Irish glass. BADA

Victor Burness
241 Long Lane, SE1. Specialist in scientific instruments.

L.& G.Burnett
(Leslie & Gladys Burnett). 290 Portobello Rd, W10 5TE. Tel 969 8899. Open Fri 7.30am-noon; Sat 7.30am-4; other times by appt. Fine linens, lace, tapestries, needlework, textiles.

The Bury Street Gallery
(Jane Abdy). 11 Bury Street St James's, SW1. Tel 930 2902. Open Mon-Fri 10-1, 2-5; other times by appt. 19thC European paintings, drawings and prints. Specialising in Danish paintings of the 19thC, works by Paul Helleu and J.J.Tissot.

Bushwood Antiques
317 Upper St, N1. Tel 359 2095. Open Mon-Fri 9.30-5.30; other times by appt. Very large stock of 17th to 19thC furniture, clocks, pictures and works of art. LAPADA

Business Art Galleries & The Upstairs Gallery
Royal Academy of Arts, Burlington House, Piccadilly, W1. Tel 734 1448 (priv 734 7763). Open Tues-Fri 10-6, Sat 10-5, Mon by appt only. Specialising in contemporary art including paintings, graphics, wall-hangings and sculpture. Also, comprehensive art service to businesses including hire scheme and commissions.

Butchoff Antiques
48 Peckham Rye, SE15. Tel 639 0736. Open Mon-Fri 9-5.30, Sat 9-1. Approx 4000 sq ft of 18th and 19thC furniture. Shipping goods. LAPADA

Butler & Wilson
189 Fulham Rd, SW3. Tel 352 3045. Open Mon-Sat 10-6. Art deco jewellery, ceramics and glassware.

The Button Queen
(Mrs Toni Frith & Mr Martyn Frith). 19 Marylebone Lane, W1M 5FF. Tel 935 1505. Open Mon-Fri 10-6, Thurs 10-7, Sat 10-1.30. Fine collection of antique buttons and buckles, Victorian jewellery and unusual cufflinks.

Helen Buxton Antiques
193 Westbourne Grove, W11. Tel 229 9997. Open Mon-Fri 10-6; other times by appt. Chinese and Japanese ceramics and works of art. LAPADA

Bygone
(J.C.Pierce). Stand M12, Antiquarius, Kings Rd, SW3. Tel 352 4690 (priv 748 6292). (Also at 68 Linacre Court, Great Church Lane, W6.) Open 11-5; Linacre Court by appt only. Commemoratives and general antiques.

Caboodle Ltd
(Ms Eleanor Hickox). Chelsea Antique Market, 253 King's Rd, SW3. Open Mon-Sat 10-6. 19th and 20thC jewellery, buttons, badges, curiosities etc.

Cadogan Gallery
15 Pont St, SW1. Tel 235 4526. 18th and 19thC decorative and sporting paintings, specialising in dog pictures.

Patric Capon

Fine Antique Clocks   Marine Chronometers   Barometers

DENT London No. 12354.
A chronometer timepiece having Dent's patent 'Z' balance.

LEFRAND Paris.
A rare and complicated perpetual calendar grande sonnerie minute repeating carriage clock.

I offer a varied range of eighteenth and nineteenth century clocks and barometers, please write or telephone for further details.

Showroom open Wednesday and Saturday

350 Upper Street, Islington, London N.1. Tel: 01-354 0487 or 01-467 5722 anytime

---

Odile Cavendish

Oriental art, Japanese screens, lacquer, bronzes, Chinese furniture, Indian paintings, unusual objects.

BY APPOINTMENT ONLY

14 Lowndes Street, London SW1X 9EX
Tel 01-235 2491

Chancery Antiques Ltd.

Dealers in fine
SATSUMA □ IVORIES □ CLOISONNÉ
and other JAPANESE WORKS OF ART

357A UPPER STREET, ISLINGTON, LONDON N.1. TEL. 01-359 9035

JACK CASIMIR LTD

SPECIALISTS IN ANTIQUE METALWARE

Three Fine Brass 18th Century Casters. The largest 8¾" tall.

We maintain an extremely large and varied selection of fine 16th. to 19th. Century English and Continental brass, copper, bronze and pewter.

23 PEMBRIDGE ROAD · LONDON W11 3HG · ENGLAND
TELEPHONE: 01-727 8643

Caelt Gallery
(Edward T Crawshaw). 182 Westbourne Grove, W11. Tel 229 9309 (priv 229 0303). Open Mon-Sat 9.30-6, other times by appt. Varied stock of over 500 17th to 20thC paintings.

Camden Antique Market
(Electric Enterprises). Corner of High St and Buck St, NW1. Tel 351 5353. Open Thurs from 7 am. (Near Camden Town tube station). Wide variety of collectables in a weekly market with over 150 stands.

Camden Auctions
The Saleroom, Hoppers Rd, Winchmore Hill, N21. Tel 886 1550. Auctioneers holding sales on alternate Thursdays at 10.30. Viewing Wed 9.30-8, Thurs 9-10.30.

Camden Passage Antiques Market
Upper Street, Islington, N1. Open Tues-Sat, but especially Wed and Sat for Antiques, Thurs - books.

Cameo Corner at Liberty
Liberty plc, Regent St, W1. Tel 734 1234. Jewellery. BADA

Camerer Cuss & Co
(The Cuss Clock Co Ltd). 17 Ryder St, St James's, SW1Y 6PY. Tel 930 1941. Open Mon-Fri 9.30-5. Antique watches and clocks. BADA

Peter Cameron
(Mr & Mrs P Cameron). 4 Grosvenor St, W1. Tel 491 8949. Silver, valuations. LAPADA

John Campbell Picture Frames Ltd
(Roy Hogben, Harry Norris, Anita Hogben). 164 Walton St, Knightsbridge, SW3 2JL. Tel 584 9268. Open Mon-Fri 9.30-5.30; early closing Sat. Period and contemporary frames, mount cutting and gilding. Also cleaning and restoring of paintings. Large selection of hand coloured engravings & original oils. Will search for particular subjects/pictures/artists. GMC

Canonbury Antiques Ltd
174 Westbourne Grove, W11. Tel 229 2786. Open Mon-Sat 10-6. Large stock of general furniture and decorative items.

Patric Capon
350 Upper St, Islington, N1. Tel 354 0487 (priv 467 5722). Open Wed & Sat; other times by appt. Fine 18th and 19thC clocks, marine chronometers and barometers with emphasis on carriage clocks. LAPADA

Michael Carleton
(M.D.C.Carleton). 77-81 Haverstock Hill, NW3 4SL. Tel 722 2277, 586 4458. Open Mon-Fri 9-1 2-5.30; other times by appt. Multifarious 18thC items. Also restoration, framing, hire and interior decoration services.

J Carlton-Smith
17 Ryder St, St James', SW1. Tel 930 6622 (priv 467 8020). Open Mon-Fri 10-5.30; other times by appt. Fine antique clocks & barometers. BADA

Carrington & Co Ltd
170 Regent St, W1R 6BQ. Tel 734 3727. Open Mon-Fri 9-5.30. Antique and modern silver, military silver, badge brooches and carriage clocks. Special orders, such as medals. Victorian and modern jewellery.

David Carritt Limited
15 Duke Street, SW1. Tel 930 8733. (Also Artemis Fine Arts.) Old Master paintings.

Olwen Carthew
(Olwen Carthew). 109 Kirkdale, SE26. Tel 699 1363. Open Mon, Tues, Wed, Fri, 10-5.30; Thurs 10-3; Sat 10-4.30; other times by appt. Pine and country furniture, Lloyd Loom and wicker bamboo tables, kitchen antiques.

Cartographia Ltd
(B.Marsden FRGS). 37 Southampton St, Covent Garden, WC2E 7HE. Tel 240 5687. Open Mon-Sat 10-7; other times by appt. Original maps, worldwide.

Carvers & Gilders
(F.Crosland, W.McCombe, A.Tyrrell, C.Palmer). Charterhouse Works, Eltringham St, SW18. Tel 870 7047. Open by appt only. Restoration of carving, gilding and gesso on important decorative pieces. Individual commissions also undertaken and limited edition designs.

Jack Casimir Ltd
(M. Casimir, R. Casimir). 'The Brass Shop', 23 Pembridge Rd, W11 3HG. Tel 727 8643. Open Mon-Sat 10-5; other times by appt. An extremely large stock of 16th to 19thC brass, copper, pewter and bronze. Fireplace accessories. Export a speciality. LAPADA

Cassio
68 Ledbury Rd, W11. Tel 727 0678. Open Mon-Fri 10-6, Sat 10-1. 18th and 19thC furniture (mainly Continental), clocks, paintings, bronzes and decorative items.

Casson Gallery
73 Marylebone High St, W1. Tel 487 5080. Porcelain, stoneware, studio glass and jewellery. Specialist craft books. Solo, group and mixed craft exhibitions held three or four times a year.

Castaside
(Mr D.E.Smith). Shop 19, Chelsea Antique Market, 253 King's Rd, SW3. Tel 352 9695. Open Mon-Sat 10-6. Theatrical books and ephemera.

Simon Castle
38B Kensington Church St, W8. Tel 937 2268. Decorative carvings, treen. LAPADA

D.B.Cater Antiques
(D.B.Cater). 173 & 175 Bermondsey St, SE1 3UW. Tel 407 2040. English furniture 1840-1930. Shipping goods. Valuations. LAPADA

Catspa
(B.R.Catley, W.J.Sparrow). Chenil Gallery, King's Rd, Chelsea, SW3. Tel 883 3992. Open by appt only. Art nouveau and art deco bronze and ivory figures.

Cavendish Rare Books Ltd
(B. Grigor-Taylor). 2-4 Princes Arcade, Piccadilly, SW1Y 6DS. Tel 734 3840. Open Mon-Fri 10-6; Sat 9.30-1.30. Antiquarian booksellers specialising in books on voyages, travel, maritime history, mountaineering & Polar exploration. Fine sets. ABA

Odile Cavendish
14 Lowndes St, SW1X 9EX. Tel 235 2491. Open by appt only. Oriental art, Japanese screens, lacquer, bronzes, Chinese furniture, Indian paintings and unusual objects.

Rupert Cavendish Antiques
(Rupert Cavendish). 561 Kings Rd, SW6 2DZ. Tel 731 7041. Open Mon-Sat 10-6. Empire and Biedermeier furniture, oil paintings, watercolours and prints. LAPADA

Elizabeth Cayzer Fine Art
Flat 8, 62 Rutland Gate. Tel 584 2952. Open by appt only. Specialist consultant in all periods of British paintings, watercolours, drawings and prints. Research and cataloguing undertaken.

Centaur Gallery
(Dinah & Jan Wieliczko). Great Expectations, 82 Highgate Village, N6. Tel 340 0087. Open Mon-Sat 11-6. Antique paintings, prints, pottery, ethnic and decorative items. Modern paintings and sculpture. Special exhibitions of modern art in garden gallery.

Chancery Antiques Ltd
22 Park Walk, SW10. Tel 352 6016. (Also 357A Upper St N1 (Tel 359 9035.) Open mainly by appt. Small pieces, 18th and 19thC porcelain, silver, etc.

Chancery Antiques Ltd
(Robert & David Rote). 357A Upper St, Islington, N1. Tel 359 9035. Open Tues, Wed, Fri, Sat; other times by appt. Oriental pottery, porcelain and works of art.

Chandeliers
166 Kensington Church St, W8. Tel 229 1338, 229 2310. Chandeliers.

Chanteau
(Mme Chanteau). 36 Cathcart Rd, SW10 9NN. Tel 352 0447. Open 10-5. Antique and high quality reproduction furniture, English and Continental.

Peter Chapman Antiques
10 Theberton St, Islington, N1 0QX. Tel 226 5565 (priv 348 4846). (Also Chapman Restorations at 133 Upper St, N1.) Open Mon-Sat 9.30-1, 2-6; other times by appt. Furniture 1700 to 1900, paintings, stained glass and objets d'art. Decorative and architectural items. Restoration service for most items. Fine quality leather upholstery. LAPADA

Graham Charge Antiques
305 Westbourne Grove, W11. Tel 229 7907. Open Mon-Sat 9.30-5.30. General and decorative English furniture.

Chatal Limited
457 Finchley Rd, NW3 6HN. Tel 203 2351. Open by appt. Clocks, watches, 19thC jewellery, 18th and 19thC silver.

Chaucer Fine Arts Inc
(Marcello Violante). 45 Pimlico Rd, SW1. Tel 730 2972. Open Mon-Fri 10-6, Sat 10-1. Dutch and Italian Old Masters, pictures and drawings; also classical sculpture.

Chelsea Antique Fairs
(Caroline Penman). 11 Kings Court South, Chelsea Manor Gardens, SW3. Tel 351 9152(priv 04447-2514). (See also Penman Antiques Fairs, Lindfield, W.Sussex.) Chelsea Antique Fair held every March and September in Chelsea Old Town Hall, King's Rd, SW3. 40 exhibitors. LAPADA

Chelsea Antique Market
245a & 253 King's Road, SW3. Tel 352 5689. Open Mon-Sat 10-6.

Chelsea Clocks
Stand Z3, Antiquarius, Kings Rd, SW3. Tel 352 8646. Antique clocks and general.

The Clock Clinic Ltd.

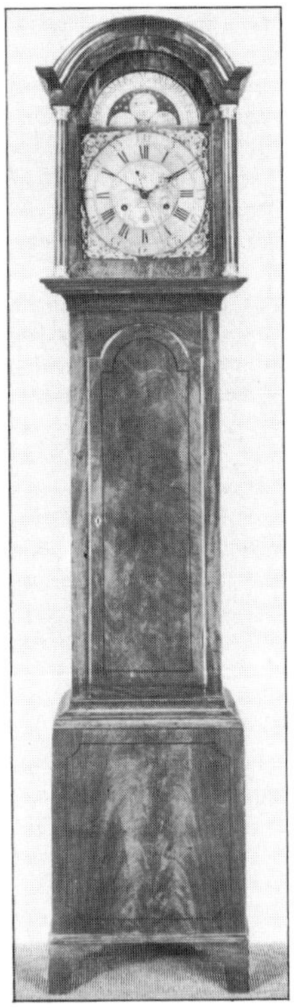

85 Lower Richmond Road,
Putney,
London SW15 1EU.
Telephone: 01-788 1407

An interesting and varied selection of all types of quality Clocks which includes Carriage, Mantel, Wall, Bracket and Longcase Clocks.

Also interesting Barometers

Repairs/Restorations undertaken on all types of quality clocks, barometers and musical boxes.

Valuations for Insurance

Enquiries Welcome

Open:
Tues. – Fri. 9—6 Sat. 9–1

The Chelsea Antiques Fair

Famous since 1951 – Twice a year, on King's Road, London S.W.3.

10–21 March 1987
8–19 September 1987

Daily 11am-8pm; Saturdays 11am-6pm; Closed Sundays

A carefully balanced selection of top English Dealers – (most B.A.D.A. members) offer their finest wares. Almost all pre 1830.

Adm: £2.50 incl, catalogue
Group rate on application

Enquiries:
Penman Fairs, P.O. Box 114
Haywards Heath, W. Sussex
Telephone 04447–2514

LONDON'S FIRST ANTIQUE MARKET

THE MOST FRIENDLY AND STILL THE BEST

245/253 KINGS ROAD,
LONDON SW3
(opposite Carlyle Square)

Chelsea Antique Market

The Famous Market where dealers from all over the world come to buy. This large Antique Centre is where there is something for the specialist and general collector.

Open from 10 am – 6 pm Monday to Saturday

Telephone: 01-352 5689

Chelsea Clocks & Antiques
(Donald Torr). 479 Fulham Road, SW6. Tel 352 8646, 731 5704. Open Tues-Fri 10-5; Sat by appt. Antique clocks, scales, brass, writing boxes and all collectable items.

Chelsea Rare Books
(Leo Bernard). 313 King's Rd, SW3 5EP. Tel 351 0950. Open Mon-Sat 9-6. 18th to 20thC English literature, travel, natural history, art and architecture. ABA

Chenil Galleries
181-183 King's Rd, Chelsea, SW3. Tel 351 5353. (Correspondence to 15 Flood St, Chelsea, SW3.) Open Mon-Sat 10-6. Wide range of antiques, especially Art Nouveau and Art Deco, also 17th and 18thC oil paintings, furniture & fine clocks, scientific instruments, antiquarian books and prints, jewellery, collector's items, golfiana, minerals, dolls & toys.

Chesterfields Etc.
(P.F. Crawford). 99 Lisson Grove, NW1. Tel 402 9728. (Also at 224 Upper Richmond Rd West, SW14 (878 6025.) Open Mon-Fri 10-6, Sat 10-5; other times by appt. Victorian upholstery, re-upholstery, repro leather chesterfields & wing chairs, etc.

Chi Mei Chai Eastern Art Gallery
40 Great Russell St, WC1. Tel 631 4868. Open Tues-Sat 10.30-5.30. Chinese paintings only and regular exhibitions.

China Repairers
(A.Drayson, P.Mair, J.Radford & H.Howard). 64 Charles Lane, NW8. Tel 722 8407. Open Mon-Fri 9.30-1, 2.15-5.30, Sat 10.30-1.30 or by appt. Specialists in porcelain restoration. LAPADA

Directory Entries are Free and ADDITIONS OR CORRECTIONS will be welcomed by *THE EDITOR, British Art and Antiques Directory, National Magazine House, 72 Broadwick Street, London W1V 2BP*

J.Christie
(P.S. Christie, M.J.Christie). 26 Burlington Arcade, Piccadilly, W1V 9AD. Tel 629 3070. Open Mon-Fri 10-5, Sat 10-1. Antique and modern silver, plate, antique Sheffield, French & Russian animalier bronze, silver and enamel boxes. Japanese and European ivories. Jewellery and objets d'art. BADA CINOA LAPADA

Christie's
8 King St, St James's, SW1Y 6QT. Tel 839 9060. Open Mon-Fri 9-4.45. Fine art auctioneers and valuers. Also open for viewing Sunday afternoons during the auction season.

Christie's in the City
(Simon Birch, Peter Arbuthnot). 56-60 Gresham St, EC2V 7BB. Tel 588 4424. Office for the fine art auctioneers and valuers.

CCA Galleries
8 Dover St, W1. Tel 499 6701. (Also in Harrods, and in New York.) 20thC prints and sculpture.

Christie's South Kensington
85 Old Brompton Rd, SW7 3JS. Tel 581 7611. Open Mon 9-7; Tues-Fri 9-5. Auctioneers of fine art and antiques including specialist sales of toys, dolls, mechanical music, photographs, textiles, scientific instruments, art nouveau, art deco, tribal art and many more.

Church Street Galleries
(G.A.Meyer & J.Meyer). 77 Kensington Church St, W8 4BG. Tel 937 2461 (priv 937 9175). Open Mon-Fri 9-6, Sat 10-4; other times by appt. Late 17th to early 19thC English furniture. BADA

Ciancimino Ltd
(J.C.Ciancimino & A.Ciancimino). 99 Pimlico Rd, SW1W 8PH. Tel 730 9950. Open Mon-Fri 10-6; Sat by appt. Oriental, English and Continental 18th and 19thC fine and decorative works of art. BADA

City Clocks
(Jeffrey Rosson, FBHI). 1B Lambs Passage, Chiswell St, EC1Y 8LE. Tel 628 6749. Open Mon-Fri 8-7; other times by appt. Longcase clocks, bracket clocks, French clocks, barometer & musical boxes. Almost any clock or watch repaired on premises. FBHI

City Fine Arts
(M. W. M. Davidson). (7th Floor) 50 Pall Mall, SW1Y 5JQ. Tel 935 6826. Open by appt only. Furniture, paintings, valuations. LAPADA

Clarendon Gallery
(Gavin Henderson). 8 Vigo Street, W1. Tel 439 4557. Open Mon-Fri 9.30-5.30. Old Master paintings, English and French 18th and 19thC paintings and architectural drawings.

Clarges Gallery
(R.J.R.McDougall). 158 Walton Street, SW3. Tel 584 3022. Open Mon-Fri 10-5.30, Sats as advertised; other times by appt. 19th and 20thC watercolours, drawings and oils of the British school, also contemporary limited edition prints. Periodic exhibitions of living and recently deceased artists.

Gerald Clark Antiques Ltd
(Gerald & June Clark). 1 High St, Mill Hill Village, NW7 1QY. Tel 906 0342. Open Tues-Sat 10-5; other times by appt. Early English & Victorian Staffordshire pottery figures, animals, cottages, groups, jugs, mugs etc. Also small furniture & watercolours. LAPADA

Clarke Fine Art
191 Chiswick High Rd, W4. Gallery specialising in new artists.

John Clay
263 New King's Rd, SW6. Tel 731 5677. Open Mon-Fri 8.30-6, Sat 10-6. Approx 500 sq ft of furniture, mainly mahogany 1740 to 1850, decorative furniture & animalier objets d'art.

Ian Clayton Ltd
4 Stainer St, SE1. Tel 403 2742. Statuary and monument conservation.

William Clayton Ltd
38 Bury St, St James's, SW1. Tel 930 1173. Open 10-5. Chinese works of art, jades, porcelain, sculptures.

The Clerkenwell Green Association for Craftsmen
Pennybank Chambers, 33-35 St John's Square, EC1. Tel 251 0276. Craftsmen practising a wide range of crafts including jewellery, watch and clockmaking, clock restoring, ceramic restoring, antique musical instruments.

Clifton Fine Art
(Edward B. Goslett). 6 Bristol Gardens, Little Venice, W9 2JG. Tel 286 9121. Open Mon-Sat 10.30-6. 19th and 20thC British and Continental paintings, with the emphasis on the 20thC. Exhibitions of established 19th and 20thC artists.

Clock Clinic Ltd
(P.Banks, R.S.Pedler FBHI). 85 Lower Richmond Rd, Putney, SW15 1EU. Tel 788 1407. Open Tues-Fri 9-6; Sat 9-1; other times by appt. Fine longcase, bracket, wall and carriage clocks, mainly 18th and 19thC. Restoration and repair services. FBHI

Clunes Antiques
(Daphne Clunes). 9 West Place, Wimbledon, SW19 4UH. Tel 946 1643. Open Tues, Thurs, Fri, Sat, 10-5; other times by appt. Staffordshire figures, theatrical items and general small antiques.

Coakley & Hayter
(T.Coakley, M.Hayter). Stand D13, Chenil Galleries, King's Rd, SW3. Tel 351 2914 (priv 0992 52907). Art Deco and Art Nouveau furniture and smalls, specialising in Bugatti furniture, Art Deco bronzes and ivories.

Cobb Antiques Ltd
(Mark West). 39b High St, Wimbledon Village, SW19. Tel 946 2811 (priv 540 7982). Open Wed, Thur, Fri 1-6; Sat 10-6; other times by appt. Large stock of table glass, decanters etc. & coloured platters and small furniture (1000 sq.ft).

Cobra & Bellamy
(Tania Hunter and Veronica Manussis). 149 Sloane St, SW1. Tel 730 2823. Open Mon-Fri 10.30-6; Sat 10.30-4. Decorative arts and jewellery of the 20thC.

Fergus Cochrane Antiques
570 Kings Rd, SW6. Tel 736 9166. Furniture.

Cocozza Antiques
208 Westbourne Grove, W11. Tel 221 1535. Open Mon-Fri 10-6; Sat 10-1; other times by appt. Fine furniture, objets d'art and decorative items. LAPADA

Coexistence Limited
(Mary Wiggin). Hobhouse Court, 13 Whitcomb St, WC2H 7HA. Tel 839 6620. (Also in Canonbury Lane and Bath.) Open Mon-Sat 10-6; other times by appt. Country furniture, textiles.

Coexistence Limited
(Mary Wiggin). 17 Canonbury Lane, N1 2AS. Tel 226 8382. (Also in WC2 and Bath, Avon.) Open Mon-Sat 10-6; other times by appt. Country furniture, textiles.

Cohen and Pearce (Oriental Porcelain)
(Michael Cohen and Rosemary Pearce). 84 Portobello Rd, W11 2QD. Tel 229 9458. Open Fri 10-4; Sat 8-4; other times by appt. Chinese export porcelain and Oriental works of art, specialists in Famille Rose, Famille Verte and other Qing porcelains. BADA

B.Cohen & Sons
35 Bury St, St James's, SW1Y 6AY. Tel 839 6466/7. Open Mon-Fri 9.30-6, but appt always advisable. Old Masters. BADA

Edward Cohen
(Edward Cohen). 40 Duke St, St James's, SW1. Tel 839 5180. Open 9.30-6; other times by appt. Master paintings.

Moira Cohen Ltd
22-23 New Bond St, W1. Tel 629 0160. Open Mon-Fri 9-6. Silver & objets d'art; antique, art nouveau, Edwardian & art deco jewellery.

Coin Exchange
153 Portobello Rd, W11. Open Sat only. Antiques, coins, silver etc.

Colefax & Fowler
39 Brook St, W1Y 1AU. Tel 493 2231. Open 9.30-1, 2-5.30. Important English and Continental 18th and 19thC antique furniture and unusual decorative works of art.

Aubrey J.Coleman Antiques
(G.D. & G.E.Coleman). 121 Kensington Church St, W8 7LP. Tel 221 6228. Open Mon-Sat 9.45-6; other times by appt. Antique furniture and objects. Large stock of chess sets and boards. LAPADA

Simon Coleman
40 White Hart Lane, Barnes, SW13. Tel 878 5037. Open Mon-Sat; other times by appt. Country furniture in oak, fruitwood and pine. French & English farm tables always in stock.

Coleridge
192 Piccadilly, W1. Tel 437 0106. (Also in Highgate Village, N6 (Tel 340 0999.) Wide selection of contemporary British glass. ICGA

Philip Colleck Ltd
(P. Colleck, S.R. Bentley). 84 Fulham Rd, SW3 6HR. Tel 584 8479. Open Mon-Fri 9.30-5.30; Sat 9.30-1; other times by appt. Fine antique English furniture and works of art. BADA

Collectables
(Mr J. Davison). 141 Greenwich South St, Greenwich, SE10. Tel 692 4047. (Also at 1 & 3 Blackheath Hill, SE10. Tel 692 5826.) Open Tues-Sat 10-6. General antiques. Old stripped pine furniture at Blackheath Hill.

Collectors Corner
Coburg Street, N1. Open Mon-Fri 9-5; Sat 9-4.30. British Rail memorabilia including station signs, nameplates, headlamps and smaller objects such as tickets and buttons. Also railway clocks.

Collectors Corner - Militaria
(James H. Joslyn). 1 Northcross Rd, East Dulwich, SE22 9ET. Tel 693 6285. Open 6 days 10.30-5.30; other times by appt. All military items bought, sold and exchanged. Also film and TV Company's supplies.

Collingwood of Bond Street
171 Bond Street, W1. Tel 734 2656. Open Mon-Fri 9-5. Fine quality modern and antique jewellery, mainly Victorian; silver, mainly Georgian. BADA

Julie Collino
15 Glendower Pl, SW7. 19th and 20thC paintings and etchings, unusual decorative items.

Frank Collins
60 Ledbury Rd, W11 2AJ. Tel 221 7108, 0502-714842. (Also same hours at Marlborough Farm, London Rd, Weston, Suffolk.) Open Mon-Sat 9.30-1 2-5.30. 17th to 19thC furniture and works of art. LAPADA

Isabelle Collins Antiques
(John Cullis & Isabelle Collins). 156 and 158 Wandsworth Bridge Rd, SW6. Tel 731 4695. (Also 115 Newbury St, Boston, Mass. 02116, USA.) Open Mon-Sat; other times by appt. Pine and decorative furniture, 18th and 19thC.

Joan Collins
153 Portobello Rd, W11. Tel (priv) 727 6848. Open Sat only. Art nouveau, art deco and decorative arts.

Peter Collins
92 Waterford Rd, SW6. Tel 736 4149. Open 10-1 & 3-6; other times by appt. 17th, 18th and early 19thC country furniture. Also decorative items.

Sylvia Collins
Unit 15, Bond St Antique Centre, 124 New Bond St, W1Y 9AE. Tel 9625. Open Mon-Fri 10-5. Antique, Edwardian and Art Deco jewellery. Chinese and Japanese works of art - netsuke, okimono, hardstone carvings.

Cecilia Colman Gallery
67 St Johns Wood High St, NW8. Tel 722 0686. Open Mon-Fri 10-5.30; Sat 2-5. Studio glass, ceramics and porcelain - contemporary British artists. ICGA

Colnaghi and Simon
(M. & J.Brookstone, R. Herner, M. Asher). 70 Pimlico Rd, SW1W 8LS. Tel 730 8673. Open Mon-Sat 10-6; other times by appt. 18th and 19thC English pictures.

P. & D. Colnaghi & Co Ltd
14 Old Bond St, W1X 4JL. Tel 491 7408. Open Mon-Fri 10-6. Old master paintings, drawings and prints, English paintings, drawings and watercolours, European sculpture, furniture, and works of art. SLAD

O. Comitti & Son Ltd
656 Forest Rd, Walthamstow, E17 3ED. Tel 509 0011. Open Mon-Fri 8.30-5.30. Manufacturers of clocks and barometers. Restorers of antique barometers. BCWMA, BJA

Commemoratives
(Frances Annesley). 3 Pierrepont Arcade, Camden Passage, Islington, N1. Tel eves only 278 2146. Open Tues 12-4; Wed 9-5; Fri 12-4; Sat 9-5; other times by appt. Commemoratives in pottery and porcelain from Queen Victoria to Prince Harry. Also commemoratives for theatre, cinema, radio, television, exhibitions.

Connaught Brown PLC
2 Albemarle St, W1X 3HF. Tel 408 0362. Open Mon-Fri 10-6; Sat 10-12.30; other times by appt. Paintings, drawings, watercolours and sculpture. Specialising in French Post Impressionists, Danish and Scandinavian (1880-1920), modern British, contemporary British.

Connaught Galleries
44 Connaught St, W2. Tel 723 1660. Open Mon-Fri 10-6, Sat 10-1. 18th and 19thC furniture, glass, porcelain, scientific instruments, also pictures.

The Connoisseur Gallery
14 Halkin Arcade, SW1X 8JT. Tel 245 6431. Specialists in Arabic manuscripts, books, maps, prints, paintings and works of art of the Middle East.

Contemporary Textile Gallery
10 Golden Square, W1R 3AF. Tel 439 9070. Open Mon-Sat 9-5.30, Thurs 9-7. Modern carpets, rugs, tapestries and textiles with emphasis on contemporary young designers. Also works to commission.

S.A.Cook & Son
(S.A., G.B. & A.W.Cook). 279 Finchley Rd, NW3. Tel 435 4543. Open Mon-Sat 9-6.30; other times by appt. Victorian and Edwardian furniture, silver, plate and china.

Mary Cooke Antiques Ltd
15 King St, SW1. Tel 839 6566. Open Mon-Fri 9.30-5.30. Wide range of antique silver, mainly pre-1830; both collectors' items and more important pieces. BADA

R. & D. Coombes
Charleville Gallery, 7 Charleville Rd, West Kensington, W14 9JL. Tel 385 3795. Open Tues-Fri 10-5; other times by appt. Oriental ceramics and works of art, Japanese prints. LAPADA

A.C.Cooper Ltd
10 Pollen St, W1R 9PH. Tel 629 7585. Photographic services.

Belinda Coote Antiques
29 Holland St, W8. Tel 937 3924. Open Mon-Fri 10-6; Sat 10-1; other times by appt. Wide range of 19thC pottery and porcelain and items of furniture, decorative items, papier mache, tole peinte. Specialising in Masons Ironstone China and reproduction French tapestries.

Coracle Press
235 Camberwell New Road, SE5. Tel 703 5201. Open Tues-Sat 11-6 and by appt. Contemporary art.

The Corner Cupboard
(Marjorie Fry, Ruth Fischelis). 679 Finchley Rd, NW2 2JP. Tel 435 4870. (See also The Trinket Box, 1 Goldhurst Terrace, NW6.) Open Mon-Sat 9.30-6. Jewellery, silver, porcelain, pottery, small furniture, prints, bric-a-brac.

Laurence Corner, Euston Gallery
(Victor Laurence (Merchants) Ltd). 126-130 Drummond St, NW1. Tel 388 6811. Open Mon-Sat 9-5.30. Oil & watercolour paintings 1800 to date, old engravings and prints, topographical work worldwide. Also Laurence Corner Militaria and Costumes at same address, selling militaria, old theatrical costumes, uniforms, ambassadorial & court dress, swords etc.

Richard Courtney Ltd
112-114 Fulham Rd, SW3 6HU. Tel 370 4020. Open Mon-Fri 9.30-6; other times by appt. Fine 18thC English furniture. BADA

Ralph Cox
53 Ledbury Rd, W11. Tel 229 6900 (priv 723 3162). Open 9.30-12.30, 2-4.30; other times by appt. Sculpture, early metalwork, decorative and architectural objects.

R.O. & F. Coyle
10 Holland St, Kensington, W8 4LT. Tel 937 3723. Open Mon-Sat 10-5.30. Folk and tribal art including weather vanes, American and European decoys, Sri Lankan masks and puppets.

Craddock & Barnard
(O.H.Barnard & Miss Audrey Gibbs). 32 Museum St, WC1A 1LN. Tel 636 3937. Open Mon-Fri 9.30-5.30. Modern and Old Master etchings, engravings, lithographs and woodcuts.

Crafts Council Shop, V & A
(Managed by Crafts Council). Victoria and Albert Museum, SW7 2RL. Tel 589 5070. Open Mon-Thurs 10-5.45; Sat 10-5.30; Sun 2.30-5.30. Sculptural ceramics, domestic pottery, glass, wood, jewellery, metalwork and textiles.

The Craftsmen Potters Shop
(Vivien Whitaker, Manager). 7 Marshall St, W1V 1FD. Tel 437 7605. Open Mon-Sat 10-5.30. Contemporary pottery - a selection of the finest work made by British potters, including domestic and individual unique pieces.

Cranbourn Antiques Ltd. (Artinterias)
(G. Fever). 32 Thanet Lodge, Mapesbury Rd, NW2 4JA. Tel 459 0782. Open by appt. 19thC French furniture, porcelain and objets d'art.

The Crane Gallery
(A. Kalman). 171A Sloane St, (1st Floor), SW1. Tel 235 2464. Open Mon-Fri 10-6, Sat 10-4; other times by appt. English and American folk art, quilts, naive paintings, furniture, decoys and Americana.

Crane Kalman Gallery
(Andras Kalman). 178 Brompton Rd, SW3. Tel 584 7566. Open Mon-Fri 10-6; Sat 10-4. 20thC modern, European & British paintings and sculpture. SLAD

Crawford & Pawle Ltd
(Alastair Crawford, Julian Pawle). 2nd Floor, Bond St Silver Galleries, 111-112 New Bond St, W1Y 9AB. Tel 499 8442. Antique silver and jewellery. Acquisition and selling on commission as well as cash basis. Also offer services including general engraving, seal engraving, restoration, repairs and valuations for insurance, division and probate.

Lesley Craze
5 Essex Rd, Islington, N1. Tel 226 3200. Modern jewellery and silversmithing. ICGA

Tony & Iris Cremer-Price
282 Westbourne Grove, W11 YT19. Open Sats only. Silver. LAPADA

Crescent Antiques
(Stephen Farrelly). 152 Fleet Rd, NW3 2QX. Tel 485 2089. (Also in London SW16.) Open 10-5.30; early closing Thurs. General stock of antique furniture, pictures, porcelain, glass, metalware, carpets. Also some secondhand items.

Crescent Furniture Stores
(Stephen Farrelly). 634 Streatham High Rd, SW16 3QL. Tel 764 4028. (Also in London NW3.) Open 9-5; early closing Wed. General stock of antique furniture, pictures, porcelain, glass, metalware, carpets. Also some secondhand stock.

Crest Antiques
(S.J. Corker). 287 Putney Bridge Rd, Putney, SW15. Tel 789 3165. (Registered Head Office: 313-315 Putney Bridge Rd, SW15.) Open Mon-Sat 10-5. English furniture 1800-1930, porcelain, glass, paintings, clocks, bronzes, silver & bric-a-brac.

John Crichton
34 Brook St, W1Y 1YA. Tel 629 7926. Open Mon-Fri 10-5. Oriental ceramics and works of art.

J. Crisp & Son
48 Roderick Rd, Hampstead, NW3 2NL. Tel 340 0668. Specialists in hand finished leathers, table linings, upholstery and panelling. Desk and table tops re-lined on premises Also embossing and leather restoration.

T.Crowther & Son Ltd
282 North End Rd, Fulham, SW6 1NH. Tel 385 1375/7. Open Mon-Fri 9-6. Oak and pine room panelling, carved wood and marble chimneypieces, garden ornaments and statues, 18thC furniture, grates, fenders, fire-irons, chandeliers and wall lights.

Csaky's Antiques
20 Pimlico Rd, SW1. Tel 730 2068. (Also at 133 Putney Bridge Rd, SW15.) Open Tues, Sat 9-12, 1.30-6. 15th to 18thC English and Continental furniture, carvings, rugs and unusual items. Pine for shipping, polishing and restoration.

Prudence Cuming Associates Ltd
28-29 Dover St, W1X 3PA. Tel 629 6430, 629 1638. Open Mon-Fri 8.30-6. Photographers of fine art - paintings, sculpture, furniture, jewellery, etc. BIPP

Cura Antiques
(Gianfranco & Mark Antichi). 34 Ledbury Rd, W11 2AB. Tel 229 6880. Open Mon-Fri 9.30-6, Sat9.30-1; other times by appt. Continental furniture, paintings and objets d'art.

Curwen Gallery
(Jane Hindley, Director). 4 Windmill St, off Charlotte St, W1. Tel 639 1459. Open Mon-Fri 10-5, Sat 10-1. Contemporary art.

Cutler Street Antique Market
Cutler St, E1. Tel 351 5353. Open Sun 7am-2. Gold, silver, jewellery, coins, stamps and medals.

R. D'Alessandro
610 Kings Rd, SW6. Tel 731 7160. Antique furniture of 18th and 19thC.

Anthony d'Offay Gallery
9 & 23 Dering St, New Bond St, W1. Tel 499 4100. Open Mon-Fri 10-5.30; Sat 10-1. 20thC British paintings, drawings and sculpture. Contemporary art at Number 23.

Daedalus
43 The Village, Charlton, SE7 8UG. Tel 858 2514. Specialists in the restoration of fine English and Continental antique clocks and watches.

John Dale Antiques
(John Dale). 87 Portobello Rd, W11. Tel 727 1304. Antique furniture.

Peter Dale Ltd
11 & 12 Royal Opera Arcade, Pall Mall, SW1Y 4UY. Tel 930 3695. Open Mon-Fri 9.30-5, Sat am by appt, but appt always advisable. Antique arms, armour and militaria for the collector.

Anthony Dallas & Sons Ltd
17 Clifford St, W1. Tel 734 7127. Open Mon-Fri 9-5.30; other times by appt. Old Master and English oils and watercolours. Also valuations and restorations.

Dalton Peett Antiques
610 Fulham Rd, SW6.

Zal Davar
26A Munster Rd, SW6. Tel 736 2559, 736 1405. Open Mon-Fri 9.30-5.30. Quality Victorian and antique furniture, barometers and selected decorative items. LAPADA

Arthur Davidson Ltd
(Arthur Davidson, Lynda Davidson). 78-79 Jermyn St, SW1. Tel 930 6687, 930 4643. Open Mon-Fri 9-5.30, Sat 9-1; other times by appt. Early furniture, scientific instruments and works of art. BADA CINOA LAPADA

Michael Davidson Antiques
52-54 Ledbury Rd, W11 2AJ. Tel 229 6088 (priv 352 4541). Open Mon-Fri 9.15-5; Sat 9.15-1; other times by appt. 18thC furniture and decorative items.

Davies Antiques
(H.Q.V.Davies). 44A Kensington Church St, W8. Tel 937 9216. Open Mon-Fri 10.30-5.30, Sat 10-3; other times by appt. Continental porcelain from the 18th to the 20thC, antique maps and prints. LAPADA

Barry Davies Oriental Art
(Barry Davies). E14/17 Grays Mews, 1-7 Davies Mews, W1. Tel 408 0207 (priv 09326 4906. Open Mon-Fri 10-6; other times by appt. Dealer in oriental art, ivories, netsuke, inro, ojime, lacquer, bronzes, porcelain, cloisonne.

J.M.Davies (Jewellers) Ltd
(J.M.Davies). Grays Antique Market, 58 Davies St, W1. Tel 493 9624. Jewellery. LAPADA

John Davies Framing Ltd
8 Bury St, St. James's, SW1. Fine reproductions of period frames specialists in North European frames; carving and gilding.

N.Davighi
117 Shepherds Bush Rd, W6. Tel 603 5357. Open Mon-Sat 9-5, other times by appt. Repair, restoration and manufacture to order of chandeliers, wall and table lights in crystal and ormolu, gilding, brass casting and rewiring.

A.B.Davis Ltd
18 Brook St, W1. Tel 629 1053. Jewellery.

Jesse Davis
16 Lower Richmond Rd, Putney, SW15. Tel 785 7155. Antiques and works of art.

Kenneth Davis
38 Bury St, SW1. Tel 930 0313. Fine antique silver and works of art.

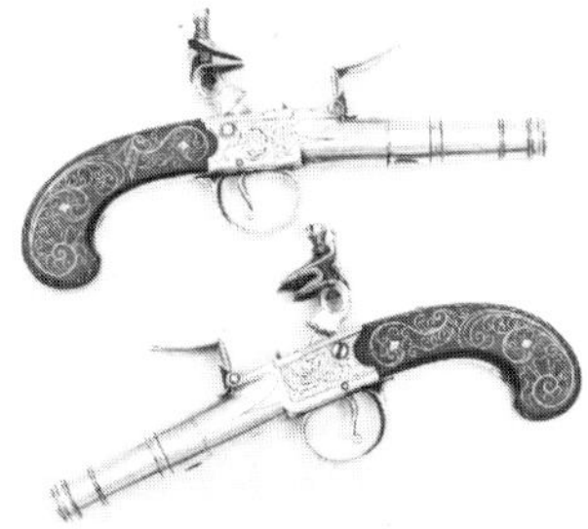

Anthony Dawson
41 Lillian Rd, Barnes, SW13. Tel 748 1306. Contemporary art.

Caroline Dawson
Tel 727 4106. Open by appt, or at Covent Garden Jubilee Market on Mondays. Inventions and patents, scientific instruments, very early metalware, early country items, kitchen and domestic equipment.

Richard Day Ltd
173 New Bond St, W1. Tel 629 2991, 493 7569. Old master drawings. SLAD

Shirley Day Ltd
91B Jermyn St, SW1Y 6JB. Tel 839 2804. Open by appt. Japanese works of art, paintings, screens, ceramics and lacquers. Also Chinese, South Asian & Korean works of art. BADA

Robin de Beaumont
25 Park Walk, Chelsea, SW10. Tel 352 3440. Open by appt only. Victorian illustrated books and bindings. 1860s illustrators and colour printing. Occasional catalogue issued.

de Havilland Antiques
(Balfour de Havilland). 48 Sloane St, SW1X 9LU. Tel 235 3534. Open Mon-Sat 9.30-5.30; other times by appt. 18thC furniture, silver and clocks. LAPADA

P.G. De Lotz
20 Downside Crescent, NW3. Military history and books on warfare. Catalogues. Postal business only. ABA

Rogers de Rin
(Victoria de Rin). 76 Royal Hospital Rd, SW3. Tel 352 9007. Open Mon-Fri 10-6, Sat 10-1, other times by appt. Specialists in Scottish Wemyss pottery, collectors' items, Staffordshire cottages, cow-creamers and objets de vertu. Also some furniture.

Delieb Antiques Ltd
31 Woodville Rd, NW11 9TP. Tel 458 2083. Open Mon-Fri by written appt only. Specialist in antique silver for collectors.

Marilyn Delion
(Marilyn Caron Delion). Wyllie Gallery, 12 Needham Rd, W11 2RP. Tel 727 0606 (priv 937 3377). Open Mon-Fri 2-6; Sat 10-1; other times by appt. English pottery & porcelain. Small antiques.

Delomosne & Son Ltd
(J.B.Perret, M.C.F.Mortimer, T.N.M.Osborne). 4 Campden Hill Rd, W8 7DU. Tel 937 1804. Open Mon-Fri 9-5.30, Sat 9.30-1. 18th and 19thC British and European pottery, porcelain and glass, including chandeliers. Also needlework. BADA

Demas
31 Burlington Arcade, Piccadilly, W1M 7HB. Tel 493 9496. Open Mon-Fri 10-5, Sat 10-1. Silver, Georgian and Victorian jewellery and Art Deco pieces; also coloured Victorian glass.

Demetzy Books
(Paul & Marie Hutchinson). 113 Portobello Rd, W11. Tel Witney (0993) 2209. Open Sat 7-4. Fine bindings and antiquarian books on a variety of subjects. Collectors' miniature books; 19thC first editions, especially Dickens. ABA, PBFA

John Denham Gallery
50 Mill Lane, NW6. Tel 794 2635. Open Tues-Fri & Sun 10-5.30; other times by appt. Oils and watercolours, etchings, engravings 17th-20thC. Full restoration service.

Denisa the Lady Newborough
1-1A-2 Whitehorse St, Shepherd Market, W1. Tel 493 3954 (priv 493 0854). Open Mon-Sat 10-5. Georgian, Queen Anne, Charles II and Victorian jewellery and silver.

Richard Dennis
(Richard Dennis). 144 Kensington Church St, W8 4BN. Tel 727 2061. Open Mon-Fri 10-6; Sat 10-2. English studio pottery 1850-1960, specialising in Doulton, Wedgwood, Martin, Moorcroft and Parian.

Colin Denny
18 Cale St, SW3 3QU. Tel 584 0240. Open Mon-Sat 9-6; Sat 9.30-1; other times by appt. Marine oil paintings, watercolours, prints, mainly of the 19thC. Some models of ships.

F.T. Dent
58 Goldhurst Terrace, NW6. Tel 624 8383. Important trade in Old Master paintings. Wholesale only.

Dernier & Hamlyn Ltd
17 Lydden Rd, Wandsworth, SW18 4LT. Tel 870 0011/2. (Showroom c/o Arnold Montrose Ltd, 47-48 Berners St, London W1.) High quality reproduction light fittings in traditional styles of the 18th and 19thC. Catalogue of standard ranges available. Restorers of traditional lighting fittings. Special commissions undertaken.

Kay Desmonde Antiques Ltd
(Kay Desmonde). 17 Kensington Church Walk, W8 4NB. Tel 937 2602 (priv 04606 3280. Open Sat 11-3; other times by appt. Antique dolls, dolls' houses, dolls' house furniture and accessories, toys. All antique, no reproductions stocked.

H.&W.Deutsch
111 Kensington Church St, W8. Tel 727 5984. Open Mon, Thurs, Fri, 10-6; other times by appt. Large stock of 18th to late 19thC silver and silver plate, Continental porcelain, glass, furniture and decorative items. LAPADA

Dickens Old Curiosity Shop
(David Goldband). 13-14 Portsmouth St, WC2A 2ES. Tel 405 9891. Open 364 days a year, closed Christmas day. Specialists in anything to do with Charles Dickens: first editions, prints, porcelain etc. Also Hogarth prints, copperware, brassware, silver and silver plate, pottery and porcelain.

Robert Dickson Antiques
(Robert Dickson). 263 Fulham Rd, SW3. Tel 351 0330 (priv 948 5825). Open daily 9.30-5.30; Sat 9.30-1; other times by appt. 18th and early 19thC furniture and works of art. BADA

Richard Digby
(R.Digby). Stand L18-21, Grays Mews, 1-7 Davies St, W1. Tel 491 0251. (Office at 63 South Molton St, W1.) Open Mon-Fri 10-6. Jewellery including cameos & intaglios. LAPADA

The Dining Room Shop
(Kate Dyson). 64 White Hart Lane, Barnes, SW13 0PZ. Tel 878 1020 (priv 876 5212). Open Mon-Sat 10-5.30; other times by appt. All kinds of antique furniture for the dining room, chairs, tables etc. Antique porcelain and pottery for the table, antique glass and decanters, silver, table linen and lace related accessories.

Discovery
(Peter Machin). Chelsea Antique Market, 245-253 King's Rd, SW3. Tel 352 9695. Open Mon-Sat 10-6. Antiquarian gramophone records, sheet music and musical and theatrical ephemera. Postcards and newspapers.

Nimrod Dix & Company
(Mr Nimrod Dix). 17 Piccadilly Arcade, SW1Y 6NL. Tel 493 5082. Open Mon-Fri 10-5. Military orders, decorations and medals, militaria, military presentation items, reference books.

Dixon's Antique Centre
(Mrs Jean Dixon). 471 Upper Richmond Road West, East Sheen, SW14. Tel 878 6788. Open Thurs-Tues 10-5.30 (incl Sun). 30 dealers selling a wide range of general antiques, art nouveau glass, 19th and early 20thC pottery and porcelain etc. Two large showrooms of good clean furniture.

Peter & Daniele Dodd
66 Ledbury Rd, W11. Tel 221 4727. Open 10-6. Continental and English furniture and paintings and decorative items of the 19thC.

Dodo
(Elizabeth Farrow). 3 Denbigh Rd, W11. Tel 229 3132. Open Fri & Sat 10-6; other times by appt. Old advertising signs, posters, labels, enamel & tin signs, display & packaging material 1880's-1930's, mostly British, American & French.

The Dolls House Toys Ltd
(Michal Morse). 29 The Market, Covent Garden, WC2E 8RE. Tel 379 7243. Open Mon-Sat 10-8. Dolls houses and hand-made miniature furniture.

Philip & Bernard Dombey
174 Kensington Church St, W8. Tel 229 7100. Open Mon-Fri 10-4, Sat 10-2. Antique clocks and clock sets, specialising in French antique clocks.

Donay Antiques
35 Camden Passage, Islington, N1. Tel 359 1880. Games boxes, compendia and old games.

Donohoe
(Mr & Mrs Edward Donohoe). 1-7 Davies Mews, W1. Tel 629 5633 (priv 455 5507). Open Mon-Fri 10-6; other times by appt. Antique silver, early jewellery, objects of vertu, European needlework. BADA LAPADA

Jack Donovan
93 Portobello Rd, W11. Tel 727 1485. Open Tues-Sat 10-6. Mechanical antiques, musical boxes, unusual clocks etc. LAPADA

Douwes Fine Art Ltd
(Evert J.M.Douwes Jnr). 38 Duke St, St James's, SW1Y 6DF. Tel 839 5795. Open Mon-Fri 9.30-5.30; other times by appt. Important 16th to 19thC Dutch, Flemish and French paintings, watercolours, drawings and prints.

Robert Douwma Prints & Maps Ltd
4 Henrietta St, The Piazza, Covent Garden, WC2. Tel 836 0771. Open Mon-Fri 10-6, Sat 10-5. Large and varied stock of antique prints and maps.

Dowell Lloyd & Co Ltd
118 Putney Bridge Rd, SW15. Tel 788 7777. Jewellery sales every Tuesday, furniture sales alternate Thursdays.

Dragons of Walton St Ltd
(Rosie B. Fisher, Mark Fisher). 19 & 23 Walton St, SW3 2HX. Tel 589 3795/0548. (Also at 6 Prince Albert St, Brighton, E.Sussex.) Open Mon-Fri 9.30-5.30; Sat 10.30-4.30. Hand-decorated children's furniture. Everything from toy boxes, beds, tables, chairs to hairbrushes, pencil boxes with a choice of Walt Disney characters. Also Dragons II for adults, including antiques and hand painted furniture.

Drescher Ltd
17 Alverstone Rd, NW2. Tel 459 5543. Open 8-8, other times by appt, but appt always advisable. Expert restorers of prints, drawings, pastels by old and modern masters and anything appertaining to paper restoration.

Alec Drew Picture Frames Ltd
7 Cale St, Chelsea Green, SW3. Tel 352 8716. Open Mon-Fri 9-5, Wed 9-6.30 & Sat 9-1. Decorative borders and pictures.

Drian Galleries
7 Porchester Place, Marble Arch, W2. Tel 723 9473. Open Mon-Fri 10-5, Sat 10-1. Fine paintings.

Drummond Antiques
110 Campden Hill Rd, W8. Open Tues-Fri 10-1, 2-5.30; other times by appt. 18th and early 19thC English and Continental furniture, engravings, glass and other decorative objects.

William Drummond
(Covent Garden Gallery), 11 Bury St, St James's, SW1. Tel 930 9696. Open by appt only. 18th and 19thC watercolours and drawings. BADA

Duits Ltd
104 Wigmore St, W1. Tel 629 5571. Open Mon-Fri 10-5.30. Dutch Old Master paintings and drawings.

E. & A. Antiques
(E. di Michele). 36 Ledbury Rd, W11. Tel 229 1823. Silver, silver plate, furniture. LAPADA

E.H.W. & Co
12 Sicilian Ave, Southampton Row, WC1A 3QD. Tel 405 5509. Open Mon-Fri 9.30-5. A wide selection of Commonwealth stamps; also British, colonial, foreign and Roman coins.

East Asia Co
103 Camden High St, NW1 7JN. Tel 388 5783. Open Mon-Sat 10-5.30. Chinese and Japanese antiquarian books, original prints and paintings, objets d'art, current books on Oriental art.

Peter Eaton (Booksellers) Ltd
(Peter & Margaret Eaton). 80 Holland Park Ave, W11. Tel 727 5211. (Also at 'Lilies', Weedon, Aylesbury, Bucks.) Open Mon-Sat 10-5; other times by appt. Antiquarian and secondhand books. ABA

Ebury Gallery
89 Ebury St, SW1. Tel 730 3341. Open Mon-Fri 10-5.30, Sat 10-1; other times by appt. Decorative objects, furniture, paintings and prints. Specialising in art deco.

Charles Ede Ltd
37 Brook St, W1Y 1AJ. Tel 493 4944. Open Tues-Fri 12.30-4.30; other times by appt. Pre-classical and classical antiquities from 5000 BC to AD 500 including Egyptian, Greek, Roman and Persian.

Owen Edgar Gallery
(Owen Edgar). 9 West Halkin St, SW1X 8JL. Tel 235 8989. Open Mon-Fri 10-6, Sat by appt. Important 18th and 19thC paintings and major Victorian works. BADA

Editions Graphiques Gallery
3 Clifford St, W1. Tel 734 3944. Open Mon-Fri 10-6, Sat 10-2. Fine and decorative arts 1880-1930, (Art Nouveau, Art Deco), graphics, paintings etc, 1880-present.

Andrew Edmunds
44 Lexington St, W1R 3LH. Tel 437 8594. Open Mon-Fri 10-6; other times by appt. Decorative prints up to the 1830s, also drawings, books and period frames. Specialist in caricatures, Gillray, Rowlandson, Cruikshank, Dighton etc.

Edward and Victoria Antiques
(M. Tillett). 7 Blackheath Hill, Blackheath, SE10. Tel 691 3062. (Also Antique Warehouse at 9-12 Deptford Broadway SE8.01-469 0295.) Open Mon-Sat 10-6, Sun 11-2. Large premises containing Victorian and Edwardian antiques for private and trade buyers.

M.Ekstein Ltd
90 Jermyn St, SW1Y 6JD. Tel 930 2024. Open 9.30-5.30; early closing Sat. Objets d'art, silver, porcelain, enamel, scientific and musical instruments. Also Russian works of art. BADA

Eldridge London
(Brian Eldridge). 99-101 Farringdon Rd, EC1. Tel 837 0379. Open Mon-Fri 9-5.30; Sat 9-1; other times by appt. Dealers in English antique furniture.

Electrum
21 South Molton St, W1. Tel 629 6325. Open Mon-Fri 10-6, Sat 10-1. New and experimental jewellery.

Elgin Antiques
121-123 Portobello Rd, W11. Tel 727 9852. General antiques, classical antiquities and primitive art.

Elmerside Ltd
85-87 Jermyn St, SW1Y 6JD. Tel 930 0138. Open by appt only. Books, prints and paintings. BADA

Emanouel Antiques Ltd
(Emanouel Naghi and Jacob Shavleyan). 64 South Audley St, W1Y 5FA. Tel 493 4350, 499 0996. Open Mon-Fri 9.30-6; other times by appt. Antiquities, European glass and porcelain, Islamic works of art, 19thC Continental works of art and furniture. Also valuations. LAPADA

L. & R. Entwistle & Co Ltd
70 South Audley St, W1Y 5FE. Tel 493 2828. Open by appt. Ethnographic, contemporary & old master paintings.

Ermitage Ltd
(Alexander von Solodkoff, Dr.Fabian Stein). 14 Hay Hill, W1X 7LJ. Tel 499 5459. Faberge, objets d'art, Continental silver.

Eskenazi Ltd
Foxglove House, 166 Piccadilly, W1V 9DE. Tel 493 5464. (Also in Milan, Italy.) Open Mon-Fri 10-6, appt advisable. Early Chinese works of art, Japanese lacquer, inro, netsuke and important works of art. BADA

Etna Antiques
81 Kensington Church St, W8 4BG. Tel 937 3754. 18th and 19thC English and Continental furniture.

Barbara Eustace Antiques
608 Kings Rd, SW6. Tel 731 3837. Open Mon-Fri 10-1, 2-6; Sat 10-12.30.

Peter Evanson
(Peter Evanson). 464 Fulham Rd, SW6. Tel 385 4185. Open Mon-Sat 9-5.30; Thurs 9-1. General furniture, bric-a-brac etc.

Eve's Lace
(Eve Stancliffe). Stand X5, Antiquarius, Kings Rd, SW3. Tel 351 0175. Antique lace and accessories.

J.F.Ewing
(J.F. & E.A.Ewing). 11 High St, Wimbledon Village, SW19. Tel 946 4700. (Also at Portobello Antique Store.) Open Tues-Sat 10-1, 2-5; closed Wed pm. Antique jewellery. LAPADA

Eyre and Greig Ltd
(Giles Eyre and Charles Greig). 38 Old Bond St, W1X 3AE. Tel 491 1445. Fine paintings.

Henry Faber Ltd
94 Southampton Row, WC1 4BB. Tel 405 0749. (Also retail business at same address.) Open Mon-Fri 11.30-6; other times by appt. Wholesaler of antique and secondhand jewellery.

Fagin's Phonograph Emporium
(Stephen Morris). 189 Blackstock Rd, Highbury, N5 2LL. Tel 359 4793 (priv 354 1212). Open Sat only 10-4; other times by appt. Specialist in talking machines and repairs thereto.

Baroukh Fahimian
(B. Fahimian). 4 Blenheim St, New Bond St, W1. Tel 493 7509 (priv 723 7179). Open Mon-Fri. Antique and Oriental carpets, specialising in antique Persian carpets.

Fairhurst Gallery
(Miles Fairhurst). 291 New King's Rd, SW6 4RE. Tel 736 9132. Open Mon-Sat 11-7; other times by appt. Art gallery showing oils, watercolours, some sculpture (British 1900-1950). Large stock of Modern British work. Specialist in British original book illustrations & related paintings of an illustrative, fantasy or cartoon type.

Jack Fairman (Carpets) Ltd
(John & Serina Page). 218 Westbourne Grove, W11 2RH. Tel 229 2262/3(priv 992 0087). Open Mon-Fri 10-6; Sat 10-2; other times by appt. Oriental carpets, rugs & tapestry. Specialists repairs & cleaning. Valuations.

Falkner Fine Art
Stands B18/C19 Grays Mews, Davies Mews, W1. Tel 629 3644 (priv 385 0174). Open Mon-Fri 10-6. Japanese sword fittings, swords, lacquer, ceramics, scroll paintings etc.

Featherston Shipping Ltd
24 Hampton House, 15-17 Ingate Place, SW8 3NS. Tel 720 0422. Packers & shippers. LAPADA

Jocelyn Feilding Fine Art Ltd
(Jocelyn Feilding). 8 Duke St, St James's, SW1. Tel 839 5040. Open Mon-Fri 10-6; other times by appt. Old master and English paintings and English watercolours. SLAD

R.Feldman Ltd
Vaults 4/6 The London Silver Vaults, Chancery Lane, WC2A 1QS. Tel 405 6111. Open Mon-Fri 9-5.30, Sat 9-12.30. Antique & modern silver, Sheffield plate, objets d'art. LAPADA

C.R.Fenton & Co Ltd
(C. Fenton, T.A.C. Richards, B.E. Bath,). Beachy Rd, Old Ford, E3 2NX. Tel 533 2711. Open Mon-Fri 9.30-5; other times by appt. Fine art packer & shippers, removers, insurance, storage. LAPADA, IFF

Fermor Antiques
80-82 Pimlico Rd, SW1. Tel 730 7004. Furniture, paintings, candelabra, clocks.

Fernandes & Marche
(J.A.Fernandes & J.Marche). 23 Motcomb St, Belgrave Sq, SW1. Tel 235 6773. Open Mon-Fri 9.30-5.30; other times by appt. Good stock of period mirrors, console tables and 18thC English furniture. LAPADA

D.J.Ferrant Antiques
21A Camden Passage, N1. Tel 359 3597. Open Mon-Sat 10.30-4. Period furniture and unusual objects.

Fiddes Watt
Studio 7, 52A Avonmore Rd, W14 8XU. Tel 603 9015. Open Tues-Sat; other times by appt. Paintings - mainly the Scottish school. Preservation, lining and cleaning of pictures, prints and watercolours.

Audrey Field
Stand 806, Alfie's Antique Market, 13 Church St, NW8. Tel 723 0449. Open 10-6; closed Mon & Wed. Collectors and costume lace.

Fieldborne Galleries
63 Queens Grove, St Johns Wood, NW8 6ER. Tel 586 3600.

Brian Fielden
(Brian Fielden). 3 New Cavendish St, W1M 7RP. Tel 935 6912. Open Mon-Fri 9.30-1, 2-5.30; Sat 9.30-1. 18th and early 19thC English mahogany and walnut furniture.

Finchley Fine Art Galleries
(Mr Greenman). 983 High Rd, North Finchley, N12 8QR. Tel 446 4848. Open Tue & Thurs-Sun 11.30-7; other times by appt. Specialist in English watercolours of 18th and 19thC. Also British paintings 18th-20thC, fine English furniture of 17th to late 19thC porcelain.

The Fine Art Society Plc
(Sir Norman Macfarlane, Andrew McIntosh Patrick MD). 148 New Bond St, W1Y 0JT. Tel 629 5116. (Also in Edinburgh and Glasgow.) Open Mon-Fri 9.30-5.30; Sat 10-1. 19th and 20thC British paintings, watercolours, drawings, sculpture and decorative arts. BADA SLAD

Fischer Fine Art Ltd
30 King St, SW1. Tel 839 3942. 19th and 20thC art.

Five Five Six Antiques
(Patricia Harvey). 556 King's Rd, SW6. Tel 731 2016 (priv 624 5173). (Also at Geoffrey Van's arcade, Portobello Rd, W11 on Sats.) Open Mon-Fri 10-5.30; Sat 10-4; other times by appt. Items of especial interest to the interior designer and decorator. Unusual pieces of furniture and architectural items, also primitive paintings, watercolours, samplers, needlework and large selection of needlework cushions. LAPADA

The Flask Bookshop
(Joseph Connolly). 6 Flask Walk, Hampstead, NW3. Tel 435 2693. Open Mon-Sat 10-6; closed Thurs. Modern first editions, art, literature.

Mario Flecha Gallery
239 Liverpool Rd, N1. Tel 607 5096. Open Mon-Fri 10-6, Sat 11-1. Art gallery.

H.M. Fletcher
(W.R., I.M., and Keith R. Fletcher). 27 Cecil Court, Charing Cross, WC2N 4EZ. Tel 836 2865. Open Mon-Fri 10-5.30. General stock of old and rare books. ABA

Fleur de Lys Gallery
(H.S.Coronel, B.S.Coronel). 8 Fulham High St, SW6 3LQ. Tel 731 7454 (priv 0372 67934). Open daily after 1 pm; closed Mon; other times by appt. 19thC oil paintings and watercolours of English, Dutch and Continental schools. Specialising in 19thC marine paintings.

Flight of Fancy
(Monica Davis, Patricia Fawkes). Chenil Galleries, 183 King's Rd, SW3. Tel 352 8653. Open Mon-Sat 10-6. Silver, majolica and general antiques.

Angela Flowers Gallery Ltd
11 Tottenham Mews, W1. Tel 637 3089. Open Mon-Fri 10.30-6; Sat 10.30-12.30. Contemporary British art.

Sam Fogg
66 Highbury Hill, N5. Books and manuscripts.

Diana Foley Antiques
(Diana Foley). Stand L18/21 Grays Mews, 1-7 Davies Mews, W1. Tel 408 1089. Open Mon-Fri 10-6. Antique jewellery (in association with Madeleine Popper and Richard Digby). LAPADA

Forget-Me-Not
(Poppy & Trisha). Chelsea Antique Market, 253 King's Rd, SW3. Tel 352 1424. Open Mon-Sat (incl) 10.30-6. Spanning a century of men's and women's clothing and accessories at affordable prices. Specialists in the sale of gents formal wear, ie dress & morning suits etc. Established (at same address) 9 years.

Forman of Piccadilly Ltd
(F.D. Forman and M.R. Forman). 92 Piccadilly, W1. Tel 493 2174. Open Mon-Fri 10-5.30. Works of art, objets d'art, orders of chivalry. Specialist in Napoleonic ships, bronzes, bone work.

W.Forster
83A Stamford Hill, N16 5TP. Tel 800 3919. Open by appt only. Secondhand and antiquarian books, particularly bibliography and kindred subjects. ABA

Fortnum & Mason Ltd
Antiques Department, 181 Piccadilly, W1A 1ER. Tel 734 8040.

Kate Foster Ltd.
(Mrs Kate Davson, Mr C.M.E.Davson). 9 Halkin Arcade, Motcomb St, SW1. Tel 245 9848 (priv Rye 222661). Open Mon-Fri 9.30-5.30; other times by appt. Fine European ceramics specialising in porcelain & faience. BADA

Michael Foster
118 Fulham Rd, SW3 6HU. Tel 373 3636. Open Mon-Sat 9-6; other times by appt. Fine 18th and early 19thC furniture, mirrors and works of art. BADA

Foto-Call
138 Sloane St, SW1. Tel 730 2764. Photographers.

Foulsham House Prints
(Hilary Chapman). Erika Brandl Gallery, 758 Fulham Rd, SW6 5SE. Tel 661837 (priv 747 0400). Open Mon-Fri 10-1. 19th & 20thC etchings, engravings and decorative prints. Large stock of medical and hospital prints.

Judy Fox Antiques
(Mrs J Fox). 81 Portobello Rd, W11. 19thC furniture, porcelain. LAPADA

Peter Francis
26 Museum St, WC1A 1JT. Tel 637 0165. Open Mon-Fri 9.30-5.30; other times by appt. 18th and early 19thC furniture and objects, old Sheffield plate, tole peint, selected glass. BADA

Franco's Antiques
(F. Chiodo). 49 Camden Passage, N1. Tel 354 1860. (Also warehouse at 69 Upper St, N1.) Open Mon-Sat 10-5; other times by appt. 18th and 19thC English furniture, also oil paintings.

Franklin's
(R.N. Franklin, M.W.H. Howroyd). Camberwell Antique Market, 161 Camberwell Rd, SE5. Tel 703 8089. Open Tues-Sat 10-6; Sun 1-6; other times by appt. General antiques. Brass, copper, garden furniture. All types of antique furniture, prints etc. Shipping goods.

Robert Franses & Son
5 Nugent Tce, St John's Wood, NW8. Tel 286 6913 (priv 328 0949). Open Mon-Fri 9-3; other times by appt. Antique Oriental and European carpets, tapestries and textiles; also saddlebags, early Turkoman, unusual Chinese, Turkish village rugs and early English needlework.

S.Franses Ltd
82 Jermyn St, St James's, SW1. Tel 235 1888/9. (Also at 11 Spring St, Paddington, W2.) Open Mon-Fri 9-5.30; other times by appt. Important European tapestries, early carpets and textiles. BADA

S.Franses Ltd
11 Spring St, Paddington, W2. Tel 262 1153/4. (Also at 82 Jermyn St, St James's, SW1.) Open Mon-Fri 9-5.30; other times by appt. Decorative carpets, rugs, needleworks and tapestries. Specialising in restoration and cleaning. BADA

Victor Franses Gallery
57 Jermyn St, SW1Y 6LX. Tel 439 6284. Open Mon-Fri 10-5.30; other times by appt. Rugs, tapestries, needlework and bronzes. BADA

C.Fredericks & Sons
92 Fulham Rd, SW3.
Tel 589 5847. Open Mon-Fri 9-5.30; other times by appt. Good stock of 18thC furniture. BADA

Gerald Freedman (Cale Antiques)
(Gerald Freedman). Box 458, Fulham, SW6 3RS. Tel 736 8666. Open by appt. Fine Chinese porcelain, European and English porcelain and pottery, including tin glazes - delft, faience and majolica. Valuations for insurance.

I. Freeman & Son, Simon Kaye Ltd
(A.C.Kauffmann). 18 Dover St, W1X 3PB. Tel 493 7658. Open Mon-Fri 9.30-5. Antique English silver, old Sheffield plate, antique medical instruments. BADA

J.Freeman
85A Portobello Rd, W11.
Tel 221 5076. Open Mon-Sat 9.30-1, 2-5.30. Victorian and modern silver, old Sheffield and Victorian plate. LAPADA

Vincent Freeman Antiques
(Vincent Freeman). 1 Camden Passage, Islington, N1.
Tel 226 6178. Open Tue 10-4;Wed 8-5;Fri 11-4;Sat 10-5; other times by appt. Specialist in musical boxes. Large stock of glass, barometers, oriental and European porcelain, decorative antiques. All high quality.

Frost & Reed Ltd
41 New Bond St, W1.
Tel 629 2457. Open 9-5.30. Fine sporting paintings, also 19th and 20thC British and European paintings. BADA, SLAD

Fry Gallery
58 Jermyn St, St James's, SW1 6LX. Tel 493 4496. Open Mon-Fri 10-5.30. 18th to 20thC British watercolours & drawings from important works to small sketches. SLAD

O.Frydman
(Mrs L.Frydman, Mr G.Barnett). Bond St Silver Galleries, 111-112 New Bond St, W1. Tel 439 4895. Open Mon-Fri 9-5. Modern and antique British silverware, old Sheffield and Victorian silver plate.

Furniture Cave
533 King's Rd, Chelsea, SW10.
Tel 352 2046. Several dealers selling a wide range of furniture.

Furniture Fair
(Janet Bates). 22 Church St, NW8.
Tel 262 1338. Antiques and re-upholstery.

Elizabeth Gage
20 Albemarle St, W1.
Tel 499 2879. Jewellery.

Robin Gage
50 Pimlico Rd, SW1W 8LP.
Tel 730 2878. Open by appt only. Specialist in antique cigar humidors and brass club fender seats.

D.Ira Gale
42c South Audley St, Adams Row, W1Y 5DH. Tel 499 2030. Old Master prints, modern prints, drawings.

Galerie George
98 George St, W1H 5RI.
Tel 935 3322, 935 9998. (Also at 50 Kensington Church St, W8.) Open Mon-Fri 10-6; other times by appt. Specialists in fine 19th and early 20thC oil paintings and watercolours by British and European artists. Kensington gallery specialising in paintings of 1870-1920.

Galerie 1900
267 Camden High St, NW1.
Tel 485 1001. Open Mon-Sat 10-6; Sun 11-4. Art nouveau, art deco.

Galerie 360
564 King's Road, SW6.
Tel 736 5160. Open Mon-Fri 10-6, Sat 11-5. Antique and decorative furniture, fine objects and accessories.

Galerie 39
96 George St, W1. Tel 487 5038. Open Mon-Fri 10-6; other times by appt. Contemporary art.

Galia Antiques
Osman Aytal). Antiquarius, 135 King's Rd, SW3. Open Mon-Sat 9.30-6. Contemporary crafts,. including 20thC pottery jewellery, silver and glass. Also art nouveau and art deco items.

Gallery of Antique Costume & Textiles Ltd
(Lionel & Alyson Segal). 2 Church Street, Marylebone, NW8.
Tel 723 9981 (priv 743 3821). Open Mon-Sat 10-5.30; other times by appt. Antique costumes and textiles, Coptic, 1930's. Chinese embroideries and wall hangings, needlework, beadwork and a large variety of items for interior decoration.

Gallery Lingard
(Timothy Lingard, Jane Lingard). 50 Pall Mall, SW1Y 5JQ.
Tel 930 1645. Open Mon-Fri 10-6.30; other times by appt. Architectural and design drawings and watercolours. SLAD

The Gallery Muswell Hill
(Carolyn Wildman). 105 Muswell Hill Broadway, N10. Open Mon-Sat 9.30-5.30; other times by appt. Original paintings, limited editions, prints. Mainly 20thC.

Gallery 10 Ltd
(Anne Marcou). 10 Grosvenor St, W1X 9FB. Tel 491 8103. Open Mon-Fri 10-5.30; Sat 10-1; other times by appt. British contemporary artists, Royal Academicians and young promising artists.

Gallery 181
(Tom Miszewski). 181 King's Rd, SW6. Tel 736 1955. Open Mon, Tues, Wed, Fri 9.30-5.30, Sat 9.30-5. Picture framers and art restorers.

Gallery 25
4 Halkin Arcade, Motcomb St, SW1. Tel 235 5178. Decorative arts 1900-1930, including glass, furniture.

Game Advice
Alick & Sheila Elithorn).
23 Holmes Road, NW5 3AA.
Tel 485 2188 (priv 485 4226). Open by appt. Chess sets, playing cards, antiquarian chess and cookery books, games and toys.

Gander & White Shipping Ltd
(Patrick White (Chairman), Gerald Divall (MD)). 21 Lillie Rd, SW6 1UE. Tel 381 0571. (Also at 14 Mason's Yard, Duke St, London, SW1. Tel 930 5383.) Open Mon-Fri 9-6; other times by appt. Shipping agents.

Garrard & Co Ltd
112 Regent St, W1A 2JJ.
Tel 734 7020. Open Mon-Fri 9-5.30, Sat 9-12.30. Antique silver, watches, clocks, jewellery, glass, objets d'art; also fine gold boxes. Military silver, modern silver. BADA

Stephen Garratt Fine Paintings
(Stephen & Felicity Garratt). Exhibiting at 146 Brompton Rd, (Knightsbridge Safe Deposit), SW3. Tel 603 0681. Open Mon-Fri 10-5.30; other times by appt. 18th and 19thC oils and watercolours of English and Continental schools. BADA

Garton & Cooke
(Robin Garton and Gordon Cooke). 9 Lancashire Court, New Bond St, W1Y 9AD. Tel 493 2820. Open Mon-Fri 9.30-5.30; other times by appt. Specialists in British etchings 1850-1940 and other modern prints: Palmer, Haden, Whistler, Bone, Cameron and Robin Tanner. Watercolours by Claude Muncaster. Publishers of art books.

Peter John Gates
2nd Floor, 94 New Bond St, W1.
Tel 629 4962. Fine art photographers.

Gay Antiques
1 Beauchamp Place, SW3.
Tel 584 9615. Continental porcelain, French furniture, clocks, bronzes and ivories.

General Antiques and Books
(Mr & Mrs Terry Hillyer).
301 Sydenham Rd, SE26.
Tel 778 6361 (priv 777 2506). Open 8.30-4.45. General antiques, furniture, china, glass, pictures, books etc.

General Trading Co
(D.C. Part and E.M. Barlow).
144 Sloane St, SW1X 9BL.
Tel 730 0411. Open Mon-Fri 9-5.30; Sat 9-2. 18th and 19thC antique furniture and reproductions; 18th and 19thC porcelain, prints, pewter and objects d'art. LAPADA

George Smith
392-396 Fulham Rd, SW6.

Georgian Village Vaults and Galleries
Camden Passage, N1.
Tel 226 2159. Shops, stalls and boutiques with a wide range of stock.

Michael C.German
(M.C.German). 38B Kensington Church St, W8. Tel 937 2771. Open Mon-Fri 10-5.30, Sat 10.30-3; other times by appt. Specialist dealer in Oriental and European arms and armour, and walking-sticks. BADA, LAPADA

Stanley Gibbons
399 The Strand, WC2.
Tel 836 8444. (Also Stanley Gibbons Auctions at this address.) Open Mon 10-5.30;Tue-Fri 9.30-5.30;Sat 10-12; other times by appt. Stamp dealers. Also postal history, postcards, banknotes and bond and share certificates. PTS

Stanley Gibbons Auctions Limited
(Stanley Gibbons International Limited). 399 The Strand, WC2R 0LX. Tel 836 8444. Open Mon-Fri 9-5. Stamp auctioneers.

Christopher Gibbs Ltd
118 New Bond St, W1Y 9AB.
Tel 629 2008. Open Mon-Fri 9.30-5.30. Old Masters and works of art.

Thomas Gibson Fine Art Limited
(Thomas H. Gibson). 9a New Bond St, W1Y 9PE. Tel 499 8572. Open Mon-Fri 9-5.30. 20thC paintings, drawings and sculpture, and selected Old Masters.

Attilio Gilberti
70 Wigmore St, W1. Tel 487 3167 & 935 4339. Fine Oriental carpets.

GOTHICK DREAM FINE ART

Arts and Crafts writing bureau. Walnut with elaborate brass furniture.

specialises in
Modern British and
Victorian Paintings,
Arts and Crafts,
Aesthetic Movement
and Victorian Gothic
Furniture and Artefacts

14 Needham Road
Westbourne Grove
London W11 2RP
Tel 01 221 0417.
Tues-Sat

"Seated Nude" oil on panel. John Melville signed and dated 1938

BIGGEST AND BUSIEST ANTIQUE MARKETS IN LONDON

1–7 DAVIES MEWS & 58 DAVIES STREET
LONDON W1 01-629 7034
(By Bond Street Station)

Open Monday–Friday 10a.m.-6p.m.

in Davies Mews
GRAYS
& Davies Street

SPECIAL OFFER
to
ANTIQUE DEALERS

The British Art & Antiques Directory
at the wholesale rate – **33%** discount.

Give your customers the chance to buy this prestigious book.
Order 5 or more copies and take advantage of our
special wholesale rate – £7 each including delivery.
No payment required now; we will invoice you on delivery.
All orders to: The British Art & Antiques Directory,
National Magazine House, 72 Broadwick Street, London W1V 2BP
(Tel. 01-439 7144).

GERALD FREEDMAN
(CALE ANTIQUES)

FINE CHINESE PORCELAIN,
ALSO EUROPEAN CERAMICS,
INCLUDING DELFT, FAIENCE
AND MAIOLICA

BOX 458, FULHAM SW6 3RS
Tel 01-736 8666
(By Appointment)

The Tony Gill Organisation-Number One
(Tony Gill). 173 Bermondsey St, SE1 3UW. Tel 403 4982. Consultancy, public relations and marketing for antiques, fine art and interior design.

G. & F.Gillingham Ltd
(George & Fryda Gillingham). 4 Crediton Hill, NW6 1HP. Tel 435 5644. Open all times. Restored & unrestored mahogany 19thC English & Continental furniture, barometers, leather upholstered chairs, armchairs, writing desks, bookcases, etc. LAPADA

Gimpel Fils
30 Davies St, W1Y 1LG. Tel 493 2488. Open Mon-Fri 9.30-5.30, Sat 10-1; other times by appt. Contemporary British European and American painting and sculpture, also South Arabian art. SLAD

Loretta Giordani
Stand B4, Antiquarius, Kings Rd, SW3. Tel 352 7989. Antique jewellery, watches.

G.Glass & Son
(H.Glass). Bond St Silver Galleries, 111-112 New Bond St, W1Y 9AB. Tel 493 5176. Open Mon-Fri 9-5. Antique silver and plate. BADA

The Glasshouse Gallery & Workshop
(A. Meech, D. Taylor, F. Tookey, C. Williams). 65 Long Acre, Covent Garden, WC2. Tel 836 9785 (priv.240 7508). Open Mon-Fri 10-5.30, Sat 11-4; other times by appt. Contemporary studio glass gallery & workshop, glass restoration, commissions welcome. Glassblowing can be viewed by the public.

M.& R. Glendale
(Ruth Sands, Monika Sears). 9a New Cavendish St, (entrance in Marylebone St), W1M 7RN. Tel 487 5348. Specialists in rare books for children, and women's interest literature. Also domestic books. ABA

Glendining & Co
(Enquiries: William French). 7 Blenheim St, New Bond St, W1Y OAS. Tel 493 2445. Auctioneers and valuers.

Godson & Coles Ltd
(Richard H. Godson & Richard D. Coles). 310 King's Rd, SW3 5UH. Tel 352 8509. Open Mon-Fri 9.30-5.30, Sat 10-4; other times by appt. 18th and early 19thC English furniture and decorative works of art. BADA

Michael Goedhuis Ltd. Colnaghi Oriental
(Michael Goedhuis, Nadia Goedhuis). 14 Old Bond St, W1X 4JL. Tel 409 3324. Open Mon-Fri 9-6; other times by appt. Fine Oriental works of art. BADA

Hilde Goldbaum Antiques
(Hilde Goldbaum). Stand X1, Antiquarius, 135 King's Rd, SW3. Open Mon-Sat 10-6. British and European silver, silver plate and Sheffield plate.

The Golden Past
(M. Oppenheimer, I. Oppenheimer). 6 Brook St, W1Y 1AA. Tel 493 6422. Open Mon-Fri 10-5; other times by appt. Antique and old jewellery of all kinds, gold, silver and pinchbeck jewellery. Also china and enamel.

Goldsmith & Perris
(Mrs G Goldsmith, E Perris). Alfies Antique Market, 13-17 Church St, NW8. Tel 723 0563. Silver, plate. LAPADA

Goodall & Co Ltd
26 Chiswick High Rd, W4. Tel 994 1729 (priv 994 2376). Open Mon-Sat 9-5; closed Thurs; other times by appt. Antique and fine reproduction furniture, maps and topographical prints.

Thomas Goode & Co (London) Ltd
(B.P. Jakins, M.J.R. Stroud, B. Brock, N.J. Spiers). 19 South Audley St, W1Y 6BN. Tel 499 2823 (7 lines). Open Mon-Fri 9-5, Sat 9-1; other times by appt. Glass decanters, chandeliers, china plaques, dessert, dinner and tea services. Also vases, antique china, glass, papier mache. BADA

Peter Goodwin Antiques
284 Westbourne Grove, W11. Tel 581 3873. Open 9-5 by appt. 24 hr answering service. Good scientific, nautical & medical instruments, works of art, unusual items, primitive art.

A. & F. Gordon
(Joseph Gordon). 120A Mount St, W1. Tel 499 5596. Open Mon-Fri 9.30-5.30; other times by appt. Antique and decorative furnishings, paintings, objets d'art and sculpture. BADA

Brian Gordon
(B Gordon). Chenil Galleries, 181-183 Kings Rd, SW3. Tel 351 5808. Silver, plate. LAPADA

Jill Gosling Ltd
104 Kensington Church St, W8. 18th and 19thC English porcelain and pottery.

Gothick Dream
(Leslie Harcourt). 14 Needham Rd, W11. Tel 221 0417. Open Mon-Sat 10-6. 20thC British paintings and related works of art & furniture. Also any good quality 18thC furniture, pictures & objects.

Lawrence Gould
(L. Gould). Harris's Arcade, 161/163 Portobello Rd, W11. Open Sats only. Enamels and watches. Valuations. LAPADA

Patrick & Susan Gould
(Mr & Mrs P Gould). Grays Mews, 1-7 Davies Mews, W1. Tel 408 0129. Art Nouveau and Art Deco glass. LAPADA

Graffiti
(Blackman Harvey). 29 Earlham St, Covent Garden, WC2. Tel 836 1904. Open Mon-Fri 9-6; Sat 10-4. Specialists in contemporary Arab art & contemporary original prints.

Graham & Oxley (Antiques) Ltd
(Michael Graham & Joseph Oxley). 101 Kensington Church St, W8 7LN. Tel 229 1850. Open Mon-Fri 10-5.30; Sat 10-5. Fine 18th and early 19thC ceramics, furniture and works of art. BADA CINOA

David Graham Antiques
2 The Mall, Camden Passage, Islington, N1. Tel 352 2112. Specialists in fine English silver from Georgian to Edwardian periods; also quality old Sheffield plate and Victorian plate.

Gavin Graham Gallery
47 Ledbury Rd, W11 2AA. Tel 229 4848. Open Mon-Fri 10-6; Sat 10-4.30. 17th to 19th & early 20thC oil paintings of English, European etc. schools. LAPADA

Imogen Graham
585 King's Rd, SW6. Tel 736 2465. English furniture, pine, painted furniture, bamboo, and oil paintings.

Michael & Diana Grainger
113 Portobello Rd, W11. Tel 858 0778. Jewellery. LAPADA

Granny's Goodies and Chelsea Lion
(Brenda Gerwat-Clark & Steve Clark). Chenil Galleries, 181 King's Rd, Chelsea, SW3. Tel 352 8653 (priv 771 1277). (Also at 290 Westbourne Grove, London W11.) Open Mon-Sat 12-5.30; other times by appt. Dolls, toys and a good selection of general antiques, lamps, clocks etc.

Graus Antiques
(Eric and Herbert Graus). 125 New Bond St, W1Y 9AF. Tel 629 6680, 629 6651. Open Mon-Fri 9.30-5. Specialists in watches, enamels, objets d'art and jewellery. LAPADA

Solveig & Anita Gray
(Solveig & Anita Gray). 58 Davies Street, W1. Tel 408 1638. Open Mon-Fri 10-6; other times by appt. Oriental art and works of art. LAPADA

Grays Antique Market & Grays Mews
58 Davies St and 1-7 Davies Mews, W1. Tel 629 7034. Open Mon-Fri 10-6. closed Sat. Two adjacent large permanent markets each with numerous dealers selling a wide range of collectable antiques.

David E.Green Gallery
(David E.Green MBE). 188 Dartmouth Rd, SE26. Tel 699 5461. Open Mon-Sat 9-5.30; Thurs to 7.30; other times by appt. Fine early British drawings and watercolours, framing, cleaning and restoration. Specialising in British watercolours 1750-1850.

Richard Green
36 & 44 Dover St, W1. Tel 493 3939. (Also at 4 New Bond St, W1X 4JQ.) Open Mon-Fri 9.30-6, Sat 9.30-12.30. Fine English and Continental paintings. BADA SLAD CINOA

Green's Antique Galleries
(Sidney Green). 117 Kensington Church St, W8 7LN. Tel 229 9618/9. Open Mon-Sat 9.30-5.30. Antique jewellery, silver, silver plate, china, glass & objets d'art.

Greenwich Antiques Market
Greenwich Market, College Approach, Greenwich, SE10. Tel 240 7405. Open Sat and Sun 10-4. Over 100 dealers offering a wide range of collectables.

Judy Greenwood
(Judy Greenwood). 657 Fulham Rd, SW6. Tel 736 6037. Open Mon-Sat 10-5; other times by appt. Country furniture, including pine, bamboo and Victoriana. Also quilts, curtains and textiles.

Nigel Greenwood Gallery and Bookshop
(Nigel Greenwood). 4 New Burlington St, W1X 1FE. Tel 434 3795/6. (Bookshop Tel No: 434 3797/8.) Open Mon-Fri 10-6; Sat 10.30-1.30. Contemporary paintings, sculptures, drawings, prints etc. The Bookshop specialises in contemporary artists books, exhibition catalogues, special editions, monographs, pamphlets and printed ephemera. SLAD

Gregory, Bottley and Lloyd
(Brian Lloyd, Mary Lloyd). 8-12 Rickett St, SW6 1RU. Tel 381 5522 (priv 878 5202). Open 9.30-5; other times by appt. Specialists in antique collections of minerals, fossils and meteorites, spar towers,spar boxes and allied objects.

Henry Gregory
(H.Gregory). Stand 335, Grays Antique Market, 58 Davies St, W1Y 1LB. Gold and silver jewellery, silver. LAPADA

Martyn Gregory
34 Bury St, St James's, SW1. Tel 839 3731. Open Mon-Fri 10-6. British watercolours and paintings and pictures relating to China and the Far East.

Gres
(David Gill). Stand 378,Grays Antique Market, 58 Davies St, W1. Tel 499 3075. Open Mon-Fri 10-6; other times by appt. Objets d'art 1850-1930, furniture, pictures.

Simon Griffin Antiques
(S.J. Griffin). 3 The Royal Arcade, 28 Old Bond St, W1. Tel 491 7367. Open Mon-Fri 10-5; Sat 10.30-12. Antique silver, Old Sheffield Plate, modern silverware.

Grimaldi
(Keith Banham, Osvaldo Patrizzi). 12 Royal Arcade, 28 Old Bond St, W1X 3HB. Tel 493 3953. Open Mon-Fri 9.30-5.30; other times by appt. Fine antique clocks, fine technical and decorative watches, wristwatches, scientific instruments and objects.

Grosvenor Antiques Ltd
(S.A.C.Lorie, E.M.H.Lorie). 27 Holland St, W8. Tel 937 8649. Open Mon-Fri 10-5.30; other times by appt. 18th and 19thC porcelain, ormolu, glass and small works of art. BADA

Directory Entries are Free and ADDITIONS OR CORRECTIONS will be welcomed by *THE EDITOR, British Art and Antiques Directory, National Magazine House, 72 Broadwick Street, London W1V 2BP*

Grosvenor Gallery
(Sevenarts Ltd and Eric & Salome Estorick). 48 South Molton St, W1Y 2JU. Tel 629 0891. Open Mon-Fri 9-5; other times by appt. Three floors of 20thC Italian, Russian and Chinese art; Art Nouveau especially Mucha, Art Deco — exclusive world representatives of Erte.

Grosvenor Prints
28 Shelton Street, WC2. Tel 836 1979. Open Mon-Fri 10-6, Sat 10-1. Prints, specialising in topographical and dogs and decorative prints.

L.Guerra
82 Portobello Rd, W11. Tel 727 0374. Open Mon-Sat 9.30-5.30; other times by appt. 18th and 19thC European furniture, ivory, silver and objets d'art.

Guinevere Antiques Ltd
578 King's Road, SW6. Tel 736 2917. Open Mon-Sat 9-6. Large showrooms of antique and decorative furniture, fine objects and accessories.

Gwyneth Antiques
(Gwyneth Lloyd). 56 Ebury St, SW1. Tel 730 2513 (priv 352 4864). Open Mon-Fri 10-1, 2.15-5; other times by appt. Oriental and decorative furniture, objects, textiles and rugs.

Hadji Baba Ancient Art
36 Davies St, W1Y 1LD. Tel 499 9363, 499 9384. Open 9.30-6; other times by appt. Ancient and Islamic art, Oriental carpets.

Hahn Gallery
(P.A. Hahn & J.A. Hahn). 47 Albemarle St, W1X 3FE. Tel 493 9196. Open Mon-Fri 9.30-5.30; Sats by appt. 17th to 19thC English and Continental paintings. Specialising in marine and landscape paintings.

John Haines Antiques Ltd
(John & Susan Haines). 59 Elm Grove Rd, Barnes, SW13 0BX. Tel 876 4215. Open by appt only. Furniture paintings and objects. BADA

M.Hakim
(W.S.Hakim, H.Hakim, J.Humphreys, F.Finburgh). 4 The Royal Arcade, Old Bond St, W1X 3HD. Tel 629 6243. Open Mon-Fri 9.30-5. Objets d'art, gold snuff boxes, antique watches and jewellery. Also Oriental and European works of art. BADA

Halcyon Days
(Susan Benjamin). 14 Brook St, W1Y 1AA. Tel 629 8811. (Also at 4 Royal Exchange, EC3. (Tel 626 1120.) Open Mon-Fri 9.15-5.30, Sat 9.30-1.30. Specialising in 18th and early 19thC English enamels and objects of vertu, papier mache, tole, treen, prints and also fine contemporary enamel boxes. BADA

Robert Hales Antiques Ltd
(Robert Hales). 133 Kensington Church St, W8 7LP. Tel 229 3887. Open Mon-Fri 10-5.30; other times by appt. Oriental, Islamic and tribal arms and armour, ethnographic art.

Georgina Hall
(Georgina Hall). H3/H4 Antiquarius, 135 King's Rd, SW3. Tel 352 8734 (priv 731 0366). Open Mon-Sat 10.30-5.30. English watercolours of the 19th and 20thC - particularly gardens and cottages.

John Hall
(John Hall). 31 Epple Rd, SW6 4DJ. Tel 736 3542. Open by appt only. Named Victorian Staffordshire portrait figures, lithographed music covers, vintage postcards, fairings, other prints including theatre. Specialists in theatrical items.

Halliday's (Antiques)
28 Beauchamp Place, SW3. Tel 589 5534. (Also in Dorchester-on-Thames, Oxon.) Specialists in reproduction 18thC mantelpieces and room panelling, together with all accessories for the fireplace. Also wide range of fenders, fire-irons etc, and antique marble mantelpieces. LAPADA

Halsey
(John Halsey, Mrs Halsey). 101 Duncan House, Dolphin Square, SW1. Tel 828 5529. Open by appt only. Private show apartment for the business based in Salcombe, Devon. BADA

Ross Hamilton Ltd
(Ross Hamilton). 73 Pimlico Rd, SW1. Tel 730 3015. Open Mon-Fri 9.30-6, Sat 11-2. Highly decorative antique furniture, paintings & objects, 17th-19thC. LAPADA

Hamlet Gallery
(R.Lee-Richardson & Dr E.Stacey Andreou). 5 Pond St, Hampstead, NW3. Tel 794 7904 (priv 452 0056). (See also Lee & Stacey, London.) Open Tues-Fri 10.30-5.30; other times by appt. Large stock of 19th and early 20thC oils and watercolours; also bronzes. Exhibitions twice a year.

Hampstead Antique Emporium
12 Heath St, NW3. Tel 794 3297. Open Tues-Sat 10-6. Approx 25 dealers offering wide range of barometers, ceramics, clocks & watches, furniture, glass, jewellery, mirrors, oils, prints (including Japanese), watercolours and silver.

Han-Shan Tang Ltd
(Christer von der Burg and Vivien Robinson). 717 Fulham Rd, SW6 5UL. Tel 731 2447. Open Mon-Fri 10-6, Sat 10-4; other times by appt. More than 20,000 books and periodicals (antiquarian, out-of-print and new) on all aspects of Asia and the Pacific. Specialising in Chinese art books, Japanese art books. ABA

Hancock Gallery
(Mark and Frances Hancock). 184 Westbourne Grove, W11. Tel 229 7827 (priv 878 5008). Open Mon-Fri 10-6.30; Sat 10-5. Oil paintings, pictures of all periods and origins.

Hancocks & Co (Jewellers) Ltd
1 Burlington Gardens, W1X 2HP. Tel 493 8904. Open Mon-Fri 9.30-5. Fine stock of antique and art deco jewellery, and cameos. Also Georgian and Victorian silver, specialising in services of spoons and forks. BADA NAG

William Handford Antiques
(W. Handford). 517 King's Rd, SW10 0TX. Tel 351 2768. Open Mon-Sat 10-5.30; other times by appt. Period & decorative furniture and accessories specialising in antique garden urns and benches.

Handweavers Studio and Gallery
29 Haroldstone Rd, Walthamstow, E17. Tel 521 2281. Open Tues-Sat 10-5, Fri 10-9. Large selection of yarns and other materials, equipment and publications on spinning and weaving. Handwoven articles for sale.

Hanover Studios
104-112 Marylebone Lane, W1. Tel 487 4431/2. Fine art photography.

Rod Hanrick
11 Church St, NW8. Tel 724 9270. Open Mon-Fri 10-6; Sat 12-6. Decorative antiques.

Harari & Johns Ltd
12 Duke Street, St James's, SW1. Tel 839 7671. Open Mon-Fri 10-6; other times by appt. Old Master paintings.

Harcourt Antiques
(John Christophe). 5 Harcourt St, W1. Tel 723 5919. Open Tues-Fri 10-4; Sat 10-1; other times by appt. Fine ceramics and works of art.

GRAHAM and OXLEY (Antiques) Ltd.

Fine Ceramics and Works of Art

Pair of fine Derby ice pails, covers and liners painted with landscapes by Zachariah Boreman and borders of roses in reserve by William Billingsley. Circa 1785.

101, KENSINGTON CHURCH STREET, LONDON W8 7LN

Telephone 01-229-1850 Cables: Gramox, London

Jackson-Stops & Staff

Chattels Auctioneers and Valuers

Contents of House Sales conducted throughout the British Isles

Valuations for Insurance, Probate, Family Division and any other purposes

14 Curzon Street, London W1Y 7FH
Telephone: 01-499 6291

ALSO IN: CHELSEA · FULHAM · CHESTER · CHICHESTER · CHIPPING CAMPDEN · CIRENCESTER · DARLINGTON · EXETER · MIDHURST · NEWMARKET · NORTHAMPTON · YEOVIL · YORK · DUBLIN

R. & J. JONES

English and European
Oil paintings (17th to 19th century)

18th century porcelain

137 KENSINGTON CHURCH STREET, LONDON W8. Tel 01-221 4026.

Jeanette Hayhurst

Fine Glass

A rare engraved composite stem glass, c.1745

A rare opaque twist stem toasting glass, c.1765

3b Burlington Gardens, London W1.
Tel: 01-437 4975

Keith Harding
(W.Keith Harding FBHI, Cliff A.Burnett CMBHI). 93 Hornsey Road, N7 6DJ. Tel 607 6181, 607 2672. Open Mon-Fri 8.30-6, Sat 10-1; other times by appt. Musical boxes, clocks, automata and their restoration. Horological books. Catalogues available.

James Hardy & Co
235 Brompton Rd, SW3 2EP. Tel 589 5050. Good stock of silver and jewellery, specialising in old and modern silver tableware.

Harmers of London Stamp Auctioneers Ltd
91 New Bond St, W1A 4EH. Tel 629 0218. (Also in New York, San Francisco and agency in Sydney.) Open Mon-Fri 9.15-5.15. International stamp auctioneers and valuers. Agents for Lloyds stamp collectors' insurance. PTS, BPF

Harrington Bros
(Peter & Adrian Harrington). Chelsea Antique Market, 253 King's Rd, SW3. Tel 352 5689. Open Mon-Sat 10-6. Antiquarian books, prints and maps, also bindings for the decorator.

Harris (Antiques) Limited
17-18 Old Bond St, W1X 3DA. Tel 499 0352. Open Mon-Fri 9.30-5. Antique silver. BADA

Essie C.Harris
(Mrs E.C.Harris, D.I.Harris, J.A.Harris). Diamond House 37-38 Hatton Garden, EC1. Tel 242 9115/1558. Open Mon-Fri 9-5. Jewellery, valuations. Trade only. LAPADA, BJA

Jonathan Harris
(Jonathan Harris). 54 Kensington Church St, W8. Tel 937 3133. Open Mon-Fri 9.30-1, 2-6. Selected fine quality European and Oriental furniture and works of art, including paintings, tapestries, ceramics and unusual objects of all kinds. BADA

M.Harris & Sons
(R.M.Harris). Gayfere House, 22-23 Gayfere St, SW1P 3HP. Tel 222 8161. Open Mon-Fri 9-5; other times by appt. Important stock of English and French antique furniture and works of art. Specialising in English 18thC furniture. BADA

Nicholas Harris
26 Conduit St, W1. Tel 499 5991. Open Mon-Fri 10.30-5; other times by appt. Decorative silver, fine jewellery and objets d'art. LAPADA, BADA

Harrods
87-135 Brompton Rd, SW1. Tel 730 1234. Open Mon-Fri 9-5, Wed 9-7, Sat 9-6. Large and varied stock of fine quality antique, Victorian and Edwardian furniture, also oil paintings, bronzes, porcelain, etc.

Hart & Rosenberg
(E.O.Hart, H.Rosenberg). 2-3 Gateway Arcade, 355 Upper St, Camden Passage, N1 0PD. Tel 359 6839. Open Tues, Fri, Sat 10.30-4.30; Wed 9-5; other times by appt. Oriental ceramics and works of art, European porcelain, glass and other miscellaneous objects.

Sheila Hart Antiques
(Mrs S P Hart). 104 Islington High St, N1. Tel 226 2315. Furniture, decorative objects mostly 19thC. LAPADA

Julian Hartnoll
14 Mason's Yard, Duke St, St James's, SW1. Tel 839 3842. Open Mon-Fri 2.30-5; other times by appt. Paintings, drawings and prints specialising in pre-Raphaelite and late 19thC English artists.

Harvey & Gore
4 Burlington Gardens, W1X 1LE. Tel 493 2714. Antique jewellery and silver. BADA

W.R.Harvey & Co (Antiques) Ltd
5 Old Bond St, W1. Tel 499 8385. (Also 67-70 Chalk Farm Rd, NW1.) Fine antique furniture and objets d'art. BADA

W.R.Harvey & Co (Antiques) Ltd
67-70 Chalk Farm Rd, NW1 8AN. Tel 485 1504, 267 2767. (Also at 5 Old Bond St, W1.) Open Mon-Sat 9.30-1, 2-5.30. 14 showrooms of 17th to early 19thC furniture, clocks, appurtenances, paintings and barometers. BADA

Harvey's Auctions Ltd
14/18 Neal Street, Covent Gdn, WC2. Tel 240 1464. Open for viewing Tues 9.30-3.30 only. Enquiries Mon-Fri 9-5. Antique & general furniture, silver, ceramics, carpets, rugs, pictures, prints, occasional bankruptcy goods.

Harwood Antiques
24 Lower Richmond Rd, Putney, SW15. Tel 788 7444.

Haslam & Whiteway
(Michael Whiteway). 105 Kensington Church St, W8 7LN. Tel 229 1145. Open Mon-Fri 10-6; Sat 10-2. Arts & Crafts movement in Britain. Specialists in 19th & 20thC furniture, metalwork, stained glass & enamels.

Nicholas Haslam
12 Holbein Place, SW1. Tel 730 8623. Open Mon-Fri 9.30-5.30. Decorative furniture & antiques. Interior design.

H.J.Hatfield & Sons Ltd
42 St Michaels St, Norfolk Place, W2. Tel 723 8265/6. Open Mon-Fri 8-5, other times by appt, but appt always advisable. Restorers of all fine art including inlaid furniture, ormolu, buhl and painted furniture.

Brian Haughton Antiques
3b Burlington Gdns, Old Bond Street, W1X 1LE. Tel 734 5491. Open Mon-Fri 10-5.30, Sat 10-1. Fine English & Continental ceramics. LAPADA

Haverstock Antiques
(Judith Newton). 78 Haverstock Hill, Hampstead, NW3 3BS. Tel 267 1627. Open Mon-Sat 10-5; other times by appt. Large stock of restored 19thC English town and country furniture on display. LAPADA

Jeanette Hayhurst Fine Glass
3b Burlington Gdns, Old Bond Street, W1. Tel 437 4975. Open Mon-Fri 10-5.30, Sat 10-1; other times by appt. 18thC English drinking glasses, 18th & 19thC decanters & table glass, scent bottles, fine 19thC decorative glass. LAPADA

Hayman & Hayman
(M.C. Hayman & Georgina Hayman). R1 & H4 Antiquarius, 135 King's Rd, SW3. Tel 351 6568 (priv 741 0959). Open Mon-Sat 10.30-5.30. Specialist in small collectors' items, photograph frames, inkwells, treen, match-strikers and seals.

Hazlitt, Gooden & Fox
(Jack Baer, Stefanie Maison, Charles Alabaster). 38 Bury St, St James's, SW1. Tel 930 6422. Open Mon-Fri 9.30-5.30. French 19thC paintings, drawings & sculpture. Italian Baroque and Rococo paintings. English 18th and 19thC paintings and drawings. SLAD

Hedleys Humpers Ltd
159 Iverson Rd, West Hampstead, NW6. Tel 624 6874 & 6981. (Also at 33 Liddell Road, Maygrove Road, NW6. Tel: 625 4551.) Open Mon-Fri 8-6; other times by appt. Packers & shippers. LAPADA

Heenglen Antiques
5 Cale St, SW3. Tel 352 8716. Decorative antiques and pictures.

Heim Gallery
(Dr A.Ciechanowiecki, Mr J.Pomian, Francois Heim). 59 Jermyn St, St James's, SW1Y 6LX. Tel 493 0688. Open Mon-Fri 10-5.30; other times by appt. Old Master paintings and sculpture.

Heirloom and Howard Ltd
(David S.Howard). 1 Hay Hill, Berkeley Sq, W1. Tel 493 5868. Open Mon-Fri 9.30-6; other times by appt. Armorial antiques, English and Chinese porcelain, coach and harness fittings, seals, dies, embroidery and Sheffield plate.

Helius Antiques
(M.Rowlands). 487-493 Upper Richmond Rd West, SW14 7PU. Tel 876 5721 (priv 940 5595). Open Mon-Fri 10-5.30, Sat 10-1; closed Wed; other times by appt. 18th, 19th and 20thC furniture, especially concerning writing.

Marina Henderson
11 Langton St, SW10. Tel 352 1667. Theatre and architectural design: fine drawings.

Thomas Heneage Art Books
(Shaunagh and Thomas Heneage). 42 Duke St, St James's, SW1 6DJ. Tel 930 9223 (priv 720 1503). Open Mon-Fri 10-6 and weekends by appt. New and out of print books on all aspects of the fine and decorative arts. ABA

Hennell Ltd
12 New Bond St, W1Y 0HE. Tel 629 6888. Open Mon-Fri 9-5; other times by appt. Silver, specialising in Hennell silver, jewellery, repairs, valuations. BADA

Lesley Hepherd Antiques
(Lesley Hepherd). SW7. Tel 244 9675. Open by appointment only. English period furniture and drinking glass, 1740-1840.

Heraldry Today
10 Beauchamp Place, SW3. Tel 584 1656. (Also at Parliament Piece, Ramsbury, Nr. Marlborough, Wilts.) Closed Fri and Sat. Books on heraldry, genealogy and topography. Catalogues quarterly. ABA

Heraz
(Malcolm Puttick, Andre Sasso). 25 Motcomb St, SW1X 8JT. Tel 235 7416. (Also at West Halkin St, 6 Halkin Arcade, SW1.) Open 10-6; other times by appt. Antique textile cushions, needlework carpets, decorative European and Oriental carpets, tapestries, table covers.

Heritage Antiques
(Anjula Daniel). 112 Islington High Street, Camden Passage, N1. Tel 226 7789. (Also neighbouring shop,'Christopher Ashton & Anjula Daniel'.) Open Wed & Sat 10-5; other times by appt. Specialist in antique metals and country furniture. LAPADA

Heritage Auctions
(Mr Draper). 101 Hoe Street, Walthamstow, E17. Tel 520 3215.

Hermitage
(Bernard Vieux-Pernon). 97 Pimlico Rd, SW1W 8PH. Tel 730 1973. Open Mon-Fri 10-6, Sat 10-3; other times by appt. French provincial furniture, Biedermeier furniture, Empire and decorative art and oil paintings.

M.Heskia
19 Mount St, W1. Tel 629 1483. Open Mon-Fri 9.30-6.30. Eastern carpets, European tapestries, antiques and works of art. Specialising in fine old Persian and Caucasian rugs. BADA

Richard Hewlett Gallery
(Richard Hewlett). 24 Cale St, Chelsea Green, SW3 3QU. Tel 584 8531. Open Mon-Fri 9.30-6; Sat 10-1; other times by appt. Architectural, natural history, sporting, topographical prints 16th-19thC, English county and world maps 16th-17thC.

A.Hicks
15 Flood St, SW3. Tel 352 8077. Open Mon-Sat 10-6. Jewellery and objects of the 1930s, specialising in art deco.

Highgate Gallery
(Julian and Miranda Halsby). 26 Highgate High St, N6. Tel 340 7564. Open Tues-Fri 10-1.30, 2.30-5.30; Sat 10-5.30; other times by appt. Fine 19thC English and Scottish watercolours. Moorcroft and art pottery, etchings.

J.K.Hill
(Janet Hill, Stuart Mansell). 151 Fulham Road, SW3 6SN. Tel 584 7529. Contemporary ceramics. ICGA

Hillyers
301 Sydenham Rd, SE26. Tel 778 6361. Open Mon-Fri 8.30-4.30; Sat 8.30-2; closed Wed. General antiques, pre-1900 furniture, china, glass, pictures, books etc. LAPADA

His Nibs
(Philip Poole). 182 Drury Lane, WC2. Tel 405 7097. Open Mon-Fri 10-5; Sat 11-2. Writing instruments and accessories including dip nibs.

Carlton Hobbs
(Carlton Hobbs). 533 Kings Rd, SW10. Tel 351 3870. Open 10-6; other times by appt. Continental and English furniture.

Hobhouse Ltd
39 Duke St, St James's, SW1 6DF. Tel 930 9308. Open Mon-Fri 10-5.30, but appt always advisable. 18th and 19thC drawings and paintings, also paintings by European artists working in India and Far East. Natural history drawings & paintings, European and Oriental. SLAD

Christopher Hodsoll Antiques
50 & 69 Pimlico Rd, SW1. Tel 730 9835. Open 10-7. 18th and 19thC furniture, pictures, large Oriental and English porcelain, carpets.

Hoff Antiques Ltd
(Mrs Ruth Hoff). 66A Kensington Church St, W8 4BY. Tel 229 5516 (priv 272 6542). Open Mon-Fri 10-6, Sat 10-4. Appt advisable for Continental porcelain. Specialist in important 18thC English and Continental porcelain. BADA

Michael Hogg
172 Brompton Rd, SW3. Tel 589 8629. Open Mon-Fri 9.30-5.30. Mainly 18th and early 19thC English and Continental furniture, works of art and Chinese porcelain.

Holland & Holland Ltd
33 Bruton St, W1X 8JS. Tel 499 4411. Open Mon-Fri 9-5.30. Large stock of modern guns and rifles. Antique guns and weapons always in stock.

Hollywood Road Antiques
1a Hollywood Road, SW10. Tel 352 5248. Country furniture, decorative antiques and quilts.

Hollywood Road Gallery
(Patrick and Catharine Kennaugh). 12 Hollywood Rd, SW10. Tel 351 1973. Open Mon-Fri 11-7.30; Sat 11-3; other times by appt. Decorative paintings, oils & watercolours, dating 1880-1940, mostly British & French £50-£2,500.

Holmes (Jewellers) Ltd
29 Old Bond St, W1X 3AB. Tel 493 1396. Open Mon-Fri 9-5.30, Sat 9-1. Jewels, antique silver and old Sheffield plate. BADA

Holmes (Silversmiths) Ltd
24 Burlington Arcade, W1. Tel 629 8380. Open Mon-Fri 9-5.30; Sat 9-4.30. Jewels, antique silver and old Sheffield plate. BADA

Brian and Lynn Holmes
Stands 304-306, Grays Antique Market, 58 Davies St, W1. Tel 629 7327. Open Mon-Fri 10-6. Antique jewellery. LAPADA

Hope and Glory (Ernest Titmuss)
131a Kensington Church Street, W8. Tel 727 8424. Open Tues-Fri 10-5, Sat 10-2. Royal commemorative china and glass.

Stephanie Hoppen
17 Walton St, SW3. Tel 589 3678. Open Mon-Fri 10-6; Sat 12-4. Botanical illustrations: birds, animals, reptiles, butterflies. Architectural design. Art Nouveau & Deco. Antique books on food and wine. BADA ABA

Jonathan Horne
66C Kensington Church St, W8 4BY. Tel 221 5658. Open Mon-Fri 9.30-5.30; other times by appt. Early English pottery. Works of art. BADA, CINOA

J.I.Horwit
94 Southampton Row, WC1 4BB. Tel 405 0749. Open Mon-Fri 11.30-6; other times by appt. Antique and secondhand jewellery of most descriptions.

Hotspur Ltd
14 Lowndes St, Belgrave Sq, SW1. Tel 235 1918. Open Mon-Fri 9-6, Sat 9-1. Good stock of 18thC English furniture. BADA

House of Buckingham
(Bruce White). 113-117 Farringdon Rd, EC1R 3BT. Tel 278 2013. Open Mon-Sat 9-5.30; other times by appt. Nautical gear, brass, boxes, games, 19thC furniture. LAPADA

How (of Edinburgh)
(Mrs G.E.P.How). 2-3 Pickering Place, St James's St, SW1A 1EA. Tel 930 7140. Open Mon-Thurs 9.45-5.15; Fri 9.45-4 but appt advisable. Fine antique British silver.

Howard Antiques
8 Davies St, W1. Tel 629 2628. English and Continental furniture.

Thomas Howard-Sneyd Ltd
35 Fursecroft, George Street, W1. Tel 723 1976. Open by appt only. Antiquities and works of art.

Derek Howard
Stand B2, Chenil Galleries, 181-183 King's Rd, Chelsea, SW3. Tel 352 2163. Antique scientific instruments, nautical, astrological items.

Eric Hudes
(Eric Hudes). 142 Portobello Rd, W11. Tel daily 0376-83767. (Also at Braintree, Essex.) Open Sat only 9-4.30, tel 727 4643. Oriental ceramics and works of art, and early English pottery. Specialising in early period Chinese and S.E.Asian ceramics - celadons, blue & white, blanc de chine etc, and later monochrome-glazed porcelain and pottery. Toby jugs, delftware, creamware. LAPADA

Paul Hughes, Antique & Ancient Textiles
(Paul Hughes). 3a Pembridge Sq, W2. Tel 243 8598. Open Mon-Sat 10-6 by appt only. Textile art of the world. Specialising in pre-Columbian & Coptic textile art. English 17thC embroidery.

Christopher Hull Gallery
17 Motcomb St, SW1. Tel 235 0500.

Human Touch
(H.Siegelmann). 533 King's Rd, SW10. Tel 352 2046. Open Mon-Sat 10-6; other times by appt. Display cabinets, restaurant fittings, selected pine, decorative furniture. Specialising in display cabinets & show pieces for restaurants.

Cyril Humphris
8 Pembroke Walk, W8. Tel 937 1719. Open Mon-Fri 10-5.30, but appt advisable. European works of art mainly 15th to 17thC sculpture, carved wood, decorative art etc. Also paintings.

Hundred And One
(Michael & Anna Selway). 101 Notting Hill Gate, W11. Tel 727 2326. Open Mon-Sat 9.30-5.30; other times by appt. Georgian to modern English silver and plate. Also some jewellery.

Sally Hunter and Patrick Seale Fine Art
(Sally Hunter and Patrick Seale). 2 Motcomb St, Belgrave Sq, SW1X 8JU. Tel 235 0934. Open Mon-Fri 10-6; other times by appt. 20thC British art.

Hurford & Scott
618-620 Kings Rd, SW6. Tel 731 4655.

Hyde Park Antiques
(G.E.&J.E.Baldwin). 191 Westbourne Grove, W11. Tel 727 1585. Open Mon-Fri 9.30-1.30, 3-5.30. Silver and silver plate, general antiques.

Hymore Hodson Antiques
181-183 King's Rd, Chelsea, SW3. Tel 352 9770. (Also at 140-142 Kensington Church St, W8 & in Godalming, Surrey.) Open Mon-Sat 10-6; other times by appt. At Chelsea: English furniture of 18th & 19thC. At Kensington: English longcase and bracket clocks from 17th, 18th and 19thC.

Iconastas
5 Piccadilly Arcade, Jermyn St, SW1. Tel 629 1433. Russian fine art. BADA

Manya Igel Fine Arts Ltd
(Mrs Manya Igel). 21-22 Peters Court, Porchester Rd, W2. Tel 229 1669/8429 (priv 6770). (Also Glencorse Antiques in Kingston, Surrey.) Open by appt only. Late 19thC and early 20thC oils and watercolours and modern British.

Brand Inglis Ltd.
(D.B. Inglis S.M. Inglis). 9 Halkin Arcade, Motcomb St, SW1. Tel 235 6604. Open Mon-Fri 9.30-6; other times by appt. Fine English & European silver. BADA

Malcolm Innes Gallery
172 Walton St, SW3. Tel 584 0575. (Also at 67 George St, Edinburgh. (031 226 4151.) Open Mon-Fri 9.30-6; other times by appt. Scottish landscape, sporting and natural history pictures. SLAD

Intercol London
(Yasha Beresiner). 1A Camden Walk, Islington Green, N1. Tel 354 2599 (priv 349 2207). Open Mon-Sat 8.45-6; other times by appt. Playing cards and books about cards, games and gambling. Maps, prints and books on cartography. Paper money, cheques and bonds. Books on economics, banking and currencies. BNTA

Iona Antiques
(Iona & Stephen Joseph). Stand 107, Gray's Antique Market, 58 Davies St, W1Y 1FH. Tel 499 2386. Open Mon-Fri 10-5.30; other times by appt. Largest selection of 19thC primitive animal paintings in England. Also British, primitive, sporting & 19thC paintings. BADA

Richard and Georgina Ivor
9 Tantallon Rd, SW12 8DS. Tel 673 7179. Open by appt only. Fine English watercolours, 18th-20thC and 18thC oil paintings.

Jackson-Stops & Staff
14 Curzon St, W1. Tel 499 6291. Chattels and fine art auctioneers and valuers. Sales of the contents of private houses conducted on the premises. Also at Chester, Chichester, Chipping Campden, Cirencester, Darlington, Exeter, Midhurst, Newmarket, Northampton, Yeovil, York, Dublin.

Olivia Jackson Antiques
(Olivia Jackson). 287 Westbourne Grove, W11. Tel 727 2817. Open 9-1 2-5.30; closed Mon. 17th to 19thC English and Dutch furniture.

Alan Jacobs Gallery
(Alan Jacobs in association with Charles Young). 8 Duke St, St James's, SW1. Tel 930 3709. Open Mon-Fri 10-6; other times by appt. 17thC Dutch and Flemish Old Master paintings. BADA; SLAD

Nicola Jacobs Gallery
9 Cork St, W1. Tel 437 3868. Open Mon-Fri 10-5.30, Sat 10-1. Contemporary art.

Bernard Jacobson Ltd
2A Cork St, W1. Tel 439 8355. Open Mon-Fri 10-6, Sat 10-1. Contemporary art.

Anthony James & Son Ltd
(James Millard). 88 Fulham Road, SW3. Tel 584 1120 (priv 385 3408). Open Mon-Fri 9.15-6, Sat 10-1; other times by appt. Fine 18th and 19thC English and Continental furniture, objects and decorative pictures. BADA

David James Fine Paintings
291 Brompton Rd, SW3. Tel 581 3399. Fine Victorian watercolours. BADA

Japanese Gallery
(Mr & Mrs C.D. Wertheim). 23 Camden Passage, N1 8EA. Tel 226 3347. (Also at 66D Kensington Church St, W8 Tel: 229 2934.) Open Mon-Sat 9-5; other times by appt. Japanese woodblock prints, paintings, scrolls, screens, kimono (Japanese clothing), Japanese porcelain, bronze.

Gillian Jason Gallery
42 Inverness St, NW1. Tel 267 4835. Open Tues-Sat 10.30-5.30. Modern British art.

Melvyn Jay Antiques
(M. Jay). 64a Kensington Church St, W8. Tel 937 6832. 19thC furniture, silver, glass, paintings. LAPADA

Tobias Jellinek
(at Alistair Sampson Antiques). 156 Brompton Rd, SW3 1HW. Tel 589 5272, 581 2267. Open Mon-Fri 9.30-5.30; other times by appt. Fine early furniture, pottery, porcelain and needlework. BADA

Charles Jerdein
38 Albemarle St, W1X 3FB. Tel 493 0291. Paintings.

Jeremy Ltd
255 King's Rd, Chelsea, SW3 5EL. Tel 352 3127, 352 0644. Open Mon-Sat 8.30-6. English and French 18th and 19thC furniture. Mirror painting and ormolu. BADA

John Jesse & Irina Laski
(John Jesse & Irina Laski). 160 Kensington Church Street, W8. Tel 229 0312. Open Mon-Sat 10-6. Art Nouveau & Art Deco objects & jewellery dating from 1880-1950.

H.R.Jessop Ltd
3 Pickering Place, St James's, SW1A 1EA. Tel 930 4696. Open Tues, Wed, Thurs 10-5; other times by appt. Fine 17th and 18thC English silver and objets d'art.

The Jewel House (Mayfair)
(James G. Aldridge). 23 Lansdowne Row, W1X 7LN. Tel 499 7936. Open Mon-Fri 9.30-6. Antique and modern jewellery, some antique silver. NAJ

S. & H. Jewell Ltd
26 Parker St, WC2B 5PH. Tel 405 8520. Open Mon-Fri 9-5.30; other times by appt. Almost 4000 sq ft of antique and reproduction furniture, specialising in desks, bookcases, boardroom furniture. Also cabinets, dining tables, chairs etc.

C. John (Rare Rugs) Ltd
(Leon Sassoon). 70 South Audley St, Mayfair, W1Y 5FE. Tel 493 5288. Open Mon-Fri 9.30-5; other times by appt. Rare & decorative carpets, rugs, tapestries & textiles. BADA

Michael John Decorative Arts Ltd
(Michael John). 25A Lowndes St, SW1. Tel 235 3154/5. Open Mon-Fri 10-6; other times by appt. Art Nouveau, Art Deco and Vienna Secession. Bronzes, furniture, glass, paintings, ceramics, metalwork. Specialising in painting and applied art from the Secession period.

John's Antiques
(John Joseph). Stands 345/346, Grays Antique Market, 58 Davies St, W1. Tel 629 1140. Open Mon-Fri 10-6. Georgian, Victorian, Art Nouveau and Art Deco jewellery.

George Johnson
(Paul George, Ian Johnson). 120 Kensington Park Road, W11 2PW. Tel 229 3119. Open Mon-Sat 9.30-5.30; other times by appt. 17th & 18thC furniture, works of art. LAPADA

Johnson, Walker & Tolhurst Ltd
64 Burlington Arcade, Piccadilly, W1. Tel 629 2615, 629 2616. Open Mon-Fri 9-5. Fine antique jewellery and silver. BADA

Belle Johnston
(Mrs. I.A. Johnston). Stands K1 & K2 Antiquarius, Kings Rd, SW3. Tel 352 7989. Open Mon-Sat 10-6. Brass, copper and metalware.

Ruth Joly
(Mrs R.R.Joly). 32 Moreton St, Pimlico, SW1V 2PD. Tel 834 8764 (priv 828 5299). Open Mon-Fri 10-5; other times by appt. Antique furniture and decorator's items.

Jones
(Judy Jones). 194 Westbourne Grove, W11. Tel 229 6866. Open Mon-Sat 10-6; other times by appt. Original old lighting 1850-1950. Large stock of old glass lamp shades, brass table lamps, wall lights, pendants, electroliers & various other ceiling lights. Victorian, Edwardian, art nouveau & art deco.

Annabel Jones
52 Beauchamp Place, Knightsbridge, SW3. Tel 589 3215. Fine antique & contemporary jewellery, silverware and old Sheffield plate.

Howard Jones
43 Kensington Church St, W8. Tel 937 4359. Open Mon-Sat 10-5. Specialising in silver of all periods. Also some porcelain and bronzes. LAPADA

Paul Jones
Stand Y6 Antiquarius, 135 Kings Rd, SW3. Tel 352 4690. Specialist in Paisley shawls, Kashmir and European textiles.

R.& J. Jones
(Robert Jones). 137 Kensington Church St, W8. Tel 221 4026. Open Mon-Fri 10-6; Sat 10-1; other times by appt. 17th, 18th, 19thC Continental and English oil paintings. 18thC ceramics. BADA

Jorgen Antiques
(A.J.Dolleris). 40 Lower Richmond Rd, Putney, SW15. Tel 789 7329. Open Tues-Fri 11-5. Antique furniture.

Visit the . . .

Open Monday-Friday 9am-5.30pm
Saturday 9am-12.30pm

LONDON SILVER VAULTS

The world's largest commercial collection of antique and modern silver and silver plate in **two floors beneath Central London**

DEALERS AND RETAIL TRADE CATERED FOR
Also JEWELLERY, GLASS, CHINA

David S Shure & Co, vault 1
Jules Golding & Co Ltd, vault 2
Wm Walter (Antiques) Ltd, vaults 3 & 5
R Feldman Ltd, vaults 4 & 6
Linden & Co (Antiques) Ltd, vault 7
L Langford & Co, vaults 8 & 10
I J Mazure & Co, vault 9
I Franks, vault 11
H Perovetz Ltd, vaults 13 & 15
H Miller (Antiques) Ltd, vaults 12 & 14
Percy's (Silver) Ltd, vaults 16 & 17
B Lampert, vault 19
B L Collins, vault 20
Nat Leslie Ltd, vaults 21, 22 & 23
Fine China (London) Ltd, vaults 20 & 24
Rare Art (London) Ltd, vault 25
E & C T Koopman & Son Ltd, vault 25
B Silverman, vaults 26 & 33

Fine silver Bright Cut tea and coffee set, dated 1801, at the London Silver Vaults.

A Bloom, vault 27
Lawrence Block (Silverware) Ltd, vault 28
Silstar Antiques, vault 29
J Mammon Antiques, vault 30
C & T Mammon, vaults 31 & 64
M J Dubiner, vault 38
Wolfe (Jewellery), vault 41
A & G Weiss Jewellery, vaults 42 & 44
Peter K Weiss Antique Watches, vaults 42 & 44
A Urbach, vault 50
J Podlewski & P Daniel, vault 51
L Brian Antiques, vault 56
Leon Antiques Ltd, vault 57
L Saunders, vault 60
Nagioff Jewellery, vaults 63 & 69
Lawrence Block & Co Ltd, vault 65

CHANCERY HOUSE, 53-63 CHANCERY LANE, LONDON WC2

DAVID KER FINE ART

85 BOURNE STREET SW1. 730 3523/8365

Decorative paintings, watercolours & drawings of the 18th Century, 19th Century & 20th Century

Antique & Old Paste Jewellery

Decorative Antiques and Objets D'Art

LARGE STOCK OF ITEMS UNDER £100

JUST DESKS

Period and reproduction pedestal desks, partners desks, writing tables, davenports and desk chairs

20 Church Street London NW8 Telephone 01-723 7976

Also at
6 Erskine Road London NW3 Tel 01-722 4902

STEPHEN LONG

18th and 19th century English painted furniture, pictures and prints, china and objects

Old chintz, *toiles*, shawls and patchwork quilts

Nursery and kitchen antiques

348 FULHAM ROAD · LONDON SW10
Tel 01-352 8226

E.Joseph & Chas. J. Sawyer
(David J.Brass, Richard Sawyer). 1 Vere St W1M 9HQ. Tel 493 8353/4/5. Open Mon-Fri 9.30-5.30; other times by appt. Fine and rare books, including standard sets in leather or cloth, illustrated books, press books, fine bindings, colour plate books and a selection of Victorian and early 20thC watercolour paintings. ABA

John Joseph
(Mr & Mrs J Joseph). Grays Antique Market, 58 Davies St, W1. Tel 629 1140. Jewellery, valuations. LAPADA

Jubilee Antiques Market
The Piazza, Covent Garden, WC2. Tel 240 7405. Open Mondays only, 5am-4pm. Over 200 individual dealers with things of interest to collectors and trade buyers.

Annely Juda
(Mrs Annely Juda and David Juda). 11 Tottenham Mews, off Tottenham St, W1P 9PJ. Tel 637 5517. Open Mon-Fri 10-6, Sat 10-1; other times by appt. Russian Constructivism, Bauhaus, de Stijl, etc. SLAD

Julian Antiques
67 Park Rd, NW1. Tel 723 0653. (Also 124 High St, Hurstpierpoint, W.Sussex.) Open Mon-Fri 10.30-4; other times by appt. French clocks, furniture, mirrors, fireplaces and general French antiques. LAPADA

Alexander Juran & Co
(Alexander Juran). 74 New Bond St, W1Y 9DD. Tel 629 2550, 493 4484. Open Mon-Fri 9-5.30. Antique Oriental rugs, textiles and tapestries. BADA

Just a Minute Antiques
27 Battersea Rise, SW11. Tel 223 5341. Antique and Victorian furniture.

Just A Second Antiques Ltd
(G.Bastillo). 40 Fulham High St, SW6. Tel 731 1919, 223 5341. Open Mon-Sat 9-6; other times by appt. Large stock of furniture, silver, pictures, porcelain and decorative items.

Just Desks
(Guy Gordon, Noelle Finch). 20 Church St, NW8 8EP. Tel 723 7976, 402 0391. (Further showrooms at 6 Erskine Rd, London NW3.) Open Mon-Sat 9.30-6; other times by appt. Manufacturers and retailers of traditional style office and study furniture. Furniture built to specification. Restorers and retailers of antique desks. LAPADA

JPL Fine Arts
(C.A.P.Neffe). 24 Davies St, W1Y 1LH. Tel 493 2630. Open Mon-Fri 10-5.30; other times by appt. Impressionist and post impressionist paintings, drawings and watercolours. SLAD

M. & A. Kaae
(Mr & Mrs A. Kaae). Grays Mews, 1-7 Davies Mews, W1. Tel 629 1200. Jewellery. LAPADA

Kaleidoscope Gallery
(Karl Barrie). 66 Willesden Lane, NW6. Tel 328 5833. Open Mon-Sat 10-5.30; other times by appt. 18th, 19th and 20thC oils, watercolours and prints.

Lewis M. Kaplan Associates Ltd
(Lewis M. Kaplan, Gordon D. Watson). 50 Fulham Rd, SW3. Tel 589 3108 or 584 6328. Open Mon-Sat 11-6; other times by appt. Art Nouveau, Art Deco, including signed Cartier jewellery. LAPADA

Keeble Ltd
13 Walton St, SW3. Tel 581 3676. Fine carpets, rugs, tapestries, needlework and furniture.

John Keil Ltd
154 Brompton Rd, SW3. Tel 589 6454. (Also in Bath, Avon.) Open Mon-Fri 9.30-6; other times by appt. Fine 17th to early 19thC furniture, mainly English. BADA

Peter W.Kemp
174A Kensington Church St, W8 4DP. Tel 229 2988. Open Mon-Fri 10-5.30; other times by appt. Oriental and European ceramics and works of art. Decorative larger 19thC Oriental porcelain and works of art for the Interior Decorating trade.

Beryl Kendall
The English Watercolour Gallery, 2 Warwick Place, W9 2PK. Tel 286 9902. Open Tues-Fri 1.30-6; other times by appt. 18th and 19thC watercolours; also living artists.

Kennedy Carpets & Kelims
9A Vigo St, W1. Tel 439 8873. Open Mon-Sat 9.30-6. Specialists in fine Oriental carpets, rugs and kelims. LAPADA

Robin Kennedy
(Robin Kennedy). 29 New Bond St, W1Y 9HD. Tel 408 1238 (priv 940 3281). Open Mon-Fri 10-6; other times by appt. Fine Japanese prints and paintings.

Kensington Carpets
98/99 Jermyn St, SW1. Tel 930 2044. Open Mon-Sat 10-6. Specialists in fine Oriental carpets, rugs and kelims. LAPADA

Kensington Furniture
(David Robinson, Libby Robinson). Troy Court, 214-216 Kensington High St, W8. Tel 937 4973. Open Mon-Sat 9-6. Over 3,000 sq ft of 19thC and Edwardian furniture, reproduction furniture, brass, copper, ceramics and pictures. Exports arranged.

Kenway Antiques
(C. & C.P. Boas). 70 Kenway Rd, SW5 0RD. Tel 373 1631. Open 10-5.30. Chinese porcelain, also English and Continental items.

David Ker Fine Art
85 Bourne St, SW1. Tel 730 8365 (priv 730 3523). Open Mon-Fri 9.30-5.30; other times by appt. Decorative paintings, watercolours and prints of the 18th, 19th & 20thC. Antique and old paste jewellery. Decorative antiques and objets d'art.

Thomas Kerr Antiques Ltd
(Thomas & Anna Kerr). 11 Theberton St, Islington, N1. Tel 226 0626. Open Mon-Sat 9.30-6; other times by appt. Three floors of Georgian mahogany and early oak furniture, clocks, oil paintings and other decorative items. LAPADA

Khachadourian Gallery
(Minas Khachadourian, Simon Khachadourian). 60 Pall Mall, St James's, SW1Y 5HT. Tel 930 3333. Open Mon-Fri 9.30-6; other times by appt. Michelin ceramic tiled panels, automobile and aeronautical art, antique tin-plate toy cars.

Khalili Gallery
(N. D. Khalili). 15c Clifford St, Bond St, W1. Tel 734 4202. Open Mon-Fri 10-5.30; other times by appt. Persian and Islamic art, ceramics, archeaological relics, ancient glass, calligraphics and miniatures. Specialising in rare Islamic items. LAPADA

Richard Kihl Ltd
(Richard Kihl). 164 Regent's Park Rd, NW1 8XN. Tel 586 3838. Open Mon-Fri 9.30-5; Sat 11-5; other times by appt. Specialist in wine antiques and accessories, including decanters, claret jugs, glasses, bottles, trays and corkscrews.

The Kilim Warehouse Ltd
(Jose Luczyz-Wyhowska). 28A Pickets St, SW12 8QB. Tel 675 3122. Open Mon-Sat 10-4; Sun 11-2; other times by appt. Importer, wholesaler & retailer of kilims from Turkey, N.Africa, Afghanistan, Persia and the Caucasus. Cleaning and restoration of kilims.

Eric King Antiques
203 New Kings Rd, SW6. Tel 736 3162. Open Mon-Sat, 10-6. Unusual decorative furniture and objects (English and Oriental), and collectors items. Specialising in bentwood, wicker, garden and pine furniture, also screens.

James Kirkman Limited
(Mr & Mrs James Kirkman). 46 Brompton Sq, SW3 2AF. Tel 589 4328,. Open by appt only. Impressionists, 19th & 20thC drawings and paintings. SLAD

Klaber & Klaber
(Mrs B. and Miss P.Klaber). 2A Bedford Gdns, Kensington Church St, W8 7EH. Tel 727 4573. Open Mon-Sat 10-5, closed 1-2. 18th and some early 19thC English and Continental porcelain and enamels. BADA

Knight's of London
(Andrew Knight). 2a Belsize Park Mews, Belsize Village, NW3 5BL. Tel 431 2490. Antique and period fireplace consultants.

Knightsbridge Coins
(S.C.Fenton). 43 Duke St, St James's, SW1. Tel 930 7597. Open Mon-Fri 10-6; other times by appt. British and United States coins. BNTA

Knoedler Kasmin
22 Cork St, W1. Tel 439 1096. Contemporary painting and sculpture.

Konig & Co
26 Talina Centre, Bagley's Lane, SW6. Tel 736 0915. Open Mon-Fri 9.30-1 2-5.30. Good quality antique furniture, objects, pictures and china.

Konig Newton Ltd
(A.de Chappuis Konig, R.J.Newton). 27 The Talina Centre, Bagley's Lane, Fulham, SW6. Tel 736 0915. Furniture painters, carvers, gilders and restorers, bespoke picture and looking glass frame makers, specialist tole manufacture and decoration.

E.& C.T.Koopman & Son Ltd
The London Silver Vaults, Chancery House, Chancery Lane, WC2. Tel 242 8365 242 7624. Open Mon-Fri 9-5; other times by appt. Antique English & Continental silver and objets d'art. BADA

L. & E. Kreckovic
62 Fulham High St, SW6. Tel 736 0753. Open Mon-Fri 9.30-5, Sat 10-5; other times by appt. Antique furniture and works of art.

Krios Gallery
305 Brompton Rd, SW3.
Tel 589 5811. Varied stock of watercolours.

Richard Kruml
P.O.Box 4LE, 47 Albemarle St, W1A 4LE. Tel 629 3017. Open 11-5 and other times by appt, but appt always advisable. Extensive selection of fine Japanese prints.

L'Acquaforte
49A Ledbury Rd, W11.
Tel 221 3388. Open Mon-Fri 9-5; Sat 9-1. Decorative prints, particularly natural history & botanical (current stock includes plates by Besler, Weinmann, Gould etc.) Also specialising in Continental watercolours & prints (especially Italian works, mainly 19thC & prints 16th to 19thC).

The Lacquer Chest
(A.V. & G.A.Andersen).
75 Kensington Church St, W8.
Tel 937 1306. Open Mon-Fri 9.30-5.30, Sat 9.30-2. 19thC country and other furniture, textiles, china and lamps. Also unusual objects.

Lacy Gallery
(Colin Lacy). 38-40 Ledbury Rd, W11. Tel 229 9105, 229 5316. (Also in Henley-in-Arden, Warwickshire.) Open Mon-Sat 10-5. Decorative and sporting 18th, 19th and early 20thC oils, watercolours amd carvings etc. Period picture frames 1700-1940. Decorative and sporting prints of the 18th and 19thC.

Fiona & Bill Laidlaw Antiques
40 Gordon Place, Holland St, W8 5JF. Tel 937 8493. Open Tues-Fri 10.30-5.30; Sat 10.30-2.30; other times by appt. Oil and watercolours 1810-1920, Biedermeier furniture, English ceramics 1810-1920 including majolica, tole and papier mache. Scandinavian painted furniture 1750-1850.

Lamont Antiques Ltd
(Neil Lamont, Frank Llewellyn, Caroline Lamont). Newhams Row, 175 Bermondsey St, SE1 3UW. Tel 403 0126. Open Mon-Fri 9-5.30; other times by appt. Architectural fixtures, fittings, leaded and stained glass, pub mirrors & signs, 19th & 20thC English & Continental furniture, painted ships furniture. LAPADA

S.Lampard & Son
32 Notting Hill Gate, W11.
Tel 229 5457. Open Mon-Fri 9-4.30. Antique jewellery, clocks and silver. BADA

Lancaster Antiques
(P. H. Smith). Harlequin, Grays Antique Market, 58 Davies St, W1. Tel 629 6502. Jewellery. LAPADA

The Landscape Ornament Co
(Rosalind Burrows,Michael Balston,David Jenkins). Voysey House, Barley Mow Passage, Chiswick, W4 4PN. Tel 995 9739. Open Mon-Fri 9.30-5.30. Design and commission of high quality stone and timber garden ornaments. Reproductions of antique statuary in stone & bronze in limited editions.

Lane Fine Art Ltd
86-88 Pimlico Road, SW1.
Tel 730 7374. Open Mon-Fri 10-6, Sat 10-1. Old Master paintings pre-1630, especially Elizabethan portraits. English 18thC sporting paintings. LAPADA, BADA

Langfords
Oldebourne House, 46-47 Chancery Lane, WC2.
Tel 405 6402. (Also in the London Silver Vaults.) Open Mon-Fri 9.30-5.30 (Sat 9.30-12.15 Vaults only). Specialising in antique and modern silver and plate. Also very large and fascinating stock of Victoriana, unusual items, furniture, marine and scientific instruments, clocks and paintings. Specialists in model ships. LAPADA

Langton Gallery Ltd
(R.S.Stuart, P.G.Bainbridge, A.E.Wolley Dod). 3 Langton St, SW10. Tel 352 9150. Open Mon-Sat 10-6. Specialising in British humorists and illustrators including Rowlandson, Cruickshank, H.M.Bateman, Heath Robinson, Pont, Fougasse etc. and related books and illustrators books.

Judith Larney
103A St John's Hill, SW11.
Tel 350 1002. Restoration and conservation of porcelain, pottery, enamels and glass.

Lasson Gallery
(Zola Lasson). 34 Duke St, St James's. Tel 930 5950. Open Mon-Fri 10.30-5.30, Sat 11-1; other times by appt. Old Masters and modern pictures.

Laurence Corner Euston Gallery
1st Floor, 126-130 Drummond St, NW1. Tel 388 6811. Open daily incl Sat 9.30-5.30. Paintings and old prints.

D.S.Lavender (Antiques) Ltd
(D.S.Lavender, P.C.Lavender). 16B Grafton St, W1X 3LA.
Tel 629 1782 (priv 409 2305). Open Mon-Fri 9.30-5.30. Fine jewels, miniatures and works of art. BADA

J.Lavian
(J.Lavian). 53-79 Highgate Rd, NW5 1TL. Tel 485 7955. Open Mon-Fri 9.30-6; other times by appt. Antique & modern oriental carpets, rugs, kelims, Aubusson & tapestry.

Ledger Antiques
(R.M.Donnelly & D.G.Ledger). 101A Fulham Rd, SW3 6RH.
Tel 581 0922. Open Mon-Sat 10-6; other times by appt. Mason's ironstone, Staffordshire pastille burners and houses, Staffordshire naval and military figures.

Ronald A.Lee (Fine Arts) Ltd
1-9 Bruton Place, W1X 7AD.
Tel 499 6266. Open Mon-Fri 10-5. Specialist in antique clocks. Important stock of early works of art, paintings, furniture, silver and other items in two large showrooms. BADA

Lefevre Gallery
30 Bruton St, W1X 8JD.
Tel 493 1572. Open 10-5. Highly important 19th and 20thC paintings, bronzes and sculpture.

The Leger Galleries Ltd
13 Old Bond St, W1.
Tel 629 3538. Paintings - old masters of the English Dutch and Flemish schools. Early English watercolours. Exhibitions. BADA

Leggatt Bros
17 Duke St, St James's, SW1Y 6DB. Tel 930 3772 and 930 3252. Important Old Master paintings particularly the English School.

Leigh Gallery
(Michael Ranson-Witt). 17 Leigh St, Bloomsbury, WC1H 9EW.
Tel 242 5177. Individual works of contemporary pottery and glass. ICGA

Leinster Fine Art
Fourth Floor, 3 Clifford St, W1X 1RA. Tel 437 4534. Open Mon-Fri 10-6; Sat 11-1. Works by modern & contemporary German expressionists, Scottish contemporary artists, contemporary European & American artists.

Nellie Lenson & Roy Smith
16 Camden Passage, N1 8ED.
Tel 226 2423 (priv 340 8767). (Also at 153 Portobello Rd, W11. Warehouse at 1 St Peters St, N1.) Open Mon-Sat 10-4.30; Wed 9-4.30. Decorative antiques.

Lenygon & Morant Ltd
30-31 Lyme St, NW1 0EE.
Tel 482 2156. Architectural items. BADA

Lev (Antiques) Ltd
(Mrs L.Lev). 97A & 97B Kensington Church St, W8 7LN. Tel 727 9248. Open Mon-Fri 10-5 and most Sats. Jewellery, silver, plate, curios, pottery. Picture restoration.

M.P.Levene Ltd
5 Thurloe Place, SW7 2RR.
Tel 589 3785. Open Mon-Fri 9.30-6, Sat 9.30-1. Antique and modern silver and old Sheffield plate. BADA

M. & D. Lewis Antiques
1 Lonsdale Rd, W11.
Tel 727 3908. Open Mon-Fri 9.30-5.30; Sat 9.30-4. Continental & English furniture & porcelain.

Liberty & Co Ltd
Regent St, W1R 6AH.
Tel 734 1234. Open Mon-Sat 9.30-6; Thurs 9.30-7. Antiques department - furniture, pewter, silver, pottery.

Libra Antiques
(Anna M. Wolsey). 131e Kensington Church St, W8 7PT. Tel 727 2990. Open Mon-Fri 10-5.30, Sat 10-4, or by appt. Blue and white pottery, early European ceramics, mainly 1720-1830.

Lighthouse Antiques
(Mrs E Kingston). 67 Ridgway, Wimbledon Village, SW19.
Tel 946 2050. Chandeliers, antique lights, small furniture. LAPADA

Lillie Antiques
(M. & E. Bargielowski). 244 Lillie Rd, SW6 7QA. Tel 385 9852. Open Mon-Fri 10-6, Sat by appt only. 17th to early 19thC oak and mahogany furniture, Continental porcelain and objets d'art. LAPADA

Limner Antiques
(B.&G.Viner). 124 New Bond St, W1Y 9AE. Tel 629 5314 (priv 493 6115). Open Mon-Fri 10-5. Portrait miniatures.

S.Linden
33 Craven St, WC2. Tel 930 3659. Open by appt only. General stock of secondhand and antiquarian books.

Lindsay Antiques
(Tristram Jellinek, Lindsay Shand). 99 Kensington Church St, W8.
Tel 727 2333. Open Mon-Fri 9.30-5.30; other times by appt. Decorative antiques, specialising in early English pottery. BADA

Eric Lineham & Son
(Peter Lineham). 62 Kensington Church St, W8 4oB.
Tel 937 9650. Open Mon-Fri; other times by appt. Glass, porcelain, art nouveau. Valuations and restorations.

J.Lipitch Ltd
(Jack Lipitch). 177 Westbourne Grove, W11. Tel 229 0783. Open 9.30-5.30; Sat 10-1.30. Fine furniture, pottery and porcelain. BADA

Michael Lipitch
(M.I. & G.R.Lipitch). 98 Fulham Rd, SW3. Tel 589 7327 (priv 440 7797). Open Mon-Fri 9.30-6, Sat 10-1.30; other times by appt. Fine quality English and Continental 18thC furniture and decorations, specialising in pairs, tables, chairs, cabinets.

Peter Lipitch Ltd
120-124 Fulham Rd, SW3. Tel 373 3328. Furniture. BADA

W. Lipka Ltd
(W. Lipka). 62 Aylestone Ave, NW6. Tel 459 4588. Jewellery, silver, works of art, metalware. LAPADA

Sanda Lipton
(Mrs S.F.V.Lipton). 35 Kenway Rd, SW5. Tel 373 9625 (shop), 407 0278. Open Mon-Fri 1.30-6.30, Sat 10-1, 2-4; other times by appt. Antique silver up to the mid-19thC. Collectable items, early English spoons, table services and general flatware. Silver repairs and engraving undertaken. LAPADA

Lisson Gallery
(Nicholas Logsdail). 66-68 Bell St, NW1 6SP. Tel 262 1539. Open Mon-Fri 10-6; Sat 10-1. Art gallery holding approximately 12 exhibitions yearly. Contemporary art by British & international artists. SLAD

Little Winchester Gallery
(Irene Berge). 36A Kensington Church St, W8 4BX. Tel 937 8444. Open Mon-Sat 11-6; other times by appt. Fine 19th and 20thC French paintings, and 19thC Dutch paintings.

Lockson Services Ltd
29 Broomfield St, E14 6BQ. Tel 515 8600. Packers & shippers. LAPADA

The London Architectural Salvage & Supply Co Ltd
('LASSCO'). The Mark St Depository, Mark St, off Paul St, EC2A 4ER. Tel 739 0448. (Also Door Store, King Johns Ct, EC2 repairs & sells period doors.) Open Mon-Sat 10-5. Specialist suppliers of architectural relics of every description, including doors, panelling, chimney pieces, ironwork, glass & ecclesiastical joinery, pews and all salvaged building materials.

The London Restoration Centre
(Mr Squatriti). 220 Westbourne Grove, W11. Tel 727 6596. Open Mon-Sat. Restoration of porcelain, ceramics, ivory, marble, enamels.

London Silver Vaults
Chancery House, Chancery Lane, WC2. Tel 242 3844. Open Mon-Fri 9-5.30, Sat 9-12.30, closed Bank Holidays. Many dealers in antique, secondhand and new silver, jewellery, fine china and objets d'art.

Stephen Long
Albion House, 348 Fulham Rd, SW10 9UH. Tel 352 8226. Open Mon-Fri 9-1, 2.15-5.30; other times by appt. English pottery, small furniture (especially painted), small decorative items. Specialists in English fabrics, paisley shawls, toys and games.

Paul Longmire Ltd
(Paul Longmire, E.J. Longmire). 12 Bury St, St James's, SW1. Tel 930 8720. Open Mon-Fri 9-5; other times by appt. Antique jewellery, objects of vertu, modern silver, works of art, 18th and 19thC furniture. Specialist in cufflinks, regimental badges and heraldry. NAG

M. & J. Longmore
(M C & J A Longmore). No 8, 284 Westbourne Grove, W11. Tel 994 6896. Open Sats only. Silver, jewellery, watches. LAPADA

Loot
(Gill Goldsmith). 76-78 Pimlico Rd, SW1. Tel 730 8097 (priv 352 0135). Open Mon-Fri 10-6, Sat 10-1. 19thC decorative furniture, objects, pictures, textiles, Oriental screens etc.

Lords Gallery
(Philip Granville). 26 Wellington Road, NW8 9SP. Tel 722 4444. Open by appt. 3,000 rare old original posters. Also paintings and sculpture.

Lots Road Chelsea Auction Galleries
(Roger Ross). 71 Lots Rd, Chelsea, SW10 0RN. Tel 351 7771, 352 2349 24 hr. Open Mon 9 am-10.30 pm; Tues 10-7; Wed 9-6; Thurs-Fri 9-5; Sat 10-1. Antique, traditional & modern furniture,carpets, silver, china, glass etc. Auction every Monday evening 6.30 pm. On view Friday 9-4, Saturday & Sunday 10-1, Monday 9-6. Quality items accepted daily. Send s.a.e. for catalogue.

N.W.Lott & H.J.Gerrish Ltd
14 Mason's Yard, Duke Street St James's, SW1. Tel 930 1353. (Also at Froxfield, Wiltshire.) Open Mon-Fri 10-6; other times by appt. 19th and 20thC etchings and engravings. Also some watercolours, paintings (usually by leading etchers and engravers), and some early photographs.

Peter Loveday Prints
46 Norland Sq, W11 4PZ. Tel 221 4479. Open by appt. Sporting art, topography prints & books. LAPADA

Clive Loveless
29 Kelfield Gdns, North Kensington, W10 6NA. Tel 969 5831. Open by appt only. Antique tribal rugs, kelims & textiles. Consultancy service; cleaning & restoration. BADA

The Lucerne Gallery
(David Barclay Ltd). 7 Kensington Mall, Kensington Church St, W8. Tel 727 1726. Open Mon-Fri 10-6. Paintings, antique furniture and works of art.

Lucky Parrot (Antiques and Things)
(Jinnie Moore & Roger Lascelles). Bellevue Rd, Wandsworth Common, SW17. Tel 672 7168. Open Mon-Sat 10-1, 2.30-5, closed Wed; other times by appt. Victorian and Edwardian patchwork, textiles, china and glass.

Lumley Cazalet Ltd
24 Davies St, W1. Tel 499 5058. Open Mon-Fri 10-6; other times by appt. Original prints by 20thC masters, including Braque, Chagall, Matisse, Miro, Picasso etc. Late 19thC French prints. Important Matisse collection of drawings and prints and occasionally paintings and collages.

Lunn Antiques Ltd
(Stephen Lunn, John Fry). 86 New King's Rd, SW6 4LU. Tel 736 4638. Open Mon-Sat 10-6; other times by appt. Antique textiles, lacework, embroidery, linens, costume.

Lynde Albury Antiques
23 Buckingham Ct (2nd floor), Kensington Park Rd, W11. Tel 229 3941. Open by appt only. General antiques, including 18th and 19thC brass, small 18thC and early 19thC furniture, Chinese and English porcelain, glass and embroideries. Wholesale and export only.

Lyons Gallery
(John Lyons, Diana Lyons). 47 Mill Lane, West Hampstead, NW6 1NB. Tel 794 3537. Open Wed-Sat 11-6; other times by appt. Specialists in Art Nouveau, Art Deco, modern British paintings, studio ceramics. Emphasis on signed and decorative items.

LPJ Antiques
(Laurence Mitchell). 27 Camden Passage, Islington, N1. Tel 359 7579. Open Tues-Sat 9-5; other times by appt. Oriental & European ceramics, English porcelain & ironstone, decorative works of art, ivories & bronzes, export porcelain from c.1700, glass, oriental and European furniture. LAPADA

M. & M. Oriental Gallery Ltd
(M.A. and M.Karimzadeh). 4th Floor, Block D, 53/79 Highgate Rd, NW5 1TL. Tel 267 5973. Open Mon-Fri 10-4; other times by appt. Old and antique Oriental carpets and rugs, many qualities and sizes including very large sizes; tapestries and needlework; large premises, supplying the trade. Valuations, repairs and cleaning.

Maas Gallery
15A Clifford St, New Bond St, W1X 1RF. Tel 734 2302. Open Mon-Fri 10-5. Victorian paintings, drawings and watercolours. SLAD

Mackinnon and Strachey
17 Savile Row, W1. Tel 734 6911. Art gallery.

The Maclean Gallery
49 Drayton Gardens, SW10. Tel 373 2867. Open by appt only. British paintings, watercolours, drawings and prints. 18thC French wallpaper.

MacConnal-Mason
14 Duke St, St James's, SW1Y 6DB. Tel 839 7693/4 and 499 6991. (Also at 15 Burlington Arcade, W1V 9AB.) Open Mon-Fri 9.30-6, Sat 9.30-12.30. 19th and 20thC English and Continental paintings. Also contemporary paintings. BADA

Finbar MacDonnell
17 Camden Passage, N1. Tel 226 0537. Open Mon-Sat 10-6. Old prints and engravings.

Sue Madden
(Sue Madden). Stall X10 Antiquarius, 135 Kings Rd, SW3. Tel 351 5757 (priv 703 4634). Open Mon-Sat 10-6. Antique white bed and table linen, with hand worked embroidery and lace. Victorian and Edwardian handworked white curtains. Antique christening robes and bonnets (19thC). Especially Ayrshire embroidery.

Maggs Bros Ltd
50 Berkeley Sq, W1X 6EL. Tel 493 7160. Open weekdays. Important general stock of antiquarian and secondhand books, manuscripts and autographs. Also Oriental miniatures. ABA, BADA

Mail Order Book Specialist
(Leon Drucker). 25 Dicey Ave, Cricklewood, NW2. Tel 452 1581. Open by appt. Modern first editions, law and legal philosophers, Prime Ministers, performing arts, collectors' books, newspapers.

C.H. Major
154 Kensington Church St, W8 4BM. Tel 229 1162. Open Mon-Fri 9-5.30; Sat 11-1.30, 3.30-5.30. English mahogany furniture.

The Mall Antiques Arcade
(Barcbourne Ltd). 359 Upper St, Camden Passage, Islington, N1. Tel 359 0825, 349 3111. Open Tues, Thurs, Fri 10-5, Wed 7.30-5, Sat 9-6. 33 dealers with a wide range of general antiques, including furniture, silver, porcelain, works of art, clocks etc.

The Mall Gallery
17 Carlton House Terrace, SW1. Tel 930 6844.

Mallett & Son (Antiques) Ltd
40 New Bond St, W1Y 0BS. Tel 499 7411. Open Mon-Fri. Specialists in fine English furniture dating from 1690 to 1835. Also works of art, clocks, needlework, lamps, decorative objects and pictures. BADA

Mallett at Bourdon House Ltd
2 Davies St, Berkeley Sq, W1Y 1LJ. Tel 629 2444/5. Open Mon-Fri. Specialists in fine French and other Continental antique furniture, including clocks, objets d'art and some 18thC sculpture. Also provincial and painted furniture. Antique garden statuary, ornaments on display in courtyard. BADA

Mangate Gallery
(Mrs Sara Beamish). 3 Chiswick Lane, W4 2LR. Tel 995 9867. Open any time by appt. English and Continental watercolours 1800-1950, also small stock of 19th and 20thC British oil paintings. Cleaning of watercolours and prints. Specialists in marine landscapes. LAPADA

A.J.Mangion Antiques
1A Phillip Walk, Peckham Rye, SE15. Tel 732 6749.

D.M.&P.Manheim (Peter Manheim) Ltd
(Peter Manheim, Pearl Manheim). 69 Upper Berkeley St, Portman Sq, W1H 7DH. Tel 723 6595 (Priv 340 9211). Open Mon-Fri 10-4.30; other times by appt. English porcelain, pottery & enamels 1680-1840. Large stock of fine items. BADA

Mrs David Manheim
69 Upper Berkeley St, Portman Sq, W1H 7DH. Tel 723 6595. English pottery, porcelain and enamels. BADA

Mansour Gallery
(M. Mokhtarzadeh). 46 Davies St, W1. Tel 491 7444. Open Mon-Fri 9.30-5.30,; other times by appt. Persian and Islamic art, ceramics, archaeological relics, ancient glass and ancient jewellery.

Manspace Gallery
64 Clifton Hill, NW8. Tel 624 4110. Full range of 20thC British architectural drawings both from students and well established architects. Also engineering, landscape and design drawings as works of art.

The Map House
(Hon C.A.Savile, Simon Pointer, Hon Mrs Z.L.Savile). 54 Beauchamp Place, Knightsbridge, SW3. Tel 589 4325, 589 9821. Open Mon-Fri 9.45-5.45, Sat 10.30-5. Large stock of antique maps of all parts of the world, antique atlases, antique engravings and antique globes. Framing and mounting. ABA

Marcella Antiques
(Jean Baillie, Julita Flaas). 290 Battersea Park Rd, SW11 3BT. Tel 2231574. Furniture, accessories and silver, old lace cushions, pictures and prints.

S.Marchant & Son
120 Kensington Church St, W8 4BH. Tel 229 5319, 229 3770. Open Mon-Fri 9.30-5.30; other times by appt. Chinese and Japanese ceramics, especially early pottery. Also jades & Chinese furniture. BADA

Mark Gallery
9 Porchester Place, Marble Arch, W2 2BS. Tel 262 4906. Open Mon-Fri 10-1, 2-6; Sat 10-1; other times by appt. 16th to 19thC Russian icons, modern lithographs and etchings. BADA

Marks Antiques Ltd
(A Marks). 49 Curzon St, W1. Tel 499 5392. Silver, plate, valuations. LAPADA

Marlborough Fine Art (London) Ltd
(Gilbert Lloyd). 6 Albemarle St, W1X 4BY. Tel 629 5161. Open Mon-Fri 10-5.30; Sat 10-12.30. Impressionists and 20thC paintings, drawings, graphics and sculpture.

Marlborough Rare Books Ltd
35 Old Bond St, W1X 4PT. Tel 493 6993. Open daily, early closing Sat. Specialists in finely illustrated books of all periods, works on fine and applied arts and bibliography. Catalogues. ABA

Michael Marriott Ltd
(M.Marriott). 588 Fulham Rd, SW6 5NT. Tel 736 3110, 381 3455. Open Mon-Fri 9.30-1, 2-6; Sat 10-1; other times by appt. 18th and 19thC furniture, accessories, 18th & 19thC original prints, restoration, upholstery.

David Martin-Taylor
56 Fulham High St, SW6. Tel 731 4135.

C.J. Martin (Coins) Ltd
85 The Vale, Southgate, N14 6AT. Tel 882 1509/4359. Open by appt only. Archaic, classical and later antiquities.

Robin Martin
44 Ledbury Rd, W11. Tel 727 1301 (priv 727 1300). Open 10.30-5.30; Sat 11-1; other times by appt. Furniture, pewter, works of art, early metalware, and scientific instruments.

Ed Mason
(Edmund Graham Mason). Shop 5 Chelsea Antique Market, 253 King's Rd, SW3. Tel 352 9695. Open Mon-Sat 10-6. Cinema memorabilia 1900-1980s.

Jeremy J. Mason
29 New Bond St, W1Y 9HD. Tel 629 3410. Open Mon-Fri 10-5; other times by appt. Oriental art.

Paul Mason
149E Sloane St, SW1. Tel 730 3683. Open Mon-Fri 9-5, Sat 9-1; other times by appt. 18th and 19thC marine, military, sporting, topographical and decorative prints and paintings. Ship portraits. Portfolio stands and old frames. BADA, LAPADA

Mason's Yard Gallery
(H.M.C. Le Brock). 6 Mason's Yard, Duke St, St James's, SW1. Tel 930 2780. Open 10-5.30; other times by appt. All schools of paintings for the trade.

Massada Antiques
(B. & C. Yacobi). 45 New Bond St, W1Y 9HB. Tel 493 4792; 493 5610. Open Mon-Fri 10-6. Specialists in fine Georgian and Victorian jewellery and objets d'art. LAPADA

Mathaf Gallery Ltd
(Brian MacDermot, chairman). 24 Motcomb St, SW1X 8JU. Tel 235 0010. Open Mon-Fri 9.30-5.30; other times by appt. 19thC and modern paintings of Arabia. LAPADA

Gerald Mathias Clocks
(Gerald Mathias). R5 & R6 Antiquarius, 135 King's Rd, SW3. Tel 351 0484 (priv 998 1049). Open Mon-Sat 10-6. Clocks and boxes.

Matt's Gallery
(Robin Klassnik, Matt E. Mulsion). 10 Martello St, London Fields, E8. Tel 249 3799, 521 4913. Open for exhibitions; other times by appt. A space which shows art, Contemporary/Experimental works made especially for Matt's. They are all installations. Non profit making gallery.

Matthiesen Fine Art Ltd
(P.D. Matthiesen). 7-8 Mason's Yd, Duke St, St James's, SW1. Tel 930 2437. Open Mon-Fri 10-6; other times by appt. Fine Italian, French and Spanish old master pictures 1350-1800 of museum quality and 19thC paintings.

Richard Maude Tools
(Richard Maude). 22 Parkfields, Putney, SW15 6NH. Tel 788 2991. Open by appt only. Old woodworking tools, ornamental turning lathes, keys and locks.

A.Maurice & Co Ltd
70 South Audley St, W1Y 5FE. Tel 629 9797. Carpets and rugs. BADA

J. & J. May
40 Kensington Church St, W8 4BX. Tel 937 3575. Open Mon-Sat, 10-6. 18th and 19thC historical and commemorative pottery, porcelain, pictures, enamels and objets d'art. BADA

The Mayor Gallery
22A Cork Street, W1. Tel 734 3558. Open Mon-Fri 10-5.30, Sat 10-1. Contemporary art specialising in American and modern British. SLAD

THE MALL

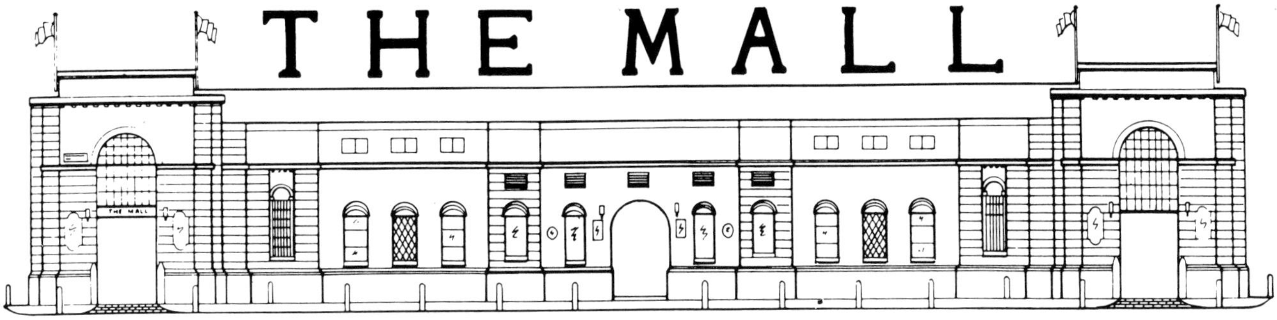

IN

CAMDEN PASSAGE

Tel: 01-359 0825 & 01-349 3111

35 GALLERIES SPECIALISING IN ANTIQUES

In the Mall you will find a comprehensive range of English and French Antique furniture, Silver Pottery & Porcelain, Pictures & Prints, Oriental Art, Antiquities, Ephemera, Militaria, Jewellery, Clocks, Dolls, and Collectors & Decorators' Items.

CLOSED SUNDAY AND MONDAY

359 UPPER STREET, ISLINGTON, LONDON N1.

H. W. NEWBY

(A.J. Waller)

Antique English, Continental and Oriental porcelain, pottery and glass

Valuations for all purposes

H. C. MOTE

Antique English, Continental and Oriental porcelain, pottery and glass

15 WALTON STREET · LONDON SW3 2HX · Tel: (01) 589 2752

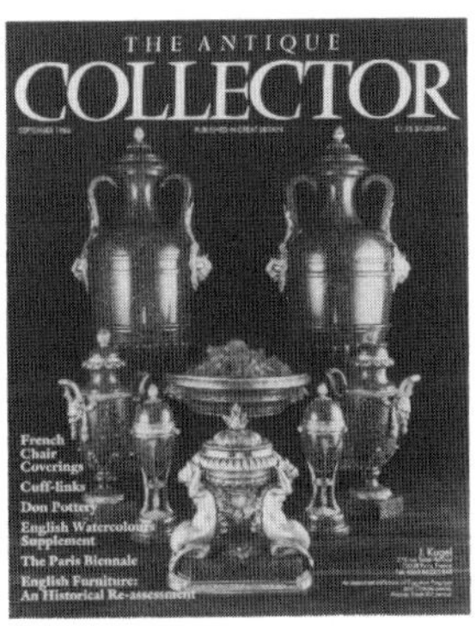

Britain's Internationally Best-selling Antiques Magazine

The beginning of a new era for The Antique Collector. A larger magazine, a more beautiful magazine, a better designed magazine and a more colourful magazine, but a magazine which is still as informed, as comprehensive, as authoritative, as well written and essential as it has always been.

For a complimentary copy and subscription details telephone or write to:
THE ANTIQUE COLLECTOR,
72 Broadwick Street, London W1V 2BP. Tel: 01-439 7144

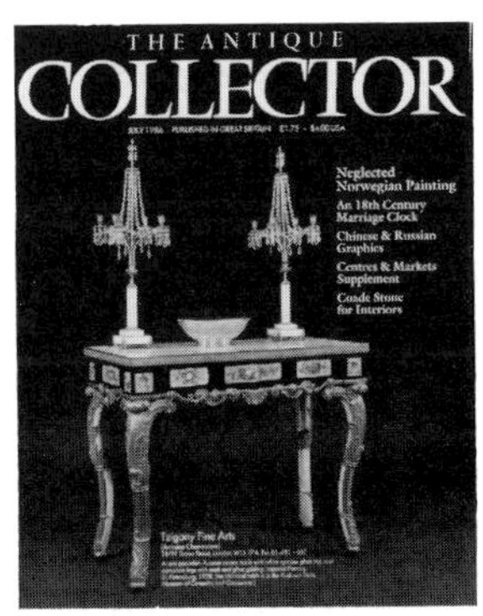

Mayorcas Ltd
(J.D., L.G.Mayorcas). 38 Jermyn St, SW1Y 6DN. Tel 629 4195. Open Mon-Fri 9.30-5.30; Sat 9.30-12.30. Specialists in antique tapestries and period fabrics, needlework, European rugs, carpets, works of art. BADA

I.J.Mazure & Co Ltd
90 Jermyn St, SW1Y 6JD. Tel 839 3101/2. Open Mon-Fri 9.30-5.30 early closing Sat. Late 19thC Russian works of art including Faberge, 18thC gold boxes, selected silver and silver gilt of 16th to 19thC, ivories, miniatures, jewellery. BADA

M. McAleer
(Mrs M.McAleer & M.J.McAleer). 32A Sussex Place, Hyde Park, W2 2TH. Tel 723 5794. Open Mon-Fri 9-5.30; other times by appt. Collectors' pieces of Irish and Scottish silver and jewellery. Also vinaigrettes, caddy spoons, wine labels and vesta cases. LAPADA

McAlpine Ancient Art
(Bruce A.McAlpine and Ingrid McAlpine). 60 Brook St, W1. Tel 629 2247. Open Mon-Thur 9.30-1, 2.30-5; Fri by appt. Greek, Roman, Egyptian and Near Eastern antiquities.

Norma McCaw Conservation
The Studio, 107 Shepherds Bush Rd, W6 7LP. Tel 602 0757. Open Mon-Fri 9-5; other times by appt. Specialist in the care of works of art on paper. Conservation of prints, watercolours, drawings, photographs, memorabilia and contemporary items. Research also undertaken.

Heather McConnell
18 St George St, Hanover Sq, W1R 9DE. Tel 493 6420. Public relations, specialising in art and antiques.

Joy McDonald
(Joy McDonald). 50 Station Rd, Barnes, SW13. Tel 876 6184. Open normal hours. Res on prem. General antiques, unusual items, some pine, large mirrors, brass etc.

R.I. McKay
(R.I. McKay). 63 South Molton St, W1Y 1HH. Jewellery, valuations. LAPADA

Rodd McLennan
24 Holbein Place, SW1. Tel 730 6330. Open Mon-Fri 9.30-1, 2-6; Sat 9.30-1. Russian, Swedish, Danish, German, Viennese, Biedermeier, Bois-Clair and mahogany furniture, 1810-1850; decorative objects, 1800-1900.

The Medici Galleries
7 Grafton St, Bond St, W1X 3LA. Tel 629 5675.

D.Mellor & A.L.Baxter Antiquarian Booksellers
(D.Mellor & A.L.Baxter). 121A Kensington Church St, W8 7LP. Tel 229 2033 221 8822. Open Mon-Fri 10-6.30; Sat 10-5. Antiquarian books 15th to 20thC, finely bound literary sets, English literature and history, travel, illustrated childrens books. LAPADA

David Mellor
26 James St, WC2. Tel 379 6947. (Also at 4 Sloane Sq. SW1(730 4259) & 66 King St. Manchester.) Open weekdays 10-6.30. Specialist kitchen shop.

Christopher Mendez
58 Jermyn St, SW1Y 6LP. Tel 491 0015. Open Mon-Fri 10-5; other times by appt. Old Master engravings, etchings and woodcuts. Also 18thC English prints sold as artists' work rather than decoration. ABA

Sybil Mendoza
2 Andora Court, Brondesbury Park, NW6. Tel 459 1705. (Also at Woburn Abbey Antiques Centre.) Fine paintings, Dutch masters.

Mercury Antiques
(Liane Richards). 1 Ladbroke Rd, Kensington, W11 3PA. Tel 727 5106. Open Mon-Sat 10-5.30. Medium sized premises. English ceramics 1745-1850, Delft and glass. Specialising in 18th and early 19thC collectors' items. BADA

Mercury Gallery Ltd
26 Cork St, W1. Tel 734 7800. 20thC paintings, drawings and sculpture by British, French, German and contemporary artists. SLAD

B.C.Metalcrafts Ltd
(F.Burnell). 69 Tewkesbury Gardens, NW9 0QU. Tel 204 2446. Open by appt only. Antique light fittings such as table lamps, candelabra, also clocks and clock sets. Satsuma lamps.

Michael Coins
(Michael Gouby). 6 Hillgate St, W8. Tel 727 1518. Open Mon-Fri 10-5; other times by appt. Coins, stamps and banknotes.

Arthur Middleton Ltd
12 New Row, Covent Garden, WC2N 4LF. Tel 836 7042. Open Mon-Fri 9.30-6.30; Sat 11-6; other times by appt. Antique instruments concerned with navigation, astronomy, surveying, medicine, weighing and measuring. LAPADA

Bernard C. Middleton
3 Gauden Rd, Clapham, SW4 6LR. Tel 622 5388. Restoration of early books.

Richard Miles Antiques
(Richard Miles). 8 Holbein Place, SW1 8NL. Tel 730 1957. (Also basement of 10 Holbein Place, SW1.) Open Mon-Fri 10-6; other times by appt. Unusual and decorative 18th and early 19thC furniture; paintings and works of art.

Roy Miles Fine Paintings Ltd
(Roy Miles). 3 Berkeley Square, W1X 5HG. Tel 491 3611. Open by appt only. Art dealer specialising in major English paintings and high Victorian art.

David Miller Antiques
198 Upper Richmond Road West, East Sheen, SW14. Tel 876 8331. Original lighting and general antiques.

Duncan R. Miller Fine Arts
(Duncan R. Miller). 11 Wedderburn Rd, NW3. Tel 435 5462 (priv 794 2119). Open 10-5; other times by appt. British and French paintings and watercolours 1840-1940, specialising in modern Scottish paintings and antique silk oriental rugs. LAPADA

H. Miller (Antiques) Ltd
Silver Vaults, Chancery Lane, WC2. Tel 242 7073. (Also at 22A Ship St, Brighton.) Open Mon-Fri 9-5; Sat 9-12; other times by appt. Antique silver, silver and silver plate, old Sheffield and jewellery. LAPADA

Milne & Moller
35 Colville Terrace, W11 2BU. Tel 727 1679. Open Sats other times by appt. 19th & 20thC watercolours.

Milne Henderson
(Sondra and John Milne Henderson). 96 Mount St, W1. Tel 499 2507. Open Mon-Fri 9.30-5.30; other times by appt. Oriental paintings, Japanese screens. BADA

Nigel Milne Ltd
(Nigel Milne). 16C Grafton St, W1X 3LF. Tel 493 9646. Open 9.30-5.30; other times by appt. Antique jewellery, silver, silver photograph frames.

John Mitchell & Sons
8 New Bond St, W1Y 9PE. Tel 493 7567. Fine paintings: 17thC Dutch, 18thC English and 19thC French. Specialist in flower paintings. BADA

Paul Mitchell
99 New Bond Street, W1. Tel 493 8732/0860. Restoration of paintings, antique frames, period framing. BADA

Mitre Frames
(C.J.Petrie). 112 Fortune Green Rd, NW6 1DH. Tel 794 9569. Open Tues-Sat 8.30-1, 2-5.30; other times by appt. Over 450 mouldings, 100 colours & types of board.

Kate Moffatt
Stand V4, Antiquarius, Kings Rd. Tel 352 5409. Oil and watercolour paintings from 1880 to 1940.

Bashir Mohamed Ltd
(Bashir Wali Mohamed). 46 Montagu Square, W1. Tel 723 1844. Open 11-5; other times by appt. Islamic works of art, painting, Indian & Moghul art, Malaysian art.

Lennox Money (Antiques) Ltd
(Lennox Money). 93 Pimlico Rd, SW1W 8PH. Tel 730 3070. Open Mon-Fri 9.45-6; Sat 11-1. Furniture, works of art and chandeliers, especially of colonial origin. Specialist in Indian colonial items.

D.C.Monk & Son
132-134 Kensington Church St, W8. Tel 229 3727. Open Mon-Fri 10.30-5; closed Sat. Antique and decorative porcelain.

Monro Heywood Ltd
(Jean Monro, Edward Heywood). 336 Kings Rd, SW3. Tel 351 1477. Open Mon-Fri 10-5; other times by appt. Antique furniture, English porcelain, prints and pictures.

Mrs Monro (Antiques) Ltd
(Miss Jean Monro, Mr Edward Heywood). 11 Montpelier St, SW7. Tel 589 5052, 821 1860. Open Mon-Fri 9.30-5.30. Georgian furniture and English 19thC porcelain. Specialist in interior decoration.

Montpelier Studio
(Bernice Sandelson). 4 Montpelier St, SW7 1EZ. Tel 584 0667. Open Mon-Fri 10-5.30, Sat 10-1. 20thC British art and contemporary exhibitions.

Monway Ltd
London House, 271-273 King St, Hammersmith, W6. Tel 741 8011. Organisers of antiques fairs.

Moreton Street Gallery
40 Moreton St, SW1. Watercolours and prints.

Robert Morley & Company Limited
(J.S.P. Morley, C.R. Morley). 4 Belmont Hill, Lewisham, SE13 5BD. Tel 852 6151. (Also workshop at 34 Engate St (318 5420, 5429.) Open Mon-Sat 9-5; other times by appt. Harpsichords, pianos and harps. Restoration. BADA

Morton Morris & Co
32 Bury St, St James's, SW1. Tel 930 2825. Open Mon-Fri 9.30-6; other times by appt. English 17th to 19thC watercolours and paintings. Old master drawings.

Richard Morris
142 Wandsworth Bridge Rd, SW6. Tel 736 1448. Open Mon-Sat 9-6. Specialist in antique and old pine furniture from linen boxes to breakfront bookcases.

Stephen Morris Shipping Ltd
89 Upper St, N1 ONP. Tel 354 1212. Freight forwarder & packer. Specialist packers & shippers of antiques. Regular consolidation services worldwide.

Guy Morrison
91C Jermyn St, SW1Y 6JB. Tel 930 8008. Art dealer.

Terence Morse & Son Ltd
(T.Morse & G.Morse). 197, 199 and 237 Westbourne Grove, W11. Tel 229 9380, 229 4059. Open Mon-Fri 9-5.30. Antiques and fine furniture.

Mortlake Antiques
69 Lower Richmond Rd, Mortlake, SW14. Tel 876 8715. Furniture and clocks.

Moss Galleries
(Brian and Rachel Moss). 2 Prebend Gardens, Chiswick, W4. Tel 994 2099. Open by appt only. 19th & 20thC watercolours and drawings. LAPADA

Sydney L. Moss Ltd
(Eileen M. Moss, Paul G. Moss). 51 Brook St, W1Y 1AU. Tel 629 4670; 493 7374. Open Mon-Fri 10-5; other times by appt. Specialists in Chinese and Japanese works of art, paintings, netsuke. BADA

A. & M. Mossowski
595 King's Rd, SW6. Tel 731 0334. Furniture, mirrors etc.

H.C. Mote
(Hugh C. Mote). 15 Walton St, SW3 2HX. Tel 589 2752. Open Mon-Fri 9.30-5.30. 18th and early 19thC Chinese and European pottery and porcelain.

Frederick Mulder
(Frederick Mulder). 83 Belsize Park Gardens, NW3 4NJ. Tel 722 2105 (priv 722 3861). Open by appt. Old master and modern prints. Original prints of Durer, Rembrandt, Goya, Renoir, Munch, Picasso etc.

Myriad Antiques
131 Portland Rd, W11. Tel 229 1709. Open Mon-Sat 11-6. Decorative objects, furniture, kitchen and bathroom fixtures. Especially painted furniture.

Peter Nahum
(P.J. Nahum). 5 Ryder St, SW1Y 6PY. Tel 930 6059 (priv 994 1501). Open 10-5.30; other times by appt. 19th and 20thC British & European paintings, drawings and bronzes including a selection of pre-Raphaelites and Symbolists.

Sylvia Napier Ltd
(Sylvia Napier). 32 Ledbury Rd, W11. Tel 229 9986 (priv 221 7247). Open Mon-Sat 10-6; other times by appt. Decorative antiques.

Nash Antiques
(M. Bennett). 183 Westbourne Grove, W11. Tel 727 3796. Open Mon-Sat 9.30-6. Chinese and Japanese furniture, porcelain, ivory and lacquer.

Peter Nash
(P. Nash). 173 Bermondsey St, SE1 3UW. Tel 407 2040. Furniture, general antiques. LAPADA

Naylers
56a Clerkenwell Rd, EC1. Tel 253 4594. Silversmiths.

R.S.& S.Necus
Stand H1, Antiquarius, 135 King's Rd, SW3. (Also at C5 Chenil Galleries, 183 King's Rd.) Silver.

Guy Nevill Pictures
10C Bramerton St, SW3 5JX. Tel 351 4292. Open by appt. Sporting paintings, drawings and prints.

New Grafton Gallery
(David Wolfers). 49 Church Rd, Barnes, SW13 9HH. Tel 748 8850. Open Tues-Sat 10-5.30. 20thC British paintings and Portrait Centre.

New Kings Road Gallery
(Amos Levy, Eric Ford). 293 New Kings Rd, SW6. 19th and 20thC European pictures.

H.W. Newby
(Arthur John Waller). 15 Walton St, SW3 2HX. Tel 589 2752. Open Mon-Fri 9.30-1, 2-5.30; other times by appt. Continental, English & Oriental ceramics & glass. BADA

Newcombe & Son
(Mike Newcombe). 89 Maple Rd, Penge, SE20 8UL. Tel 778 0816. Open Tues-Fri 9-5.30; Sat 9-4.30; other times by appt. Clock case maker, cases or complete clocks made to order, special one-off items of furniture, inlaid boxes & wooden toys, repair & restoration of clocks & antique furniture. GMC

Newman & Cooling Ltd
(J.H.Cooling, B.G.Hart, Mrs B.Benzimra,Mrs A.Hart). 38 Albemarle St, W1X 4QJ. Tel 629 5224, 930 6068. Open Mon-Fri 9.30-5.30; other times by appt. Fine 19thC paintings. SLAD

Nicolaus Antiques
(Boston Brothers). Chenil Galleries, 181-183 King's Rd, Chelsea, SW3. Tel 352 8790. Open six days 10-6. Fine period furniture, decorators items, Chippendale. Premier specialist in majolica.

Nihon Token
(Michael & Hiroko Tsuji Dean). 23 Museum St, WC1A 1JT. Tel 580 6511. Open Mon-Sat 10-5; other times by appt. Japanese antiques, including arms and armour, lacquer, paintings, sculpture, pots, metalwork, inro, netsuke, screens.

Ning Ltd
(P.C.Grant). 58 Cambridge St, SW1. Tel 834 3292. Open Mon-Fri 10-6; other times by appt. Decorating, fine art and antiques.

Nonesuch Antiques
(Eva Michelson). Stand3, Bond St Antique Centre, 124 New Bond St, W1. Tel 629 6783. Open Mon-Fri 10-5.30. Antique jewellery.

Noortman (London) Ltd
(Robert Noortman). 40-41 Old Bond St, W1X 3AF. Tel 491 7284. Open Mon-Fri 9.30-5.30; Sat by appt. 17thC Dutch and Flemish paintings, French paintings of the mid-19thC to Post-Impressionism.

Sue Norman
(Sue and Nick Alloway). Stand L4, Antiquarius, 135 King's Rd, SW3. Tel 352 7217 (priv 870 4677). Open Mon-Sat 10.30-5.30. Early 19thC blue and white transfer ware, Masons and other ironstone china.

North London Clock Shop Ltd
(Mr D.S.Tomlin). 72 Highbury Park, N5. Tel 226 1609. Open Mon-Fri 9-6. Clocks and barometers - sales and restorations. Also horological books. BHI, BWCMG

North West London Auctions
9-17 Lodge Lane, Finchley, N12. Tel 445 9000. Weekly sales of general antiques on Monday at 5pm. Viewing Sun 10-5, Mon 9.30-5.

Stephen O'Donnell Antiques
(S O'Donnell). Grays Antique Market, 58 Davies St, W1. Tel 491 8852. Victorian boxes, scientific instruments, valuations. LAPADA

John C. O'Mahony
Flat 10, 15 Westbourne Terrace, W2 3UN. Tel 724 0277. Open by appt only. Oriental rugs and textiles.

Hal O'Nians Ltd
(H.M.O'Nians, Mrs.E.W.O'Nians). King Street Galleries, 17 King St, St James's, SW1Y 6QU. Tel 930 9392/3993. Open Mon-Fri 10-5.30; Sat 10-1; other times by appt. Fine old master and British paintings 1550-1900. Specialist in Dutch & Italian 17th and 18thC paintings. Also regular exhibitions of contemporary artists.

O'Shea Gallery
(Raymond O'Shea). 89 Lower Sloane St, Belgravia, SW1 8DA. Tel 730 0081, 730 0082. Open Mon-Fri 9.30-6, Sat 9.30-1; other times by appt. Very large collection of original maps, topographical and decorative prints. Decorative mounting and framing. ABA, BADA

Octavia Antiques
(Mrs S. Daly). 1 Wandon Rd, New Kings Rd, SW6 2JF.
Tel 736 1196. Open Mon-Sat 10-5.30; other times by appt. General antiques.

October Gallery
(Corinna MacNeice, Mary Evans). 24 Old Gloucester St, WC1.
Tel 242 7367. Open Tues-Sat 12.30-4.30 and by appt. Contemporary art gallery showing contemporary art from around the world.

Oddiquities
(S.A.Butler). 61 Waldram Park Rd, SE23. Tel 699 9574. (Also 20 Sunderland Rd, SE23.) Open Mon-Fri 10-5; closed Thurs; Sat 9.30-4; other times by appt. General antiques, fire furniture & early light fitments and decorative items.

L'Odeon
(Noel C.Tovey and David Sarel). 173 Fulham Rd, SW3.
Tel 581 3640 (priv 736 4216). Open Mon-Sat 11-6. Art nouveau and art deco items, including furniture, glass, jewellery, paintings and pottery.

Odin Antiques
(Audun Sjovold). Chenil Galleries, 181 King's Rd, SW3.
Tel 352 9066. Open Mon-Sat 10-6. Interesting general antiques, including furniture, paintings, boxes and metalware.

Richard Ogden Ltd
28 & 29 Burlington Arcade, Piccadilly, W1V 0NX.
Tel 493 9136/7. Open Mon-Fri 9.30-5.30; Sat 9-1. Fine and traditional jewellery. BADA

Old Drawings Gallery
(G.T.Siden). 15 King St, St James's, SW1Y 6QU.
Tel 930 7462 (priv 624 9045). Open Mon-Fri 10-5; other times by appt. 16th-19thC drawings and Old Master drawings.

Old Maps and Prints
(Collectors Treasures Ltd). 4th floor, Harrods, Knightsbridge, SW1. Tel 730 1234 ext 2124. Open Mon-Fri 9-5 (Wed till 7); Sat 10-6. Antiquarian maps and prints from 16thC to 1880, old watercolours & oil paintings also now available. LAPADA

Old Pine
(B.Rippingale). 594 King's Rd, SW6. Tel 736 5999. (Also Old Pine's Painted Furniture, 571 King's Rd,SW6 01-736 5999.) Open Mon-Sat 10-5.30; other times by appt. Renovated antique and Victorian pine, including dressers, cupboards, tables and decorative items.

Old World Trading Company
(R.J. Campion). 565 Kings Rd, SW6. Tel 731 4708. Open Mon-Sat 9.30-6; other times by appt. Antique & decorative furniture. Chimney pieces, hearths & grates. English & French mirrors.

Oliver-Sutton Antiques
(Anthony Oliver & Peter Sutton). 34C Kensington Church St, W8. Tel 937 0633. Open Mon-Fri 10-6, Sat 10-4; closed all August. Large collection of Staffordshire portrait figures, Prattware, potlids and early 19thC British pottery. BADA

Omell Galleries
43A Duke St, St James's, SW1. Tel 930 7744. (See also other shops in London and Windsor.) Open 10-5.30; Sat 10-1; other times by appt. 19thC Continental, English and Old Master paintings especially marine & still life paintings. LAPADA

Omell Galleries
22 Bury St, St James's, SW1. Tel 839 4274/5. (See also other branches in London and Windsor.) Open Mon-Fri 10-5.30. 19thC Continental and English paintings. LAPADA

Omell Galleries
40 Albemarle St, W1.
Tel 499 3685/6. (See also other branches in London and Windsor.) Open Mon-Fri 10-5.30; other times by appt. Contemporary British and French paintings. LAPADA

N.R. Omell
6 Duke Street, St James's, SW1. Tel 839 6223/4. Open Mon-Fri 9.30-5.30; Sat 10-1. 18th and 19thC paintings. Specialising in marine and Victorian paintings. SLAD

Oola Boola Antiques
(R. Scales). 166 Tower Bridge Rd, SE1. Tel 403 0794. Open 9-5.30. Furniture, - Victorian, Edwardian mahogany. LAPADA

Carol Orford Antiques
(Mrs C. Orford). Bond Street Antique Centre, 124 New Bond St, W1. Tel 493 2654. Jewellery. LAPADA

Anatol Orient Ltd
318 Portobello Rd, W10.
Tel 969 4119. Open Wed-Sat 10.30-5.30; Tues by appt. Modern textiles and ceramics by designers and craftsmen. ICGA

Oriental Carpet Centre
(Vigo Carpet Gallery). 10 Golden Sq, W1R 3AF. Tel 439 9070. (Also in Nottingham, Bristol and Ilford.) Open Mon-Sat 9-5.30; Thurs 9-7. Modern Oriental carpets, rugs and kelims from China, Turkey, Pakistan, Iran, India and Rumania. Also cleaning and restoration.

Ormonde Gallery
(Westbourne Antiques Ltd). 156 Portobello Rd, W11.
Tel 229 9800, 042482-226. Specialists to the trade in Oriental sculpture, paintings and ceramics.

Stephen Orton Antiques
(Stephen Orton, B.Sc). 72 Upper St, Islington, N1 0NY.
Tel 226 2770 (priv 508 1023). Open Mon-Sat 9-5; other times by appt. Suppliers of period, Georgian, Victorian & Edwardian quality furniture (& some decorative items) to home and overseas trade buyers (5,000 sq.ft of showrooms). LAPADA

Osborne Gallery
(S.J.Fenemore, R.W.Fenemore). 21 Grosvenor St, W1X 9FE.
Tel 409 3599. Open Mon-Fri 10.30-5.30. Fine English watercolours, paintings and watercolours of Arabian interest.

Alec Ossowski
83 Pimlico Rd, SW1.
Tel 730 3256. Open Mon-Fri 8-6, Sat 9.30-1; other times by appt. Gilt mirrors and wood carvings. Also Continental furniture.

A.& H.Page
(G. & B. Leyens). 66 Gloucester Rd, Kensington, SW7.
Tel 584 7349. Antiques, jewellery and silver. NAG

Pageant Antiques
(Mr A.Kopriva). 122 Dawes Rd, W14. Tel 385 7739. Open Mon-Fri 9.30-5.30, Sat 10-2. Architectural antiques, including chimneypieces.

Park Galleries
(M.M.Lynn, J.R.Lynn). 20 Hendon Lane, Finchley, N3 1TR.
Tel 346 2176. Open Tues-Sat 9.30-6; early closing Thurs; other times by appt. Art gallery specialising in English watercolours.

The Parker Gallery
12A & 12B Berkeley St, Piccadilly, W1X 5AD.
Tel 499 5906/7. Open Mon-Fri 9.30-5.30; other times by appt. Specialists in nautical, military, topographical and sporting prints and paintings. Also ship models, old and new naval and military relics. Catalogues periodically. (Estab 1750). BADA, SLAD, FATG

Michael & Margaret Parker
24 Cheval Place, SW7.
Tel 589 0133. Open Mon-Fri 10-1, 2-5; other times by appt. 18th and 19thC French and English furniture, English lacquer, papier mache and painted furniture.

Michael Parkin Fine Art Ltd
11 Motcomb St, SW1.
Tel 235 8144, 235 1845. Open Mon-Fri 10-6, Sat 10-1; other times by appt. Modern British art 1860-1950, paintings, watercolours, prints and drawings. Specialising in works by Sickert, Wadsworth, Claude Flight School, Walter Greaves, J.E. Laboureur.

Partridge (Fine Arts) Ltd
144-146 New Bond St, W1.
Tel 629 0834. Open Mon-Fri 9.30-5.30; other times by appt. Fine furniture, clocks, silver, paintings, porcelain and works of art.

David Paskin Antiques (London) Ltd
(D.Paskin). Grays Antique Market, 58 Davies St, W1. Tel 408 1129. Jewellery, silver, watches. Valuations. LAPADA

The Patchwork Dog and the Calico Cat Ltd
(Mrs Joen Zinni-Lask). 21 Chalk Farm Road, NW1. Tel 485 1239. Open Tues-Sun 10-6. Antique English & American patchwork quilts.

Paton Gallery
2 Langley Court, Long Acre, WC2E 9JY. Tel 379 7854. Open Tues-Sat 11-6; other times by appt. New generation British painters including Chris Baker, H.D.Pietsch, John Monks, Andrew Stahl, Mary Mabbutt, Peter Howson and others.

W.H. Patterson Fine Arts Ltd
(W.H.Patterson, Mrs P.M. Patterson, John White).
19 Albemarle St, W1X 3HA.
Tel 629 4119. Open Mon-Fri 9.30-6; other times by appt. Specialist in Dutch and European masters of the 19thC and 20thC. Modern masters, Jan H. Eversen, Andrew Coates, Helen Bradley M.B.E., Willem Dolphyn. BADA, SLAD

M.Pauw Antiques
569 Kings Rd, SW6 2EB.
Tel 731 4022. Open Mon-Fri 9-6. Decorative antiques.

Pawsey & Payne
4 Ryder St, SW1. Tel 930 4221. Open Mon-Fri 9-5.30; other times by appt. English and Continental paintings, watercolours, drawings and engravings; specialising in English sporting pictures. BADA

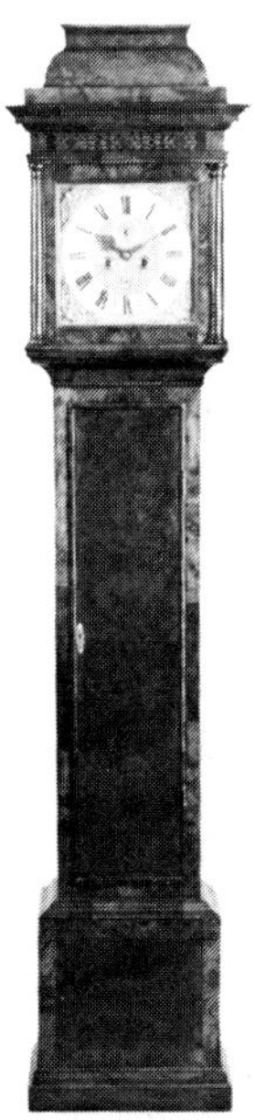

Fine walnut longcase clock by Jonathan Lowndes, London.

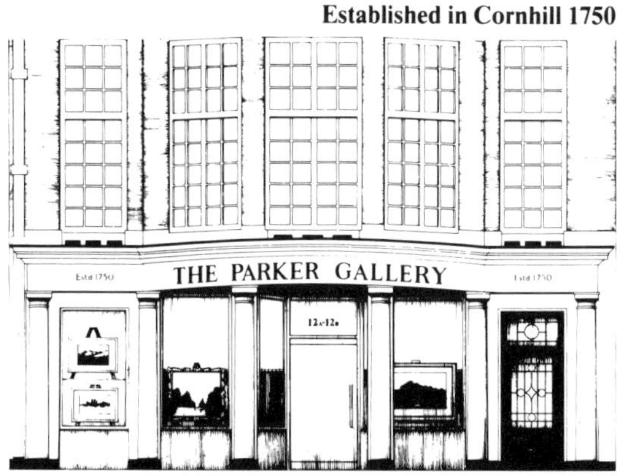

Pearl Cross Ltd
(D.E. Strange). 35 St Martin's Court, St Martin's Lane, WC2N 4AL. Tel 836 2814, 240 0795. Open Mon-Fri 9.30-4.45. Jewellers, silversmiths, clocks and pocket watches.

Vic Pearson & Co Ltd
7 Munton Rd, SE17 1PR. Tel 703 8351. Open Mon-Fri 8.30-5.30; other times by appt. Packers and shippers, specialising in fine art.

Peel Antiques
(Douglas & Marjorie Ladd). 131D Kensington Church St, W8 7LP. Tel 727 8298. Open weekdays 9.30-1, 2-5.30. General antiques, 18th and 19thC small furniture, pottery, porcelain and metal. Domestic antiques.

Pelham Galleries (Est 1927)
(E.W., V. & A. Rubin). 163-165 Fulham Rd, SW3. Tel 589 2686. Open Mon-Fri 9-5.30; Sat 10-1. Important stock of antique English and Continental furniture, clocks, works of art, screens, lacquer, early keyboard instruments. BADA

Penfriend Ltd
The Arcade, Bush House, Aldwych, WC2. Current and vintage writing equipment.

Penny Farthing Antiques
177 Bermondsey St, SE1 3UW. Tel 407 5171. Open Mon-Fri 10-5. Large stock on 3 floors of antique & shipping furniture. Also small items, clocks & mirrors.

Peoples Gallery Limited
71 & 73 Prince of Wales Rd, NW5 3LT. Tel 267 0433. Open Tues-Fri 11-6; other times by appt. Contemporary art, mostly unknown artists.

Percy's Silver Ltd
London Silver Vaults, 53 Chancery Lane, WC2. Silver, plate. LAPADA

H. Perovetz
50/2 Chancery Lane, WC2. Tel 252 5857 and 242 5820. Open Mon-Fri 9-6, Sat 9-1. Large export trade in Victorian and Georgian silver and Sheffield plate. LAPADA BADA

Persian Carpet Gallery
(Karel Weijand). 3 Motcomb St, SW1. Tel 245 6564. (Also Lion & Lamb Courtyard, Farnham (Tel: 0252 726215.) Open Mon-Fri 10-5; other times by appt. Oriental carpets and rugs. Fine silks.

The Persian Market
(A. Zacaim). 48 Upper St, Islington, N1. Tel 226 7927. Glass, porcelain, silver, carpets. LAPADA

Oscar & Peter Johnson Ltd
Lowndes Lodge Gallery, 27 Lowndes St, SW1. Tel 235 6464,. Open Mon-Fri 9-5.30, by appt Sat 9.30-12. Fine English 18th and 19thC oil paintings, drawings and watercolours. BADA

David Pettifer Ltd
269 King's Rd, SW3 5EN. Tel 352 3088. Open Mon-Sat 9.30-5.30. Large stock of 18thC English furniture, mainly mahogany but also some oak and walnut. Pictures, including Chinese rice-paper pictures. BADA

Michael Phelps Antiquarian Books
(Michael Phelps). 19 Chelverton Rd, Putney, SW15 1RN. Tel 785 6766. Open Mon-Fri. Books on medicine, science, technology, natural history. ABA, PBFA

Trevor Philip & Sons Ltd
(Trevor Waterman, Rina Waterman). 75a Jermyn St, St James's, SW1Y 6NP. Open Mon-Sat 9-5.30; car park at rear for clients. Scientific, medical and philosophical antique instruments. LAPADA

Phillips Fine Art Auctioneers
Blenstock House, 7 Blenheim St, W1Y 0AS. Tel 629 6602. Open daily and Sat morning. Fine art auctioneers. SOFAA

Phillips Marylebone
Hayes Place, Lisson Grove, NW1 6UA. Tel 723 2647. Auctioneers.

Phillips West 2
2 Salem Road, W2 4BU. Tel 221 5303. Auctioneers.

Henry Phillips
2 Campden Street, W8 7EP. Tel 727 4079. Open Mon-Fri 10-6; other times by appt. English 18thC and Regency furniture and unusual objects. BADA

Howard Phillips
(Howard Phillips). 11A Henrietta Place, W1M 9AG. Tel 580 9844. Open Mon-Fri 9.30-5.15. Antique glass from all countries, from its earliest years to 1840. Also French paperweights. BADA

John F.C. Phillips
92 Rossiter Rd, SW12. Tel 673 5150. Open by appt only except during exhibitions (March & October). English watercolours (especially topographical and figure), drawings and prints, mostly pre-1850 and under £300. Average stock 200, usually including Cox, Goodwin, Hayter, Prout and Uwins. Mail order & approval service (Catalogues).

Ronald Phillips Ltd
26 Bruton St, W1X 8LH. Tel 493 2341. Open Mon-Fri 9-5.15. Fine quality 18th and early 19thC English furniture. BADA

S.J. Phillips Ltd
(Martin, Jonathan, Nicolas and Francis Norton). 139 New Bond St, W1A 3DL. Tel 629 6261, 629 6262. Open Mon-Fri 10-5. Important antique Continental and English silver. Gold and gold enamel snuff boxes, objets d'art, 16th-17thC watches, portrait miniatures and jewellery. BADA

Richard Philp
59 Ledbury Rd, W11. Tel 727 7915. Open 10-6; other times by appt. Works of art, fine paintings. Interiors. BADA

The Photographers' Gallery
5 & 8 Great Newport St, WC2. Tel 240 5511. Open Tues-Sat 11-7.

The Piccadilly Gallery
16 Cork St, W1X 1PF. Tel 629 2875. Open daily 10-5.30, Sat 10-12.30 (not July to Sept & Jan to Feb). Symbolist paintings, drawings and objects. Also drawings and watercolours by British and Continental artists from 1900. Paintings by young figurative artists. SLAD

Pickering and Chatto Ltd, inc Dawsons of Pall Mall
(Sir William and Lady Rees-Mogg). 17 Pall Mall, SW1Y 5NB. Tel 930 2515. Open Mon-Fri 9.30-5.30. Antiquarian books - English literature, economics, science and medicine, manuscripts and autographs. ABA

Mr Pickwick Antiques
(J. Sturton). 137 Bermondsey St, SE1 3UW. Tel Wickford (03744) 63741. Victorian & Edwardian furniture, clocks. Trade only. LAPADA

The Pine Mine
(Crewe Read). 100 Wandsworth Bridge Rd, SW6. Tel 736 1092. Open Mon-Fri 9.45-5.45, Sat 9.45-4.30. Antique pine dressers, chests of drawers, tables, sets of chairs, wardrobes and architectural items.

The Pine Village
162 Wandsworth Bridge Road, SW6. Tel 736 2753. Open Mon-Sat 9.30-6, Sun 10-6. Also showroom at 21-22 Chepstow Corner, 1 Pembridge Villas, W2 (221 7044); 195 Upper Richmond Rd West, SW14 (876 4053); 19,Chalk Farm Rd, NW1 (485 4034). Old and reproduction pine, Victorian, Georgian, Edwardian periods. Some oak, satinwood etc.

Pitt & Scott Ltd
20-24 Eden Grove, N7 8ED. Tel 607 7321. Packers and shippers of antiques and fine art. Shipping and forwarding and airfreight agents. Comprehensive service provided for visiting antique dealers. Insurance arranged. LAPADA

Peter Place
636 Kings Rd, SW6. Tel 736 9945. Open Mon-Sat 9-5.30; other times by appt. Specialising in metalware, decorative items and unusual objects.

The Plazzotta Studio
22 Cathcart Rd, SW10 9NN. Tel 352 7493. Open by appt. Wide selection of bronze sculpture, etchings, reliefs and medallions by the late Enzo Plazzotta on display and for sale.

Plowden & Smith Limited
(Anna Plowden, Peter Smith). 190 St Ann's Hill, Wandsworth, SW18 2RT. Tel 874 4005. Restoration and conservation centre. 25 craftsmen working in bronze, precious metals, stonework, marble, wood, ceramics, waxes and lacquer. Bases and stands made. FIIC

Polak Gallery
21 King St, St James's, SW1Y 6QY. Tel 930 9245, 930 3911. Open Mon-Fri 9.30-5.30. Dealers in 19th and 20thC paintings and watercolours. BADA

Edwin Pollard Gallery
(Edwin Pollard). 23 Church Rd, Wimbledon Village, SW19 5DQ. Tel 946 4114. Open Tues-Sat 10-6. Contemporary works of art - oil paintings and watercolours, including Rowland Hilder, F.Donald Blake, John Bratby, Edward Dawson, Peter Newcombe and Richard Bolton.

Jonathan Poole Gallery
915 Fulham Rd, SW6. Tel 736 1404. Fine art - watercolours, pastels, sculpture.

John Pope & Hunts Ltd
(S. Shamoon). 91 Old Brompton Rd, SW7. Tel 581 5375, 584 2229. Open Mon-Fri 10-6. English & Continental furniture, clocks & works of art. LAPADA

Annabel Popovic
15 Ranelagh Grove, SW1. Tel 730 3327. Old master drawings, decorative watercolours and antique French wallpapers. Catalogue available.

Madeleine Popper FGA, Diana Foley, Richard Digby
Stand L18-L21, Grays Mews, 1-7 Davies Mews, W1. Tel 408 1089. Open Mon-Fri 10-6. Antique jewellery, cameos, cut steel, objets de vertu, coloured gold and gem stone jewellery. Antique paste and Berlin iron. LAPADA

Henry Pordes Ltd
529B Finchley Rd, NW3. Tel 435 9878/9. (Also at 58-60 Charing Cross Rd, WC2.) Open 9.45-6. Books- secondhand, art, bibliography, Judaica, reference books for libraries, learned and scientific periodicals.

Henry Pordes Ltd
58/60 Charing Cross Rd, WC2H 0BB. Tel 836 9031. (Also at 529B Finchley Rd, NW3.) New condition bargain books, secondhand books, art, bibliography, Judaica.

Portal Gallery Ltd
16a Grafton St, W1. Tel 493 0706 & 629 3506. Specialists in self-taught fantasy painting - Beryl Cook, Kit Williams and many others.

The Portland Gallery
(John Thompson, Tom Hewlett). 2 Holland Park Terrace, Portland Rd, W11. Pictures 1880-1950 and furniture.

Portmeirion Antiques
(S. Beazley & A. Barker). 62 White Hart Lane, Barnes, SW13. Tel 876 2367. Open Mon-Fri 10.30-5.30; Sat 10.30-1; other times by appt. Continental and English furniture, china, glass and objects of all kinds. Biedermeier furniture occasionally in stock.

Portobello Antique Store
(D.H.P.Gregory & J.F.Ewing). 79 Portobello Rd, W11 2QB. Tel 221 1994. Open Mon-Fri 10-4; Sat 8-4. General antiques, silver plate, objets d'art, jewellery, luggage, silver.

Portobello Antiques Markets
(Red Lion and World Famous Markets). 165-169 & 177 Portobello Rd, W11. Tel 431 2875 (24 hours). Open Fri and Sat. Antiques, antiquities, collectors' jewellery, coins and stamps. European and Oriental ceramics, metalware, arms, lace, militaria, statuary. Facilities include valuations, shipping, bureaux de change etc.

Jonathan Potter
1 Grafton St, W1X 3LB. Tel 491 3520. Open Mon-Fri 9.30-5.30; Sat 10-12. Specialising in antique maps, prints, atlases, travel books, illustrated books, globes and geographical curiosities. ABA BADA

H.W.Poulter & Son
(H.W.Poulter & D.W.Poulter). 279 Fulham Rd, SW10 9PZ. Tel 352 7268 (priv 603 7398). Open Mon-Fri 9-6; appt advisable. Marble chimney pieces, fire grates, dogs, fenders etc. Brass chandeliers, wood mantelpieces. Sculpture.

Prashina Ltd
(S. Byron). Bond Street Antique Centre, 124 New Bond St, W1. Jewellery. LAPADA

Prides of London
15 Paultons House, Paultons Square, SW3. Tel 586 1227. Open by appt only. Furniture.

Princedale Antiques
(G.M. Sykes, G.N. Atley). 70 Princedale Rd, Holland Park, W11. Tel 727 0868. Open Thurs, Fri, Sat 10-6.30; other times by appt. Pine furniture 1800-1930, country furniture, large supplier to USA trade.

Princedale Antiques Workshop
(G.M.Sykes, G.N.Atley). 56 Eden Grove, N7. Tel 607 6376. (Also at 70 Princedale Rd, W11.) Open Mon-Fri 10.30-6; other times by appt. Antique English pine and country furniture. Supplier to U.S. trade.

Arthur Probsthain
41 Great Russell St, WC1B 3PH. Tel 636 1096. Book specialist. ABA

The Pruskin Gallery
(Michael and Jacqueline Pruskin). 183 King's Rd, SW3. Tel 352 9095, (priv)243 1939. (Also at 73 Kensington Church St, W8. Tel:937 1994.) Open (King's Rd) Mon-Fri 10-6; (Kensington) Tues-Sat 10-6; other times by appt. Art Nouveau, Art Deco and 1950s - furniture, paintings, Lalique, bronzes, ceramics, glass, jewellery and silver. Also Rolex and Cartier wristwatches.

Pryce and Brise Antiques
(Nella Pryce, Jan Brise). 79 Moore Park Rd, SW6. Tel 736 1864. Open Mon-Sat 10-6; other times by appt. 18th & 19thC English glass, furniture and decorative items.

The Purple Shop
(A.J.Gardner & O.M.Becker). 15 Flood St, Chelsea, SW3 5ST. Tel 352 1127. Open Mon-Sat 10-6. Antique and period jewellery, specialising in art nouveau and art deco.

Pym's Gallery
(A.E.& M.A. Hobart). 13 Motcomb St, Belgravia, SW1X 8LB. Tel 235 3050. Open Mon-Fri 10-6; other times by appt. Fine art dealers stocking British, Irish, European and modern British paintings, drawings and watercolours.

Bernard Quaritch Ltd
5-8 Lower John St, Golden Sq, W1. Tel 734 2983. Antiquarian books.

Quevedo
(J.F.T.Rodgers). 25 Cecil Court, WC2N 4EZ. Tel 836 9132. Open Mon-Fri 10-5.30. Antiquarian and rare books. ABA

Barrie Quinn Antiques
(Barrie Quinn). 3 & 4 Broxholme House, New King's Rd, SW6. Tel 736 4747. Open Mon-Sat 10-5.30; other times by appt. Specialist in jardinieres, pottery, polished steel, copper and brass. 2000 sq ft of Queen Anne to Victorian furniture, oak, mahogany etc. Oriental works of art. Large range of decorative objects and decorative furniture.

Quinton Green Fine Art
(Amanda Green, Lindy Quinton Cosh). 5/6 Cork St, W1. Tel 734 9179. Contemporary art.

Rabbitz Antiques
121 Portobello Rd, W11. Oriental and European items.

Rabi Gallery
94 Mount St, W1. Tel 499 8886. Open 9-6. Ancient art and oriental rugs. LAPADA

Nigel Raffety
34 Kensington Church St, W8. Tel 938 1100. (Also in Shere, Surrey.) Open Mon-Fri 10-1, 2-5; Sat 10-1; other times by appt. English and Continental longcase bracket clocks, watches and barometers. Restoration. LAPADA

Rankin Best & Green Ltd
(C.E.& P.M.Rankin). 24-36 Pearson St, E2 8JD. Tel 729 4200. (Also at The Mall, Camden Passage (359 0654) Open Tues-Sat 10-5.) Open Mon-Fri 9-5. Specialist glass for safety purposes. Also replacements for antiques made from flat or mirror glass. Specialising in show-cases.

J.S.Rasmussen Fine Arts
(Jens Salen Rasmussen). 5 Logan Mews, Logan Pl, W8. Tel 373 6527. Open by appt. Japanese 18th & 19thC netsuke and inro. Continental furniture and works of art.

Redfern Gallery
(John M Synge, Margaret Thornton, Gordon Samuel). 20 Cork St, W1X 2HL. Tel 734 1732/734 0578. Open Mon-Fri 10-5.30; Sat 10-12.30; other times by appt. 20thC paintings, drawings, sculpture and graphics. SLAD

William Redford
9 Mount St, W1. Tel 629 1165. Open 9.30-5.30. French furniture and works of art. BADA

Redmile
(J.A. Redmile). 95 Pimlico Rd, SW1W 8PH. Tel 730 0557. Open Mon-Fri 9.30-6; Sat 10-3. Unusual decorative objects - antique and modern.

Anthony Reed Gallery
(Anthony Reed). 3 Cork St, First Floor, W1X 1HA. Tel 437 0157. Open Mon-Fri 10-5; other times by appt. English drawings and watercolours, 18th to 20thC.

M. Rees
Stand E2, Antiquarius, Kings Rd, SW3. Tel 352 8734. Specialist in Quimper and Mason's ironstone.

Paul Reeves
(Paul Reeves). 32B Kensington Church St, W8 4HA. Tel 937 1594 (priv 968 7413). Open Mon-Sat 10-6; other times by appt. Furniture and artefacts 1860 to 1960, specialising in English arts and crafts furniture. Also design consultancy service related to the period.

William Reeves Bookseller Ltd
1A Norbury Cres, SW16 4JR. Tel 764 2108. Rare and secondhand books, specialising in music. ABA

Alex Reid & Lefevre Ltd
30 Bruton St, W1. Tel 493 1572. Open Mon-Fri 10-5. 19th and 20thC paintings and sculpture and drawings. SLAD

John Reid
40A Kensington Church St, W8. Tel 937 3379. Old prints and engravings.

Relcy Antiques
(R.Challis). 9 Nelson Rd, Greenwich, SE10. Tel 858 2811/2. Open Mon-Sat 10-6; other times by appt. Good quality 17th, 18th and 19thC furniture; all marine articles and pictures; fine instruments.

PORTMEIRION ANTIQUES

Interesting, varied collection of English and Continental antique furniture and innumerable small decorative items

62 WHITE HART LANE, BARNES, LONDON SW13 0PZ
Tel 01-876 2367

This advertisement was written by our clients – unasked

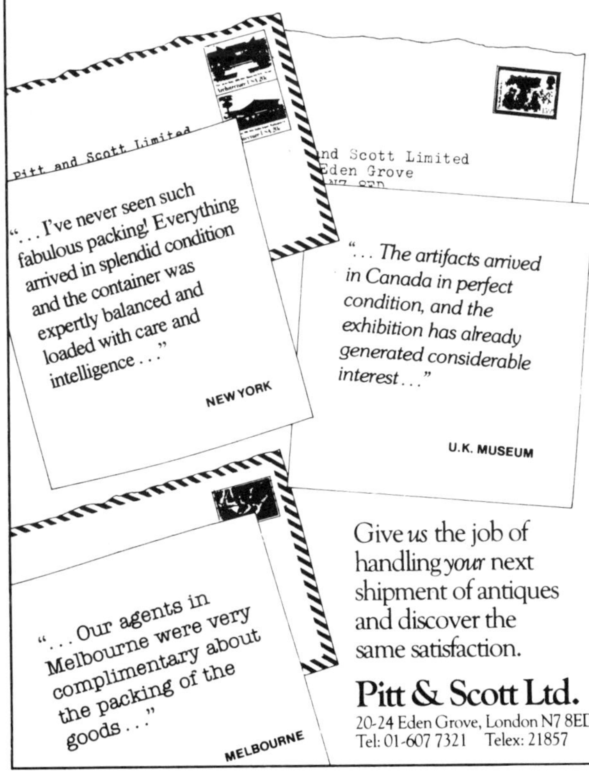

Give *us* the job of handling *your* next shipment of antiques and discover the same satisfaction.

Pitt & Scott Ltd.
20-24 Eden Grove, London N7 8ED
Tel: 01-607 7321 Telex: 21857

H. W. POULTER & SON

18th and early 19th century marble and pine mantelpieces, steel and brass fire grates, fenders, fire irons and old brass chandeliers

279 FULHAM ROAD, LONDON SW10 9PZ
Tel 01-352 7268

Relic Antiques
(Grierson Gower & Malcolm Gliksten). 1 Camden Walk, Islington, N1. Tel 359 6755. (Also at 248 Camden High St, NW1 (485 8072) & Malmesbury, Wilts.) Open Tues-Sat 10-5.30. Camden High St: Thurs-Sun 10-5.30. Trade warehouse and offices at 127 Pancras Rd, London NW1 (388 2691), Mon-Fri 10-5.30. Decorators and collectors items; naive and fairground art, architectural antiques, shop fittings, early advertising, English and French country pieces, garden items.

Reg and Philip Remington
(Reg and Philip Remington). 14 Cecil Ct, WC2. Tel 836 9771. (Also offices at Suite 33, 26 Charing Cross Rd, WC2.) Open Mon-Fri 10-5; other times by appt. Antiquarian and secondhand books: voyages and travels, natural history, maps and prints. ABA

Renaissance
9A Trevor Place, SW7. Biedermeier furniture, patchwork, decorative items and hand-made Moroccan goods.

Rendall
(Richard & Lesley Rendall). 572 King's Rd, SW6. Tel 736 2520 (priv 948 4400). Open Mon-Sat 9.30-6; other times by appt. Fine furniture and decorative items, early 18th to mid-19thC.

Rendlesham & Dark
498 Kings Rd, SW10. Tel 351 1442. Open 10-6. 18thC & 19thC English and Continental furniture and works of art.

Peter Reynolds Antiques
(Peter Reynolds). 67 New King's Rd, SW6. Tel 736 7797. Open Mon-Fri 10-5.30; Sat 10-4; other times by appt. Decorative pine, Oriental and country furniture and unusual decorative objects.

David Richards and Sons
(M., H. & E. Richards). 12 New Cavendish St, W1. Tel 935 3206. Open Mon-Fri; other times by appt. Silver, Old Sheffield plate & Victorian plate & reproductions. LAPADA

Paul Richards Antiques
(Paul Richards). 16 Fulham High St, SW6 3LQ. Tel 736 0976. Open Mon-Sat 9.30-5.30. Decorative furniture, objects, glass, lighting, framed prints.

The Richmond Gallery
(Timothy Pringle, John Moloney, Charles Mayes). 8 Cork St, W1. Tel 437 9422. Impressionist and Post-Impressionist paintings.

Gwen Riley Antiques
(Gwen Riley). 135-141 Kings Rd, SW3. Tel 352 4739. Open Mon-Sat, 10-6. 18th & 19thC pottery & porcelain and stamps.

L.J. Roberton Ltd
Marlborough House, Cooks Rd, Stratford, E15 2PW. Tel 519 2020. Packers & shippers. LAPADA

Jane Roberts & Robert Alderman
2nd Floor, 180 New Bond St, W1Y 9PD. Tel 491 0168. Open by appt only. 18th and 19thC European paintings, drawings and watercolours, and decorative works of art. Indian and Islamic works of art, from miniatures to metalwork.

Robson Lowe at Christie's
47 Duke St, St James's, SW1Y 6QX. Tel 839 4034/5. Auctioneers of stamps and postal history.

Rochefort Antiques
(Mr & Mrs L.W.Stevens-Wilson). 32-34 The Green, Winchmore Hill, N21. Tel 886 4779 (priv 363 0910). Open Mon-Fri 10-1, 2-6; Sat 10-7; closed Wed. General antiques, specialising in porcelain, silver, glass, Georgian and Victorian furniture, watercolours and oils, oil lamps, antique brass and jewellery.

J. Roger (Antiques) Ltd
(Joan Roger, Carolyn Bayley). 17 Uxbridge St, W8. Tel 727 2227 (priv 603 7627). Open Tues-Fri 2.30-5; other times by appt. Late 18thC & early 19thC furniture, especially small elegant pieces of Sheraton and Regency periods. Also mirrors, prints, porcelain and boxes. BADA

Rogers Antiques Gallery
65 Portobello Rd, W11. Tel (enquiries) 351 5353. (Office at 15 Flood St, Chelsea.) Open 7am-5pm every Sat. Antique centre with over 60 dealers including specialists in Moorcroft, majolica, advertising, silver and jewellery.

T. Rogers & Co (Packers) Ltd
(R.E.&R.J.Pepprell). PO Box 8, 1A Broughton St, SW8 3QL. Tel 622 9151. Open Mon-Fri 9-5.30. Security storage - packing and shipping, forwarding of antiques and works of art. Import and export.

Roman Antiques
76 Peckham Rye, SE15. Tel 732 4967.

Rona Gallery
1-2 Weighhouse St, W1. Art gallery.

Geoffrey Rose Ltd
77 Pimlico Rd, SW1W 8PH. Tel 730 3004. Open Mon-Fri 9.30-1 2.15-6; most Sats a.m.; other times by appt. Late 18thC and early 19thC English furniture. BADA

R.E.Rose
(R.E. Rose). 731 Sidcup Rd, Eltham, SE9. Tel 859 4754 (priv 464 2653). Open Mon 8.30-6; Tues 8.30-4.30; Wed-Sat 8.30-5.30; other times by appt. Restoration of antique clocks and barometers. Supplier of materials for restoration of clocks, barometers and watches. Clock sales. FBHI, BWCMG

Simon Leigh Rose Fine Decorative Antiques
(S.L. & P.D. Rose). 569 Kings Rd, Chelsea, SW6. Tel 731 7356. Open Mon-Sat 10-6; other times by appt. Lacquer, papier mache and fine decorative antiques.

Juda Rowan Gallery
(Ian Barker, Annely & David Juda, Alex Gregory-Hood). 11 Tottenham Mews, Off Tottenham St, W1P 9PJ. Tel 637 5517/8. Open Mon-Fri 10-6, Sat 10-1; other times by appt. Contemporary paintings and sculpture. SLAD

Royal Exchange Art Gallery
(Roger & Jill Hadlee). 14 Royal Exchange, EC3V 3LL. Tel 283 4400. Open Mon-Fri 10.30-5.15; other times by appt. Oils, watercolours, etchings, 19th and early 20thC.

Royal Garden Antiques
63 Kensington Church St, W8 4BA. Tel 937 7375. Open Mon-Sat 10-6. International dealers in fine art, antiques, English and Continental porcelain, furniture, oil paintings, clocks etc.

Rutland Gallery & Co
32a St George St, W1. Tel 499 5636. 20thC English and American pictures, English 18th and 19thC primitives, 18thC Indian paintings and China Coast pictures.

Sabin & Vanderkar (Fine Paintings) Ltd
43 Duke St, St James's, SW1. Tel 839 1091. Open by appt. Old master paintings. BADA

Sabin Galleries Ltd
(Sidney F.Sabin, Evelyn Patricia Sabin). Campden Lodge, 82 Campden Hill Rd, W8 7AA. Tel 937 0471. Open by appt only. Fine paintings, specialising in 16th-early 19thC. SLAD, BADA

Barry Sainsbury Oriental Art
(Barry Sainsbury). 145 Ebury St, SW1. Tel 730 3393. Open Mon-Fri 10-1, 2-5; other times by appt. Chinese and Japanese furniture and lacquer.

Edward Salti Ltd
(Edward Salti). 77 Wellesley Court, Maida Vale, W9. Tel 286 3106. Open by appt only. Continental porcelain, English enamels.

Samiramis Ltd
(H Ismail). Grays Mews, 1-7 Davies St, W1. Tel 629 1161 or 439 5106. Islamic art, valuations. LAPADA

Alistair Sampson Antiques (inc Tobias Jellinek)
156 Brompton Rd, SW3 1HW. Tel 589 5272, 581 2267. Open Mon-Fri 9.30-5.30; other times by appt. Very large stock of 17th,18th and 19thC English pottery, needlework and metalwork. 17th,18th and 19thC furniture, especially oak and country furniture, primitive pictures and decorative items. BADA

Patrick Sandberg Antiques
(Patrick Sandberg). 791 Fulham Rd, SW6 5HD. Tel 736 9454. Open Mon-Fri 9.30-6.30; Sat 10-1.30; other times by appt. 18th and early 19thC English furniture and decorative antiques. BADA

Robin Sanders & Sons
590 Fulham Rd, SW6. Tel 736 0586. Open Tues-Fri 10-6; Sat 10-2. Furniture, Staffordshire pottery, old Sheffield plate and glass pictures. BADA CINOA

Sanford Books
(S.A.Wallach). Chelsea Antique Market, 253 King's Rd, SW3. Tel 352 5581. Open 10-6. Antiquarian bookseller. ABA

Sangorski & Sutcliffe
1 Poland St, W1. Tel 437 2252. Bookbinders.

A.V. & M.R. Santos
1 Campden St, W8. Tel 727 4872. 17th & 18thC Chinese porcelain. LAPADA

G. Sarti Antiques Ltd
(G.Sarti). 186 Westbourne Grove, W11. Tel 221 7186. Continental and English furniture, specialising 17th and 18thC cabinets and marble tables, also paintings and objets d'art. LAPADA

Sarum Antiquarian Maps
(Ericsson & Christoph). 10 Chapel St, Belgrave Sq, SW1. Tel 235 6744. Open by appt only. 16th, 17th, 18thC maps.

DRUSKIN GALLERY.

ART & DECORATION 1880–1960

LONDON'S LEADING SPECIALISTS IN ART DECO & ART NOUVEAU

73 KENSINGTON CHURCH STREET
LONDON W8 · TELEPHONE 01 937 1994

HOURS: MON–FRI 10AM TO 6PM · WKNDS BY APPT.

WE ARE ALSO OPEN MON–SAT. 10–6 AT OUR PREMISES AT 183 KINGS ROAD · SW3
TEL 01 352 9095 · HOME TEL 01 243 1939

Barrie Quinn Antiques

Two showrooms: Light and darkwood furniture, decorative objects, bronze and steelware, gardenware and the unusual

Open 10am–5.30pm Monday–Saturday

Trade and Export Welcome

American Express

3 & 4 Broxholme House, New Kings Road, Fulham, London SW6. Telephone: 01-736 4747

ROCHEFORT ANTIQUE GALLERY

A group of dealers specialising in 18th and 19th century silver, English and Continental porcelain, jewellery, furniture, pictures, fine antique clothes and lace, oil lamps, and a wide variety of other antiques.

32/34 The Green,
Winchmore Hill, London N21.

Open 10-1 and 2-6 (Closed Wednesday) *Tel. (01) 886 4779*

Alistair Sampson

ANTIQUES

Incorporating Tobias Jellinek Antiques

Specialist dealers in
17th & 18th Century
English Pottery,
Oak and
Country Furniture,
Metalwork, Needlework,
Primitive Paintings,
Treen and
Decorative Items.

MEMBER OF THE BRITISH ANTIQUE DEALERS' ASSOCIATION

156 BROMPTON ROAD
LONDON SW3 1HW
TELEPHONE: 01-589 5272

South Audley Art Galleries Ltd

ANTIQUES, ENGLISH & CONTINENTAL PORCELAIN, IVORIES, FRENCH FURNITURE, PICTURES, CHANDELIERS, CLOCKS

Trade welcomed

36 South Audley Street, London W1

Phone 01-499 3178 & 01-499 3195 Monday to Friday 10am to 6pm

Gerald Sattin Ltd
25 Burlington Arcade, Piccadilly, W1V 9AD. Tel 493 6557. Open Mon-Fri 9-5.30, Sat 9-1; other times by appt. English and Continental porcelain, English glass, collectors' silver, paintings and small furniture. Specialising in unusual items of 18th and 19thC silver and 18thC glass. BADA

Savile Pine
560 Kings Rd, SW6. Tel 736 3625. Pine furniture.

Scallywag
(John A. Butterworth). The Old Church, Wren Rd, Camberwell Green, SE5 8QS. Tel 701 5353. (Also at 22 High St, Beckenham, Kent.) Open Mon-Fri 9-6; Sat, Sun 10-6. Antique and old country pine furniture, pine stripping, architectural items.

Scarlet Pimpernel Antiques
(Mrs J. Findlay, P. Wright). Grays Antique Market, 58 Davies St, W1. Silver, jewellery. Valuations. LAPADA

Christine Schell
15 Cale St, SW3 3QS. Tel 352 5563. Open Mon-Fri 10-5.30; Sat 10-1. Late 19thC decorative objects including tortoiseshell pique, ivory, enamel, shagreen etc.

Schidlof Galleries
1 Holland Park Ct, Holland Park Gdns, W14. Tel 603 9480. Open by appt only. Drawings, portrait-miniatures and objects of vertu.

Thomas E. Schuster
(Thomas E.Schuster). 9 Gillingham St, SW1. Tel 828 7963. Open Mon-Fri; other times by appt. Antiquarian books and prints, decorative flower & bird prints, specialising in topography and colour plate books. ABA

Schwartz Sackin & Co Ltd
89 Portobello Rd, W11. Tel 727 3857. General. Shipper. LAPADA

Directory Entries are Free and ADDITIONS OR CORRECTIONS will be welcomed by *THE EDITOR, British Art and Antiques Directory, National Magazine House, 72 Broadwick Street, London W1V 2BP*

Scope Antiques
(Karl Barrie). 64-66 Willesden Lane, NW6. Tel 328 5833. Open Mon-Sat 10-6; other times by appt. Shipping and general antiques, brass and copper.

Philippa Scott
30 Elgin Crescent, W11. Tel 229 8029. Open by appt only. Textiles, embroideries, costumes (Middle Eastern and Central Asian) objects, ancient jewellery (classical and Islamic), oriental rugs. Sometimes books on the above subjects. Dealing, consultancy and conservation of textiles and tapestries.

B.A. Seaby Ltd
8 Cavendish Sq, W1M 0AJ. Tel 631 3707. Open Mon-Fri 9.30-5. Large stock of ancient, medieval and modern coins, antiquities and numismatic new and antiquarian books. Also commemorative medals struck and company histories published. Catalogues and lists available on request.

Arthur Seager Antiques
(A.A. Seager). 25a Holland St, Kensington, W8. Tel 937 3262. Open Mon-Sat 10-6; other times by appt. 18th & 19thC country and decorative furniture, paintings, treen & lacquer, also brass decorative items, 17th & 18thC.

Seago
(Tim and Lindy Seago). 16 Lower Richmond Rd, Putney, SW15. 17th-19thC decorative, rare and unusual furniture and works of art.

Searle & Co Ltd
(Mrs P Bird, R.G.J.Bird, S.F.Redknap, R.J.Bridges). 1 Royal Exchange, EC3V 3LL. Tel 626 2456. Open Mon-Fri 9-5.30. Antique and modern jewellery, silver. NAG

H.& M. Sedler
(Henry Sedler, Michael Sedler). Stand F2, Antiquarius, Kings Rd, SW3. Tel 351 5000 (priv 226 2418). Open Mon-Sat 10-6. Silver, plate, writing equipment, treen. Specialising in travelling inks, early spectacles. LAPADA

Sekmet Galleries Ltd
(Alan Jacobs & Silvia Duran). 47 Camden Passage, Islington, N1 8EA. Tel 359 1755. Open Mon-Sat 10-5; other times by appt. Decorative arts and antiques, specialising in cat objects.

M. & D. Seligmann
(David & Maja Seligmann). 37 Kensington Church St, W8 4LL. Tel 937 0400 (priv 722 4315). Open Mon-Fri 10-6, Sat 11-2.30; other times by appt. Country furniture from 16th to early 19thC, mainly oak. 18thC English pottery. Treen, objets d'art and bygones. BADA

Sensation Ltd
(Maita Fenwick). 66 Fulham High St, SW6 5LQ. Tel 736 4135 (priv 584 9414). Open Mon-Fri 8.30-5; other times by appt. 18th and 19thC furniture, pottery, porcelain, valuations a speciality.

Jean Sewell (Antiques) Ltd
(Robert & Jean Sewell). 3 Campden St, Kensington Church St, W8 7EP. Tel 727 3122. Open Mon-Sat 10-5.30. Large stock of antique porcelain and pottery, specialising in 18th and 19thC tableware. BADA

David Seyfried
759 Fulham Rd, SW6. Tel 731 4230. Antique and decorative furniture. Also papier-mache and works of art.

Shapland
207 High Holborn, WC1. Tel 405 3507. Open Mon-Fri 9-5. Antique and secondhand jewellery, silver, objets d'art.

David Shaw Silverware Ltd
231-235 Liverpool Rd, Islington, N1 1LX. Tel 609 9091. Manufacturing silversmiths. Silver repairers.

Sheppard & Cooper Ltd
(Christopher Sheppard). 35 St George St, W1. Tel 629 6489. Open Mon-Fri 10-5.30; other times by appt. Antique glass, especially from 1400 BC to 1800 AD. Also works of art and Roman and Greek antiquities.

Sylvia Sheppard
71 Kensington Church St, W8 4BG. Tel 937 0965. Open 9.30-5.30, Sat 9.30-1; other times by appt. Queen Anne, Georgian and Regency furniture.

Sheraton Antiques Ltd
192 Westbourne Grove, W11. Tel 229 8748. Specialise in making long sets of chairs in varying styles and Regency dining tables of any length.

George Sherlock
588 King's Rd, SW6. Tel 736 3955. Decorative and unusual items.

Shield & Allen
(Don Shield & Michael Allen). 584-586 King's Rd, SW6. Tel 736 7145. Open Mon-Sat 9.30-6; other times by appt. Good stock of 16th to 18thC English and Continental furniture, pictures and works of art; specialising in French provincial furniture.

Shipley
70 Charing Cross Road, WC2. Tel 836 4872. Specialist art book seller.

S.J.Shrubsole Ltd
43 Museum St, WC1. Tel 405 2712. (Also in New York.) Open Mon-Fri 9-5.30. Important specialists in antique silver and old Sheffield plate. BADA

M. & L.Silver Co Ltd
2 Woodstock St, W1R 1HD. Tel 499 5392. Open Mon-Fri 9-5.30; other times by appt. Antique silver, silver plate, old Sheffield and shipping plate. LAPADA

B. Silverman
London Silver Vaults, 63 Chancery Lane, WC2A 1QS. Tel 242 3269. Silver. BADA

Simeon
19 Burlington Arcade, Piccadilly, W1V 9AB. Tel 493-3353. Open Mon-Fri 10-5; Sat 10-1. Estate & period jewellery, English and Continental miniatures, netsuke, snuff bottles and objets d'art. NAG

Simpsons
(Sharon Simpson Yardy). 17 Girdlers Rd, W14. Tel 603 8625. Res on prem. Period carved and plain pine mirrors.

Sims, Reed and Fogg Ltd
58 Jermyn St, SW1 6LX. Tel 493 5660/0952. Open Mon-Fri 10-6. Rare and out of print books on the fine and applied arts. Books illustrated with original graphics. ABA

Robin Sims
7 Camden Passage, N1. Tel 226 2393. Open Tues-Sat 10-4. General antiques.

Sinai Antiques Ltd
(M. Sinai). 221 Kensington Church St, W8. Tel 229 6190. Open 10-7. Decorative antiques and works of art. LAPADA

The Singing Tree
(Thalia Sanders and Anne Griffith). 69 New King's Rd, SW6. Tel 736 4527. Open Mon-Sat 10-5.30; trade by appointment. Dolls' houses and accessories, old and new. Mail order catalogue £3.

Keith Skeel
94 Islington High St, N1 8EG. Tel 359 9894. Open always, res on prem. Specialist in decorators' antiques including brass, papier mache, bamboo, Irish & Scottish furniture. LAPADA

The Sladmore Gallery
(Edward Horswell & Julia Hazandras). 32 Bruton Place, off Berkeley Sq, W1X 7AA. Tel 499 0365. Open Mon-Fri 10-6; other times by appt. 19th and 20thC animal sculptures, sporting and wildlife paintings and prints.

Peta Smyth - Antique Textiles
42 Moreton St, Pimlico, SW1. Tel 630 9898. Open Mon-Fri 10-5.30. 17th-19thC European textiles & needlework.

Sneath, Kent and Stuart (Insurance Brokers) Ltd
Dorriston House. 21/25 Earl St, EC2A 2AL. Tel 377 9866. Specialists in antiques and fine art dealers' insurances.

The Solomon Gallery
(Dorothy and Philip Solomon). 31 Bruton Place, W1X 7AB. Tel 499 4701/2. 20thC paintings, sculptures and ceramics.

Somerville & Simpson Ltd
11 Savile Row, W1. Tel 437 5414. Old Master paintings, drawings and prints, English watercolours and paintings. SLAD

Sotheby's
34-35 New Bond Street, W1A 2AA. Tel 493 8080. Open Mon-Fri 9-4.30. Fine art auctioneers.

Henry Sotheran
(Managing director R.D.Kirkman). 2-5 Sackville St, W1X 2DP. Tel 734 1150, 734 0308. Open Mon-Fri 9-5.30. Large stock of antiquarian books and prints. ABA

South Audley Art Galleries Ltd
(A.J.Singer). 36 South Audley St, W1Y 5DH. Tel 499 3178, 499 3195. Open Mon-Fri 10-6; other times by appt. Antiques, including English and Continental porcelain, ivories, French and English furniture, pictures, chandeliers, clocks, enamels. LAPADA

South London Art Gallery
Peckham Rd, SE5. Open Tues-Sat 10-6, Sun 3-6. Contemporary art.

John Sparks Ltd
(Michael Gillingham & David Davenport). 128 Mount St, W1Y 5HA. Tel 499 2265 and 499 1932. Open Mon-Fri 9.30-5; other times by appt. Specialists in Chinese works of art with an important stock of porcelain, jades, bronzes and other items. BADA

A. & J. Speelman
129 Mount St, W1. Tel 499 5126. Oriental ceramics and works of art. BADA

Edward Speelman Ltd
(Anthony A. Speelman). Empire House, 175 Piccadilly, W1V 0NP. Tel 493 0657. Open Mon-Fri 10-5; other times by appt. Highly important picture specialist. Mainly Dutch and Flemish Old Masters but also fine early paintings and Impressionists.

George Spencer Decorations Ltd
(M.Laurie, D.A.Laurie, A.C.M.Hay). 36 Sloane St, SW1. Tel 235 1501. Open Mon-Fri 9.30-5.30; other times by appt. Interior decorators, exclusive fabrics, wallpapers, furniture, pictures, carpets, lamps, shades, objets d'art etc.

Spenser S A
(N.C. Meares). 16b Grafton St, Bond St, W1X 3LF. Tel 723 9149. Open Mon-Fri 9.30-5.30, Sat by appt. Fine 19th and 20thC paintings and watercolours. Also some works by contemporary artists, wildlife and marine subjects.

Simon Spero
109 Kensington Church Street, W8. Tel 727 7413. Open Tues-Fri 10-5; Sat 10-1; other times by appt. 18thC English porcelain. Also 18thC English enamels, Continental porcelain and watercolours.

Spice
2 Wandon Rd, Stanley Bridge, SW6. Tel 736 4619. Pine furniture.

Aubrey Spiers Antiques
Stand C5, Chenil Galleries, King's Rd, Chelsea, SW3. Tel 352 7384. Open Mon-Sat from 10.30. Oriental, English, Continental porcelain & pottery, 17th & 18thC.

H.J. Spiller Ltd
37-39 Beak St, W1R 3LD. Tel 437 4661. Open Mon-Fri 9.30-5.30. Antique carved wood frames and Old Master paintings. BADA

Spink & Son Ltd
5, 6 & 7 King St, St James's, SW1. Tel 930 7888. Open Mon-Fri 9.30-5.30. Fine art, coin and medal dealers. English paintings and watercolours, English silver and jewellery, antique paperweights; Chinese, Japanese, Indian, South-East Asian, Persian and Islamic art, coins, medals, decorations. BADA

Marshall Spink Ltd
18 Albemarle St, W1X 3HA. Tel 493 2575 and 493 5280. Open Mon-Fri. Important Old Master paintings and drawings. Sculpture.

Spread Eagle Antiques
(Richard F.Moy). 22-23 Nelson Rd, SE10. Tel 858 9713, 692 1618. (Also 8 Nevada St, SE10.) Open Mon-Sat 10-5.30; early closing Thurs. Nelson Rd: period furniture and decorations, oil paintings, watercolours and large decorative items. Nevada St: Victoriana, books, postcards and printed ephemera, period costume and curios.

Spyer & Son (Antiques) Ltd
(Gerald Spyer). 18 Motcomb St, Belgrave Sq, SW1X 8LB. Tel 235 3348. Open Mon-Fri 10-6; other times by appt. Four showrooms with 18th and early 19thC English furniture. Also good stock of gilt period mirrors.

St George's Gallery Books Ltd
8 Duke St, St James's, SW1. Tel 930 0935. Open Mon-Fri 10-6; Sat 10-1. Good stock of reference works from all countries concerning the arts and antiques.

St Jude's Antiques
(Stephen Boyd, Philip Graham). 107 Kensington Church St, W8. Tel 727 8737. Open Mon-Sat 10-1, 2-5; other times by appt. 18th & 19thC English pottery & porcelain, small period furniture, decorative items. LAPADA

The Stable Shop and Gallery
(John Lawrence, Philip Arnott). 22B Bellevue Rd, Wandsworth Common, SW17. Tel 767 4688 (priv 673 1642). Open Mon-Sat 9-5; closed Wed; other times by appt. Contemporary and period paintings and prints, mounting and framing, greetings cards.

Stair & Company Ltd
120 Mount St, W1Y 5HB. Tel 499 1784, 499 1785. (Also in New York. Established 1912.) Open Mon-Fri 9-5.30; other times by appt. English 18thC furniture and works of art, barometers, clocks, chandeliers, mirrors, needlework and architectural engravings. BADA, CINOA

Stanley Studios
(Peter & Georgette Collins). Park Walk, Chelsea, SW10. Tel 352 4353, 352 9996. (Also in Balcombe, W.Sussex.) Open by appt. Early oak, pine, country furniture, paintings, antique and modern.

Louis Stanton
(L.R.Stanton, S.A.Stanton). 299 Westbourne Grove, W11. Tel 727 9336. Open Mon-Sat 9.30-5.30; other times by appt. Early English oak and fine 18thC furniture, tapestries, clocks, metalware, works of art, unusual decorative items. BADA, CINOA, LAPADA

Anne Steele Antiques
60 Fulham High St, SW6 3LQ. Tel 736 2387. Furniture and decorative objects.

Robert Stephenson Oriental Carpets
42 Fairfax Rd, NW6 4HA. Tel 722 4043. (Also at Kirkwood, North Church Walk, Newark-on-Trent, Notts.) Open by appt only. Oriental and European decorative carpets and textiles.

Stern Art Dealers Co
(D. & M. Stern). 46 Ledbury Rd, W11 2AB. Tel 229 6187. Open Mon-Sat 10-6. Large stock of 19thC paintings at trade prices.

Constance Stobo
(Constance Stobo). 31 Holland St, W8 4LX. Tel 937 6282 (priv 373 4709). Open Mon-Fri 10-5.30; Sat 10-2; other times by appt. English lustreware and pottery, Mason's ironstone, Staffordshire animals and small furniture - 18th & 19thC. BADA

Peter Stockham at Images
16 Cecil Court, Charing Cross Rd, WC2. Tel 836 8661. Open Tues-Fri 11-6.15; 1st Sat in month 11-2.30; other times by appt. Antiquarian and new books, art and illustrated books, graphic ephemera, children's books and toys, reference works and monographs. Large stock of books on children's games, toys and dolls. ABA

Stockspring Antiques
Stand J23, Grays Mews Market, Davies Mews, W1. Tel 629 3788. Fine English porcelain and pottery. LAPADA

Carolyn Stoddart-Scott
Tel 727 5045. Open by appt. 18th and 19thC pottery and porcelain.

BY APPOINTMENT TO
H. M. QUEEN ELIZABETH
THE QUEEN MOTHER
ANTIQUARIES OF CHINESE ART

BY APPOINTMENT TO
HER LATE MAJESTY QUEEN MARY
ANTIQUARIES OF CHINESE ART

BY APPOINTMENT TO
HIS LATE MAJESTY KING GUSTAF VI. OF SWEDEN
ANTIQUARIES OF CHINESE WORKS
OF ART

JOHN SPARKS

LIMITED

An early 18th-century Chinese figure
of a European in polychromed plaster,
signed AMOY CHINQUA. Height: 9″

128 MOUNT STREET, LONDON W1Y 5HA
Telephone 01-499 2265

Sotheran's
OF SACKVILLE STREET

Many of the world's most beautiful books pass through our hands

Rare books have been both our business and our pleasure for over 200 years. Many great libraries have passed through our hands, including those of Charles Dickens and a selection from the library of Sir Winston Churchill, and we have assisted in building up private collections throughout the world. Our famous bookshop in Sackville Street contains one of London's finest collections of rare old books. Also new books suitable for collection or presentation, standard works in fine bindings, antiquarian engravings, maps and autograph letters.

Visit us soon and browse amongst the world's most beautiful books.

HENRY SOTHERAN LIMITED
2, 3, 4 & 5 SACKVILLE STREET · PICCADILLY · LONDON W1X 2DP
TEL: 01-734 1150

Jean Sewell (Antiques) Ltd

3 Campden Street,
Kensington Church Street,
London, W8 7EP
Tel: 01-727 3122

Rockingham Squirrel—3″ high—impressed mark

For 18th–19th century porcelain and pottery

Jacob Stodel Antiques
(Jacob Stodel). 116 Kensington Church St, W8 4BH.
Tel 221 2652. Open Mon-Fri 10-6; other times by appt. European furniture, works of art, pottery & porcelain to the 18thC. Oriental porcelain & pottery. BADA, LAPADA

Alan Stone Antiques
(Alan Stone). 3 Wadham Rd, Putney, SW15. Tel 870 1606 (priv 642 6877). Open 9-6 (variable). Early 19thC furniture, davenports, desks & collectors items. Also restoration to same, public & trade.

Stoppenbach & Delestre Ltd
25 Cork St, W1X 1HB.
Tel 734 3534. 19th and 20thC paintings, drawings and sculpture.

Harold T.Storey
(Mr Kingswood). 3 Cecil Court, WC2N 4EZ. Tel 836 3777. Open Mon-Fri 10-6; Sat 10.30-5.30. Fine bindings of books in general. Prints and engravings.

Stratton Quinn Antiques Etc
(N.J. Quinn). 164 Thames Rd, Strand-on-the-Green, Chiswick, W4 3QS. Tel 994 3140. Open daily including most Sundays, 11-6; other times by appt. 18th and 19thC furniture and mirrors restored on the premises. Emphasis on English, Irish and Scandanavian pine but also attractive, practical furniture in other woods.

Pamela Streather
(Pamela Streather). 4 Studio Place, Kinnerton St, SW1.
Tel 235 3450. (Also Stable Cottage, Chilton, Aylesbury (0844 208859.) Open by appt in London Mon-Fri, Chilton by appt weekends. 17thC furniture, objects, works of art. CINOA, BADA

Directory Entries are Free and ADDITIONS OR CORRECTIONS will be welcomed by *THE EDITOR, British Art and Antiques Directory, National Magazine House, 72 Broadwick Street, London W1V 2BP*

Strike One (Islington) Ltd
(J.G.Mighell). 51 Camden Passage, N1 8EA. Tel 226 9709 (priv 359 6459). Open Mon-Sat 9-5; other times by appt. Longcase, bracket, lantern, wall, skeleton, Act of Parliament, Vienna regulators, carriage clocks. Barometers and chronometers. BADA, LAPADA

Louise Stroud
3, Cale Street, Chelsea Green, SW3. Tel 351 5988. (With Walker Galleries of Harrogate.) Open Tues-Fri 10-5.30, Sat 10-1. Antique jewellery. Valuations and restorations. FGA LAPADA

L.&M.Sutton
91 Portobello Rd, W11.
Tel 727 0386. Silver and Sheffield plate, antiques, Chinese porcelain, English and Continental pottery, bygones, early metalware, pictures and furniture.

Swan Fine Art
Camden Passage, Islington, N1.
Tel 226 5335. Large stock of 19thC paintings including animal, sporting, marine subjects, still life, landscape and portraits.

Oliver Swann Galleries
(Oliver Swann). 117A-119 Walton St, SW3 2HP. Tel 581 4229. (Also at 170 Walton St, SW3.) Open Mon-Fri 10-6, Sat 10-4; other times by appt. Regular exhibition of contemporary work at 117a-119 Walton St. At 170 Walton St, stock of 19th and early 20thC watercolours and oils, especially marine subjects.

David Swanson
186 Wandsworth Bridge Rd, SW6. Oak, fruitwood and pine from 17th to early 19thC.

E.Swonnell (Silverware) Ltd
(E., P., & N.W. Swonnell). Bond St Silver Galleries, 111-112 New Bond St, W1. Tel 629 9649. Open 10-5. Antique silver, old Sheffield plate.

Robin Symes
3 Ormond Yard, Duke of York St, St James's, SW1. Tel 930 9856/7. (Also at 94 Jermyn St, SW1. Tel:930 5300.) Open Mon-Fri 10-5.30. Ancient art and antiquities, specialising in sculpture. Old master drawings at Jermyn St.

SPS Shipping
Unit 3, Osiers Industrial Estate, Osiers Rd, SW18. Tel 871 1223. Open Mon-Fri 8.30-6.30; Sat 10-1. Packers and shippers.

Tadema
(D. & S. Newell-Smith).
10 Charlton Place, Camden Passage, N1. Tel 359 1055. Open Tues-Sat 10-5.30; other times by appt. Modern British & Continental paintings also decorative arts, including jewellery, ceramics, glass, silver, bronzes, furniture etc.

Talar Oriental Carpets
23 North End Parade, North End Rd, West Kensington, W14.
Tel 602 0046. Specialists in repairs and cleaning and lining tapestries and Aubussons.

The Talent Store Gallery
(Berta J. Pinnell, Jane Penruddock). 11 Eccleston St, SW1W 9LX. Tel 730 8117. Open Mon-Fri 9.30-5.30; other times by appt. Contemporary landscapes, oil paintings, graphic art, silkscreen paintings and collages.

Talisman
(Lesley Schiff). 363/4 Gray's Antique Market, 58 Davies St, W1. Tel 409 2743. Open Mon-Fri 10-6. Antique tribal and European jewellery. LAPADA

John Tanous Ltd
115a & 115b Harwood Rd, Fulham, SW6 4QL. Tel 736 7999. Open Mon-Fri 8-5. Fine art picture frame makers, gilders, restorers.

Taranman Ltd
236 Brompton Rd, SW3 2BB.
Tel 589 7838. Open 10-6, Sat 10-4. Etchings, drawings, pottery and fine books.

Taurus Gallery
(Maurice Bull). 5 Wadham Rd, Putney, SW15 2LS. Tel 874 2534. Open Tues, Wed, Thurs, Fri noon-5.30; Sat 10-5.30; other times by appt. Antique engravings and prints, picture framing, posters, decorative items, ephemera, greeting cards. Searches undertaken for publishers, museums, television, private collectors etc.

Pamela Teignmouth & Son
108 Kensington Church St, W8.
Tel 229 1602. Open Mon-Fri 10-6; Sat 10-4. English 18th and 19thC furniture and decorative items. Specialists in papier-mache and toleware.

M. & C. Telfer-Smollett
88 Portobello Rd, W11.
Tel 727 0117 (priv 370 1860). Open Wed-Sat 10-5. Oriental and natural history items, also fabrics.

F.Teltscher Ltd
17 Crawford St, W1H 1PF.
Tel 935 0525. Open Mon-Fri 10-5. Fine paintings, wood carvings and works of art.

Temple Gallery
4 Yeomans Row, Brompton Rd, SW3. Tel 589 6622. Open Mon-Fri 10-6, other times by appt, but appt always advisable. Extremely fine and large stock of early Russian and Greek icons. BADA

Tempus Antiques Ltd
(Louis Lawrence, J.J. Francis). 2-4 King St, St James's, SW1Y 6QL. Tel 839 5144. Open Mon-Fri 10-6 by appt. Japanese works of art. LAPADA

Tessiers
26 New Bond St, W1Y 0JY.
Tel 629 0458. Open Mon-Fri 9.30-5. Fine antique and modern reproduction silver, antique and modern jewellery, gold and enamel snuff boxes and etuis. BADA

Textile Conservation Studio
(Ksynia Marko). The Limehouse Cut, Morris Rd, Poplar, E14 6NT. Tel 538 4314. Open by appt only. A conservation workshop providing comprehensive services for the preservation of fine textiles. Specialist in tapestries and embroideries.

The Textile Gallery
(Michael and Jacqueline Franses). 4 Castellain Rd, Little Venice, W9 1EZ. Tel 286 1747. Open strictly by appt only. Rare and decorative textile art, prior to 1800 from all over the world. BADA

Themes & Variations
(Liliane Fawcett & Giuliana Medda). 231 Westbourne Grove, W11. Tel 727 5531. Open daily 10-6; closed Sun; other times by appt. 20thC decorative arts, furniture, glass, ceramics, carpets, lamps, jewellery, Art Nouveau, Art Deco, 1950s. contemporary.

The Thimble Society of London
(Bridget McConnell). Grays Antique Market, 58 Davies St, W1. Tel 493 0560. Thimbles, needlework tools.

This & That (Furniture)
(R.P.Schanzer). 50 & 51 Chalk Farm Rd, NW1. Tel 267 5433. Open Tues-Sat 10.30-6; Sun 11-5.30; other times by appt. 3000 sq ft of stripped pine, oak and country furniture at No.50; Victorian and Edwardian, oak, mahogany and walnut furniture at No.51. Shipping goods.

Nicholas Thomas
57 Ledbury Rd, W11 2A. Open Mon-Sat 9.45-5.45; other times by appt. Paintings, decorative furniture.

Sue & Alan Thompson
15 Flood Street, SW3.
Tel 352 3494. Silver and enamel vesta cases, frames, pin cushions and collectables.

Murray Thomson Ltd
141 Kensington Church St, W8 7LP. Tel 727 1727, 727 1825. (Also at 233 Westbourne Grove W11 2SE. Tel:221 8174.) Open Mon-Fri 9-6, Sat 10-1. Large stock of 18th and 19thC English and Continental furniture, objets d'art, Oriental furniture and works of art. Also a large warehouse of stock. LAPADA

Thornhill Galleries Ltd
76 New Kings Rd, SW6.
Tel 736 5830. Open 10-5. Marble, stone and wooden chimneypieces. Fire-grates and fenders. Architectural features, wood carvings, panelled rooms.

Thornton Associates
(Jill Thornton). 27 Henniker Mews, SW3. Tel 351 5242/3. Public relations.

Three Centuries Antiques
152 Kensington Church St, W8 4BN. Tel 221 1045. Good quality general antiques.

Through the Looking Glass Ltd
(J.J. & D.A. Pulton). 563 King's Rd, SW6. Tel 736 7799. Open Mon-Sat 10-5.30; other times by appt. Large stock of 19thC mirrors.

William Thuillier
10a West Halkin St, SW1.

Thumb Gallery
20-21 d'Arblay St, W1.
Tel 434 2931. Open Mon-Fri 10-6, Sat 11-4. Watercolours, drawings, paintings and limited edition prints by contemporary artists.

Brian Tipping
Stand U6, Antiquarius, Kings Rd, SW3. Tel 352 3315. Antique pipes.

Tobias and the Angel
(Tobias Ray & Angel Hughes). 68 White Hart Lane, Barnes, SW13. Tel 878 8902. Open Mon-Sat 10-6. Country furniture, textiles including bed linen, table cloths, especially North Country quilts, pottery, country objects, kitchen antiques.

Igor Tociapski
39-41 Ledbury Rd, W11.
Tel 229 8317. Open Mon-Fri 10-6; early closing Fri; other times by appt. Specialist in antique clocks and scientific instruments.

Michael Tollemache Ltd
78 Cadogan Pl, SW1.
Tel 235 5107. Old Masters and British 18th and 19thC paintings, drawings, watercolours, prints and sculptures. SLAD

Ferenc Toth
(F.I. Toth & Mrs. E. Toth). 598A Kings Rd, SW6 2DX.
Tel 731 2063 (priv 602 1771). Open 9-6; other times by appt. 19th and some 18thC mirrors, decorative furniture, paintings (general subjects).

Tower Bridge Antique Warehouse Ltd
(Mr.I.C. Kaufman). 163 Tower Bridge Rd, SE1. Tel 403 3660 (3 lines). Open Mon-Thurs 8.30-5.30; Fri 8.30-4.30; other times by appt. Largely antique furniture. Also some porcelain, glass, painting, prints, watches, silver plate, clocks, painted furniture. Repro leather. LAPADA

Townsends
(Matt Townsend). 1 Church St, NW8. Tel 724 3746 & 624 4756. (Also 81 Abbey Rd and 36 New End Square, Hampstead NW3.) Open Tues-Sat 10-6. Church St: large selection of original Victorian tiles and stained glass windows. Abbey Rd: reconditioned fireplaces and accessories, glazed doors.

Townsends
(Matt Townsend). Showroom: 36 New End Square, Hampstead Village, NW3.
Tel 794 5706/5707. (Also at 1 Church St, NW8 & 81 Abbey Rd, NW8.) Open Mon-Sat 10-6. Stained glass workshop. Showroom for period architectural fittings. Consultancy. Specialists in tiles, stained glass, fireplaces and doors.

Clifford J. Tracy
6-40 Durnford St, Seven Sisters Rd, N15 5NQ. Tel 800 4773. Antique furniture restoration, marquetry, boulle, ivory work, turning, carving, wax polishing, copy chairmaking, upholstery, caning, furniture hand made to customer's requirements.

Traditio Antiques
38A Kensington Church St, W8. Tel 937 9532. Open Mon-Fri 10-6; Sat 10-1. 17th and 18thC Chinese export porcelain.

Trafalgar Galleries
35 Bury St, St James's, SW1Y 6AU. Tel 839 6466/7. Open 9.30-6. Old Master paintings. BADA

Trafford Gallery
(C.A.Hardings). 119 Mount St, W1Y 5HB. Tel 499 2021. Open Mon-Fri 10-1, 2-5.30, Sat 10-1. Contemporary paintings.

Trans Euro Worldwide
Fine Art Division, Drury Way, Brent Park, NW10 0JN.
Tel 459 8080. Antique and fine art shippers and packers.

David Tremayne Ltd
320 King's Rd, SW3.
Tel 352 1194. Open Mon-Fri 10-5. Works of art and fine furniture, including Oriental and lacquer items. BADA

Triangle Bookshop
36 Bedford Sq, WC1.
Tel 631 1381. New and out of print books on architecture and architectural history.

Trianon
(Mrs I.Flowerdew-Horton). Grays Antique Market, 58 Davies St, W1. Tel 491 2764. Jewellery, objects of vertu. Valuations. LAPADA

The Trinket Box
(Marjorie Fry, Ruth Fischelis). 1 Goldhurst Terrace, NW6 3XH. Tel 624 4264. (Also The Corner Cupboard, 679 Finchley Rd, NW2 2JP.) Open Mon-Fri 9.30-6; Sat 9.30-5. Jewellery, silver, porcelain, pottery, small furniture, prints, bric-a-brac.

David Tron (Antiques) Ltd
275 King's Rd, Chelsea, SW3.
Tel 352 5918. 17th and 18thC furniture. BADA

Trove
(Peter Roe & Jim Smith).
71 Pimlico Rd, SW1.
Tel 730 6514. Open Mon-Fri; early closing Sat. Furniture, bronzes, sporting paintings and decorative items.

The Tryon and Moorland Gallery
23-24 Cork St, W1X 1HB.
Tel 734 6961/2256. Open Mon-Fri 9.30-5.30. Specialists in sporting and natural history pictures, prints, bronzes and books. SLAD

Tugwell & Thomas Antiques
(P.Tugwell, R.Thomas). Grays Antique Market, 58 Davies St, W1 Tel 499 1337. Animal-related oil paintings, porcelain and bronzes. LAPADA

Turn On Ltd
(Janet Holdstock).
116-118 Islington High St, Camden Passage, N1 8EG.
Tel 359 7616. Open Tues-Sat 10.30-5.30; other times by appt. Antique lighting, especially Victorian, Art Nouveau, Edwardian and 1920s lighting. Valuations and prop hire. Consultancy service available.

Rogers Turner Books Ltd
(P.J.Rogers, A.J.Turner).
22 Nelson Rd, Greenwich, SE10. Tel 853 5271. (Also at 24 Rue du Buisson Richard, 78600 Le Mesnil-Le-Roi, Paris.) Open daily 10-6; early closing Thurs. Antiquarian and secondhand books specialising in books about clocks, watches, scientific instruments. (Paris phone no. 3-912-11-91). ABA

M.Turpin
21 Manson Mews, Queensgate, SW7. Tel 736 3417. Open by appt only. Fine antiques and objets d'art, specialist in English and Continental 18thC furniture, high class furniture restoration and gilding. LAPADA

Twentieth Century Gallery
(Gregory Guest, David Sim).
821 Fulham Rd, SW6 5H6.
Tel 731 5888. Open Tues-Fri 10-6; Sat 10-1; other times by appt. Modern British oils & watercolours.

Tzigany Fine Arts
(Antoine Cheneviere). 28-29 Dover St, W1X 3PA. Tel 491 1007. Russian, Austrian, German, Swedish and Italian 18th and 19thC furniture and objets d'art.

J.S.Ullmann
10 Hatton Gdn, EC1N 8AH.
Tel 405 1877. (Also A.R.Ullmann Ltd at same address.) Open Mon-Fri 9-5.30. Antique and second hand jewellery. Repair and valuation service. Also watches and clocks.

Leigh Underhill Gallery
100 Islington High St, Camden Passage, Islington, N1.
Tel 226 5673. Open Tues-Sat 9-6. Paintings, prints, sculpture - 20thC British. Works of art.

Doris Urquhart Antiques
28 Church St, NW8.
Tel 258 3748. Country antiques.

Vale
(H.J. & R.P. Varnham).
21 Tranquil Vale, Blackheath, SE3 0BU. Tel 852 9817. Open Mon-Sat 10-5.30; closed Thurs; other times by appt. Stamps, coins and medals, antiquities, postcards and ephemera. PTS ADA

David Tron Antiques

275 Kings Road
Chelsea
London SW3
01-352 5918

Works of Art
Fine Antique
Furniture

Member of the British
Antique Dealers' Association

A fine French drawleaf table (circa 1800), and eight oak chairs (circa 1720)

Antique Furniture Restoration

MARQUETRY BOULLE IVORYWORK
TURNING CARVING WAXPOLISHING
COPYCHAIRMAKING UPHOLSTERY
CANING FURNITURE HAND MADE TO
CUSTOMERS REQUIREMENTS

Private enquiries welcome

Collection and delivery

Overseas enquiries invited

CLIFFORD J. TRACY
6–40 Durnford Street,
Seven Sisters Road,
London N15 5NQ
Telephone 01-800 4773/4774

MURRAY THOMSON LTD.

141 KENSINGTON CHURCH STREET
LONDON W8 7LP
Telephone 01-727 1727 & 01-727 1825

Large and varied stock in new premises at:

233 WESTBOURNE GROVE
LONDON W11 2SE
Tel. 01-221 8174

Rafael Valls Gallery
(Rafael Valls). 6 Ryder St, St James's, SW1Y 6QB.
Tel 930 0029. Open Mon-Fri 10-6. Specialists in 17thC Old Master paintings and 19thC paintings.

Jan van Beers
Stand K24/25, Gray's Mews, 1-7 Davies Mews, W1. Tel 408 0434. Open Mon-Fri 10-6. Oriental ceramics and works of art. BADA

Johnny Van Haeften Ltd
(John Henry Van Haeften, Sarah Anne Van Haeften). 13 Duke St, St James's, SW1Y 6DB.
Tel 930 3062. Open Mon-Fri 10-7; other times by appt. 16th and 17thC Dutch and Flemish old master paintings. BADA

Edric Van Vredenburgh
(Edric Van Vredenburgh). 37 Bury St, SW1. Tel 839 5818. Open Mon-Fri 10-5.30; closed 1-2; other times by appt. Bronzes, carvings, ivories, European furniture, needlework, hardstone cabinets and table tops.

Geoffrey Van Ltd
105 and 107 Portobello Rd, W11. Tel 229 5577. Open Mon-Sat 10-1, 2-6; other times by appt. Specialist in woodcarvings of all periods (large stock); also early furniture, tapestries, maiolica, and objets d'art.

Earle D.Vandekar of Knightsbridge Ltd
(Nicholas M.Vandekar & Paul R.Vandekar). 138 Brompton Rd, SW3. Tel 589 8481, 589 3398. (Also 15 East 57th St, New York NY10022, USA.) Open Mon-Fri normal business hours; other times by appt. Fine antique ceramics - English, European and Oriental. BADA, CINOA, LAPADA

C.J.Vander (Antiques) Ltd
Dunstan House, 14a St Cross St, EC1. Tel 831 6741. Large stock of antique silver and old Sheffield plate. Wholesale only. BADA

Vane House Antiques
15 Camden Passage, N1.
Tel 359 1343. Open Mon-Sat. 18th and early 19thC furniture.

Vaseroy
(H. Fazeli, M.R. Amini). Unit 16 Bond St Antique Centre, 124 New Bond St, W1. Tel 491 4942. Open Mon-Fri 10-5. Art Nouveau and Art Deco objects, glass and bronzes. Specialising in Art Nouveau and Art Deco.

Venners Antiques
(Mrs S.Davis). 7 New Cavendish St, W1. Tel 935 0184. (Also at Littlewick Green, Maidenhead, Berks.) Open Mon-Fri 10.15-4.30; Sat 10-1; other times by appt. 18th and 19thC pottery and porcelain.

Ventura-Pauly Ltd
(M.Ventura-Pauly). Grays Antique Market, 58 Davies St, W1.
Tel 408 1057. Jewellery. Valuations. LAPADA

Vigo Carpet Gallery
6A Vigo St, W1. Tel 439 6971. Open Mon-Fri 9-5.30; other times by appt. Antique and semi-antique Oriental and European rugs, carpets, tapestries and textiles. Also cleaning and restoration. LAPADA

Vigo-Sternberg Galleries
37 South Audley St, W1.
Tel 629 8307. Open 9-5.30. Large stock of period tapestries and rugs. BADA

Vinci Antiques
(Armando Vinci). Shop 456, Bond St Antique Centre, 124 New Bond St, W1. Tel 499 1041. Objets d'art, jewellery, silver, porcelain, glass, objects of vertu. LAPADA

Vintage Cameras Ltd
(John Victor Jenkins). 254-256 Kirkdale Corner, Sydenham, SE26 4NL.
Tel 778 5416. Open Mon-Sat 9-5. Vintage cameras and photographica, also scientific instruments. LAPADA

Lydia von Kubowski Antiques
(Mrs Carla Kavanagh-Genuth). Stand V 22, Antiquarius, 135 King's Rd, SW3. Tel 352 7989. Open Mon-Sat 10-6. Anything to do with cats and illustrated children's books.

Vortex Gallery
139-141 Church St, Stoke Newington, N16. Tel 254 6516. Art gallery, art shop and book shop.

W.13 Antiques
10 The Avenue, Ealing, W13 8PH. Tel 998 0390. Open Tues, Thurs, Fri, Sat; other times by appt. Furniture, porcelain and general antiques.

Waddington Galleries Ltd
(L. Waddington, H. van Royen, A. Cristel, T. Lighton). 2,4,11 & 34 Cork St, W1. Tel 437 8611. Open Mon-Fri 10-5.30; Sat 10-1. Paintings, sculpture and prints by 20thC British & foreign artists.

Wade Galleries
(S.Harris, P.J.Pierce). 12B Camden Passage, Charlton Place, N1. Tel 226 3803. (Also in Deal, Kent.) Open Wed and Sat only. Books and antiques.

Barrie Waiting
7 New Cavendish St, W1.
Tel 935 0186. Porcelain, miniatures and paintings.

Walker Galleries of Harrogate Ltd
(David and Ian Walker). 3 Cale St, Chelsea Green, SW3.
Tel 351 5988. (With Louise Stroud.) Open Tues-Sat 10-5.30; Sat 10-1; other times by appt. 18thC English and continental oil paintings, watercolours and works of art, woodcarvings, early Chinese ceramics and 18th and 19thC furniture. Also valuations and restorations.

W.E.Walker
(W.E.Walker, R.A.Walker, A.R.Walker). 277/9 Camden High St, NW1 7BX. Tel 485 6210 (priv 485 4433). Open Mon-Fri 10-6, Sat 10-1; other times by appt. 17th to 19thC furniture specialising in furniture with musical connections.

Walker-Bagshawe
(Caryl Walker, Nicholas Bagshawe). 73 Walton St, SW3.
Tel 589 4582 (priv 381 2172). Open Mon-Sat 10-6; other times by appt. Edwardian paintings, good English oils & watercolours 1870-1930. Framing service. Valuations.

John Walker
64 South Molton St, W1Y 1DY.
Tel 629 3487. Restoration of clocks, watches & jewellery. GMC

William Walter
Silver Vaults, Chancery House, Chancery Lane, WC2A 1QS.
Tel 242 3248/9. Fine and large stock of antique silver and old Sheffield plate. Also objets d'art and other items. Wholesale and export only. BADA

Leigh Warren
566 Kings Rd, SW6.
Tel 736 2485. General antiques.

Wartski Ltd
14 Grafton St, W1.
Tel 493 1141/2/3. Open Mon-Fri 9.30-5. Fine stock of antique jewellery, silver, snuffboxes and other items. Also the foremost specialist in Faberge. BADA

Warwick Arts Trust
33 Warwick Square, St George's Drive, SW1V 2AQ. Tel 834 7856. Art gallery.

The Warwick Leadlay Gallery
5 Nelson Rd, Greenwich, SE10 9JB. Tel 858 0317 (priv 852 7484). Open Mon-Sat 9.30-5.30; Sun 11-5.30; other times by appt. 18th and 19thC maps, prints, illustrated antiquarian books and atlases. Specialist in SE London and NW Kent material. Expert mounting & framing serivice carried out on the premises. Cleaning, restoration & colouring service available.

B.G.Watson Antiques
(B.G.Watson). 173 Bermondsey St, SE1. Tel 407 2040. Victorian furniture.

Watts & Christensen
(C.E.H.Watts, H.O.Christensen). 54 Cambridge St, SW1.
Tel 834 3554. Open Mon-Fri 9-6; other times by appt. Decorative antiques.

Waveney Antiques
(G.E. Breeze). 58 & 68 Peckham Rye, SE15. Tel 732 1251. Open Mon-Fri, 9-5.30; Sat, 9-1. Good quality furniture of all periods. LAPADA

Wylma Wayne Fine Art
17 Old Bond St, W1.
Tel 629 4511. Open Mon-Fri 10.30-6. 17th-19thC English and Continental paintings.

Weinreb Architectural Gallery
36 Store Street, WC1E 7BS.
Tel 636 4895. (Also architectural prints at 34 Museum St, WC1.) Open Mon-Fri 10-6; Sat 10-1. Modern & antiquarian architectural books.

The Weiss Gallery PLC
(Mark Weiss, Joan Weiss). 1B Albemarle St, W1X 3HF.
Tel 409 0035 (priv 212 481). Open Mon-Fri 10-6; other times by appt. Paintings, furniture & works of art. Specialising in Elizabethan & Jacobean portraits. BADA

Welbeck Gallery
(D. & S. Spellman). 18 Thayer St, W1M 5LD. Tel 935 4825 (priv 340 7130). Open Mon-Fri 10-5.30, Sat 10.30-12.30; other times by appt. Prints, etchings, engravings, lithographs etc. Topography, natural history, cartoons, military, birds and plants. Vanity Fair cartoons and Victorian music covers.

Wellington Gallery
(Mr & Mrs K.Barclay). 1 St Johns Wood High St, NW8.
Tel 586 2620. General antiques. LAPADA

Westenholz Antiques Ltd
(Piers von Westenholz).
68 Pimlico Rd, SW1.
Tel 730 2151. (Also larger shop at 80-81 Pimlico Road.
Tel 730 9264.) Open Mon-Fri 10-6. 18th & 19thC furniture, pictures, lamps, objects, prints etc.

Westleigh Antiques
(Mrs P.Sneath). Croesus, Grays, 58 Davies St, W1. Tel 493 0624. Victorian, Edwardian & art deco jewellery. LAPADA

Westminster Group
(P.Bates, C.Forbes, B.Lankester). Stand 150, Grays Antique Market, 58 Davies St, W1Y 1HH.
Tel 493 8672. Open Mon-Fri 10-6. Antique and second hand jewellery.

David Weston Ltd
44 Duke St, St James's, SW1.
Tel 839 1051. Scientific instruments and marine antiques.

William Weston Gallery Ltd
(William Weston). 7 Royal Arcade, Albemarle St, W1X 3HD.
Tel 493 0722. Open Mon-Fri 9.30-5; Sat 10.30-1 (closed Sat in Aug). Specialist dealer in 19th and early 20thC original prints and drawings. SLAD

Andrew White
Shop 17, The Quadrant, Kilburn Lane, W10. Restorer and upholsterer.

Richard White and Peter Howlett
911 Fulham Rd, SW6. Decorative furniture.

Whitehead & Lightfoot
(D. Bailie, D. Lightfoot). Blocks 2 & 4 Avon Trading Estate, Avonmore Rd, W14 8TS.
Tel 603 4237. Open Mon-Fri 8-6.30; other times by appt. Specialist furniture makers & joiners - fitted cabinets, panelled rooms etc. GMC

Edna Whiteson Ltd
66 Belmont Ave, EN4 9LA.
Tel 449 8860. (Also at Dolphin Arcade, 157 Portobello Rd W11. Sats only.) Open by appt only. Modern firsts, literature, illustrated travel, art and general books. Also a collection of original maps and pre-1850 prints. Framing service. ABA PBFA

Whiteway & Waldron
305 Munster Rd, SW6.
Tel 381 3195. Open Mon-Fri 10-6; other times by appt. Specialist in stained glass and architectural fittings.

Robert Whitfield Antiques
(R J Whitfield). 173 Bermondsey St, SE1 3UW. Tel 407 2040. Victorian & Edwardian furniture. Valuations. LAPADA

Whitford & Hughes
(Adrian Mibus, David Hughes). 6 Duke St, St James's, SW1.
Tel 930 9332. Open Mon-Fri 10-6; Sat 10-1 by appt. Paintings from the Post-Impressionist, Symbolist, Vienna Secession, Salon, Academy 1900, Belle Epoque, Abstract, Orientalist and Australian schools. SLAD

Neil Wibroe Antiques Ltd
185 Westbourne Grove, W11. 18th and early 19thC English furniture and works of art.

Arnold Wiggins & Sons Ltd
30-34 Woodfield Place, Harrow Rd, W9 2BJ. Tel 286 9656. Open 9-5.30. Extensive stock of fine antique frames of all periods. Picture frame makers, carvers & gilders, reproductions, restorations and alterations.

Wildenstein & Co Ltd
(Alec Wildenstein, Max Harari). 147 New Bond St, W1Y 0NX.
Tel 629 0602. (Also in New York, Tokyo and Buenos Aires.) Open Mon-Fri 10-5.30. Impressionist and Old Master paintings and drawings. SLAD

Wilkins & Wilkins
(Bartholomew & Mary Anne Wilkins). 1 Barrett St, St Christopher's Place, W1.
Tel 935 9613. Open Mon-Fri 11-5. 17th, 18th and early 19thC decorative paintings and portraits.

R. Wilkinson & Son
(David J. Wilkinson).
43-45 Wastdale Rd, Forest Hill, SE23 1HN. Tel 699 4420. Open Mon-Fri 10-1, 2-4; other times by appt. Antique & fine quality reproduction chandeliers, wall lights, candelabra, general tableware, replacement chandelier pieces. Restoration of antique glass. GMF

Willcocks Antiques
(Yvonne and Clive Willcocks). Chenil Galleries, 183 King's Rd, Chelsea, SW3. Tel 352 8653. Open Mon-Sat 10-6. Illustrated & children's books, silver, porcelain & pottery, fine fans, decorative prints.

Williams & Son
2 Grafton St, W1X 3LB.
Tel 493 5751, 493 4985. Open Mon-Fri 9-6. 19thC British and European oil paintings and watercolours.

Catherine Williams
Stand A1, Antiquarius, Kings Rd, SW3. Tel 352 7989. General antiques and interesting collectors' items.

Temple Williams
(Joan K. Williams, Caroline T. Williams). Kensington.
Tel 876 4726. Open by appointment only, goods in store. Fine Regency furniture and works of art.

Winifred Williams
3 Bury St, St James's, SW1.
Tel 930 4732. Fine English and Continental ceramics and enamels. BADA

Henry Willis (Antique Silver)
(Henry Willis). 4 Grosvenor St, W1. Tel 491 8949. Open Mon-Fri 10-6; other times by appt. Antique & early silver, mostly British, 16th to 19thC. Always a small selection of early English spoons before 1700. LAPADA

Althea Wilson
(Althea Wilson). 43 Burnaby St, Lots Rd, SW10. Tel 352 9394. Open by appt only. Restoration of antique painted furniture. Painted furniture to style required. Interior decor.

Ian Wilson Antiques
70-72 Peckham Rye, SE15.
Tel 639 5068 (priv 732 5349). Open Mon-Fri 9-5; closed 1-2; other times by appt. Victorian, Edwardian, period furniture. Also good decorative furniture including pine, art deco etc. Also spectacular shipping goods for export market. Specialising in carved oak, good shipping pieces.

O.F.Wilson
(O.F. Wilson, P.Jackson, M.E.Tushingham). Queen's Elm Parade, Fulham Rd, SW3 6EJ.
Tel 352 9554 (priv 373 4602). Open Mon-Fri 9.30-5.30; Sat 10.30-1; other times by appt. English and Continental furniture, chimney pieces and other decorative items. BADA, LAPADA

Wingate & Johnston Ltd
(R.Pateman). 78 Broadway, Stratford, E15 1NG. Tel 555 8123. Open Mon-Fri 9-5.30; other times by appt. Offices in all major provincial UK ports. Shipping and forwarding agents, air-freight agents, export packers specialising in the packaging of antique and fine arts with worldwide coverage; also insurance agents.

The Winter Palace
69 Kensington Church Street, W8. Tel 937 2410. Open Mon-Fri 10-5.30, Sat 10.30-2. Icons, silver, enamels, porcelain, glass, papier mache, specially Russian works of art.

Mary Wise Antiques
(Elizabeth Wise). 27 Holland St, W8. Tel 937 8649 (priv 352 7334). Open Mon-Fri 10-5.30; other times by appt. Specialist in 18thC English porcelain, Chinese ceramics and jade. BADA

The Witch Ball Print & Map Shop
2 Cecil Court, Charing Cross Rd, WC2. Tel 836 2922. (Also in Brighton.) Open Mon-Sat 10.30-6; other times by appt. Marine, sporting, theatrical and topographical engravings, caricatures and maps.

Barry M. Witmond
5A Mill St, W1. Tel 409 2335. Restorer of antique English & Continental plate. Maker of hand wrought gold & silver plate.

J.Wolff & Son Ltd
82 Troutbeck, Albany St, NW1. Tel 388 3588. (Also at Woburn Abbey Antiques Centre, Shop 25.) English and Continental furniture, mirrors, clocks, etc. carving, gilding and fine restorations undertaken. LAPADA GMC

Christopher Wood Gallery
(Christopher Wood). 15 Motcomb St, SW1. Tel 235 9141 (priv 828 1092). Open Mon-Fri 9.30-5.30; other times by appt. Victorian paintings; drawings, sculpture, photographs, 19th and 20thC ceramics. SLAD, BADA

W.J. Woodhams
182 Munster Rd, SW6.
Tel 736 6293/6371. Antique furniture.

H. Woods Wilson Ltd
103 Pimlico Rd, SW1.
Tel 730 2558. Open Mon-Fri 10-6, other times by appt. Specialist in Oriental art including Japanese screens, lacquer, porcelain and bronze, and Chinese porcelain and furniture.

Christopher Wray's Lighting Emporium
Tiffany Shop & Lamp Workshop, 600-606 King's Rd, SW6.
Tel 736 8434. Open Mon-Sat 10-6. Decorative lighting of the 1880s, replacement parts for gas, oil and early electric lights. Specialist in Victorian and Edwardian lamps and decorative ceiling fans.

Christopher Wrays Lamp Workshop
(C.J.D. Wray). 579/581 King's Rd, SW6 2DX. Tel 736 8434. Open Mon-Sat 10-6. Replacement shades and spare parts for oil and gas lamps.

Wren Antiques
49B Church Rd, Barnes, SW13. Period furniture, with some silver and porcelain.

Linda Wrigglesworth
Stand B17/A23, Gray's Mews, 1-7 Davies Mews, W1. Tel 408 0177. Open Mon-Fri 10-6. Early 18th to late 19thC Chinese textiles, robes and embroideries. LAPADA

Clifford Wright
104/106 Fulham Rd, SW3. Tel 589 0986. Open Mon-Fri 9-6, Sat 9-3. 18th and early 19thC decorative period mirrors, gilt furniture. BADA

Andrew Wyld
17 Clifford St, W1X 1RG. Tel 734 5575/5576. Open 10-6. English watercolours, drawings and oil paintings.

The Wyllie Gallery
(John Wyllie). 12 Needham Road, W11. Tel 727 0606 (priv 584 6024). Open Mon-Fri 9-6; Sat 10-1; other times by appt. 19th/20thC Marine paintings & engravings.

Harriet Wynter Ltd
(M.R.Freeman, A.P & P.M.Freeman). 50 Redcliffe Rd, SW10 9NJ. Tel 352 6494. Open only by appointment. Scientific instruments and related objects - paintings, folk art, carvings, books etc. Marine & medical items. Free catalogue on request. BADA

Wynyards Antiques
5 Ladbroke Rd, W11. Tel 221 7936, 727 5106. Open Mon-Fri 10-5.30; Sat 10.30-5.30. Treen, small furniture and objects of art. Decorator items.

Yesterday Child
(D.J.& J.C.Barrington). 24 The Mall, Camden Passage, N1. Tel Milton Keynes (0908) 583403. Open Wed, Fri 9-4, Sat 9-1; other times by appt. Specialists in juvenilia with large stock of rare dolls; also automata. LAPADA

Young Stephen Ltd
(Stephen & Janie Burton). 1 Burlington Gdns, New Bond St, W1X 1LD. Tel 499 7927. Open Mon-Fri 9.30-5.30, Sat 10.30-3.30; other times by appt. Edwardian, art nouveau and art deco jewellery of high quality with a few specially designed modern pieces. Valuation and repairs undertaken. LAPADA

Robert Young Antiques
(Robert Young). 68 Battersea Bridge Rd, SW11. Tel 228 7847. Open Tues-Fri; closed Mon; other times by appt. Antique oak and country furniture, treen, English and European folk art and objects.

Robert Yuen
105 Pimlico Road, SW1. Tel 730 9257. Open Mon-Fri 10-6, Sat 11-2. Period furniture, ceramics, glass, objects of interest from East and West.

Zadah Persian Carpets Ltd
(A. Zadah). 20 Dering St (First Floor), (Off New Bond St), W1R 9AA. Tel 493 2622, 493 2673. Open Mon-Fri 9.30-5.30; other times by appt. Old and antique Oriental rugs and carpets.

Zaehnsdorf Ltd
175 Bermondsey St, SE1. Tel 407 1244. Craft bookbinding, conservation & restoration of books and papers.

Zamana Gallery Ltd
1 Cromwell Gardens, SW7 2SL. Tel 584 6612/3. Islamic art.

Ziggurat
(Judy Daniels). Chenil Galleries, 183 King's Rd, SW3. Tel 352 2123. Open Mon-Sat 10-6. Art nouveau, art deco and 1950s items. Jewellery and silver, including a selection of Georg Jensen, art glass, studio pottery, Clarice Cliff.

A.Zwemmer Ltd
24 Litchfield St, WC2. Tel 836 1749. Open Mon-Sat. (Off Charing Cross Rd.) New, old and out-of-print books on collecting subjects, art, architecture and painting. ABA

ENGLAND

How to Use This Book
After the editorial articles the book is divided into five main sections:

1 Directory (*begins on page 37*)
Dealers, auctioneers, packers, restorers, trade suppliers and so on are all listed here, with address, telephone number, opening hours, and type of business or area of specialisation. Entries are listed in alphabetical order under town or village, within the relevant county and geographical area.

2 Gazetteer (*begins on page 265*)
This is an alphabetical list of the towns and villages mentioned in the Directory, showing the counties and geographical areas under which they are listed.

3. Index to Specialists
(*begins on page 270*)
Directory entries are here listed under type of business or nature of stock.

4. Index to Business Names
(*begins on page 363*)
All business names in the Directory are listed alphabetically with their town or village, county and geographical area.

5 Maps (*begin on page 391*)
Showing villages and towns listed in the Directory.

Note
Counties and geographical areas are listed with page references under 'Contents' on page 3.
Auctioneers are listed both in the main Directory under the relevant town or village, and in the Specialists index under 'Auctioneers'.
Abbreviations and names and addresses of useful organisations are listed on page 4.

Avon

Banwell STD 0934

John H. Collings
Antique Village, Knightcott, BS24 6HS. Tel 823181 (priv 812030). Open as available, and by appt. General shipping furniture. Paintings, particularly 19thC landscapes.

Bath STD 0225

Abbey Galleries
(C.Dickson). 9 Abbey Churchyard, BA1 1LY. Tel 60565. Open Mon-Sat 10.30-5; other times by appt. Antique jewellery & Chinese works of art.

Alderson & Alderson
23 Brock St. Tel 21652. Open Mon-Sat 9.30-1, 2-5.30; other times by appt. 18thC and Regency furniture and accessories. BADA

Aldridges of Bath
The Auction Galleries, 130-132 Walcot St. Tel 62830, 62839. Auctioneers of art and antiques.

Antique Interiors
Great Western Antique Centre, 50-52 Bartlett St, BA1 5HR. Tel Bradford-on-Avon (02216) 4717. Open Mon-Fri 9.30-5; Sat 9.30-5.30. 18th and 19thC furniture, decorative items, oils and watercolours.

Arts of Living Gallery
18 Green St. Tel 64270. Open Mon-Sat 10-5.30. 1000 sq ft of fine and antique Oriental rugs.

Aspidistra
(J.T.Waggoner). 46 St James Parade. Tel 61948. Open Mon-Sat 10.30-5; other times by appt. Interesting stock of general antiques, prints and books, old music & musical instruments.

C.G. Baker
Forester Rd, BA2 6QE. Tel 64095. Modern first editions, private presses illustrated books and typography. ABA

Bartlett Street Antique Market
7-10 Bartlett St. Tel (office) 66689. Open Mon-Sat 9.30-5, Wed 8-5. (Stallholders Tel:310457 & 330267). Over 50 dealers selling a wide variety of antiques and collector's items.

Bath Antique Market
(Mrs Mary Johnson). Guinea Lane, Lansdown Rd. Tel 858467, 60909. Open Wed 7-3. Indoor market with 90 stalls and restaurant.

Bath Galleries
33 Broad St, BA1 5LP. Tel 62946. Open Mon-Sat 9.30-5; other times by appt. Derby porcelain, Wedgwood and Chinese ware, jewellery, silver, furniture and pictures.

Bath Saturday Antique Market
Walcot St. Tel 317837, 858467. An open market of 50 stalls for antiques, bric a brac, secondhands.

Bath Stamp & Coin Shop
(J.H. & E.A. Swindells). Pulteney Bridge. Tel 63073. Open Mon-Sat 9-5.30. Stamps, coins, postcards, medals, medallions and all necessary collectors' accessories. We also run Pulteney Auctions,which are held six times a year, and include all collectables. PTS, BNTA

George Bayntun
(C.M. & H.H. Bayntun-Coward). Manvers St, BA1 1JW. Tel 66000. Open Mon-Fri 9-1, 2.15-5.30; other times by appt. Good stock of fine bindings and rare books. ABA

Beaux Arts Ceramics
(Reg and Patricia Singh). 13 York St, BA1 1NG. Tel 64850. Studio ceramics. ICGA

Blyth Antiques
(Brian and Sylvia Blyth). 28 Sydney Buildings, BA2 6BZ. Tel 69766. Open by appt. 18thC yew-tree and fruitwood furniture, fine 18thC samplers and English domestic brass.

J. Brett
The Old Malthouse, 7A Angelo Terrace, Walcot. Open Mon-Sat 10-5. Antique curios and bygones.

David Bridgwater
14 Fountain Buildings, Lansdown Road. Tel 63652. Open 9.30-5.30, early closing Thurs; other times by appt. Eclectic stock, architectural antiques, pine and marble fireplaces, garden ornaments, bathroom fittings, stained glass, mirrors and other decorative items.

Bryers Antiques
(Sheila Haines and Peter Bryers). 12A Manvers St. Tel 60535, 66352. Open 10-6; other times by appt. Silver and silver plate. Interesting and decorative furniture, glass, ceramics, metalware and unusual items of quality.

Coexistence
(Mary Wiggin). 10 Argyle Street. Tel 61507 (priv 314846). (Also in London.) Open Mon-Sat, 10-6; other times by appt. Country furniture, textiles.

Robin and Jan Coleman Antiques
27B Belvedere, Lansdown. Tel 316216. Open 9-6; early closing Sat. Range of decorative items, from period pieces to primitive paintings and exotic paraphernalia.

Colleton House Gallery
(Mym and Richard Biddle). 8a Quiet St, BA1 2JU. Tel 28806. Open Mon-Sat 10-6; other times by appt. Mid-17th to mid-19thC oils and watercolours for collectors and investors; bronzes; decorative French furniture. Flower paintings and transport art as additional specialities.

Brian & Caroline Craik Ltd
(Brian Craik, Caroline Craik). 8 Margaret's Buildings, Brock St, BA1 2LP. Tel 337161. Open daily 9.15-5.30; other times by appt. Decorative items, metalware of all descriptions, furniture (mainly 19thC) and architectural items. LAPADA

Crawford-Holden
(Mr and Mrs Crawford-Holden). 1-3, Palace Yard Mews. Tel 335338 (eves 079371 310). Open by appointment. 18th and early 19thC English and Continental furniture and mirrors.

John Croft Antiques
(John Croft). 3 George St, BA1 2EH. Tel 66211. Open Mon-Sat 9.30-5.30; other times by appt. 17th to 19thC furniture, clocks, paintings and objets d'art. LAPADA

Andrew Dando
(Gordon A.Dando). 4 Wood St, Queen Sq, BA1 2JQ. Tel 22702. Open Mon-Fri 9.30-5.30, Sat 10-1. Specialist in 18th and early 19thC English, Chinese and Continental porcelain. Large stock of porcelain and pottery; antique furniture and general antiques. Valuations. BADA

Michael Danny
The Manor House, Wellow. Tel Combe Down (0225) 832027. Open any time by appt. Fine English watercolours.

Gerald Deacon
2 Wood St, Queen Sq, BA1 2JQ. Tel 25907. Open 10-5, Sat 10-1; other times by appt. 18th and 19thC furniture and antique porcelain of most factories. Mirrors and small decorative objects. BADA

Devonshire House Antiques
143 Wellsway. Tel 312495. Open Mon-Fri 10-5.30; other times by appt. General antiques.

D. & B. Dickinson
22 & 22A New Bond St, BA1 1BA. Tel 66502. Open Tues-Fri 9.30-1, 2.15-5, Sat 9.30-1; other times by appt. Antique silver, old Sheffield plate and jewellery. BADA

Dollin & Daines Ltd
2 Church St, York St. Tel 62752. Musical instruments. Valuations. BADA

Brian & Angela Downes Antiques
(Brian & Angela Downes). 9 Broad St, BA1 5LJ. Tel 65352. Open Mon-Sat 9-5.30. 18th and 19thC furniture, mahogany, walnut & rosewood, mirrors, clocks, metalware, decorators items. Also a large stock of fine early 19thC porcelain 1800-1840. LAPADA

Focol Photography
(P.E. Skeffington). 7 The Corridor, BA1 5AP. Tel 66343. Open Mon-Sat 9-5.30; closed Thurs; other times by appt. Photographers.

Gene & Sally Foster (Antiques)
(Gene & Sally Foster). 27A Belvedere, Lansdown Rd, BA1 5HR. Tel 28256 (priv 28058). Open Mon-Fri 9-6;Sat 9-1;closed Thurs; other times by appt. Decorative antiques, country furniture, primitive paintings, needlework, painted furniture, folk art.

Fotowest
(Gary Brothers, LBIPP, LRPS). 19 Westgate St, BA1 1EQ. Tel 63195. Open Mon-Sat 9.30-5.30; 24hr answering service; other times by appt. Industrial and commercial photographers specialising in photographing furniture and objets d'art.

Simon and Claire Freeman Antiques
27B Belvedere, Lansdown, BA1 5HR. Tel 316216. Open 9-5.30; early closing Sat; other times by appt. Highly decorative items of humour and interest for local and overseas tastes.

G.C.W.Antiques
(G.C.Withers). 2 Lower East Hayes, London Rd. Tel 334228 (priv 66497). Open Mon-Sat 10-6; other times by appt. Furniture, porcelain and curios.

Sven Gahlin
Tel 313032. Open by appt only. Indian and Persian miniature paintings.

Brian and Angela Downes Antiques

9 BROAD STREET
BATH, AVON BA1 5LJ
Telephone BATH (0225) 65352

Old Established Firm
Valuations for Probate and Insurance

We carry a Large Stock of 18th, 19th century Furniture, early 19th century English Porcelain. Also Metalware and Items for the Interior Decorator.

A worthwhile call when you visit this area.

George III mahogany bow front chest, upon which stands a fine pair of Minton vases, c.1860

JOHN CROFT ANTIQUES

Fine 18th and early 19th century
Furniture
Decorative Objects

3 GEORGE STREET, BATH BA1 2EH
Tel. 0225 66211

T. E. ROBINSON ANTIQUE DEALER

Member of the BADA

Interesting collection of period furniture, old drinking glasses, unusual and rare items

3 & 4 BARTLETT STREET, BATH BA1 2QZ
Tel 0225-63982 Close to the Assembly Rooms

Somervale Antiques

Wing Cdr. R. G. Thomas M.B.E. R.A.F. (Ret'd)

6 Radstock Road,
Midsomer Norton,
Bath, BA3 2AJ.
Tel: (STD 0761)
Midsomer Norton 412686

SHOP OPEN ONLY BY APPOINTMENT

Resident on premises

TRAINS TO BATH MET BY ARRANGEMENT

24 hour telephone service

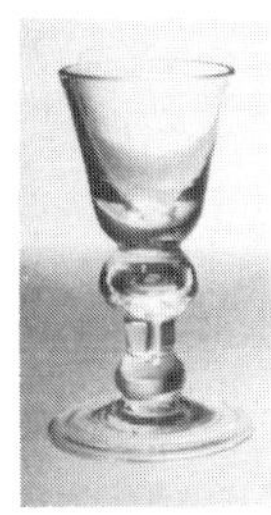

Specialist in 18th and early 19th century English drinking glasses, decanters, cut and coloured Bristol and Nailsea glass, etc. Also bijouterie, scent bottles etc.

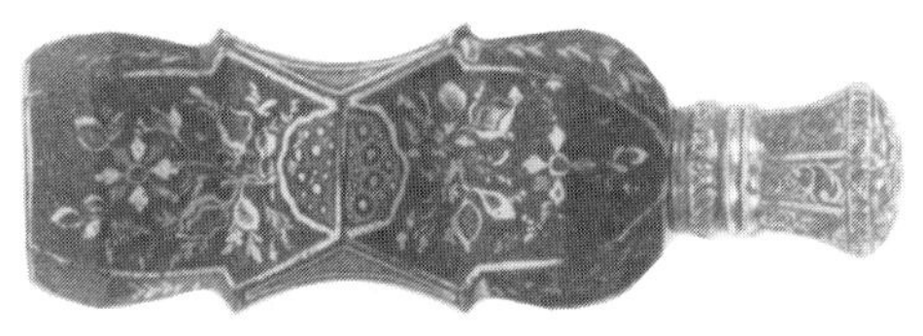

Member of the British Antique Dealers' Association
Member of the London and Provincial Antique Dealers' Association

The Galleon
(David L.Gwilliam, Michael J.Wren). 33 Monmouth St, BA1 2AN. Tel 312330. Open Mon-Fri 10-5.30, Sat 10-6; other times by appt. Jewellery, silver, china, copper, brass, small furniture, small collectables and general antiques.

Valentine Gould
33 Belvedere, BA1 5HR. Tel 312367. Open Mon-Sat 9-5.30. Furniture, paintings, metalwork, bygones and decorations.

Great Western Antique Centre Ltd
(J.R. & E.J. Capstick-Dale). Bartlett St, BA1 2QZ. Tel (office) 24243. (Tel (stallholders): 20686, 310388, 28731.) Open Mon-Sat 9.30-5; one-day market 7.30-4.30 every Wed. Furniture, porcelain and pottery, watches and clocks, jewellery, paintings & prints, toys, buttons, costumes and accessories, copper & brass, fine inlaid boxes, photographica, radio and gramophones, postcards & stamps, dolls, commemorative china etc.

George Gregory
(H.Bayntun-Coward). Manvers St, BA1 1JW. Tel 66055. Old books, maps, prints. ABA

Helena Hood and Co
(Lynette Hood). 3 Margarets Buildings, Brock St, BA1 2LP. Tel 24438. Open Tues-Fri 9.30-5.30; Sat 10-1. Antique dealer and interior decorator. Specialist in silk pictures, creamware and decorative furniture.

M.A.& D.A.Hughes
(Mrs D.A.Hughes). 11 Pulteney Bridge. Tel 65782. Silver, jewellery. LAPADA

Images Antiques
4 Cleveland Terrace, London Rd. Tel 26806. Open Mon-Sat 9.30-5; closed Thurs; other times by appt. Victorian and Edwardian furniture, clocks, china and metalware.

Jadis Ltd
(N.A.Mackay, J.B.Creese-Parsons). The Old Bank, 17 Walcot Buildings, London Rd. Tel 338797. Open Mon-Sat 9.30-6; other times by appt. English & Continental country furniture, decorative items and painted furniture.

John Keil Ltd
10 Quiet St, BA1 2JU. Tel 63176. Open Mon-Fri 10.30-1; Sat 2.30-4.30. 17th to early 19thC furniture, also metalware and objects. BADA

Kimono
(Mrs Katie Page). 4 Belvedere, Lansdown Rd, BS8 5ED. Tel 315987. Open Mon-Sat; closed Thurs; other times by appt. Antique and vintage clothes; Oriental robes and embroideries.

Ann King
38 Belvedere, Lansdowne Rd. Tel 336245 (priv 0373 864747). Open Mon-Sat 11-4; closed Thurs; other times by appt. Antique and pre 1950 clothes, linen and lace.

Lansdown Antiques
(Christopher and Ann Kemp). 23 Belvedere, Lansdown Rd, BA1 5ED. Tel 313417. Open Mon-Sat 9-6; Tues till 8 pm; closed Thurs; other times by appt. 17th to 19thC furniture, metalware and decorative items.

Lantern Gallery
(Anne Campbell Macinnes). 9 George St, BA1 2EH. Tel 63727. Open Mon-Fri 9.30-5.30; Sat 10-4.30; other times by appt. Old decorative, botanical & natural history prints. Local topography. BADA

Mac Humble Antiques
(William McAdam Humble, Barbara Jean Humble). 11 Queen St, BA1 2Jo. Tel 62751 (priv 022122 3594). Open Mon-Sat 9.30-5.30; other times by appt. 17th-19thC furniture, metalware, treen, samplers & needlework, decorative objects. BADA

E.P.Mallory & Son Ltd
1-4 Bridge St, BA2 4AP. Tel 65885. (Also at 5 Old Bond St, Bath.) Open Mon-Fri 9-5, Sat 9-1. Antique silver and Sheffield plate, clocks and jewellery. BADA CINOA

Mendip Antiques
(W.G.Selwyn & J.V.M.Selwyn). Great Western Antiques Centre, Bartlett St. Tel 310388. Open Mon-Sat 9.30-5. 18th and 19thC furniture in mahogany, rosewood and walnut, in good clean condition, silver collectors' pieces. LAPADA

Nash Antiques
10 Fountain Buildings, Lansdown Rd. Tel 313584. Open Mon-Sat 9.30-6. English furniture, European and Oriental porcelain, including good stock of Regency furniture.

Nevill Gallery
2A York St, BA1 1NG. Tel 66904. (Also at 43 St Peter's St, Canterbury, Kent.) Contemporary paintings, watercolours and prints by well known British artists.

David & Penny Newlove Antiques
70/71/102 Gt Western Antique Centre, Bartlett St. Tel 28731 & 310388. (Also in Bruton and Wincanton, Somerset.) Open Mon-Sat 9.30-5. Mahogany, oak and walnut furniture and stripped and well-finished pine. Also clocks, silver and plate, general small antiques.

No.Twelve Queen Street
(Carole Roberts, Keith Stables). 12 Queen St. Tel 62363 (priv 314846). Open Mon-Sat 9.30-5.30; other times by appt. Oak and country furniture, 17th - early 19thC, textiles, needlework, silk pictures, samplers, period brass, painted furniture, decorative objects. Interior decoration and design service.

The Old Curiosity Shop
(V.Lewis & L.R.Lewis). 33 Walcot St. Tel 60974. Open Tues 2-5, Wed and Sat 10-5. Jewellery and small items.

Oriental Antiques
(Francis Page). 4 Belvedere, Lansdown Rd. Tel 315987. Open Mon-Sat 10-5; closed Thurs; other times by appt. Oriental ivories, carvings, hardstones, porcelain, costume & embroideries.

Paragon Antiques Market
3 Bladud Buildings, The Paragon. Open Weds.

Richard Parker Ltd
(C.R.J. Parker, J.R.J. Parker & D.C.A. Parker). Trim Bridge, 1 Queen St, BA1 1HE. Tel 330257 (priv 330585). Open Mon-Sat 9.30-6; other times by appt. 17th-19thC furniture, objets d'art. BADA

Phillips & Jollys
(Phillips, Son & Neale). 1 Old King St, BA1 1DD. Tel 310609/310709. Open Mon-Fri 8.30-5; Sat 9-12. Auctioneers. SOFAA

Piccadilly Antiques
(Stuart King). 1/2 Piccadilly, London Rd, BA1 6AN. Tel 332779. Open 10-5.30; other times by appt. Folk art, country furniture and allied accessories. Painted pine in the American taste, samplers, trade signs etc, all with naive accent.

Pineapple
(Norman Kemp). Fountain Buildings, Lansdown Rd, BA1 2JQ. Tel 65223. Open 9-6; other times by appt. Good country furniture, decorative items. Also design and manufacture of large architectural bookcases and dressers.

Mark J.Poole
3 Percy Place. Tel 317957. Specialist in unusual English silver, Sheffield and electroplate.

Queens Parade Antiques
(E.A.Quinton (BADA), S.Isbell). 35 Gay St. Tel 20337. Open Mon-Fri 9.30-5.30; Sat 9.30-5. 18th and early 19thC English furniture, decorative objects, architectural items and paintings.

Quiet Street Antiques
(R. Windebank & K. Hastings-Spital). 3 Quiet St. Tel 315727 (priv 332399). Open Mon-Sat 10-6; other times by appt. English furniture, clocks especially carriage and longcase, mirrors, bronzes, boxes and decorative items including brass candlesticks. BHI

Ernest Quinton Antiques
7 Princes Buildings, George St, BA1 2ED. Tel 66309. Furniture. BADA

T.E.Robinson Antiques
(Thomas Ernest Robinson). 3A 3 & 4 Bartlett St, BA1 2QZ. Tel 63982 (priv 832307). Open Mon-Sat 9.30-6; other times by appt. Good period furniture from the 17thC to the early 19thC, drinking glasses and other glass ware, a variety of other period and decorative objects. Some silver. BADA

Sheila Smith Antiques
10A Queen St. Tel 60568 (priv 0373 830217). Open Mon-Sat 11.30-6; other times by appt. Specialist in fans, needlework tools and accessories, period glass and treen. Wide variety of fans always in stock. LAPADA

St James's Gallery
(Ron and Susan Sloman). 9 Margarets Building, BA1 2LP. Tel 319197. Studio ceramics. ICGA

Trim Bridge Galleries
2 Trim Bridge. Tel 66390. Open Mon-Sat 9.30-5.30; closed Thurs. 18th and 19thC watercolours and drawings, some oils and 18thC prints.

Walcot Reclamation
(Richard Knapp, David Bridgwater, Marcus Olliff). 108 Walcot St, BA1 5BG. Tel 66291/2. Open Mon-Sat 9-5.30. Architectural antiques, including period bathrooms, fireplaces, marble, stone & pine chimney pieces, doors, garden statuary. Also traditional roofing, timber, ironwork, gates, railings, paving, decorative stonework, chimney pots etc.

Derek & Glenda Wallis
6 Chapel Row, Queen Sq. Tel 24677. Open Mon-Sat 10-5.30; other times by appt. Antiquarian and secondhand books, especially children's and illustrated books. ABA

Widcombe Antiques
(Mrs J.Winter, Mrs C.Wix, Mr M.Winter). 8-9 Claverton Buildings, Widcombe. Tel 28767. Open Mon-Sat 10.30-5.30; other times by appt. Period stripped pine and old brass and copper.

Robert Wilkes Antiques
(Robert Wilkes). 2 Lansdown Rd, BA1 5EE. Tel 315860. Open Mon 6pm-9pm; Tues 8am-9pm; Wed 8am-6pm; other times by appt. A wide variety of general stock including many small items.

G.C.Withers Antiques
The Grange, Bathampton, BA2 6SY. Tel 334228. Open 10-5; other times by appt. General stock of antique furniture and small items. Accommodation and courier service available.

Woodbridge
(C.F.Rogers, N.S.Woodbridge). 15A George St, BA1 2EN. Open Tues, Wed, Fri 10-5. 18th and 19thC paintings, watercolours and works of art. Special interest in topographical works, marine paintings, artefacts, naive and primitive works of all subjects.

Bristol STD 0272

Abbas Combe Pine
(Ian Robert Sinnott). 4 Upper Maudlin St, BS2. Tel 299023. Open Mon-Sat 10-6; other times by appt. Period & Victorian pine country furniture. Also reproductions in old pine and oak. Stripping and restoration work undertaken. Large selection of clocks, Dinky & tin toys, wine accessories, decanters, corkscrews etc. Large selection of Devon pottery.

Affordable Arts
(Nicholas Hankinson, Moira Hankinson). 76 Colston St, BS1 5BB. Tel 24838. Open Tues-Sat 10-6; other times by appt. English watercolours circa 1790-1950, contemporary printed & original work by West Country artists. Picture framing service available.

Antiques & Crafts Market
(Market Superintendent, M.L. Watkins). The Exchange, Corn St, BS1 1JQ. Tel 20021. Open daily 9-4; Office 9-5. 50 traders dealing in a variety of antiques and bric-a-brac. Now part of a 6 day miscellaneous market with snack bars etc.

Bellevue
(A.J.Colley). 48 Alpha Rd, Southville, BS3 1DH. Tel 662010. Open Mon-Sat but telephone first. Small furniture, brass, copper, collectors items, musical boxes. Specialist in restoration of cylinder musical boxes.

Blantern & Davis
(Ian Blantern ABIPP). 11 Wetherell Place, Clifton, BS8 1AR. Tel 741747. Photographers. BIPP

Blatchpack Ltd
22-24 Smyth Rd, Ashton. Tel 665996. Shippers.

The Bristol Gallery
12 Princess Victoria St, Clifton. Tel 734134. Open by appt only. The works of the late Jack Hartert, removed from his studio. No other works.

Robin Butler
9 St Stephen's St, BS1. Tel 276586 (priv 662167). Open Mon-Fri 9.30-5.30; Sat 10-4. Period furniture, silver, bygones and wine related antiques. BADA

Carnival Antiques
(A.J.Williams). Griffen Court, 19 Lower Park Row, BS1 5BN. Tel 297754. Furniture, glass, china, metalware. LAPADA

Clifton Antiques Ltd
12-13 Waterloo St, Clifton. Tel 36038. Open Mon-Sat 9.30-6; other times by appt. Large stock of furniture and general antiques, shipping goods, clocks and smalls. Trade warehouse by appt.

Clifton Antiques Market
(A.J.S.Begbie & M.W. Stein). 26-28 The Mall, Clifton, BS8. Tel 741627 734531 738504. Open Tues-Sat 10-6. Sixty antique dealers under one roof showing antiques and collectors items. Restoration workshops. Coffee lounge.

Derek Cornwell
(D.M. Cornwell). 14 The Mall, Clifton, BS8 4DR. Tel 743765 (priv 735493). Open Tues-Sat 10.30-5.30; appt advisable. 18th and early 19thC English furniture, works of art, silver and oil paintings.

Cotham Books
59A Cotham Hill, Cotham. Tel 732344.

Cotham Galleries
(David Jury). 22 Cotham Hill, Cotham, BS6 6LF. Tel 736026 (priv 687393). Open Mon-Fri 9.30-5.30; Sat 9.30-12.30. Furniture, jewellery, glass, silver and general antiques.

Cotham Hill Antiques
(David Hudson). 18 Cotham Hill, BS6 6LF. Tel 744033. Open Mon-Sat 9.30-5.30; other times by appt. Furniture, rugs, decorative & general antiques, Art Nouveau, Art Deco and modernist objects.

Cottage Antiques
(Margaret M.Hind). The Old Post Office, Langford, BS18 7BP. Tel Wrighton (0934) 862597. Open Mon-Sat 10-6; other times by appt. (200 yards west of A38, Lower Langford turn, 11 miles south of Bristol.) Specialists in brass and copper, including kitchen equipment. Early oak and country furniture, ironwork and treen.

David Cross Gallery
(David Cross). 3A Boyces Ave, Clifton, BS8 4AA. Tel 732614. Open Mon-Fri 9.30-6; Sat 9.30-5.30. Paintings, drawings and prints. British topographical, landscape, marine and sporting art. Craftsmen framers and restoration adjoining premises.

An Englishman's Home
(Andre & Rose Busek). 56 Stokes Croft. Tel 424257. (Also Architectural Antiques, New Rd, South Molton,Devon.) Open Mon-Sat 9-6; other times by appt. Specialising in marble & wooden surrounds, highly decorative items for interior designers.

Richard Essex
(Richard Essex). 41 Alma Vale Rd, BS8 2HL. Tel 733949. Open Mon-Fri 10-5.30; other times by appt. 18th and 19thC furniture, china, glass, and decorative items.

Wm.George's Sons Ltd
89 Park St, BS1 5PW. Tel 276602. Open Mon-Sat 9-5.30. Large and general stock of new, secondhand and antiquarian books, especially topography. ABA

Grey-Harris & Co
12 Princess Victoria St, Clifton. Tel 737365. Open Mon-Sat 9.30-5.30. Jewellery, silver, Sheffield plate and watches. BADA

P.G. Kydd
(P.G.Kydd). 70 Colston St, BS1 5AZ. Tel 299265. Open Mon-Sat 9.30-5.30; other times by appt. Pewter, brass, iron & silver. Also restoration of these materials.

Lalonde Bros & Parham
(Fine Art Dept). 71 Oakfield Road, Clifton, BS8 2BE. Tel 734052. (Also at Station Rd, Weston-super-Mare. (Tel 0934-33174.) Fortnightly auctions of Victorian and later furniture and objects. Specialist and fine art sales every two months.

Michael and Amanda Lewis Oriental Carpets and Rugs
23 Small St, BS1 1DW. Tel 264246. (Also at 8 North St, Wellington, Somerset.) Open Tues-Fri 10-5.30; other times by appt. Oriental & European carpets and rugs, antique, old and new, bought and sold. Valuations, commission sales and purchases executed. Specialist restorations, repairs and cleaning on the premises. Hanging, mounting, framing etc.

Susan Liddiard Antiques
(Susan Liddiard). Lodway Croft, Pill. Tel 2315. Open Thurs, Fri, Sat 10-5; other times by appt. (1 mile from Junction 19, M5) Victorian and Edwardian furniture, smalls.

The Old Lantern
(I.T.M.W.&E.M.Cox). 20 Cotham Hill, BS6 6LF. Tel 734397. Open Mon-Sat 10.30-6.30. Silver, glass, china, clocks, watches and antique jewellery. LAPADA

The Oriental Carpet Centre
Maples, 3 Queens Rd, Clifton, BS8 1QS. Tel 290165. Open Mon-Sat 9-5.30; Thurs 9.30-5.30. Oriental carpets & rugs.

Osmond Tricks
Regent St Auction Rooms, Regent St, Clifton, BS8 4HG. Tel 737201. Monthly auctions of antiques & objets d'art. Specialist auctions throughout the year, fortnightly auctions of Victorian & general household furniture & effects. Auction calendar available on request.

Pelter/Sands Fine Paintings
(R.J.Pelter, S.R.Sands, A.R.Bush). 19 The Mall, Clifton, BS8 4JG. Tel 741830. Open Mon-Fri 10-1 2-5, Sat 10-1; other times by appt. 18th, 19th and 20thC oil paintings and watercolours, specialising in landscapes.

Potters - Colston Street Antiques
(Brian C Potter). 60 Colston Street. Tel 22551. Open Mon-Sat 10.30-5.30; other times by appt. Brass, copper, commemoratives, coins, small furniture & antiquities.

Leigh Rice Antiques
(L.F.Bentham-Rice). 29 The Mall, Clifton. Tel 730975. 18th & 19thC English furniture, interior furnishings, valuations. LAPADA

S. & S. TIMMS ANTIQUES LTD

(LAPADA MEMBER)

Over 1,500 sq. feet of pre-1880 Furniture for the Trade and Private Buyer

Including

Queen Anne Walnut
Mahogany
Oak and Yewwood
Victorian Walnut
and some Inlaid Furniture

OPENING HOURS

Monday–Friday
9 am–6 pm

Saturday
10 am–4 pm

Any other time by appointment ring Sue or Steve on

0525–403067

(resident on premises)

16–20 DUNSTABLE STREET · AMPTHILL · BEDFORDSHIRE

Michael Danny

English Watercolours

Frederick Augustus Sandys 1829–1904
Binham Priory, Norfolk
Pencil and Watercolour, $6\frac{1}{4}$ × 14 inches

The Manor House, Wellow, Bath
Telephone 0225 832027

Open at any time by appointment

The Collectors Gallery

SPECIALISTS in 18th and 19th CENTURY FINE ART PAINTINGS

'ARTISTS STUDIO'
Signed R. Craeyvanger 1866.
Watercolour 18″ × 21″

Come and see our extensive selection of paintings at:-

8 Bridge Street
Caversham, Reading, Berkshire
Telephone: (0734) 483663

John Roberts Bookshop
43 Triangle West, Clifton, BS8 1ES. Tel 28568. Open Mon-Sat 9-5.30. General literature, natural history and topography. Specialists in antiquarian topographical prints to the trade.

Ruskin's
(Louis M.Raskino). 426-428 Wells Rd, BS14 9AL. Tel 776456. Silver and art pottery.

Taviners
Prewett St, Redcliffe. Tel 25996. Auctioneers.

Triangle Antiques
9 Byron Place, Clifton, BS8 1JT. Tel 292502. Open Mon-Sat 10-5.30. Stock of general antiques.

West of England Restoration Studio
(Richard Pelter, S.R.Sands). 19-21 The Mall, Clifton, BS8 4JG. Tel 741830. Restorers and conservators of paintings and murals.

Christopher Wray's Lighting Emporium
62 Park St. Tel 278537. (Main branch in London.) Decorative lighting of the 1880s. Victorian and Edwardian lamps.

Clevedon STD 0272

Folio (Clevedon Books & Clevedon Fine Arts)
(G. & W.E.C. Douthwaite). The Gallery, Cinema Buildings, Old Church Rd, BS21 6NN. Tel 875862 (priv 872304). Open 6 days 11-5.30 (open 10 Sat); other times by appt. Antique maps, antiquarian books, decorative and antique prints, secondhand books, etchings.

Hoddell Pritchard
Clevedon Salerooms, Six Ways, BS21 7NT. Tel 876699. Fine art auctioneers and valuers.

Clutton

Ian McCarthy
Arcadian Cottage, 112 Station Rd. Tel Temple Cloud (0761) 53188. Open anytime - subject only to availability. Antique and decorative lamps of all types. Restoration of lamps and metalware. Lamp spares and shades.

Hinton Charterhouse

Raphael at Homewood Park
Homewood Park. Tel Limpley Stoke (022 122) 3586. Open by appt any time. 17th and 18thC Continental furniture, English Regency furniture, clocks and decorative items.

Midsomer Norton STD 0761

Somervale Antiques
(Wing Commander R.G.Thomas MBE, RAF retd). 6 Radstock Rd, BA3 2AJ. Tel 412686. (Situated on A362 between Midsomer Norton & Radstock.) Open by appt only, (res on prem); 24 hr telephone service. (Trains to Bath met by arrangement). Specialist in all types of English 18th and early 19thC glass including drinking glasses, decanters, cut and coloured Nailsea and Bristol glass. Also bijouterie, glass scent bottles. BADA CINOA LAPADA

Thornbury STD 0454

Thornbury Antique Framers and Restorers
(James Liddiard). 32 High St, BS12 2A. Tel 413595. Open Mon-Sat 10-5.30; Thurs 10-1; other times by appt. Small antique furniture, prints and framing materials. Restoration of small antique furniture. Framing of pictures.

Weston-super-Mare STD 0934

Harwood Westend Antiques
(Anthony Harwood). 13 West St, BS23 1JR. Tel 29874 (priv 24992). Open Mon-Sat 9-5; half day Thurs; other times by appt. General antiques and militaria jewellery. LAPADA

Sterling Books
(D.Nisbet). 43A Locking Rd, BS23 3DG. Tel 25056. Open Mon-Sat 9-6; closed 1-2; early closing Thurs; other times by appt. Antiquarian & secondhand books on all subjects, especially travel & topography at home & abroad, leather bindings, bibles & prayer books and books for the collector. ABA

Winters' Antiques
(R.N. & L.Winters). (Trade and Export Warehouse), 62 Severn Rd. Tel 20118 (priv 814610). Open 9-12, 2-4; closed Thurs and Sat pm; other times by appt. LAPADA

Wrington STD 0934

Sir William Russell Flint Galleries
Georgian House, Broad St, BS18 7LA. Tel 863149. (Also at Michael Stewart Fine Art, Guildford, Surrey.) Open Mon-Fri 9-5; other times by appt. Books, signed proofs, limited editions, watercolours and engravings by the artist.

Wrington Antiques
Tanners, BS18 7QQ. Tel 862200. Open Mon-Sat 10-6; other times by appt. (A38, 12 miles from Bristol.) Country furniture and pieces, some Victoriana.

Yatton STD 0934

Glenville Antiques
120 High St, BS19 4DH. Tel 832284. Open Mon-Sat 10.30-1, 2.15-5; other times by appt. Victorian glass, porcelain, small furniture, silver, jewellery. LAPADA

Bedfordshire

Ampthill STD 0525

Ampthill Antiques Centre
(Alex Olney). Market Square. Tel 403344. Open daily 10-5.30 except Monday. General stock including antique & pine furniture, bric-a-brac, jewellery.

Ampthill Emporium
6 Bedford St. Tel 402131. Open every day 10-5. Large selection of old and antique furniture and small items displayed on two floors.

Pat Bently Antiques
7 King's Arms Yard. Tel 404939. Open Tues-Sat 11-5; Sun 2-5. Antique and shipping furniture, especially pine. Also small items. Displayed in shop and large barns.

Robert Harman Antiques
11 Church St. Tel 402322. Fine 18th and early 19thC furniture.

Thistledome Antiques
Kings Arms Yard, MK45. Tel 403394 (priv 717368). Open Tues-Sat 11-4.30; Sun 2-5. Antiques up to 1940s, furniture, brass & copper, specialising in fenders, fireirons, cast iron etc. firebaskets, firetools.

S. & S. Timms Antiques Ltd
(Stephen Timms & Mrs. Susan Timms). 16,18,20 Dunstable St, MK45 2JT. Tel 403067. Open Mon-Fri 9-6; after hours ring bell; weekends by appt. All furniture 1700-1900. New large showrooms now open. LAPADA

Tricia Timms Antiques
82A Dunstable St. Tel 403030. Open every day 9-6. Antique and shipping furniture and small collectables.

Yesterday's Pine
(Neville E. Chesters). 13 Dunstable St. Tel 402260. Open Wed-Sat 10-6, Sun 2-6; other times by appt. Head Office and Workshop: The Old Chapel, Leighton St, Woburn, Beds, Tel Woburn 536. Another showroom at 61 High St, Berkhamsted, Herts. Tue-Sat 10-6, Sun 2-6. Stripped pine furniture, kitchenalia, decorative ceramics. Hand-made furniture from old pine.

Bedford STD 0234

Christine Barratt Antiques
84 Bromham Rd.

The Bazaar
(F.A. Doyle). 96 High Street. Tel 54957 (priv 56933). Open Mon-Sat 9.30-5.30; closed Thurs. Jewellery, silver, furniture, brass, clocks etc.

Foster Hill Road Antiques Centre
(R.H.Tingey). 84-84A Foster Hill Rd, MK40 2ET. Tel 53318. Open Mon-Sat 10.30-7.30; Sun 11.30-2.30 by appt. General antiques.

Greenfield

Mary Collins Furniture Ltd
Unit 8, Sinclair Estate, Pulloxhill Rd. Tel Ampthill (0525) 717555. Open Mon-Sat 10-5. Warehouse with an extensive stock of Victorian and pre 1920s furniture, particularly oak. Also reproduction furniture and fitted kitchens.

Haynes STD 023 066

Gatward Fine Arts
(G.B.& L.M.Pheazey). 50 Northwood End Rd, MK45 3PT. Tel Hitchin (0462) 33759(priv 023066 348). Open by appt. Mainly 19thC watercolours, some early 20thC, antique maps & some oils. FATG

Hagen (Restorations)
(Richard & Ann Hagen). Bakehouse Cottage, Northwood End Rd, MK45 3QD. Tel 424. Open usually, res on prem. Specialists in woodworm treatment and conservation, repair and restoration of antique furniture, non-structural woodwork, metalwork and pictures. Painted furniture also restored. UKIC

Heath and Reach STD 052 523

Charterhouse Antiques
(Mrs S.Berkeley). 14 Bird's Hill. Tel 532 379. Open daily, except Thurs, 9.30-5.30; other times by appt. General antique furniture and metalwares. Metal restoration undertaken on the premises.

Woburn Abbey Antiques Centre

One of the largest Antiques Centres under one roof in England, with 50 independent shops and showcases with established dealers, some of whom are members of B.A.D.A. and L.A.P.A.D.A., is situated in the magnificent South Court of Woburn Abbey.

We are pleased to offer the dealer and private collector a wide range of Antiques: Clocks, Porcelain and Glass, Paintings, Prints, Furniture, Silver, Works of Art, Painted Furniture, Jewellery, Objets d'Art and Kitchenalia, at competitive prices.

One of the streets on the ground floor

Within one hour's drive of London, via M1, Exit 12 (signposted Woburn Abbey). Trains from St. Pancras to Flitwick can be met by prior arrangement. Dealers admitted free and their park entrance refunded at the Antiques Centre. Visiting dealers' car park adjacent to the Antiques Centre.

OPEN EVERY DAY OF THE YEAR including Sundays and Bank Holidays. Closed for Christmas 25th–26th December inclusive.
Easter to October 10–6pm.
November to Easter 11–5pm

An interior of one of the shops on the first floor

WOBURN ABBEY ANTIQUES CENTRE, WOBURN ABBEY BEDFORDSHIRE MK43 0TP. Telephone Woburn (052525) 350.

Helton Antiques
26A Birds Hill. Tel 474. Open Mon-Sat 10-6; Sun 2-6. Good quality furniture and general antiques.

Luton STD 0582

David Ball Antiques
(David Ball). 126A Leagrave Rd, LU4 8HX. Tel 417560 (priv 0525-210753). (Also at 6-8 Bridge St, Leighton Buzzard:Tel 0525 38294.) Open Mon, Tues, Thurs, Fri; other times by appt. 18th-20thC furniture, clocks, barometers etc. Valuations. LAPADA

J.Denton (Antiques)
(Mrs J.Denton). Rear of 440 Dunstable Rd, (Corner Arundel Rd), LU4 8DT. Tel 582726. Open Mon-Fri 10-2.45; other times by appt. Shipping goods; Edwardian and Victorian furniture, glass, china, brassware, clocks and bric-a-brac.

Foye Gallery
15 Stanley St, LU1 5AL. Tel 38487. Open Mon-Sat 9.30-5; other times by appt. General stock of maps and topography, engravings, etchings, drawings, paintings and watercolours. Specialist in topography of Beds and Herts. Also small stock of antiquarian and secondhand books.

Leaside Antiques
(T.G. & M.W.R.Pepper). 44 Gordon St, LU1 2QP. Tel 27957. Open Mon-Sat 10-5; early closing Wed. Appt please. Jewellery, silver, furniture and china. LAPADA

The Old Pine Loft
Kingham Way, Reginald St. Tel 459001. Open Mon-Sat 9-5. Specialising in old & antique pine, old pine doors, pine stripping service. Sand blasting service for cast iron and metalwork.

Melchbourne

Peter Hempson
Melchbourne Park. Tel Riseley (023063) 8872. Open by appt only. Continental furniture and works of art.

Shefford

F. & M. Odell
35 & 37 High St. Tel 0462-813940. Open Mon-Sat 9-6. 18th and 19thC furniture, pictures, clocks etc. Probate and insurance valuations. Restorations.

Toddington STD 052 55

Cobblers Hall Antiques
(Bert & Noreen Huckett). 119-121 Leighton Rd, LU5 6AR. Tel 2890. Open by appt only. 18th and early 19thC pottery and porcelain, small 18th and 19thC silver. Georgian and Victorian boxes, also late Georgian & Regency glass.

Wilshamstead

Manor Antiques
(Mrs S. Bowen). The Manor House, Cottonend Rd, MK45 3BT. Tel Bedford (0234) 740262. Open Mon-Sat 10-5; other times by appt. Antique to Edwardian furniture, copper, brass, oil lamps, lighting and decorative items in seven showrooms.

Woburn STD 052 525

Atrium Antiques Ltd
(Mrs A.Fluitman). 19 Market Place, NK17 9PZ. Tel 444. Open Mon-Sat 9.30-5.45; Sun 2-5.45; other times by appt. Georgian furniture, early oak and stripped pine furniture. Decorative items such as lamps, rugs, paintings, prints, porcelain and maps.

Beacon Gallery
(Roy Chase). Woburn Abbey Antiques Centre, Woburn Abbey. Tel (priv) 062187-607. Antique silver and period furniture.

Christopher Sykes Antiques
(Christopher & Margaret Sykes). The Old Parsonage, Bedford St, MK17 9QL. Tel 259 (priv 467). Open Mon-Sat 9-6, Sun 11-6. Scientific, nautical and medical instruments, pottery, porcelain and early metalware. Illustrated 100 page catalogue of corkscrews & wine related antiques, £4 or US$10 sent air mail. BADA, LAPADA

Woburn Abbey Antiques Centre
Woburn Abbey, MK43 0TP. Tel 350. Open daily Easter to Oct, 10-6; Nov-Easter, 11-5. Fifty independent shops stocking a variety of antiques including clocks, porcelain and glass, paintings, prints, furniture, silver, painted furniture, works of art etc.

Woburn Fine Arts
(Zdzislaw Bieganski). 12 Market Place, MK17 9PZ. Tel 624. Open Mon-Fri 2-5.30 (Except Thur); Sat & Sun 11-5.30; other times by appt. Oil paintings, especially by Gaston Pierre Galey, Emile Bernard, Emanuel Levy, Alfred Daniels and George Large. Also watercolours, bronzes, sculptures, ivory carvings, and oriental fine arts.

Woburn Sands

See Buckinghamshire

Berkshire

Ascot STD 0990

Austin/Desmond Fine Art Ltd
Brookside Farm, Winkfield Row. Tel Winkfield Row (0344) 886147. 20thC British art.

Chancellors Hollingsworths
31 High St, SL5 7HG. Tel 27101. (Also at Westcombe House,56-58 Whitcomb St,London WC2.01-839 1875.) Open 9-5.30. Auctioneers holding auction sales of general antiques and all types of household contents; also quarterly specialist sales.

Caversham

The Collectors Gallery
8 Bridge St, Caversham Bridge. Tel Reading (0734) 483663.

Cookham

Phillips & Sons
(Jean & Peter Phillips). The Dower House, SL6 9SN. Tel Bourne End (06285) 29337. Open by appt only. Large selection of 19th and 20thC English paintings, particularly Staithes group.

Datchet

Manor House Antiques
(Mrs J.A.Gibbs). The Green. Tel Slough (0753) 42164 & 41460. 18th & 19thC furniture, Oriental porcelain, silver, plate. Valuations. Upholstery restoration. LAPADA

Charles & Jane Toller
20 High St, SL3 9EQ. Tel Windsor (0753) 42903. Open Mon-Sat 9.30-5; other times by appt. 17th and 18thC oak and fruitwood furniture; also fine treen, 18th and early 19thC samplers. BADA

Eton

Alden & Blackwell (Eton) Ltd
High St. Tel Windsor (0753) 863849. Open Mon-Fri 9-1, 2-5.30; Sat 9-5.30. New books specialising in antiques and fine arts. Also brass rubbing equipment.

Roger Barnett
(R.Barnett). 91 High St. Tel Windsor (0753) 867785. (Also at 52 Hill Rise, Richmond, Surrey.) Open Mon-Sat 9-5.30, Sun 2.30-5.30; other times by appt. General antiques, mainly furniture.

Eaton's of Eton Ltd
(Mr & Mrs Paul Eaton). 62-63 High St. Tel Windsor (0753) 860337 (priv 0628 27413). Open Mon-Sat 9-5, Sun, 1-5; other times by appt. 17th to 19thC furniture, porcelain, paintings and clocks. LAPADA

Eton Antique Book Shop
88 High St. Tel Windsor (0753) 855534. Open Mon-Sat 10-5.30, Sun 2-5. Antiquarian books and prints.

Eton Cottage Antiques
60 High St. Tel Windsor (0753) 856329. Open Mon-Sat 9.30-5.30, Sun afternoons. Porcelain, silver, furniture, general antiques.

Eton Gallery
(Josephine Smith). 116 High St. Tel Windsor (0753) 865147 (priv 860963). Open Tues-Sat 10.30-5; early closing Wed; other times by appt. 18th and early 19thC furniture.

J.Manley & Thames Gallery
(R. Devonside). 27 High St. Tel Windsor (0753) 865647. Open Mon-Sat 9-5. 18th, 19th and 20thC watercolours. Picture framing, cleaning and restoration of prints, oils and watercolours.

Peter J. Martin
40 High St, SL4 6BD. Tel Windsor (0753) 864901 (priv 863987). Open Mon-Sat 9-5 (closed 1-2); other times by appt. 18th, 19thC furniture & decorative items. Also shipping goods to 1930.

John A.Pearson Ltd
(Jillian Sinclair-Hill). 127-128 High St, SL4 6AR. Tel Windsor (0753) 860850. Open 10-5 or 5.30; other times by appt. 18th and 19thC English furniture, decorative items and works of art. Also valuations. BADA

Ulla Stafford
65 High St, SL4 6AA. Tel 0753-859625. 18thC furniture and porcelain. Valuations.

Studio 101 High St. Tel Windsor (0753) 863333. Open Mon-Sat 10-5.30; other times by appt. 18th and 19thC furniture, pottery, glass, prints and metalware.

Maurice Taffler Ltd
17 High St. Tel Windsor (0753) 864711. General antiques.

Times Past Antiques Ltd
(Phillip Jackson). 59 High St. Tel Windsor (07535) 57018. Open Mon-Sat 10.30-5.30, Sun 12-5; other times by appt. Specialist in 18th and 19thC clocks; also watches, small furniture, silver and porcelain. LAPADA

Turks Head Antiques
98 High St. Tel Windsor (0753) 863939. Open Tues-Sat 10.30-5, Sun 2-5 in summer. Georgian and Victorian silver, plate, lace, jewellery.

Windsor Antiques
(Alan & Helga Procter). 80 High St, SL4 6AF. Tel Windsor (0753) 860752. Open 7 days a week 9.30-6; other times by appt. 18thC longcase clocks, 18th and early 19thC furniture, mahogany and rosewood, Victorian oil paintings. LAPADA

Hermitage STD 0635

Richard Barder Antiques
(Richard and Philippa Barder). Crossways House, RG16 9SU. Tel Newbury (0635) 200295. Open Tues-Sat 9.30-5.30; other times by appt. Fine antique clocks: longcase, lantern, bracket and carriage. Antiquarian horological books. Restorations.

Hungerford STD 0488

Ashley Antiques and Restoration
(Robert A.C. Duff). 129 High St. Tel 82771. Open Mon-Sat 10-1, 2-5; other times by appt. Furniture, furniture restoration, pictures, clocks.

Mary Bellis Antiques
(Edwin Willson, David Gill). Charnham Close (A4 Highway), RG17 0EJ. Tel 82620. Open Mon-Sat 10-5; other times by appt. Five showrooms with large stock of fine quality 16th and 17thC oak furniture and related works of art. BADA

Below Stairs
(S. & L.Hofgartner). 103 High St, RG17 0NB. Tel 82317. Open Mon-Sat 10-6; Sun 2-6. Kitchen antiques, quality 19thC beds & bedroom furniture, craftsmen's tools & country items, old decorative garden items and other interesting collectables.

Collectors Shop
(Violet Lawson). 27-32 Charnham St. Tel 83519 (priv 023 587 536). Open Mon-Sat 10-5.30; Sun afternoons; other times by appt. Collectables, furniture, silver, glass, porcelain and brass and pine old kitchenware, tins.

The Craftsman
(C.J.B. & E.A.Jarrett). 16 Bridge St, RG17 0EG. Tel 82262. Open Mon-Wed, Fri, Sat 10-5. Large stock of old stripped pine and country furniture.

The Fire Place (Hungerford) Ltd
(E.B. Smith, E.M. Smith). Hungerford Old Fire Station, RG17 0EP. Tel 83420. Open Mon-Sat 10-1, 2.15-5; other times by appt. Items associated with fires and fire-sides, grates, fenders, mantels, coal scuttles, fire irons, fire screens.

Thomas Franklin (Antiques)
(T.G.Franklin). 28 Charnham St, RG17 OEJ. Tel 82404. Open Mon-Sat 9.30-5.30; closed 1-2; other times by appt. 18th & early 19thC English and Continental furniture.

Bibi Harris Antiques
(Mrs B. Harris). The Saleroom, Church St. Tel 83382 (priv 84616). Open Mon-Fri 8.30-6; Sat 10-6; other times by appt. Decorative antiques for the trade, 2000 sq.ft. LAPADA

Hungerford Arcade
(Wynsave Investments Ltd). 26 High St. Tel 83701. Open Mon-Sat 9.30-5.30, Sun 10-6. More than 120 stand-holders selling a wide range of antiques, period furniture. Specialist dealers in collectors' items.

Roger King Antiques
(R.F. King). 111 High St. Tel 82256. Open Mon-Sat 9.30-5.30; other times by appt. Large general stock of 18th and 19thC furniture. LAPADA

Jack Knight
20 Bridge St. Tel 2902. Photographer.

Medalcrest Ltd
(Douglas H.Farrow, FSVA, FFS). Charnham House, 29-30 Charnham St, RG17 0EJ. Tel 84157. Open Mon-Fri 9.30-5.30; Sat 10-6; other times by appt. Eight rooms of 18th & 19thC furniture, clocks, barometers, barographs, Persian rugs,prints, oil paintings, many interesting small items & early metalware, specialising in bracket, carriage, Vienna regulators, longcase clocks, barometers.

Neates
(I.V.Scull FRICS FRVA). 108 High St, RG17 0NB. Tel 82808. (Also in Newbury, Marlborough, Swindon and Winchester.) Open Mon-Fri 9-5, Sat 9-12. Chartered surveyors, estate agents, auctioneers, valuers.

The Old Malthouse
(Peter Foyle Hunwick). 15 Bridge St (A4), RG17 0EG. Tel 82209 (priv 83647). Open Mon-Sat; other times by appt. Clocks and barometers; 18th and 19thC English furniture. BADA

Pandora's Box
(Joan Gleave). Bridge St. Tel Marlborough (0672) 810468. Open Mon-Sat 10-4.30; other times by appt. General antiques and smalls and collectors items. Specialist in Staffordshire figures.

Principia Fine Art
Hungerford Antiques Arcade. Tel Marlborough (0672) 55275. Scientific instruments, treen, commemorative medals, clocks, watches, collectors items, early metalware, portraits of professional men and women.

Riverside Antiques Ltd
(Margaret Stockland). Riverside House, Charnham St. Tel 82314. Open Mon-Sat 10-5.30; other times by appt. 18th and 19thC furniture, decorative items and upholstered furniture.

Styles
(P.C.Styles). 12 Bridge St. Tel 83922. Open Mon-Sat 10-5.30; other times by appt. Silver of all periods, small collectables, and silver plate.

Maidenhead STD 0628

Lowe & Pomfrett
63 Queen St. Tel 20759. Open Mon-Sat 9.30-5; Sat 9.30-1 May-Oct, closed Thurs. General antiques. Specialising in jewellery & silver.

Samman Antiques
(Francoise Daniel). 71 St Marks Rd. Tel 23058 (priv 72974). Open Mon-Sat 10-5.30; Fri 8.30 pm; other times by appt. Furniture, porcelain, glass, metalwork, jewellery, silver, collectables.

Newbury STD 0635

John Baker
20 George St, Kingsclere. Tel Kingsclere (0635) 298744. Open Mon-Sat 9-6.30; other times by appt. 17th to 19thC furniture and paintings for the trade. Restoration of fine antiques only.

Dreweatts
Donnington Priory, Donnington, RG13 2JE. Tel 31234. Chartered surveyors and fine art auctioneers and valuers. Regular sales of antique furniture, clocks, ceramics etc. SOFAA

Griffons Court
(Trevor & Audrey Jackson). Highclere, RG15 9QS. Tel Highclere (0635) 253247. Open by appt. 18thC mahogany furniture, Victorian desks, decorative items, paintings and watercolours.

Neates
8 St Mary's Hill, Cheap St, RG14 5DF. Tel 42961. (Also in Hungerford, Marlborough and Swindon.) Open Mon-Fri 9-5; Sat 9-12. Chartered surveyors, estate agents, auctioneers, valuers.

Reading STD 0734

Bracher & Sydenham
(Northern Goldsmiths Co Ltd). 24 Queen Victoria St, RG1 1TG. Tel 583265, 53724. Open Mon-Sat 9-5. Antique silver and jewellery, clocks and pocket watches. NAG

Ann Bye Antiques
88 London Rd, RG1 4SJ. Tel 582029. Open Mon-Sat 9-5.30; other times by appt. Mainly pine and country furniture and furnishings. Also some silver and unusual items.

John E. Davis Antiques
21 Wokingham Rd, RG6 1JG. Tel 663108. Open Mon-Sat, Sun by appt (trade only). Always a large number of clocks of all descriptions in stock. Also musical boxes, furniture and antiques in general.

Eliot Antiques
(Lady Cathleen Hudson). Stanford Dingley, RG7 6LX. Tel Bradfield (0734) 744649 (priv 744346). Open mornings only; other times by appt. Objects of vertu, 18thC English enamels. BADA

Graham Gallery
(J.Steeds). Highwoods, Burghfield Common. Tel Burghfield Common(073529) 2320. Open any time, any day but by appt only. 19th and early 20thC watercolours, oils and prints.

Hymor Photographers Ltd
41-43 Prospect St, Caversham. Tel 475656, 479450. Photographers.

Simmons and Lawrence
114 London St. Tel 500575. Auctioneers.

William Smith (Booksellers) Ltd
(D.H.R. La'Porte). 35-39 London St, RG1 4PU. Tel 595555. Open Mon, 10-5.30; Tues-Sat 9-5.30. Bookselling. ABA

Streatley

Holloway's
(T.J. Holloway, FRICS). 12 High St, RG8 9HY. Tel Goring-on-Thames (0491) 872318 (priv 0295 811297). (Also at 49 Parsons St, Banbury, Oxon.) Open Mon-Fri 9-5.30; other times by appt. Auctioneers & valuers. RICS

18th & 19th Century Furniture, objets d'art, fine antiques

Riverside Antiques Ltd

Margaret Stockland

RIVERSIDE HOUSE, CHARNHAM STREET, HUNGERFORD, BERKSHIRE
Exit 14, M4 Tel Hungerford (STD 0488) 82314

Hungerford Arcade

OVER 70 SHOPS and SHOWCASES

OPEN SEVEN DAYS A WEEK

26 HIGH STREET, HUNGERFORD, BERKS.
Telephone: Hungerford 83701

P. F. HUNWICK

TELEPHONE (0488) 82209

THE OLD MALTHOUSE

George I walnut veneered lowboy on cabriole legs. English, c. 1740

18TH CENTURY ENGLISH FURNITURE CLOCKS & BAROMETERS

15 BRIDGE STREET, HUNGERFORD, BERKSHIRE

Guy Bousfield

Buyer and Vendor of GEORGIAN furniture

58 Thames Street,
Windsor, Berks.
Tel. Windsor (STD 0753) 864575

Robust mid-18th-century architect's table in mahogany. Note the double lift drawing surface above the pull out centre section which has a baize covered writing surface concealing a well of divided compartments and secret drawers. 38½in wide × 23in deep × 28½in to top of writing surface.

PETER A. CROFTS

Member BADA Ltd

Antique Dealer and Exporter

BRIAR PATCH, HIGH ROAD, ELM, WISBECH
Tel (STD 0945) 584614 Appointment Suggested

Thatcham STD 0635

John Whybrow
The Crown House, High St, RG13 4JD. Tel 63335. Open Mon-Sat 2-6; other times by appt. Furniture, china, silver, Persian rugs, violins and jewellery.

Twyford STD 0734

Biggs of Maidenhead
(F.R. & M. H. Stamp). Hare Hatch Grange, RG10 9SK. Tel Wargrave (073 522) 3281 (priv 3104). Open daily except Sun & Mon. (Leave M4 at Junction No 8/9 and take A423(M) to A4, turn left, then 3.5 miles on right) Fine period furniture, clocks, paintings and works of art. BADA CINOA

Twyford Antiques Centre
(Gail Spence). 1 High St. Tel 342161 (priv 473011). Open Mon-Sun 9.30-5.30; closed Wed. General antiques.

White Waltham

Braemar Antiques Ltd
Waltham Rd. Tel Littlewick Green(062 882) 3741. Furniture and shipping goods.

Windsor STD 075 35

Guy Bousfield
(Guy Bousfield). 58 Thames St. Tel 864575. Open Mon-Sat 9-6, sometimes closed Mon. Good stock of Georgian furniture and items of that period. BADA

Greengrass Antiques
(Mr & Mrs D.Greengrass). 34 Frances Rd. Tel 65627. General. Shipper. LAPADA

Lupin Antiques Ltd
134 Peascod St. Tel 56244. Porcelain, glass, silver and furniture.

Omell Galleries
(Omell Galleries (Windsor) Ltd). Goswell Hill, 134 Peascod St, SL4 1DR. Tel 852271. (Also three galleries in London.) Open Mon-Sat 10-5.30; other times by appt. Fine original paintings by contemporary English & French artists, 19thC works also available. Contemporary original artists etchings. Oils and watercolours restored and reframed. LAPADA FATG

Wokingham STD 0734

Paul Thomas Fine Paintings
(Paul A.Thomas). 27 Glebelands Rd, RG11 1DY. Tel 794671. Open by appt only. 19th and 20thC oil paintings and watercolours, British and Continental.

Woolhampton STD 0734

The Old Bakery
Bath Rd. Tel 712116. Open Mon-Sat 9-6; other times by appt. General antiques.

Wraysbury STD 078 481

Wyrardisbury Antiques
(C.W. Tuffs). 23 High St. Tel 3225. Open Tues, Wed, Fri, Sat 10-5. Clocks and small furniture, porcelain, silver, watercolours.

Buckinghamshire

Amersham STD 024 03

Amersham Antique Centre
(Mr Green, Mr King). 20-22 Whielden St, Old Amersham. Tel 3939. Open Mon-Sat 9-6. Nine full time dealers selling furniture, porcelain, glass, watercolours, books etc.

Antique Lovers Coterie at Ingram Warwick Ltd
(John S.Ingram & Trudi Ingram). 20A High St, Amersham Old Town, HP7 ODJ. Tel 21033. Open Tues-Sat 9.30-5.30; other times by appt. Jewellery, objets d'art, unusual antiques, prints, maps and books. Parking facilities.

Benedict Jewellers
(William Bennett, Kenneth Smith). 37 High St, Old Amersham, HP7 0DP. Tel 22803. Open Mon-Sat 9.30-5.30. Antique, secondhand and new jewellery, silver and glass. NAG,LAPADA

Crispin Antiques
(Sarah Newfield). 10 The Broadway, HP7 0HP. Tel 21779. Open Mon-Sat; other times by appt. Res on prem. 18th and 19thC English country furniture, English and Continental porcelain and Belleek.

The Cupboard Antiques
(Mrs C.Lucas, N.S. Lucas). 80 High St, Old Amersham. Tel 22882. Open 10-5; other times by appt. Georgian furniture & antiques, interior decorators items.

Hetheringtons, Pretty & Ellis
125 Station Rd. Tel 29292. Open Mon-Fri 9-5.30; Sat 9-12. Fine art auctioneers & valuers.

Mon Galerie
(A.R. & D.E.Guy). 49 High St. Tel 21705. Open Mon-Sat 10.15-5; closed Thurs; other times by appt. 19thC watercolours, antique maps etc.

Old Amersham Antiques Centre
20-22 Whielden St, Old Amersham. Tel 3939. Open Mon-Sat.

Old Amersham Auctions
(office) 2 School Lane, Old Amersham. Tel 22758. Auctions of antiques and general goods on alternate Saturdays.

Sundial Antiques
(Andrew D.G. Macdonald & Mrs. M.J. Macdonald). 19 Whielden St, HP7 0HU. Tel 7955. Open Mon-Sat 9.30-5.30, closed Thurs; other times by appt. Metalware, small period furniture, oil lamps, porcelain, glass and unusual items. LAPADA

Aylesbury STD 0296

Peter Arnold Gallery
(Peter Arnold). 3 Knolls Close, Castle St, Wingrave, HP22 4PY. Tel 681568. Open by appt, except during exhibitions. British watercolours and paintings (1820-1980). Usually examples of W. Langley, Sylvester Stannard, W.L. Wyllie, W. Tyndale, G.G.Kilburne, etc. available. Additional viewing facilities in Dover St. London, W1.

Paul D. Lipson
67 Cambridge St. Tel 89535. Open Mon, Tues, Sat 10.30-5; other times by appt. Collectors items especially prints, ephemera, silver, jewellery.

Weatherheads Bookshop
(Pentos Retailing Group Ltd). 58 Kingsbury, HP20 2JG. Tel 23153, 24985. Open Mon-Sat 9-5.30. New and secondhand booksellers.

Beaconsfield STD 049 46

Christopher Cole (Fine Paintings) Ltd
1 London End, HP9 2HN. Tel 71274. Open Mon-Sat 9.30-1, 2-5.30; other times by appt. Fine 18th, 19th & early 20thC watercolours and oil paintings, especially British.

Grosvenor House Interiors
(T.I.Marriott). 51 Wycombe End. Tel 77498. Open Mon-Sat, 9-1, 2-5.30. 18th & 19thC furniture, pictures, clocks. Specialist in fireplaces and all accompaniments.

Norton Antiques
(Tony & Norma Hepburn). 56 London End, HP9 2JH. Tel 3674. Open Mon-Sat 10-1, 2-5.30; closed Wed. 18th and early 19thC furniture, decorative antiques, clocks, paintings, woodworking tools and general antiques. Also pine stripping service for trade & private customers.

Old Curiosity Shop
(David J. Barker). 47/49 Wycombe End, Beaconsfield Old Town, HP9 1LZ. Tel 4473. Open Tues-Sat 9.45-5.30; closed Mon; closed for lunch; other times by appt. General antiques (mainly small items) including some furniture.

Old Town Clock Shop
(Frank Lord). 1-3 Aylesbury End, HP9 1LU. Tel 6783. Clocks and watches.

Charles Sale Ltd
Crosskeys, 18 Wycombe End. Tel 4012. Open Mon-Sat. Furniture, mirrors, glass, china and brassware.

Spinning Wheel
(Sarah Margaret Royle). 86 London End. Tel 3055 (priv 024 07 3294). Open Mon-Sat 10-5; closed Wed; other times by appt. Georgian furniture, porcelain, pictures, glass.

Buckingham STD 0280

Adrian Hornsey Ltd
Chandos Rd, MK18 2AO. Tel 816363. Open by telephone appt only. Trade only - import/export and general antiques.

Lennard Antiques
(Gill Meddings). The Laurels, Tingewick, MK18 4NN. Tel Finmere (02804) 371. (Also at Woburn Abbey Antique Centre, Woburn, Beds.) Open Tues, Wed, Sat 10-6; other times by appt. 17th, 18th and early 19thC furniture and accessories.

Chalfont St Giles STD 024 07

Aquarelle of St Giles
8 The Lagger, HP8 4DG. Tel 5592. Open 9.30-12.30, 2-4; other times by appt. Watercolours and drawings of all periods, specialising in English watercolours.

Bucks House Antiques
High St. Tel 5711. Open Mon-Sat 10-5. General antiques.

Chesham STD 0494

Albert Bartram
177 Hivings Hill. Tel 783271. Open by appt only. Res on prem. Antique pewter, important early metalwork and 16th and 17thC works of art.

Chess Antiques
(M.Wilder). 85 Broad St, HP5 3EF. Tel 783043. 18th and 19thC furniture, period clocks. Also restorations. LAPADA

Peter Farrow
(Peter Farrow). Hillbury House, Missenden Road, HP5 1JZ. Tel 784138. Open by appt. Buyer & acquirer of antique furniture on commission basis. Valuations of furniture for insurance, probate etc.

Omniphil Ltd
(A.R.T.Muddiman). Germains Lodge, Fullers Hill (office). Tel 771851. (Shop at 113 Grays Antique Market, Davies St, London W1.) Open 9-5.30. Dealers in rare prints, stamps and Illustrated London News.

Pednor Antiques
(Lady Caroline Simmonds). 44 Church St.

Queen Anne House
(Miss A.E.Jackson). Queen Anne House, 57 Church St, HP5 1HY. Tel 783811. Open Wed, Fri and Sat 9.30-5; other times by appt. Antiques and decorative furniture, objets d'art, bric-a-brac and Oriental rugs.

Denham STD 0895

Antiquities
(K. & J. Carpenter). Village Rd, Denham Village. Tel 833340 (priv 09274 25125). Open Tues, Wed, Fri 12-5, Sat 12-5.30; other times by appt. Victorian/Edwardian furniture, silver, jewellery, pictures, small amount of porcelain.

Margaret Elmes Antiques
(Mrs M.J. Elmes). Denham Gallery, UB9 5BE. Tel 832244. Open Mon-Sat 10-12.30, 2.30-5; closed Wed; other times by appt. 18th & 19thC furniture. English pottery & porcelain, metal and some pictures, watercolours, prints etc. Restoration & upholstery undertaken.

Directory Entries are Free and ADDITIONS OR CORRECTIONS will be welcomed by *THE EDITOR, British Art and Antiques Directory, National Magazine House, 72 Broadwick Street, London W1V 2BP*

Dorney

The Old School Antiques
(Lt-Col & Mrs V.O.F. Wildish). The Old School, SL4 6QW. Tel Burnham (06286) 3247. Open daily 10-5; other times by appt. Res on prem. Antique porcelain, also 17th to early 19thC oak and mahogany furniture. LAPADA

Gerrards Cross STD 0753

Aristocat Antiques
(H.James). 19 Packhorse Rd. Tel 888011. Open Mon-Sat 10-5; Wed 10-1; other times by appt. Furniture, copper, brass, silver, jewellery and decorative items. LAPADA

Ethorpe Antiques
2b Ethorpe Crescent, SL9 8PN. Tel 887499. Good quality 18th and 19thC Continental and English porcelain, particularly Meissen, fine jewellery, glass, silver and interesting objets d'art, some furniture.

Greensleeves Galleries
(Monika Tejwani). 3 Bulstrode Way. Tel 886160. Open Tues-Sat 10-5; closed Wed; other times by appt. Oil paintings & watercolours by contemporary artists, watercolours and prints, etchings etc. 18th to early 20thC, small sculptures.

H.S.Wellby Ltd
Ponders, Hedgerley Lane, SL9 8SY. Tel 887957. (Also at Haddenham.) Open by appt only. Antique Continental silver and 18th and 19thC paintings.

Great Missenden STD 024 06

Basia
(Basia Watson-Gandy). Squirrel Court, Hare Lane, Little Kingshill, HP16 0EF. Tel 5441. Open by appt only. Commemorative ware individually designed. Icons, lustrework, goldwork, miniatures, thimbles. Specialising in individually hand-painted china & porcelain. Lustrework - modern and traditional techniques.

E. & R. Cooper
(Evelyn and Reginald Cooper). 99a High St. Open Tues, Wed, Fri & Sat 10-5; other times by appt. Fine watercolours, small antique furniture, porcelain, glass and objects. LAPADA

Heritage Antiques & Restoration
(John & Silviane Wilshire). 36b High St. Tel 5710.

W.E.Hill & Sons
Havenfields, HP16 9LS. Tel 3655. Open Mon-Fri 10-4. Specialists in antique instruments and accessories for the violin family. BADA

M.V. Tooley, Antiquarian Horologist
The Guildroom, The Lee. Tel 463. Open Sat or by appt. Antique clocks including dial, bracket, lantern but specialising in longcase and Vienna. CMBH, MBWG

Haddenham STD 0844

Sally Turner Antiques
(Sally Turner). Church End, HP17 8AH. Tel 290346. Open by appt only. General antiques, including furniture, porcelain, glass, pictures, decorative items etc. LAPADA

H.S.Wellby Ltd
(C.S.Wellby). The Malt House, 4 Church End. Tel 290036. (Also at Gerrards Cross.) Open by appt only please. 18th and 19thC oil paintings. ABPR

High Wycombe STD 0494

Wycombe Cane and Rush Works
(P.J. Gilbert, J.A. Gilbert). Victoria St, HP11 2QR. Tel 442429. Open Mon-Fri 9-5.30; Sat 10-12.30. Cane and rush chair seating repairs. All types of canework undertaken, including bergere suites, fan and spider-back patterns.

Iver Heath

Pine Dealers
(Paul Jones & Mark Twine). Blanchards Farm, Seven Hills Rd. Tel Fulmer (028 16) 2540 (priv 024 026 3184). Open Mon-Sun 7 days 10-6; other times by appt. Mainly pine.

Little Brickhill

Baroq Antiques
(Brian & Barbara Dawson). Watling St, MK17 9LY. Tel Great Brickhill (052 526) 401 (priv 561). Open Tue-Fri 2-5; Sat 1-5; other times by appt. Pottery & porcelain, watercolours & oils, furniture, mainly mahogany & oak, Edwardian & earlier.

Long Crendon STD 0844

Hollington Antiques
(J.& V. Asta). Bicester Rd, HP18 9EF. Tel 208294. Open Mon-Sun incl. Victoriana, badges, militaria, china, glass, prints, drawings, watercolours and books.

Marlow STD 062 84

Bishop (Marlow) Ltd
(L. & P. Bishop). 8 & 10 West St, SL7 1AJ. Tel 3936. Open Mon-Thurs 9-1; Sat 9-1; other times by appt. 18th and early 19thC English furniture, Georgian silver and English porcelain.

Angela Hone
The Garth, 31 Mill Rd. Tel 4170. Watercolours and paintings.

David Messum Ltd
(David Messum, M.D.L. Child). The Studio, Lords Wood, SL7 2QS. Tel 6565/6 (priv 4169). Open by appt Mon-Sat. British paintings 1880 onwards - Plein Air (Newlyn School); 18thC English paintings. Specialising in Newlyn School and 18thC marine paintings. BADA

Paul Rich Fine Art
Brick Cottage, Lower Woodend, SL7 2HN. Tel 2665. Open by appt. Paintings and drawings of all periods and schools.

Milton Keynes STD 0908

Fenny Lodge Gallery
(Sophie Rathsach). Simpson Rd, Bletchley, MK1 1BD. Tel 642207. Contemporary crafts: ceramics, glass, wood, wall hangings, jewellery, sculpture, paintings, limited edition prints. ICGA

Greville Antiques & Design Ltd
(O. Greville). The Square, Aspley Guise, MK17 8DF. Tel 584466 (priv 583408). Open Mon-Sat, 9-6; other times by appt. Primitive and country furniture, pictures, prints, decorative objects. We also have an interior design service encompassing fabrics, carpets, soft furnishings, paint finishes. Design consultancy service.

Knobs
(B.Raine). 155 North Ninth St, MK9 3AW. Tel 605465. Brass cabinet handles. Mail order only. Free catalogue.

Jeanne Temple Antiques
(J.R. Temple). Stockwell House, Wavendon, MK17 8LS. Tel 583597. Open Mon-Sat 9-5; other times by appt. Georgian and Victorian furniture, brass and copper items. Specialising in Victorian, Edwardian and 1930s light fittings.

Monks Risborough

Tudor Antiques
(B.T. & G.E.Thornley). Tel Princes Risborough(08444) 3523. Open Mon-Sat 9-5.30; closed Wed; other times by appt. 18thC mahogany & oak furniture and decorative prints of the same period.

Naphill STD 024 024

A. & E. Foster
Little Heysham, Forge Rd. Tel 2024. Open by appt only. Specialists in treen, also other antiques and works of art. BADA

Olney

Iris Martin Lacemaking Supplies
(Iris Martin). 62 High St.
Tel Bedford (0234) 712446. Open Mon-Sat 9.30-5.30; other times by appt. Antique & modern lace bobbins, books, patterns, threads, hand made lace and other lacemaking items.

Olney Antique Porcelain Company
(R.F.Soul). 21 High Street South. Tel Bedford (0234) 711263. Open Mon-Sat 10-1, 2.15-6; early closing Wed; other times by appt. 18th to 20thC pottery and porcelain, especially potlids, Prattware and fairings.

Rose Court Studios Antiques
(John Overland). Rose Court, Market Place. Tel Bedford (0234) 712351 (priv Oakley 4876). Open 7 days 10-5; other times by appt. Antique pine, clocks, brass ware, silver, country oak, mahogany furniture, oil, watercolour paintings, tin plate unusual items.

Penn STD 049 481

The Country Furniture Shop
3 Hazelmere Rd. Tel 2244. Open Mon-Sat 10-1, 2-5; half day Thurs. General antiques including furniture, china, glass, copper, brass, also carved pine mantelpieces.

Francis Wigram Antiques
Cotters Barn, PN10 8LB.
Tel 3266. Open Mon-Sat 9-5; Wed 9-12.30; other times by appt. Good stock of Jacobean, Queen Anne and Georgian furniture, porcelain and silk pictures. BADA

Princes Risborough
STD 084 44

Antique Centre
20-22 Bell St.

Vine House Antiques
(Mrs S.Stallabrass). Market Square, HP17 9AA. Tel 5485. Open Thurs, Fri & Sat 10-5; other times by appt. Porcelain, glass, metalware and small furniture.

The White House Antiques
(Martyn Amor). 3 High St.
Tel 6976. Open by appt. Chandeliers, marble statuary. Specialist in insurance valuations for antique and modern household contents.

Waddesdon

Collectors' Corner
(Mrs Kitty Good, Mrs Valerie Grant). 106 High St, HP18 0JF. Tel Aylesbury (0296) 651563. Open Mon-Sat 9-5; other times by appt. Porcelain, silver, jewellery, metalware, paintings, watercolours and furniture.

Wendover STD 0296

Art Distribution Ltd
Hogarth House, High St, HP22 6DU. Tel 624402. Open Mon-Sat 9.30-5.30; other times by appt. Antique wallpaper roller lamps.

Bowood Antiques
(Peggy Peyton-Jones). Wendover Dean Farm, Bowood Lane, HP22 6PY. Tel 622113. Open 9-5.30, appt always preferable. 17th,18th and 19thC furniture and objets d'art.

Collectors Treasures
(S.D. Paessler). Hogarth House, High St, HP22 6DU. Tel 624402. Open Mon-Sat 9.30-5.30; other times by appt. 16th to 19thC maps and prints of all parts of the world and of every description, old watercolours and oils. Also incorporating Hogarth Framing. Christie's Contemporary Graphics (signed limited editions), sporting prints and restrikes. LAPADA

West Wycombe

Browns of West Wycombe
(Mr.D.A. Hines). Church Lane, HP14 3AH. Tel High Wycombe (0494) 24537 (priv 0895 39163). Open Mon-Fri 8.30-5.30; other times by appt. Specialist furniture makers. Antique repair and restoration. Specialising in chairmaking - copying to complete or extend existing sets.

Weston Turville

Sonia Halliday Photographs
Primrose Cottage. Tel Stoke Mandeville(029 661) 2266. Photographer.

Woburn Sands

Forty Three
(Gerry & Meryl Tyrrell). High St. Tel Milton Keynes (0908) 582447. (Also at Haydon House, Station Rd.) Open Tues, Fri, Sat 10.30-1 2.30-5; other times by appt. Copper, brass and metal items, oak, elm, pine country furniture, boxes, prints and decorative and interesting items.

Haydon House Antiques
(Gerry & Meryl Tyrrell, D.Missenden). Haydon House, Station Rd, MK17 8RX. Tel Milton Keynes (0908) 582447. (Also at Forty Three, High St.) Open Mon-Sat 10-5.30; closed Thurs; other times by appt. Large comprehensive stock of antiques and interesting and decorative items. LAPADA

Neville's Antiques
64-66 Station Rd, MK17 8RQ. Tel Milton Keynes (0908) 584827 (priv 583024). Open Tues-Sat 10-5; closed Wed; other times by appt. Georgian, Victorian and Edwardian furniture, oil paintings, porcelain and glass.

Cambridgeshire

Brampton

Brampton Mill Antiques Centre
Brampton Mill. Tel Huntingdon (0480) 55593. Open Mon-Sat 10.30-6.30, Sun 2-6; other times by appt. Country furniture, 17th and 18thC oak, 19thC mahogany and clocks.

Burwell

Peter Norman Antiques
57 North St, CB5 0BA.
Tel Newmarket (0638) 742197. Open Mon-Sat 9-12.30, 2-5.30; other times by appt. Furniture, clocks, arms, silver, china, copper and collectors items.

Cambridge STD 0223

The Antique Home
(Paul Farmar). 15 Gwydir St.
Tel 311203. Open 9.30-5.30; closed Thurs. General antiques, specialising in stripped pine and Victorian furniture.

Jess Applin Antiques
(Jess Applin). 8 Lensfield Rd, CB2 1EG. Tel 315168 (priv 246851). Open Mon-Sat 10-5.30; other times by appt. Furniture 17th to 19thC and decorative items. BADA

John Beazor & Sons Ltd
(Keith Beazor and Martin Beazor). 78-80 Regent St, CB2 1DP.
Tel 355178. Open Mon-Sat 9.15-1, 2-5; other times by appt. Mainly English furniture - 18th and early19thC. BADA

Benet Gallery
(G.H.Criddle & J.Criddle).
19 King's Parade. Tel 353783 (priv 248739). Open Mon-Sat 9-5; other times by appt. Antique maps and prints of Cambridge and general topography. Specialists in reproduction playing cards from all parts of the world.

D.Bickersteth
38 Fulbrooke Rd, CB3 9EE.
Tel 352291. Volumes on English literature, economics, science and medicine. ABA

Buckie's Jewellers, Valuers & Silversmiths
(Mrs G.McC. Buckie, P.R. Buckie). 31 Trinity St, CB2 1TB.
Tel 357910. Open Tues-Sat 9.45-5. Specialising in antique and secondhand jewellery & silverware, glass, porcelain, clocks and works of art. Specialists in appraising and restoring antique jewellery. LAPADA NAG GA GMC

Cambridge Fine Art Ltd
(Mr R.Lury, Mrs J.Lury). 'Priesthouse', 33 Church St, Little Shelford, CB2 5HG. Tel 842866 (priv 843537). (Also at The Studio, 33 Church St, Little Shelford, Cambs..) Open by appt only. British & European oil paintings 1800-1900, modern British paintings, 1880-1950, portraits 1600-1940. Picture restorers. LAPADA

Cheffins, Grain and Chalk
The Cambridge Saleroom, Cherry Hinton Rd. Tel 358721. Auctioneers.

Malcolm G.Clark
3 Pembroke St, CB2 3QY.
Tel 357117. Good stock of old English furniture, china and glass. BADA

Collectors Market
Dales Brewery, Gwydir St. Open Mon-Fri 9-5; Sat 9-5.30. Several dealers selling antiques, furniture, bric-a-brac, pictures, glass etc.

Collins & Clark
(J.G. & O. Collins). 81 Regent St, CB2 1AW. Tel 353801. Fine antique furniture, English and Oriental porcelain, silver and old glass.

Cottage Antiques
(Mrs Anna Yandell& Mrs Anne Owen). 16-18 Lensfield Rd.
Tel 316698. Open Mon-Sat 9.30-5; other times by appt. Glass, china, country furniture, Oriental porcelain.

G.David
3, 4 & 16 St Edward's Passage, CB2 3PJ. Tel 354619. Open Mon-Sat 9-5. General stock of secondhand, antiquarian and new reduced books. ABA

Deighton Bell & Co
(Wm Dawson & Sons). 13 Trinity St, CB2 1TD. Tel 353939. Open Mon-Fri, 9-5.30; Sat 9-1. Antiquarian rare and fine books. Specialising in travel, topography, English literature and classics. ABA

Dolphin Antiques
(L. Aldred & R. Bramwell). 33 Trumpington St. Tel 354180. Open 9.30-5.30; other times by appt. 18th and 19thC furniture, boxes, glass and metalware.

Rodney T.Firmin
(R.T.& C.J. Firmin). 16 Magdalene St. Tel 67372. Open Tues-Sat 10.30-12.30, 1.30-5. Clocks and watches.

Gabor Cossa Antiques
(Mrs Joan Eve). 34 Trumpington St, CB2 1QY. Tel 356049. Open daily 10-1, 2-5.15. Early English & Oriental porcelain, pottery, delftware, 18thC drinking glasses, objets d'art, Japanese woodblock prints. General prints, local topography.

Galloway & Porter Ltd
30 Sidney St. Tel 67876. Open Mon-Fri. Large general stock of secondhand and antiquarian books. ABA

P.R.Garner (Antiques)
(P.R. & R.J. Garner). Willow Farm, 104 High St, Landbeach. Tel 860470. Open by appt. Shipping goods, 19th and 20thC furniture, musical boxes, gramophones, vintage and veteran cars. Also at Norfolk House, 15 Norfolk St, Cambridge (open Mon-Sat 9-5, closed Thurs), selling good pre-1900 furniture, mechanical antiques, clocks, china etc.

The Haunted Bookshop
(Derek Gibbons). 9 St Edward's Passage, CB2 3PJ. Tel 312913 (priv 68169). Open daily 9.30-5. Antiquarian bookseller. ABA

W. Heffer & Sons Ltd
20 Trinity St, CB2 3NG. Tel 358351. Open Mon-Sat. Large stock of books in all fields.

Lensfield Antiques
(Paul Farmar, Digby Cayley). 12 Lensfield Rd, CB2 1EG. Tel 357636. Open Mon-Sat 9.30-5.30; other times by appt. English period furniture and decorative items. Specialising in treen & wood carvings.

Michael's Antiques
(Michael Smith). 5-7 Norfolk St. Tel 357558. Open Mon-Sat 9-5. Furniture, china, clocks. Gallery for early 20thC paintings, watercolours, prints, antique lighting.

Jean Pain Gallery
7 King's Parade, CB2 1SJ. Tel 313970. Open Mon-Sat 9.30-5. Antique maps, prints and art posters. ABA

Phillips Cambridge
(P. Brittain). 42 Newnham Rd. Tel 66523. Office for Phillips fine art auctioneers.

Quinto of Cambridge
34 Trinity St, CB2 1TB. Tel 358279. Open Mon-Sat 9-6, Sun 11-5; other times by appt. Antique maps and prints. Antiquarian and second hand books, specialising in classic and foreign language books. ABA

Dorothy Radford (Antiques and Interiors)
132 Trumpington Rd, CB2 2NE. Tel 840179 (priv 357966). Open daily. Antiques and decorative objects.

S.J.Webster-Speakman
(F.P. & S.J. Webster-Speakman). 79 Regent St. Tel 315048 (priv 354089). Open Mon-Sat 10-5.45; other times by appt. Georgian furniture, Staffordshire animals, fine brass inlaid Regency furniture. Bracket, longcase and French clocks, carriage clocks. BADA

Croydon

Penny Farthing
(G.&G.Sole). High St. Tel Cambridge (0223) 207331. Open weekends and by appt. British 18th, 19th and 20thC furniture, reproductions, shipping goods.

Doddington STD 079 586

Doddington House Antiques
(B.A.Frankland). 2 Benwick Rd, PE15 0TG. Tel March (0354) 740755. Open Mon-Sat 10-6; closed Wed; other times by appt. Furniture, mainly Victorian, barometers, clocks, craft tools, treen, bygones, mirrors and unusual items of interest. Barometers restored; chairs recaned.

Duxford

Riro D.Mooney
4 Moorfield Rd. Tel Cambridge (0223) 832252. Large stock of furniture of all periods.

Ely STD 0353

Comins
(E.S.Legge FRICS;P.L.Ambrose FRICS;E.W.Lee ARICS). 25 Market Place, CB7 4NP. Tel 2265. Open Mon-Sat 9-5. Chartered surveyors, auctioneers and estate agents.

The Furniture Station Ltd
(Miss A.Lanham). The Kelterment Antique Market, Fordham. Open daily. Georgian and Victorian furniture and shipping goods, copper and brass.

W.A.Lee
90 St Mary's St. Tel 3483. Books on arts and crafts, early printing, old science and technics. ABA

Fordham

Phoenix Antiques
(K.& A. Bycroft). 1 Carter St. Tel Newmarket (0638) 720 363. Open 9-6, except Sun & Wed pm; other times by appt. Early English and Continental furniture, carpets, metalware, pottery.

Harston

Antique Clocks
(C.J.Stockes). 1 High St, CB2 5PX. Tel Cambridge (0223) 870264. Open 9-6; other times by appt. Antique clocks of all types.

Histon STD 022 023

C.P.Stockbridge Ltd
47 Impington Lane. Tel 4031. Open 9.30-5. Furniture, silver, porcelain, clocks, oil paintings and watercolours, musical boxes.

Little Abington

Abington Books
(J.Haldane). 29 Church Lane, CB1 6BQ. Open by appt only. World's largest stock of books on Oriental rugs and on classical tapestries. Also fair number on related subjects . Inspection facilities in North London, please phone 01-267 2701 for appt. ABA

March STD 035 42

Gallery Three
(John Burn). 96-98 High St, PE15 9LP. Tel 53484 (priv 52262). Open Wed, Fri, Sat10-12.30, 2.30-5; other times by appt. Silver, porcelain, small furniture and some paintings and clocks.

Melbourn

P.N.Hardiman
62 High St, SG8 6AJ. Tel Royston (0763) 60093. Open Mon-Sat 9-6. Good stock of period furniture.

Orwell

West Farm Antiques
(Jean Kershaw). High St, SG8 5QN. Tel Cambridge (0223) 207464. Open Thurs, Sat, Sun; other times by appt. Country furniture, oak and pine, 18th and 19thC mahogany and walnut furniture, decorative items, metalware, large tables. LAPADA

Outwell

Langhorn Antiques
(Philip Grant). Langhorn Lane, PE14 8SL. Tel Wisbech (0945) 772668. Open daily; closed Wed morning; other times by appt. General stock.

Peterborough STD 0733

Christie's
(The Hon. Lady Hastings, Mrs William Proby). The Stables, Milton Hall, PE6 7AA. Tel Castor (073121) 781. Open Mon-Fri 9-1, 2-4. Regional office for the auctioneers and valuers.

Ivor & Patricia Lewis Antique & Fine Art Dealers
(Mr and Mrs I. Lewis). Westfield, 30 Westwood Park Rd. Tel 44567. Open by appt only. English and French furniture (some signed). Porcelain, bronzes. LAPADA

Studio Antiques
31 Lincoln Rd, PE1 2RH. Tel 54394. Open Tues, Wed, Fri 10.30-5; Sat 10.30-4; other times by appt. Antiques, furniture, china, glass, silver, jewellery and coins.

Sydney House Antiques
14 Elton Rd, Wansford. Tel Stamford (0780) 782786. English pottery and porcelain, European antique and Edwardian furniture, English and French clocks.

Ramsey STD 0487

Abbey Antiques
(John and Rita Smith). 63 Great Whyte, PE17 1HL. Tel 814753, 812758. Open Tues-Sun 10-5. Victorian & Edwardian furniture, pine, porcelain, Goss and crested china, copper, brass and collectables.

Jackson's
(James Jackson). Hill Villa, Bury, PE17 1AB. Tel 812361. (Also at The Old Post Office, High St, Ramsey and in Isle of Man.) Open by appt only. Clocks, silver, china, glass, arms, medals, coins, brass and copper ware, ivory, pictures, unusual antiques, furniture and treen.

Reach

Cladgild Ltd
(A.F. & J.A.Dudley). Vine House, Fair Green, CB5 0JD. Tel Newmarket (0638) 742171. (Also 13 High St, Newmarket & 4-18 Mill St, Mildenhall, Suffolk.) Open Mon-Sat 9-6; other times by appt. Cabinet makers and antique restorers. Antique furniture, bygones, chaise longues, Victorian chairs, chests of drawers, desks, display cabinets etc. Also shipping stock. Antique restorations, woodwork repairs, polishing, re-leathering, upholstery. GMC

Dudley's Home Interiors
(A.F. Dudley & J.A. Dudley). Vine House, Fair Green. Tel Newmarket (0638) 741989. (Also Cladgild Ltd and at 13 High St, Newmarket.) Open Mon-Sat 9-6; other times by appt. Antique restoration of all types: woodwork, polishing, carving, turning, upholstery, caning, veneering. Also clock and barometer restoration. Cabinet maker.

Soham

Audraw Ltd
(L. Audus). 64 Fordham Rd. Tel Ely (0353) 720342. Open daily except Wed. Large varied stock of furniture, china, glass, brass, copper and other items.

St Ives STD 0480

Adams Antiques
Houghton Rd. Tel 300455. Open Mon-Fri 8.30-5.30; other times by appt. Also at The Old Bus Station, North Rd. St Ives. 47 Chalk Farm Rd, London NW1 and 53-55 Fulham High St, London SW6. Trade warehouse of pine furniture.

Ekins, Fine Art Auctioneers
The Salerooms, The Market. Tel 68144. Open Mon-Fri 9-5.30; other times by appt. Auctioneers holding three weekly fine art & antique auctions on Tuesdays; fortnightly auction sales of general goods.

B.R.Knight & Sons
4 The Quay, PE17 4AS. Tel 68295. Open Mon-Sat 10.30-5; closed Thurs & Sun. Porcelain, pottery, pictures, paintings by artists from Huntingdon, Bedfordshire and Cambridge, jewellery, art nouveau, pewter, art deco ceramics, small antiques and decorative metalware, period costume & lace. LAPADA

Timecraft
(Mr F.K.Hemmings CMBHI). 6 Crown Street Mews, PE17 4EB. Open Mon, Wed, Fri, Sat 9-1, 2.30-5; other times by appt. Specialists in antique clock and barometer repairs and restoration.

Trumpington

Sotheby's
(Representative: Christopher Myers). 56 High St, CB2 2LS. Tel Cambridge (0223) 8452225. Open 9.30-5.30. Auctioneers & valuers.

Warboys

The Golden Drop Antiques
(Maggie Clarke). Chatteris Rd (A141). Tel Chatteris (03543) 2990. Open Mon-Sat 10-6, Sun 2-6; other times by appt. Pine, shipping goods, oak, mahogany, and walnut furniture. Private and trade welcome. Large selection of polished pine.

Waterbeach

Reeve Photography
Denny Industrial Centre. Tel Cambridge (0223) 861824. Photographers.

Whittlesford

Guildhall Antiques
(Maurice Finlinson (Resident)). The Guildhall, CB2 4NZ. Tel Cambridge (0223) 833943. Open by prior appt only.

Wisbech STD 0945

Attic Gallery
(D. & B. Ransome). 88 Elm Rd. Tel 583734. Open by appt only. Limited edition prints, pre-1900 oil paintings and watercolours, antique silver and porcelain.

Coach House Antiques
(Mrs Joan Ing). 55 Elm Rd, PE13 2TB. Tel 583129. Open Mon-Fri 9-5; other times by appt. Silver, prints, Victorian jewellery and general antiques. LAPADA

Peter A. Crofts
(P.A. Crofts & Pat L. Crofts). Briar Patch, 117 High Rd, Elm, PE14 0DN. Tel 584614. Open Mon-Fri 8-5; closed Sat; other times by appt. English antique furniture, china, silver, jewellery and books. BADA

Grounds & Co
2 Nene Quay, PE13 1AG. Tel 585041. Open 9-5.30. Fine art auctioneers, 1700 lot fine art sales, two 2-3 day events held in May and Nov each year.

Leverington Hall Gallery
(A. & G. Thompson). Leverington, PE13 5DE. Tel 582055. Open any time by appt. Victorian & Edwardian paintings, watercolours & bronzes.

Cheshire

Alderley Edge STD 0625

Alderley Antiques
17 London Rd, SK9 7JT. Tel 583468. LAPADA

Anthony Baker Antiques
(G.D.A.Price). 14 London Rd, SK9 7JS. Tel 582674. 17th to 19thC furniture, barometers, glass and porcelain. LAPADA

Bridgfords Ltd
1 Heyes Lane, SK9 7LA. Tel Wilmslow (0625)585347. Open Mon-Fri 9-5.30. Auctioneers - fine art & general.

Brook Lane Antiques
(G.M. Broadbridge, M.Goodwin). 93 Brook Lane, SK9 7RU. Tel Wilmslow (0625) 582717. (Also at 3 Knutsford Rd., Alderley Edge, Cheshire, SK9 7RU.) Open Tues-Sat 10.30-5; other times by appt. Stripped pine, general antiques, Victoriana, Edwardiana, brass & iron bedsteads.

Shirley Eaton Antiques
15 London Rd, SK9 7JT. Tel 582522. Open Mon-Fri 10-5.30; Sat 10-1; other times by appt. Art deco, 30s and 40s.

Aldersey

Wellesley Wilson Antiques
(Richard Talbot Wilson). Aldersey Manor, CH3 9EH. Tel Broxton (082 925) 500. Open by appt only. 17th to 19thC English furniture and oil paintings.

Altrincham

See Greater Manchester

Cheadle

See Greater Manchester

Cheadle Hulme

See Greater Manchester

Chester STD 0244

Adams Antiques of Chester
(Bruce Adams Ltd). 65 Watergate Row. Tel 319421. Open Mon-Sat 10-5; other times by appt. 18th and 19thC decorative and traditional furniture, clocks and objets d'art. LAPADA

Antique Exporters of Chester
Tel Tarvin (0829) 41001 (priv 0244-570069). Open by appt only. 50,000 sq ft of varied merchandise for export only. Full packing facilities.

Boodle & Dunthorne Ltd
52 Eastgate St, CH1 1LE. Tel 26666. (Also in Liverpool and Manchester.) Open 6 days a week. Fine jewels. Antique and Victorian jewellery and silver. Antique and genuine period French clocks and carriage clocks. NAG

Christina Chance Antiques
Windsor Lodge, Mickle Trafford. Tel 300442.

Chester Antiques
(R. & M. Davison). 49 Watergate Row. Tel 311768 (priv 532208). Open Mon-Sat 9.30-5; other times by appt. Longcase clocks, dolls.

Chester Furniture Cave
(G.A. & R.G. Hadley, J.O. & H.M. Phillips). Old Congregational Church, 97A Christleton Rd. Tel 314798. Open Mon-Sat 9-5; other times by appt. Antiques & decorative items. (Large warehouse 4000 sq.ft).

Grosvenor Antiques of Chester
22 Watergate St. Tel 315201. Open Mon-Sat 9-6; other times by appt. Jewellery, silver, porcelain, furniture, glass, Oriental items, paintings, clocks, watches and dolls.

Erica & Hugo Harper
27 Westgate Row, CH1 2LE. Tel 23004. Open daily 10-5; early closing Wed; other times by appt. Victorian and Edwardian furniture, Staffordshire china, bric-a-brac and Victoriana.

Jackson-Stops & Staff
(G.C.Adnitt FRICS). 25 Nicholas St. Tel 28361. Open Mon-Fri 9-5.30, Sat 9-12; other times by appt. Auctioneers.

Laurel Bank Interiors
Farndon. Tel Farndon (0820) 270704. Oak furniture, wooden bowls, turned accessories, brass and copper reproductions, copies of old master drawings.

Look Around Antiques
61 Watergate Row. Tel 49826. Open Mon-Sat 10-5.30. Large stock of 18th and 19thC furniture, metalware, clocks, barometers and oil paintings.

Lowe & Sons Ltd
(A.J.Thompson). 11 Bridge St Row, CH1 1PD. Tel 25850. Open Mon-Sat 9-5.30. Antique, modern and secondhand silver and jewellery. Also wrist and pocket watches. Large stock of Chester silver and jewellery. LAPADA

Made of Honour
(Eric Jones). 11 City Walls, CH1 1LD. Tel 314208. Open Mon-Sat. Small decorative antiques, books, ceramics, Staffordshire figures.

Mappin & Webb Ltd (Butt & Co)
32 Eastgate Row, CH1 1LF. Tel 25938. (Also in London.) Open daily 9-5.30. Silver; antique and modern jewellery.

Richard A.Nicholson
25 Watergate St, CH1 2LB. Tel 26818. Open Mon-Sat 9.30-5. Antique maps and prints of all parts of the world; framed and unframed. Efficient postal service. Catalogues issued.

Old Schoolhouse Antiques
(Mr & Mrs M. Melody). 41-43 Lower Bridge St. Tel 28968. 17th-19thC furniture, small items. LAPADA

Phillips in Chester
(Robert G. Gowland, FRICS, Director, Chester). New House, 150 Christleton Rd, CH3 5TD. Tel 313936. Open Mon-Fri 8.30-5, Sat 9-12. Fine art auctioneers and valuers. SOFAA

Christopher Pugh Antiques
(Christopher Pugh). 68 Watergate St, CH1 4JE. Tel 314137 (priv 0492 48162). Open Mon-Sat 10-5; other times by appt. Early English furniture, ceramics, glass, metalware, paintings, works of art. LAPADA

Sotheby's Chester
(G.H.S. Bailey, ARICS). Booth Mansion, 28 Watergate St, CH1 2NA. Tel 315531. Open Mon-Fri 9.30-4.30. Auctioneers & valuers.

St Peter's Fine Art Gallery
St Peters Churchyard, Northgate St. Pictures 1840-1940.

Tilston-Woolley Antiques
(Gerald Tilston, Graham Woolley). Hatton Hall Farm, Heath. Tel Farndon (0829) 270827. Open by appt only. Wide range of services including auctioneering, valuation and restoration.

J.W.Tranter
Market Hall. Tel 23614. Open Mon-Sat 10-5. Antiques, jewellery, Victoriana etc.

Bernard Walsh Ltd
11 St Michael's Row, CH1 1EF. Tel 26032. Open Mon-Sat 9.30-5.30. General antiques, including silver and jewellery.

Watergate Antiques
56 Watergate St. Tel 44516. Open Mon-Sat 9.30-5.30. Silver, plate, metalware, porcelain, pottery and militaria.

Disley STD 066 32

The Antique Shop
(Eleanor Brindley). 4 Market St, SK12 2AA. Tel 3297. Open Mon-Sat 10-5.30, early closing Wed; other times by appt. Oak furniture, brass and copper, porcelain. General antiques.

Mill Farm Antiques
(F. Berry). 50 Market St, SK12 2DT. Tel 4045. Open 7 days a week 9-8; other times by appt. Clocks, music boxes, general antiques, pianos, shipping goods.

Farndon STD 0829

Derek Rayment Antiques
Orchard House, Barton Rd, Barton, SY14 7HT. Tel 270 429. Antique barometers of all periods including marine and stick barometers, Fitzroy barometers and barographs. Also specialists in the repair and restoration of these instruments. GMC

Hale

See Greater Manchester

Knutsford STD 0565

David Bedale Antiques
(D.F.W.Bedale). 5 Minshull St. Tel 53621. Open Mon-Sat 9.30-5.30; other times by appt. 17th, 18thC furniture, decorative items.

Cranford Galleries
(M.Bentley). 10 King St. Tel 3646. Open Mon-Sat 10-5; other times by appt. Pictures, prints, Victoriana and pine items.

Arthur Lee Antiques
(Mr and Mrs V.A.Wragg). Hollingford House, Toft Rd. Tel 3134. Open Mon-Sat 9-5.30; early closing Wed; other times by appt. 17th to 19thC English furniture, porcelain, silver, copper, brass.

Lion Gallery & Bookshop
(Raymond P.Hepner). 15A Minshull St, WA16 6HQ. Tel 52915. Open Thurs, Fri, Sat 10-4.30; other times by appt. Large stock of antique maps and prints. Fine antiquarian books.

Frank R. Marshall & Co
Church Hill, WA16 6DH. Tel 53284. Auctioneers.

Michael Wisehall Antiques
Minshull Gallery, 7 Minshull St. Tel 4901. 18th and 19thC furniture, glass, porcelain and decorative items mainly for the trade. BADA

Little Budworth STD 082 921

Greenwoods of Oulton Mill
(Mrs B Oulton). Oulton Mill, Park Rd. Tel 282. Pine furniture. LAPADA

Macclesfield STD 0625

Brocklehursts
Auction Rooms, King Edward St, SK10 1AQ. Tel 27555. Open Mon-Fri 9-5.30. Auctioneers - sales every two weeks.

S.E. Christie - Antiques
(S.E. Christie). 56 Mill Lane. Tel 23929. Open Mon-Sat 10-6. Clean decorative furniture, 1780-1920. Decorative objects, 1780-1920. Furnishing rather than collectors items.

Robert Copperfield Antiques
(Robert Copperfield). 47-49 Mill Lane, SK10 7NP. Tel 26620. Open Mon-Sat 10-6; other times by appt. 17th, 18th and 19thC furniture, Oriental rugs and carpets, metalware, textiles, paintings, works of art, ethnographica.

Gatehouse Antiques
72 Chestergate. Tel 26476. Open Mon-Fri 9-5; early closing Wed. 17th to 19thC furniture, brass, copper, silver, pottery and clocks. Specialising in glass, brass and copper. LAPADA

Macclesfield Antiques
(Paula Bolton). 85 Chestergate, SK10 1DU. Tel 33033 (priv 72281). Open Mon-Sat 10-6; other times by appt. Decorative furniture and small antiques,18th-20thC including silver, jewellery, glass, also large stock paintings. Emphasis on decorative or unusual items.

Morten's Bookshops Ltd
(E.J. Morten, S. Pryce). Chestergate. Tel 23679. Open Mon-Sat 9.30-5.30. New, secondhand and antiquarian books on all subjects. ABA

Malpas STD 0948

Stewart Evans
Church St Antique Shop. Tel 883214. (Also in High St.) Res on prem. Mostly early Welsh and English dressers.

Well House Antiques
(Mrs Sarah Helena French-Greenslade). The Well House, Tilston, SY14 7DP. Tel Tilston (08298) 332. Open Wed, Thurs, Fri, Sat 9.30-5; other times by appt. Country antique shop selling mainly small furniture, silver, porcelain, pottery, glass and many collectors' items.

Nantwich STD 0270

Rex Boyer Antiques
(Rex Boyer). Townwell House, 52 Welsh Row, CW5 5EJ. Tel 625953. Open Mon-Sat 9-6; other times by appt. 19thC furniture. Some shipping. LAPADA

Bridge House Antiques
(Len & Val Tait). The Old Police Station, 96 Welsh Row, CW5 5ET. Tel 624035. Open Mon-Sat 9-5.30; early closing Wed. 19thC furniture, clocks, china and bric-a-brac. Shipping goods.

Farthings Antiques
(P.&A.S.Jones). 50-52 Hospital St, CW5 5RP. Tel 625117. Open 9.30-5.30; early closing Wed; other times by appt. General antiques specialising in silver. Also stocking porcelain, glass, jewellery and furniture.

Nantwich Antiques Centre
(Len Tait). The Old Police Station, 94/96 Welsh Row, CW5 5 ET. Tel 624035. (Also Bridge House Antiques, The Old Police Station, Welsh Row.) Open Mon-Sat 10-5; half day Wed. Wide variety of Victoriana, art deco, glass, china, silver, small furniture.

Townwell House Antiques
(R.Boyer). 52 Welsh Row, CW5 5EJ. Tel 65953. 18th and 19thC furniture. LAPADA

Peter Wilson & Co
The Victoria Gallery, Market St, CW5 5DG. Tel 623878. Auctioneers.

Wyche House Antiques
(Miss J.Clewlow, H.Clewlow). 22 Pepper St. Tel 626803. Open Mon-Sat 9.30-5; closed Wed. Fine furniture, silver, jewellery, china. LAPADA

Neston

Peggy Prothero
(Margaret Mary Prothero). Vine House, Parkgate Rd, L64 9XE. Tel 051-336 2423. Open daily 9-5.30. Res on prem but appt always advisable. Silver, glass, furniture, porcelain and some shipping goods.

Vine House Antiques
(Peggy and R.M.Prothero). Vine House, Parkgate Rd. Tel Liverpool (051) 336 2423. Open daily 10-5; other times by appt. British pottery, porcelain, furniture and silver. Also carpets and rugs. Valuations.

Parkgate STD 038 786

The Green Bottle Antiques
(Mrs Joan Williams). The Parade. Tel Liverpool (051) 336 2823. Open Mon, Tues, Thurs 11-1, 2.30-5; Wed 11-1; Fri 2.30-5; Sat 12.30-5; other times by appt. Porcelain, silver, glass and small furniture.

Plumley

Coppelia Antiques
(Valerie and Roy Clements). Holford Lodge, Plumley Moor Rd, WA16 9RS. Tel Lower Peover (056 581) 2197. Open 7 days by appt. Longcase, Vienna, wall, bracket and carriage clocks. Period oak and mahogany furniture. Victorian soft furnishings - suites, chairs, smalls. Copper and brass. GMC

Poynton STD 0625

Derbyshire Antiques Ltd
(Maureen and Robert Derbyshire). 159 London Road South, SK12 1LQ. Tel 873110. Open Mon-Sat 10-5.30; Wed 10-12.30; other times by appt. Mainly furniture and decorative items of 16th, 17th, 18th and early 19thC, early oak and walnut pieces and Georgian furniture to the Regency period. Only high quality stocked.

Prestbury STD 0625

Artizana
(Jemila and Ramez Ghazoul). The Village, SK10 4DG. Tel 827582. Cross section of British crafts with emphasis on studio glass. ICGA

Prestwich

See Greater Manchester

Sale

See Greater Manchester

Stockport

See Greater Manchester

Tarporley STD 082 93

Brenda Arden Antiques
(Mrs B. Arden). Hulgrave Hall, Tiverton, CW6 9UQ. Tel 2427. 18thC English furniture. Valuations. LAPADA

Wright-Manley
(W.T.Witter (Department Manager). 63 High St, CW6 0DR. Tel 2151. (Also at Chester, Crewe, Nantwich, Whitchurch and Wem.) Auctioneers, valuers, surveyors, land & estate agents. Sales at Beeston Furniture & Fine Art Saleroom. Tel: 0829 260318.

Warrington STD 0295

The Magpie's Nest
(Mrs V.K.Woolley). 665 Knutsford Rd, Latchford. Tel 37079. Open Mon & Thurs 10.30-4.30; closed Sun am. Furniture, china, glass, silver, copper, brass.

Whitegate

The Antiques Shop, Whitegate
(T.H.&B.A.Rogerson). Cinder Hill. Tel Northwich (0606) 882215. Open daily 9.30-6.30 except Mon 2-6 and Thurs 3.30-6.30; other times by appt. General antiques and restoration of paintings, watercolours and prints.

Wilmslow STD 0625

Peter D. Bosson
(Peter Bosson). 10B Swan St, SK9 1HE. Tel 525250 (priv 527857). Open Tues, Thurs-Sat 10.30-5.30; other times by appt. Antiquarian horologist dealing in clocks, barometers, scientific instruments and barographs. Clock & barometer restoration and repairs. Specialist in early electrical horology.

Knutsford Road Antiques
(Frank & Paula Casey). 48 Knutsford Rd, SK9 6JB. Tel 531829 (priv 526043). Open Tues-Sat 10.30-1 2.30-5; early closing Wed; other times by appt. Furniture, glass, porcelain, metalware and general antiques

Cleveland

Billingham

Margaret Bedi Antiques
The Antique Shop, 5 Station Rd, TS23 1AG. Tel Stockton-on-Tees (0642) 607296. Open any time by appt. Fine quality furniture from 1720-1920 and collector's items including Staffordshire figures, local pottery, silver, brass and all metalware. Watercolours and Victorian prints always in stock.

Guisborough STD 0287

Atrium Antiques
(W.L.&M.G.Richardson). 53-55 Church St. Tel 32777. Open Tues, Thurs, Fri,Sat 10-12, 2.30-4.30; other times by appt. Furniture, silver, pottery, porcelain and jewellery.

Middlesbrough STD 0642

E.&N.R.Charlton
69 Cambridge Ave, Marton, TS7 8EG. Tel 319642. Fine English porcelain, including Royal Worcester. LAPADA

Emporia Antiques
(Ronald Freeman, Jill Freeman, K. Wrigglesworth). 279 Linthorpe Rd, TS1 4AS. Tel 242956 (priv 812991). Open Mon-Fri 9-5; Sat 9-1; other times by appt. Jewellery, silver, pottery, paintings, prints, small furniture. NAG

Saltburn-by-the-Sea

Mariners Antiques
High St, Staithes. Tel Whitby (0947) 840565. Open Easter to end Sept:Sat, Sun, bank hols; daily July and Aug; other times by appt. Good selection of general antiques.

Stockton-on-Tees STD 0642

T.B. & R. Jordan
(Tom & Rosamund Jordan). Aslak, Aislaby, Eaglescliffe, TS16 0QN. Tel 782599. Open by appt only. 19thC and early 20thC oil paintings and watercolours. Some contemporary work. LAPADA

Thornaby

Alan Ramsey Antiques
(A.Ramsey). 4A Thornaby Place. Tel Middlesbrough (0642) 603181. Victorian and shipping goods. LAPADA

Cornwall

Bude STD 0288

Bude Antiques
(F.G. & G.E. Palmer). 39 Ocean View Road, EX23 8NH. Tel 3509. Open by appt only. Copper, brass, coloured glass, bric-a-brac and small furniture.

Callington

Chattels
(Peter Lightbody). 6 Saltash Rd, PL17 7BA. Tel Liskeard (0579) 83184. Open Mon-Sat 9.30-5.30; other times by appt. General antiques, selling entirely on commission.

Lorelle Art & Antiques
Fore Street. Open Mon-Sat 10-5. Specialists in pottery,porcelain, glass & small furniture.

Camborne STD 0209

The Old Chair and Wheel Antiques
(Mrs M.V.Major). 32 Wellington Rd, TR14 7LQ. Tel 713700. Open Mon-Sat 9-9; other times by appt. Victoriana, china, glass, books, pictures and furniture.

Flushing

Graham Dark
Carleen, Trefusis Rd. Tel Penryn (0326) 75460. Furniture, works of art and antiquities. BADA

Hayle STD 0736

A.W. Glasby & Son
(D.E. Glasby). 'Antiques', The Stores, Leedstown, TR27 6BE. Tel Leedstown (0736) 850303. Open 10-12.45, 2.15-5; other times by appt. Furniture, porcelain, clocks.

Paul Jennings Antiques
(Paul Jennings). Millbrook House, Angarrack, TR27 5HZ. Tel 754065. Open Mon-Sun 9-5; other times by appt. All types of antique clocks, antique and Victorian furniture.

Indian Queens

The Collectors Trail
(Mrs B.M.Hester). St Francis Rd. Tel St.Austell (0726) 860338. Open Mon-Sat 9-6; other times by appt. Art pottery of early 1900s-Torquay, Brannam, Elton, Bretby; art nouveau/deco metalware; 19thC watercolours, oils, etchings.

Launceston STD 0566

Tamar Gallery
(Norman Preston & Irene Preston). 5 Church St. Tel 4233 (priv 2740). Open Mon by appt; Tues-Sat 10-5; early closing Thurs. 18th to 20thC watercolours, especially British, oil paintings, glass, porcelain and pottery (especially blue and white), jewellery, small furniture.

Westward County Pine
(N.C.Parsonson). 10 Church St. Tel Canworthy Water (056 681) 309 or (0566) 5605. 18th & 19thC English country furniture.

Looe STD 050 36

Ian Barrett's Furniture Workshop
(Ian Barrett). Pink Cottage, Widegates, PL13 1QL. Tel Widegates (05034) 258. Open Mon-Sat 9.30-5.30 and most Suns; other times by appt. All types of furniture restoration. Stock of restored, mainly Victorian & Edwardian to 1930's furniture and small items of copper, brass, china and glass.

Lostwithiel

Old Palace Antiques
(D.V.Bryant). Quay St. Tel Bodmin (0208) 872909. Open Mon-Sat 10-5.30; other times by appt. General antiques and Victoriana. 19th and 20thC furniture, porcelain, postcards, jewellery.

D.W.Patterson Antiques
(D.W.Patterson). 20 Queen St, PL2 0AD. Tel Bodmin (0208) 872879. Open Mon-Sat 10-5.30; other times by appt. General antiques, pine furniture, arms, militaria, instruments, brass, ivories and toys.

Tickle & Bragger & Co Ltd
(K.Tickle, E.M.Greenhouse). Great Western House and Warehouse. Tel Bodmin (0208) 873027 (priv 0503-20504). Open by appt only. Late Victorian, Edwardian, pine and shipping goods.

Mousehole

Vanity Fayre
(Mr J.L.Gillingham). Commercial Rd. Open Mon-Sat 10-1, 2-5; closed Thurs; other times by appt. Interesting and collectable items of all types and from all periods.

Newquay STD 063 73

The Attic
(Miss M. Dixon). Station Approach.

Padstow STD 0841

The Curiosity Shop
(Miss Susan Schofield). West Quay. Tel St Mawgan (0637) 860567. (Home address: Highcove Farm, Trenance, Mawgan Porth,Newquay.) Open 10.30-5.30; 8-10 (April - Nov). Small antiques, pottery, porcelain and metalware, including commemorative wares and crested ware. Many small collectables including postcards and militaria.

Mayflower Antiques
(Miss Cynthia Hoskin). 15 Duke St, PL28 8AB. Tel 532308. Open Mon Sat (summer)10-1 2-5;(winter)10-1; other times by appt. Small antiques and secondhand goods, including commemoratives, jewellery, pottery and porcelain.

Penzance STD 0736

All Things Bright and Beautiful
(Christine & David Brown). The Old Sunday School, Cape Cornwall St, St Just, TR19 7JZ. Tel 788444. Open Mon-Sat 10.30-5.30; other times by appt. Stripped pine furniture, 19thC furniture, general items of copper, brass, lamps, mirrors, china and glass etc.

Charles Jackson Antiques
48-50 Market Jew St, TR18 2HZ. Tel 4388 and 3774. Open daily 8.30-5.30; closed Sun. Clocks, antique glass, china, period oak, French and English furniture.

Melbourne Antiques
48 Market Jew St. Tel 3774. (Assoc. Charles Jackson Estab 1891.) Specialist in antique and modern jewellery. Trade enquiries welcome.

Newton Antiques
(William Nicholas Newton). 85A Market Jew St. Tel 61905. Open Mon-Sat 10.30-1, 2.30-5.30; closed Wed; other times by appt. Jewellery, watches, antique topographical prints and maps, silver, pottery & porcelain, copper & brass, coins, glass, commemoratives etc.

Penzance Pine Centre
(Terry Saunders). 13-14 Bread St. Tel 64027. Open Mon-Sat 10-5.30; half day Wed & Sat; other times by appt. Antiques & pine furniture, silver, silver plate, copper & brass.

Tony Sanders Antiques and New Gallery
(Tony Sanders). 14 Chapel St, TR18 4AW. Tel 66620 (priv 68461). Open Mon-Sat 9-5.30; evenings in Summer; other times by appt. 18th and 19thC general stock, furniture, porcelain, pottery (especially Doulton), silver, glass, prints, paintings. Specialising in 19th & 20thC watercolours and oils including many local artists.

Probus

Rose Linden Antiques
(Stanley Hounsell). Fore St. Tel St Austell (0726) 882055. Open daily in summer, 10-6; closed Thurs and Sun in winter; other times by appt. Porcelain, glass, potlids and Prattware, Staffordshire figures, silver, Victoriana, commemoratives, jewellery and small furniture.

St Austell STD 0726

Ancient and Modern
(Mr & Mrs P.J.Watts). 32-34 Polkyth Rd. Tel 3983. General. Valuations. Restorations. LAPADA

Margaret Chesterton
33 Pentewan Rd. Tel 72926. Open Mon-Sat; other times by appt. Res on prem. Small decorative items, Victoriana, glass and porcelain, some furniture and clocks. Also some old dolls. Mainly trade.

Christie's
(Representative: Christopher Petherick). Tredeague, Porthpean. Tel 64672. Auctioneers & valuers.

London Apprentice Antiques
(R.&J.Noble). PL26 7AR. Tel 63780. Open Mon-Sat 9.30-6; other times by appt. Oriental porcelain & Oriental works of art. English furniture.

Poldark Antiques
(Mrs J Langran). Market House. Tel 72818. Open Mon-Sat 9.30-5; closed Thurs.

St Ives

Artist
(Miss L.Stamiland Roberts ARMS). Zelah Studio, Portgwidden, TR26. Tel 795941. Open occasionally in summer and by appt. Artist - miniatures and portraits in oils, pastels, landscapes, flowers. Restoration of miniatures.

New Craftsman
24 Fore Street. Tel 795652. Open Summer: Mon-Fri 10-10, winter: Mon-Fri 10-5 except Thurs. Pots by leading makers, woven rugs, studio glass, paintings as well as some sculpture including carved and painted objects.

Truro STD 0872

Alan Bennett
(Alan Bennett). 15/16 St Mary's St, TR1 2AF. Tel 73296. Open Mon-Sat 9-5.30. 18th and 19thC furniture, porcelain, silver and jewellery.

Old Barn
(Messrs Campbell and Marsh). Perran-ar-worthal, TR3 7NY. Tel 863831. Open Mon-Fri. 18th and 19thC furniture, copper, brass, ethnographica, especially West African. Weapons - edged and long arms (percussion and flintlock). Longcase clocks.

Peter Stanton Antiques
The Old Pottery, Chapel Hill, TR1 3BN. Tel 70262. Open Mon-Sat 9-5.30. 18th and 19thC furniture, paintings and porcelain. Furniture restoration.

Strickland & Dorling
(Mrs P.Strickland and Mr R.Dorling). 3 River St. Tel 72345. Open Mon-Sat 10.30-4.30; closed Thurs. 18th and 19thC porcelain and pottery, glass, silver, jewellery, pictures and maps, furniture, rugs and collectors items, Staffordshire. Specialising in nautical things and early silver spoons.

Wadebridge STD 020 881

Camel Antiques
(J.S. & B.C.Murphy). J.Young's Market, Molesworth St. Tel 2833 (priv 0840 212476). Open Mon-Sat 10-5; other times by appt. General items, including postcards, porcelain, glass, silver, jewellery, collectors' items.

St Breock Gallery
(Newmark Industrial Securities Ltd). St Breock Churchtown, St Breock, PL27 7JS. Tel 2543 (priv 3451). Open Mon-Sat 10-5; other times by appt. 19th and 20thC watercolours, general antiques, reproduction and antique furniture.

Cumbria

Ambleside STD 0966

B.P. Dennison (Antiques)
(B.P. Dennison). Dwarf Hall, Chapel Hill, LA22 9EB. Tel 32651. (Sats only at 288 Westbourne Grove,London W11(Portobello Market.) Open by appt only. Quality smalls, scientific, medical, nautical instruments, early metalware, treen, bijouterie, oriental and ethnic items, musical instruments, decorators items etc. Specialising also in lighting, electric, gas, oil & candle. LAPADA

The Singing Birds
(Mr R.S.E.Gifford). Michael's Nook, Grasmere, LA22 9RP. Tel Grasmere (09665) 496. Open by appt. English furniture and prints, some silver, brass and porcelain.

The Stables
(Kay & Andrew Saalmans). College St, Grasmere. Tel Grasmere (096 65) 453. Open daily March-Oct 10-6; other times by appt. Country antiques, including metalware, pottery and treen. Also a selection of local maps and prints.

Appleby STD 0930

The Black Boy (incorp Au Bon Souvenir)
1-2 High Wiend. Tel 51491. General antiques.

Brampton STD 069 77

Mary Fell Antiques
(Mary Fell). Collectors Corner, 32/34 Main St. Tel 2685 (priv 0228 22224). Open Tues, Wed, Fri, Sat 11-6; other times by appt. Antique furniture, porcelain, paintings, silver, objets d'art and jewellery. Brass & copper.

Geoffrey Nanson Antiques
25 Front St. Tel 3000. Open Mon-Sat 9-12, 1-5.30, closed Thurs; other times by appt. Watches, carriage clocks, silver, porcelain, brass and copper.

Sotheby's
(Representative: The Earl of Carlisle). Market Place, CA8 1NW. Tel 3722.

Brough STD 093 04

Augill Castle Antiques Ltd
(Michael Hogarth). Augill Castle, CA17 4AY. Tel 412. Open daily 10-6; other times by appt. English & Continental furniture, Chinese porcelain, old master paintings.

Carlisle STD 0228

James W. Clements
19 Fisher St, CA3 8RF. Tel 25565. Open 9-12.30, 1.45-5.30, closed Thurs. Antiques generally.

Maurice Dodd (Booksellers)
(G.W. & V.A.Keates, R.J.McRoberts). 112 Warwick Rd. Tel 22087. Open Mon-Fri 9-5; other times by appt. Antiquarian and general books, paintings, prints and a small stock of antiques. PBFA

Thomson Roddick & Laurie Ltd
24 Lowther St. Tel 28939. (Also in Dumfries, Scotland.) Open Mon-Fri 9-5. Auctioneers of furniture, fine art and antiquarian books.

Cartmel STD 044 854

Norman Kerr
(N.M. Kerr and H. Kerr). Priory House, Priest Lane, LA11 6PX. Tel Cartmel (044 854) 247. Postal business only. Secondhand and antiquarian books on aeroplanes, ships, railways, trams and other subjects. ABA

Cockermouth STD 0900

Cockermouth Antique Market
Main St. Open Mon-Sat, and on Thurs & Sun by appt.

Coniston STD 0966

The Old Man Antiques
Yewdale Rd, LA21 8DU. Tel 389. Open 10-5; other times by appt. Barometers as available, porcelain, silver, glass, coins, jewellery, prints, paintings and furniture.

Fenwick Pattison
(Fenwick Pattison). Bowmanstead, LA21 8HB. Tel 41235. Open Mon-Sat 9.30-5.30; other times by appt. (Half a mile south of Coniston village on Torver Rd.) Early oak and country furniture, some walnut and mahogany, treen, metalware, glass, paintings, carvings.

Grange-over-Sands STD 044 84

Shire Antiques
(Brian and Jean Shire). The Post House, High Newton, Newton-in-Cartmel. Tel Newby Bridge (0448) 31431. Open 9.30-5.30 inc Sun; closed Tues; other times by appt. Early oak and country furniture, treen and copper; early ironwork.

Kendal STD 0539

Cumbria Antiques
(Mr & Mrs P.I.Phillips). 26 Kirkland. Tel 24676. 17th-19thC furniture, paintings, clocks. Valuations. Rush and cane seating. LAPADA

Dower House Antiques
38-40 Kirkland. Tel 23835. Antiques and works of art.

Keith D Edwards Antiques
Crosscrake Farm, Crosscrake, LA8 0LB. Tel Sedgwick (0448) 60313. Open Mon-Fri 9-5; other times by appt. General antiques (period and shipping), smalls and decorative items.

Gerrard Antiques
The Old Cottage, 54 Branthwaite Brow. Tel 23881. Small oak furniture, brass, copper and porcelain. LAPADA

Highgate Antiques
(David Jones & Pat Gunson). 99 and 181 Highgate, LA9 5AA. Tel 24527 (priv 0448 31343). Open Mon-Sat; other times by appt. Large stock of period oak and mahogany furniture, Victorian furniture, clocks, treen, silver, paintings, jewellery etc.

Kendal Studio Pottery
2-3 Wildman St, LA9 6EN. Tel 23291. Open Mon-Fri 10.30-1, 3-6; Sat 10-30-1, 3-5; other times by appt. Oak, silver, glass, jewellery and modern studio pottery. Specialising in paintings, oils and watercolours, drawings, portraits and landscapes. Picture restoration service for oils and watercolours, cleaning, mounting and framing.

Ewen Kerr Books
1 New Rd, LA9 4AY. Tel 20659. Open Mon-Sat 10-5; closed Thurs. Large stock of general and antiquarian books, specialising in modern first editions, natural history and the Lake District. ABA

Multum-In-Parvo & Tools Past
Kirkland. Tel 25168. Open Mon-Sat 10.30-5, closed Thurs; other times by appt. Antique ironmongery, craftsmen's tools, items of folk interest and rural industries, pine. Cabinet makers' tools.

Keswick STD 0596

Holmes Antiques
(Claude & Simone Holmes). 15 and 26b St John's St, CA12 5AS. Tel 73605 (priv 82364). Open Mon-Sat 9.30-5.30; winter closed Wed; other times by appt. Furniture, paintings, collectors' items, objets d'art.

J.Young & Son (Antiques)
12-14 Main St, CA12 5JD. Tel 73434. Open Mon-Sat 9-5.30; closed Wed mid-Winter; other times by appt. Large stock of mainly 18th and 19thC furniture, pottery, metalware & glass.

Kirkby Lonsdale STD 0468

Alexander Adamson Antiques
(Nigel & Piers Adamson, Diana Adamson (Ptnrs)). Tearnside Hall, LA6 2PU. Tel 71989. Open Mon-Fri 10-1, 2-5; Sat 10-5.30. Decorative items, some 18th & early 19thC furniture.

Cumbrian Fine Art Galleries
(Peter Haworth). Lane House, Cow Brow, (postal address:Via Carnforth,Lancs). Tel Crooklands (044 87) 208. Open any time by appt. English & Scottish watercolours 1800-1950, paintings 1880-1950. Exhibitions in April and October; catalogues posted on request.

James Thompson
(James Thompson FSVA, James Thompson FRICS). 64 Main St, LA6 2AJ. Tel 71555. Open Mon-Fri 9-12.30, 1.30-5; other times by appt. Monthly sales of antique and reproduction furniture, silver, glass and china, collectables etc. Quarterly sales of oil paintings and watercolours. Valuations.

Kirkby Stephen STD 0930

Beckfoot Antiques
(Mr & Mrs A.C.B. Ford). Beckfoot Hall. Tel 71348. Open by appt. Small unusual items of Georgian and Victorian jewellery and silver for the collector.

The Book House
(Chris and Mary Irwin). Grey Garth, Ravenstonedale, CA17 4NQ. Tel Newbiggin-on-Lune (05873) 634. Open most times by appt. Antiquarian books, specialising in industrial archaeology and transport history. ABA

Haughey Antiques
(D.M.Haughey). 28-30 Market St, CA17 4QW. Tel 71302. Open Mon-Fri 10-5, Sat noon-5; other times by appt. Period and good quality Victorian furniture, longcase clocks, country furniture and garden statuary. LAPADA

Milburn

Netherly Cottage Antiques
(John & Joy Heelis). Tel Kirkby Thore (0930) 61403. Open daily except Tues morning. Turn off M6 at Penrith, take A66 Penrith-Appleby road to Temple Sowerby. Turn off for Milburn. (Postal address Netherley, Milburn, Penrith, Cumbria.) Bygones, treen, old kitchen items, pottery, porcelain, blue and white, watercolours, books.

Newby Bridge STD 0448

Townhead Antiques
(C.H., E.M. & C.P. Townley). Townhead, LA12 8NP. Tel 31321. Open Mon-Sat 9-5.30; other times by appt. Large stock of antique furniture, porcelain, glass, silver, Victoriana, garden ornaments and arms and armour.

Penrith STD 0768

Antiques of Penrith
(E. & L. Mildwurf & Partners). 4 Corney Sq, CA11 7PX. Tel 62801. Open Mon-Fri 10-12, 1.30-4.45, Sat 10-12; closed Wed. Appt advisable for trade. Large and varied stock of early oak, mahogany, Victorian and Edwardian furniture, brass and copper, glass, china, Staffordshire figures and silver plate. Trade welcome.

Archer Antiques
(V.W.K.Archer). 58 Castlegate. Tel 63446 (priv 0930 51813). Open Mon-Sat 10.30-5, closed Wed; other times by appt. 18th and 19thC furniture and general antiques.

Christie's
(Representative: Victor Gubbins). Eden Lacy, Lazonby, CA10 1BZ. Tel 8800. Open Mon-Fri 9-5. Fine art auctioneers and valuers.

Corney House Antiques
Corney House, Corney Square. Mostly stripped pine furniture and a few small items.

Pelican Antiques
(Mrs Jean Kirkby). The Pelican, Church Rd, Greystoke, CA11 0TW. Tel Greystoke (085 33) 477. Open all day every day but safer to phone first. Small antiques and some furniture.

Jane Pollock Antiques
(Jane Pollock). 4 Castle Gate. Tel 67211. Open Mon-Sat 9.30-5; closed Wed. Silver, pottery, porcelain, boxes.

Sedbergh STD 0587

Merlin Antiques & Restorations
(R.Udall). Howgill Lane. Tel 20301 (priv 20719). Open Mon-Fri 9-5; Sat & Sun by appt. All types of furniture restoration, metal cleaning, pine stripping, French polishing. Period furniture, clocks, brass and copper items, mechanical music instruments, pine furniture stocked. Interested in shipping antiques abroad.

Stable Antiques
(Miss M.Thurlby). Oakdene Country Hotel, Garsdale Rd, LA10 5JN. Tel 20280. Open 7 days, 9-9; other times by appt. Brass, small silver items, treen, small furniture and prints.

Ulverston STD 0229

The Antique Shop & Sale Room
(J.C.Jackson). 11-13 Union St. Tel 52983 (priv 52319). (Also The Sale Room, Fountain St.) Open daily, except Wed; other times by appt. General antique furniture, brass and copper, pottery,china and pictures.

AIA Antiques and Joseph W.Thornton Antiques
59B Market St. Tel (022988) 745. (Also Joseph W. Thornton Antiques in Windermere.) Open by appointment. (Also at 4 Victoria St, Windermere, Tel 09662 2930; saleroom supermarket at North Terrace, Bowness on Windermere.) Fine art, antiques, shipping goods, clocks, paintings, bric-a-brac.

Directory Entries are Free and ADDITIONS OR CORRECTIONS will be welcomed by *THE EDITOR, British Art and Antiques Directory, National Magazine House, 72 Broadwick Street, London W1V 2BP*

Whitehaven STD 0946

Owen Kelly
(V.C.Kelly). 10 & 11 New St, CA28 7DY. Tel 2879. Open by appt. Large stock of various 18thC and later furniture, china, metals, glass etc.

Windermere STD 096 62

Serpentine Antiques
(Mrs M.Worsley). Lake Rd, Bowness-on-Windermere. Tel 4770 (priv 2189). Open Mon, Tues, Wed, Fri, Sat 10-12.30, 2-5; other times by appt. General antiques.

Joseph W.Thornton Antiques
4 Victoria St. Tel 2930 & 022988 745. (Saleroom at North Terrace, Bowness; also AIA Antiques,Ulverston.) Open Sat & Sun by appt. Any item bought or sold. Antiques, Victoriana, shipping goods, bric-a-brac, pictures, clocks, silver plate etc.

H.V. Wilkinson
25-37 Crescent Rd. Tel 815. Large stock of new, secondhand and antiquarian books. Also antique furniture and pictures.

Derbyshire

Ambergate STD 077 385

P.W. Gottschald
(P.W., D.J. & C.R. Gottschald). 32 Derby Rd, DE5 2GE. Tel 6428. Open daily 10-6; other times by appt. Antiques and fine art, European porcelain, 18th & early 19thC furniture, watercolours, engravings, drawings.

Ashbourne STD 0335

John Brown Antiques
38 Church St. Tel 43470. Open Mon-Sat 9-5, closed Wed. General furniture.

Pamela Elsom Antiques
5 Church St. Tel 43468. Open Mon-Sat 10-5; closed Wed; other times by appt. 17th to 19thC furniture; metalware, pottery, glass, general antiques. Separate secondhand book department. LAPADA

P.J.Fradley
Ellastone Old House, Ellastone, DE6 2GU. Tel Ellastone (033 524) 291. Open most days; res on prem. 16th to 19thC furniture and general antiques, including pottery, pewter and ironwork.

Manion Antiques
(Mrs Vivyan J.Manion). 23 Church St, DE6 1AE. Tel 43207. Open Thurs, Fri & Sat 10-5; other times by appt. General antiques with the emphasis on quality.

Old Farmhouse Furniture
(Rod Beech). Alsop en le Dale. Tel Parwich (033525) 473. Large stock of antique and reproduction pine comprising 10 000 sq ft workshops and showrooms. Over 200 pieces of good quality pine in stock. Container packing and courier service.

Out of Time Antiques
21 Church St. Tel 42096. Open Mon-Sat 10-5, closed Wed. Antiques and collectables.

Spurrier-Smith Antiques
(I.Spurrier-Smith). 28 & 41 Church St. Tel 43669 (priv 077 389 368). Open Mon-Sat; closed Wed; other times by appt. 17th, 18th & 19thC furniture, antiques, paintings, porcelain, metalware, architectural items, pine, early oak. Specialist in cork-screws.

Kenneth Upchurch
(Kenneth Upchurch). 30B Church St. Tel Derby (0332) 754499. Open Thurs-Sat 11-5.15; other times by appt. 18th-20thC oil paintings and watercolours, specialising in Victorian landscape oils. 18th-20thC porcelain and pottery, especially Derby.

Yew Tree Gallery
(Gill Wyatt Smith). Ellastone, DE6 2HA. Tel 033 524 341. Contemporary crafts: ceramics, glass and textiles. ICGA

Bakewell STD 062 981

Antiques Coffee House
(Peter Cassidy). Buxton Rd. Tel 3544. Open Mon-Sat 10-5, Sun 2-5; other times by appt. 18th, 19th, 20thC furniture, books, antiquities.

Beedham Antiques Ltd
Holme Hall. Tel 3285. Open by appt only. 16th-17thC English furniture.

K.Chappell Antiques & Fine Art
(Mrs K.Chappell & Mr W.N.Chappell). King St, DE4 1DZ. Tel 2496 (priv 2960). (Also in Baslow, Derbyshire.) Open Mon-Sat 9-6; other times by appt. Fine period functional furniture in walnut, oak, mahogany & yew, clocks, porcelain, treen & objets d'art, oil paintings and watercolours. BADA, CINOA

Maurice Goldstone & Son
(Michael Goldstone). Avenel Court, King St. Tel 2487. (Also The Old Town Hall.) Open daily 9-6. Specialist in English and Continental oak and early period furniture in 18 showrooms. Also decoration. BADA

Water Lane Antiques
(Joy Shaw). Water Lane.

Baslow STD 024 688

K.Chappell Antiques & Fine Art
(Mrs K.Chappell & Mr W.N.Chappell). Goose Green, DE4 1SR. Tel 3311. (Also in Bakewell, Derbyshire.) Open by appt only. Period furniture, fine art and porcelain. BADA

Radcliffe House Antiques
Nether End, DE4 1SR. Tel 2262/2141. 18th & 19thC furniture, desks, bureau bookcases, tables, chairs,china cabinets, clocks, etc. Shipping and deliveries arranged.

Buxton STD 0298

West End Galleries
(A. & A. Needham). 8 Cavendish Circus. Tel 4546 (priv 6632). Open Mon-Fri 9.30-5; other times by appt. Furniture, bronzes, oils and works of art.

Castleton STD 028 76

Ann Capon Antiques
Market Place, S30 2WG. Tel Hope Valley (0433) 20270. Open daily except Tues 1.30-5; other times by appt. General antiques, including pottery, porcelain, brass and copper.

Chesterfield STD 0246

Brian Bingham Antiques
420 Chatsworth Rd, Brampton. Tel 208441. 17th and 18thC oak furniture, early metalware, pictures, some mahogany furniture.

Chesterfield Antiques Centre
(C.B.Sheppard). 195 Chatsworth Rd. Tel 205614. Open Mon-Sat 9.30-5.30, closed Wed & Sun. Eight showrooms of quality antiques, collectors items and paintings of all descriptions.

Westfield Antiques
(Mrs Dorothea Pugh). Freebirch Cottage, Eastmoor, S42 7DQ. Tel Baslow (024 688) 3153. Open by appt only. Early 19thC porcelain, Chinese embroidery, maps and prints.

K. Chappell Antiques and Fine Art

Vendors & Purchasers of Fine Quality Antiques

Always a Large Selection of period functional Furniture from the 17th century to the 19th century, in Oak, Walnut, Mahogany & Fruitwood stocked in our Nine Showrooms

Open 9am to 6pm, Monday to Saturday

Car Parking at Rear

Antiques Trade Warehouse Now open

King Street Bakewell Derbyshire

TELEPHONE 062981 2496 AND 4531 (BUSINESS HOURS) OR BY APPOINTMENT CALL 062981 2960
20 MINUTES FROM JUNCTION 28 ON M1, OR OUR CAR WILL COLLECT FROM LOCAL RAIL STATIONS

Kendal Studio Pottery

ANTIQUES

WILDMAN STREET
KENDAL LA9 6EN
Tel (STD 0539) 23291

Monday–Friday 10.30–1; 3–6
Saturday 10.30–1; 3–5

Access, Barclaycard,
Diners, American Express

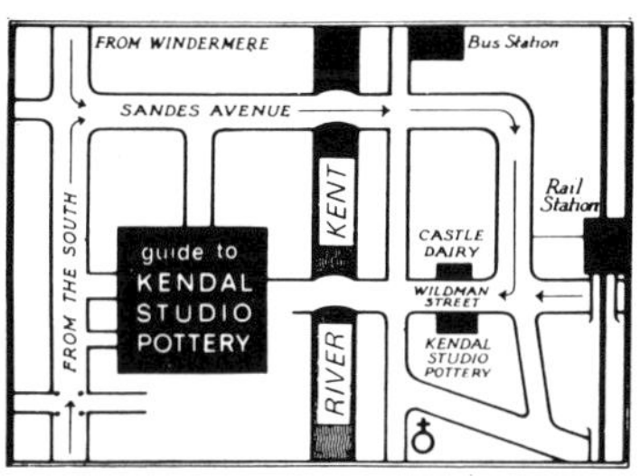

The sign of
THE BRITISH ANTIQUE DEALERS' ASSOCIATION

The nearest you will get to a guarantee
in the world of antiques.
Ring Sally Tunley on 01-589 4128
for a free list of members

HAUGHEY ANTIQUES

KIRKBY STEPHEN, CUMBRIA CA17 4QW
Tel: (07683) 71302

Extensive showrooms of 17th, 18th and 19th century furniture, clocks, barometers, decorative items and garden furniture and statuary.

Good trade call en route to Scotland, 10 mins from Junction 38, M6.

Derby STD 0332

Antique Exporters (Derby) UK
(R. Allsebrook). The Warehouse, Britannia Mills, Mackworth Rd. Tel 32487. Victorian furniture, specialising in large tables. Restorations. Shipping. Trade only.

Richard Flavell Antiques
(Richard Flavell). 9 Curzon St. Tel 367727. Open Mon 12.30-4; Tues-Sat 10-4; closed Wed; other times by appt. 19th and 20thC antique curios & objets d'art.

Neales Innes Nichols
(Brian Nichols). Becket St, DE1 1HW. Tel 43286. (Branch of Neales of Nottingham.) Auctioneers.

Eyam

Antiques
(N.S.Oxley). Main St. Tel Baslow (024 688) 3265. Open Fri, Sat, Sun noon-5; other times by appt. 18thC furniture, Staffordshire figures, 18thC porcelain, brass and copper prints, watercolour drawings.

Glossop STD 045 74

Chapel Antiques
(Nicholas Greenbank, E.Annal). Brookfield. Tel 5195. Open 10.30-6.30; other times by appt. Large stock of 17thC to Edwardian furniture. Also paintings, dolls, European & Oriental porcelain, glass, clocks and silver.

Matlock STD 0629

Temple Antiques
(D.J.Mitchell). Glenwood Lodge, Temple Walk, Matlock Bath.

Melbourne STD 033 16

C.Reynolds Antique Clock and Watch Specialist
(C.Reynolds, Esq). The Spindles, Tonge. Tel 2609. Open Mon-Sat 9-5; other times by appt. Unusual clocks and watches, including longcase and bracket clocks.

Old Glossop

Seymour Galleries
(Patricia Seymour). Church St South. Tel 04574-62555. Open Wed-Sun 10-5.30; other times by appt. Early oak and decorative items.

Quarndon

Friary Antiques
(N.W.Jackson). Tel Derby (0332) 552160. Open by appt only. General antiques. LAPADA

Sandiacre STD 0602

Ian H.R.Cowley
(Ian Cowley). The Book Shop, 4 Station Rd, NG10 5BG. Tel 393379. Open Mon-Sat 9.30-5; closed Wed. (Sandiacre is at Junction 25 on the M1.) Books on most subjects, including literature, art, antiques, theology. New books to order.

Ticknall

Sam Savage Antiques
(C.A.J.Savage and Mary Savage). Hayes Farm, DE7 1JZ. Tel Melbourne (033 16) 2195. Open Mon-Sat 10-5.30; other times by appt. 17th-19thC furniture, walnut, mahogany and oak. Also decorative antiques. LAPADA

Whaley Bridge STD 066 33

The Antique Home Ltd
(Christopher Howarth Robert Waterhouse). 3 Lower Macclesfield Rd. Tel 3078. English and Continental furniture, clocks, porcelain, bronzes. LAPADA

Richard Glass
Hockerley Old Hall, SK12 7AS. Tel 4320. Open Fri, Sat & Mon; please telephone first. 17thC oak furniture and decorative items from various periods.

Martin Marsh Militaria
(Martin Marsh). 114 Buxton Rd, SK12 7JF. Tel 3267. Open daily 10-5; other times by appt. British military badges. Mainly mail order. Catalogue with sample badge £1.

Devon

Ashburton STD 0364

Ashburton Marbles
(Adrian Ager & Alyson Ager). 6 West St, TQ13 7DU. Tel 53189 (priv 0626 833934). Open Mon-Sat 9.30-5; half day Wed & Sat; other times by appt. Period fireplaces & accessories, decorative antique furnishings (overmantles, fenders, scuttles etc) all stocked.

Brocanteuse Gallery
11 North St. Tel 53389. Period painted furniture, oak, primitives, needlework, metalware, country, decorative objects, early pine.

Edward Cassassa
The Gallery, East St.

Margerie Collinge Gallery
20 West St.

Atherington

Hilton Restorations
East View Cottage. Tel High Bickington (0769) 60253. Restoration of metal antiques, including pewter, bronzes and ormolu.

Axminster STD 0297

The Old Curiosity Shop (Antiques)
(N.A.& C.J.Love). South St, EX13 5AD. Tel 33016. Open 8.30-5.30; other times by appt. General antiques & curios, silver, clocks, furniture & secondhand books.

Bampton STD 0398

Robert Byles
7-9 Castle St, EX16 9NS. Tel 515. Open Mon-Sat 10-5.30. Early oak, country furniture, unstripped pine, Delft, slipware and metalwork.

Barnstaple STD 0271

Mark Parkhouse Antiques & Jewellery
(Mark Parkhouse). 106 High St, EX31 1HP. Tel 74504-5. Open Mon-Sat 9.30-5; half day Wed. General antiques and jewellery.

John Smale & Co
(R.Wonnacott FRICS, A.M.Evans FRICS). 19 Cross St. Tel 42000, 42916. Open Mon-Fri 9-5.30; Sat 9-12. Auctioneers. Auction sales of antique and other furniture and effects in private houses in the North Devon area at irregular intervals.

Bideford STD 023 72

Chandlers
(R.J.Lloyd). 65 High St, EX39 2AN. Tel 72331. Open Mon-Sat 9.30-5; closed Wed; other times by appt. Books, prints, etchings, paintings, pottery and general antiques.

J. Collins and Son (Est.1953)
(John, John Collin and Pamela Biggs). The Studio, 63 & 28 High St, EX39 2AN. Tel 73103 (priv 76485). Open 9.30-5; closed Wed; other times by appt. Five extensive showrooms of furniture and general antiques. Also two large galleries of fine 19thC oil paintings and watercolours. Shipping goods.

A.C.Littlejohns
43 Lower Gunstone. Tel 2478. Photographers.

Petticombe Manor Antiques
(O. Wilson). Petticombe Manor, Monkleigh, EX39 5JR. Tel 75605. Open daily, incl Sun; closed Wed. Large stock of dining chairs, easy chairs, dining tables, chests, bookcases, desks, bureaux, extensive stock of general antiques, brass, copper, watercolours and oils.

Braunton STD 0271

Eileen Cooper Antiques
(Mrs Mary B. Chugg). Challoner's Rd, EX33 2ES. Tel 813320. Open Tues-Sat 10.30-1, 2-5; Wed 10.30-1; other times by appt. Pottery and porcelain, silver, jewellery, metalware, small furniture, paintings and prints, lace, fine linen, textiles, embroideries, costume.

Timothy Coward Fine Silver
Marisco, Saunton. Tel 890466. Fine antique silver.

Brixham STD 080 45

Courtney Beer
Milton House. Tel 3195. 18thC English furniture.

John Prestige Antiques
1/2 Greenswood Court, Greenswood Rd. Tel 6141, 6723 (priv 3739). Open Mon-Fri 8.45-6; other times by appt. Large stock of Victorian and period furniture, paintings, metalware and smalls. Shipping goods.

Buckfastleigh STD 0364

D.& D.R.Pope
(Dennis and Dorothy Pope). Woodview House, 114 Plymouth Rd, TQ11 0DB. Tel 43552. Open 10-5.30 (7 days a week); other times by appt. Small furniture, early silver, paintings and porcelain.

Budleigh Salterton
STD 039 54

Just Judy Antiques
High St.

New Gallery
(Major J.G. Hull). Abele Tree House, 9 Fore St, EX9 6NG. Tel 3768. Open Tues-Sat 10-5; other times by appt. Oils, watercolours, antique prints 17th to 19thC. Signed proofs of limited editions, sculpture. Valuations for insurance and probate. Restoration.

Quinney's
High St. Tel 2793. Open 9.15-12.45, 2.15-5.15, closed Thurs and Sat pm. General antiques.

Maurice Goldstone & Son

MICHAEL GOLDSTONE

AVENEL COURT
BAKEWELL
DERBYSHIRE DE4 1DZ
Telephone 062 981-2487

Early Period
Furniture and
Decoration

A small oak one flap table with double gates, c. 1690.

THE ANTIQUE CENTRE, HONITON

(Abingdon House, 136 High St., Honiton)

Situated in a Devon High Street with 18 antique shops, the Centre offers a wide range of antiques on behalf of 12 dealers. Specialisms include Mason's Ironstone, Blue and White, stripped pine, woodworking and agricultural tools, and jewellery. Open Mon–Sat 9.30–5.00. Enquiries about fully managed rented units welcome.

Tel: (0404) 2108 or (after hours) (0404) 850464

Antique Jewellery Bought and Sold

Large stock of interesting items from Victorian and Edwardian to 20's and 30's Art Deco. Our selection is constantly being updated so telephone or visit our Poole showrooms and find out more.

D.J. JEWELLERY

166-168 ASHLEY ROAD, PARKSTONE, POOLE, DORSET. BH14 9BY. TEL: (0202) 745148

ASHBURTON MARBLES

6 West Street, Ashburton, Devon
0364-53189

A fine Victorian Sicilian marble fire surround with twin pink marble ¼-columns + pink marble inlays – £850 – a Victorian rococo cast iron interior c 1850 – £375

Just one example from the extensive and varied stock of marble and timber fire surrounds, c 1790-1910, decorative cast iron interiors and antique fireplace accessories.

"7,000 sq feet of desirable fireplaces at buyable prices"

B. & T.Thorn & Son
2 High St, EX9 6LQ. Tel 2448. Open Mon-Sat 9.30-5.30; early closing Thurs; other times by appt. English ceramics. BADA

Chagford STD 064 73

John Meredith Antiques
(Avril and John Meredith). 36 The Square. Tel 3474 (priv 3405). Open Mon-Sat 10-5; other times by appt. Oak furniture and Oriental furniture, ethnic items, carved wood and stone, metalware and weapons.

Mary Payton Antiques
The Old Market House, TQ13 8DD. Tel 2428 (priv 2388). Open Tues-Sat 10-5; closed Wed; other times by appt. English pottery and porcelain, specialising in Staffordshire; English glass, maps and prints of Devon and Baxter prints.

Colyton STD 0297

Brookfield Gallery
Market Place. Tel 52038. Open Tues, Thurs-Sat 10-5; other times by appt. English and Continental watercolours.

Ch-Art
(Philip Wadsworth). Marine House, St Andrew Sq. Tel 53335. Chattels and fine art valuations and sales advisory service.

Crediton STD 036 32

Taylor-Halsey Antiques
(Maureen and Richard Halsey). Strangs, Sandford, EX17 4EL. Tel 3408. Open most business hours. 17th-19thC oak, country and other furniture and associated items. Also books on collecting and similar subjects. PBFA

Cullompton STD 0884

Mills Antiques
(G.&V.Mills). 39 Fore St. Tel 33266. Open Mon-Fri 9.15-5.30; Sat 9.15-1;closed Thurs. Furniture and general antiques.

Kimberley Snow & Son
(A.L.Snow). Verbeer Manor, Willand, EX15 2PE. Tel 33312. Open by appt only. 18th, 19th and 20thC British furniture. Also art nouveau and art deco items.

Sunset Strip
(Miller & Reeves). The Old Forge, Higher Mill Lane. Tel 32689. Stripped pine.

Dartington

Dartington Cider Press Centre
(Dartington Trading Company). Shinners Bridge, TQ9 6JE. Tel Totnes (0803) 864171. Open Mon-Sat 9.30-5.30; also Sun in summer. Domestic ware by Dartington Pottery Workshop, toys, glass, woven rugs, knitware and jewellery in precious metals. Ten shops situated in Old Cider Press Centre.

Dartmouth STD 080 43

Agincourt House
(R.L.Bowes). Lower Ferry, TQ6 9AN. Tel 2472. Open daily, including Sun pm. Good stock of antique furniture of all periods and general curios, prints and paintings.

Chantry Book Shop
(M.P. Merkel). 11 Higher St, TQ6 9RB. Tel 2796 (priv) 4208. (Also showrooms at Burnley Rd.) Open Mon-Sat 10.30-5.30; other times by appt. Rare prints & books, watercolours, oils, antiquarian maps, sea charts & town plans.

Simon Drew Gallery
(Simon and Caroline Drew). 13 Foss St, TQ6 9DR. Tel 2832. Ceramics and fine arts. ICGA

Georgian House Antiques
(Anthony Burden). 2 Anzac St, TQ6 9DL. Tel 2723. Open Mon-Sat 10-5.30, closed Sun; other times by appt. Small Georgian & Victorian furniture, pottery, porcelain, clocks, brass, copper, etc.

East Budleigh

The Old Bakery
Tel Budleigh Salterton (03954) 3289. Porcelain, furniture, silver and copper.

Exeter STD 0392

Wm Bruford & Son Ltd
1 Bedford St, EX1 1LU. Tel 54901. (Also in Eastbourne, E.Sussex.) Open Mon-Fri 9-5.30, Sat 9-1. Specialists in fine old English silver and silver spoons, antique and secondhand jewellery. BADA

Drummer Antiques
(John & Shirley Durn). Nr Exeter Airport, Clyst Honiton. Tel Exeter (0392) 66279. (Also in South Molton.) Open Mon-Fri 9-5. 19thC furniture, oak, walnut, mahogany, rosewood and pine. Shipping goods.

Brian Mortimer Antiques
87 Queen St, EX4 3RP. Tel 79994. Open Mon-Sat 9.30-5. Jewellery & silver.

John Nathan
153/154 Cowick St. Tel 78216. Open Mon-Sat 9-5.30; Wed 9-1. Silver, clocks, furniture and jewellery.

Palace Gate Gallery
1 Deanery Place, Palace Gate, EX1 1HU. Open Mon-Sat 10-1, 2-5.30. Ceramics, studio glass and wood.

Phillips in Exeter
(Christopher Hampton, Manager). Alphin Brook Rd, Alphington, EX2 8TH. Tel 39025/6. Open Mon-Fri 8.30-5; Sat 9-12. Fine art auctioneers, holding regular specialised sales of antique furniture, Victoriana, ceramics, glass, metalware, paintings, prints, silver, jewellery, sporting and collectors items. SOFAA

C. Samuels & Sons Ltd
17-18 Waterbeer St, Guildhall Shopping Centre, EX4 3EH. Tel 73219. Open Mon-Sat 9-5.30. Antique prints and maps. Specialising in topographical (UK & world) fashion, flowers, portraits, Vanity Fair prints, Japanese woodblock prints & others. FATG

Sotheby's
(Representative: John Tremlett). Bickham House, Kenn, EX6 7XL. Tel 833416. Auctioneers and valuers.

Stockwell Antiques
(D.L.Biggs). Exeter Antique Wholesalers, Exeter Airport, Clyst Honiton, EX5 2LL. Tel 66279. Period English furniture, shipping goods. LAPADA

The Tudor Gallery
(Leonard J.Smith Esq). 2nd floor, 93 Sidwell St, EX4 6PH. Tel 77659. Open 10-1, 3-5 usually but appt always advisable. Restorer of old oil paintings. ABPR

Peter Wadham
The Antique Shop, 5 Cathedral Close. Tel 39741. Open Mon-Sat 10-6; other times by appt. Small furniture,(small tables, corner cupboards, desks etc), mirrors, glass, pottery, topographical prints and unusual pictures. Specialising in boxes, needlework pictures, treen and glass.

Waterwheel Pine and Antiques
Cricklepit Mill, The Quay. Tel 217076. Selection of pine and country furniture plus an extensive range of quality reproduction furniture.

Exmouth STD 0395

Michael & Jean Vaughan (Devon) Ltd
5 High St. Tel 71528. General and 18thC furniture.

Hatherleigh STD 0837

Hatherleigh Antiques
(Sally & Mike Dann). 51 Market St. Tel (priv) 810500. Open Mon, Tues, Fri, Sat 9-5; other times by appt. Country furniture, pottery, oak.

Honiton STD 0404

Abingdon House - The Antique Centre
(J.J.Butler & M.V. Melliar-Smith). 136 High St, EX14 8JP. Tel 2108/86300 (priv 850464). Antique centre with fifteen dealers.

J. Barrymore & Co
(F.J.Ogden, Mrs M.R. Ogden). 73-75 High St. Tel 2244. Open Mon-Sat 10-5.30; early closing Thurs. Antique and modern silver, old Sheffield plate, Victorian electro-plate and Victorian jewellery. Specialising in cutlery and old Exeter hall-marked silver.

Roderick P.Butler
Marwood House, EX14 8PY. Tel 2169. Open Mon-Sat 9.30-5.30; other times by appt. 17th and 18thC furniture and early metalwork. Specialising in rare and unusual items. BADA

Christopher J. Button-Stephens
(C.J. Button-Stephens). Plympton House, 59 High St. Tel 2640. Open Mon-Fri 9.30-1, 2-5; closed Thurs; other times by appt. 18th, 19thC furniture, metalware including brass, copper & pewter.

The Honiton Lace Shop
(Jane, Neil & Jonathan Page). 44 High St. Tel 2416 (priv 2629). Open Mon-Sat 9.30-1. 2-5; other times by appt. Antique lace, linens, European & Oriental textiles, needleworks and rugs.

L.J.Huggett & Son
Bramble Cross, Exeter Rd. Tel 2043. Res on prem. English and Continental furniture and works of art.

Kings Arms Antiques
(Mark Griffiths). 56 High St, EX14 8PQ. Tel 3659. Open 10-5. Furniture, pottery, porcelain, Persian rugs, copper & brass.

Michael Matthews
Auction Rooms. Tel 41872. Auctioneer.

Geoffrey M. Woodhead
Monkton House, 53 High St. Tel 2969. Open 9.30-1, 2.15-5.20; early closing Thurs, Sat; other times by appt. Antique and furnishing pieces of all periods; also small stock of secondhand books.

Horrabridge

Robert Howes Antiques
The Olde Saddlers Shoppe, PL20 6ED. Tel Yelverton (0822) 853929 (priv 852109). Open Mon-Sat; other times by appt. General antiques and collectors' items.

Ilfracombe STD 0271

Old Britannia
(S.L. Malsom). Castle Street, Combe Martin. Tel Combe Martin (027 188) 3610. Open daily 10-5.30; other times by appt. Stripped pine, oak, mahogany, shipping and architectural goods. Also smalls. Brass & copper.

Retrospect Antiques
(L.M.McCulley). King St, Combe Martin. Tel Combe Martin (027188) 2346. Open Mon-Sat 9.30-5.30; also Sun in summer; other times by appt. General antiques and bric-a-brac, including metalware, clocks and watches, silver, furniture, oddities and occasionally collectors cars & motorcycles.

Ivybridge

Thomson Antiques
(Alex & Sheila Thomson). Ermefield House, Western Rd, PL21 9AL. Tel Plymouth (0752) 892304. Open by appt only. High quality period furniture including mahogany, oak, walnut, country furniture. Selected smalls.

Kingsbridge STD 0548

A. Halsey Antiques
(Angela Halsey). Boffins Boft, Bowcombe Creek. Tel 2440. (Also by appt in Pimlico, London SW1.) Open Mon-Fri 9.30-5; Sat 9.30-12; other times by appt. Important stock of 17th & 18thC English & Continental oak & fruitwood furniture & works of art. Antique purchasing service, courier service, art appreciation courses. Interiors created internationally. Valuations for insurance & probate. BADA, CINOA

Charles Head & Son
(C.W.A. Head, A.C. Head & R.J. Cattell). 113 Fore St, TQ7 1BG. Tel 2352. Open Mon-Fri 9-5.30, Sat 9-4; other times by appt. Auctioneers.

Moretonhampstead STD 0647

Herbert Clark
2/4 Ford St, TQ13 8LN. Tel 40334. Open 9.30-1; 2.15-5.30; closed Thurs; other times by appt. Glass, china, metal, few pieces of furniture. Specialising in 18thC pottery.

Newton Abbot STD 0626

Calver Associates
(George & Florence Calver). TQ12 4QE. Tel 3263 (pm only). Open by appt only. Consultants on antique sewing machines (International). Largest world records of antique sewing machines and Keats stardiscs. With requests for help please enclose photographs and data, and two SAEs.

David & Charles
(Nigel Hollis). Brunel House, Ford Road.

Julian Antiques
(J.V.S. Goode). Aller Vale Buildings, Market Park Rd, Kingskerswell, TQ12 5AZ. Tel Kingskerswell (08047) 2629 (priv 0803 24934). Open Mon-Fri 8.30-5; other times by appt. Large trade warehouse. Victorian furniture.

Newton Abbot Antiques Centre
(Paul Stockman). 55 East St. Tel 4074. Open Tues 9-4; Shop only Sat & Mon 10-12. Over 50 dealers every Tuesday with wide range of goods. Half a mile from Newton Abbot by-pass roundabout.

Old Treasures
(John & Brenda Gordon). 126A Queen St, TQ12 2EU. Tel 67181. Open Mon-Sat 9.30-4.45; early closing Thurs. Period jewellery, porcelain, glass, portrait miniatures.

Northam

H.A. & D.M. Hale
5A Cross St. Tel Bideford (02372) 77216. Open Mon,Tues, Thurs, Fri 9-5; other times by appt. Silver, silver plate, porcelain, antiques and fine art generally.

Tooley Antiques
5 Cross St. Tel Instow (0271) 860851. Open Mon-Sat 10.30-5, closed Wed. Specialists in longcase barometers; also general antiques including glass, ceramics, silver, brass and small furniture.

Okehampton STD 0837

Alan Jones Antiques
Fatherford Farm. Tel 2970. English furniture, small items. Valuations. Shipping furniture - 30 000 sq ft. Trade only. LAPADA

Skeaping Gallery
(Nicholas Skeaping). Townend House, Lydford, EX20 4AR. Tel 383. Open by appt only. 19th and early 20thC oil paintings and watercolours, specialising in West Country scenes and artists.

Ottery St Mary STD 040 481

Georgian House Antiques
(Peter & Sandie Hampshire). 13 Silver St. (Also at Honiton Antiques Ltd.)

Plymouth STD 0752

Alvin Antiques
148 Union St. Tel 665628. Large stock of 18thC furniture and 18th and 19thC porcelain.

N. & P. Bennett
16 Southside St, Barbican, PL1 2LB. Tel 68676. Open Mon-Sat 9.30-6; other times by appt. General antiques including ceramics, jewellery and silver.

Christie's
(George Lopes). Gnaton Estate Office, Yealmpton. Tel 880636. Agent for auctioneers and valuers.

Circa Fine Art
(Philip Saunders). Island House, Barbican, PL1 2LS. Tel 663318. Open Tues-Sat 10-5; other times by appt. Oil paintings & watercolours, 1550-1930.

Galaxy Arts
38 New St, Barbican, PL1 2NA. Tel 667842. Open Mon-Sat 9.30-5.30. General antiques specialising in scientific instruments.

Luella Antiques
(Peter Gray). 40 North Hill, PL4 8ET. Tel 667536. Open Mon Tues Thurs Fri 9.30-5.30; Wed 9.30-1; Sat 10.30-1, 2.30-5.30. Antique furniture, ceramics, objets d'art, jewellery.

Michael Newman (Fine Art Auctioneer & Valuer)
(Michael H. Newman, FRICS). Central Auction Rooms, St Andrews Cross, PL1 2DQ. Tel 669298 (priv 892144). Open 9-5; Sat 9-12; other times by appt. Auctioneer and valuer of pictures, paintings, prints & maps, furniture, porcelain, silver, jewellery and the whole range of antiques and paintings. Specialising in sunken treasure. RICS, SOFAA

Colin Rhodes Antiques
(C.J.Rhodes & B.R.C.Rhodes). Collier House, 53 Southside St. Tel 669079 (priv 42761). Open Mon-Sat 10-1, 2-5; other times by appt. Oil paintings and watercolours, metalware, 18th and early 19thC furniture, clocks etc. Valuations for probate and insurance undertaken. LAPADA

Taylor Lane & Creber
38 North Hill, PL4 8EQ. Tel 670700. Fine art and chattels auctioneers.

Priestacott Meshaw

Thomas & Dymond
(Roger Thomas & Jane Dymond). EX36 4NG. (Also at Bartlett St. Antique Centre, 7-10 Bartlett St, Bath.) English furniture, Masons Ironstone, blue & white transfer ware and decorative items. LAPADA

Salcombe STD 054 884

Windjammer Crafts
2 Russell Court. Tel 2979. Open Mon-Sat 10-5, Thurs 10-1. Nov to March shop closes at 1. Ceramics, studio glass, woven textiles, turned wood. Exhibitions held four times a year.

Seaton STD 0297

Etcetera
Beer Rd, EX12 2PA. Tel 21965. Open Mon-Sat 10-5, early closing Thurs. General antiques.

Tantalus Antiques & Books
(A.A.& B.K.Dunstan-Smith). Holly Cottage, Watercombe, Branscombe, EX12 3BT. Tel Branscombe (029780) 457. Open by appt only. Paintings, books and small furniture. PBFA

Sidmouth STD 039 55

Copperfields
(Mrs H.Halkes). 1 Church St. Tel 2145. Open Mon-Sat 10-1, 2.15-5; early closing Thurs; other times by appt. Specialists in silver and jewellery. LAPADA

Peter Eley F.S.V.A.
(P.J.Eley, K.M. Eley, S.W. Eley, R.J.Eley). Western House, 98-100 High St, EX10 8EF. Tel 2552. Open Mon-Fri 9-1, 2.15-5.30; Sat 9-12.30. Fine art and general auctioneer. FSVA

Fox Antiques
(J. & B. Napier-Fenning). 70 High St. Tel 3485. Open Mon-Fri 10-5, Thurs & Sat 10-1; other times by appt. 19thC furniture, porcelain, glass, curios.

John Lyle
Harpford, EX10 0NH. Tel Colaton Raleigh (0395) 68294. Open daily by appt only. On Exeter to Sidmouth Rd, near Newton Poppleford, lane marked Higher Way, corner with Knapps Lane. Early books on wine and food, 1470-1900. ABA

Sefton Antiques
(A.M.& A.Miller). Old Fore St, EX10 8LP. Tel 2842 (priv 3923). Open Mon-Sat 10-5; other times by appt. Centre of Sidmouth near Market Square. Furniture, metalwork, treen, glass, porcelain, silver, old Sheffield plate, pictures. Antiques for the country home.

South Brent STD 036 47

Philip Andrade Ltd
(Philip Andrade, Margaret Andrade). White Oxen Manor, Rattery, TQ10 9JX. Tel 2454. Open Mon-Fri 9-6 & Sat am; other times by appt. Large stock of period furniture, antiques and works of art. BADA

Fine Pine Ltd
(Nick and Lorraine Gildersleve). Zeaston Farm. Tel 2505. (Also in Totnes.) Good selection of old pine & country furniture, & furnishing pieces in oak and mahogany.

P.M.Pollak Fine Scientific and Medical Books
(Dr P.M.Pollak). Moorview, Plymouth Road, TQ10 9HT. Tel 3457. Open by appt. Select stock of antiquarian and rare books, manuscripts, prints and photographs with emphasis on medicine, science and natural history, occasional surgical and scientific instruments. Free catalogues issued about 3-4 p.a. ABA PBFA

South Molton STD 076 95

Architectural Antiques
(Andre & Rose Busek). The New Savoy Show Rooms, New Road. Tel 3342 (priv 4167). (Also "An Englishman's Home", 56 Stokes Croft, Bristol.) Open Mon-Sat 9-6; other times by appt. Architectural antiques, panelling, fire surrounds, doors, stained & leaded glass, Victorian bathroom fittings, pub and shop interiors. Trade warehouse of 6000 sq ft at Ley Farm, South Molton. Tel 07695-2059.

Drummer Antiques
(John D.Durn). 100 East St, EX36 3DF. Tel 2521. (Trade warehouse at Exeter Airport, Clyst Honiton, Exeter.) Open Mon-Sat; early closing Wed; other times by appt. Large stock of Victorian and Edwardian items and others up to 1930. Also pine goods.

Norman Antiques
113 East Street. Tel 3055.

Tavistock STD 0822

Archways
(Geoffrey, Claire & Kay Mallinson). Abbey Arch, Bedford Sq, PL19 0AE. Tel 2773. Open Mon-Sat 10-4; early closing Wed & Sat; other times by appt. Porcelain, jewellery, small furniture, paintings. GMC

King Street Curios
(Tony and Patricia Bates). 5 King St, PL19 0DS. Tel 5193. Open Mon-Sat 9-5.30. General antiques, specialising in art nouveau, art deco, 19th and 20thC British porcelain, postcards, pine furniture.

Milton Abbot Antiques
(James Cant). Venn Hill, Milton Abbot. Tel 392. Open most days, res on prem. General antiques, including furniture, boxes and tea caddies.

Ward & Chowen
(R.G.Woolcock, FRICS, Mrs A.F. Woolcock). 1 Church Lane. Tel 2458/9. (Also at Auction Rooms, Market Rd, Tavistock (Tel. 0822 2603.) Open Mon-Fri 9-5, Sat 9-4; other times by appt. Quarterly sales of antique furniture, pictures, silver, jewellery, etc at The Town Hall, Tavistock. Fortnightly sale of household and lesser value shipping goods at Auction Rooms.

Teignmouth STD 062 67

Charterhouse Antiques
(A.J. & S.N.Webster). 1B Northumberland Place. Tel Newton Abbot (0626) 4592. Open Tues, Wed, Fri 11-1, 2.30-5; Sat 10.30-1, 2.30-5; other times by appt. Commemorative pottery, early pottery and porcelain, silver, collectors' items, Victorian jewellery.

Curio Shop
(Barbara C.Wale). 11 Northumberland Place. Tel (priv)Exeter(0392)54166. Open Mon-Sat; closed Thurs. Militaria.

Peter Dryden Ltd
(P.H.C.Dryden, J.Dryden). Teign Court, TQ14 8AY. Tel 78095 (priv 78392). Open by appt only. English & Continental furniture & works of art. BADA

Extence Antiques
2 Wellington St. Tel 3353. Open Mon-Sat 9.30-5.30, closed Thurs; other times by appt. 17th to early 19thC furniture, Sheffield plate and silver.

Teign Gallery
2 Northumberland Place, TQ14 8DD. Tel 3089. Open Mon-Sat 10-5, closed Thurs in winter; other times by appt. Furniture, oil paintings and watercolours, glass, pottery and porcelain.

Tiverton STD 0884

Bygone Days
(Neville Park). 40 Gold St, EX16 6PY. Tel 252832. Open Mon-Sat 9.30-1 2-5; closed Thurs; other times by appt. Furniture, mainly Victorian and Georgian; also later furniture of good quality. Watercolours and oils.

Chancery Antiques
(Charles, Helen, Richard & Michael Bowyer). 8-10 Barrington St, EX16 6PU. Tel 252416 (priv 253190). Open 5 days a week 9-5; closed Thurs & Sun; other times by appt. Massive stock of stripped pine and country furniture. Some pieces of early oak furniture. Retail, trade and export. Shipping easily arranged.

Grey House Antiques
(Angela Peters). 8 Newport St, EX16 6NH. Tel 255846. Open Mon-Sat 9.30-5.30; other times by appt. Period furniture.

R.E. Martin
40 Gold St. Tel 252832. Open Mon-Sat 9.30-5.30. Period and Victorian furniture, china and silver.

Trevor Micklem, Antiques
(Mr & Mrs Trevor Micklem, T.J.M.Micklem). Withywine Farm, Morebath, EX16 9BZ. Tel Bampton (0398) 31409. Open normal business hours and weekends by appt. Fine early furniture specialising in oak & walnut, needlework, tapestries, metalwork. English delftware and pottery a speciality. BADA

Townend Antiques
24 Silver St. Tel 254250. Open Mon, Tues, Wed and Sat; other times by appt. Silver, porcelain, coins and Victoriana.

Topsham STD 039 287

Elizabeth Allnutt
13 Fore St. Tel 4224. Open 9.30-5.30; early closing Wed; other times by appt. Small furniture, china, glass and jewellery.

The Clock Shop
(Basil Palmer). 40 Fore St.

Don Warren Antiques
High St. Tel 4703. Open Mon-Fri 10-5; other times by appt. Pottery, porcelain, clocks and furniture.

Torquay STD 0803

Bearnes
Rainbow, Avenue Rd, TQ2 5TG. Tel 26277. Open Mon-Fri 9.30-1, 2.15-5; other times by appt. Auctioneers and valuers of fine art and jewellery. SOFAA

Birbeck Antiques
(S.J. Birbeck, H.H. Birbeck, K.A. Birbeck). 219 Union St, TQ1 4BZ. Tel 23318 (priv 214836). (See also Devonshire Gallery.) Open Mon-Fri 10-1, 2-5; Sat 10-1; other times by appt. English, Oriental, European, china, glass, metalware & works of art. English & Oriental furniture, English & Continental oil paintings, watercolours and prints.

Derby House Antiques
(B. & Mrs M.E.Ward). 48 South St, Torre, TQ2 5AA. Tel 212335. Open Mon-Fri 10-1, 2-5; Wed, Sat 10-1; other times by appt. Small furniture and silver. English and Continental pottery and porcelain. Collector's items.

The Devonshire Gallery
45 Abbey Rd, TQ2 5NQ. Tel 27144. (See also Birbeck Antiques.) Open Mon-Sat 10-1, 2-5.30; other times by appt. Oil paintings, watercolours, engravings, statuary and works of art. LAPADA BADA

Jennings Antiques
215 Higher Union St, TQ1 4BZ. Tel 23165. Open Mon-Sat 10-5; other times by appt. Furniture, clocks, silver, pottery and porcelain.

Laburnum Antique Galleries
3 Laburnum Row, TQ2 5QX. Tel 26983. Open Mon-Sat 9.30-5.30. 18th and 19thC English and Continental furniture, arms and shipping goods.

Russell's (Antiques) Ltd
64 Fleet St. Tel 22781. Open Mon-Sat 9-5.30. French and English furniture, jewellery, china, glass, silver, chandeliers and other items.

Sheraton House Antiques
(K. Goodman). No.1 Laburnham Row, Torre. Tel 23334. Open 10-4.30; other times by appt. English & Continental furniture (18th & 19thC). Pictures & decoration.

Spencers Antiques
187 Higher Union St, Torre. Tel 26598. Open Mon-Fri 11-4; closed Wed; other times by appt. Silver, jewellery, china, glass, pictures, furniture, etc.

Torquay Antique Centre
177 Union St. Tel 26621. Open Mon-Fri 9.30-5, Sat 9.30-1; other times by appt. Several dealers with a wide range of stock.

Torre Antique Traders
(Jane Birbeck). 266 Union St, TQ1 4ET. Tel 22184 (priv 34449). Open Mon-Fri 10-5, Sat 10-1; other times by appt. Antiques centre with eight stallholders selling items of all kinds.

Totnes STD 0803

Butterwalk House
55 The Old Butterwalk, High St. Tel 863044. Open 10-5; early closing Thurs, Sat; other times by appt. 17th-19thC small furniture, decorative items, Oriental art and bronzes, porcelain, treen, samplers and paintings.

Collards Bookshop
(Mrs Belle Collard). 4 Castle St, TQ9 5NU. Tel (priv) 0548 550246. Open Mon-Sat 10-5 (Summer); Thurs 10-1 (Winter); other times by appt. Old and rare books.

Fine Pine Ltd
(Nick and Lorraine Gildersleve). Woodland Rd, Harbertonford. Tel Harbertonford (080 423) 465. (Also at 85 High St, Totnes and Zeaston Farm, South Brent.) Open Mon-Sat 9-5; other times by appt. Pine and country furniture, other general antiques and decorative items, paintings and nautical items.

David C.Golby
2 Queens Terrace. Tel 862048. Photographer.

Tony Grey Antiques and Fine Arts
19 Leechwell St, TQ9 5SX. Tel 862841. Antiques, fine arts and unusual items. Trade welcome, but appt advisable.

Hugh Mendl Antiques
(Hugh Mendl). Collard's Bookshop, 4 Castle Street, TQ9 5NU. Tel 863970. Open Mon-Sat 10-1, 2.15-5; early closing Thurs in winter; other times by appt. Pottery and porcelain, small decorative antiques and decorative prints,childrens' plates, blue & white transfer ware.

John Tuckey, Bogan House Gallery
43 High St. Tel 862025. Open Mon-Sat 10-5.30; early closing Thurs; other times by appt. Antiques, early English watercolours, paintings and drawings.

Whimple STD 0404

Anthony James Antiques
Brooklyn Cottage, The Square, EX5 3BD. Tel 822146. Open Mon-Sat 9-6; other times by appt. 17th and 18thC furniture, metalware and small items.

Winkleigh STD 083 783

M.Webb Antiques
(Mrs M.Webb). Nine Beeches, EX19 8HR. Tel 983 209. Open all times. Varied stock, furniture, brass, copper, porcelain, clocks, collectors items.

Dorset

Abbotsbury STD 030 587

Old Post Office Antiques
(E.W.&S.B.Harris). Tel 383. Open Mon-Sat 9.30-5.30; closed Thurs; other times by appt. 18th and 19thC furniture and silver; clocks and watches.

Beaminster STD 0308

Beaminster Antiques
(Mrs T. Frampton, P. Frampton). 4 Church St, DT8 3AZ. Tel 862591 (priv 093589 395). Open Mon-Sat 9.30-5.30; closed all day Wed; other times by appt. General silver & gold jewellery, silver plate, porcelain, glass, brass, copper, samplers, sewing items, furniture & collectables.

Daniels House Antiques
(Carl & Gloria Hennessy). Hogshill St, DT8 3AG. Tel 862635. Open Mon-Sat 9.30-6; other times by appt. English, Continental & Irish antique pine & country furniture. Some period oak & decorative items. LAPADA

Good Hope Antiques
(Mr D.Beney). 2 Hogshill St. Tel 862119. Open Mon-Sat 9.30-5.30; closed Wed; other times by appt. Longcase, bracket and wall clocks; also period furniture and barometers.

Jill Maxwell-Hyslop
The Manor house, Toller Whelme, DT8 3NU. Tel Buckland Newton (030 05) 224 (priv 030 862339). Open by appt. Fine watercolours of 19th and early 20thC.

Raleigh Antiques
(L.A.F.& J.Holland). 17 The Square. Tel 862136. Open Mon-Sat,closed Wed; other times by appt. Small antiques, lace and linen, furniture and collectables.

Blandford Forum STD 0258

Zona Dawson Antiques
(J.T. & J.H.Dawson). The Old Club House, 2 The Close, Charlton Marshall. Tel Blandford (0258) 53146. Open Tues-Sat; other times by appt. Res on prem. 18th and 19thC furniture, longcase and other clocks.

Priory Antiques
(E.Peters). 37 East St. Tel 53472. Open Mon-Sat 9-5.30; other times by appt. Period furniture and restoration.

Peter Strowger of Blandford Forum Antiques
13 East St. Tel 53567 & 54374. Open Tues-Sat 10-1, 2.30-6; other times by appt. 16th to 19thC English furniture, porcelain, glass, oil paintings, watercolours, engravings, metalwork. LAPADA

Bournemouth STD 0202

Antiques Trade Warehouse
(Mrs A.L.Williams). 28 Lorne Park Rd, BH1 1JL. Tel 292944. Open Mon-Fri 9-5; other times by appt. Victoriana, shipping goods pre-1930s, art deco, pine, bric-a-brac.

Richard Batsford Antiques
(R.Batsford). Antique Trade Warehouse, 29 Lorne Park Rd. Tel 292944 (priv 25485). Open Mon-Fri 9-5; other times by appt. Oriental, British and European furniture, garden furniture and statuary. Trade suppliers. Also shipping goods.

Arthur Bircumshaw
(Mr & Mrs A. Bircumshaw). 250 Charminster Rd, BH8 9RR. Tel 511541. Open by appt only. Furniture, china, boxes, restorations. Shipping. Wedgwood.

Christie's Robson Lowe
(Charles Leonard, Director). 39 Poole Hill. Tel 292740. Fine art valuers & stamp auctioneers. PTS

Commin's Bookshop
(Peter Kennedy). 100 Old Christchurch Rd. Tel 27504. Open Mon-Sat 9-5.30; other times by appt. Large stocks of antiquarian, collectors and secondhand books, plus antique maps and prints. ABA

Charles Fox (Jewellers) Ltd
21 & 22 The Arcade, BH1 2AH. Tel 27633 & 28196. Open 9-5.30. Jewellery, silver, watches, clocks, objets d'art.

Hampshire Gallery
18 Lansdowne Rd. Tel 21211. Open Mon-Fri 9.30-1, 2.15-5.30, Sat 10-12; other times by appt. 17th to 19thC English and Continental paintings and watercolours.

Litchfield Gallery
1062 Christchurch Rd, East Boscombe. Tel 45454. Open Mon-Sat 9-1, 2-5.30; early closing Wed. 17th to 19thC maps and prints, limited edition modern prints and etchings.

Marneys
(M. Lumb). 813 Christchurch Rd, Boscombe. Tel 423907. Open Mon-Sat 10-5; early closing Wed, Sat; other times by appt. Furniture, china.

G.B.Mussenden & Son
24 Seamoor Rd, Westbourne, BH4 9AR. Tel 764462. Open 9-5.30; closed Wed. Antiques, jewellery and silver.

R.E. Porter
2/4 Post Office Rd, BH1 1BA. Tel 24289. Open 9.30-5; half day Wed. Antique silver, Baxter prints and antique jewellery.

Portique
(E.J.C. Mundy & J.E.A. Mundy). 17 Criterion Arcade, BH1 1BU. Tel 22979. Open Mon-Sat 9.30-5.30. Antique jewellery and silver and paperweights.

S.H. & W.P.Reynolds
888 Christchurch Rd, Boscombe, BH7 6DJ. Open Mon-Sat 9-5.30; early closing Wed. General antiques, including grandfather clocks and curios. Trade welcome.

Riddetts of Bournemouth
The Auction Galleries, Richmond Hill, The Square, BH2 6EJ. Tel 25686 (4 lines). Open Mon-Fri 9-5.30; Sat 9-11.30. Auctioneers of fine art and antiques. Auctions fortnightly include 18th & 19thC English, Continental and Oriental furniture, pottery & porcelain, English & Continental oil paintings & watercolours, silver plate, jewellery, Persian & Oriental rugs. SOFAA

Sainsburys of Bournemouth
(Thomas E.F. Sainsbury). 23-25 Abbott Rd, BH9 1EU. Tel 529271 (priv 763616). Open Mon-Fri 8-1, 2-6; Sat 8-12; other times by appt. Georgian furniture. LAPADA

Sloane Galleries
49 Poole Rd, Westbourne, BH4 9BA. Tel 764684. 17th to 20thC oils and watercolours.

Sotheby's
(Representative: George Kidner). 42 Holdenhurst Rd, BH8 8AF. Tel 294425. Auctioneers & valuers.

Peter Stebbing Ltd
7 Post Office Rd. Tel 22587. Open six days 9.30-5. Business established 26 years, dealing with all aspects of the antique trade.

Sterling Coins
2 Somerset Rd, Boscombe. Tel 423881. Open Mon-Sat 10-1, 2-5, closed Wed. Coins, medals and militaria.

Stuarts Antiques
(D.C.Stuart). 336 Holdenhurst Rd. Tel 34218. Open Mon-Fri 9-5.30; other times by appt. Victorian quality furniture, silver etc.

R.A.Swift & Sons
(S.R.Swift). St Andrews Hall, 4c Wolverton Rd, Boscombe, BH7 6HT. Tel 34470. Open Mon-Fri 9-5.30; Sat 9-4; other times by appt. English and Continental furniture, porcelain, paintings, decorative items and works of art. LAPADA

Christopher Williams (inc Culmus Books)
(Christopher and Pauline Williams). 23 St Leonard's Rd, BH8 8QL. Tel 519683. Open by appt only. Antiquarian and secondhand bookseller. Volumes on the arts, bibliography, topography, cookery, wine and finely illustrated books. ABA

Christopher Wray's Lighting Emporium
Gervis Place. Tel 22660. (Main branch in London.) Decorative lighting of the 1880s. Victorian and Edwardian lamps.

Sidney Wright
12-13 Royal Arcade, Boscombe. Tel 37153. Antiquarian books. ABA

Bridport STD 0308

Croft Antiques
(Miss R.C. Ross). 3 Barrack St, DT6 3LX. Tel 22552 (priv 0308-68352). Open Tues, Wed, Sat 10-4; other times by appt. General antiques and jewellery.

Hobby Horse Antiques
(J. Rodber). 29 West Allington, DT6 5BJ. Tel 22801. Open 10-1, 2.30-5, closed Thurs; other times by appt. Collectors items - railway, marine, music boxes, automata. Silver, glass, jewellery, brass, copper, porcelain, furniture.

Little Bric a Brac Shop
(Isabel Caddy). The Green, Morcombelake. Tel Chideock (0297) 89346. Open Mon-Fri, 10-1, 2-5; closed Wed & Sat; other times by appt. Brass, copper, porcelain, bygones, curiosities, patchwork cushions, quilts and clothes.

Tudor House Antiques
(P.&V.Knight, A.&D.Burton). 88 East St. Tel 27200. Open Mon-Sat 9-5; other times by appt. General antiques. LAPADA

Cerne Abbas STD 030 03

Cerne Antiques
(Irene Pulliblank). 2 Duck St. Tel 490. Open Mon-Thurs 10-1, 2-5; closed Fri; other times by appt. Furniture, silver and bric-a-brac.

Charlton Horethorne

David & Rosemary White
(David & Rosemary White). The Forge, DT9 4PB. Tel Corton Denham (096 322) 347. Open Mon-Fri 8.30-6; other times by appt. 18th & 19thC furniture, decorative items, oil paintings, pine furniture, clocks. LAPADA

Christchurch STD 0202

J.L. Arditti
88 Bargates. Tel 485414. Open Mon-Sat 9-5.30; other times by appt. Old oriental rugs and carpets.

H.L.B. Antiques
(H.L. Blechman). 139 Barrack Rd, BH23 2AW. Tel 429252. Open Mon-Sat 10-5; other times by appt. General antiques.

Gerald Hampton
12 Purewell, BH23 1EP. Tel 699. 18th and early 19thC English and Continental furniture, clocks, china, plated wares, glass and decorative items.

Compton Abbas

David Lane Antiques
(D.L.Lane). The Old Forge, Fanners Yard. Tel Shaftesbury (0747) 811881. 17th, 18th, early 19thC English & Continental furniture, metalware, decorative items. Furniture restorer. Valuations.

Dorchester STD 0305

Christie's
(Representative: Nigel Thimbleby). Wolfeton House. Tel 68748. Fine art auctioneers and valuers.

County Antiques
(Michael J.T. Naylor). Colliton Antique and Craft Centre, Colliton St. Tel 62444(workshop 69398). (Warehouse at Site 22, Casterbridge Industrial Estate, London Rd.) Open 6 days 9-5.30; other times by appt. Antique and period furniture, metalware, collectors items.

H.V. Day
The Old Roman Catholic Church, 25 High West St, DT1 1UW. Tel 64904. Maps, prints, watercolours, old and rare books and Dorset items. ABA

Hy. Duke & Son
(C.J.Hillier A.S.V.A, Guy Schwinge). Fine Art Salerooms, Weymouth Ave, DT1 1QR. Tel 65080. (Also in Weymouth.) Open Mon-Fri 9-5.30, closed 1-2. Fine art auctioneers (Estab 1823).Regular specialist sales of pottery and porcelain, silver and jewellery, paintings and drawings, oriental ceramics and works of art. SOFAA

Michael Legg Antiques
15 High East St. Tel 64596. (Also at the Old Malthouse, Bottom-o-Town.) Large stock of antiques generally with some fine items.

Plume of Feathers Antiques
(Anne Elwin). Princes St. Tel 67729. Open Mon-Fri 9.30-4; early closing Thurs & Sat. Particularly small antiques, Victorian jewellery, bric-a-brac.

Gillingham STD 074 76

Talisman Antiques
(Ken Bolan). The Old Brewery, Wyke, SP8 4NW. Tel 4423. Open Mon-Fri 9-6; Sat 10-4; other times by appt. Large quantity of antiques and decorative items. LAPADA

Poole STD 0202

Allen's (Branksome) Ltd
(D.L.Dardenne). 449 Poole Rd, Branksome, BH12 1DH. Tel 763724. Open Mon-Sat 9-1, 2.15-6. (200 yards from Branksome Station.) Tables, chairs, chests, bookcases, desks, reconditioned furniture. Specialising in large bookcases.

D.J.Jewellery
(Dennis & Patti O'Sullivan). 166-168 Ashley Rd, Parkstone, BH14 9BY. Tel 745148. Open Mon-Fri 9-6; Sat 9-1; other times by appt. Victorian & Edwardian jewellery and small silver items. Specialising in Russian enamels & jewellery. NAG BWCMG GA

Guildhall Antiques
(Mrs G.P.Robinson). 7-9 Old Orchard. Tel 675962 (priv 698636). Open Mon-Sat 10-4; closed Wed in winter; other times by appt. Miscellaneous display of Victorian and Edwardian furniture and bric-a-brac. Trade welcome.

Antiques by Nikki
(N.Medd). 123A Commercial Rd, Lower Parkstone, BH14 0JD. Tel Parkstone (0202) 740939. Open Mon-Sat 10-5; closed Wed; other times by appt. 19thC porcelain, small furniture, pine and country items, watercolours and decorative items.

Shaftesbury STD 0747

John Jeffery & Son
(D. Jeffery). Minster House, The Commons, SP7 8JL. Tel 3331. Open Mon-Fri 9-5.30. Auctioneers of antique furniture and effects, vintage machinery, coins and medals.

G.E. Johnson & Son (Shaftesbury) Ltd
41-45 High St, SP7 8JF. Tel 2113. Open Mon-Sat 8-5, Wed 8-1; other times by appt. General antiques.

Sherborne STD 0935

Country Pine & Antiques
(Simon Dodge). 3 The Green. Tel 5216. Open Mon-Sat 9-5.30; other times by appt. A good selection of pine furniture all well stripped and finished. All our stock is clean and ready to be used.

Dodge & Son
(A.R.K.Dodge Snr, S.Dodge, A.Dodge). 28 & 33 Cheap St, DT9 3PU. Tel 5151. Open Mon-Sat 9-5.30; other times by appt. All types of antique furniture for export and the home market displayed over 4,000 sq ft.

Greystoke Antiques
(F.L.& N.E. Butcher). Swan Yard, off Cheap St, DT9 4EP. Tel 812833 (priv 813484). Open Mon-Sat 9.30-5; other times by appt. Georgian, Victorian and later silver, pottery and porcelain especially blue transfer ware, furniture, needlework.

Johnson's of Sherborne Ltd
South St, DTG 3NF. Tel 812585. Open Mon-Sat 8-1, 2-5; other times by appt. 18th and 19thC furniture, decorative items and shipping goods.

The Nook Antiques
(M.B. & B.C. Bruton). South St, DT9 3LX. Tel 813987. Open Mon-Sat 10-5; closed Wed; other times by appt. Small furniture, brass, copper, china, general Victoriana.

Old Barn Antiques Co
(G.W.Mott, T.E. Haines). Flamberts, Trent, DT9 4SS. Tel 850648. Open by appt only. Fine 18th and 19thC furniture. Restoration and valuation service.

Phillips
(P.W.Allan, ASVA). Long Street Salerooms, Long St, DT93BS. Tel 815271. Fine art auctioneers.

Sherborne Antiques Ltd
(Edwin Roxburgh, T.H.Mayer). At The China Gallery, Long St, DT9 3BS. Tel 812978. Open Mon-Sat 9-5.30; other times by appt. 17th to 19thC furniture and clocks.

Sherborne Arcade
(Mattar Antique Galleries). 17 Newlands. Tel 813464. Period building housing several small antique shops with goods for trade and collectors.

Sturminster Newton
STD 0258

Peter Brazier
Nash Court Farmhouse, Marnhull, DT10 1JZ. Tel Marnhull (0258) 820255. Restoration of period furniture including casting of missing mounts and hardware. Trade and private commissions. Regular London collections. BAFRA

Quarter Jack Antiques
(H.C. & A.B.Neilson). Bridge St, DT10 1BZ. Tel 72558. Open Mon-Sat 9-5.30; Wed 9-1; other times by appt. A wide selection of 18th to 20thC glass, including 18thC drinking glasses, wine glasses, decanters, ale glasses and rummers. Also English porcelain, copper, brass, walking sticks and small antique furniture.

Swanage STD 0929

Georgian Gems
(Brian Barker). 28 High St, BH19 1HA. Tel 424697. Open Mon-Sat 9-1, 2.30-5; other times by appt. Antique jewellery & silver. Valuations. (Repairs, antique jewellery a speciality). NAG, FGA JAC

The Old Forge
(Mrs L.P. Sprigg). 273A High St, BH19 2NH. Tel 423319. Open Mon-Sat; closed Thurs. General antiques.

Wareham STD 092 95

S.W. Cottee & Son
(C.J. Quick & J. Egglestone). The Market, East St, BH20 4NR. Tel 2826. Open normal office hours. Auctioneers and valuers.

Weymouth STD 0305

Hy. Duke & Son
(Manager: Robert Bover). Weymouth Saleroom, St Nicholas St. Tel 783488. Open 9-1 2-5.30. Regular sales of Victorian and later furniture and effects. No buyer's premium. SOFAA

Roderic Antiques
(Rodney Arnoldi & Eric Gunawardena). Westbrook House, Upwey. Tel Upwey (030 581) 2929, 3022. Open Tues-Sat 9-5; other times by appt. Georgian, Victorian and Edwardian furniture and clocks.

Wimborne Minster
STD 0202

Antiquatat Antiques Ltd
(Mr D.W.Schwier). The Old Civic Centre, Hanham Rd. Tel 887496. Furniture, porcelain, silver, shipper, restorer. LAPADA

The Antique Shop
(N.Wrigley). 6 West St. Tel 880297. 19th & 20thC porcelain, 17th & 18thC oak & mahogany furniture. LAPADA

Hicklenton & Phillips Ltd
Colborne Ave. Tel 882040. Open by appt only. Antique and modern silver, jewellery and regalia. Specialist in goods made to order.

Metcalfe Jackson
(Mr&Mrs B.Metcalfe Jackson). 24A West St, BH21 1JS. Tel 883327. Open Mon-Fri 10-5. Early furniture, Chinese ceramics, Oriental rugs, old master drawings.

Wimborne Antiques
(J.F.Mason). 46 High St, BH21 1HT. Tel 887863 (priv 883686). Open Mon-Sat 9.30-5.30; other times by appt. Paintings, jewellery, weapons, china, glass, brass, clocks, furniture and restoration. Also pine and shipping goods in warehouse.

Durham

Barnard Castle

The Collector & The Collector (Restorations)
(Robert A.Jordan). Douglas House, 23-25 The Bank, DL12 8PH. Tel Teesdale (0833) 37783. Open Wed & Sat 10.30-6; other times by appt. Unusual objects both small & large. Period & Victorian furniture. Specialist in restoration of metalwork, cabinetwork & clockwork.

The Doll Shop
(Mrs K. Ashton). 6 Newgate.

Gibberd and Grant Antiques
(Marten Gibberd and Stephanie Grant). 40 The Bank, DL12 8PN. Tel Teesdale (0833) 37437. Open Summer: Mon-Sat 9-6; Winter: Mon-Sat 9-5;closed Thurs; other times by appt. Oak, mahogany and pine furniture 1600-1900. Glass, pottery, porcelain, treen, kitchenalia, oil & watercolours, pewter, needlework, brass, copper, cast iron and many other interesting objets d'art. Good trade discounts.

Stephanie Grant Antiques
(Stephanie Grant). 38 The Bank. Tel Teesdale (0833) 37437. Open Mon-Sat 9-6; other times by appt. Paintings, prints, early oak furniture, needlework, pottery, treen.

Mrs S. Hanford
25 The Bank.

Jackson's Antiques
(Alan Jackson, Elizabeth M. Jackson). Neville House, 10 The Bank. Tel Teesdale (0833) 37412. Open weekdays and Saturdays; other times by appt. Period & Victorian furniture, pottery, porcelain, glass and decorative works. Specialist in Victorian coloured glass.

Newgate Curios
(Elizabeth Sidaway). 12 Newgate. Tel 0833-38163. Open Wed, Fri, Sat 11-5; other times by appt. Silver, jewellery and decorative items.

Bishop Auckland STD 0388

G.H.Edkins & Son
(Denis Edkins FSVA, ACIArb). 122 Newgate St, DL14 7HE. Tel 603095. (Also at Shildon, Durham.) Open Mon-Fri 9-5, Sat 9-4; other times by appt. General auctioneers with regular sales of furnishings,and periodic sales of antiques.

Darlington STD 0325

Carousel Antiques
(J. & R. Winram). The Red House, Church Lane, Middleton St George. Tel Dinsdale (0325) 332093. Exhibitor at major antiques fairs throughout the country. Quality 18th and 19thC furniture, jewellery, and small silver.

Ronald Richardson
(Mrs I.K.Richardson, Mrs K.B.M.Cooper). 28 Post House Wynd, DL3 7LP. Tel 464860 (priv 0325 332388). Antique silver and Sheffield plate. Also clocks, jewellery and other items.

Durham STD 0385

Bridge Antiques
(R.A.&M.V.Graham). 93 Elvet Bridge. Tel 45530. Open 9.30-5; closed Wed; other times by appt. General antiques and stringed musical instruments and small art gallery.

J.Shotton
(John Shotton). 89 Elvet Bridge, DH1 3AG. Tel 64597. Open normal business hours. Antique books, prints and maps. ABA

Ferryhill STD 0740

Robin Shield Antiques
(W.R. and P.E.Shield). Great Chilton Farm, DL17 0JY. Tel Bishop Auckland (0740) 720237. Open any time - appt advisable. Furniture, paintings, works of art, metalware, garden furniture.

Seaham STD 0783

Past & Present
(Mr & Mrs E.Patrickson). 13 Lord St. Tel 813888. Open Mon-Sat 9.30-5; other times by appt. Res on prem. Books and general antiques.

Essex

Abridge STD 037 881

Abridge Antique Clock Centre
Market Place.

Abridge Antiques Centre
Market Place. Tel Theydon Bois (037 881) 3113. Open 10-5. 9 shops offering a wide range of antiques.

Battlesbridge

Battlesbridge Antique Centre
Tel Wickford (03744) 63344. Open most days. Over 40 dealers in 4 interesting old buildings, Bridgebarn, Cromwell House, Haybarn and The Old Granary. Buying and selling furniture, clocks, china, glass, brass, copper, maps, prints, jewellery, silver, musical boxes, toys and automata.

James Gallie
(J.F.Gallie). 1 Maltings Rd. Tel Wickford (03744) 63344. Post-1860 furniture.

The Old Granary
(J. Gallie). Battlesbridge Antique Centre, Hawk Hill (by the "Barge" pub). Tel Wickford (037 44) 63344. Open 7 days a week 8-6; other times by appt. Craft and antique centre housing craftsmen skilled in restoring and repolishing furniture, upholstery, stripped pine, brasswork,solid wood kitchens, woodburning stoves, oak reproduction furniture & craftwork. Good stock of antique & pre-war furniture.

Audrey Wallace Antiques
Room 11, Cromwell House. Tel Wickford (037 44) 62612. 18th and early 19thC porcelain, paintings and small furniture.

Billericay STD 027 74

Andrew Hawkins
74 High St.

J. Collins and Son

(ESTABLISHED 1953)

Antiques and Fine Paintings

THE STUDIO, 63 HIGH STREET
BIDEFORD, NORTH DEVON. EX39 2AN

TEL. BIDEFORD (02372) 73103

OPENING HOURS 9.30 to 5 p.m.
CLOSED ALL DAY WEDNESDAY AND SUNDAY.

FIVE EXTENSIVE SHOWROOMS OF ANTIQUES AND TWO GALLERIES OF FINE 18th and 19th CENTURY OIL PAINTINGS AND WATERCOLOURS.

Brandler Galleries

SOLD

Pictures selling fast
Private and Trade clients
Twentieth century British paintings wanted.
C. WEIGHT, BUHLER, CASSON, GORDON BUTLER
PIPER, METHUEN, SUDDABY etc.
Free car park for clients

1 Coptfold Road, Brentwood, Essex CM14 4BM
Telephone: Brentwood (0277) 222269

MARGERY DEAN ANTIQUES

ESTABLISHED 1947

Large stock of 17th, 18th and 19th century furniture also pine and country.
Dealers especially welcome.

THE GALLERIES
ALMA STREET.
(left off High St.)
WIVENHOE. NR. COLCHESTER

Telephone Wivenhoe 2523 and evenings Colchester 250485
12 capacious showrooms

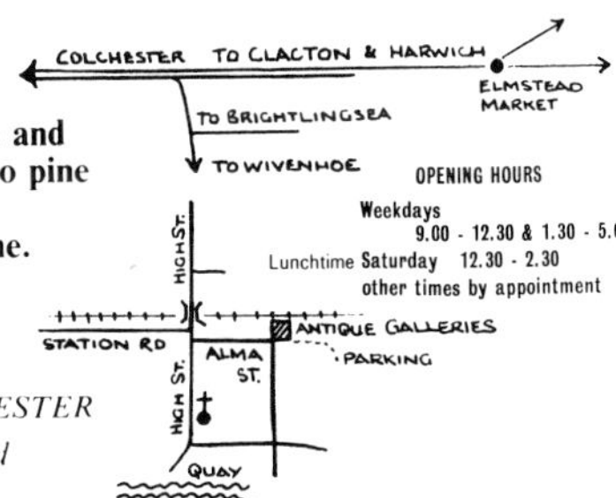

OPENING HOURS
Weekdays
9.00 - 12.30 & 1.30 - 5.00
Lunchtime Saturday 12.30 - 2.30
other times by appointment

ANTIQUES, PICTURES
and
FURNITURE OF QUALITY

S. BOND & SON

Established over 120 years

14–15 NORTH HILL · COLCHESTER
Tel 572925

Trinity Antiques Centre

7 TRINITY ST., COLCHESTER, ESSEX
Colchester 577775. Opposite New Library
Open 6 days per week

16th Century building with 8 dealers in fine silver, unusual Victorian jewellery, small furniture, porcelain & china. Upstairs for Militaria, pine and collectors items.

Sheredays Antiques
22 High St, CM12 9BQ. Tel 22323/4356. Open Mon-Sat 10-4.30; closed Thurs; other times by appt. Several dealers specialising in a range of antiques.

Braintree STD 0376

The Golden Sovereign
(C.P. & W.G.M. Leitch). Old Police House, High St, Gt Bardfield. Tel Great Dunmow (0371) 810507. Open Mon, Tues, Thurs, Fri 10-6, Sat 12-6; other times by appt. General antiques, mainly small items.

Eric Hudes
Paigles, Perry Green, Bradwell, CM7 8ES. Tel Silver End (0376) 83767. (Also at 142 Portobello Rd, London W11 on Sats.) Open by appt only. Specialist in Oriental ceramics, particularly early Chinese and South East Asian wares, plus later blue and white and decorative wares. Also English pottery 1700 to 1820, with emphasis on delftware, creamware and Toby Jugs. LAPADA

Markswood Gallery
Great Bardfield. Tel 810106.

Brentwood STD 0277

Brandler Galleries
(John Brandler). 1 Coptfold Rd, CM13 4BM. Tel 222269. Open Tues-Sat 10-5.30; other times by appt. 20thC British art and modern masters.

Louis Lipman Antiques
33-35 Kings Rd. Tel 222380. Open Mon-Sat 9-5.30 closed Thurs; other times by appt. Georgian and Victorian furniture and decorative items.

Directory Entries are Free and ADDITIONS OR CORRECTIONS will be welcomed by *THE EDITOR, British Art and Antiques Directory, National Magazine House, 72 Broadwick Street, London W1V 2BP*

Burnham-on-Crouch

Gough Antiques
(Thelma Gough). 111 Station Rd. Tel Maldon (0621) 784322. Open Mon-Sat 10-5; closed Wed. Furniture, brass, copper, glass, china, original silver, silver plate, general antiques.

Quai Antiques
(Mrs Catherine McMullan). 1 Crouch Rd, CM0 8DX. Tel Maldon (0621) 782863. Open Easter to end Oct, Mon-Sat 10-5; closed Wed. Antique jewellery, small furniture, porcelain, glass.

Castle Hedingham

Orbell House Gallery
(Edward & Inka Greene). Orbell House, 8 St James's St, Co9 3EJ. Tel Hedingham (0787) 60298. Open Tues-Fri 2-6, Sat 10-6; other times by appt. Old & antique oriental rugs. Repairs and cleaning undertaken. Lectures given. Specialising in Persian, Afghan, Caucasian, Anatolian rugs and runners.

Chelmsford STD 0245

Chelmsford Antiques and Collectors Market
Chancellor Hall, Market Rd. Tel 71079 & 466952. Open 2nd Sat in month 10-3.45. Many dealers with a wide range of antiques. Organisers: Heirloom Antiques, 33 Galleywood Rd, Great Baddow.

Chelmsford Auction Rooms
(S.H.Rowland). 42 Mildmay Rd. Tel 354251. Open Mon-Fri 9-5.30, Sat 10.30-1.30; other times by appt. Antique and modern furniture, china, glass etc.

Cooper-Hirst
(R. Cooper-Hirst, R.L. Cooper-Hirst). Goldlay House, Parkway, CM2 7PR. Tel 58141. Open office hours including Sats. Auctioneers.

The Stores
(Mollie Webster). Great Waltham. Tel 360277 (priv 0376 26997). Open Mon-Sat 10-5; closed Tues & Sun; other times by appt. Stripped pine.

Coggeshall STD 0376

Antique Metals
(R.M. & S.V. Chaplin). 12 East St, Co6 1SH. Tel 62252. Open 7 days a week, 9-6. Specialists in Victorian and period metalware, brass beds and fenders.

Coggeshall Antiques
(Olive Mabey). 1 Doubleday Corner. Tel 62646 (priv 0245 56027). Open Mon-Sat 10-5; other times by appt. 18th, 19th & early 20thC furniture, paintings, silver plated ware etc.

Dolphyn
(Mr T.H.Disley). 8 Market End, CO6 1NP. Tel 61608. (Workshop/office at The Old Brewery, Bridge St.) Open Mon-Sat 9.30-5.30; Sun 11-4; other times by appt. Bespoke picture framing, restoration of paintings, repair of swept frames, gilding. General antiques, maps and prints, mirrors.

Lindsell Chairs
(T.J.L. and A.M. Martin). 11 Market Hill, CO6 1TS. Tel 62766 (priv 0371-84 222). (Office at The Glebe House, Lindsell, Gt.Dunmow, Essex CM6 3QN.) Open daily 10-6; Sun 2-6. Chairs and seating of all kinds from the 18thC to 1914. Stock of 1000 items.

Lion Antiques
(M.Rojo & M.Mills). 10 Bridge St, CO6 1NP. Tel 61530. (Also at 6 East St.) Open Mon-Fri 9-5.30; other times by appt. 18th and 19thC furniture, porcelain, paintings, silver, silver plate and glass.

Mark Marchant, Antiques
(Mark Marchant). Market Square, CO6 1T6. Tel 61188. Open Mon-Sat 10-5, Sun 2.30-5.30; other times by appt. Mostly grandfather clocks, mantle, & music boxes. LAPADA FBHI

J.P.Smith Auctions
(John Playle Smith). 1 Church St. Tel 62051. Open Mon-Sat 9.30-5; other times by appt. Auctions of pictures and general antiques.

John Smith Antiques
(John Playle Smith). 1 Church St, CO6 1TU. Tel 62051. Open Mon-Sat 9.30-5; other times by appt. Antique furniture, pictures, curios.

Colchester STD 0206

S.Bond & Son
(M.W.&R.W.Bond). 14-15 North Hill, CO1 1DZ. Tel 572925. Open Mon-Sat; early closing Thurs; other times by appt. Antique furniture, paintings, watercolours, prints, china, glass and silver.

Castle Bookshop
(A.B. Doncaster). 37 North Hill. Tel 577520 (priv 34 204). Open Mon-Sat 9-5; closed Thurs. Bookseller, secondhand & antiquarian books, maps and prints. ABA

The Coin & Stamp Centre
(R.B.Field). 13 Centurion House (1st floor), St John's St, CO2 7AH. Tel 41232 (priv 579345). Open Mon-Sat 9-5; closed Thurs. Coins, stamps, medals, cigarette cards, post cards, military badges.

Margery Dean Antiques
(Judy Dean & Evelyn Dean). The Galleries, Alma St, Wivenhoe. Tel 222523 (priv 250485). Open Mon-Fri 9-5; Sat 10.30-12.30, 2.30-5; other times by appt. Nine large showrooms of early 17th to 19thC furniture. Also country pine furniture. LAPADA

John Drury Rare Books Ltd
(D.R.D.Edmunds). PO Box 77, CO1 1EL. Tel Ramsey (0255) 886260. Open by appt only. Small specialist stock of books on economics, social history, philosophy, politics, law & numismatics. ABA

Partner & Puxon
(S.H.Partner, Minette Partner, J.G.Partner). 7&16 North Hill, Co1 1DZ. Tel 573317. Open Mon-Sat 9-1, 2.15-5.30; early closing Thurs. Trade by appt at other times. 17th to early 19thC English furniture, period metalware, brass, copper, silver, pottery, porcelain and rugs. BADA

Pughs' Porcelains
(John & Jane Pugh). Layer Fields House, Fields Farm Rd, Layer de la Haye, CO2 0JW. Tel Layer de la Haye(020634) 8170. Open by appt only. 18th and early 19thC English & Welsh porcelain.

Elfreda Rowley
(James and Elfreda Dilley). 7 East Stockwell St, CO1 1TS. Tel 577337. Res on premises, appointment preferred. 19thC and fine furniture, mirrors, old lighting and decorative items. Specialising in conversion of old lamps.

Trinity Antiques Centre
7 Trinity St. Tel 577775. Open Mon-Sat 9,30-5. 8 dealers in fine silver, Victorian jewellery, porcelain, militaria and a wide range of other antiques.

Earls Colne STD 078 75

Compton-Dando (Fine Arts) Ltd
(Ashley and Joanna Compton-Dando). Berewyk Hall, White Colne. Tel 2200 (priv 0787 312610). (Also at Hall St, Long Melford, Suffolk.) Open by appointment, res on prem. Full-period English and Continental furniture, also a wide and interesting range of decorative fixtures and fittings for the interior designer, all adapted from the antique. Packing, insurance and transport arranged.

Epping STD 0378

Epping Galleries
(P.Hellmers & C.Hellmers). 64-66 High St. Tel 73023. Open Mon-Sat 10-5; closed Wed. Furniture, bygones, curiosities, toys, pictures, linens, contemporary crafts. Also coffee shop. Flea market on Sat.

Felsted

Janet Howard
Argyll House. Tel Great Dunmow (0371) 820682. Open Mon-Sat, 10-5; closed Wed & Sun; other times by appt. Res on prem. Furniture, china, metalware and bric-a-brac.

The Venture
Causeway End. Tel Great Dunmow (0371) 820248. Open Tues-Sat 9.30-5.30. 18th and 19thC furniture, glass and metalware.

Finchingfield

Andrew Tate Pine
(Andrew Tate). Great Wincey Farm, Brent Hall Rd, CM7 4NP. Tel Great Dunmow (0371) 810004 (priv 0371 810280). Open Mon-Fri 9-5, Sat 9-1; other times by appt. Pine of all descriptions.

Frinton-on-Sea STD 025 56

Bow Window
(Jasmine R.Faiers). 58 Connaught Ave. Tel 4607. Open Mon, Tues, Thurs, Fri, Sat, 9-1, 2-5. Porcelain, pottery, jewellery, silver and plate, glass, watercolours, oils, prints, small furniture & mirrors.

Dickens Curios
(Miss Margaret Wilsher). 151 Connaught Ave. Tel 4134. Open Mon-Sat; early closing Wed; other times by appt. China, copper, brass, furniture, pictures, glass, fountain pens. Louis Wain cat pictures.

Frinton Antiques
(K.J. & G.M. Pethick). 5 Old Rd. Tel 71310 (priv 71894). Open Mon-Sat 9.30-5.30, closed Wed; other times by appt. Quality antique furniture, porcelain, silver, pictures, etc.

Great Baddow

The Antique Brass Bedstead Co Ltd
(Ian Rabin (Director)). Gt. Baddow Antique Centre, Church St. Tel Chelmsford (0245) 71137 (priv 0621 741941). Open Mon-Sat 10-5; Sun 12-5. Fine selection of Victorian bedsteads; 150 always on show.

Baddow Antiques and Craft Centre
(Ian Rabin, David de Ferry, Tony Finch). The Bringy. Tel Chelmsford (0245) 76159. Open Mon-Sat 10-5; Sun 12-5. Antique centre with 22 units and dealers. General stock. Trade warehouse of shipping and Victorian goods.

Great Bardfield

Markswood Gallery
(Eric W.Goodwin). Brook St, CM7 4TY. Tel Great Dunmow (0371) 810106 (priv 810329). Open Tues, Thurs, Sats 11-5; Sun 2.30-5; other times by appt. Watercolours, paintings and small furniture. LAPADA

Great Chesterford

Great Chesterford Antiques
(C.C. & S.J.Mortimer). School St, CB10 1NN. Tel Saffron Walden (0799) 30249. Open Mon-Fri - phone to confirm. General antiques and some later goods.

Charles & Joan Mortimer & Sons
Sugar House, School St, CB10 1NN. Tel Saffron Walden (0799) 30261. Open Thurs, Sun 2.30-5, Sat 11-1, 2.30-5; other times by appt. Specialists in 16th to 18thC oak and 16th and 17thC portraits (oils).

Great Dunmow STD 0371

Church End Antiques
Church End. Tel 3431. Open Mon-Fri 10-6; closed Wed; other times by appt. General antiques, stripped pine etc.

Simon Hilton
(Simon Hilton). Flemings Hill Farm, Great Easton, CM6 2ER. Tel Bishops Stortford (0279) 850107. Open any time by appt. Fine art of all periods, Barbizon school and 20thC British art.

J.M.Welch & Son
(C.J. Welch, Saleroom Manager). The Old Town Hall, CM6 1AU. Tel 2117/2118. Regular sales of antique furniture & effects. (All entries from private, non trade sources).

Great Wakering

Books and Things
(Maurice Sherman). 195 High St. Tel Southend (0702) 219752 (priv 218088). Open daily 1.30-5.30. General antiques and collectables.

Halstead STD 0787

Helen Blomfield
(Miss Helen Blomfield). Hampers, Little Maplestead. Tel 2159. Open by appt only. Georgian and Victorian silver and Sheffield plate. Valuations.

Tempus Fugit
Trinity House, Trinity St. Tel 475409. Open by appt only. On main Halstead to Braintree Rd, opp Park. Antique clocks. Also repairs and restoration.

Harlow STD 0279

Rundells Antiques
(M & R Cox). London Rd (B 1393), CM17 9LH. Tel 22906. Open Mon-Sat 9.30-5; other times by appt. Eight showrooms containing 17th, 18th & 19thC furniture and porcelain, silver, silver plate, bric-a-brac etc.

Stone Hall Antiques
Down Hall Rd, Matching Green. Tel 731440. Open Mon-Fri 9-5.30; other times by appt. Large stock of furniture, both restored and unrestored, suitable for American, Australian and European markets.

Harwich STD 025 55

Mayflower Antiques
(John W.Odgers). 180-182 High St, Dovercourt. Tel 504079. (Also on Sats at 117 Portobello Rd, W11.7-3.Tel:727 0381.) Open Tues-Fri 10-5; other times by appt. Clocks, Victorian and Georgian furniture, and general antiques. Specialist in mechanical music and automata, scientific and nautical instruments. Shipping goods.

Ilford

Gift House Antiques
(Mrs R. & Mr C.Stevens). 3 Highview Parade, Redbridge Lane. Tel 01-550 5168. Open Mon-Wed 9-5; Thurs 9-1; Fri, Sat 9-6; other times by appt. General antiques and fine art reproductions.

Ingatestone STD 0277

Meyers Gallery
(Mrs J Meyers). 66 High St. Tel Brentwood (0277) 355335 (priv 215446). Open 10-5; closed Sun & Wed; other times by appt. Antiques & paintings. Picture restoration. Furniture and clocks.

Kelvedon STD 0376

Dial House Antiques
(D.E.Mason). High St. Tel (priv) 70706. Open Mon-Sat 10.30-5.00; other times by appt. Victorian pine furniture, porcelain, linen, clothes, etc.

Falcon House Antiques and Old Book Shop
32 High St. Tel 70451. Open Mon, Wed, Sat 10-6, Tues 2.30-6; other times by appt. Paintings, small furniture, old books, curios, bric-a-brac and metalware.

Kelvedon Antique Centre
(Diana Mason). 139 High St. Tel 70896 (priv 0206 573938). Open Mon-Sat 10-5; other times by appt. Ten dealers. Furniture, silver, porcelain, jewellery, linen, art deco etc.

Kelvedon Antiques
(James Billings). 90 High St, CO5 9AA. Tel Braintree (0376) 70557. Open Mon-Sat 9.30-1 2-5.30; other times by appt. 18th and early 19thC period furniture. BADA

Millers Antiques, Kelvedon
(R.C.Miller). 46 High St. Tel 70098. Open Mon-Fri 9-6, Sat 10-4; other times by appt. A very large selection of 17th,18th and 19thC mahogany, oak and walnut furniture, both English and French. Especially wholesale and export. LAPADA

G.T.Ratcliff Ltd
(D.V.Ratcliff & W.D.Boyd Ratcliff). Durwards Hall. Tel 70234. Open Mon-Fri 9-5. Trade and export only. Enormous stock of antique furniture in 40,000 sq ft of showrooms, all in excellent condition and mainly 18th and 19thC.

Riverside Antiques
180 High St. Tel 70549. Open Mon-Sat 9.30-5.30. Furniture, clocks, china, brass, copper items, general objets d'art and bric-a-brac.

Thomas Sykes Antiques
16 High St, CO5 9AG. Tel 71969 (priv 0787 477617). Open Mon-Sat 9.30-5.30; other times by appt. 18th to early 19thC furniture. LAPADA

Leigh-on-Sea

Antiques Objets D'Art & Curios
(J. Streamer). 86 The Broadway. Tel Southend-on-Sea (0702) 72895 & 711633. (212 Leigh Road.) Open Mon-Fri 9.30-5.30; closed Wed. Antiquities, clocks and watches, bygones and curiosities and jewellery.

Stephen Charles Antiques
3 Leigh Hill, SS9 2DR. Tel Southend-on-Sea (0702) 714649 (priv 0268 774977). Open Mon, Fri, Sat, 12.30-6; other times by appt. Small items antiques and art deco. Shipping furniture & general items. Antique fairs organisers.

Gems
(Betty & Eric White). 11 Rectory Grove. Tel Southend-on-Sea (0702) 53835. Open Mon-Sat 10.30-5.30; early closing Wed. Jewellery, coins, postcards and general antiques.

Leigh Auction Rooms
(P.J.,F.C.&J.Stacey). 88-90 Pall Mall. Tel Southend-on-Sea (0702) 77051. Open Mon-Fri 9-5.30, Sat 9-1; other times by appt. Auctioneers of antiques and works of art. Mainly executors' estates. Transporters of furniture and works of art in the UK and Europe.

Pall Mall Antiques
(Maurice Sherman). 104c & 104d Elm Rd. Tel Southend-on-Sea (0702) 77235. (Also at Books & Things, Great Wakering, Essex.) Open daily. Copper, cottage and country antiques, domestic items and ephemera.

Loughton

Ambrose
149 High Rd. Tel 01-508 2121. Auctioneers and surveyors.

Maldon STD 0621

Beeleigh Abbey Books
(W. & G. Foyle Ltd). Beeleigh Abbey. Tel 56308. Travel and topography, English literature, fine bindings and illustrated books. ABA

Maldon Antiques & Collectors Market
(D.J. Major). United Reformed Church Hall, Market Hill. Tel Earls Colne (07875) 2826. Open 1st Sat every month, 10-5. Antiques and collectors market.

The Plume Porcelain Co Ltd
West Bowers Hall, Woodham Walter, CM9 6RZ. Tel Danbury (024 541) 2562. Open by appt only. Specialists in antique English and Continental dinner, dessert and tea and coffee services.

Trident Coins Ltd
Great Totham. Tel 891858. Open 9-5.30; other times by appt. English, foreign and Roman coins.

Newport

Brown House Antiques
(Jean and Brian Hodgkinson). High St, CB11 3QY. Tel Saffron Walden (0799) 40238. Open Mon-Sat 10.5.30; Sun 1-5.30. Wide range of antique pine and Victorian style reproduction pine.

Galerie Appenzell
(Lester Simms). High St, CB11 3QZ. Tel Saffron Walden (0799) 40623. Open daily 10-5.30; closed Wed & Sun. A large stock of 18th, 19th & 20thC watercolours, oils & prints.

The M11 Antiques Centre
(Deborah Hodgkinson). High St, CB11 3QY. Tel Saffron Walden (0799) 40321 (priv 40238). Open Mon-Sat 10-5; other times by appt. Eight dealers selling mainly 18th & 19thC darkwood furniture, also silver, china, pictures.

Rayleigh STD 0268

F.G. Bruschweiler (Antiques) Ltd
(F.G. Bruschweiler). 41-67 Lower Lambricks, SS6 7EN. Tel 773761, 773932. Open Mon-Fri 9-5; other times by appt. Large warehouse and showrooms of Victorian furniture and smalls, continental and Edwardian furniture. Shipping goods. LAPADA

Romford STD 0708

Geo Copsey & Co Ltd
Danes Rd. Tel 24213. Packers & shippers. LAPADA

Saffron Walden STD 0799

Antiques
(Jane Sumner). 9 Market Square. Tel 23611 (0672 870727). Open Mon-Sat 9.30-5; other times by appt. 17th, 18th and early 19thC oak, walnut, rosewood and mahogany furniture. Antique jewellery. Early metalware.

Michael Beaumont Antiques
(M.J. Beaumont). Hempstead Hall, Hempstead, CB10 2PR. Tel Steeple Bumpstead (044084) 239. Open 7 days, 10.30-5. Fifteen large showrooms mainly of furniture in oak, mahogany, rosewood and walnut of the 17th, 18th and 19thC.

The Church Street Gallery
(Mrs Patricia M. Pickard). 17 Church St, CB10 1JW. Tel 24422 (priv 0279-850423). Open Mon-Sat 10-5; closed Thurs; other times by appt. Specialising in 18th-20thC watercolours, 19th & 20thC paintings, sculpture, studio pottery. LAPADA

Lankester Antiques & Books
Old Sun Inn, Church St and Market Hill. Tel 22685. Open Mon-Sat 9.30-5.30;. Good stock of furniture, general antiques and books, maps, prints, Victoriana and metalware.

Littlebury Antiques
58/60 Fairycroft Rd. Tel 27961. Open Mon-Fri 9-5, weekends by appt. Marine antiques and paintings, clocks and chronometers, barometers, walking sticks and chess sets.

Norfolk Antiques
16 Market Row, CB10 1HB. Tel 27633. Open Mon-Sat 10.30-1, 2-5.30, closed Thurs. Furniture, jewellery, silver, glass and some porcelain.

R.B. Walkyier & Son
17 High St. Tel 3430. Open Mon-Sat 9-6; early closing Thurs; other times by appt. Large range of all types of antique weapons, pistols, guns, rifles, swords and armour.

Watsons
1 Market St. Tel 22058. Open Mon-Fri 9-5.30. Auctioneers.

Sible Hedingham

W.A.Pinn & Sons
(K.H., W.J. & C.Pinn). 124 Swan St, CO9 3HP. Tel Hedingham (0787) 61127. Open Mon-Sat 9-6; other times by appt. 17th to 19thC furniture and works of art. BADA

South Ockendon STD 0708

Alfred S.Allen & Co
(Alfred S.Allen). PO Box 4, RM15 4JE. Tel Purfleet (0708) 866075. Wholesalers and retailers of coin jewellery, coins and numismatic accessories.

Stanford le Hope STD 0375

Barton House Antiques
(L. & J. Pigney). Barton House, 48 Wharf Rd, SS17 0DY. Tel Stanford-le-Hope (0375) 672494. Open by appt only. Specialists in 18thC English blue and white porcelain; also 17th, 18th and 19thC English furniture, copper, brass, glass and interesting items.

Stansted Mountfitchet

F.J. Harris
(F.J. Harris). 23 Silver St. Tel Bishops Stortford (0279) 813371. Open Mon-Sat 9.30-5.30; other times by appt. 18th and 19thC furniture, clocks, silver, porcelain, brass and copper. LAPADA

Linden House Antiques
(A.W.Sargeant). Linden House, 3 Silver St, CM24 8HA. Tel Bishops Stortford (0279) 812372. Open Mon-Sat 9-6; other times by appt. 18thC & 19thC English furniture, dining tables & sets of chairs, bookcases, desks and good selection of fine antique oak furniture.

Valmar Antiques
(Marina, John & Nicola Orpin). Croft House, High Lane, CM24 8LQ. Tel Bishops Stortford (0279) 813201. Open Mon-Sat 8-5; other times by appt. Large stock of selected antiques - furniture, decorative items and pictures for the home and overseas trade only.

Wiskin Antiques
(K. Wiskin & Mrs M. Wiskin). 18 Silver St. Tel Bishops Stortford (0279) 812376. Open Mon-Sat 10-5.30; other times by appt. Furniture including Georgian, Victorian, mahogany, oak & walnut and well stripped period pine.

Stock STD 0277

Sabine Antiques
(Celia E.Sabine). 38 High St, CM4 9BW. Tel 840553. Open Tues -Sat 10-5; other times by appt. Furniture and porcelain. Restorations and valuation.

Thaxted STD 0371

Guildhall Galleries
Tel 395. (Also at Turpins Antiques.) Fine selection of 17th and 18thC furniture.

Turpins Antiques
(John F.Braund). 4 Stoney Lane. Tel 830495 (priv 830059). Open Mon-Sat 10-5; other times by appt. 17th and 18thC oak, walnut and mahogany furniture, early metalware. Restoration undertaken. BADA

Theydon Bois STD 037 881

A.F. Allbrook
22 Morgan Crescent, CM16 7DX. Tel 2344. Open by appt only. Specialist in 17th and 18thC English pottery.

Thorpe-le-Soken

Le Soken Antiques
High Street. Tel Clacton (0255) 861 337. Open Thur, Fri, Sat 10-6; other times by appt. General antiques and collectors items. 18th and 19thC furniture, Tunbridge ware, tea caddies, writing slopes, treen, boxes, copper and brass. LAPADA

Wakes Colne

Janet Gordon
(Janet Gordon). Wakes Colne House. Tel Earls Colne (07875) 2402. Open daily but Sunday by appt. Mainly pre-1900 furniture. Re-upholstery, curtains, loose covers, fabrics.

Westcliff-on-Sea

David, Jean & John Antiques
(David Howard, Jean & John Swainsbury). 587 London Rd. Tel Southend (0702) 339106. Open Mon-Sat 9.30-5.30; closed Wed; other times by appt. 18th and 19thC clocks, watches, jewellery, Victorian furniture and smalls. Also shipping goods. BWCMG

Its About Time
(R.&V.Alps). 863 London Rd, SS26 6BA. Tel Southend (0702) 72574 (priv 205204). Open daily except Wed and Sun; other times by appt. Antique clocks, 18th & 19thC longcase & Vienna wall clocks. 19thC furniture & barometers.

Witham STD 0376

Witham Antiques
(Deirdre E. Gann). Tel 512416. Open by appt only. Period furniture, antique silver, gold and jewellery, porcelain, brass, copper, coins.

Woodford Green

Shirley King Antiques
2 Johnston Rd. Tel 01-505 5774. Open Mon, Wed, Fri 11.30-5; Sat 9.30-5; other times by appt. Victoriana, porcelain, glass, jewellery and small furniture.

Gloucestershire

Barnsley

Denzil Verey Antiques
(Mrs Denzil Verey). The Close, Barnsley House. Tel Bibury (0285 74) 402 (priv 028585 495). Open Mon-Fri 9.30-5.30; Sat 10.30-5.30; other times by appt. 18th and 19thC country furniture, pine, treen, unusual and decorative items. CADA

Berkeley

Berkeley Antiques
(Peter and Roslyn Dennis). Marybrook St. Tel Dursley (0453) 810 391. Open Mon-Sat 10-6; closed Wed; other times by appt. A good cross section of furniture, brass and copper. LAPADA

Sylvia Harris
13 High St, GL13 9BH. Open Mon-Sat 10-6; closed Wed. Porcelain and jewellery.

Michael R. Mathews
(Airclass Designs Ltd). 13 High St, GL13 9BH. Tel Dursley (0453) 811120. Open Mon-Sat 10-6; closed Wed; other times by appt. 17th, 18th and early 19thC furniture; also porcelain and silver.

Newcomb Antiques
(John Newcomb Cryer, Wendy Newcomb Cryer). 17 & 19 High St, GL13 9BH. Tel Dursley (0453) 810338. Open Mon-Fri 9.30-5.45; Sat 10-1 closed Wed & Sun; other times by appt. 18th and 19thC furniture, porcelain and pine.

Blockley STD 0386

Pamela Rowan Antiques
(Pamela and Maurice Rowan). High St, GL56 9ET. Tel 700280. Open Wed-Sat 9.30-5.30; other times by appt. 18th and 19thC English and Chinese porcelain, also some Continental. Small oak and mahogany furniture and smalls. BADA, CADA

Bourton-on-the-Water
STD 0451

Chestnut Gallery
(Mary & Peter O'Connor). High Street. Tel 20017. Open Mon-Sat 10-5; Sun 2-5; closed Mon & Wed in winter; other times by appt. Permanent stock of pottery, glass, turned wood etc. Specialising in contemporary studio pottery. 2 or 3 exhibitions each year. Selected for quality by the Crafts Council. ICGA

Henry-Brett Galleries
(Martyn Riley). Halford House. Tel 20443 (priv 028 574 433). Open daily in summer 10.30-5.30; closed Wed during winter; other times by appt. Sporting, wildlife and landscape art. Oils, watercolours, etchings, prints, pastels and sculptures. Restoration and framing services.

Studio Antiques Ltd
GL54 2BX. Tel 20352. Open at any time, and by appt. Quality antiques of all periods. Furniture, porcelain, silver, copper, brass, pottery - garden items. CADA

Cheltenham STD 0242

Antiques Cheltenham
(Mrs J. Turner). 22 Montpellier Walk, GL50 1SD. Tel 522939. Open 10-4.30; other times by appt. General antiques. LAPADA

Architectural Heritage of Cheltenham
(Tania Wyman, Adrian Puddy). Boddington Manor, Boddington, GL51 OTJ. Tel Coombe Hill (024268) 741. Open Mon-Fri 10-5; Sat 10.30-1; other times by appt. Architectural antiques, panelled rooms, chimney pieces, garden ornaments and statues, pub and shop interiors, stained glass, doors.

Archway Gallery
43 North St, Winchcombe. Tel 603058. Antique prints & maps. Res on premises.

Armada Exports
(Kenneth J.Shave). 50 Suffolk Rd. Tel 29812, 32615. (Also at the Antique Market, 54 Suffolk Rd, Cheltenham.) Open Mon-Sat 9-5.30; other times by appt. Victorian mahogany, walnut and carved oak and general antiques for trade and export. LAPADA

Barrie's Bookshop
4 Montpellier Walk, GL50 1SD. Tel 515813. Open by appt Mon-Sat. Travel, bindings, fore-edge paintings. Showroom above Mrs B's coffee shop. ABA

Benson Antiques
(H.F.& F.Benson). 13 Suffolk Parade. Tel 578366. Open Tues-Sat 10-5 (Summer 9.30-5.30). Late Georgian, Regency & early Victorian mahogany & rosewood furniture. Decorative items, antique bed covers and table linens.

Borbaletta
(C.G.R.Pollard). Cheltenham Antique Market, 54 Suffolk Rd. Tel 29812. Open Mon-Sat 9.30-5.30. General antiques.

Bottles & Bygones
(John M. Brown). 96 Horsefair St, Charlton Kings. Tel 236393. Open Wed, Thurs, Fri, Sat 10-5.30; other times by appt. Specialist dealers in old bottles, pot-lids, enamel advertising, tins, dolls' heads, claypipes, postcards. General antiques and collector's items.

David Cambridge
13 Rotunda Terrace. Tel 42178. Open Mon-Sat 9-5. 17th and 18thC oil paintings, Continental furniture and works of art.

Cameo Antiques
(Roger Chitty). 31 Suffolk Parade. Tel 33164. Open Mon-Sat 10-1, 2-5; early closing Wed; other times by appt. Victorian, Edwardian inlay, art nouveau and art deco, art pottery, porcelain and brassware . Also 18thC furniture.

Castle Antiques
(T.C. Germain). 15 Commercial St. Tel 524563. (Also Cheltenham Spa Restorations, 33 Imperial Sq, Cheltenham.) Open by appt. Silver, furniture, clocks, barometers. Restorations of all kinds connected with the antique business. LAPADA

Cheltenham Antique Centre
(The Antique Forum (Birmingham) Ltd). 1A Crescent Place. Open Tues-Sun 10-6. 60 dealers with a range of general antiques.

Cheltenham Antique Market
54 Suffolk Rd. Tel 529812. Open 9.15-5.30 6 days a week.

Cheltenham Spa Restorations
(T.C. & N.G. Germain). 33 Imperial Square. Tel 581919. (Also at Castle Antiques, 15 Commercial St, Cheltenham.) Open 10-4; other times by appt. Silver, furniture, clocks, barometers. Restorations of all kinds connected with the antique business.

China Doll
31 Suffolk Parade. Tel 33164. Antique dolls and accessories.

Christie's
(Viscount Ebrington, Annette Gough,Rupert de Zoete). 111 The Promenade. Tel 518999. Fine art auctioneers & valuers.

Cloud Hill Antiques
(Mrs Sue Teale). 8 High St, Winchcombe. Tel 602015. Stripped pine, linen & lace, bric-a-brac.

Danny Cox
(Daniel G.Cox). Cheltenham Antique Market, 54 Suffolk Rd. Tel 29812. Open Mon-Sat 9-5.30; other times by appt. Quality furnishing items.

George Curtis
(George Curtis). 14 Suffolk Parade, GL50 2AB. Tel 513828. Open Mon-Sat 9.30-6; other times by appt. 17th and 18thC English and Continental clocks and occasionally period furniture. BADA, LAPADA

Colin Elliott
4 Great Norwood St. Tel 528590. Open daily 10-5.30; other times by appt. Antique watches and clocks.

Gladys Green Antiques
(Yvonne Reynolds, Stephen Reynolds). 15 Montpellier Walk, GL50 1SD. Tel 512088 (priv 525054). Open 9-5; early closing Wed; other times by appt. 18th and 19thC porcelain, jewellery, silver and furniture. Antiquarian & secondhand books.

J.P.J.Homer Oriental Rugs
Stoneleigh, Parabola Rd, GL50 3BD. Tel 34243. Open any time by appt. Antique and old Oriental rugs, mainly tribal.

Martin Ellis Jones
15 Suffolk Parade. Tel 516670. Open Mon-Fri 10-6; other times by appt. General stock with bias to the unusual and small.

MARKSWOOD GALLERY

Eric Goodwin

Great Bardfield,
Braintree Essex.
Gallery (0371) 810106
Home (0371) 810329

Two examples of many fine English watercolours and paintings to be found at this well established country gallery within easy reach of London

Above:
William Woodhouse
Signed oil on canvas
"The White Cattle of Chillingham"

Left:
Robert Hills, O.W.S.
Watercolour
"Donkeys at Rest"

Watercolours and Paintings
Antiques and Restoration

Tuesdays, Thursdays & Saturdays 11a.m.–5p.m.
Sundays 2.30–5p.m. All other times by appointment.

W. A. PINN & SONS

Antiques and Works of Art
17th & 18th century Furniture & Accessories

Extremely fine Regency mahogany bookcase of unusual design, c1810, 60" wide.

124 SWAN STREET, SIBLE HEDINGHAM,
Nr. HALSTEAD, ESSEX CO9 3HP.
Tel. 0787-61127

GLADYS GREEN ANTIQUES MONTPELLIER

FINE VICTORIAN JEWELLERY, ANTIQUE SILVER, PORCELAIN & GLASS
SOME FURNITURE

Constantly changing Stock suitable for the Home and Overseas Trade

15 Montpellier Walk, Cheltenham, Gloucester 0242 512088/525054

RANKINE TAYLOR ANTIQUES

(Mrs. Leslie Taylor)

Interesting collection of Antique Furniture, Silver, Glass and Rare Items.

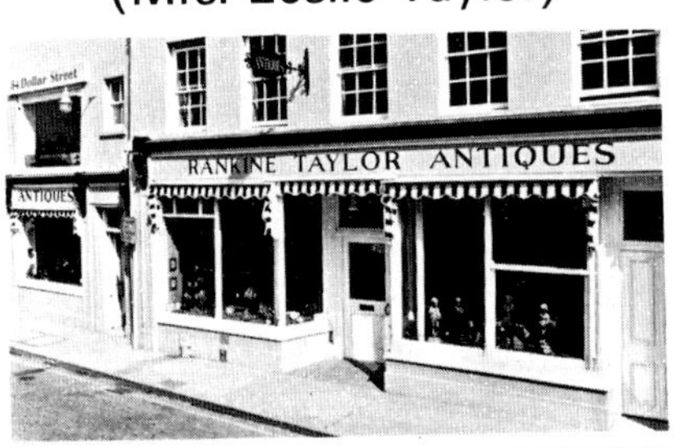

34 Dollar Street,
Cirencester, Glos.
Tel. Cirencester 2529

H.W. Keil (Cheltenham) Ltd
(P.J.W. Keil). 129-131 The Promenade, GL50 1NW. Tel 522509, 527974. Open Mon-Sat 9.15-1, 2.15-5.30; other times by appt. Large stock of 17th-early 19thC furniture. 18th and 19thC watercolours and oil paintings. General antiques, including glass chandeliers, glass, pewter. Interior decoration. BADA

Mallams
(M.R.V.Lear, B.J.Lloyd). 26 Grosvenor St. Tel 35712. (Also in Oxford.) Open Mon-Fri 9-1 2-5.30. Auctioneers of fine art and antiques. Monthly sales, including specialist sales of pictures, silver, jewellery, Eastern rugs and porcelain.

Manor House Antiques
42 Suffolk Rd. Tel 32780. Open Mon-Fri 9.30-5.30; other times by appt. Victorian furniture, quality mahogany and walnut. Shipping goods.

Martin & Co Ltd
(M.A. Dimmer). 19 The Promenade. Tel 522821. Antique silver and Sheffield plate, jewellery. BADA

Janet Maund
Cheltenham Antique Market, GL3 1HA. Tel 529812 (priv 0452 712286). Open Mon-Sat 9.15-5.30; other times by appt. Fans, small furniture, silver and plate, china, porcelain and glass.

Jeannette Meager
Cheltenham Antique Market, 54 Suffolk Rd. Tel 29812. Open Mon-Sat 9-5.30. General stock including mirrors and mirror pictures.

T.Mercer Chronometers
16A Lansdown Place Lane, GL50 2LB. Tel 516022. Makers of chronometers since 1858; also antique chronometers and restorations.

Anne Newman
Cheltenham Antique Market, 54 Suffolk St. Tel 29812, 32615. Open Mon-Sat 9-5.30. Furniture, silver.

Elizabeth Niner Antiques
(Mrs G.E.Niner). 53 Great Norwood St. Tel 516497 (priv 520066). Open Mon-Fri 9.30-5. 17th to 19thC furniture, mainly mahogany, and decorative items. Specialist in four-poster beds.

Ogle Fine Arts
(Jenny & Douglas Ogle). Ogle Gallery, 12 Rotunda Terrace, Montpellier St. Tel 518605 (priv 31011). Open Tues-Sat 10-5; other times by appt. Exhibition gallery for contemporary British paintings, artists' prints, sculpture, glass, ceramics, jewellery, silver and wood.

Patrick Oliver Antiques Ltd
(D.P.& M.D.Oliver). 4 Tivoli St, GL50 2UW. Tel 513392/519538. General. Valuations. LAPADA

A. Oram
Cheltenham Antique Market, 54 Suffolk St. Tel 29812 (priv 512539). Open Mon-Sat 9.30-5.30; other times by appt. General trade stock.

Eric Pride Oriental Rugs
(Eric Pride). 8 Imperial Sq, GL50 1QB. Tel 580822 (priv 521057). Open Mon-Fri 10-6; Sat 9.30-4; other times by appt. Buying, selling, valuation, cleaning and restoration of handwoven old carpets, rugs, flatweaves, and collectors' items from Persia, Anatolia, Caucasus and Central Asia. GMC

Priory Gallery
(Ric & Elizabeth James). The Priory, Station Rd, Bishops Cleeve. Tel Bishops Cleeve (024 267) 3226. Open by appt. Quality oil paintings and watercolours of late 19th and early 20thC origin. Specialising in figurative and genre of the Edwardian period. Restoration and framing service.

P.J. Reynolds Antiques
(Paul John Reynolds). Cheltenham Antique Market, 54 Suffolk Rd. Tel 529812 (priv 513382). Open Mon-Sat 9-5.30. Victorian, Edwardian & pre-1930s shipping furniture.

Scott Cooper Ltd
52 The Promenade, GL50 1LY. Tel 522580. Fine antiques and 19thC jewellery, bijouterie, silver, Sheffield plate, miniatures, Battersea enamels and objects of vertu. BADA

Sotheby's
(Representative: John Harvey). 18 Imperial Sq, GL50 1QZ. Tel 510500. Open Mon-Fri 9.30-1, 2-5.30. Fine art auctioneers.

J.P.Townsend Antiques
(John Patrick Townsend). Cheltenham Antique Market, 54 Suffolk Rd. Tel 29812. Open Mon-Sat 9.30-5.30; other times by appt. Pine.

Turtle Antiques
(Patricia Field). 29 Suffolk Parade, GL50 2AE. Tel 41646. Open Mon-Sat 9-6; other times by appt. Furniture, porcelain, silver. Oils, watercolours and prints. Jewellery, glass, decorative items etc.

Winchcombe Gallery
(Jenny & Tony White). 7 Hailes Street, Winchcombe. Tel 603578. 18th & 19thC furniture, porcelain.

Chipping Campden

Circa Antiques
(T.G. Ball). The Square, GL55 6AL. Tel Evesham (0386) 840851. Open Mon-Sat 10-1, 2.30-5; early closing Thurs; other times by appt. 18th and 19thC English porcelain specialising in Doulton Lambeth wares.

Saxton House Gallery
(S.D. & J. Coy). High St, GL55 6HQ. Tel Evesham (0386) 840278. Open Mon-Sat 9.30-5.30; closed Thurs; other times by appt. Clocks, barometers, English furniture, pre-1830, oil paintings & watercolours. Antique jewellery.

Swan Antiques
High St, GL55 6HB. Tel Evesham (0386) 840759. Open Mon-Sat 9-1, 2-5; Thurs 9-12.30; other times by appt. 17th and 18thC furniture, china silver & jewellery.

Cinderford

Francis J. Grogan
Brayne Court Gallery, Little Dean. Tel Dean (0594) 22163. Open anytime by appt. Paintings and watercolours, British and European, 19th and 20thC.

Puzzle House Antiques
(S.J.Jones). Trafalgar. Tel Dean (0594) 60653. (Also at 16A,St Mary's St, Chepstow, Gwent. Tel 02912-3314.) Open Mon-Sat. Small antiques, furniture 1800-1930, boxes, pictures. LAPADA

Cirencester STD 0285

At the Sign of the Herald Angel
(Thomas & Pamela Hudson). 19 Park St, GL7 2BX. Tel 2972. Open Mon-Sat 9-1, 2-5.30; other times by appt. Small antiques, mainly pre-1840. Specialising in old Sheffield plate, snuffboxes, early spoons, fans, needlework tools and workboxes. CADA

Jonathan Beech
Workshop 7a, The Cirencester Workshops. Tel 67630. Antique clock restorer.

Walter Bull & Son (Cirencester) Ltd
10 Dyer St, GL7 2PF. Tel 3875. Open Mon-Sat 9-5. Silver, jewellery, porcelain and other items.

Cirencester Antique Market
Market Square. Open Fri 9-4.50. Dealers with general antiques.

Cirencester Antiques Ltd
(Richard Chester-Master). 17 Dyer St, GL7 2PP. Tel 2955 (priv 3066). Open Mon-Sat 9-5.30; other times by appt. Large stock of fine quality English & Continental furniture and works of art, 17th-early 19thC. CADA

Cirencester Workshops
Brewery Court. Tel 61566. 20 full-time professional craftsmen: willow baskets, leatherwork and saddlery, embroidered textiles, jewellery, bookbinding and restoration, stained glass, furniture making and restoration, antique clock and clock-face restoration. Also exhibitions.

Fraser Glennie & Partners
(Fraser R. Glennie, ARICS). The Old Rectory, Siddington, GL7 6HL. Tel 3938. Open Mon-Fri 9-5.30; Sat 9-12; other times by appt. Auctioneer - Surveyor. RICS

Jay Gray Antiques
Syrena House, 1 Cheltenham Rd, GL7 2HS. Tel 2755. Open Mon-Sat 9-6; other times by appt. General antiques and works of art, 18th and 19thC French and English furniture, pictures, glass, Victorian jewellery and Oriental, English and Continental porcelain.

Hobbs & Chambers
At the Sign of the Bell, Market Place, GL7 1QQ. Tel 4736 (priv 0672 20018). (Also at 15 Royal Crescent, Cheltenham. Tel: 0242 513722.) Open Mon-Fri 9-5.30; Sat 9-1. Fine arts & chattels auctioneers & valuers. Specialist sales of antiques held.

W.W.Holzgrave
7 Gosditch St. Tel 69351. Open Mon-Sat 9.15-5.30. 17th-early 19thC mahogany. Also metalware and works of art. CADA

Jackson-Stops & Staff
Dollar St. Tel 3334. Land and estate agents, surveyors and valuers.

E.C.Legg & Son
(C.A.Legg). The Old School House, Somerford Keynes, GL7 6DJ. Tel 861420. Open Mon-Fri 9-5, Sat 9-12.30. General furniture and restoration work.

The William Marler Gallery
36/38 Dyer St, GL7 2PF. Tel 68526. Open Mon-Sat 9.30-5.30. Specialist in natural history and sporting paintings-predominantly early 20thC. Also watercolours and prints. Framing, restoration and valuations.

Moore Allen & Innocent
33 Castle St. Tel 61831. Auctioneers.

A.J.Ponsford Antiques and Restorations
(Alan & Ruth Ponsford). 51-53 Dollar St, GL7 2AS. Tel 2355. Open Mon-Fri 8-5.30; other times by appt. Est 25 years. Large showroom with clean, restored antique furniture in oak, walnut, mahogany etc 1700-1900. Brass cabinet fittings. Quality reproductions to order.Restoration of furniture and pictures; upholstery; framing.Leather tops with gold tooling.

Rankine Taylor Antiques
(Mrs Leslie Taylor). 34 Dollar St, GL7 2AN. Tel 2529. Open Mon-Sat 9-5.30; other times by appt. 17th, 18th & early 19thC furniture, silver, glass, porcelain and rare interesting objects. CADA, LAPADA

John D.Rivers
1 Ashcroft Rd. Tel 67616. Jewellery. LAPADA

William H.Stokes
(W.H.Stokes & P.W.Bontoft). Roberts House, Siddington, GL7 6EX. Tel 67101. (Siddington is about 1 mile south of Cirencester off A19 to Swindon.) Fine early oak furniture and works of art. BADA CADA

Thornborough Galleries
(Richard Purdon, Alan du Monceau). 28 Gloucester St, GL7 2DH. Tel 2055 (priv 099386 367). Open Mon-Fri 9-5, Sat 9-1; other times by appt. Old and antique Eastern and European carpets, tapestries and needlework. BADA

Coleford

St John's Studio
(A.E.D. & D.D.Young). 18 St John's St, GL16 8AR. Tel Dean (0594) 32368. Open 10-1, 2-5; closed Thurs. 19thC furniture, antiquarian books, brass, copper and metalware, 18thC paintings and 19thC pottery, porcelain and glass.

Dowdeswell

Geoffrey Stead
The Old Rectory, GL54 5LX. Tel Cheltenham (0242) 820571. Open Mon-Sat 8.30-7 appt advisable. English and Continental period furniture,decorative items, primitive paintings, prints, architectural items, garden furniture and statuary.

Eastleach

Guy Holland
Shepbridge Barn, GL7 3PS. Tel Southrop (036785) 296. Open by appt only. Fine 17th and 18thC English furniture. Early walnut. BADA

Fairford

Gloucester House Antiques Ltd
(Mr & Mrs Chester-Master). Market Place, GL7 4AB. Tel Cirencester (0285) 712790 (priv 3066). Open Mon-Sat 9-5.30; other times by appt. English and French country furniture (restored on premises), pottery, treen, decorative items from the 17th, 18th and 19thC. Large showrooms, and barn by appt. CADA

Charles Woodward Antiques
(Charles Woodward). Market Place, GL7 4AB. Tel Cirencester (0285) 712094. Open Mon-Fri 10-5; Sat 9.30-1, 2-4.30; other times by appt. 17th to 19thC furniture, brass and smalls.

Gloucester STD 0452

Antique Restoration
(C.A. Cook, E.J. Cook, P. Overthrow). Antique Centre, 1 Severn Rd. Tel 29716 (priv 20911). Open Mon-Fri 9-5; Sat 9-4.30; Sun 1-4.30; other times by appt. Restorers and conservators of antique furniture. Mobile workshop for overseas work.

Douglas Bartrick - Antiques
(Douglas & Steven Bartrick). Gloucester Antiques Centre, Severn Rd, GL1 2LE. Tel 29716 (priv 618465). Open Mon-Fri 9-5; Sat 9-4.30; Sun 1-4.30. General antiques, small furniture, silver, oils, prints, clocks, bronzes plus a miscellany of Art Nouveau and Art Deco. Specialist in antique maps.

Bruton Knowles & Co
Albion Chambers, 55 Barton St. Tel 21267. (Also at 10a Castle St, Cirencester.) Fine art auctioneers and valuers. House and collective sales held.

E.J.Cook & Son Antiques
The Antique Centre, 1 Severn Rd. Tel 29716. Open Mon-Fri 9-5, Sat 9-4.30, Sun 1-4.30. Large stock of 18th and 19thC furniture, both restored and unrestored, also furnishing goods. Export services.

The Gloucester Antiques Centre
(E.J.Cook). 1 Severn Rd. Tel 29716. Open Mon-Fri 9.30-5, Sat 9-4.30, Sun 1-4.30; other times by appt. 65 antique dealers in 30,000sq ft. Very wide range of all types of antiques. Full restoration services. Export goods.

Hayes and Newby Antique Export
(Paul Hayes). The Pit, Hare Lane. Tel 31145, 24722. Open Mon-Fri 9-6, Sat 10-4; closed Sun. Architectural antiques, church interiors. French and English furniture.

HQ84
(Mrs Barbara Williams). Southgate St. Tel 27716. Open Mon-Fri 9.30-5.30; other times by appt. Mainly militaria, old and new medals, badges, coins, small antiques. Plenty of government surplus. Trade welcome. No furniture.

Kimbrose Antiques
78 Southgate St. Tel 27310. Open Mon-Fri 9-5; Sat 9-1; other times by appt. 18th and 19thC furniture, clocks, pictures.

Hartpury STD 045 270

Jan Carter
Tel 628. Open daily by appt. Specialist in New Hall porcelain.

Lechlade

Peter Bell Fine Arts
(Rosemary A Bell). High St, GL7 3DL. Tel Faringdon (0367) 52987 (priv 52255). Open Mon-Sat 10-5.30; other times by appt. Good early country oak furniture, English glass pre 1830, carvings, metalwork, oils, contemporary etchings.

Gerard Campbell
(J. & G. Campbell). Maple House, Market Place, GL7 3AB. Tel Faringdon (0367) 52267. Open by appt only. Clocks, Viennese regulators. Watercolours.

Moreton-in-Marsh STD 0608

The Antiques Centre
London House, High St. Tel 51084. Open Mon-Sat 9.30-5.30; other times by appt. Ten dealers selling period English furniture, treen, oil painting & watercolours, rugs, decorative items, porcelain.

Astley House - Fine Art
(David and Nanette Glaisyer). Astley House, High St, GL54 0LL. Tel 50601. Open Mon-Sat 9-5.30; other times by appt. 19th & 20thC oil paintings, especially large Victorian oils. Specialist framing of all types including porcelain. Cleaning & restoration of oils and watercolours. CADA

Simon Brett
(S.A. Brett and E.C.C. Brett). Creswyke House, High St, GL56 0LH. Tel 50751. Open Mon-Sat 9.30-5.30; other times by appt. 17th to early 19thC English and Continental furniture, works of art and portrait miniatures. Also old fishing tackle and related items. BADA

Paul Cater Antiques
High St, GL56 0AD. Tel 51888. 17th - 19thC oak, mahogany and walnut furniture, metalware, treen and carvings

Franfam Ltd
(J. and S. Franses). High St, GL56 0LH. Tel 50648. Open Mon-Sat 9-6. Country antiques including furniture, metalware, pottery, porcelain and paintings. CADA LAPADA

Grimes House Antiques
(S. & V. Farnsworth). Grimes House, High St, GL56 0AT. Tel 51029. Open Mon-Sat 9.30-1, 2-5.30; closed Wed; other times by appt. Good quality Victorian furniture, watercolours, porcelain and general antiques. Trade picture framing; specialist in watercolour framing.

M.K.Nielsen
(M.K. Nielson). Seaford House, High St, GL56 0AD. Tel 50448. (Also at Grimes House, High St.) Open Mon, Thurs, Fri, Sat 9.30-5. Porcelain, specialising in Derby and Worcester, including signed pieces; also furniture, glass and metalware. LAPADA

Elizabeth Parker Antiques
High St, GL56 0LL. Tel 50917. Open Mon-Sat 9-5.30; other times by appt. 18thC English and Continental furniture, silver and plate.

Primrose Antiques
(Mrs B. Stickland). High St, GL66 0LL. Tel 50591. Period oak, walnut & mahogany furniture, brass, copper etc. CADA

Peter Roberts Antiques
(Paul Martain). High St, GL56 0LM. Open 10-6; other times by appt. Decorative furniture, beds, objets d'art, garden furniture.

THORNBOROUGH GALLERIES

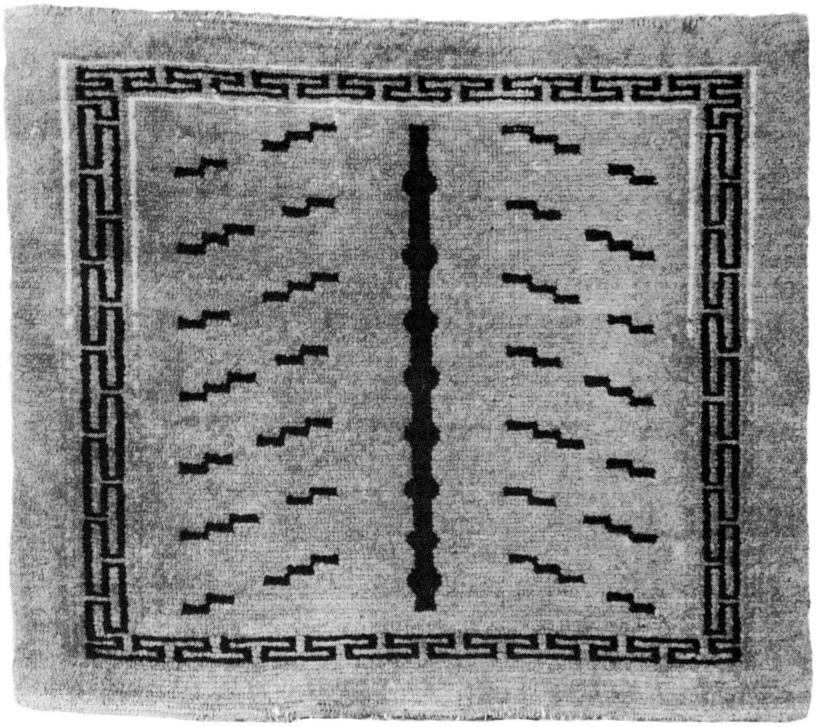

Member of
the British Antiques Dealers' Association

This rare Tibetan saddle cover is part of our stock of antique and decorative old eastern carpets displayed in five showrooms

Richard Purdon – Alan du Monceau
28 GLOUCESTER STREET,
CIRENCESTER GL7 2DH
TELEPHONE (0285) 2055

Upton Lodge Galleries

Specialists in British Impressionists and Post Impressionists

Avening House, Avening, Tetbury,
Gloucestershire GL8 8NH
Telephone: Nailsworth (045 383) 4048

Landscape by John Anthony Park, ROI, RBA (1880–1962)
Oil, 24″ × 28″, signed

Exporters of 19th and early 20th century British and Continental oils and watercolours

Photographs and details can be sent with condition, provenance and quality of paintings guaranteed. Any gallery interested, please contact Josephine Grant at the above address (if from USA or Canada, by AIRMAIL please) or by telephone.

Gastrell House,
33 Long St. Tetbury,
Gloucestershire
Tetbury 52228

John Morris

Fine Period Furniture
Clocks and Paintings

Anthony Sampson
(Anthony Sampson). Dale House, High St, GL56 0AD. Tel 50763. Open Mon-Sat 9-1, 2-5.30; other times by appt. Res on premises. Mainly 18thC & early 19thC furniture, walnut mahogany, satinwood & rosewood - a little oak & country furniture. Decorative items. BADA

Nailsworth STD 045 383

John Barry
Barton End Hall, GL6 0QQ. Tel 3471. Open Mon-Sat 9.30-5.30; other times by appt. (1 mile south of Nailsworth on the A46 Bath Rd) Fine 18th and early 19thC furniture, paintings and objects of art. BADA LAPADA

Painswick STD 0452

Hamand Antiques
(Major F.N.L.Chapman). Friday St, GL6 6QJ. Tel 812310. Open Mon-Sat but appt. advisable. Oriental and other pottery and porcelain. Some furniture, glass and general antiques.

Heather Newman Gallery
(Heather Newman, Derek Newman). Milidduwa, Cranham, GL6 6TX. Tel 812230. Open 7 days a week by appt. Fine 18th-19thC, early 20thC British watercolours and drawings. Major exhibitions during May and November.

Painswick Antiques
(Mr & Mrs J. Hutton-Clarke). Beacon House, New St, GL6 6UN. Tel 812578. Open Mon-Sat 9-5.30; other times by appt. Good quality period furniture, oak, fruitwood, yew, mahogany, walnut, rosewood, some early pine. CADA

Regent Antiques
Dynever House, New St. Tel 812543. Open Mon-Fri 10-5.30, Sat 10-1; other times by appt. 17th and 18thC furniture in oak, walnut and mahogany and works of art.

Stone House Antiques (and Design & Craft Gallery)
(W.R. Large). St Mary's St, GL6 6QB. Tel 813540 (priv 045286 2343). Open 10-1, 2-5.30; Sat 10-1; other times by appt. Country furniture (18thC yew and oak furniture), plus contemporary in our Craft and Design Gallery. Also a large range of 19thC Japanese antiques. CADA

Red Marley

John Nash Antiques
(J.Nash, L.Calleja). The Coach House, Drury Lane. Tel Bromsberrow (053181) 616. 18th & 19thC English furniture & decorative antiques. Interior decor.

Stow-on-the-Wold STD 0451

Baggott Church Street Ltd
(D.J. Baggott, C.M. Baggott). Church Street, GL54 1BB. Tel 30370. (Also Huntsmans Yard and The Square.) Open Mon-Sat, 10-6; other times by appt. Fine 17th-19thC English, oak, mahogany, walnut & yew furniture, portrait paintings, metalwork, treen, decorative items and pottery. CADA

D.J. Baggott
(D.J.Baggott). Huntsmans Yard, Sheep Street. Tel 30662. (Also at The Square and Church St.) Open Mon-Fri 9-5; other times by appt. Large stock of 17th-19thC English and Continental furniture in 'as found' condition. Trade only. CADA

Duncan J. Baggott
(D.J.Baggott). The Square, GL54 1AB. Tel 30662. (Also at Huntsmans Yard and Church St.) Open Mon-Sat, 10-6; other times by appt. 17th to 19thC English oak and country furniture, domestic items, brass, copper, lighting, needlework and primitive paintings. CADA

D.Bryden Antiques
(D.Bryden). Sheep St. Tel 30840. Open Mon-Sat 10-12.30, 2-5; closed Wed; other times by appt. Antique and modern silver and silver plate, Victorian and Edwardian furniture and porcelain.

J. & J. Caspall Antiques
(John and Josie Caspall). Sheep St. Tel 31160. Open Mon-Sat 9.30-5.30; other times by appt. Specialist in 17th and 18thC oak and elm 1600 to 1750, early ironwork especially lighting and hearth items, early carvings and treen.

Chantry House Antiques
(Hon Mrs B.M.Davis, Mrs G.Ewart, Mr A.J.Ewart). Sheep St, GL54 1AA. Tel 30450. (See also Gavina Ewart, Broadway, Hereford & Worcester.) Open 9.30-1, 2-5.30. Maps and prints of the 16th-19thC. 18th and 19thC porcelain & furniture.

Annarella Clark Antiques
11 Park St. Painted and country furniture, needlework, quilts and decorative items.

Christopher Clarke
(Christopher Clarke). The Fosse Way, GL54 1JS. Tel 30476. Open Mon-Sat 9.30-6; other times by appt. English and Continental furniture and works of art. BADA, CADA

Cotswold Galleries
(Richard & Cherry Glaisyer). The Square, GL54 1AB. Tel 30586. Open Mon-Sat 9-5.30; other times by appt. Extensive premises displaying large stock of Victorian and contemporary oil paintings. A first class framing and restoration service is offered. CADA

Country Life Antiques
(David & Ann Rosa). Sheep St, GL54 1JS. Tel Cotswold (0451) 30776. (Also at Grey House, The Square.) Open Mon-Sat 10-5; other times by appt. Specialising in pewter, scientific instruments, decorative accessories, collectors' items, brass, copper and occasional pine and oak furniture.

Country Life Antiques
(David and Ann Rosa). Grey House, The Square, GL54 1AF. Tel 31564. (Also in Sheep St.) Open Mon-Sat 10-6; other times by appt. General antique furniture of 17th, 18th and 19thC. Longcase clocks, paintings, decorative accessories and scientific instruments.

John Davies (Fine Paintings)
(John Davies). The Church Street Gallery, Church St, GL54 1BB. Tel 31698 (priv 31790). Open Mon-Sat 9-6; other times by appt. Fine British paintings 1875-1950, significant British artists from the late 19thC, Post Impressionist, Edwardian, Modern British, Newlyn and St Ives schools.Also earlier decorative & sporting works. Top class restoration & conservation of all works.

Fosse Gallery
The Square. Tel Cotswold (0451) 31319. Open Mon-Sat 10-5.30. British post-impressionism and modern British paintings.

R.H. & E.M.Freeman
4 Park St, GL54 1AQ. Tel 31184. Open Mon-Sat 9-5.30; other times by appt. Antiques & Oriental works of art.

Lynn Greenwold
Digbeth, Digbeth St. Tel 30398. Open Mon-Sat 10-5; other times by appt. Jewellery, English porcelain and pottery, Oriental porcelain,silver. BADA,CADA

Keith Hockin Antiques Ltd
(Keith and Pat Hockin). The Square, GL54 1AF. Tel 31058. Open Mon-Sat 9-6; other times by appt. Res on premises. Specialist dealer in 17th and early 18thC oak furniture and country furniture in elm, yew, fruitwoods etc of 18th to early 19thC. BADA, CADA

Huntington Antiques Ltd
(M.F. and S.P.Golding). The Old Forge, Church St. Tel 30842. Open Mon-Sat 9-6; other times by appt. Period oak, walnut and country furniture (esp. yew wood), tapestries, treen, metalware, carpets & rugs. Usually some medieval, Gothic and Renaissance pieces. Complete range of ironwork to complement our furniture. CADA

Lilian Middleton's Antique Doll Shop
(Lilian Middleton A.D. Ltd.). Days Stables, Sheep St, GL54 1AA. Tel 30381. Open daily 9.30-5; Sun 1.30-5; other times by appt. Antique dolls, dresses & accessories, dolls houses & miniatures, antique doll collection on display. Antique doll repairs and restoration. CADA, ADDA

Richard Moult Antiques
(L.R. & I.M. Moult). The Square. Tel 30377. Open 9.30-5.30. Large general stock, oak furniture, country chairs, brass. Licensed firearms dealer (Martin Mann) on premises.

Simon W.Nutter
(Simon W.Nutter). Wraggs Row, Fosse Way. Tel 30658. Open Mon-Sat 9.30-5.30; other times by appt. 17th to early 19thC furniture; small amount of pottery, porcelain and metalware. BADA

Rudolph Otto
The Little House, Sheep St. Open Mon-Sat 9.30-6; other times by appt. 17th to 19thC mahogany and oak furniture.

Park House
Park St. Tel 30159. 19thC watercolours and oils.

Antony Preston Antiques Ltd
(Antony Preston, Prudence Preston). The Square, GL54 1AB. Tel 31586 (priv 31406). Open Mon-Sat 9.30-5.30; other times by appt. 18th and 19thC English and Continental furniture, barometers and clocks. BADA, CADA, LAPADA

South Bar Antiques
Digbeth St. Tel 30236. Specialising in clocks, porcelain, furniture, jewellery and paintings.

Touchwood Antiques
(Kenneth & Linda Dixon). 9 Park St., GL54 1AQ. Tel 30221. Open Mon-Sat 9-6; other times by appt. Oak, walnut, fruitwood and other timbers associated with early furniture. Also iron and metalware, carvings. Touchwood wax polishes and polishing for collections and museums. CADA, LAPADA

GLOUCESTER HOUSE ANTIQUES

MARKET PLACE, FAIRFORD, GLOS. GL7 4AB Telephone Cirencester (STD 0285) 712790

English and French country furniture, pottery and decorative accessories

Restoration is done in our own workshop and unrestored goods may be viewed in our barns by appointment

1½ hrs from London by M4 or M40

Examples of 18th and 19th century French faience and pottery on an 18th century English pine dresser

COTSWOLD CURIOS

John Smith

1 MIDDLE STREET
STROUD
GLOUCESTERSHIRE

Tel 04536 5956 and 77628
(after hours 0453 882564)

All kinds of English and Continental period furniture, some clocks, paintings etc

PERSONAL CONTINENTAL COLLECTION AND DELIVERY SERVICE LARGE AND SMALL QUANTITIES

Christopher Clarke Antiques

Fine English Furniture and Works of Art

**THE FOSSE WAY,
STOW-ON-THE-WOLD, GLOS. GL54 1JS
Tel (0451) 30476**

Van Riemsdijk Fine Art
(B.M.L. van Riemsdijk). Digbeth St. Tel Cotswold (0451) 30424 (priv 0908 582621). Open Mon-Sat 10-5; closed 1-2; other times by appt. 19th and early 20thC oil paintings and watercolours. LAPADA

Vanbrugh House Antiques
(John & Monica Sands). Park St, GL54 1AQ. Tel 30797. Open Mon-Sat 10-6; other times by appt. 17th to early 19thC furniture and silver. Early maps, arms and armour, music boxes, square pianos and clocks.

Wye Antiques
(Charles & Sheila Wye). The Square, GL54 1AB. Tel Cotswold (0451) 31004. Open Mon-Sat 9.30-5.30; other times by appt. Antique oak, mahogany & pine furniture, china including Staffordshire figures, blue & white, majolica, glass, metalware, garden troughs and decorative items. CADA

Stroud STD 045 36

Cotswold Curios
(J.T. Smith). 1 Middle St. Tel 5956 (priv 77628). Open Mon-Fri 10-1, 2-4.30; early closing Thurs; other times by appt. General English and Continental antiques. Personal collection and delivery service anywhere in Europe. LAPADA

Daisy Dawkins Antiques
Bearpools, Rodborough Common.

A.W. England & Sons
54 Lower St. Tel 3262. Open 9-5. General antiques especially furniture and shipping goods.

Gnome Cottage
(Mrs Ivy McGrane). 55-57 Middle St, GL5 1DZ. Tel 3669. Open Mon-Sat 9-6; closed Wed. Antique and secondhand furniture and bric-a-brac.

Clifford & Joan Silcocks
(C.G.&J.M.Silcocks). Pitchcombe View, Pitchcombe, GL6 6LW. Tel Painswick (0452) 812225. Open during exhibitions in April and October; other times by appt. British watercolours 1750-1950.

Tetbury STD 0666

Alderley House Antiques
(Michael Orr). Alderley House, 53 Long St, GL8 8AA. Tel 53667. Open Mon-Sat 10-6; other times by appt. Antiques, furniture, Oriental rugs, decorative items, stringed musical instruments.

George S.Bolam
Oak House, The Chipping. Tel 52211. Open Mon-Fri 9.15-5.30; other times by appt. 17th to early 19thC furniture, works of art, oriental porcelain. BADA CADA

Breakspeare Antiques
(Mr & Mrs M.Breakspeare). 36 Long St, GL8 8AQ. Tel 53122. 18th & early 19thC mahogany furniture, country longcase clocks. LAPADA

J. & M. Bristow Antiques
28 Long St, GL8 8AQ. Tel 52222. Open Mon-Sat 9.30-1, 2-5.30, closed Thurs; other times by appt. 17th and 18thC furniture. Specialising in English country clocks, mainly longcase and barometers. BADA

The Chest of Drawers
(A.& P.Bristow). 24 Long St, GL8 8AQ. Tel 52105. Open Mon-Sat 9-5.30; closed Thurs; other times by appt. Furniture, English 17th to 19thC.

Joane Crarer Antiques
The Fuller's Cottage, 18 Long St. Tel 52660. Open mornings only; other times by appt. General antiques.

Gastrell House
(John Morris). 33 Long St, GL8 8AA. Tel 52228. Open Mon-Sat 10-6; other times by appt. Fine furniture 17th to 19thC; clocks and paintings. Also restoration of clocks, furniture and paintings and photographic service.

Long Street Gallery
(Serina Butler-Henderson). 50 Long Street, GL8 8AQ. Tel 53722. Contemporary crafts: mixed media - ceramics, glass, wood; contemporary material jewellery, limited edition prints, paintings. ICGA

Paul Nash
(Paul and Ana Gifford Nash). The Barn House, Cherington. Tel Rodmarton (028 584) 215. Open by appt only. Fine 18thC English furniture. BADA

John Nicholls Antiques
27 Long St. Tel 52781 (priv 08893 2383). Open Mon-Sat; other times by appt. Good 17th and 18thC oak and country furniture, also complementary items. CADA

Silver Corner
23 Market Pl. Tel 52766. Antique and modern silver and jewellery.

Tetbury Antiques
(C.Parsons). 39A Long St. Tel 52748. Open Mon-Sat 9-6; other times by appt. 17th and 18thC English and Continental country furniture.

Upton Lodge Galleries
(Josephine Grant). Avening House, Avening, GL8 8NH. Tel Nailsworth (045 383) 4048. Open by appt. Specialists in British Impressionists & post Impressionist oils & watercolours c1880-1940. Export services available.

Wain Antiques
(Janet & Peter Wain). 45 Long Street. Tel 52440. Open Mon-Fri 9.30-5; Sat 10-4. Chinese & English pottery & porcelain of the 18th & 19thC.

Yeo Antiques
(B.G. & B.D. Ackrill). 8 Springfields, GL8. Tel 521300. Open by appt only. 17th & 18thC furniture, clocks, pottery, porcelain, metalware. Restorations. Valuations. LAPADA

Tewkesbury STD 0684

Abbey Antiques
62 Church St. Tel 2378. General antiques and shipping goods.

Auriol House Antiques
124 High St, GL20 5JU. Tel (priv) 038689-351.

Gainsborough House Antiques
81 Church St. Tel 293072. 18th and early 19thC furniture and general antiques.

F.W.Taylor
Waite House, 71 Church St. Tel 295990. Open Mon-Sat 9-5; other times by appt. Fine 18th and 19thC porcelain and pottery, small period furniture, small antique silver and flatware, 18th and 19thC glass, antique maps & prints.

Uley

Old Chapel Antiques
(B. & L.Narbeth). Fop St. Tel Dursley (0453) 860656 (priv 860396). (Also at the Street.) Open 9.30-5; other times by appt. Large and fast-changing stock of general antiques, country items, pine, shipping goods and smalls. Furniture restored in own workshops. LAPADA

Ullenwood

J.P.Townsend
(J.P.Townsend). Ullenwood Park Farm. Tel Coberley (024 287) 223. (Also at Cheltenham Antique Market.) Open by appt Ullenwood; Mon-Sat at the Antique Market. Antiques, stripped pine, shipping goods.

Whelford

Bowmoore Gallery
GL7 4DT. Tel 0285-712651. Open 7 days a week; appt preferred. Good range of watercolours and oils.

Winchcombe STD 0242

Kenulf Gallery
(Eric & Jean Ford). High St, GL54 5LJ. Tel 602124. Open Mon-Sat 9.30-1, 2-5.30; other times by appt. Late 18th to 20thC oil & watercolour paintings & prints, sculpture & furniture. Services - valuations, restoration of oils & watercolours, period framing. CADA

Muriel Lindsay
(D.J. and M.E.Lindsay). Queen Anne House, High St. Tel Cheltenham (0242) 602319. Open Mon-Sat 9.30-5.30; other times by appt. Large stock of small goods especially brass, glass and country goods suitable for the American trade. Est. 21 years.

Wotton-under-Edge

Bell Passage Antiques
(Mrs D.V.Brand). 36-38 High St, Wickwar, GL12 8NP. Tel Wickwar (045 424) 251. (Also at 1 Arnolds Field Estate.) Open Tues-Sat 8-6; other times by appt. Period furniture, prints, clocks, porcelain, early drinking glasses, 18th and 19thC watercolours and oils. General stock and shipping goods. LAPADA, GMC

G.M.S. Restorations
(G.M.St.G.Stacey). 36 High Street, Wickwar, GL12 8NP. Tel Wickwar (045424) 251. (Workshops at Arnolds Field Estate, Wickwar.) Open Mon-Fri 8-5. Restorers of antique & modern furniture, specialists in French polishing, picture restoration, gilding, inlay work & metalwork. Traditional & modern re-upholstery. Collection & delivery service. GMC

Sandoe Luce Panes
1 High St. Tel 843193. Open Mon-Sat 9-5. Fine art auctioneers. SOFAA

Greater Manchester

Altrincham STD 061

Cottage Antiques
(J. & J.M. Gholam). Hasty Lane, Ringway, Hale Barns, WA15 8UT. Tel 980-7961. Open Mon-Sat 9-6; Sun by appt. Good quality furniture, brass, ceramics & general antiques.

L.H. Gilliard
64 Manchester Rd, WA14 4PJ. Tel 928 2943. Open Mon, Tues, Thurs, Fri 10-6; Wed & Sat 10-5. General antiques & shipping goods.

Halo Antiques
(Major & Mrs Philip Oulton). 97 Hale Rd, WA15 9HL. Tel 941 1800. Open Tues-Sat 10-5; other times by appt. Complete range of current trade goods from period furniture to pine & shipping goods for the American market.

The South Manchester Gallery
(Mrs Audrey Love). 140 Ashley Rd, Hale Village, WA14 2UQ. Tel 061-941 6244. Contemporary crafts: glass, ceramics, jewellery, metals, wood, textiles. ICGA

Bolton STD 0204

Astley Bridge Antiques
(J.G.&D.Taylor). 419-421 Blackburn Rd, Astley Bridge, BL1 8NJ. Tel 51160 (priv 53390). Open Mon-Fri 10-4; other times by appt. Antique and secondhand furniture, clocks, porcelain and glass; 7 showrooms.

Gallery 77
(Michael L. Wayne). 18 Princess St, Bradshawgate, BL1 1EJ. Tel 35252. Open Mon-Sat 9-5.30; other times by appt. 19th and 20thC watercolours, 19th and 20thC oil paintings, framing and restoration. FATG

G.Oakes & Son (Bolton) Ltd
(J.A.Shacklady). 160 Blackburn Rd, BL1 8DR. Tel 26587. Open Mon, Tues, Thurs, Fri 9-5. General furniture.

Park Galleries Antiques, Fine Art and Decor
(Mrs S.Hunt). 167 Mayor St, BL1 4SJ. Tel 29827 (priv 061 764 5853). Open Thurs, Fri, Sat, 10.30-5; other times by appt. Antique and period furniture, clocks, brass and copper, glass, works of art, collectors and decorative items.

Directory Entries
are Free and
ADDITIONS OR
CORRECTIONS
will be welcomed by
THE EDITOR,
British Art and Antiques Directory,
National Magazine House,
72 Broadwick Street,
London W1V 2BP

Bramhall

Small Antiques Ltd
45 St Michael's Ave. Tel Manchester (061) 439 4308. Toilet mirrors, decorative boxes and small furniture.

Bury STD 061

The Antique Shop
(Mr & Mrs R.Salisbury). 17 Market St, Edenfield, BL0 0JA. Tel Ramsbottom (070682) 2351. Open Mon-Sat, trade Sun 1.30-4.30. Antiques, fine art, shipping, bric-a-brac, etc.

Paul Quentin Antiques
(D. & P. Eccleston). 626 Manchester Rd, BL9 9SU. Tel 766 6673. Open Mon-Sat 9-7; other times by appt. Militaria, metalware, pottery, porcelain, lamps and furniture. Also shipping goods.

Cheadle STD 061

Malcolm Frazer Antiques
19 Brooklyn Crescent. Tel 428 3781. 18th and 19thC marine and scientific instruments together with a range of decorative related items.

Cheadle Hulme

Den of Antiquity
69 Station Rd. Tel 061-485 8713. Open Mon-Sat 12-5.30; other times by appt. General, some militaria, jewellery and silver.

Didsbury

E.J. Morten (Booksellers) Ltd
(Eric J.Morten & Shirley Pryce). 2, 4, 6, 8, 9 Warburton Street, M20 0RA. Tel 061-445 7629. (Also in Macclesfield, Cheshire.) Open 10-5.30; other times by appt. Large stock of antiquarian, secondhand, and new general literature, old and rare books, topography. ABA

Hale

Anne Kerr Antiques
(Mrs A.B. Kerr). 191A Ashley Rd, SK9 4ZY. Tel (061) 928 0091. Open Tues-Sat 10.30-1; 2.15-5; closed Wed; other times by appt. Small decorative antiques. Some silver & art nouveau silver, jewellery. No repro.

Manchester STD 061

Artingstall & Hind
(J.H.Norris). 378/380 Deansgate, Knott Mill, M3 4NA. Tel 834 4559. Open Mon-Fri 9-5.15. Auctioneers.

Baron Antiques
373 Bury New Rd. Tel 773 9929. Open Mon-Sat 9.30-6. 18thC English furniture, clocks, porcelain, shipping goods. Restorations. LAPADA

James Briggs & Sons Ltd
Lion Works, Old Market St, Blackley, M9 3DU. Tel 795 8410. Open Mon-Thurs 9-5; Fri 9.30-5. Manufacturers and distributors of the Antiquax range of furniture, silver, copper and brass polishes and accessories.

Britannia Antiques
(George Zammit & Sons). 754 Stockport Rd, Longsight, M12 4GD. Tel 224 8350, 224 6425. Open Mon-Fri 9-5.30; Sat 9-12; other times by appt. Mainly Victorian & Georgian plus shipping goods.

Capes Dunn & Co
38 Charles St, M1 7DB. Tel 273 1911. Open Mon-Fri 9-5. Fine art and chattel auctioneers and valuers. ISVA

Clarendon Gallery
(R.J.Proctor-Pearson). 20 Albert Square. Tel 980 6343. Open Mon-Fri 10.30-5.30; Sats during exhibitions; other times by appt. English and Continental paintings and watercolours, contemporary works by local artists and bronzes.

The Connoisseur
(S. Cohen). 528 Wilmslow Rd, Withington. Tel 445 2504. Open Mon-Sat 10.12-6; closed Mon & Wed am; other times by appt. Antiques & objets d'art especially Continental porcelain & furniture, paintings and automata. LAPADA

Craft Centre
Royal Exchange Theatre, St Ann's Square. Tel 833 9333. Open Mon, Tues, Thurs, Fri 11-7.30; Wed 11-2.30; Sat 11-4. Contemporary British craft work of quality.

Dickinson Deansgreen Ltd
(D.H.Dickinson). 17/19 John Dalton St. Tel 834 1042. English & Continental furniture, decorative items. LAPADA

Henry Donn Galleries
(H.& D.Donn). 138-142 Bury New Rd, Whitefield, M25 6AD. Tel 766 8819. Open Mon-Sat, 9.30-5.30. Oils and watercolours from 1900; limited editions by prominent contemporary artists.

The Ginnel
(Keith and Irene Mottershead). Lloyds House, 16 Lloyd Street. Tel 833 9037. Open Mon-Fri 9-5.30; other times by appt. Antiques, including furniture, pottery and porcelain, and also modern art. LAPADA

Frank Hill (Removals & Storage) Ltd
(P.A. Hill, P.L.Hill, M.R.Purvis, A.G.Purvis). Cambridge St Industrial Estate, Salford 7, M7 9UT. Tel 834 1317 (priv 766 3260). Open Mon-Fri 8-5, Sat 8-noon usually; other times by appt. International packers and shippers. Road hauliers and customs assent. Courier service.

Kenworthys Ltd
(C.J.Collins, Mrs M.Collins, Mrs E.Kenworthy). 226 Stamford St, Ashton-under-Lyne, OL6 7LW. Tel 330 3043. Open Mon-Sat 9-5.30; closed Tues. Large stock of antique and modern silver, Sheffield plate and Victorian jewellery. BADA

E. & C.T.Koopman & Son Ltd
John Dalton House, John Dalton St, M2 6JP. Tel 834 2402, 832 9036. (Also see Chancery House and Silver Vaults in London.) Open Mon-Fri 10-5; other times by appt. Antique silver, silver plate, antique jewellery and objets d'art. BADA

John Long Antiques
(John Long). St Mary's Old Church, 915 Stockport Rd, Levenshulme. Tel 224 7923. Open Mon-Sat 9-6. Period furniture and shipping goods. Specialising in clocks.

Gibb's Bookshop Ltd
(A.& A.Gibb). 10 Charlotte St, M1 4FL. Tel 236-7179. Open Mon-Sat 9.30-5.30. Medium size general stock of secondhand & antiquarian books. ABA

Royal Exchange Antiques Gallery
(Mike Gilbert, Information Officer). Royal Exchange Shopping Centre, 2. Tel 834 5765/1427. Open Mon-Sat 10-5. Twenty antique dealers selling a wide range of antiques and fine art.

Shaw's Bookshop Ltd
11 Police St, M2 7LQ. Tel 834-7587. Open Mon-Sat 9.30-5.30. Antiquarian and secondhand books, maps, prints. Framing and restorations. ABA

St James Antiques
41 South King St. Tel 834 9632. Open Mon-Fri 11-5; other times by appt. Silver, jewellery, furniture, Oriental porcelain, china and objets d'art. Buying and valuations.

Tameside Antiques
(B.Boyle & D.Downworth). Cavendish Mill, Cavendish St, Ashton-under-Lyne. Tel 344 5477 (priv 308 4445). (Also at 1092 Stockport Rd, Levenshulme. Tel:432 1619.) Open Mon-Sun 9-6; other times by appt. Antiques and shipping furniture. At Stockport Rd, antique and period pianos.

Oldham STD 061

Abbey Antiques
(D. Mullin). 299-301 Manchester Rd, Hollinwood, OL8 4RF. Tel 681 6538. Open Mon-Sat 10-6, Sun 12-3; other times by appt. Pine, shipping goods, clocks, paintings and bric a brac.

Ace Antiques
(Raymond, John and Jean O'Brien). 40 Huddersfield Rd, OL4 2AE. Tel 620 5755 (priv 626 2062). Open Mon-Fri 9-6, Sat 9-11; other times by appt. Antique furniture, shipping furniture and pianos.

Marks Antiques
(B.J.Mark & S.Mark). 16 Waterloo St, OL8 3DT. Tel 624 5975. Open Mon-Sat 10-5; closed Tues; other times by appt. A wide range of jewellery, pottery and period furniture.

Waterloo Antiques
16 Waterloo St. Tel 624 5975. Open daily 10-5; other times by appt. Antique and fine art specialising in jewellery, silver and period furniture.

Peter Young Antiques
Friarmere School House, 47 Huddersfield Rd. Tel Saddleworth (04577) 70467. (See also Peter Young at Darwen, Lancs.) Open any time by appt. 18th and 19thC furniture, shipping goods, unusual and decorative items. Trade only.

Prestwich STD 061

David Friend Antiques
(David and Gail Friend). 23 Guest Rd, M25 7DJ. Tel 773 1382. Open strictly by appt. English, Continental & Oriental ceramics & works of art. Specialist in signed Worcester, Derby, Coalport, Minton etc. Canton, Satsuma, Imari, cloissonne, ivory.

St Margarets Antiques
(A.Page). 3 St Margarets Rd. Tel 773 1864 (priv 427 2412). Open Mon, Tues, Thurs, Fri, Sat 10.15-1, 2-5; other times by appt. Furniture, clocks, brass, copper and china.

Rochdale STD 0706

Antiques and Fine Arts (Prestwich) Ltd
(D.Falk). Tel 44946. Open by appt only. English period furniture. LAPADA

Stephen Falk
OL12 6LE. Tel 44946. Open strictly by appointment. Fine English period furniture. LAPADA

Owen Antiques
(J.G.T.Owen). 189-193 Oldham Rd. Tel 48138 (priv 353270). Open Mon-Sat 12-6.30; Sun 2-6; other times by appt. Clock, watches, orreries, scientific and nautical instruments. Paintings, prints and maps. Some furniture. Also early wireless equipment. Clock restoration service.

Sale STD 061

Leslie Davey Antiques
(C.S.Rubin & Mrs E.Rubin). 80 School Rd, M33 1XB. Tel 962 9303. Open Mon-Sat 9-5; Wed 9-1. Jewellery, silver, EPNS, glassware. BWCMG

Eureka Antiques
(Noel Gibson). 18 Northenden Road, M33 3BR. Tel 962 5629. Open Mon-Sat 10-5, closed Wed; other times by appt. Period furniture, clocks, porcelain, metalwork, patchboxes and mother of pearl.

Reeds Rains
Trinity House, 114 Northenden Rd, M33 3HD. Tel 962 9237 969 7173. Open Mon-Fri 9-5.30; Sat 9-12.30; other times by appt. Auctioneers of fine art and antiques. Sales held every two weeks. Victorian and general sales held twice monthly on Weds, specialist sales of clocks, watches, pictures, silver, jewellery, glass, ceramics and furniture on Thurs.

Salford STD 061

AS Antiques
(Audrey Sternshine). 26 Broad St, Pendleton. Tel Manchester (061) 737 5938. Open Mon-Fri 10-5.30 closed Tues; Sat 11-5; other times by appt. (On A6 next to Salford College of Technology, 1 mile from Manchester city centre.) Art Nouveau and Art Deco specialist with large stock. Also comprehensive stock of general antiques. Valuations and restorations.

Fulda Gallery
(M.J.Fulda). 19 Vine St, M7 0NY. Tel 792 1962. Open by appt only. Fine paintings and watercolours of all periods and schools.

Stockport STD 061

The Antique Shop
(Mr Norgrove). 23-25 Middle Hillgate. Tel 061-477 8970. Open Mon-Fri 12.30-5.30; Sat 10-5; other times by appt. Good stock of longcase and wall clocks.

Garrick Bookshop
(Peter Stephenson Aird). 20A Wellington Road South, SK4 1AD. Tel 480-4346. (Also at 142 Buxton Rd, Heaviley, Stockport. (061-483 6391.) Open Mon-Sat 10-5. Large general stock plus postcards. PBFA

Gay's Antiques Ltd
(G.A.Yeo). 34-38 London Rd, Hazel Grove. Tel 061-483 5532. 18th and 19thC furniture, decorative items. 10 000 sq ft. Trade only. LAPADA

Gemini Antiques Ltd
(P.J.Wilkinson). 408/412 Buxton Rd, Great Moor. Tel Manchester (061) 456 4566. Furniture, clocks, paintings, general. Restorations. Valuations.

Imperial Antiques
(A.Todd). 295 Buxton Rd, Great Moor. Tel Manchester (061) 483 3322. Furniture, silver, plate, Oriental items, Persian carpets. Valuations. LAPADA

Lower Fold Antiques
(Geoffrey Douglas). 23-25 Lower Fold, Marple Bridge, SK6 5DU. Tel 427 4699. Open Mon-Sat 10-6-6; other times by appt. General stock. Also furniture and clock repair and restoration, painted dial restoration.

G.R. Naisby & Son
65 Wellington Road North. Tel 480 6445 (priv 432 8737). Open 10.30-5; other times by appt. Large stock of paintings, prints and general antiques.

Page Antiques
(Denis Page). 424 Buxton Rd, Great Moor. Tel 483 9202 (priv 427 2412). Open Mon-Sat 10-4; closed Wed; other times by appt. Antique furniture, pictures, art deco, metalware, clocks, pine furniture.

Regent House Antiques
(G.T.Allcroft). 8 Buxton Rd, New Town, New Mills. Tel 42684. Open Mon-Thurs 10.30-5, Sat 2-5; other times by appt. Antique and Victorian furniture, Oriental porcelain, clocks, oil paintings and watercolours.

Woodford Antiques
(Terry and Margie Cooper). 382 Buxton Rd, Great Moor. Tel Manchester (061) 483 9917 (priv 0625 582074). Open any time by appt but closed Weds. Georgian & Victorian furniture. LAPADA

Wigan STD 0942

Clifton Books
(D.M. Shaw). 5A Dicconson St. Tel 36716 (priv 726319). Open Mon 10-4; Tues to Sat 10-5. Books, antique maps and prints, occasional watercolours. PBFA

Jimmy Collins Antiques Ltd
136 Standishgate, WN1 1XP. Tel 48180 (priv 41484). Open Mon-Fri 9-5. Trade only, wholesale and export. Large stock of clocks, furniture, English, Continental and Oriental porcelain. Packing, shipping and container services. LAPADA

Lancashire Bygones
(Mrs M.Rathbone). 12 Parliament St, Up Holland, WN8 0LN. Tel Up Holland (0695) 625624 (priv 0695 622458). Open Wed, Fri, Sat, 10-5; other times by appt. Large selection of antique fenders and other fire furniture.

John Robinson Antiques
(John Robinson). 172-176 Manchester Rd, WN2 2EA. Tel 47773 (priv 41671). Open Mon-Fri 8.30-5; Sat 9-noon. Wholesale shop & three large warehouses of interesting stock. Packing & shipping goods.

Worsley STD 061

H.& M.J.Burke
(Henry Burke). Packet House Buildings, M28 4PA. Tel 794 2093. Open Mon-Fri 10-4; other times by appt. 17th and 18thC English furniture, including oak and walnut, also porcelain and paintings. ADA

Hampshire

Alresford STD 096 273

Alresford Gallery
(Keith E. Bell). Livingstone House, 7 Broad St. Tel 3002 (priv 3556). Open Mon-Sat 9-5; other times by appt. Specialising in 18th-19thC watercolours.

Artemesia
(D.T.L.Wright). 16 West St. Tel 2277. Open Mon-Sat 9.30-5.30; other times by appt. Chinese and Japanese porcelain and works of art. Mainly Ming and Ching but some earlier. LAPADA

The Candover Gallery
(Barbara and John Ling). 22 West St, SO24 9AE. Tel 3200. Contemporary crafts - ceramics, glass, wood, watercolours. ICGA

Evans & Evans
(Alresford Clocks Ltd, N.C.Evans, D.M.W. Evans). 40 West St, SO24 9AU. Tel 2170. Open Tues-Sat 9.30-5.30; other times by appt. English clocks of all periods, French decorative and carriage clocks, musical boxes and barometers.

Rogers of Alresford
(Tom and Vasanti Rogers). 16 West St, SO24 9AT. Tel 2277, 2862. Open Mon-Sat 10-5.30; other times by appt. English country furniture and collectors' items. Specialist in English pottery, including Sunderland lustre, delft, Staffordshire blue and white, and commemorative wares. Also Oriental porcelain, works of art & rugs. Exhibit at major antique fairs. LAPADA

Studio Bookshop and Gallery
(Laurence Oxley). 17 Broad St, SO24 9AW. Tel 2188. Open daily, early closing Wed. Secondhand and antiquarian books and maps. Specialising in India. ABA

Winchester House Antiques
(Daphne & Peter Thompson). 39 Broad St. Tel 3110. Open Mon-Sat 9-5; other times by appt. General antiques.

Alton STD 0420

Collectors Cases
(R.J.Graham). Alderney House, 58 Normandy St, GU34 1EL. Tel 83366. Open by appt. Display cases of all types, new and antique glass domes.

Messrs Martin & Stratford
(G.D. Stratford - Snr. Partner). 70 High St, GU34 1EX. Tel 84402. (Sale room at the Auction Mart, Market Sq, Alton.) Open Mon-Fri 9-5.30; Sat 9-4. Chartered surveyors & auctioneers.

Andover STD 0264

Country Cottage Bedsteads
(Susan M. Wilson). Park House, Penton Mewsey, SP11 0RW. Tel Weyhill (026477) 2527. Open by appt only, 7 days a week. Antique brass and iron bedsteads.

May & Son
(Frank W.May FSVA, John F.May FNAEA). 18 Bridge St, SP10 1BH. Tel 63331. Open weekdays 9-5; Sat 9-1. Auctioneers, established 1925. Executors, trustees, private goods (no trade items). Monthly sales held 3rd Wed in month (except August). House sales on premises.

Titley Antiques Ltd
Linkenholt Manor, Linkenholt. Tel Linkenholt (026487) 222. Open by appt. Furniture. BADA

Basingstoke STD 0256

Ewhurst Gallery
(Richard Mayfield). Ramsdell, RG26 5RG. Tel 850051. Open any time by appt. 18th to early 20thC watercolours and drawings. LAPADA

The Morris Singer Foundry Ltd
(D.J. Vallance). Bond Close, Kingsland Industrial Park, RG24 0PT. Tel 24033. Open 8.30-5; other times by appt. Restoration of antique metalwork, bronze, lead, iron etc, architectural metalwork & sculpture casting.

Beaulieu STD 0590

Beaulieu Fine Arts
(Mr F.Cookson). High St. Tel 612089. Open daily 9-1, 2-5.30; other times by appt. Mainly good quality watercolours, oil paintings, drawings and etchings by 19th and 20thC artists of repute.

Bishops Waltham STD 048 93

C.P.A. Antiques
(David Beale). Newtown Lodge, Tangier Lane, SO3 1BU. Tel 5176. Open by appt only. 18th and 19thC furniture, shipping goods. Specialising in Australian market goods (both furniture and smalls).

Bordon STD 042 03

Bristow Antiques
(Dudley Robin Bristow). Lindford Rd, Lindford, GU35 0PY. Tel 2301. Open Mon-Fri 10-6, Sat 9-12; early closing Wed; other times by appt. 18th and 19thC British furniture. Also furniture restoration.

Botley STD 048 92

Prudence Battersby Antiques
(Prudence Battersby). 8 Winchester St, So3 2EB. Tel 2354. Open Mon, Tues, Fri, Sat 10-5; other times by appt. Small pieces of antique furniture, fine porcelain and collectables.

Cadnam

C.W.Buckingham
(C.W. Buckingham and family). Twin Firs, Southampton Rd, SO4 2NP. Tel Southampton (0703) 812122. (Also in Fulham, London.) Open Mon-Sat; closed Thurs; other times by appt. Antique furniture and pine furniture, over 2,000 sq.ft. LAPADA

Eastleigh STD 0703

Geoffrey Lanham Antiques
96 Chalvington Rd, Chandler's Ford, SO5 3EH. Tel Chandler's End (042 15) 65541. Specialist in antique French paperweights.

Emsworth STD 024 34

Trentham Gallery Ltd
(M.Davis & M.T.D.Davis-Shaw). 1 Tower St. Tel Havant (0705) 484935 (priv 02434 2551). (Also 40 North St, Havant, Hants.) Open by appt. Small antiques, maps, paintings, prints, pottery, porcelain, silver.

Fareham STD 0329

The Elizabethans
(Mrs Elizabeth Keeble). 58 High St. Tel 234964(answering machine). Open Mon, Tues, Thurs, Sat 10-4.30; other times by appt. Small general antiques - furniture, paintings, jewellery, silver etc. Porcelain restorations. Houses cleared. Est.25 years in Fareham.

Gaylords
(Donald L.Hebbard). 75 West St, Titchfield. Tel 43402 (priv 662606). Open Mon-Sat 9.30-5.30; other times by appt. Furniture, paintings and clocks. Also timber polishing and preservation; cabinet makers, restorers and upholsterers.

Farnborough STD 0252

Martin & Parke
(J. Martin, N.S. Carter). 97 Lynchford Rd. Tel 515311 (priv 511388). Open Mon-Fri 9-5; Sat 9-4; other times by appt. Shipping goods and general antiques. LAPADA

Fleet STD 025 14

Pearsons of Fleet
1-3 Fleet Rd. Tel 29211. (Also in Winchester.) Auctioneers of antique and general furniture and fine art.

Fordingbridge STD 0425

Avon Lodge Antiques
(G.M. & J.Pearce). Southampton Rd, SP6 1AB. Tel 53275. Open Mon-Fri 10-1, 2-5.30; other times by appt. 17th, 18th and 19thC mahogany, oak and pine furniture, metalware, plate, and general items.

Mark Collier
24 The High St. Tel 52555. Open Mon-Sat; other times by appt. Large stock of period English furniture, porcelain, jewellery and objects. BADA NAG FGA

Duveen Antiques
(Clive and Irma Aston). Burgate, SP6 1LX. Tel 53309. Open daily. Res on prem. 16th, 17th and 18thC oak furniture, also longcase clocks, sculpture, carvings, treen and metalware.

Fox & Sons
(M. Carpenter Jeyre). 5, Salisbury St, SP6 1AD. Tel 52121. Open Mon-Fri 9-4; other times by appt. Auctioneers selling furniture, silver, pictures, books etc.

Gosport STD 0705

E. Cooper Antiques
(E. Cooper). 20 Stoke Rd. Tel 585032. Open Mon-Fri, 9-12, 1-5; Sat, 9-1, 2-5; closed Wed. Furniture, bric-a-brac, silver, china, glass, mechanical music, fairground items.

Hartley Wintney
STD 025 126

Nicholas Abbott
(Christopher Nicholas Abbott, Anthea Frances Abbott). High St, RG27 8NY. Tel 2365 (priv 3509). Open Mon-Sat 9.30-5.30. English furniture 1680-1830. Mainly Georgian mahogany.

Andwells
High St. Tel 2305. Open Mon Sat 9.30-5.30. 18th and early 19thC furniture. LAPADA

Cedar Antiques
(Derek Green). High St, RG27 8NY. Tel 3252. Open Mon-Sat 9-6; other times by appt. Large showrooms of English 17th and 18thC yew wood, fruitwood, oak and walnut. Specialists in fine country furniture. Large selection of carefully chosen French provincial furniture and accessories. BADA

Bryan Clisby - Antique Clocks
at Andwells Antiques, High Street. Tel 2305. Specialist in fine clocks and barometers.

Just The Thing
(Mrs S.P.Carpenter). High St. Tel 3393. 18th & 19thC furniture, brass, copper, jewellery. LAPADA

David Lazarus
High St. Tel 2272. Open Mon-Sat 9.30-5.30; other times by appt. 17th to 19thC English and Continental furniture and objets d'art.

Morris Singer will repair, refurbish, repatinate any Antique Metalwork.

THE MORRIS SINGER FOUNDRY LTD.
Bond Close, Kingsland, Basingstoke, Hants
RG24 0PT Tel Basingstoke (0256) 24033
Telex 858704 MSF Ltd, Basingstoke

FACILITIES Design, Manufacture, Installation, Repair
SCOPE OF WORK UNDERTAKEN We can manufacture the items listed. Also we have a casting capacity of 1,000 kgs in bronze, 300 kgs in aluminium and 10 kgs in precious metal
DOORS AND DOOR FURNITURE Ornamental, Entrance Security
PANELS Wall Cladding
SCULPTURE Lost Wax, CO_2, Sand Process
HAND RAIL Decorative, Functional, Balustrade
GARDEN Pots, Seats, Planters, Sculpture
SCREENS Ornamental
MURALS Wall Cladding Pictorial
GATES Ornamental, Security, Railings
PLAQUES Coats of Arms Crests, Lettering, Signs
FOUNTAINS Interior, Exterior

Copy of renaissance fountain at Woolbeding House, nr. Midhurst

18th and early 19th century furniture

ANDWELLS

HIGH STREET, HARTLEY WINTNEY
HAMPSHIRE

Tel Hartley Wintney 2305

CEDAR ANTIQUES

DEREK GREEN

HIGH STREET · HARTLEY WINTNEY · HAMPSHIRE
Tel: 025126 3252

Specialist in Fine Walnut,
Early Oak,
Country Furniture & Metalwork

Phoenix Green Antiques
(John Biles). London Rd, Phoenix Green, RG27 8RT. Tel 4430. Open Mon-Fri 8.30-5.30; Sat 9.30-5; other times by appt. Traditional English and Continental country furniture 18th-19thC in about 2000 sq ft of showrooms. Also Georgian and Regency mahogany furniture and an additional 2000 sq ft of warehousing. Valuations.

A.W. Porter & Son
(M.A. Porter). High St, RG278NY. Tel 2676. Open Mon-Fri 9-5.30; Sat 9-4.30; closed Wed pm; other times by appt. Clocks, mainly longcase, mahogany furniture, silver & jewellery. BHI, NAG

Anthony Willson
22 High St. 18thC furniture and paintings.

Havant STD 0705

Parvo
10 North St. Tel 4813. Open Tues-Sat 10-5.30, closed Wed. Period furniture, Oriental carpets and rugs, pottery, pewter, brass, bric-a-brac.

Trentham Gallery Ltd
(M. Davis, M.T.D.Davis-Shaw). 40 North St. Tel 484935 (priv 02434 2551). (Also at Tower St, Emsworth, Hants (02434-2551.) Open 9.30-5.30; other times by appt. Small antiques, maps,paintings and prints, pottery and porcelain, silver and small furniture. Specialising in county maps and views of Sussex and Hampshire.

Hayling Island STD 0705

Celia Gray
The Old Post Office, 85 Havant Rd, Stoke. Tel 464062. Furniture restoration.

Hook STD 025 672

Forster Ritchie
The Acorn, London Rd, RG27 9DY. Tel 2309. (Also at Vann Place, Eversley Cross, Hants. Tel 0734-733408.) Open Mon-Sat 9.30-6; other times by appt. Period furniture, silverware, glass and jewellery. LAPADA

Hordle

Rod & Sue Peacock
(Rod & Sue Peacock). Minia, Ashley Lane. Tel priv 0425-616000. Open by appt only. General antiques.

Horndean STD 0705

Goss & Crested China Ltd
(N.J. Pine, L.J. Pine). 62 Murray Rd, PO8 9JL. Tel 597440. Open 8.30-5.30, 6 days a week; other times by appt. Large stock of heraldic porcelain. Also the full range of books and related publications about Goss and crested china.

Liss STD 0730

Brian Walton
Farnham Rd. Tel (priv) 0252-710367.

Lymington STD 0590

Corfield of Lymington
(M.C. Corfield). 120 High St, SO4 9SQ. Tel 73532, 75359. (Also at the Old School, Pennington, Lymington, Tel 77872.) Open Mon-Sat 9.15-5.30; other times by appt. Good quality English 18th & early 19thC furniture, brass, porcelain,pictures and glass. Probably the largest stock of quality furniture in the South West. Well displayed in 12 showrooms. BADA

The Old Alarm
Quay Hill, SO4 9AR. Tel 77100. Marine antiques, nautical instruments and items of nautical interest.

Old Solent House Galleries
(Mrs Mary Brook-Hart). Quay St, SO41 9AR. Tel 75511. Open Sat; other times by appt. Specialising in 19th and 20thC British marine paintings.

Lyndhurst STD 042 128

Lita Kaye of Lyndhurst
(Lita, Sidney and Stephen Ferder). 13 High St, SO43 7BB. Tel 2337. Open Mon-Sat 9.30-5; other times by appt. Large stock of fine period furniture. Also antique and decorative clocks and porcelain. BADA

Old Pump House
20 High St, SO4 7BD. Tel 2137. Glass, Staffordshire pottery and small period furniture. Specialists in 19thC paintings.

Meonstoke

W.D.Trivess
Heathfield House, SO3 1ND. Tel Droxford (0489) 877326. Open by appt only. Antique maps & topographical prints.

Middle Wallop

Roger Wilson
The Old George. Tel Wallop (0264) 781422. Open most times, res on prem. Antique furniture.

New Milton STD 0425

The Churchill Group of Companies
(Corporate Publicity Services). Hoopers Hill, Lymington Rd, BH25 5PZ. Tel 620400,620123. Open Mon-Fri; other times by appt. Advertising, PR, marketing, design & commercial photography & processing laboratory. BIPP

Odiham STD 025 671

Woodgoods
(Geoff Brown). High St, Tel 2676. Open Mon-Sat; other times by appt. Stripped pine.

Petersfield STD 0730

Abacus Antiques
(James O. Crawford). 58 Winchester Rd, Stroud. Tel 61935. Open daily 10-6; closed Sun; other times by appt. English oak and country furniture, some mahogany. English delft.

Clinkers Antiques Ltd
c/o Island Farm, Steep. Tel 62319. Open by appt only. Early oak furniture and early works of art prior to 1680. BADA

Cull Antiques
(Jonathan Cull). 14 Dragon St, GU31 4JN. Tel 63670. Open Mon-Fri 10-5 Sat 10-1; other times by appt. 18thC English furniture.

Dragon Antiques
(Mrs L.Kirkland & L.R.Kirkland). 9 Dragon St (A3), GU31 4JN. Tel 62570 (priv 64427). Open Mon-Sat 10-5.30; other times by appt. Period furniture, porcelain, silver, glass, metals and curios.

Folly Antiques Centre
College St. Antique centre with several dealers selling a wide range of antiques.

House of Antiques
4 College St, GU31 4AD. Tel 62172. Open Mon-Sat 9.30-5; early closing Thurs. Expert dealers on two floors, including specialists in quality furniture, treen, boxes, porcelain, pottery, metalware, medical instruments, jewellery, silver, oils and watercolours. Restoration of gilding, papier mache and lacquer.

Jacobs & Hunt
(C.H. Jacobs). Auction Rooms, Lavant St, GU32 3EF. Tel 62744. Open Mon-Sat 9-5. Auctioneers. Auctions every 6-8 weeks.

The Petersfield Bookshop
16A Chapel St, GU32 3DS. Tel 63438. Open Mon-Sat 9-5.30. Good books, old & modern, 15th-20thC. Maps & prints. Catalogues. ABA, BADA

Joy Warren at The House of Antiques
4 College St. Tel 2172. Open Mon-Sat; early closing Thurs. English blue and white transfer ware and small pieces of furniture.

Whiteheads
(C.A. Wiltow-Smith, N.J. Gibson). 34 High St, GU 3JL. Tel Portsmouth (0705) 820701. (Auction Office: 111/113 Elm Grove, Southsea. 40 branches.) Open Mon-Fri 9-5.30; Sat 9-4. Auctioneers valuers and estate agents.

Plaitford

Plaitford House Galleries
(William Yeo). Tel West Wellow (0794) 22221. Open most days, any time by appt. Very large stock of oil paintings, watercolours and bronzes 1800 to 1950.

Portsmouth STD 0705

A.Fleming (Southsea) Ltd
Clock Tower, Castle Rd. Tel 822934. Open Mon-Fri 8.30-5, Sat 8.30-1; other times by appt. Extensive stock of antiques, silver, jewels, furniture and china. BADA

D.M.Nesbit & Co. Auctioneers
7 Clarendon Rd, Southsea, PO5 2ED. Tel 864321. Open 9-5.30. Auctioneers.

Osborne Jewellers
(D. & D.Garcia). 55 Osborne Rd, Southsea, PO5 3LS. Tel 825101. Open 9.30-5. Antique and secondhand jewellery, 19th and 20thC silver, clocks, china and bric-a-brac.

Pretty Chairs
(Mrs J.Ruffell). 189/191 Highland Rd. Tel 731411. Victorian furniture, chairs. LAPADA

Ringwood STD 042 54

Millers of Chelsea Antiques Limited
(Alan & Carole Miller). Netherbrook House, 86 Christchurch Rd, BH24 1DR. Tel 2062. Open Mon-Fri 9-5.30, Sat 9-1; other times by appt. Over 7000 sq ft of showroom space and trade warehouse. English & Continental furniture, 19thC mahogany, decorative and amusing items. LAPADA

Tyrrell Bookshop & Gallery
(Nigel Owen). 80 Christchurch Rd, BH24 1DR. Tel 474489. Open Tues-Fri 9.30-1, 2-5; Sat 9.30-1, 2-4.30; closed Mon; other times by appt. Rare books, pictures and small antiques.

LITA KAYE of LYNDHURST

LITA, SIDNEY AND STEPHEN FERDER

A William and Mary period Oystershell veneered and inlaid Side Table, Circa 1690, from our large collection

Largest Collection in the District of Fine Period Furniture from the William and Mary to the Regency Periods.

13 HIGH STREET, LYNDHURST, HAMPSHIRE

Telephone: LYNDHURST 2337

GERALD E MARSH

"Time Honoured Clocks"

JOHN CLOWES, LONDON

8-day striking movement with verge escapement and pull quarter repeating on 5 bells, ebony veneered double basket top case, 15½ inches high excluding the handle.

32A The Square, WINCHESTER, Hants SO23 9EX

Telephone Winchester (0962) 54505

CORFIELD of Lymington Ltd

Members of the BADA

Large Showroom of English Furniture, Porcelain and Pictures for trade and the public

120 HIGH STREET, LYMINGTON, HAMPSHIRE SO4 9AQ. Tel Lymington 73532 and 75359

New showrooms and restoration at:

THE OLD SCHOOL, PENNINGTON, Tel LYMINGTON 77872

Burns & Graham

Good quality 17th, 18th and early 19th century Furniture

Decorative Items of the Period

4 ST. THOMAS STREET, WINCHESTER, HANTS.

Tel 0962-53779

MILLERS

of

CHELSEA ANTIQUES LTD.

Merchants to the International Antiques Trade

Vast stock of antiques and decorative items

Netherbrook House, Christchurch Road RINGWOOD Hants.

04254 2062

MEG CAMPBELL

English Domestic Silver and Collectors' Pieces

Illustrated Catalogue with prices sent on request, $3 by air

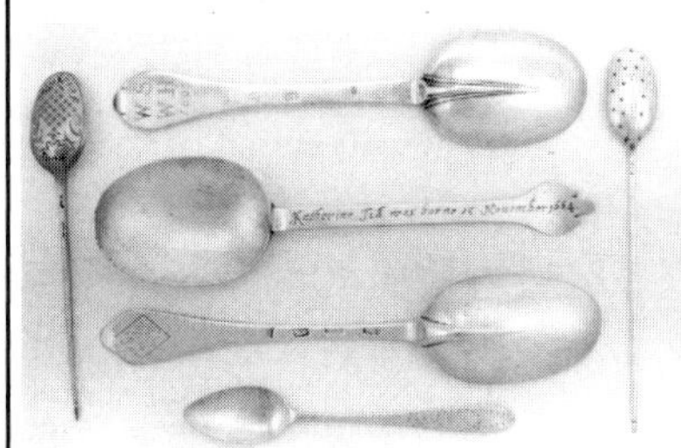

SPOONS FOR COLLECTORS including caddy spoons, mote spoons, trifid spoons, dognose spoons and Scottish and Irish Provincial spoons

Approval Service

10 Church Lane, Highfield, Southampton SO2 1SZ

Tel: 0703 557636

By appointment only

Romsey STD 0794

Bell Antiques
(Mike Gay & Berni Gay). 8 Bell St, SO51 8GA. Tel 514719. Open Mon-Sat 9.30-1, 2.15-5.30; Wed & Sat closed 1-2.15. General antiques, including art nouveau and art deco items; 19th and 20thC furniture, glass, pottery and porcelain. Also topographical prints, and 19th and 20thC jewellery.

Charles Antiques
(T.R.Cambridge). 101 The Hundred, SO5 8BZ. Tel 512885. Open Mon-Sat 9-6, closed Wed; other times by appt. 18th and 19thC furniture, porcelain, pictures, metalware, clocks and books. LAPADA

Selborne STD 042 050

David Clark
The Plestor. Tel 274. Open Mon-Sat 9.30-5.30; other times by appt. Country furniture, brass, copper and primitive paintings.

Southampton STD 0703

Meg Campbell
10 Church Lane, Highfield, SO2 1SZ. Tel 557636. Open by appt only. Antique silver, silver flatware, small collectables and old Sheffield plate.

H.M.Gilbert & Son
(B.L. & R.C.Gilbert). 2½ Portland St, SO1 0EB. Tel 26420. (Also at 19 The Square, Winchester.) Open Mon-Sat 8.30-5. Large stock of general antiquarian and secondhand books. Catalogues. ABA

Hingstone's
(Nick & John Hingstone). 13 & 15 Northam Rd. Tel 20180 (priv 0703-812301). Open Mon-Sat; closed Wed & Fri afternoon; other times by appt. Large stock of 1930s and Victorian shipping goods.

R.K.Leslie Antiques
(Raymond K.Leslie). 23 Northam Rd, SO2 0NZ. Tel 224784. Open Mon, Tues, Thurs, Fri 10-12.30, 2-4; Wed 10-12.30; other times by appt. Buying and selling antiques; jewellery, silver, furniture, clocks and watches.

L. Moody
(J. & A.H. Gubb). 70 Bedford Place, SO1 2DS. Tel 333720 (priv 29718). Open Mon-Sat. Antique furniture, porcelain, silver.

Parkhouse & Wyatt Ltd
(J.R.Parkhouse). 96 Above Bar, SO9 4FF. Tel 226653. Open Tues-Sat 9-5.30. Antique and secondhand jewellery and silver. NAG

Southsea

R.C.Dodson Antiques
(Mr & Mrs R.Dodson). 85 Fawcett Rd. Tel 0705-829481. (Also at 117 New Road, Portsmouth.) 18thC to Edwardian period furniture. Valuations. LAPADA

The Gallery
(Mrs Ivana Murphy). 11 & 19 Marmion Rd. Tel Portsmouth (0705) 822016. (Also at 85-87 Albert Rd, Southsea. Tel: 734102.) Open Mon-Fri 9-1. 2.30-5.30; other times by appt. Chairs, armchairs, chaise longues, Chesterfields, settees in general, already upholstered.

Hiscock Gallery
11 Stanley St. Tel 0705-825330. Open Tues-Sat 10-5. Continuous exhibitions of paintings, original prints, reproduction prints, picture framing, artists materials.

Colin Macleods Antique Centre
(Colin Macleod, David Arthur). 159/161 Goldsmith Ave, PO4 8BL. Tel Portsmouth (0705) 734173. Open Mon-Fri 8.30-5.30; Sat 9-2.30; other times by appt. 65,000 sq ft of antiques and shipping goods.

Stockbridge

Douglas Gordon Antiques
(Lord & Lady Douglas Gordon). The Old Rectory, SO20 6EU. Tel 0264-810662. Open Mon-Sat 10-5.30; other times by appt. Fine quality 18thC furniture. BADA

George Hofman Antiques
(George Hofman). Brookside, High St, SO20 6EY. Tel 0264-810570. Open Mon-Fri 10.30-5.30, Sat 10.30-4; other times by appt. General antiques, including furniture, wooden items, metalware, bygones and prints.

Victor Mahy Ltd
(John V. Mahy & John H. Parnaby). Mulberry House, SO20 6EY. Tel 0264-810466. Open Mon-Sat 9.30-5; Sun by appt only. 17th and 18thC English furniture and works of art. BADA

Philip & Anne Merridale
Bridge House. Tel 673. Open Mon-Fri 9-5, Sat & Wed 9-1. General antiques including late 18th and 19thC furniture; also pictures. Gallery of late 18th and 19thC watercolours.

Victor Needham Antiques
Hinwood House, High St, Broughton. Tel Broughton (0794) 301205. Extensive stock of fine 17th and 18thC furniture, works of art and garden ornaments. BADA

Stockbridge Antiques
High St. Tel 0264-810 829. Open Mon-Sat, Sun by appt. General antiques, watercolours, porcelain, silver, embroidery.

Elizabeth Viney
Jacob's House, High St. Tel 0264 810761. Open Mon-Sat 9-5; sometimes closing Mon and Wed. Antiques of 18th and 19thC, English furniture, treen, objets d'art and unusual items. BADA

Tichborne

Barlow Antiques
(Stephen & Prue Barlow). Sevington Manor, SO24 0NF. Tel Alresford (096 273) 4800. Open by appt. 17th and 18thC furniture and works of art.

Titchfield STD 0329

Titchfield Antiques Ltd
(George Alexander). 15 South St, PO14 4DL. Tel 45968. Open Tues-Sun 10-5.30. Art Nouveau, Art Deco, silver, general furniture.

Upham

Susanna Fisher
(Susanna Fisher). Spencer, SO3 1JD. Tel Durley (04896) 291. Open by appt only. Navigational charts, sailing directions and pilot books, 16th-19thC. Mainly mail order. 3 catalogues a year, no charge.

Wickham STD 0329

The Shambles
(Helen Penry). Southwick Rd (A333), Wickham Common. Tel 832250. Open daily except Wed and Sun. General antiques, porcelain, jewellery, glass, furniture of all kinds.

Winchester STD 0962

Antiques & Interiors
(W.Todd and G.Austin). 6 Andover Rd, SO23 7BS. Tel 69824. Open Mon-Sat. 18th-20thC pottery, porcelain, glass, mirrors, boxes, furniture & cabinets. Also decorating and unusual antique items for the home.

J.W.Blanchard Ltd
(J.W.Blanchard, O.D.F.Harris). 12 Jewry St. Tel 54547 (priv 52041). Open Mon-Sat 9-5. Large selection of general antiques. LAPADA BADA

Burns & Graham
4 St Thomas St. Tel 53779. Open Mon-Sat 9.30-5; other times by appt. Good quality 18th and 19thC furniture and decorative items, fabrics and furnishings, brass and copper, also upholstery.

Close Antiques
(Caryl Baron). 19 Little Minster St, SO23 9HA. Tel 64763. Open Mon-Sat 9-5; other times by appt. 17th and 18thC country furniture, English pottery (especially Delftware), samplers, tiles, early metal, treen. BADA

Polly de Courcy-Ireland
(P.A. de Courcy-Ireland). 16 Chilbolton Ave, SO22 5HD. Tel 65716. Open by appt only. Specialising in treen and unusual objects. BADA

Gallery Antiques Ltd
Avebury House, 6 Peter St, SO23 8BN. Tel 62161. (Also extensive showroom premises at 16 Jewry St, Winchester.) Open by appt. Georgian period items.

Henry March Gilbert
19 The Square, SO23 9RY. Tel 52832. Open Mon-Sat 9-5.30. Large wide-ranging stock of secondhand and antiquarian books available. Books bought.

Jeffery Hammond Antiques
(J. & E.Hammond). 18-19 High St, Twyford, SO21 1RF. Tel Twyford (0962) 714036. Open Mon-Sat 8.30-6.30; other times by appt. British & European 17thC, 18thC & 19thC furniture, some clocks, barometers and paintings.

The Hampshire Bookshop
Kingsgate Arch. Tel 64710. Open Mon-Sat. Good general antiquarian stock including illustrated books, natural history and antique prints and maps.

M. Harrington Ltd
74 Parchment St, SO23 8AT. Tel 53608. Open Mon-Sat 9-5.30; other times by appt. New books and large selection of secondhand/antiquarian theatrical books.

Itchen Gallery
(Lawson E.Bell). 29 Middle Brook St. Tel 61309. Open Mon-Sat 9.30-5.30. Specialising in 19thC oils and watercolours.

G.E. Marsh (Antique Clocks)
32A The Square, SO23 9EX. Tel 54505. Open 9-5; other times by appt. Antique clocks, watches and barometers, some modern stock. Restoration of antique clocks, watches and barometers. BADA BHI

Pearsons
Tower House Saleroom St, Tower St, SO23 8TA. Tel 62515/64444. Open Mon-Fri 9-1, 2-5; Sat 9-12. Auctioneers of general antiques with specialist sales.

The Pine Cellars
38 Jewry St, SO23 8RY. Tel 67014. Antique pine and country furniture. Suppliers of old pine panelled rooms. Expert stripping service available. Also trade enquiries - 20000 sq ft of traditional British furniture.

Printed Page
(Christopher & Jean Wright). 2-3 Bridge St, SO23 9BH. Tel 54072 (priv 62995). Open Tues-Fri 9.30-5.30; Sat 10-6; other times by appt. Prints 1750 to 1890; maps 1600 to 1890; small selection of Victorian watercolours. Valuations carried out. Restoration and conservation of pictures. Also framing. GMC, FATG

Ships and Sealing Wax Antiques
(Daly, Peter M.). 20a Jewry St. Open Fri, Sat 10-5 and usually Mon or Wed. General antiques specialising in books on natural history, travel, exploration and field sports.

SPCK Bookshops
24 The Square. Tel 66617. Open Mon-Sat 9-5.30. Large stock of books including antiquarian.

Todd & Austin Antiques & Fine Art
(W.Duncan-Todd, G.Austin). 2 Andover Rd, SO23 7BS. Tel 69824. Open Mon-Sat 9.30-5.30; other times by appt. Pottery and porcelain services, glass paperweights, boxes, table glass and clocks. Also 18th & 19thC glass, porcelain, barometers, ivory, furniture, decorative items, cased sets of cutlery, decorative silver, snuff boxes, tea caddies. Oriental art.

Hereford & Worcester

Bewdley STD 0299

James Geddie Ltd (Bewdley Auctions)
22 Load St, DY12 2AE. Tel 2187. Open 9.30-5; other times by appt. General antiques.

Broadway STD 0386

Blinkhorn & Company
(Michael L. Blinkhorn and Brian L. Gusterson). 41-43 High St, WR12 7DP. Tel 852456 (priv 853686). Open Mon-Sat 9-1, 2.15-5.30. Chartered surveyors and auctioneers. RICS

Broadway Antique Arcade
(R.G.Brown). 13 Leamington Rd, WR12 7EQ. Tel 853035. Open Tues-Sun 10-5. Porcelain, copper, brass, furniture, pictures, linen & lace, clocks, objets d'art, glass.

Gavina Ewart
60 High St. Tel 853371. (Also at Chantry House, Sheep St, Stow-on-the-Wold.) Open Mon-Sat 9.30-1, 2-5.30. Res on prem. Antique silver, especially flatware and cutlery; glass; porcelain, especially early Worcester and Derby. Prattware, clocks and Georgian to mid-Victorian furniture, especially mahogany and walnut. BADA CADA

Fenwick and Fisher Antiques
(George Fenwick, Diana Fisher). 88 High St. Tel 853227 (priv 853228). Open daily 10-6 including Sundays; other times by appt. 17th to early 19thC furniture in oak, mahogany and walnut. Treen, boxes, samplers, pewter, lace bobbins and needlework tools, toys, games and country furniture.

Richard Hagen Ltd
(R.L.W.Hagen, G.B. Hagen). Yew Tree House, WR12 7DT. Tel 853624. Open Mon-Sat 9-6; Sun by appt. Victorian & Edwardian watercolours, contemporary watercolours & late 19th & 20thC oils.

Hay Loft Gallery
(Jane Pitt & Sally Pitt). Berry Wormington, WR12 7NH. Tel Toddington (024 269) 202. Open 10-5.30; other times by appt. Paintings, specialising in Victorian oils & watercolours.

H.W.Keil Ltd
(V.M.Keil & P.J.W.Keil). Tudor House, WR12 7DP. Tel 852408. Open daily; early closing Thurs. Extensive showrooms of fine 17th and 18thC English furniture, especially oak, walnut and mahogany. BADA

John Noott
(John Noott). Picton House Gallery, High St, WR12 7AL. Tel Evesham (0386) 852787. Open Mon-Sat 9-5.30; other times by appt. Large stock of paintings, watercolours 1850-1950. Specialising in oils, smalls and jewellery. CADA

Olive Branch Antiques
(Sylvia and Peter Riley). 80 High St, WR12 7AJ. Tel 853440. Open daily 9.30-5.30; other times by appt. Specialising in clocks and Victoriana.

Brobury

Brobury House Gallery
(E. Okarma). Brobury House, HR3 6BS. Tel Moccas (09817) 229. (Also The Corner Shop, Hay-on-Wye.) Open Mon-Sat 9-4.30 (winter 9-4); other times by appt. Large stock of old prints, mainly 19thC. Also late 19th and early 20thC watercolours.

Droitwich STD 0905

Grant Books
(Bob & Shirley Grant). Victoria Sq. Tel 778155. Open 9-5; other times by appt. Books - general stock, golf books, new and out-of-print. Golfing memorabilia.

H. & B.Wolf Antiques Ltd
(H.G. & Mrs B.J.Wolf). 128 Worcester Rd (A38), WR9 8AN. Tel 772320. Open Mon-Sat 9.30-5.30; closed Thurs. 18th & 19thC porcelain, pottery & glass and other collectors items.

Eardisley STD 054 46

Arboyne Antiques
Arboyne House. Tel 218. Open always. Country furniture, 18th to 20thC porcelain, Oriental porcelain, Doulton, copper, brass and decorative items.

Evesham STD 0386

D.J. Chapman & Son (Antiques)
Hampton House, Hampton. Tel 830216. Open daily 9-6; other times by appt. Period furniture, longcase clocks. Trade, retail and export. LAPADA

Gordon & Brenda Knight
3 Waterside, WR11 6BS. Tel 2953. (Also in Broadway.) Furniture, china, glass, copper and bric-a-brac.

Magpie Antiques & Jewellers
(R.J. & E.R. Bunn). 61 High St. Tel 41631. (Also at 2 Port St,Evesham.) Open Mon-Sat 9.30-5.30; early closing Wed at Port St; other times by appt. At High St, gold, silver, jewellery, furniture, brass & copper, porcelain etc. At Port St, Silver, gold, jewellery, porcelain,brass & copper etc. LAPADA

Hay-on-Wye STD 0497

John Allott Abrahams
(John Allott Abrahams CMBHI). The Bear, 2 Bear St. Tel 820085. Open Mon-Sat 10-6; other times by appt. Antique clock sales, restorations, hand-crafted replica clocks.

Richard Booth's Bookshop
(Richard Booth). 'The Limited', Lion St, HR3 5AA. Tel 820322 (priv 820503). (Also The Print Shop & Hay Castle Barn.) Open daily 9-8; Sun 10.30-7.30; other times by appt. Thousands of books including all subjects. Hay Castle Barn specialises in sports & pastimes. Specialist in military books.

The Corner Shop
(D. Raven). 5 St John's Place. Tel 820045. (Also The Brobury House Gallery, Brobury.) Open Mon-Sat 10-5 in summer; winter hours variable. 19thC prints and watercolours, contemporary watercolours and etchings.

The Hay Galleries Ltd
4 High Town, HR3 5AE. Tel 820356 (priv 820852). Open Mon-Fri 8.30-5.30; Sat 10-4.30; other times by appt. 18th and 19thC pine, country & decorative furniture, limited stock of textiles, metalware and decorative items. LAPADA

Hereford STD 0432

I. & J.L. Brown
(Ian & Joyce Brown). 58 Commercial Rd, HR1 2BP. Tel 58895 (priv 0432 70 674). (Also 636 Kings Rd, London SW3.) Open Mon-Sat 9-5.30; other times by appt. Matched sets of country chairs, also tables, dressers, desks, etc. Specialising in English country and French provincial furniture.

Great Brampton House Antiques Ltd
(P.B. Howell). Great Brampton House, Madley, HR2 9NA. Tel Golden Valley (0981) 250244. Open Mon-Sat 9-5; other times by appt. Furniture, pictures, carpets and rugs. Interior design and decoration. LAPADA

Jennings
(John Richard Jennings & Ray Kingsley-Taylor). 36 Aubrey St, HR4 OBU. Tel 276564 (priv 850752). Open Mon-Sat 10.30-5; other times by appt. Antique furniture, jewellery, silver, copper & brass. Porcelain.

Pierpoint Gallery
(A.G. & H.L. Beaver). 10 Church St, HR1 2LR. Tel 267002. Open Mon-Sat 9.30-5.30; closed Thurs. Antiquarian and general books, original maps and prints.

G.E.Richards & Son (Antiques)
(G.E.Richards, P.J.Richards). 57 Blueschool St, HR1 2AR. Tel 267840 (priv 268827). Open Mon-Sat 9-5.30; other times by appt. Period furniture, porcelain, Victoriana, barometers and reproductions. LAPADA

Ledbury STD 0531

Collection
13 The Southend. Tel 4641. Open Mon-Fri 9-1; 1.45-5.30; Sat 10-5.30. Work of leading contemporary makers, particularly in ceramics and wood, studio glass, jewellery and prints.

Gavels
(Gary K.Blissett). Bramble Cottage, 40 Ashperton Rd, Ashperton, HR8 2RY. Tel Trumpet (053183) 270. Open by appt only. Quality 19th and 20thC watercolours, etchings, cartoons and illustrations.

Leominster STD 0568

Architectural Antiques
Chatelaine House, New Street. Tel 611958. Open Mon-Sat 9-5. All types of restorational requirements.

Barometer Shop
Waterway Galleries. Tel 3652. Open Mon-Fri 9-5.30; other times by appt. Clocks, watches, barometers and restoration.

The Bird in Hand
44 Broad St. Tel 3160. Open Mon-Sat 9-5.30. General antiques, bygones (wooden and iron).

Bliss Antiques
19 Broad St. Tel 4444. Open Tues, Wed, Fri, Sat 10-5; Mon & Thurs by appt. General antiques, mahogany, country pine, textiles and pictures.

Books and Things
Burgess Street. Tel 5902. Open Mon-Fri 10-4. Children's books, toys and bygones. Musical instruments, paintings and prints.

Boyne House Antiques
Lion Yard, Broad Street. Tel 5596. Open Mon-Sat 10-5.30. General antiques, restoration and re-upholstery of all furniture.

Coltsfoot Gallery
(Edwin Collins). Hatfield, HR6 0SF. Tel Steensbridge (056 882) 277. Open by appt. 19th and 20thC landscape, wildlife and sporting watercolours' 18th and 19thC sporting and wildlife prints. Restoration and conservation of all works of art on paper. Member of Institute of Paper Conservation.

Country Antique Market
14 Broad St. Tel 2189. Open Tues-Fri 10-5. Furniture, textiles, ceramics, treen, pictures, postcards, copper & brass.

Courts Miscellany
48 Bridge St. Open Mon-Sat 9.30-5. General small items and interesting bygones.

Geoffrey Crofts Limited
29/31 South Street. Tel 611580 (priv 0568). Open Mon-Fri 10-4. Wide range of country and period furniture, porcelain, pottery, metalware and objets d'art.

Eardisley Antiques
(W.E. & J.E. Kinch). Leominster Antique Market, 14 Broad St. Tel 2189 (priv 05446 310). (Home address: Oakwood, Eardisley, Hereford.) Open Mon 10-5 Trade only; Tues-Fri 10-5; other times by appt. 19thC pottery and porcelain, small furniture, Victoriana, 19thC coloured glass.

P. & S.N. Eddy
(P.&S.N.Eddy). 22 Etnam St, HR6 8AQ. Tel 2813. Open Mon-Sat 9-6; other times by appt. Res on prem. 18th and 19thC furniture, metalware, treen , bygones and blue and white pottery.

Half-a-Living
3 Bridge St. If not open contact 48 Bridge St. Small antique furniture and silver. Staffordshire pottery figures, gold and silver coins.

Hubbard Antiques
The Golden Lion, Bridge St. Tel 4362. Period oak, mahogany, walnut, early brass, metal. LAPADA

Jennings Antiques
Bridge St. Open Mon-Sat 9-5.30. Furniture, pottery and porcelain.

Just-a-Living
5 Bridge St. Tel 81556. Open Mon-Fri 10-5; other times by appt. Antique country furniture and effects.

La Barre Ltd
The Place, 116 South St, HR6 8LE. Tel 4315. Large quantity of 18th and 19thC antique furniture, pine and country furniture and interesting small objects.

Leominster Antiques
(Ken & Julia Watherington). 87 Etnam St. Tel 3217. Open Mon-Sat 9-6; other times by appt. 18th and early 19thC furniture, mahogany, walnut, oak, pine. Some pottery & porcelain. LAPADA

Lighthouse Antiques
2 Bridge St. Tel 611838. Open Mon-Sat 10-5; other times by appt. Furniture, samplers, needlework and pottery.

Pitcher Pine Antiques
Lion Yard, Broad Street. Tel 3361. Open Mon-Sat 8,30-6. Pine furniture and general antiques. Victorian type knobs, feet, brass handles, leaded lights. Also stripping of all types of pine.

David Robert
Waterway Galleries, 25 Broad St. Tel 2988. Open Mon-Sat 9-5.30; other times by appt. Period oak, walnut, mahogany and country furniture.

Russell Baldwin & Bright
The Fine Art Saleroom, Ryelands Rd. Tel 3897. Auctioneers.

Michael Stewart Antiques
Lion Yard, Broad Street. Tel 4946. Open Mon-Sat 10-5.30. Country furniture, Georgian chests, quality mahogany and general antiques.

Wheelbarrow Castle Antiques
Stoke Prior. Tel 2219. Open daily but appt advisable at weekends. Period furniture of good quality with bias to early oak, also some mahogany.

Lugwardine

Newcourt Park
Tel Hereford (0432) 850752. English and Continental period furniture, valuations, interior design and construction, curtains, carpets and upholstery.

Malvern STD 068 45

Aladdin's Cave
Church Street. General antiques, furniture. Also restoration and recaning service.

Joan Coates
26 St Ann's Rd. Tel 5509. General antiques.

The Great Malvern Antiques Arcade
(Leonard Sutton, Robert Rice). Salisbury House, 6 Abbey Rd, WR14 3HG. Tel 5490. Open Mon-Sat 9.30-5.30; other times by appt. Over 2000 sq ft of decorative antiques and garden furniture.

E.M.Kimber & Son
(E.M.Kimber). 6 Lower Howsell Rd, Malvern Link. Tel 2000. Open Mon-Fri 9-1, 2-5; other times by appt. 18th and 19thC furniture and other items.

The Malvern Bookshop
(R.A.H. & A.J. Lechmere). 5-7 Abbey Rd. Tel 5915 (priv 0684-40340). Open Mon-Sat 9.15-1, 2.15-5.30; early closing Wed. Large general stock of antiquarian and secondhand books.

Malvern Studios
(L.M. Hall). 56 Cowleigh Rd, North Malvern, WR14 1QD. Tel 4913. Open Mon-Thurs 9-5.15; Fri & Sat 9-12.45, 2-4.45; other times by appt. Large stock of Edwardian, Victorian and Georgian furniture. Antique restoration workshops within the premises capable of all types of restoration. Reproduction mirrors, chandeliers, wall-lights, brass cabinet fittings, plaster mouldings, etc. LAPADA

Revivals
Cowleigh Road. General antiques.

Tinderbox
Church Street. General antiques, textiles, costumes.

Whitmore
(John & Stella Whitmore). Teynham Lodge, Chase Rd, Upper Colwall. Tel Colwall (0684) 40651. Open by appointment only. British and foreign coins, tokens and medallions. Catalogue of 10,000 items published twice a year. BNTA

Woodstock
Unicorn Yard, Rear of 6/8 Bellevue Terrace, WR14 4EZ. Tel 60297. Open Mon-Sat 8.30-6. Antique pine furniture. Also kitchen and bathroom interiors incorporating antique wood; pub interiors.

Pershore STD 0386

Penoyre Antiques
9 - 11 Bridge St. Tel 3522. Open Mon-Sat 9.30-5.30; other times by appt. 17th to early 19thC furniture, specialising in Georgian dining room furniture, mirrors and chandeliers.

S.W.Antiques
Abbey Showrooms, Newlands. Stripped pine and 19th-20thC furniture.

I+JL Brown Ltd

Major suppliers of English country and French provincial antique furniture, decorative objects and metalware.

Over 50,000 sq. ft. of merchandise available.

Specialists in tables, chairs, Welsh dressers, buffets, armoires, desks, lowboys & side tables.
Also selected hand crafted reproduction furniture.

HEAD OFFICE: 58 COMMERCIAL ROAD, HEREFORD, HR1 2BP. Telephone: **Business (0432) 58895**
Private (0432) 70 674
ALSO AT : 636 KINGS ROAD, CHELSEA, LONDON SW6 2DU. Telephone: (01) 736 4141

WHEN IN HEREFORDSHIRE

Gerald and Vera Taylor are an essential stop for buyers of Long Case Clocks and period furniture. Always a comprehensive stock of fully restored clocks available, with the emphasis on 8-day mahogany painted dials. Trade and private customers welcome: preferably telephone first for an appointment.

Winforton Court, Winforton, Herefordshire, tel. 05446 226

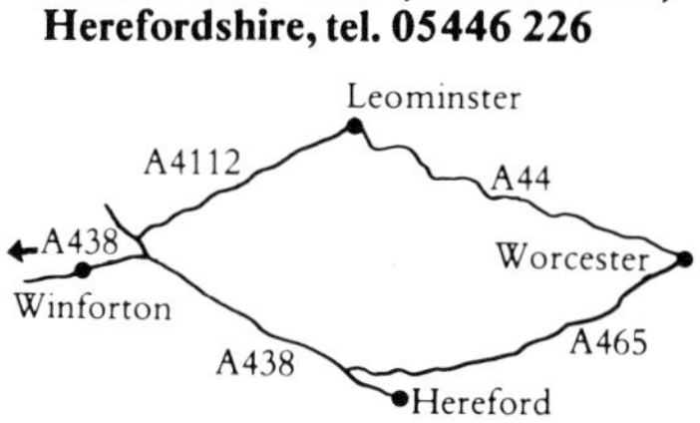

Free delivery to London and modest charges for delivery elsewhere in the UK. Export orders also arranged. New showroom opening soon.

Example of current stock: Scottish clock in mahogany case, 8-day movement, c.1810.

Park Street Antiques

350 High Street, Berkhamsted
Hertfordshire HP4 1HT
Berkhamsted (04427) 4790

Extensive stock of
Period Furniture, Barometers & Works of Art

Also Large Trade Only Area

Times Past
(Judith K.Pollitt). 84 High St, WR10 1DU. Tel 554258. Open Mon-Sat 10-1, 2-5; closed Thurs; other times by appt. Small antiques including pottery, silver, jewellery, glass, treen, needlework tools, samplers, silk pictures, bygones, buttons. Specialising in blue and white transfer pottery, and needlework tools.

Two Windows
(Alec Nelmes). 18A Bridge St, WR10 1AT. Tel 552121. Open Mon-Sat 9.30-4.30; closed Thurs. Mainly restoration of clocks and barometers.

Powick

The Barn Gallery
(Martin D. Ham). Sandpits Farm, Colletts Green Rd, WR2 4RY. Tel Worcester (0905) 830029. Open for exhibitions April and October; other times by appt. Victorian paintings and watercolours.

Redditch STD 0527

Alan Morris
503 Evesham Rd, Crabbs Cross, B97 5JJ. Tel 45084. Open Mon-Sat 10-6; other times by appt. Reproduction wholesalers - warehouse and mail order. Oil lamp spares and reproductions - callers only. Plate stands and hangers, and Tobies - mail order.

Ross-on-Wye STD 0989

Antique Centre
Brookend. Tel 62752. Open Mon-Sat 9.30-5.30. 8 stalls of various specialities; mainly country items & Staffordshire figures.

Baileys Architectural Antiques
The Engine Shed, Ashburton Industrial Estate, HR9 7BW. Tel 63015. Open Mon-Sat 9.30-5; other times by appt. Large fast changing stock of original and reproduction fireplaces, bathrooms, stained glass, pews, doors, shop fittings, garden furniture.

Fritz Fryer
Greenway Cottage, Glewstone. Tel Llangarron (098984 512. (Old Pine Shop,27 Gloucester Rd. Ross-on-Wye.Tel:0989 64738.) Decorative antique lighting specialist & consultant. Entire lighting schemes devised and executed.

Robin Lloyd Antiques
23-24 Brookend St. Tel 62123. Open Mon-Sat 10-5.30. Oak furniture for the country cottage - gatelegs, dressers, windsor and spindleback chairs, brass and copper, all pre-1850. Also offer service of furnishing any property with oak furniture copied from originals using 17th and 18thC timber.

Old Pine Shop
(Barbara Miller). 27 Gloucester Rd, HR9 5BU. Tel 64738 (priv 0594 543349). Open Mon-Sat 10-5.30; Wed by appt. Large stock of quality antique pine furniture, new kitchen chairs & reproduction furniture to order. 1st floor - antique lighting.

Serendipity
(Mrs R.J. Ford). Brookend. Tel 63836 (priv 053184 245). Open Mon-Sat 9.30-5; other times by appt. Large stock of 18th & 19thC oak & mahogany furniture, plus a new range of reproduction oak furniture made from 17thC timber including four poster beds.

Trecilla Antiques
(Lt Col & Mrs I.G.Mathews). 36 and 36A High St, HR9 5HD. Tel 63010 (priv 0981 540274). Open Mon-Sat 9-5.30; early closing Wed. General antiques, period furniture, prints, arms and militaria. ABA

Winforton

Gerald and Vera Taylor
Winforton Court, HR3 6EA. Tel Eardisley (05446) 226. Open any time by appt. Long case clocks and period furniture specialising in longcase clocks of 1790-1830.

Woolhope

Bridge End Gallery
(Walenty Pytel NDD, Mary Pytel, Jeremy Pytel). Terrace Hall, HR1 4QJ. Tel Fownhope (043277) 373. Open any time by appointment. Bird and animal sculptures in steel and bronze by Walenty Pytel. Mary Pytel: antique clothes and textiles. Jeremy Pytel:antique dealer and restorer specialising in small Georgian furniture especially tripod tables.

Worcester STD 0905

Banks & Silvers
(D.G.F.Banks). 66 Foregate St, WR1 1EB. Tel 23456. Open Mon-Fri; other times by appt. Fine art auctioneers of private goods only. House and collective sales of any items.

Andrew Boyle (Booksellers) Ltd
21 Friar St. Tel 611700. Stock of antiquarian and secondhand books on many topics. ABA

Bygones of Worcester
(Gabrielle Doherty Bullock, FGA). 55 Sidbury, WR1 2HU. Tel 23132 and 25388. (Also Bygones by the Cathedral, Deansway.) Open Mon-Sat 9.30-1 2-5.30; other times by appt. Jewellery and silver, porcelain and pottery, art glass, furniture and paintings. Specialising in jewellery and Worcester porcelain. FGA LAPADA

Edgar Davis Antiques
The Old Bakery, Fernhill Rd.

Andrew Grant Fine Art Auctions
(Andrew Grant, FRICS). 59/60 Foregate St. Tel 52310. Open Mon-Sat 9-8; other times by appt. Fine art auctioneers and valuers. Offices at Droitwich, Malvern, Kidderminster, Redditch and Stourbridge.

Jean Hodge
Peachley Manor, Hallow Lane, Lower Broadheath, WR2 6QL. Tel 640255. Open every day including Sunday. (Between A443 and B4204, 3 miles NW of Worcester.) Res on prem. 18th and 19thC furniture and general items. LAPADA

M.Lees & Sons
(M. Lees & I.M. Lees). Tower House, Severn St. Tel 26620 (24 hours). Open Mon-Sat 9-5; closed Thurs; other times by appt. English and Continental period furniture, porcelain, silver and metalware. Specialising in 19thC signed Worcester porcelain. LAPADA

Keith Robinson Antiques
(Keith Robinson). 49 Upper Tything. Tel 25357 (priv 068 481 599). Open Mon-Sat 9.30-5.30; other times by appt. 4,500 sq ft of showroom and warehouse on 3 floors stocking 17th, 18th, 19th and 20thC furniture and accessories for home and export market. LAPADA

Simons Antiques
61 The Tything. Tel 25152. Open Mon-Sat 9.30-6, Thurs 9.30-1; other times by appt. Worcester porcelain and other porcelain; also jewellery and some glass.

T. Tolley
26 College St, WR1 2LS. Tel 26632. Pictures, prints, maps, hardstones, jade, coral, loose minerals and objets d'art. Also antiques generally.

Hertfordshire

Baldock STD 0462

The Attic
(Pat Sheppard). 20 Whitehorse St. Tel 893880 (priv 33113). Open Tues, Wed, Fri, Sat 10-4.30; other times by appt. Small furniture, bygones, antiques and curiosities.

Anthony Butt Antiques
7-9 Church St. 17th-19thC furniture and works of art.

Howard & Reeves
38 Whitehorse St. Tel 892385. (Also in Hitchin.) Open Mon-Sat 9.30-5; closed Thurs. Clocks, barometers & jewellery.

Ralph and Bruce Moss
(Messrs R.A. & B.A.Moss). 26 Whitehorse St, SG7 6QQ. Tel 892751. Open Mon-Sat 9-6; other times by appt. 17th to 19thC furniture and a wide range of other antiques. LAPADA

Graham Porter Antiques
(Graham Porter). 31 Whitehorse St. Tel 895351. Open Mon-Sat 9.30-6; other times by appt. 18th and 19thC pine furniture and decoration.

The Wheelwright
1 Mansfield Rd. Tel 893876. Open Mon-Sat 10-5.30; closed Thurs. Antiques & bric-a-brac.

Barnet STD 01

Barnet Antiques & Fine Art
(R.J.Gerry, C.J.Hawkins, B.J.Miller). 236 High St, EN5 5TD. Tel 01-440 3620. (Also 1180 High Rd, Whetstone, London N20 Tel: 445 9695.) Open Mon-Sat 9.30-1 2-5;Thurs 9.30-1; other times by appt. Retail, wholesale, and export of fine Georgian and Regency furniture, pictures and objets d'art. BADA

C.Bellinger Antiques
(Carl Bellinger). 91 Wood St, EN5 4BX. Tel 449 3467. Open Thurs, Fri, Sat 10-5; other times by appt. Victorian furniture, silver, plate, jewellery and bric-a-brac.

Chandos Books
(Stanley J. Brett). 111 Park Rd, New Barnet, EN4 9QR. Tel 449 9457. PBFA

Berkhamsted STD 044 27

M. & S. Armson Ltd
(Michael Armson). 370 High St. Tel 2241. Open Tues, Wed, Thurs, Sat 8.30-1; other times by appt. 17th, 18th and 19thC furniture.

Castle Gallery
87 High St. Tel 4814. Open 10-5.30, closed Mon and Wed; other times by appt. Mainly English 18th and 19thC oil paintings.

J. & J. Hutton
123 High St, HP4 2DJ. Tel 5979 (priv 5576). Open 1 Oct to 24 Dec: Mon-Sat 9.30-5.30; closed Wed; other times by appt. 18th and 19thC glass.

Park Street Antiques
(Mark Shanks). 350 High St (on A41), HP4 1HT. Tel 4790 (priv 024029 255). Open Mon-Sat 9.30-5.30; other times by appt. 17th to 19thC English and Continental furniture, barometers, clocks and works of art. BADA

Bishop's Stortford STD 0279

M.W. Bush
7 Dane St. Tel 3198. General stock, mainly furniture.

Sworder Salerooms
19 North St. Tel 52441. Auctioneers.

Watsons
Water Lane. Tel 52361. Auctioneers.

Windhill Antiquary
4 High St. Tel 51587. Appointment advisable. 17th and 18thC English and Continental furniture.

Bushey STD 01

Yesterday's Antiques
(M. Isenberg). 13 Sparrows Herne. Tel 950 7600. Open Mon & Thurs 9.15-2.30; Sat 9.15-4; other times by appt. 18th-19thC furniture, interesting smalls, metalware, boxes. Mainly trade. Good selection; stock changes daily.

Directory Entries are Free and ADDITIONS OR CORRECTIONS will be welcomed by *THE EDITOR, British Art and Antiques Directory, National Magazine House, 72 Broadwick Street, London W1V 2BP*

Harpenden STD 058 27

Hammersley Galleries
(Stanley & Joyce Hammersley). 12 Roundwood Lane, AL5 3BZ. Tel 4053. Open by appt any time. 18th & 19thC English & Continental oil paintings.

Hatfield STD 070 72

The Antiques Book Centre
(J.S. and S.D. Smith). 93 Bradmore Green, Brookmans Park, AL9 7QT. Tel Potters Bar (0707) 44426. Open 10-3.30; closed Mon & Wed. Specialist suppliers of old and new books on antiques and collecting and general stock of secondhand books on all subjects. Catalogues issued twice yearly on antiques.

Old Hatfield Galleries
(A. Smith). 1-3 Park St. Tel 71500. Open 9.30-5; other times by appt. Paintings and antiques.

Hemel Hempstead STD 0442

Abbey Antiques and Arts
(Elizabeth, Leonard & Simon Eames). 97 High St, HP1 3AH. Tel 64667. Open Mon-Sat 9.30-5.30; early closing Wed; other times by appt. 18th to early 20thC English watercolours, silver, plate, jewellery, furniture & glass. LAPADA

Cherry Antiques
(A.& R.S.Cullen & J.& J.M.Payne). 101-103 High St. Tel 64358. Open Mon-Fri 9.30-4.30; Wed 9.30-1; Sat 9.30-5. A deceptively large shop containing constantly changing stock of furniture, porcelain, silver, jewellery, needlework tools, dolls, fans, decorative and collector's items.

Rene Dolton Antiques
15a High St. Tel 64329. Open Mon, Thurs-Sat 10-4. Specialist in 19thC jewellery.

Frame One Photographic
23 Old High St. Tel 57028. Photographers.

Georgina Antiques
100 High St. Tel 56957. General and Oriental antiques.

G.B. Kent & Sons
Tel 251531. Brushmakers since 1777 offering a renovation service for antique brushes.

Linaire Antiques
136 Piccotts End. Tel 56729. General small antiques.

Hertford STD 0992

Beckwith & Son
St Nicholas Hall, St Andrew St, SG14 1HZ. Tel 52079. Open Mon-Sat 9-1, 2-5.30. Extensive stock of antiques, works of art and Victoriana, including furniture, glass, pottery, porcelain, metalwork, silver, prints and paintings.

Georgian House Antiques
(Mr & Mrs P. Hale). 42 St Andrew St. Tel 53508. Open Mon-Sat 9-1, 2-5.30; early closing Thurs; other times by appt. 17th to 19thC furniture, clocks, brassware and bric-a-brac.

Robert Horton Antiques
(Robert Horton). 13 Castle St, SG14 1ER. Tel 57546. Open Mon-Sat 9-5.30. Large variety of clocks of all types, barometers, furniture and general antiques. BWCMG

Neale Antiques
(S.C.Neale, A.J.Neale). 21 Old Cross, SG14 1RE. Tel 52519 and 51347. Open Mon-Sat; closed Thurs. Large stock of general antiques, silver, jewellery, and especially musical boxes and polyphons. Valuations. NAG

L. Partridge Antiques
(Perline & Alexander Hodgkinson). 25 St Andrew St, SG14 1JA. Tel 584385. Open Mon-Sat 10-5.30, closed Thurs; other times by appt. Large selection of furniture, pottery and porcelain, silver and metalware, objets d'art, collectables and prints.

Something New
(Roy Roberts). 3 Old Cross. Tel 551530. (Also Something Old at 6-8 Old Cross, Hertford.) Open Mon-Sat 9.30-5.30; closed Thurs. Reproduction items.

Something Old
(Roy Roberts). 6-8 Old Cross, SG14 1RB. Tel 551530. (Also Something New, 3 Old Cross, Hertford.) Open Mon-Sat 9.30-5.30; closed Thurs. Dolls, automata, furniture, pictures, music.

Village Green Antiques
(Norman & Pat Petre & Sons). 6/8 Old Cross St. Tel 57698 (priv 56994). (Also at 21/23 St Andrew St.) Open Mon-Sat 9.30-5.30; other times by appt. Large stock of selected antique & decorative furniture in 11 showrooms.

Hitchin STD 0462

The Aspidistra
(Mary M.Plant). 29 Sun St. Tel 53817. Open Mon-Sat 9.30-5.30; closed Wed; other times by appt. Victoriana, bric-a-brac and curios.

Bexfield Antiques
13-14 Sun St. Tel 32641. Open Mon-Sat 9.30-5. Variety of changing stock.

Courtyard Antiques
(Joan Savitsky). Rear of 23 Bancroft. Open Tues, Thurs, Sat 10-4.30. Silver, jewellery, porcelain and small furniture.

Michael Gander
10 Bridge St. Tel 32678. Open 9-6. Period furniture, metalware.

George Jackson & Son
(P.J. Smyth). Paynes Park House, Paynes Park. Tel 55212. Open Mon-Fri 9-5.30; Sat 9.30-1. Auctioneers of antiques and general household goods.

Hitchin Antiques Gallery
(Ronald Perry). 37 Bridge St. Tel 34525. Open six days a week, 10-5.30. Antique centre with 15 dealers selling a variety of antiques including furniture, clocks, silver, jewellery, porcelain and metalware.

Howard & Reeves
1 The Arcade. Tel 35454. (Also in Baldock.) Open Mon-Sat 9-5; closed Wed. Clocks, barometers & jewellery.

Eric T.Moore
(E.T.Moore). 24 Bridge St. Tel 50497. Open Mon-Sat; closed Wed. Antiquarian and secondhand books, antiquarian prints, maps. ABA

R.J.Perry Antiques
(Ronald Perry). 38 Bridge St, SG5 2DF. Tel 34525 (priv 0582-25546). (Also at Woburn Antiques Centre.) Open Mon-Sat 10-5.30; other times by appt. Metalware, especially fireplace furniture, small furniture and decorative items. LAPADA

Phillips of Hitchin (Antiques) Ltd
(Jerome Phillips). The Manor House, Bancroft (main street), SG5 1JW. Tel 32067. Open Mon-Sat 9-1, 2-5.30. Important stock of 17th and 18thC furniture and specialist art book department with current and out-of-print books on collecting. Specialist annual exhibitions. BADA

Roslyn House Galleries Ltd
7 Sun St, SG5 1AE. Tel 34774. Open Mon-Sat 9-1, 2.30-5; early closing Wed; other times by appt. Furniture, silver, china, clocks and barometers. LAPADA

Carole Thomas Fine Arts
First Floor, 32A Sun St, SJ5 1AH. Tel 36077. Open Mon-Sat 10.30-5.30; closed Wed. 19thC English watercolours, Victorian and Edwardian oil paintings, etchings and prints.

Wheldon & Wesley Ltd
Lytton Lodge, Codicote, SG4 8TE. Tel 820370. Open Mon-Fri 9-5; other times by appt. Large stock of books on natural history, particularly fine illustrated and out-of-print books. ABA

Hoddesdon STD 0992

The House of Whiting
66 High St. Tel 63483. Open Wed & Sat 10-5; other times by appt. General antiques, furniture and porcelain.

Kings Langley STD 092 77

Frenches Farm Antiques
(I. Cross). Frenches Farm, Tower Hill, Chipperfield. Tel 65843. Open Mon-Sat afternoons; other times by appt. (On right, 500 yds along road to Bovingdon from Chipperfield.) 18th-19thC furniture, pine, porcelain, copper, brass. Also Victoriana.

Much Hadham STD 027 984

Lynton Porcelain Company & Keith Arden
(Keith Williams, BA, Mary Arden-Davis, BA). Morris Cottage, High St, SB10 6BY. Tel 2297. Open by appt. 18th to 20thC porcelain & watercolours, small furniture, hand made, painted & gilded fine bone china by Stefan Nowacki, Alan Telford. LAPADA

Puckeridge

Puckeridge Antiques
25 Buntingford Road.

St Ouen Antiques
(Messrs Blake). Vintage Corner, Old Cambridge Rd. Tel Ware (0920) 821336. Open 10.30-5; other times by appt. 17th and 18thC English and Continental furniture, pictures and tapestries. Restorations. Valuations. LAPADA

Radlett STD 092 76

J.F.Foster & Son
21 High Firs, Gills Hill. Furniture, pottery, porcelain.

Hasel-Britt Ltd, Antiques
(Mrs D.Britton). 157 Watling St, WD7 7NQ. Tel 4477. Open Mon-Sat 10-5.45,closed Wed. General antiques: furniture, china,glass, prints, silver, brass and copper etc.

Redbourn STD 058 285

J.N.Antiques
(M.Brunning). 86 High St. Tel 3603 or 4544. English furniture, general. LAPADA

George Large Gallery
47-49 High St. Tel 3140. Fine pictures.

Questor Antiques
47-49 High St. Tel 3140. Open Mon-Sun 10-5; other times by appt. Antique furniture, maps and prints.

Tim Wharton Antiques
24 High St. Tel 4371. Open Tues, Wed, Fri 10-5; Sat 10-4. Thurs by appt. Good quality 18th and early 19thC furniture in oak, mahogany and elm. Antique brass, copper and metalware and a selection of small items. Unrestored furniture also sold.

Rickmansworth STD 0923

Clive A. Burden Ltd
(Clive A. Burden, Pauline E. Burden). 46 Talbot Rd. Tel 772387. (Also 13 Cecil Court, WC2 & PO Box 2792 Naples, Florida, USA.) Open 8-4; other times by appt. Antique maps and prints (topographical, natural history, caricatures, Vanity Fair) and antiquarian books. ABA

Royston STD 0763

Greenbury Antiques
(Iris Cornwell & Janet Carr). Corn Exchange, Market Place. Tel 45019 (priv 84362). Open Wed and Sat all day; other times by appt. Antiques including jewellery, china, furniture, curios and bric-a-brac.

Mel Antiques
(J.I. Moore). 5 Mortlock Street, Melbourn. Tel 61538 (priv 0767 51384). Open Mon, Wed, Fri, Sat 10-5; other times by appt. General antiques.

Royston Antiques
(John & Margaret Newnham). 27-29 Kneesworth St. Tel 43876. Open Mon-Sat 9.30-5, closed Thurs; other times by appt. Mainly Georgian, Victorian and Edwardian furniture, pottery, porcelain, metalware and cottage furniture.

Sawbridgeworth

The Herts & Essex Antiques Centre
(Western Associates Ltd). The Maltings, Station Rd, CM21 9JX. Tel Bishops Stortford (0279) 725809. Open daily, except Mon, 10.30-6. More than 30 antique shops under one roof with a wide range of antiques including furniture, pictures etc.

Graham Portlock
Unit D2, The Maltings, Station Rd. Tel Bishop's Stortford (0279) 722992. Photographer.

St Albans STD 0727

Bereston Antiques
Tel 55258. Open by appointment. Antique furniture.

The Clock Shop St Albans
(Mr Setterfield). 161 Victoria St, AL1 3TA. Tel 56633. Open Mon-Sat 10.30-6.30; closed Thurs. Clock, watch and barometer repairs. We also buy and sell old clocks and watches.

Dolphin Antiques
(C.Constable). 13 Holywell Hill, AL1 1EZ. Tel 63080 (priv 61941). Open Mon-Fri 9-5; other times by appt. General antiques, Victorian and Edwardian furniture, clocks, porcelain, glass, metalware and collectors' items. LAPADA

L.A.James
(Stephen James, Wendy James). 11 George St. Tel 56996. Open Mon-Sat 10-5. 18th and 19thC furniture, metalware, 19thC glass and topographical prints and maps of St Albans & Hertfordshire.

Mariposa
108 Holywell Hill. Tel 50469. Open Mon-Sat 10-5; other times by appt. Victorian furniture, silver, metalware, butterflies and paintings.

Pamela & Barry Auctions
(L.B. Vinton). 75 Chiltern Rd, Marshalswick, AL4 9ST. Tel 61180. Auctioneers of antiques and collectors' items. Auctions held fortnightly at Sandridge Village Hall, High Street, Sandridge, St Albans, Herts.

St Albans Antiques Market
Town Hall. Tel 50427. Open every Mon 9.30-4. 34 dealers selling a selection of small antiques and jewellery.

Stevenage STD 0438

Jefferies Antiques
The Ivy House, 36 High St, Old Stevenage. Tel 52239. Open Mon-Sat 9-6; other times by appt. Furniture,old silver, plate, china, pictures, prints and many other items.

Tring STD 044 282

John Bly
50 High St, HP23 5AG. Tel 3030. Open Mon-Sat 9-5.30; early closing Wed. Large stock of mahogany, oak and other furniture pre-1850, metalware, decorative items, silver and china. BADA

Waltham Cross STD 0992

John de Haan
12A Seaforth Drive, EN8 8BU. Tel 763111 (priv 0920 2534). Open any time by appt. 18thC furniture, mirrors, barometers.

Ware STD 0920

Old Tavern Antiques
Watton Rd. Tel 68644. Open Mon-Sat 10-6. Country furniture and general antiques.

Robin Sanders
The Pond House, Dane End. Tel Dane End (092084) 265. Fine antique furniture and works of art.

Watford STD 0923

Copper Kettle Antiques
(Robert & Colleen Barton). 172 Bushey Mill Lane. Tel 48877. General antiques.

Wheathampstead STD 058 283

F.G. & C. Collins Ltd (Collins Antiques)
Corner House, Church St, AL4 8AP. Tel 3111 & 3483. (Also at Barton House, Brewhouse Hill.) Open Mon-Fri 9-1, 2-6; Sat 9.30-1, 2-5.30; other times by appt. 25,000 sq ft of 18thC mahogany furniture and oak, walnut and 19thC furniture.

Humberside

Beverley

Raymond Hawley
5 North Bar Within, HU17 8AP. Tel Hull (0482) 883193. Furniture, porcelain, paintings and silver.

Ladygate Antiques
8A Market Place, HU17 8BB. Tel Hull (0482) 881494. Open Mon-Sat 9.30-5.30; other times by appt. General antiques, shipping goods, antique jewellery, brass and copper.

Bridlington STD 0262

Lesley Berry Antiques
The Manor House, Flamborough, YO15 1PD. Tel 850943. Open most days incl Sun 10-6; appt advisable. Brass, copper, treen, pictures, prints, beads, especially amber & jet, pottery, small furniture, linen.

Sweets Antiques
(Sheila Sweet). 24 West St, YO25 7DF. Tel 677396. Open Mon-Fri 10-6; 7 days summer 10-8; other times by appt. Antique furniture, Victoriana, porcelain, glass, pewter, copper, brass also specialising in art deco.

Brigg STD 0652

Dickinson, Davy & Markham
10 Wrawby Street. Tel 53666. Open Mon-Fri 9-5.30; Sat 9-12. Auctioneers and valuers.

Burstwick

John Corlyon (Furniture) Ltd
The Workshop. Tel Patrington (0964) 70701. Furniture designer, cabinet maker, and maker of fine reproduction furniture.

Driffield STD 0377

Carlton Gallery
60A Middle South St. 19thC pictures.

Dee & Atkinson
The Exchange. Tel 43151. Auctioneers.

Grimsby STD 0472

Kenneth Harvey Antiques and Fine Art
21-23 South St Mary's Gate. Tel 49370. Open Mon-Sat 10-5.30. Large showrooms of fine quality antiques, including 17th and 18thC clocks and 18th and 19thC furniture.

P.K. & R.H. Leigh
42 Friargate, Riverhead Centre. Tel 42597 (priv 77739). Open Mon-Sat 9-5; Thurs 9-4. General antiques. FATG

Scarthoe Antiques
(P.Bridges). 38A Louth Rd, Scartho, DN32 8PP. Tel 77394. Open Tues, Wed, Fri, Sat 10-5; other times by appt. Victorian and later jewellery, silver, plate, porcelain, linen, prints, maps, etc.

Hull STD 0482

55 Antiques
55 Spring Bank, HU3 1AG. Tel 224510. Open Mon-Sat 10-5; other times by appt. Period antiques, including marine items, oil paintings, garden furniture and good quality Victoriana.

Bank House Antiques
(Beryl & Maurice Taylor). 175 Spring Bank. Tel 227337. General antiques.

Brunswick Antiques
(Philip Allison). 64A Beverley Rd. Tel 20874 (priv 847653). Open Mon-Fri 9.30-4.30; other times by appt. General stock, including shipping goods, 20thC glass, pottery and porcelain.

R.P. Carmichael & Co.Ltd
George St, HU1 3BH. Tel 23439 (6 lines). Open Mon-Sat 9-5.30, Fri until 7. Antique, reproduction and modern furniture, jewellery, gifts.

De Grey Antiques
(Mr G.Dick). 96 De Grey St, Beverley Rd, HU5 2SE. Tel 442184. Open Mon-Sat 10-1, 2.15-5.40; other times by appt. China, pottery, glass, pewter, copper & brassware, paintings, watercolours, small furniture.

H. Evans & Sons
(H. Evans). 1 Parliament St, HU1 2AR. Tel 23033. Auctioneers.

David K.Hakeney Antiques
(David K.Hakeney). 64 George St, HU1 3AB. Tel 228190 (priv 668634). Open Mon-Sat 10-6; other times by appt. Georgian, Victorian and Edwardian furniture and bric-a-brac - trade and retail. Stock changing daily. LAPADA

Hull Pine Co
338 Wincolmlee. Tel 227169. Antique pine furniture. Stripping service.

Imperial Antiques
397 Hessle Rd. Tel 27439. General antiques and furniture.

Lesley's Antiques
329 Hessle Rd, HU3 4BL. Tel 23986 (priv 646280). Open Mon-Sat 9.30-3.30; other times by appt. General antiques, Victoriana and shipping goods.

Geoffrey Mole Antique Exports
(Geoffrey Mole). 400 Wincolmlee. Tel 27858. Open Mon-Fri 9-5; Sat 9-1; other times by appt. 12,500 sq ft of shipping and general antiques. LAPADA

Sandringham House Antiques
476 Beverley Road. Tel 43013 (priv 847653). General antiques.

James H.Starkey Galleries
49 Highgate, Beverley, HU17 9ON. Tel 881179. Open Mon and Fri 10-12, Tues-Thurs 10-2; other times by appt. 15th to 20thC quality paintings. Also a selection of other paintings and drawings.

Paul Wilson, Old, Antique & Reproduction Pine
(Paul & Ann Wilson). Perth Street West, HU5 3UB. Tel 447923/448607/48251. Open Mon-Fri 8-5.30; Sat 8-12; other times by appt. All types of British & European pine furniture, also manufacturers of a wide range of top quality reproduction pine tables, dressers, bureaux, desks, corner cupboards, beds etc. LAPADA GMC

Little Weighton

Rowley Restorations
(Mr & Mrs B.Levine). Station House, Rowley Rd. Tel 0482-844531. 19thC mahogany furniture. Restorations. LAPADA

Market Weighton STD 0696

Grannies Attic
(G.A.& P. Drysdale). Kiplingcotes Station. Tel Dalton Holme (069 64) 284. Antique and modern furnishings.

Houghton Antiques
(M.Watson, F.Cottrell). Houghton Hall, Sancton, YO4 3RE. Tel 73234. Open Mon-Sat 9-5; other times by appt. (From Market Weighton it is 1 mile on Cliffe Rd and 5 miles from M62). Furniture, paintings, china, objets d'art.

Isle of Wight

Bembridge STD 098 387

Vectis Fine Arts Gallery
(Terence Bruce-Joyner). 41 High St. Tel 852316. Open Tues-Sat. Specialists in marine watercolours, from 19th to 20thC.

Windmill Antiques
(E.J.de Kort). 1 Foreland Rd. Silver, jewellery, china, glass, small furniture. LAPADA

Worlds End Watercolours
(Mrs Joan Morton). Shern Lodge, Northclose Rd, PO35 5XP. Tel Isle of Wight (0983) 872307. Watercolours 1850-1950 and some oils. British watercolours and oils fully reframed and, if required, restored. Details of artists and the background of the pictures given. Photographs & details of stock pictures available. External exhibitions.

Cowes STD 0983

Colin Campbell Fine Paintings
(Colin Campbell). Bath Road. Tel 200 124 (priv 855 300). (Also in Yarmouth, I.o.W..) Contemporary and antique fine marine paintings and watercolours. Signed limited edition prints.

Finishing Touches
(Martin Scadgell). 42 High St, PO31 7RS. Tel 294875 (priv 521057). (Also 14 Scarrots Lane, Newport, PO30 1JA.) Open Mon-Sat 9.30-5; other times by appt. 19th & 20thC oil paintings, drawings and prints, newly manufactured furnishings, fine rugs, objets d'art.

York House Antiques
(H.W. Paul). 11-13 York St. Tel 295746. Open Mon-Sat 10-5; early closing Wed; other times by appt. Clocks, barometers and scientific instruments, oil paintings.

Ryde STD 0983

Hayter's
(R.W. and F.L. Hayter). 19-20 Cross St, PO33 2AD. Tel 63795. Open Mon-Sat 9-5.30; closed Thurs, Sun. Antique, Victorian and shipping furniture.

The Snuff Box
(John and Barbara Van Praagh). 10 High St. Tel 67722 (priv 63403). Open Mon-Sat 10-1, 2.30-5.30; early closing Thurs. Small furniture, Victoriana and objets d'art.

Uriah's Heap
(F.Cross). 9 Royal Victoria Arcade, Union St. Tel 64661. Open daily except Tues, Thurs & Sun; other times by appt. General antiques, jewellery and silver.

Shanklin STD 098 386

Collectors Centre
(Keith Shotter). 81 Regent St, PO37 7AP. Tel 862334. Open Mon-Sat 9.30-4.30; other times by appt. Antique glass and stoneglaze bottles 1630-1930. Coins, stamps, old postcards, military badges and medals, dolls, old and new jewellery, other small collectables.

Ventnor STD 0983

Bygones
(I.W.Mercury Ltd. Mrs Jill Wearing). 33 Pier St. Tel 852 138. Open Mon-Fri; Sat in summer; other times by appt. Antiques and bric-a-brac.

A. & S. Keen
(Alec and Sheila Keen). 19 Pier St, PO38 1ST. Tel 853706. Antiquarian and secondhand books (especially literary), small antiques. ABA

Yarmouth STD 0983

Colin Campbell Fine Paintings
(C.H.Campbell). The Gallery, The Square, PO41 0NS. Tel 760784. (Also The Marine Gallery, Cowes.) Open Mon-Sat 10-5; other times by appt. Watercolours, oils with a marine bias, and signed limited edition marine prints.

Marlborough House Antiques
(Peter A. Webb & Victoria K. Webb). 86 High St. Tel 760498. (Also 2 The Square, Yarmouth.) Open Mon-Sat 10-6; other times by appt. Period furniture, silver, antique prints and maps, jewellery, glass, porcelain, copper, brass, clocks and watches.

CHEVERTON'S

OF EDENBRIDGE LTD

LAPADA Registered Member

ONE OF THE LARGEST
AND MOST VARIED
STOCKS OF FURNITURE
IN THE SOUTH OF ENGLAND

ONE HOUR'S DRIVE FROM LONDON

Car park on premises

OPEN MONDAY – FRIDAY 9am–5.30pm

TAYLOUR HOUSE, HIGH STREET, EDENBRIDGE, KENT
Telephone (0732) 863196 and 863358

HAYTER'S

Dealers in Antique and
Victorian Furniture

Trade welcomed

(seven minutes by Hovercraft from Southsea)

19-20 CROSS STREET, RYDE
ISLE OF WIGHT PO33 2AD TELEPHONE 63795

SPECIAL OFFER
to
ANTIQUE DEALERS

The British Art & Antiques Directory
at the wholesale rate – **33%** discount.

Give your customers the chance to buy this prestigious book.
Order 5 or more copies and take advantage of our
special wholesale rate – £7 each including delivery.
No payment required now; we will invoice you on delivery.
All orders to: The British Art & Antiques Directory,
National Magazine House, 72 Broadwick Street, London W1V 2BP
(Tel. 01-439 7144).

Derek Roberts Antiques

FINE CLOCKS
Period Furniture
Tunbridge Ware

24/25 Shipbourne Road
Tonbridge, Kent TN10 3DN
Tel (0732) 358986

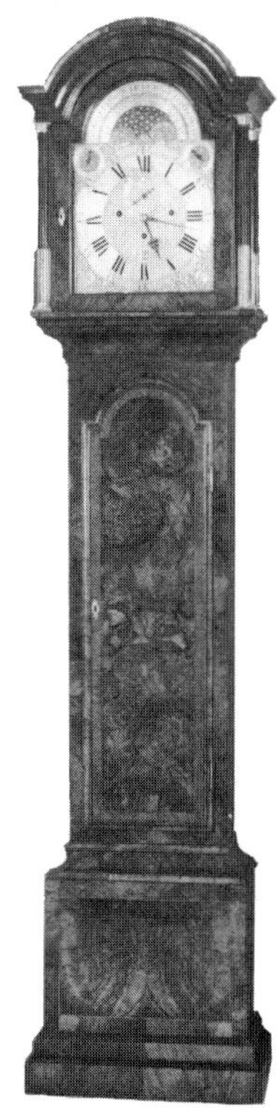

A fine musical and quarter chiming walnut longcase clock by Joseph Barber, London, circa 1740. One of numerous fine longcase, bracket, table, mantel, skeleton, carriage and precision clocks currently available.

Illustrated catalogues in colour and black and white available either singly price £5, post & packing 75p U.K., £2 Overseas Airmail, or on annual subscription, price £20, post & packing £3 U.K., £8 overseas airmail.

Kent

Ashford STD 0233

Cobbs, Burrows & Day
39-41 Bank St, TN23 1DJ. Tel 24321. Open Mon-Fri 9-5.30. Auctioneers of antiques and fine art. RICS

Mill House Antiques
(Mrs T.Fitzgerald-Moore). George House, Bridge St, Wye. Tel Wye (0233) 812035. Open 10-1, 2-5.30; closed Wed; other times by appt. 18th and early 19thC furniture, silver, ceramics, decorative and collectors items.

Martin Orskey Ltd
Little Gains House, Elmsted. Tel Elmsted (023 375) 204. Colour plate books, decorative prints, general science, Oriental miniatures, photography. ABA

Beckenham STD 01

Henry Flack (1860) Ltd
P.O.Box 78, BR3 4BL. Tel 01-658 2299. Suppliers of Briwax - wax polish for antique and other fine furniture. Beeswax polish for pine and oak. Various shades available to tone with a variety of woods.

Scallywag
(John A.Butterworth). 22 High St, BR3 1AY. Tel 658 6633. (Also in Camberwell Green, London SE5.) Open Mon-Sat 9.30-6. Antique and old country pine furniture, pine stripping, architectural items.

Valion Antiques
(Bob & Mollie Valentine). 42 Chancery Lane. Tel 462 9190. Open Tues, Thurs, Sat 10.30-5.30; other times by appt. Antique furniture, 1700 to 1930 and decorative items of porcelain, glass, plate, copper and brass.

H.S.Walsh & Sons Ltd
243 Beckenham Rd, BR3 4TS. Tel 01-778 7061. (London Showrooms at 12-16 Clerkenwell Rd, EC1. Tel:01-253 1174.) Clock material and movements. Replacement clock parts of all sorts. Horological books.

Norman Witham Antiques
(N.Witham). 2-2A High St. Tel 650 9096 (priv 650 4651). Open all day Fri & Sat; Mon & Wed pm; other times by appt. Small 18th, 19th, 20thC antique furniture also glass, china and watercolours.

Bexley

Argentum Antiques
(L.T. Laklia). 18-20 High St, DA5 1AD. Tel Crayford (0322) 527915. Open Mon-Sat, 9-5; Thurs, 9-1; other times by appt. Antique & modern silver & jewellery. Sheffield plate, curios, porcelain, clocks etc. English & Continental furniture. Paintings (oils & watercolours).

Biggin Hill STD 0959

Joan E. Allen & Co.
184 Main Rd. Tel 4234. Open Tues-Fri 10-5, Sat and Sun 2-6; other times by appt. High quality English coins and numismatic accessories.

Birchington

Silvesters
2 Station Rd. Tel Thanet (0843) 41524. (Also at Wingham.) Open Mon-Fri 9.30-5, Sat 9-1; other times by appt. Period, Victorian and some Edwardian furniture, Victorian and modern silver, good quality and decorative smalls and glass. Shipping goods. LAPADA

Borough Green STD 0732

Markland Antiques
Western Rd. Tel 4152. Open Tues-Sat 9.30-6; other times by appt. Oak furniture, 17thC glass, copper and other items.

William Tillman Ltd
(William F. Tillman). Crouch Lane, TN15 8LT. Tel 883278. Open Mon-Fri 8-5. Fine English reproduction furniture in mahogany.

Boughton

Philip Faithfull Antiques
202 The Street, ME13 9AL. Tel Canterbury (0277) 750395. Open Mon-Sat 9-5.30; other times by appt. General antiques & furniture. Restoration business attached to shop.

Hansen Antiques
(S.L.Hansen). 119 The Street. Tel Canterbury (0277) 751 421. Open all day. Small furniture, chairs, pewter.

Brasted

Attic (Sevenoaks) Ltd
(J.&R.Brydon). The Village House, TN16 1HU. Tel Westerham (0959) 63507. Open by appt preferably. Books on topography, travel and military subjects and general antiquarian books. ABA

David Barrington
The Antique Shop. Tel Westerham (0959) 62537. Open Mon-Sat 9-6; other times by appt. Antique furniture and china.

The Blacksmiths Shop
(L.Van den Bussche). High St. Tel Westerham (0959) 63114 (priv 62589). Open Mon-Sat 10-6, closed Wed. English and Continental furniture, especially oak, metalware, Delft.

Nigel Coleman Antiques
High St. Tel Westerham (0959) 64042. Open Mon-Sat 9.30-5.30; other times by appt. 18th and 19thC furniture, barometers, tea caddies, porcelain and decorative items. BADA

Keymer Son & Co Ltd
Swaylands Place, The Green, TN16 1JY. Tel Westerham (0959) 64203. Antique furniture and clocks.

Mandeys Antiques
Mandeys, High St. Tel Westerham (0959) 62408. Open Mon-Fri 8.30-5.30; Sun by appt. English and Continental furniture, occasionally good porcelain, glass, bronze and small decorative items.

Southdown House Antique Galleries
(R.H.Thomas). Southdown House, High St, TN16 1JE. Tel Westerham (0959) 63522 (priv 0732 455533). Open Mon-Sat 9.30-5.30; other times by appt. Varied general dealer, specialising in 19th/early 20thC furniture (not oak), oil and watercolour pictures.

Dinah Stoodley
High St, TN16 1JJ. Tel Westerham (0959) 63616. Open Mon-Sat 9.30-5.30. Period oak & country furniture. Pottery.

Swans Antiques
High St. Open Mon-Sat 10-5, closed Wed. Furniture, porcelain, silver, paintings, jewellery and brass.

Tilings Antiques
(Liz Matthews, Penny Fawcett, Helen Loveland). High St. Tel Westerham (0959) 64735. 18th & 19thC porcelain, furniture & decorative items.

The Village Gallery
(Mr & Mrs J. Key). High St, TN16 1JA. Tel Westerham (0959) 62503. Open Mon pm-Sat 5.30; other times by appt. Victorian pine furniture and general antiques.

W.W. Warner (Antiques) Ltd
(Mrs. C.U. Warner). The Green, TN16 1JL. Tel Westerham (0959) 63698. Open Mon-Sat 10-5, Sun by appt. 18th and early 19thC pottery and porcelain, furniture and glass. BADA

Weald Gallery
(S.J. Turley & N.V. Turley). Southdown House, High St. Tel Westerham (0959) 32728. Open Mon-Sat 9.30-5.30. British watercolours 1840-1940, fine collectors watercolours & decorative pictures. Restoration service.

Broadstairs

Broadstairs Antiques
49 Belvedere Rd. Tel Thanet (0843) 65600. Open Mon-Sat 10-5; closed Wed; other times by appt. Small furniture, porcelain,china and bric-a-brac.

Bromley STD 01

Bugatti
173 Widmore Rd, BR1 3AX. Tel 460 9979. Open by prior appointment. Fine antique carriage clocks.

Taurus Antiques Ltd
(Paul Quastel). 145 Masons Hill, BR2 9HY. Tel 464 8746. Open Mon-Sat; closed Wed; other times by appt. 18th and 19thC furniture, porcelain, pottery, copper, brass, clocks, and many miscellaneous items. LAPADA

William Whitfield Antiques
(William Whitfield). 51-53 Beckenham Lane, Shortlands, BR2 0DA. Tel 466 6506 (priv 650 3558). Open Mon-Sat 9.30-5; other times by appt. Furniture, paintings, bronzes, ivories, silver. Trade supplied. LAPADA

Canterbury STD 0227

Coach House Antiques
(James Donoghue). Duck Lane, Northgate, St Radigands. Tel 463117. Open Mon-Sat 10-5; closed Sun; other times by appt. Two floors of constantly changing general antiques, including period furniture and pine.

G.W. Finn & Sons
Brooklands, Fordwich. Tel 710200. Auctioneers. RICS

Five Centuries Antiques
18 Palace St. Tel 463379. General furniture, copper, silver, brass and clocks.

Forge House Antiques
4 & 5 Best Lane. Tel 65654. Open Mon-Fri 11-5, closed Thurs. Furniture, porcelain and pictures.

Hoodeners Antiques & Collectors Market
(A.W.& E.M.Garratt). The Red Cross Centre, Lower Chantry Lane, CT4 6EN. Tel Petham (022770) 437. Open every first and third Saturday in month. Up to 20 dealers with general stock.

Nevill Gallery
(John Nevill, A.M.M.Nevill, D.Smithers,D.Nevill). 43 St Peter's St, CT1 2BG. Tel 65291. (Also at 2A York St, Bath, Avon.) Open daily 10-1, 2-5. Contemporary paintings, watercolours and prints by well known British artists.

Northgate Antiques
(Mrs M.E.Chilver). 37 North Gate, CT1 1BL. Tel 464773. Open Mon-Sat 9.30-5; early closing Thurs; other times by appt. Porcelain, watercolours, furniture. Also porcelain & furniture restorers.

Parker-Williams Antiques
(L.Parker, Mrs E.Williams). 22 Palace St, CT1 2DZ. Tel 468341. Open Mon-Sat 10-6, Thurs 10-1; other times by appt. Fine English 18th & 19thC furniture. Wide selection of porcelain, silver, bronzes, copper & brass. Oil & watercolours. Always in stock good selection of restored longcase, bracket, wall, skeleton, mantel and carriage clocks. LAPADA

Saracen's Lantern Antiques
(W.J.Christophers). 9 The Borough, CT1 2DR. Tel 451968. Open Mon-Fri 10-5; closed Thurs. General antiques and collectors' items.

West Gate Fine Art
(P. Faulkner). 16 St Peter St, CT1 2BQ. Tel 453636 (priv 03043 62093). Open Mon-Thurs. 10-1.30, 2.30-5.30; Fri, Sat 9.30-5.30; other times by appt. 20thC oils & watercolours, etchings, drawings. International limited edition prints, Old Master modern prints, bronze figurines, rapid bespoke framing service. FATG

The Westgate Towers Antique & Collectors Market
Sidney Cooper Centre, St Peters St. Tel 451755 (ext 389). Open every Saturday.

Worsfolds of Canterbury
Auction Galleries, 40 Station Road West. Tel 68984. Auctioneers of antiques.

Charing STD 023 371

Bygones
(Mrs O. Dodgson). Peirce Cottage, High St. Tel 2494. Open Tues-Sat 9.30-5.30; other times by appt. 18th century porcelain, silver, small pieces of furniture. Specialising in 18thC blue and white porcelain and pottery.

Chatham STD 0634

Baldwin & Partners
26 Railway St, ME4 4JT. Tel Medway (0634) 400121. Open Mon-Sat 9-5.30; other times by appt. Auctioneers and valuers with a photographic coverage service devised in conjunction with Kent Police. House auctions arranged in Kent, Surrey & Sussex.

John Chawner
44 Chatham Hill. Tel Medway (0634) 811147. Open Mon-Sat 9.30-12.30, 1.30-4.30; other times by appt. Large selection of clocks and furniture.

Chilham

Chilham Art Galleries
The Square. Tel Canterbury (0227) 730250, 730565. Open by appt. Period furniture, fine paintings and decorative items. Fine art consultants always in attendance.

Peacock Antiques
The Square. Tel Canterbury (0227) 730219. Open Mon-Sat 9-6, Sun 2-5.30; other times by appt. 18th and 19thC furniture, metalware and unusual items.

Chislehurst

Chislehurst Antiques
(Mrs M Crawley & Mrs R Gosnell). 7 Royal Parade. Tel London (01) 467 1530. English furniture 1760-1900. Valuations. LAPADA

Easdens Antiques
4 Royal Parade. Tel 01-467 3352. Open Mon-Sat 9-5.30; early closing Wed. Furniture, glass, pottery and porcelain, clocks, gold and silver and metalware.

Michael Sim
1 Royal Parade, BR7 5PG. Tel 01-467 7040. Open Mon-Sun 9-6; other times by appt. Georgian and Regency furniture, longcase, bracket, mantel and carriage clocks, regulators, barometers, Oriental works of art, paintings.

Cranbrook STD 0580

Bridge House Antiques
(Dr H.Canham, Mrs S.Canham). 2 Bridge Buildings, Stone St, TN17 3HJ. Tel 712573. Open Mon-Sat 9.30-5.30 closed Wed. General antiques.

Cranbrook Antiques
(Derek Harwood). 23 Stone St. Tel 712173.

Deacon & Sandys
Hill Crest Farm Oast, Hartley. Tel 713775. English oak furniture.

Ann Morris Antiques
Cranehurst. Tel 713296. Interesting objets d'art, 18th and early 19thC ceramics.

The Old Bakery Antiques
(Douglas Bryan). St David's Bridge, TN17 3HL. Tel 713103. Open 9-5.30; Wed 9-1; other times by appt. 17th and 18thC oak furniture.

Old Saddlers Antiques
(Sylvia M.Curd). Church Rd, Goudhurst, TN17 1BH. Tel 211458. Open 10-12.30, 2.30-5.30; closed Tues and Sun; other times by appt. Porcelain, paintings and prints, small silver, copper, pewter, horse brasses, antique jewellery, small furniture.

Swan Antiques
(Robert White). Stone St. Tel 712720. Open Mon-Sat 9.30-5.30; closed Wed; other times by appt. Country furniture, decorative items, treen, English pottery, rustic items, pine, English painted furniture. Specialists in applied finishes such as marbleising, graining, stencilling, etc.

Crayford STD 0322

Alberts Auctions & Co
(P.E.Waghorn & A.T.Waghorn). Farm Buildings, Maiden Lane. Tel 528868. General auction held each Wed, commencing 10am. Viewing Tues 4.30-8.30pm.

Watling Antiques
(J.C. Leith). 139 Crayford Rd, DA1 4AS. Tel 523620. Open Mon-Sat 9-5. Bric-a-brac, shipping goods.

Dartford STD 0322

Christie's
(Christopher Proudfoot). The Old Rectory, Fawkham. Tel Longfield (04747) 2854. Agent for the auctioneers and valuers.

Deal STD 0304

Wade Galleries
(S. Harris, P.J.Pierce). Globe House, 191 Beach St. Tel Deal (0304) 362856. (Also in London N1.) Open Mon-Sat 10-4 by appt only. General, decorative and unusual antiques. Leather-bound books.

Dunton Green STD 073 273

Gladstone Antiques
London Rd. Tel 416. Open 9-6; early closing Wed. General, furniture and Victoriana.

East Peckham STD 0622

Desmond and Amanda North
(Desmond and Amanda North). The Orchard, Hale St, TN12 5JB. Tel 871353. Open any reasonable time by appt. Several hundred old & antique oriental tribal & village rugs, carpets, runners, prayer rugs, camel & saddle bags, kelims, embroideries, hangings, cushions. Valuations, cleaning, restoration (reweaving, re-edging, patching). LAPADA

Edenbridge STD 0732

Cheverton's of Edenbridge Ltd
(David Adam). Taylour House, 69 High St, TN8 5AL. Tel 863196. Open Mon-Fri 9-5.30. 18th and 19thC furniture, large selection. LAPADA

Barbara Lane Antiques
(Mrs E.B.Avery). Tudor Cottage, Chiddingstone. Tel Penshurst (0892) 870577. Open Mon-Sat 11-5; Sun pm; other times by appt. General antiques: china, glass, silver, copper, brass etc and furniture.

Farnborough STD 0689

Farnborough (Kent) Antiques
(Janet Dewdney & Celia Jennings). 10 Church Rd, BR6 7DB. Tel 51834. Open Sat; other times by appt. Specialists in wood carvings - medieval and Renaissance, northern European, particularly secular. Also 17th and 18thC oak furniture. BADA

Pembroke Antiques Ltd
(P.Kingston, R.Kingston). 3 Church Rd, BR6 7DB. Tel 62846 (priv 0732 460697). Open Mon-Sat 10-1, 2.30-5.30; other times by appt. Period furniture both mahogany and oak.

Farningham STD 0322

Peter T. Beasley
(Peter T.Beasley & Mrs.R. Beasley). Forge Yard, High St, DA4 0DB. Tel 862453. Open 9-6; closed Tues. English period furniture and general antiques.

Faversham STD 0795

Clockshop Antiques
(Stanley G. Fowler). 187 The Street, Boughton, ME13 9BH. Tel Canterbury (0227) 751258. Open Mon-Fri 10-6; other times by appt. Antique clocks.

Gunpowder House Antiques
(Elizabeth Platt). 78 West St. Tel 534208. Open 9.30-5.30 but best to phone. General antiques, Victoriana, mostly small items. Valuations.

Folkestone STD 0303

Antiques Etcetera (Mostly Etcetera)
(H. & M.F. Brown). 93 High St, Sandgate, CT19 6HL. Tel 39389 (priv 52683). Open every day (incl Sun) 11-1, 2-5.30; other times by appt. 19th and 20thC furniture, books, mirrors, ephemera.

Beaubush House Antiques
(Jane Winikus). 95 Sandgate High St. Tel 39099. Open Mon-Sat 9.30-5.30; other times by appt. Specialising in 18th & 19thC European porcelain and pottery, jewellery, pictures and small period furniture. LAPADA

M.W. Fitch Ltd
(M.W.Fitch). 99 Sandgate High St. Tel 39600 (priv 30839). Open Mon-Sat 10-6. English furniture 1750-1900. LAPADA

Freeman and Lloyd
(Mr K.Freeman and Mr M.R.Lloyd). 44 Sandgate High St, Sandgate, CT20 3AP. Tel 38986. Open Mon-Sat, 9.30-6; other times by appt. 17th to early 19thC English furniture, antique clocks, silver, paintings, bronzes and porcelain. LAPADA

Howard Godfrey Antiques Ltd
(R. Howard Godfrey & Barry Crunden). 56/60 Sandgate High St. Tel 39133. Open Mon-Sat. Furniture, clocks, silver and paintings. NAG, BADA

Jonathan Greenwall Antiques
(Jonathan Greenwall). Sandgate Antiques Centre, 61-63 Sandgate High St. Tel 38987. Open 7 days a week 10-6; other times by appt. Six showrooms with a large varied stock. Specialising in 18th and 19thC furniture, antique jewellery, watercolours, objets d'art, watches, clocks, silver, porcelain, pottery and paintings. LAPADA

Eric Hill
3 Sandgate High St. Tel 39556. Open 10-6, Sun 10-12.30; other times by appt. Furniture, silver and paintings.

Clare Hutchison
(Clare Hutchison). 1 Sandgate High St, Sandgate. Tel Hythe (0303) 64864. Open Mon-Sat 10-6; other times by appt. Period frames, 19thC paintings.

David M. Lancefield (Antiques)
(David M. Lancefield). Sandgate Antiques Centre, 61/63 Sandgate High St. Tel 38987 (priv 0303-81 3565). Open Mon-Sat 10-6; Sun 11-6. 18th & 19thC furniture, silver, ceramics and jewellery.

Alan Lord Antiques
(Alan, Julie & Russell Lord). 71 Tontine St, CT20 1JR. Tel 53674 (priv 59205). Open normal hours; closed Wed 1 pm; Sat 1-30 pm. General antiques.

Marrin & Sons
(Patrick, John and D.I.Marrin). 149 Sandgate Rd. Tel 53016. Open 9.30-1, 2.30-5.30; other times by appt. Antiquarian books, maps and prints. ABA

Noble Antiques
(F.G. Noble). 59A Sandgate High St. Tel 39466. Open daily 10-5.30. Furniture, clocks, silver, jewellery, porcelain, pottery, glass, collectors' items.

Nordens
43 Sandgate High St, CT20 3AH. Tel 38443. Open Mon-Sat 10-12, 2-6; early closing Wed. Furniture, china, glass, metals, bric-a-brac, pictures.

Phillips Fine Art Auctioneers
(Michael Shortall ARICS FSVA). Bayle Place, 11 Bayle Parade, CT20 1SQ. Tel 45555. (Sussex office at 120 Marina, St Leonards-on-Sea. Tel:0424-434854.) Open Mon-Fri 9-5; Sat 9-12. Fine art auctioneers and valuers. Valuations for probate, insurance & tax purposes.

J.T.Rutherford & Son
55 Sandgate High St, CT20 3AH. Tel 39515 (priv 60822). Open 8.30-6; other times by appt. 17th to 19thC oak and mahogany furniture, longcase and bracket clocks of 17th and 18thC. High class restorations.

Sandgate Antiques Centre
(Jonathan Greenwall). 61-63 Sandgate High St, Sandgate, CT20 3AH. Tel 38987. Open Mon-Sat 10-6, Sun 11-6; other times by appt. Seven dealers (including 2 members of LAPADA) with eleven showrooms of period furniture, silver, clocks, jewellery, paintings, porcelain and objets d'art.

Tontine Antiques
(William Patrick). 75-81 Tontine St. Tel 53077 (priv 0303 89 3157). Open Mon-Sat 9-5.30. Antique furniture, book cases, desks, pictures, and decorative items. Trade and export. Cabinet work undertaken.

Gillingham

Coxsmith UK
(C.D.Cox). 96A Shakespeare Rd, ME7 5QJ. Tel Medway (0634) 575983. Open 9-5. Export shippers. LAPADA

Hadlow STD 0732

Langold Antiques Ltd
Oxon Hoath. Tel Plaxtol (0732) 810577. Open Mon-Fri 9-5.30; early closing Sat. 18th and 19thC English furniture.

Hawkhurst STD 058 05

John Atkins Antiques Galleries
Cranbrook Rd. Tel 2033/4. (Also in Brussels.) Specialist in 17th and 18thC Continental oak and walnut furniture and English antique furnishings.

Dymoke House
Highgate. Tel 3265. Open Mon-Fri 9.30-6; other times by appt. General antiques and 18thC drinking glasses.

Hollingbourne STD 062 780

The Old Forge
Pilgrims Way, ME17 1UW. Tel 360. Open daily 10.30-6; closed Thurs, Sun; other times by appt. Early oak furniture, Staffordshire pottery, glass, metalware and pot lids.

Horsmonden

Chilstone Architectural Ornaments
Sprivers Estate. Tel Brenchley (089272) 3553. Open every day. Hand made garden ornaments in traditional styles and architectural items.

Hythe STD 0303

The Front Parlour
(A.G.Douglass). 252A Seabrook Rd, Seabrook. Open daily 10-6. Small antiques, collectors items. Unusual carnival glass.

Hera Fine Art
252 Seabrook Rd, Seabrook. Tel 39046. Period frames and paintings.

Hythe Galleries
(David Arthy, Anita Pratt). 125 High St, CT21 5JJ. Tel 69339. Open Mon-Sat 10-1 2-5.30; Weds 10-1; other times by appt. Antiques: Victorian jewellery, silver, china, brassware, small furniture. Antiquarian prints, Victorian watercolours, picture framing and restoration.

Radio Vintage
(Les Riches). 250 Seabrook Rd, Seabrook, CT21 5RQ. Tel 30693.

Samovar Antiques
(Mrs Clutterbuck). 158 High St. Oriental rugs, clocks etc.

Seabrook Antiques
256 Seabrook Rd, Seabrook. Antique to 1930s furniture.

Traditional Furniture
248 Seabrook Rd, Seabrook. Tel 39931. Antique pine wholesale and retail.

What a Pity Antiques
244 Seabrook Rd, Seabrook. Pottery, porcelain and furniture.

Lamberhurst STD 0892

The China Locker
(Godfrey O.H.R.Wilson). Bedwyn Cottage, The Slade, TN3 8HN. Tel 890555. No formal opening hours, owner res on prem. 18th and 19thC engravings and small stock of 19thC pottery and porcelain.

Leigh

Anthony Woodburn Ltd
Orchard House, High Street. Tel Hildenbrough (0732) 832258. 17th, 18th and early 19thC English clocks, French and English carriage clocks from the 19thC. English barometers and chronometers. BADA, LAPADA

Maidstone STD 0622

Charles International Antiques
(Mr & Mrs C Bremner). 3 Market St. Tel 682882. Victorian, Edwardian & shipping goods. Valuations. LAPADA

Sutton Valence Antiques
Sutton Valence. Tel 843333. (Also at Unit 4, Haslemere Park Wood.) Open Mon-Sat 10-5.30; other times by appt. Furniture, porcelain, copper, brass, silver and pictures. Shipping goods. Valuations. LAPADA

Mrs. M. Turk
4 Clarendon Place, King St, ME14 1BQ. Tel 51284. Open Mon-Sat 9.30-5.30, closed Wed. Victorian, Edwardian furniture, glass, china, copper, brasses, oil lamps, furniture, linen and other items.

Minster STD 0795

Michael Lamb Antiques
White Horse Inn, 2 Church St, CT12 4BX. Tel Thanet (0843) 821666. Open usually Mon-Fri 10-6; other times by appt. General antiques and decorative items.

New Romney STD 0679

East Kent Antiques
(R.Massingham). Cheriton Lodge, West St. Tel 62630. Open 9.30-5. Period furniture, oak and mahogany, marquetry, clocks and watches. LAPADA

Nonington STD 0304

Southdown House Antiques
(D.&V.Mowatt). Southdown House, Easole St, CT15 4HE. Tel 840987. Open Mon-Sat; closed Wed; other times by appt. General antiques and restoration of antique upholstered furniture.

Otford STD 095 92

The Darenth Bookshop
8 High St, TN14 5PQ. Tel 2430. Open Mon-Sat 9-5.30; closed Wed. Antiquarian, secondhand and new books, antique maps and prints, watercolours.

Hofman & Freeman Ltd
8 High St, TN14 5PQ. Tel 2430. Open by appt. 16th to 19thC English literature, literary and historical manuscripts, Kent books. ABA

Penshurst STD 0892

Bridge House Antiques
(R.G.J. Binning & R.M. Binning). TN11 8BQ. Tel 870209. Open Tues-Sat 10-5; other times by appt. Country furniture in oak, elm, yew and mahogany - all period items. Some copper, brass and pewter. LAPADA

Rainham

Rainham Antiques
(Maurice Hamlyn & Arthur Walkers). 295 High St. Tel Medway (0634) 31037. Open Mon-Sat 10-6. Jewellery, furniture, glass, china etc.

Ramsgate

Patricia Antiques
(J.Pratt). 2 Grange Rd, CT11 9NA. Tel Thanet (0843) 591222. Open 10-1; other times by appt. 18th and 19thC furniture. LAPADA

Rochester

Castle Antiques
(Stuart Smith and Andrew Smith). 88 High St. Tel Medway (0634) 409148 (priv 576565). Open Mon-Sat 9-6; other times by appt. General antiques including furniture, jewellery, silver, porcelain, clocks, pictures.

Joyce Hynds Ceramics
Tel 0634-723461. Open by appt. Fine English porcelain and pottery including blue and white transfer printed ware and Masons Ironstone.

Francis Iles
(Mr & Mrs John Iles). Rutland House, La Providence, High St. Tel Medway (0634) 43081, 43082. (Also specialist shops at 62,73,103 High St, Rochester.) Open Mon-Sat 9.30-5.30, Wed 9.30-1. Art gallery. Also stockists of artists materials, tapestry wools, embroidery silks etc at our specialist shops.

Langley Galleries
(Mr K.J.Cook). 153 High St. Tel Medway (0634) 811802. Open Mon-Sat 9-5.30. Art dealers with a stock of 19th and 20thC paintings, watercolours and oils. Framing and restoration.

Northgate Antiques
48 High St. Tel Medway (0634) 408534. Open Mon-Sat 9.15-5.30. Shipping furniture, smalls.

Rolvenden

T.H. Boughton
White Ladies, 26 High St. Tel 058084-36163/67. Open 10-6; early closing Wed. General antiques, furniture, copper, brass, glass, china etc.

Sandwich STD 0304

James Atkinson Gallery
38 King St, CT13 9BL. Tel 617216 (priv 613298). Open daily 10-12.30, 2.15-5; closed Wed; other times by appt. Specialists in 19thC paintings and watercolours. Also fine marine paintings by T.F.R.Thompson. A varied selection of work by contemporary artists. Restoration and framing. Art reference books.

John Hogbin & Son
15 Cattle Market. Tel 611044. Auctioneers.

Noah's Ark Antiques Market
(Mr & Mrs R.M. Maytone Graham). 5 King St. Tel 611144 (priv 613270). Open Mon, Tues, Thurs, Fri, Sat 10-5; other times by appt. General antiques, including pottery, porcelain, furniture, jewellery etc. Staffordshire figures.

James Porter
5 Potter St. Tel 612218. Open daily; early closing Wed. General stock of copper, china, furniture, glass and brass.

Sevenoaks STD 0732

Charles R.P.Allix
(trading as Malcolm Gardner). Bradbourne Farmhouse, Bradbourne Vale Rd, TH13 3DH. Tel 451311. Open by appt only. Founded in 1934. Specialist in rare and antique books about clocks and watches. Also modern titles. Unique catalogue free on request. Horological consultant attending auctions.

The Antiques Centre
(Ruth Harrison). 120 London Rd. Tel 52104. Open Mon-Sat 9-1, 2-5.30; other times by appt. 12 stands offering a selection of 17th to 19thC mahogany, oak, pine and Oriental furniture, paintings, porcelain, dolls, silver, brass and decorative items.

Ibbett Mosely
125 High St, TN13 1UT. Tel 452246. Open Mon-Fri 9-5.30; Sat 9-12.30. Auctioneers of fine art and antiques.

Parsons Welch & Cowell
49 London Rd. Tel 451211. Open Mon-Fri 9-5.30; Sat 9-12.30. Antique auctioneers. SOFAA

The Sevenoaks Furniture Gallery
(Mr & Mrs M.N. Carmichael). 140 High St. Tel 453030. Open Mon-Sat 9.30-5.30. Antique pine furniture and decorative items.

Lydia Wimbleton
(Mrs L.Wimbleton). at The Antique Centre, 120 London Rd. Tel 52104 (priv 0732 832184). 18th-19thC furniture, Victorian dolls, paintings, tapestry, copper, china, boxes. Valuations. Doll restoration. Shipping. LAPADA

Shoreham

The Porcelain Collector
(D.J. Porter). The Old Pony Stable Antiques, High Street, TN14 7TD. Tel Otford (09592) 3416. Open Mon-Sat by appt. Antique and 20thC fine English and Continental porcelain, objects of vertu, furniture, jewellery, metalware and collectors' items. Valuations. Also modern limited edition porcelain subjects. Railwayana. Specialists in the restoration of porcelain.

Sidcup STD 01

Bygones
(Bruce & Mary Woodcock). 2 Sidcup Hill, DA4 6HH. Tel 300 3178. Open 10.30-5; closed Monday; other times by appt. Bygones, books, china, furniture, metalware.

Godfrey New Photographics Ltd
195 Faraday Ave. Tel 300 7637. Photographers.

Sissinghurst

Milkhouse Antiques
(Nigel & Sandra Crockett). The Street. Furniture of all periods and unusual objects.

Sittingbourne STD 0795

Halstow Antiques
(I.P.Harvey, J.L.Harvey). Green Farm House, The Green, Lower Halstow, ME9 7DS. Tel 842016. Open daily 9-7; other times by appt. Oak and country furniture, copper, brass, ironwork, bygones and curiosities.

Steppes Hill Farm Antiques
(W.F.A.Buck). Steppes Hill Farm, Stockbury, ME9 7RB. Tel 842205. Open Mon-Sat 10-6; appt advisable. 18th-20thC English porcelain, silver and furniture with emphasis on fine quality pieces. Specialising in Worcester porcelain, silver wine labels, spoons and collectables. BADA

Smeeth

S.G.Child & Son
The Water Mill Antiques. Tel Aldington (023 372) 234. Res on prem. Furniture and general antiques. Restorers of fine furniture.

Snodland STD 0634

Aaron Antiques
(R.J.Goodman). 90 High St, ME6 5AL. Tel 241748. Open Mon-Fri 9-1, 2-5; closed Wed; other times by appt. General antiques, including antiquarian books, Oriental porcelain, British furniture, clocks and watches.

South Darenth

Kent Sales - Auctioneers
(A.J.Marriott-Smith, Mrs J.A. Marriott-Smith). Kent House, New Rd, DA4 9AR. Tel Farningham (0322) 864919. Open Mon-Fri 10-5; other times by appt. Auctioneers specialising in military collectables, antiques, theatrical costume. Imperial German & 3rd Reich memorabilia.

Sundridge

Old Hall Antiques/Sphinx Gallery
(L.Van Den Bussche). The Old Hall. Tel Westerham (0959) 62589. (Also at The Blacksmiths Shop, High St, Brasted.) Open Mon-Sat 9-6; other times by appt. Early English and Continental furniture, especially oak, metalware, Delft. LAPADA

Sundridge Antiques
9 Church Rd. Tel Westerham (0959) 64104. Open any time, res on premises. Furniture, porcelain, silver plate and objects of interest. LAPADA

Tenterden STD 058 06

John Hogbin & Son
53 High St. Tel 2241. Auctioneer.

Keith Hogg
82 High St, TN30 6JJ. Tel 2050. Bibliography, typography, printing, book design, publishing and book trade. ABA

John McMaster
(Ian F.J.McMaster). 5 Sayers Square, Sayers Lane, TN30 6BW. Tel Hastings (0424) 814671. Open Mon-Sat 9.30-5.30; other times by appt. 18th and 19thC furniture, prints and objets d'art. BADA

Tonbridge STD 0732

C. & A.J.Barmby
68 Judd Rd. Tel 356479. Open to callers by appt; mainly mail order. Accessories for trade and collectors including all sorts of display stands and plate wires, ultra violet lamps, magnifiers, spring balances, silver polishing mitts, security marker pens, precious metal testing kits etc.

Codex Art Ltd
2 Lyons Crescent, TN9 1EX. Tel 358274. 17th to 20thC prints, chalcographic plates, books, curiosa.

Edmund Eldridge Antiques
(E.A.W. Eldridge). 167 High St, TN9 1BX. Tel 361921. Open Mon-Fri 9-5; Sat 10-11; other times by appt. Antique clocks and period furniture. Restoration of antique clocks.

Derek Roberts Antiques
(Mr & Mrs Roberts). 24/25 Shipbourne Rd, TW10 3DN. Tel 358986. Open Mon-Sat 9.30-1, 2.15-5.30; other times by appt. Extensive range of clocks of all types. Illustrated catalogue issued quarterly, available either singly or on annual subscription. Some furniture kept and also Tunbridgeware. BADA

Tudor Cottage Antique Centre
22 Shipbourne Rd. Tel 351719. Open Mon-Sat 9.30-1 2.15-5.30. A good quality antique centre shared by seven dealers.

Tunbridge Wells STD 0892

Annexe Antiques
33 The Pantiles. Seven dealers offering a variety of small antiques.

Annique Antiques
(Mrs Ann Boanas, N.Holland). 13 Nevill St, TN2 5RU. Tel 26776. Open Mon-Sat 10-5; other times by appt. 18th and 19thC furniture, needlework, porcelain and prints.

L.J. Arditti & E.M. Arditti
29A The Pantiles. Tel 43361. Open by appt only. Oriental rugs, Oriental pottery, Oriental art and antiques, needlework and small items.

Henry Baines
(Henry Baines). 14 Church Rd, Southborough, TN4 0RX. Tel 32099. Open Mon-Fri 8.30-4.30; Sat 10-4.30; other times by appt. 17th and 18thC oak and country furniture, especially matched sets of chairs.

The Chair Shop
6 London Rd. Tel 27364. Open Mon-Sat 10-1, 2-5.30; early closing Wed. Antiques, antiquarian books and objets d'art, French and Italian spoken.

Chapel Place Antiques
(Anne Clare). 9 Chapel Pl. Tel 46561 (priv 04353 2624). Open Mon-Sat 10-6. Good quality antiques: furniture, jewellery, silver and plate, good stocks of old cutlery.

Clare Gallery
(Gallery Laraine Ltd). 21 High St. Tel 38717. (Also see Stewart Gallery in Bexhill and Eastbourne.) Open Mon-Sat 8.30-5.30; other times by appt. Original paintings, ceramics, glass and giftware and occasional furniture; framers, restorers and valuers.

Cowden Antiques
(Angela Linstead). 24 Mount Ephraim Rd. Tel 20752. Open 9.30-5; other times by appt. Period mahogany, oak, pine, general antiques, porcelain and other decorative items.

Franca Antiques
(Franca Spurgeon). 2 Castle St. Tel 25779 (priv 29785). Open Tues, Thurs, Fri, Sat 10-5; other times by appt. Maps, prints, furniture, cloisonne, pottery and jewellery . Postal history.

Geering & Colyer
(Auctioneer-M.F.P.Carey). 22/24 High St, TN1 1XA. Tel 25136. Open Mon-Fri 9-5.30. Fine art auctioneers and valuers, and estate agents.

Gore-Langton Gallery
5 Castle St, TN1 1XT. Tel 26373. Open Mon-Sat 10-5, closed Wed. Oil paintings and watercolours.

Hadlow Antiques
(M. & L.L.Adler). No 1 The Pantiles. Tel 29858. Open Mon-Sat 10-5; Wed & Sat 10-1; other times by appt. Clocks, watches, scientific and medical instruments, dolls & automata. Repairs to all of the above.

Hall's Bookshop
(Sabrina Izzard). 20 Chapel Place. Tel 27842. Open Mon-Sat 9.30-5. Antiquarian and secondhand books.

Oliver Hanson
19 Crescent Rd. Tel 23043. Jewellery, silver, objets d'art, metalware, porcelain and small furniture.

Leonard Lassalle
(Leonard Lassalle). 21 The Pantiles, TN2 5TD. Tel 31645. Open Mon-Sat 9-1, 2-5.30; other times by appt. Specialist in 17thC English and Continental furniture, works of art, paintings and statues; Delft, faience, maiolica, & early pottery. Early metalwork; early fabrics, embroidery & tapestry. Oriental rugs. Frescoes.Interior specialists 16th/17thC houses. BADA

Charles A. Lusted Ltd
96A Calverley Rd. Tel 25731. Open Mon-Fri 9-5; Sat 9-5.30. British and foreign campaign medals, gallantry awards and orders of chivalry. British and foreign coins, ephemera and photographs with military connections. Antique jewellery, Georgian to 1920s.

Angela Page Antiques
(Angela Page). Sion House, 15 Mount Sion, TN1 1OD. Tel 22217. Open anytime by chance or prior appt. Res on premises. 17th and 18thC oak and country furniture, treen, textiles & objects of folk art.

Pantiles Antiques
31 The Pantiles. Tel 31291. Open Tues-Sat 10-5, closed Wed. Furniture, brass, bronze, copper, ivory and lamps.

Pennink & Owers Ltd
(Adrian Owers). 23-25 The Pantiles, TN2 5TD. Tel 35051. Open Mon-Sat 9-1, 2-5.30; other times by appt. Large stock of general antiques and good prints.

Strawson Antiques
(Mr & Mrs Meredith Broad). 39-41 The Pantiles, TN7 5TE. Tel 30607. Open Mon-Sat 9.30-5.30. 18th and 19thC furniture - mahogany, walnut, rosewood. Silver plate, Sheffield plate, jewellery. Specialising in Tunbridge ware and glass. Valuations. LAPADA

White Horse Antiques
(Judith and Bryan Dilliway). 7 Chapel Place, TN1 1YQ. Tel 25810. Open Thurs, Fri, Sat 10-6; other times by appt. 18th and 19thC furniture and paintings. Also pottery, porcelain and glass.

G.R.Wimsett
Old House, 30 Hastings Rd, Pembury, TN2 4PD. Tel 2807. Open Mon-Fri 9-6; closed Sat; other times by appt. General antiques - mainly trade.

York Gallery, Tunbridge Wells Ltd
(Mr D.L.Alcock, Mrs J.E.Alcock). No 6 Castle St. Tel 22326 (4 lines). Open Mon-Sat 9-5.30. Contemporary watercolours and oils; Victorian oils, watercolours and prints.

West Malling STD 0732

The Old Clock Shop
(Mrs Sacha Luck). 63 High St. Tel 843246 (priv 840345). Open 9.30-5; other times by appt. English and Continental longcase, bracket, mantel, carriage, wall clocks.

West Wickham

Swansong Antiques
(Gill Coe & Angela Dees). 91 Station Rd. Tel 01-777 5990. Open Mon-Fri 10-5; Sat 9-5. Victoriana and decorative antiques including furniture, porcelain, linen, glass etc.

Westerham STD 0959

Cosmo Antiques (inc Jolie Jewellery)
(Peter and Maggie Cosmos). Westerham Antiques Centre, 18 Market Sq, TN16 1AR. Tel 62080. (Also at 18 High St, Westerham (trade only.) Open Mon-Sat 9.30-5; other times by appt. Furniture, jewellery, plate, silver, china, brass, copper, rugs etc. Suppliers to the trade and public. Shipping goods.

Dunsdale Lodge Antiques
(Mr & Mrs A.C.Scott). Dunsdale Lodge, Brasted Rd, TN16 1LJ. Tel 62160. Open every day, 9-6; other times by appt. Specialist in 18th and 19thC English pottery and porcelain figures, early Staffordshire portrait figures, cottages, Toby jugs and lustre. BADA

Sally Fullers Antiques
(Gerald & Sheila Lee). Fullers Hill. Tel 63412. Open Mon-Sat 10-5, closed Wed; other times by appt. (Next to Post Office.) General antiques, including furniture, copper, brass, porcelain, collectables etc.

Henry Hall
19 Market Sq. Tel 62200. Quality antique clocks, including English table clocks, marquetry long case clocks and English regulators. LAPADA

Anthony J.Hook
(Anthony J.Hook). 3 The Green. Tel 62161 (priv 0892-870552). Open Mon 4-5.30; Tues, Wed, Thurs, Fri 9-5.30. 18th and 19thC furniture.

B.& A.Marks
(A.Marks & B.Marks). London House, 4 Market Square, TN16 1AW. Tel 64479. Open 9-6; other times by appt. 18th & 19thC furniture. Restorer of clocks, barometers and some metalware. LAPADA

D.H.Sargeant
21 The Green, TN16 1AX. Tel 62130. Open Tues-Sat 9-5; closed Wed; other times by appt. Specialist in glass, chandeliers, candelabra, lustres, decanters and general glass, brass chandeliers, candelabra, wall lights and other items.

Twenty-One Antiques
(Mrs M. Richardson). 21 High St. Tel 63055. Open Mon-Sat 10-5.30; other times by appt. Furniture, porcelain,silver, pewter, paintings & collectors' items.

Stewart Ward (Coins) Ltd
(M.S.Millward). 16 High St, TN16 1RF. Tel 63997. Open Mon-Fri 9.30-5. 2,000sq ft of bullion coins, English silver and copper, hammered coins, foreign coins, medals and medallions. Shipping goods.

Westerham Galleries
(R.R.Wood). The Green (on A25). Tel 63359. Open every day including Sun; Fri by appt. 18th-19thC original paintings. (Large stock). Also small 19thC furniture.

Directory Entries are Free and ADDITIONS OR CORRECTIONS will be welcomed by *THE EDITOR, British Art and Antiques Directory, National Magazine House, 72 Broadwick Street, London W1V 2BP*

Wingham

Lloyd's Bookshop
(Mrs Jane Morrison). 27 High St, CT3 1AW. Tel Canterbury (0227) 720774. Open daily 9.30-5; closed Sun; other times by appt. General antiquarian and secondhand books, prints, watercolours, ephemera, maps, music. ABA

Silvesters Antiques
(Mrs J.E.Wallis, Mr G.M.A.Wallis, Mr S.N.Hartley). 33 High St. Tel Canterbury (0227) 720278. (Also in Birchington.) Open Mon-Sat 9.45-5. Period, Victorian and some Edwardian furniture, Victorian and modern silver, good quality and decorative smalls, paintings and glass. LAPADA

Lancashire

Accrington STD 0254

J.Bridgeman Coins
(J.Bridgeman). The Coin Shop, 129A Blackburn Rd. Tel 384757 (priv 382049). Open Mon-Sat 10-5.30; closed Wed; other times by appt. Coins, medals etc. Antique and modern jewellery. Also old post cards and cigarette cards.

Bickerstaffe

E.W. Webster Antiques
(K.M. Webster). Wash Farm, Rainford Rd. Tel Skelmersdale (0695) 24322. Open by appt anytime. Oak, walnut & country furniture 1650-1840 only. Some mahogany, metalware, samplers and decorative objects. No shipping goods or bric-a-brac. BADA

Blackburn STD 0254

The Abbey Antique Shop
(A.D. & E. Austin). 43-45 King St, Whalley, BB6 9SP. Tel Whalley (0254) 3139. Open Mon-Fri 9-5; Sat 9-12; other times by appt. General and export goods. 18th and 19thC furniture. Trade and overseas buyers welcome.

T.& D.Brindle Antiques
(T.H. Brindle, D.Brindle, P.Brindle, I.Brindle). 4-8 Lynwood Rd, BB2 6HP. Tel 670714; 53628. Open Mon-Fri 9-5; other times by appt. English and Continental furniture, works of art and porcelain, Oriental ivories, vases etc. LAPADA

Lock Antiques
(S. Mitchell). 76 Bolton Rd. Tel 664663. (Also Mitchells Antique Centre.) Open Mon-Fri, 10-5. Varied stock general antiques.

Blackpool STD 0253

Neville Bates Antiques and Fine Art Gallery
208 Dickson Rd, FY1 2JS. Tel 53552. Open Mon-Sat 10-5.30, Wed 10-1; other times by appt. Furniture and 18th and 19thC oil paintings and watercolours. Trade and shipping goods.

Capricorn Collections
(Tom Walsh). 48 St Anne's Rd, South Shore, FY4 2AS. Tel 49766. Open Sat 10-6; other times by appt. Vintage wind-up horn gramophones, phonographs, polyphons, music boxes. Vintage wireless components. Oil lamps, 78 records, discs, cylinders. Pottery and other general antiques. Refurbishing, repairs. World War II RAF clothing, equipment, model aircraft.

The Golden Age
7-9 Metropole Buildings, FY1 1RF. Tel 22969. Antique and reproduction furniture, light fittings, paintings, French clock sets. Interior decoration.

Hobsons Choice
(J.D.Hobson & E.Hobson). 85 Bispham Rd. Tel 56979. Open Thurs-Sun; other times by appt. Model trains and antiques.

Tom Owen Antiques
18 Rawcliffe St. Tel 33008. Open Mon-Sat 10.30-5.30. General small antiques, shipping goods and metalware.

R. & L. Coins (Coin & Bullion Investments Ltd)
(A.Holloway). 521 Lytham Rd, FY4 1RJ. Tel 43081. Open Mon-Fri 9-5; other times by appt. Gold bullion, ancient and medieval coins, English silver and bronze coins and tokens, both hammered and milled. BNTA

Bolton

See Greater Manchester

Brierfield

J.H. Blakey & Sons Ltd
Church St, BB9 5AD. Tel Nelson (0282) 63593/602493. (Also Burnley Rd, Emporium.) Open Mon-Fri 8-12, 1.30-5, Sat 8-12. Furniture, pictures, organs and pianos, clocks, brass, copper, pewter, locks and bygones. Specialised restoration services.

Burnley STD 0282

Mrs E.Falik
Plantation Cottage, Greenhead Lane, Fence, BB12 9DX. Tel 65172. Open by appointment only. Early English and Continental porcelain and pottery. BADA, LAPADA

Ralph A.Sutcliffe Antiques
(Ralph & Barbara Sutcliffe). Harle Syke Mill, Harle Syke. Tel 31412. Open Mon-Fri 8-5; other times by appt. Antiques and Victoriana to the shipping trade. Packers and shippers. Trade only. LAPADA

Burscough STD 0704

West Lancs Antique Exports
(W. & R. Griffiths). Black Horse Farm, 123 Liverpool Road South. Tel 894634. 18000 sq ft warehouse, stocked with oak, mahogany & pine for USA, Australia & Continental market. Full shipping, documentation and courier service available. LAPADA

Bury

See Greater Manchester

Carnforth STD 0524

M.& I. Finch
(Mark and Isobel Finch). 15 Yealand Rd, Yealand Conyers. Tel 732212. Open mostly 9-6; other times by appt. Varied stock of antique and trade goods. Decorative items.

Wm Goodfellow (Antiques)
(Wm Goodfellow). The Green, Over Kellet, LA6 1BU. Tel 733030. Open daily 10.30-6; closed Wed; other times by appt. Small period furniture, pre-1870 pottery and porcelain, glass, silverware, collector's and decorative items.

Clitheroe STD 0200

Castle Antiques
(J. & B. Tomkinson). 15 Moor Lane. Tel 26568 (priv 0254 35820). Open Tues, Thurs, Fri, Sat 10-4.30; other times by appt. Clocks, furniture, leaded coloured glass windows, shipping goods in large warehouse.

Harrop Fold Clocks
(F.Robinson). Harrop Fold, Bolton by Bowland, BB7 4PJ. Tel Bolton by Bowland (02007) 665. Open any time by appointment. Turn left 3 miles north of Grindleton, on Clitheroe-Slaidburn road. British clocks, longcase, bracket, wall, 17th-19thC; barometers, stick, wheel, 17th-19thC. Sales, restorations, repairs.

Sotheby's
(Representative: Susan Yorke). Hall Foot, Worston, BB7 1QA. Tel 41520. Auctioneers & valuers.

Darwen STD 0254

K.C. Antiques
538 Bolton Rd. Tel 772252. Furniture and shipping goods.

Barronfield Gallery

47 FRIARGATE, PRESTON, PR1 2AT
Telephone: (0772) 563465

Fine 19th and 20th Century

ENGLISH WATERCOLOURS

Also a Collection of Royal Worcester Porcelain by:
Stinton, Townsend, Shuck, Powell, Freeman, Austin, Sebright and others.

OPEN MONDAY – SATURDAY
10.00 a.m. – 5.00 p.m.
THURSDAY AND SUNDAY BY APPOINTMENT

The drop-leaf table illustrated is of Walnut with Vase shaped standard with super patine. Italian (Tuscan) Circa. 1600.

H. & M. J. Burke

Worsley, Lancashire
Tel: 061–794–2093

Member of the Antiquity Dealers Association

Leycester Map Galleries Limited

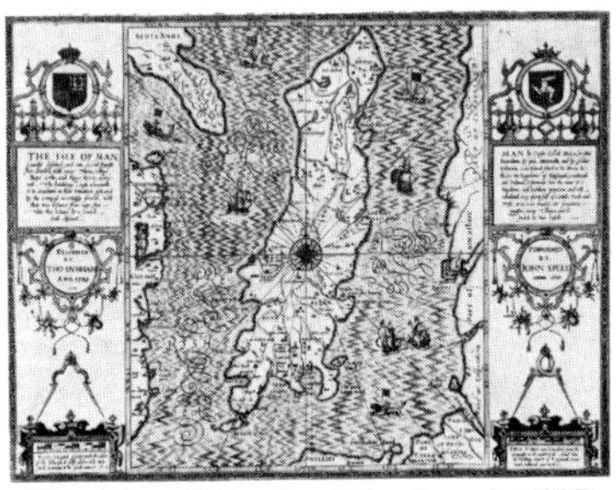

The Isle of Man by John Speed, 1627

Authentic Antique Maps: XVIth – XIXth Century

WELL HOUSE, ARNESBY, LEICESTER LE8 3WJ

Telephone: Peatling Magna (053 758) 462

MAIL-A-MAP
service for collectors and the trade.

Timothy Kendrew Antiques

A superb quality Flight Barr & Barr Worcester vase painted with a panel of shells in the manner of Baxter, on a rich blue and gold ground – $7\frac{1}{8}$ ins high.

Tel:
0780-56072
08012-2325 A/H

18th and early 19th century porcelain, silver, furniture and objets d'art

Valuations Undertaken

Mon-Sat
9.30-5.30

5-8 GEORGE HOTEL MEWS
STAMFORD, LINCOLNSHIRE

Telephone Leicester 606682

Richard Green

J. Green & Son
Antiques

1 Coppice Lane,
Queniborough, Leicester.

Peter Young Antiques
(Peter Young). Earcroft School, Blackburn Rd. Tel 73521 (priv 04577-70467). (See also Peter Young in Oldham, Gtr.Manchester.) Open Mon-Fri 9-5.30; other times by appt. Furniture, general antiques, shipping goods.

Didsbury
See Greater Manchester

Haslingden
Clifton House Antiques
198 Blackburn Rd, Rossendale. Tel Rossendale (0706) 214895. Open Mon-Fri 9-6; other times by appt. Antiques and curios.

Kirkby Lonsdale
See Cumbria

Lancaster STD 0524
GW Antiques
47 North Rd. Tel 32050. Large stock of antique pine furniture. Specialists in early pine and larger pieces.

Longton STD 0772
Longton Hall Antiques
(Mrs Betty Easterby). Longton Hall, Liverpool Rd, PR4 7HA. Tel 613324. Open Mon-Fri 9.30-5.30. Georgian, Victorian and Edwardian furniture, longcase clocks. Trade only. LAPADA

Manchester
See Greater Manchester

Oldham
See Greater Manchester

Ormskirk STD 0695
Oasis Fine Arts Ltd
(Mrs S. Forbes). Tel 421080. Open by appt only. 18th and 19thC furniture and decorative items. LAPADA

Preston STD 0772
Ages Ago Antiques
(A.W.Shalloe). 47-49 New Hall Lane. Tel 798606. Furniture, general. LAPADA

Donald Allison Antiques
(Donald Allison). 115-119 New Hall Lane. Tel 701916 (priv 615946). Open Mon-Sat 9-6; other times by appt. Furniture, paintings, sculpture, ceramics and decorative works of art from all periods. Large stock. LAPADA

The Antique Shop
(W. & E.M. Parker). Garstang Rd, PR3 5DQ. Tel 862204. Open weekdays; other times by appt. General antiques.

Barronfield Gallery
(J.R. Tomlinson). 47 Friargate, PR1 2AT. Tel 563465. Open Mon-Sat 10-5; Thurs, Sun & other times by appt. Victorian and Edwardian watercolours.

Jack Blackburn
105 New Hall Lane. Tel 791117. Open Mon-Fri; other times by appt. General antiques and shipping goods.

Halewood & Sons
37 Friargate, PR1 2AT. Tel 52603. Large stock of antiquarian books. Specialists on New Zealand, Australia, Canada, South Africa and South America. Catalogues. ABA

North Western Antique Centre
New Preston Mill (Horrockses Yard), New Hall Lane, PR1 5UH. Tel 794498. Open Mon-Fri 8.30-5.30. Trade only. Large stock of period furniture and shipping goods, pottery, porcelain etc.

Norwin Photographics
65 Fishergate, PR1 8BJ. Tel 54214. Industrial and commercial photographers.

Tom Owen (Antiques)
(Tom Owen). 111 Newhall Lane. Tel 792950. Open Mon-Fri 9.30-5.30; other times by appt. Mixed stock of general antiques and shipping goods.

Ralph A.Sutcliffe Antiques
(Ralph & Barbara Sutcliffe). 274-278 New Hall Lane. Tel 700216. (Also in Preston.) Open Mon-Sat 9-5. Antiques and Victoriana. LAPADA

Swag
(Marcella Fletcher). 24-26 Leyland Rd, Penwortham, PR1 9XS. Tel 744970. Open Mon-Fri 9.30-6; other times by appt. Dolls - 1830 to 1939, furniture, pottery and porcelain, watercolours and clocks.

Frederick Treasure Ltd
(J.F. Treasure). The Treasure House, 274 New Hall Lane, PR1 4SU. Tel 700216. Open Mon-Fri 9.30-5.30; Sat 10-4. 18th and 19thC furniture and general antiques. LAPADA

Rochdale
See Greater Manchester

Salford
See Greater Manchester

St Anne's STD 0253
Curios
(Mrs C.A. Yates). 12 St Albans Rd, FY8 1UB. Tel 724187. Open Mon-Sat 10-5.30; closed Wed. General antiques, decorative items including silver, brass & copper, treen etc.

Georgian House
37 Wood St. Tel 23029. Oil paintings, porcelain and general antiques.

Howison-Haworth
14-14a Alexandria Drive, Lytham. Tel 720956. Open Mon-Sun 9-6; other times by appt. Oil paintings, watercolours, furniture, guns, carpets, general antiques.

Spinning Wheel Antiques
(Maj and Mrs C.M.Yates). 12 St Albans Rd. Tel 724187. (Also 16 St Davids Rd.) Open Mon-Sat 10-5.30; closed Wed; other times by appt. General antiques including ivories, guns and weapons, maps, prints, Oriental and English porcelain and small furniture.

Tunstall STD 046 834
Godfrey M.Simpson (Antiques)
(Godfrey M.Simpson). Thurland Castle. Tel 360, 371. Open Mon-Fri 9-5; other times by appt. Antiques, pine and decorative goods.

Whalley STD 025 482
Davies Antiques
(Gloria and Edmund Davies). 32 King St, BB6 9SL. Tel 3764. Open Mon-Sat 10-5; other times by appt. Furniture, longcase clocks, jewellery.

Wigan
See Greater Manchester

Worsley
See Greater Manchester

Leicestershire

Anstey
Antiques in Charnwood
(V.N.Bonfield FSVA, Mrs B. Whadcock). 68 Bradgate Rd. Tel 350708. English furniture 1700-1910, silver. LAPADA

Arnesby
Leycester Map Galleries Ltd
Well House, Arnesby. Tel Peatling Magna (053758) 462. Open by appt. Mail service for collectors and the trade. Antique maps and atlases.

Ashby de la Zouch STD 0530
Ashby Antiques
(William & Marie Allen). 51 Market St. Tel 415004. Open Mon-Sat 10-5; closed Wed; other times by appt. Furniture, porcelain, glass, silver, pewter, jewellery, metalware and shipping goods.

Ivanhoe Antiques
(John and Ann Mansfield). 53 Market St. Tel 415424. Open 10-5; closed Wed; other times by appt. 18th and 19thC furniture, porcelain, oil paintings, some silver, copper and brass. LAPADA

Ropers Hill Antiques
(S.&R.Southworth). Ropers Hill Farm, Staunton Harold. Tel 413919. Open Mon-Fri 9-5; other times by appt. Shipping goods, silver, plate and metalware.

Blaby
Blaby Gallery
5 Leicester Rd. Tel Leicester (0533) 772877. Open Mon-Sat 9.30-6; other times by appt. Jewellery, small furniture, carvings, porcelain, ivory etc.

Coalville STD 0530
Charnwood Antiques
(Miss P.Moorhouse, Miss R.A.Ward). Tel 38530. Open by appointment only. 18thC English porcelain, including Worcester, Caughley, Liverpool, Bow, Chelsea, Lowestoft. All stock undamaged and unrestored. Georgian and Victorian watercolours and Baxter prints.

Keystone Antiques
(Mrs I. & Miss H. McPherson FGA). 9 Ashby Rd, LE6 2LF. Tel 35966. Open Mon-Sat 10-5; closed Wed. Georgian and Victorian silver and jewellery. Valuations. LAPADA

Hinckley STD 0455
Castle Galleries
(J.L.Wilmot). 122 Castle St. Tel 39209. Open Mon-Sat 9-5.30; closed Thurs; other times by appt. Furniture restorers.

Kegworth STD 050 97
Kegworth Antiques
2 Market Place, DE7 2EE. Tel 2852. Open Mon-Sat 10-5. Varied stock antiques.

Kibworth Beauchamp
STD 053 753

The Kibworth Antiques Centre
(Reginald Wheatley). 5 Weir Rd, LE8 0LR. Tel 2761. Open Tues-Sat 10-6, Sun 2-6; other times by appt. Antique centre with wide range of furniture, paintings, prints, silver,porcelain and jewellery.

Leicester STD 0533

The Antiques Complex
St Nicholas Place. Tel 26596. Open Mon-Sat 9.30-5.30, Sun 2-5. Antique centre with professional dealers in 16000 sq ft area stocking 17th, 18th and 19thC furniture, clocks and porcelain.

Corner Cottage Antiques
(J.M. Roberts, Mrs G. Roberts). 64 Narborough Rd. Tel 548488. Open Mon-Sat 10-5; other times by appt. Georgian & Victorian furniture, general antiques & shipping goods. Pottery, porcelain, silver etc.

County Auctions
(Paul S. Ross, Victor S. Berridge). Pilot House, King Street, LE1 6RN. Tel 556199 (priv 0509 413590). (Salerooms at Duke St, Leicester.) Open Mon-Fri 9-5.30. Auctioneers - antique & shipping, industrial & commercial. Sales held every 2 or 3 weeks on Tuesdays.

John Desmond Antiques
Haddon House, 1 Dunbar Rd, LE4 7JL. Tel 769126. Open by appt only. 18thC Worcester, oil paintings, 19thC furniture (small items).

Graeme & Jennifer Gittings
White House, 1 Oakfield Ave, Birstall. Tel 674760.

Richard Green
1 Coppice Lane, Queniborough, LE7 8DR. Tel 606682. Open : Res on premises, but appt preferable. 18thC furniture.

Hammond Smith
Beaumont House, 24 Knighton Drive, LE2 3HB. Tel 709020. British watercolours, etchings and art reference books.

Heathcote Ball & Co
(J.E.H.Ball FRICS). Castle Auction Rooms, 78 St Nicholas Circle, LE1 5NW. Tel 536789. Open Mon-Fri 9-5.30. Fine art auctioneers and valuers.

Leicester Antique Centre Ltd
16-26 Oxford St. Tel 553006. Open Mon-Sat 10-5.30. 120 stalls selling all kinds of antiques. Shipping goods.

Lettys Antiques Ltd
(I. Dubberley & M.M. Dubberley). 6 Rutland St, LE1 1RA. Tel 26435. Open Mon-Sat 9.15-5; closed Thurs. Gold, silver, platinum jewellery, silverware, plated ware, brass and copper.

Walter Moores & Son
89 Wellington St, LE1 6HJ. Tel 551402 (priv 704992). Open 8.30-6.30. Good stock of furnishing antiques of most periods.

Murray's Ltd
23 Loseby Lane, LE1 5DR. Tel 20360. Antiquarian and new booksellers. ABA

Robert Neville Antiques
The Old Dairy, Western Boulevard. Shipping goods, pine and smalls.

Percival Restoration
53A Wellington St. Tel 545061. Specialising in old and reproduction pine.

E. Smith (Leicester) Ltd
(K.W. Sansom). The Antique Complex, 9 St. Nicholas Place, LE1 5LB. Tel 533343. Open Mon-Sat 9.30-5.30; other times by appt. 16000 sq ft of antiques, Victorian & Edwardian furniture, collectables & smalls, Australian, USA & European markets catered for. Container facility. LAPADA

Warner Sheppard & Wade
16-18 Halford St, LE1 1JB. Tel 21613. Fine art auctioneers.

White House Antiques
1 Oakfield Ave, Birstall. Tel 674760. English porcelain.

Withers of Leicester
(Simon Frings). 142A London Rd, LE2 1EB. Tel 544836 (priv 708968). Open Mon-Sat 9-5.30; early closing Thurs, Sat; other times by appt. 17th to 19thC furniture, occasionally antique china, silver and oil paintings.

Loughborough STD 0509

Copperfield Antiques
(Betty Gardner). 221A Derby Rd, LE11 0HJ. Tel 232026 (priv 239281). Open Tues-Fri 10-5; Sat 10-1; other times by appt. Small furniture, fine porcelain, pottery, brass, copper, pewter, glass (late 18th-late 19thC).

Sylvia Hawkins Antiques
Willoughby-on-the-Wolds. Small general antiques, silver, pictures & glass.

Charles Lowe & Sons Ltd
(R.C.Lowe, J.M. Lowe). 37-40 Church Gate. Tel 217876. Open Mon-Fri. Large stocks of early walnut, oak and mahogany, 1600-1900. Sixteen showrooms of furniture & furnishings of all periods. Oak dressers, gatelegs, refectories and Windsors, and sets of chairs. Also upholstery of all periods, interior design.

Stable Antiques
(Mrs Peter Wilkinson). 14 Loughborough Rd, Hoton, LE12 5SF. Tel Wymeswold (0509) 880208. Open Mon-Fri 9-6, Sat 9-1; other times by appt. Georgian to Edwardian furniture, boxes, claret jugs and decanters. Specialists in 18th, 19th and 20thC field sports prints, Baxter and Le Blond prints.

Lyddington

Lapwing Antiques
(Derek L.Jones Ltd). Lapwing House, 115 Main St, LE15 9LS. Tel Uppingham (057282) 2852. (Also Shop 13, Woburn Abbey, Bedfordshire.) Open Mon-Sat 10-5.30; other times by appt. Period furniture, also porcelain and pottery.

Market Harborough
STD 0858

Brown Jack Bookshop
(R.L.Leete). 78 Main St, Lubenham. Tel 65787. (Also at Leicestershire Sporting Gallery, Lubenham.) Open Mon-Sat 10.30-5.30; other times by appt. Books on English Civil War bought and sold, Cromwell, Charles I. Ephemera. Also books on cricket, sports, jockeys and legal subjects, Vanity Fair cartoons.

Leicestershire Sporting Gallery
(R.L.Leete). The Old Granary, Lubenham, LE16 9DG. Tel 65787. (Also Brown Jack Bookshop, Market Harborough.) Open Mon-Sat 10.30-5.30; other times by appt. 5 showrooms. Furniture, militaria, model railway engines, books, engravings, oil paintings, maps and views. Specialising in antiquarian books, Vanity Fair cartoons.

St Mary's Mart
(Mr Bowley). 3 St Mary's Road, LE16 7LN. Tel 32251. Wide range of antiques and collectables.

Oakham STD 0572

Rutland Antiques and Coins
(W.R.Lynn). 27 Mill St. Tel 3364 (priv 2408). Open Mon-Fri 9-12, 1-5; Sat 9-12; other times by appt. Good stock, mainly furniture and clocks pre-1820.

David Smith Antiques
(G.D.M.Smith and R.N.C.Bingley). The Old Cottage, Manton. Tel Manton (057 285) 244 (priv 473 or 314). Open Mon-Sat 9-1, 2-5; other times by appt. 18th and 19thC antiques, mostly furniture. Restorations and valuations also undertaken.

Walker, Walton & Hanson
4 Market Place. Tel 2681. Auctioneers.

Quorn STD 0509

David E. Burrows
4 High St. Tel 412191. (Also warehouse at 29 Loughborough Rd.) Oak, mahogany and walnut furniture of 17th-19thC, clocks, paintings, and porcelain. LAPADA

Mill on the Soar Antiques Ltd
(J.York). 1-3 High St, LE12 8DS. Tel 414218. Open Mon-Sat; other times by appt. 17th and 18thC furniture and general antiques. Specialising in pre-1830 period furniture.

Ratcliffe-on-the-Wreake

Pavilion Antiques
(Mrs M. Collins). Long Gable. Tel 0664-74209. Furniture. LAPADA

Redmile

Evelyn Buckle
The Villa, Main St, NG13 0GA. Tel Bottesford (0949) 42057. Open by appt please. 18th and 19thC furniture and miscellaneous items.

Redmile Studio
NG13 0GA. Mainly painted furniture & restorations.

Rothley

John A.Brooks
2 Knights Crescent. Tel Leicester (0533) 302625. Open by appt only. Antique glass.

Shepshed STD 0509

G.K. Hadfield
(G.K. & J.V. Hadfield). Blackbrook Hill House, Tickow Lane, LE12 9EY. Tel 503014. Open Mon-Sat 9-5; other times by appt. Specialists in fine antique clocks, primarily restored but some unrestored. Main stock includes longcase, English dial and bracket clocks. Also horological books - more than 400 titles. Large selection of materials for the restoration of antique clocks.

Thurnby

J.A. Morrison Ltd
43 Grange Lane, LE7 9PH. Tel Leicester (0533) 413750. Open daily 9-6. Militaria, weapons and associated items specialising in Scottish dress & weapons. GTA

Wymeswold STD 0509

N.Bryan-Peach Antiques
28 Far St. Tel 880425. Clocks, barometers and watches.

Lincolnshire

Boston STD 0205

James Eley & Son
(D.A.Bryant, C.B.Mather). 1 Main Ridge West, PE21 6QQ. Tel 61687. Open Mon-Fri 9-5.30, Sat 9-12; other times by appt. Auctioneers. RICS

Geoff Parker Antiques Ltd
(Geoff Parker). Haltoft End,Freiston, PE22 0PG. Tel 760444. Open Mon-Sat 9-5. Large stock - 9000 sq ft furniture from 1700-1920; also large stock of smalls. Specialising in Victorian furniture, clocks and smalls. LAPADA

Bourne STD 0778

Bourne Antiques
The Old Mill, North Rd. Tel 425323 (priv 423781). Period and Victorian furniture and general antiques.

Lyall & Co
(G.H.Clay; N.P. Webster; C.G.Richardson; T.R.R.Walmsey). Auction Rooms, Spalding Rd, PE10 9LE. Tel 422431(4 lines);422686. Open Mon-Fri 9-1 2-5; Sat 9-12. Auctioneers.

Colsterworth

Clive Underwood Antiques
46 High St. Tel Grantham (0476) 860689. Open Mon-Sat 9.30-5.30. 17th and 18thC furniture, treen, copper and brass.

Coningsby STD 0526

Laurence Shaw Antique Centre
Sandy Bank Road, New York. Tel 42578. (Also at Spilsby Rd, Horncastle, Lincs.) Open Mon-Sat 9-5. 17th to 20thC furniture including stripped pine, decorative objects and rustic bygones.

Donington-on-Bain

Lindum Antiques
(D.G. & M. Wilby). Main Rd. Tel Stenigot (050 784) 639. Open by appt only. Pottery, porcelain and small furniture.

Gosberton

Mary King
Victoria House, 2 Wargate Way. Tel Spalding (0775) 840317. Open by appt. Furniture, oil paintings, general antiques.

Grantham STD 0476

The Antique Shop
(Mr & Mrs Cunningham). Off West Gate.

Antiques Shop
(Anthony Barlow). 10 North Parade. Tel 68748. Open Tues-Sat; other times by appt. Antique furniture, clocks and general stock.

William H.Brown
Westgate Hall, Westgate, NG31 6LT. Tel 68861. Open Mon-Fri 9-5.30. Auctioneers. SOFAA

J.Dobie (Antiques) Ltd
(James Dobie). 44 North Parade. Tel 78810. Open Tues, Wed, Fri 8.30-6 Sun 1-5; other times by appt. 18th & 19thC furniture, porcelain, paintings, decorative items.

Escritt & Barrell
Elmer House, NG31 6RD. Tel 65371. (Also in Sleaford, Lincs. Tel:0529-302271.) Auctioneers holding periodic sales of antique and general furniture, china, silver, paintings etc.

Anthony W.Laywood
(A.W.Laywood). Knipton, NG32 1RF. Tel 870224. Open normal shop hours; other times by appt. Antiquarian books. 4,000 books before 1850, also bibliography and reference. Secondhand books. ABA

J. & J. Palmer Ltd
42-44 Swinegate. Tel 70093. Open Tues, Thurs, Fri, Sat 10-6; Wed 10-1. Fine collection of country pine furniture and bric-a-brac.

Horncastle STD 065 82

Lincolnshire Antique Centre
Bridge Street, LN9 5HZ. Open Mon-Sat 9-5. 7000 sq ft of showrooms stocking furniture and general antiques.

Laurence Shaw Antiques
(L.D. & K.P.Shaw). Spilsby Rd, LN9 5DQ. Tel 7638 (priv 065 888 600). (Also at Sandy Bank Rd, New York, Lincs.) Open Mon-Sat 8.30-5; other times by appt. Furniture, china, glass, clocks and decorative objects from the 17th to 19thC. Exporters, importers, container packing facilities.

Kirton

Kirton Antiques
(Alan R.Marshall). 3 High St, PE21 DR. Tel Boston (0205) 722595 (priv 722134). Open 8.15-6, 6 days a week; other times by appt. Decorative arts, Victorian & Edwardian furniture. LAPADA

Lincoln STD 0522

Castle Gallery
(Alexander Buchanan). 61 Steep Hill, LN2 1LR. Fine paintings, watercolours and longcase clocks.

Anthony Cotton
(A.Cotton). 26-27 Steep Hill. Tel 25838 (priv 0673 60562). Open Mon-Sat; other times by appt. 17th, 18th and 19thC furniture, longcase clocks and decorative items.

Designs on Pine
(Mr R.G. & Mrs J.Chesterton-North). 27 The Strait. Tel Market Rasen (0673) 29252 (warehouse 858789). (Also Tealby Pine at Goltho Hall, Wragby, Lincs.) Open 10-5; closed Mon and Wed. Original pine furniture.

Eastgate Antique Centre
(Nan Marris). Black Horse Chambers, 6 Eastgate. Tel 44404 (priv 754327). Open Mon-Sat 9.30-5; other times by appt. 12 dealers selling good quality period furniture, oil and watercolour paintings, silver, jewellery, porcelain, brass, copper, instruments, clocks & quality collectors items.

Fockerby Hall Antiques
(John C.Wraith). 6 Eastgate, LN2 1QA. Tel 41470. Open Mon-Fri 10-1, 2-5; also Sat; other times by appt. General decorative antiques, including jewellery, silver, furniture, brass, porcelain and watercolours.

David J. Hansord
(David Hansord & Anne Hansord). 32 Steep Hill. Tel 3004. Open Mon-Sat 10-1, 2.15-5. English & Continental furniture, pre-1850, objects, clocks, barometers & scientific instruments. BADA

Harlequin Gallery
22 Steep Hill. Tel Wragby (06734) 294. Antiquarian books, old prints and ethnography.

Lincoln Fine Art
(Mrs D Glen-Doepel). 33 The Strait. Tel 33029. Open Mon-Sat 10.30-5; other times by appt. Fine oil paintings and watercolours, including portrait miniatures and drawings.

Nan Marris
1 Eastgate. 17th-19thC furniture.

Thos Mawer & Son
63 Monks Rd. Tel 24984. Open Mon-Fri 9-1, 2-5; other times by appt. Auction rooms, holding sales every fortnight.

Pinfold Antiques
(J. Ballinger & J.D. Harman). 28 Steep Hill. Tel 44716 (priv 0526 832057). (Also at 3 Pinfold Lane, Ruskington, Lincs. Tel 0526-832200.) Open Mon-Sat 10-5; other times by appt. English longcase, bracket & lantern clocks. Continental mantel clocks, pre-1840 English & Continental furniture.Also weapons, scientific instruments, prints and maps. LAPADA

C. & A.E. Sinclair
(Charles Sinclair). No 10 The Avenue. Business by mail order only. All types of stands for the display of antiques etc. Wire coated or acrylic plastic.

The Strait Antiques
5 The Strait. Tel 23130. Open Mon 2-4.15, Tues, Thurs & Fri 10-4.15, Sat 10-5. English pottery and porcelain and all antiques.

Market Deeping STD 0778

Church Street Antiques
(Mrs Margaret Roth). 68 Church St, PE6 8AA. Tel 342660. Open Wed-Sat 10-5; other times by appt. Victorian jewellery, silver, collectors items, small furniture and porcelain. Services: picture framing, custom-made lampshades.

Market Rasen STD 0673

Country Life Antiques
Queen Street Passage.

Harwood Tate
(J. Harwood Tate). Church Mill, Caister Rd, LN8 3HX. Tel 843579. Open Mon-Fri 9.30-5.30; other times by appt. Large showrooms displaying English furniture, clocks, pictures, bronzes and other ornamental items.

Navenby

The Pedlar
High St. Tel Lincoln (0522) 810410. Open Wed-Fri 10-1, 2-4.30, Sat & Sun 2-4.30. 18th and 19thC furniture and porcelain, watercolours and prints, copper and brass.

Osbournby

Audley House Antiques
(Miss S.Wood). North St.
Tel Culverthorpe (05295) 251.
Open Mon-Sat 9-5.30; Sun 11-2; other times by appt. 18th to 20thC furniture, clocks, pictures, silver, plate, glassware, ornamental items, upholstered Victorian furniture. Large showroom. Easy parking.

Sleaford STD 0529

Earl & Lawrence
55 Northgate, NG34 7AB.
Tel 302946. Open Mon-Fri 8-5.30.
Fine art and general auctioneers.

Spalding STD 0775

Bridge Antiques
(A.E.Gittins). 22-100 Bridge Rd, Sutton Bridge. Tel Holbeach (0406) 350704 (priv 350535).
Open 9-6; other times by appt.
Very large stock of Victorian furniture on 4 floors and in warehouse. Also china, glass, copper oil lamps.

Betty Dean Antiques
The Walnuts, Weston St Mary's, PE12 6JB. Tel Holbeach (0406) 370429 (priv 371067).
Open daily. Furniture, Victoriana, farm tools, bygones, brass, copper, bric-a-brac.

Spilsby STD 0790

Shaw Antiques
(Jean Shaw). High St, PE23 5JE.
Tel 52317 (priv 52297). Open 10-5; closed Tues; other times by appt. China, glass, silver, furniture pine.

Stamford STD 0780

O.M. & R.D.Cox Antiques
(Olive May and Ralph Dennis Cox). 5 St Mary's Hill. Tel 64159.
Open Mon-Sat 9.30-5; closed Thurs; other times by appt. 16th to 19thC furniture, carvings, antique jewellery, silver, and decorative items. Also linen, lace and kitchen antiques.

Dickenson and Thomas
(W.A. Dickenson & A.M. Thomas).
Old Granary, 10 North St, PE9 2YN. Tel 62236 (priv 55093).
Open Mon-Sat 9.30-6; other times by appt. Mainly pine and country furniture and architectural fitments.

Timothy Kendrew Antiques
5-8 George Hotel Mews.
Tel 56072 (priv 08012 2325).
Open Mon-Sat 9.30-5.30; other times by appt. 18th and 19thC antiques, silver, porcelain, furniture, objets d'art and paintings. LAPADA

Sotheby's
(Representative: Lady Victoria Leatham). George Hotel Mews, Station Rd, PE9 2LB. Tel 51666.
Auctioneers & valuers.

Henry Spencer & Sons
38 St Mary's St. Tel 52136. Open Mon-Fri 8-1,2-5, Sat 9-noon; other times by appt. Fine art auctioneers. FRICS

St George's Antiques
(G.H.Burns). St George's Sq.
Tel 54117 (priv 0778 423781).
(Warehouse in Wharf Rd.) Open Mon-Sat 10-4.30 (phone call advisable); other times by appt.
Period & Victorian furniture, shipping goods, metalware, clocks and general smalls.

Stapleford

Allens
Moor Farm. Tel Bassingham (052 285) 392. Quality Victorian style sanded wooden knobs and feet for furniture. Phone or write for samples and price list.

Wainfleet

The Antique Centre
1 Spilsby Rd, PE24 4EH.
Tel Skegness (0754) 880489.
Open 10-6; other times by appt.
18th and 19thC furniture, paintings, copper, brass and unusual items.

Woodhall Spa STD 0526

Kirkby Antiques Ltd
(J.F., M.F., R.& A.E. Carter).
Highfield, Kirkby on Bain, LN10 6YN. Tel 52119 & 53461.
Open Mon-Fri 8-5; other times by appt. Extensive stock of furniture in restored condition, from Georgian to shipping. Restoration and furniture conversion facilities. LAPADA

V.O.C. Antiques
27 Witham Rd. Georgian mahogany, old oak, copper, brass and porcelain.

Wragby STD 0673

Tealby Pine
(Mr R.G. & Mrs J.Chesterton-North). Goltho Hall, Goltho. Tel 858789. (Also Designs on Pine, shop in Lincoln.) Open at all times to trade. Original pine furniture. Trade suppliers.

Merseyside

Birkenhead STD 051

Richard Baker and Thomson
9 Hamilton St. Tel 647 9104.
(Also 24 Cooks Rd, Crosby, Merseyside.) Open Mon-Fri 9-5.30.
Auctioneers and valuers.

William Courtney & Sons
(R.W.Courtney, Mrs B.Bratley).
Cross St, Tunnel Entrance, L41 5DR. Tel 647-8693. Open 10-5, Thurs pm & Sun by appt.
Large shops with adjoining warehouse of general antiques, small items and shipping goods (to trade). LAPADA

Hoylake STD 051

The Clock Shop
(Kevin & Diane Whay). 7 The Quadrant, L47 2EE. Tel 632 1888 (priv 632 3818). Open Mon-Sat 9.30-6; other times by appt.
Clocks and watches, jewellery, restoration and repair. BHI, BWCG

Market Antiques
(W.M.Bateman). 80 Market St, L47 3BB. Tel 632 4059 (24 hrs).
Open Thurs, Fri, Sat 10-4.30; other times by appt. 18th to 20thC furniture and furnishing items, pictures and prints. Also shipping goods.

Liverpool STD 051

Antiques Gallery
(W.Blanchflower). 37 Hanover St, L1 3DN. Tel 709 9529. Open Mon-Fri 9-5, Sat 10-1; other times by appt. 18th and 19thC furniture, clocks, watches, general antiques and reproductions.

Bluecoat Display Centre
Bluecoat Chambers, School Lane.
Tel 709 4014. Open Tues-Fri 10.30-5.30, Sat 10.30-2.30.
Mondays only in December.
Pottery, textiles, glass and jewellery.

Bluecoat Gallery
School Lane, L1 3BX.
Tel 709 5689. Open Tues-Fri 10.30-5, Sat 10.30-5.
Contemporary art.

Boodle & Dunthorne Ltd
35 Lord St. Tel 227-2525. (Also at Chester and Manchester.) Open Mon-Sat 9-5. Fine jewels, antique and Victorian jewellery and silver, antique and genuine period French clocks and carriage clocks. NAG

Philip Cowan Antiques
(Philip Cowan). 33 Parliament St.
Tel 709 1217. Open Mon-Fri 9-5; other times by appt. Mostly furniture, some shipping goods.

Davies, Turner & Co Ltd
Unit 9 & 10, Brickfields Trading Estate, Huyton, L36 6HY.
Tel 480 8118. Shippers.

Eldon Worrall
15 Seel Street. Auctioneer & valuer.

Gostin of Liverpool Ltd
Portway, off 2a Higher Rd, Halewood, L25 0QQ.
Tel 486 1703/6175. Makers of fine period style English furniture.

Alan Leonard Antiques
(Alan Leonard). 503 Smithdown Rd, L15 5AE. Tel 733 5277 (priv 722 4766). Open Mon-Sat 9.30-5.30; other times by appt.
Antique furniture, 18thC to early 20thC, pottery, porcelain, antique and modern silver and plate. 19th and 20thC watercolours and paintings.

The Lyver and Boydell Galleries
(Paul Breen (Fine Art) Ltd).
15 Castle St, L2 4SX.
Tel 236 3256. Open Mon-Fri 10.30-5.30; other times by appt.
Pictures for all tastes, including antique maps and prints, watercolours and oil paintings 18th-20thC, modern graphics and reproductions. Restoration and framing. LAPADA FATG

Maggs Antiques
(Mr & Mrs G.Webster).
26-28 Fleet St, L1 4AR.
Tel 708 0221. 18th and 19thC furniture, shipping goods, courier service. Shipper. Restorations. LAPADA

John Mason (Wavertree)
127 High St, L15 8JT.
Tel 722 2352. Shippers. LAPADA

Outhwaite & Litherland
(R.B., R.M. & P.S. Litherland).
Kingsway Galleries, Fontenoy St, L3 2BE. Tel 236 6561. Open Mon-Fri 9-5; other times by appt.
Fine art auctioneers and valuers. SOFAA

Harriet Owen Hughes
(Harriet Owen Hughes). 41 Blue Coat Chambers, School Lane, L1 3BX. Tel 708 6808 (priv 427 2008). Open Mon-Fri 9-4.30; other times by appt. No stock; conservation and restoration of oil paintings. IIC ICOM APBR UKIC

Richard Baker & Thomson
24 Cooks Rd, Crosby.
Tel 647 9104. Auctioneers.

Savoy Antiques
(Brian Coleman). 7 Bridgewater St. Tel 708 9159. Open Mon-Fri 9-5; other times by appt. (Incorporating Savoy Antiques International, California.) Buyers, packers, shippers and restorers. 7-floor warehouse with 20,000 sq ft of shipping goods and antiques, mainly furniture.

Theta Gallery
(Mr John Matson). 31 Parliament St. Tel 709 1217. Open Mon-Fri 9-5; other times by appt. General antiques.

Trentini International Antiques
(J Trentini). The Old Police Station, 80 Lark Lane. Tel 733 9357. Paintings, works of art. LAPADA

Ryan Wood Antiques
(Francis Ryan & Peter Woods). 102 Seel St, L1 9AR. Tel 709 7776 (priv 709 3203). Open Mon-Sat 9.30-5; other times by appt. General antique and secondhand dealers with a good cross-section of stock.

New Brighton

Arbiter
(W.D.L. Scobie & P.D. Ferrett). 10 Atherton St, L45 2NY. Tel 051- 639 1159. Open Tues-Fri 11-6; other times by appt. Decorative items of all periods, including ethnic & Oriental & original graphics.

Southport STD 0704

R.W.Baxter
(R.W.Baxter). 43 Hoghton St, PR9 0PG. Tel 37377. Open Mon, Wed, Fri 9-5.30; other times by appt. Restoration of antique clocks, repairs to modern clocks and watches. Reproduction longcase clocks, made to order only. Longcase painted dials restored. Brass dials resilvered and restored, wheels cut. Parts made for antique clocks. FBHI, BWCMG

C.K.Broadhurst & Co Ltd
5-7 Market St. Tel 32064, 34110. Open Mon-Sat; early closing Tues. Large stock of books on travel, natural history, literature and modern first editions. Catalogues, topography. ABA

W. & R. Griffiths
(William & Robina Griffiths). 19 Market St. Tel 38056 (priv 35720). Open Mon-Sat 9-5; other times by appt. Stripped pine & antique furniture. LAPADA

Jays Fine Art Dealers
(Alan & Barbara Joseph). Cambridge Gallery, 4 Cambridge Arcade, PR8 1AS. Tel 34488 (priv 69500). Open Mon-Sat 10-1, 2.15-5.30; closed Tues; other times by appt. Watercolours & oil paintings, 18thC to early 20thC. Also a few high quality works of contemporary artists, e.g. Ruth Gibbons. LAPADA

Little Thatch Antiques
(John & Brenda Jebb). 54 Botanic Rd, Churchtown. Tel 27096. Open daily 9-5; closed Tues; other times by appt. Victorian and Edwardian paintings, pottery, brass, copper and postcards.

Tony Sutcliffe Antiques
(Tony Sutcliffe). 130 Cemetery Rd. Tel 47968 (priv 33465). Open Mon-Sat 9.30-12.30, 1.30-5.30; other times by appt. Quality antiques, Georgian and Victorian furniture, porcelain and glassware.

H.S.Walne Jewellers Ltd
(Mr H.S.Walne, Mrs M.Walne). 183 Lord St. Tel 32469. Open Mon, Wed, Thurs, Fri, Sat 10.15-5.30; other times by appt. Diamond rings, gold and silver jewellery, silver articles. All secondhand.

Weldon Antiques and Jewellery
(Mr Nigel C.Weldon, Mr Herbert W.Weldon). 655 Lord St, PR9 0AW. Tel 32191. Open Mon-Sat 9.15-5.45; other times by appt. Antique furniture, silver, porcelain, clocks, watches, ivories, bronzes etc. Antique and modern jewellery.

St Helens STD 0744

Colin Stock
8 Mossborough Rd, Rainford. Tel 2246. Open by appt only. Furniture. BADA

Wallasey

Robbies Antiques
(Mrs R.I.Dalby). 140 Seabank Rd. Tel 051 638 3848. Open afternoons 2-5 except Wed; other times by appt. 18th and 19thC furniture, ceramics, glass and most other antique items.Also restorations (furniture) and re-upholstery.

West Kirby STD 051

Oliver and Helen Horswill Antiques
62 Grange Rd. Tel 625 7111 (priv 625 6182). Open Mon-Sat 10-5.30; early closing Wed; other times by appt. 17th to 19thC furniture and decorative items.

Jane Thomas Antiques
15A Westbourne Rd. Tel 625-6080. Open Mon-Sat 10-4.30, closed Wed; other times by appt. Old maps and prints of local interest, small furniture, china, glass and bric-a-brac.

Wirral STD 051

M.Fearn
(Marion Fearn). 124A Market St, Hoylake, L47 3BH. Tel 632 3839. Open Mon-Sat 11-1 2.30-4.30; closed Wed; other times by appt. Old dolls, jewellery, copper, brass, furniture.

Middlesex

Eastcote STD 01

Madeleine Adams
Tel London (01) 868 5075. Open by appt only. Early English porcelain. LAPADA

Feltham STD 01

J.H.Bachmann (UK) Ltd
Unitair Centre, Gt South West Rd, TW14 8NT. Tel 844 1771. Packing and shipping of antiques, paintings and objets d'art.

James Bourlet & Sons Ltd
(C.C.Vaughan, D.T.N.Wetmore, T.S.Lock, J.Parr). 3 Space Waye, TW14 0TY. Tel 751 1155 (24 hours). Open Mon-Fri 8.30-5.30; other times by appt. International transporters to the art world - import and export. Specialists in collection and delivery of works of art. Expert packing, freighting by air and sea. Own road transport fleets in UK and Europe. Full documentation service.

Burlington Fine Arts
(B.J.Bedingfield, A.Morton-Hunte Ltd). Unit 8, Ascot Rd, Clockhouse Lane, TW14 8QS. Tel Ashford (07842) 48183. Open Mon-Fri 9-5.30; other times by appt. Fine art packers and forwarders.

Hampton STD 01

Ian Sheridan's Bookshop
(Ian Sheridan). Thames Villa, 34 Thames St. Tel 979 1704. Open daily 10-7 incl. Sun; other times by appt. Antiquarian and secondhand books.

Hampton Hill STD 01

The Hampton Hill Gallery Ltd
(Robert Crewdson & Bruce Mitchell). 203-205 High St, TW12 1NP. Tel 977 1379. Open Tues-Sat 9-5.30; other times by appt. 19th & 20thC watercolours & prints,fine art framers, mounters. Restorers of watercolours & paintings. Specialists in the cleaning & restoration of watercolours. FATG

Harrow on the Hill STD 01

Kathleen Mann Antiques
49 High St, HA1 3HT. Tel 422 1892. Open Mon, Tues, Thurs, Fri, Sat 9-5.30. 18th and 19thC furniture and decorative items. LAPADA

Winston Galleries
(R. Weston, P. Weston). 68 High St, HA1 3LL. Tel 422 4470. Open 9.30-5.30; closed Wed; other times by appt. 18th and 19thC furniture, clocks, porcelain, prints, watercolours and general antiques.

Heathrow STD 01

W.B. Airfreight Ltd
69/70 G Building 521, Cargo Terminal, London Airport. Tel 01-897 2551. Packers & shippers. LAPADA

Hillingdon STD 01

J.A.Fredericks & Son
99 Hercies Rd. Tel Uxbridge (0895) 55462. Open by appt only. Furniture. BADA

Hounslow STD 01

Worldwide Autographs Ltd
(I.K.T. Sayer, M.C. Sayer). 68 Staines Rd, TW3 3LS. Tel 572 3606. Open Mon-Fri 10-5; Sat 10-1; other times by appt. Autographed letters, documents, photographs & books. Also framed items.

Isleworth STD 01

Crowther of Syon Lodge
(Derek Crowther, Chairman, Barry Perry M.D.). Syon Lodge, Busch Corner, London Rd, TW7 5BH. Tel 560 7978, 560 7985. Open Mon-Fri 9-5; Sat, Sun 11-4. (Next to Syon House, entrance on London Rd. 20 minutes from Hyde Park corner by car, en route to London Airport.) Very large and important stock of garden ornaments, chimneypieces, panelled rooms, wrought ironwork and period architectural features.

Pinner STD 01

Artbry's Antiques
(A.Davies & B.Hill). 44 High St, HA5 5PW. Tel 868 0834. Open Mon-Sat 9-5.30; early closing Wed. 18th and 19thC furniture, all types of clocks. Antique brass, copper and porcelain.

Staines STD 0784

K.W.Dunster Antiques
(Mr & Mrs K.Dunster). 23 Church St. Tel 53297. Jewellery, furniture, clocks. LAPADA

Teddington STD 01

Binsted Antiques
(C.J.Wills ARICS). 21 Middle Lane, TW11 0HQ. Tel 943 0626. Open Mon-Sat 9-6; (phone in advance if poss); other times by appt. 17th, 18th and 19thC English furniture, English pottery and porcelain. Restored square pianos prior to 1810. Oil paintings and prints, antique glass.

Joan Jarman Antiques
81A High St. Tel (priv) 977 4260. Open Tues, Sat 10-5; Mon, Thurs, Fri 2-5; other times by appt. Furniture, porcelain, prints and Tunbridge ware.

Church Lane Restorations
(R.S.Vincent & C.Evans). 1 Church Lane. Tel 977 2526. Open Mon-Fri 8-5.30. Antique furniture restorers. Cabinet making and French polishing.

Twickenham STD 01

Anthony C.Hall
30 Staines Rd. Tel 898 2638. Open Mon-Fri 9-5.30 (closed Wed pm); other times by appt. Volumes on Russia, Eastern Europe, Middle East, Africa and world history. ABA, PBFA

John Ives Antiquarian Books
5 Normanhurst Drive, St Margarets, TW1 1NA. Tel 892 6265. Open anytime by appt. Scarce and out-of-print books on antiques and collecting. Catalogues issued.

Marble Hill Gallery
(D.L. & L.T. Newson). 72 Richmond Rd, TW1 3BE. Tel 892 1488. Open Mon-Sat 10-5.30. Over 200 Victorian watercolours always in stock. Antique French marble mantels in Louis XV & XVI style. Antique clocks, fenders and brass ware, pine & white Adam style fireplaces, antique style firebaskets.

Onslow Clocks
(M. Onslow-Cole). 48 King Street, TW1 3SH. Tel 892 7632. Open Mon-Sat 9-5; closed Wed; other times by appt. Early English longcase clocks, also bracket, French, English dial clocks. Restoration of quality clocks. Valuations. LAPADA

Phelps Ltd
(R.C.Phelps & W.J.Phelps). 133-135 St Margaret's Rd, TW1 1RG. Tel 892 1778, 892 7129. Open Mon-Fri 9-1, 2-5.30; Sat 9-5; other times by appt. Very large stock of Victorian, Edwardian and pre-war furniture, specialising in tables, chairs, desks, bookcases and conversion furniture for trade and export. LAPADA

S & S Antiques
64 Hampton Rd. Antiques and good quality shipping goods.

Rita Shenton
148 Percy Rd, TW2 6JG. Tel 894 6888. Open for callers by appt, mainly business by post. Specialist in horological books with a large stock of new, out-of-print and antiquarian books on clocks, watches, sundials and bells. Descriptive catalogue available. MBHI

Zafer Antiques
(R.D.Zafer). 36 Church St. Tel 891 3183. Open Mon-Sat 10-5; closed Wed. 18th and 19thC furniture, silver and jewellery, paintings, 17thC oak.

Uxbridge STD 0895

The Antiques Warehouse
(Michael Allenby). 34-36 Rockingham Rd, UB8 2TZ. Tel 56963 & 71012. Open Mon-Sat 9.30-5.30. Antique furniture, particularly 19th and 20thC, and shipping goods.

Wealdstone

Abadjian Ltd
Palmerston Rd. Tel 01-863 1141. Specialist carpet washers. Also retailing of Oriental rugs.

Norfolk

Attleborough STD 0953

F. & T.King and Everyman Antique Fairs
(Terry King, Faith King). Victorian Cottage, High St, NR17 2BT. Tel 453285. Open Tues-Sat 9.30-5.30. Georgian and Victorian furniture, glass, porcelain, needlework, etc. Goods suitable for Continental buyers.

Aylsham STD 0263

G.A.Key
(G.A. Key, D.J. Lines, A.M. Bond, P.E. Barker). 8 Market Place, NR11 6EH. Tel 733195 (priv 732477). Open Tues-Fri 9-5. Antique furniture sale, picture sales, book sales, general furniture sales.

Maltings Antiques
(T.W. Bishop). Sixty Millgate. Tel 732291. Open Sat & Mon 10.30-1, 2-5; other times by appt. Furniture (mainly pine), domestic items, hand tools & smaller items of agriculture & various trades.

White Hart Gallery
3 White Hart St, NR11 6HG. Open 10-5 Mon, Tues, Thurs (Summer) Fri & Sat; other times by appt. Furniture, paintings, ceramics etc.

Blakeney STD 059 451

Providence House Antiques
(J.S. Macpherson, FSVA). High St, NR25 7NX. Tel Sheringham (0263) 740403. (Also at Fakenham Antiques Centre.) Open most days. Antique and shipping furniture, clocks, china, silver.

Burnham Market

M. & A. Cringle
The Black Horse. Tel Fakenham (0328) 738456. Open 9-5; closed Wed & Sun. General antiques. Country furniture, oak, elm, mahogany. Glassware, china & pottery. Maps & prints. No modern reproductions. No rubbish.

Market House Antiques
(Mrs David Maufe). Market House, PE31 8HF. Tel Fakenham (0328) 738475. Open 9-6; other times by appt. Fine quality period furniture and works of art. BADA

Coltishall

Eric Bates & Sons
High St. Tel Norwich (0603) 738716. General antiques, shipping furniture. Upholstery and cabinet making.

Coltishall Antiques Centre
(E.M. Allport). High St, NR12 7HU. Tel Norwich (0603) 738306 (737631). Open Mon-Sat 10-5; other times by appt. Ten dealers specialising in antiques from guns, glass, swords, porcelain, postcards, silver, jewellery, pictures, art deco to small furniture and collectors items.

Corner Antiques
(Elizabeth Allport). Coltishall Antiques Centre, High St, NR12 7HV. Tel Norwich (0603) 738306 (priv 737631). Open Mon-Sat 10-5; other times by appt. Collectors' items, 18th and 19thC porcelain, small furniture. Specialising in snuff boxes and sewing accessories. LAPADA

Gwendoline Golder
(Gwendoline Golder). The Little Shop. Tel Norwich (0603) 737404. Open Mon-Sat 2-5.30; other times by appt. General antiques, bygones, collectors' items and crested ware.

Cromer STD 0263

Bond Street Antiques
(M.R.T. Jones, J.A. Jones). 6 Bond St, NR27 9DA. Tel 513134. (Also at Jas.J.Briggs Jewellers, 38 Church St, Cromer.Tel 512379.) Open 9-1, 2.30-5.30 daily except Sun; other times by appt. Modern and antique jewellery, old porcelain, clocks, bronzes, silver, gold, objets d'art, watches, small furniture, oriental. NAG FGA

Kees & Co
(C.A.J.Woerkom). Tandridge, Top Common, West Runton, NR27 9LT. Tel 8109. Open daily 10-5; other times by appt. Packers and shippers, trade suppliers, restorers and conservators. Leathering service. Antique and pine furniture.

E.D.Levine
The Antique Gallery, Church St. Tel 512335. Open mainly by appt on most Sats. English and Chinese porcelain, furniture, drawings, paintings, objets d'art. Specialising in 18thC English china and Norwich school paintings.

Past & Present
28 Louden Rd. Tel 512894. Open Mon-Sat 10-1, 2.30-5; early closing Wed; other times by appt. Brass, copper, porcelain, Victoriana, some small furniture, clocks, pictures and bric-a-brac.

A.E. Seago
(D.C. Seago). 15 Church St. Tel 512733. Open Mon-Sat 9.30-1, 2.15-5; closed Wed; other times by appt. Furniture, general antiques and maps and medals, old postcards.

Dereham STD 0362

Antiques and Collectables
(L.I.Wells). 8 Aldiss Court, High St. Tel 447. Open Mon-Sat 9.30-5; other times by appt. Pine, oak and mahogany furniture. Fine porcelain of all periods, pictures, plate, silver, jewellery, and collectors' items etc. Specialising in wall plates and figurines.

Norfolk Polyphon Centre
(Norman Vince). Wood Farm, Bawdeswell, NR20 4RX. Tel Bawdeswell (036 288) 230. Open weekends 10-4.30; other times by appt. Mechanical music, sales, purchases, repairs.

Diss STD 0379

The Angel Antiques
(Mr and Mrs J.R.Saxon). Crown Hill, Botesdale, IP22 1BU. Tel 898894. Open Tues-Sun 9.30-6. Antique furniture including pine, silver, silver watches, jewellery, clocks, china, glass and collectables. Furniture restoration service.

Brockdish Antiques
(M.&L.Palfrey). Commerce House, Brockdish. Tel Hoxne (037975) 498. Open Mon-Sat 9-5.30; early closing Wed; other times by appt. On A143 Bury St Edmunds to Great Yarmouth Rd. Antique and secondhand furniture and miscellanea. Antique restorations and upholstery on the premises.

Diss Antiques
(Brian Wimshurst). 2 Market Place & 23 St Nicholas St. Tel 2213 (priv 51369). Open Mon-Sat 9.30-1, 2-5; closed Tues; other times by appt. 1500 sq ft of antiques, pre 1920. Specialists in barometer restoration, general restorations, restoration materials supplies wholesale/retail, brass furniture supplied wholesale/retail.

The Falcon Gallery
(Nicholas Smith). Honeypot Farm, Wortham, IP22 1PW. Tel Mellis (037 983) 312. Open 7 days a week by appt. Res on premises. Watercolours & oil paintings 1840-1920, plus old masters. Annual mixed exhibitions of Victorian works every November. Catalogues available. Specialising in every facet of Victorian art to include sporting, landscapes, portraits, seascapes & primitives.

Thos. Wm. Gaze & Son
10 Market Hill, IP22 3JZ. Tel 519313. Antique and cottage furniture from house clearances. Auction sales every Friday 11.30 am.

Glennie Middleton and Bullock
3 Church St, IP22 3DD. Tel 51617. Open Mon-Fri 9-5. Auctioneers and valuers specialising in antiquarian books, maps, prints, manuscripts, early photographic images and equipment, small collectors items including coins, stamps, postal history, postcards, medals, corkscrews, sporting equipment.

Idears
(P.B.Benton). 1 Chapel St, IP22 3AN. Tel 51521. Open Mon-Sat 9.30-5. 18th & 19thC furniture and country antiques, interior design, fabrics, upholstery, pottery, porcelain and lighting.

Market Hill Art & Antiques
(H. & B.V.Cox). 13 Market Hill. Tel 3315 (priv Botesdale 612). Open Mon-Sat 10-5.15; closed Tues; other times by appt. Early 19thC furniture, porcelain, fine art etc; specialising in collectors' items.

John Oliver & Co
(J.Oliver, T.Meldrum). 41 Mere St, IP22 3AG. Tel 2662. Jewellery, silver, porcelain. LAPADA

East Dereham

Wynyard R.T. Wilkinson, FSA Scot, Fine Silver
(Wynyard Wilkinson). Bylaugh Park, NR20 4RL. Tel Bawdeswell (036 288) 200 (priv 01-788 6953). Open by appt any time. British and Colonial silver c.1650-1850 with a speciality in small items and provincial makers.

Fakenham STD 0328

Great Ryburgh Antiques (Pine Centre)
(M.E.Allison). 39 Fakenham Rd, Gt Ryburgh. Tel Great Ryburgh (032 878) 447. Country pine, porcelain etc.

Great Yarmouth STD 0493

David Ferrow
77 Howard St South. Tel 843800 (priv 662247). Open 9.30-1, 2.30-5.30; Thurs by appt. Antiquarian and modern books on all subjects. ABA

Malcolm & Joy Ferrow & Son
6-7 Hall Quay, NR30 1HX. Tel 4630. Open Mon-Sat 9.15-1, 2.15-6; early closing Thurs. General antiques, paintings and watercolours.

Barry Howkins Antiques
(Barry Howkins). 35 King St. Tel 2713. (See also John Howkins, 145 King St.) Open Mon-Sat 9-5.30; other times by appt. Antique jewellery, porcelain, silver, pictures. LAPADA

John Howkins Antiques
(John Howkins). 145 King St. Open by appt only. Furniture and shipping goods.

Rodney & Michael Wheatley
16A Northgate St, White Horse Plain. Tel 857219. (Also secondhand bookshop 7 White Horse Plain.) Open 9.30-5.30; Thurs 9.30-1.30; other times by appt. Old books, post cards etc.

Harleston STD 0379

Grange Gallery
Withersdale Lodge, Withersdale. Tel 852254. Open by appt. Res on premises. Specialising in fine Victorian watercolours and small furniture.

George Sneed Woodwork
(George Sneed). Old Orchard, Church Rd, Alburgh, IP20 ODA. Tel Homersfield (098 686) 472. Open by appt only. Rush, cane and willow seat, back and bed end repairs in all patterns, also associated structural repairs. Virtually all kinds of non-upholstered woven seating undertaken, but upholstery carried out where necessary to complete restoration.

Heacham STD 0485

Peter Robinson
Pear Tree House. Tel 70228. Open Mon-Sat 9-5, appt advisable. Large stock of English furniture of all periods, copper, pottery and porcelain.

Holt STD 026 371

Simon Gough Books
(Simon Gough). 3 Fish Hill. Tel 2650. Open Mon-Sat. Books: antiquarian and secondhand, all subjects, especially Norfolk natural history, art, bindings. ABA

Peter Hammond
(P.Hammond). Church House, Thornage. Tel 861352. Open Mon-Sat 10-5; other times by appt. 17th, 18th and 19thC country furniture.

Humbleyard Fine Art
(James Layte). 3 Fish Hill. Tel 713362(priv 036 283 793). Open Mon-Sat 10-5; closed Fri; other times by appt. Scientific and medical instruments, nautical, decorative antiques, samplers, needlework, pottery, prints, painted furniture, all unusual items.

New Street Antiques
(Barrie James Adams). 33 New St. Tel 3089. Open Mon-Sat 10-5.30; other times by appt. Large stock of stripped pine and Victorian furniture.

Richard Scott Antiques
(R.A.Scott). 30 High St. Tel 2479. Open 10-1, 2-5; closed Thurs. General antiques and many rare objects. Specialising in china repairs and conservation.

Hunstanton STD 048 53

Old Bakery Antiques
(A. & J. Fairhead). 1 Church St. Tel Brancaster (0485) 210396. Open Mon, Fri, Sat 11-1; other times by appt. Textiles, samplers, embroideries, lace and dolls.

Kenninghall

Tony Cardy
The Market Place, NR16 2AH. Tel Quidenham (095 387) 643. Open Sats and other days as sales allow. General antiques, specialising in motoring, motorcycling and cycling collectables including literature, prints, lamps, horns, bells, instruments, clocks etc.

King's Lynn STD 0553

Antiques
23 St James' St. Tel 3931. Open 9-5.30; early closing Wed. Small stock of furniture, porcelain and objets d'art.

Priory Antiques
Litcham Priory, Litcham. Tel Litcham (0328) 701262. Open 10-5; other times by appt. Country furniture, old craft and farming implements, stripped pine, copper, cast iron and secondhand books.

Anthony Reed
(Anthony Reed). The Old Granary Studio, Kings Staith Lane. Tel 5509. (Also at 21 St John Maddermarket, Norwich (0603-612894.) Open Mon-Sat 9.30-5.30; other times by appt. Antiques market with a general stock, plus pictures and prints. FATG

Steed-Croft Antiques
(John M.Tate). Marshlands, Cross Lane, Brancaster, PE31 8AE. Tel Brancaster (0485210) 812. Open by appt only. Period furniture & decorative items.

The Tower Gallery
Middleton Tower. Tel 840203. Open daily. (3.5 miles from King's Lynn toward Norwich on A47.) General antiques, including furniture, porcelain, paintings and Victoriana.

Treasures
(H. & M. Merckel). Mileham. Tel Fakenham (03286) 701234. Open 9-6 in summer; 9-4 in winter; other times by appt. 18th and 19thC British furniture, glass, potlids and Prattware, cottage antiques and jewellery.

Long Stratton STD 0508

Newcomen Gallery
Church Cottage, Forncett St Mary. British pictures.

Melton Constable STD 0263

Sharrington Antiques
(Peter Coke). Sharrington, NR24 2PQ. Tel 861411 (priv 860719). Open 9.30-5.30; closed Jan, Feb & March; other times by appt. Interesting and unusual small antiques, furniture, pictures, papier-mache, etc.

North Walsham STD 0692

North Walsham Antique Gallery
(Mr & Mrs M.B. Hicks). 29 Grammar School Rd. Tel 405059. (Also in Stalham - See Stalham Antique Gallery.) Open Mon-Fri 9.15-1, 2.15-5; Sat 9.15-1; other times by appt. Silver, porcelain, small furniture and collectors' items.

Solus Marketing (Norfolk)
Cromer Rd, Felmingham, NR28 OJS. Buyer and exporter of silver. LAPADA

Norwich STD 0603

Arthur Brett & Sons, Ltd
40-44 St Giles St, NR2 1LW. Tel 628171. Open Mon-Fri 9.30-4; other times by appt. 18thC English furniture. Also restoration and reproduction. BADA

E. & G. Briere
(Edna & Gilbert Briere). Keeper's Cottage, Suffield, NR11 7ER. Tel Aylsham (0263) 732651. Open by appt only. Res on prem. 17th to 19thC English furniture, paintings, garden furniture and statuary, mirrors.

Christie's
(Representative: Iain Henderson Russell). Old Bank of England Court, Queen St, NR2 4BX. Tel 614546. Open Mon-Fri 9-5. Fine art auctioneers and valuers.

Directory Entries are Free and ADDITIONS OR CORRECTIONS will be welcomed by *THE EDITOR, British Art and Antiques Directory, National Magazine House, 72 Broadwick Street, London W1V 2BP*

Thomas Crowe
77 Upper St Giles St. Tel 21962. Open Mon-Fri; early closing Sat. Large stock of books, including old and rare items, voyages and travel, English literature, natural history. ABA

D'Amico Antiques Ltd
(J.E.Wrightson). 20 Highland Rd. Tel 52320. (Also at 30 Hillside, Pitmedden, Aberdeen.) Open daily; res on prem. Clocks, glass, china, small furniture and shipping goods. Clocks restored. LAPADA

J. & T.J.Fairhurst
The Art Gallery, 7 Parsonage Sq, Bedford St, NR2 1A5. Tel 614214. Open Mon-Sat 10-5. 17th to 19thC oils and watercolours. Also modern oils and antique furniture. Shipping goods.

George & Dragon Gallery
(Denis King). Reepham. Tel 870360. Open Mon-Fri 9-5.30; Sat 9-12; other times by appt. (Reepham road leaves Norwich ring road at Appollo.) Antique maps, prints and watercolours.

Michael Hallam Antiques
(Michael Hallam). 17 Magdalen St. Tel 21163 (priv 413692). (Also Norwich Antique Centre, The Quayside, Norwich.) Open 10.30-4, closed Sun; other times by appt. General stock of furniture, small prints & paintings, porcelain pottery & collectors items.

Ann Hathaway
(Peter Shreeve). 345 Aylsham Rd, NR3 2RU. Tel 412730. Open Mon-Fri 10.30-4.30; closed Thurs. Furniture, porcelain, oil paintings, crested china, copper & brass.

Denis King
George & Dragon Gallery, Reepham. Tel 870360. Open Mon-Fri 9-5.30; Sat 9-12; other times by appt. Antique maps & prints, some watercolours. Cleaning, restoration, mounting & framing & print colouring.

Levine, Henry & Co
55 London St, NR2 1HL. Tel 628709. Open usual hours; closed Thurs. Antique silver, jewels and objects of vertu. BADA

Maddermarket Antiques
7 St John's Alley, Maddermarket. Tel 620610. Open Mon-Sat 9.30-5. Jewellery, silver, plate, china, brass, copper, medals and weapons.

Mandell's Gallery
Elm Hill, NR3 1HN. Tel 626892, 629180. (Also at Polak Gallery, 21 King St, St James's. 01-930 9245.) Open Mon-Sat 9-5.30. 18th and 19thC watercolours and oils, particularly the Norwich School. Also a selection of contemporary local and Continental artists. BADA

Norwich Antique & Collectors Centre
(R.A.Dazeley, I.J.Ford). No 1 Quayside, NR3 1RQ. Tel 612582. Open Mon-Sat 10-5 and Bank Holidays. 40 dealers in 3 large showrooms. Trade warehouse. Exhibitions. Coffee bar.

Phillips
(Enquiries: Stephen Kaye). 3 Opie St, NR1 3DP. Tel 616426. Auctioneers & valuers.

Rackheath Hall
Rackheath Park. Tel 720326. (Off Norwich-Wroxham road.) Large stock of general antiques, especially furniture.

The Scientific Anglican Bookshop
30-30A St Benedict St. Tel 24079. Open Mon-Sat 10-6; closed Thurs. Large stock of books on three floors, specialising in antiquarian and secondhand.

Oswald Sebley
(P.H.Knights). 20 Lower Goat Lane. Tel 26504. Open Mon-Sat 9-5; closed Thurs; other times by appt. Antique and secondhand silver and jewellery.

St Giles Antiques and Period Fashion
(G. Matthews). 51 St Giles St, NR2 1JR. Tel 628535. Open Mon-Sat 10-5. General antiques, porcelain, glass, silver, jewellery, collectors items. Pre-1950 clothes, shipping furniture by appt. Phone 0603 506348. Overseas buyers welcome.

Kevin Taylor
24 Shipfield, NR3 4QN. Tel 402869. Photographer. Specialising in brochure and catalogue work.

James & Ann Tillett
(James and Ann Tillett). Tombland House, 12-13 Tombland, NR3 1HF. Tel 624914. Open Mon-Sat 9.30-5.30. Antique and modern jewellery, silver, clocks and pewter. LAPADA, NAG

Treasure House Antiques & Crafts Gallery
(P.R. Pennington & Mrs G.S.Swannack). St Gregory's Alley, Lower Goat Lane. Tel (priv) 0777-818494. Open Tues-Sat 10-5. (Also Treasure House Antiques & Antiques Centre, 6-10 Swan St, Bawtry, S.Yorks). General antiques.

William G.Wells
20 St John Maddermarket. Tel 21260. Open Mon-Sat 10-5.30; closed Thurs; other times by appt. General antique furniture, also gallery of prints and fine old paintings. Specialising in Oriental porcelain.

Wensum Antiques Ltd
(Kenneth and Margaret Blacklock). 20 Wensum St, NR3 1HY. Tel 616867. Open Mon-Sat 9.30-5.30. Glass, china, copper, brass and small furniture.

The Whatnot
(T.J.Watts). 10 Unthank Rd, NR2 2RA. Tel 25614. Open Mon-Sat 9.30-5.30; other times by appt. Antique and Edwardian furniture, porcelain, pottery, silver, copper, brass, weapons, books and prints.

Robert Young Antiques
(Mr & Mrs R.Young). 4A Exchange St, NR2 1AT. Tel 618605. Jewellery, & silver, valuations. LAPADA

Old Costessey

The Coach House
(Judy Hines). The Coach House, Townhouse Rd, NR8 5BX. Tel Norwich (0603) 742977. Open any time by appt. Res on premises. 20thC paintings. East Anglian watercolours. Fast framing service. Specialists in original 19th and 20thC prints. Other stock includes primitives, Baxter and Le Blond prints. Decorative and the 'Illustrators'. FATG

Costessey House Antiques
(Mrs Vicki Shortis). Costessey House, The Street, NR8 5DG. Tel Norwich (0603) 742012. Telephone first for opening times. Stripped pine and general antiques.

Reepham

The Chimes
(Peter & Eunice Elphick). Market Place, NR10 4JJ. Tel Norwich (0603) 870480. (Also at Norwich Antique Collectors Centre.) Open Mon-Sat 9.30-5.30; Thurs 9.30-1; Sun 10.30-4; other times by appt. General antiques including small furniture and collectors' items. Specialising in nautical antiques, nautical pictures & prints including Captains paintings; scientific instruments.

Ewings
(K.J. Ewing). Market Place, NR10 4JJ. Tel Norwich (0603) 870473. Open Mon-Fri 9-1, 1-5.30; Sat 9-1, 2-4. Auctioneers.

Orchard House, Oriental Rugs
(Mrs S. Aitchison). Orchard House, Ollands Road. Tel 870234. Open 7 days, (resident); other times by appt. Old and antique Oriental rugs, carpets, embroideries, restoration and repairs.

Reymerston

Xanthus Gallery
September Cottage, NR9 4AG. Tel Dereham (0362) 850862. Open any time by appt. British watercolours, drawings and oil paintings especially Norwich school and British orientalists.

Sheringham STD 0263

Dorothy's Antiques
(Mrs D.E.Collier). 23 Waterbank Rd, NR26 8RB. Tel 822319 (priv 823018). Open daily 11-5.30; other times by appt. Cranberry glass, Royal Worcester, Meissen and other porcelain, Staffordshire figures, commemoratives, Goss and crested china, small furniture, clocks, cased birds, brass & copper and other collectable items.

South Walsham STD 060 549

Leo Pratt & Son
Curiosity Shop, NR13 6EA. Tel 204. Open Tues-Sat 9-5.30; other times by appt. Antique, Victorian & shipping furniture, porcelain, glass, clocks, metalware, pictures.

Stalham STD 0692

Stalham Antique Gallery
(Mr & Mrs M. B. Hicks). High St. Tel 80636. (Also in North Walsham, see North Walsham Antique Gallery.) Open 9.15-1, 2.15-5; Sat 9.15-1; other times by appt. 17th to 19thC furniture, some paintings.

Stoke Ferry STD 0366

Farmhouse Antiques
(Peter Philpot). Whites Farm House, Barkers Drove, Off Oxborough Rd. Tel 500 588. Complete restoration service including French polishing, cabinet making, pine stripping, wood carving and gilding, upholstery and caning.

Swaffham STD 0760

The Antique Shop
(Ralph Cross). 66-68 London St, PE37 7DJ. Tel 21697. Open Tues-Sat; other times by appt. Period furniture, Chinese porcelain, paintings and silver. Victorian shipping furniture.

Manor Farm Antiques & Garden Ornaments
Manor Farm. Tel 21395. Open mornings, Mon-Fri; other times by appt. (On old A47, 200 yds from George Hotel.) Marble and stone type figures, garden urns and statuary. Victorian buttoned back chairs, sofas and Chesterfields. Also pine, beds, general antiques and shipping goods. Good parking facilities.

Swaffham Antiques Centre
(Keith & Rosaline Buckie). Market Place. Eight dealers, trading mainly in small antiques and collectors' items.

Watton STD 0953

Clarence House Antiques
High St. Tel 767. Large selection of antique furniture, china, glass, weapons and curios. Direct shipping to Belgium.

Wells

Marshfield Antiques
(Mr & Mrs C.R.Waters). 51-53 High St. Tel Fakenham (0328) 710552. Open Mon-Sat 9-5; closed Thurs. Fine furniture, porcelain, silver and collectors' pieces.

Wroxham STD 060 53

T.C.S.Brooke
(T.C.S. Brooke, M.A. Brooke, S.T. Brooke). The Grange, NR12 8RX. Tel 2644. Open 9.30-5.30, Mon, Tues, Thurs, Fri, Sat. Valuations: Stock - general antiques, including 18thC furniture, silver, glass and ceramics; fine mahogany reproductions and Oriental rugs. BADA

Wymondham STD 0953

Irelands Hall & Palmer
11 Market Place. Tel 603031. (Also at Norwich, Aylsham, North Walsham, Attleborough, Watton and Long Stratton.) Periodic sales of antiques furniture, china, glass, pictures and quality household effects. Regular catalogue sales held at the Royal Hotel,Norwich for coins,medals etc.

Margaret King Antiques & Curios
(Margaret King). 16 Market Place, NR18 0AX. Tel 604758 (priv 602427). Open Tues, Thurs, Fri & Sat; other times by appt. Furniture, porcelain, pottery, jewellery, silver, brass and copper. Interesting glass, bygones and curios.

Turret House
(Dr & Mrs D.H.Morgan). 27 Middleton St, NR18 0AB. Tel 603462. Open most days and any time by appt. 18th and 19thC scientific instruments; antiquarian books and barometers. Expert on microscopes. PBFA

Northamptonshire

Ashley STD 063 087

J.E.Hoffman
Owsley House, LE16 8HF. Tel Medbourne Green (085883) 315. Specialist in English and Continental clocks; also period furniture. BADA

Brackley STD 0280

Peter & Heather Jackson Antiques
3 Market Place. Tel 703259. Open Mon-Sat 10.30-1, 2-5; closed Wed & Sun; other times by appt. Res on prem. 18th and 19thC furniture, pictures and porcelain.

Brenda Nutting Antiques
(Brenda Nutting). Hollywood House, 69 High St, NN13 5BW. Tel 703362. Open Mon-Sat 10-5.30; Wed 10-2; other times by appt. General antiques, furniture (especially chairs), porcelain, pottery, collectables.

Cosgrove

Restall, Brown & Clennell Ltd
(Simon Brown, Adrian Frazer). Cosgrove Hall, MK19 7JB. Tel Milton Keynes (0908) 565888 (priv 563336). Open Mon-Fri 9-5.30; other times by appt. (Leave M1 at Junction 9, continue up A5. Take A508 (Northampton) turn right after ¼ mile.) Large stock 17th, 18th and 19thC English furniture. Also showrooms for the Restall Brown & Clennell reproduction range. Valuation and restoration. LAPADA

Finedon

Simon Banks Antiques
(Simon Banks). Quaker Lodge, 28A Church St, NN9 5NA. Tel Wellingborough (0933) 680371. Open Mon-Thur 9.30-5.30; Sat 10-1; other times by appt. Changing stock of mainly 18th and 19thC furniture, Staffordshire and a wide range of smalls.

Jean Burnett Antiques
(Jean Burnett). 3a Church St. Tel Wellingborough (0933) 680430. Open Mon-Sat 10-1, 2-6.30 unless at Fairs; other times by appt. Needlework tools, needlework accessories, samplers, embroidered pictures, decorative items & pine furniture.

Finedon Antiques Centre
(Denis Burnett). 3 Church St. Tel Wellingborough (0933) 680430. Open Weds only for antiques market 10-4.30; other times by appt. Various dealers offering wide range of antiques and collectables of all types. Good parking. Light refreshments available.

Thorpe Antiques
(Michael Clow). 51 High St, NN9 5JN. Tel Wellingborough (0933) 680196. Open Mon-Thurs 10.5.30; Sat 3-5.30; other times by appt. Period to Edwardian 19thC furniture in shop, pine and oak shipping furniture in warehouse at rear.

Flore

Flore House Antiques Ltd
(P.G. Norman). Flore House, NN7 4LZ. Tel Weedon (0327) 40585. Open Mon-Fri 9.30-6.30; other times by appt. Period & decorative antiques, 18th & 19thC and accessories. No jewellery or silver.

Higham Ferrers

Thorpe Antiques
(Peter, Stacey and Michael Clow). 3 High St. Tel Wellingborough (0933) 59747. (Also at Finedon.) Open Mon-Sat 9.30-6; other times by appt. 19thC furniture and shipping goods. LAPADA

Kettering STD 0536

H.J.Benford
14-16 Wellington St. Tel 513793. Open 9-6. Manufacturer of high quality clock cases, all hand made. Reproductions and new designs.

Alexis Brook
(Alexis Brook). 74 Lower St, NN16 8DL. Tel 513854. Open Mon-Sat 10am-10pm (if in); other times by appt. Mainly small antiques and decorator's items.

Rockingham Road Antiques
103 Rockingham Road. Tel 511842.

Southam and Sons
(W.J.Southam, N.Croskell, R.J.Eaton). Corn Exchange, Thrapston. Tel Thrapston (080 12) 4486. Open Mon-Fri 9-5.30, Sat 9-4. Auctioneers.

Stamford Road Antiques
127 Montague Street. Open Mon-Sat 10.30-5.30; closed Thurs. Jewellery, Art Deco and general antiques.

C.W.Ward Antiques
(Colin Mason). Deene House, 40 Lower St. Tel 513537. Antiques, soft furnishings & paintings.

Northampton STD 0604

Cave's of Northampton
(Gillian and Allan Cave). 111 Kettering Rd, NN1 4BA. Tel 38278. Open Mon-Sat 9-5.30; closed Thurs; other times by appt. (On A43 near centre. Easy parking. Send for sketch map.) 17th to 19thC English furniture, Continental furniture, decorative furniture, oil paintings.

Four Seasons Gallery
(George & Phyllida Hammerschmidt). 39 St Giles St, NN1 1JF. Tel 32287. Open Mon-Sat 9.30-5.30. Broad range of contemporary crafts, inc. ceramics, jewellery, wood, glass. Contemporary original prints. Picture framing.

Michael Jones Jeweller
(Michael Jones, Tony Clarke, William Craghill). 1 Gold St, NN1 1SA. Tel 32548. Open Mon-Sat 9-5.30; other times by appt. Victorian and Edwardian jewellery, precious gems and diamonds, silver, old watches and clocks. NAG

Lennard Antiques
(Gill Meddings). Poplars House, Rothersthorpe. Tel 830423. (Also at Woburn Abbey Antiques Centre.) Open by appt. Furniture, 17th, 18th and early 19thC porcelain, prints and objets d'art. LAPADA

Regent House Antiques
(Gillian Cave). Royal Terrace, NN1 3RF. Tel 37992. Open Mon-Fri 9-5.30; Sat 9-1. 18th and early 19thC furniture, especially mahogany; Continental furniture; oil paintings. Large Georgian house furnished with antiques which are for sale. Unrestored area for trade only.

R.S.J. Savage & Son
(Michael J. Savage). Alfred St, NN1 5EY. Tel 33852 (priv 405482). Open Mon-Fri, 9-5.15; Sat, 9-12.30; other times by appt. Fine art dealer, picture framer and restorer. FATG LAPADA

Wootton-Billingham
(David J. Veryard). 79 St Giles St, NN1 3HR. Tel 34531. Open Mon-Sat 10-5; other times by appt. Secondhand collectable and antiquarian books, local county maps and prints. PBFA

Oundle STD 0832

Howard Antiques
(Malcolm C.Taylor). 46-46A West St. Tel 74239 (priv 0234 711106). Open Tues-Sat 10-5; other times by appt. Large stock general antiques, furniture, metalwork, china, glass etc from 17th-19thC.

Paulerspury STD 032 733

The Antique Galleries
(Malcolm Cameron). Watling St. Tel 238. Open Mon-Sat 9-6. (3 miles south of Towcester on A5.) Good stock in 12 showrooms of English period furniture. BADA

Potterspury

Reindeer Antiques Ltd
(J.W. Butterworth). 43 Watling St, NN12 7QD. Tel Yardley Gobion (0908) 542407. Open Mon-Sat 9-6; other times by appt. 35,000 sq ft of period furniture and accessories, mainly pre-1830. BADA, LAPADA

Thrapston STD 080 12

Chancery Antiques
(Bob Andrews). 24-26 High St. Tel 2434. Open Mon, Wed, Fri 10-1, 2-6; other times by appt. General antiques, clocks & watches, decorative pieces.

Towcester STD 0327

Acorn Antiques
(Ian Porter). The Old Mill, Moat Lane, NN12 7AD. Tel 52788. Open Mon-Fri 8.30-5; Sat 10-4; other times by appt. Country furniture from all of Europe, Gt. Britain & Ireland. Architectural bookcases & items.

Ron Green Antiques
(Michael, Nicholas & Christopher Green). 209, 227 & 239 Watling St, NN12 7BX. Tel 50387. Open Mon-Sat 9-6; other times by appt. English and Continental furniture, decorative items, shipping goods and paintings.

R. & M. Nicholas
161 Watling St. Tel 50639. Open Mon-Sat 9.30-6; other times by appt. Porcelain, glass, silver.

Weedon STD 0327

Antiqva
(John and Joan Parker). 36 High St.

Thirty Eight Antiques Ltd
(E.A.Saunders). 25-27 High St, NN7 4QD. Tel 40766. Open by appt only. English, French, Spanish and Irish furniture in pine and fruitwood. Room panelling and architectural fittings.

The Village
62 High St. Tel 42015. Open Mon-Sat 9.30-5.30; Sun & bank holidays 10.30-5.30. 40 stalls stocking antique furniture and general antiques.

Wellingborough STD 0933

W.F.Knight Ltd (Silversmiths)
(B.F.Knight & I.A.Knight). 2 Park Rd. Tel 222463. Open Mon-Sat 9-5; other times by appt. General stock of modern, reproduction and antique jewellery. Paintings, art nouveau and art deco items. Medals and porcelain.

West Haddon STD 078 887

Antiques
9 West End. Tel 772. Open Mon-Sat 10-5.30; other times by appt. Country and cottage furniture, treen and early metalwork.

Paul Hopwell Antiques
(Paul Hopwell & Anne Hopwell). 30 High St, NN6 7AP. Tel 636. Open Mon-Sat 9-6; other times by appt. Res on premises. Specialists in 17th & 18thC oak, country furniture and metalware. Also in stock, pictures, rugs and clocks. BADA

Northumberland

Alnwick STD 0665

Fine Arts Traders & Shippers and Bondgate Antiques
(P. & B. Marshall). Hill House, 39 Bondgate Within, NE66 1SX. Tel 603394 (priv 0665 830816). Open Mon-Sat 10-12.30 2-5; closed Wed pm; other times by appt. General antiques, Victoriana, silver, plate, china, clocks and small pieces of furniture, shipping goods. LAPADA

Ian A.Robertson
(I.A.Robertson). Narrogate. Furniture, porcelain, prints, metalware. Restorations. Valuations.

Berwick-upon-Tweed STD 0289

Bridge End Antiques
(Robert Goodfellow). 8-12 Bridge End, Next to Old Bridge, TD15 1AL. Tel 308702 (priv 066-84 433). Open Mon-Sat 10-4.30; other times by appt. Antiques, shipping furniture.

J.& D.Stewart (Antiques)
6 West Street, Norham, TD152LB. Tel 82376. Open Mon-Sat 9-6; res on premises; other times by appt. General smalls, china, glass, collectors items etc. Parking outside.

Corbridge STD 043 471

Christie's
(Representative: Aidan Cuthbert). Eastfield House, Main St. Tel 3181. Auctioneers & valuers.

Gallery 26
(Dorothy & Maurice Williamson). 26 Middle St. Open Wed, Fri, Sat; other times by appt. Silver, antiques and marine items.

Haltwhistle STD 0498

Sotheby's
(Representative: The Earl of Carlisle). Market Place, NE49 0BU. Tel 20363. Auctioneers & valuers.

Hexham STD 0434

Beaufort Gallery
(Judith Essenhigh, Caroline Braithwaite). Beaumont St. Fine 19th and 20thC paintings, watercolours and drawings, antique silver and a small selection of oriental rugs.

Arthur Boaden Antiques
(Richard J.Boaden). 29-30 Market Place, NE46 3PB. Tel 603187 (priv 604265). Open Mon-Sat 9-5; closed Thurs. Eight showrooms with antique, Victorian and second-hand furniture, china, glass, silver, jewellery, paintings etc. LAPADA

Colman's of Hexham, Saleroom and Antique Fair
15 St Mary's Chare. Tel 3812 day,4662 or 3944 eve. Open Mon-Sat 9-5.30; other times by appt. Several dealers with a wide variety of stock.

Hallstile Antiques
(Mrs E. Elliott). 17 Hallstile Bank, NE46 1UF. Tel 602239. Open 10-5, closed Thurs. Georgian, Victorian and Edwardian furniture, assorted small antiques, pine, linen and quilts.

Haydon Bridge Antiques
(J . & J. Smith). 3 Shaftoe St, Haydon Bridge. Tel Haydon Bridge (043484) 200 (priv 461). Open Mon-Sat 9-6; closed Thurs; other times by appt. Large premises, includes stripped pine, showrooms, art gallery, Victorian oils, watercolours and general antiques.

J.A. & T. Hedley
3 St Mary's Chare. Tel 602317. Open 9-5; Thurs 9-12. Furniture, glass and porcelain. Furniture restoration.

Hexham Antiques
(John and Dorothy Latham). 6 Rear Battle Hill. Tel 604813. Open Mon, Tues, Wed, Fri 10.30-5, Sat 9.30-5; other times by appt. General antiques, clocks, pictures and collectors items.

Prudhoe Cottage Antiques
(James and Myrtle Hall). Hexham Antique Market, 15 St Mary's, Chare. Tel 603812 (priv 0661 33421). Open Mon-Sat 10-5; closed Thurs. 18th and 19thC furniture, mainly mahogany. 18th and 19thC clocks, English glass, porcelain, pottery, oil lamps. Clock repairs.

Trevor-Venis Antiques
13 Hencotes, NE46 2EQ. Tel 607458. 18th and 19thC furniture and works of art.

Tynedale Antiques
Overstone House, Elvaston Rd. Tel 4662. (See also Coleman's.) Open Mon-Sat 9-5.30. Mainly furniture and a large stock of clocks and general antiques.

Rothbury STD 0669

The Jackdaw
(Mrs S.G.Taylor). Townfoot. Tel 0669 20785. Open Tues-Sat 10-5.30; other times by appt. General antiques, curios, paintings and prints.

Wooler STD 0668

Glendale Antiques
Peth Head. Tel 81396. Open 10-5; other times by appt. Clocks, furniture, silver and porcelain. Trade and shipping goods.

W.J. Miller & Son
(William James Miller, Kathleen Miller). 1-5 Church St. Tel 81500 (priv 06687 281). (Also at 6-8 High St, warehouse at 12 Station Rd.) Open any time by appt. Large stock Georgian & Victorian furniture, clocks, oil paintings, shipping goods.

Nottinghamshire

Annesley Woodhouse

Stonecourt Antiques
(Peter W. Miller). Stonecourt, Salmon Lane. Tel Mansfield (0623) 751710. Fine furniture and paintings.

Askham

Sally Mitchell Fine Arts
(Sally Mitchell). Thornlea, NG22 0RN. Tel Gamston (077783) 234. Open by appt. Sporting paintings, sporting prints, portraits and general paintings. Writer on sporting paintings, valuations, framing and restoration.

Aslockton

East Bridgford Antiques
(M. & M. Thompson). Aslockton Grange. Tel (0949) 50204. (Also East Bridgford Antiques Centre in East Bridgford, Notts.) Open by appt only. (On main A52 road one mile past Bingham towards Grantham). Furniture, paintings and decorative objects.

Bingham STD 0949

E.M. Cheshire Antiques
(E.M. Cheshire). The Manor House, Market Place. Tel 38861 (priv 38455). (Also Shop 34, Woburn Abbey, Beds.) Open Mon-Sat 10-5.30; early closing Wed. 18thC oak, 18th and 19thC mahogany and early metalwork. BADA LAPADA

East Bridgford STD 0949

East Bridgford Antiques Centre
(M. & M. Thompson). Main St. Tel 20741. (Also at Aslockton Grange, Aslockton, Notts..) Open daily. 7 dealers in furniture, treen and collectors' items.

Eastwood

Stonecourt Antiques
(P.W.Miller, D.J.Mitchell). 20 Mansfield Rd. Furniture, clocks and paintings.

Elton STD 083 24

Mary Mackie Antiques
General antiques & painted furniture.

Kirton

Homestead Antiques
(Harry and Glenis Lowe). The Homestead, Main St. Tel 0623-861679. 17th-19thC furniture.

Langford

Terry Baker
(Terry Baker). Langford House Farm. Tel Newark-on-Trent (0636) 704026. Open Mon-Fri 8-6; other times by appt. Good Victorian and period furniture.

Long Eaton STD 0602

Goodacre Engraving Ltd
(John Skeavington, Philip Frearson). Trumpton Ave, Meadow Lane, NG10 2GB. Tel 734387 (priv 05097-3082). Open Mon-Fri 8.30-5.30; other times by appt. Hand engravers of complete dials and parts thereof. Brass and painted dial restoration, high quality longcase and bracket clock parts and castings in stock - old movements usually available. BHI

Mansfield STD 0623

Fair Deal Antiques
138 Chesterfield Rd North. Tel 653768. General antiques.

Mansfield Antiques
(W. & L.M. Pedley). 49-51 Ratcliffe Gate. Tel 27475 (Priv 32108). Open Mon-Sat 9-5; other times by appt. Period & shipping goods.

John B.Sheppard Antiques
(J.B.Sheppard). 122-124 Chesterfield Rd North. Tel 31691. Open 9.30-5.30; closed Wed; other times by appt. Res on prem. Antiques and Victorian furniture suitable for most markets, also a few clocks and furnishing antiques.

Newark-on-Trent STD 0636

Edward Bailey & Son
17 Northgate, NG24 1EX. Tel 77154. Open Mon-Fri 9-5.30; other times by appt. Weekly auction sales of antique and Victorian furniture, silver, oil paintings, pottery and porcelain, etc.

Castle Antiques
(Roger Key). Bairds Malt, Northgate. Tel 704290 (priv 707764). (Also at Northgate House, Northgate.) Open Mon-Fri 8-5; other times by appt. 18th, 19th and 20thC goods including English and imported pine & decorators items. Specialising in country furniture.

Castle Gate Antique Centre
55 Castlegate. Tel 700076. Open Mon-Sat 9-5; other times by appt. Antiques centre with 12 participating dealers offering 18th and 19thC furniture, paintings and watercolours, silver and old Sheffield plate, metalware, treen and ceramics etc. Trade warehouse at rear of centre.

Corner House Antiques
(B.R. & B. Wigglesworth). Farrar Clse, Brunel Dr, Northern Rd Industrial Estate, NG24 2EQ. Tel 79014 (priv 892628). Open Mon-Fri 9-5; other times by appt. Manufacturers of good quality reproduction pine furniture made entirely from old timbers.

Curiosity
(Sheila Dyson). Newark Art & Antiques Centre, Market Place, NG24 1DU. Tel 703959 (priv 0777 870537). Open Mon-Sat 9.30-5; Thurs 9.30-12. Antiques, curios and collectors' items.

F.J.McCarthy Ltd
(Frederick J. & Irene McCarthy). The Grange, Normanton on Trent, NG23 6RQ. Tel 821382. Open Mon-Sat 9-6; other times by appt. Early to 19thC British and European furniture, Oriental pottery, porcelain and works of art.

Newark Art & Antiques Centre
(G. Jacobs). The Market Place and Chain Lane. Tel 703959. Open 9.30-5; early closing Thurs. Thirty shops dealing in furniture, porcelain, pictures, militaria, bygones, jewellery, uniforms, brass, copperware, stamps, coins, glass, silver, dolls, costumes.

Newton

Sally Burt Antiques
The White House. General antiques.

Nottingham STD 0602

Berkley Antiques
Trent Bridge, West Bridgford.

Breck Antiques
(P.H.K. Astill). 726 Mansfield Rd, Woodthorpe. Tel 605263 (priv 621197). Open Sat only; other times by appt. General antiques.

Joan Cotton Antiques
(Joan Cotton). 5 Davies Rd, West Bridgford. Tel 813043. Open 9-5, except Wed. Jewellery, silver, general smalls.

Heather Cowley Bookshop & Galleries
235-237 Mansfield Rd. Tel 473836. Open Mon-Sat 9-6. Antiquarian, art and collectors' books, topographical prints. Framing. FATG

Alastair Fraser Antiques
(Alastair & Eleanor Fraser). 2A Rushworth Ave, West Bridgford. Tel 821835. Open 10.30-5 closed Thurs; other times by appt. Dealer in pine, mahogany and oak, shipping furniture, antiques and curios.

Friar Antiques and Collectors' Centre
(Roy Morris-Cooke). 12-18 Friar Lane. Tel 417857. Open Mon-Sat 9.15-5. New antiques centre with many shops with a wide range of stock.

ANTONY DAVENPORT

Good 17th, 18th and 19th
Century English Furniture
and Decorative Items

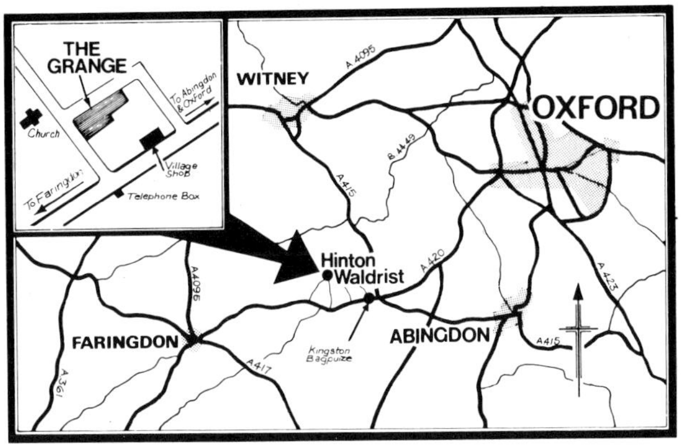

THE GRANGE, HINTON WALDRIST
Near FARINGDON, Oxon
(opposite the Church)
TELEPHONE LONGWORTH (STD 0865) 820227

HALLIDAYS

Fine Antiques for the Connoisseur

Behind this name lies the
world of Antiques.

HALLIDAYS

Fine Antiques for the Connoisseur

24 spectacular Antique showrooms

HALLIDAYS

Fine Antiques for the Connoisseur

Mostly William & Mary, Queen
Anne, Georgian & Regency furniture,
pictures, porcelain and silver.

HALLIDAYS

Fine Antiques for the Connoisseur

In beautiful Dorchester-on-Thames.
London only 52 miles. Do come and
see us, or send for
colour brochure.

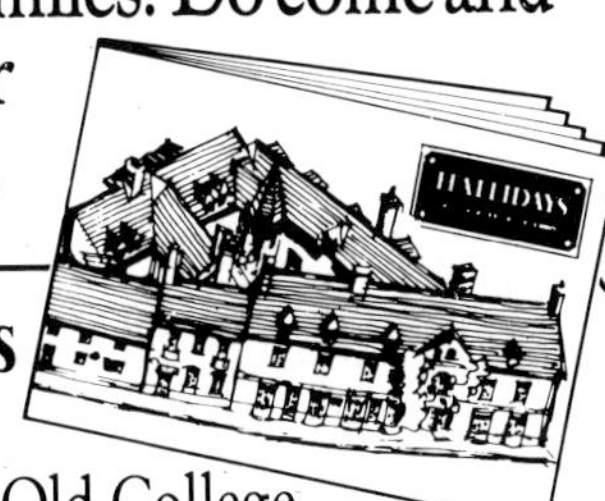

**HALLIDAYS ANTIQUES
LIMITED.**

Dept. A/BAA07, The Old College,
Dorchester-on-Thames, Oxfordshire OX9 8HL.
Tel: Oxford (0865) 340028/68

LEO PRATT & SON

*Large selection of
antiques in six showrooms*

**OLD CURIOSITY SHOP
SOUTH WALSHAM, NORFOLK**

Telephone South Walsham 204

Castle Gate Antique Centre

**55, CASTLE GATE, NEWARK-ON-TRENT,
NOTTINGHAMSHIRE TEL 0636 700076
(Situated on the A46)**

*Twelve dealers offering a good range of quality
antiques and collectors items*

A Dateline Antique Centre

Open Monday-Saturday 9.00am-5.00pm

Other times by appointment

A good trade call and well worth a visit
Also
Quality Trade Warehouse

Golden Cage
(Jill Pearson). 99 Derby Rd, Canning Circus. Tel 411600 (priv 254984). Open 10-5; closed Thurs & Sun; other times by appt. Antique clothes, beaded dresses, linen & lace, 20's & 30's dresses, mens wear, jewellery.

Arthur Johnson & Sons Ltd
(R.A. Johnson). Cattle Market, London Rd. Tel 869128. Open Mon-Fri 9-1, 2.15-5; Sat 8.30-2. Auctioneers with weekly sales on Sat (3 salerooms); antique, shipping and modern furniture, silver, porcelain, glass, metalware and collectors' items. Around 1500 lots weekly.

Melville Kemp Ltd
89-91 Derby Rd, NG1 5BB. Tel 417055. Open Mon-Fri 9.30-5.30; early closing Sat; closed Thurs; other times by appt. Old silver and plate, jewellery, china and glass.

Lustre Metal Antiques Ltd
Canning Circus, Derby Rd. Tel 704385. Open Mon-Sat 9-5. Antique metalware.

Matsell Antiques Ltd
(B.M. Matsell & P.D. Matsell). 2 & 4 Derby St, Off Derby Rd, NG1 5FP. Tel 472691 (priv 288267). Open Mon-Fri 10-5; closed Thur; other times by appt. Antiques of all periods, decorative and decorators objects, ironstone & oriental ceramics. Large showrooms & warehouse mainly directed towards home and export trade.

Neales of Nottingham
192/194 Mansfield Rd, NG1 3HX. Tel 624141. Chartered Auctioneers and Valuers. Specialist and fine art sales. Weekly sales of antique, Victorian and other furniture and decorative goods. Country house sales.

Michael Pollock Antiques
(Michael Pollock). 110 Derby Rd. Tel 474266 (priv 504027). Open Mon-Sat 10.30-2.30; other times by appt. Antiques, collectors' items, furniture and clocks.

David & Carole Potter (Antiques)
76 Derby Rd, NG1 5FD. Tel 417911. Open Mon-Sat 10-5 (closed Thurs); other times by appt. 18th and 19thC English and Continental furniture including a selective stock of scientific instruments, paintings, maps, pottery, porcelain, glass and metalware. Also a good selection of clocks.

Top Hat Antiques Centre & Fine Art Gallery
(Mr Bowley). 72 Derby Rd. Tel 419143. Open Mon-Sat 9.30-5. Wide range of antiques, paintings and watercolours. Restoration service for porcelain, jewellery and furniture. Picture framing.

Trade Winds Antiques
2 Queens Rd. Tel 8628850. Open Mon-Sat 12-4, closed Thurs. Clocks and general antiques.

Trident Arms
(Mike Long, Mike Scott, Herman Otten). 74 Derby Road, NG1 5FD. Tel 474137. Open Mon-Fri, 9.30-5.15; Sat, 10-4; other times by appt. Arms, armour, militaria, antique and modern.

Turner Fletcher & Essex
(R.H.Chatterton). Cattle Market, London Rd. Tel 865041. Open Mon-Fri 9-5. Auctioneers.

The Vintage Wireless Shop and Hockley Antiques
(Mr & Mrs D.A.Yates). 16 Hockley. Tel 57097, 205441. Open Mon-Sat 9.30-4.30; other times by appt. Vintage wireless sets from 1900 to 1950. Also horn gramophones, phonographs and collectors' items, plus general antiques.

Walker Walton & Hanson
Byard Lane, Bridlesmith Gate. Tel 586161. Auctioneers.

D.Wise Antiques
(D.Wise). 78 Derby Rd, NG7 1AY. Tel 472132. Open Mon-Sat 10-5.30; other times by appt. General antiques and shipping goods. Silver.

Retford STD 0777

Henry Spencer & Sons
20 The Square. Tel 708633. Open Mon-Fri 8.30-5. Fine art auctioneers holding regular specialist sales of art and antiques.

Southwell STD 0636

Strouds of Southwell Antiques
(V.N. and J. Stroud). 3 Westgate. Tel 815001. (Also at King St. Gallery, 7 King St, Southwell (813176.) Open Mon-Sat, 10-5; other times by appt. Caning of chairs, early 17th to 19thC furniture, mirrors, pewter.

Tuxford STD 0777

Dukeries Antiques
(John & Judy Coupe). Newcastle Cottage, 74 Newcastle St. Tel 871506. (Also at Castle Gate Antique Centre, Newark, Notts.) 18th and 19thC furniture and decorative pieces.

Worksop STD 0909

Worksop Antiques
(J.W.Dench). 20 Park St. Tel 476384. (Also trade warehouse at 85 William St, Sheffield.) Open Mon-Sat 10-5; other times by appt. Antique furniture and Staffordshire figures. LAPADA

Oxfordshire

Abingdon STD 0235

Checker Books
2 Checker Walk. Tel 28172. Bowls, bowling clubs, Berkshire, Oxfordshire. ABA

Banbury STD 0295

Holloway's
(T.J. Holloway, FRICS). 49 Parsons St, OX6 8PF. Tel 53197 (priv 811297). (Also at 12 High St, Streatley, Berks.) Open Mon-Fri 9-5.30; Sat 9-12.30; other times by appt. Auctioneers and valuers. RICS

Weaves and Waxes
(Laurie and Mary Grayer). 53 Church St, Bloxham, OX15 4ET. Tel 721535. Open Tues-Sat 9-1, 2-5.30; other times by appt. Purveyors of antique furniture restoration materials, glues, stains, polishes, chemical wood treatments, veneers, bandings cabinet brassware, traditional upholstery requisites, leather desk/box skivers, books, etc. GMC

Benson

Bygones
(M.&J.Cleland). Paddock House, 8 Brook St, OX9 6LQ. Tel Wallingford (0491) 38307. Open Mon-Sat; closed Wed; other times by appt. Good mixed stock furniture, porcelain, glass, plate, metals. Repairs.

Sarum Antiques
(M.J.Hatton). Castle Square, OX9 6SD. Tel Wallingford (0491) 38527. Open 10-5.30; early closing Wed; other times by appt. 19thC and Edwardian furniture, clocks, brassware and china.

Bicester STD 0869

Messengers
27 Sheep St, OX6 7JF. Tel 252901. Auctioneers.

Tollgate Antiques
(D. & M. Palmer). 31 North St. Tel 24196. Open Mon-Sat 9.30-6; other times by appt. Furniture, glass, china, plate, copper, brass, books and militaria.

Bladon

Blenheim Antiques
OX7 1RW. Tel Woodstock (0993) 811841. Open Mon-Sat 9.30-5.30. Res on prem. 18th and 19thC furniture, clocks and smalls.

Blewbury STD 0235

Blewbury Antiques
London Rd, OX11 9NX. Tel 850366. Open Mon-Sun 10-6, closed Wed; other times by appt. General antiques, Victoriana, books, garden and outdoor items, bric-a-brac. Specialising in country items.

Burford STD 099 382

The Burford Gallery
(Brian Etheridge). Classica House, High Street, OX8 4QA. Tel 2305. Open Tues-Sat 10-6, most Suns 12-5; other times by appt. 18th, 19th and early 20thC British watercolours.

Clement House Antiques
(Derrick Stevens). High St, OX8 4QE. Tel 3172. Open Mon-Sat 9.30-5.30; other times by appt. 17th, 18th, 19thC Town & Country furniture & 19thC glass. BADA

The Crypt Antiques
(Peter Matthey, Manfred Schotten). London House, High St. Tel 2302. Open Mon-Sat 9.30-1, 2-5.30; other times by appt. 18th & 19thC oak & mahogany furniture, some pine, antique fishing tackle & golfing collectables. CADA

Jonathan Fyson Antiques
(J.R. & J. Fyson). High St. Tel 3204 (priv 0865 880943). (Also in Cassington, Oxon.) Open Mon-Sat 9.30-5.30. English & Continental furniture, pine, brass & decorative items including jewellery. CADA

Horseshoe Antiques & Gallery
(Mr & Mrs B.Evans). High St, OX8 4RJ. Tel 3244. 17th & 18thC oak furniture, watercolours, oil paintings, 18th & 19thC Staffordshire figures and animals. Period copper & brass. LAPADA

Jubilee Books Ltd
18 High St, OX8 4QE. Tel 2209. Open Mon, Tues, Thurs, Sat 9.30-1, 2-5.30. General secondhand and antiquarian books. Literature, history, theology. ABA

Anthony Nielsen Antiques
(Anthony Nielsen). High St, OX8 4QQ. Tel 2014 (priv 0451 21710). Open Mon-Sat 9.30-1, 2-5.30; other times by appt. Quality English furniture and selected brass and copper.

Anthony Scaramanga Antiques

SAMPLERS

Colour prints of samplers and needlework pictures from our extensive stock available on request. Samplers crated and sent airmail to all parts of the world at reasonable rates.

Fine sampler 11" × 14" worked by Mary Downing 1771. It features a lady holding a rose in a country scene with hills, trees and deer. A border in shaded eyelet stitch and lozenge shapes containing flowers, birds and her name. Above are two verses and further border patterns. Colour and condition extremely good.

Orphanage sampler from Bristol. 13" × 16", 1877, worked by Alice Pitt. It has a great variety of alphabets, numbers and repeat border patterns, a verse on Home, sweet Home, and a house. All worked in fine red crossstitch. Colour and condition excellent.

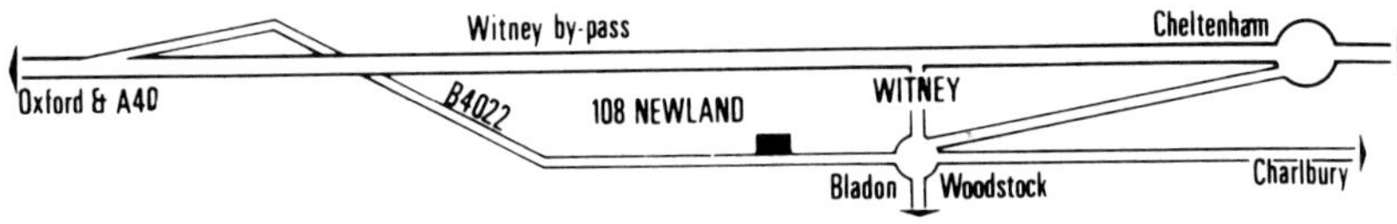

108 NEWLAND, WITNEY, OXON. Telephone Witney (0993) 3472

Closed Fridays

ANTIQUES MARKET

10 – 4.30
Trade 9.15

A good trade call

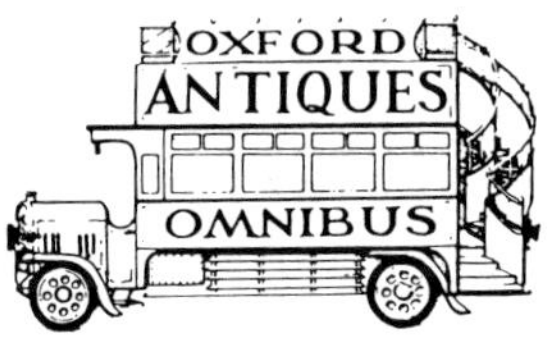

Every Wednesday

Every Saturday

The Basement, OMNI STORE, George Street, OXFORD

(near bus, rail stations and car parks, loading/unloading in George St. Mews)

Stalls include Clocks, Furniture, Watercolours, Books, Jewellery, Silver & Brass, Curios & Collectables, Ceramics, 20's-60's Clothes. Also an inexpensive good picture framing and clock repair service.

Oxford Antiques Omnibus – Oxford 739071, Didcot 817076

Thame Antique and Art Galleries

Fine Antique Furniture
Victorian Water-colours and Oil paintings

Premises established over 100 years as a centre for antiques

11–12 HIGH STREET, THAME, OXFORDSHIRE
Telephone Thame 2725

OXFORD

NORTH PARADE ANTIQUES

75 BANBURY ROAD, OX2 6PE. (Corner of North Parade Avenue & Banbury Road)

Tel: (0865) 59816 Home 880923.

Open 9.30 am to 6 pm Monday to Saturday

MICHAEL BULL BUYS & SELLS 19th CENT. FURNITURE AND ASSOCIATED SMALLS FOR HOME & EXPORT

Best approach is via Northern By-pass (A40 North) & turn into the city at the Banbury Road Roundabout. The shop is one mile down on the right.

Peter Norden Antiques
(Peter and Jenny Norden). High St, OX8 4XX. Tel 2121 (priv 0993 830064). Open Mon-Sat 9.30-5.30; other times by appt. Early oak and country furniture, period mahogany and walnut furniture, pewter, brass, copper, delft, treen and coloured glass. Some pistols and blunderbusses. CADA

Brian Sinfield (Gallery)
(B. Sinfield). The Studio, High St, OX8 4ST. Tel 2402. Open 10-5.30; other times by appt. British watercolours 1750-1950 and Edwardian and 20thC oil paintings.

Zene Walker
(Patrick Walker). The Bull House Antiques, High St. Tel 3284. Open Mon-Sat 9-1 2-5; other times by appt. Oriental, Islamic, English & European ceramics and works of art. English oak & walnut, mahogany and rosewood furniture, 17th-18thC. BADA

Cassington

Jonathan Fyson Antiques
The Old School House. Tel Oxford (0865) 880943. (Also in Burford,Oxon.) English and Continental furniture, pine, brass and decorative items.

Chipping Norton STD 0608

Bugle Antiques
(M. & D. Harding-Hill). 9 Horsefair. Tel 3322. Open 9-6; other times by appt. English country furniture, Windsor chairs. Also large trade showrooms at 80 yds distance. LAPADA

G. & E. Cashmore Antiques
50 West St.

Gillian Dickerson
Packer House, 28 High St. Tel 3255 (priv 41717). Open Tues-Sat 9.30-5.30. Secondhand and rare books.

C.B.Gardner Antiques
(C.B.Gardner). 31 High St. Tel 3913. Open Mon-Sat 9-6; other times by appt. Country furniture, some mahogany and smalls. CADA

Horsefair Antiques
(R.K.Walker). 21 Horsefair. Tel 3089. Open Mon-Sat 9.30-5.45; other times by appt. Country furniture, especially Windsor chairs, clocks, barometers, early ironware, some Victoriana and curios.

Jonathan Howard
21 Market Place. Clocks.

Key Antiques
(D. & M.Robinson). 11 Horsefair, OX7 5AL. Tel 3777. Open Mon-Sat 9.30-6; other times by appt. Oak and country furniture, 16th to 19thC; antique metalware and lighting, primitive paintings, candlesticks. CADA

Lion House/Robert Croot Antiques
(Robert & Hilary Croot). 16 New St, OX7 5LJ. Tel 3294. Open Mon-Sat 9-6; other times by appt. Country furniture, tables, sets of chairs, desks, bureaux, cupboards, dressers, corner cupboards, clocks. CADA

Packer House
(Ted & Sheila Jones). 28 High St, OX7 5AD. Tel 3255. Open Mon-Sat 9.30-6; other times by appt. Oak country furniture, copper & brass.

Keith Platt
4 West St.

Harry Smith
The Studios, Hitchman Mews, West St, OX7 5AA. Tel 2624 (priv 61612). Photographer.

Peter Stroud Antiques
(Peter & Sylvia Stroud). Station Yard Industrial Estate, OX7 5HX. Tel 41651 (priv 3103). Open Mon-Sat 9-5.30; other times by appt. Large stock of English 18th & 19thC oak & mahogany furniture, French country furniture and decorative items. CADA

Church Enstone

Warrack & Perkins
Rectory Farm House, OX7 4NN. Tel Enstone (060 872) 572. Open by appt only. 19th and 20thC illustrated books, prints, drawings, posters, private press books. ABA

Culham

Colin & Charlotte Franklin
Home Farm. Tel Abingdon (0235) 22544. Fine and rare printing, manuscripts, illustrated books and bindings. ABA

Deddington STD 0869

The Antiques Centre
(Mrs June Hope). Laurel House, Bull Ring, OX4 5TT. Tel 38968 (priv 0934 412069). Open Wed-Sat; other times by appt. Nine rooms of antiques from 1780-early 20thC. Paintings, watercolours, furniture, silver, porcelain & metalware. Pine furniture, linen & many collectables.

Old Noah Antiques
(A.G.Enstone). Featherton House, Chapel Square. Tel 38259. Open by appt. Clocks, period furniture, shipping goods, Victorian, country oak, bric-a-brac.

Didcot STD 0235

E.M.Lawson & Co
Kingsholm, East Hagbourne, OX11 9LN. Tel 812033. Open by appt only. Antiquarian books, specialising in 17th and 18thC English literature, voyages and travel, early science, economics. ABA

Dorchester

Dorchester Galleries
(Doreen Knipe). Rotten Row, OX9 8LJ. Tel Oxford (0865) 341116. Open daily 10-6, except Wednesdays; other times by appt. Watercolours, prints, maps, porcelain, pottery and furniture.

Hallidays Antiques Ltd
The Old College, High St. Tel Oxford (0865) 340028. (Also at 28 Beauchamp Place, London SW3.) Open Mon-Sat 9.15-5.15. Large premises, 8,000sq ft. 17th to 19thC furniture and paintings; period and reproduction wood and marble fireplaces; period style room panelling. All accessories for the period fireplace. LAPADA

Mike Ottrey Antiques
28 High St. Tel Oxford (0865) 340079. Open Mon-Thurs 9.30-1 2-5.30; other times by appt. 17th,18th and 19thC furniture, mainly country, but some mahogany. Also copper and brass and some oil paintings. Unusual items also stocked. (Also trade warehouse).

Eynsham

David John Ceramics
(John Twitchett,David Holborough & Roy Beeston). 11 Acre End St, OX8 1PE. Tel Oxford (0865) 880786. Open Tues-Sat 10-5; other times by appt. 18th, 19th & early 20thC porcelain, small furniture, pictures and books on pottery and porcelain. CADA

Redthorne Cottage Antiques
1 Newland St, OX8 1LB. Tel Oxford (0865) 880641. Open Mon-Thurs 10-6, Fri-Sun by appt.

John Wilson (Autographs) Ltd
(John Wilson). 50 Acre End St, OX8 1PD. Tel Oxford (0865) 880883. Open Mon-Fri 9-6; other times by appt. Autograph letters, documents and manuscripts. ABA

Faringdon STD 0367

A.& F. Partners
(F.P.& Mrs A.M. Bench). 20 London St, SN7 7AA. Tel 20078. Open Mon-Sat 9.30-6; other times by appt. 17th to 19thC English and European furniture, oak, walnut & mahogany, collectors items, treen and delftware. BADA

Classey Ltd
Park Rd, SN7 7DR. Tel 20911. Natural history. ABA

Antony Davenport
The Grange, Hinton Waldrist. Tel Oxford (0865) 820227. Good 18th & early 19thC English furniture and decorative items.

The Faringdon Galleries
79 London St. Tel 20344. Open Fri & Sat; other times by appt. Fine 17th to 19thC oak, 18th to 19thC mahogany, also walnut furniture.

Betty Haslam
4 Market Pl. Tel 21574. Open Mon-Sat. Oils, watercolours and sporting prints from 1800. Also small furniture, silver and porcelain.

La Chaise Antique
(Roger Clark). 30 London St, SN7 7AA. Tel 20427. Open Mon-Sat 10-6; other times by appt. 18th and 19thC chairs, furniture, upholstery and soft furnishings. Specialist in leather restoration, leather desk and table tops. Wide range of reproduction leather chairs available. Stockists of fine modern fabrics and wallpapers.

Fyfield STD 027 785

Blackwell's Rare Books
Fyfield Manor, OX13 5LR. Tel Frilford Heath (0865) 390692-3. Open Mon-Sat 8.30-5.15. (On A420 Oxford -Swindon.) Antiquarian and rare modern books on most subjects. ABA

WITNEY ANTIQUES

L. S. A. & C. J. Jarrett

96–98 Corn Street, Witney, Oxon. OX8 7BU
Tel. Witney (0993) 3902 or 3887

You are invited to visit our spacious period showrooms in Witney where we have for sale an important collection of fine 17th and 18th cent. furniture, longcase and bracket clocks and works of art.

We are able to offer specialist restoration and conservation services for fine antique furniture. All work carried out in our own workshops by highly trained and experienced craftsmen.

SPECIALISTS IN FINE ENGLISH FURNITURE AND CLOCKS

PRIESTS

Antiques and Fine Arts
60 North Street Thame Oxfordshire
Telephone Thame 4461

Good quality late 18th century mahogany bureau. Circa 1780. Size: 43″ High, 40″ Wide, 19½″ Deep. Price £1650

The Lamb Antiques Centre

HIGH STREET,
WALLINGFORD,
OXON.

Open 10 a.m. to 5 p.m. – Monday-Saturday (excluding Wednesday)

The Lamb houses probably the largest collection of Antiques, Fine Arts and Collectable items in the Thames Valley.

Located mid-way between Oxford and Reading; approx. one hour's drive Central London.

Coffee lounge and Wine Bar/Restaurant

Antique Furniture Restorer on Premises

Further enquiries to Graham Pack on 01-349-3111

Henley-on-Thames
STD 0491

The Antique Galleries
(E.G.L.Mackie, O.C.Bond, H.C.P.Mackie, H.G.Bond). 16 Hart St, RG9 2AU. Tel 572181 (priv 073522 2100). Open Mon-Sat 9.30-5; closed Wed; other times by appt. General antiques, including furniture, silver, glass, pottery, metalware, clocks and watches.

The Barry M. Keene Gallery
(B.M. Keene, J.S. Keene). 12 Thameside, RG9 1RY. Tel 577119. Open Mon-Sat 9.30-5.30; other times by appt. Fine 18thC, 19thC and early 20thC watercolours, paintings, etchings, maps & prints, Master picture frame maker, restorer, carver & gilder. Pictures cleaned, relined & restored. Valuations. FATG

Richard J.Kingston
(R.J.Kingston). 95 Bell St, RG9 2BD. Tel 574535. Open Mon-Fri 9-5.30, Sat 9.30-5; other times by appt. 17th-19thC furniture and general antiques, including silver, porcelain and antiquarian and other books. BADA

Market Place Antiques
(Elisabeth Whittaker). 35 Market Place, RG9 2AA. Tel 572387. Open Mon-Sat 10-1, 2-6; other times by appt. Large general stock, decorative and unusual items, metalware, tools, needlework and treen. Large stock of pine and country furniture. LAPADA

B.R.Ryland
75 Reading Rd, RG9 1AX. Tel 573663. Open 9-5.30. Victorian, Edwardian and reproduction furniture, brass, copper, china.

Simmons & Lawrence (Chartered Surveyors)
32 Bell Street, RG9 2BH. Tel 571111. Open Mon-Fri 9-5.30; Sat 9-12.30. Auctioneers and valuers of fine art antiques and chattels.

Thames Gallery
Thameside, RG9 2LT. Tel 572449. Open Mon-Sat 10-5. Specialists in English silver of the Georgian and Victorian periods.

Long Hanborough

Antiques
(D.Strong). 127 Main Rd. Tel Oxford (0865) 881484. Open Tues-Fri 10-5; Sun 2-6; closed Mon. Country furniture, brass, copper, rural and domestic bygones.

Nettlebed STD 0491

Harvey Ferry, William Clegg Antiques
(Harvey Ferry, William Clegg). The Barns, 1 High St, RG9 5AA. Tel 641533. Open Mon-Fri 9-5.30, Sat 10-4; other times by appt. A large stock of English furniture 1600 to 1850. LAPADA

Oxford STD 0865

The Antiquary
50 St Giles. Tel 59875. Old English silver, Sheffield plate, china, glass and jewellery. BADA

P.Audley-Miller
46 High St, OX1 4AP. Tel 247952. Open 9.30-5 daily. General antiques, art pottery.

Reginald Davis (Oxford) Ltd
34 High St, OX1 4AN. Tel 248347. Open Mon-Sat 9-5, closed Thurs. Antique silver, jewellery, old Sheffield plate, Continental silver. BADA

The Desk Shop
(James Devereux). 41 St Clements. Tel 245524. Open Mon-Fri 9-5.30, Sat 9-5; other times by appt. Antique pedestal desks; restoration service and releathering. Contract furnishing service for period offices.

C.T.Legge Oriental Carpets
(Christopher Legge). Oakthorpe Rd, Summertown. Tel 57572 (priv 0993 831298). Open Mon-Sat 10-5; other times by appt. Old Oriental carpets. Also cleaning service.

Laurie Leigh Antiques
36 High St. Tel 244197. Open Mon-Sat 11-6, closed Thurs. 17th and 18thC longcase and bracket clocks. Early keyboard instruments, fortepianos, harpsichords, clavichords, etc.

Magna Gallery
(Brian Kentish). 41 High St. Tel 245805. Open Mon-Sat. Antique maps and prints, especially English county maps and Oxford views. ABA

Mallams
(M.R.V.Lear, B.J.Lloyd). 24 St Michael's St. Tel 241358,57250. (Also at Cheltenham.) Auctioneers of fine art and antiques. Monthly sales including specialist sales of pictures, silver, jewellery, Eastern rugs and porcelain.

Nicholas Meyjes Photography
(Nicholas Meyjes, ABIPP). 12 Forge Close, Horton-cum-Studley, OX9 1BL. Tel Stanton St John (086 735) 496. Open Mon-Fri; other times by appt. Photography of antiques and paintings, architecture and other subjects for publication. ABIPP

North Parade Antiques
(Michael Bull). 75 Banbury Rd (A423). Tel 59816 (priv 880923). (Warehouse (strictly trade only) 2 Oxford Rd, Eynsham.) Open Mon-Sat 9.30-6. General stock of European and Oriental antiques. 19thC and shipping furniture. CADA

Oxford Antiques
(Polly Clewett). Number Ten, North Parade, OX2 6LX. Tel 512816. Open Mon-Sat 10-1.30 also afternoons in the Autumn; other times by appt. Small antiques, mainly porcelain, expecially 19thC English porcelain.

Oxford Antiques Omnibus
The Basement, Omni Store, George St. Tel 739071. Open every Wed & Sat 10-4.30 (trade 9.15). 26 dealers offering a wide range of antiques including furniture, clocks, watercolours, silver, brass, ceramics. Picture framing and clock repair service.

Oxford Gallery
(M.D.:Dr Peter Shahbenderian). 23 High St, OX1 4AH. Tel 242731. Open Mon-Sat 10-5. Contemporary fine art and craft gallery specialising in studio ceramics, jewellery and metalwork and original prints. Important collection of 20thC British studio ceramics including Rie, Cooper, Leach etc. ICGA

D. Parikian
The Old Rectory, Waterstock, OX9 1JR. Tel Ickford (084 47) 603. Open by appt only. Continental books before 1800, mythology, iconography, emblemata. ABA

Payne & Son (Goldsmiths) Ltd
(G.N. Payne, E.P. Payne, J.D. Payne). 131 High St, OX1 4DH. Tel 243787. Open Mon-Sat 8.30-1, 2-5. Antique, secondhand & modern silver & jewellery. BADA

Phillips
(Enquiries: Michael Welch). 39 Park End St, OX1 1JD. Tel 723524. Auctioneers & valuers.

Rosemary & Time
(Tom Fletcher). 42 Park St.

A. Rosenthal Ltd
9-10 Broad St, OX1 3AP. Tel 243093. Fine books and manuscripts; Continental literature, autograph letters. Judaica. ABA

Sanders of Oxford Ltd
(R.W.Mills, managing director). 104 High St, OX1 4BW. Tel 242590. Open Mon-Fri 9-1, 2.15-5.15, Sat 9-1. Antiquarian prints and maps, rare books and watercolours. ABA

The Ship Street Antique Gallery
5 Ship St, OX1 3DA. Tel 248130. Open Mon-Sat 9-5.30. Antique furniture, china, silver and other items.

A. & J.Stuart-Mobey & Daughter
Bedford House, Lower Wolvercote, OX2 9PF. Tel 50170. (Also at Span Antiques, Market St, Woodstock, Oxon.) Open daily 10-5; closed Wed; other times by appt. 18th to 20thC furniture, pottery, watercolours, treen, metalware and barometers.

Studio Edmark
Wheatsheaf Yard, High St. Tel 24186. Photographers.

Studio One Gallery
(Mrs Betty Clark). 214 Banbury Rd, OX2 7BY. Tel 511637. Open 9.30-5.30 (Thurs pm by appt). 19thC watercolours and prints, 20thC wood engravings.

The Talbot Gallery
290 Woodstock Rd, OX2 7NN. Tel 59049. Open Tues-Sat 10-1, 2.30-5.30. 19th and 20thC watercolours and oils, studio pottery 1870-1930, Art Nouveau and small antiques.

Thomas-Photos Oxford
1 Collingwood Close, Headington. Tel 61350. Photographers.

Thornton's of Oxford Ltd
(W.A.Meeuws, J.S.Meeuws). 11 Broad St, OX1 3AR. Tel 242939. Open Mon-Sat 9-6. Antiquarian and new booksellers. Rare and bibliophile department. ABA

Shipton-under-Wychwood STD 0993

Ye Olde Junk Shoppe
(B.Hill). St Michael's College. Tel 830576. Open Mon-Sat 10-7; closed Thurs. Large stocks of country furniture, mostly pine and oak, brass, copper, iron, wood, bygones, militaria, books, clocks, pottery, glass and jewellery.

Standlake STD 086 731

Cottage Antiques
Bracken Cottage, High St. Tel 421. Open daily. Antique furniture and some small items.

Manor Farm Antiques
(Mrs M.Leveson-Gower). Manor Farm, OX8 7RL. Tel 303. Open Mon-Sat 10-6; other times by appt. Brass and iron beds, country furniture, stripped pine, copper and bric-a-brac. Victorian beds always in stock. Some shipping goods.

Thame STD 084 421

Peter Fell of Thame
(Peter and Katherine Fell). 81 High St. Tel 4487. Open daily 9.30-5.30; closed Mon; other times by appt. Antique clocks, especially English longcase and bracket clocks and French mantel clocks. Some furniture. BADA

Priests Antiques & Fine Arts
(Michael G.Priest). 60 North St. Tel 4461. Open Mon-Sat 10-5. Specialists in high quality English antique furniture and fine paintings.

Telling Time Antiques
(Shirley Telling). 57 North St, OX9 3BH. Tel 3007. Open Mon-Sat 10-1, 2.15-5; other times by appt. Clocks, watches, jewellery, furniture & general antiques.

Thame Antique Galleries
11-12 High St. Tel 2725. Open Mon-Sat 9-5.30; other times by appt. 17th - 19thC furniture.

Wallingford STD 0491

The Antique Shop
6 St Peter's St. Tel 39345. Open 9.30-5; closed Mon & Wed. Clocks, Victorian furniture and ornamental items.

Eagle House
(W. Ottrey & Son). 16 High St. Tel 36429. Open Mon-Sat 8-6. Antique English furniture and general antiques.

The Lamb Antiques Centre
High St. Tel 735166. Open Mon-Sat 10-5; closed Wed. Wide range of antiques including furniture, maps, glass, pottery, porcelain, metalware, jewellery and many other items.

MGJ Antiques
(Mrs M.Jane). 1A, St Martins St. Tel 34336. Jewellery. LAPADA

Erik Pelham
P.O.Box 28, OX10 0ED. Tel 33568 24hr ans phone. Photographers specialising in interiors, location photography and lighting.

Pennyfarthing Antiques
Crowmarsh Gifford, OX10 8EA. Tel 37470. Open Mon-Sat 9-6; other times by appt. Antiques, including horse drawn vehicles, carts and curios.

Summers, Davis & Son Ltd
(Mr M.S.Baylis & Mr G.Wells). Calleva House, 6 High St, OX10 0BP. Tel 36284. Open Mon-Fri 8-6, Sat 9-1 2-5; other times by appt. English and Continental decorative furniture and objects from 17th to 19thC. BADA, LAPADA

Wantage STD 023 57

Green & Co
(G.Green FRICS). 33 Market Place, OX12 8AL. Tel 3561/2. Open Mon-Fri 9-5.30; Sat 9-5. Chartered surveyors, auctioneers and valuers.

Jack F.W.King
(Jack King, Zena King). 33 Wallingford St. Tel 2676. Open Mon-Fri 10.30-5.30; other times by appt. Furniture, bronzes, sculpture, paintings, prints, watercolours, silver, scientific instruments, mirrors, objects of vertu, porcelain, pottery, clocks, glass, brass, copper - with emphasis on the unusual.

Watlington STD 049 161

Thimbles Antiques
42 Couching St. Tel 2238. Open Mon-Sat 10-5.30; other times by appt. English porcelain prior to 1830.

Weston-on-the-Green

Julie Strachey
Southfield Farm, North Lane. Tel Bletchington (0869) 50833. Open anytime by appt. Country furniture, specialising in stripped pine.

Witney STD 0993

Robin Bellamy Ltd
(P.R.G. & J.M. Hornsby). 97 Corn St, OX8 7DL. Tel 4793. Open by appt or chance. Antique pewter, metalware and works of art, medieval to 1830. BADA

C.Greenway Antiques
90 Corn St. Tel 5026. Open Mon-Sat 9.30-5; other times by appt. 17th-19thC furniture, metalware, clocks and shipping items.

Ian Pout Antiques
99 High St. Tel 2616 (priv 0869 40205). Open Mon-Sat 10-5.30; other times by appt. Pine, country and decorative furniture, metalware and unusual objects. CADA

Anthony Scaramanga Antiques
108 Newland. Tel 3472. Open daily 10-5.30; closed Fri; other times by appt. 17th to 19thC samplers,needlework pictures, Staffordshire figures, blue & white pottery, small furniture. BADA CADA

Wantage Antiques
42-44 Newbury St. Tel 67872. Open Tues-Sat 10-1, 2-5.30; Sun 2-5.30; other times by appt. Furniture, bygones, collectables and general antiques.

Joan Wilkins Antiques
158 Corn St. Tel 4749. Open Mon-Sat 9.30-5; early closing Tues. Selection of good quality 18th and 19thC English furniture, metalware, glass & jewellery.

Witney Antiques
(L.S.A. & C.J.Jarrett). 96-98 Corn St, OX8 7BU. Tel 3902. (See also Witney Restorations.) Open Mon-Sat 9.30-5; other times by appt. Large stock of fine 17th & 18thC furniture, longcase & bracket clocks. Pewter and watercolours, objets d'art. BADA, CADA

Witney Restorations Ltd
(C.S.Jarrett, L.S.A.Jarrett, A.M.Smith). 96-98 Corn St, OX8 7BU. Tel 3902 or 3887. Restoration and conservation of fine antique furniture.

Woodstock STD 0993

Fox House
30-32 Oxford St. Open 9.30-5.30. General antiques.

Span Antiques
(Hugh Haig & Maureen Haig). 6 Market Place, OX7 1TA. Tel 811332. Open Sun-Sat 10-1, 2-5; closed Wed; other times by appt. Multi-dealer shop occupied by 8 dealers. Middle range furniture from Georgian to 20thC, English & Oriental porcelain, metalware & domestic bygones, textiles, collectors items.

Woodstock Antiques
(Clive Mason-Pope). 11 Market St, OX7 1SU. Tel 811494. Open 9-5.30 inc Sun; early closing Wed; other times by appt. Victorian Staffordshire figures and pottery, decorative objects, pictures and small furniture.

Shropshire

Bridgnorth STD 074 62

John Astill Antiques
(John Astill). 4 St John St, Low Town, WV15 6AG. Tel 3440. Open all day, every day. General antiques.

Christie's
(Representative: Michael Thompson). Stanley Hall. Tel 61891. Auctioneers and valuers.

English Heritage
(J.I.White, B.M.White). 2 Whitburn St. Tel 2097. Open Mon-Sat 9-5.30; Thurs 9-2; other times by appt. Antiques, specialising in maps; also furniture, silver, pictures, prints, china; also giltware and reproductions.

Church Stretton STD 0694

Old Barn Antiques
(Lt Col (Rtd) D.W. & Mrs S.K.Witting). High St, SY6 6BX. Tel 723742 (priv 722294). Open Tues, Thurs, Fri, Sat 10-12.45, 2.15-5.15; other times by appt. Georgian, Victorian and Edwardian furniture, porcelain, silver, metalware and general antiques. LAPADA

Craven Arms STD 058 82

Cartwright & Co
(W.L. Cartwright). Stokesay Antiques, Ludlow Rd. Tel 2263. Open Mon-Sat 8-5.30; other times by appt. General antiques, furniture restorers.

Partridge Restorations
(Ian and Jane Way). Peaton Lodge, Peaton, SY7 9DL. Tel Munslow (058 476) 639. Open Mon-Sat 9.30-5.30; other times by appt. Furniture restoration, all aspects but specialising in Jacobean and Georgian pieces. Porcelain restoration, all aspects but specialising in modelling on figures. Regular collection and delivery to London. Free estimates including 'ready-by' dates.

Pym Antiques
(John Pym). 6 Market St. Tel 2497. Open Tues-Fri 10-5; Sat 9.30-1. General antiques.

Dorrington STD 074 373

Singing Bird Antiques
13 Main Rd. Tel 208. Open Mon-Fri 10.30-5; other times by appt. Furniture 1700-1900, pewter, copper, brass, porcelain and pottery.

D.J.Wakeman & Co Ltd
(P.D.Simmonds, P.A.Simmonds). Grove Farm House. Tel 388. Open Mon-Fri 9-5; other times by appt. 18th and 19thC English and Continental furniture, clocks and general antiques. Restoration of antique furniture. LAPADA

Ellesmere STD 069 171

White Lion Antiques
(Dorothy Wheeldon). 4 Market St. Tel 2335. Open Mon-Sat 9-6; other times by appt. Mixed general stock.

Ludlow STD 0584

The Antique Centre
(K.L. Morris). Pepper Lane. Tel 6494 (priv 074 632 292). Open Mon-Sat 10-5; closed Thurs; other times by appt. Furniture, furnishings, paintings, prints, jewellery, porcelain and other collectable and antique items.

Directory Entries are Free and ADDITIONS OR CORRECTIONS will be welcomed by *THE EDITOR, British Art and Antiques Directory, National Magazine House, 72 Broadwick Street, London W1V 2BP*

Antique Corner
(A.J. Sciville & J. Clegg). 5 Corve St. Tel 3176 (priv 0584 77 468). Open Mon-Fri 10-6, closed Thurs. Country furniture, unstripped pine, related small goods, treen, china, metalware and general antiques.

D.W. & A.B. Bayliss & Son
(Donald Bayliss & Alice Begg Bayliss). 22-24 Old St. Tel 3634. Open Mon-Sat 9-6; other times by appt. Quality furniture, silver, silver plate, paintings, jewellery, glass.

Castle Lodge
(D.G. & H.G.Pearce). Castle Square. Tel 2833. Open Mon-Sat 10-5.30; appt advisable. Early furniture and furnishings, including large stock of oak and walnut. Specialists in 17th and 18thC dressers, tables and chairs.

R.G.Cave & Sons Ltd
17 Broad St. Tel 3568. Open Mon-Sat 9.30-5.30; other times by appt. Specialist in good period furniture and fine clocks; also paintings, needlework, porcelain, glass, Persian carpets, brass and copper. BADA LAPADA

William Marler Gallery
Dawes Mansion, Church St. Tel 4160. (Also 36/38 Dyer St, Cirencester,Glos.) Open Mon-Sat 9.30-5; closed Thurs pm. Sporting and natural history paintings, watercolours and prints. Framing & restoration.

McCartneys
(J.L. Talbor, MA, ARICS). Portcullis Hall Salerooms. Tel 2636. Open Mon-Fri 9-1, 2-5.30. Auctioneers fine art. SOFAA

Olivia Rumens
30 Corve St. Tel 3952. Open 10-1, 2-5; closed Thurs; other times by appt. Fine art dealer and restorer. Res on prem. Large stock of 17th and 18thC oil paintings and some Continental furniture. BADA

Audrey Silk Antiques
(Mrs Audrey Hosmer). 23 Bull Ring, SY8 1AA. Tel 5124 (priv 054 74 613). Open Mon-Sat 10-5.30; closed Thurs; other times by appt. Silver, jewellery, porcelain, pictures, furniture, specialising in unusual articles, antique textiles and decorative furnishings.

Paul Smith
(P. & B. Smith). The Old Chapel, Old St, SY8 1NP. Tel 2666. Open usually but appt advisable. Res on prem. 17th and 18thC oak and mahogany furniture. BADA

St Leonard's Antiques Centre
St Leonard's Church, Corve St. Tel 5573. Open Mon-Sat 9-5. General antiques and restoration of furniture.

M. & R. Taylor Antiques
(Mr & Mrs Michael Taylor). 53 Broad St, SY8 1NH. Tel 4169. Open anytime, res on premises. Furniture, mahogany, oak and walnut, 17th-19thC, rugs, brass, copper and treen.

Teme Valley Antiques
(Christopher Harvey). No.1 The Bull Ring, SY8 1AD. Tel 4686. Open usually Mon-Sat 10-5.30; other times by appt. English & European porcelain (18th-early 20thC), furniture, oil & watercolour paintings (17th-early 20thC) & silver, plate & metalware (18th-19thC).

Stanley Woolston
29 Broad St, SY8 1NJ. Tel 3554. Open normal hours. Early closing Thurs; other times by appt. Good antique furniture from 17th, 18th & 19thC and accessories. Also a gallery of modern fabrics, interior decoration & design. BADA, LAPADA

Market Drayton STD 0630

A.J. & L.Onions
(A.J. & L. Onions). White Cottage, 8 Tern Hill, TF9 3PR. Tel Tern Hill (063 083) 222. Open Mon-Sat 9-6; other times by appt. 17th & 18thC oak and walnut furniture.

Much Wenlock STD 0952

Wenlock Antiques
(K.C.Howard). 61 High St, TF13 6AE. Tel 727271. Open Mon-Sat 9-5.30; other times by appt. Cottage and country antiques, brass, copper and metalware, 18th and 19thC furniture, clocks, pottery and porcelain and prints.

Newport STD 0952

Classic Furniture Ltd
(David Tringham, Anne Tringham). Audley Avenue. Tel 813311. Open Mon-Fri 9-5; Sat 9-12; other times by appt. Reproduction antique cast iron furniture.

Norwood House Antiques
Norwood House, Pave Lane. Tel 811544. Open Tues-Sat 9-6; other times by appt. Antique furniture, clocks, metalware and objets d'art.

St Mary's Antiques and Cabinet Makers
(Ray & Dot Edwards). 2 Lower Bar. Tel 811549. Open Mon-Sat; other times by appt. Cabinet makers, wood carvers, clock makers & restorers. GMC

Oswestry STD 0691

Little Raven
(George and Betty Fogg). 11 Albion Hill. Tel 652172. Open Mon-Sat 10-4; closed Thurs; other times by appt. Jewellery and small items.

Trefor-Jones Antiques
(P.Trefor-Jones). The Old Poste House, Whittington. Tel 662312. Open Tues, Wed, Fri 11-4; other times by appt. China, dolls, small furniture, brass, copper, silver etc.

Shifnal

Broadway Antiques
(Mrs E.Onions). 25 Broadway, TF11 8BB. Tel Telford (0952) 460997. Open Mon-Sat 9-6; other times by appt. Oak and country furniture, 17th to 19thC, brass and copper.

Doveridge House of Neachley
(Cdr & Mrs H.E.R. Bain). Neach Hill, Long Lane. Tel Albrighton (090 722) 3131, 3132. Open everyday 10-6.30; other times by appt. Res on prem. Specialist in period English, French and oak furniture. Also paintings, clocks, fireplaces, porcelain and silver. LAPADA BADA

Southgate Gallery
(John Constable, Nigel Collins). 20 Market Place. Tel Telford (0952) 460351. Open Tues, Wed, Fri 10-4.30, Sat 10-1; other times by appt. British watercolours 1900-1950 and British oils of the same period. Shop incorporates Nigel Collins (Fine Books) - new and secondhand art and illustrated books.

Martin & Ruth Taylor
6 Broadway. Tel Telford (0952) 461504. Open Mon-Sat 9-6; other times by appt. 17th to 19thC English furniture, including oak and mahogany. Also shipping goods and good quality interesting curios. LAPADA

Shrewsbury STD 0743

Candle Lane Books
(John Thornhill). 28-31 Princess St, SY1 1LW. Tel 65301. Open Mon-Sat 9.30-5. Books, pictures and prints.

Hall Wateridge & Owen
Welsh Bridge. Tel 60212. Open 9-5.30. (Also at Oswestry, Ellesmere, Wem, Wrexham, Telford and Bishops Castle.) Antique and fine arts salerooms. Household furniture sales every Friday.

Hutton Antiques
18 Princess St. Porcelain and silver.

Lantern Antiques
(Margaret A. & Albert Love). 5-6 Milk St, (side door entrance, no shop front). Tel 3783. Open daily 9.30-1, 2.30-5; closed Thurs; other times by appt. General antiques including mahogany furniture, glass, porcelain, clocks, oil lamps, silver, dolls, pewter, brass and copper. Also cigarette cards and post cards.

F.C.Manser & Son Ltd
(G.F.D. Manser, J.C. Manser, M.A. Manser). 53-54 Wyle Cop, SY1 1XJ. Tel 51120 (priv 68899). Open Mon-Fri 9-5.30; Sat 9-5; other times by appt. 17th-20thC furniture, also china, glass, silver & plate, jewellery. Textiles, oriental, lighting, rugs. 1150 sq.ft show rooms.

Mill House Antiques
(Tom & Daniel Callaghan). 139 Abbey Foregate. Tel 240328. Open Mon-Fri 9-5, Sat 9-12. 18thC furniture, porcelain, silver. 19thC paintings, rugs, firearms. Also at same address, Fine Art Services Ltd: valuers of antiques and fine art for insurance, probate and sale. Tel:240327.

Mytton Antiques
(M.A. & E.A. Nares). Norton Crossroads, Atcham. Tel Uppington (095286) 229. Open Mon-Sat 10.30-5; Sun 2-5; other times by appt. Located on the A5 road between Wellington (Shrops) and Shrewsbury. General antiques, especially clocks and small ivories, longcase clocks usually in stock. 24 hr answering service.

Nevill Antiques
(Rosemary Evason). 9-10 Milk St, SY1 1SZ. Tel 51013 (priv 62877). Open Mon-Sat 9.30-1, 2-5; closed all day Thurs; other times by appt. 18th-20thC silver, glass, 18th-20thC porcelain, 18th & 19thC furniture.

Severn Fine Art
(Gordon Hancock). 77 Wyle Cop. Tel 247514. Open Mon-Sat 9-5; other times by appt. 19th and early 20thC paintings and watercolours.

Shrewsbury Antique Centre
Princess St. Tel 247704. Open 7 days a week 9.30-5.30. 40 dealers in 5,000 sq.ft. offer a wide range of antiques and collectables.

Michael Smith Antiques
39 St Johns Hill, SY1 1JQ. Tel 56439. Open Mon-Sat 10-1, 2-5; other times by appt. 17th to 20thC furniture & decorative objects.

Robin Smith
(Robin Smith). 23 Belle Vue Rd, SY3 7LN. Tel 50357. Open 9-6; other times by appt. 17th to early 19thC furniture, clocks, watches, barometers, scientific instruments.

Telford STD 0952

Dale End Antiques
(J. & M. Wilson). Dale End, Coalbrookdale. Tel 452145. Open almost always. Porcelain, pottery, glass, metals, furniture, bric-a-brac, pictures.

Bill Dickenson
(William Jack Dickenson). Tudor House, 11 Tontine Hill, Ironbridge, TF8 7AL. Tel Ironbridge (095245) 3783. Open Mon-Sat 10-5.30;Sun 2.30-5.30. English porcelain & pottery.

Ironbridge Antique Centre
(F.G. Cooke). Dale End, Ironbridge, TF8 7DS. Tel Ironbridge (095245) 3784 (priv 0952 51507). Open Mon-Fri 10-5; Sat 10-6; Sun 2-6; other times by appt. Furniture, jewellery, porcelain, prints, pictures,bric-a-brac and shipping goods.

West Felton

West Felton Antique Market
Tel Queens Head (069 188) 335. Open Mon-Sat 9-6, Sun 2-5. (On A5, 12 miles North of Shrewsbury.) Dealers in period furniture, shipping goods, silver, china etc.

Whitchurch STD 0948

F.W.Hancock
Moss Side, 4 Brownlow St. Tel 2567. Furnishing items, dressers, metalware, grandfather clocks and other items.

Somerset

Axbridge STD 0934

The Corner House Gallery
(N.J. Arlidge). The Square, BS26 2AP. Tel 732757. Specialising in 19th & 20thC British marine paintings and watercolours.

Bridgwater STD 0278

Tamlyn & Son
High St, TA6 3BN. Tel 58241/2. Auctioneers.

Bruton STD 074 981

Bruton Gallery Limited
(Michael and Sandra Le Marchant, Directors). High St, BA10 0AB. Tel 812697 & 812205. Open Mon-Fri 10-5.30; other times by appt. Source of European 19th and 20thC sculpture and contemporary paintings. Specialising in European sculpture including Rodin, Bourdelle, Maillol, Bernard, Carton.

Marksdanes Antiques Ltd
(P.Landers). Station Rd. Tel 3267. Open Mon-Fri 9-6; Sat 9-1; other times by appt. Victorian and Edwardian furniture, shipping goods, decorative items. Shipping. Restorations. Valuations.

David & Penny Newlove Antiques
Unit 3, The Old Mill, Station Rd. Tel 32672. (Also in Wincanton and Bath.) Open Mon-Fri 8.30-6; Sat 8.30-12. (By arrangement with Dovecot Antiques). Mahogany, oak, walnut furniture and comprehensive stock of stripped pine.

Burnham-on-Sea STD 0278

Adam Antiques
(Mr & Mrs H.S. & R. Coombes). 30 Adam St, TA8 1PQ. Tel 783193. Open Mon-Sat; other times by appt. Large stock of furniture, jewellery, china, clocks, shipping goods.

C.T.Culverwell
Vicarage Chambers, Victoria St. Tel 2307. Open Mon-Sat 9-1, 2-6; other times by appt. Large general stock of furniture, silver, jewellery, china, glass and bric-a-brac.

Terence Kelly Antiques
(T. & M. Kelly). 1 Cross St. Tel 782129 (priv 785052). Open Mon-Fri 9.30-5, Sat 9.30-12.30; other times by appt. 18th and 19thC furniture, brass, copper and metalware, pottery and interesting collectors' items.

Castle Cary STD 0963

Domus
(Mr Pearson). Woodcock St, BA7 7BL. Tel 50912 (priv 50489). Open Mon-Sat 10-5.30; Early closing Thurs; other times by appt. Pine furniture 18th & 19thC. Selected items silver & glass.

Longley's Antiques
(J.Longley). 1 High St. Tel 51259. Open 10-5. Furniture, glass, silver, porcelain.

John Martin Antiques
Woodcock St. Tel 50733. Open Mon-Sat 9.30-5.30; other times by appt. Near town centre. Clocks, watches, jewellery, copper and brass, decorative items and country furniture.

Crewkerne STD 0460

Julian Armytage
The Old Rectory, Wayford, TA18 8QG. Tel 73449. Fine sporting, marine and decorative prints.

Crewkerne Furniture Emporium
(Anthony Bucke & Julie Wells). 20-22 East St. Tel 75319. Open Mon-Sat 9-5.30; other times by appt. All types of furniture, including antiques. Periodic sales by auction. 30-35 bric-a-brac stalls on bank holiday Mondays.

Colin Jeffrey Associates
(Colin Jeffrey, Mrs K.Jeffrey). 9 East St, TA18 7AB. Tel 73242. Open Mon-Sat 9-5.30; other times by appt. Commercial and industrial photography and all photographic supplies and services specialising in fine art and antiques including paintings, silver, jewellery, china and furniture. Reproduction of historic photographs.

Lawrence Fine Art of Crewkerne
(M.A.Bartlett, R.M.F.Gold ARICS J. Pearn BA). South Street, TA18 8AB. Tel 73041. Open Mon-Fri 9-5.30; other times by appt. Fine art auctioneers. SOFAA

Oscars Antiques
(Bryan John Hall & Helen Hall). 13-15 Market Square. Tel 72718. Open Mon-Sat 9.30-5.30; other times by appt. Full range of furniture, china and books.

Curry Rivel

Chalon Ltd
(Nicholas, Michael and Timothy Chalon). Old Hambridge Mill, Hambridge, TA10 0BP. Tel Langport (0458) 252374 (priv 0460 67715). Open Mon-Fri 8-5; Sat 8-1; other times by appt. Wholesale 18th and 19thC European furniture, country, decorative and architectural. LAPADA

Dulverton STD 0398

Dulverton Antique Centre
(David Gregory). Lower Town Hall.

Frome STD 0373

Ray Coggins Antiques
3 Keyford. Tel 72286. (Also in Bradford-on-Avon, Wilts.) Open Mon-Fri 9.30-5.30; Sats by appt. Period pine furniture and carvings, decorated furniture.

ANTIQUE DEALERS INTERNATIONAL plc

★**25,000 sq. ft showroom** of good antique English and Continental furniture – walnut, mahogany, rosewood, marquetry and decorated furniture

★**4,500 sq. ft shop** in London

★Paintings, bronzes, tapestries, clocks, mirrors, carpets and porcelain

★Decorative and designer items

★Excellent trade call suitable for all markets: UK, USA, Australia and Europe

★**Goods packed and shipped** to any part of the world

★**Courtesy courier** and chauffeuring service available

STOCK CHANGING DAILY

MAIN SHOWROOM:
BOW STREET, LANGPORT, SOMERSET
Telephone: 0458 252977 Telex 885194

LONDON SHOP:
57-58 UPPER STREET, LONDON N.1.
(Opposite Camden Passage)

Tom Hickman
10 Bath St. Tel 73076.

Richard & Pamela Nadin
(Richard & Pamela Nadin). 12 Paul St, BA11 1DT. Tel 64957. (Also at 5 Woolley St, Bradford-on-Avon, Wilts.) Open six days; other times by appt. Unusual decorations and furniture, rugs and carpets, ethnographical, folk and primitive art, painted furniture.

Sutton & Sons
15 & 33 Vicarage Street, BA11 1PX. Tel 62062. Open daily; early closing Thurs. General stock of antiques and furnishings.

Whisstock's
(P.&.D.Whisstock). 9 Catherine Hill. Tel 63289. Open Mon-Sat 9-5; early closing Thurs; other times by appt. Art materials, picture framing, maps and porcelain.

Glastonbury STD 0458

Abbey Antiques
(C.R.G. Browning). 52-54 High St, BA6 9DY. Tel 31694 (priv 32795). Open Mon-Sat 8.15-1, 2-5.30; early closing Wed; other times by appt. 17thC to early 19thC furniture, Georgian and Victorian glass.

The Flintlock
(Francis Laver). 17A High St, BA6 9DR. Tel 31525 (priv 32813). (Also at Paragon Antique Centre, Bath. Wed only.) Open 9.30-5 except Wed; other times by appt. Antique and modern firearms and restoration, militaria, valuations etc.

Monarch Antiques
(John A.Badman). 15 High St. Tel 32498. Open Mon-Sat 10-5.30; other times by appt. Militaria, bygones and curiosities, coins and medals. Antiquities, ethnographical and pre-Columbian items. Also early to 17thC pottery and porcelain.

Highbridge

Colin Dyte Exports Ltd
(C.W.E.Dyte). Huntspill Rd. Tel Burnham-on-Sea (0278) 788590 (priv 683761). Open 8-6; other times by appt. Antique dealers - comprehensive range Georgian, Victorian, Edwardian, etc. LAPADA

Highbridge Antique Centre
Huntspill Rd. Tel Burnham-on-Sea (0278) 781395. Open all day Mon-Sat. On main A38 2 miles from M5. Twenty antique dealers selling a variety of antiques.

Treasure Chest Ltd
(Roger J.Rumble, Valerie Rumble). The Jays, 19 Alstone Lane, TA9 3DS. Tel Burnham-on-Sea (0278) 787267. (Also at Highbridge Antique Centre, Huntspill Rd, Highbridge.) Open anytime to traders. Best to phone first. Trade only. Stock varies with trends but always good smalls-oriental, Worcester, coloured glass, caddies, boxes etc. Clocks, watches, silver & plate, musical boxes etc. Furniture. Courier service & commission buyer.

Ilminster STD 046 05

Ray Best Antiques
North Street House. Tel 2194. Open Mon-Fri 9.30-6; other times by appt. 17th to 19thC furniture, metalware, pottery, paintings, objets d'art and general antiques.

County Antiques Centre
21-23 West St. Antique centre.

Moolham Mill Antiques
(Rona Cropper). Moolham Mill, Moolham Lane, TA19 0PD. Tel 2834. Open Mon-Fri 9-7; other times by appt. Res on prem. Antique furniture, especially early oak, country furniture, 18thC mahogany, pewter, delft, metalwork, clocks, textiles and needlework. BADA

J.A.Stancomb
Bullen Court, Broadway, TA19 9QY. Tel 2640. Open any time and by appt. Res on premises. Antique & secondhand silver.

Stuart Interiors
(Peter Russell, Ken Peterkin). Barrington Court, Barrington, TA19 0NQ. Tel South Petherton (0460) 40349. Open Mon-Sat 10-5.30. Design and decoration for the age of oak in England. Manufacture of handmade furniture and architectural joinery including staircases, doors and panelling. High standard of authenticity, handcarving, polishing etc. Also large stock of antiques.

Langport STD 0458

Antique Dealers International PLC
Bow Street. Tel 252977. Open Mon-Fri 8-6; other times by appt. Antique dealers and interior designers. Primarily English and Continental antique furniture and works of art. Also a range of designer and decorative items. Furniture restoration.

Bow House
(Mrs Gladstone). Bow House, Bow Street.

Kings House Antiques
(Mrs Desmond). Bow Street.

Shirleys Antiques
(S.A.Hollard). Bow St. Tel 250064. Open Tues-Sat; closed Mon morning and all day Wed. Smalls and furniture, shipping goods.

Limington

Genges Farm Antiques
(Roy and Pam Gilbert). Genges Farm. Tel Ilchester (0935) 840464. Res on prem: available weekends and evenings. Interesting English, Irish, Welsh and French pine and country furniture. Original painted pieces.

Milverton STD 0823

Milverton Antiques
(Audrey Waymouth). Fore St, TA4 1JU. Tel 400597. Open Mon-Sat 9-6; other times by appt. Oak and pine country furniture, longcase clocks, copper, brass and china.

Charles Read Georgian Furnishing
(Charles Read). Bathealton Court, Bathealton, TA4 2AJ. Tel Wiveliscombe (0984) 23225. Open any time by appt. Good quality Georgian furniture, mainly mahogany, and oriental rugs. Georgian interior decorating service. Decorative objects. All services, including elegant accommodation offered for overseas visitors.

Minehead STD 0643

Zwan Antiques
(Mr & Mrs M.van Zwanenberg). Timberscombe, TA24 7TG. Tel Timberscombe (064384) 621 (priv 608). Open Tues, Wed, Thurs, Sat & Sun afternoons; other times by appt. Sporting pictures & prints, jewellery & smalls - some furniture.

Shepton Mallet STD 0749

Bristol Antiques Ltd
(J.P.A.Peeters). Cumhill Farm, Pilton. Tel Pilton (074 989) 240. Victorian and Edwardian furniture. Purchaser and shipper only. LAPADA

Peter Coe Fine Paintings
The Priory. Tel 2412. Open by appt only. 18thC and pre-Victorian paintings and watercolours, predominantly landscapes.

Pennard House Antiques
(Martin Dearden). East Pennard, BA4 6TP. Tel Ditcheat (074986) 266. Open any time Mon-Sat. Specialist in pine furniture; 18th and 19thC French farmhouse furniture. LAPADA

Somerton STD 0458

London Cigarette Card Co Ltd
(Ian A.Laker). Sutton Rd, TA11 6QP. Tel 73452. Mail order only. Cigarette and trade cards. Catalogues, albums and reference books.

Taunton STD 0823

C.W.Atkins & Co. Antiques
92 Wellington Rd, TA1 5LA. Tel 72660. (Also N. Meade, 90 Wellington Rd.) Open afternoons, Mon-Sat; other times by appt. Furniture including garden furniture, ivory figures, pewter, porcelain, bronzes and penny farthing cycles. Guns and pistols, some cased.

The Granary Galleries
(Mr R.H.Hall). Court House, Ash Priors, near Bishops Lydeard, TA4 3NQ. Tel Bishops Lydeard (0823) 432402 (priv 432816). Open 6 days a week 8.30-5.30. Large stock of period English, Continental and Oriental furniture, country oak and pine, oil paintings and watercolours, general antiques and shipping goods.

Grange Court Antiques
(Mr & Mrs P.M.Halliday Hawker). Corfe. Tel Blagdon Hill (082 342) 498. Open Mon-Thurs 10-5. 17th to 19thC country furniture in stripped pine, oak, elm and fruitwood. Large collection of treen.

William Morley Antiques
(William Morley). Musgrave's Old Farm, West Monkton, TA2 8NW. Tel West Monkton (0823) 412751. Open Mon-Sat 9.30-6; other times by appt. Fine 17th and 18thC strictly period English furniture. Early metalware, china and glass. Decorative items for the country house.

Old Buttons (UK)
Buttons, West Lyng. Tel North Curry (0823) 629. Mail order only. Buttons for mail order export to the USA and for sale by distributers in the UK.

Sotheby's
(Representative: Robert Dalgety). Magdalene House, Magdalene St, TA1 1SB. Tel 88441. Auctioneers & valuers.

Staplegrove Lodge Antiques
(T.J.Atkins). Staplegrove. Tel 81153. (Mon 9-4 at Stand 41, Taunton Antique Centre, Silver St. Taunton.) Open Tues-Sat 10-5; other times by appt. Res on prem. Furniture, mainly oak and mahogany, china, silver and general items.

PENNARD HOUSE

EAST PENNARD, SHEPTON MALLET, SOMERSET BA4 6TP
Telephone: DITCHEAT 074986 266
Martin and Susie Dearden

LAPADA Registered Member

We carry large stocks of period pine and French provincial furniture. At present we have over 60 sets of French rush-seated chairs, and many fruitwood tables

Ray Best

ANTIQUES
NORTH STREET HOUSE
ILMINSTER Somerset

Constantly changing stock of 17th to 19th century English and Continental furniture, metalware, porcelain, objets d'art and general antiques.

George III mahogany secretaire bookcase and a pair of George III walnut side chairs

Resident on premises **Ilminster (04605) 2194**

CHARLES READ

Georgian Furniture, Oriental Rugs
Elegant and luxurious accommodation available

Bathealton Court
Taunton, Somerset TA4 2AJ
Tel. Wiveliscombe (0984) 23225

Open: By appointment

Taunton Antique Centre
(S.M. Lowe, M. & P.A. Carter). 27-29 Silver St. Tel 89327. Open Mon 9-4. An antique market with 100 stalls under one roof. Stall holders stock a complete range of goods. Market 1.5 miles from junction 25 on the M5.

Edward Venn Antiques
52 Long St, Williton, TA4 4QU. Tel Williton (0984) 32631. Open 10-5. General antiques and restoration of furniture,longcase clocks and barometers.

Williton Antiques
(H.W. & Mrs J.E.Root). 26 High St, Williton. Tel Williton (0984) 32393 (priv). Open Mon, Wed, Fri 9.30-5; other times by appt. Metalware, including brass and copper, treen, country bygones and small general antiques including some ceramics and glass.

Taunton Lydeard

Hall's Antiques
(A.R. & J.M. Hall). Court House, Ash Priors, TA4 3NQ. Tel Bishops Lydeard (0823) 432402. Open Mon-Sat 9-5.30; other times by appt. Full variety of English and Continental antiques and quality reproductions of every description. Paintings, decorative items, jewellery. Some shipping goods. Established 40 years.

Templecombe STD 0963

Christie's
(Representative: Richard de Pelet). Monmouth Lodge, Yenston, BA8 0NH. Tel 70518. Auctioneers.

Wellington STD 082 347

Michael and Amanda Lewis Oriental Carpets and Rugs
(Michael and Amanda Lewis). 8 North St, TA21 8LT. Tel 7430. (Also at 23 Small St, Bristol.) Open Tues-Sat 10-5.30; other times by appt. Oriental & European carpets and rugs, antique, old and new, bought and sold. Valuations, commission sales and purchases executed. Specialist restorations, repairs and cleaning on premises. Hanging, mounting, framing etc.

Wellington Salerooms
(Raymond Cooper). Mantle St, TA21 8NR. Tel 4815. Open 9-5 weekdays only. General chattel auctioneers.

Yesterday's Paper
(Fiona Clewlow). 5 Cornhillgate. Open by appt only. General stock of printed ephemera, postcards, periodicals, antiquarian and second-hand books etc. Catalogues issued on children's books, annuals & comics. Also vintage glamour, pin-up and naturist material, general books and ephemera. PBFA

Wells STD 0749

Cherub Antiques
(Mr & Mrs J.O. Newsam). 9 Sadler St, BA5 2RR. Tel 72503 (priv 73893). Open Mon-Sat 9-5.30; other times by appt. Furniture, objets d'art, clocks and silver.

Mitre Antiques
(B.G. & M. House). The Market Place. Tel 72607. Open Mon-Sat 10-1, 2-5; early closing Wed. Furniture, scientific instruments and general stock. Specialist in barometers. Also miniature and child's furniture.

E.A. Nowell & Sons
(E.A. Nowell, M. Nowell, J. Nowell). 21-23 Market Place, BA5 2RF. Tel 72415, 78738, 76915. Open Mon-Sat 9.15-1, 2.15-5.30. Extensive showrooms of 17th, 18th, early 19thC furniture, silver, old Sheffield plate & jewellery. BADA

Wincanton STD 0963

Mattar Arcade
(Mattar Antique Galleries). South Street. Tel 34154. Arcade of antique shops.

Moorland-Coon
8 Bennetts Field. Furniture, paintings, porcelain and silver.

David & Penny Newlove Antiques
28 High St, BA9 9JF. Tel 32672. (Also in Bath, Avon and Bruton, Somerset.) Open Mon-Sat 9-6; other times by appt. Mahogany, oak & walnut furniture plus a large selection of interesting, well-finished pine. Also clocks and small antiques. Experienced in export to all markets.

Wiveliscombe STD 0984

Brownsells Granary
(John White). 9 High St, TA4 2JX. Tel 23117 (priv 0823 400427). Open Mon-Fri 9.30-5, Sat 9.30-1. Country furniture, period furniture.

Yeovil STD 0935

Brimsmore House Antiques
(Wendy Rose). Brimsmore House, BA21 3NZ. Tel 74959. Open Mon-Sat 9-6; other times by appt. General antiques, bric-a-brac. House clearance.

Fox & Co
30 Princes St. Tel 72323. Open Mon-Sat 9-5.30. Antiquities, badges, coins, medals and medallions, stamps and ephemera. BNTA, PTS

Murdoch MacTaggart
Little Brympton, Brympton d'Evercy. Tel West Coker (093 586) 2609. Open by appt only. Antiquarian books and prints. Fine arts, humanities, early printing, Japanese and old master prints. ABA

Paul Watson
Orchard Cottage, Sparkford. Tel 40259. Open by appt only. Fine English watercolours.

Staffordshire

Burton upon Trent
STD 0283

Ashley House Antiques
(Mrs P.A.Benton). 61 High St, Measham, DE12 7HR. Tel Measham (0530) 73568 (priv 0543 373655). Open Thurs, Fri, Sat 10.30-5; other times by appt. Longcase and wall clocks, small furniture, copper and brass, ribbon and lace plates, original horse brasses.

Cottage Antiques (Bollington) Ltd
The Old Rectory, Tatenhill. Tel 63015. Furniture.

John German
The Rotunda, High St, DE14 1LN. Tel 42051. Auctioneers; also valuations and occasional sales of complete house contents.

Eccleshall STD 0785

Horsley Antiques Ltd
Horsley Hall. Tel 850332. Open daily 9-5.30. 18th and 19thC furniture, pictures and objets d'art.

Hanley

Norman Jones (Industrial Photography) Ltd
Bethesda Building, 11 Bethesda St, ST1 3DE. Tel Stoke-on-Trent (0782) 268548. Photographer.

Tunnicliffes Antiques
(A.J.Tunnicliffe). Five Towns Antique Shop, 17 Broad St, ST1 4HS. Tel Stoke-on-Trent (0782) 272930 (priv 657899). Open Mon-Sat 10-4; closed Thurs. Pottery, brass, prints and furniture.

Leek STD 0538

Anvil Antiques
The Old School, Alsop St. Tel 385280. (Showrooms in London, Hanley and San Francisco.) Open Mon-Sat; other times by appt. Fine pine and decorative items. 20 000 sq ft warehouse.

Aspleys Antique Imports & Exports
(John Aspley). Compton Mill, Compton. Tel 373346-96. (Also at Uttoxeter.) Open Mon-Sat 9-6. 38000 sq ft of stripped pine and shipping furniture, with the emphasis on pine, lots of original pieces.

Brook Street Antiques
(N.Grosvenor). 4-6 Brook St, ST13 5JE. Tel 384506 (priv 382976). Open Mon-Sat 9-5; other times by appt. General antiques. Shipper. LAPADA

Country Cottage Interiors
(J.& L.Salmon). The Co-op, Compton. Tel 386621. Open Mon-Sat 9-5. Pine furniture etc.

Gemini
The Old Church School, Compton. Tel 387834. 5000 sq ft of pine and bric-a-brac.

J.S. & R.Hine
Fowlchurch Farm, Ball Haye Green. Tel 372699. Craftsman-made furniture in pine, oak, elm and yew. Gun cabinets made to order.

Lichfield STD 054 32

Corridor Antiques and Perdy's Junk Shop
(Perdita J. Mellor & Thelma J.A. Bosworth). 53-55 Tamworth St. Tel 263223 (priv 251489). Open Mon-Sat 10-4.30; closed Wed; other times by appt. Primarily suppliers to the trade, also cheap secondhand furniture and re-saleable antique junk.

Exquisite Arts Ltd
(David Holderness, Helen Holderness). 22 Bore St. Tel 253626, (priv 253697). (Also at 147 High St, Henley in Arden, Warwickshire.) Open Mon-Sat 9.30-5.30. 20thC oils and watercolours. Quality framing and restoration.

Anne Hall - Prints
19 Dam St, WS13 6AE. Tel 263263. Framed and unframed antique maps and prints.

Directmoor
LTD

THE COPPICE FARM
Nr MOORCOURT, OAKAMOOR
STAFFORDSHIRE

English, Irish, and Continental Furniture available at stages of Restoration from fully restored and carefully finished to unstripped.

Why not give us a try?

Approx. 8 miles from Leek, near to Alton Towers. We would be only too pleased to arrange transport from Airport (Manchester) or Rail Station (Derby or Stoke)

A telephone call is advised. **Call Dave Johnson (0538) 702419**

LAPADA

E. W. Cousins & Son

Established since 1910

27 High Street
Ixworth, Bury St. Edmunds,
Suffolk

Tel: Pakenham 30254

Specialist in Georgian and Victorian furniture.
Large selection of clocks and barometers.

15,000 sq. ft. of selected furniture.
Export trade welcome. Containers packed.
Wholesale and retail trade.

THE CLARE COLLECTOR

1 Nethergate Street, CLARE, (nr. Long Melford), Suffolk.
Tel: Clare (0787) 277909

An exciting Antique Shop in a 15th century Hall House. Stocking a wide variety of good 17th, 18th and 19th century furniture (Walnut, Fruitwood, Mahogany, Oak and Elm), pottery & porcelain, prints & watercolours, oriental and tribal rugs, and unusual items of every kind.

Wintertons Fine Arts
(A.J.Winterton, A.J.Ridgway, M.Smedley). St Mary's Chambers, WS13 6LQ. Tel 263256. (Auction rooms at Church St. (The Smithfield) Lichfield.) Open Tues-Fri 9-5; closed lunch 1-2. Bi-monthly antique furniture & picture sales. Bi-monthly silver, jewellery, ceramics & collectors items. Monthly Victorian & shipping sales.

Newcastle-under-Lyme STD 0782

Hood and Broomfield Lyme Galleries
(J.Hood & G.H.Broomfield). 29 Albert St, ST5 1JP. Tel 626859. Open Mon-Fri 10-5.30; Sat 10-4; Thurs by appt. 19th & early 20thC oils & watercolours. Framing & picture restoration. Valuations. LAPADA

Oakamoor STD 0538

Directmoor Ltd
(David Johnson). Coppice Farm, Farley Rd, Moorcourt. Tel 702419. Appointment advised. Pine and country furnishings. Container loading and shipping service world wide.

Rugeley STD 088 94

Rugeley Antiques Centre
(D.&N.Edwards). 161-163 Main Rd, Brereton. Tel 77166. Open Mon-Sat 10-5.30; other times by appt. A wide range of general antiques.

Stafford STD 0785

Colin Davies Antiques International
385 Eccleshall Road. Tel 55433. French furniture, clocks, clock sets, watches, enamels, porcelain, cameo glass, Oriental objets d'art, bronzes, carriage clocks and fine art.

Weston Antique Gallery
(Frank Rabone). Boat Lane, Weston, ST18 0HU. Tel Weston (0889) 270450. Open Wed-Sat 10-5.30; other times by appt. Maps, prints, Staffordshire pottery and porcelain, glass, silver and small collectors items.

Stoke-on-Trent STD 0782

Alpha Antiques
(Martin and Dorothy Harper). Church Lane, Checkley, ST10 4NJ. Tel Tean (0538) 722149. Open daily, res on prem. 18th and 19thC furniture and decorative items. Also a re-upholstery service.

Esme Antiques 'Marelle'
(Esme Elizabeth Howell). Street Lane, Rode Heath. Tel Alsager (09363) 5603. Res on premises. Fine art porcelain, signed pieces. Specialist in Royal Worcester.

The Little Antique Shop
(Peter & Sheila Lumley). 167-169 Stone Rd, Hanford. Tel 657674. Open Mon-Sat 10-7 (res on premises). Large stock of clean furniture, specifically inlaid furniture, dining tables and sets of chairs. Especially 'Sheraton Revival' furniture,(1870-1910). Also silver and jewellery.

Lowen Gallery
(Claire Lowen). 471 Hartshill Rd, Hartshill, ST4 6AA. Tel 623762. Contemporary crafts: glass, ceramics, woven textiles painted knitwear, wood, precious and non-precious jewellery, paintings, prints. ICGA

Stone STD 0785

Stone Antique Centre
Bridge House, 56 Newcastle Rd. Tel 818218. Furniture, ceramics, glass, silver, jewellery, pictures, prints, clocks and collector's items.

Stone-Wares Antiques
(Graham Wheeler). 24 Radford St. Tel 815000. Long-cased clocks.

Uttoxeter STD 08893

Aspleys Antique Imports & Exports
18 Carter St. Tel 5291. (Also in Leek.) Open Mon-Sat 9.30-5.30, closed Thurs. 2000 sq ft of furniture, smalls and prints.

Pine Antiques
52 Bridge St. Tel 5374. 7 showrooms containing pine and country furniture, pottery, linen and kitchenalia.

Yoxall STD 0543

J.C.E. & N.I. Armson - Antiques
(Roger Armson). The Hollies, DE13 8NH. Tel 472352 (priv 028371-2052). Open Mon-Fri 9-5; other times by appt. Mainly furniture 17th-19thC, mostly trade and overseas buyers. LAPADA

H.W.Heron & Son Ltd
(E.M. Heron, H.N.M. Heron, J. Heron). 1 King St. Tel 472266. Open Mon-Fri 9-6; Sat, Sun 10.30-6. Antiques generally, old English furniture, china and glass. LAPADA

Suffolk

Aldeburgh STD 072 885

Aldeburgh Antiques
(Howard Royall). The Corner Shop, Wentworth Rd. Tel 2977 (priv 0502 722201). Open Fri & Sat 10.30-1, 2.30-5; other times by appt. Porcelain, small furniture, mirrors, fabrics, copper & brass, glass, period clothes.

Guillemot
134/136 High St. Tel 2361. Country furniture and antiques.

Mole Hall Antiques
102-104 High St. Tel 2361. Open Mon-Sat 9.30-5.30 and by appt. Country furniture and unusual decorative items.

Thompson's Gallery
175A High St. Tel 3743 (priv 2488). Antique & contemporary paintings & furniture.

Beccles STD 0502

Art & Antiques
6 The Walk. Tel 713561. Open Mon-Sat 10-5; early closing Wed. General antiques.

Saltgate Antiques
(Mrs A.Ratcliffe). 11 Saltgate, NR34 9AN. Tel 712776. Open Mon-Sat 10-5; Wed 10-1; other times by appt. 18th, 19th & early 20thC furniture. Watercolours, metalware, bygones & curiosities. Shipping goods. Pottery & porcelain.

Waveney Antiques Centre
Saltgate. Tel 716147. Open Mon-Sat 10-5.30. 24 dealers offering a variety of antiques.

Bildeston STD 0449

Oswald Simpson Antiques
Market Place, IP7 7EP. Tel 740030. Open Mon-Sat 9.30-5.30; other times by appt. Large stock of 17th to 19thC period furniture, specialising in country, oak and fruitwood and decorative pieces. LAPADA

Blythburgh STD 050 270

E.T. Webster
Westwood Lodge. Tel 539. Open by appt only. New, secondhand and antiquarian books relating to English literature from the 16th to 20th centuries. Also large quantities of period oak beams & floor boarding, panelling for house and furniture restoration.

Boxford STD 0787

The Corner Cupboard
(Victoria Davidson). At the Old Bakery, Next to the Fleece, CO6 5DX. Tel 210123. Open Tues-Sat 10-5; other times by appt. Antiques and Victoriana, papier mache, amusing decorative items, needlework, beadwork and small furniture.

Laurimore Gallery
(Jon and Jill Laurimore). The Mews, 29 Swan St, CO6 5NZ. Tel 210138. One-off contemporary crafts: ceramics, glass, wood, stitch and fibre, metal, furniture. ICGA

Bungay STD 0986

Country House Antiques
(G.R.Searle). 30 Earsham St. Tel 2875 (priv 0508-58144). Open Mon-Sat, closed 1-2 and Weds; other times by appt. Antique furniture and collectibles. Mahogany 18th and 19thC furniture, and a small amount of blonde wood and oak, some period.

John Derham Ltd/Earsham Hall Pine
(John Derham). Earsham Hall, NR35 2AN. Tel 3423. Open Mon-Sat 9-5; other times by appt. Large stock of old pine furniture & architectural antiques. Also reproduction pine furniture & fire surrounds.

Bures STD 0787

Bures Antiques
(Mrs P.Holme and Mrs J.Way). 1 Bridge St, CO8 5AD. Tel 227858 (priv 0206 210215). Open Mon-Sat 9.30-5.30; other times by appt. Varied stock from 17thC to Art Deco. Large tables, sets of chairs, mahogany and farmhouse furniture, porcelain and glass.

Bury St Edmunds STD 0284

Brookes Forge Flempton
(Brian R. Brookes, Erica K. Brookes). Flempton, IP28 6EN. Tel Culford (028484) 473 (priv 0449 781376). Open Mon-Fri 2-5.30; other times by appt. Castings in ferrous & non ferrous metals, antique metalwork restoration, chemical formulations created to suit customers requirements, e.g.for ebonising, patination etc.

Bullivant Antiques
(P.T. Bullivant). Whitegates, Great Ashfield, IP31 3HH. Tel Elmswell (0359) 40040. Open 9-6; other times by appt. 17th, 18th & 19thC oak, walnut & fruitwood furniture, longcase and other clocks.

Guildhall Gallery
(P.Hewes). 1 Churchgate St. Tel 62366. Open daily 10-5.30; closed Thurs. 18th and 19thC English and Continental paintings. LAPADA

J.C.Heather Antiques
Clandore House, Woolpit, IP30 9SA. Tel Elmswell (0359) 40297. Open daily 9-6. 17th, 18th & 19thC furniture. Trade suppliers.

Lacy Scott
Fine Art Dept and Saleroom, 10 Risbygate St, IP33 1LS. Tel 63531. Open Mon-Fri 9-5.30; other times by appt. Auctioneers.

Peppers Period Pieces
(Michael Pepper). 22/23 Churchgate St. Tel 68786 (priv 0359 50606). (Also at Park Farm, Wattisfield, by appt (Tel 0359 50606.) Open Mon-Sat 10-5; other times by appt. 16th-19thC country furniture, 17th-19th English domestic implements in brass, copper, lead, iron, pewter and treen.

Eileen Ryley
104 Risbygate St. Tel 67377. Open Tues, Wed, Fri, Sat 11-5. General antiquarian and out-of-print books. Also children's books of the 19th and early 20thC.

Graham K.Scott
68-69 St John's St, IP33 1SJ. Tel 3933. Books on East Anglia, military subjects, architecture and biography. ABA

St Edmunds Antique Centre
(R.Chapman). 30 St Johns St. Tel 64469 (priv 0842 878286). Open Mon-Sat 9.30-5.30; other times by appt. 18 dealers selling silver, militaria, fine furniture, paintings, glass, porcelain, pottery, stamps, coins,medals, prints, maps,radios, tools, toys & collectables. 7 dealers selling books.

R.N.Usher
(R.N.Usher). 42 Southgate St, IP33 2AZ. Tel 4838. Open 9-5.30; other times by appt. 18th and 19thC furniture, china, glass, silver and mantelpieces. Gilding and chair caning.

Clare STD 0787

P.Carrington
(P.Gansell). Well Lane. Tel 277 440. Open Mon-Sat 10-5; other times by appt. Clocks, china and decorative items.

The Clare Collector
(Jan Verney). 1 Nethergate St. Tel 277909 (priv 277494). Open Mon-Sat 10-1, 2-5.30; Sun by appt. Four rooms of 17th, 18th and 19thC English and Continental furniture, pottery, porcelain, prints and watercolours. Oriental and tribal rugs. Unusual items of every kind at reasonable prices.

Granny's Attic
(Margaret Sadler). 22 High St, CO10 8NY. Tel 277740. Open Sats 11-4.30; also March-Dec, Tues, Thurs, Fri 2-5. Victorian-1940's clothing, linens, cottage glass, china; collectables, no furniture.

Half Moon Antiques
(Mrs C.E. Dyson). Half Moon House, High St. Tel 277993. Open 11-5; closed Wed & Sun; other times by appt. Antique, reproduction & secondhand furniture, Victorian, Edwardian & shipping furniture. Good stock of quality stripped pine.

Michael Moore Antiques
The Old Court, Nethergate St, CO10 8NP. Tel 277510. Open Mon-Fri; other times by appt. Quality antique pine, some country furniture, decorative items, upholstery.

Debenham STD 0728

Bygones of Debenham
(Christopher & Anne Bigden). 1 High St. Tel 860707. Open Mon-Sat 9.30-5.30; other times by appt. Mainly 17th-19thC furniture & paintings. Large and decorators items a speciality. Very varied and large stock, 6 showrooms & trade warehouse.

Flemings Antiques
(Norman Kelvin & David Ball). High St, IP14 6QJ. Tel 860422. Open Mon-Sat 10-6; other times by appt. Specialising in oak and walnut furniture and garden ornaments.

Foresters Hall Antiques
High St. Tel 777. Open Mon-Sat 9.30-5; other times by appt. Period oak, walnut, mahogany and pine furniture, longcase and other clocks, smalls, silver plate and pictures.

N.A.J. Lanchester
(N.A.J. Lanchester). 21 High St. Tel 860756. Open Sun-Sat, 9-5.30; other times by appt. Antique furniture, china, shipping furniture, bric-a-brac.

Felixstowe STD 0394

Diamond Mills & Co
(G.W. Mills, FSVA, N.J. Papworth, ASVA). 117 Hamilton Rd. Tel 282281. (Also saleroom at the Orwell Hall, Orwell.) Open Mon-Fri 9-1, 2-5.30. Regular sales of antiques, furniture & objets d'art etc.

Framlingham STD 0728

Goodbrey Antiques
29 Double St. Tel 723756. Open Mon-Sat 9-1, 2-5.30; other times by appt. 18th and 19thC English and Continental furniture and decorative items. Specialising in good quality pieces in unusual woods especially lightwood & Biedermeier furniture, antique beds in brass, iron & wood.

Mrs A.M.Ponsonby Antiques
Upham House, Ashfield, IP14 6LT. Tel Earl Soham (072 882) 200. Open by appt. 18th & 19thC furniture, pictures and decorative pieces. Fine linen.

Grundisburgh STD 047 335

Sotheby's
(Representative: Lord Cranworth). IP13 6TW. Tel 581. Auctioneers & valuers.

Hacheston

The Antique Shop
Tel Wickham Market (0728) 746485. Open Mon-Sat 10-6; other times by appt. Country furniture, including stripped pine, refectory tables, dressers, chests, bookshelves etc. Also period oak and mahogany and general antiques.

Hadleigh STD 0473

Barn End Antiques & Firearms
(P.M.Skoulding). Barn End, High St. Tel 823164. Open most days; other times by appt. Small furniture, silver, china, glass, metalware. Reg. Firearms Dealer, No.43 Suffolk Const. GTA

Church Street Antiques
(Martin Hart). 4 Church St. Tel 822418. Open Mon-Sat 9.30-5.30; other times by appt. Period mahogany, clocks, barometers, some oak & decorative items.

Randolph
(Baden F.Marston, Mrs H.M.Marston & Mrs V.M.Brett). 97-99 High St, IP7 5EJ. Tel 823789. Open Mon-Sat 9-5.30; other times by appt. Mainly very good quality 17th to early 19thC English furniture and accessories. Some furniture restoration and valuations, also undertaken. BADA

Isobel Rhodes
69-73 Angel St. Tel 823754. Open Mon-Sat 10-5; other times by appt. General stock, including oak and country furniture and metalware.

Gordon Sutcliffe
105 High St, IP7 5EJ. Tel 823464. Specialists in 18thC furniture. BADA

Haverhill STD 0440

Boardman Fine Art Auctioneers
(Neil A.Lanham FRICS). Station Rd Corner, CB9 0EY. Tel 703784. Open Mon-Fri 9-1, 2.15-5. 6-weekly sales of fine furniture and paintings. Chartered surveyor and fine art auctioneer.

C.C.A.W. Ltd
(Major & Mrs Noel Corry). Gunhouse, Steeple Bumpstead. Tel Steeple Bumpstead 044084 275. Open by appt only. Antique and modern reproduction guns and pistols. Kits to make into weapons.

Suffolk House Antiques
Barton Place, Kedington. Tel 3803. Open Wed-Fri 12-6; other times by appt. Interesting mixed stock, including early walnut chests of drawers, Victorian Chesterfields, chairs etc.

Ipswich STD 0473

Barrett & Butler
The Old Bull Furniture Workshops, Key St. Specialist chair makers.

Brownhouse Antiques
(Sue and Graham Bradley). 1 Ipswich Rd, Claydon. Tel 830130. Open Mon-Sat 10-5; other times by appt. Specialising in stripped pine furniture, silver, Victoriana, bric-a-brac.

Paul Bruce Antiques & Pine Shop
(P.Bruce). 25-27 St Helens St. Tel 55400. (Pine Dept: (0473 212794.) Open Mon-Sat 9-5; other times by appt. Oak, walnut, mahogany furniture. Restoration work. Shipping. Large stock of antique pine in Pine Department. LAPADA

College Gateway Bookshop
(Claude Cox). 3 Silent St, IP1 1TF. Tel 54776. Open 10-5 daily; closed Wed. Secondhand and antiquarian books especially printing and arts of the book, literature and Suffolk topography. ABA

Cordell Antiques
13 St Peter's St. Tel 219508. Open Mon-Fri 10-4; other times by appt. Small silver collectables, especially needlework tools and thimbles. Also pictures, small furniture, mauchlineware, tartanware, and treen.

Robert Dove & Partners
(Jonathan Snook). Dover House, Wolsey St. Tel 55137. Fine art auctioneers.

The Edwardian Shop
(Joe Hodgson). 556 Spring Rd. Tel 712890. Open Mon-Sat 10-5.30; other times by appt. Mainly pre-war furniture.

Elm Studios Ltd
42 Princes St. Tel 52069. Photographers.

G.M.B. Auctions
Box No. 5534, 30 Lower Brook St. Tel 662655. Auctioneers.

Hubbard Antiques
(R.J.&J.E.Hubbard). 16 St Margarets Green. Tel 226033. (Also shop at 47 St Nicholas St, Ipswich. Tel. 211344.) Open Mon-Sat 9-5.30; other times by appt. 5000 sq ft showroom containing Georgian mahogany & walnut furniture suitable for USA & Germany, making & restoration on premises, leathering, marble supplied. Decorative items.

Ipswich Pianos
45 Graham Rd. Tel 50740. Open by appt. Fine reconditioned upright and grand pianos and interesting collection of beds, including oak, four-posters, Victorian brass and inlaid mahogany.

R.W.Paul
(J.J.Duggan). 20A Fore St. Tel 51696. Open Mon-Fri 9.30-5; other times by appt. Furniture, china, copper, brass, plated ware, glass and silver.

Phillips Ipswich
Dover House, Wolsey St, IP1 1UD. Tel 55137. (Also at Garrod Turner Rooms,50 St Nicholas St, Ipswich.Tel.54664.) Open Mon-Fri 8.30-5; Sat 9-12; other times by appt. Valuers & auctioneers selling furniture, silver, jewellery, pictures. SOFAA

Tom Smith Antiques
(Thomas Smith). 33A St Peters St. Tel 210172. (Also at Lavenham, Suffolk.) Open Mon-Sat 10-6; other times by appt. General antiques, mainly furniture. Four-poster and half tester beds. Silver of all periods.

Gerald Weir Antiques
(G.I.Weir). Hepplewhite House, 7 Vermont Rd. Tel 52606. Open by appt only. Georgian & Victorian furniture. LAPADA

Ixworth

E.W.Cousins & Son
(E.Cousins). 27 High St. Tel Pakenham (0359) 30254. Open Mon-Fri 9-5; Sat 9-12.30; other times by appt. Georgian and Victorian furniture. Shipper. Valuations. LAPADA

Lavenham STD 0787

R.G.Archer
(R.G.Archer). 7 Water St, CO10 9RW. Tel 247229. Open Mon-Sat 9-5.30; Sun 10-5.30. Antiquarian and secondhand books plus remainders.

J. & J. Baker
(Mr C.J. and Mrs B.A.J.Baker). 12-14 Water St. Tel 247610. (Also 3A High St.) Open Mon-Sat 9-1, 2-5.30. Quality 17th, 18th and early 19thC furniture, 19thC oils and watercolours, pottery and porcelain (perfect examples only) 1780-1840, metalware, collectors' items.

Phoenix Gallery Ltd
(Jill & Noel Oddy; Gallery Director:Jane Thorpe). 97 High St, CO10 9PZ. Tel 247356. Open Mon-Fri 10-5.30; Sat 10-6; Sun 2-6. Contemporary art. New exhibitions every 4 weeks.

Long Melford

R. Bell
Coconut House. Tel Sudbury (0787) 79860. Open Mon-Sat 9-6; other times by appt. Antiques, furniture, contemporary paintings.

The Chater-House Gallery
(A.D.Chater-House). Foundry House, Hall St. Tel Sudbury (0787) 79831. Open 7 days 10-5; other times by appt. 17th-20thC furniture, jewellery, clocks, pianos, paintings, silver, ceramics.

Compton-Dando (Fine Arts) Ltd
Hall St, CO10 9JL. Tel Sudbury (0787) 312610. (Also at Berewyk Hall, White Colne, Essex.) Period English and Continental furniture, also a wide and interesting range of decorative fixtures and fittings for the interior designer, all adapted from the antique. Packing, insurance and transport arranged.

Country Antiques
(Ilona Bury). 10 Westgate St. Tel Sudbury (0787) 310617. Open 11-5 except Wed & Sun. Country and kitchen bygones, woodworking tools, curiosities and collectors' items. Also linen, lace & Victorian clothing.

The Enchanted Aviary
(C.C.Frost). 63 Hall St. Tel 0787-78814. Open usually Mon-Sat 9.30-5.30 but appt advisable. Mounted birds, animals, fish, mainly pre-1900, also other natural history items.

The Goff Galleries
(Mr B.Goff Gillings). Hall St, CO10 9JQ. Tel Sudbury (0787) 78228. Open Mon-Fri 9.30-5.30; Sat 9-5; other times by appt. 18thC mahogany furniture. Valuations.

Denzil Grant Antiques Ltd
(Denzil Grant). Hall Street. Tel 75470 (priv 04493 576). Open Mon-Sat 10-5.30; other times by appt. 17th, 18th and early 19thC furniture, tapestries and objects.

Long Melford Antiques
Chapel Maltings, High St. Tel Sudbury (0787) 79287. Open Mon-Sat 9.30-5.30; other times by appt. Fine country oak and pine, wholesale and trade.

Jessica Longhurst
Magill Antiques, Chestnut House, CO10 9HZ. Tel 78088. Open Mon-Sat 9-5.30; other times by appt. Res on prem. Mainly 18th and 19thC furniture.

W.C.Nunn & Son Antiques and Valuations
(B.D.Nunn). Cross Keys Lt St Marys. Tel Sudbury (0787) 75787 (priv 74782). (Also at 67 Friars St, Sudbury, Suffolk CO10 6AJ.) Open Mon-Sat 2-6; other times by appt. Antique furniture, china, glass, pictures. Most stock pre-1835.

Old Forge Antiques
(Mr & Mrs C.Chilton). Old Forge, Bridge St. Tel Sudbury (0787) 247083. Open Tues-Sun 9.30-5; other times by appt. 18th to 20thC pine, mahogany, oak and walnut furniture.

Old George Antiques
(W.M.Wild). at R. Bell, Coconut House, Hall Street. Open Mon-Sat 9-6; other times by appt. 17th and 18thC English and Continental furniture and decorative items.

Pauline Peretz Antiques
(Mrs P.Peretz). Linden House, Hall St, CO10 9JF. Tel Sudbury (0784) 70534. Silver 1600-1860, antique prints, furniture and decorative items. LAPADA

Sun House Antiques
(Maureen Thompson). Hall St, CO10 9HZ. Tel Sudbury (0787) 78252. Open Thur-Sat 10-5; other times by appt. Specialist dealer in 18th and 19thC glass; also needlework and 18th & 19thC furniture & decorative items. BADA

Suthburgh Antiques
(R.P.Alston). Red House, Hall St. Tel Sudbury (0787) 74818. Open Mon-Sat 10-5. English furniture, including Georgian mahogany and early oak and walnut pieces. Antiquarian maps and prints.

Tudor Antiques
(A.H. & S.J.Denton Ford). CD10 9HY. Tel Sudbury (0787) 75950. Open Mon-Sat 9.30-5.30; Sun 2-5. General antiques; very large range of quality small items, bygones and furniture in ten showrooms.

Ward Antiques
Hall St. Tel Sudbury (0787) 78265. Open Mon-Sat 10-1 2-5.30; other times by appt. Wide range of English furniture.

Lowestoft STD 0502

Charles Hawkins
Notleys Salerooms, Royal Thoroughfare. Tel 2024. Open Mon-Fri 9-1, 2-5.30; Sat 9-12. Auctioneers -General antique and modern furniture.

Kessingland Antiques
(T.A.Hammond & P.J.M.Utting). 36A High St, Kessingland. Tel 740562 (priv 740285/74139. Open daily including Sun 9-5.30; other times by appt. General antiques, furniture. 1400 sq ft of showrooms.

Royal Thoroughfare Gallery
(R.H.Sprake). 6 Pier Terrace, NR33 0AB. Tel 82006. Open Thurs & Fri only 10-11.30; other times by appt. Lowestoft porcelain & general antiques on commission.

Nayland STD 0206

Hugh Arnold Antiques
(Hugh Arnold). 20 High St. Tel 262486 (priv 262422). Open Mon-Sat 9-5.45; other times by appt. All types of antiques, 1700-1940.

Templar Antiques
(Pamela Wilson). The Corner House, 2 Bear St, CO6 4HX. Tel 262520. Open weekdays 9.30-5.30; other times by appt. Period glass, porcelain, small items of furniture, paintings, etc. Specialising in period drinking glasses, Bristol & Nailsea ware, Doulton, Staffordshire, early transfer ware.

Needham Market STD 0449

Roy Arnold
77 High St. Tel 720110. Open Mon-Sat 9-5.30; appt preferable. Specialist in tools and books about tools. Woodworker, clockmaker, also medical and other instruments.

COMPTON-DANDO

(FINE ARTS) LIMITED

HALL STREET, LONG MELFORD, SUFFOLK

Telephone: Sudbury (0787) 312610

Messages can be received at any hour by Ansafone

A good selection of English and Continental Antique Furniture of the 17th, 18th and early 19th Centuries

We continue to carry stock at

BEREWYK HALL, WHITE COLNE, ESSEX

TELEPHONE: EARLS COLNE (07875) 2200

where we are resident and will be pleased to see you at any reasonable hour by prior appointment

PAULINE PERETZ ANTIQUES

Linden House Hall Street
Long Melford
Suffolk CO10 9JF

Telephone Sudbury (0787) 70534

A pair of silver tea caddies, 1722, by Gundry Rood

We carry a wide Selection of 18th and early 19th century Silver, Furniture and Antique Prints

Opening hours 10a.m.–5p.m. daily

E. T. MANSON

(CLOCKS)

8 Market Hill · Woodbridge · Suffolk

Tel. Woodbridge (STD 03943) 7226

Needham Market Antique Centre
(S. & R. Abbott). The Old Town Hall, High St. Tel 720773 (priv 0473 41145). Open Mon-Sat 10-5. General antiques, jewellery workshop, clock repairer.

The Relic Shop
(Carole Russell). 106A High St, IP6 0EN. Tel 721245 (priv 0473 830858). Open Mon-Fri 10-1; closed Thurs; open all day Sat; other times by appt. Bygones, curiosities, 19th and 20thC jewellery, needlework, silver, dolls, toys, country antiques.

Uvedale Hall Reproductions
Uvedale Hall. Tel 720262.

Newmarket STD 0638

Clock Tower Antiques
(Mrs W. Thurston). 2, Old Station Rd, CBB 8DN. Tel 664915. (Also at 12/14 Old Station Rd.) Open Mon-Sat 10.30-5.30; other times by appt. General antique dealer, one shop having porcelain, brass, copper, pictures, objets d'art, antique dolls, costume, etc; the other, furniture from 18thC to late 19thC, paintings, furnishing items, etc. Large varied stock.

Jemima Godfrey Antiques
(Miss A. Lanham). 5 Rous Rd. Tel 663584. Open Thurs, Fri 10-1, 2-4.30; other times by appt. Brass, copper, linen, jewellery, sporting prints and general collectors' items.

R.E. & G.B.Way
(M.G. Way). Brettons Burrough Green. Tel 217. Open Mon-Sat 9-5. Antiquarian and other books on hunting, horses, racing and field sports. ABA

Orford STD 039 45

Castle Antiques
(Brenda M.Bennett). Market Hill, IP12 2LQ. Tel 450388. Open daily 12-4.30; other times by appt. General small antiques, bric-a-brac, furniture and clocks.

Peasenhall STD 072 879

Peasenhall Arts & Antiques Gallery
The Street. Tel 224. Open 7 days. Paintings, furniture and clocks.

Saxmundham STD 0728

Market Place Antiques
The Market Place. Tel 2503. Open Mon-Sat 9-5. Res on prem. 19thC furniture, pottery, porcelain and general antiques.

Southwold STD 0502

D. & D. Lee
21 High St, IP18 6AS. Tel 722795 (priv 722576). Open Mon-Sat 10-1, 2.30-5; closed Wed except July-Sept 10-1. General antiques and Victoriana.

Stoke-by-Nayland

Country Bygones
(Michael Everett). Half Moon House. General stock. Clock restoration service.

Stowmarket STD 0449

Chelsea House Antiques
(David Cordon). 27 Station Rd. Tel Elmswell (0359) 40895. (Also at Woolpit, Suffolk.) Open 10-5 every day except Tues; other times by appt. General antiques and pine. Many decorative items in china, glass, textiles. Good quality pine, country elm, oak furniture and small mahogany pieces.

Trench Enterprises
(Kevin Holmes). Three Cow Green, Bacton, IP14 4HJ. Tel Bury St Edmunds (0284) 60909. (Display in Hildreth's Arcade,139-151 Portobello Rd,London W11.) Open Sats only 8-4. Antique (pre 1900) and old (pre 1945) wooden & card jigsaw puzzles & dissected maps for sale by mail order. Restoration work & replacement pieces (wooden) undertaken. Annual subscription for catalogue £2. Individual wooden puzzles made to order.

Sudbury STD 0787

Magpie Antiques
(Norma Horsefield). 53 Station Rd.

Olivers
23-24 Market Hill, CO10 6EN. Tel 72247. Auctioneers and valuers. FRICS

Weston

Frank Collins
Marlborough Farm, London Rd. Tel Beccles (0502) 714842. (Also in London.) Open Mon-Sat 9.30-1 2-5.30; other times by appt. 17th - 19thC furniture and works of art. LAPADA

Wickham Market STD 0728

Abbotts
The Hill, IP13 0QX. Tel 746321. Open Mon-Fri 9-1, 2-5.15, Sat 9-12. Auctioneers.

Crafers Antiques
(Elizabeth Davies). The Hill. Tel 747347. Open Mon-Sat 9.30-5.30; closed for lunch Tues & Thurs. 18th and 19thC English pottery and porcelain, glass, furniture, and collector's items, silver and jewellery.

Morris Antiques & Bygones
(Mr & Mrs V.Taylor). 70 High St. Tel 746275. Open Mon-Sat 10-1, 2.30-5.30; other times by appt. Furniture and general antiques.

Woodbridge STD 0394

The Antique Furniture Warehouse
Old Maltings, Crown Place. Tel 7222. Open Mon-Fri 9-5; other times by appt. 12,000 sq ft of showroom and warehouse containing furniture, general antiques and shipping goods.

Simon Carter Gallery
23 Market Hill, IP12 4LX. Tel 2242. Open Mon-Sat 9-5.30; other times by appt. Oil paintings, watercolours & drawings. Oak and mahogany furniture, decorative objects. Specialising in portraits, primitives,20thC British paintings.

Peter Downing
Alde House, Single St, IP12 3BE. Tel 411873. Open by appt only. General antiques. LAPADA

David Gibbins Antiques
(D.W.L.Gibbins). 21 Market Hill, IP12 4LX. Tel 3531 (priv 2685). Open Mon-Sat 9.30-5.30; other times by appt. Late 17th to early 19thC furniture, 18thC English porcelain, specialising in Lowestoft porcelain. BADA, CINOA

Hamilton Antiques
8 Church St. Tel 7222. (Also The Antique Furniture Warehouse, Old Maltings, Crown Place.) Open Mon-Sat 9.30-1 2-5; Wed 9.30-1. 18th and 19thC mahogany, rosewood, walnut and oak furniture.

Anthony Hurst Antiques
(A.H.B.&C.Hurst). 13 Church St. Tel 2500. Open Mon-Sat 9.30-1, 2-5.30; early closing Wed; other times by appt. A large stock of changing 18th and 19thC furniture. Valuations. LAPADA

Lambert's Barn
24a Church St. Tel 2380. Open Mon-Sat, half day Wed. 19th and 20thC furniture.

Edward Manson
8 Market Hill. Tel 7226. Fine clocks.

Neal Sons & Fletcher
26 Church St, IP12 1DP. Tel 2263/4 (priv 0728 723877). (Also at 33 Market Hill, Framlingham.) Open Mon-Fri 9-5.30, Sat 9-1. Fine art auctioneers and valuers. All types of antiques and chattels sold in regular sales at the Theatre St Saleroom, Woodbridge. RICS

Top Floor Studio
(John Roberts). Quayside, IP12 1BH. Tel 3627. Open Mon-Fri 9-6; Sat 9-12.30; other times by appt. Photographers. Also marine prints.

A.G. Voss Antiques
16 Market Hill, IP12 4LU. Tel 5830. Open 9.30-1, 2-5.30 early closing Wed. 17th to 19thC oak, walnut and mahogany furniture, clocks and barometers. BADA

Woolpit

Woolpit Antiques
(David Cordon). The Old Butchers Shop, The Street. Tel Elmswell (0359) 40895. (Also at Stowmarket, Suffolk.) Open Mon-Sat 10-5.30; other times by appt. General antiques, decorative items in china, glass, textiles. Good quality pine, country elm, oak furniture and small mahogany pieces.

Wrentham STD 050 275

The Old Reading Room Antiques
(Sarah Jane Bradbear). 7 High St. Tel 376. Open Mon-Sat 10-5.30, Sun 2-5.30. Victorian china, glass, bric-a-brac, pre-1940 clothes, bygones, collectors items, jewellery.

Wren House Antiques
(Janet and William Pipe). 1 High St. Tel 276. Open Tues, Thurs, Sat 10-5; other times by appt. Clocks, antique maps and prints, quality china, glass and collectors items.

Yoxford STD 072 877

Yoxford Bazaar
(Mrs F.R.Rush). High St. Tel 448. Open Mon, Thurs, Fri, Sat; other times by appt. Small interesting decorative antique items, period clothes, textiles, i.e. bed covers, cushions & embroideries etc.

Surrey

Abinger Hammer STD 0306

Stirling Antiques
(V.S.Burrell). Aberdeen House, Guildford Rd, RH5 6RY. Tel Dorking (0306) 730706. Open Mon-Sat 9.30-6.30, closed Thurs; other times by appt. Metalware, stained glass, furniture, curios, lighting.

Ashtead STD 037 22

Gadsby's Antiques
88-90 The Street. Tel 72305. Open Mon-Sat 9.30-1, 2.15-5.30; other times by appt. Georgian and Victorian furniture, silver, brass, copper, pewter, glass, porcelain, clocks and barometers.

Banstead

The Pug Antiques
35a Nork Way.

Bletchingley STD 0883

John Anthony Antiques
(John & Nancy Hart). 71 High St. Tel Godstone (0883) 843197. Open Mon-Fri 10-6; other times by appt. Desks, general 18th, 19thC furniture. LAPADA

The Cider House Galleries Ltd
Norfolk House, 80 High St, RH1 4PA. Tel Godstone (0883) 842198. Open Mon-Fri 9.30-5.30, Sat 10-1; other times by appt. More than 700 fine quality oil paintings, 17th to early 20thC. Specialists in export for trade and collectors.

Elias Clark Antiques Ltd
(David and Jackie Clark). 1 The Cobbles, High Street, RH1 4PB. Tel Godstone (0883) 843714. Open Tues-Sat 10-1, 2.30-5; other times by appt. English pottery of the 18th and early 19thC, particularly figures, groups & animals, Delft, prattware, creamware and pearlware cottages, toby jugs, country furniture, naive and primitive paintings. BADA, LAPADA

Simon Marsh Antiques
(Mr Simon Marsh). The Old Butchers Shop, High St. Tel Godstone (0883) 843350. Live on prem. 18th and 19thC furniture, clocks. Also furniture restoration, clock restoration and re-upholstery.

Directory Entries are Free and ADDITIONS OR CORRECTIONS will be welcomed by *THE EDITOR, British Art and Antiques Directory, National Magazine House, 72 Broadwick Street, London W1V 2BP*

Post House Antiques
(P.Bradley). High St. Tel Godstone (0883) 843317. Antique furniture, decorative items, mirrors, fenders, lamps & general goods. LAPADA

Byfleet STD 093 23

Ronald A. Lee (Fine Arts) Ltd
The Manor House. Tel 43346. Open strictly by appt only. Specialist in antique clocks with an important stock, also paintings, works of art and furniture. BADA

Camberley STD 0276

The Antique Home
247 London Rd. Tel 26412. Four dealers specialising variously in 18th and 19thC furniture, silver, 18thC and early 19thC porcelain and jewellery.

Benmuir Photographic Services Ltd
(T.J. Chapman, Managing Director). 475 London Rd, GU15 3JA. Tel 26267. Open Mon-Fri 9-5.30. Commercial, industrial & advertising photographers.

Clarke's Antiques (Camberley)
(J.E.Clarke, D.P.Clarke FGA). 311 London Rd, GU15 3HE. Tel 22677. Open Mon-Sat 9-6; other times by appt. General antiques and secondhand items - furniture, jewellery, porcelain, glass, medals etc.

J. Goddard & Sons Ltd
(Johnson Wax Ltd). Frimley Green, GU16 5AJ. Tel 63456. Manufacturers of all types of silver and fine metal polishes.

Carshalton

Carshalton Antiques Galleries
(B.A., J.M.&M.E.Gough). 5 High St, SM5 3AP. Tel 01- 647 5664. Open Mon-Sat 9-5; closed Wed; other times by appt. Large stock of period, Victorian, Edwardian furniture and shipping goods. Clocks, bric-a-brac etc.

Cheam STD 01

Rogers Antiques
(Christine and Michael Rogers). 22 Ewell Rd. Tel 643 8466. Open daily 10-5.30; closed Wed, Sun. 18th and 19thC furniture with the best of reproduction pieces made from solid woods, i.e. William Tillman, interior design service for private homes, offices, boardrooms. LAPADA

Chertsey STD 093 28

The Love Affair - Antiques
(Brian and Patricia Love). 8 Windsor Street. Tel 63565. Furniture, porcelain, glass, clocks, pictures, objets d'art.

Surrey Antiques Centre
(Patricia Lee Allen). 10 Windsor St. Tel 63313 (priv 0932 41097). Open Mon-Sat 10-5. Twelve dealers. Ethnic art, pictures, clocks, furniture, glass, pottery, and porcelain; also clothes, books and records.

Chobham STD 099 05

Chobham Antiques Market
The Old Print House, Rear of 62 High St, GU24 8AA. Tel 6227. Period furniture, art, antiques and ephemera.

Michael Hedgecoe Antique Furniture Restoration
(M. Hedgecoe). 21 Burrow Hill Green, GU24 8QS. Tel 8206. Open Mon-Fri, 8-6; other times by appt. Fine restoration and upholstery, chair copying, upholstery fabrics. Weekly London delivery. Carriage countrywide. LAPADA, GMC

The Tarrystone
40-42 High St. Tel 7494. Open Mon-Fri 9-1, 2-5, Sat 9.30-1; other times by appt. 18th and early 19thC English furniture, porcelain, paintings and prints. IDDA

Cobham STD 0932

Antics
(K.J.Needham). 44 Portsmouth Rd. Tel 5505. Open Mon-Sat 9.30-5.30; closed Wed; other times by appt. Pine and 20thC furniture, also shipping goods.

Shepherds Antiques
65 Portsmouth Rd. Tel 7909. Specialists in Georgian and earlier furniture. Trade and overseas buyers welcome.

Alanna Staton Antiques
(Mrs E.Staton). 4 Anyards Rd, KT11 2JZ. Tel 63407 (priv 04864 2407). Open Mon-Sat, 9.30-4.30; Wed, 9.30-1; other times by appt. Furniture (1780-1860), small decorative items. LAPADA

Cranleigh STD 0483

David Mann & Sons Ltd
High St, GU6 8AY. Tel 273777. Open Mon-Sat. Antique furniture of all periods. Oriental carpets and rugs.

Croydon STD 01

Apollo Galleries
(G.W.Barr). 61, 65 and 67 South End, CR0 1BF. Tel 681 3727, 680 1968. Open Mon-Sat 9.30-6; other times by appt. 19th and early 20thC paintings, English furniture, French bronzes, clocks, porcelain and silver. LAPADA

Keith Atkinson Antiques
(Keith Atkinson). 59 Brighton Rd, CR2 6ED. Tel 688 5559. Open Mon-Sat 9-6; other times by appt. 5000 sq ft of antique furniture & shipping goods for trade & export. LAPADA

Brazil Antiques Ltd
(N.A. Brazil). 145 Brighton Rd. Tel London (01) 680 2707. Victorian furniture. LAPADA

Frederick Grace
91 South End. Tel 680 6966. Period and Victorian antiques.

G.E.Griffin
43a Brighton Rd, CR2 6EB. Tel 688 3130. Open Mon-Fri 8-5.30, Sat 9-5. Antique furniture for trade and export. Restoration work.

A.W. John Simmons & Son
77 South End, CR0 1BF. Tel 688 0990. Open Mon-Sat 9-5.30, Wed 9-1; other times by appt. 19th and 20thC oil paintings. FATG LAPADA

Brian Trengove Antiques and Picture Gallery
46 South End, CR0 1DP. Tel 688 2155. Open daily 9.30-5. 18th and 19thC furniture. English, Continental and Oriental porcelain. Also period silver and 19thC paintings. BADA

The Whitgift Galleries
(A.W.J.Simmons, P.J.Simmons). 77 South End. Tel 01-688 0990. Oil paintings, watercolours. Valuations. LAPADA FATG

Dorking STD 0306

R. Bennett Antiques
6 West St, RH4 1BL. Tel 882828. Open Mon-Sat 9-5.30; other times by appt. Desks, dining tables, chairs, bureaux and bookcases. Restorations.

Dorking Antiques
58 West Street. Tel 883777. 18th and 19thC glass, small antiques, needlework tools and silver plate.

The Dorking Desk Shop
(J.G.Elias). 20 West St. Tel 883327. Open Mon-Fri 8-5.30, Sat 10-5. Pedestal, cylinder, roll top, partners desks, bureaux, library tables, davenports, secretaires, clerks desks and writing boxes.

J.G.Elias Antiques
(J.G.Elias). 37 West St. Tel 880535 and 883327. Open Mon-Fri 8-5.30, Sat 10-5. Desks and general antique furniture. Also Dorking Desks, rear of store in Junction Rd, by appointment only: Tel:887697. Specialist in pedestal and partners desks.

Hampshires of Dorking
51/52 West St. Tel 887076. Open Mon-Sat 9.30-6. Large stock of 17thC and 18thC furniture.

E. Hollander Ltd
(D.J. Pay, B. Pay). The Dutch House, Horsham Rd, South Holmwood, RH5 4NF. Tel 888921. Open by appt only. Antique clocks & barometers, English silver and old Sheffield plate (mainly 1750-1825). All types of restoration. BADA

Eleanor Hutton
59 West Street. Tel 883777. Antique silver and jewellery.

Kennedy & Spooner Antiques
(Stephen Kennedy & Philip Spooner). 1 Meadowbrook Rd. Tel 881773 (priv 0372-52877). Open 10-1 2.15-5.15. 17th-19thC furniture.

C.C. Kohler
12 Horsham Rd. Tel 881532. Assembling of special collections. English literature, George Gissing. ABA

Loft Antiques
(Maureen Hicks). Old Kings Head, 11 High St. Pine and country furniture.

Lyons Court Antiques
(Mrs Nonie Cellier). 1-2 Lyons Court, High St. Tel 883582. Open Mon, Tues, Fri, Sat 10-5. General antiques, pine and watercolours.

The Old House Antiques
(Reginald & Ronald Harman). 9-10 West St, RH4 1QH. Tel 887278. Open Mon-Sat 9.30-5.30; early closing Wed; other times by appt. 18th and 19thC mahogany and oak furniture, brass, copper, and bric-a-brac. Trade only.

Reflections
(Babs Wilby). 54 West St, RH4 1BS. Tel 881775 (priv Shere 2502). Open Mon-Sat 9.30-5.30; other times by appt. 19thC furniture, porcelain, glass and bric-a-brac.

Michael Schryver Antiques Ltd
(M.R.P.Schryver, A.V.Schryver). The Granary, North St, RH4 1DN. Tel 881110. Open Mon-Fri 8.30-5.30; Sat 8.30-12.30. Restoration of fine period furniture, contemporary and period upholstery, brass work. Specialising in 18thC English furniture. GMC

Sheengate Galleries
(Miles S.Lamdin). Henhurst House,Henhurst Cross Lane, Beare Green, Nr.Ockley, RH5 4PX. Tel 712184. Open 9.30-6.30. 19th and early 20thC watercolours and oils.

The Stable Antiques
Old Kings Head Court, 11 High St. Tel 885452. Open Mon-Sat 9.30-5.30; other times by appt. Georgian and early Victorian mahogany and rosewood, period oak and country furniture.

Swan Antiques
(Maj & Mrs J.R.Grogan, Mr R.M.Douglas). 62A West St. Tel 881217 (priv 01-394 2361). Open 10-5.30; other times by appt. 17th to early 19thC furniture, metalware and decorative items.

Thorpe & Foster Ltd
49 West St. Tel 881029. (See also Hampshires of Dorking.) Open Mon-Sat 9.30-6. Large stock of 17thC and 18thC furniture.

Tucker & Langs
(John Lang & Colin Tucker). Kings Head Court, High St. Tel 882203. Open Mon-Sat 9-5.30. Brass & copper fire furniture including fenders & coal buckets. Also candlesticks, kettles, jam pans, jardinieres etc.

West Street Antiques
63 West Street.

P.F. Windibank
18-20 Reigate Rd. Tel 884556. Auctioneers.

Patrick Worth
11 West St. Tel 884484. Open Mon-Sat 9.30-5.30; closed Wed. 18th and 19thC furniture and decorative items. BADA

East Horsley STD 048 65

A.E.Gould & Sons (Antiques) Ltd
(D & P Gould). Old Rectory Cottage, Ockham Rd South, KT24 6QJ. Tel 3747. 18th & 19thC English furniture, barometers, clocks, brass. LAPADA

East Molesey STD 01

The Antique Centre
(Mr & Mrs R.V.Rumble). 46 Bridge Rd. Tel 979 4969(priv 0372 64034). Open 10-5; closed Wed; other times by appt. Staffordshire, porcelain, jewellery, silver.

The Arcade
(Louie Abbott). 77 Bridge Rd, KT8 9HN. Tel 979 7954. Open Mon-Sat 10-5. Eleven individual shops offering a variety of stock.

The Court Gallery
(Judy Clark). 16 Bridge Rd. Tel 941 2212. Open 10-5.30; closed Wed; other times by appt. 19th and 20thC oils, watercolours, drawings, prints and maps. Complete framing service and restoration on the premises.

Hampton Court Revival Antiques Centre
(Paytons Galleries Ltd). 52-54 Bridge Rd. Tel 979 3552. Open 10-5; closed Wed & Sun. Large antiques centre with 50 dealers selling furniture, silver, jewellery, prints, pine and smalls.

Nicholas Antiques
(Nicholas Wallace). 31 Bridge Rd. Tel 979 0354. Open Mon-Sat 9.30-5.30; closed Wed pm; other times by appt. Georgian, Victorian and Edwardian furniture and decorative items.

The Textile Conservation Centre
Apartment 22, Hampton Court Palace, KT8 9AU. Tel 977 4943.

Egham STD 0784

Stampantique
(A.S. Carlyon-Gibbs). 86 High St, TW20 9DP. Tel 36290. Open Mon-Sat 10-5.30; other times by appt. Large stock of stamps of all countries, especially West Indies, good USA and Germany, pictures,many watercolours, clocks & pocket watch specialists. Antique furniture & interesting silver.

Esher STD 0372

Kensington Galleries
(John S Bates). Badgers Wood, West End Lane, KT10 8LB. Tel 64407. Open by appt only. 18th and 19thC sporting oil paintings. LAPADA

Ewell

J.W.McKenzie, Bookseller
12 Stoneleigh Park Rd, KT19 0QT. Tel 01- 393 7700. Theatre and cricket books.

Farnham STD 0252

G.E.Day
(J.L.Day and J.E.Ross). 82 West St, GU9 7EN. Tel 715 043. (Parking adjacent to shop.) Open 9.30-1, 2.15-5; early closing Wed; other times by appt. Three rooms of 17th and 18thC oak and mahogany furniture, copper, brass, glass, silver and porcelain. Also reproduction cabinet handles.

Horn Antiques
(Paula Hardwick). Churt, GU10 2JA. Tel Headley (0428) 714298. Open Wed-Sat 9.30-5.30. Antique horn items. Pre-1830 small oak and fruitwood furniture. Topographical framed prints. BADA

P. & B.Jordan
90 West St, GU9 7EN. Tel 716272. Open Mon-Fri 9.30-1, Sat 9.30-1, 2-5.30; other times by appt. Furniture, prints, paintings, maps, china and glass. BADA

New Ashgate Gallery
(Elfriede Windsor). Wagon Yard, GU9 7JR. Tel 713208. Open Tues-Sat 10-1, 2-5. Contemporary paintings, prints, sculpture, ceramics, jewellery. Also gallery for contemporary crafts. ICGA

R. & M. Putnam
(Ronald Putnam, Maureen Putnam). 60 Downing St, GU9 7PN. Tel 715769 (priv 715485). Open 9.30-1, 2-5; half day Wed; other times by appt. 18th to 19thC furniture, metalware, pictures and paintings.

Henry Stevens, Son & Stiles
4 Upper Church Lane. Tel 715416. Maps, atlases and Americana, Canadiana, the West Indies and the polar regions. ABA

Karel Weijand
Lion & Lamb Courtyard. Tel 726215. (Also the Persian Carpet Gallery, London.) Open Mon-Fri 9.30-5; Sat 9.30-1; other times by appt. Oriental carpets and rugs. Fine silks. LAPADA

Godalming STD 048 68

Andrew Cottrell Galleries
(Andrew Cottrell). 7-9 Church St. Tel 7570. Open Mon-Sat. Wide range of antiques in 15 showrooms including furniture, pictures, china, silver, glass, bric-a-brac, linen, lace and metalware. Also specialists in old toys, models and games, firearms and weapons, oriental ceramics.

Godalming Galleries Ltd
(Andrew G.L. Goolding). 3 Wharf St, GU7 1NN. Tel 22254. Open Mon-Sat 9.30-5.30 (5.00 Sat); other times by appt. Original paintings by leading contemporary artists, including oils & watercolours, limited edition prints, sculpture, quality framing, cleaning & restoration. Specialising in pictures of animals, wildlife, birds, landscape, sporting subjects. FATG

Hawkley Studio Associates Ltd
(Nick Nicholson). 3 Weston Close, Ballfield Rd, GU7 2EY. Tel 22366. Photographers of antiques and works of art or craft for publishers, dealers and collectors.

Heath-Bullock
8 Meadrow, GU7 3HN. Tel 22562. Open 9-5 Mon-Sat. (On A3100, on left coming from Guildford to Godalming.) Large stock of English and Continental furniture, garden ornaments and works of art. Exhibitors at and organisers of Buxton, Surrey and Kensington Antiques Fairs. BADA

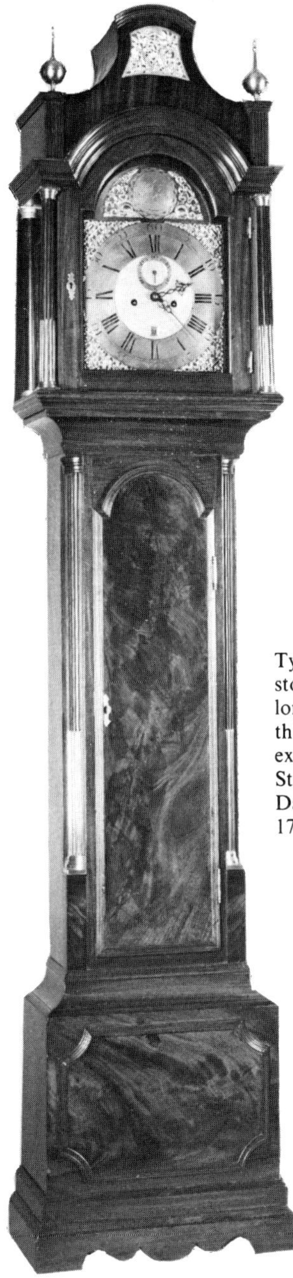

Hymore Hodson & Potts Restorations
Town End Street. Tel 25626. (Also Hymore Hodson (clocks and furniture) in London.) Open Mon-Fri 8.30-5. Entire antique clock and furniture restoration service; specialist in the restoration of longcase, bracket and skeleton clocks.

Messenger May Baverstock
93 High St, GU7 1AL. Tel 23567. Open Mon-Fri 9-5.30; Sat 9-12.30; other times by appt. Auctioneers of antiques and fine art. SOFAA

The Nice Little Shop
13 Wharf St. Tel 23025. 20thC toys and models.

Priory Antiques
29 Church St. Tel 21804. Small items from late 19thC, including china, brass, old clothes etc.

The Reid Gallery Ltd
(Mr & Mrs Graham Reid). Mousehill House, Milford, GU8 5BL. Tel 6990. Open by appt. 19th and early 20thC watercolours and a few oil paintings. A number of living artists in both oil and watercolours. Valuations and restorations.

Great Bookham

Roger A. Davis
19 Dorking Rd. Tel 0372 57655/53167. Antiquarian horologist.

Guildford STD 0483

The Antiques Centre
(Mrs J.S.Voke). 22 Haydon Place, GU1 4LL. Tel 67817. Open Tues, Thurs, Fri, Sat 10-5. The centre houses 7 dealers stocking jewellery, silver, sewing items, lace, prints, ceramics, glass, dolls, lace bobbins, fans and other items.

Churchill Antique Galleries Ltd
65 Quarry St, GU1 3UA. Tel 506662. Specialists in 18th and 19thC desks.

Cubitt & West Fine Art Auctioneers
Cubitt & West Auction Galleries, Millmead, GU2 5BE. Tel 504030. Fine art auctioneers and valuers.

Denning Antiques
(C.A.Denning). 1 Chapel St. Tel 39595. Lace, linen and textiles.

Gillinghams Antiques
(D.M. Shepherd, J.P.M. Hobbs). 148 London Rd, GU1 2UF. Tel 61952. Open Mon-Fri 9.30-5; other times by appt. Antique period furniture.

Guildford Galleries Ltd
(Brian Mills). Cranley Court, 59 Cranley Rd, GU1 2JW. Tel 61646. Open by appt only. Oils and watercolours cleaned and restored and individually framed at our private studios. LAPADA FATG

Horological Workshops
(M.D.Tooke, B.R.Ward J.P.). 204 Worplesdon Rd, GU2 6UY. Tel 576496. Open Mon-Fri 8.30-5.30, Sat 9-12.30; other times by appt. Antique clocks, including longcase, French carriage, skeleton, mantel and bracket, also box chronometers, watches and barometers. BHI

G.Oliver & Sons
St Catherine's House, Portsmouth Rd. Tel 575427. Open daily. Large and important stock of old English and French furniture. A few fine pictures. Also specialising in antique garden statues and furniture. BADA

Michael Spratt Watercolours
Kingfishers, East Shalford Lane, Shalford, GU4 8AS. Tel 504607. Open daily by appt. (2 miles south of Guildford on A281 Horsham Rd). 18th and 19thC watercolours.

Geoffrey G.Stevens
26-28 Church Rd, GU1 4NG. Tel 504075. Open Mon-Sat; early closing Wed. Antique clocks and barometers - also repairs.

Michael Stewart Fine Art Galleries Ltd
(inc. Sir William Russell Flint Galleries). 61 Quarry Street. Tel 504359. Works of living British artists. Books, signed proofs, limited editions, watercolours and engravings pertaining to Sir William Russell Flint.

Thomas Thorp
170 High St, GU1 3HP. Tel 62770. Open Mon-Sat 9-5. Large stock of new, out-of-print and antiquarian books. ABA

Charles W. Traylen
(Charles W. & Nigel C.R.Traylen). Castle House, 49 Quarry St. Tel 572424. Open Tues-Sat 9-5. Very large stock in 21 rooms of fine books, manuscripts, prints and maps. Catalogues. ABA

Haslemere STD 0428

Fine Art Petworth PLC
(H. Lack, W. Minns). Fernhurst Gallery, Crossways, Fernhurst. Tel 56177 (priv 0252-711923). Open Mon-Sat 9-5.30, Sat 9-1; other times by appt. Fine 19th and 20thC oils and watercolours. LAPADA, FATG

Julia Holmes Antique Maps and Prints
(Mrs Julia Holmes). Muirfield Place, Bunch Lane, GU27 1AE. Tel 2153. Open anytime, but only by appt. Maps 1575-1880, particularly of the British Isles. Engravings 1700-1880, with the emphasis on country life, sports and animals.

Surrey Clock Centre
(S. Haw & C.Ingrams). 3 Lower St. Tel 4547. Open 9-4.45; early closing Wed and Sat. Grandfather and carriage clocks, barometers. Trade repairers & dial silvering and repainting.

Wood's Wharf Antiques Bazaar
(D.M.Brindle-Wood-Williams). 56 High St. Tel 2125 (priv Midhurst 6500). Open Mon-Sat 9.30-5; other times by appt. Furniture, porcelain, silver, jewellery etc.

Hindhead STD 042 873

Albany Antiques
(T.&E.D.Winstanley). 8-10 London Rd. Tel 5528. Open Mon-Sat 9-6; other times by appt. Antique furniture, carpets, china and brass items.

M.J.Bowdery
12 London Rd. Tel 6376. Open Mon-Fri 9-5.30; Sat 9-1; other times by appt. 18th & early 19thC English and Continental furniture.

Oriel Antiques
(J. Gear). 3 Royal Parade, GU26 6TD. Tel 6281. Open Tues-Sat, 9-5.30; Wed 9-1; other times by appt. 18th and 19thC English furniture and watercolours.

Secondhand Rose
(Simon & Sue Ridout). Portsmouth Rd, Bramshot Chase, GU26 6DB. Tel 4880. Open Mon-Sat 9.30-6; other times by appt. 18th & 19thC furniture, pictures and metal, 20thC and modern furniture (wood and upholstered), general accessories (i.e. Georgian, Regency, Victorian, Edwardian & modern furniture).

Horley STD 029 34

The Hinton Gallery
(S.F.Waley). Crutchfield Farm, Hookwood, RH6 0HT. Tel 862417. 19thC oils and watercolours especially of Middle East subjects. LAPADA

Kingston upon Thames
STD 01

Glencorse Antiques
(Mrs Manya Igel,Mr B. Prydal). 321 Richmond Rd, Ham Parade. Tel 541 0871. Open Mon-Sat 10-5.30; other times by appt. Quality 18th and 19thC furniture, specialising in Canterburys.

Kingston Antiques
138 London Rd. Tel 546 2221. Fine 17th, 18th, 19thC clocks.

Richard Lyon Oriental Art Books
PO Box 150, KT2 5AY. Tel 546 6149. Books, specialising in oriental art books & primitive art books.

Margaret McCloy Antiques
(Margaret McCloy). 49 Surbiton Rd, KT1 2HG. Tel 549 6423. Open Mon-Sat 10-5; closed Wed. Antique pine furniture.

Warner's Military Specialists
(G.G.Warner). 2 The Apple Market, Eden St, KT1 1JE. Tel 546 7527(24 hr answering). Everything connected with the armies of the past bought and sold. Business by mail order only. Catalogue £1 (fully illustrated).

Leatherhead STD 0372

Fire and Iron Limited
(Richard Quinnell). Rowhurst Forge, Oxshott Rd, KT22 0EN. Tel 375148. Contemporary craft metalwork. ICGA

Merstham STD 073 74

Michael & Margaret Baker
6 High St. Tel 2658. Open Mon, Wed, Fri 10-5; other times by appt. General antiques and decorative items specialising in textiles, samplers & quilts.

Rayne Antiques
34 High St, RH1 3EA. Tel 3443. Decorative furniture, clocks, boxes and paintings.

Milford

Michael Andrews Antiques
(Michael Andrews). Portsmouth Rd. Tel Godalming (04868) 20765. Open Mon-Sat. Fine period furniture.

Thursley Textile Designs
(Zoe O'Brien). 1 Moushill Lane, (at junction with A3). Tel Godalming (04868) 24769. Open Mon-Sat. Original textiles, mostly handmade by craftsmen throughout the world, ranging from fine oriental embroidery to chunky knitwear, and from antique lace to modern furnishing fabrics.

Scott Antiques

67 WALTON STREET,
WALTON-ON-THE-HILL,
SURREY, KT20 7RZ.
TADWORTH 2097

FINE PERIOD FURNITURE
PAINTINGS. PORCELAIN

Open Monday-Saturday 10.00 am-1.00 pm; 2.30 pm-5.00 pm;
Closed Wednesday

The sign of
THE BRITISH ANTIQUE DEALERS' ASSOCIATION

The nearest you will get to a guarantee
in the world of antiques.
Ring Sally Tunley on 01-589 4128
for a free list of members

Ripley Antiques

HEATHER DENHAM

A very attractive French oak provencial marriage armoire, the panels carved with foliage and birds, first half of the 19th Century

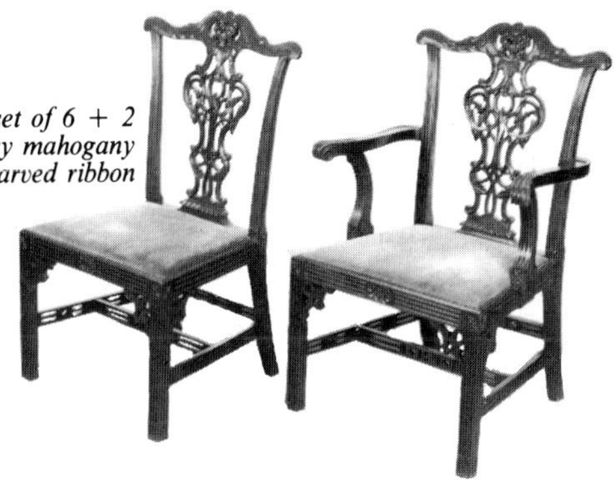

A superb set of 6 + 2 19th century mahogany chairs, finely carved ribbon backs, with drop in seats and fretted stretchers.

A very fine 18th century mahogany tallboy, crossbanded drawers in satinwood with cantered corners, on ogee bracket feet. Height 75", width 43", depth 22".

Specialising in 18th and 19th century English and Continental Furniture for Trade and Export. Also decorative items.

67 HIGH STREET, RIPLEY, SURREY
Telephone: Guildford (0483) 224981.

2 mins from Junction 10 on the M25 and 30 mins from London on the A3.

Morden STD 092 945

A.Burton-Garbett
(Arthur Burton-Garbett). 35 The Green, SM4 4HJ. Tel 540 2367. Open by appt only. Books from the 15th to the 20thC on South and Central America, Mexico and the Caribbean; also Spain and Portugal.

Old Hall Gallery Ltd
(Andrew Merkler). Crown Lodge, Crown Rd, SM4 5BY. Tel 540 9918. Open by appt only. 17th to 19thC original oil paintings.

Oxted STD 088 33

The Chair Shop
83 High St. Tel 2122. Open Tues-Sat 10-1, 2.15-5; other times by appt. Victoriana, silver, pictures, plate, furniture and clocks.

Treasures
151 Station Road East. Antique centre.

Redhill STD 0737

English Street Furniture Company
Somers House, Linkfield Corner, RH1 1BB. Tel 60986. Open Mon-Fri 9-5.30; other times by appt. Victorian lamp-posts.

Irene & Alan Holmes & Grant
(Mr & Mrs A.Holmes). 83A & 87 Brighton Rd. Tel 71146. Open Mon-Fri 10-5. 19thC English furniture, silver, jewellery, porcelain, copper, brass, glass. Shipping goods.

F.G.Lawrence & Sons
(S.A. & C.R. Lawrence). 89 Brighton Rd, RH1 6PS. Tel 64196/7. Open Mon-Fri 9-1, 2-5; Sat 10-1; other times by appt. General antiques and Victoriana.

Reigate STD 073 72

Bourne Gallery
(John Robertson). 31-33 Lesbourne Rd. Tel 41614. Open Mon-Sat 10-5.30. Victorian and 19thC Continental paintings, also watercolours and drawings. Specialist in English paintings and watercolours. LAPADA

Heath Antiques
(Jon & Paul Gibson). 15 Flanchford Rd, RH2 8AB. Open normally 9.30-5 seven days; other times by appt. Small furniture, silver, porcelain, specialising in Moorcroft & Worcester porcelain.

Esmond Holden Ltd
53A High St, White Post Hill, RH2 9AF. Tel 44754. Open Mon-Sat 9-5; Wed 9-1. Antiquarian books, paintings and antiques. ABA

Lewis & Lloyd Ltd
(J.D. & P.C.Lewis). 13 West St. Tel 21509. Open Mon-Sat 9.30-5; closed Wed; other times by appt. 18th and 19thC English furniture. LAPADA BADA

Bertram Noller (Reigate)
(A. Noller). 14A London Rd. Tel 42548. Open Mon, Thur, Fri, Sat 9.30-5; other times by appt. Brass and copper - good stock of fenders. Small collectors items. Small furniture. Pine and marble mantelpieces. Specialising in clock repairs, furniture repairs and french polishing.

Reigate Antique Arcade
(Terry & Berene Willcocks). 57 High St. Nine dealers selling a range of stock.

Victoriana Dolls
(Mr and Mrs C. Bond). Tel 49525. Open by appt only. Antique dolls and accessories. LAPADA

Richmond STD 01

The Antique Mart
(Y. & G. Katz). 72-74 Hill Rise, TW10 6UB. Tel 940 6942. Open daily 11-1, 3-6; closed Wed; Sun 3-6; other times by appt. Top quality 19th century furniture, exclusive stock.

Colin Bodner
24 Hill Rise, TW10 6UA.

Mollie Evans
84 Hill Rise. Tel 948 0182 (priv 940 3720). Open Thurs, Fri, Sat 10.30-5.30; Sun 2.30-5.30; other times by appt. Period furniture - early country and decorative. Interesting bygones and unusual bold decorative items up to the 1930s.

Peter and Debbie Gooday
20 Richmond Hill. Tel 940 8652. Open Tues, Thurs, Sat 11-5.30; Fri, Sun 2-5.30; other times by appt. Art nouveau and art deco objects & jewellery. Liberty pewter and other decorative items 1880-1950.

Hamilton Weston Wallpapers
(Robert Weston & Georgina Hamilton). 11 Townshend Rd, TW9 1XH. Tel 940 4850. Open Mon-Fri 9-6; other times by appt. Hand-printed wallpapers. Documentary reproductions from original fragments. 'Old Paradise' range contains designs from the 17th, 18th and 19thC. IDDA

Hill Rise Antiques
(Patrick Hinde, Dietmar Milewski). 26 Hill Rise, TW10 6UA. Tel 948 1140. Open Mon-Sat 10.30-5.30; Sun 2.30-5.30; closed Wed; other times by appt. 18th and 19thC English mahogany and walnut furniture and longcase clocks, silver and plate. LAPADA

Giulia Irving
(Mrs G.Irving). PO Box 29, TW10 6HY. Tel 940 0368. English porcelain. LAPADA

Kingaby's
(Mrs P.B.Kingaby, Miss A.Glazebrook). 15-17 Paved Court. Tel 940 6533 (priv 894 1731). Open 10-5.30. Antique and secondhand jewellery, pictures, silver, glass, weapons and general antiques. NAG

F. & T. Lawson, Antiques
(T.A. Lawson, Mrs F.M. Lawson). 13 Hill Rise. Tel 940 0461. Open Mon-Sat 10-5.30; Sun 2.30-5.30; closed Wed; other times by appt. Clocks and watches, furniture, paintings, prints.

Layton Antiques
(Lady Layton). 1 Paved Court, The Green. Tel 940 2617. Open Mon, Tues, Thurs-Sat 10-5; other times by appt. 18th and early 19thC furniture, silver, china and glass.

Nigel B. Mendes da Costa
Tel 940 4525. Open by appt only. Fine 17th, 18th and early 19thC furniture. Valuations. LAPADA

Palmer Antiques
(David and Valerie Palmer). 10 Paved Court. Tel 948 2668. Fine Georgian and Victorian furniture.

Piano Nobile Fine Paintings
26 Richmond Hill, TW10 6QX. Tel 01-940 2435. Open Thurs-Sun 10-8; other times by appt. Specialists in fine 19th and 20thC English and Continental oil paintings for collectors and investors.

Richmond Antique Traders
30-32 Hill Rise, TW10 6UA. Wide variety of antiques including furniture, costumes, objects, china and glass.

Ripley

J. Hartley Antiques Ltd
186 High St. Tel Guildford (0483) 224318. Large stock of 18th and early 19thC furniture, paintings and bric-a-brac for trade and export.

Manor House Antiques
High St. Tel Guildford (0483) 225350. Open Mon-Sat 9-5; other times by appt. 18th and 19thC English and Continental furniture, porcelain, reproduction metalware and garden ornaments.

Ripley Antiques
(Heather Denham). 67 High St, GU23 6AQ. Tel Guildford (0483) 224981. Open Mon-Sat 9.30-1, 2-5.15; Wed 9.30-1; other times by appt. 18th and 19thC furniture for export and trade also decorative items, mirrors, chandeliers etc. LAPADA

Sage Antiques & Interiors
(Howard & Chrissie Sage). High St, GU23 6BB. Tel Guildford (0483) 224396. Open Mon-Fri 9.30-12.30, 2-5.30; Sat all day; other times by appt. Antique furniture, pre-1830, walnut, mahogany, oak, decorative items, oil paintings, watercolours, silver, silver plate, interior design, fabrics, wall coverings, carpets etc. LAPADA, GMC

Anthony Welling Antiques
(Anthony Welling). Broadway Barn, High St, GU23 6AQ. Tel Guildford (0483) 225384. Open 9.30-1, 2-5.30 daily; other times by appt. 17th & 18thC oak and country furniture, brass, copper and pewter. BADA

Shackleford

F.F.Hill
The Gate House, Lombard St, GU8 6AR. Tel Guildford (0483) 810330. Open Mon, Wed, Fri; other times by appt. Clocks and watches: restoration and repairs. Church and chamber barrel organs: repairs and tuning.

Shere STD 048 641

Dial Antiques
(Nigel Raffety). Dial Cottage, GU5 9HS. Tel 2722. (Also at 34 Kensington Church St, London, W8.) Open Mon-Sat 9.30-5.30; other times by appt. English and Continental longcase & bracket clocks, watches and barometers. Restoration.

Shirley

Spring Park Jewellers (inc The Clock Shop)
(D.Ashton, D.R.Horton). 284 Wickham Rd. Tel 01-656 2800. Open Mon-Sat 10-5.30, early closing Wed. 18th and 19thC clocks, antique jewellery, silver, furniture and collectables. BHI

Surbiton STD 01

Raymond Fortt Studios Ltd
(C.A.Fransella, Mrs A.D.Fransella). 95 Ewell Rd, KT6 6AH. Tel 399 6765. Open Mon-Fri 9.30-6. 24-hour answerphone. Specialist photographers of antiques and works of art.

House of Mallett
(Katie Mallett). 67-69 Brighton Rd, KT6 5NF. Tel 390 3796. Open Mon, Fri, Sat 10-5; Sun 10-1; other times by appt. Porcelain and pottery of all types, silver, metalware, furniture (mostly Victorian mahogany etc), oil paintings, watercolours. Specialist in Art Deco porcelain, furniture, mirrors etc.

B.M.Newlove
139-141 Ewell Rd. Tel 339 8857. Open Mon-Sat 9.30-5.30; closed Wed. 17th to 19thC furniture, especially early oak and Georgian mahogany. Also china, paintings and clocks. LAPADA

Quested Antiques
62 Brighton Rd, KT6 5NF. Tel 390 3566. Open Mon, Fri, Sat 10-5; Sun 10-1. Specialists in pine furniture. Also oak and kitchenalia.

Sutton STD 01

Whittington Galleries
(M. Wakely). 22 Woodend, SM1 3LT. Tel 644 9327. Open by appt only. 18th and 19thC English and European porcelain, blue and white transferware. LAPADA

Tadworth STD 073 781

Ian Caldwell
(Ian W.R.Caldwell). 9A The Green, Dorking Rd, KT20 5SQ. Tel 3969. Open Mon-Sat 9.30-6; other times by appt. Antique furniture, mainly 18th and early 19thC, and mainly mahogany although some oak, walnut etc. Valuations for insurance, probate; restoration services. LAPADA

Virginia Water

Wentworth Auction Gallery
22 Station Approach. Tel Wentworth (09904) 3711. Auctioneers.

Walton on the Hill

Moorhen Antiques
(Mr & Mrs B.Page). 9 Walton St. Tel Tadworth (073 781) 2272. Open Tues, Thurs, Fri 10-5; Sat 11-5; other times by appt. General antiques, collectors' items, pine furniture.

J.P.Raison
Sturt House, Chequers Lane, KT20 7RQ. Tel Tadworth (073781) 3557. Open by appt only. 18thC English porcelain, especially first period Worcester; also Chelsea, Bow and Derby.

Scott Antiques
(G.P.H. & A.E. Graves, A.T. Clarke). 67 Walton St, KT20 7RZ. Tel Tadworth (073781) 2097 (priv 0396 882431). Open Mon-Sat 10-1, 2.30-5; closed Wed; other times by appt. Fine period furniture, oil paintings and watercolours and porcelain. BADA

Walton-on-Thames STD 0932

The Boathouse Gallery
(Bernard E.Clark). The Towpath, Manor Rd, KT12 2PG. Tel 242718. Open Tues-Sat 9.15-5. Picture & frame restoration, artists materials, picture framing and mounting. Gallery of paintings, i.e. originals and limited editions.For exhibitions we are open seven days. FATG

West Byfleet

Academy Antiques
WTS House, Camphill Industrial Estate. New and antique billiard tables.

Weybridge STD 0932

Church House Antiques
(R.W.Foster). 42 Church St. Tel 42190. Open Mon-Sat 10-5.30; other times by appt. 18th and 19thC furniture, 19th and 20thC jewellery, silver, decorative boxes, clocks, china and glass. LAPADA

The Clock Shop
64 Church St. Tel 40407, 55503. Open Mon-Sat 9.30-6; other times by appt. Antique clocks. Restoration.

Edward Cross Fine Paintings
128 Oatlands Drive, KT13 9HL. Tel 51093. English and Continental paintings and watercolours.

R. Saunders
71 Queens St. Tel 42601. Antique English furniture, silver, porcelain, glass, paintings, barometers. BADA

Witley

Malcolm Ellis
(Patricia & Malcolm Ellis). Petworth Rd. Tel Wormley (042879) 2896. Open by appt only. Buyers (nationwide collection service) of coins, medals, old bonds and gold and silver.

Woking STD 048 62

Chattels
(John Kendall). 156 High St, Old Woking, GU22 9JH. Tel 71310. Open 9-5. Small stock, consisting of English dial, bracket and longcase clocks, and barometers. Specialists in the restoration of English clocks and barometers.

Elsdon Antiques
152 High St, Old Woking, GU22 9JH. Tel 62651. Open Mon-Sat 9-6; other times by appt. Trade and export furniture 1690-1900.

Knaphill Antiques
(P.W.Bethney and J.A.Bethney). 38 High Street, Knaphill. Tel Brookwood (048 67) 3179. Open Tues-Sat 8.30-6. 18th and 19thC mahogany and some pine furniture and some objects of vertu.

Wych House Antiques
(A.C.Perry). Wych Hill. Tel 64636. 18thC furniture. LAPADA

Wonersh

M. Odell Foster
Millmead. Tel Guildford (0483) 892375. Open daily 9.30-6. Egyptian, Greek, Roman and other antiquities. Islamic, South-East Asian art, icons. Catalogues available.

E.Sussex

Alfriston STD 0323

Alfriston Antiques
(J.A.Tourell). The Square, BN26 5UD. Tel 870498. Open Tues-Sun 10.30-5.30; other times by appt. Silver, jewellery, clocks, brass, copper and reproduction and wholesale goods.

Old Paint Shop
(N.Barnard). High St, BN26 5TD. Open Mon-Sun 11-5; other times by appt. Small furniture, all metals, firearms, china and old glass.

Battle STD 042 46

Duncan Campbell
The Prior's Lodge, Upper Lake. Tel 2888. Open Thurs & Fri 9-5, Sat 9-4; other times by appt. Large selection of antique weapons, also small pieces of furniture,copper, brass, silver, glass and porcelain.

Bexhill STD 0424

Barclay Antiques
(Roger & Mary Barclay). 7 Village Mews, Little Common. Tel Rye (0797) 222734. Open Mon-Sat 10-4.30; closed Wed. 18th & 19thC furniture, ceramics, paintings & treen together with interesting and unusual decorative items. LAPADA

The Old Mint House
(J.C.Nicholson). 45 Turkey Rd. Tel 216056 (priv 0323 761251). (Main shop at Pevensey, near Eastbourne.) Open Mon-Fri 9-5; other times by appt. All shipping goods. LAPADA

David & Sarah Pullen Antiques
(D. & S. Pullen). 29-31 Sea Rd, TN40 1EE. Tel 222035. Open Mon-Fri 10-1, 2-5; Sat 10-1; other times by appt. Antique clocks, longcase, wall & mantel clocks, barometers, 18th & 19thC furniture of good quality, decorative items. Most clocks & furniture are restored. LAPADA

Stewart Gallery
(Gallery Laraine Ltd). 48 Devonshire Rd. Tel 223410. (Also in Eastbourne, and see Clare Gallery, Tunbridge Wells.) Open Mon-Sat 9-5.30; other times by appt. Original paintings, ceramics, glass and giftware. Framers, restorers and valuers.

Tamar Gallery
(Mrs G.T.Mills). 17 Wickham Ave. Tel 221835. Open 9-1, 2.30-5.30; closed Wed; other times by appt. 19thC watercolours and paintings, general antiques.

Village Antiques
(Mr & Mrs D.C.M. Cowpland). 2 Cooden Sea Rd, Little Common. Tel Cooden (04243) 5214. Open Mon-Sat 9.30-5.30; other times by appt. Large showrooms of furniture, barometers, clocks, jewellery, porcelain, metalware, vintage and veteran cars and shipping goods.

Brighton & Hove STD 0273

Adrian Alan Ltd
15c Prince Albert St. Tel 25015. (Head office & warehouse: 4 Frederick Place, Brighton Tel:25277.) Open Mon-Fri 10-5, Sat 10-4 at shop. Warehouse open Mon-Fri 8.30-5.30, Sat 9-1; other times by appt. 17th to 19thC English and Continental furniture, clocks, bronzes, porcelain etc. LAPADA

Angel Antiques
(P. Angel). 16 Church Rd, BN3 2FL. Tel 737955. Open Mon-Fri 9-12.30, 2.15-4; Sat 9-12.30; other times by appt. All kinds, no repro. LAPADA

Ashtons Furniture Centre
(R.Neish). 1-3 Clyde Rd, BN1 4NN. Tel 605253. Open Mon, Tues, Thurs, Fri 9.30-5; Wed 10.30-1; Sat 9.30-2. Shipping goods and general antiques.

Attic Antiques
(Mr & Mrs F.B.Moorhead). 23 & 32 Ship St, BN1 1AD. Tel 29464 (priv 551594). (See also Patrick Moorhead Antiques, 59a Ship St.) Open Mon-Fri 10.30-1, 2.45-5; Sat 11.30-1. Clocks, music boxes, brass and copper, writing boxes, caddies, silver and plate etc. Specialising in Oriental porcelain, furniture, bronzes, ivories and American shipping goods and paintings. Victorian glass. LAPADA

Hugo Barclay
(Hugo Barclay). 7 East St, BN1 1HP. Tel 21694. Open Mon-Sat 10-1. 2-5.30. Contemporary work from British ceramicists, jewellers and glassmakers. ICGA

Barnetts Antiques
(Mr & Mrs M.Barnett). Tel 502706. Open by appt only. Silver, silver plate. LAPADA

Ron Beech
(R.E.Beech). 150 Portland Rd, BN3 5QL. Tel 724477. Open Tues-Sat 10.30-1.30, 3.30-6.30; other times by appt. Victorian Staffordshire figures and potlids. LAPADA

John Bird/Annette Puttnam
44 Upper North St, BN1 3FH. Tel 739425. Open Mon-Fri 9.30-5.30; other times by appt. Country, painted, lacquered & primitive furniture, boxes, baskets, needlework, pottery & treen.

Brighton Antiques Gallery
(B.Collie, Esq). 41 Meeting House Lane. Tel 26693, 21059. Open Mon-Sat 10-5.30. Twenty stallholders exhibiting Georgian, Victorian and Edwardian jewellery and silver, brass, copper, small furniture, dolls, coins and militaria.

Bruton-Brighton
(H.B. & B.C.Bruton). 31-32 Meeting House Lane, BN1 1HB. Tel 26591. Open Mon-Sat 10-5. General Victorian furniture, brass, copper, militaria, pewter, china. LAPADA

Caroline Buxton Interiors
(Caroline Buxton). 22 Victoria Rd, BN1 3FS. Tel 771200. Open Mon-Fri 10-5.30; other times by appt. Decorative antiques and interior design.

Peter Carmichael
(Hal Mileham). 33 Upper North St, BN1 3FG. Tel 28072. Open Mon-Sat 9-1, 2.15-6; Sat 9-1; other times by appt. General antiques, specialising in antique barometers. Trade and exporters welcome. LAPADA

Chattels
172 Church Rd, Hove. Antiques, textiles and jewellery.

Compton Antiques
60A Middle St. Tel 774229. Open Mon-Fri 9.30-5.30; other times by appt. Chinese and English porcelain, ivory and hardstone carvings, snuff bottles, small period furniture, general antiques.

David Crook Antiques
(David Crook). 16 Bond St, BN1 1RD. Tel 26040. Open Mon-Sat 10-30-5.30; half day Thurs; other times by appt. Furniture, glass, china, jewellery and Victorian needlework, specialising in lace, tablecloths, bedspreads etc.

Dawes & Billings
176A Old Shoreham Rd. Tel 722971. Photographers.

Graham Deane Antiques
5 Market St. Tel 24526. Open Mon-Fri 9.30-5.30, Sat 10-1; other times by appt. 19thC furniture, clocks, barometers, scientific and marine instruments.

Mike Deasy Ltd
108-114 Eastern Road. Tel 688523/687237. Open Mon-Fri 8-6; Sat 8-1. Antiques, garden ornaments and fine reproductions.

Diamond Antiques
(Dane Carlos Henty). 156 Portland Rd. Tel 739064. Open Mon-Sat 9-6. Good quality jewellery and Victoriana.

Harry Diamond & Son
Barclays Bank Chambers, 26 North St, BN1 1EB. Tel 29696 (priv 507689). Open Mon-Sat 9-5; other times by appt. Antique jewellery, silver and French clocks.

Iain Downe Antiques
(Iain Fraser Downe). 28 North Rd, BN1 1YB. Tel 697496. Open 9.30-5.30; other times by appt. 18th and 19thC oak and mahogany furniture. Mainly trade and export.

Dupont Galleries
33 Grand Parade. Tel 738257 and 695094. Open Mon-Sat 11-6. Oriental rugs, carpets, kelims, Islamic and early European textiles.

D.H.Edmonds Ltd
27-28 Meeting House Lane, BN1 14B. Tel 27713, 28871. Open Mon-Sat 9.45-6; other times by appt. Antique jewellery and silver.

Gee-Pemberton Macphail
(Peter Gee-Pemberton, Gordon Macphail). 52 Upper North St. Tel 774224. Open anytime. Decorative antique furniture and paintings.

Graves Son & Pilcher Fine Arts
71 Church Road. Tel 735266. Auctioneers.

Hallmarks
4 Union St, The Lanes. Tel 725477. Silver, jewellery, clocks.

Simon Hatchwell Antiques
(Simon Hatchwell). 64-65 Middle St, BN1 1AL. Tel 27663. Open Mon-Fri 9-1.30, 2-5.30; other times by appt. English and Continental furniture, paintings, barometers, clocks, carpets. Chandeliers.

David Hawkins (Brighton) Ltd
15B Prince Albert St, The Lanes. Tel 21357. Open Mon-Sat 9-5.30; other times by appt. English, Continental and oriental furniture, pottery, porcelain, clocks, lamps, arms and armour. Postal service. Shipping arranged. LAPADA

Holleyman & Treacher Ltd
(M.G. Kadwell & D.J. Plumtree). 21A & 22 Duke St, BN1 1AH. Tel 28007. Open Mon-Sat 9-5.30. Large stock of secondhand and antiquarian books on all subjects, together with prints & maps, and a large stock of music & music books. ABA

The House of Antiques
(A.Margiotta). 25 Meeting House Lane. Tel 27680, 24961. (Also at 17 Prince Albert St.) Open Mon-Sat, closed 1-2 for lunch; other times by appt. Antique jewellery, silver, furniture, china and general stock. LAPADA

Dudley Hume
46 & 50 Upper North St, BN1 3PH. Tel 23461. Open Mon-Fri 9.30-6; other times by appt. Furniture, metalware and garden furniture. Warehouse with some shipping goods.

Raymond P.Inman
(R.P. Inman, M.H. Inman). 35 & 40 Temple St, BN1 3BH. Tel 774777. Open Mon-Fri, 9-1, 2-5; other times by appt. Auctioneers and valuers.

Lennox Antiques
(M. Lennox Cato). 53 Upper North St, BN1 3FH. Tel 29409 (priv 563104). Open Mon-Fri 9.30-6; other times by appt. Good quality Georgian and Victorian furniture, porcelain, pottery, glass and pictures. Decorative items. Oriental works of art.

Ruth Macklin Smith Antiques
Tel 689668 and 05516-350. Open by appt only. Small pieces of 18th and 19thC furniture, needlework pictures, copper, brass and decorative items.

H. Miller (Antiques) Ltd
22A Ship St. Tel 26255. (Also at The London Silver Vaults, Chancery Lane, London, WC2.) Open Mon-Fri 10-2.30; other times by appt. Antique silver, and silver plate, old Sheffield, jewellery. LAPADA

Patrick Moorhead Antiques
(P. Moorhead). 59A Ship St, BN1 1AD. Tel 28209 (priv 551594). Open Mon-Sat 10.30-1 3-5; other times by appt. Old paintings, good Victorian porcelain, pottery, writing boxes, desks and inkwells, dolls and bears. Specialist in Oriental porcelain.

Michael Norman Antiques Ltd
15 Ship St, BN1 1AD. Tel 29253/4 26712. (Also at 18-19 Bond St. Tel 697716.) Open Mon-Sat 9-5.30; other times by appt. Ship St: pre-1840 English furniture and works of art. Bond St: furniture, general antiques and shipping goods. BADA

Page & Hawkes
(B.J.Page & D.H.Hawkes). 30 Trafalgar St, BN1 4ED. Tel 609310 (priv 553879). Open Mon-Sat 10-5.30; other times by appt. English & Continental art nouveau furniture and decorative arts 1870-1940, Japanese works of art including colour prints & block printed books.

Colin Page Antiquarian Books
36 Duke St, BN1 1AG. Tel 25954. Open Mon-Sat 10-5.30; other times by appt. Antiquarian booksellers. Wide range of subjects including travel, topography, natural history, art & antiques. Large stock of leather bound volumes, plate books. ABA

Dermot & Jill Palmer Antiques
(Dermot & Jill Palmer). 7-8 Union St, The Lanes. Tel 28669. Open Mon-Sat 9-6; Sun by appt. Decorative furniture and objects, primitive paintings, lacquer and unusual and interesting items. Rocking horses.

Pandora's Box
112 St Georges Rd, Kemptown. Tel 603305. Open Mon-Sat 10-2; other times by appt. Porcelain, pottery and small furniture; specialising in British art pottery.

Park Galleries
215/217 Preston Rd, BN1 6SA. Tel 504057 (priv 29466). Open Mon-Sat 10-6; other times by appt. Antiques and interior decorations. Specialist in lacquer, beds, bergere furniture, bamboo.

The Pine Shop
(Michael Thornber). 3 Dukes Ct, Duke St, BN1 1AR. Tel 253365 (priv 501110). Open Tues-Sat 10-5; other times by appt. Interesting pine and country furniture and decorative items. Specialising in Irish and English country furniture.

Resners
(Mr S. Resner, Mrs G.R.Resner, Mr M. Daniels). 1 Meeting House Lane. Tel 29127. Open Mon-Sat 10-5.30. Antique jewellery, specialising in Georgian, Victorian and signed jewellery. Also Art Deco, objets d'art and silverware. BADA

Robinson's Bookshop (Brighton) Ltd
(Mr & Mrs T.Brown). 11 Bond St, BN1 1JL. Tel 29012. Open daily 9-5.30. New books only. Specialist in reference books on antiques and works of art. Lists.

Clive Rogers Oriental Rugs
(Clive Rogers). 22 Brunswick Rd, Hove, BN3 1DG. Tel 738257. Open by appt only. Persian and other Oriental carpets and rugs, ancient and ethnographic textiles, Islamic objects.

J.& A.Savery
Tel 501601. Open by appt only. Porcelain, glass, silver. LAPADA

Frank Semus Ltd
(F.& I.Semus). 20 Middle St. Tel 28883. Open Mon-Fri 9.30-5; other times by appt. Reproduction Queen Anne style furniture, especially with walnut veneer, made for American market.

Shelton Mounting Service
(D.F.Saw). 4 Islingword Rd, BN2 2SE. Tel 698345. Open Mon-Fri 9-6; other times by appt. Oils,watercolours, prints. Specialising in framing, dry mounting, fine art restoration and mount cutting.

S. & L. Simmons
(S.L.Simmons, L.M.Simmons). 9 Meeting House Lane, BN1 1HB. Tel 27949. Open 9.30-5.30. 19th and 20thC jewellery and silver. LAPADA, NAG

South Coast Antiques Ltd
(W.E.Collins). 3 Kensington Place. Tel 609828. General. LAPADA

Sussex Commemorative Ware Centre
(Mrs R.Prior). 88 Western Rd, Hove, BN3 1JB. Tel 773911. Open Mon-Sat 9.30-12.30, Sat also 2-3.30; other times by appt. 19th and 20thC commemorative ware and collectors' items in ceramics and teapots.

Talbot Antiques
(K.B. Talbot). 60 Middle St. Tel 26758 (priv 724352). Open Mon-Fri 9.30-5; other times by appt. Furniture, paintings, porcelain, metalware, clocks, general antiques.

Tapsell Antiques
(Alistair P.R.Tapsell, Christopher R.C.Tapsell). 59, 59A Middle St. Tel 28341 (priv 553249). (Also at 10 Ship Street Gardens.) Open Mon-Sat 9-1, 2-5.30; other times by appt. Large stock including 18th and 19thC English and Continental furniture, clocks and porcelain. Separate rooms of antique Chinese blue and white and antique Japanese imari. LAPADA

Toby Antiques
(Daphne Elverson). Dukes Arcade, 32 Duke St. Tel 25800. Open Mon-Sat 9.30-5.30. Silver, copper, brass, toys and collectors items e.g. thimbles, hatpins, dolls house furniture, boxes etc.

Margot Tyldesley Antiques
Tel 21307. Open by appt only. English furniture, clocks, general antiques.

Graham Webb
(Graham Webb). 59 Ship St, BN1 1AE. Tel 21803 (priv 772154). Open Tues-Sat 10-5; other times by appt. All forms of mechanical musical instruments, including large stock musical boxes.

Weiner aus Wien Military Antiques
(George Weiner). 2 Market St, The Lanes, BN1 1HH. Tel 729948. Open 10-5 daily incl Sats; other times by appt. Antique arms, armour, edged weapons, uniforms, accoutrements, flags, guns, helmets and all worldwide militaria. British militaria of the Victorian to modern periods. Third Reich and Imperial German war memorabilia. Catalogue available, 50p or £1 abroad.

The Witch Ball Print & Map Shop
48 Meeting House Lane, BN1 1HB. Tel 26618. (Also at 2 Cecil Court, Charing Cross Rd, London WC2.) Open Mon-Sat 10.30-6; other times by appt. Marine, sporting, theatrical and topographical engravings, caricatures and maps, especially of the home counties.

Yellow Frog (Brighton) Ltd
(Julian Chalcraft, Mrs N.E.Lynn). 10 & 11 Meeting House Lane. Tel 25497. Open Mon-Sun 9-6; other times by appt. Antique jewellery, silver, ivory, English porcelain, watches, jade, unusual items.

Yellow Lantern Antiques Ltd
(B.R.&E.A.Higgins). 34 & 65B Holland Rd, Hove, BN3 1JL. Tel 771572 (priv 0273 455476). Open Mon-Fri 9-1, 2.15-5.30; Sat 9-1; other times by appt. English period furniture, ormolu, bronzes, porcelain, paintings, miniatures etc.

19 Middle Street Antiques
19 Middle St. Tel 727791. China, glass, furniture and decorative antiques.

Burwash STD 0435

Chateau Briand Antique Centre
High St. Tel 882535. Open 7 days a week 10-5; Sun 12-5. 11 stands selling antique furniture, fine porcelain, copper, brass, fine lace and linen, ethnic textiles, country antiques, ivories, bronzes and old prints.

Lime Tree Antiques
(S.& A.Vickery). High St, TN19 7ET. Tel 882 385. Open every day;on Sun ring door bell or phone. Furniture, oil paintings, watercolours, porcelain, rugs, silver, prints etc.

Small Antiques
(Mrs J.M.Murley). Lobbs Cottage, High St.

M. Walsh
Chaunt House, High St.

Ditchling

Nona Shaw
(Nona Shaw). 4 & 8 West St, BN6 8TS. Tel Hassocks (079 18) 3290 (priv 0273 27398). Open Mon, Tues, Thurs, Fri 10.30-5, Sat 12-6. Two well-stocked showrooms of quality antiques.

Eastbourne STD 0323

B & T Restorations
Unit 6 Commercial Mews South, 42 Commercial Rd. Tel 646457. High quality antique furniture restoration , clocks and instrument repairs.

Douglas Barsley Antiques
(Douglas Barsley). 44 Cornfield Rd, BN21 4QH. Tel 33666. (Also at 214-216 Seaside, Eastbourne, BN22 7QP (Tel: 26834.) Open Mon-Sat 9-1.30, 2-5. Antique furniture, silver, porcelain, jewellery, collectors' items. LAPADA

Wm Bruford & Son Ltd
(L.G.N.Bruford, E.R.Bruford-Davies). 11-13 Cornfield Rd, BN21 3NA. Tel 25452. (Also in Exeter, Devon.) Open Mon-Sat 9-1, 2.30-5.30; early closing Wed. Specialists in English silver, antique and secondhand jewellery, clocks and objets d'art. BADA

John Cowderoy Antiques (The Musical Box Centre)
(J.H., Mrs R., D.J. & R.A.Cowderoy). 40/42 South St, BN21 4X. Tel 20058 (priv 645353). Open Mon-Sat 9.30-1, 2.30-5; early closing Wed; other times by appt. Musical boxes, antique clocks, fine antique furniture, jewellery, gold, silver, brass, copper, porcelain, dolls and collectors items. Specialists in the repair and restoration of musical boxes and clocks. LAPADA

Roderick Dew-Antiquarian Books
(R.F.&K.A.Dew). 29 South St. Tel 646206 (priv 20239). Open Mon-Sat, closed Wed; other times by appt. General antiquarian stock, especially books on art, architecture and antiques.

Eastbourne Antique Market
(Charles French). 80 Seaside. Tel 20128 (priv 37730). Open Mon-Sat 10-5.30; other times by appt. 30 stalls, furniture, bric-a-brac, postcards, militaria, brass, copper etc.

Eastbourne Fine Art
(R.J.Day). 9 Meads St, BN20 7QY. Tel 25634. Open Mon-Sat 10-5; early closing Wed & Sat; other times by appt. 19th and 20thC English and Continental oils and watercolours. Specialists in the Norwich and Suffolk schools. Publishers of fine art reference books. Expert restoration of oil paintings and old frames.

Edgar Horn
(M.B.Allen FRICS). 47 Cornfield Rd, BN21 4QS. Tel 22801. Open Mon-Fri 9-1 2.15-5.30; Sat 9-12.30. Regular auction sales of antique and reproduction furniture, paintings, silver, rugs, collectors' items. (10 sales per year) at 46-50 South St. FRICS

Raymond Smith
30 South St, BN21 4XB. Tel 34128. Open Mon-Sat 9-5.30, closed Wed. Antiquarian and secondhand books, English and foreign literature, railways, the arts, history, theology, natural history, science, etc. ABA

E. Stacy-Marks Ltd
24 Cornfield Rd, BN21 4QH. Tel 20429 or 32653. Open Mon-Sat 9-5.30; early closing Wed; other times by appt. 19th & 20thC English, Dutch and Continental paintings. BADA

Stewart Gallery
(Gallery Laraine Ltd). 25 Grove Rd. Tel 29588. (Also in Bexhill and see Clare Gallery, Tunbridge Wells.) Open Mon-Sat 8.30-5.30; other times by appt. Original paintings, ceramics, glass and giftware. Framers, restorers. Valuations.

W.H.Weller & Son
(D.G.Ricketts). 12 North St, BN26 3H6. Tel 23592. Open Mon-Fri 10-12.30, 2-4; other times by appt. Brass, copper and bric-a-brac. Cleaning and restoration of brass and copper items undertaken on the premises.

Eridge

S.& O. Mathews
Stitches Farm House, TN3 9JB. Tel Rotherfield (089 285) 2848. Photographic services.

Flimwell STD 058 087

Graham Lower
(Graham Lower). Stonecrouch Farmhouse, TN5 7QB. Tel 535. Open Mon-Sat 9-6; other times by appt. 16th to 18thC English & Continental oak and country furniture.

Forest Row STD 034 282

Crosby Books
(A.S.B.Crosby). Orlingbury House. Tel Hartfield (089277) 4545. Open any time but by appt only. Books for collectors of glass and Oriental carpets.

Hailsham STD 0323

Camelot Antiques
(Mrs B.C.Chambers). Boreham St, BN27 4SH. Tel Herstmonceux (0323) 833460. Open Mon-Sat 10-5.30; closed Wed. Small furniture, silver, plate, porcelain, pottery, glass, brass, copper etc. Mirrors, prints, boxes, fans, jewellery, polishes and treen.

Hartfield Wells

Richard Macnutt Ltd
Hamm Farm House, Withyham, TN7 4BJ. Tel Groombridge (089276) 218. Open by appt only. Antiquarian music and music literature, autographs, manuscripts, musical and theatrical ephemera. ABA

Hastings STD 0424

Crossbow Antiques
38 High St. Tel 31878. Open Mon-Sat 10.30-5.30; early closing Wed; other times by appt. Pictures, furniture, china, weapons, bric-a-brac, antiques.

Howes Bookshop
(Raymond Kilgarriff). Trinity Hall, Braybrooke Terrace, TN34 1HQ. Tel 423437. Open Mon-Fri 9.30-1, 2.15-5, Sat 9.30-1. Antiquarian books and books on the humanities. ABA

Heathfield STD 043 52

Heathfield Furniture Salerooms
(E.Watson & Sons, manager Graham J.Foster). The Market, Burwash Rd. Tel 2132. Open Mon-Fri 8.30-5.30; other times by appt. Auctioneers.

Heffle Corner Antiques
(Ralph Willatt). Heffle Corner, Station Approach, Station Rd, TN21 8LG. Tel 3381. Open Mon-Sat 9.30-1, 2-5; early closing Wed; other times by appt. Arms, armour, militaria, china, coins, medals and small furniture, specialising in firearms, edged weapons & medals.

Herstmonceux STD 0323

New Malthouse Antiques
(Jacqueline Foyle Hunwick). New Malthouse, Hailsham Rd. Tel 833542. Open Mon-Sat 10-6; other times by appt. 18thC small furniture, treen, porcelain and silver.

Hurst Green STD 058 086

Delmas Antiques
(P.D.Stimpson). TN19 7PN. Tel 345. Open Mon-Sat 10-6.30; closed Wed; other times by appt. English and Continental furniture, Victorian landscapes , marine paintings and 18thC portraits.

Pigeon House Antiques
(D.K. & R.M. Wiltshire). 52 London Rd, TN19 7PN. Tel 474. Open any time, res on prem. 18th and 19thC British and European furniture, Regency, Biedermeier and Empire. Also decorative items. LAPADA

Lewes STD 079 16

Bow Windows Book Shop
128 High St, BN7 1XL. Tel 472839. Open Mon-Fri 9-5.30, Sat am by appt. Natural history, travel, topography and general English literature. ABA

Celia Charlotte's
(Mrs C.C. Russell). 7 Malling St, BN7 2RA. Tel 473303. Open Thurs-Sat 10-6; other times by appt. Antique linen & collectors lace, textiles, period costume, childrens clothes, embroideries, high class accessories etc.

Cliffe Antiques Centre
(Miss P. Harrison). 47 Cliffe High St, BN7 2AN. Tel 473266. Open Mon-Sat 9.30-5. 16 dealers with varied stock including silver, paintings, watercolours, furniture, jewellery, coins and medals, smalls, china etc.

Coombe House Antiques
(Mrs Marjorie Grinling). Malling St. Tel 473862. Open Mon-Sat 10-5. 18th & 19thC English & Continental furniture and small items. Garden furniture & ornaments.

Clifford Dann Auction Galleries
20/21 High St. Tel 477022. Auctioneers.

H.P.Dennison & Son
(D.H.Dennison). 22 High St, BN7 2LN. Tel 473665. Open 9-5; other times by appt. Antique furniture and works of art.

Felix Gallery
(W.S.H. Whitehead & M.M. Whitehead). 2 Sun St, BN7 2QB. Tel 472668. Open Mon-Sat 10-6; Sun 12-6; other times by appt. Specialising only in cats. Porcelain, pottery, enamels, woodcarvings, bronzes, silverware, jewellery, pictures etc. English, Continental, oriental.

Fifteenth Century Bookshop
(Eric Blundell). 99 High St, BN7 1XH. Tel 474160. Open Mon-Sat 9.30-5.30; Wed 9.30-1. General antiquarian and second-hand books.

Gorringes
15 North St. Tel 472503. Auctioneers.

Renee and Roy Green
Ashcombe House, Lewes Rd. Tel 474794. Open Mon-Fri 10-5.30; other times by appt. Six showrooms of quality period furniture and objects for trade only. BADA

Lewes Auction Rooms (Julian Dawson)
(Julian Dawson). 56 High St. Tel 478221. (Also auction rooms at Garden St, Lewes.) Open Mon-Fri 9-5.30, Sat 9-12.30; other times by appt. Antique & general furniture and effects. Auctioneers.

Stephen Moore Ltd
(S M Moore). 103 High St, BN7 1XH. Tel 474158. Open Mon-Sat 10-5; Wed 10-1; other times by appt. Fine quality furniture, also jewellery and pictures. BADA

Edward Reeves
(T.E.Reeves BSC LBIPP LRPS). 159 High St, BN7 1XU. Tel 473274. Photographer.

Southdown Antiques
48 Cliffe High St. Tel 472439. Open Mon, Tues, Thurs 10.30-1 only; other times by appt. General, small antiques.

Trevor
(M. Trevor-Venis). Trevor House, 110 High St. Tel 471975. Furniture. BADA

Tyne House of Lewes Ltd
140 High St. Tel 477446. Open Mon-Sat 10-6. Antique country furniture.

Wallis & Wallis
West Street Auction Galleries, West St, BN7 2NJ. Tel 473137. Open 9-1, 2-5.30. Auctioneers specialising in militaria, arms and armour, also coins and medals.

Lionel Young Antiques
(Berkeley L.Young). 1 South St, Cliffe Corner, BN7 2BT. Tel 472455. Open 11-5; closed Mon & Wed; other times by appt. Antique furniture, Georgian and Victorian china, glass, silver, plate, paintings and prints.

Mayfield STD 0435

W.J.Gravener Antiques
(Mr and Mrs Gravener). High St, TN20 6AA. Tel 873389. Res on prem. Longcase clocks, 18th and 19thC furniture.

Newhaven STD 0273

Leonard Russell
21 Kings Avenue, BN9 0NB. Tel 515153. Open by appt only. English pottery figures, groups, Toby jugs,porcelain, pastille burners & cottages; prattware, money boxes, cow creamers of the period 1750-1850. (Victorian 'flat-back' chimney ornaments not stocked). LAPADA

Ninfield STD 0424

Martin Hutton
Luxford House, Standard Hill, TN33 9NJ. Tel 892088. Open by appt only. 18th and 19thC furniture, porcelain. BADA

Northiam STD 079 74

Northiam Antiques
(K.W.Clarke). Main St. Tel 2182. Open daily 9.30-6; closed Fri; other times by appt. Oak & country furniture, small stock of 18thC porcelain and weapons.

Pevensey

The Old Mint House
(J.C.Nicholson). High St, BN24 5LF. Tel Eastbourne (0323) 762337 (priv 761251). (Also large warehouse at Bexhill, E.Sussex.) Open Mon-Sat 9-5; other times by appt. Furniture, clocks, metalware and porcelain. Antiques and shipping goods. LAPADA

Polegate STD 032 12

John Botting
(J.F.Botting). A27 Antiques Warehouse, Chaucer Industrial Estate. Tel 7167. Victorian furniture, shipping goods. LAPADA

BBC Antiques
(Bobby & Janice Morley). A27 Antiques Warehouse, Unit 2 Chaucer Industrial Estate. Tel 5301 (priv 0273-477446). Open Mon-Fri 9-6; other times by appt. Country chairs especially Windsors, and oak and pine country furniture.

Graham Price Antiques
A27 Antiques Warehouse, Dittons Rd. Tel 7167 (priv 0435-882553). Comprehensive stock of pine.

Directory Entries are Free and ADDITIONS OR CORRECTIONS will be welcomed by *THE EDITOR, British Art and Antiques Directory, National Magazine House, 72 Broadwick Street, London W1V 2BP*

Radford Antiques
(Mrs P.J. Radford). Twytton House, Alfriston, BN26 5TD. Tel Alfriston (0323) 870440. Open everyday from 10 am; Sat & Sun from 2 pm. Mixed stock antique furniture, plate, jewellery, weapons, maps and decorative prints. ABA

Portslade STD 0273

I.Blatt
17 Bampfield St. Tel 416641. Open Mon-Fri 9-1, 2-5; other times by appt. Antique and reproduction barometers and thermometers.

London & Southern Shipping
The Warehouse, Gladstone Rd, BN4 1LJ. Tel 420154/202989. Open 6 days 8-6; other times by appt. Packing & shipping service, overseas removals.

Peter Marks Antiques Warehouse
(Peter Marks & Sylvia Marks). 1-11 Church Rd. Tel Brighton (0273) 415471 (priv 501978). Open Mon-Fri 9.30-5.30, Sat 9.30-12.30; other times by appt. General antiques and shipping goods. LAPADA

J.Powell (Hove) Ltd
(J.Powell). 20 Wellington Rd. Tel 411599. Open Mon-Fri 8-6, Sat 8-1; other times by appt. Furniture, shipping goods. Mainly trade and export.

Semus Lewis Containers Ltd
69-77 North St. Tel 420154 and 415078. (Also 19 Prince Albert St.) Open Mon-Fri 9.30-5.30, Sat 9.30-12. Massive stock of shipping goods. Containers to all destinations. Couriers, collection and packing.

Robertsbridge STD 0580

de Montfort
(A.A.Sloane, E.D.Sloane,). 49 High St, TN32 5AN. Tel 880698 (priv 082 584 243). Open Mon-Sat 10-5; other times by appt. Early English and Continental furniture including country pieces. European sculpture, antiquities, Islamic ceramics.

Robertsbridge House Antiques
High St, TN32 5AN. Tel 880291. 17th to 19thC furniture.

Rottingdean

Trade Wind
(Richard Morley Smith). 15A Little Crescent, BN2 7GF. Tel Brighton (0273) 31177. Open by appt only. Small dainty pieces of 18th and 19thC furniture, silver, porcelain, treen, pictures, prints, watercolours and maps.

Rye STD 0797

Bragge & Sons
(N.H. & J.R. Bragge). Landgate House. Tel 223358. Open 9-5; early closing Tues. (Opp town gate.) Specialising in English furniture, silver, paintings and works of art.

David Cooke Fine Paintings
Old Post House, Playden. Tel Iden (07978) 303. Fine paintings. Specialising in English portraits.

H.G. Gasson
(T.J.Booth). Lion Galleries, Lion St, TN31 7LB. Tel 222208. Open Mon-Sat 9-5.30; early closing Tues afternoon; other times by appt. Early oak furniture, mahogany furniture, walnut furniture.

Ann Lingard
(Ann Lingard). Rope Walk Antiques, Rope Walk, TN31 7NA. Tel 223486. (Also at 62 Cinque Port Street (corner of Rope Walk.) Open Mon-Sat 9-5.30; Sun by appt. 7000 sq ft of well finished pine furniture, kitchenalia, antiques. LAPADA

The Rye Auction Galleries
(Vidler & Co). Cinque Ports St, TN31 7AL. Tel 222124. Open Mon-Fri 9-5.30, Sat 9-1. Auctioneers. RICS

Seaford STD 0323

Richard Alexander
Crouch House, Crouch Lane. Tel 896577. Open by appt. Antiquities, oil paintings, watercolours and collectors' items, including Oriental pieces.

The Barn Collectors Market
(Lynn Price). Church Lane (off High St), BN25 1HL. Tel 890010. Open Tues, Thurs, Sat 10-4.30. A complex of 4 shops selling collectables, bric a brac, ephemera, furniture, brass & copper, books, militaria, stamps, etc. Also studio bookshop upstairs, large wide ranging stock.

The Old House (Seaford) Ltd
(P.R. Barrett & S.M. Barrett). 15-17 High St, BN25 1PD. Tel 892091, 892204, 892934. Open Mon-Sat 9-5; other times by appt. General antiques, restoration, packers & shippers, valuations.

St Leonards STD 0424

Chapel Antiques
(Robert Alff). 18 Gensing Rd, TN38 0SE. Tel Hastings (0424) 440025 (priv 425487). (Workshops at 66 Southwater Rd, St Leonards.) Open Mon-Sat 9-5.30; other times by appt. Period furniture, paintings, china, glass, furniture restorers.

Galleon Galleries
42 Westfield Lane. Tel 440974. (Also 19 Marina.) Open Mon-Sat 9.30-6. Early oak, mahogany and Victorian rosewood furniture. Specialists in Chinese and Japanese lacquered and hardwood furniture, carvings, ivories, porcelain, silks and bronzes.

The Granary & Rene Antiques and Art
(Mr R.Struik, Derek Ashby). 17A Kings Rd, TN37 6DU. Tel 432610 (priv 71586). Open Mon-Sat 9.30-1 2-6; other times by appt. Period and shipping furniture, clocks, pine, china, metalware and upholstery.

Sherwood Antiques
9 Marine Court, TN38 0DN. Tel 428204. Open Mon-Fri 9.30-5.30; Sat 9.30-1. Jewellery and general antiques.

Ticehurst STD 0580

Arita Antiques
(Clive Holmes). 1 High St, TN5 7AL. Tel 200015. Open on request at any time. Furniture, paintings, glass, porcelain, silver, fine jewellery, Oriental works of art.

Uckfield STD 0825

Nicholas Bowlby
(Nicholas Bowlby). Owl House, Poundgate, TN22 4DE. Tel Crowborough (08926) 3722. Open 7 days a week by appt. Over 150 British watercolours from 1780-1930. Also early 20thC oil paintings and prints.

Georgian House Antiques
(Mrs I. Crouch). 222 High St, TN22 1RE. Tel 5074. Open Mon-Sat 10-6; sometimes closed Wed; other times by appt. English domestic oak & country furniture and related decorative items.

Ringles Cross Antiques
(Colin & Jennifer Dunford). Ringles Cross. Tel 2909. Open Mon-Sat 9-6; other times by appt. Specialists in Chinese furniture and Oriental art in general. Also English country furniture.

St John Smith
194/198 High St, TN22 1RH. Tel 4111. (Also at Brighton, Crowborough, Heathfield & Tunbridge Wells.) Auctioneers.

Wadhurst STD 089 288

Art and Antiques
(Mrs D M Maskell). High St, TN5 6AA. Tel 2091. Open Thurs, Fri, Sat 10-5; other times by appt. Pewter, old English pottery, dolls, lace, porcelain, brass, copper, textiles, period clothes, small furniture.

P.B.Pollington
(P.B.& G.K. Pollington). 4 Central Parade, High St, TN5 6AL. Tel 2866. Open Mon-Sat 9-1, 2.15-5; other times by appt. Specialist in the hire of antique vehicles and associated items for period street scenes for television, film and theatre.

Aldo Broccardi Schelmi (Fine Arts)
(Belmont Galleries Ltd). Dewhurst Lodge. Tel 3519. Important stock of English & French 18thC furniture. LAPADA

Whatlington

Chapel Antiques
(Meyrick Browne). TN33 0NL. Tel Sedlescombe (042 487) 272. Res on prem. 18thC mahogany and oak furniture, Persian rugs and runners. General antiques.

Winchelsea

Thomas Crispin
(Thomas Crispin). The Little Manor, TN36 4EJ. Tel Rye (0797) 226699. Open only by appt. Specialising only in early English oak. BADA

W.Sussex

Arundel STD 0903

Armstrong-Davis Gallery
High St. Tel 882752. Open Mon-Sat 10-6. Fine sculpture and bronzes of all periods.

Arundel Antique & Collectors' Market
51 High St. Tel 883590. Open 7 days 10-5. Several stalls and shops with a wide variety of antiques.

Arundel Antiques Market
The Shipyard, River Rd. Open Sat only 9-5.30. Stalls of antiques and bric-a-brac.

Baynton-Williams
Maltravers House, 49 Maltravers St, BN18 9BQ. Tel 882898. Old maps and atlases, prints and books. ABA,BADA

Frean Antiques
(Mrs E.Frean). 25 Tarrant St, BN18 9DG. Tel 882350. Open Mon-Sat 10-1, 2-5; closed Wed; other times by appt. Mainly Georgian furniture.

Victoria Fry
25B High St, BN18 9AD. Tel 883293. Open Mon-Sat 10-5; closed Wed. Pottery, porcelain, clocks and furniture.

Pat & David Golding
6 Castle Mews, Tarrant St. 18th-20thC porcelain, pottery and glass.

Grey Gables
16a Tarrant St, BN18 9DJ. Tel 883903. Antiques and interiors.

Old Stable Antiques
(Mrs B.Driver). Tarrant Sq, Tarrant St. Tel 882921. Open Mon-Sat 10-1, 3-5; Sun 3-5; other times by appt. Furniture, paintings, porcelain, glass and silver.

Spencer Swaffer Antiques
33 High St, BN18 9AB. Tel 882132. (Also at 30 High St with traditional and decorative antiques.) Open Mon-Sat 9-6; other times by appt. Pine and country furniture.

Treasure House
(D.R.Henderson). 31 High St. Tel 883101. (Also Treasure House Antiques Market, Crown Yard, & 7 Tarrant St.) Open daily (shop); market Sat 9-5. General antiques, including porcelain, pottery, silver, lace, jewellery, gramophones and commemoratives. Clocks, woodworking and domestic bygones, brass, copper, small furniture.

Balcombe STD 044 483

Balcombe Galleries
(Peter & Georgette Collins). RH17 6NF. Tel 811439 or 811415. (Also at Stanley Studios, Park Walk, Chelsea, SW10.) Open 9-5.30 daily; other times by appt. Early oak, pine, country furniture, paintings, antique and modern.

Billingshurst STD 040 381

Sotheby's
Summers Place, RH14 9AD. Tel 040 381 3933. Auctioneers.

Burgess Hill STD 044 46

British Antique Exporters Ltd
Queen Elizabeth Ave, RH15 9RX. Tel 45577. Open Mon-Fri 8-5.30. Large stock of goods, including brass, copper and metalware, clocks, watches, furniture, porcelain and Victoriana. Container loads for export. LAPADA

James Buckingham
School Close, Queen Elizabeth Ave. Tel 45577. Large selection of 19th and 20thC dining tables and 18th-20thC office furniture.

Chichester STD 0243

Peter Hancock
40-41 West St, PO19 1RP. Tel 786173. Open Tues-Sat 9.30-5.30; other times by appt. Furniture, china, glass, jewellery, weapons, coins, silver, pictures and ethnographical items and books.

Meynell's Bookshop
(Offord & Meynell Ltd, Vivian & Patsy Meynell). 11 The Hornet, Eastgate Square. Tel 782018 (priv 512798). Open Tues-Sat 10-1, 2.15-5. Secondhand and antiquarian books, some new books, old prints and watercolours. ABA

J. & M. Riley
(James & Marion Riley). Antique Shop, Frensham House, Main Road B2145, Hunston, PO20 6NX. Tel 782660. Open 6 days 9-6; other times by appt. 18th & early 19thC English furniture, bureaux, sofa tables, dining chairs, work tables, dining tables.

West Dean College
(The Edward James Foundation). West Dean, PO18 0QZ. Tel Singleton (0243 63) 301. Restoration of antique furniture, clocks, ceramics and porcelain.

Wyatt & Son
Baffins Hall Saleroom, Baffins Lane, PO19 1HN. Tel 787548. Fine art auctioneers.

Cuckfield

John Hopkins
((Hopkins Antiques Ltd)). 1 The Courtyard, Ockenden Manor, RH17 5LD. Tel Haywards Heath (0444) 454323. Open by appointment only. 17th-19thC furniture, watercolours, pottery, porcelain and barometers. BADA

Peter Jeeves Antiques
(P.&T.Jeeves). High St. Tel Haywards Heath (0444) 454420. Open Mon-Sat 10-5.30. (Off A23 towards Haywards Heath.) 18th and 19thC English and Continental furniture, china, glass and treen, painted furniture and decorative items. LAPADA

B. & C.Seago
(B. & C. Seago). Whitemans Green, RH17 5BY. Tel Haywards Heath (0444) 456111. Open Mon-Sat 10-1, 2-5.30; other times by appt. Antiquarian and secondhand booksellers and valuers. PBFA

East Grinstead STD 0342

Turner Rudge & Turner
29 High St. Tel 24101. Auctioneers with bi-monthly sales.

Eastergate STD 024 368

Granville Antiques
(Ian Miller). Mount Pleasant Farm, Level Mare Lane. Tel 2293. Open by appt. (5 miles east of Chichester, off A27.) Period furniture (mainly English pre-1840), works of art. LAPADA

Felpham

Antiquarius
(Mark Reeves). 45 Felpham Rd. Tel 0243-821056 (priv 821616). (Also in Chichester.) Open Mon-Sat 10-3.30; closed Wed; other times by appt. General antiques, silver, pictures, furniture.

Haywards Heath STD 0444

Sussex Auction Galleries
(Hedley F. Vaughan). 59 Perrymount Rd, RH16 3DS. Tel 414935. Open Mon-Fri 9-1, 2-5.30; Sat 9-12 by appt. Antique and fine art auctioneers.

Henfield STD 0273

Alexander Antiques
(Mrs Judith Goodinge). Post House, Small Dole. Open Mon-Fri mornings, Sat 11-7. General antiques, including brass, copper, treen, samplers, country furniture and unusual items.

Horsham STD 0403

Christie's
(Representative: Robin Loder). Leonardslee Gardens, Lower Beeding, RH13 6PP. Tel Lower Beeding (040 376) 305. Auctioneers & valuers.

Garth Denham and Associates
Horsham Auction Galleries, Carfax. Tel 53837. Open Mon-Fri 9-5.30. Auctions at least monthly throughout the year. Each sale contains antique furniture, silver jewellery, ceramics, pictures, metalware and other collectors items. Always a sale on the 3rd Wed in each month. Viewing preceding Tues, 10-7. FSVA

Hurstpierpoint STD 0273

Julian Antiques
124 High St. Tel 832145. (Also 67 Park Rd, London NW1.) Open Mon-Fri 9-5; other times by appt. French clocks, furniture, mirrors, fireplaces and general French antiques. LAPADA

Michael Miller
The Lamb, 8 Cuckfield Rd, BN6 9RU. Tel 834567. Open Thurs, Fri, Sat; other times by appt. Arms, armour, militaria. GTA

John Hopkins (*Hopkins Antiques Ltd.*)

By appointment only:

**1, THE COURTYARD,
OCKENDEN MANOR,
CUCKFIELD, SUSSEX
RH17 5LD**

A fine pair of Regency mahogany cabinets, in the manner of Gillows, circa 1820

For all appointments: Telephone 0444-454323

INTRODUCTION TO

BRITISH ANTIQUE EXPORTERS LTD

MEMBER OF: LAPADA, GUILD OF MASTER CRAFTSMEN

£7,500 to £10,000
will give you

Variety

Selection

Value

Wholesale exporters

Container loads of antique furniture, porcelain & decorative items of Georgian, Victorian, Edwardian & 1930's periods

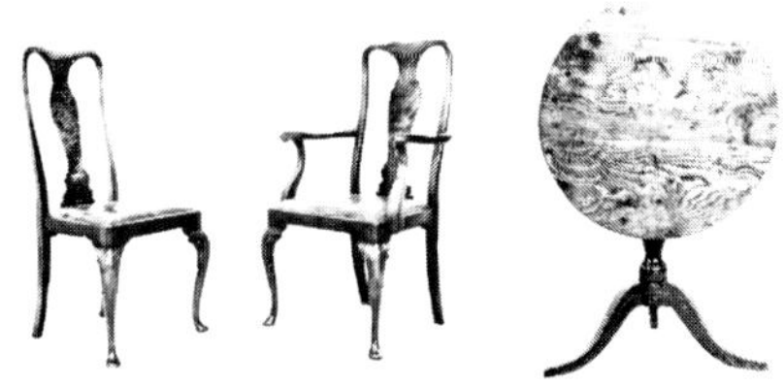

If for any reason our choice does not come up to your expectations we will refund your money

QUEEN ELIZABETH AVENUE, BURGESS HILL, WEST SUSSEX RH15 9RX, ENGLAND

Tel: Burgess Hill (04446) 45577 Telex: 87688

Lancing STD 0903

Curiosities
(J.D. Van Dam). 152 South St, BN15 8AU. Tel 752670 (priv 0273 454669). Open every day 10-1, 3-5; other times by appt. Cameras, scientific, nautical instruments, prints and paintings, clocks and watches, picture framing and restorations.

Lindfield STD 044 47

David Adam Oriental Carpets
59 High Street. Tel 73817. Open Mon-Fri 9-5.30. Fine Oriental carpets and rugs from 1850 onwards and tapestries from 16thC onwards.

Alma Antiques
(Mrs Alma Wright). 79 High St. Open daily 10.30-5; closed Sun & Wed and for lunch; other times by appt. Small furniture, porcelain, prints, copper and brass, silver and clocks.

David Burkinshaw Antique Desks
66 High St, RH16 2HL. Tel 2826. Partners and pedestal desks.

Hillside Antiques
(P.C.Becker & C.C.Becker). Units 12-13 Lindfield Enterprise Pk, Lewes Rd, RH10 4SX. Tel 3042 (priv 0444 811003). Open Mon-Fri 9.30-5.30; other times by appt. Pine & country furniture, decorative items, 18th-19thC furniture.

Lindfield Galleries Ltd
(F.E.Williams & D.C. Adam). 59 High St, RH16 2HN. Tel 2817. Open 9.30-5.30; other times by appt. Fine Oriental carpets and rugs, European tapestries, oil and modern paintings and small furniture. Specialist in antique Persian rugs. BADA

Penman Antiques Fairs
(Caroline Penman). Cockhaise Mill, RH16 2QP. Tel 2514. (See also Chelsea Antique Fairs, London.) Open by appt. Organisation of Antiques Fairs - Chelsea, West London, Ardingly, Brighton etc. LAPADA

Midhurst STD 073 081

Campbell Walchli Antiques Ltd
(Angela Campbell, Susan Walchli). Church Hill, GU29 9NX. Tel 4233. Open Mon-Sat; half day Wed; other times by appt. Georgian mahogany furniture, copper, brass, plate, local prints.

Dean House Antiques
Dean House, Bepton Rd, GU29 9LY. Tel 2277. Clocks, barometers and scientific instruments. BADA

Eagle House Antiques
(J.H.Brown, BEM). Eagle House Antiques Market, Market Square. Tel 2718 (priv 0705 326620). Open Mon-Sat 9-5; 9-5.30 in summer. Furniture, silver, porcelain, brass, copper & general antiques.

Foord Antiques
(Gay and Simon Foord). Tel Graffham (07986) 351. Open by appt only. 18th and early 19thC furniture, boxes, treen, metalware and decorative items. LAPADA

Gauntlett Antiques
(P.A. & P.K. Gauntlett). Grange Rd. Tel 3101 (priv 0428 724274). Open Mon-Fri 9-1, 2-5; other times by appt. Large stock antique furniture, painting, china, glass, metalware.

Midhurst Antiques Market
(Mrs I. Brindle-Wood). Curfew Garden Ct, Knockhundred Row. Tel 4231. Open Mon-Sat all day. Stall-holders selling a wide variety of stock.

Michael Toone
Tudors, Church Hill, GU29 9NX. Tel 2519. Open by appt only. Furniture. BADA

Petworth STD 0798

Angelshades Antiques
Angel St.

The Antique Centre
(J.C. & B.D. Tutt). Angel St, GU28 0BQ. Tel 43221. Open Mon-Sat 10-1, 2-5.30; other times by appt. Eight dealers with a range of antique furniture, paintings, porcelain & accessories.

The Ballroom Antiques
(N.P. Roberts). Swan House, Market Square. Tel 43638. Open Mon-Sat 10-5.30; other times by appt. 16th, 17th, 18th, 19thC furniture and small items, works of art.

Boss Antiques
(A.J.and J.F.Boss). Hells Bells Corner, GU28 0DD. Open daily 9-6; other times by appt. Interesting good quality varying stock of carvings, furniture, ceramics, paintings, prints and metalware.

Lesley Bragge Antiques
Fairfield House, High St. Tel 42324. Open Mon-Sat 10-5; other times by appt. 18th and 19thC furniture and objets d'art, brass, copper, silver plate, silver, and decorative items. Garden furniture, textiles, porcelain.

Mark Chapman Antiques
New Street. Tel 42283. Open Mon-Sat 10-5.30; other times by appt. Large selection of 17th & 18thC oak & country furniture and 18th & 19thC mahogany. Large stock of brassware including 18thC base metal candlesticks. 19thC pictures, decorative items, garden furniture. Services:metal & painting restoration, wood carving.

Richard Davidson
Lombard St, GU28 0AG. Tel 42508. Open Mon-Sat 9.30-5.30; other times by appt. Good stock of fine antique furniture, mostly 18thC and Regency but some selected Victorian and decorative pieces. BADA

Flora Dora Antiques
(John and Pamela Waldy). Dales House, Lombard St, GU28 0AG. Tel 43109. Open Mon-Sat, 10-1, 2.15-5.30; other times by appt. Furniture, copper and brass, porcelain, glass, prints and pictures.

Frith Antiques
(H.A.Frith & Mrs M.A.Frith). New St. Tel 43155 (priv 079881 606). Open Mon-Sat 10-5.30; other times by appt. Country style antiques especially oak period furniture and treen. Specialising in antique woodworking tools and cut steel jewellery.

Griffin Antiques
(Rodney & Catherine Wilson). Church St, GU28 0AD. Tel 43306. Open Mon-Sat 10-5.30; res on premises. General antiques and collectors items.

William Hockley Antiques
(Derek and Valery Thrower). East Street, GU28 0AB. Tel 43172 (priv 048 649 331). Open Mon-Sat 10-5; other times by appt. Fine 18th and early 19thC furniture and decoration. Early English pottery. LAPADA

Howes Gallery
(B.K.Wigg). Market Square, GU28 0AH. Tel 43523. Open Mon-Fri 10-1 2-5.15. Fine 18th, 19th and 20thC oil paintings and drawings.

Humphry Antiques
(John & Marion Humphry). East St, GU28 0AB. Tel 43053 (priv 42944). Open Mon-Sat 10-1 2-5.30; other times by appt. Early oak and walnut and country furniture and associated items from 16th to 18thC. Specialising in wood carvings and sculpture from 15th-18thC. Metalware and stoneware.

Loewenthal Antiques
Tillington Cottage, Tillington. Tel 42969. Open Mon-Sat; closed Wed; appt advisable. (1 mile from Petworth on A272.) 18thC furniture and objets d'art.

Millhouse
(C.F. & E.G. Rawnsley). The Square, GU28 9BP. Tel 43080. (Administration:Halfway Bridge, Nr Petworth. Tel:07985-406.) Open Mon-Sat 10-5. Fine 18th and early 19thC furniture and works of art. Also tea caddies and boxes, and wine relics.

Millhouse Fine Arts
(E.G. & C.F.Rawnsley). The Square. Tel 43080. (Administration: Halfway Bridge, Nr Petworth. Tel:07985-406.) Open Mon-Sat 10-5. 18th & 19thC oil paintings and watercolours.

John G.Morris Ltd
(J.G. & L.Morris). Market Square, GU28 0AH. Tel 42305. Open Mon-Sat 10-5.30; early closing Wed; other times by appt. Specialists in 17th, 18th and early 19thC English furniture. Also clocks, bronzes and associated decorative items. BADA

O'Neill
(M.J.O'Neill). Swan House, Market Square. Tel 42616. Fine furniture and clocks, 17th to early 19thC. LAPADA

Persian Carpet Gallery
(Majid Amini). North Street, GU28 0DD. Tel 43344. Open Mon-Sat 9.30-5. Specialist in antique and rare oriental rugs. Restorations, valuations, selling, buying, exchange.

Petworth Antique Market
East St. Tel 42073. Open Mon-Sat 10-5.30. More than 35 dealers selling a wide variety of antiques.

Petworth Antiques Warehouse
(Rob Macwhirter, John Harris). Colhook Industrial Park. Tel Northchapel (042 878) 667. Open Mon-Fri 9-1 2-5. (2 miles North of Petworth on A283). Antique and decorative furniture, architectural and garden items. Trade only.

E. Streeter & Daughter
(Anne M. Simmons). Clock House, Lombard St. Tel 42239. Open 9-1, 2-5; closed Wed. Jewellers with secondhand & antique jewellery and some silver.

THE FAMOUS GIANT

ARDINGLY

ANTIQUES TRADE & COLLECTORS' FAIRS

South of England Showground, Sussex.
5 miles N. of Haywards Heath.

January 28 –Indoors 180 stalls
April 22 –Indoors 200 stalls, outside 400
July 15 –Indoors 75 stalls, outside 300
September 23 –Indoors 200 stalls, outside 600
November 4 –Indoors 180 stalls

Free Transport from Haywards Heath Station
Bureau de Change,
Shipper.

Enquiries:
PO Box 114
Haywards Heath, W. Sussex
Tel: 04447-2514

Penman Antiques Fairs

Humphry ANTIQUES,

Early Oak · Carvings & Decorative Items

EAST STREET · PETWORTH
W. SUSSEX · GU28 0AB
Tel. Petworth (0798) 43053

The sign of
THE BRITISH ANTIQUE DEALERS' ASSOCIATION

MEMBER OF THE BRITISH ANTIQUE DEALERS' ASSOCIATION

The nearest you will get to a guarantee
in the world of antiques.
Ring Sally Tunley on 01-589 4128
for a free list of members

O'Neill

PETWORTH LTD

Fine Antique Furniture and Clocks

Very fine Geo I Burr Yewwood
chest on chest of superb colour
and patination
(CIRCA 1720)
Height $65\frac{1}{2}''$ (167 cm), width $41\frac{1}{4}''$ (105 cm)

Enquiries welcome, photos sent on request.

SWAN HOUSE, MARKET SQUARE,
PETWORTH, WEST SUSSEX
TELEPHONE (0798) 42616

Member of the London and Provincial Antique Dealers Association

Michael Wakelin and Helen Linfield
(Helen Linfield and Michael Wakelin). 10 New St. Tel 42417. Open Mon-Sat 10-5; other times by appt. Period formal, country and decorative furniture, metalware, pottery, naive paintings, woodcarvings, painted pine, treen, lightings, textiles, mirrors, decorative accessories. LAPADA

Jeremy Wood Fine Art
East St, GU28 0AB. Tel 43408. Open Mon-Sat 10-1 2-5; other times by appt. Oil paintings, watercolours 1880-1930, illustrated colour plate books, art, reference and motoring books 1900-1950.

Pulborough STD 079 82

Roy Barton
(Roy Barton). Myrtle Cottage, Codmore Hill, RH21 1BQ. Tel 2730. Open by appt, res on prem. On A29, 1 mile north of Pulborough. Quality 17th, 18th and early 19thC furniture, longcase clocks and some pictures. BADA

Mare Hill Galleries
Mare Hill. Tel 2006. Open Mon-Fri 10-5.30. (On A283 1 mile east of Pulborough.) Antique furniture, porcelain, glass, 19thC paintings and watercolours.

Mulberry House Galleries
(Mr & Mrs D. Golledge). Codmore Hill, RH20 1BQ. Tel 2463. Open Tues-Sat 9.30-6; closed Wed. Antique linen and lace. Contemporary British and some antique paintings.

Pine and Country Antiques
(G. Wilmshurst, P. Blackaby, S. Donnelly). Sandhill Barn, Washington. Tel Ashington (0903) 892888 (priv 892210). Open Mon-Sat 9.30-5.30; other times by appt. Pine furniture, large stock of all country things.

Martin Scadgell Fine Art
Mulberry House Galleries, Codmore Hill. Tel 2463. British art 1840-1940, oil paintings, watercolours, valuations, cleaning and restoration of oils and watercolours.

Rudgwick STD 040 372

Kings Antiques
(Margaret and Peter Larcombe). Guildford Rd, Bucks Green. Tel 2084. Open Mon-Sat 9.30-1, 2-5; other times by appt. 18th and 19thC English furniture.

Shoreham-by-Sea
STD 079 17

Studio Arts & Antiques
(N.O. & Mrs S.Harvey). Tudor Cottage, 457 Upper Shoreham Rd, Old Shoreham. Tel 453554. Open Mon-Sat 10-6; evenings in summer; other times by appt. A variety of stock, including furniture, silver, jewellery and small antiques.

Sussex Antiques (Southdown) Ltd
(Mrs T.A.Lawson). 11 Western Rd. Tel 2727. Open Mon-Sat 10-5. General antiques. LAPADA

Washington

Chanctonbury Antiques
(G.D. Troche). Clematis Cottage, RH20 4AP. Tel Ashington (0903) 892233. Open daily 10-6; closed Tues; Suns by appt only. Furniture, china and other small antiques with some unusual and rare items. Specialists in English porcelain and needlework.

Worthing STD 0903

Antique and Collectors Market
(F.H.Henderson). 4 Warwick Place. Open every Mon. General antiques, militaria, porcelain, silver, jewellery, commemoratives, bygones.

Broadwater Bookroom
(Ursula Powell). 20 Broadwater St East, BN14 9AD. Tel 39708. Open Mon-Sat 9.30-5 (closed Wed). General books, postcards, pictures.

Chloe Antiques
(Mrs Dorothy Peters). 61 Brighton Rd. Tel 202697. Open Mon-Sat 9.30-12.30 2-4. Antiques, bric-a-brac, jewellery and collectors' items.

Frances Books
(Mr & Mrs M.J. Lee). 54A Homefield Rd, BN11 1RL. Tel 36437 (priv 31169). Open by appt only. Small selection of antiquarian books. ABA, PBFA

Godden of Worthing Ltd
(J. Godden & G. Godden). 17 Crescent Rd, BN11 1RL. Tel 35958. Open Mon-Fri 9-1, 2.15-5. English porcelain and pottery. BADA

Geoffrey Godden, Chinaman
(Retail division of Godden of Worthing Ltd). 17-19 Crescent Rd, BN11 1RL. Tel 35958. Open Mon-Fri 9-1, 2.15-5. Wide and interesting collection of British pottery and porcelain of all periods.

The Terrace Gallery
(Margrit Avon). 7 Liverpool Terrace, BN11 1TA. Contemporary crafts: pottery, porcelain, glass, wood, jewellery and silverware, fine art prints. ICGA

Walter Gardiner Photography
Southdownview Rd, BN14 8NL. Photographer.

H.Wilson & Son
(F.Wilson, H.Wilson). 28 High St, BN11 1NT. Tel 202059. Open Mon-Sat 8.30-5.30; other times by appt. 18th, 19th and early 20thC English furniture & decorative antiques. Retail, trade, export. LAPADA

Worthing Auction Galleries
(Fox & Sons). 31 Chatsworth Rd, BN11 1LY. Tel 205565. Open Mon-Fri 8-1, 2-5; Sat 9-12. Auctioneers and valuers.

Tyne & Wear

Newcastle upon Tyne
STD 0632

Abercrombies
(C.N.Stell). 140 Manor House Rd, Jesmond, NE2 2NA. Tel Tyneside (091) 2817182. Open Tues-Sat 10-6; other times by appt. Victorian and Edwardian furniture, fabrics, fittings and china. Specialists in restoration and renovation of furniture and architectural antiques.

Anderson and Garland
Fine Art Salerooms, Anderson House, Market St. Tel 326278. Auctioneer.

Corbitt's of Clayton Street
(A.P. Corbitt). 105 Clayton St, NE1 5PZ. Tel 324356 (priv 2521301). Open Mon-Sat 9-5; early closing Wed. Coins, medals, militaria, Victorian jewellery, small silver.

Cradlewell Antiques
244 Jesmond Rd. Tel 810691. Open Mon-Fri 10.30-4, early closing Wed and Sat. Antique furniture, glass, gold, silver, copper, brass and porcelain bought and sold. Exporters.

Davidson's The Jewellers
94-96 Grey St. Tel 22551, 22895. Specialists in antique jewellery and silver.

The Dean Gallery
(Mr A.P.Graham). 42 Dean St, NE1 1PG. Tel 321208. Open Mon-Fri 9-5, Sat 9-12.30. 19th and early 20thC paintings, etchings and drawings. FATG

Anna Harrison Antiques
49 Great North Road, Grange Park, Gosforth. Specialists in furniture, early English porcelain, Victorian watercolours. LAPADA

Hazel Cottage Clocks
(Edward & Margaret Charlton). Hazel Cottage, Eachwick, Dalton. Tel Wylam (066 14) 2415. Open daily 9.30-6; other times by appt. Specialising in good longcase, wall and skeleton clocks. Also barometers.

Owen Humble
(Owen Humble). 11,12,13 Clayton Rd, Jesmond, NE2 4RP. Tel 2810882. Open Mon-Sat 10-5.30. Furniture, general smalls, shipping goods. LAPADA

Lyndhurst Antiques
(William & Joyce Walker). 231 Jesmond Rd, Jesmond, NE2 1LA. Tel 2817286. Open 10-5. Furniture, clocks, pictures & bric-a-brac.

Robinson (Newcastle) Ltd
49-53 Grainger Market. Tel 22978. New and secondhand books. ABA

S.R.Antiques
(Rose Branskey). 13 High Bridge. Tel 326739. Open 9-3.45 except Mon. Jewellery, mostly antique, apart from diamond engagement rings, old silver and plate, small amount of china and brass.

P.& D.Smith Antiques
(Patrick and Dinah Smith). 6 Ashburton Rd, Gosforth. Tel 2856455. Open Mon, Tues, Thurs, Fri 10-5; Sat 10-1; other times by appt. Silver, silver plate, early paintings and drawings, Oriental porcelain. Also valuations.

Robert D.Steedman
9 Grey St, NE1 6EE. Tel 326561. Open Mon-Sat, early closing Sat. English literature and history, sets and first editions of standard authors, fine bindings, sport and natural history. ABA

North Shields STD 0632

Alyn House Antiques
(Mrs Hazel Jean Danskin). Alyn House, 8-10 Queen Alexandra Rd. (584868.) Open 10-5; closed Wed; other times by appt. General antiques, bric-a-brac, jewellery, pictures, furniture.

MARK CHAPMAN

17th and 18th century English furniture and metalware, including large selection of English 18th century candlesticks, oil paintings and decorative items

NEW STREET
PETWORTH, WEST SUSSEX
Tel 0798 42283

RICHARD DAVIDSON

FINE ANTIQUE FURNITURE

A superb Sheraton West Indian satinwood side cabinet, original throughout, 48″ wide, c.1785.

Situated 1 hour from Central London

0798 42508

LOMBARD STREET, PETWORTH
WEST SUSSEX GU28 OAG

Holly House Gallery
(Timandra Gustafson). 14 Front Street, Tynemouth, NE30 4DX. Tel 592753. Contemporary crafts: ceramics, glass, wood, textiles, jewellery, leather, original prints. ICGA

Pattersons Antiques
(J. Chester, P. Chester). 1 Grey St. Tel 572118. Furniture, art nouveau & art deco, clocks, watches & jewellery, pottery & porcelain, costume, lamps, shipping goods & container service available. Buys & sells at auction.

Station Antiques
(Julia Crompton Brenchley). 1 Camp Terrace. Tel 571800. LAPADA

South Shields STD 0632

The Curiosity Shop
(Thomas Harvey Davies, Glen David Davies). 16 Frederick St, NE34 0SF. Tel 4565560 (priv 4552861). Open Mon-Sat; Wed 9-1; other times by appt. Oil paintings, watercolours, furniture, jewellery, all collectors items.

Sunderland STD 0783

Peter Smith Antiques
(Peter Smith). 2 Tunstall Rd. Tel 77842 (priv 40008). (Warehouse at 12 Borough Rd. Tel: 0783 673537.) Open 11-5.30 daily; closed Wed; other times by appt. Antiques and shipping goods. LAPADA

Washington

Harry Carr Antiques
(H.J.Carr). Field House, Rickleton. Tel Chester-le-Street (0385) 886442. Furniture, general. LAPADA

Swanbridge Art Company Ltd
(W.G. Lowe). Tower Rd, Glover West Industrial Est, District 11, NE37 2SH. Tel Tyneside (091) 415-0080. Open Mon-Fri 9-5; other times by appt. Interior decor consultants, fine arts and architectural antiques.

Whitley Bay

Bric-a-Brac Ltd
(O.W., R.W. & Mrs C.Rawes). 195 Park View, NE26 3RD. Tel Tyneside (091) 2526141 (priv 2528508). Open Mon-Sat 9.30-1, 2.30-5; other times by appt. General antiques and good-quality reproductions.

Warwickshire

Alcester STD 0789

Coughton Galleries Ltd
(SirRobert &Lady Isabel Throckmorton,W.S.L.Guinness). Coughton Court, B49 5JA. Tel 762642. Open Wed,Thur,Sat,Sun 10-5.30; other times by appt. Mainly 19th and 20thC oil paintings, watercolours and prints, specialising in Midland artists.

High Street Antiques
(Mrs P.A.Payne). 11A High St, B49 5AE. Tel 764009. Open Mon, Tues, Thurs, Sat 11-1, 2.30-5; other times by appt. Victorian glass, china, brass, copper, books, small selection art deco.

Bidford-on-Avon STD 0789

Brook Farm Antiques
(Thelma Hughes). Bidford Antique Centre, High St. Tel 773680. Open Tues-Sat 10-5; Sun 2-5.30; other times by appt. Furniture, paintings, jewellery, porcelain, silver, copper, brass.

Churchover

Mawby's International
(P.J. Mawby). Old Village Hall, School St, CV23 0EG. Tel Rugby (0788) 832600 (priv 0788 75305). Open Mon-Fri 8.30-5.30; other times by appt. 3500 sq ft stripped pine.

Dunchurch

The Little Bizarre
(Mrs Florence Sharpe). Kildin Antique Centre. Tel Rugby (0788) 817147. (Correspondence to 18 High St, Harpole, Northampton (0601-830540.) Open daily except Fri; other times by appt. Jewellery and silver.

Henley-in-Arden STD 056 42

The Arden Gallery
(G.B.Horton). 54 High St, B95 5AN. Tel 2520. Open Mon-Fri afternoons; appt preferable. 19th & early 20thC oils, watercolours. Also portrait miniatures.

Colmore Galleries Ltd
52 High St. Tel 2938. Open Mon-Sat 11-5.30; other times by appt. 19th & 20thC fine oil paintings & watercolours.

Ferneyhough
(M.H.Ferneyhough, A.R.Ferneyhough). Brook House, Beaudesert, B95 5QR. Tel 2451. Open Mon-Sat 8.30-6. 18th and early 19thC furniture, decoration and works of art. BADA, LAPADA

Lacy Gallery
(Colin Lacy). 56 High St. Tel 3073. (Also at 38 & 40 Ledbury Rd, London, W11.) Open Mon-Fri 10-1, 2-5.30. 18th, 19th and early 20thC decorative art and period picture frames.

Jasper Marsh
3 High St. Tel 2088. (Also at 3 The Chipping, Tetbury, Glos.) Period furniture and porcelain, chinoiserie and Oriental art. BADA

Charles R.Phillips
(Charles R.Phillips FSVA, Patricia A. Alldridge). 48 High St. Tel 4330/1/2. (Also in Stratford-upon-Avon and Banbury.) Open Mon-Fri 9-5.30, Sat 9-1, Sun 10.30-3.30; other times by appt. Auctioneers, valuers, estate and land agents.

Lapworth STD 056 43

Gerald Buxton Gooding - Lapworth Clocks
(Gerald & Elsie Gooding). 160 Station Lane, B94 6JJ. Tel 3243. Open 9-5; other times by appt. Longcase clocks, restorations to movements and cases.

Leamington STD 0926

Hague Antiques
(Jonathan Hague). 2 Regent St. Tel 37236. Open Mon-Sat 9.30-5.30; other times by appt. General antiques but a large stock of unstripped pine.

Locke and England Auctioneers
18 Guy St. Tel 27988. (Also salerooms at Walton House, The Parade.) Weekly general sales Victorian, Edwardian & later furniture & effects. Fine art sales every five/six weeks. All sales held on Thursday, starting 11 am.

V. & C. Madeira
(Mr & Mrs V.M.R. Madeira). The Grange, 16 Guys Cliffe Ave. Tel 25012. Open any time, by appt please. Furniture, metalware, scientific, nautical and medical instruments, bygones and curiosities.

Percy F.Wale Ltd
(B.A., P.G. & G.S.Barton). 32-34 Regent St, CV32 5EG. Tel 21288. Open Mon-Sat 9-1,2-6; no lunchtime closing on Sat. Stock of antique and old furniture and silver, together with antique maps, prints, silver plate etc. Specialists in furniture restoration.

Nuneaton STD 0203

Harper's Hill Farm Antiques
(Evelyn Dickinson). Main Street, Stoke Golding, CV13 6HZ. Tel Hinckley (0455) 212418. Open Tues-Thurs 2-5; Sat, Sun 2-5; other times by appt. Furniture, mirrors, metalware etc.

John Speed (Maps)
(Jeffery John Speed & Hilary Anne Speed). Drove House, Bilstone, CV13 6NG. Tel Tamworth (0827) 880439. Open any time by appt. Antiquarian books, maps and atlases.

Sport & Country Gallery
(Robert Hill). Northwood House, Bulkington, CV12 9RX. Tel 314335. Open anytime by appt. Sporting, animal, bird & military pictures, bronzes, 19th & 20thC oils and watercolours. LAPADA

Priors Marston

Daneby House Antiques
(Daneby Antiques Ltd). Daneby House, CV23 8SA. Tel Byfield (0327) 60347. Open 9-6; closed Tues and Thurs; other times by appt. Period and general antique furniture, silver, glass and china.

Rugby STD 0788

Alan Grant
Clifton. Tel 71165. Decorative silver items and interesting smalls.

Linnets Nest Antiques & Mawby's International
(P.J.Mawby). 50 Church St. Tel 61393 &832600 priv75305. (Warehouse at School St. Churchover, Nr.Rugby.) Open (shop & warehouse) Mon-Fri 9-5; other times by appt. Shop sells mainly small furniture including pine, oak, mahogany. Warehouse carries large stock of stripped pine, especially large dressers & bookcases. Also Victorian shipping goods.

Shipston on Stour STD 0608

Birmingham House Antiques
(John Bolton, Vera Bolton-Van de Weij). Birmingham House, 8-10 Church Street, CV36 4AP. Tel 62037 (priv 029588 439). Open Mon-Fri 10-5.30, Sat 10-4; other times by appt. 17th 18th and 19thC furniture, specialising in country furniture.

Fine-Lines (Fine Art)
(L.W. & R.M. Guthrie). The Old Rectory, at 31 Sheep St, CV36 4AE. Tel 62323. Open any social hour, but by appt, please. Watercolours, broadly 1850-1950. Fine decorative works.

JOHN G. MORRIS LTD.

You are cordially invited to visit our constantly changing stock of 17th, 18th & 19th century English & Continental furniture together with many associated items of interest at our showrooms in the centre of Petworth.

MARKET SQUARE,
PETWORTH, SUSSEX GU28 0AH

TELEPHONE: 0798 42305

Patrick and Gillian Morley Antiques

8 Jury Street, Warwick

Tel: Warwick (0926) 492963

(formerly in Kenilworth — Member LAPADA)

10 Showrooms of fine antiques, sculptures and works of art

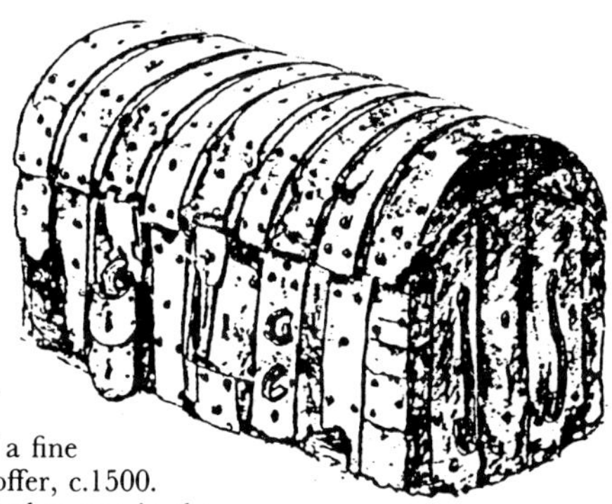

An artist's impression of a fine iron bound coffer, c.1500. Almost identical to one in the Gruuthuse Museum, Bruges. (Ex Earl of Stafford Collection).

Always something rare and unusual in stock

A. T. Silvester & Sons Limited

2-4 HIGH STREET
WARWICK
Tel 0926-492972

Antiques ~ Silver ~ Jewellery

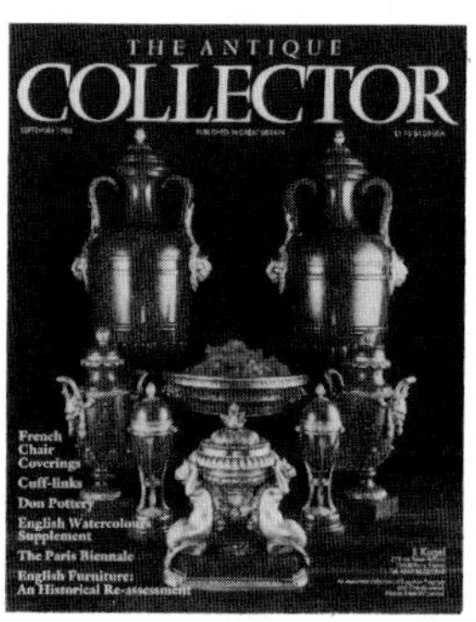

Britain's Internationally Best-selling Antiques Magazine

The beginning of a new era for The Antique Collector. A larger magazine, a more beautiful magazine, a better designed magazine and a more colourful magazine, but a magazine which is still as informed, as comprehensive, as authoritative, as well written and essential as it has always been.

For a complimentary copy and subscription details telephone or write to:
THE ANTIQUE COLLECTOR,
72 Broadwick Street, London W1V 2BP. Tel: 01-439 7144

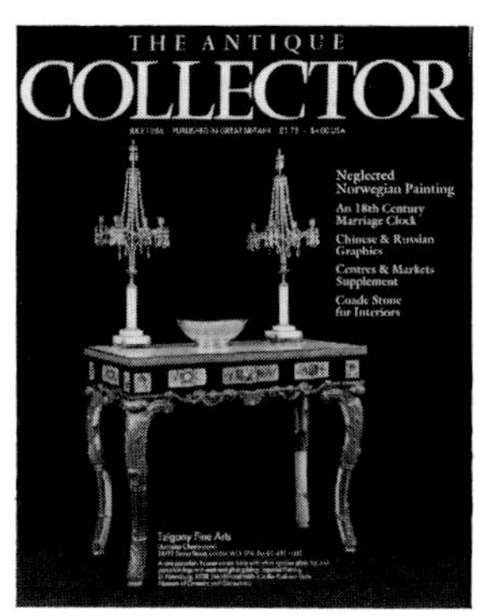

Time in Hand
(Francis Bennett). 11 Church St, CV36 4AP. Tel 62578. Open Mon-Sat 9-5.30; closed 1-2; Thurs 9-1; other times by appt. Wide range of longcase clocks, wall clocks, barometers, barographs etc. and some table clocks. Repair of clocks & barometers.

Wigington Partners
(Diana Coupland, Marc Miller, Henry Wigington). 22 New St, CV36 4EN. Tel 61205. Open Mon-Sat 10-1, 1.30-6; other times by appt. Furniture, mainly 18th & 19thC mahogany, small quantity of oak, some walnut, no pine. Oil paintings and prints. Restoration of paintings and framing.

Stratford-upon-Avon
STD 0789

Abode
(Mrs Ann Bannister). 40 Sheep St, CV37 6EE. Tel 68755. Open Mon-Sat 9-5.30; other times by appt. Antiques, pine furniture, brass and copperware, interior design.

Arbour Antiques Ltd
(Robin J. Wigington). Poet's Arbour, Sheep St, CV37 6EF. Tel 293453 (priv 204095). Open Mon-Fri 9-5.30; other times by appt. Antique arms and armour. BADA

Arden Antiques
(K.G.Whateley). 7 Greenhill St, CV37 6LF. Tel 67067. Open Mon-Sat 9.30-5. Copper, brass, bygones, curiosities, small furniture.

Jean A.Bateman Antiques
41 Sheep St. Tel 298494. Antique jewellery. NAG, LAPADA

Bow Cottage Antiques
(R.Harvey-Morgan). Antique Arcade, Sheep St. Tel 297249 (priv 205883). Open Mon 10.30-5.30; Tues-Sat 10-5.30; other times by appt. China, glass, prints, maps, pictures, furniture, stamps, coins, silver and jewellery.

Robert Garrett Antiques
Guild St, CV37 6UB. Tel 292795. Open Mon-Sat 9.30-5. 3,500 sq ft warehouse of Georgian and Victorian furniture, fine arts and antiques.

Peter Hillary Ltd
54 Henley St. Tel 5669. Open Mon-Sat 10-5.30; other times by appt. Furniture, porcelain, glass, music boxes, silver and general items.

Rosemary Antiques & Paper Moon Books
(Mrs R.E.Fletcher). 4 Sheep St. Tel 297249 (priv 038677-472). Open Mon 10.30-5.30; Tues-Sat 10-5.30. Pottery and porcelain up to 1940 including Royal Doulton and Shelley. Small furniture. Sewing machines. Children's books, illustrated books, English literature.

Soft Surround
(Andrew & Sarah Maxwell-Wood). 2 Centre Craft Yard, 43 Henley St, CV37 6QW. Tel 295070 (priv 0608-62181). Open Mon-Sat 10-5.30. Contemporary crafts - cushions, wall-hangings, embroidered pictures, contemporary jewellery, ceramics, accessories, dolls, prints, treen.

Stratford-upon-Avon Antiques Centre
59-60 Ely Street. Tel 204180. Open Mon-Sun 10-5. Over 60 dealers selling jewellery, porcelain, silver, pictures, collectables, militaria etc. Also large furniture galleries.

Robert Vaughan Antiquarian Booksellers
(R.Vaughan, C.M.Vaughan). 20 Chapel St, CV37 6EP. Tel 205312. Open weekdays 9-6; other times by appt. Fine, rare and out-of-print books, maps, prints. ABA

J.Wigington & Sons
(J. Wigington). 'Winchester 73', 276 Alcester Rd. Tel 293881. Open by appt only. Arms, armour and sporting equipment. Also 19thC furniture, tools, bygones and treen.

Chris Wright Photography
The Old Granary, 19A Greenhill St. Tel 299766. Photographer.

Studley STD 052 785

Prospect Antiques
(R.T.Felix). Chester House, Alcester Rd, B80 7NJ. Tel 2494 (priv 078976 4539). Open Mon-Fri 10-5; Sat 9.30-12.30. General 19thC furniture, china, bronzes, clocks and decorative items.

Tanworth-in-Arden
STD 056 44

Peter Montagu-Williams
Gilberts Green. Tel 2314. Open normal business hours and by appt. Fine paintings, also specialising in quality furniture and ornaments for house and garden.

Warwick STD 0926

Duncan M.Allsop
(Duncan M.Allsop). 26 Smith St, CV34 4HS. Tel 493266. Open Mon-Sat 9.30-5.30. Antiquarian and modern books. ABA

Apollo Antiques Ltd
(R.H.Mynott & C.B.J. Mynott). 62 West St. Tel 494746. Open Mon-Fri 9.30-5.30; other times by appt. Extensive stock of 18th and 19thC English & Continental furniture, decorative & architectural items, oriental, bronzes, marble & wooden sculpture, decorative oil paintings & watercolours as well as general shipping goods from warehouse. LAPADA

H.H.Bray Ltd
(N.A.Harper). 9 Jury St. Tel 492791. Open Mon-Sat 9.30-5.30; other times by appt. Jewellery 1840 to present day, specialising in gem jewellery and silver from 1700, Sheffield plate and porcelain. LAPADA

Gordon's Antiques
(Gordon Fernhead). 7 Cattell Rd. Tel 490461. Mainly trade. Shipping furniture.

Tim Harrison Trade & Export Antiques
(Tim Harrison). 36 Market St. Tel 491400. Open Mon-Fri; other times by appt. Victorian and shipping furniture.

Nevil and Betty Malin
Swan Lane Antiques, Swan Lane, CV34 4BJ. Tel 400040. Open Mon-Sat 10-5. Specialists in commemorative and crested china (Goss etc). Also other china, porcelain etc.

P.and G. Morley
8 Jury Street, CV34 4EN. Tel 492963 (priv 0926 54191). Open Mon-Fri 9-5.30; Sat 9-12; other times by appt. 10 showrooms of 17th-19thC furniture, works of art, decorative items, rare and unusual pieces. LAPADA

James Reeve
9 Church St. Tel 498113. Open Mon-Sat; early closing Sat. 17th to 19thC English furniture in the finest condition.

A.T.Silvester & Sons Ltd
(Mr C.A.Silvester). 2-4 High St, CV34 4AP. Tel 492972. Open Mon-Sat 9-1, 2-5.30; Thurs 9-1. Antique silver and jewellery as well as a large stock of general antiques, period furniture, mirrors, and china. LAPADA

Swan Lane Antiques
Swan St. Tel 400040. Open Mon-Sat 10-5.30. Antiques centre.

Turtons
Smith Street Antique Centre, 7 Smith St. Watches & jewellery.

Warwick & Warwick Ltd
(D.Talbot, C.Rowcliffe, C.Such). Arbon House, 21 Jury St. Tel 499031. Open by appt Mon-Fri 9-5. Auctioneers of stamps, postcards, ephemera. PTS

Warwick Antique Centre
22 High St. Tel 495704. Open Mon-Sat 10-5.30. 25 specialised dealers with a wide variety of antiques.

Warwick Antiques
16 & 18 High St, CV34 4AP. Tel 492482. Open Mon-Fri 9-5.30; Sat 9-1; other times by appt. (Parking at rear.) Metalware, pewter, copper, brass and bronze; also porcelain, glass and curios, decorative items, lighting, continental porcelain, large furniture showrooms, pictures, prints, oriental rugs.

W.Midlands

Birmingham STD 021

Ashleigh House Antiques
(Ron & Pauline Hodgson). 5 Westbourne Rd, Edgbaston, B15 3TH. Tel 454 6283. Open by appt any reasonable time. Fine period furniture, clocks and objets d'art and paintings.

B.E.L.Products Ltd Inc.B.E.L.Tradepoint
(A.R.Newton, M.J.Newton). 302 Windsor St, Nechells, B7 4DW. Tel 359 7791. Open Mon-Fri 8.30-4.30; Sat 8.30-11.30; 26 Oct-14 Dec 8-11.30; other times by appt. Reproduction brassware, cabinet fittings, fireside accessories, oil lamps and glass shades.

Biddle and Webb
Icknield Sq, Ladywood Middleway. Tel 455 8042. Auctioneers.

Birmingham Antique Centre
(R.E.C. Dufty). 141 Bromsgrove Street, B5 6RQ. Tel 692 1414. Open every Thurs 9-3. Varied antiques, approx 30 stands.

Bright Willis
677 Warwick Rd, Solihull. Tel 705 6491. Auctioneers.

Cariss Residential
(Peter L. Cariss). 20-22 High St, Kings Heath, B14 7JU. Tel 444 0088/8579. Open seven days a week 9-7. Auctioneers holding regular executors sales, specialist fine art and collectors sales.

Peter Clark Antiques
(P.N.Clark). 36 St Marys Row, Moseley. Tel 449 8245. 18th-early 20thC English furniture, silver, restorations. LAPADA

Fellows & Sons
88 Hagley Rd, B16 8LU. Tel 454 1261. Auctioneers & valuers of jewels & silver. (Established 1876.).

Ray & Diane Ginns
39 Norman Rd, Northfield, B31 2ES. Tel 476 8319. Open by appt. Specialist in fine Toby Jugs and 18th and 19thC pottery.

Bob Harris & Sons
(R.E., R.M. & I.J.Harris). 2071 Coventry Rd. Tel 743 2259. Open Mon-Sat 10-5; other times by appt. (On A45,2 miles from Birmingham airport, 4 miles from M6) 18th and 19thC furniture, brass, copper and shipping goods. LAPADA

Samuel Heath & Sons PLC
Cobden Works, Leopold St, B12 0UJ. Tel 772 2303. Reproduction antique candlesticks.

John Hubbard Antiques
(John & Pauline Hubbard). 224-226 Court Oak Rd, Harborne, B32 2EG. Tel 426 1694. Open Mon-Sat 9-5.30. 18th, 19th and early 20thC furniture, silver and paintings. Specialising in desks and library furniture. LAPADA

Martin & Co Ltd
97 Camden St. Tel 233 2111. Open Mon-Fri 9-5.30. Reproduction antique brass and other metal furniture fittings for old and new furniture. Handles, hinges etc based on classic designs. GMC

The Moseley Gallery
Woodbridge Rd, Moseley, B13 8EH. Tel 449 9456. 18th, 19th and 20thC watercolours.

Nathan & Co (Birmingham) Ltd
31 Corporation St. Tel 643 5225. Open Mon-Sat 9-5. Antique silver and jewellery, modern jewellery and giftware.

Stuart House Fine Art
(J.Hubbard). 123 Queens Park Rd, Harborne. Tel 426 3300. Open Mon-Sat 9-5.30. 18th & early 19thC furniture, paintings & objets d'art. LAPADA

Tilley's Antiques
(S.A.Alpren). Tel 704 1813. (Also at Birmingham Thursday Antique Market, Bromsgrove St.) Open by appt only. Victoriana, prints, maps, silver, watches, clocks, jewellery, furniture, porcelain and musical boxes. LAPADA

Treasure Trove
1852-1854 Pershore Rd, Cotteridge, Kings Norton. Tel 4582219. Open Mon-Sat, early closing Wed. (On main Redditch rd 5 miles from city centre.) Mainly secondhand and 1930s furniture.

Weller and Dufty Ltd (Est 1835)
141 Bromsgrove St. Tel 692 1414. Auctioneers specialising in arms, armour and militaria. Ten two day sales per annum.

Christopher Wray's Lighting Emporium
Bartholomew Row. Tel 233 3364. (Main branch in London.) Decorative lighting of the 1880s. Victorian, Edwardian and Art Deco period lights.

Coventry STD 0203

Barn Antiques
(N. Green). Binley Common Farm, Rugby Rd. Tel 447628, 453878. Open Mon-Sun 9.30-5.30. Antique furniture, Victorian and Edwardian furniture, oak, clocks, copper, brass, desks etc.

Centre Crafts
(Mary O'Donovan and Gerry O'Donovan). 169 Spon St. Tel 27200. Open Mon-Sat 9-5.30. Small gallery retaining British crafts and contemporary limited edition prints.

Memories Antiques
(R.Seymour). 400A Stoney Station Rd. Tel 687994. Open Mon, Tues, Thurs, Fri, Sat; other times by appt. Porcelain, china, bric-a-brac, militaria, silver, furniture, paintings and jewellery.

Neil Spencer Antiques
(Robert Simmons). 29 St Osburgs Rd, Stoke. Tel 441182. Open Mon 5.30-7.30; Tues, Wed, Fri, Sat 10.30-5.30; other times by appt. General antiques, pine furniture (unstripped), gramophones, radios and bygones.

Spon End Antiques
(Mrs S.Halliday). 115-116 Spon End, CV1 3HF. Tel 28379. Open Mon-Sat 10-5.30; other times by appt. General antiques and pre-1960 clothes and accessories. Also jewellery, crested and commemorative china, pottery, porcelain, bygones and ephemera.

Dorridge

Ashton Antiques
(R.B. & B.A. Ashton). 12 Arden Buildings, Station Rd. Tel 05645 3040. Open 9-5.30; other times by appt. Antique furniture, clocks, of all kinds. Restoration.

Erdington STD 021

Kestrel House Antiques
72 Gravelly Hill North. Tel 021-373 2375. Open Mon-Sat 10-6; other times by appt. 18th and 19thC oil paintings, watercolours and curios.

Kinver STD 0384

David Quimby
Wellbeck, White Hill. Tel 872564. Open by appt only. 18th and early 19thC pottery and porcelain.

Knowle STD 056 45

Phillips
(Enquiries: John Haycraft). The Old House, Station Rd, B93 0HT. Tel Knowle (05645) 6151. Auctioneers & valuers.

Oldswinford

Oldswinford Antiques
(Antony R. Harris). 106 Hagley Rd, DY9 0HB. Tel Stourbridge (038 43) 5577. Open Mon-Sat 9.30-5. Oil paintings, watercolours, prints 19th-20thC, picture framing, restoration of oils and watercolours.

Stourbridge STD 0384

Meriden House Antiques
(J. & T. Taplin). Meriden House, 75 Market St. Tel 395384. Open Mon-Sat 10-5.30; closed Thurs; other times by appt. Small 18th & 19thC furniture, antique jewellery, dolls, silver, boxes, porcelain, glass, brass & copper. Samplers.

Robert Wilkes Antiques and Traditional Furniture
Norton Rd. Tel 393539. Open Sat 10.30-6. Good pre-war furniture, glass, china, bric-a-brac. Specialist in Victorian glass.

Sutton Coldfield STD 021

Kenneth W. Allen
Moor Old Lodge, 6 Moor Hall Park, Four Oaks, B75 6LP. Tel 308 1685. Specialist in chess sets of all materials, particularly ivory. Ivory restoration, especially chessmen. Consultant/sculptor.

Thomas Coulborn & Sons
Vesey Manor, 64 Birmingham Rd, B72 1QP. Tel 354 3974, 354 3139. Open Mon-Sat 9-1, 2-5.30. Good stock of 17th and 18thC English and Continental furniture and works of art. BADA

Driffold Gallery
(David Gilbert). The Smithy, 78 Birmingham Rd. Tel 021-355 5433. Open 10-6, closed Thurs. 19th and 20thC oils and watercolours.

H.& R. Parry Ltd
(H. Parry & R.L. Parry). 23 Maney Corner, B72 1QL. Tel 354 1178. Open 10-5.30; other times by appt. 18th & 19thC furniture, silver (all periods), jewellery (all periods). BADA

Walsall STD 0922

Antique Centre
The Royal Hotel, Ablewell St. Open Mon-Sat 10-5; poss Sun 2-5. 18 stands with general stock ranging from furniture to collector's items.

Midas Antiques
(Alan Tuckley). 181 High St, Brownhills, WS8 6HG. Tel Brownhills (0543) 377719. Open Mon-Sat 9-6; closed Thurs; other times by appt. Furniture, household goods, pottery and porcelain, pictures, metalware, silver, clocks and watches, coins, stamps.

Willenhall STD 0902

Josiah Parkes & Sons Ltd
Union Works, Gower St, WV13 1JX. Tel 66931. Open Mon-Fri 9-5, but appt always advisable. Manufacturers of locks and architectural ironmongery.

Wolverhampton STD 0902

Dam Mill Antiques
(Gwilym and Hilary Bassett). 6 Birches Rd, Codsall. Tel Codsall (09074) 3780. (Also at Ironbridge Antique Centre.) Open Mon, Wed, Fri 10-1, 2.30-5.30; Sat 10.30-6; other times by appt. General antiques; good selection of pottery and porcelain. Late 19th and 20thC paintings, Victorian and Edwardian furniture.

Melbourne Antiques
(Mr R.G.Smart). Rock House Antique Centre, Tettenhall. Tel 754995. Open Mon-Sat 10-5. Antique clocks and watches, jewellery, small furniture, copper and brass. General antiques. Antique clock repairs and restorations.

Martin Quick Antiques Ltd
(C.R.Quick & W.D.M.Quick). 321-323 Tettenhall Rd, WV6 0JZ. Tel 754703 (priv 752908). Open Mon-Fri 9-6, Sat 9.30-12.30; other times by appt. (One mile from town centre on A41 towards Newport.) 20,000 sq ft 18th and 19thC furniture and shipping goods. LAPADA

K. Stuart Swash
(K. Stuart Swash, FSVA). 2 Waterloo Rd, WV1 4BL. Tel 710626. Auctioneers and valuers.

Thomas Coulborn & Sons

Vesey Manor
Sutton Coldfield,
West Midlands B72 1QP
021-354 3974/3139

Antiques, Fine Arts, Fine Clocks, Silver and Works of Art

Fine and rare 18th century
burr and walnut bachelors chest
Height 31″, width 37¼″, depth 17¾″

Bob Harris & Sons

ANTIQUE DEALERS

2071 Coventry Road, Sheldon
Birmingham B26 3DY
021-743 2259
Resident on premises

Showrooms & Warehouse

Antiques & Victoriana, General Trade & Shipping Goods.

CROSS HAYES ANTIQUES

The Antique and Furniture Warehouse
19 Bristol Street, Malmesbury, Wilts.

Antique and Shipping Furniture, Oak, Mahogany, Walnut, and Pine. Over 200 pieces always in stock displayed on 2 floors.

Open Saturday to Monday 9 a.m. – 5 p.m.

Large Selection of China, Glass, Prints, Frames, Books, Metalware and Bric-A-Brac

Enquiries Contact
DAVID BROOKS (06662) 4260 Day 2062 Evenings

Rupert Gentle

Dealer in Antiques and Works of Art

The Manor House,
Milton Lilbourne,
Nr. Pewsey, Wiltshire
SN9 5LQ
Telephone: Marlborough 63344 (STD 0672 63344)

17th and 18th century furniture, needlework and all domestic accessories of the period. Specialising in English and Continental domestic brass, 1600-1800.

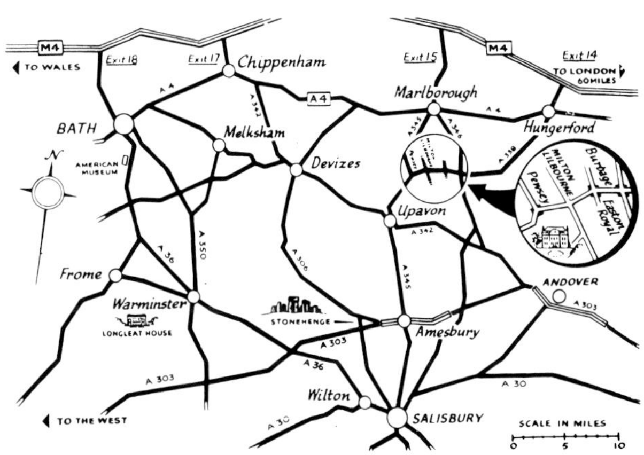

A.E.Wakeman & Sons Ltd
140B Tettenhall Rd, WV6 0BQ. Tel 751166. Open Mon-Fri 8.30-5.30; other times by appt. Victorian and other antique furniture. Trade only. LAPADA

Walker, Barnett and Hill (Auctioneers)
3-5 Waterloo Rd, WV1 4DL. Tel 771511, 772771. Open Mon-Fri 9.15-5.30; other times by appt. Auctioneers. Also insurance and valuation services.

Wiltshire

Box STD 0225

Frogmore House Antiques
Frogmore House, Market Place. Tel 2550. Open Mon-Sat 10-5.30; closed Tues; other times by appt. Galle, Martin pottery, Lalique, Loetz; also furniture, pottery, potlids and silver.

Bradford-on-Avon STD 022 16

Avon Antiques
(V. & A. Jenkins). 26-27 Market St. Tel 2052. Open Mon-Sat inclusive 9.45-5.30; other times by appt. Large stock of English furniture 1600-1830; brass, pewter, treen, clocks, barometers, some painted and lacquer furniture. Also English textiles. BADA

Bradford Furniture Workshops
(Peter K.Scott and Ian Blackshaw). Unit 20, Longs Yard, off Trowbridge Rd, BA15 1EE. Tel 4551. Open Mon-Fri 8.30-5.30; other times by appt. Restoration of old country furniture. Also furniture stripping.

The China Hen
(Miss M.E.Stephenson). 9 Woolley St, BA15 1AD. Tel 3369. Open Mon-Sat 10-6; other times by appt. Country furniture, pottery & porcelain, prints, watercolours, oil paintings.

Ray Coggins Antiques
The Old Brewery, Newtown. Tel 3431. (Also at Frome, Somerset.) Specialists in period pine furniture and architectural interior fittings.

Country Interiors
(Peter K.Scott, Ian Blackshaw). 12 Frome Rd, BA15 1LE. Tel 4000 (priv 4551). Open Tues-Sat 10.30-5; other times by appt. Old country furniture, specialising in kitchen dressers, locally made oak furniture, antiquarian prints.

Harp Antiques
17 Woolley St, BA15 1AD. Tel 5770. Open 9-6; other times by appt. Four showrooms of mainly 18th and early 19thC mahogany furniture (no oak or pine). Also good stock of early English pottery and porcelain, some silver and decorative items.

Jose Hornsey
3 Silver St. Tel 4333 (priv 0380 870764). Open Mon-Sat 10.15-5.45; other times by appt. Country furniture, treen, metals and decorative objects.

Moxhams Antiques
(Roger & Jill Bichard). 17 Silver St. Tel 2789 (priv 038 082-677). Open 9-1, 2.15-5.30; other times by appt. Large stock of period oak and mahogany furniture, English and Oriental pottery, clocks and unusual items. Trade welcome. Parking behind shop.

Richard & Pamela Nadin
5 Woolley St, BA15 1AD. Tel 2476. (Also at 12 Paul St, Frome, Somerset.) Open Mon-Sat, res on prem. Unusual decorations and furniture, carpets, folk and primitive art, painted furniture.

Photography West
37 Silver St. Tel 2719. Photographers.

Brinkworth STD 066 641

North Wilts Exporters
(M.W. Thornbury). Farm Hill House. Tel 423 and 625. Open any time but trade only. Shipping goods for America and Europe, stripped pine, 18th and 19thC antiques.

Calne STD 0249

Roy Carter Antiques
Park View, 205 Quemerford. Tel 2270. Open usually, res on prem. Unusual objects and 17th to 19thC furniture.

Hilmarton Manor Press
(Charles & Sarah Baile de Laperriere). Hilmarton, SN11 8SB. Tel Hilmarton (024976) 208. Open Mon-Sat 9-6; other times by appt. Art and antiques reference and photography books.

P.A. Oxley, Antique Clocks and Barometers
(P.A. Oxley). The Old Rectory, Cherhill. Tel 816227 (priv 812742). Open Mon-Sat 9.30-2.30; closed Wed; other times by appt. Clocks, barometers and some furniture. LAPADA

Castle Combe STD 0249

Combe Cottage Antiques
(Brenda and Adrian Bishop). SN14 7HU. Tel 782250. Open daily 10-1, 2-5.30; closed Sun; other times by appt. Country furniture, formal and primitive, early lighting, treen, ironwork, stone sculpture, fireplace furniture. BADA

Michel Le Coz
(M.&R.E.LeCoz). High St, SN14 7HU. Tel 782223. Open Mon-Sat 10-6; other times by appt. Antique and decorative furniture.

Chippenham STD 0249

Berry Powell & Shackell
(M.A.E.Powell, J.E.Dutch, A.R.West). 46 Market Place. Tel 653361. Auctioneers and valuers.

Harley Antiques
(G.J.Harley & Gary Low). The Comedy, Christian Malford. Tel 720112. Open daily 10-6, Sun by appt. Large stock of quality traditional and country antique furniture, decorative objects, period brass and glass. LAPADA

Harley Two
(Geoffrey Harley & Gary Low). The Chimneys, Christian Malford. Tel 720112. (Also at The Comedy, Christian Malford.) Open any time by appt. Selected country, pine & fruitwood furniture, baskets & country crafts. LAPADA

Corsham STD 0249

Robin and Matthew Eden
Pickwick Village. Tel 713335. Open daily except Sundays. Antique furniture, garden furniture, many interesting and decorative items, Lutyens garden seats.

Cricklade

Edred A.F. Gwilliam
Candletree House, Bath Rd, SN6 6AX. Tel 0793-750241. Specialist in antique arms and armour.

Devizes STD 0380

R.L.Cook
Belmont House, Little Horton. Tel Cannings (038 086) 214. Antiquarian and fine books. ABA

Elizabeth Newby-Vincent
Nursteed Place. Tel 3844. Open by appt only. 18th and early 19thC furniture, decorative things, garden things.

Saville Antiques
(B.S. & P.Bruce). 37 Long St. Tel 3559. Open Mon-Sat 9-6; other times by appt. 17th to 19thC oak and mahogany, metalware, paintings and porcelain.

Froxfield

N.W.Lott & H.J.Gerrish Ltd
The Old Rectory, SN8 3JY. Tel Hungerford (0488) 82188. (Also in London.) Open by appt. 19th and 20thC British etchings and engravings. Also some watercolours, paintings (usually by leading etchers and engravers), and some early photographs.

Andrew Ross Antiques
Thacketts. Tel Hungerford (0488) 82087. Open Mon-Sat 9.30-6; other times by appt. English and Continental furniture - 18th and early 19thC. Oil paintings and watercolours.

Hindon STD 074 789

Monkton Galleries
(J. & B. Dempsey). High St, SP3 6DR. Tel 235. Open Mon-Fri 9.30-6.30, Sat 9.30-1. Early oak and country furniture, clocks, pottery and metalware. BADA

Malmesbury STD 066 62

The Antique Shop
22 Gloucester St.

Andrew Britten
(T.A.Freeman, T.M.Tyler). 48 High St, SN16 9AT. Tel 3376. Open Mon-Sat 9.30-6; other times by appt. (Res.on prem.) Furniture 1700-1900 and decorative icons, especially of metal. LAPADA

Cross Hayes Antiques
(David Brooks). The Antique and Furniture Warehouse, 19 Bristol St. Tel 4260 (priv 2062). Open Mon-Sat 10-5; other times by appt. Furniture 1780 to 1920 also china, glass, copper & brass items, pictures, prints, general smalls. LAPADA

J.P.Kadwell
Silver St. Tel 3589. Open Mon-Sat 9-5. Antiques and country furniture.

The Keyser Gallery
Quarry House, Corston, SN16 0HJ. Tel 2429. Specialists in sporting and wildlife pictures.

M.J.Lympany
34 Cross Hayes. Tel 3086.

Malmesbury Antiques and Interiors
(Paul von Fullman). 100 Lower High St. Tel 4656. Open Mon-Sat 9.30-1, 2-5.30; other times by appt. 18th & 19thC furniture, lamps, fabrics & objects.

Rene Nicholls Antiques
(Mrs Irene Nicholls). 56 High St, SN16 9AL. Tel 3089. Open daily 10-6; other times by appt. British pottery and porcelain, small pieces of furniture.

Ramshead Gallery Studio
(June Randall). 125 Lower High St, SN16 9AL. Tel 2505. Open Tues-Sat 10-6; other times by appt. Giltwood furniture and frames, both antique and reproduction. Lacquerwork. Paintings and prints.

Relic Antiques
(Malcolm Gliksten & Grierson Gower). Brillscote Farm, Lea, SN16 9PF. Tel 2332. (Also in London.) Open Mon-Fri 9-5.30; other times by appt. Country warehouse of Relic Antiques, London N1. Decorators and collectors items, fairground art, old pub and shop fittings, early advertising. One annual auction of architectural antiques.

Restorations Unlimited
(David Ellis, Peter Knapp). Pinkney Park. Tel 840888 (priv 840437). Open Mon-Thur 9-5.30; Fri 9-1 2-5; Sat 9-1; other times by appt. Craftsmen restoring all periods of antique furniture, ceramics and metalwork. Oil paintings cleaned, restored and re-varnished.Regular weekend residential courses in ceramic & furniture restoration. (5 miles from Malmesbury on B4040 Bristol Rd). GWW

Marlborough STD 0672

Nigel Cracknell Antiques Ltd
(N.O. & B.M.Cracknell). 138 High St, SN8 1HN. Tel 52912. Open 10-6; other times by appt. Fine quality furniture, 17th to early 19thC oak, walnut & mahogany & related items. Specialist in Mason's Ironstone. BADA

Directory Entries are Free and ADDITIONS OR CORRECTIONS will be welcomed by *THE EDITOR, British Art and Antiques Directory, National Magazine House, 72 Broadwick Street, London W1V 2BP*

Dormy House Antiques
(Denys & Ann Bellerby). 43 Kingsbury St, SN8 1JE. Tel 52703. Open weekdays, closed weekends, appt advisable. 18thC English drinking glasses, lace-makers' bobbins and general antiques.

Jonathan Gaunt
5 Cold Corner Cottages, Oare, SH8 5JL. Photographer.

Robert Kime Antiques
(Robert D. Kime). Dene House, Lockeridge, SN8 4EQ. Tel Lockeridge (067 286) 250. Open Mon-Fri 10-6; other times by appt. (4 miles west of Marlborough on A4, turn right to Lockeridge, last large house on right.) Period European furniture and good quality decorative items and works of art.

Kingsbury Gallery
5 Kingsbury St. Tel 52896. Open Mon-Sat 10-5; early closing Wed, Sat. Period furniture, silver, smalls.

London House Antique Centre
(John & Rita Watkins). High St. Tel 52331. Open Mon-Sat 9.30-5.30. 18th and 19thC furniture, clocks, pottery and porcelain, small collectable silver and jewellery, brass and copper, watercolours and prints.

Marlborough Antiques
18 The Parade. Tel 54818. Oak furniture 1600-1700. Also metalware, treen and decorative objects.

Marlborough Sporting Gallery & Bookshop
(Rupert Collens). 6 Kingbury St. Tel 54074. Open Tues-Sat 10-5; closed Mon. Sun by appt. Gallery specialising in prints, watercolours and oils of British Sport and Country pastimes. In particular works by Cecil Aldin, Lionel Edwards, Snaffles, G.D.Armour, etc. Also a medium sized bookshop devoted to sporting books and Modern Firsts.

Neates
93 High St, SN8 1HD. Tel 54916. (Also in Hungerford, Newbury, and Swindon.) Auctioneers and chartered surveyors.

Objects
(Nicholas Mitchell). 77 High St.

Melksham STD 0225

A.R.Jaffray
(Alan & Iris Jaffray). 16 Market Place, SN12 6EX. Tel 702269. Open Mon-Fri 10-5.30; Sat by appt. Res on prem. Large stock of furniture and metalware, mainly for the trade.

Paul Wansbrough
Seend Lodge, Seend. Tel Seend (038 082) 213. Open Mon-Fri 9.30-5; Sat 9.30-1 but phone first; other times by appt. Fine 18th and early 19thC furniture and objects.

Pewsey

Rupert Gentle Antiques
(Mrs R. Gentle). The Manor House, Milton Lilbourne, SN9 5LQ. Tel Marlborough (0672) 63344. Open Mon-Sat 9-6; other times by appt. 18thC English furniture, 16th-18thC brass, steel & ironwork. 17th & 18thC needlework. Domestic accessories of the period. BADA

Potterne

V.K. and R. Antiques
(Mrs V.J. Morris). 8 High St. Tel Devizes (0380) 3933. Open Thurs-Sun 10-6; other times by appt. Oak, fruitwood, pine furniture and metalware including Victorian & Edwardian fireplaces.

Salisbury STD 0722

D.M. Beach
(Anthony Pearce). 52 High St, SP1 2PG. Tel 333801. Open Mon-Sat 9-5.30. Old and rare books, fine bindings and prints. ABA

Derek Boston Antiques
(D.A.Boston). 223 Wilton Rd. Tel 22682. Open Mon-Sat 9-5.30; other times by appt. Fine period furniture, decorators items, Chippendale, premier specialist in majolica. LAPADA

Robert Bradley
71 Brown St. Tel 333677. Open Mon-Fri 9.30-5.30; Sat 9.30-1.30. Good quality 17th and 18thC English furniture and decorative objects.

Castle Galleries
(John C. Lodge). 79 Castle St, SP1 3SP. Tel 333734. Open Mon-Fri 9.30-5; Sat 9.30-1; closed Wed; other times by appt. Coins, medals, small antiques, gold, silver.

Courcoux and Courcoux
(Ian and Linda Courcoux). 90-92 Crane St, SP1 2QD. Tel 333471. Contemporary crafts: ceramics, studio glass, wood, sculpture, wall-hangings. ICGA

Anne Davenport Antiques
(Mrs Anne Davenport). 61 Milford St. Tel 336905. Open Mon-Fri 9.30-4.30; Sat 10.30-12.30; closed Wed; other times by appt. General antiques and small furniture.

Gard Books (Music)
(Philip Lawson). 52 The Close, SP1 2EL. Tel 23565. Sheet music and scores. Postal business only. Free catalogues issued.

Ian G.Hastie
46 St Ann St. Tel 22957. Open Mon-Sat 9-6; other times by appt. Large general stock with much 17th, 18th and early 19thC English and Continental antique furniture. Also silver, clocks and other items. BADA

John & Judith Head, The Barn Book Supply
(John & Judith Head). 88 Crane St. Tel 27767. Open Mon-Fri 9-4.30; other times by appt. Antiquarian books on field sports. ABA

Patrick Mullins
5 St John St. Tel 22570. Open Mon-Fri 9.30-5.30, Sat 9.30-12; other times by appt. 17th to 19thC furniture, English and Oriental pottery and porcelain and works of art.

Salisbury Bookbinders
(Alan Winstanley). 213 Devizes Rd. Tel 334998. Open Mon-Fri 8.15-12.30 1.45-5.30; other times by appt. Restoration of antiquarian books and allied materials, leather table tops inlaid and tooled, new leather tooled bindings, limited editions and library bindings. Specialist in original designed bindings and music box books.

Jeremy Warner
St Ann St. Tel 22842. Open by appt only. 18th and 19thC oak, walnut and mahogany furniture.

Woolley & Wallis
Castle Auction Mart, Castle St, SP1 3SU. Tel 21711. Valuers & auctioneers.

Sherston

Sherston Antiques
(P.O.Hawkins). The Old Pharmacy House. Tel 0666- 840291. Open 9-5.30; other times by appt. Silver, plate, English porcelain. LAPADA

Swindon STD 0793

The Old Bakehouse Antiques
Lydiard Millicent.

Victoria Bookshop
(S. Austin). 30 Wood St, Old Town, SN1 4AB. Tel 27364. Open Mon-Sat 9-5.30. New and secondhand books, old postcards.

Tisbury STD 0747

Rectory Antiques
(Mrs G.E.Whitworth). 4 High St, SP3 6PS. Tel 870710. Open 10-5; closed Mon. Silver, porcelain, jewellery, glass and small furniture.

Warminster STD 0985

Bishopstrow Antiques
55 East Street.

Century Antiques
10 Silver St.

P. Gale Shipping
Furlong House, East St. Shippers.

Obelisk Antiques
(P.R.Tanswell). 2 Silver St, BA12 8PS. Tel 216874. Open Mon-Sat 10-1 2-5.30; other times by appt. English and Continental 18th and 19thC furniture, mirrors, pictures, decorative items etc.

Sotheby's
(Representative: Lord Seymour). Maiden Bradley, BA12 7HW. Tel Maiden Bradley (098 53) 525. Open Mon-Fri 9-6; other times by appt. Auctioneers & valuers.

Warminster Antiques
(Thelma Mullen). 4a Silver St. Tel 212536. Open Mon-Sat 10-5.30. Antique furniture, glass, Oriental and decorative items and porcelain.

K. & A. Welch
(K.J. & A.L. Welch). 1A Church St. Tel 214687 (priv 213433). Open Mon-Fri 8-6; Sat 9-12; other times by appt. Large stock (10,000 sq ft) Victorian, Edwardian and shipping furniture, for the export market.

Westbury STD 0373

Ancient & Modern
(Mrs Anne Curtis). 17 Mariston St.

Bratton Antiques
(Tony & Felicity Hyde). Market Place, BA13 3DE. Tel 823021. Open Mon-Fri 10.15-5, Sat 10.15-1; sometimes closed Mon and Wed; other times by appt. English pottery, particularly Staffordshire. Rural and domestic treen and metalware. Mahogany and country furniture. LAPADA

Wilton

Ian J. Brook
(Ian & Ann Brook). 26 North St, SP2 OHJ. Tel Salisbury (0722) 743392. Open daily 8.30-6; other times by appt. Good quality furniture, fine oil paintings & watercolours, plus good quality small items, silver, copper, brass, porcelain etc.

A.Earle
47 North St. Tel 0722-3284. Open 9-6, closed Wed, Sun. Brass, copper, small furniture, old guns, revolvers and pistol weapons of all kinds. Military items.

Pamela Lynch
18 West St. Tel 0722-4113. Small furniture, needlework pictures, decorative items and objets de vertu.

Norman Newport
The Old Thatched House, 37-39 West St. Tel 0722-3340. English and Continental antiques. Some unusual and early items.

Wealden House Antiques
(Lynda and Peter Constable). 25 North St. Tel Salisbury (0722) 744902. Porcelain, small silver and furniture, paintings.

Wootton Bassett

Stonedge Antiques
(Dr A. Stebbens). 137 High St, SN4 7AY. Tel Swindon (0793) 853296. Open Mon-Sat 9-5.30; closed Wed; other times by appt. Furniture, porcelain, copper & brass.

N.Yorkshire

Bedale STD 0677

W.Greenwood
(W.Greenwood). 7 Church Wynd, Burneston. Tel 24830. Open by appt. 18th, 19th & 20thC paintings & watercolours & frames.

Thornton Gallery
(Mr & Mrs W.H.Turnbull). Snape, DL8 2TR. Tel 70318. Open by appt. 19th & early 20thC oil paintings and watercolours.

Boroughbridge STD 090 12

John Boddy's Fine Wood & Tool Store Ltd
(F.S.Boddy & E.J. Boddy). Riverside Sawmills, YO5 9LJ. Tel 2370. Open Mon-Fri 8-5; Sat 8-4. Veneers, bandings, brass cabinet fittings, wood finishes and waxes, carving, turning and general tools together with many other items complementary to a stock of over 60 species of British, imported and exotic timber available in kiln dried boards.

Country Antiques
High St. 18th-19thC furniture and silver.

Joan Eyles Antiques
(John C.H.Eyles and Joan M.Eyles). The Stone Yard, Fishergate, YO5 9QY. Tel 3357 (priv 2487). Open Mon-Sat 11-5.30; closed Thurs; other times by appt. 18th and 19thC British furniture, lace, samplers, textiles, treen, metalware and sewing requisites. BADA

R.S. Wilson & Sons
(J.D. & G.R.Wilson). High St, YO5 9AW. Tel 2417 (priv 2654). Open Mon-Sat 9-5.30, Thurs 9-12.30; other times by appt. 18th & 19thC mahogany & oak furniture, copper, brass, glass & china.

Gargrave STD 075 678

Andrew and Linda Blackburn Antiques
12 West St, BD23 3RD. Tel 403. Open by appt, anytime. Period mahogany and oak furniture and metalware.

Bernard Dickinson Antiques
(Bernard Dickinson). 88 High St, BD23 3LX. Tel 285 and 8257. Open Mon-Sat 9-5.30. Small family business selling furniture with restoration workshop. BADA

Myers Galleries
(Jean M. Myers). Endsleigh House, High St, BD23 3LX. Tel 587. Open Mon-Sat 9-5.30; other times by appt. 18thC furniture, pottery, porcelain, glass, metalware and silver. BADA

Harrogate STD 0423

Alexander Galleries
(A.G. Jackson). 81 Station Parade, HG1 1ST. Tel 55430. Open Mon-Fri 10-6; Sat 9.30-5.30. Small stock of antique Yorkshire prints.

Antique and Furniture Centre
(Jan and Richard Maynard). 46/48 Kings Rd. Tel 509708. Open Tues-Sat 10.30-5; other times by appt. Good selection of mahogany, oak and pine furniture, collectables, linens and shipping goods.

Antique Pine Furniture, Michael Green
Library House, Regent Parade. Tel 60452. Open Mon-Sat 9-6. Country and kitchen antiques, collectors' items and treen. Stripping and restoration service.

Armstrong Antiques
(Mark & Tina Armstrong). 10 & 11 Montpellier Parade. Tel 506843. Open Mon-Sat 9.30-5.30; other times by appt. Fine quality furniture, decorative objects and early English glass. LAPADA BADA

Shirley Baguley Antiques
West Park Antique Pavilion, 20 West Park. Tel 61758 (priv 65512). Open Tues-Sat 10-5. Antique jewellery, silver and small furniture.

C.W. Bateson
51 Woodlands Drove. Tel 889937 58595. Telephone appt required. Repairs and restoration of brass, copper, bronze, pewter, iron and steel. Casting service. Lamp and vase conversion.

Church View Antiques
34B Leeds Rd. Tel 502694. Open Mon-Sat 9-5. General furniture, smalls and decorative items.

Cold Bath Antiques
(Mrs S.R.Houlgate). 20 Cold Bath Rd, HG2 0NA. Tel 62331. Open Mon-Sat 9.30-5.30; other times by appt. Mainly small Victorian and Edwardian furniture; some porcelain, chrystoleums, inlaid writing and other boxes, jardinieres etc.

Cottage Antiques
West Park Antiques Pavilion, 20 Westgate. LAPADA

Cottage Antiques
(Sandra J. Evans). 3 Devonshire Place, Skipton Rd, HG1. Tel 68195 (priv 0937 72694). Open Mon-Sat 10-5, closed Fri; other times by appt. Period oak, country furniture, pine, kitchen and dairy antiques, domestic cast iron, copper, brass, pewter and delftware. LAPADA

Daleside Antiques
(Simon & Cheryl Evans). St Peter's Sq, Cold Bath Rd, HG2 0NP. Tel 60286 (priv 509618). Open Mon-Fri 8-5; other times by appt. Specialists in old and period pine furniture & architectural features & fittings & decorative accessories.

Dragon Antiques
(G.Broadbelt). 10 Dragon Rd, HG1 5DF. Tel 62037. Open daily 9-6; other times by appt. General stock, specialising in art glass, art pottery, art nouveau and art deco.

Duncalfe Antiques & Fine Arts
(John Duncalfe). 34 Montpellier Parade. Tel 521452. Open Mon-Sat 9.30-5.30. Fine furniture, porcelain and paintings. BADA

Elizabeth Finlay
131 High St, Starbeck. Tel 886389. Open Mon-Sat 1-5; closed Fri. Small antique furniture and collectors' items.

Godfrey & Twatt
(Alex Twatt). 7 Westminster Arcade, Parliament St, HG1 2RN. Tel 525300. Contemporary crafts: jewellery, glass, ceramics, textiles, wood. ICGA

Michael Green
Library House, Regent Parade. Tel 60452. Country and kitchen antiques, collectors items and treen. Also quick stripping and professional restoration of doors and furniture.

W.F.Greenwood & Sons Ltd
(C.F., R.G., M.V., M.R., R.M. Greenwood, M.C.Watson). 2&3 Crown Place, HG1 2RY. Tel 504467. Open Mon-Sat 9-1, 2.15-5.30; early closing Wed. Antique furniture, silver, jewellery, pottery, porcelain and metalware. BADA

Harewood Antiques
(Andy and Mavis Daniel). West Park Antique Pavilion, 20 West Park. Tel 61758 (priv 0532-813650). Open Tues-Sat 10-5. Victorian lamps, brass, copper, clocks, porcelain and 19thC furniture.

Haworth Antiques
(June & Glynn White). Stand 5A West Park Antiques Pavilion, 20 West Park. Tel 61758 (priv 74293). (Also shop at Huby, N.Yorks.) Open Tues-Sat 10-5. Clocks of all kinds, clock repairs, dial restoration, furniture and collectables.

Irene Kelly
38 Forest Lane Head, Starbeck. Tel 889832. Open Mon-Sat 10-5; closed Tues. Small antique furniture, porcelain, glass and needlework. Copper and brass, old and unusual boxes.

Rodney Kent
(Rodney Kent, Joanna Kent). West Park Antiques Pavilion, 20 West Park. Tel 60352 (priv 523766). Open 10-5; other times by appt. Oil paintings, watercolours, drawings, prints. 17th, 18th & 19thC. LAPADA

J.K.Layton
Fawcett Yard, off Tower St, back Belford Place. Tel 68809. Open Mon-Fri 8-5; closed 12-1. All types of furniture upholstered.

David Love
10 Royal Parade. Tel 65797. Open Mon-Sat 9-1, 2-5.30; other times by appt. 18thC furniture, European and Oriental pottery and porcelain. BADA

Charles Lumb & Sons Ltd
(Frank Lumb, A.R.Lumb). 2 Montpellier Gardens, HG1 2TF. Tel 503776 (priv 863281). Open Mon-Sat 9-1, 2-6; other times by appt. Pre-1830 fine English furniture, metalware, period accessories. CINOA, BADA

J.Marlow Antiques
(Mrs J. Marlow). West Park Antique Pavilion, 20 West Park. Tel 61758 (priv 0642 781529). Open Tues-Sat 10-5. Art nouveau, art deco, jewellery and general antiques.

McTague of Harrogate
17/19 Cheltenham Mount. Tel 67086 (priv 884400). Open Mon-Sat 9.30-5.30; closed Wed. Fine antique prints and paintings. Restoration undertaken.

Mews Antiques
(Mrs Fisher). 2 John St. Tel 57549 (priv 883092). Open Mon-Fri 10-4; Sat 10-12. English and Oriental porcelain, small furniture, oils and watercolours.

Archie Miles Bookshop
(Mrs C. M. Linsley). 54 High St, Pateley Bridge, HG3 5JZ. Tel 711294 (priv 711166). Open Tues-Sat 10-5; Sun 1-5; other times by appt. General secondhand, out-of-print and antiquarian books, specialising in English literature, fine illustrated books and topography. Also jewellery and bric-a-brac. PBFA

Morphets
(J.Sorrell FSVA, J.C.Tyreman FRICS, M.Verity ARICS). 4-6 Albert St, HG1 1JL. Tel 502282. Open Mon-Fri 9-5.15; Sat 9-12.30. Fine art auctioneers and estate agents.

Nidd House Antiques
Nidd House, Bogs Lane. Tel 884739. All types of furniture restoration, polishing, inlay and carving, upholstery, metalwork, clock repairs, gilding and oxidised finishes. GMC

Ogden of Harrogate Ltd
38 James St, HG1 1RQ. Tel 504123. Open Mon-Sat 9.30-5. Jewellery, occasional silver and paintings. BADA, NAG

Omar (Harrogate) Ltd
(Miss R.Wolfe & P.McCormick). 8 Crescent Rd, HG1 2RS. Tel 503675. Open Mon-Sat 9-5.30; early closing Wed; other times by appt. Large stock of Oriental carpets and rugs. Cleaning and restoration of same.

Past Times
Rear of 46 Cold Bath Rd. Tel 60896 63846. Open Mon-Thurs 10-4. Traditional French polishing and upholstery.

Paul M. Peters Antiques
(Paul Peters). 15 Bower Rd. Tel 60118. Open Mon-Fri 9.30-5.30; other times by appt. 17th to 19thC Chinese and Japanese ceramics and other Oriental works of art. European ceramics and metalware. Also scientific instruments, 19thC Continental glass and decorative items.

Elaine Phillips Antiques Ltd
2 Royal Parade. Tel 69745. Open 9.30-5.30; other times by appt. Early oak & country furniture, metalware and allied decoration. BADA

Pine Finds
(Geoffrey & Janette Pitt, Gilbert & Betty Harrison). The Old Cornmill, Bishop Monkton, HG3 3QN. Tel Ripon (0765) 87159. Open Mon-Sat 9-5, Sun and bank hols 10-5; other times by appt. Over 800 pieces English, Irish, Bavarian & Scandinavian pine.

Regency Fine Art
123 Wetherby Rd, HG2 7SH. Tel 883178. Open all times by appt only. Good quality English and Continental paintings at keen trade prices.

Renton & Renton
(H.C. Bigg, FRICS, FSVA). 16 Albert St. Tel 61531. (Also at Knaresborough, Ripon, Thirsk, Northallerton, Richmond.) Open 9-5.30. Auctioneers and valuers of chattels & fine arts.

Norman C.Sanderson
The Coach House, Montpellier St. Tel 502687 (priv 56502). Open daily; early closing Wed. 18thC English furniture and porcelain.

Sandler Fine Arts with Bill Bentley
16 Montpellier Parade. Tel 64084. Open Mon-Sat 9-6; other times by appt. 17th, 18th and 19thC oak furniture, Continental and English ceramics, brass, copper and treen.

F.B.Shaftoe
(F.B.&P.J.Shaftoe). 17-18 Regent Parade, HG1 5AW. Tel 502151. Open Mon-Sat 9-6; other times by appt. 18th and 19thC furniture only; wholesale furniture exports. Trade only.

Shaw Bros
21 Montpellier Parade. Tel 67466. Open Mon-Sat 9.30-5.30; early closing Wed. Porcelain, silver, antique jewellery, objets d'art.

The Singing Bird
(Alice M.Sagar). 19 Knaresborough Rd. Tel 888292. Open Mon-Fri 10-5; other times by appt. Small furniture, porcelain, silver and metalware.

Smith's The Rink Ltd
Dragon Rd. Tel 503217. Open Mon-Sat 9-5.30. 18th and 19thC English and Continental furniture, good quality shipping furniture.

Sotheby's
(Representative: R J Phillips). 8-12 Montpellier Parade, HG1 2TJ. Tel 501466/7. Auctioneers & valuers.

Sutcliffe Galleries
8 Albert St. Tel 62976. Open 10-5, closed Wed. 17th to 20thC paintings, including landscapes, marine, topographical and sporting. Specialists in restoration, reframing and valuation of period oil paintings. BADA

T.L. Phelps
Unit 2, Rear of 17 York Place. Tel 524604. Open Mon-Fri 8.30-5.45; closed 1-2. Fine furniture restoration.

Thorntons of Harrogate
(Mr R.H.Thornton). 1 Montpellier Gdns, HG1 2TF. Tel 504118. Open Mon-Sat 9.30-5.30; other times by appt. 17th, 18th, 19thC furniture, silver, porcelain, clocks, metalware, arms, armour, prints & paintings particularly sporting. LAPADA

Walker Galleries Ltd
(Ian & David Walker). 6 Montpellier Gdns. Tel 67933. (Also at 3 Cale St, London SW3.) Open Mon-Sat 9.30-1, 2-5.30; other times by appt. 19thC English and Continental oil paintings and watercolours. Early Chinese ceramics, and 18th and 19thC English furniture. LAPADA BADA

Christopher Warner
(C.C.Warner Esq, I.P.Legard Esq). 15 Princes St, HG1 1NG. Tel 503617. Open Mon-Sat 9.30-5. Antique silver, jewellery and valuations. BADA

John Weatherell & Sons Antiques
(J.D.Weatherell). Westmorland House, 13-19 Westmorland St, HG1 5AY. Tel 60038/69718. Open Mon-Sat 9-5.30. Large stock on three floors of antique and good quality English and Continental furniture. Also good quality smalls and pictures. LAPADA

West Park Antiques Pavilion
20 West Park. Tel 61758 (priv 60352). Open Tues-Sat 10-5. 16 quality antique dealers under one roof stocking a wide variety of items.

Westmorland Antiques
25/27 Westmorland St. Tel 56721. Open Mon-Sat 8.30-5.30; early closing Wed. General antiques and specialist shipping goods.

Huby

Haworth Antiques
(June & Glynn White). Harrogate Rd, LS17 0EF. Tel Harrogate (0423) 74293. (West Park Antiques Pavilion, 20 West Park. Tel:61758.) Open Tues-Sat 9-6; other times by appt. Clocks - all styles and periods from £10-£1,000. Also small furniture and collectables. BWCMG

Killinghall

Norwood Cottage Antiques
(Mr & Mrs J Davies). 88 Ripon Rd. Tel 0423-56468. Open Mon-Sat 10-6; other times by appt. 18th and 19thC furniture, porcelain.

Knaresborough STD 0423

Robert Aagaard Ltd
Frogmire House, Stockwell Rd, HG5 0JP. Tel Harrogate (0423) 864805. Open Mon-Fri 9-5; Sat 9.30-5; other times by appt. Antique mantels, marble interiors, hand-carved mantels, fireplace restoration & design. BADA, GMC

Gordon Reece Gallery
Finkle Street. Tel 866219 866502. Open Mon-Sat 10.30-5; Sun 2-5; closed Thurs. Large stock of tribal rugs, early oak carving, treen, metalware, etc.

Milton Holgate Antiques
(Milton Holgate). 4 Market Place. Tel Harrogate (0423) 863205. Open Mon-Sat 10-5; closed Thurs; other times by appt. 17th and 18thC furniture. BADA

Home of Antiques
(D. Lee). 104-106 High Street. Tel 864563. Open Mon-Sat 9-5; closed Thurs. Large stock of mixed general antiques, copper and brass.

Kelly's of Knaresborough
(Mr D.C.Kelly). Rear, 96 High St. Tel Harrogate (0423) 862041 (24 hr answering). Open Fri, Sat, Mon 10-5; other times by appt. Complete old lighting specialist offering comprehensive range of chandeliers, wall lights, candelabra, lustres and lamps. Also full restoration service.

T.E.& S.Kindon Antiques
(T.Kindon). St John's House, Station Rd. Tel 867554. Furniture, shipping goods, shipping & packing. Trade only. LAPADA

Provincial Antiques Ltd
(A.D.Allinson). 8 Shorthill Lane, Coneythorpe. Tel Harrogate (0423) 865136. Furniture.

Charles Shaw
12 Market Place. Tel 867715. Open Mon-Sat. Taxidermy, old books, sporting and country pictures, small antiques and English guns.

John Thompson Antiques
(Mr & Mrs J.Thompson). Swadforth House, 5 Gracious St. Tel 864698. General. Valuations. LAPADA

Vollans Photography
26/28 Cheapside. Tel 862626. Open any time by telephone appt. Specialist photographers of all types of antiques and fine art.

Leyburn

Tennants
(J.E. & R.M. Tennant). 26-27 Market Place. Tel Wensleydale (0969) 23451. (Also 27a Market Pl. Richmond (0748 2149) & 33 North End, Bedale.) Open all offices Mon-Fri 9-5; Sat 9-12; other times by appt. Auctioneers.

Melmerby STD 076 584

Simon Greenwood Antiques
(Simon and Chloe Greenwood). 23 Melmerby Industrial Estate, Green Lane, HG4 5HP. Tel 571 (priv: 0677-22554). Open Tues-Fri 9.30-12.30; Sat 9.30-12. (Off A61 between Ripon and A1; 15 miles north of Harrogate.) 4000 sq ft warehouse of furniture, decorative items and shipping goods. LAPADA

Northallerton STD 0609

Alverton Antiques
(Mrs M. Matson). 7 South Parade. Open Wed, Fri & Sat; other times by appt. Antique clocks of all kinds and period furniture.

Antique and Art
(D.M.Willoughby). 7 Central Arcade. Tel 2051. Open Mon-Sat 10-4.30. General antiques and small items.

Collector Corner
(Mrs J. Wetherill). 145-146 High St (South). Tel 5199. Open Wed-Fri 10-12.30, 2-4; Sat 10-12.30, 2-5; also Tues April-Oct; other times by appt. Ceramics, glass, general small antiques, art pottery, Northern pottery, collectables (tools, instruments, postcards, costume etc), small silver, jewellery, paintings, prints and books (over 1000).

Pateley Bridge

Brian Loomes
(Brian Loomes). Calf Haugh Farm. Tel Harrogate (0423) 711163. Open Mon-Sat 10-5; other times by appt. Res on prem. Antique clock dealers. Specialist dealer with large stock of antique British clocks, mainly longcase. No watches.Author of numerous reference books on antique British clocks.

Pickering STD 0751

John Hague Antiques
45 Market Place. Tel 72829. Open Mon-Sat 1-3.30; other times by appt. Furniture, ceramics, prints, oils, watercolours, glass, brass, copper, curios.

Richmond STD 0748

Brown's
2 New Road, DL10 4QS. Tel 4095. Georgian and Victorian furniture, silver, plate, porcelain.

St Trinians Antiques
(T. & M. Bosman). St Trinians Hall, Easby, DL10 7ET. Tel 2560. Open daily 10-5; Sat 10-6; other times by appt. Furniture from 1660-1900, rugs, china, paintings. Trade welcome.

Ripon STD 0765

J.W.Bentall & Sons
(J.W.Bentall). The Coach House, Sharow Cross, Sharow. Tel 2551 (priv 4336). Open by appt only. China, furniture, glass, pewter, silver, jewellery and general antiques. Shipping goods. Oil paintings, objets d'art, weapons, armour.

Jeremy A. Fearn
The Old Rectory, Winksley. Tel Kirkby Malzeard (0765 83) 625. Open Mon-Sat 9-1, 2-5.30, respectfully with appt please. Mainly 18th and 19thC English furniture, though some fine Victorian and Edwardian pieces usually in stock. Also silver, silver plate and some porcelain. Restoration work of furniture undertaken. Detailed valuations for probate & insurance purposes.

Duncan Grimmond
The Old Granary, Upper Court Terrace. Tel 700982. Open Thurs 10-4 and by appt. Repairs to jewellery, hollow and flatware. Restoration of ivory, mother of pearl, tortoiseshell and bronze.

Sigma (Antiques & Fine Art)
(David Thomson). Water Skellgate. Tel 3163. Open Mon-Sat 9-5.30; other times by appt. Large stock quality furniture, smalls and jewellery etc. LAPADA

Scarborough STD 0723

H.C.Chapman & Son
The Auction Mart, North St. Tel 372424. Auctioneers.

Lindy Lou Antiques
(Julien Brett and John Roberts). 138 Victoria Rd, YO11 9SL. Tel 63348 (priv 862985). Open Mon-Sat 9.30-5.30; other times by appt. General antiques, including pictures, furniture, ceramics, glass, jewellery, watercolours. Also 1930s items.

Settle STD 072 92

Jay Davis Antiques
Bishopsdale Court. Tel 2764. Country furniture and antiques, needlework, metalware, treen and pottery.

David Dean Antiques
(David Dean). Pen-Y-Ghent View, Church St. Tel 3702 (priv 3660). Open any time including Sundays; appt always advisable. Genuine antiques of all periods except late Victorian. Bias towards Georgian furniture, mahogany, oak etc. Also earthenware, treen, metalware, decorative items & carvings.

H. I. Milnthorpe
Kirkgate. Tel 2331. Furniture, ceramics, metalware.

Nanbooks
(Mrs N.M.Midgley). Undercliffe Cottage, Duke St, BD24 9DJ. Tel 3324 (priv 04685-551). Open Tues, Fri, Sat 11-5.30; other times by appt. Small antiques, English pottery and porcelain, glass, coins, ephemera, some books and prints.

The Pen-y-Ghent Gallery
(Mrs A.Cox). Devonshire House, Duke St. Tel 2405. Open Tues, Thurs, Fri, Sat 10-12.30, 2-5; other times by appt. Small antiques and collectable items, including pottery, porcelain, glass, metalware and country antiques.

The Philip S.Walden Collection of Antiques
(Philip S.Walden). The Folly. Tel 2312. Open Mon-Sat 10-5, closed Wed; other times by appt. Quality 18th and 19thC furniture, 18th to 20thC smalls, plus a selection of secondhand and antique jewellery and some painting.

Skipton STD 0756

Amy Egan
3A & 7 Mill Bridge, High St. Tel Halifax (0422) 201203. Open Wed & Sat 10-5; other times by appt. Victoriana, silver, jewellery, collectors' items, needlework & textiles.

Gadzooks
(H.Blackburn). 21 Otley St. Tel 3323. Open Mon-Sat 9-5.30; other times by appt. 18th, 19th and 20thC furniture, metalware, pottery, porcelain, clocks, pictures etc. Courier service for overseas buyers.

Stokesley STD 0642

Three Tuns Antiques
Three Tuns Wynd. Tel 711377 (priv 724284). Open Mon-Sat 10.30-5. Furniture, pottery and porcelain, glass, silver and jewellery.

Thirsk STD 0845

Seth Kirby & Sons
Lloyds Bank Chambers, Market Place. Tel 22218. Auctioneers.

Kirkgate Picture Gallery
(Richard Bennett). 18 Kirkgate, YO7 1PQ. Tel 24085. Open Mon, Thurs, Sat 9.30-5; other times by appt. Oil paintings and watercolours up to early 20thC. Oil paintings and gilt frames restored.

Pandion Books
(L. & P.L. Wray). 10 Carr Close, Rainton, YO7 3PS. Tel 578224. Open by appt. Private premises. Fine secondhand books on natural history and related subjects; books illustrated by BB and Tunnicliffe always in stock. Catalogues issued. Selection of stock at Jack Duncan Books, York. PBFA

Potterton Books
(Mrs C. Jameson). The Old Rectory, Sessay. Tel 401218. Open Mon-Fri 9.30-5.30; other times by appt. Leading suppliers of out-of-print and modern reference books on Antiques and Collecting, Art and Architecture. Catalogues issued. Free book searches undertaken. PBFA

Whitby STD 0947

Coach House Antiques
(Carolyn Rea). 75 Coach Rd, Sleights, Yo22 5BT. Tel 810313. Open Mon-Sat 10-5; closed Thurs; other times by appt. Furniture, silver, porcelain, glass, copper, brass, pewter, paintings, prints, jewellery & linen.

Hanover Books
(E.M. & G.E. Shipley). 8 Hunter St. Tel 603587 (priv 602795). Open daily, except Wed; also closed Mon in Winter. Books and postcards.

The Mount Antiques
(B.Bottomley). Khyber Pass. Tel 604516. Open Mon-Sat 9-5. General antiques specialising in fireplaces.

York STD 0904

Jenny Aste & Richard Smith
7 Grape Lane. Tel 21243. Open Mon-Fri 9-6. All kinds of binding work undertaken. Specialising in restoration and conservation of antiquarian books.

Barbican Bookshop
24 Fossgate. Tel 53643. (Also at 12 Main St, Fulford, by appt.) Open Mon-Sat, 9-5.30. 14 rooms of secondhand and antiquarian books on most subjects. Specialities include theology, British topography, angling. Catalogues issued in certain fields. Mail order service. 'Visa' and 'Access' cards acceptable. PBFA

Barkes & Richardson
38 High Petergate, YO1 2HW. Tel 51080. Open Mon-Sat 10-5.30, closed Wed; other times by appt. 19th and 20thC oil paintings and watercolours and late 19thC Japanese woodblock prints.

Christie's
(Representative: Sir Nicholas Brooksbank, Bt). 46 Bootham. Tel 30911. Auctioneers & valuers.

A. Clewlow (Books)
(Allan Clewlow). 24 Fishergate, YO1 4AB. Tel 27715. Open by appt only. General secondhand books and prints.

Pamela Davies
(P A Davies). 56-58 Long St, Easingwold, YO6 3HT. Tel 21251. Open Mon-Sat 10-6; other times by appt. Oil paintings, watercolours, books, small furniture, miscellaneous antiques.

Gate Antiques
(D.Butler). 29 St Saviour's Gate, YO1 2NQ. Tel 27035. Open by appt only. Victorian and Georgian furniture, named Staffordshire figures, brass, copper and glass.

Thomas C.Godfrey Ltd
21 Stonegate, YO1 2AP. Tel 24531. New, secondhand and antiquarian booksellers. Literature, local history, archaeology, history. ABA

Goodramgate Books, Maps and Prints
58 Goodramgate. Tel 51275 (priv 0484 46833). Open Mon-Sat 10.45-4.15. Antiquarian and secondhand books on topography and travel, natural history and the sciences, art and literature. Fine bindings. Antique prints, views and maps.

Henry Hardcastle Ltd
51 Stonegate, YO1 2AW. Tel 23401. Open Mon-Sat 9-5.30, closed Wed. Large and fine stock of old English silver and Sheffield plate. BADA

Helperby Antiques
(D. & K.V. Simpson). Main Street, Helperby, YO6 2PL. Tel Helperby (09016) 692. Open by appt. Mainly trade: Georgian, Victorian & shipping furniture, pottery, metalware & general antiques. Location A1 Boroughbridge 5 miles A19 Easingwold 6 miles.

John Henderson
(John & Margaret Henderson). 70 Micklegate, YO1 1LF. Tel 24414. Open Mon-Sat 9-5.30; other times by appt. Craft bookbinders and antiquarian book restorers, specialising in sympathetic rebinding and repairs. Volumes also bound to customers' specifications.

Inch's Books
(Peter Inch and Janette Ray). 3 St Paul's Sq, YO2 4BD. Tel 27082 (priv 29770). (Bookroom at 39 Low Petergate York; 2nd & 3rd floors.) Open Thurs & Fri 11-5; other times by appt. 20thC art, architectural and design history, photography, town planning and social history. No general stock held. Catalogues issued. PBFA

Kershaw Studios
15 Davygate, YO1 2QR. Tel 55190. Photographer. LBIPP

Lawson Larg
(A.G.Black FRICS, CAAV & J.Stansfield FRICS, CAAV). St Trinity House 3-4 King's Sq. Tel 21532. (Also at Norton (Malton), Thirsk and Tadcaster.) Open Mon-Fri 9-5.15, Sat 9-1. Chartered valuation surveyors, auctioneers and estate agents holding frequent sales of furniture and effects at Fulford Church Hall & Thirsk Town Hall. Also country house sales. House clearance. Occasional auctions of other antiques. No buyers premium.

Philip Martin Music Books
(Martin Dreyer). 36 Fossgate, YO1 2TF. Tel 641389. (Office at 22 Huntingdon Rd, York YO3 7RL. Tel 36111.) Open Mon-Sat 10-5.30. Large stock of secondhand music and books on music. Also new books. Catalogues quarterly. Selection of stock on view at Jack Duncan Books, York.

McDowell & Stern Ltd
3 & 5 Grape Lane. Tel 22000. Open Mon-Sat, 9-12.30, 1.45-5. Two floors of antiquarian books and one of secondhand. Specialising in science, technology, medicine, natural history and economics but with some stock in all fields. Catalogues issued. Antiquarian maps and prints.

The Minster Gates Bookshop
8 Minster Gates. Tel 21812. Open Mon-Sat 9.30-5.30. Large general stock of secondhand and antiquarian books. Good selection of illustrated and children's books, history, literature, folklore. Catalogues issued.

Robert Morrison & Son
Trentholme House, 131 The Mount, Yo2 2DA. Tel 55394. Open Mon-Fri 9-5.30, Sat 9-12; other times by appt. Important stock of English furniture, porcelain and clocks. BADA

O'Flynn Antiquarian Books
35 Micklegate, YO1 1DD. Tel 641404. Open 9-5.30; other times by appt. Very large stock of secondhand and antiquarian books on most subjects, especially early printing, Scottish and classical texts.

Nicola B. Pirozek, Dip. Cons
9 Minster Yard, YO1 2HH. Tel 35609. Open Mon-Fri 10-1, 2-5.30; other times by appt. Qualified paper conservationist and restorer. Specialist in 19thC watercolours, antiquarian books and maps of all types of prints and drawings.

William Sissons Gallery
23 Market Place, Helmsley, YO6 5BS. Tel 71385. Art gallery.

Ken Spelman Booksellers
(P.B.Miller). 70 Micklegate, YO1 1LF. Tel 24414. Open Mon-Sat 9-5.30. 50,000 secondhand and antiquarian books on most subjects with the emphasis on fine arts, history and literature. Also prints, maps and watercolours. Regular exhibitions. Catalogues issued. ABA PBFA

Colin Stillwell (Books)
25 Fossgate, YO1 2TA. Tel 27467. Open Mon-Sat 12-5.30. Good selection on history, literature & art. Catalogues issued irregularly on history. PBFA

Symington Bookbinders - York
(Douglas and Charles Symington). 3 Coffee Yard, Off Stonegate, YO1 2AR. Tel 633995. Open Mon-Fri 9-5.30, Sat 9.30-4.30. Restoration of antiquarian books and manuscripts. Full and half bindings in morocco and calf. Repair, respining and rebinding in cloth, buckram and rexine available.

Bernard Dickinson

**The Estate Yard,
West Street,
Gargrave,
Skipton, Yorks.**

*Set of four walnut chairs
Circa 1700.*

Telephone Gargrave 285 and 8257

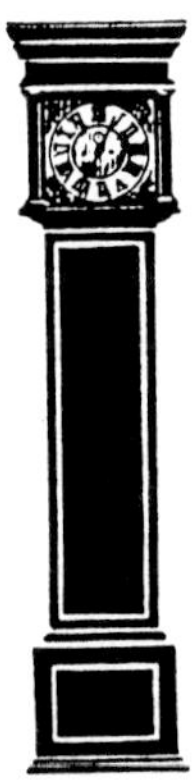

Brian Loomes

Specialist dealer in antique British clocks. Large stock of over fifty longcase plus usually some lantern clocks and wall clocks. Established 19 years. Internationally recognised authority and author of numerous reference books.

**Calf Haugh Farm, Pateley Bridge,
North Yorks.
Tel. 0423-711163** *(Prior phone call advisable)*

CERAMICS BY
**CLARICE CLIFF,
CHARLOTTE RHEAD,
SHELLEY AND OTHERS**
ALSO FURNITURE, LAMPS,
MIRRORS ETC.

MUIR HEWITT

**HALIFAX ANTIQUES CENTRE
Queens Road/Gibbet Street
Halifax HX1 4LR**
Open Tues–Sat 10am–5pm
Tel (0422) 66657

THIRTY–SEVENTH NORTHERN ANTIQUES FAIR

THE ROYAL BATHS
ASSEMBLY ROOMS
HARROGATE
24–30 SEPTEMBER 1987

All enquiries to:- The Secretary
NORTHERN ANTIQUES FAIR
Manor House, High Birstwith, Harrogate
HG3 2LG
Telephone 0423 770385

One of the most prestigious Antiques Fairs in Britain

ESTABLISHED 1951

Taikoo Books Ltd.
(D.A. Chilton, A. Chilton, S. Chilton). 29 High Petergate, YO1 2HP. Tel 641213 (priv 36636). Open Mon-Sat 10-5.30; other times by appt. Fine secondhand and antiquarian stock of Oriental, African, mountaineering, polar, big game hunting & general travel.

John D. Thornton & Family (Antiques) Ltd
123 The Mount, YO2 2DA. Tel 23264. Open Mon-Fri 9-5. Antiques, Victoriana and general shipping goods.

L.L.Ward & Son
(Richard K. Ward). Bar House, Brandsby, YO6 4RQ. Tel Brandsby (034 75) 651. Open Mon-Sat 9-5; other times by appt. Restored pine furniture.

York Antiques Centre
2A Lendal. Tel 641582. Open Mon-Sat 9.30-5.30. Over 50 dealers offering a full and varied range of antiques and collectables.

S.Yorkshire

Barnsley STD 0226

Angela Charlesworth
(J.B. & A. Charlesworth). 99 Dodworth Rd, S70 6HB. Tel 282097 (priv 203688). Open Mon, Tues, Wed, Fri 1-5; Sat by appt. 18th & 19thC furniture, English pottery & porcelain, particularly Yorkshire factories and collectors items.

Mallglade Antiques
(Adrian & Dianne Alexander). Haigh Hall, Haigh, S75 4BT. Tel Bretton (0924 85) 516. Open by appt - trade only. Furniture, 18th-20thC.

Bawtry STD 0302

Treasure House - M.J.M. Enterprises
(Messrs. Jackson, Smith, Robinson). 6 Swan St. Tel Doncaster (0302) 710621 (priv 0909 732153). Open 7 days a week, 9.30-5; other times by appt. General antiques, collectables, furniture.

Timothy D.Wilson
(Timothy D.Wilson). No.1 Swan St, DN10 6JQ. Tel Doncaster (0302) 710040. Open Mon-Sat 9-5; other times by appt. 17th and 18thC English oak furniture, 18th and 19thC Windsor chairs. BADA

Doncaster STD 0302

Antique & Bargain Stores
(M.N.Hunter). 6 Sunny Bar. Tel 4857. Open 9.30-5. Porcelain, furniture, dolls, toys, clocks, watches and antique jewellery.

Barnard Gallery
(F.B.&R.Poynter). Grange Farm, Everton, DN10 5BG. Tel Retford (0777) 817324. Open by appt only. Specialists in old prints and engravings, also maps, watercolours, oil paintings and books;(postal business only for books).

Bryan Bowden
199 Carr House Rd. Tel 65353. English pottery and porcelain and small furniture.

Doncaster Sales & Exchange
(M.H.Hunter). 20 Copley Rd, DN1 2PF. Tel 4857. (Also at Antiques and Bargain Stores, 6 Sunny Bar, Doncaster.) Open Mon-Sat; closed Thurs. Antiques and general goods, including porcelain, toys, dolls, furniture, jewellery, clocks and watches.

Francis Sinclair Ltd
Georgian House, 39 Hallgate. Tel 67260. Open Mon-Sat 9-5.30, Thurs 9-1. Antiques, longcase clocks.

Stanilands
28 Netherhall Rd. Tel 27121. Auctioneers.

Hoyland

Charisma Antiques Trade Warehouse
(John & Christine Simmons). Market St. Tel Barnsley (0226) 747599 (priv 790482). Open Mon-Sat 10.30-4. Furniture and smalls.

Rotherham STD 0709

Roger Appleyard Ltd
(Roger Appleyard). Fitzwilliam Rd, Eastwood Trading Estate, S65 1SL. Tel 67670. Open Mon-Fri 8.30-5; other times by appt. Trade and shipping goods. Container packing. LAPADA

Wickersley Antiques
(Mr & Mrs N.Butler). 3 Broad St, Parkgate. Tel 525595. Period & Victorian furniture, items up to 1920. Restorations. Shipping arranged. LAPADA

George Wright (Rotherham) Ltd
The Crofts, S60 2DJ. Tel 63871. Open Mon-Fri 9.30-5.30, Sat 9.30-12.30. Old marble and pine chimney pieces. Also reproduction fireplaces and dog grates, period light fittings, reeded cast iron panels and decorative firebacks.

Sheffield STD 0742

Diva Antiques
379 Abbeydale Rd. Small items, general antiques.

Eadon, Lockwood & Riddle Auctioneers
Weston Saleroom, Crookes, S1 1XJ. Tel 686294. Auctioneers, surveyors and valuers.

G.W.Ford & Son Ltd
(I.G.F. Thomson). 290 Glossop Rd, S10 2HS. Tel 22082. Open Mon-Fri 8.30-5.30; Sat 10-5; other times by appt. Period English furniture (mainly 18th & early 19thC),general items including Old Sheffield plate, porcelain, silver and paintings. BADA

Fulwood Antiques
(Mrs H.J.Wills). 7 Brooklands Ave, Fulwood, S10 4GA. Tel 307387 (priv 301346). Open Wed, Fri 10-5; Sat 10-1; other times by appt. General stock. Small furniture, porcelain, silver and metalwork. Also oils and watercolours.

Hinson Fine Paintings
679 Ecclesall Rd, S11 8TG. Tel 665927. Open Mon-Fri 9.30-5; Sat 9.30-1. English and Continental paintings. Also cleaning, restoration and re-framing of oil paintings.

A.E.Jameson & Co
(P.Jameson). 257 Glossop Rd, S10 2GZ. Tel 23846 (priv 26189). Open Mon-Fri 9-6, Sat 9-1; other times by appt. 17th, 18th and 19thC furniture. Prints, silver, repairs and valuations. LAPADA

Many Things
(Mrs J.H.Leslie). 259 Fulwood Rd. Tel 665459 (priv 664786). Open Mon-Sat 10.30-5; half day Thurs. 18th and 19thC furniture, glass, silver and silver-plated goods.

Marron Coins
(Mr R.H.Fyfe). 7 Beacon Close, Grimsthorpe, S11 8ZG. Tel 433500. Open by appt only. Coins and medals.

Martins Antiques
379 Abbeydale Rd, S7 1FS. Tel 581278 (priv 553932). Open Mon-Sat 10-4. Furniture, Victorian onwards (occasionally a few period pieces) some porcelain and glass.

A.D.Moorhouse Ltd
(A.D.Moorhouse, J.Oxley). 2 Barmouth Court, Barmouth Rd, Abbeydale, S7 2DH. Tel 582160. Open to trade only. 3000 sq ft of 18th and 19thC furniture. Valuations, packing, shipping and courier services. LAPADA

Paraphernalia
(W.K.Keller). 66-68 Abbeydale Rd. Tel 550203 (priv 664135). Open Mon-Sat 9.30-5; other times by appt. General antiques and bric-a-brac.

Porter Prints
(Mr A.Sedgwick). 205 Whitham Rd, Broomhill, S10 2SP. Tel 685751. Open Mon-Sat 9-5.30; other times by appt. Antiquarian maps & prints, engravings.

N.P. & A. Salt Antiques
(Norman Salt and Annette Salt). Abbeydale House, Barmouth Rd, S1 2DH. Tel 582672. Open Mon-Fri 9.30-4.30. A large stock of shipping furniture, changing daily. Trade only. LAPADA

Paul Ward Antiques
(Paul Ward). 150 Abbeydale Rd, S7 1FH. Tel 583004 (priv 335980). Open Mon-Sat 10-4; other times by appt. General antiques, matched sets of Victorian kitchen and dining chairs (balloon backs).

Wharf Antiques
(Michael Housley). 85 William St. Tel 29321 (Priv 307639). Open Mon-Fri 9.30-5; other times by appt. Antique furniture. LAPADA

John R. Wrigley
185 The Wheel, Ecclesfield, S30 3ZA. Tel 460275. Postal business only. Publishers of 'The Green List' monthly.

W.Yorkshire

Addingham STD 0943

Addingham Antiques
(Gerald J. Estevez). 70-72 Main St. Tel 830788. Open Tues, Thurs, Fri 10-5; Sat 9-noon; other times by appt. A wide variety of antiques including period furniture, clocks, barometers, scientific instruments, musical boxes, oil paintings, Doulton studio pottery. LAPADA

Batley STD 0924

Leon Cooper Antiques
(L.Cooper). 10A Commercial St. Tel 475057. Period furniture, metalware, porcelain, silver, miniatures. Restorations. Valuations. LAPADA

Bingley

The Bingley Antiques Centre
(John and Jennifer Poole). Keighley Rd. Tel Bradford (0274) 567316. Open Mon-Sat 9.30-5; Sun 2-5, early closing Tues, 12.30; other times by appt. General stock. Also container packing service available. Nearby trade warehouse with shipping goods.

E.Carrol (Fine Arts)
(E. Carrol). 5 Rushworth Hall, Keighley Rd, Crossflats, BD16 2EL. Closed Tues, Sat & Sun. General.

J.V.T. Antiques
(J. Van Der Tol). 76-78 Old Main St. Tel Bradford (0274) 566188. Open Mon-Sat 9.30-5; other times by appt. Antique & reproduction pine shipping furniture and some brass and copper.

Juliana
(Julie & Tina Capstick). 92 Main St. Tel Bradford (0274) 562994. Open Mon-Sat 10-5; other times by appt. General antiques.

Bradford STD 0274

Coach House Antiques
(Diane Rhodes). 27 Thackley Rd, Thackley, BD10 0RT. Tel 616789. Open by appt only. Large quantity of painted pine furniture, English, Irish, Welsh.

Collector's Corner
(C.S. & G.M.Douthwaite). 5-7 Frizinghall Rd, BD9 4LA. Tel 487098. Open daily 2-6pm; closed Thurs; other times by appt. Bygones and curios, clocks, gramophones, postcards, commemoratives, tins.

Early Music Shop
(R.H. Wood). 28 Sunbridge Rd, BD1 2AE. Tel 393753. Open Mon-Sat 9-5.30. Antique & reproduction musical instruments and kits for musical instruments.

John H.Raby & Son
(Michael E. Lewis, FRICS, Keith McLelland, FSVA). St Mary's Rd, BD8 7QL. Tel 491121/2/3. Open Mon-Fri 9-5.30; Sat 9-12. Auctioneers, estate agents, surveyors & valuers. Auctioneering, weekly sales (up to 500 lots). Antique auctions once a month.

Burley in Wharfedale
STD 0943

Richard Greene Antiques
(Richard Greene). 87 Main St, LS29 7JX. Tel 862156. Open Mon-Fri 9.30-5; Sat 9.30-12.30; other times by appt. Mainly furniture, 17th to mid 19thC.

Elland STD 0422

Andy Thornton Architectural Antiques Ltd
(Andy Thornton, Mrs Thornton, J.Bagshaw, F.Standbrook). Ainleys Industrial Estate, HX5 9JP. Tel 78125 (priv 0484 712636). Open Mon-Fri 8-5; Sat 8-12. Large stocks of architectural antiques including panelling, doors, etched, cut and stained glass, pew seating, panelled rooms, whole church and shop interiors, and decorative pub items, barfitters and suppliers of reproduction lighting.

Halifax STD 0422

Collectors Old Toys and Antiques
(John Haley). 89 Northgate, Northbridge. Tel 822148. Open Mon-Sat 10.30-5. Large selection on 3 floors. Collectors' toys, general and shipping antiques. Small antiques: china, glass, clocks etc. Always interested to receive offers of old toys.

Peter Gould
101 Northgate. Early furniture, metalware and decorative items.

Halifax Antiques Centre
(Marjorie E.Sykes, Muir Hewitt, Betty Stafford). Queens Road Mills, Queens Rd/ Gibbet St, HX1 4LR. Tel 66657. Open Tues-Sat 10-5. Antiques and collectors items - eighteen dealers with a wide selection of goods. Shipping warehouse. Cafe.

Muir Hewitt
(Mr Muir Peter Hewitt). Halifax Antiques Centre, Queens Rd Mills, Queens Rd/Gibbet St, HX1 4LR. Tel 66657 (priv 0274 882051). Open Tues-Sat 10-5; other times by appt. Art Deco pottery, porcelain, lamps and furniture, some Art Nouveau pewter, ceramics etc.

Hebden Bridge STD 0422

James Harrison
(George Ian Colmer Peace, ARICS). The Estate Office & Auction Room, 35 West End, HX7 8UQ. Tel 842007. Auctioneers - fortnightly sales on Tuesdays, antique, Victorian & Edwardian furnishings, china, glass, metalwares etc.

Huddersfield STD 0484

Bygones
(V. & H. Akroyd). 710 Manchester Rd, Cowlersley, HD4 5SP. Tel 842852. Open Mon & Fri, 2-4.45; Tues, Wed, Thurs, Sat, 10-4.45; other times by appt. General antiques, bric-a-brac, art pottery, Doulton, books, some prints.

David W.Dyson
Holme Court, New Mill. Specialist in arms and armour.

Eddisons Auctioneers
4-6 High St, HD1 2LS. Tel 533151. Auctioneers and chartered surveyors. Fortnightly auction sales of furnishings & effects. Quarterly collective sales of antiques, silver, jewellery, porcelain etc.

Fillans Antiques
(I.Fillan & G.Neary). 2 Market Walk, HD1 2QA. Tel 531609. Open Mon-Sat 9-5.30. Antique and secondhand jewellery, silver and old Sheffield plate. NAG

Ilkley STD 0943

Butterfields
(Jonathan Butterfield). The Auction Galleries, Riddings Rd, LS29 9LU. Tel 603313 (priv 0274-594068). Open Mon-Fri 9-5.30; Sat 9-12; other times by appt. Monthly sales of antique furniture, porcelain, pictures, silver.

J.H. Cooper & Son (Ilkley) Ltd
(Charles Cooper Snr. Charles Cooper Jnr). 33-35 Church St, LS29 9DR. Tel 608020. (Works at 50 Leeds Rd.) Open Mon-Sat 9-5.30; other times by appt. English and French furniture, silver, porcelain, copper, pewter and pictures. Valuations. LAPADA

Dacre, Son & Hartley
(A.D.Hartley). 1-5 The Grove, LS29 9HS. Tel 600655. (Salerooms at Victoria Hall, Little Lane, Ilkley.) Open Mon-Fri 9-5.30; Sat 9-12.30. Auctioneers holding approx 25 sales per year of general furnishings and shipping goods, catalogued sales of antiques, fine arts, silver, ceramics etc every two months. RICS

Manor Barn Pine
(Rose Farm Furniture Ltd). Burnside Mill, Main St, Addingham, LS29 0PJ. Tel Addingham (0943) 830176. Open Mon-Sat 8-6; other times by appt. Very large collection of high quality antique pine shipping goods.

Jack Shaw & Co Antique Silver
(Jon Shaw and Kay Shaw). The Old Grammar School, Skipton Rd, LS29 9EP. Tel 609467. Open 9.30-12.45, 2-5.30. Antique and modern silver, specialising in cutlery. Also some furniture.

J. & W. Tweed (H. Tweed)
4 Corn Mill, Menston, LS29 6BY. Tel 73964. Open by appt only. Furniture, clocks and silver. BADA

Wharfedale Galleries
(F.Bryan Ayers, Margaret J Ayers). Antiques & Pine, 17 Rupert Rd, Middleton, LS29 0AQ. Tel 602676. Open by appt only-Sat 10-5.30. 19thC - early 20thC oil paintings and watercolours.

Keighley STD 0535

Antiques & Pine
(M.Kelly & B.Ellison). Unit 6 Eastburn Mills, Eastburn, BD20 7SJ. Tel 53002. Open Mon-Sat 9-5; other times by appt. 12,000 sq ft finished & unfinished English & European pine and general antiques. Containers supplied and shipped.

Barleycote Hall Antiques
(R.Hoskins). 2 Janet St, Crossroads. Tel 44776. Open 7 days 11-5; other times by appt. Furniture, metalwork, clocks, porcelain. LAPADA

Real Macoy
(Janet Street). Crossroads. Tel 44776. Dealing exclusively in textiles including samplers, costume & linens.

Smith-Albany Antiques
(G. Waite). 60a Keighley Rd, Cowling. Tel Nelson (0282) 64356. Open Mon, Wed, & Thurs; Sat morning; other times by appt. General small antique shop dealing in whatever arises from quality antiques to general secondhand shipping goods.

Leeds STD 0532

The Antique Shop
226 Harrogate Rd, LS7 4QD. Tel 681785. Open Mon-Fri 9.30-5; other times by appt. Furniture, china, pictures, clocks, all types antique weapons.

Henson's Antiques
(H.J.S. Henson). 7A Chapel Place, North Lane, Headingley, LS6 3HY. Tel 751914. Open Mon-Thurs 9-6; Fri 9-4; Sat 9-1. Antique dealer.

Phillips Fine Art Auctioneers & Valuers
17A East Parade, LS1 2BU. Tel 448011. Open Mon-Fri 9-5, Sat 9-12. Valuation and auction of fine and decorative arts. SOFAA

P.D. & S. Solden
65 Mabgate, LS9 7DR. Tel 452229. Open Mon-Fri 9.30-12.30, 1.45-5; other times by appt. Large stock antiques & secondhand jewels.

St Paul's Gallery
Stowe House, 5 Bishopgate St. Art gallery.

Kingsway Antiques
(Terry Waddington). 223 New Road Side, Horsforth, LS18 4DR. Tel 587674. Open by phoning for appt; closed Wed. Jewellery, clocks, glass etc.

Wharf Salerooms
(Gary Donoughue, Elizabeth Donoughue). Canal Wharf, Water Lane, LS11 5PS. Tel 434464 (priv 667434). Open Mon 2pm & Tues 7pm; other times by appt. Auctioneers of antiques and household goods.

Windsor House Antiques (Leeds) Ltd
(D.K. Smith). 18/20 Benson St, LS7 1BL. Tel 444666. Open Mon-Fri 9-5, Sat 9-1. 18th and 19thC furniture, metalware, silver and plate, porcelain, Staffordshire pottery, clocks and oil lamps. LAPADA

Christopher Wray's Lighting Emporium
16 Headingly Lane. Tel 782653. Decorative lighting of the 1880s. Victorian and Edwardian lamps.

Mirfield STD 0924

Carol Brooke
9A Pratt Lane, WF14 9LX. Tel 492483. Open by appt. Royal commemorative ware, lace and linen, glassware.

Morley STD 0532

Phillips Auctioneers
20 Fountain St, LS27 9EH. Tel 523888. Open Mon-Fri 9-5.30. Valuation and auction of Victorian and reproduction furniture, household effects. SOFAA

Otley STD 0943

H. & M. Suttle
(Mrs D.M. Allott & Mrs S.M. Tankard). 18 Market Place, LS21 2AQ. Tel 462313. Open 10-5; other times by appt. Antique jewellery, china, silver.

Pudsey STD 0532

N. Geary Ltd
(J.A. Geary). 114 Richardshaw Lane. Tel 564122. Open Mon-Sat 10-5.30; closed Wed. Antique and 20thC furniture and shipping goods.

Thorpe Arch

Mavis Daniel Antiques
The Green, Thorpe Arch Village. Tel Leeds (0532) 813650. Open Thurs, Fri and Sat 2-5; other times by appt. 19thC small furniture, lamps, brass, copper etc.

Wakefield STD 0924

Marie Jordan Gallery
(Marie Jordan-Cooke). 659 Barnsley Rd, WF2 6HJ. Tel 255419. Contemporary crafts: ceramics, jewellery, original prints, glass, wood, textiles and watercolours. ICGA

Laidlaws
Crown Court Saleroom, Crown Court, off Wood St, WF1 2SU. Tel 375301. Open Mon-Fri 9-5.20; other times by appt. Auction saleroom (chartered surveyors).

Wetherby STD 0937

Raymond Tomlinson (Antiques) Ltd
(R.Tomlinson, C.Tomlinson). Northfield Buildings, Northfield Place, LS22 4TB. Tel 64866, 64870. Open Mon-Fri 8-5; other times by appt. Antique and shipping furniture dealers and exporters. Packing and shipping organised on premises. LAPADA

ISLANDS

How to Use This Book
After the editorial articles the book is divided into five main sections:
1 Directory *(begins on page 37)*
Dealers, auctioneers, packers, restorers, trade suppliers and so on are all listed here, with address, telephone number, opening hours, and type of business or area of specialisation. Entries are listed in alphabetical order under town or village, within the relevant county and geographical area.
2 Gazetteer *(begins on page 265)*
This is an alphabetical list of the towns and villages mentioned in the Directory, showing the counties and geographical areas under which they are listed.
3. Index to Specialists
(begins on page 270)
Directory entries are here listed under type of business or nature of stock.
4. Index to Business Names
(begins on page 363)
All business names in the Directory are listed alphabetically with their town or village, county and geographical area.
5 Maps *(begin on page 391)*
Showing villages and towns listed in the Directory.

Note
Counties and geographical areas are listed with page references under 'Contents' on page 3.
Auctioneers are listed both in the main Directory under the relevant town or village, and in the Specialists index under 'Auctioneers'.
Abbreviations and names and addresses of useful organisations are listed on page 4.

CHANNEL ISLANDS

Guernsey STD 0481

St Peter Port

Armatura
Sydney Vane House, Rue du Commerce. Tel 21625. Antique arms and armour.

Peter Cherry Antiques
17 Tudor House Shopping Centre, Mill St/Bordage. Tel 26808 (priv 711080). Open 10-1, 2-5; early closing Thurs. Old furniture, grandfather clocks, silver, brass, copper, china, glass, Victoriana & marine antiques. 1500 sq.ft.

J.& J.Hubbard Antiques
(J.A.& J.M.Hubbard). 11A Mill St. Tel 28462 (priv 28540). Open Mon-Sat 10-12.45, 2.15-5; other times by appt. Oriental works of art, including Chinese & Japanese porcelain, bronzes, wood & metalware from 1600-1900 & Japanese netsuke, inro & ivory carvings.

St Sampson's

The Old Curiosity Shop
(Mrs Adele Stevens-Cox). Commercial Rd. Tel 45324. Open Mon & Wed 9.30-4; Tues 9.30-12; Sat 9.30-2. Mixed stock, items of interest from 2000BC to 20thC, Channel Island silver.

Jersey STD 0534

St Helier

Christie's
(Representative: Richard de la Hey). 58 David Place. Tel 77582. Auctioneers and valuers.

Directory Entries are Free and ADDITIONS OR CORRECTIONS will be welcomed by *THE EDITOR, British Art and Antiques Directory, National Magazine House, 72 Broadwick Street, London W1V 2BP*

Dodo Antiques
(Jacqueline Harvey). 23 Peter St. Tel 71497 (priv 62275). Open Mon-Sat 10-12.30, 2-5; early closing Thurs; other times by appt. Dolls, toys, jewellery, china, glass, medals, militaria.

William C.Fox & Co Ltd
(Michael Sinel). 41 New St. Tel 22708 (priv 79001). Open 9-5.30 Mon-Sat; other times by appt. Minerals and fossils.

The Grange Gallery & Fine Arts Ltd
39 New St. Open Mon-Sat 9-5.30; other times by appt. 19thC oil paintings and watercolours, period and reproduction swept frames. Also restorers of paintings. Coin dealers.

Langlois Ltd
(A.G.Langlois, A.P.Langlois, J.A.Langlois). Don St. Tel 22441. (Also in St Peter Port, Guernsey.) Open Mon-Fri 9.5.30; other times by appt. Auctioneers and valuers. All types of antiques.

F. Le Gallais
Bath St. Tel 30202. Auctioneer.

Union Street Antique Market
(Arthur L.Thomson). 8 Union St. Tel 73805. Open Mon-Sat 10-5.30; other times by appt. General antiques.

St Lawrence

David Hick Antiques
(David & Rosemary Hick). Alexandra House, Carre Four Selous. Tel 62965. Open Mon-Sat 10-5; other times by appt. An interesting old property with an original Victorian shop selling quality period and Victorian furniture and smalls. Also a large trade warehouse including shipping goods. Goods can be exported to the mainland at competitive rates.

St Ouen

St Helier Galleries Ltd
(J.H.&M.A.Appleby, R.S.du Feu). Les Ormes, Ville au Bas. Tel 82332. Open by appt only. Oil paintings, watercolours, drawings and prints. BADA

ISLE OF MAN

Castletown STD 0624

J.& H.Bell Antiques
(Jessie Bell). 22 Arbory St. Tel 823132 (priv 822414). Open Mon, Wed, Fri, Sat 10-5. Furniture, silver, metalware, china, glassware, jewellery. LAPADA

Douglas STD 0624

Charles Alexander Ltd
(C.G.&S.J.Alexander). 41 Strand St. Tel 21527 (priv 822907). Open Mon-Sat 9-5.30. Antique and secondhand jewellery and silver. New jewellery in silver, gold and silver plate. Clocks and watches. In-house manufacturing and repair facility. NAG

Chrystals Auctions
(John Keefe). Athol St. Tel 3986. Open Mon-Fri 9-5. Auctioneers. Sale every week of general household furniture and effects, plus three general antique sales per year.

Kirk Michael STD 062 487

Church View House Antiques
(Philip Morrison). Tel 0624 87433. Late 18th and 19thC furniture, porcelain, silver etc. LAPADA

Peel STD 062 484

Castle Antiques
(Mr F.Quayle). 5 Castle St. Tel 3105. Open Mon, Wed, Sat; other times by appt. Antique and Manx items, including paintings, prints, maps and books.

The Golden Past
(Dorothea M.Horn, Lesley McPherson). 18A Michael St. Tel 2170. Open winter 2-4.30; summer 10.30-4.30; other times by appt. A large stock of general antiques, jewellery, silver, bric-a-brac, collectables & bygones. Also second hand and antiquarian books.

Jackson's
(James Jackson). 9 Castle St. (Also in Ramsey, Cambridgeshire.) General antiques.

Lesley McPherson Antiques
2 Crown St. Tel 2767. Open summer only Mon-Fri 1.45-5, Sat 10.30-5; other times by appt. Kitchenalia, pine, secondhand books, bric-a-brac.

ISLE OF WIGHT

See England

IRELAND

How to Use This Book
After the editorial articles the book is divided into five main sections:
1 Directory (*begins on page 37*)
Dealers, auctioneers, packers, restorers, trade suppliers and so on are all listed here, with address, telephone number, opening hours, and type of business or area of specialisation. Entries are listed in alphabetical order under town or village, within the relevant county and geographical area.
2 Gazetteer (*begins on page 265*)
This is an alphabetical list of the towns and villages mentioned in the Directory, showing the counties and geographical areas under which they are listed.
3. Index to Specialists
(*begins on page 270*)
Directory entries are here listed under type of business or nature of stock.
4. Index to Business Names
(*begins on page 363*)
All business names in the Directory are listed alphabetically with their town or village, county and geographical area.
5 Maps (*begin on page 391*)
Showing villages and towns listed in the Directory.

Note
Counties and geographical areas are listed with page references under 'Contents' on page 3.
Auctioneers are listed both in the main Directory under the relevant town or village, and in the Specialists index under 'Auctioneers'.
Abbreviations and names and addresses of useful organisations are listed on page 4.

EIRE

Co Clare

Shannon Airport

Mike McGlynn Antiques
Bunratty. Tel (061) 62011. Furniture, ceramics and general antiques. IADA

Co Cork

Castle Lyons

Mrs J. Benson
Tim's House, Ballyvolane. Tel (025) 36251. Furniture, ceramics and objects of art. IADA

Cork

The Antique Shop
(J.Feehan & A.Feehan). 43 McCurtain St. Tel (021) 504079. Open Mon-Fri 10-5.30; other times by appt. Furniture, paintings, prints, silver, books. IADA

Diana O'Mahony
8 Winthrop St. Tel (021) 276599. Silver, jewellery and small period furniture. Specialising in Georgian and Cork silver. IADA

Co Donegal

Donegal Town

Thomas Antiques and Fine Arts
(Sean & Noreen Thomas). Antique Shop, Diamond. Tel 21144 (priv 35024). Open 10-6; Wed 10-1 except Nov-April when closed Wed. Belleek specialists, jewellery, paintings & prints, general items of interest. IADA

Directory Entries
are Free and
ADDITIONS OR
CORRECTIONS
will be welcomed by
THE EDITOR,
British Art and Antiques Directory,
National Magazine House,
72 Broadwick Street,
London W1V 2BP

Co Dublin

Blackrock

Peter Linden
10 Rock Hill. Tel Dublin 885875. Oriental rugs and carpets. IADA

John O'Reilly
17 Greygates, Stillorgan Rd. Tel 882327. Open at all times by telephone appt. Consultant on valuations, commissions, family division etc. Will travel anywhere, regularly to Britain. Specialising in antique jewellery, silver, paintings, watercolours etc. IADA

Cloghran

Kilronan Antiques
(G.Dawson). Tel Dublin 403499. Period pine specialists with many interesting country pieces.

Dublin

James Adam and Sons
26 St Stephens Green. Tel 760261. Open Mon-Fri 9-1, 2-5.30. Fine art auctioneers and valuers. IAVI

Alexander Antiques
(Malcolm Alexander). 10 Duke St. Tel 718676. Open Mon-Sat 9.30-5.30. 18th and 19thC furniture, clocks, porcelain, glass etc. IADA

Anthony Antiques
7 Molesworth St. Tel 777222. Open Mon-Sat 9-6; other times by appt. Oil paintings, English and French furniture, copper, brass and chandeliers.

Antiqcurios & Irene Fine Art
(William Kearney & Irene O'Sullivan). 33 Clarendon St. Tel 714932. Open Mon-Sat 8.30-6; other times by appt. Antique furniture, porcelain, silver, Sheffield plate and antique jewellery. Fine glass. IADA

Balfes
(William Flynn). 4 Lower Ormond Quay. Tel 741263. 18th & 19thC furniture. IADA

Beaufield Mews Antiques
(Mrs Jill Cox). Woodlands Ave, Stillorgan. Tel 880375. 18th and 19thC furniture and general antiques. IADA

Patrick F. Brown
15 South William St. Tel 719013. Open Mon-Fri 10-5.30; other times by appt. Old master & 19thC paintings, 20thC Irish school paintings. IADA

Edward Butler
(Peter J. Butler-Bateman). 14 Bachelors Walk. Tel 730296. Open Mon-Fri 10.30-4.45. 17th to 19thC furniture, glass, porcelain, paintings and works of art. IADA

Cooke Antiques
(Paul Cooke). 79/85 Francis St. Tel 751885, 751250, 752251. Open Mon-Sat 9-6; other times by appt. Victorian and Georgian furniture and chimney-pieces. Also restorations. IADA

Courtville Antiques
(Grainne & Miriam Pierse). Powerscourt Townhouse Centre, South William St. Tel 710028. (Also in Tipperary.) Antique jewellery, silver, porcelain and objets d'art. IADA

Coyle Fine Art
(P.Coyle). 6 Lower Merrion St. Tel 762506. Open Mon-Fri 10-5.30, Sat 10-1. Fine 19thC European oils and watercolours.

H.Danker
10 South Anne St. Tel 774009. Open 9-5.30; early closing Sat; other times by appt. Silver, silver plate, paintings and jewellery. IADA

Dillon Antiques Ltd
(Anne Dillon, Helen Dillon, Val Dillon). 27 South Anne St. Tel 772142. Open Mon-Fri 9.30-5.30; Sat 9.30-1; other times by appt. 18th and 19thC Irish and English furniture. Also glass, china and silver, watercolour and oil paintings. IADA

John Duffy
(Michael P. Duffy). 10 Parnell St. Tel 747470. Open Mon-Fri 10-5.30; other times by appt. Furniture, paintings, silver brass and copper. Specialising in Victorian furniture and Irish pine.

Elizabeth Antiques
11 Patrick St, Dunlaoghaire. Tel 882092. Open 10.15-1, 2.30-5.30. Old silver, 18thC and Victorian glass, china, jewellery, curios, stamps and small furniture. IADA

European Fine Arts
(Dr Marie-Theres Schmitz). 6 Lower Merrion St. Tel 762506. Old Master paintings & drawings from the 16th-18thC. Continental prints.

Francis Street Antique Gallery
59 Francis St. Open Mon-Sat 11-5.30. 14 dealers in furniture, glass, china, jewellery, linen, silver, books etc,.

Fred Hanna Ltd
28 & 29 Nassau St. Tel 771255/6. Open 9-5.30; early closing Sat. New and secondhand books and old prints and maps of Irish interest.

Johnston Antiques
15 Castlepark Rd, Sandycove. Tel 801406. Shippers of fine furniture, Georgian and Victorian antiques, mirrors and objets d'art. IADA

Gerald A. Kenyon
Powerscourt Townhouse Centre, South William St. Tel 977345. (Also at 10,Great Strand St, Dublin. Tel 730625/730488.) Open Mon-Sat 10-6. Fine Georgian and Victorian furniture, china, paintings and works of art. IADA

Kildare Antiques
(Norah Breen). 19 Kildare St. Tel 763576 (priv 688194). Open Mon-Fri 10-6; early closing Sat; other times by appt. Furniture, porcelain, silver, paintings.

R.McDonnell Ltd
16 Kildare St. Tel 762614. Open Mon-Fri 10-5. Antiques, including furniture, paintings, porcelain, silver, glass and curios. IADA

Mitchell Antiques Ltd
(Mr and Mrs Lionel Mitchell). 40 Clarendon St. Tel 773922. Open Mon-Fri 9.30-5, Sat 9.30-1. Furniture, light fittings, marble and pine mantlepieces, clocks, brass, Sheffield plate, art objects etc. IADA

T.J.Mitchell Antiques Ltd
1a Lower Pembroke St. Tel 766881. Furniture, cabinet making, upholstering, french polishing, antique restoring.

John Morton Ltd
48/49 Nassau St. Tel 774462. Antique and secondhand jewellery and silver, also modern silver and souvenir jewellery. IADA

Neptune Gallery
(Bruce Arnold, Andrew Bonar). 41/42 South William St. Tel 715021. Open Mon-Fri 10-6, Sat 10-1; other times by appt. Antiquarian prints, maps, oils, watercolours, books. Specialising in anything to do with Ireland. IADA

Cynthia O'Connor & Company Ltd
(Sir Robert Goff, Lady Goff, Cynthia O'Connor). 17 Duke St. Tel 792198/792177. Open Mon-Fri 10-5.30; other times by appt. 18th, 19th & 20thC Irish paintings & watercolours. IADA

Oriel Gallery
(Oliver Nulty). 17 Clare St. Tel 763410, 684152. Open Mon-Fri 10-5.30, Sat 10-1; other times by appt. 19th to 20thC Irish paintings.

S.B.&J.Orken
33b Mill St. Tel 758707. Regency furniture, ceramics, brass and works of art. IADA

Ormond Antiques
32 Lower Ormond Quay. Tel 741569. Open Mon-Fri 10-5.30; other times by appt. 18th and 19thC furniture, glass, porcelain, including Belleek. Also pewter, copper, lamps, clocks and pictures. IADA

Rembrandt Antiques
(Mrs Phyllis Jackson). 24 South Anne St. Tel 779374. Open Mon-Fri 10-5.30; Sat 10-1; other times by appt. 18th and 19thC silver, porcelain, glass, jewellery, copper, pewter and objets d'art. IADA

M.Samuels (Antiques)
(Melvyn Samuels, Avril Samuels). 17 South Anne St. Tel 711262. Open Mon-Sat 9.30-5.30. (Also at 23 Powerscourt Townhouse Centre, Clarendon St, Dublin 2 and 4346 Lovers Lane, Dallas, Texas 75225 USA. Tel 214-739-009). Silver, jewellery, plated ware, Belleek, porcelain. IADA

Saskia Antiques
43 South William St. Tel 779711. Open Mon-Fri 10-5; other times by appt. 17th, 18th, 19thC furniture, fine rugs, carpets & paintings. IADA

The Silver Shop
23b Powerscourt Townhouse Centre, South William St. Tel 715093. Antique silver, porcelain, miniatures, objects of vertu. IADA

Sotheby's
(William Montgomery). 123a Upper Abbey St. Tel 734811. Open Mon-Fri 10-4. Main branch of Sotheby's (fine art auctioneers) in Ireland offering an advisory service with valuation for probate & insurance, and advice on purchase, sale, transport & shipping.

Weir & Sons (Antiques) Ltd
(D.A.N. Andrews, G.P.Moss, A.A.Kilpatrick, T.Jenkinson). 97 Grafton St. Tel 779678. Open Mon-Sat 9-5.30. Fine antique and secondhand silverware and jewellery, clocks and watches, paintings, furniture, objets d'art. Specialising in Irish silver. IADA, NAG

J.W.Weldon
55 Clarendon St. Tel 771638, 772742. (Also 18 South Anne St.) Open Mon-Fri 9.30-5.30, Sat 9.30-1. Antique silver and jewellery, specialising in provincial Irish silver. IADA

Malahide

Malahide Castle Antiques
(Matt McNulty). Malahide Castle. Tel Dublin 952655. Irish furniture, bygones, country furniture & country items. IADA

Sandycove

The Georgian Shop
(Paul and Chris Johnston). 15 Castlepark Rd. Tel 801406. Shippers for fine furniture, Georgian and Victorian antiques, mirrors, and objects of art. IADA

Co Galway

Oughterard

Oughterard Antiques
Main St. Tel 45. Open 10-5.30. Early Georgian furniture, silver and pictures. IADA

Co Kerry

Killorglin

The Antique Shop
(Henry W. de Courcy Dodd). Main St. Tel (064) 31234. (Also at The Antique Shop, College Sq, Killarney.) Small period furniture, sporting prints, oil paintings, watercolours, silver, pewter, glass etc. IADA

Co Kilkenny

Kilkenny

Christopher Wray's Lighting Emporium
26 Patrick St. Tel 22776. (Main branch in London.) Decorative lighting of the 1880s. Victorian and Edwardian lamps.

Co Limerick

Adare

George Stacpoole
(George H.Stacpoole). Tel (061) 94409. (Also at 35 Cecil Street, Limerick Tel 061 45433.) Open Mon-Sat 10-5.30; other times by appt. 18th and 19thC furniture, silver, porcelain, paintings ,prints and objets d'art. At Cecil Street shop: Antiquarian & secondhand books and prints. IADA

Glin

Christie's
(Representative : Desmond Fitz-Gerald). Glin Castle. Tel (priv) Dublin 680585. Auctioneers and valuers.

Limerick

Antiques
95 Lower Henry St. Tel 45949. Open Mon-Sat; other times by appt. Silver, glass, porcelain, pictures and works of art.

John Dunphy Antiques
(John Dunphy). 83-84 Upper Henry St. Tel (061) 316732 (priv 52673). Open Mon-Sat 10-5.30; other times by appt. Good quality 18th and 19thC furniture, clocks, mirrors and works of art. IADA

George Stacpoole
35 Cecil Street. Tel (061) 45433. (Also in Adare, Co Limerick.) Open Mon-Fri 10-5.30; other times by appt. 18th and 19thC furniture, silver, porcelain, prints, paintings and objets d'art. IADA

Co Louth

Drogheda

Greene's Antique Galleries
(Austin Greene). The Mall. Tel (041) 36212, 38286. Open Mon-Sat 9-6; closed Wed. Extensive Victorian/Edwardian furniture. Large collection Irish silver. Irish watercolours. IADA

Co Mayo

Westport

Earl of Altamont
Westport House. Tel Westport 308. Items of general interest; books. IADA

Co Offaly

Ferbane

The Antique Shop
Upper Main St. Open 10-10. Silver, copper, brass, glass, pewter and furniture.

Co Tipperary

Roscrea

Victor Mitchell Exports Ltd
(Victor Mitchell). Mount Butler. Tel (0505) 21396. Open Mon-Sat. Georgian & Victorian furniture, pine furniture, brass, copper, porcelain, glass, pictures, curios. IADA

Tipperary

Courtville Antiques
(Catherine Pierse). The Corner House, St Michael's St. Tel (062) 51249. (Also in Dublin.) Open 10-6; early closing Wed; other times by appt. Antique jewellery, silver, porcelain and objets d'art. IADA

Co Waterford

Ballyduff

The Lodge
Flower Hill. Tel 6 and 29. Open 11-6; other times by appt. Small antiques, including glass, silver, furniture, china, prints, Irish crafts.

Tramore

The Antique Shop
(Thomas O'Neill). Main St. Tel (051) 81548. Open 7.30pm-9pm. 18th and 19thC furniture, silver, china and glass. IADA

Co Wexford

Enniscorthy

Warren Gallery
(Mrs B. Warren). Castle Hill. Tel (054) 33721. Open Mon-Fri 9-6, Sat 10-1, 2-5; appt preferred. Mainly 19th and 20thC oil paintings, watercolours and bronzes. IADA

Co Wicklow

Avoca

Thomas Murtagh Antiques
Tinnahinch House. Silver, jewellery, general. IADA

NORTHERN IRELAND

Belfast

Belfast STD 0232

The Bell Gallery
(James Nelson Bell). 13 Adelaide Park, off Malone Rd. Tel 662998. Open Mon-Fri 9-5; 9-1 Sat except June, July, Aug; other times by appt. Paintings and drawings, particularly 18th and 19thC Irish and Victorian English. Also small furniture and bronzes. FATG

Tom Caldwell Galleries Ltd
(Tom Caldwell, Christopher Caldwell, Molly Caldwell). 40/42 & 56 Bradbury Place, BT7. Tel 223226 (priv 0846 621352). Open Mon-Fri 10-5; Sat 10-1; other times by appt. 18th & 19thC English & Irish furniture, also ceramics & paintings. IADA

Emerald Isle Books
(John A. Gamble & Mrs J.E.Gamble). 539 Antrim Rd, BT15 3BU. Tel 771798. Open Mon-Fri 9-5; other times by appt. Antiquarian booksellers, mainly books relating to Ireland, also theology, travel, illustrated and reference works. ABA

Kavanagh Antiques
(Joseph Kavanagh). 27 Smithfield, BT1 1JE. Tel 220000. Open 9-5. Large stock of all kinds of antiques, including coins, medals, pistols, silver, glass, Victoriana and other items.

Charlotte and John Lambe
41 Shore Rd. Tel 777761. 19thC English and French furniture, pictures and works of art. IADA

Osborne King & Megran
(J.R.B.Williams-Ellis). Castle Arcade Buildings, 17 Castle Arcade, BT1 5DG. Tel 240332. Open 9.15-5; other times by appt. Auctioneers of fine art. Estate agents and surveyors.

Treasure House
(Thomas Harper Kearney, Marie Kearney). 123 University St, BT7 1HP. Tel 231055. Open Mon-Sat 10-6; other times by appt. Antiques and reproduction furniture. Main business: restoration of all types of furniture, polishing and upholstery.

Ulster Coin Centre & William Rodman
83 Dublin Rd. Tel 40052. Open Mon-Fri 9-5, Sat 9-1. Large stock of coins, medals and banknotes.

Co Antrim

Bushmills STD 026 57

Brian R. Bolt Collector's Antiques
(Brian R. Bolt). 88 Ballaghmore Road, Portballintrae, BT57 8RL. Tel 31129. Open by appt only. Antique smallware, including all types of snuff-boxes, small & large antique silver, any unusual collector's items including vestas, vinaigrettes, scent bottles, wine labels, spoons & treen items. Overseas & trade enquiries welcome.

Dunluce Antiques
(Mrs J.C.Ross & W.P.Ross). 33 Ballytober Rd. Tel 31140. Open Mon-Sat 2-6; closed Fri & Sun; other times by appt. General stock of antiques, specialising in 18th and 19thC British porcelain and furniture. Restorers of porcelain and furniture.

Carrickfergus STD 096 03

The Antique Shop
(Robert Huffam). Glynn Park, Taylors Ave. Tel 63284. Open Tues-Sat 10-1, 2-5. Furniture, 18th and 19thC silver, quilts and patchworks, natural history items. IADA

Larne STD 0574

Albert Graham Ltd
(A.M.Graham). 98-100 Main St. Tel 76655 (priv 73134). Open 9.30-5.30; closed Tues; other times by appt. Georgian to Edwardian furniture. Mainly shipping and wholesale. LAPADA

Newtownabbey

New Abbey Antiques
(Anne MacHenry & Rupert MacHenry). Caragh Lodge, Glen Rd, BT37 0RY. Tel Whiteabbey (0231) 62036. Open any time. Furniture, paintings, pottery and porcelain. BADA, IADA

Portrush STD 0265

Alexander Antiques
(Mr & Mrs R. Alexander & D. Alexander). 108 Dunluce Rd, BT56 8NB. Tel 822783. Open Mon-Sat 10-6; other times by appt. Georgian, Victorian and Edwardian furniture, British porcelain, 18th to 20thC British & Irish silver.

Seaview Antiques
(Mrs B Macafee). 110 Dunluce Road, BT56 8NB.

Co Down

Bangor STD 0247

Hugh Greer
29 Hamilton Rd. Tel 5014. Irish literature and topography. ABA

Downpatrick STD 0396

Christie, Manson and Woods Ltd
(Representative: John Lewis-Crosby). Marybrook House, 9 Raleagh Rd, Crossgar, BT30 9JG. Tel 830574. Open 9-5 weekdays. Fine art auctioneers and valuers.

Groomsport

The Gallery No.10
(W.A. McFadden). 10 Bangor Rd. Tel Bangor (0247) 464376. Open 9.30-5.30, except Thurs; other times by appt. Picture framer, restorer, retailer of original paintings and of engravings and etchings. FATG

Helen's Bay STD 0247

Maypole Antiques
(Mrs Margaret Kerr). Horse Rock, 18 Grey Point. Tel 853640. Open by appt. China, glass, silver, brass, pewter and furniture.

Hillsborough STD 0846

Stonewall Antiques
(R.J.Johnson). 21 Lisburn St. Tel 682117. Open Tues-Sat 11-5; other times by appt. A small shop in a conservation area stocking small silver items, porcelain, ironstone, linens and laces, jewellery, bric-a-brac etc.

Holywood STD 023 17

Hamilton Antiques
(Mr & Mrs H.D.Deering). 19 Shore St. Tel 4404. Open Tues-Sat 9.30-5. Period silver, porcelain, glass, furniture, Victorian jewellery, paintings, jade and ivory. BADA, IADA

Newry STD 0693

Downshire House Antiques
(H. & R. McCabe). 63 Downshire Rd, BT34. Tel 66689. (Also McCabes Antiques, Newry.) Open Mon-Sat 9-1 2-6; Sun 2-6. 18th and 19thC furniture. LAPADA

McCabes Antiques
(Hugh and Raymond McCabe). 11-12 St Marys St. Tel 2695 (priv 5178). (Also at Downshire House Antiques, Newry.) Open Mon-Sat 9.30-1, 2-5.30; closed Wed; other times by appt. 18th and 19thC furniture. LAPADA

Newtownards STD 0247

The Antique Shop
(Marjorie McAuley). 7 Main St, Greyabbey, BT22 2RP. Tel Kirkcubbin (024 771) 333. Open Wed 2-5.30; Fri, Sat 11.30-5.30. General antiques.

Old Cross Antiques
(Clifford J. Auld). 3-5 Main St, Greyabbey, BT22 2NE. Tel Greyabbey (024 774) 346. Open Mon 2-5.30; Tues-Sat 10.30-5.30; closed Thurs; other times by appt. 18th, 19th & 20thC furniture, silver, porcelain. Also bric-a-brac.

Sotheby's
(Representative: William Montgomery). The Estate Office, Greyabbey. Tel Greyabbey (024 774) 668. Auctioneers & valuers.

Co Tyrone

Cookstown STD 064 87

The Saddle Room Antiques
(Christopher J.Leitch). 4 Coagh St, BT80 8NQ. Tel 64045 (priv 62033). (Home:Rosecroft, Lower Claggan, Cookstown.) Open Tue & Thurs 10-5.30; Fri & Sat 10-6; other times by appt. Jewellery, silver, porcelain, furniture, general antiques.

SCOTLAND

How to Use This Book
After the editorial articles the book is divided into five main sections:
1 Directory (*begins on page 37*)
Dealers, auctioneers, packers, restorers, trade suppliers and so on are all listed here, with address, telephone number, opening hours, and type of business or area of specialisation. Entries are listed in alphabetical order under town or village, within the relevant county and geographical area.
2 Gazetteer (*begins on page 265*)
This is an alphabetical list of the towns and villages mentioned in the Directory, showing the counties and geographical areas under which they are listed.
3. Index to Specialists
(*begins on page 270*)
Directory entries are here listed under type of business or nature of stock.
4. Index to Business Names
(*begins on page 363*)
All business names in the Directory are listed alphabetically with their town or village, county and geographical area.
5 Maps (*begin on page 391*)
Showing villages and towns listed in the Directory.

Note
Counties and geographical areas are listed with page references under 'Contents' on page 3.
Auctioneers are listed both in the main Directory under the relevant town or village, and in the Specialists index under 'Auctioneers'.
Abbreviations and names and addresses of useful organisations are listed on page 4.

Borders

Coldstream STD 0890

Coldstream Antiques
(John and Ann Trinder). 44 High St, TD12 4AS. Tel 2552. Open Mon-Sat 9-6; other times by appt. Res on prem. 17th to 19thC furniture and small items.

Jedburgh STD 0835

R. & M. Turner Ltd, Antiques and Fine Art
(Mr & Mrs R.J.Turner). 34/36 High St. Tel 63445. Open Mon-Sat 10-5; closed Thurs; other times by appt. Large general stock of furniture, paintings, porcelain and jewellery of the 18th to 20thC. General shipping warehouse. LAPADA

Kelso STD 0573

The Curiosity Shop
(H. & B.V. Cox). 27 Horsemarket. Tel 24541. Open Mon-Sat 10-5; other times by appt. Jewellery, silver, porcelain, glass,furniture, paintings & watercolours, decorative antiques & curios of all descriptions.

Christopher Wood
(Christopher Wood). Harlaw Farmhouse, TD5 7RA. Tel Stichill (05737) 321. Open by appt only. Antique clocks, watches, chronometers, scientific and navigational instruments, regulators and precision electrical clocks.

St Boswells STD 0835

William Bruce & Co
(William Bruce, Diana Bruce). Mainhill, Charlesfield, TD6 0HG. Tel 23628 23788. Open Tues-Fri 10.30-5.30; Sat 10.30-12.30; other times by appt. European & British paintings and watercolours, also contemporary.

Chriscotts Antiques
Dall House, The Crescent.

Directory Entries are Free and ADDITIONS OR CORRECTIONS will be welcomed by *THE EDITOR, British Art and Antiques Directory, National Magazine House, 72 Broadwick Street, London W1V 2BP*

West Linton STD 0968

Alex M. Frizzell
Castlelaw, EH46 7AA. Tel 60450. Scottish books, typography and antiquarian books. ABA

Central

Bannockburn STD 0786

Elizabeth Paterson Antiques
(Mrs Paterson). 1A Main St. Tel Stirling (0786) 816392. LAPADA

Killin STD 056 72

Maureen H.Gauld
(James A. & Maureen H. Gauld). Main Street. Tel 475. Open 10-5, April-Oct; other times by appt. General goods of the 18th, 19th, 20thC.

Dumfries & Galloway

Castle Douglas STD 0556

R.& L. Hampshire Antiques
(Mr & Mrs R. Hampshire). Rutherford Hall, Gatehouse of Fleet, DG7 4HS. Tel Gatehouse (05574) 616. Large stock of furniture including shipping goods. Valuations. LAPADA

Dumfries STD 0387

Thomson Roddick & Laurie Ltd
60 Whitesands. Tel 5366. (Also in Carlisle, Cumbria, England.) Open Mon-Fri 9-5. Auctioneers of furniture, fine art and antiquarian books.

Moffat STD 0683

T.W.Beaty
22 Well St. Tel 20380. (Also at Academy Rd.) Open Mon-Sat 9.15-5; other times by appt. 18th and 19thC furniture, china, glass, silver, pictures etc. Also large warehouse of shipping furniture. LAPADA

Fife

St Andrews STD 0334

Bookranger
(J.W.B. Laing). 14 Hepburn Gardens. Tel 75066. Modern first editions, English literature, art, illustrated books and biography. ABA

Mortimer & Hughes
13 Queens Gardens.

Grampian

Aberdeen STD 0224

Antiques
(James Benzie). 651 George St, AB2 3XQ. Open Mon-Sat 1-4. Glass, china, silver plate, silver, pictures and all small objects of vertu.

Atholl Antiques
(Gordon Murray). 322 Great Western Rd. Tel 593547. Open 10.30-1, 2.30-6; other times by appt. 19th and 20thC Scottish paintings, 18th and 19thC furniture, china, rugs.

John Bell of Aberdeen Ltd
Balbrogie, by Blackburn. Tel 79209. Open Mon-Fri 9-5; other times by appt. Georgian antique furniture. BADA

George Bewes & Co
235 George St. Tel 635830. Open 6 days. Fine art dealers, paintings, prints and watercolours.

James G.Bissett Ltd
99 High St, Old Aberdeen. Tel 46102. Antiquarian books.

John Milne
(R.J.F.Milne, A.D.Milne). The Bon-Accord Auction Rooms, 9-11 North Silver St. Tel 639336. Auctioneers.

The Rendezvous Gallery
100 Forest Ave. Tel 323247. Open Mon-Thurs 10-6, Sat 10.30-6; other times by appt. Art nouveau, art deco, glass, jewellery and furniture, Scottish oils and watercolours. LAPADA

Studio Morgan. Commercial Photography Co
6-7 Queens Gardens. Tel 631250. Open Mon-Fri 8.30-5.30; other times by appt. General commercial and production of transparencies for reproduction of paintings. BIPP

Thistle Antiques
(Mrs P.Bursill). 28 Esslemont Ave. Tel 634692. Open Mon-Fri 10-5; Sat 10-1, Wed 10-1. General antiques and jewellery. LAPADA

J.R.Webb
23 Bon Accord Terrace. Tel 26709. Jewellery, silver and furniture. Specialist in export, mainly to the trade.

Colin Wood Antiques Ltd
(Colin Wood). 25 Rose St, AB1 1TX. Tel 643019. Open Mon-Fri 10-12.30, 2.15-5; Sat 10-12, 2.15-4; other times by appt. Antique furniture, Scottish paintings, Scottish silver, metalwork, ceramics and bygones.

J.H.Wood
Thistle Antiques, 2D Thistle St, AB1 1XJ. Tel 645008. General antiques, furniture, china, jewellery and brass.

William Young (Antiques) Ltd
1 Belmont St, AB1 1JR. Tel 644757. Open Mon-Fri; early closing Sat. Large stock of 18th and 19thC furniture and fine art, silver and glass. BADA

Aboyne STD 0339

Sotheby's
(Representative: Earl of Aboyne). Aboyne Castle. Tel Banchory (03302) 4007. Auctioneers and valuers.

Alford STD 0336

R.S. Gordon Antiques
Main St. Tel 2404. General antiques, clocks, musical boxes and bric-a-brac.

Ballater STD 0338

The McEwan Gallery
(Dr & Mrs P.J.McEwan). The Bridge of Gairn (on A939), AB3 5UB. Tel 55429. Open daily. Paintings, watercolours and prints. Old Scottish, Polar and sporting books. LAPADA

Banchory STD 033 02

Sunfield Cottage Antiques
(H.B. Henderson & Mrs Lorna Henderson). Sunfield Cottage, Inchmarlo, AB3 4AT. Tel 2703. Open Mon-Sat 9-6; Sun 1.30-5; other times by appt. Porcelain, clocks and watches, glass, silver. Small furniture, copper and brass. Antique clocks and watches repaired.

Bieldside

Bieldside Antiques
(Mr & Dr James). 85 North Deeside Rd. Tel Aberdeen (0224) 867339. Open Mon-Sat 9.30-5; other times by appt. Silver, china, glass, furniture and jewellery. LAPADA

Elgin STD 0343

West End Antiques
(Frank Stewart). 35 High St. Tel 7531 (priv 3216). Open 9.30-5 Mon-Sat; other times by appt. Silver, watches, jewellery, furniture, brass, copper, china and general bric-a-brac. HADA

Inverurie STD 0467

Christie's
(Agent: Lord Inverurie). The Stables, Keith Hall, AB5 0LD. Tel 24366. Auctioneers and valuers.

Highland

Beauly STD 0463

Iain Marr Antiques
(Iain & Avril Marr). 3 Mid St, IV4 7DP. Tel 782372. Open Mon-Sat 10.30-5.30 (closed Thurs); other times by appt. Silver, especially Georgian and Scottish, jewellery, glass, scientific instruments, oil lamps, oil paintings and watercolour paintings, small furniture, firearms and porcelain. HADA

Dingwall STD 0349

Claisabhrea Antiques
Tulloch St. Tel 2228. Open Mon-Fri 10-1, 3-6; other times by appt. Large stock, including Victorian reproduction furniture, jewellery.

Drumnadrochit STD 045 62

Joan Frere Antiques
Drumbuie House. Tel 210. Open 9-8 May-Oct; other times by appt. English oak furniture prior to 19thC and general antiques, specialising in interior decoration and design.

Fearn STD 086 283

Christie's
(Agent: John Douglas-Menzies). Mounteagle. Tel 2866. Auctioneers and valuers.

Fortrose STD 0381

Black Isle Antiques
Tel 20988. Clocks, china, silver. HADA

Inverness STD 0463

The Attic
Newmarket Close, 34 Church St. Period clothes, linen, textiles & art deco & jewellery. HADA

Past and Present
(Mr & Mrs L.Weurman). 19 Market Brae. Tel 226185 (priv 223583). Open Mon-Sat 10-5; other times by appt. Porcelain, brass, prints, jewellery, silver, bygones and curios. HADA

Kiltarlity by Beauly STD 046 374

Old Pine Furniture and Jouet
(Alison and John Jeorrett). 8 Kinerras, IV4 7JL. Tel Kiltarlity (046374) 261. Open all week, by appt only. Manufacture of wooden toys and small items of pine furniture. Any item in pine can be made to order. Traditional designs.

Kingussie STD 054 02

Colin Murdoch
56 High St, PH21 1HZ. Tel 552. Open Mon-Sat 9.30-1, 2.15-5.30; early closing Wed. (Appt advisable in winter months.) Oil paintings, watercolours, drawings, prints, maps, books and some antique furniture.

Muir of Ord STD 0463

Beauly Antiques
Achnasoul, Marybank. Tel Urray (09973) 254. Furniture and shipping goods.

Nairn STD 0667

Donald Ellis Antiques
St Ninian Rd. Tel 53303. Open 10-1, 2-5.30; closed Wed, Sun. 18th and early 19thC furniture, china, glass, silver.

Highland Antiques
2 Bridge St. Tel 53614. 19thC furniture and paintings. General antiques. HADA

Newtonmore STD 054 03

The Antique Shop
Main St, PH20 1DD. Tel 272 (priv 05402 487). Open Mon-Sat 9-6; other times by appt. General antiques. HADA

Thurso STD 0847

J.Miller Calder
12 Traill St. Tel 2002. Open 9-1, 2-6; early closing Thurs; other times by appt. Antique furniture, silver, china, pictures and maps. Also modern furniture.

The Ship's Wheel
(Mr A.H. & Miss H.E.Monro). 2 Traill St, KW14 8EJ. Tel 62485 (priv 62018). Open Mon-Sat 9-1, 2-5; Thurs 9-1; Oct-May 10-12, 2-4, closed Thurs. General antiques, specialising in furniture, pottery, porcelain, prints, maps and export goods. HADA

Thurso Antiques
(G. Atkinson, J. Atkinson). Drill Hall, Sinclair St. Tel 63291 (priv 66202). Open Mon-Sat 10-1, 2-5; early closing Thurs; other times by appt. Antique jewellery, silver, porcelain, coins, oil paintings & watercolours. Restoration of paintings, jewellery repairs. HADA

Lothian

East Linton STD 0620

Straight Lace
(Nina Salkovskis). 9 High St, EH40 3AA. Tel 860017 (priv 062088 284). Open by appt or luck. Lace, linen, crochet. Collectors items, tiles, tin boxes, domestic pottery & wood ware.

Edinburgh STD 031

Another World
(Dorothy E. Harrison). 25 Candlemaker Row, EH1 2QG. Tel 661 0723. Open Wed, Fri & Sat 12-5; other times by appt. Netsuke and oriental art.

Antique Market
(R.A. Mitchell). 72 St Stephen St. Tel 225 6016. Open Tues-Sat 10-12.30, 2-5.30. Furniture.

Avarice Antiques
(Gordon Fleming). 24 St Stephen St. Tel 225 7237. Open Mon-Sat 11-4; other times by appt. Mainly 19th & early 20thC furniture.

Joseph Bonnar
(Joseph Bonnar). 72 Thistle St. Tel 226 2811. Open Mon-Sat 10.30-5; other times by appt. Antique and period jewellery, objects of vertu.

Bourne Fine Art Ltd
(P.S.Bourne). 4 Dundas St, EH3 6HZ. Tel 557 4050. (Also at Bourne Frames & Restoration, 79 Cumberland St.) Open Mon-Fri 10-6, Sat 10-1. British paintings 1800-1950 and The Decorative Arts.

Bourne Frames & Restoration Ltd
(P.S.Bourne, N. McGill Duncan). 79 Cumberland St, EH3 6RD. Tel 557 4874. Suppliers of modern and reproduction handmade frames; suppliers, restorers and gilders of antique frames. Oil painting and watercolour restoration.

Margaret Brown Antiques
14-16 St Stephen St. Tel 661 3764. Open Mon-Sat 12-5.30; closed Wed. Furniture, glass, porcelain, jewellery.

Calton Gallery
(Andrew & Sarah Whitfield). 10 Royal Terrace, EH7 5AB. Tel 556 1010. Open Mon-Sat 10-6; other times by appt. Wide selection of fine 19th and early 20thC British and European paintings and watercolours by over 100 artists. Some sculpture.

The Carson Clark Gallery
(A.Carson Clark FRGS). (Scotiamaps - Mapsellers), 173 Cannongate, The Royal Mile, EH8 8BN. Tel 556 4710. Open Mon-Sat 10.30-5.30; other times by appt. Antique maps, atlases, sea charts and topographic prints. Books on travel and discovery.

Castle Antiques
(Harry Parry). 330 Lawnmarket, ME1 1JT. Tel 225 7615. Open Mon-Fri 9.30-5.30. Antique furniture, porcelain, silver, glass and pewter.

Christie's
(Representative: Michael Clayton). 5 Wemyss Place. Tel 225 4756/7. Auctioneers and valuers.

Paul Couts Ltd
101-107 West Bow, Victoria St. Tel 225 3238. Open Mon-Fri 9-1, 2.30-5.30; Sat 9.30-1; other times by appt. Good stock of 18thC English furniture and furnishings; Continental and Oriental items. BADA

M.J.Dareau
66 Cumberland St. Tel 556 9352 & 0968 73028. Open by appt. Clocks of all periods but especially collectors', early and unusual items, barometers, watches, musical boxes and scientific instruments.

Eric Davidson (Antiques) Ltd
(Eric Davidson). 4 Grassmarket, EH1 2JU. Tel 225 5815. Open Mon-Fri 9-5.30, Sat 9-1; other times by appt. English and Continental antique furniture, oil paintings, grandfather clocks, Persian rugs, silver and plate.

John Dewar
2 North East Circus Place, EH3 6SP. Tel 225 2691. Photographer. LBIPP

A.F.Drysdale
(James Thomson, Angus Williamson & David Gillon). 35 North West Circus Place, EH3 6TW. Tel 225 4686. Open Mon-Fri 10-1, 2-5; Sat 10-1; other times by appt. Interior decorators. Also decorative furniture and selected antiques.

Dunedin Antiques Ltd
(David Ingram, Graham Niven). 4 North West Circus Place. Tel 226 3074. Open Mon-Sat 9.30-5.30. Furniture and architectural items. Associated interior design business.

Edinburgh Antiques Market
(Peter and Julia London). 5A Johnston Terrace. Open daily 10-6. A variety of individual dealers with comprehensive stocks of all types of antiques.

Donald Ellis Antiques
(Donald Ellis). 9 Bruntsfield Place. Tel 229 1819. Open Mon-Sat 9.30-5.30; other times by appt. General antiques, including furniture, china, silver, glass, jewellery, Scottish pottery.

Fine Art Gallery
(P.G.Ross). 41 Dundas St, EH3 6QQ. Tel 557 4569. Open Mon-Sat 10-5.30; other times by appt. Drawings, paintings, watercolours.

The Fine Art Society Plc
12 Great King St, EH3 6QL. Tel 556 0305. (Also in Glasgow and London.) Open Mon-Fri 9.30-5.30, Sat 10-1. 19th and 20thC British paintings and watercolours, with an emphasis on Scottish artists.

Fyfe's Antiques
(H.P.Fyfe & A.M.Fyfe). 41 & 48 Thistle St, EH2 1DY. Tel 225 4287. Open Mon-Fri 10.30-5; other times by appt. Fine stock of paintings, furniture and shipping goods.

Georgian Antiques
19 Windsor Place. Tel 661 0249.

Grange Bookshop
(David & Kristina McNaughton). 186 Causewayside, EH9 1PN. Tel 667 2759 (priv 03617 311). Open Mon-Sat 10-5. General secondhand and antiquarian books, folk-lore and general. ABA

John Grant
9A & 13C Dundas St. Tel 556 9698. Open Tues-Sat 9.30-5.30; other times by appt. Early prints, maps, antiquarian books and fine bindings. ABA

Hand in Hand
(Mr & Mrs O.F. Hand). 3 North West Circus Place, EH3 6ST. Tel 226 3598. Open Tues-Sat 10-5.30. Period costumes, Victorian furnishings, antique lace wedding gowns, paisley & embroidered shawls, textiles & linen.

Herrald Antiques
38 Queen St. Tel 225 5939. Open Mon-Fri 9-5, Sat 9-1. Antique and reproduction furniture. Persian rugs, brass and copper, general items.

E. Humphrey
38 Victoria St, EH1 2HH. Tel 226 3625. Open mornings or by appt. Paintings, etchings, collectors' items, postcards, china and glass.

A.G.Ingram Ltd
74 Broughton St. Tel 556 7824. Photographers.

Malcolm Innes Gallery
67 George St. Tel 226 4151. Open Mon-Fri 9.30-6; Sat 10-1; other times by appt. Scottish landscape, sporting and natural history pictures.

Kenneth Jackson (Antiques)
66 Thistle St. Tel 225 9634. Open Mon-Sat 9.30-5; other times by appt. Paintings. Specialists in French, Provincial, lacquer and oak furniture. Also 17th and 18thC English and Continental furniture.

Letham Antiques
(Mrs J.Letham). 20 Dundas St, EH3 6HZ. Tel 556 6565. Open Tues-Sat 10-5.30; other times by appt. General antiques, including furniture, Victorian jewellery, objects of vertu, paintings and watercolours, silver.

David Letham
(David Letham). 17A Dundas St. Tel 557 4466 (priv 225 7399). Open Mon-Sat 11-6; other times by appt. Antique furniture and decorative objects. BADA

Greig Linton Antiques
95 West Bow. Tel 226 6946. Open Mon-Sat 10-5.30. Pictures, art nouveau, bronzes, porcelain and decorative items.

Michael Maclaren Photography
322 Webster's Land, EH1 2RU. Tel 228 6895. Photographer.

William MacAdam
86 Pilrig St, EH6 5AS. Tel 553 1364. Open strictly by appt. 18th & early 19thC glass, collectors pieces, coloured glass, usable glass, glass curiosities. BADA

William MacIntosh & Co
(Peter and Julia London). 5 Johnston Terrace, EH1 2PW. Tel 225 6113. Open Mon-Sat 10-7, Sun 11-6; other times by appt. Architectural brassmongery, brassware and general antiques. Trade supplied.

John Mathieson & Co
48 Frederick St. Tel 225 6798, 225 6686. Open Mon-Fri 9-5.30, Sat 9-4.30. Fine art dealers, paintings, prints, watercolours.

McNaughtan's Bookshop
(Elizabeth A.Strong). 3A & 4A Haddington Place, EH7 4AE. Tel 556 5897. Open Tues-Sat 9.30-5.30; other times by appt. Scottish and general literature, general juvenile, topographical and travel books, art & architecture. ABA

D. & N.Nairne Antiques
(David Nairne, Norma Nairne). 25A Dundas St, EH3 6QQ. Tel 557 0978(priv 0764 70298). Open Mon-Fri 10-5.30; other times by appt. 18th-19thC furniture, ceramics, paintings, objets d'art. LAPADA

John Nelson
22-24 Victoria St, EH1 2JW. Tel 225 4413 (priv 667 5275). Open Mon-Fri 10-12, 1.30-5, Sat 10-1, 2-5; other times by appt. Good stock of old maps and prints, specialising in Scotland and watercolours.

Old Golf Shop Inc
13 Albany St, EH1 3PY. Tel 556 1944 (priv 663 7647). (Also 325 West Fifth St, Cincinnati, Ohio 45202, USA.) Largest dealer in golf memorabilia in the world. Also tennis items.

The Penny Farthing
7-8 Beaufort Rd. Tel 447 2410. Open Mon-Sat 10-12.30, 2.30-5.30. General antiques, specialising in upholstered furniture.

Phillips
65 George St, EH2 2JL. Tel 225 2266. Fine art auctioneers and valuers. SOFAA

Quadrant Antiques
5 North West Circus Place, Stockbridge. Tel 226 7282. Nautical antiques, furniture and shipping goods.

Alan Rankin
72 Dundas St. Tel 556 3705. Open regularly but appt advisable. General antiquarian and 18thC Scottish books. Catalogues.

Royal Mile Curios
363 High St. Tel 226 4050. Open Mon-Sat 10.30-5; other times by appt. Silver, jewellery and objets d'art.

James Scott
43 Dundas St, EH3 6JN. Tel 556 8260. Open Mon-Sat 11.30-1, 2.30-5.30. Large stock of bric-a-brac, furniture, silver & jewellery etc.

Daniel Shackleton
23 Dundas St, EH3 6QQ. Tel 557 1115. Open Mon-Fri 10-4; Sat 10-1. Paintings, prints and works of art, especially those connected with Scottish history. Childrens book illustrators.

Sotheby's
(Representative: John Robertson). 112 George St, EH2 4LH. Tel 226 7201. Open Mon-Fri 9.30-1, 2-5. Auctioneers and valuers.

James Thin
54 South Bridge. Tel 536 6743. Open Mon-Fri, early closing Sat. Wide range of antiquarian, secondhand and new books. Catalogues issued. ABA

This & That
(Jane Millar). 22 Argyle Place, EH9 1JJ. Tel 229 6069 (priv 447 1309). Open Mon, Thurs-Sat 2.30-5. Furniture, silver, bric-a-brac.

The Three Estaits
49 Dundas St, EH3 6RS. Tel 556 7084. Open Tues-Sat 10-1, 2.30-5.30. Collectors' items including pottery, porcelain, treen and many unusual and decorative items.

John Updike (Rare Books)
7 St Bernard's Row, EH4 1HW. Tel 332 1650. Rare books, first editions, private presses and fine bindings. ABA

Whytock & Reid
(J.Campbell Reid & David C.Reid). Sunbury House, Belford Mews, EH4 3DN. Tel 226 4911. Open Mon-Fri 9-5.30; Sat 9-12.30. 18th & 19thC furniture, old Eastern rugs and carpets. Restoration of furniture & rugs. Cabinet making, upholstery and interior decorating.

Wildman's Antiques
(Ian Wildman & Mark Wildman). 48 St Stephen St, EH3 5AL. Tel 225 7310 (priv 449 3038). Open Mon-Sat 10-4.30; other times by appt. Silver, silver plate, china, jewellery, art nouveau, small furniture.

Aldric Young
49 Thistle St. Tel 226 4101. Open Mon-Fri 9-6; early closing Sat. General antiques, mainly furniture and pictures.

Haddington STD 062 082

Elm House Antiques
(Mrs Irene Macdonald). Elm House, Church St. Tel 3413. Open Sat 10-1, 2-5; by appt most weekdays. 18th and 19thC English porcelain and pottery, blue and white earthenware, Scottish pottery, boxes, small pieces of furniture.

North Berwick STD 0620

Fraser Antiques
119 High St, EH39 4HB. Tel 2722. Open Mon-Sat, 10-5; closed Thurs; other times by appt. Porcelain, glass, silver, pictures, furniture and other small items.

Strathclyde

Coatbridge STD 0236

Quality Antiques
(Michael Stewart). 6 Hornock Cottages. Tel 22532. Open by appt only. General stock and shipping goods etc.

Galston STD 0563

De Fresnes (Antiques)
(The Baron de Fresnes). Cessnock Castle. Tel 829314. 17thC oak, general objets d'art and other items such as silver, glass and pictures. Interior decoration and furnishings. Also a permanent picture gallery for modern and 19thC work.

Glasgow STD 041

Albany Antiques
(P.J. O'Loughlin). 1351 Argyle St, G3 8AD. Tel 3394267 (priv 3341880). Open Mon-Fri 9.30-5; other times by appt. Decorative furniture, shipping goods, Chinese & Japanese ceramics and works of art. LAPADA

Michael Alexander Fine Arts Ltd
147 Bath St. Tel 221 3539. Furniture, paintings, china, silver etc. LAPADA

Barclay Lennie Fine Art
(S.B.Lennie). 203 Bath St. Tel 226 5413. Oil paintings and watercolours. LAPADA

Daniel Brewster
182 West Regent St. Tel 226 3406. Open Mon-Fri 10-5; other times by appt. Pre-1830 furniture, clocks and scientific instruments.

Browns Clocks Ltd
(John & Alison M. Wilson). 203 Bath St, G2 4HZ. Tel 248 6760. Open Mon-Fri 10-5; Sat 10-1. All types antique clocks. FBHI

Robert A.Campbell
The Kelvin Gallery, 117 Bath St, G2 2SZ. Tel 221 1367. Paintings and watercolours, fine arts and furniture.

Carronade
(R.I.Frame). 63 West Regent St. Tel 332 5600 (priv 649 3655). Open Mon-Fri 10-5. Militaria, scientific, nautical and medical instruments, coins and medals, bygones, photographic items and cameras.

Christie's Scotland
164-166 Bath St, G2 4TG. Tel 332 8134;. Open Mon 9-7; Tues-Fri 9-5. Auctioneers.

Corner House Antiques
217 St Vincent St, G2. Tel 221-1000. Open Mon-Sat 10-5. Six dealers with a wide range of silver, china, glass, furniture, collector's items, postcards, etc.

Duophone Antiques
(J.E.Cavanagh Esq). Victorian Village, 57 West Regent St. Tel 332 9802. Open Mon-Fri 10-5; Sat 10.30-1. General antique furniture, clocks, gramophones, brassware and general smalls.

The Fine Art Society Plc
134 Blythswood St, G2 4EL. Tel 332 4027. (Also in Edinburgh, Lothian and in London.) Open Mon-Fri 9.30-5.30; Sat 10-1. Dealers in fine art.

George & Helen Gardiner
105 West Regent St, G2 2BA. Tel 332 1264. Open Mon-Fri 10-5.30. Antiques and decorative objects, tapestries, samplers, treen, country furniture, unusual smart and topical items.

Golightly Restoration
(John Smith & Son Ltd). 69 Kent Rd, G3. Tel 221 7472. Open 9-5. Furniture restoration and antique repair work, upholstery.

David Gray Antiques
284 Woodlands Rd. Tel 334 3047. Open Tues-Thurs 10-4.30; other times by appt. Antique furniture, paintings, decorative items and curios. LAPADA

Chisholm Hunter
27 Trongate. Tel 552 0717. General antiques.

Jocelyn Antiques
(John McChesney). 161 West George St. Tel 248 3024. General antiques.

Keep Sakes Antiques
(Mrs R.Currie). 27 Gibson St. Tel 334 2264. Open 10-5; Mon 10-2. General antiques, jewellery, silverware. Also coffee shop.

I.E.Lovatt Antiques
(Ivor Lovatt). 100-102 Torrisdale St., G46 6RG. Tel 423 6497 (priv 638 0302). Open Mon-Fri 9.30-5.30; other times by appt. Georgian, Victorian shipping furniture, bric-a-brac. LAPADA

Iain MacKinnon Antiques
The Victorian Village, 57 West Regent St. Tel 332 9802. Open Mon-Fri 10-5; Sat 10-1. General dealer, furniture, porcelain, silver, paintings and 19thC Scottish pottery.

Jean Megahy
(Mr Halliday). 481 Great Western Rd. Tel 334 1315. Open Mon and Fri; other times by appt. Period furniture, furnishing and other decorative items.

Mercat Antiques
(J.Jack, P.Hughes). 246 West George St, G2 4QY. Tel 204 0851. Open Mon-Fri 10-5.30; other times by appt. Large stock of furniture, porcelain, silver, jewellery, shipping goods, clocks and watches.

Muirhead Moffat & Co
182 West Regent St. Tel 226 4683 and 226 3406. Open Mon-Fri 10-5 by appt. Fine quality 18th and early 19thC furniture, clocks, barometers, jewellery, objects of vertu.

Ewan Mundy Fine Art
(Ewan Mundy). 48 West George St, G2 1BP. Tel 331 2406. Open Mon-Sat 9.30-5.30; other times by appt. 19th & 20thC Scottish artists.

Robert Paterson & Son
8 Orchard St, Paisley. Tel 889 2435. Auctioneers.

Pettigrew & Mail
(C.Pettigrew, Mrs S.Mail). Giffnock. Tel 639 3292. Open by appt only. 19th and 20thC oil paintings. LAPADA

Phillips (Glasgow)
98 Sauchiehall St, G2 3DQ. Tel 332 3386. Fine art auctioneers and valuers.

Scott Packing & Warehousing Co Ltd
Kilsyth Road, Kirkintilloch. Tel 776 7191. (Also in Edinburgh, Aberdeen, Montrose, London, Birmingham, Leeds.) Packers and shippers. LAPADA

John Smith & Son (Glasgow) Ltd
57-61 St Vincent St. Tel 221 7472. Open Mon-Sat 9-5.30. Antiquarian and secondhand books. Scottish literature, prints and maps. ABA

Jeremy Sniders
(Jeremy Sniders). Victorian Village, 57 West Regent St. Tel 332 2424. Open Mon-Fri 10-5, Sat 10-1. Antique and quality jewellery. Also furniture, objets d'art, silver, clocks and watches. Repair work undertaken.

Sotheby's
(Representative: Anthony Weld Forester). 146 West Regent St, G2 2RQ. Tel 221 4817. Auctioneers & valuers.

Victorian Village
53,57 & 63 West Regent St. Tel 332 0703. Open daily 9.30-5; Sat 9.30-1. Market with about 30 dealers with wide range of period and collectable antiques.

Vintage & Value
220-224 Woodlands Rd, G3 6LN. Tel 332 0495. Furniture, clocks, ceramics, paintings, brass, barometers, jewellery, musical instruments, bric-a-brac.

Wellington Fine Art
(Anthony F.Armstrong). 14 Park Circus, G3 6AX. Tel 331 2896. Open by appt. Agent for antique and 20thC pictures. Restoration & framing.

Tim Wright Antiques
(T.& J.M.Wright). 147 Bath St. Tel 221 0364. Open Mon-Fri 9.30-5; other times by appt. Good quality small items, particularly ceramics & glass, also extensive range of metalware, bronzes, boxes, plate, treen, etc. Also quality furniture, prints & samplers. LAPADA

High Blantyre

Crossbow House Antiques
Stoneymeadow Rd. Tel Blantyre (0698) 823106, 822378. A large amount of shipping goods, furniture, brass, general antiques, garden ornaments, militaria and clocks.

Inveraray STD 0499

Christie's
(Agent for Argyll: Sir Ilay Campbell Bt). Cumlodden Estate Office, Crarae, PA32 8YA. Tel Minard (0546) 86633 (priv 86274). Open usual office hours; other times by appt. Agent for the fine art auctioneers and valuers.

Kilbarchan STD 050 57

Corrigan Antiques
(John Corrigan). The Cross, PA10 2JG. Tel 2229. Open Mon-Fri, 10-5; closed Sat; other times by appt. Antique furniture, oak, brassware, porcelain, rugs and textiles and decorative items. Specialist in Paisley shawls. LAPADA

Gardner's, The Antique Shop
(D.F. Gardner, G.D. Gardner, R.K.F.Gardner). Wardend House, Milliken Park, PA10 2PN. Tel 2292. Open Mon-Fri 10-1, 2-6; Sat 10-1; other times by appt. Large stock of furniture, Victoriana, porcelain, glass, brass, silver, pictures and interesting items. Also shipping. Mostly trade. LAPADA

W. & P. McQuade Antiques
7 Shuttle St. Tel 4249. Open Mon-Fri 10-5.30, Sun 2-5.30. Clocks, brass, copper, Victoriana.

Killearn STD 0360

Country Antiques
(Lady Edmonstone). Main Street. Tel 70215. Open 9.30-5; other times by appt. Small antiques, ceramics, silver, jewellery, Victoriana.

Kilmacolm STD 050 587

Kilmacolm Antiques Ltd
(Mrs Hilary Maclean). Stewart Place. Tel 3149. Open Mon-Sat 10-12.30, 2.30-5; closed Wed; other times by appt. Georgian and Victorian furniture and jewellery, silver, clocks, pictures and prints.

Maybole STD 0655

Christie's
(Representative: James Hunter Blair). Blairquhan. Tel Straiton (06557) 239. Auctioneers and valuers.

Tayside

Aberfeldy STD 0887

Denis Young Antiques
(Denis Young, Mrs J.M.Young). 3 Kenmore St. Tel Glenlyon (08877) 232. English and Oriental porcelain and glass, and paintings. Also books, especially children's books. HADA

Auchterarder STD 076 46

The Hayes Gallery
(Paul & Maria Hayes). 71 High St, PH3 1BN. Tel 2320 (priv 3442). Open Mon-Sat 9.30-5; closed Wed; other times by appt. 18th, 19th & 20thC fine paintings, English & Scottish, marine, sporting, and Scottish landscape paintings. PADA

Susan Procter
(Susan Procter). 47-51 The Feus, PH3 1DG. Tel 2532. Open most days 9-6; other times by appt. Scottish & English pottery & porcelain, Staffordshire figures, samplers, Paisley shawls, books, decorative country items. PADA

Stuart Antiques
4 High St. Tel 2410. Open Mon-Sat 9.30-5. Antique furniture, paintings, silver, plate and porcelain. Specialising in Scottish paintings.

John Whitelaw & Sons
(John, Ian & Alan Whitelaw). 120 High St, PH3 1AD. Tel 2482. Open Mon-Sat 9-5.30; other times by appt. One of the largest trade stocks of period furniture in Scotland.

Blairgowrie STD 0250

Roy Sim Antiques
(Roy Sim). 21 Allan St, PH10 6AB. Tel 3860 (priv 3700). Open Mon-Sat 9-1, 2-5.30; other times by appt. Furniture, clocks, silver and plate, jewellery, metalware, scientific and nautical instruments, weapons, oriental items and decorative china. Over 3000 items in stock. Also 5000 sq ft shipping warehouse. PADA

Bridge of Earn STD 0738

Imrie Antiques
(Mr & Mrs I.Imrie). Back St. Tel 812784. Open Mon-Sat 10-5.30; other times by appt. Victorian and Georgian shipping goods. LAPADA

Dundee STD 0382

Angus Antiques
(Stanley Paget). 4 St Andrews St. Tel 22128. Open Mon-Fri 10-4; closed Sat; other times by appt. Decorative & curious items, militaria & weapons, jewellery, silver, gold, collector's items, advertising items, art deco & art nouveau.

Cooper of Dundee (Furniture) Ltd
(A.& Y.Middleton). 131 Seagate, DD1 2HW. Tel 24286. Open Sat 9.30-12.30. Furniture, china, glass and brass.

Nethergate Gallery
(Neil Livingstone). 140 Nethergate (shop & office), DD1 4ED. Tel 21751. (Warehouse in Brewery Lane.) Open Mon-Sat 9-5; other times by appt. Exporters & packers of antiques; trade warehouse, retail gallery. LAPADA

Silver Tay Trading Company Ltd
(Neil Peter Livingstone). St Colmes, 496 Perth Rd, DD2 1LS. Tel 21751 (priv 67454). Open by appt. Packers and exporters of antiques to anywhere in the world.

Westport Ltd
3 Old Hawkhill, DD1 5EU. Tel 25517. Open by appt only. Antique furniture, paintings and works of art. Very little under £1000.

Dunning STD 076 484

Dunning Antiques
(Alexander McDonald Forsyth). Tron Square. Tel 224. (Also in Perth.) Open Mon-Sat 10-5; other times by appt. Silver, jewellery and Monart glass.

Errol STD 082 12

Errol Antiques
(A.Knox). The Cross. Tel 391. Open Mon-Fri 8.30-12 1-4.30; other times by appt. 18th and 19thC furniture, paintings. PADA

Inchture STD 0828

C.S. Moreton (Antiques)
(Paul M. Stephens). Inchmartine House, PH14 9QQ. Tel 86412. Open Mon-Fri 9-5.30. Good 17th, 18th & 19thC furniture in mahogany, walnut, oak, rosewood & satinwood, Persian carpets & rugs, metalware, ceramics & objets d'art. PADA

Killiecrankie

Christie's
(Representative: Sebastian Thewes). Strathgarry House. Tel Blair Atholl (079681) 216. Auctioneers and valuers.

Perth STD 0738

Walter S.Beaton
(William Beaton). 75 Kinnoull St, PH1 5EZ. Tel 28127. Open Mon-Fri 9-1, 2-5.30; early closing Sat; other times by appt. Good stock of 18th and early 19thC furniture, porcelain, paintings and other items. BADA

Beveridge (Antiques)
(Barbara Beveridge). 1-2 South St John's Place, PH1 5SU. Tel 35055(priv 030786 212/209. Open Mon-Sat 9.30-5; other times by appt. 17th and 18thC furniture; 18th and 19thC Scottish oil paintings. BADA

Coach House Antiques Ltd
(John Walker). 77 Kinnoull St. Tel 29835 (priv 073882 627). (Also at 7 Atholl St.) Open Mon-Sat 9.30-5.30; other times by appt. Period furniture, furnishings, metalware, large selection of sporting prints. PADA

A.S.Deuchar & Son
10-12 South St. Tel 26297 (priv 51452). Open Mon-Fri 10-1, 2-5.30; other times by appt. Antiques and Victoriana. Trade welcome.

Fair Maids House Scottish Crafts
(Mrs Eva McDonald). North Port. Tel 25976. Open Mon-Sat 10-5; other times by appt. Contemporary Scottish crafts; unusual knitwear, pottery, silver, horn, wood and glass.

Forsyth Antiques
(Alexander McDonald Forsyth). 8 St Paul's Sq. Tel 22173. Open Mon-Sat 10-5; other times by appt. Silver, jewellery, Monart glass, general antiques.

Hardie Antiques
(Timothy Hardie). 25 St John St. Tel 33127. Open Mon-Fri 9.30-5; Sat 9.30-1. Fine jewellery & silver, mainly Victorian & Edwardian. PADA

W.T.C.Henderson
5 North Methven St. Tel 24836. Open 9.30-5.30; early closing Wed. Antiques, jewellery, stamps, coins and medals.

Thomas Love & Sons Ltd
(Thomas Love & Miss Elizabeth Love). 53 South St, PH2 8PD. Tel 24111 (4 lines). Open Mon-Fri 9-5.30; Sat 9-12.30. Large stock of antique furniture, pottery, porcelain, glass, pictures, prints, carpets, rugs, silver, Sheffield plate, mirrors and bibelots.

Ian Murray Antiques Warehouse
(Ian Murray). 21 Glasgow Rd. Tel 37222 (priv 0250-2508). (Also Curio Corner, 38 George St, Perth.) Open Mon-Fri 9-5; other times by appt. 12,000 sq ft of antique, Victorian and shipping items.

Robertson and Cox
(Michael Cox, Caryl Robertson). 60 George St, PH1 5JL. Tel 26300. Open Mon-Fri 9.30-5.30; Sat 9.30-1; other times by appt. Period furniture, small antiques, porcelain, paintings, watercolours & oriental rugs. PADA

John Scott-Adie
16 St John St, PH1 5SP. Tel 25550. Paintings.

R.M.Sinclair & Son
58 South William St. Tel 29666. Open by appt. Large and varied stock of Victorian furniture, antiques and shipping goods.

Tay Street Gallery
(Ian Ingram). 70 Tay St. Tel 20604. Open Mon-Fri 9.30-1, 2-5; early closing Wed; other times by appt. Period furniture, pictures by Scottish & other artists, sporting prints & selected ornaments.

Pitlochry STD 0796

Blair Antiques
14 Bonnethill Rd, PH16 5BS. Tel 2624. Open 9-5; closed Thurs pm. Period furniture, Scottish oil paintings, silver, clocks, pottery and porcelain. PADA

Phone: INCHTURE (0828) 86412

On A85 Perth-Dundee Trunk road

LARGE STOCK OF PERIOD FURNITURE

C. S. MORETON

at

Inchmartine House

INCHTURE · PERTHSHIRE · PH14 9QQ

Prop. PAUL STEPHENS

ALSO ORIENTAL CARPETS and RUGS

—

METALWARE and CERAMICS

ANTIQUE FURNITURE AND DECORATIVE ITEMS

David Keith

Antiques

Rait by Perth

Telephone: 08217 339

When in Scotland . . .

Carse Antiques

RAIT, PERTHSHIRE

(Halfway between Perth and Dundee off the A85)

4 Showrooms and 10,000 sq. feet of period furniture and furnishings. Specialising in 17th and 18th Century Oak, fine Georgian pieces, metalware, treen and decorative items.

Open 10 to 5.30 Monday through Saturday and by appointment

Telephone Rait (082 17) 205
Home (082 17) 227

The sign of
THE BRITISH ANTIQUE DEALERS' ASSOCIATION

MEMBER OF THE BRITISH ANTIQUE DEALERS' ASSOCIATION

The nearest you will get to a guarantee in the world of antiques.
Ring Sally Tunley on 01-589 4128 for a free list of members

ROY SIM ANTIQUES

Large Stock Of

FURNITURE, CLOCKS, SILVER, SILVER PLATE, JEWELLERY, BRASS AND COPPER WARE, ORIENTAL ITEMS, SCIENTIFIC AND NAUTICAL INSTRUMENTS, WEAPONS

Also SHIPPING WAREHOUSE

21 ALLAN STREET, BLAIRGOWRIE, PERTHSHIRE

Tel 0250 3860, Evenings 3700 Open Monday to Saturday

Rait, by Perth STD 082 17

Carse Antiques
(M.S.M.& M.J.M. Threipland). PH2 7RT. Tel 205 (priv 227). Open Mon-Sat 10-1 2-5.30; other times by appt. (One mile north of A85 between Perth and Dundee.) Four showrooms of period furniture and furnishings. Specialising in early oak, brass, copper, metalware, walnut, treen, paintings, cottage and country antiques. PADA

David Keith Antiques
Tel 339 or 245. Open Mon-Sat 9-5.30; other times by appt. Antique furniture and decorative items.

Rait Antiques
(David Terence Pickett & Mrs June Pickett). Rait Farmhouse, PH2 7RT. Tel 287. PADA

WALES

Abergavenny	Gwent
Aberystwyth	Dyfed
Anglesey	Gwynedd
Bala	Gwynedd
Bangor	Gwynedd
Barmouth	Gwynedd
Barry	S. Glamorgan
Beaumaris	Gwynedd
Bethesda	Gwynedd
Brecon	Powys
Bridgend	Mid Glamorgan
Caerleon	Gwent
Caernarvon	Gwynedd
Cardiff	S. Glamorgan
Cardigan	Dyfed
Carmarthen	Dyfed
Chepstow	Gwent
Colwyn Bay	Clwyd
Cowbridge	S. Glamorgan
Deeside	Clwyd
Gilwern	Gwent
Haverfordwest	Dyfed
Henllan	Dyfed
Kidwelly	Dyfed
Knighton	Powys
Laugharne	Dyfed
Llandeilo	Dyfed
Llandogo	Gwent
Llandovery	Dyfed
Llandudno	Gwynedd
Llanelli	Dyfed
Llangefni	Gwynedd
Llanrwst	Gwynedd
Machynlleth	Powys
Mold	Clwyd
Monmouth	Gwent
Moylegrove	Dyfed
Neath	W. Glamorgan
Newport	Gwent
Newtown	Powys
Northop	Clwyd
Pembroke	Dyfed
Pen-y-Lan	S. Glamorgan
Portmeirion	Gwynedd
Presteigne	Powys
Pwllheli	Gwynedd
Rhos-on-Sea	Clwyd
Rhuddlan	Clwyd
Ruthin	Clwyd
Shotton	Clwyd
St Asaph	Clwyd
Swansea	W. Glamorgan
Tenby	Dyfed
Tintern	Gwent
Usk	Gwent
Welshpool	Powys
Wolvesnewton	Gwent
Wrexham	Clwyd

How to Use This Book
After the editorial articles the book is divided into five main sections:
1 Directory (*begins on page 37*)
Dealers, auctioneers, packers, restorers, trade suppliers and so on are all listed here, with address, telephone number, opening hours, and type of business or area of specialisation. Entries are listed in alphabetical order under town or village, within the relevant county and geographical area.
2 Gazetteer (*begins on page 265*)
This is an alphabetical list of the towns and villages mentioned in the Directory, showing the counties and geographical areas under which they are listed.
3. Index to Specialists
(*begins on page 270*)
Directory entries are here listed under type of business or nature of stock.
4. Index to Business Names
(*begins on page 363*)
All business names in the Directory are listed alphabetically with their town or village, county and geographical area.
5 Maps (*begin on page 391*)
Showing villages and towns listed in the Directory.

Note
Counties and geographical areas are listed with page references under 'Contents' on page 3.
Auctioneers are listed both in the main Directory under the relevant town or village, and in the Specialists index under 'Auctioneers'.
Abbreviations and names and addresses of useful organisations are listed on page 4.

Clwyd

Colwyn Bay STD 0492

North Wales Antiques
(F.Robinson). 58 Abergele Rd. Tel 30521. Shipping goods, oak, mahogany & pine. LAPADA

Phillips
(Enquiries: George Forrester). 9 Conwy Rd, LL29 7AF. Tel 33406. Fine art auctioneers & valuers. SOFAA

Deeside STD 0244

Rocking Chair Antiques
(G.Baines). Antique Exporters, 27 Gladstone Way, Hawarden. Tel 537250.

Mold STD 0352

Dodds Property World
(K. Hugh Dodd & Partners). Victoria Auction Galleries. Tel 2552. Weekly general sales; periodical antique sales.

G.A.Thomas
4 New St. Tel 55466. Open by appt. Silver and jewellery. BADA FGA NAG

Tom Lloyd-Roberts
(Tom Lloyd-Roberts). Old Court House, Caerwys, CH7 5BB. Tel 720276. Open Mon-Fri 10-1, 2.15-6. Large stock of antiquarian and new books on topography, travel, history, literature and books on Wales. ABA

Northop STD 035 286

James H.Morris & Co
(James H. Morris). Old Village School, The Green, CH7 6BD. Tel 508. Appt advisable. Period oak and mahogany furniture, also longcase and other clocks.

Rhos-on-Sea

Shelagh Hyde
11 Rhos Rd. Tel Colwyn Bay (0492) 48879. Res on prem. Small mahogany furniture, china, glass and decorative items.

Rhuddlan STD 0745

Rhuddlan Antiques
(J Griffiths). High St. Tel 590705 (priv 07456 6222). Open Tues-Sat 10-4; other times by appt. General antiques, furniture, silver, brass, copper.

Ruthin STD 082 42

Northeast Wales Antiques
(Mr & Mrs H.J.Northeast). 15 Well St, LL15 1AE. Tel 2782 (priv 2154). Open Mon-Sat 10-5.30. Furniture, oil paintings, silver, porcelain, clocks and barometers. LAPADA

Shotton

Angharads Antiques
(Mrs J.Buckley). 106 Chester Rd West. Tel Deeside (0244) 812240. Open Tues, Thurs, Fri, Sat 10-5; other times by appt. Small furniture, weapons, general antiques and collectors items, specialising in portrait miniatures. Appointment necessary for antique guns and accessories including Colt revolvers.

St Asaph STD 0745

John Trefor Antiques
(John & Barbara Trefor). Rhuallt Hall Farm, Rhuallt, LL17 0TR. Tel 583604. (Location: on A55 3 miles east of St.Asaph.) Open at all times. 6 showrooms with a varied stock of furniture, longcase clocks and small antiques. Fine selection of shipping goods and pine furniture.

Wrexham STD 0978

Renaissance Furniture
(Philip L. Grassie). Providence Chapel, Tan y Lan, Ruabon. Tel Ruabon (0978) 824202. Open Mon-Fri. Hand made solid oak reproduction furniture.

Dyfed

Aberystwyth STD 0970

Howards of Aberystwyth
(Mr & Mrs J. Howard). 10 Alexandra Rd. Tel 4973. Jewellery, English and Welsh pottery, 18th and 19thC furniture. Valuations. LAPADA

Cardigan STD 0239

The Cardigan Book Centre
(Mrs Frances Mason). 1 Royal Oak, Quay St, SA43 1HR. Tel 612704. Antiquarian books, prints, maps, theology, childrens, general subjects, books. Specialising in Welsh and other British History books.

Vernon Smith & Son
(Mr R.L.V.Smith, Mr G.V.Smith). Bayvil House, High St, SA43 1HE. Tel 612654. Open Mon-Sat 9-5.30; Wed 9-1. Brass, copper, metalware, 19thC furniture and porcelain.

Carmarthen STD 0267

John Francis
(Capt. P.G. Francis, D.L.). Curiosity Sale Rooms, King St. Tel 233456. Auctioneers. SOFAA

Haverfordwest STD 0437

Gerald Oliver Antiques
(Gerald & Sylvia Oliver). 14 Albany Terrace, St Thomas Green, SA61 1RH. Tel 2794. Open 9.30-1, 2.15-5; 9.30-1 Thurs; other times by appt. 18th & 19thC furniture, small silver, metalwork, unusual & decorative bygones, ceramics & glass.

Pine Corner Antiques
(John Palmer). 19 & 21 Bridgend Square. Open daily 10-5. Stripped 18th and 19thC pine furniture. Modern decorative items.

Henllan

Richard Lloyd
(Richard Lloyd). Dolhaidd Mansion. Tel Velindre (0559) 370791. Open Mon-Sat 9-6. Trade only. Large stock of pine, oak and mahogany furniture. Also shipping goods, pottery, brass, copper and country bygones.

Kidwelly STD 0554

Country Antiques
(R.J.& L. Bebb). Castle Mill, The Bridge. Tel 890534. Open Tues-Sat 10.15-5.15; other times by appt. 17th to 19thC furniture in oak, pine, mahogany & walnut. General small items. Valuations. LAPADA

Laugharne STD 099 421

Neil Speed Antiques
(Neil Speed, Glynda Speed). The Strand, SA33 4SZ. Tel 412. Open winter Fri, Sat; most days in summer; other times by appt. General antiques, with the emphasis on British country furniture of all periods.

Llandeilo STD 0558

James Ash Antiques
(James and Patricia Ash). The Warehouse, Station Rd. Tel 823728 (priv 0269 850119). Open Mon-Fri 9-5; other times by appt. Welsh country furniture, shipping goods, Victorian and antique furniture. Largest warehouse of oak, mahogany and pine furniture in Wales.

Llandovery STD 0550

The Curiosity Shop
(J.B.Luffman & Sons). High St. Tel 20390. Country furniture, clocks, paintings, militaria.

Llanelli STD 055 42

Alice's Antiques
(Mrs Alice Davies, Mr George Davies). 24 Upper Park St, SA15 3YN. Tel 773045 (priv 750533). (Also at 58-60 Wern Rd, Llanelli.) Open Mon-Fri, closed Tues; other times by appt. Silver, china, clocks, furniture, local and Victorian paintings.

Memories Antiques
(George Davies). 58-60 Wern Rd. Antique jewellery and coins.

Robert Graham Pugh
Tel 772613. Open by appt only. Pottery and country antiques. LAPADA

Moylegrove STD 023 986

Dibley Antiques
(Jeanne and Peter Dibley). Ffynnon Watty. Tel 668. (Also at Cardigan Guildhall, Lower Floor, Stand No.12,Thurs & Sat.) Open by appt. Specialising in fine silver and small antiques.

Pembroke STD 0646

Northgate Antiques
(J.P. & J. Howells). 10 Northgate St, SA71 5LF. Tel 684416 (priv 672388). Open Mon-Sat 10-6; early closing Wed; other times by appt. 18th and 19thC furniture, oak, pine, prints and maps, pottery & porcelain. LAPADA

Tenby STD 0834

Audrey Bull
15 Upper Frog St. Tel 3114 (priv 0834 813425). Open Mon-Sat 10-1, 2.30-5; closed Wed; other times by appt. Period and Welsh country furniture, jewellery and general antique items.

Mid Glamorgan

Bridgend STD 0656

Davies's
48 Nolton St. Tel 4983. Open 9-5.30; other times by appt. Small furniture, china, glass, silver, brass, copper.

S.Glamorgan

Barry STD 0446

Antique Shop
114 Broad St. Tel 733602. Open 10.15-5; early closing Wed. General stock.

Olde Worlde Trading Company
282 Holton Rd. Tel 744850. Open Mon-Sat 10-5.30. General antiques, country items, stripped pine, shipping goods and smalls.

Cardiff STD 0222

Adam Antiques
(Rhys & Ellen Davies). 12 Sneyd St, Canton. Tel 40022 (priv 0222 883415). Open Mon-Fri 9.30-6; Sat by appt. 18th and 19thC Welsh and English furniture, silver, metalware, decorative objects. General shipping goods.

Alice Lighting
3 Wellfield Rd. Tel 499156. Open 9.30-1, 2-5.30; early closing Wed. Period and other furniture, other items and decorative lighting.

Antiques Unlimited
(Mrs B. Williams, Eric B. Williams). 34 Church Rd, Whitchurch, CF4 2EA. Tel 693748. (Also at Stall 47 Jacobs Market, West Canal Wharf, Cardiff centre.) Open by appt at Church Rd; market open Thurs and Sat. Second-hand and antique jewellery and silver, small antiques etc.

Broadway Antiques
(S.C.Hughes). 185, 185A, 187 Broadway, Roath. Tel 24470. English & Continental furniture, English & Oriental porcelain, silver, glass. Restorer. Valuations. LAPADA

Cottage Antiques
(P.Grimwade). 9 Kings Rd, Canton. Tel 24484. General. Valuations. LAPADA

K.A.Davies Antiques
248 Cowbridge Rd East. Tel 29989. Coins, medals, guns, furniture, china, glass, pewter, brass and copper.

Gazebo
27 Penylan Rd. Tel 498720. Open Mon-Sat 10-6; other times by appt. Furniture of all periods, glass, china, brass, pewter and other items.

Llewelyn Antiques
(Miss S.H.Llewelyn). 64 Monthermer Rd, Cathays, CF2 4RA. Tel 43367. Open Mon-Sat 10-5.30; other times by appt. Small furniture, bygones and curiosities.

Maindy Fine Antiques
(C.M.W.Heath). 17 Pont Canna St. Tel 382072. Open Mon-Sat 10-5.30; other times by appt. Mostly Victorian and Edwardian furniture and art nouveau, art deco, porcelain, glass, metalwork, picture, prints, modern signed limited edition prints.

Miles Antiques
151 Albany Rd. Tel 31485. Open daily 9-5.30; early closing Wed; other times by appt. Period Welsh oak, paintings, silver and porcelain.

John Owen Gallery
(John Owen). 20 Salisbury Rd, CF2 4AD. Tel 45868 (priv 04463 2767). Open Mon-Sat 10-6; other times by appt. 18th, 19th & 20thC oil paintings, drawings & watercolours. Quality contemporary prints. Also restoration and framing.

Phillips in Wales
(Hugh Bulmer). 9-10 Westgate St, CF1 1DA. Tel 396453. Fine art auctioneers and valuers.

Cowbridge STD 044 63

Brenin
(S.M. King). Old Wool Barn, Verity's Court, CF7 7AJ. Tel 3893 (priv 0443 223553). Open Thurs, Fri, Sat pm; other times by appt. Fine 18th and 19thC English and Welsh porcelain and pottery. Also collectors' books.

Eastgate Antiques
85 Eastgate, CF7 7AA. Tel 5111. (Also at Thicke Galleries, Swansea.) 19thC oils & watercolours. General antiques, furniture, silver etc.

Matthews & Davies Fine Art Ltd
(Mrs I.F.M.Davies, Mr J.H.C.Davies). 85-87 Eastgate, CF7 7AA. Tel 4340. Open Tues-Sat 9.30-5; other times by appt. 18th and 19thC oil paintings, watercolours and prints. Selected antiques, porcelain and silver. Restoration, valuation and framing services.

Pen-y-Lan

Peter Philp
(Peter & Pamela Philp). 77 Kimberley Rd, CF2 5DP. Tel Cardiff (0222) 493826. Open Sat only, 9-5; other times by appt. Small pieces of British and Continental furniture, pottery, metalwork, treen, watercolours.

W.Glamorgan

Neath STD 0639

P.R. George (Antiques)
(P.R. George). 64 Briton Ferry Rd. Tel 4677. Open afternoons only; other times by appt. Prints, maps, antiques.

Georgian Antique Company
24B Briton Ferry Rd. Tel 4677. Open 9-5.30. 17th to 19thC furniture, English and Welsh porcelain and Victorian jewellery.

Swansea STD 0792

Roger Hughes Antique Gallery
13 Dillwyn St. Tel 52584. Open Mon-Fri 9.30-5.30; closed Thurs. Period Welsh oak and mahogany furniture, china, glass and silver.

The Old Clock Shop
49 St Helen's Rd. Tel 53334. Open Mon-Fri 10-5. Clocks of all types, including grandfather, wall clocks and carriage clocks.

Thicke Galleries Swansea
(T.G.Thicke). 26 St Andrews Close, Mayals, SA3 5DX. Tel 401656. (Also at 85 Eastgate, Cowbridge, S.Glamorgan.) 19thC oils and watercolours. LAPADA

West Wales Antiques
(H.Davies). 18 Mansfield Rd, Murton, Gower. Tel Bishopston (044128) 4318. 18th & 19thC pottery, porcelain, furniture, silver, dolls. Valuations. LAPADA

Yates Antiques
21a Woodfield St, Morriston. Tel 781422. Antique furniture, glass, china, pianos, shipping goods.

Gwent

Abergavenny STD 0873

Henry H.Close
36 Cross St. Tel 3583. Open 9-5.30; closed Thurs; other times by appt. 18th and 19thC furniture, porcelain, pottery and glass.

Morris's
(Mark, Hugh, Patricia, Paul & Sonya Morris). Brecon Rd Antiques, 34 Brecon Rd. Tel Crickhowell (0873) 810246. Open Mon-Sat 10-5; early closing Thurs; other times by appt. Period furniture, glass, militaria, shipping goods and bric-a-brac.

Tower Antiques
(Paul A.Long). 11 Market St. Tel 4283 (priv 2146). Open 10-5; Thurs 9-1. General antiques.

Caerleon STD 0633

Marc Rhys
The Mynde House, High St. Tel 420535. Open by appt only. Fine quality furniture, Welsh oak, Staffordshire figures and decorative items.

Chepstow STD 029 12

Chepstow Antiques
(G.Wall). 11 Lower Church St. Tel 6500. Open Mon-Sat 10-5. General antiques specialising in period furniture. Also postcards.

Davies Antiques
(J.F.Davies, M.Davies,J.C.Davies, D.M.Davies). 12 St Mary St, NP6 5EW. Tel Dingestow (060 083) 343. Open 6 days 10-5; other times by appt. Fine furniture, general and shipping. LAPADA

Davis & Sons
Manor House, Bank Sq. Tel 4908. Auctioneers.

Esther Jones Antiques
(Esther and Steve Jones). 16A St Mary's St. Tel 3314 (priv 0594-60653). Open Mon-Fri 9.45-5.15; Sat 11-4.30. Furniture 1750-1910, boxes, silver plate.

Nash Antiques
(C. & D. Huish). 5 & 6 Lower Church St. Tel 4150. Open Mon-Sat 9.30-5.30. Furniture, mainly old oak.

Plough House Interiors
Upper Church St. Tel 5200. Open Mon-Sat 9.30-5.30. General antiques, fine Victorian and Edwardian furniture, accessories.

Gilwern STD 0873

Gilwern Antiques
(D.Powell & W.J.Powell). Main Road, NP7 0AS. Tel 830276 (priv 830384). Open Tues-Sat; other times by appt. General antiques of the Victorian/Edwardian period, also some Georgian.

Llandogo

Llandogo Antiques
(Rob and Jan Hall). NP5 4TA. Tel Dean (0594) 530213. Open 10-1, 2-5.30 daily except Tues; other times by appt. Ceramics, jewellery and decorative items.

Monmouth STD 0600

Lawrence Musgrove Antiques
(L.Musgrove). Dixton Lodge, Hadnock Rd. Tel 3656. 18th & 19thC furniture, clocks. Valuations. LAPADA

Newport STD 0633

Antiques of Newport
(Mrs T.R. Morgan, Mr & Mrs J.M.Duggan). 82 Chepstow Rd, NP9 8ED. Tel 59935. Open Mon-Sat 9.30-5.30, closed Thurs; other times by appt. General antiques, furniture, pottery, porcelain, silver, jewellery, maps, prints & pictures.

The Ceramic Book Co
St John's and Chepstow Rd. Tel 71561. Large stock of all reference works of collectors and the antique trade. Catalogues.

Charles St Antiques
(Ryan Richards, Geoff Wall). 35 Charles St. Tel 55530. Open Mon-Sat 9-5.30. Silver jewellery, 18th & 19thC furniture.

Derek S. Hutchings
The Annexe, 210 Chepstow Rd. Tel 65511. Open by appt. English and Welsh pottery and porcelain.

Tintern STD 029 18

Abbey Antiques
(David & Hermione Ford). NP6 6SF. Tel 233. Open daily 9.30-5.30; other times by appt. Antique jewellery, silver, brass, copper, shipping furniture and country oak furniture.

Usk STD 029 13

Old Market Antiques
37 Old Market St. Tel 2813. Open Tues, Thurs, Fri 10-5, Wed 10-12.30, Sat 2-5.30; other times by appt. 18th and early 19thC furniture, porcelain, oil paintings and watercolours.

Three Salmons Antiques
Three Salmons Hotel Ltd. Tel 2133, 2134. Open 9-5; other times by appt. Jacobean and early English furniture.

Betty Williams
The Gallery, Tyr Eglwys, Tredunnock, NP5 1LY. Tel Tredunnock (063349) 301. Open by appt only. Fine watercolours.

Wolvesnewton STD 029 15

Rex Moreton
The Model Farm, NP6 6NZ. Tel 231. Photographer.

Gwynedd

Anglesey

Museum of Childhood
(Robert & Joan Brown). 1 Castle St, Beaumaris. Tel 0248-810448 (priv 712498). Open 10-6; other times by appt. Collectors toys and children's memorabilia.

Michael Webb Fine Paintings
(Michael Webb). Cefn-Llwyn, Llangristiolus, Bodorgan, LL62 5DN. Tel Bodorgan (0407) 840336. Open by appt only. Victorian oil paintings & watercolours. Restorations. Framing. Valuations. LAPADA

Bala STD 0678

Wynnstay Galleries
Druid House. Tel 219. Open Mon-Fri 10-6. Varied stock.

Bangor STD 0248

David Windsor Gallery
(Mrs E. Creathorne). 201 High St. Tel 364639. Open Mon-Sat 10-5.30; closed Wed. Oils, watercolours, limited editions, etchings, antique maps, engravings and lithographs. We also restore, mount & frame oils, watercolours etc & restore antique frames.Specialising in antique maps and prints of Wales - particularly North Wales. FATG

Barmouth STD 0341

E.Evans & Partners Ltd
Tyn-y-Coed, High St. Tel 538. Antiques, curios, prints, jewellery and books.

Ron Jones Antiques
(R.W.Jones). Tri Brynwcws, Llanaber, LL42 1RR. Tel 280691. (3 miles on Barmouth-Harlech Rd).Preliminary phone call appreciated. General antiques, including photographic equipment and cameras, pottery and porcelain, metalware, bygones and curiosities.

Beaumaris STD 0248

Mona Antiqua & Tudor Rose
(Hendrik Lek & Son - Karel Lek). 31-32 Castle St. Tel 810203. Open Mon-Sat 9-1, 2-5.30; early closing Wed in off season; other times by appt. Antique furniture, pottery, porcelain, glass, works of art, miscellanea, objects of vertu. Large stock of antiquarian prints including topography, satire (Spy, Ape etc), historical and natural history, theatre. Sheet music, old photographs, games, toys.

A Stitch in Time
(Elizabeth Bradley). 1 West End. Tel 811055. Open by appt. Antique samplers and embroidered pictures. Woolwork cushions, rag rugs and quilts.

Bethesda STD 0248

Ogwen Antiques
(Joy and Roy Ostle). 10 High St. Tel 600460 (priv 600549). Open Mon-Sat 10.30-5.30; other times by appt. Victoriana, Edwardiana, art nouveau, art deco, old tools, furniture, pine, clocks, bottles, postcards, toys and paintings. Specialist in prints of North Wales. Above shop Mrs Bunns refreshment rooms run by Joy Ostle.

Caernarvon STD 0286

Caernarfon Antiques
(Mrs E.C.Dyson). 18 Bangor St. Tel 5739. Furniture, Victorian and Edwardian jewellery. LAPADA

W.W. Griffiths
(W.W. Griffiths). Ivy Cottage, Bethel, LL55 1UW. Tel Port Dinorwic (0248) 670 556. Open Mon-Fri 9-5; other times by appt. Clocks and watches, furniture, metalware, pottery and porcelain, decorative prints, shipping goods.

Llandudno STD 0492

C.G.Lee
The Antique Shop, 24 Vaughan St, LL30 1AH. Tel 75575. Open daily 9-5.30. Res on prem. Large stock of porcelain, glass, ivories, jewellery and silver. Also furniture, metal and shipping goods.

Madoc Antique & Art Gallery
(Harold & Louise Aldridge). 48 Madoc St. Tel 79754 (priv 79760). Open Mon-Sat 9-5.30; other times by appt. 18th and 19thC furniture, 19thC silver and paintings, barometers, clocks, watches and pianos.

Llangefni STD 0248

Owens Gwynedd & Co
(G.E.&M.Owens). Llanerchymedd Auction Centre. Tel 722950 (priv 0248-76 482). (Office at 56 High St, Llangefni, Isle of Anglesey, LL77 7NA.) Auctioneers, estate agents, surveyors and valuers. Sales of antiques & quality household effects.

Llanrwst STD 0492

Snowdonia Antiques
(Jeffrey Collins). Station Rd, LL26 0EP. Tel 640789 (priv 640027). Open 10-5; other times by appt. Period furniture and grandfather clocks, particularly Llanrwst clocks. LAPADA

Portmeirion

Angel Arcade
(Sylvia Jones). Tel Penrhyndeudraeth (0766) 770 228. Open daily except Tues. Antique furniture, jewellery, Staffordshire figures, ceramics and Welsh items.

Pwllheli STD 0758

Rodney Adams Antiques
Hall Place, 10 Penlan St, LL53 5DH. Tel 613173 (priv 614337). Open Mon-Sat 9-5; other times by appt. Period furniture and grandfather clocks.

Mayfair Antiques
11A, Goal St. Tel 613033. Furniture, 19thC ceramics, brass, copper. LAPADA

Powys

Brecon STD 0874

D.G. & A.S. Evans
7 The Struet, LD3 7LL. Tel 2714. Open daily; early closing Wed. Maps and prints specialising in Welsh topography.

Knighton STD 0547

Walkmill Antiques
(A.J. & C.Beirne). 2 Broad St, LD7 1AT. Tel 528002. (Also at 7 High St.) Open Mon, Tues, Thurs, Fri, Sat 10-5; other times by appt. General antiques.

Machynlleth STD 0654

Colin S.Hughes
36 Penrallt St. Tel 2363. Open Mon-Sat 9-6; other times by appt. Three showrooms of 18thC oak, country furniture, pine, mahogany, walnut, Victoriana, shipping goods. Mainly trade.

G. & M.Hughes
6 Penrallt St. Tel 2053. Victorian jewellery and general antiques. Welsh dressers a speciality.

Newtown STD 0686

Severn Antiques
11-12 Severn St. Tel 26265. Open Mon-Sat; early closing Sat. Furniture, porcelain, pictures and glass.

Presteigne STD 0544

Christie's
(Representative: Sir Andrew Duff Gordon, Bt). Downton House, New Radnor. Tel Cheltenham (0242) 518999. Auctioneers and valuers.

Welshpool STD 0938

F.E.Anderson & Son
(David Anderson, Ian Anderson). 5 High St, SY21 7JF. Tel 3340 (priv 3324 or 75509). Open Mon-Fri 9-5, Sat 9-2; other times by appt. Good antique furniture of the 16th, 17th, 18th & mid 19thC. Some porcelain, paintings, glass, metalwork, etc. LAPADA

Waterloo Antiques
(Ruth & Nigel Robinson). 1-2 Waterloo Place, Salop Rd. Tel 3999. Furniture, porcelain, metalwork and paintings. LAPADA

Tudor Rose and Mona Antiqua

Beaumaris, Anglesey

Antiques and Objects of Art

Hendrik Lek & Son

31 & 32 CASTLE STREET

Collectors will find the largest stock of antique furniture, china, glass, curios, antiquarian prints and paintings in North Wales in our two attractive buildings one of which is scheduled as an ancient monument. *To view stock in 'Tudor Rose' apply at 'Mona Antiqua' across the road.*

We specialise in antiquarian prints of all counties of Gt. Britain, and other parts of the world. Also prints of animals, birds, flowers, famous people, historical, satirical, naval and theatrical subjects. Also maps and paintings, ephemera, objets d'art and vertu, treen, ethnography

Telephone Beaumaris (STD 0248) 810203

During January and February it is advisable to make a telephone appointment before calling.

THE TUDOR ROSE
A.D. 1400
Proprietor:
KAREL LEK, ATD, RCA

Curiosity Shop

Specialising in Oak, Mahogany and Walnut Furniture and Militaria

Always a large selection of Oils, Watercolours and Clocks

Open 7 days per week

An excellent Trade Call

For further details and catalogue contact:

High Str., Llandovery, Dyfed, West Wales

Telephone: 0550 20390
Evenings: 0550 20984

FINE QUALITY WATERCOLOURS

BETTY WILLIAMS

THE GALLERY, TYR EGLWYS TREDUNNOCK, USK, GWENT

Reginald Mills, R.A., R.B.A. Exhibited 1921–1958
Cottages in Stoke Gabriel on the River Dart, South Devon.

OTHER ARTISTS IN STOCK:—

W. W. Ball, T. Campbell, W. Cook, A. D. Fripp, G. A. Fripp, H. Hammond, Parker Hagarty, C. Hayes, C. S. Lidderdale, W. Mathison, J. McDougal, Warren Williams, G. Whyatt, A. C. Wyatt, J. Yardley

EXHIBITIONS HELD IN MAY AND NOVEMBER

Open throughout the year by appointment

PLEASE TELEPHONE TREDUNNOCK (063349) 301

SPECIAL OFFER
to
ANTIQUE DEALERS

The British Art & Antiques Directory
at the wholesale rate – **33%** discount.

Give your customers the chance to buy this prestigious book. Order 5 or more copies and take advantage of our special wholesale rate – £7 each including delivery. No payment required now; we will invoice you on delivery.

All orders to: The British Art & Antiques Directory, National Magazine House, 72 Broadwick Street, London W1V 2BP (Tel. 01-439 7144).

HIGH STREET, CAERLEON, GWENT
Telephone 0633-420535

MARC RHYS

CAERLEON

By Appointment

BRITISH ART & ANTIQUES DIRECTORY 1987

GAZETTEER OF TOWNS AND VILLAGES

How to Use This Book
After the editorial articles the book is divided into five main sections:
1 Directory (*begins on page 37*)
Dealers, auctioneers, packers, restorers, trade suppliers and so on are all listed here, with address, telephone number, opening hours, and type of business or area of specialisation. Entries are listed in alphabetical order under town or village, within the relevant county and geographical area.
2 Gazetteer (*begins on page 265*)
This is an alphabetical list of the towns and villages mentioned in the Directory, showing the counties and geographical areas under which they are listed.
3. Index to Specialists
(*begins on page 270*)
Directory entries are here listed under type of business or nature of stock.
4. Index to Business Names
(*begins on page 363*)
All business names in the Directory are listed alphabetically with their town or village, county and geographical area.
5 Maps (*begin on page 391*)
Showing villages and towns listed in the Directory.

Note
Counties and geographical areas are listed with page references under 'Contents' on page 3.
Auctioneers are listed both in the main Directory under the relevant town or village, and in the Specialists index under 'Auctioneers'.
Abbreviations and names and addresses of useful organisations are listed on page 4.

Abbotsbury, Dorset, England.
Aberdeen, Grampian, Scotland.
Aberfeldy, Tayside, Scotland.
Abergavenny, Gwent, Wales.
Aberystwyth, Dyfed, Wales.
Abingdon, Oxfordshire, England.
Abinger Hammer, Surrey, England.
Aboyne, Grampian, Scotland.
Abridge, Essex, England.
Accrington, Lancashire, England.
Adare, Co Limerick, Eire.
Addingham, W.Yorkshire, England.
Alcester, Warwickshire, England.
Aldeburgh, Suffolk, England.
Alderley Edge, Cheshire, England.
Aldersey, Cheshire, England.
Alford, Grampian, Scotland.
Alfriston, E.Sussex, England.
Alnwick, Northumberland, England.
Alresford, Hampshire, England.
Alton, Hampshire, England.
Altrincham, Greater Manchester, England.
Ambergate, Derbyshire, England.
Ambleside, Cumbria, England.
Amersham, Buckinghamshire, England.
Ampthill, Bedfordshire, England.
Andover, Hampshire, England.
Anglesey, Gwynedd, Wales.
Annesley Woodhouse, Nottinghamshire, England.
Anstey, Leicestershire, England.
Appleby, Cumbria, England.
Arnesby, Leicestershire, England.
Arundel, W.Sussex, England.
Ascot, Berkshire, England.
Ashbourne, Derbyshire, England.
Ashburton, Devon, England.
Ashby de la Zouch, Leicestershire, England.
Ashford, Kent, England.
Ashley, Northamptonshire, England.
Ashtead, Surrey, England.
Askham, Nottinghamshire, England.
Aslockton, Nottinghamshire, England.
Atherington, Devon, England.
Attleborough, Norfolk, England.
Auchterarder, Tayside, Scotland.
Avoca, Co Wicklow, Eire.
Axbridge, Somerset, England.
Axminster, Devon, England.
Aylesbury, Buckinghamshire, England.
Aylsham, Norfolk, England.

Bakewell, Derbyshire, England.
Bala, Gwynedd, Wales.
Balcombe, W.Sussex, England.
Baldock, Hertfordshire, England.
Ballater, Grampian, Scotland.
Ballyduff, Co Waterford, Eire.
Bampton, Devon, England.
Banbury, Oxfordshire, England.
Banchory, Grampian, Scotland.
Bangor, Co Down, Northern Ireland.
Bangor, Gwynedd, Wales.
Bannockburn, Central, Scotland.
Banstead, Surrey, England.
Banwell, Avon, England.
Barmouth, Gwynedd, Wales.
Barnard Castle, Durham, England.
Barnet, Hertfordshire, England.
Barnsley, Gloucestershire, England.
Barnsley, S.Yorkshire, England.
Barnstaple, Devon, England.
Barry, S.Glamorgan, Wales.
Basingstoke, Hampshire, England.
Baslow, Derbyshire, England.
Bath, Avon, England.
Batley, W.Yorkshire, England.
Battle, E.Sussex, England.
Battlesbridge, Essex, England.
Bawtry, S.Yorkshire, England.
Beaconsfield, Buckinghamshire, England.
Beaminster, Dorset, England.
Beaulieu, Hampshire, England.
Beauly, Highland, Scotland.
Beaumaris, Gwynedd, Wales.
Beccles, Suffolk, England.
Beckenham, Kent, England.
Bedale, N.Yorkshire, England.
Bedford, Bedfordshire, England.
Belfast, Belfast, Northern Ireland.
Bembridge, Isle of Wight, England.
Benson, Oxfordshire, England.
Berkeley, Gloucestershire, England.
Berkhamsted, Hertfordshire, England.
Berwick-upon-Tweed, Northumberland, England.
Bethesda, Gwynedd, Wales.
Beverley, Humberside, England.
Bewdley, Hereford & Worcester, England.
Bexhill, E.Sussex, England.
Bexley, Kent, England.
Bicester, Oxfordshire, England.
Bickerstaffe, Lancashire, England.
Bideford, Devon, England.
Bidford-on-Avon, Warwickshire, England.
Bieldside, Grampian, Scotland.
Biggin Hill, Kent, England.
Bildeston, Suffolk, England.
Billericay, Essex, England.
Billingham, Cleveland, England.
Billingshurst, W.Sussex, England.
Bingham, Nottinghamshire, England.
Bingley, W.Yorkshire, England.
Birchington, Kent, England.
Birkenhead, Merseyside, England.
Birmingham, W.Midlands, England.
Bishop Auckland, Durham, England.
Bishop's Stortford, Hertfordshire, England.
Bishops Waltham, Hampshire, England.
Blaby, Leicestershire, England.
Blackburn, Lancashire, England.
Blackpool, Lancashire, England.
Blackrock, Co Dublin, Eire.
Bladon, Oxfordshire, England.
Blairgowrie, Tayside, Scotland.
Blakeney, Norfolk, England.
Blandford Forum, Dorset, England.
Bletchingley, Surrey, England.
Blewbury, Oxfordshire, England.
Blockley, Gloucestershire, England.
Blythburgh, Suffolk, England.
Bolton, Greater Manchester, England.
Bordon, Hampshire, England.
Borough Green, Kent, England.
Boroughbridge, N.Yorkshire, England.
Boston, Lincolnshire, England.
Botley, Hampshire, England.
Boughton, Kent, England.
Bourne, Lincolnshire, England.
Bournemouth, Dorset, England.
Bourton-on-the-Water, Gloucestershire, England.
Box, Wiltshire, England.
Boxford, Suffolk, England.
Brackley, Northamptonshire, England.
Bradford, W.Yorkshire, England.
Bradford-on-Avon, Wiltshire, England.
Braintree, Essex, England.
Bramhall, Greater Manchester, England.
Brampton, Cambridgeshire, England.
Brampton, Cumbria, England.
Brasted, Kent, England.
Braunton, Devon, England.
Brecon, Powys, Wales.
Brentwood, Essex, England.
Bridge of Earn, Tayside, Scotland.
Bridgend, Mid Glamorgan, Wales.
Bridgnorth, Shropshire, England.
Bridgwater, Somerset, England.
Bridlington, Humberside, England.
Bridport, Dorset, England.
Brierfield, Lancashire, England.
Brigg, Humberside, England.
Brighton & Hove, E.Sussex, England.
Brinkworth, Wiltshire, England.
Bristol, Avon, England.
Brixham, Devon, England.
Broadstairs, Kent, England.
Broadway, Hereford & Worcester, England.
Brobury, Hereford & Worcester, England.
Bromley, Kent, England.
Brough, Cumbria, England.
Bruton, Somerset, England.
Buckfastleigh, Devon, England.
Buckingham, Buckinghamshire, England.
Bude, Cornwall, England.
Budleigh Salterton, Devon, England.
Bungay, Suffolk, England.
Bures, Suffolk, England.
Burford, Oxfordshire, England.
Burgess Hill, W.Sussex, England.
Burley in Wharfedale, W.Yorkshire, England.
Burnham Market, Norfolk, England.
Burnham-on-Crouch, Essex, England.
Burnham-on-Sea, Somerset, England.
Burnley, Lancashire, England.
Burscough, Lancashire, England.
Burstwick, Humberside, England.
Burton upon Trent, Staffordshire, England.
Burwash, E.Sussex, England.
Burwell, Cambridgeshire, England.
Bury, Greater Manchester, England.
Bury St Edmunds, Suffolk, England.
Bushey, Hertfordshire, England.
Bushmills, Co Antrim, Northern Ireland.
Buxton, Derbyshire, England.
Byfleet, Surrey, England.

Cadnam, Hampshire, England.
Caerleon, Gwent, Wales.
Caernarvon, Gwynedd, Wales.
Callington, Cornwall, England.
Calne, Wiltshire, England.
Camberley, Surrey, England.
Camborne, Cornwall, England.
Cambridge, Cambridgeshire, England.
Canterbury, Kent, England.
Cardiff, S.Glamorgan, Wales.
Cardigan, Dyfed, Wales.
Carlisle, Cumbria, England.
Carmarthen, Dyfed, Wales.
Carnforth, Lancashire, England.
Carrickfergus, Co Antrim, Northern Ireland.
Carshalton, Surrey, England.
Cartmel, Cumbria, England.
Cassington, Oxfordshire, England.
Castle Cary, Somerset, England.
Castle Combe, Wiltshire, England.
Castle Douglas, Dumfries & Galloway, Scotland.
Castle Hedingham, Essex, England.
Castle Lyons, Co Cork, Eire.
Castleton, Derbyshire, England.
Castletown, Isle of Man.
Caversham, Berkshire, England.
Cerne Abbas, Dorset, England.
Chagford, Devon, England.
Chalfont St Giles, Buckinghamshire, England.
Charing, Kent, England.
Charlton Horethorne, Dorset, England.
Chatham, Kent, England.
Cheadle, Greater Manchester, England.
Cheadle Hulme, Greater Manchester, England.
Cheam, Surrey, England.
Chelmsford, Essex, England.
Cheltenham, Gloucestershire, England.
Chepstow, Gwent, Wales.
Chertsey, Surrey, England.
Chesham, Buckinghamshire, England.
Chester, Cheshire, England.
Chesterfield, Derbyshire, England.
Chichester, W.Sussex, England.
Chilham, Kent, England.
Chippenham, Wiltshire, England.
Chipping Campden, Gloucestershire, England.
Chipping Norton, Oxfordshire, England.
Chislehurst, Kent, England.
Chobham, Surrey, England.
Christchurch, Dorset, England.
Church Enstone, Oxfordshire, England.
Church Stretton, Shropshire, England.
Churchover, Warwickshire, England.
Cinderford, Gloucestershire, England.
Cirencester, Gloucestershire, England.
Clare, Suffolk, England.
Clevedon, Avon, England.
Clitheroe, Lancashire, England.
Cloghran, Co Dublin, Eire.
Clutton, Avon, England.
Coalville, Leicestershire, England.
Coatbridge, Strathclyde, Scotland.
Cobham, Surrey, England.
Cockermouth, Cumbria, England.
Coggeshall, Essex, England.
Colchester, Essex, England.
Coldstream, Borders, Scotland.
Coleford, Gloucestershire, England.
Colsterworth, Lincolnshire, England.
Coltishall, Norfolk, England.
Colwyn Bay, Clwyd, Wales.
Colyton, Devon, England.
Compton Abbas, Dorset, England.
Coningsby, Lincolnshire, England.
Coniston, Cumbria, England.
Cookham, Berkshire, England.
Cookstown, Co Tyrone, Northern Ireland.
Corbridge, Northumberland, England.
Cork, Co Cork, Eire.
Corsham, Wiltshire, England.
Cosgrove, Northamptonshire, England.
Coventry, W.Midlands, England.
Cowbridge, S.Glamorgan, Wales.
Cowes, Isle of Wight, England.
Cranbrook, Kent, England.
Cranleigh, Surrey, England.
Craven Arms, Shropshire, England.
Crayford, Kent, England.
Crediton, Devon, England.
Crewkerne, Somerset, England.
Cricklade, Wiltshire, England.
Cromer, Norfolk, England.
Croydon, Cambridgeshire, England.
Croydon, Surrey, England.
Cuckfield, W.Sussex, England.
Culham, Oxfordshire, England.
Cullompton, Devon, England.
Curry Rivel, Somerset, England.

Darlington, Durham, England.
Dartford, Kent, England.
Dartington, Devon, England.
Dartmouth, Devon, England.
Darwen, Lancashire, England.
Datchet, Berkshire, England.
Deal, Kent, England.
Debenham, Suffolk, England.
Deddington, Oxfordshire, England.
Deeside, Clwyd, Wales.
Denham, Buckinghamshire, England.
Derby, Derbyshire, England.
Dereham, Norfolk, England.
Devizes, Wiltshire, England.
Didcot, Oxfordshire, England.
Didsbury, Greater Manchester, England.
Dingwall, Highland, Scotland.
Disley, Cheshire, England.
Diss, Norfolk, England.
Ditchling, E.Sussex, England.
Doddington, Cambridgeshire, England.
Doncaster, S.Yorkshire, England.
Donegal Town, Co Donegal, Eire.
Donington-on-Bain, Lincolnshire, England.

Longton, Lancashire, England.
Looe, Cornwall, England.
Lostwithiel, Cornwall, England.
Loughborough, Leicestershire, England.
Loughton, Essex, England.
Lowestoft, Suffolk, England.
Ludlow, Shropshire, England.
Lugwardine, Hereford & Worcester, England.
Luton, Bedfordshire, England.
Lyddington, Leicestershire, England.
Lymington, Hampshire, England.
Lyndhurst, Hampshire, England.

Macclesfield, Cheshire, England.
Machynlleth, Powys, Wales.
Maidenhead, Berkshire, England.
Maidstone, Kent, England.
Malahide, Co Dublin, Eire.
Maldon, Essex, England.
Malmesbury, Wiltshire, England.
Malpas, Cheshire, England.
Malvern, Hereford & Worcester, England.
Manchester, Greater Manchester, England.
Mansfield, Nottinghamshire, England.
March, Cambridgeshire, England.
Market Deeping, Lincolnshire, England.
Market Drayton, Shropshire, England.
Market Harborough, Leicestershire, England.
Market Rasen, Lincolnshire, England.
Market Weighton, Humberside, England.
Marlborough, Wiltshire, England.
Marlow, Buckinghamshire, England.
Matlock, Derbyshire, England.
Maybole, Strathclyde, Scotland.
Mayfield, E.Sussex, England.
Melbourn, Cambridgeshire, England.
Melbourne, Derbyshire, England.
Melchbourne, Bedfordshire, England.
Melksham, Wiltshire, England.
Melmerby, N.Yorkshire, England.
Melton Constable, Norfolk, England.
Meonstoke, Hampshire, England.
Merstham, Surrey, England.
Middle Wallop, Hampshire, England.
Middlesbrough, Cleveland, England.
Midhurst, W.Sussex, England.
Midsomer Norton, Avon, England.
Milburn, Cumbria, England.
Milford, Surrey, England.
Milton Keynes, Buckinghamshire, England.
Milverton, Somerset, England.
Minehead, Somerset, England.
Minster, Kent, England.
Mirfield, W.Yorkshire, England.
Moffat, Dumfries & Galloway, Scotland.
Mold, Clwyd, Wales.
Monks Risborough, Buckinghamshire, England.
Monmouth, Gwent, Wales.
Morden, Surrey, England.
Moreton-in-Marsh, Gloucestershire, England.
Moretonhampstead, Devon, England.
Morley, W.Yorkshire, England.
Mousehole, Cornwall, England.
Moylegrove, Dyfed, Wales.
Much Hadham, Hertfordshire, England.
Much Wenlock, Shropshire, England.
Muir of Ord, Highland, Scotland.

Nailsworth, Gloucestershire, England.
Nairn, Highland, Scotland.
Nantwich, Cheshire, England.
Naphill, Buckinghamshire, England.
Navenby, Lincolnshire, England.
Nayland, Suffolk, England.
Neath, W.Glamorgan, Wales.
Needham Market, Suffolk, England.
Neston, Cheshire, England.
Nettlebed, Oxfordshire, England.
New Brighton, Merseyside, England.
New Milton, Hampshire, England.
New Romney, Kent, England.
Newark-on-Trent, Nottinghamshire, England.
Newbury, Berkshire, England.
Newby Bridge, Cumbria, England.
Newcastle upon Tyne, Tyne & Wear, England.
Newcastle-under-Lyme, Staffordshire, England.
Newhaven, E.Sussex, England.
Newmarket, Suffolk, England.
Newport, Essex, England.
Newport, Gwent, Wales.
Newport, Shropshire, England.
Newquay, Cornwall, England.
Newry, Co Down, Northern Ireland.
Newton, Nottinghamshire, England.
Newton Abbot, Devon, England.
Newtonmore, Highland, Scotland.
Newtown, Powys, Wales.
Newtownabbey, Co Antrim, Northern Ireland.
Newtownards, Co Down, Northern Ireland.
Ninfield, E.Sussex, England.
Nonington, Kent, England.
North Berwick, Lothian, Scotland.
North Shields, Tyne & Wear, England.
North Walsham, Norfolk, England.
Northallerton, N.Yorkshire, England.
Northam, Devon, England.
Northampton, Northamptonshire, England.
Northiam, E.Sussex, England.
Northop, Clwyd, Wales.
Norwich, Norfolk, England.
Nottingham, Nottinghamshire, England.
Nuneaton, Warwickshire, England.

Oakamoor, Staffordshire, England.
Oakham, Leicestershire, England.
Odiham, Hampshire, England.
Okehampton, Devon, England.
Old Costessey, Norfolk, England.
Old Glossop, Derbyshire, England.
Oldham, Greater Manchester, England.
Oldswinford, W.Midlands, England.
Olney, Buckinghamshire, England.
Orford, Suffolk, England.
Ormskirk, Lancashire, England.
Orwell, Cambridgeshire, England.
Osbournby, Lincolnshire, England.
Oswestry, Shropshire, England.
Otford, Kent, England.
Otley, W.Yorkshire, England.
Ottery St Mary, Devon, England.
Oughterard, Co Galway, Eire.
Oundle, Northamptonshire, England.
Outwell, Cambridgeshire, England.
Oxford, Oxfordshire, England.
Oxted, Surrey, England.

Padstow, Cornwall, England.
Painswick, Gloucestershire, England.
Parkgate, Cheshire, England.
Pateley Bridge, N.Yorkshire, England.
Paulerspury, Northamptonshire, England.
Peasenhall, Suffolk, England.
Peel, Isle of Man.
Pembroke, Dyfed, Wales.
Pen-y-Lan, S.Glamorgan, Wales.
Penn, Buckinghamshire, England.
Penrith, Cumbria, England.
Penshurst, Kent, England.
Penzance, Cornwall, England.
Pershore, Hereford & Worcester, England.
Perth, Tayside, Scotland.
Peterborough, Cambridgeshire, England.
Petersfield, Hampshire, England.
Petworth, W.Sussex, England.
Pevensey, E.Sussex, England.
Pewsey, Wiltshire, England.
Pickering, N.Yorkshire, England.
Pinner, Middlesex, England.
Pitlochry, Tayside, Scotland.
Plaitford, Hampshire, England.
Plumley, Cheshire, England.
Plymouth, Devon, England.
Polegate, E.Sussex, England.
Poole, Dorset, England.
Portmeirion, Gwynedd, Wales.
Portrush, Co Antrim, Northern Ireland.
Portslade, E.Sussex, England.
Portsmouth, Hampshire, England.
Potterne, Wiltshire, England.
Potterspury, Northamptonshire, England.
Powick, Hereford & Worcester, England.
Poynton, Cheshire, England.
Prestbury, Cheshire, England.
Presteigne, Powys, Wales.
Preston, Lancashire, England.
Prestwich, Greater Manchester, England.
Priestacott Meshaw, Devon, England.
Princes Risborough, Buckinghamshire, England.
Priors Marston, Warwickshire, England.
Probus, Cornwall, England.
Puckeridge, Hertfordshire, England.
Pudsey, W.Yorkshire, England.
Pulborough, W.Sussex, England.
Pwllheli, Gwynedd, Wales.

Quarndon, Derbyshire, England.
Quorn, Leicestershire, England.

Radlett, Hertfordshire, England.
Rainham, Kent, England.
Rait, by Perth, Tayside, Scotland.
Ramsey, Cambridgeshire, England.
Ramsgate, Kent, England.
Ratcliffe-on-the-Wreake, Leicestershire, England.
Rayleigh, Essex, England.
Reach, Cambridgeshire, England.
Reading, Berkshire, England.
Red Marley, Gloucestershire, England.
Redbourn, Hertfordshire, England.
Redditch, Hereford & Worcester, England.
Redhill, Surrey, England.
Redmile, Leicestershire, England.
Reepham, Norfolk, England.
Reigate, Surrey, England.
Retford, Nottinghamshire, England.
Reymerston, Norfolk, England.
Rhos-on-Sea, Clwyd, Wales.
Rhuddlan, Clwyd, Wales.
Richmond, N.Yorkshire, England.
Richmond, Surrey, England.
Rickmansworth, Hertfordshire, England.
Ringwood, Hampshire, England.
Ripley, Surrey, England.
Ripon, N.Yorkshire, England.
Robertsbridge, E.Sussex, England.
Rochdale, Greater Manchester, England.
Rochester, Kent, England.
Rolvenden, Kent, England.
Romford, Essex, England.
Romsey, Hampshire, England.
Roscrea, Co Tipperary, Eire.
Ross-on-Wye, Hereford & Worcester, England.
Rothbury, Northumberland, England.
Rotherham, S.Yorkshire, England.
Rothley, Leicestershire, England.
Rottingdean, E.Sussex, England.
Royston, Hertfordshire, England.
Rudgwick, W.Sussex, England.
Rugby, Warwickshire, England.
Rugeley, Staffordshire, England.
Ruthin, Clwyd, Wales.
Ryde, Isle of Wight, England.
Rye, E.Sussex, England.

Saffron Walden, Essex, England.
Salcombe, Devon, England.
Sale, Greater Manchester, England.
Salford, Greater Manchester, England.
Salisbury, Wiltshire, England.
Saltburn-by-the-Sea, Cleveland, England.
Sandiacre, Derbyshire, England.
Sandwich, Kent, England.
Sandycove, Co Dublin, Eire.
Sawbridgeworth, Hertfordshire, England.
Saxmundham, Suffolk, England.
Scarborough, N.Yorkshire, England.
Seaford, E.Sussex, England.
Seaham, Durham, England.
Seaton, Devon, England.
Sedbergh, Cumbria, England.
Selborne, Hampshire, England.
Settle, N.Yorkshire, England.
Sevenoaks, Kent, England.
Shackleford, Surrey, England.
Shaftesbury, Dorset, England.
Shanklin, Isle of Wight, England.
Shannon Airport, Co Clare, Eire.
Sheffield, S.Yorkshire, England.
Shefford, Bedfordshire, England.
Shepshed, Leicestershire, England.
Shepton Mallet, Somerset, England.
Sherborne, Dorset, England.
Shere, Surrey, England.
Sheringham, Norfolk, England.
Sherston, Wiltshire, England.
Shifnal, Shropshire, England.
Shipston on Stour, Warwickshire, England.
Shipton-under-Wychwood, Oxfordshire, England.
Shirley, Surrey, England.
Shoreham, Kent, England.
Shoreham-by-Sea, W.Sussex, England.
Shotton, Clwyd, Wales.
Shrewsbury, Shropshire, England.
Sible Hedingham, Essex, England.
Sidcup, Kent, England.
Sidmouth, Devon, England.
Sissinghurst, Kent, England.
Sittingbourne, Kent, England.
Skipton, N.Yorkshire, England.
Sleaford, Lincolnshire, England.
Smeeth, Kent, England.
Snodland, Kent, England.
Soham, Cambridgeshire, England.
Somerton, Somerset, England.
South Brent, Devon, England.
South Darenth, Kent, England.
South Molton, Devon, England.
South Ockendon, Essex, England.
South Shields, Tyne & Wear, England.
South Walsham, Norfolk, England.
Southampton, Hampshire, England.
Southport, Merseyside, England.
Southsea, Hampshire, England.
Southwell, Nottinghamshire, England.
Southwold, Suffolk, England.
Spalding, Lincolnshire, England.
Spilsby, Lincolnshire, England.
St Albans, Hertfordshire, England.
St Andrews, Fife, Scotland.
St Anne's, Lancashire, England.
St Asaph, Clwyd, Wales.
St Austell, Cornwall, England.
St Boswells, Borders, Scotland.

St Helens, Merseyside, England.
St Helier, Jersey, Channel Islands.
St Ives, Cambridgeshire, England.
St Ives, Cornwall, England.
St Lawrence, Jersey, Channel Islands.
St Leonards, E.Sussex, England.
St Ouen, Jersey, Channel Islands.
St Peter Port, Guernsey, Channel Islands.
St Sampson's, Guernsey, Channel Islands.
Stafford, Staffordshire, England.
Staines, Middlesex, England.
Stalham, Norfolk, England.
Stamford, Lincolnshire, England.
Standlake, Oxfordshire, England.
Stanford le Hope, Essex, England.
Stansted Mountfitchet, Essex, England.
Stapleford, Lincolnshire, England.
Stevenage, Hertfordshire, England.
Stock, Essex, England.
Stockbridge, Hampshire, England.
Stockport, Greater Manchester, England.
Stockton-on-Tees, Cleveland, England.
Stoke Ferry, Norfolk, England.
Stoke-by-Nayland, Suffolk, England.
Stoke-on-Trent, Staffordshire, England.
Stokesley, N.Yorkshire, England.
Stone, Staffordshire, England.
Stourbridge, W.Midlands, England.
Stow-on-the-Wold, Gloucestershire, England.
Stowmarket, Suffolk, England.
Stratford-upon-Avon, Warwickshire, England.
Streatley, Berkshire, England.
Stroud, Gloucestershire, England.
Studley, Warwickshire, England.
Sturminster Newton, Dorset, England.
Sudbury, Suffolk, England.
Sunderland, Tyne & Wear, England.
Sundridge, Kent, England.
Surbiton, Surrey, England.
Sutton, Surrey, England.
Sutton Coldfield, W.Midlands, England.
Swaffham, Norfolk, England.
Swanage, Dorset, England.
Swansea, W.Glamorgan, Wales.
Swindon, Wiltshire, England.

Tadworth, Surrey, England.
Tanworth-in-Arden, Warwickshire, England.
Tarporley, Cheshire, England.
Taunton, Somerset, England.
Taunton Lydeard, Somerset, England.
Tavistock, Devon, England.
Teddington, Middlesex, England.
Teignmouth, Devon, England.
Telford, Shropshire, England.
Templecombe, Somerset, England.
Tenby, Dyfed, Wales.
Tenterden, Kent, England.
Tetbury, Gloucestershire, England.
Tewkesbury, Gloucestershire, England.
Thame, Oxfordshire, England.
Thatcham, Berkshire, England.
Thaxted, Essex, England.
Theydon Bois, Essex, England.
Thirsk, N.Yorkshire, England.
Thornaby, Cleveland, England.
Thornbury, Avon, England.
Thorpe Arch, W.Yorkshire, England.
Thorpe-le-Soken, Essex, England.
Thrapston, Northamptonshire, England.
Thurnby, Leicestershire, England.
Thurso, Highland, Scotland.
Ticehurst, E.Sussex, England.
Tichborne, Hampshire, England.
Ticknall, Derbyshire, England.
Tintern, Gwent, Wales.
Tipperary, Co Tipperary, Eire.
Tisbury, Wiltshire, England.
Titchfield, Hampshire, England.
Tiverton, Devon, England.
Toddington, Bedfordshire, England.
Tonbridge, Kent, England.
Topsham, Devon, England.
Torquay, Devon, England.
Totnes, Devon, England.
Towcester, Northamptonshire, England.
Tramore, Co Waterford, Eire.
Tring, Hertfordshire, England.
Trumpington, Cambridgeshire, England.
Truro, Cornwall, England.
Tunbridge Wells, Kent, England.
Tunstall, Lancashire, England.
Tuxford, Nottinghamshire, England.
Twickenham, Middlesex, England.
Twyford, Berkshire, England.

Uckfield, E.Sussex, England.
Uley, Gloucestershire, England.
Ullenwood, Gloucestershire, England.
Ulverston, Cumbria, England.
Upham, Hampshire, England.
Usk, Gwent, Wales.
Uttoxeter, Staffordshire, England.
Uxbridge, Middlesex, England.

Ventnor, Isle of Wight, England.
Virginia Water, Surrey, England.

Waddesdon, Buckinghamshire, England.
Wadebridge, Cornwall, England.
Wadhurst, E.Sussex, England.
Wainfleet, Lincolnshire, England.
Wakefield, W.Yorkshire, England.
Wakes Colne, Essex, England.
Wallasey, Merseyside, England.
Wallingford, Oxfordshire, England.
Walsall, W.Midlands, England.
Waltham Cross, Hertfordshire, England.
Walton on the Hill, Surrey, England.
Walton-on-Thames, Surrey, England.
Wantage, Oxfordshire, England.
Warboys, Cambridgeshire, England.
Ware, Hertfordshire, England.
Wareham, Dorset, England.
Warminster, Wiltshire, England.
Warrington, Cheshire, England.
Warwick, Warwickshire, England.
Washington, Tyne & Wear, England.
Washington, W.Sussex, England.
Waterbeach, Cambridgeshire, England.
Watford, Hertfordshire, England.
Watlington, Oxfordshire, England.
Watton, Norfolk, England.
Wealdstone, Middlesex, England.
Weedon, Northamptonshire, England.
Wellingborough, Northamptonshire, England.
Wellington, Somerset, England.
Wells, Norfolk, England.
Wells, Somerset, England.
Welshpool, Powys, Wales.
Wendover, Buckinghamshire, England.
West Byfleet, Surrey, England.
West Felton, Shropshire, England.
West Haddon, Northamptonshire, England.
West Kirby, Merseyside, England.
West Linton, Borders, Scotland.
West Malling, Kent, England.
West Wickham, Kent, England.
West Wycombe, Buckinghamshire, England.
Westbury, Wiltshire, England.
Westcliff-on-Sea, Essex, England.
Westerham, Kent, England.
Weston, Suffolk, England.
Weston Turville, Buckinghamshire, England.
Weston-on-the-Green, Oxfordshire, England.
Weston-super-Mare, Avon, England.
Westport, Co Mayo, Eire.
Wetherby, W.Yorkshire, England.
Weybridge, Surrey, England.
Weymouth, Dorset, England.
Whaley Bridge, Derbyshire, England.
Whalley, Lancashire, England.
Whatlington, E.Sussex, England.
Wheathampstead, Hertfordshire, England.
Whelford, Gloucestershire, England.
Whimple, Devon, England.
Whitby, N.Yorkshire, England.
Whitchurch, Shropshire, England.
White Waltham, Berkshire, England.
Whitegate, Cheshire, England.
Whitehaven, Cumbria, England.
Whitley Bay, Tyne & Wear, England.
Whittlesford, Cambridgeshire, England.
Wickham, Hampshire, England.
Wickham Market, Suffolk, England.
Wigan, Greater Manchester, England.
Willenhall, W.Midlands, England.
Wilmslow, Cheshire, England.
Wilshamstead, Bedfordshire, England.
Wilton, Wiltshire, England.
Wimborne Minster, Dorset, England.
Wincanton, Somerset, England.
Winchcombe, Gloucestershire, England.
Winchelsea, E.Sussex, England.
Winchester, Hampshire, England.
Windermere, Cumbria, England.
Windsor, Berkshire, England.
Winforton, Hereford & Worcester, England.
Wingham, Kent, England.
Winkleigh, Devon, England.
Wirral, Merseyside, England.
Wisbech, Cambridgeshire, England.
Witham, Essex, England.
Witley, Surrey, England.
Witney, Oxfordshire, England.
Wiveliscombe, Somerset, England.
Woburn, Bedfordshire, England.
Woburn Sands, Buckinghamshire, England.
Woking, Surrey, England.
Wokingham, Berkshire, England.
Wolverhampton, W.Midlands, England.
Wolvesnewton, Gwent, Wales.
Wonersh, Surrey, England.
Woodbridge, Suffolk, England.
Woodford Green, Essex, England.
Woodhall Spa, Lincolnshire, England.
Woodstock, Oxfordshire, England.
Wooler, Northumberland, England.
Woolhampton, Berkshire, England.
Woolhope, Hereford & Worcester, England.
Woolpit, Suffolk, England.
Wootton Bassett, Wiltshire, England.
Worcester, Hereford & Worcester, England.
Worksop, Nottinghamshire, England.
Worsley, Greater Manchester, England.
Worthing, W.Sussex, England.
Wotton-under-Edge, Gloucestershire, England.
Wragby, Lincolnshire, England.
Wraysbury, Berkshire, England.
Wrentham, Suffolk, England.
Wrexham, Clwyd, Wales.
Wrington, Avon, England.
Wroxham, Norfolk, England.
Wymeswold, Leicestershire, England.
Wymondham, Norfolk, England.

Yarmouth, Isle of Wight, England.
Yatton, Avon, England.
Yeovil, Somerset, England.
York, N.Yorkshire, England.
Yoxall, Staffordshire, England.
Yoxford, Suffolk, England.

INDEX TO SPECIALISTS: ALPHABETICAL LIST OF HEADINGS

BRITISH ART & ANTIQUES DIRECTORY 1987

INDEX TO SPECIALISTS

How to Use This Book
After the editorial articles the book is divided into five main sections:
1 Directory (*begins on page 37*)
Dealers, auctioneers, packers, restorers, trade suppliers and so on are all listed here, with address, telephone number, opening hours, and type of business or area of specialisation. Entries are listed in alphabetical order under town or village, within the relevant county and geographical area.
2 Gazetteer (*begins on page 265*)
This is an alphabetical list of the towns and villages mentioned in the Directory, showing the counties and geographical areas under which they are listed.
3. Index to Specialists
(*begins on page 270*)
Directory entries are here listed under type of business or nature of stock.
4. Index to Business Names
(*begins on page 363*)
All business names in the Directory are listed alphabetically with their town or village, county and geographical area.
5 Maps (*begin on page 391*)
Showing villages and towns listed in the Directory.

Note
Counties and geographical areas are listed with page references under 'Contents' on page 3.
Auctioneers are listed both in the main Directory under the relevant town or village, and in the Specialists index under 'Auctioneers'.
Abbreviations and names and addresses of useful organisations are listed on page 4.

Americana

Clive A.Burden Ltd. 13 Cecil Court, London, WC2N 4EZ. Tel 836 2177.

The Crane Gallery. 171A Sloane St, (1st Floor), London, SW1. Tel 235 2464.

Gene & Sally Foster (Antiques). 27A Belvedere, Lansdown Rd, Bath, Avon, BA1 5HR. Tel 28256 (priv 28058).

Rutland Gallery & Co. 32a St George St, London, W1. Tel 499 5636.

Antique Markets and Centres

London

Alfies Antique Market. 13-25 Church St, London, NW8. Tel 723 6066.

Antiquarius. 135-141 King's Rd, Chelsea, London, SW3. Tel 351 5353.

Bermondsey Antique Market Ltd. 251-255 Long Lane, London, SE1.

Bond Street Antique Centre. 124 New Bond St, London, W1Y 9AE. Tel 351 5353.

Camden Antique Market. Corner of High St and Buck St, London, NW1. Tel 351 5353.

Camden Passage Antiques Market. Upper Street, Islington, London, N1.

Chelsea Antique Market. 245a & 253 King's Road, London, SW3. Tel 352 5689.

Chenil Galleries. 181-183 King's Rd, Chelsea, London, SW3. Tel 351 5353.

Cutler Street Antique Market. Cutler St, London, E1. Tel 351 5353.

Dixon's Antique Centre. 471 Upper Richmond Road West,East Sheen, London, SW14. Tel 878 6788.

Georgian Village Vaults and Galleries. Camden Passage, London, N1. Tel 226 2159.

Grays Antique Market & Grays Mews. 58 Davies St and 1-7 Davies Mews, London, W1. Tel 629 7034.

Greenwich Antiques Market. Greenwich Market, College Approach,Greenwich, London, SE10. Tel 240 7405.

Hampstead Antique Emporium. 12 Heath St, London, NW3. Tel 794 3297.

Jubilee Antiques Market. The Piazza,Covent Garden, London, WC2. Tel 240 7405.

The Mall Antiques Arcade. 359 Upper St, Camden Passage,Islington, London, N1. Tel 359 0825, 349 3111.

Portobello Antiques Markets. 165-169 & 177 Portobello Rd, London, W11. Tel 431 2875 (24 hours).

Rogers Antiques Gallery. 65 Portobello Rd, London, W11. Tel (enquiries) 351 5353.

Regions

Abingdon House - The Antique Centre. 136 High St, Honiton, Devon, EX14 8JP. Tel 2108/86300 (priv 850464).

Abridge Antiques Centre. Market Place, Abridge, Essex. Tel Theydon Bois (037 881) 3113.

Amersham Antique Centre. 20-22 Whielden St,Old Amersham, Amersham, Buckinghamshire. Tel 3939.

Annexe Antiques. 33 The Pantiles, Tunbridge Wells, Kent.

Antique and Collectors Market. 4 Warwick Place, Worthing, W.Sussex.

Antique and Furniture Centre. 46/48 Kings Rd, Harrogate, N.Yorkshire. Tel 509708.

The Antique Centre. Angel St, Petworth, W.Sussex, GU28 0BQ. Tel 43221.

Antique Centre. 20-22 Bell St, Princes Risborough, Buckinghamshire.

Antique Centre. Brookend, Ross-on-Wye, Hereford & Worcester. Tel 62752.

Antique Centre. The Royal Hotel,Ablewell St, Walsall, W.Midlands.

Antique Market. 72 St Stephen St, Edinburgh, Lothian. Tel 225 6016.

Antiques & Crafts Market. The Exchange, Corn St, Bristol, Avon, BS1 1JQ. Tel 20021.

The Antiques Centre. Laurel House, Bull Ring, Deddington, Oxfordshire, OX4 5TT. Tel 38968 (priv 0934 412069).

The Antiques Centre. 22 Haydon Place, Guildford, Surrey, GU1 4LL. Tel 67817.

The Antiques Centre. London House, High St, Moreton-in-Marsh, Gloucestershire. Tel 51084.

The Antiques Centre. 120 London Rd, Sevenoaks, Kent. Tel 52104.

The Antiques Complex. St Nicholas Place, Leicester, Leicestershire. Tel 26596.

The Arcade. 77 Bridge Rd, East Molesey, Surrey, KT8 9HN. Tel 979 7954.

Arundel Antique & Collectors' Market. 51 High St, Arundel, W.Sussex. Tel 883590.

Arundel Antiques Market. The Shipyard, River Rd, Arundel, W.Sussex.

Baddow Antiques and Craft Centre. The Bringy, Great Baddow, Essex. Tel Chelmsford (0245) 76159.

The Barn Collectors Market. Church Lane (off High St), Seaford, E.Sussex, BN25 1HL. Tel 890010.

Bartlett Street Antique Market. 7-10 Bartlett St, Bath, Avon. Tel (office) 66689.

Bath Antique Market. Guinea Lane, Lansdown Rd, Bath, Avon. Tel 858467, 60909.

Bath Saturday Antique Market. Walcot St, Bath, Avon. Tel 317837, 858467.

Battlesbridge Antique Centre. Battlesbridge, Essex. Tel Wickford (03744) 63344.

The Bingley Antiques Centre. Keighley Rd, Bingley, W.Yorkshire. Tel Bradford (0274) 567316.

Birmingham Antique Centre. 141 Bromsgrove Street, Birmingham, W.Midlands, B5 6RQ. Tel 692 1414.

Brighton Antiques Gallery. 41 Meeting House Lane, Brighton & Hove, E.Sussex. Tel 26693, 21059.

Castle Gate Antique Centre. 55 Castlegate, Newark-on-Trent, Nottinghamshire. Tel 700076.

Chateau Briand Antique Centre. High St, Burwash, E.Sussex. Tel 882535.

Chelmsford Antiques and Collectors Market. Chancellor Hall, Market Rd, Chelmsford, Essex. Tel 71079 & 466952.

Cheltenham Antique Centre. 1A Crescent Place, Cheltenham, Gloucestershire.

Cheltenham Antique Market. 54 Suffolk Rd, Cheltenham, Gloucestershire. Tel 529812.

Chesterfield Antiques Centre. 195 Chatsworth Rd, Chesterfield, Derbyshire. Tel 205614.

Chobham Antiques Market. The Old Print House,Rear of 62 High St, Chobham, Surrey, GU24 8AA. Tel 6227.

Cirencester Antique Market. Market Square, Cirencester, Gloucestershire.

Cliffe Antiques Centre. 47 Cliffe High St, Lewes, E.Sussex, BN7 2AN. Tel 473266.

Clifton Antiques Market. 26-28 The Mall, Clifton, Bristol, Avon, BS8. Tel 741627 734531 738504.

Cockermouth Antique Market. Main St, Cockermouth, Cumbria.

Collectors Market. Dales Brewery,Gwydir St, Cambridge, Cambridgeshire.

Colman's of Hexham, Saleroom and Antique Fair. 15 St Mary's Chare, Hexham, Northumberland. Tel 3812 day,4662 or 3944 eve.

Coltishall Antiques Centre. High St, Coltishall, Norfolk, NR12 7HU. Tel Norwich (0603) 738306 (737631).

Country Antique Market. 14 Broad St, Leominster, Hereford & Worcester. Tel 2189.

County Antiques Centre. 21-23 West St, Ilminster, Somerset.

Dulverton Antique Centre. Lower Town Hall, Dulverton, Somerset.

East Bridgford Antiques Centre. Main St, East Bridgford, Nottinghamshire. Tel 20741.

Eastbourne Antique Market. 80 Seaside, Eastbourne, E.Sussex. Tel 20128 (priv 37730).

Eastgate Antique Centre. Black Horse Chambers, 6 Eastgate, Lincoln, Lincolnshire. Tel 44404 (priv 754327).

Edinburgh Antiques Market. 5A Johnston Terrace, Edinburgh, Lothian.

Finedon Antiques Centre. 3 Church St, Finedon, Northamptonshire. Tel Wellingborough (0933) 680430.

Folly Antiques Centre. College St, Petersfield, Hampshire.

Francis Street Antique Gallery. 59 Francis St, Dublin, Co Dublin.

Friar Antiques and Collectors' Centre. 12-18 Friar Lane, Nottingham, Nottinghamshire. Tel 417857.

The Gloucester Antiques Centre. 1 Severn Rd, Gloucester, Gloucestershire. Tel 29716.

The Great Malvern Antiques Arcade. Salisbury House,6 Abbey Rd, Malvern, Hereford & Worcester, WR14 3HG. Tel 5490.

Great Western Antique Centre Ltd. Bartlett St, Bath, Avon, BA1 2QZ. Tel (office) 24243.

Halifax Antiques Centre. Queens Road Mills,Queens Rd/ Gibbet St, Halifax, W.Yorkshire, HX1 4LR. Tel 66657.

Hampton Court Revival Antiques Centre. 52-54 Bridge Rd, East Molesey, Surrey. Tel 979 3552.

The Herts & Essex Antiques Centre. The Maltings, Station Rd, Sawbridgeworth, Hertfordshire, CM21 9JX. Tel Bishops Stortford (0279) 725809.

Highbridge Antique Centre. Huntspill Rd, Highbridge, Somerset. Tel Burnham-on-Sea (0278) 781395.

Hitchin Antiques Gallery. 37 Bridge St, Hitchin, Hertfordshire. Tel 34525.

Hoodeners Antiques & Collectors Market. The Red Cross Centre,Lower Chantry Lane, Canterbury, Kent, CT4 6EN. Tel Petham (022770) 437.

House of Antiques. 4 College St, Petersfield, Hampshire, GU31 4AD. Tel 62172.

Hungerford Arcade. 26 High St, Hungerford, Berkshire. Tel 83701.

Kelvedon Antique Centre. 139 High St, Kelvedon, Essex. Tel 70896 (priv 0206 573938).

The Kibworth Antiques Centre. 5 Weir Rd, Kibworth Beauchamp, Leicestershire, LE8 0LR. Tel 2761.

The Lamb Antiques Centre. High St, Wallingford, Oxfordshire. Tel 735166.

Leicester Antique Centre Ltd. 16-26 Oxford St, Leicester, Leicestershire. Tel 553006.

London House Antique Centre. High St, Marlborough, Wiltshire. Tel 52331.

Colin Macleods Antique Centre. 159/161 Goldsmith Ave, Southsea, Hampshire, PO4 8BL. Tel Portsmouth (0705) 734173.

Maldon Antiques & Collectors Market. United Reformed Church Hall,Market Hill, Maldon, Essex. Tel Earls Colne (07875) 2826.

Mattar Arcade. South Street, Wincanton, Somerset. Tel 34154.

Midhurst Antiques Market. Curfew Garden Ct, Knockhundred Row, Midhurst, W.Sussex. Tel 4231.

The M11 Antiques Centre. High St, Newport, Essex, CB11 3QY. Tel Saffron Walden (0799) 40321 (priv 40238).

Nantwich Antiques Centre. The Old Police Station,94/96 Welsh Row, Nantwich, Cheshire, CW5 5 ET. Tel 624035.

Needham Market Antique Centre. The Old Town Hall, High St, Needham Market, Suffolk. Tel 720773 (priv 0473 41145).

Newark Art & Antiques Centre. The Market Place and Chain Lane, Newark-on-Trent, Nottinghamshire. Tel 703959.

Newton Abbot Antiques Centre. 55 East St, Newton Abbot, Devon. Tel 4074.

Noah's Ark Antiques Market. 5 King St, Sandwich, Kent. Tel 611144 (priv 613270).

Norwich Antique & Collectors Centre. No 1 Quayside, Norwich, Norfolk, NR3 1RQ. Tel 612582.

Old Amersham Antiques Centre. 20-22 Whielden St,Old Amersham, Amersham, Buckinghamshire. Tel 3939.

Oxford Antiques Omnibus. The Basement, Omni Store,George St, Oxford, Oxfordshire. Tel 739071.

Paragon Antiques Market. 3 Bladud Buildings,The Paragon, Bath, Avon.

Petworth Antique Market. East St, Petworth, W.Sussex. Tel 42073.

Anthony Reed. The Old Granary Studio,Kings Staith Lane, King's Lynn, Norfolk. Tel 5509.

Reigate Antique Arcade. 57 High St, Reigate, Surrey.

Richmond Antique Traders. 30-32 Hill Rise, Richmond, Surrey, TW10 6UA.

Royal Exchange Antiques Gallery. Royal Exchange Shopping Centre, Manchester, Greater Manchester, 2. Tel 834 5765/1427.

Rugeley Antiques Centre. 161-163 Main Rd, Brereton, Rugeley, Staffordshire. Tel 77166.

Sandgate Antiques Centre. 61-63 Sandgate High St, Sandgate, Folkestone, Kent, CT20 3AH. Tel 38987.

Laurence Shaw Antique Centre. Sandy Bank Road,New York, Coningsby, Lincolnshire. Tel 42578.

Sherborne Arcade. 17 Newlands, Sherborne, Dorset. Tel 813464.

Shrewsbury Antique Centre. Princess St, Shrewsbury, Shropshire. Tel 247704.

Span Antiques. 6 Market Place, Woodstock, Oxfordshire, OX7 1TA. Tel 811332.

St Albans Antiques Market. Town Hall, St Albans, Hertfordshire. Tel 50427.

St Edmunds Antique Centre. 30 St Johns St, Bury St Edmunds, Suffolk. Tel 64469 (priv 0842 878286).

St Leonard's Antiques Centre. St Leonard's Church,Corve St, Ludlow, Shropshire. Tel 5573.

Stone Antique Centre. Bridge House, 56 Newcastle Rd, Stone, Staffordshire. Tel 818218.

Stratford-upon-Avon Antiques Centre. 59-60 Ely Street, Stratford-upon-Avon, Warwickshire. Tel 204180.

Surrey Antiques Centre. 10 Windsor St, Chertsey, Surrey. Tel 63313 (priv 0932 41097).

Swaffham Antiques Centre. Market Place, Swaffham, Norfolk.

Swan Lane Antiques. Swan St, Warwick, Warwickshire. Tel 400040.

Taunton Antique Centre. 27-29 Silver St, Taunton, Somerset. Tel 89327.

Top Hat Antiques Centre & Fine Art Gallery. 72 Derby Rd, Nottingham, Nottinghamshire. Tel 419143.

Torquay Antique Centre. 177 Union St, Torquay, Devon. Tel 26621.

Torre Antique Traders. 266 Union St, Torquay, Devon, TQ1 4ET. Tel 22184 (priv 34449).

Treasures. 151 Station Road East, Oxted, Surrey.

Trinity Antiques Centre. 7 Trinity St, Colchester, Essex. Tel 577775.

Tudor Cottage Antique Centre. 22 Shipbourne Rd, Tonbridge, Kent. Tel 351719.

Victorian Village. 53,57 & 63 West Regent St, Glasgow, Strathclyde. Tel 332 0703.

The Village. 62 High St, Weedon, Northamptonshire. Tel 42015.

Warwick Antique Centre. 22 High St, Warwick, Warwickshire. Tel 495704.

Waveney Antiques Centre. Saltgate, Beccles, Suffolk. Tel 716147.

West Felton Antique Market. West Felton, Shropshire. Tel Queens Head (069 188) 335.

West Park Antiques Pavilion. 20 West Park, Harrogate, N.Yorkshire. Tel 61758 (priv 60352).

The Westgate Towers Antique & Collectors Market. Sidney Cooper Centre,St Peters St, Canterbury, Kent. Tel 451755 (ext 389).

Woburn Abbey Antiques Centre. Woburn Abbey, Woburn, Bedfordshire, MK43 0TP. Tel 350.

York Antiques Centre. 2A Lendal, York, N.Yorkshire. Tel 641582.

Antiquities

Richard Alexander. Crouch House, Crouch Lane, Seaford, E.Sussex. Tel 896577.

Antiques Objets D'Art & Curios. 86 The Broadway, Leigh-on-Sea, Essex. Tel Southend-on-Sea (0702) 72895 & 711633.

Apollo Gallery. 75A Ridgmount Gardens, London, WC1. Tel 580 6241.

The Arcade Gallery. 15 Royal Arcade, 28 Old Bond St, London, W1X3HD. Tel 493 1879 (priv 492 1706).

Ian Auld. 1 Gateway Arcade, Camden Passage, London, N1. Tel 359 1440.

Berkeley Galleries Ltd. 82 The Hall, Foxes Dale, London, SE3. Tel 852 0586.

de Montfort. 49 High St, Robertsbridge, E.Sussex, TN32 5AN. Tel 880698 (priv 082 584 243).

Charles Ede Ltd. 37 Brook St, London, W1Y 1AJ. Tel 493 4944.

Elgin Antiques. 121-123 Portobello Rd, London, W11. Tel 727 9852.

Emanouel Antiques Ltd. 64 South Audley St, London, W1Y 5FA. Tel 493 4350, 499 0996.

M. Odell Foster. Millmead, Wonersh, Surrey. Tel Guildford (0483) 892375.

Fox & Co. 30 Princes St, Yeovil, Somerset. Tel 72323.

Hadji Baba Ancient Art. 36 Davies St, London, W1Y 1LD. Tel 499 9363, 499 9384.

Thomas Howard-Sneyd Ltd. 35 Fursecroft,George Street, London, W1. Tel 723 1976.

Mansour Gallery. 46 Davies St, London, W1. Tel 491 7444.

McAlpine Ancient Art. 60 Brook St, London, W1. Tel 629 2247.

Monarch Antiques. 15 High St, Glastonbury, Somerset. Tel 32498.

Potters - Colston Street Antiques. 60 Colston Street, Bristol, Avon. Tel 22551.

Rabi Gallery. 94 Mount St, London, W1. Tel 499 8886.

B.A. Seaby Ltd. 8 Cavendish Sq, London, W1M 0AJ. Tel 631 3707.

Sheppard & Cooper Ltd. 35 St George St, London, W1. Tel 629 6489.

Robin Symes. 3 Ormond Yard,Duke of York St, St James's, London, SW1. Tel 930 9856/7.

Architectural Items

see also Fireplaces, Stained Glass

Robert Aagaard Ltd. Frogmire House, Stockwell Rd, Knaresborough, N.Yorkshire, HG5 0JP. Tel Harrogate (0423) 864805.

Acquisitions (Fireplaces) Ltd. 269 Camden High St, London, NW1 7BX. Tel 485 4955.

George Amos & Sons (CB) Ltd. 73 Leonard St, London, EC2. Tel 739 0448.

Architectural Antiques. The New Savoy Show Rooms,New Road, South Molton, Devon. Tel 3342 (priv 4167).

Architectural Antiques Ltd. 133 Upper St, London, N1. Tel 226 5565.

Architectural Heritage of Cheltenham. Boddington Manor, Boddington, Cheltenham, Gloucestershire, GL51 0TJ. Tel Coombe Hill (024268) 741.

D.J. Baggott. Huntsmans Yard, Sheep Street, Stow-on-the-Wold, Gloucestershire. Tel 30662.

Baileys Architectural Antiques. The Engine Shed,Ashburton Industrial Estate, Ross-on-Wye, Hereford & Worcester, HR9 7BW. Tel 63015.

David Bridgwater. 14 Fountain Buildings,Lansdown Road, Bath, Avon. Tel 63652.

Carse Antiques. Rait, by Perth, Tayside, PH2 7RT. Tel 205 (priv 227).

Chalon Ltd. Old Hambridge Mill, Hambridge, Curry Rivel, Somerset, TA10 0BP. Tel Langport (0458) 252374 (priv 0460 67715).

Peter Chapman Antiques. 10 Theberton St, Islington, London, N1 0QX. Tel 226 5565 (priv 348 4846).

Chilstone Architectural Ornaments. Sprivers Estate, Horsmonden, Kent. Tel Brenchley (089272) 3553.

Ray Coggins Antiques. The Old Brewery, Newtown, Bradford-on-Avon, Wiltshire. Tel 3431.

Ralph Cox. 53 Ledbury Rd, London, W11. Tel 229 6900 (priv 723 3162).

Crowther of Syon Lodge. Syon Lodge, Busch Corner,London Rd, Isleworth, Middlesex, TW7 5BH. Tel 560 7978, 560 7985.

T.Crowther & Son Ltd. 282 North End Rd, Fulham, London, SW6 1NH. Tel 385 1375/7.

Daleside Antiques. St Peter's Sq,Cold Bath Rd, Harrogate, N.Yorkshire, HG2 0NP. Tel 60286 (priv 509618).

Dickenson and Thomas. Old Granary, 10 North St, Stamford, Lincolnshire, PE9 2YN. Tel 62236 (priv 55093).

Dunedin Antiques Ltd. 4 North West Circus Place, Edinburgh, Lothian. Tel 226 3074.

Five Five Six Antiques. 556 King's Rd, London, SW6. Tel 731 2016 (priv 624 5173).

Halliday's (Antiques). 28 Beauchamp Place, London, SW3. Tel 589 5534.

Hallidays Antiques Ltd. The Old College, High St, Dorchester, Oxfordshire. Tel Oxford (0865) 340028.

Hayes and Newby Antique Export. The Pit, Hare Lane, Gloucester, Gloucestershire. Tel 31145, 24722.

Lamont Antiques Ltd. Newhams Row,175 Bermondsey St, London, SE1 3UW. Tel 403 0126.

Lancashire Bygones. 12 Parliament St, Up Holland, Wigan, Greater Manchester, WN8 0LN. Tel Up Holland (0695) 625624 (priv 0695 622458).

Lenygon & Morant Ltd. 30-31 Lyme St, London, NW1 0EE. Tel 482 2156.

The London Architectural Salvage & Supply Co Ltd. The Mark St Depository, Mark St,off Paul St, London, EC2A 4ER. Tel 739 0448.

William MacIntosh & Co. 5 Johnston Terrace, Edinburgh, Lothian, EH1 2PW. Tel 225 6113.

The Morris Singer Foundry Ltd. Bond Close,Kingsland Industrial Park, Basingstoke, Hampshire, RG24 0PT. Tel 24033.

Old Britannia. Castle Street, Combe Martin, Ilfracombe, Devon. Tel Combe Martin (027 188) 3610.

Pageant Antiques. 122 Dawes Rd, London, W14. Tel 385 7739.

Petworth Antiques Warehouse. Colhook Industrial Park, Petworth, W.Sussex. Tel Northchapel (042 878) 667.

H.W.Poulter & Son. 279 Fulham Rd, London, SW10 9PZ. Tel 352 7268 (priv 603 7398).

Relic Antiques. 1 Camden Walk, Islington, London, N1. Tel 359 6755.

Relic Antiques. Brillscote Farm, Lea, Malmesbury, Wiltshire, SN16 9PF. Tel 2332.

Scallywag. 22 High St, Beckenham, Kent, BR3 1AY. Tel 658 6633.

Scallywag. The Old Church, Wren Rd,Camberwell Green, London, SE5 8QS. Tel 701 5353.

Spurrier-Smith Antiques. 28 & 41 Church St, Ashbourne, Derbyshire. Tel 43669 (priv 077 389 368).

Geoffrey Stead. The Old Rectory, Dowdeswell, Gloucestershire, GL54 5LX. Tel Cheltenham (0242) 820571.

Swanbridge Art Company Ltd. Tower Rd, Glover West Industrial Est,District 11, Washington, Tyne & Wear, NE37 2SH. Tel Tyneside (091) 415-0080.

Thirty Eight Antiques Ltd. 25-27 High St, Weedon, Northamptonshire, NN7 4QD. Tel 40766.

Thornhill Galleries Ltd. 76 New Kings Rd, London, SW6. Tel 736 5830.

Andy Thornton Architectural Antiques Ltd. Ainleys Industrial Estate, Elland, W.Yorkshire, HX5 9JP. Tel 78125 (priv 0484 712636).

Townsends. 1 Church St, London, NW8. Tel 724 3746 & 624 4756.

Townsends. Showroom: 36 New End Square,Hampstead Village, London, NW3. Tel 794 5706/5707.

Walcot Reclamation. 108 Walcot St, Bath, Avon, BA1 5BG. Tel 66291/2.

E.T. Webster. Westwood Lodge, Blythburgh, Suffolk. Tel 539.

Whiteway & Waldron. 305 Munster Rd, London, SW6. Tel 381 3195.

George Wright (Rotherham) Ltd. The Crofts, Rotherham, S.Yorkshire, S60 2DJ. Tel 63871.

Armorial Antiques

Heirloom and Howard Ltd. 1 Hay Hill, Berkeley Sq, London, W1. Tel 493 5868.

Arms, Armour and Militaria

see also Coins and Medals, Insignias

Angharads Antiques. 106 Chester Rd West, Shotton, Clwyd. Tel Deeside (0244) 812240.

Angus Antiques. 4 St Andrews St, Dundee, Tayside. Tel 22128.

The Antique Shop. 226 Harrogate Rd, Leeds, W.Yorkshire, LS7 4QD. Tel 681785.

Arbour Antiques Ltd. Poet's Arbour, Sheep St, Stratford-upon-Avon, Warwickshire, CV37 6EF. Tel 293453 (priv 204095).

Armada Antiques. Stand 122 Gray's Antiques Mkt,58 Davies St, London, W1. Tel 499 1087.

Armatura. Sydney Vane House, Rue du Commerce, St Peter Port, Guernsey. Tel 21625.

Armoury Antiques. Unit 123, Grays Antique Market,58 Davies St, London, W1. Tel 408 0176.

C.W.Atkins & Co. Antiques. 92 Wellington Rd, Taunton, Somerset, TA1 5LA. Tel 72660.

Bruton-Brighton. 31-32 Meeting House Lane, Brighton & Hove, E.Sussex, BN1 1HB. Tel 26591.

C.C.A.W. Ltd. Gunhouse, Steeple Bumpstead, Haverhill, Suffolk. Tel Steeple Bumpstead 044084 275.

Duncan Campbell. The Prior's Lodge, Upper Lake, Battle, E.Sussex. Tel 2888.

Carronade. 63 West Regent St, Glasgow, Strathclyde. Tel 332 5600 (priv 649 3655).

The Coin & Stamp Centre. 13 Centurion House (1st floor),St John's St, Colchester, Essex, CO2 7AH. Tel 41232 (priv 579345).

Collectors Corner - Militaria. 1 Northcross Rd, East Dulwich, London, SE22 9ET. Tel 693 6285.

Laurence Corner, Euston Gallery. 126-130 Drummond St, London, NW1. Tel 388 6811.

Andrew Cottrell Galleries. 7-9 Church St, Godalming, Surrey. Tel 7570.

Crossbow House Antiques. Stoneymeadow Rd, High Blantyre, Strathclyde. Tel Blantyre (0698) 823106, 822378.

Curio Shop. 11 Northumberland Place, Teignmouth, Devon. Tel (priv)Exeter(0392)54166.

Peter Dale Ltd. 11 & 12 Royal Opera Arcade,Pall Mall, London, SW1Y 4UY. Tel 930 3695.

K.A Davies Antiques. 248 Cowbridge Rd East, Cardiff, S.Glamorgan. Tel 29989.

Den of Antiquity. 69 Station Rd, Cheadle Hulme, Greater Manchester. Tel 485 8713.

Nimrod Dix & Company. 17 Piccadilly Arcade, London, SW1Y 6NL. Tel 493 5082.

David W.Dyson. Holme Court,New Mill, Huddersfield, W.Yorkshire.

A.Earle. 47 North St, Wilton, Wiltshire. Tel 3284.

The Flintlock. 17A High St, Glastonbury, Somerset, BA6 9DR. Tel 31525 (priv 32813).

Michael C.German. 38B Kensington Church St, London, W8. Tel 937 2771.

Edred A.F. Gwilliam. Candletree House,Bath Rd, Cricklade, Wiltshire, SN6 6AX. Tel 750241.

Robert Hales Antiques Ltd. 133 Kensington Church St, London, W8 7LP. Tel 229 3887.

Peter Hancock. 40-41 West St, Chichester, W.Sussex, PO19 1RP. Tel 786173.

Heffle Corner Antiques. Heffle Corner, Station Approach,Station Rd, Heathfield, E.Sussex, TN21 8LG. Tel 3381.

Holland & Holland Ltd. 33 Bruton St, London, W1X 8JS. Tel 499 4411.

Laburnum Antique Galleries. 3 Laburnum Row, Torquay, Devon, TQ2 5QX. Tel 26983.

Martin Marsh Militaria. 114 Buxton Rd, Whaley Bridge, Derbyshire, SK12 7JF. Tel 3267.

Michael Miller. The Lamb, 8 Cuckfield Rd, Hurstpierpoint, W.Sussex, BN6 9RU. Tel 834567.

Monarch Antiques. 15 High St, Glastonbury, Somerset. Tel 32498.

J.A. Morrison Ltd. 43 Grange Lane, Thurnby, Leicestershire, LE7 9PH. Tel Leicester (0533) 413750.

Nihon Token. 23 Museum St, London, WC1A 1JT. Tel 580 6511.

Old Barn. Perran-ar-worthal, Truro, Cornwall, TR3 7NY. Tel 863831.

Old Paint Shop. High St, Alfriston, E.Sussex, BN26 5TD.

Pinfold Antiques. 28 Steep Hill, Lincoln, Lincolnshire. Tel 44716 (priv 0526 832057).

Paul Quentin Antiques. 626 Manchester Rd, Bury, Greater Manchester, BL9 9SU. Tel 766 6673.

Roy Sim Antiques. 21 Allan St, Blairgowrie, Tayside, PH10 6AB. Tel 3860 (priv 3700).

Spinning Wheel Antiques. 12 St Albans Rd, St Anne's, Lancashire. Tel 724187.

Sterling Coins. 2 Somerset Rd, Boscombe, Bournemouth, Dorset. Tel 423881.

Sundial Antiques. 19 Whielden St, Amersham, Buckinghamshire, HP7 0HU. Tel 7955.

Thorntons of Harrogate. 1 Montpellier Gdns, Harrogate, N.Yorkshire, HG1 2TF. Tel 504118.

Townhead Antiques. Townhead, Newby Bridge, Cumbria, LA12 8NP. Tel 31321.

Trident Arms. 74 Derby Road, Nottingham, Nottinghamshire, NG1 5FD. Tel 474137.

R.B. Walkyier & Son. 17 High St, Saffron Walden, Essex. Tel 3430.

Wallis & Wallis. West Street Auction Galleries,West St, Lewes, E.Sussex, BN7 2NJ. Tel 473137.

Warner's Military Specialists. 2 The Apple Market,Eden St, Kingston upon Thames, Surrey, KT1 1JE. Tel 546 7527(24 hr answering).

Watergate Antiques. 56 Watergate St, Chester, Cheshire. Tel 44516.

Weiner aus Wien Military Antiques. 2 Market St, The Lanes, Brighton & Hove, E.Sussex, BN1 1HH. Tel 729948.

Weller and Dufty Ltd (Est 1835). 141 Bromsgrove St, Birmingham, W.Midlands. Tel 692 1414.

J.Wigington & Sons. 'Winchester 73', 276 Alcester Rd, Stratford-upon-Avon, Warwickshire. Tel 293881.

Art Nouveau and Art Deco

Angus Antiques. 4 St Andrews St, Dundee, Tayside. Tel 22128.

The Antique Trader. 357 Upper St,Camden Passage, London, N1. Tel 359 2019.

Astoria. 73A Kensington Church St, London, W8. Tel 937 0105.

AS Antiques. 26 Broad St, Pendleton, Salford, Greater Manchester. Tel Manchester (061) 737 5938.

K.Barlow Ltd, Decorative Arts 1900-1950. 27 Conduit St, London, W1R 9TA. Tel 629 1653.

R.A.Barnes Antiques. 26 Lower Richmond Rd, Putney, London, SW15 1JP. Tel 789 3371.

Bell Antiques. 8 Bell St, Romsey, Hampshire, SO51 8GA. Tel 514719.

Bizarre. 24 Church St, London, NW8. Tel 724 1305.

Bourne Fine Art Ltd. 4 Dundas St, Edinburgh, Lothian, EH3 6HZ. Tel 557 4050.

Butler & Wilson. 189 Fulham Rd, London, SW3. Tel 352 3045.

Cameo Antiques. 31 Suffolk Parade, Cheltenham, Gloucestershire. Tel 33164.

Catspa. Chenil Gallery, King's Rd, Chelsea, London, SW3. Tel 883 3992.

Coakley & Hayter. Stand D13, Chenil Galleries,King's Rd, London, SW3. Tel 351 2914(priv 0992 52907).

Cobra & Bellamy. 149 Sloane St, London, SW1. Tel 730 2823.

The Collectors Trail. St Francis Rd, Indian Queens, Cornwall. Tel St.Austell (0726) 860338.

Joan Collins. 153 Portobello Rd, London, W11. Tel (priv) 727 6848.

Dragon Antiques. 10 Dragon Rd, Harrogate, N.Yorkshire, HG1 5DF. Tel 62037.

Shirley Eaton Antiques. 15 London Rd, Alderley Edge, Cheshire, SK9 7JT. Tel 582522.

Ebury Gallery. 89 Ebury St, London, SW1. Tel 730 3341.

Editions Graphiques Gallery. 3 Clifford St, London, W1. Tel 734 3944.

Galerie 1900. 267 Camden High St, London, NW1. Tel 485 1001.

Galia Antiques. Antiquarius, 135 King's Rd, London, SW3.

Gallery 25. 4 Halkin Arcade, Motcomb St, London, SW1. Tel 235 5178.

Peter and Debbie Gooday. 20 Richmond Hill, Richmond, Surrey. Tel 940 8652.

Patrick & Susan Gould. Grays Mews,1-7 Davies Mews, London, W1. Tel 408 0129.

Gres. Stand 378,Grays Antique Market,58 Davies St, London, W1. Tel 499 3075.

Grosvenor Gallery. 48 South Molton St, London, W1Y 2JU. Tel 629 0891.

Haslam & Whiteway. 105 Kensington Church St, London, W8 7LN. Tel 229 1145.

Muir Hewitt. Halifax Antiques Centre,Queens Rd Mills, Queens Rd/Gibbet St, Halifax, W.Yorkshire, HX1 4LR. Tel 66657 (priv 0274 882051).

A.Hicks. 15 Flood St, London, SW3. Tel 352 8077.

House of Mallett. 67-69 Brighton Rd, Surbiton, Surrey, KT6 5NF. Tel 390 3796.

John Jesse & Irina Laski. 160 Kensington Church Street, London, W8. Tel 229 0312.

Michael John Decorative Arts Ltd. 25A Lowndes St, London, SW1. Tel 235 3154/5.

John's Antiques. Stands 345/346, Grays Antique Market,58 Davies St, London, W1. Tel 629 1140.

Jones. 194 Westbourne Grove, London, W11. Tel 229 6866.

Lewis M. Kaplan Associates Ltd. 50 Fulham Rd, London, SW3. Tel 589 3108 or 584 6328.

King Street Curios. 5 King St, Tavistock, Devon, PL19 0DS. Tel 5193.

W.F.Knight Ltd (Silversmiths). 2 Park Rd, Wellingborough, Northamptonshire. Tel 222463.

Liberty & Co Ltd. Regent St, London, W1R 6AH. Tel 734 1234.

Greig Linton Antiques. 95 West Bow, Edinburgh, Lothian. Tel 226 6946.

Lyons Gallery. 47 Mill Lane,West Hampstead, London, NW6 1NB. Tel 794 3537.

Maindy Fine Antiques. 17 Pont Canna St, Cardiff, S.Glamorgan. Tel 382072.

J.Marlow Antiques. West Park Antique Pavilion,20 West Park, Harrogate, N.Yorkshire. Tel 61758 (priv 0642 781529).

Nigel Milne Ltd. 16C Grafton St, London, W1X 3LF. Tel 493 9646.

L'Odeon. 173 Fulham Rd, London, SW3. Tel 581 3640 (priv 736 4216).

The Pruskin Gallery. 183 King's Rd, London, SW3. Tel 352 9095, (priv)243 1939.

The Purple Shop. 15 Flood St,Chelsea, London, SW3 5ST. Tel 352 1127.

Paul Reeves. 32B Kensington Church St, London, W8 4HA. Tel 937 1594 (priv 968 7413).

The Rendezvous Gallery. 100 Forest Ave, Aberdeen, Grampian. Tel 323247.

Kimberley Snow & Son. Verbeer Manor, Willand, Cullompton, Devon, EX15 2PE. Tel 33312.

Sweets Antiques. 24 West St, Bridlington, Humberside, YO25 7DF. Tel 677396.

The Talbot Gallery. 290 Woodstock Rd, Oxford, Oxfordshire, OX2 7NN. Tel 59049.

Themes & Variations. 231 Westbourne Grove, London, W11. Tel 727 5531.

Titchfield Antiques Ltd. 15 South St, Titchfield, Hampshire, PO14 4DL. Tel 45968.

Vaseroy. Unit 16 Bond St Antique Centre,124 New Bond St, London, W1. Tel 491 4942.

Young Stephen Ltd. 1 Burlington Gdns, New Bond St, London, W1X 1LD. Tel 499 7927.

Ziggurat. Chenil Galleries, 183 King's Rd, London, SW3. Tel 352 2123.

Auctioneers

London

Bainbridges Fine Art & General Chattel Auctioneers. 2 Chapel Rd,Ealing, London, W13. Tel 579 2966.

Bloomsbury Book Auctions. 3-4 Hardwick St, London, EC1R 4RY. Tel 636 1945, 833 2636/7.

Bonhams. Montpelier Galleries, Montpelier St,Knightsbridge, London, SW7. Tel 584 9161.

Bonhams Chelsea. 65-69 Lots Rd, Chelsea, London, SW10. Tel 352 0466, 351 1380.

Camden Auctions. The Saleroom, Hoppers Rd,Winchmore Hill, London, N21. Tel 886 1550.

Christie's. 8 King St, St James's, London, SW1Y 6QT. Tel 839 9060.

Christie's in the City. 56-60 Gresham St, London, EC2V 7BB. Tel 588 4424.

Christie's South Kensington. 85 Old Brompton Rd, London, SW7 3JS. Tel 581 7611.

Dowell Lloyd & Co Ltd. 118 Putney Bridge Rd, London, SW15. Tel 788 7777.

Stanley Gibbons. 399 The Strand, London, WC2. Tel 836 8444.

Stanley Gibbons Auctions Limited. 399 The Strand, London, WC2R 0LX. Tel 836 8444.

Glendining & Co. 7 Blenheim St, New Bond St, London, W1Y OAS. Tel 493 2445.

Harvey's Auctions Ltd. 14/18 Neal Street,Covent Gdn, London, WC2. Tel 240 1464.

Jackson-Stops & Staff. 14 Curzon St, London, W1. Tel 499 6291.

Lots Road Chelsea Auction Galleries. 71 Lots Rd,Chelsea, London, SW10 0RN. Tel 351 7771, 352 2349 24 hr.

North West London Auctions. 9-17 Lodge Lane,Finchley, London, N12. Tel 445 9000.

Phillips Fine Art Auctioneers. Blenstock House,7 Blenheim St, London, W1Y OAS. Tel 629 6602.

Phillips Marylebone. Hayes Place,Lisson Grove, London, NW1 6UA. Tel 723 2647.

Phillips West 2. 2 Salem Road, London, W2 4BU. Tel 221 5303.

Robson Lowe at Christie's. 47 Duke St,St James's, London, SW1Y 6QX. Tel 839 4034/5.

Sotheby's. 34-35 New Bond Street, London, W1A 2AA. Tel 493 8080.

Regions

Abbotts. The Hill, Wickham Market, Suffolk, IP13 0QX. Tel 746321.

James Adam and Sons. 26 St Stephens Green, Dublin, Co Dublin. Tel 760261.

Alberts Auctions & Co. Farm Buildings, Maiden Lane, Crayford, Kent. Tel 528868.

Aldridges of Bath. The Auction Galleries,130-132 Walcot St, Bath, Avon. Tel 62830, 62839.

Ambrose. 149 High Rd, Loughton, Essex. Tel 01-508 2121.

Anderson and Garland. Fine Art Salerooms, Anderson House,Market St, Newcastle upon Tyne, Tyne & Wear. Tel 326278.

Artingstall & Hind. 378/380 Deansgate, Knott Mill, Manchester, Greater Manchester, M3 4NA. Tel 834 4559.

Edward Bailey & Son. 17 Northgate, Newark-on-Trent, Nottinghamshire, NG24 1EX. Tel 77154.

Richard Baker and Thomson. 9 Hamilton St, Birkenhead, Merseyside. Tel 647 9104.

Baldwin & Partners. 26 Railway St, Chatham, Kent, ME4 4JT. Tel Medway (0634) 400121.

Banks & Silvers. 66 Foregate St, Worcester, Hereford & Worcester, WR1 1EB. Tel 23456.

Bath Stamp & Coin Shop. Pulteney Bridge, Bath, Avon. Tel 63073.

Bearnes. Rainbow, Avenue Rd, Torquay, Devon, TQ2 5TG. Tel 26277.

Berry Powell & Shackell. 46 Market Place, Chippenham, Wiltshire. Tel 653361.

Biddle and Webb. Icknield Sq, Ladywood Middleway, Birmingham, W.Midlands. Tel 455 8042.

Blinkhorn & Company. 41-43 High St, Broadway, Hereford & Worcester, WR12 7DP. Tel 852456 (priv 853686).

Boardman Fine Art Auctioneers. Station Rd Corner, Haverhill, Suffolk, CB9 0EY. Tel 703784.

Bridgfords Ltd. 1 Heyes Lane, Alderley Edge, Cheshire, SK9 7LA. Tel Wilmslow (0625)585347.

Bright Willis. 677 Warwick Rd, Solihull, Birmingham, W.Midlands. Tel 705 6491.

Brocklehursts. Auction Rooms, King Edward St, Macclesfield, Cheshire, SK10 1AQ. Tel 27555.

William H.Brown. Westgate Hall, Westgate, Grantham, Lincolnshire, NG31 6LT. Tel 68861.

Bruton Knowles & Co. Albion Chambers, 55 Barton St, Gloucester, Gloucestershire. Tel 21267.

Butterfields. The Auction Galleries,Riddings Rd, Ilkley, W.Yorkshire, LS29 9LU. Tel 603313 (priv 0274-594068).

Capes Dunn & Co. 38 Charles St, Manchester, Greater Manchester, M1 7DB. Tel 273 1911.

Cariss Residential. 20-22 High St, Kings Heath, Birmingham, W.Midlands, B14 7JU. Tel 444 0088/8579.

Chancellors Hollingsworths. 31 High St, Ascot, Berkshire, SL5 7HG. Tel 27101.

H.C.Chapman & Son. The Auction Mart, North St, Scarborough, N.Yorkshire. Tel 372424.

Cheffins, Grain and Chalk. The Cambridge Saleroom,Cherry Hinton Rd, Cambridge, Cambridgeshire. Tel 358721.

Chelmsford Auction Rooms. 42 Mildmay Rd, Chelmsford, Essex. Tel 354251.

Christie, Manson and Woods Ltd. Marybrook House, 9 Raleagh Rd,Crossgar, Downpatrick, Co Down, BT30 9JG. Tel 830574.

Christie's. Stanley Hall, Bridgnorth, Shropshire. Tel 61891.

Christie's. 111 The Promenade, Cheltenham, Gloucestershire. Tel 518999.

Christie's. Eastfield House, Main St, Corbridge, Northumberland. Tel 3181.

Christie's. The Old Rectory,Fawkham, Dartford, Kent. Tel Longfield (04747) 2854.

Christie's. Wolfeton House, Dorchester, Dorset. Tel 68748.

Christie's. 5 Wemyss Place, Edinburgh, Lothian. Tel 225 4756/7.

Christie's. Mounteagle, Fearn, Highland. Tel 2866.

Christie's. Glin Castle, Glin, Co Limerick. Tel (priv) Dublin 680585.

Christie's. Leonardslee Gardens,Lower Beeding, Horsham, W.Sussex, RH13 6PP. Tel Lower Beeding (040 376) 305.

Christie's. Cumlodden Estate Office, Crarae, Inveraray, Strathclyde, PA32 8YA. Tel Minard (0546) 86633 (priv 86274).

Christie's. The Stables,Keith Hall, Inverurie, Grampian, AB5 0LD. Tel 24366.

Christie's. Strathgarry House, Killiecrankie, Tayside. Tel Blair Atholl (079681) 216.

Christie's. Blairquhan, Maybole, Strathclyde. Tel Straiton (06557) 239.

Christie's. Old Bank of England Court,Queen St, Norwich, Norfolk, NR2 4BX. Tel 614546.

Christie's. Eden Lacy,Lazonby, Penrith, Cumbria, CA10 1BZ. Tel 8800.

Christie's. The Stables,Milton Hall, Peterborough, Cambridgeshire, PE6 7AA. Tel Castor (073121) 781.

Christie's. Gnaton Estate Office,Yealmpton, Plymouth, Devon. Tel 880636.

Christie's. Downton House, New Radnor, Presteigne, Powys. Tel Cheltenham (0242) 518999.

Christie's. Tredeague, Porthpean, St Austell, Cornwall. Tel 64672.

Christie's. 58 David Place, St Helier, Jersey. Tel 77582.

Christie's. Monmouth Lodge, Yenston, Templecombe, Somerset, BA8 0NH. Tel 70518.

Christie's. 46 Bootham, York, N.Yorkshire. Tel 30911.

Christie's Robson Lowe. 39 Poole Hill, Bournemouth, Dorset. Tel 292740.

Christie's Scotland. 164-166 Bath St, Glasgow, Strathclyde, G2 4TG. Tel 332 8134;.

Chrystals Auctions. Athol St, Douglas,. Tel 3986.

Cobbs, Burrows & Day. 39-41 Bank St, Ashford, Kent, TN23 1DJ. Tel 24321.

Comins. 25 Market Place, Ely, Cambridgeshire, CB7 4NP. Tel 2265.

Cooper-Hirst. Goldlay House, Parkway, Chelmsford, Essex, CM2 7PR. Tel 58141.

S.W. Cottee & Son. The Market, East St, Wareham, Dorset, BH20 4NR. Tel 2826.

County Auctions. Pilot House,King Street, Leicester, Leicestershire, LE1 6RN. Tel 556199 (priv 0509 413590).

Cubitt & West Fine Art Auctioneers. Cubitt & West Auction Galleries,Millmead, Guildford, Surrey, GU2 5BE. Tel 504030.

Dacre, Son & Hartley. 1-5 The Grove, Ilkley, W.Yorkshire, LS29 9HS. Tel 600655.

Clifford Dann Auction Galleries. 20/21 High St, Lewes, E.Sussex. Tel 477022.

Davis & Sons. Manor House, Bank Sq, Chepstow, Gwent. Tel 4908.

Dee & Atkinson. The Exchange, Driffield, Humberside. Tel 43151.

Garth Denham and Associates. Horsham Auction Galleries,Carfax, Horsham, W.Sussex. Tel 53837.

Diamond Mills & Co. 117 Hamilton Rd, Felixstowe, Suffolk. Tel 282281.

Dickinson, Davy & Markham. 10 Wrawby Street, Brigg, Humberside. Tel 53666.

Dodds Property World. Victoria Auction Galleries, Mold, Clwyd. Tel 2552.

Robert Dove & Partners. Dover House, Wolsey St, Ipswich, Suffolk. Tel 55137.

Dreweatts. Donnington Priory, Donnington, Newbury, Berkshire, RG13 2JE. Tel 31234.

Hy. Duke & Son. Fine Art Salerooms, Weymouth Ave, Dorchester, Dorset, DT1 1QR. Tel 65080.

Hy. Duke & Son. Weymouth Saleroom,St Nicholas St, Weymouth, Dorset. Tel 783488.

Eadon, Lockwood & Riddle Auctioneers. Weston Saleroom,Crookes, Sheffield, S.Yorkshire, S1 1XJ. Tel 686294.

Earl & Lawrence. 55 Northgate, Sleaford, Lincolnshire, NG34 7AB. Tel 302946.

Eddisons Auctioneers. 4-6 High St, Huddersfield, W.Yorkshire, HD1 2LS. Tel 533151.

G.H.Edkins & Son. 122 Newgate St, Bishop Auckland, Durham, DL14 7HE. Tel 603095.

Ekins, Fine Art Auctioneers. The Salerooms, The Market, St Ives, Cambridgeshire. Tel 68144.

Eldon Worrall. 15 Seel Street, Liverpool, Merseyside.

James Eley & Son.. 1 Main Ridge West, Boston, Lincolnshire, PE21 6QQ. Tel 61687.

Peter Eley F.S.V.A.. Western House, 98-100 High St, Sidmouth, Devon, EX10 8EF. Tel 2552.

Escritt & Barrell. Elmer House, Grantham, Lincolnshire, NG31 6RD. Tel 65371.

H. Evans & Sons. 1 Parliament St, Hull, Humberside, HU1 2AR. Tel 23033.

Ewings. Market Place, Reepham, Norfolk, NR10 4JJ. Tel Norwich (0603) 870473.

Fellows & Sons. 88 Hagley Rd, Birmingham, W.Midlands, B16 8LU. Tel 454 1261.

G.W. Finn & Sons. Brooklands, Fordwich, Canterbury, Kent. Tel 710200.

Fox & Sons. 5, Salisbury St, Fordingbridge, Hampshire, SP6 1AD. Tel 52121.

John Francis. Curiosity Sale Rooms, King St, Carmarthen, Dyfed. Tel 233456.

Fraser Glennie & Partners. The Old Rectory, Siddington, Cirencester, Gloucestershire, GL7 6HL. Tel 3938.

G.M.B. Auctions. Box No. 5534, 30 Lower Brook St, Ipswich, Suffolk. Tel 662655.

Thos. Wm. Gaze & Son. 10 Market Hill, Diss, Norfolk, IP22 3JZ. Tel 519313.

Geering & Colyer. 22/24 High St, Tunbridge Wells, Kent, TN1 1XA. Tel 25136.

George Jackson & Son. Paynes Park House, Paynes Park, Hitchin, Hertfordshire. Tel 55212.

John German. The Rotunda, High St, Burton upon Trent, Staffordshire, DE14 1LN. Tel 42051.

Glennie Middleton and Bullock. 3 Church St, Diss, Norfolk, IP22 3DD. Tel 51617.

Gorringes. 15 North St, Lewes, E.Sussex. Tel 472503.

Andrew Grant Fine Art Auctions. 59/60 Foregate St, Worcester, Hereford & Worcester. Tel 52310.

Graves Son & Pilcher Fine Arts. 71 Church Road, Brighton & Hove, E.Sussex. Tel 735266.

Green & Co. 33 Market Place, Wantage, Oxfordshire, OX12 8AL. Tel 3561/2.

Grounds & Co. 2 Nene Quay, Wisbech, Cambridgeshire, PE13 1AG. Tel 585041.

Hall Wateridge & Owen. Welsh Bridge, Shrewsbury, Shropshire. Tel 60212.

James Harrison. The Estate Office & Auction Room,35 West End, Hebden Bridge, W.Yorkshire, HX7 8UQ. Tel 842007.

Charles Hawkins. Notleys Salerooms,Royal Thoroughfare, Lowestoft, Suffolk. Tel 2024.

Charles Head & Son. 113 Fore St, Kingsbridge, Devon, TQ7 1BG. Tel 2352.

Heathcote Ball & Co. Castle Auction Rooms,78 St Nicholas Circle, Leicester, Leicestershire, LE1 5NW. Tel 536789.

Heathfield Furniture Salerooms. The Market, Burwash Rd, Heathfield, E.Sussex. Tel 2132.

Hetheringtons, Pretty & Ellis. 125 Station Rd, Amersham, Buckinghamshire. Tel 29292.

Hobbs & Chambers. At the Sign of the Bell,Market Place, Cirencester, Gloucestershire, GL7 1QQ. Tel 4736 (priv 0672 20018).

Hoddell Pritchard. Clevedon Salerooms, Six Ways, Clevedon, Avon, BS21 7NT. Tel 876699.

John Hogbin & Son. 53 High St, Tenterden, Kent. Tel 2241.

John Hogbin & Son. 15 Cattle Market, Sandwich, Kent. Tel 611044.

Holloway's. 49 Parsons St, Banbury, Oxfordshire, OX6 8PF. Tel 53197 (priv 811297).

Holloway's. 12 High St, Streatley, Berkshire, RG8 9HY. Tel Goring-on-Thames (0491) 872318 (priv 0295 811297).

Edgar Horn. 47 Cornfield Rd, Eastbourne, E.Sussex, BN21 4QS. Tel 22801.

Ibbett Mosely. 125 High St, Sevenoaks, Kent, TN13 1UT. Tel 452246.

Raymond P.Inman. 35 & 40 Temple St, Brighton & Hove, E.Sussex, BN1 3BH. Tel 774777.

Irelands Hall & Palmer. 11 Market Place, Wymondham, Norfolk. Tel 603031.

Jackson-Stops & Staff. 25 Nicholas St, Chester, Cheshire. Tel 28361.

Jacobs & Hunt. Auction Rooms, Lavant St, Petersfield, Hampshire, GU32 3EF. Tel 62744.

John Jeffery & Son. Minster House, The Commons, Shaftesbury, Dorset, SP7 8JL. Tel 3331.

Arthur Johnson & Sons Ltd. Cattle Market, London Rd, Nottingham, Nottinghamshire. Tel 869128.

Kent Sales - Auctioneers. Kent House, New Rd, South Darenth, Kent, DA4 9AR. Tel Farningham (0322) 864919.

G.A.Key. 8 Market Place, Aylsham, Norfolk, NR11 6EH. Tel 733195 (priv 732477).

Seth Kirby & Sons. Lloyds Bank Chambers, Market Place, Thirsk, N.Yorkshire. Tel 22218.

Lacy Scott. Fine Art Dept and Saleroom,10 Risbygate St, Bury St Edmunds, Suffolk, IP33 1LS. Tel 63531.

Laidlaws. Crown Court Saleroom, Crown Court,off Wood St, Wakefield, W.Yorkshire, WF1 2SU. Tel 375301.

Lalonde Bros & Parham. 71 Oakfield Road,Clifton, Bristol, Avon, BS8 2BE. Tel 734052.

Langlois Ltd. Don St, St Helier, Jersey. Tel 22441.

Lawrence Fine Art of Crewkerne. South Street, Crewkerne, Somerset, TA18 8AB. Tel 73041.

Lawson Larg. St Trinity House 3-4 King's Sq, York, N.Yorkshire. Tel 21532.

F. Le Gallais. Bath St, St Helier, Jersey. Tel 30202.

Leigh Auction Rooms. 88-90 Pall Mall, Leigh-on-Sea, Essex. Tel Southend-on-Sea (0702) 77051.

Lewes Auction Rooms (Julian Dawson). 56 High St, Lewes, E.Sussex. Tel 478221.

Locke and England Auctioneers. 18 Guy St, Leamington, Warwickshire. Tel 27988.

Lyall & Co. Auction Rooms,Spalding Rd, Bourne, Lincolnshire, PE10 9LE. Tel 422431(4 lines);422686.

Mallams. 26 Grosvenor St, Cheltenham, Gloucestershire. Tel 35712.

Mallams. 24 St Michael's St, Oxford, Oxfordshire. Tel 241358,57250.

Frank R. Marshall & Co. Church Hill, Knutsford, Cheshire, WA16 6DH. Tel 53284.

Messrs Martin & Stratford. 70 High St, Alton, Hampshire, GU34 1EX. Tel 84402.

Michael Matthews. Auction Rooms, Honiton, Devon. Tel 41872.

Thos Mawer & Son. 63 Monks Rd, Lincoln, Lincolnshire. Tel 24984.

May & Son. 18 Bridge St, Andover, Hampshire, SP10 1BH. Tel 63331.

McCartneys. Portcullis Hall Salerooms, Ludlow, Shropshire. Tel 2636.

Messenger May Baverstock. 93 High St, Godalming, Surrey, GU7 1AL. Tel 23567.

Messengers. 27 Sheep St, Bicester, Oxfordshire, OX6 7JF. Tel 252901.

John Milne. The Bon-Accord Auction Rooms,9-11 North Silver St, Aberdeen, Grampian. Tel 639336.

Moore Allen & Innocent. 33 Castle St, Cirencester, Gloucestershire. Tel 61831.

Morphets. 4-6 Albert St, Harrogate, N.Yorkshire, HG1 1JL. Tel 502282.

Neal Sons & Fletcher. 26 Church St, Woodbridge, Suffolk, IP12 1DP. Tel 2263/4 (priv 0728 723877).

Neales of Nottingham. 192/194 Mansfield Rd, Nottingham, Nottinghamshire, NG1 3HX. Tel 624141.

Neales Innes Nichols. Becket St, Derby, Derbyshire, DE1 1HW. Tel 43286.

Neates. 108 High St, Hungerford, Berkshire, RG17 0NB. Tel 82808.

Neates. 93 High St, Marlborough, Wiltshire, SN8 1HD. Tel 54916.

Neates. 8 St Mary's Hill, Cheap St, Newbury, Berkshire, RG14 5DF. Tel 42961.

D.M.Nesbit & Co. Auctioneers. 7 Clarendon Rd,Southsea, Portsmouth, Hampshire, PO5 2ED. Tel 864321.

Michael Newman (Fine Art Auctioneer & Valuer). Central Auction Rooms,St Andrews Cross, Plymouth, Devon, PL1 2DQ. Tel 669298 (priv 892144).

Old Amersham Auctions. (office) 2 School Lane,Old Amersham, Amersham, Buckinghamshire. Tel 22758.

Olivers. 23-24 Market Hill, Sudbury, Suffolk, CO10 6EN. Tel 72247.

Osborne King & Megran. Castle Arcade Buildings,17 Castle Arcade, Belfast, Belfast, BT1 5DG. Tel 240332.

Osmond Tricks. Regent St Auction Rooms,Regent St, Clifton, Bristol, Avon, BS8 4HG. Tel 737201.

Outhwaite & Litherland. Kingsway Galleries, Fontenoy St, Liverpool, Merseyside, L3 2BE. Tel 236 6561.

Owens Gwynedd & Co. Llanerchymedd Auction Centre, Llangefni, Gwynedd. Tel 722950 (priv 0248-76 482).

Pamela & Barry Auctions. 75 Chiltern Rd, Marshalswick, St Albans, Hertfordshire, AL4 9ST. Tel 61180.

Parsons Welch & Cowell. 49 London Rd, Sevenoaks, Kent. Tel 451211.

Robert Paterson & Son. 8 Orchard St, Paisley, Glasgow, Strathclyde. Tel 889 2435.

Pearsons. Tower House Saleroom St,Tower St, Winchester, Hampshire, SO23 8TA. Tel 62515/64444.

Pearsons of Fleet. 1-3 Fleet Rd, Fleet, Hampshire. Tel 29211.

Phillips. 9 Conwy Rd, Colwyn Bay, Clwyd, LL29 7AF. Tel 33406.

Phillips. 65 George St, Edinburgh, Lothian, EH2 2JL. Tel 225 2266.

Phillips Ipswich. Dover House,Wolsey St, Ipswich, Suffolk, IP1 1UD. Tel 55137.

Phillips. The Old House, Station Rd, Knowle, W.Midlands, B93 0HT. Tel Knowle (05645) 6151.

Phillips. 3 Opie St, Norwich, Norfolk, NR1 3DP. Tel 616426.

Phillips. 39 Park End St, Oxford, Oxfordshire, OX1 1JD. Tel 723524

Phillips. Long Street Salerooms,Long St, Sherborne, Dorset, DT93BS. Tel 815271.

Phillips (Glasgow). 98 Sauchiehall St, Glasgow, Strathclyde, G2 3DQ. Tel 332 3386.

Phillips & Jollys. 1 Old King St, Bath, Avon, BA1 1DD. Tel 310609/310709.

Phillips in Chester. New House,150 Christleton Rd, Chester, Cheshire, CH3 5TD. Tel 313936.

Phillips in Exeter. Alphin Brook Rd, Alphington, Exeter, Devon, EX2 8TH. Tel 39025/6.

Phillips in Wales. 9-10 Westgate St, Cardiff, S.Glamorgan, CF1 1DA. Tel 396453.

Phillips Auctioneers. 20 Fountain St, Morley, W.Yorkshire, LS27 9EH. Tel 523888.

Phillips Fine Art Auctioneers. Bayle Place,11 Bayle Parade, Folkestone, Kent, CT20 1SQ. Tel 45555.

Phillips Fine Art Auctioneers & Valuers. 17A East Parade, Leeds, W.Yorkshire, LS1 2BU. Tel 448011.

Charles R.Phillips. 48 High St, Henley-in-Arden, Warwickshire. Tel 4330/1/2.

John H.Raby & Son. St Mary's Rd, Bradford, W.Yorkshire, BD8 7QL. Tel 491121/2/3.

Reeds Rains. Trinity House, 114 Northenden Rd, Sale, Greater Manchester, M33 3HD. Tel 962 9237 969 7173.

Renton & Renton. 16 Albert St, Harrogate, N.Yorkshire. Tel 61531.

Richard Baker & Thomson. 24 Cooks Rd, Crosby, Liverpool, Merseyside. Tel 647 9104.

Riddetts of Bournemouth. The Auction Galleries, Richmond Hill,The Square, Bournemouth, Dorset, BH2 6EJ. Tel 25686 (4 lines).

Russell Baldwin & Bright. The Fine Art Saleroom, Ryelands Rd, Leominster, Hereford & Worcester. Tel 3897.

The Rye Auction Galleries. Cinque Ports St, Rye, E.Sussex, TN31 7AL. Tel 222124.

Sandoe Luce Panes. 1 High St, Wotton-under-Edge, Gloucestershire. Tel 843193.

Simmons & Lawrence (Chartered Surveyors). 32 Bell Street, Henley-on-Thames, Oxfordshire, RG9 2BH. Tel 571111.

Simmons and Lawrence. 114 London St, Reading, Berkshire. Tel 500575.

John Smale & Co. 19 Cross St, Barnstaple, Devon. Tel 42000, 42916.

J.P.Smith Auctions. 1 Church St, Coggeshall, Essex. Tel 62051.

St John Smith. 194/198 High St, Uckfield, E.Sussex, TN22 1RH. Tel 4111.

Sotheby's. Aboyne Castle, Aboyne, Grampian. Tel Banchory (03302) 4007.

Sotheby's. Summers Place, Billingshurst, W.Sussex, RH14 9AD. Tel 040 381 3933.

Sotheby's. 42 Holdenhurst Rd, Bournemouth, Dorset, BH8 8AF. Tel 294425.

Sotheby's. Market Place, Brampton, Cumbria, CA8 1NW. Tel 3722.

Sotheby's. 18 Imperial Sq, Cheltenham, Gloucestershire, GL50 1QZ. Tel 510500.

Sotheby's. Hall Foot, Worston, Clitheroe, Lancashire, BB7 1QA. Tel 41520.

Sotheby's. 123a Upper Abbey St, Dublin, Co Dublin. Tel 734811.

Sotheby's. 112 George St, Edinburgh, Lothian, EH2 4LH. Tel 226 7201.

Sotheby's. Bickham House,Kenn, Exeter, Devon, EX6 7XL. Tel 833416.

Sotheby's. 146 West Regent St, Glasgow, Strathclyde, G2 2RQ. Tel 221 4817.

Sotheby's. Grundisburgh, Suffolk, IP13 6TW. Tel 581.

Sotheby's. Market Place, Haltwhistle, Northumberland, NE49 OBU. Tel 20363.

Sotheby's. 8-12 Montpellier Parade, Harrogate, N.Yorkshire, HG1 2TJ. Tel 501466/7.

Sotheby's. The Estate Office,Greyabbey, Newtownards, Co Down. Tel Greyabbey (024 774) 668.

Sotheby's. George Hotel Mews, Station Rd, Stamford, Lincolnshire, PE9 2LB. Tel 51666.

Sotheby's. Magdalene House, Magdalene St, Taunton, Somerset, TA1 1SB. Tel 88441.

Sotheby's. 56 High St, Trumpington, Cambridgeshire, CB2 2LS. Tel Cambridge (0223) 8452225.

Sotheby's. Maiden Bradley, Warminster, Wiltshire, BA12 7HW. Tel Maiden Bradley (098 53) 525.

Sotheby's Chester. Booth Mansion, 28 Watergate St, Chester, Cheshire, CH1 2NA. Tel 315531.

Southam and Sons. Corn Exchange, Thrapston, Kettering, Northamptonshire. Tel Thrapston (080 12) 4486.

Henry Spencer & Sons. 20 The Square, Retford, Nottinghamshire. Tel 708633.

Henry Spencer & Sons. 38 St Mary's St, Stamford, Lincolnshire. Tel 52136.

Stanilands. 28 Netherhall Rd, Doncaster, S.Yorkshire. Tel 27121.

Sussex Auction Galleries. 59 Perrymount Rd, Haywards Heath, W.Sussex, RH16 3DS. Tel 414935.

K. Stuart Swash. 2 Waterloo Rd, Wolverhampton, W.Midlands, WV1 4BL. Tel 710626.

Sworder Salerooms. 19 North St, Bishop's Stortford, Hertfordshire. Tel 52441.

Tamlyn & Son. High St, Bridgwater, Somerset, TA6 3BN. Tel 58241/2.

Taviners. Prewett St, Redcliffe, Bristol, Avon. Tel 25996.

Taylor Lane & Creber. 38 North Hill, Plymouth, Devon, PL4 8EQ. Tel 670700.

Tennants. 26-27 Market Place, Leyburn, N.Yorkshire. Tel Wensleydale (0969) 23451.

James Thompson. 64 Main St, Kirkby Lonsdale, Cumbria, LA6 2AJ. Tel 71555.

Thomson Roddick & Laurie Ltd. 24 Lowther St, Carlisle, Cumbria. Tel 28939.

Thomson Roddick & Laurie Ltd. 60 Whitesands, Dumfries, Dumfries & Galloway. Tel 5366.

Turner Fletcher & Essex. Cattle Market,London Rd, Nottingham, Nottinghamshire. Tel 865041.

Turner Rudge & Turner. 29 High St, East Grinstead, W.Sussex. Tel 24101.

Duncan Vincent Fine Art & Chattel Auctioneers. 105 London St, Reading, Berkshire, Tel 594748.

Walker Walton & Hanson. Byard Lane, Bridlesmith Gate, Nottingham, Nottinghamshire. Tel 586161.

Walker, Barnett and Hill (Auctioneers). 3-5 Waterloo Rd, Wolverhampton, W.Midlands, WV1 4DL. Tel 771511, 772771.

Walker, Walton & Hanson. 4 Market Place, Oakham, Leicestershire. Tel 2681.

Wallis & Wallis. West Street Auction Galleries,West St, Lewes, E.Sussex, BN7 2NJ. Tel 473137.

Ward & Chowen. 1 Church Lane, Tavistock, Devon. Tel 2458/9.

Warner Sheppard & Wade. 16-18 Halford St, Leicester, Leicestershire, LE1 1JB. Tel 21613.

Warwick & Warwick Ltd. Arbon House, 21 Jury St, Warwick, Warwickshire. Tel 499031.

Watsons. Water Lane, Bishop's Stortford, Hertfordshire. Tel 52361.

Watsons. 1 Market St, Saffron Walden, Essex. Tel 22058.

J.M.Welch & Son. The Old Town Hall, Great Dunmow, Essex, CM6 1AU. Tel 2117/2118.

Weller and Dufty Ltd (Est 1835). 141 Bromsgrove St, Birmingham, W.Midlands. Tel 692 1414.

Wellington Salerooms. Mantle St, Wellington, Somerset, TA21 8NR. Tel 4815.

Wentworth Auction Gallery. 22 Station Approach, Virginia Water, Surrey. Tel Wentworth (09904) 3711.

Wharf Salerooms. Canal Wharf, Water Lane, Leeds, W.Yorkshire, LS11 5PS. Tel 434464 (priv 667434).

Whiteheads. 34 High St, Petersfield, Hampshire, GU 3JL. Tel Portsmouth (0705) 820701.

Peter Wilson & Co. The Victoria Gallery,Market St, Nantwich, Cheshire, CW5 5DG. Tel 623878.

P.F. Windibank. 18-20 Reigate Rd, Dorking, Surrey. Tel 884556.

Wintertons Fine Arts. St Mary's Chambers, Lichfield, Staffordshire, WS13 6LQ. Tel 263256.

Woolley & Wallis. Castle Auction Mart, Castle St, Salisbury, Wiltshire, SP1 3SU. Tel 21711.

Worsfolds of Canterbury. Auction Galleries,40 Station Road West, Canterbury, Kent. Tel 68984.

Worthing Auction Galleries. 31 Chatsworth Rd, Worthing, W.Sussex, BN11 1LY. Tel 205565.

Wright-Manley. 63 High St, Tarporley, Cheshire, CW6 0DR. Tel 2151.

Wyatt & Son. Baffins Hall Saleroom,Baffins Lane, Chichester, W.Sussex, PO19 1HN. Tel 787548.

Autographs

Bertram Rota Ltd. 30-31 Long Acre, London, WC2E 9LT. Tel 836 0723.

John Hall. 31 Epple Rd, London, SW6 4DJ. Tel 736 3542.

Richard Macnutt Ltd. Hamm Farm House,Withyham, Hartfield Wells, E.Sussex, TN7 4BJ. Tel Groombridge (089276) 218.

Maggs Bros Ltd. 50 Berkeley Sq, London, W1X 6EL. Tel 493 7160.

Mail Order Book Specialist. 25 Dicey Ave, Cricklewood, London, NW2. Tel 452 1581.

Pickering and Chatto Ltd, inc Dawsons of Pall Mall. 17 Pall Mall, London, SW1Y 5NB. Tel 930 2515.

A. Rosenthal Ltd. 9-10 Broad St, Oxford, Oxfordshire, OX1 3AP. Tel 243093.

Tyrrell Bookshop & Gallery. 80 Christchurch Rd, Ringwood, Hampshire, BH24 1DR. Tel 474489.

Warwick & Warwick Ltd. Arbon House, 21 Jury St, Warwick, Warwickshire. Tel 499031.

John Wilson (Autographs) Ltd. 50 Acre End St, Eynsham, Oxfordshire, OX8 1PD. Tel Oxford (0865) 880883.

Worldwide Autographs Ltd. 68 Staines Rd, Hounslow, Middlesex, TW3 3LS. Tel 572 3606.

Automata

see also Dolls and Toys

The Connoisseur. 528 Wilmslow Rd, Withington, Manchester, Greater Manchester. Tel 445 2504.

Jack Donovan. 93 Portobello Rd, London, W11. Tel 727 1485.

Hadlow Antiques. No 1 The Pantiles, Tunbridge Wells, Kent. Tel 29858.

Keith Harding. 93 Hornsey Road, London, N7 6DJ. Tel 607 6181, 607 2672.

Hobby Horse Antiques. 29 West Allington, Bridport, Dorset, DT6 5BJ. Tel 22801.

Mayflower Antiques. 180-182 High St, Dovercourt, Harwich, Essex. Tel 504079.

Something Old. 6-8 Old Cross, Hertford, Hertfordshire, SG14 1RB. Tel 551530.

Yesterday Child. 24 The Mall, Camden Passage, London, N1. Tel Milton Keynes (0908) 583403.

Automobile and Aero Art

Tony Cardy. The Market Place, Kenninghall, Norfolk, NR16 2AH. Tel Quidenham (095 387) 643.

Norman Kerr. Priory House,Priest Lane, Cartmel, Cumbria, LA11 6PX. Tel Cartmel (044 854) 247.

Khachadourian Gallery. 60 Pall Mall,St James's, London, SW1Y 5HT. Tel 930 3333.

Jeremy Wood Fine Art. East St, Petworth, W.Sussex, GU28 0AB. Tel 43408.

Badges

see Buttons and Badges

Barometers

Addingham Antiques. 70-72 Main St, Addingham, W.Yorkshire. Tel 830788.

Anthony Baker Antiques. 14 London Rd, Alderley Edge, Cheshire, SK9 7JS. Tel 582674.

David Ball Antiques. 126A Leagrave Rd, Luton, Bedfordshire, LU4 8HX. Tel 417560 (priv 0525-210753).

Blake Antiques. 216 Westbourne Grove, London, W11 2RH. Tel 229 3232.

I.Blatt. 17 Bampfield St, Portslade, E.Sussex. Tel 416641.

Peter D. Bosson. 10B Swan St, Wilmslow, Cheshire, SK9 1HE. Tel 525250 (priv 527857).

J. & M. Bristow Antiques. 28 Long St, Tetbury, Gloucestershire, GL8 8AQ. Tel 52222.

Aubrey Brocklehurst. 124 Cromwell Rd, South Kensington, London, SW7 4ET. Tel 373 0319.

N.Bryan-Peach Antiques. 28 Far St, Wymeswold, Leicestershire. Tel 880425.

Patric Capon. 350 Upper St,Islington, London, N1. Tel 354 0487 (priv 467 5722).

J Carlton-Smith. 17 Ryder St, St James', London, SW1. Tel 930 6622 (priv 467 8020).

Peter Carmichael. 33 Upper North St, Brighton & Hove, E.Sussex, BN1 3FG. Tel 28072.

Chattels. 156 High St, Old Woking, Woking, Surrey, GU22 9JH. Tel 71310.

Bryan Clisby - Antique Clocks. at Andwells Antiques,High Street, Hartley Wintney, Hampshire. Tel 2305.

Nigel Coleman Antiques. High St, Brasted, Kent. Tel Westerham (0959) 64042.

O. Comitti & Son Ltd. 656 Forest Rd, Walthamstow, London, E17 3ED. Tel 509 0011.

M.J.Dareau. 66 Cumberland St, Edinburgh, Lothian. Tel 556 9352 & 0968 73028.

Zal Davar. 26A Munster Rd, London, SW6. Tel 736 2559, 736 1405.

John de Haan. 12A Seaforth Drive, Waltham Cross, Hertfordshire, EN8 8BU. Tel 763111 (priv 0920 2534).

Diss Antiques. 2 Market Place & 23 St Nicholas St, Diss, Norfolk. Tel 2213 (priv 51369).

Doddington House Antiques. 2 Benwick Rd, Doddington, Cambridgeshire, PE15 0TG. Tel March (0354) 740755.

Evans & Evans. 40 West St, Alresford, Hampshire, SO24 9AU. Tel 2170.

Vincent Freeman Antiques. 1 Camden Passage, Islington, London, N1. Tel 226 6178.

Good Hope Antiques. 2 Hogshill St, Beaminster, Dorset. Tel 862119.

A.E.Gould & Sons (Antiques) Ltd. Old Rectory Cottage,Ockham Rd South, East Horsley, Surrey, KT24 6QJ. Tel 3747.

W.R.Harvey & Co (Antiques) Ltd. 67-70 Chalk Farm Rd, London, NW1 8AN. Tel 485 1504, 267 2767.

Simon Hatchwell Antiques. 64-65 Middle St, Brighton & Hove, E.Sussex, BN1 1AL. Tel 27663.

Hazel Cottage Clocks. Hazel Cottage, Eachwick, Dalton, Newcastle upon Tyne, Tyne & Wear. Tel Wylam (066 14) 2415.

E. Hollander Ltd. The Dutch House,Horsham Rd, South Holmwood, Dorking, Surrey, RH5 4NF. Tel 888921.

John Hopkins. 1 The Courtyard,Ockenden Manor, Cuckfield, W.Sussex, RH17 5LD. Tel Haywards Heath (0444) 454323.

Horological Workshops. 204 Worplesdon Rd, Guildford, Surrey, GU2 6UY. Tel 576496.

Horsefair Antiques. 21 Horsefair, Chipping Norton, Oxfordshire. Tel 3089.

Howard & Reeves. 38 Whitehorse St, Baldock, Hertfordshire. Tel 892385.

Howard & Reeves. 1 The Arcade, Hitchin, Hertfordshire. Tel 35454.

Its About Time. 863 London Rd, Westcliff-on-Sea, Essex, SS26 6BA. Tel Southend (0702) 72574 (priv 205204).

Paul Jennings Antiques. Millbrook House,Angarrack, Hayle, Cornwall, TR27 5HZ. Tel 754065

Littlebury Antiques. 58/60 Fairycroft Rd, Saffron Walden, Essex. Tel 27961.

Look Around Antiques. 61 Watergate Row, Chester, Cheshire. Tel 49826.

Madoc Antique & Art Gallery. 48 Madoc St, Llandudno, Gwynedd. Tel 79754 (priv 79760).

G.E. Marsh (Antique Clocks). 32A The Square, Winchester, Hampshire, SO23 9EX. Tel 54505.

Medalcrest Ltd. Charnham House,29-30 Charnham St, Hungerford, Berkshire, RG17 OEJ. Tel 84157.

Mitre Antiques. The Market Place, Wells, Somerset. Tel 72607.

Muirhead Moffat & Co. 182 West Regent St, Glasgow, Strathclyde. Tel 226 4683 and 226 3406.

North London Clock Shop Ltd. 72 Highbury Park, London, N5. Tel 226 1609.

The Old Malthouse. 15 Bridge St (A4), Hungerford, Berkshire, RG17 OEG. Tel 82209 (priv 83647).

The Old Man Antiques. Yewdale Rd, Coniston, Cumbria, LA21 8DU. Tel 389.

Onslow Clocks. 48 King Street, Twickenham, Middlesex, TW1 3SH. Tel 892 7632.

P.A. Oxley, Antique Clocks and Barometers. The Old Rectory, Cherhill, Calne, Wiltshire. Tel 816227 (priv 812742).

Park Street Antiques. 350 High St (on A41), Berkhamsted, Hertfordshire, HP4 1HT. Tel 4790 (priv 024029 255).

Antony Preston Antiques Ltd. The Square, Stow-on-the-Wold, Gloucestershire, GL54 1AB. Tel 31586 (priv 31406).

Nigel Raffety. 34 Kensington Church St, London, W8. Tel 938 1100.

Derek Rayment Antiques. Orchard House,Barton Rd, Barton, Farndon, Cheshire, SY14 7HT. Tel 270 429.

G.E.Richards & Son (Antiques). 57 Blueschool St, Hereford, Hereford & Worcester, HR1 2AR. Tel 267840 (priv 268827).

Michael Sim. 1 Royal Parade, Chislehurst, Kent, BR7 5PG. Tel 467 7040.

Robin Smith. 23 Belle Vue Rd, Shrewsbury, Shropshire, SY3 7LN. Tel 50357.

Stair & Company Ltd. 120 Mount St, London, W1Y 5HB. Tel 499 1784, 499 1785.

Geoffrey G.Stevens. 26-28 Church Rd, Guildford, Surrey, GU1 4NG. Tel 504075.

Strike One (Islington) Ltd. 51 Camden Passage, London, N1 8EA. Tel 226 9709 (priv 359 6459).

Surrey Clock Centre. 3 Lower St, Haslemere, Surrey. Tel 4547.

Time in Hand. 11 Church St, Shipston on Stour, Warwickshire, CV36 4AP. Tel 62578.

Tooley Antiques. 5 Cross St, Northam, Devon. Tel Instow (0271) 860851.

Turret House. 27 Middleton St, Wymondham, Norfolk, NR18 0AB. Tel 603462.

Vanbrugh House Antiques. Park St, Stow-on-the-Wold, Gloucestershire, GL54 1AQ. Tel 30797.

Village Antiques. 2 Cooden Sea Rd, Little Common, Bexhill, E.Sussex. Tel Cooden (04243) 5214.

A.G. Voss Antiques. 16 Market Hill, Woodbridge, Suffolk, IP12 4LU. Tel 5830.

Anthony Woodburn Ltd. Orchard House, High Street, Leigh, Kent. Tel Hildenbrough (0732) 832258.

York House Antiques. 11-13 York St, Cowes, Isle of Wight. Tel 295746.

Beds

And So To Bed Ltd. 638-640 King's Road, London, SW6. Tel 731 3593.

The Antique Brass Bedstead Co Ltd. Gt. Baddow Antique Centre,Church St, Great Baddow, Essex. Tel Chelmsford (0245) 71137 (priv 0621 741941).

Antique Metals. 12 East St, Coggeshall, Essex, Co6 1SH. Tel 62252.

Below Stairs. 103 High St, Hungerford, Berkshire, RG17 0NB. Tel 82317.

Brook Lane Antiques. 93 Brook Lane, Alderley Edge, Cheshire, SK9 7RU. Tel Wilmslow (0625) 582717.

Country Cottage Bedsteads. Park House,Penton Mewsey, Andover, Hampshire, SP11 0RW. Tel Weyhill (026477) 2527.

Goodbrey Antiques. 29 Double St, Framlingham, Suffolk. Tel 723756.

Great Brampton House Antiques Ltd. Great Brampton House, Madley, Hereford, Hereford & Worcester, HR2 9NA. Tel Golden Valley (0981) 250244.

Ipswich Pianos. 45 Graham Rd, Ipswich, Suffolk. Tel 50740.

Manor Farm Antiques. Manor Farm, Standlake, Oxfordshire, OX8 7RL. Tel 303

Manor Farm Antiques & Garden Ornaments. Manor Farm, Swaffham, Norfolk. Tel 21395.

Elizabeth Niner Antiques. 53 Great Norwood St, Cheltenham, Gloucestershire. Tel 516497 (priv 520066).

Park Galleries. 215/217 Preston Rd, Brighton & Hove, E.Sussex, BN1 6SA. Tel 504057 (priv 29466).

Peter Roberts Antiques. High St, Moreton-in-Marsh, Gloucestershire, GL56 0LM.

Serendipity. Brookend, Ross-on-Wye, Hereford & Worcester. Tel 63836 (priv 053184 245).

Tom Smith Antiques. 33A St Peters St, Ipswich, Suffolk. Tel 210172.

Birds and Birdcages

The Enchanted Aviary. 63 Hall St, Long Melford, Suffolk. Tel 78814.

M. & C. Telfer-Smollett. 88 Portobello Rd, London, W11. Tel 727 0117 (priv 370 1860).

Book Illustrators

L.W.Bondy. 16 Little Russell St, London, WC1A 2HN. Tel 405 2733.

Robin de Beaumont. 25 Park Walk,Chelsea, London, SW10. Tel 352 3440.

Demetzy Books. 113 Portobello Rd, London, W11. Tel Witney (0993) 2209.

Fairhurst Gallery. 291 New King's Rd, London, SW6 4RE. Tel 736 9132.

Harrington Bros. Chelsea Antique Market,253 King's Rd, London, SW3. Tel 352 5689.

E.Joseph. 1 Vere St (3rd floor), London, W1M 9HQ. Tel 493 8353/4/5.

Langton Gallery Ltd. 3 Langton St, London, SW10. Tel 352 9150.

Archie Miles Bookshop. 54 High St, Pateley Bridge, Harrogate, N.Yorkshire, HG3 5JZ. Tel 711294 (priv 711166).

Pandion Books. 10 Carr Close,Rainton, Thirsk, N.Yorkshire, YO7 3PS. Tel 578224.

Chas J. Sawyer. 1 Grafton St, London, W1X 3LB. Tel 493 3810.

Daniel Shackleton. 23 Dundas St, Edinburgh, Lothian, EH3 6QQ. Tel 557 1115.

Sims, Reed and Fogg Ltd. 58 Jermyn St, London, SW1 6LX. Tel 493 5660/0952.

Warrack & Perkins. Rectory Farm House, Church Enstone, Oxfordshire, OX7 4NN. Tel Enstone (060 872) 572.

Willcocks Antiques. Chenil Galleries, 183 King's Rd,Chelsea, London, SW3. Tel 352 8653.

Bookbinders

see Restorers

Bookbindings

George Bayntun. Manvers St, Bath, Avon, BA1 1JW. Tel 66000.

D.M. Beach. 52 High St, Salisbury, Wiltshire, SP1 2PG. Tel 333801.

Robin de Beaumont. 25 Park Walk,Chelsea, London, SW10. Tel 352 3440.

Demetzy Books. 113 Portobello Rd, London, W11. Tel Witney (0993) 2209.

Colin & Charlotte Franklin. Home Farm, Culham, Oxfordshire. Tel Abingdon (0235) 22544.

Goodramgate Books, Maps and Prints. 58 Goodramgate, York, N.Yorkshire. Tel 51275 (priv 0484 46833).

Simon Gough Books. 3 Fish Hill, Holt, Norfolk. Tel 2650.

John Grant. 9A & 13C Dundas St, Edinburgh, Lothian. Tel 556 9698.

Harrington Bros. Chelsea Antique Market,253 King's Rd, London, SW3. Tel 352 5689.

E.Joseph. 1 Vere St (3rd floor), London, W1M 9HQ. Tel 493 8353/4/5.

Robert D.Steedman. 9 Grey St, Newcastle upon Tyne, Tyne & Wear, NE1 6EE. Tel 326561.

Harold T.Storey. 3 Cecil Court, London, WC2N 4EZ. Tel 836 3777.

John Updike (Rare Books). 7 St Bernard's Row, Edinburgh, Lothian, EH4 1HW. Tel 332 1650.

Books, Antiquarian

London

Anglebooks Ltd. 2 Cecil Court,Charing Cross Rd, London, WC2. Tel 836 2922.

Ash Rare Books. 25 Royal Exchange, Threadneedle St, London, EC3. Tel 626 2665.

Bertram Rota Ltd. 30-31 Long Acre, London, WC2E 9LT. Tel 836 0723.

Bloomsbury Book Auctions. 3-4 Hardwick St, London, EC1R 4RY. Tel 636 1945, 833 2636/7.

L.W.Bondy. 16 Little Russell St, London, WC1A 2HN. Tel 405 2733.

Joanna Booth. 247 King's Rd, London, SW3. Tel 352 8998.

Clive A.Burden Ltd. 13 Cecil Court, London, WC2N 4EZ. Tel 836 2177.

Cavendish Rare Books Ltd. 2-4 Princes Arcade, Piccadilly, London, SW1Y 6DS. Tel 734 3840.

Chelsea Rare Books. 313 King's Rd, London, SW3 5EP. Tel 351 0950.

Demetzy Books. 113 Portobello Rd, London, W11. Tel Witney (0993) 2209.

Peter Eaton (Booksellers) Ltd. 80 Holland Park Ave, London, W11. Tel 727 5211.

H.M. Fletcher. 27 Cecil Court, Charing Cross, London, WC2N 4EZ. Tel 836 2865.

Sam Fogg. 66 Highbury Hill, London, N5.

W.Forster. 83A Stamford Hill, London, N16 5TP. Tel 800 3919.

Han-Shan Tang Ltd. 717 Fulham Rd, London, SW6 5UL. Tel 731 2447.

Harrington Bros. Chelsea Antique Market,253 King's Rd, London, SW3. Tel 352 5689.

Heraldry Today. 10 Beauchamp Place, London, SW3. Tel 584 1656.

Stephanie Hoppen. 17 Walton St, London, SW3. Tel 589 3678.

E.Joseph. 1 Vere St (3rd floor), London, W1M 9HQ. Tel 493 8353/4/5.

S.Linden. 33 Craven St, London, WC2. Tel 930 3659.

Maggs Bros Ltd. 50 Berkeley Sq, London, W1X 6EL. Tel 493 7160.

Marlborough Rare Books Ltd. 35 Old Bond St, London, W1X 4PT. Tel 493 6993.

D.Mellor & A.L.Baxter Antiquarian Booksellers. 121A Kensington Church St, London, W8 7LP. Tel 229 2033 221 8822.

Michael Phelps Antiquarian Books. 19 Chelverton Rd, Putney, London, SW15 1RN. Tel 785 6766.

Pickering and Chatto Ltd, inc Dawsons of Pall Mall. 17 Pall Mall, London, SW1Y 5NB. Tel 930 2515.

Jonathan Potter. 1 Grafton St, London, W1X 3LB. Tel 491 3520.

Arthur Probsthain. 41 Great Russell St, London, WC1B 3PH. Tel 636 1096.

Bernard Quaritch Ltd. 5-8 Lower John St, Golden Sq, London, W1. Tel 734 2983.

Quevedo. 25 Cecil Court, London, WC2N 4EZ. Tel 836 9132.

William Reeves Bookseller Ltd. 1A Norbury Cres, London, SW16 4JR. Tel 764 2108.

Reg and Philip Remington. 14 Cecil Ct, London, WC2. Tel 836 9771.

Sanford Books. Chelsea Antique Market,253 King's Rd, London, SW3. Tel 352 5581.

Chas J. Sawyer. 1 Grafton St, London, W1X 3LB. Tel 493 3810.

Thomas E. Schuster. 9 Gillingham St, London, SW1. Tel 828 7963.

B.A. Seaby Ltd. 8 Cavendish Sq, London, W1M 0AJ. Tel 631 3707.

Henry Sotheran. 2-5 Sackville St, London, W1X 2DP. Tel 734 1150, 734 0308.

Peter Stockham at Images. 16 Cecil Court, Charing Cross Rd, London, WC2. Tel 836 8661.

Rogers Turner Books Ltd. 22 Nelson Rd, Greenwich, London, SE10. Tel 853 5271.

Wade Galleries. 12B Camden Passage, Charlton Place, London, N1. Tel 226 3803.

The Warwick Leadlay Gallery. 5 Nelson Rd, Greenwich, London, SE10 9JB. Tel 858 0317 (priv 852 7484).

Harriet Wynter Ltd. 50 Redcliffe Rd, London, SW10 9NJ. Tel 352 6494.

A.Zwemmer Ltd. 24 Litchfield St, London, WC2. Tel 836 1749.

Regions

Duncan M.Allsop. 26 Smith St, Warwick, Warwickshire, CV34 4HS. Tel 493266.

The Antique Shop. 43 McCurtain St, Cork, Co Cork. Tel (021) 504079.

The Antiques Book Centre. 93 Bradmore Green, Brookmans Park, Hatfield, Hertfordshire, AL9 7QT. Tel Potters Bar (0707) 44426.

Aspidistra. 46 St James Parade, Bath, Avon. Tel 61948.

Attic (Sevenoaks) Ltd. The Village House, Brasted, Kent, TN16 1HU. Tel Westerham (0959) 63507.

C.G. Baker. Forester Rd, Bath, Avon, BA2 6QE. Tel 64095.

Barbican Bookshop. 24 Fossgate, York, N.Yorkshire. Tel 53643.

Richard Barder Antiques. Crossways House, Hermitage, Berkshire, RG16 9SU. Tel Newbury (0635) 200295.

Barnard Gallery. Grange Farm,Everton, Doncaster, S.Yorkshire, DN10 5BG. Tel Retford (0777) 817324.

Barrie's Bookshop. 4 Montpellier Walk, Cheltenham, Gloucestershire, GL50 1SD. Tel 515813.

Baynton-Williams. Maltravers House, 49 Maltravers St, Arundel, W.Sussex, BN18 9BQ. Tel 882898.

George Bayntun. Manvers St, Bath, Avon, BA1 1JW. Tel 66000.

D.M. Beach. 52 High St, Salisbury, Wiltshire, SP1 2PG. Tel 333801.

Beeleigh Abbey Books. Beeleigh Abbey, Maldon, Essex. Tel 56308.

D.Bickersteth. 38 Fulbrooke Rd, Cambridge, Cambridgeshire, CB3 9EE. Tel 352291.

James G.Bissett Ltd. 99 High St,Old Aberdeen, Aberdeen, Grampian. Tel 46102.

Blackwell's Rare Books. Fyfield Manor, Fyfield, Oxfordshire, OX13 5LR. Tel Frilford Heath (0865) 390692-3.

The Book House. Grey Garth, Ravenstonedale, Kirkby Stephen, Cumbria, CA17 4NQ. Tel Newbiggin-on-Lune (05873) 634.

Andrew Boyle (Booksellers) Ltd. 21 Friar St, Worcester, Hereford & Worcester. Tel 611700.

Brown Jack Bookshop. 78 Main St, Lubenham, Market Harborough, Leicestershire. Tel 65787.

A.Burton-Garbett. 35 The Green, Morden, Surrey, SM4 4HJ. Tel 540 2367.

The Cardigan Book Centre. 1 Royal Oak, Quay St, Cardigan, Dyfed, SA43 1HR. Tel 612704.

The Carson Clark Gallery. (Scotiamaps - Mapsellers),173 Cannongate, The Royal Mile, Edinburgh, Lothian, EH8 8BN. Tel 556 4710.

Castle Bookshop. 37 North Hill, Colchester, Essex. Tel 577520 (priv 34 204).

The Chair Shop. 6 London Rd, Tunbridge Wells, Kent. Tel 27364.

Chantry Book Shop. 11 Higher St, Dartmouth, Devon, TQ6 9RB. Tel 2796 (priv) 4208.

Checker Books. 2 Checker Walk, Abingdon, Oxfordshire. Tel 28172.

Classey Ltd. Park Rd, Faringdon, Oxfordshire, SN7 7DR. Tel 20911.

Clifton Books. 5A Dicconson St, Wigan, Greater Manchester. Tel 36716 (priv 726319).

Collards Bookshop. 4 Castle St, Totnes, Devon, TQ9 5NU. Tel (priv) 0548 550246.

College Gateway Bookshop. 3 Silent St, Ipswich, Suffolk, IP1 1TF. Tel 54776.

Commin's Bookshop. 100 Old Christchurch Rd, Bournemouth, Dorset. Tel 27504.

R.L.Cook. Belmont House, Little Horton, Devizes, Wiltshire. Tel Cannings (038 086) 214.

Heather Cowley Bookshop & Galleries. 235-237 Mansfield Rd, Nottingham, Nottinghamshire. Tel 473836.

Thomas Crowe. 77 Upper St Giles St, Norwich, Norfolk. Tel 21962.

The Darenth Bookshop. 8 High St, Otford, Kent, TN14 5PQ. Tel 2430.

G.David. 3, 4 & 16 St Edward's Passage, Cambridge, Cambridgeshire, CB2 3PJ. Tel 354619.

H.V. Day. The Old Roman Catholic Church,25 High West St, Dorchester, Dorset, DT1 1UW. Tel 64904.

Deighton Bell & Co. 13 Trinity St, Cambridge, Cambridgeshire, CB2 1TD. Tel 353939.

Roderick Dew-Antiquarian Books. 29 South St, Eastbourne, E.Sussex. Tel 646206 (priv 20239).

Gillian Dickerson. Packer House,28 High St, Chipping Norton, Oxfordshire. Tel 3255 (priv 41717).

Maurice Dodd (Booksellers). 112 Warwick Rd, Carlisle, Cumbria. Tel 22087.

John Drury Rare Books Ltd. PO Box 77, Colchester, Essex, CO1 1EL. Tel Ramsey (0255) 886260.

E.M.Lawson & Co. Kingsholm, East Hagbourne, Didcot, Oxfordshire, OX11 9LN. Tel 812033.

Emerald Isle Books. 539 Antrim Rd, Belfast, Belfast, BT15 3BU. Tel 771798.

Eton Antique Book Shop. 88 High St, Eton, Berkshire. Tel Windsor (0753) 855534.

David Ferrow. 77 Howard St South, Great Yarmouth, Norfolk. Tel 843800 (priv 662247).

Fifteenth Century Bookshop. 99 High St, Lewes, E.Sussex, BN7 1XH. Tel 474160.

Susanna Fisher. Spencer, Upham, Hampshire, SO3 1JD. Tel Durley (04896) 291.

Folio (Clevedon Books & Clevedon Fine Arts). The Gallery, Cinema Buildings,Old Church Rd, Clevedon, Avon, BS21 6NN. Tel 875862 (priv 872304).

Foye Gallery. 15 Stanley St, Luton, Bedfordshire, LU1 5AL. Tel 38487.

Frances Books. 54A Homefield Rd, Worthing, W.Sussex, BN11 1RL. Tel 36437 (priv 31169).

Colin & Charlotte Franklin. Home Farm, Culham, Oxfordshire. Tel Abingdon (0235) 22544.

Alex M. Frizzell. Castlelaw, West Linton, Borders, EH46 7AA. Tel 60450.

Galloway & Porter Ltd. 30 Sidney St, Cambridge, Cambridgeshire. Tel 67876.

Garrick Bookshop. 20A Wellington Road South, Stockport, Greater Manchester, SK4 1AD. Tel 480-4346.

Wm.George's Sons Ltd. 89 Park St, Bristol, Avon, BS1 5PW. Tel 276602.

H.M.Gilbert & Son. 2 1/2 Portland St, Southampton, Hampshire, SO1 0EB. Tel 26420.

Henry March Gilbert. 19 The Square, Winchester, Hampshire, SO23 9RY. Tel 52832.

Thomas C.Godfrey Ltd. 21 Stonegate, York, N.Yorkshire, YO1 2AP. Tel 24531.

Simon Gough Books. 3 Fish Hill, Holt, Norfolk. Tel 2650.

Grange Bookshop. 186 Causewayside, Edinburgh, Lothian, EH9 1PN. Tel 667 2759 (priv 03617 311).

John Grant. 9A & 13C Dundas St, Edinburgh, Lothian. Tel 556 9698.

Hugh Greer. 29 Hamilton Rd, Bangor, Co Down. Tel 5014.

George Gregory. Manvers St, Bath, Avon, BA1 1JW. Tel 66055.

Halewood & Sons. 37 Friargate, Preston, Lancashire, PR1 2AT. Tel 52603.

Anthony C.Hall. 30 Staines Rd, Twickenham, Middlesex. Tel 898 2638.

Hall's Bookshop. 20 Chapel Place, Tunbridge Wells, Kent. Tel 27842.

The Hampshire Bookshop. Kingsgate Arch, Winchester, Hampshire. Tel 64710.

Hanover Books. 8 Hunter St, Whitby, N.Yorkshire. Tel 603587 (priv 602795).

Harlequin Gallery. 22 Steep Hill, Lincoln, Lincolnshire. Tel Wragby (06734) 294.

M. Harrington Ltd. 74 Parchment St, Winchester, Hampshire, SO23 8AT. Tel 53608.

The Haunted Bookshop. 9 St Edward's Passage, Cambridge, Cambridgeshire, CB2 3PJ. Tel 312913 (priv 68169).

John & Judith Head, The Barn Book Supply. 88 Crane St, Salisbury, Wiltshire. Tel 27767.

W. Heffer & Sons Ltd. 20 Trinity St, Cambridge, Cambridgeshire, CB2 3NG. Tel 358351.

Hilmarton Manor Press. Hilmarton, Calne, Wiltshire, SN11 8SB. Tel Hilmarton (024976) 208.

Hofman & Freeman Ltd. 8 High St, Otford, Kent, TN14 5PQ. Tel 2430.

Keith Hogg. 82 High St, Tenterden, Kent, TN30 6JJ. Tel 2050.

Esmond Holden Ltd. 53A High St,White Post Hill, Reigate, Surrey, RH2 9AF. Tel 44754.

Holleyman & Treacher Ltd. 21A & 22 Duke St, Brighton & Hove, E.Sussex, BN1 1AH. Tel 28007.

Howes Bookshop. Trinity Hall, Braybrooke Terrace, Hastings, E.Sussex, TN34 1HQ. Tel 423437.

Jubilee Books Ltd. 18 High St, Burford, Oxfordshire, OX8 4QE. Tel 2209.

A. & S. Keen. 19 Pier St, Ventnor, Isle of Wight, PO38 1ST. Tel 853706.

Ewen Kerr Books. 1 New Rd, Kendal, Cumbria, LA9 4AY. Tel 20659.

C.C. Kohler. 12 Horsham Rd, Dorking, Surrey. Tel 881532.

Anthony W.Laywood. Knipton, Grantham, Lincolnshire, NG32 1RF. Tel 870224.

Lion Gallery & Bookshop. 15A Minshull St, Knutsford, Cheshire, WA16 6HQ. Tel 52915.

Tom Lloyd-Roberts. Old Court House, Caerwys, Mold, Clwyd, CH7 5BB. Tel 720276.

Lloyd's Bookshop. 27 High St, Wingham, Kent, CT3 1AW. Tel Canterbury (0227) 720774.

John Lyle. Harpford, Sidmouth, Devon, EX10 0NH. Tel Colaton Raleigh (0395) 68294.

Murdoch MacTaggart. Little Brympton, Brympton d'Evercy, Yeovil, Somerset. Tel West Coker (093 586) 2609.

The Malvern Bookshop. 5-7 Abbey Rd, Malvern, Hereford & Worcester. Tel 5915 (priv 0684-40340).

Marrin & Sons. 149 Sandgate Rd, Folkestone, Kent. Tel 53016.

McNaughtan's Bookshop. 3A & 4A Haddington Place, Edinburgh, Lothian, EH7 4AE. Tel 556 5897.

Meynell's Bookshop. 11 The Hornet, Eastgate Square, Chichester, W.Sussex. Tel 782018 (priv 512798).

Archie Miles Bookshop. 54 High St, Pateley Bridge, Harrogate, N.Yorkshire, HG3 5JZ. Tel 711294 (priv 711166).

The Minster Gates Bookshop. 8 Minster Gates, York, N.Yorkshire. Tel 21812.

Eric T.Moore. 24 Bridge St, Hitchin, Hertfordshire. Tel 50497.

E.J. Morten (Booksellers) Ltd. 2, 4, 6, 8, 9 Warburton Street, Didsbury, Greater Manchester, M20 0RA. Tel 445 7629.

Morten's Bookshops Ltd. Chestergate, Macclesfield, Cheshire. Tel 23679.

Murray's Ltd. 23 Loseby Lane, Leicester, Leicestershire, LE1 5DR. Tel 20360.

O'Flynn Antiquarian Books. 35 Micklegate, York, N.Yorkshire, YO1 1DD. Tel 641404.

Colin Page Antiquarian Books. 36 Duke St, Brighton & Hove, E.Sussex, BN1 1AG. Tel 25954.

D. Parikian. The Old Rectory, Waterstock, Oxford, Oxfordshire, OX9 1JR. Tel Ickford (084 47) 603.

The Petersfield Bookshop. 16A Chapel St, Petersfield, Hampshire, GU32 3DS. Tel 63438.

Pierpoint Gallery. 10 Church St, Hereford, Hereford & Worcester, HR1 2LR. Tel 267002.

P.M.Pollak Fine Scientific and Medical Books. Moorview,Plymouth Road, South Brent, Devon, TQ10 9HT. Tel 3457.

Quinto of Cambridge. 34 Trinity St, Cambridge, Cambridgeshire, CB2 1TB. Tel 358279.

Alan Rankin. 72 Dundas St, Edinburgh, Lothian. Tel 556 3705.

Gibb's Bookshop Ltd. 10 Charlotte St, Manchester, Greater Manchester, M1 4FL. Tel 236-7179.

John Roberts Bookshop. 43 Triangle West, Clifton, Bristol, Avon, BS8 1ES. Tel 28568.

Robinson (Newcastle) Ltd. 49-53 Grainger Market, Newcastle upon Tyne, Tyne & Wear. Tel 22978.

A. Rosenthal Ltd. 9-10 Broad St, Oxford, Oxfordshire, OX1 3AP. Tel 243093.

Eileen Ryley. 104 Risbygate St, Bury St Edmunds, Suffolk. Tel 67377.

Sanders of Oxford Ltd. 104 High St, Oxford, Oxfordshire, OX1 4BW. Tel 242590.

The Scientific Anglican Bookshop. 30-30A St Benedict St, Norwich, Norfolk. Tel 24079.

Graham K.Scott. 68-69 St John's St, Bury St Edmunds, Suffolk, IP33 1SJ. Tel 3933.

B. & C.Seago. Whitemans Green, Cuckfield, W.Sussex, RH17 5BY. Tel Haywards Heath (0444) 456111.

Shaw's Bookshop Ltd. 11 Police St, Manchester, Greater Manchester, M2 7LQ. Tel 834-7587.

Ian Sheridan's Bookshop. Thames Villa, 34 Thames St, Hampton, Middlesex. Tel 979 1704.

J.Shotton. 89 Elvet Bridge, Durham, Durham, DH1 3AG. Tel 64597.

John Smith & Son (Glasgow) Ltd. 57-61 St Vincent St, Glasgow, Strathclyde. Tel 221 7472.

Raymond Smith. 30 South St, Eastbourne, E.Sussex, BN21 4XB. Tel 34128.

William Smith (Booksellers) Ltd. 35-39 London St, Reading, Berkshire, RG1 4PU. Tel 595555.

John Speed (Maps). Drove House,Bilstone, Nuneaton, Warwickshire, CV13 6NG. Tel Tamworth (0827) 880439.

Ken Spelman Booksellers. 70 Micklegate, York, N.Yorkshire, YO1 1LF. Tel 24414.

Sterling Books. 43A Locking Rd, Weston-super-Mare, Avon, BS23 3DG. Tel 25056.

Studio Bookshop and Gallery. 17 Broad St, Alresford, Hampshire, SO24 9AW. Tel 2188.

SPCK Bookshops. 24 The Square, Winchester, Hampshire. Tel 66617.

Taikoo Books Ltd.. 29 High Petergate, York, N.Yorkshire, YO1 2HP. Tel 641213 (priv 36636).

Taylor-Halsey Antiques. Strangs,Sandford, Crediton, Devon, EX17 4EL. Tel 3408.

James Thin. 54 South Bridge, Edinburgh, Lothian. Tel 536 6743.

Thornton's of Oxford Ltd. 11 Broad St, Oxford, Oxfordshire, OX1 3AR. Tel 242939.

Thomas Thorp. 170 High St, Guildford, Surrey, GU1 3HP. Tel 62770.

Charles W. Traylen. Castle House, 49 Quarry St, Guildford, Surrey. Tel 572424.

Turret House. 27 Middleton St, Wymondham, Norfolk, NR18 0AB. Tel 603462.

Tyrrell Bookshop & Gallery. 80 Christchurch Rd, Ringwood, Hampshire, BH24 1DR. Tel 474489.

John Updike (Rare Books). 7 St Bernard's Row, Edinburgh, Lothian, EH4 1HW. Tel 332 1650.

Robert Vaughan Antiquarian Booksellers. 20 Chapel St, Stratford-upon-Avon, Warwickshire, CV37 6EP. Tel 205312.

Derek & Glenda Wallis. 6 Chapel Row, Queen Sq, Bath, Avon. Tel 24677.

R.E. & G.B.Way. Brettons Burrough Green, Newmarket, Suffolk. Tel 217.

Weatherheads Bookshop. 58 Kingsbury, Aylesbury, Buckinghamshire, HP20 2JG. Tel 23153, 24985.

E.T. Webster. Westwood Lodge, Blythburgh, Suffolk. Tel 539.

Wheldon & Wesley Ltd. Lytton Lodge, Codicote, Hitchin, Hertfordshire, SG4 8TE. Tel 820370.

Christopher Williams (inc Culmus Books). 23 St Leonard's Rd, Bournemouth, Dorset, BH8 8QL. Tel 519683.

Wootton-Billingham. 79 St Giles St, Northampton, Northamptonshire, NN1 3HR. Tel 34531.

Sidney Wright. 12-13 Royal Arcade, Boscombe, Bournemouth, Dorset. Tel 37153.

John R. Wrigley. 185 The Wheel, Ecclesfield, Sheffield, S.Yorkshire, S30 3ZA. Tel 460275.

Yesterday's Paper. 5 Cornhillgate, Wellington, Somerset.

Books, Art

Alden & Blackwell (Eton) Ltd. High St, Eton, Berkshire. Tel Windsor (0753) 863849.

The Antiques Book Centre. 93 Bradmore Green, Brookmans Park, Hatfield, Hertfordshire, AL9 7QT. Tel Potters Bar (0707) 44426.

James Atkinson Gallery. 38 King St, Sandwich, Kent, CT13 9BL. Tel 617216 (priv 613298).

Blackwell's Rare Books. Fyfield Manor, Fyfield, Oxfordshire, OX13 5LR. Tel Frilford Heath (0865) 390692-3.

Bookranger. 14 Hepburn Gardens, St Andrews, Fife. Tel 75066.

Richard Booth's Bookshop. 'The Limited', Lion St, Hay-on-Wye, Hereford & Worcester, HR3 5AA. Tel 820322 (priv 820503).

Bow Windows Book Shop. 128 High St, Lewes, E.Sussex, BN7 1XL. Tel 472839.

Chelsea Rare Books. 313 King's Rd, London, SW3 5EP. Tel 351 0950.

Heather Cowley Bookshop & Galleries. 235-237 Mansfield Rd, Nottingham, Nottinghamshire. Tel 473836.

Ian H.R.Cowley. The Book Shop, 4 Station Rd, Sandiacre, Derbyshire, NG10 5BG. Tel 393379.

Roderick Dew-Antiquarian Books. 29 South St, Eastbourne, E.Sussex. Tel 646206 (priv 20239).

Maurice Dodd (Booksellers). 112 Warwick Rd, Carlisle, Cumbria. Tel 22087.

E.M.Lawson & Co. Kingsholm, East Hagbourne, Didcot, Oxfordshire, OX11 9LN. Tel 812033.

East Asia Co. 103 Camden High St, London, NW1 7JN. Tel 388 5783.

The Flask Bookshop. 6 Flask Walk, Hampstead, London, NW3. Tel 435 2693.

Garton & Cooke. 9 Lancashire Court, New Bond St, London, W1Y 9AD. Tel 493 2820.

Goodramgate Books, Maps and Prints. 58 Goodramgate, York, N.Yorkshire. Tel 51275 (priv 0484 46833).

Simon Gough Books. 3 Fish Hill, Holt, Norfolk. Tel 2650.

Hammond Smith. Beaumont House, 24 Knighton Drive, Leicester, Leicestershire, LE2 3HB. Tel 709020.

Han-Shan Tang Ltd. 717 Fulham Rd, London, SW6 5UL. Tel 731 2447.

W. Heffer & Sons Ltd. 20 Trinity St, Cambridge, Cambridgeshire, CB2 3NG. Tel 358351.

Thomas Heneage Art Books. 42 Duke St,St James's, London, SW1 6DJ. Tel 930 9223 (priv 720 1503).

Heraldry Today. 10 Beauchamp Place, London, SW3. Tel 584 1656.

Hilmarton Manor Press. Hilmarton, Calne, Wiltshire, SN11 8SB. Tel Hilmarton (024976) 208.

Inch's Books. 3 St Paul's Sq, York, N.Yorkshire, YO2 4BD. Tel 27082 (priv 29770).

S.Linden. 33 Craven St, London, WC2. Tel 930 3659.

Richard Lyon Oriental Art Books. PO Box 150, Kingston upon Thames, Surrey, KT2 5AY. Tel 546 6149.

Marlborough Rare Books Ltd. 35 Old Bond St, London, W1X 4PT. Tel 493 6993.

Philip Martin Music Books. 36 Fossgate, York, N.Yorkshire, YO1 2TF. Tel 641389.

McDowell & Stern Ltd. 3 & 5 Grape Lane, York, N.Yorkshire. Tel 22000.

Martin Orskey Ltd. Little Gains House, Elmsted, Ashford, Kent. Tel Elmsted (023 375) 204.

Colin Page Antiquarian Books. 36 Duke St, Brighton & Hove, E.Sussex, BN1 1AG. Tel 25954.

Phillips of Hitchin (Antiques) Ltd. The Manor House,Bancroft (main street), Hitchin, Hertfordshire, SG5 1JW. Tel 32067.

Henry Pordes Ltd. 529B Finchley Rd, London, NW3. Tel 435 9878/9.

Henry Pordes Ltd. 58/60 Charing Cross Rd, London, WC2H 0BB. Tel 836 9031.

Potterton Books. The Old Rectory, Sessay, Thirsk, N.Yorkshire. Tel 401218.

Sanford Books. Chelsea Antique Market,253 King's Rd, London, SW3. Tel 352 5581.

Shipley. 70 Charing Cross Road, London, WC2. Tel 836 4872.

Sims, Reed and Fogg Ltd. 58 Jermyn St, London, SW1 6LX. Tel 493 5660/0952.

Raymond Smith. 30 South St, Eastbourne, E.Sussex, BN21 4XB. Tel 34128.

Southgate Gallery. 20 Market Place, Shifnal, Shropshire. Tel Telford (0952) 460351.

Ken Spelman Booksellers. 70 Micklegate, York, N.Yorkshire, YO1 1LF. Tel 24414.

St George's Gallery Books Ltd. 8 Duke St, St James's, London, SW1. Tel 930 0935.

Robert D.Steedman. 9 Grey St, Newcastle upon Tyne, Tyne & Wear, NE1 6EE. Tel 326561.

Sterling Books. 43A Locking Rd, Weston-super-Mare, Avon, BS23 3DG. Tel 25056.

Colin Stillwell (Books). 25 Fossgate, York, N.Yorkshire, YO1 2TA. Tel 27467.

Peter Stockham at Images. 16 Cecil Court, Charing Cross Rd, London, WC2. Tel 836 8661.

Trefoil Books Ltd. 15 St Johns Hill, London, SW11. Tel 223 7037.

Edna Whiteson Ltd. 66 Belmont Ave, London, EN4 9LA. Tel 449 8860.

Christopher Williams (inc Culmus Books). 23 St Leonard's Rd, Bournemouth, Dorset, BH8 8QL. Tel 519683.

Jeremy Wood Fine Art. East St, Petworth, W.Sussex, GU28 0AB. Tel 43408.

A.Zwemmer Ltd. 24 Litchfield St, London, WC2. Tel 836 1749.

Books, Collectors

London

Ash Rare Books. 25 Royal Exchange, Threadneedle St, London, EC3. Tel 626 2665.

A.H.Baldwin & Sons Ltd. 11 Adelphi Tce, London, WC2N 6BJ.

Bertram Rota Ltd. 30-31 Long Acre, London, WC2E 9LT. Tel 836 0723.

Tony Bingham. 11 Pond St, London, NW3 2PN. Tel 794 1596.

Clive A.Burden Ltd. 13 Cecil Court, London, WC2N 4EZ. Tel 836 2177.

Cavendish Rare Books Ltd. 2-4 Princes Arcade, Piccadilly, London, SW1Y 6DS. Tel 734 3840.

Chelsea Rare Books. 313 King's Rd, London, SW3 5EP. Tel 351 0950.

Robin de Beaumont. 25 Park Walk,Chelsea, London, SW10. Tel 352 3440.

P.G. De Lotz. 20 Downside Crescent, London, NW3.

Demetzy Books. 113 Portobello Rd, London, W11. Tel Witney (0993) 2209.

East Asia Co. 103 Camden High St, London, NW1 7JN. Tel 388 5783.

The Flask Bookshop. 6 Flask Walk, Hampstead, London, NW3. Tel 435 2693.

H.M. Fletcher. 27 Cecil Court, Charing Cross, London, WC2N 4EZ. Tel 836 2865.

W.Forster. 83A Stamford Hill, London, N16 5TP. Tel 800 3919.

M.& R. Glendale. 9a New Cavendish St,(entrance in Marylebone St), London, W1M 7RN. Tel 487 5348.

Han-Shan Tang Ltd. 717 Fulham Rd, London, SW6 5UL. Tel 731 2447.

Heraldry Today. 10 Beauchamp Place, London, SW3. Tel 584 1656.

Stephanie Hoppen. 17 Walton St, London, SW3. Tel 589 3678.

E.Joseph. 1 Vere St (3rd floor), London, W1M 9HQ. Tel 493 8353/4/5.

Langton Gallery Ltd. 3 Langton St, London, SW10. Tel 352 9150.

S.Linden. 33 Craven St, London, WC2. Tel 930 3659.

Mail Order Book Specialist. 25 Dicey Ave, Cricklewood, London, NW2. Tel 452 1581.

Marlborough Rare Books Ltd. 35 Old Bond St, London, W1X 4PT. Tel 493 6993.

Michael Phelps Antiquarian Books. 19 Chelverton Rd, Putney, London, SW15 1RN. Tel 785 6766.

Henry Pordes Ltd. 529B Finchley Rd, London, NW3. Tel 435 9878/9.

Henry Pordes Ltd. 58/60 Charing Cross Rd, London, WC2H 0BB. Tel 836 9031.

Quevedo. 25 Cecil Court, London, WC2N 4EZ. Tel 836 9132.

William Reeves Bookseller Ltd. 1A Norbury Cres, London, SW16 4JR. Tel 764 2108.

Reg and Philip Remington. 14 Cecil Ct, London, WC2. Tel 836 9771.

Sanford Books. Chelsea Antique Market,253 King's Rd, London, SW3. Tel 352 5581.

B.A. Seaby Ltd. 8 Cavendish Sq, London, W1M 0AJ. Tel 631 3707.

St George's Gallery Books Ltd. 8 Duke St, St James's, London, SW1. Tel 930 0935.

Peter Stockham at Images. 16 Cecil Court, Charing Cross Rd, London, WC2. Tel 836 8661.

Triangle Bookshop. 36 Bedford Sq, London, WC1. Tel 631 1381.

Lydia von Kubowski Antiques. Stand V 22, Antiquarius,135 King's Rd, London, SW3. Tel 352 7989.

Edna Whiteson Ltd. 66 Belmont Ave, London, EN4 9LA. Tel 449 8860.

A.Zwemmer Ltd. 24 Litchfield St, London, WC2. Tel 836 1749.

Regions

Abington Books. 29 Church Lane, Little Abington, Cambridgeshire, CB1 6BQ.

Alden & Blackwell (Eton) Ltd. High St, Eton, Berkshire. Tel Windsor (0753) 863849.

Charles R.P.Allix. Bradbourne Farmhouse,Bradbourne Vale Rd, Sevenoaks, Kent, TH13 3DH. Tel 451311.

The Antiques Book Centre. 93 Bradmore Green, Brookmans Park, Hatfield, Hertfordshire, AL9 7QT. Tel Potters Bar (0707) 44426.

Barrie's Bookshop. 4 Montpellier Walk, Cheltenham, Gloucestershire, GL50 1SD. Tel 515813.

D.Bickersteth. 38 Fulbrooke Rd, Cambridge, Cambridgeshire, CB3 9EE. Tel 352291.

Blackwell's Rare Books. Fyfield Manor, Fyfield, Oxfordshire, OX13 5LR. Tel Frilford Heath (0865) 390692-3.

Bookranger. 14 Hepburn Gardens, St Andrews, Fife. Tel 75066.

Richard Booth's Bookshop. 'The Limited', Lion St, Hay-on-Wye, Hereford & Worcester, HR3 5AA. Tel 820322 (priv 820503).

Bow Windows Book Shop. 128 High St, Lewes, E.Sussex, BN7 1XL. Tel 472839.

Brenin. Old Wool Barn,Verity's Court, Cowbridge, S.Glamorgan, CF7 7AJ. Tel 3893 (priv 0443 223553).

C.K.Broadhurst & Co Ltd. 5-7 Market St, Southport, Merseyside. Tel 32064, 34110.

Broadwater Bookroom. 20 Broadwater St East, Worthing, W.Sussex, BN14 9AD. Tel 39708.

The Carson Clark Gallery. (Scotiamaps - Mapsellers),173 Cannongate, The Royal Mile, Edinburgh, Lothian, EH8 8BN. Tel 556 4710.

The Ceramic Book Co. St John's and Chepstow Rd, Newport, Gwent. Tel 71561.

Checker Books. 2 Checker Walk, Abingdon, Oxfordshire. Tel 28172.

A. Clewlow (Books). 24 Fishergate, York, N.Yorkshire, YO1 4AB. Tel 27715.

Collards Bookshop. 4 Castle St, Totnes, Devon, TQ9 5NU. Tel (priv) 0548 550246.

Commin's Bookshop. 100 Old Christchurch Rd, Bournemouth, Dorset. Tel 27504.

Heather Cowley Bookshop & Galleries. 235-237 Mansfield Rd, Nottingham, Nottinghamshire. Tel 473836.

Ian H.R.Cowley. The Book Shop, 4 Station Rd, Sandiacre, Derbyshire, NG10 5BG. Tel 393379.

Crosby Books. Orlingbury House, Forest Row, E.Sussex. Tel Hartfield (089277) 4545.

David John Ceramics. 11 Acre End St, Eynsham, Oxfordshire, OX8 1PE. Tel Oxford (0865) 880786.

Roderick Dew-Antiquarian Books. 29 South St, Eastbourne, E.Sussex. Tel 646206 (priv 20239).

E.M.Lawson & Co. Kingsholm, East Hagbourne, Didcot, Oxfordshire, OX11 9LN. Tel 812033.

Fifteenth Century Bookshop. 99 High St, Lewes, E.Sussex, BN7 1XH. Tel 474160.

Fox & Co. 30 Princes St, Yeovil, Somerset. Tel 72323.

Wm.George's Sons Ltd. 89 Park St, Bristol, Avon, BS1 5PW. Tel 276602.

Simon Gough Books. 3 Fish Hill, Holt, Norfolk. Tel 2650.

Grant Books. Victoria Sq, Droitwich, Hereford & Worcester. Tel 778155.

Halewood & Sons. 37 Friargate, Preston, Lancashire, PR1 2AT. Tel 52603.

Anthony C.Hall. 30 Staines Rd, Twickenham, Middlesex. Tel 898 2638.

M. Harrington Ltd. 74 Parchment St, Winchester, Hampshire, SO23 8AT. Tel 53608.

W. Heffer & Sons Ltd. 20 Trinity St, Cambridge, Cambridgeshire, CB2 3NG. Tel 358351.

Hofman & Freeman Ltd. 8 High St, Otford, Kent, TN14 5PQ. Tel 2430.

John Ives Antiquarian Books. 5 Normanhurst Drive, St Margarets, Twickenham, Middlesex, TW1 1NA. Tel 892 6265.

Norman Kerr. Priory House,Priest Lane, Cartmel, Cumbria, LA11 6PX. Tel Cartmel (044 854) 247.

C.C. Kohler. 12 Horsham Rd, Dorking, Surrey. Tel 881532.

W.A.Lee. 90 St Mary's St, Ely, Cambridgeshire. Tel 3483.

Tom Lloyd-Roberts. Old Court House, Caerwys, Mold, Clwyd, CH7 5BB. Tel 720276.

John Lyle. Harpford, Sidmouth, Devon, EX10 0NH. Tel Colaton Raleigh (0395) 68294.

Marlborough Sporting Gallery & Bookshop. 6 Kingbury St, Marlborough, Wiltshire. Tel 54074.

The McEwan Gallery. The Bridge of Gairn (on A939), Ballater, Grampian, AB3 5UB. Tel 55429.

J.W.McKenzie, Bookseller. 12 Stoneleigh Park Rd, Ewell, Surrey, KT19 0QT. Tel 01- 393 7700.

McNaughtan's Bookshop. 3A & 4A Haddington Place, Edinburgh, Lothian, EH7 4AE. Tel 556 5897.

Meynell's Bookshop. 11 The Hornet, Eastgate Square, Chichester, W.Sussex. Tel 782018 (priv 512798).

Archie Miles Bookshop. 54 High St, Pateley Bridge, Harrogate, N.Yorkshire, HG3 5JZ. Tel 711294 (priv 711166).

Morten's Bookshops Ltd. Chestergate, Macclesfield, Cheshire. Tel 23679.

Martin Orskey Ltd. Little Gains House, Elmsted, Ashford, Kent. Tel Elmsted (023 375) 204.

Colin Page Antiquarian Books. 36 Duke St, Brighton & Hove, E.Sussex, BN1 1AG. Tel 25954.

Pandion Books. 10 Carr Close,Rainton, Thirsk, N.Yorkshire, YO7 3PS. Tel 578224.

The Petersfield Bookshop. 16A Chapel St, Petersfield, Hampshire, GU32 3DS. Tel 63438.

Phillips of Hitchin (Antiques) Ltd. The Manor House,Bancroft (main street), Hitchin, Hertfordshire, SG5 1JW. Tel 32067.

P.M.Pollak Fine Scientific and Medical Books. Moorview,Plymouth Road, South Brent, Devon, TQ10 9HT. Tel 3457.

Potterton Books. The Old Rectory, Sessay, Thirsk, N.Yorkshire. Tel 401218.

Quinto of Cambridge. 34 Trinity St, Cambridge, Cambridgeshire, CB2 1TB. Tel 358279.

Robinson's Bookshop (Brighton) Ltd. 11 Bond St, Brighton & Hove, E.Sussex, BN1 1JL. Tel 29012.

Raymond Smith. 30 South St, Eastbourne, E.Sussex, BN21 4XB. Tel 34128.

Robert D.Steedman. 9 Grey St, Newcastle upon Tyne, Tyne & Wear, NE1 6EE. Tel 326561.

Sterling Books. 43A Locking Rd, Weston-super-Mare, Avon, BS23 3DG. Tel 25056.

Colin Stillwell (Books). 25 Fossgate, York, N.Yorkshire, YO1 2TA. Tel 27467.

Taikoo Books Ltd.. 29 High Petergate, York, N.Yorkshire, YO1 2HP. Tel 641213 (priv 36636).

Thomas Thorp. 170 High St, Guildford, Surrey, GU1 3HP. Tel 62770.

Charles W. Traylen. Castle House, 49 Quarry St, Guildford, Surrey. Tel 572424.

Derek & Glenda Wallis. 6 Chapel Row, Queen Sq, Bath, Avon. Tel 24677.

Wheldon & Wesley Ltd. Lytton Lodge, Codicote, Hitchin, Hertfordshire, SG4 8TE. Tel 820370.

Christopher Williams (inc Culmus Books). 23 St Leonard's Rd, Bournemouth, Dorset, BH8 8QL. Tel 519683.

Jeremy Wood Fine Art. East St, Petworth, W.Sussex, GU28 0AB. Tel 43408.

Yesterday's Paper. 5 Cornhillgate, Wellington, Somerset.

Denis Young Antiques. 3 Kenmore St, Aberfeldy, Tayside. Tel Glenlyon (08877) 232.

Books, Horological

Charles R.P.Allix. Bradbourne Farmhouse,Bradbourne Vale Rd, Sevenoaks, Kent, TH13 3DH. Tel 451311.

Richard Barder Antiques. Crossways House, Hermitage, Berkshire, RG16 9SU. Tel Newbury (0635) 200295.

G.K. Hadfield. Blackbrook Hill House, Tickow Lane, Shepshed, Leicestershire, LE12 9EY. Tel 503014.

Keith Harding. 93 Hornsey Road, London, N7 6DJ. Tel 607 6181, 607 2672.

North London Clock Shop Ltd. 72 Highbury Park, London, N5. Tel 226 1609.

P.M.Pollak Fine Scientific and Medical Books. Moorview,Plymouth Road, South Brent, Devon, TQ10 9HT. Tel 3457.

Rita Shenton. 148 Percy Rd, Twickenham, Middlesex, TW2 6JG. Tel 894 6888.

Rogers Turner Books Ltd. 22 Nelson Rd, Greenwich, London, SE10. Tel 853 5271.

H.S.Walsh & Sons Ltd. 243 Beckenham Rd, Beckenham, Kent, BR3 4TS. Tel 01-778 7061.

Books, Secondhand

R.G.Archer. 7 Water St, Lavenham, Suffolk, CO10 9RW. Tel 247229.

Barbican Bookshop. 24 Fossgate, York, N.Yorkshire. Tel 53643.

Castle Bookshop. 37 North Hill, Colchester, Essex. Tel 577520 (priv 34 204).

A. Clewlow (Books). 24 Fishergate, York, N.Yorkshire, YO1 4AB. Tel 27715.

Commin's Bookshop. 100 Old Christchurch Rd, Bournemouth, Dorset. Tel 27504.

Gillian Dickerson. Packer House,28 High St, Chipping Norton, Oxfordshire. Tel 3255 (priv 41717).

Peter Eaton (Booksellers) Ltd. 80 Holland Park Ave, London, W11. Tel 727 5211.

Pamela Elsom Antiques. 5 Church St, Ashbourne, Derbyshire. Tel 43468.

Fifteenth Century Bookshop. 99 High St, Lewes, E.Sussex, BN7 1XH. Tel 474160.

W.Forster. 83A Stamford Hill, London, N16 5TP. Tel 800 3919.

Galloway & Porter Ltd. 30 Sidney St, Cambridge, Cambridgeshire. Tel 67876.

Garrick Bookshop. 20A Wellington Road South, Stockport, Greater Manchester, SK4 1AD. Tel 480-4346.

Wm.George's Sons Ltd. 89 Park St, Bristol, Avon, BS1 5PW. Tel 276602.

Henry March Gilbert. 19 The Square, Winchester, Hampshire, SO23 9RY. Tel 52832.

Goodramgate Books, Maps and Prints. 58 Goodramgate, York, N.Yorkshire. Tel 51275 (priv 0484 46833).

Simon Gough Books. 3 Fish Hill, Holt, Norfolk. Tel 2650.

Grange Bookshop. 186 Causewayside, Edinburgh, Lothian, EH9 1PN. Tel 667 2759 (priv 03617 311).

Hall's Bookshop. 20 Chapel Place, Tunbridge Wells, Kent. Tel 27842.

Fred Hanna Ltd. 28 & 29 Nassau St, Dublin, Co Dublin. Tel 771255/6.

M. Harrington Ltd. 74 Parchment St, Winchester, Hampshire, SO23 8AT. Tel 53608.

Holleyman & Treacher Ltd. 21A & 22 Duke St, Brighton & Hove, E.Sussex, BN1 1AH. Tel 28007.

Anthony W.Laywood. Knipton, Grantham, Lincolnshire, NG32 1RF. Tel 870224.

S.Linden. 33 Craven St, London, WC2. Tel 930 3659.

McDowell & Stern Ltd. 3 & 5 Grape Lane, York, N.Yorkshire. Tel 22000.

Archie Miles Bookshop. 54 High St, Pateley Bridge, Harrogate, N.Yorkshire, HG3 5JZ. Tel 711294 (priv 711166).

The Minster Gates Bookshop. 8 Minster Gates, York, N.Yorkshire. Tel 21812.

E.J. Morten (Booksellers) Ltd. 2, 4, 6, 8, 9 Warburton Street, Didsbury, Greater Manchester, M20 0RA. Tel 445 7629.

Morten's Bookshops Ltd. Chestergate, Macclesfield, Cheshire. Tel 23679.

O'Flynn Antiquarian Books. 35 Micklegate, York, N.Yorkshire, YO1 1DD. Tel 641404.

Pandion Books. 10 Carr Close,Rainton, Thirsk, N.Yorkshire, YO7 3PS. Tel 578224.

P.M.Pollak Fine Scientific and Medical Books. Moorview,Plymouth Road, South Brent, Devon, TQ10 9HT. Tel 3457.

Henry Pordes Ltd. 529B Finchley Rd, London, NW3. Tel 435 9878/9.

Henry Pordes Ltd. 58/60 Charing Cross Rd, London, WC2H 0BB. Tel 836 9031.

Quinto of Cambridge. 34 Trinity St, Cambridge, Cambridgeshire, CB2 1TB. Tel 358279.

Gibb's Bookshop Ltd. 10 Charlotte St, Manchester, Greater Manchester, M1 4FL. Tel 236-7179.

The Scientific Anglican Bookshop. 30-30A St Benedict St, Norwich, Norfolk. Tel 24079.

B. & C.Seago. Whitemans Green, Cuckfield, W.Sussex, RH17 5BY. Tel Haywards Heath (0444) 456111.

Shaw's Bookshop Ltd. 11 Police St, Manchester, Greater Manchester, M2 7LQ. Tel 834-7587.

John Smith & Son (Glasgow) Ltd. 57-61 St Vincent St, Glasgow, Strathclyde. Tel 221 7472.

Raymond Smith. 30 South St, Eastbourne, E.Sussex, BN21 4XB. Tel 34128.

Ken Spelman Booksellers. 70 Micklegate, York, N.Yorkshire, YO1 1LF. Tel 24414.

Sterling Books. 43A Locking Rd, Weston-super-Mare, Avon, BS23 3DG. Tel 25056.

Colin Stillwell (Books). 25 Fossgate, York, N.Yorkshire, YO1 2TA. Tel 27467.

Studio Bookshop and Gallery. 17 Broad St, Alresford, Hampshire, SO24 9AW. Tel 2188.

Rogers Turner Books Ltd. 22 Nelson Rd, Greenwich, London, SE10. Tel 853 5271.

Derek & Glenda Wallis. 6 Chapel Row, Queen Sq, Bath, Avon. Tel 24677.

Weatherheads Bookshop. 58 Kingsbury, Aylesbury, Buckinghamshire, HP20 2JG. Tel 23153, 24985.

Christopher Williams (inc Culmus Books). 23 St Leonard's Rd, Bournemouth, Dorset, BH8 8QL. Tel 519683.

Geoffrey M. Woodhead. Monkton House, 53 High St, Honiton, Devon. Tel 2969.

Wootton-Billingham. 79 St Giles St, Northampton, Northamptonshire, NN1 3HR. Tel 34531.

Bottles

Bottles & Bygones. 96 Horsefair St, Charlton Kings, Cheltenham, Gloucestershire. Tel 236393.

Boxes

see also Tea Caddies

At the Sign of the Herald Angel. 19 Park St, Cirencester, Gloucestershire, GL7 2BX. Tel 2972.

Barham Fine Arts. 83 Portobello Rd, London, W11 2QB. Tel 727 3845.

John Bird/Annette Puttnam. 44 Upper North St, Brighton & Hove, E.Sussex, BN1 3FH. Tel 739425.

The Box Shop. Chenil Galleries, King's Rd,Chelsea, London, SW3. Tel 352 2163.

J.Christie. 26 Burlington Arcade, Piccadilly, London, W1V 9AD. Tel 629 3070.

Cobblers Hall Antiques. 119-121 Leighton Rd, Toddington, Bedfordshire, LU5 6AR. Tel 2890.

Dolphin Antiques. 33 Trumpington St, Cambridge, Cambridgeshire. Tel 354180.

Donay Antiques. 35 Camden Passage,Islington, London, N1. Tel 359 1880.

Eureka Antiques. 18 Northenden Road, Sale, Greater Manchester, M33 3BR. Tel 962 5629.

Foord Antiques. Midhurst, W.Sussex. Tel Graffham (07986) 351.

Garrard & Co Ltd. 112 Regent St, London, W1A 2JJ. Tel 734 7020.

David Gibbins Antiques. 21 Market Hill, Woodbridge, Suffolk, IP12 4LX. Tel 3531 (priv 2685).

M.Hakim. 4 The Royal Arcade, Old Bond St, London, W1X 3HD. Tel 629 6243.

House of Antiques. 4 College St, Petersfield, Hampshire, GU31 4AD. Tel 62172.

House of Buckingham. 113-117 Farringdon Rd, London, EC1R 3BT. Tel 278 2013.

Esther Jones Antiques. 16A St Mary's St, Chepstow, Gwent. Tel 3314 (priv 0594-60653).

Irene Kelly. 38 Forest Lane Head,Starbeck, Harrogate, N.Yorkshire. Tel 889832.

Le Soken Antiques. High Street, Thorpe-le-Soken, Essex. Tel Clacton (0255) 861 337.

Millhouse. The Square, Petworth, W.Sussex, GU28 9BP. Tel 43080.

Milton Abbot Antiques. Venn Hill, Milton Abbot, Tavistock, Devon. Tel 392.

Jane Pollock Antiques. 4 Castle Gate, Penrith, Cumbria. Tel 67211.

Puzzle House Antiques. Trafalgar, Cinderford, Gloucestershire. Tel Dean (0594) 60653.

Quiet Street Antiques. 3 Quiet St, Bath, Avon. Tel 315727 (priv 332399).

Sharrington Antiques. Sharrington, Melton Constable, Norfolk, NR24 2PQ. Tel 861411 (priv 860719).

Stable Antiques. 14 Loughborough Rd, Hoton, Loughborough, Leicestershire, LE12 5SF. Tel Wymeswold (0509) 880208.

Alanna Staton Antiques. 4 Anyards Rd, Cobham, Surrey, KT11 2JZ. Tel 63407 (priv 04864 2407).

Straight Lace. 9 High St, East Linton, Lothian, EH40 3AA. Tel 860017 (priv 062088 284).

Todd & Austin Antiques & Fine Art. 2 Andover Rd, Winchester, Hampshire, SO23 7BS. Tel 69824.

Treasure Chest Ltd. The Jays, 19 Alstone Lane, Highbridge, Somerset, TA9 3DS. Tel Burnham-on-Sea (0278) 787267.

Peter Wadham. The Antique Shop, 5 Cathedral Close, Exeter, Devon. Tel 39741.

Tim Wright Antiques. 147 Bath St, Glasgow, Strathclyde. Tel 221 0364.

Brass Rubbing Equipment

Alden & Blackwell (Eton) Ltd. High St, Eton, Berkshire. Tel Windsor (0753) 863849.

Gough Antiques. 111 Station Rd, Burnham-on-Crouch, Essex. Tel Maldon (0621) 784322.

Brass, Copper and Metalware

see also Fire-Irons and Fenders, Ironwork, Pewter

London

Janet & Robert Bateman Antiques. 92 Waterford Rd, London, SW6 2HA. Tel 736 4149.

Jack Casimir Ltd. 'The Brass Shop', 23 Pembridge Rd, London, W11 3HG. Tel 727 8643.

Ralph Cox. 53 Ledbury Rd, London, W11. Tel 229 6900 (priv 723 3162).

Caroline Dawson. London. Tel 727 4106.

Heritage Antiques. 112 Islington High Street,Camden Passage, London, N1. Tel 226 7789.

Belle Johnston. Stands K1 & K2 Antiquarius, Kings Rd, London, SW3. Tel 352 7989.

W. Lipka Ltd. 62 Aylestone Ave, London, NW6. Tel 459 4588.

Robin Martin. 44 Ledbury Rd, London, W11. Tel 727 1301 (priv 727 1300).

Peter Place. 636 Kings Rd, London, SW6. Tel 736 9945.

Barrie Quinn Antiques. 3 & 4 Broxholme House, New King's Rd, London, SW6. Tel 736 4747.

Alistair Sampson Antiques (inc Tobias Jellinek). 156 Brompton Rd, London, SW3 1HW. Tel 589 5272, 581 2267.

Keith Skeel. 94 Islington High St, London, N1 8EG. Tel 359 9894.

Louis Stanton. 299 Westbourne Grove, London, W11. Tel 727 9336.

Regions

Abode. 40 Sheep St, Stratford-upon-Avon, Warwickshire, CV37 6EE. Tel 68755.

Alexander Antiques. Post House, Small Dole, Henfield, W.Sussex.

Antique Metals. 12 East St, Coggeshall, Essex, Co6 1SH. Tel 62252.

Antiques. 9 Market Square, Saffron Walden, Essex. Tel 23611 (0672 870727).

Antiques. 9 West End, West Haddon, Northamptonshire. Tel 772.

Avon Lodge Antiques. Southampton Rd, Fordingbridge, Hampshire, SP6 1AB. Tel 53275.

Baggott Church Street Ltd. Church Street, Stow-on-the-Wold, Gloucestershire, GL54 1BB. Tel 30370.

Duncan J. Baggott. The Square, Stow-on-the-Wold, Gloucestershire, GL54 1AB. Tel 30662.

Albert Bartram. 177 Hivings Hill, Chesham, Buckinghamshire. Tel 783271.

J.& H.Bell Antiques. 22 Arbory St, Castletown,. Tel 823132 (priv 822414).

Robin Bellamy Ltd. 97 Corn St, Witney, Oxfordshire, OX8 7DL. Tel 4793.

Berkeley Antiques. Marybrook St, Berkeley, Gloucestershire. Tel Dursley (0453) 810 391.

Brian Bingham Antiques. 420 Chatsworth Rd, Brampton, Chesterfield, Derbyshire. Tel 208441.

Andrew and Linda Blackburn Antiques. 12 West St, Gargrave, N.Yorkshire, BD23 3RD. Tel 403.

The Blacksmiths Shop. High St, Brasted, Kent. Tel Westerham (0959) 63114 (priv 62589).

J.H. Blakey & Sons Ltd. Church St, Brierfield, Lancashire, BB9 5AD. Tel Nelson (0282) 63593/602493.

John Bly. 50 High St, Tring, Hertfordshire, HP23 5AG. Tel 3030.

Blyth Antiques. 28 Sydney Buildings, Bath, Avon, BA2 6BZ. Tel 69766.

Bridge House Antiques. Penshurst, Kent, TN11 8BQ. Tel 870209.

British Antique Exporters Ltd. Queen Elizabeth Ave, Burgess Hill, W.Sussex, RH15 9RX. Tel 45577.

Broadway Antiques. 25 Broadway, Shifnal, Shropshire, TF11 8BB. Tel Telford (0952) 460997.

Brocanteuse Gallery. 11 North St, Ashburton, Devon. Tel 53389.

Bruton-Brighton. 31-32 Meeting House Lane, Brighton & Hove, E.Sussex, BN1 1HB. Tel 26591.

Burns & Graham. 4 St Thomas St, Winchester, Hampshire. Tel 53779.

Roderick P.Butler. Marwood House, Honiton, Devon, EX14 8PY. Tel 2169.

Christopher J. Button-Stephens. Plympton House,59 High St, Honiton, Devon. Tel 2640.

Robert Byles. 7-9 Castle St, Bampton, Devon, EX16 9NS. Tel 515.

Carse Antiques. Rait, by Perth, Tayside, PH2 7RT. Tel 205 (priv 227).

J. & J. Caspall Antiques. Sheep St, Stow-on-the-Wold, Gloucestershire. Tel 31160.

Mark Chapman Antiques. New Street, Petworth, W.Sussex. Tel 42283.

Charles Antiques. 101 The Hundred, Romsey, Hampshire, SO5 8BZ. Tel 512885.

Charterhouse Antiques. 14 Bird's Hill, Heath and Reach, Bedfordshire. Tel 532 379.

E.M. Cheshire Antiques. The Manor House, Market Place, Bingham, Nottinghamshire. Tel 38861 (priv 38455).

David Clark. The Plestor, Selborne, Hampshire. Tel 274.

Close Antiques. 19 Little Minster St, Winchester, Hampshire, SO23 9HA. Tel 64763.

Coach House Antiques Ltd. 77 Kinnoull St, Perth, Tayside. Tel 29835 (priv 073882 627).

Cottage Antiques. The Old Post Office, Langford, Bristol, Avon, BS18 7BP. Tel Wrighton (0934) 862597.

Country Life Antiques. Sheep St, Stow-on-the-Wold, Gloucestershire, GL54 1JS. Tel Cotswold (0451) 30776.

Jay Davis Antiques. Bishopsdale Court, Settle, N.Yorkshire. Tel 2764.

David Dean Antiques. Pen-Y-Ghent View, Church St, Settle, N.Yorkshire. Tel 3702 (priv 3660).

Eardisley Antiques. Leominster Antique Market,14 Broad St, Leominster, Hereford & Worcester. Tel 2189 (priv 05446 310).

P. & S.N. Eddy. 22 Etnam St, Leominster, Hereford & Worcester, HR6 8AQ. Tel 2813.

Pamela Elsom Antiques. 5 Church St, Ashbourne, Derbyshire. Tel 43468.

Flora Dora Antiques. Dales House, Lombard St, Petworth, W.Sussex, GU28 OAG. Tel 43109.

Gene & Sally Foster (Antiques). 27A Belvedere, Lansdown Rd, Bath, Avon, BA1 5HR. Tel 28256 (priv 28058).

Franfam Ltd. High St, Moreton-in-Marsh, Gloucestershire, GL56 oLH. Tel 50648.

The Furniture Station Ltd. The Kelterment Antique Market,Fordham, Ely, Cambridgeshire.

Jonathan Fyson Antiques. The Old School House, Cassington, Oxfordshire. Tel Oxford (0865) 880943.

Gadsby's Antiques. 88-90 The Street, Ashtead, Surrey. Tel 72305.

Michael Gander. 10 Bridge St, Hitchin, Hertfordshire. Tel 32678.

Gatehouse Antiques. 72 Chestergate, Macclesfield, Cheshire. Tel 26476.

Rupert Gentle Antiques. The Manor House,Milton Lilbourne, Pewsey, Wiltshire, SN9 5LQ. Tel Marlborough (0672) 63344.

Gerrard Antiques. The Old Cottage, 54 Branthwaite Brow, Kendal, Cumbria. Tel 23881.

Gibberd and Grant Antiques. 40 The Bank, Barnard Castle, Durham, DL12 8PN. Tel Teesdale (0833) 37437.

Peter Gould. 101 Northgate, Halifax, W.Yorkshire.

W.F.Greenwood & Sons Ltd. 2&3 Crown Place, Harrogate, N.Yorkshire, HG1 2RY. Tel 504467.

Halstow Antiques. Green Farm House, The Green,Lower Halstow, Sittingbourne, Kent, ME9 7DS. Tel 842016.

Harley Antiques. The Comedy, Christian Malford, Chippenham, Wiltshire. Tel 720112.

Bob Harris & Sons. 2071 Coventry Rd, Birmingham, W.Midlands. Tel 743 2259.

F.J. Harris. 23 Silver St, Stansted Mountfitchet, Essex. Tel Bishops Stortford (0279) 813371.

Keith Hockin Antiques Ltd. The Square, Stow-on-the-Wold, Gloucestershire, GL54 1AF. Tel 31058.

W.W.Holzgrave. 7 Gosditch St, Cirencester, Gloucestershire. Tel 69351.

Paul Hopwell Antiques. 30 High St, West Haddon, Northamptonshire, NN6 7AP. Tel 636.

Horsefair Antiques. 21 Horsefair, Chipping Norton, Oxfordshire. Tel 3089.

Horseshoe Antiques & Gallery. High St, Burford, Oxfordshire, OX8 4RJ. Tel 3244.

Janet Howard. Argyll House, Felsted, Essex. Tel Great Dunmow (0371) 820682.

Dudley Hume. 46 & 50 Upper North St, Brighton & Hove, E.Sussex, BN1 3PH. Tel 23461.

A.R.Jaffray. 16 Market Place, Melksham, Wiltshire, SN12 6EX. Tel 702269.

John Keil Ltd. 10 Quiet St, Bath, Avon, BA1 2JU. Tel 63176.

Terence Kelly Antiques. 1 Cross St, Burnham-on-Sea, Somerset. Tel 782129 (priv 785052).

Key Antiques. 11 Horsefair, Chipping Norton, Oxfordshire, OX7 5AL. Tel 3777.

P.G. Kydd. 70 Colston St, Bristol, Avon, BS1 5AZ. Tel 299265.

Lancashire Bygones. 12 Parliament St, Up Holland, Wigan, Greater Manchester, WN8 0LN. Tel Up Holland (0695) 625624 (priv 0695 622458).

Leonard Lassalle. 21 The Pantiles, Tunbridge Wells, Kent, TN2 5TD. Tel 31645.

Muriel Lindsay. Queen Anne House, High St, Winchcombe, Gloucestershire. Tel Cheltenham (0242) 602319.

Little Bric a Brac Shop. The Green, Morcombelake, Bridport, Dorset. Tel Chideock (0297) 89346.

Robin Lloyd Antiques. 23-24 Brookend St, Ross-on-Wye, Hereford & Worcester. Tel 62123.

Charles Lumb & Sons Ltd. 2 Montpellier Gardens, Harrogate, N.Yorkshire, HG1 2TF. Tel 503776 (priv 863281).

Lustre Metal Antiques Ltd. Canning Circus, Derby Rd, Nottingham, Nottinghamshire. Tel 704385.

Mac Humble Antiques. 11 Queen St, Bath, Avon, BA1 2JO. Tel 62751 (priv 022122 3594).

William MacIntosh & Co. 5 Johnston Terrace, Edinburgh, Lothian, EH1 2PW. Tel 225 6113.

Manor House Antiques. High St, Ripley, Surrey. Tel Guildford (0483) 225350.

Markland Antiques. Western Rd, Borough Green, Kent. Tel 4152.

Marlborough Antiques. 18 The Parade, Marlborough, Wiltshire. Tel 54818.

W. & P. McQuade Antiques. 7 Shuttle St, Kilbarchan, Strathclyde. Tel 4249.

John Meredith Antiques. 36 The Square, Chagford, Devon. Tel 3474 (priv 3405).

Trevor Micklem, Antiques. Withywine Farm,Morebath, Tiverton, Devon, EX16 9BZ. Tel Bampton (0398) 31409.

Moolham Mill Antiques. Moolham Mill, Moolham Lane, Ilminster, Somerset, TA19 0PD. Tel 2834.

William Morley Antiques. Musgrave's Old Farm, West Monkton, Taunton, Somerset, TA2 8NW. Tel West Monkton (0823) 412751.

Anthony Nielsen Antiques. High St, Burford, Oxfordshire, OX8 4QQ. Tel 2014 (priv 0451 21710).

Peter Norden Antiques. High St, Burford, Oxfordshire, OX8 4XX. Tel 2121 (priv 0993 830064).

Old Barn Antiques. High St, Church Stretton, Shropshire, SY6 6BX. Tel 723742 (priv 722294).

The Old Forge. Pilgrims Way, Hollingbourne, Kent, ME17 1UW. Tel 360.

Old Hall Antiques/Sphinx Gallery. The Old Hall, Sundridge, Kent. Tel Westerham (0959) 62589.

The Old House Antiques. 9-10 West St, Dorking, Surrey, RH4 1QH. Tel 887278.

Old Paint Shop. High St, Alfriston, E.Sussex, BN26 5TD.

Mike Ottrey Antiques. 28 High St, Dorchester, Oxfordshire. Tel Oxford (0865) 340079.

Tom Owen Antiques. 18 Rawcliffe St, Blackpool, Lancashire. Tel 33008.

Packer House. 28 High St, Chipping Norton, Oxfordshire, OX7 5AD. Tel 3255.

Pall Mall Antiques. 104c & 104d Elm Rd, Leigh-on-Sea, Essex. Tel Southend-on-Sea (0702) 77235.

Partner & Puxon. 7&16 North Hill, Colchester, Essex, CO1 1DZ. Tel 573317.

Peppers Period Pieces. 22/23 Churchgate St, Bury St Edmunds, Suffolk. Tel 68786 (priv 0359 50606).

R.J.Perry Antiques. 38 Bridge St, Hitchin, Hertfordshire, SG5 2DF. Tel 34525 (priv 0582-25546).

Phoenix Antiques. 1 Carter St, Fordham, Cambridgeshire. Tel Newmarket (0638) 720 363.

Pine and Country Antiques. Sandhill Barn, Washington, Pulborough, W.Sussex. Tel Ashington (0903) 892888 (priv 892210).

Principia Fine Art. Hungerford Antiques Arcade, Hungerford, Berkshire. Tel Marlborough (0672) 55275.

Priory Antiques. Litcham Priory, Litcham, King's Lynn, Norfolk. Tel Litcham (0328) 701262.

Paul Quentin Antiques. 626 Manchester Rd, Bury, Greater Manchester, BL9 9SU. Tel 766 6673.

Isobel Rhodes. 69-73 Angel St, Hadleigh, Suffolk. Tel 823754.

D.H.Sargeant. 21 The Green, Westerham, Kent, TN16 1AX. Tel 62130.

Saville Antiques. 37 Long St, Devizes, Wiltshire. Tel 3559.

A.T.Silvester & Sons Ltd. 2-4 High St, Warwick, Warwickshire, CV34 4AP. Tel 492972.

Stable Antiques. Oakdene Country Hotel, Garsdale Rd, Sedbergh, Cumbria, LA10 5JN. Tel 20280.

Alanna Staton Antiques. 4 Anyards Rd, Cobham, Surrey, KT11 2JZ. Tel 63407 (priv 04864 2407).

Stirling Antiques. Aberdeen House,Guildford Rd, Abinger Hammer, Surrey, RH5 6RY. Tel Dorking (0306) 730706.

Studio Antiques Ltd. Bourton-on-the-Water, Gloucestershire, GL54 2BX. Tel 20352.

Sundial Antiques. 19 Whielden St, Amersham, Buckinghamshire, HP7 0HU. Tel 7955.

Swan Antiques. 62A West St, Dorking, Surrey. Tel 881217 (priv 01-394 2361).

Christopher Sykes Antiques. The Old Parsonage, Bedford St, Woburn, Bedfordshire, MK17 9QL. Tel 259 (priv 467).

Thistledome Antiques. Kings Arms Yard, Ampthill, Bedfordshire, MK45. Tel 403394 (priv 717368).

Turpins Antiques. 4 Stoney Lane, Thaxted, Essex. Tel 830495 (priv 830059).

Clive Underwood Antiques. 46 High St, Colsterworth, Lincolnshire. Tel Grantham (0476) 860689.

Vernon Smith & Son. Bayvil House, High St, Cardigan, Dyfed, SA43 1HE. Tel 612654.

Michael Wakelin and Helen Linfield. 10 New St, Petworth, W.Sussex. Tel 42417.

Warwick Antiques. 16 & 18 High St, Warwick, Warwickshire, CV34 4AP. Tel 492482.

E.W. Webster Antiques. Wash Farm, Rainford Rd, Bickerstaffe, Lancashire. Tel Skelmersdale (0695) 24322.

W.H.Weller & Son. 12 North St, Eastbourne, E.Sussex, BN26 3H6. Tel 23592.

Anthony Welling Antiques. Broadway Barn, High St, Ripley, Surrey, GU23 6AQ. Tel Guildford (0483) 225384.

Wenlock Antiques. 61 High St, Much Wenlock, Shropshire, TF13 6AE. Tel 727271.

Tim Wharton Antiques. 24 High St, Redbourn, Hertfordshire. Tel 4371.

Widcombe Antiques. 8-9 Claverton Buildings, Widcombe, Bath, Avon. Tel 28767.

Williton Antiques. 26 High St, Williton, Taunton, Somerset. Tel Williton (0984) 32393 (priv).

Tim Wright Antiques. 147 Bath St, Glasgow, Strathclyde. Tel 221 0364.

Bronzes

see also Sculpture, Casting

Apollo Galleries. 61, 65 and 67 South End, Croydon, Surrey, CR0 1BF. Tel 681 3727, 680 1968.

Armstrong-Davis Gallery. High St, Arundel, W.Sussex. Tel 882752.

The Bell Gallery. 13 Adelaide Park, off Malone Rd, Belfast, Belfast. Tel 662998.

Bluett & Sons Ltd. 48 Davies St, London, W1Y 1LD. Tel 629 4018, 629 3397.

Butterwalk House. 55 The Old Butterwalk, High St, Totnes, Devon. Tel 863044.

Cassio. 68 Ledbury Rd, London, W11. Tel 727 0678.

J.Christie. 26 Burlington Arcade, Piccadilly, London, W1V 9AD. Tel 629 3070.

Clarendon Gallery. 20 Albert Square, Manchester, Greater Manchester. Tel 980 6343.

Colleton House Gallery. 8a Quiet St, Bath, Avon, BA1 2JU. Tel 28806.

Forman of Piccadilly Ltd. 92 Piccadilly, London, W1. Tel 493 2174.

Victor Franses Gallery. 57 Jermyn St, London, SW1Y 6LX. Tel 439 6284.

Freeman and Lloyd. 44 Sandgate High St, Sandgate, Folkestone, Kent, CT20 3AP. Tel 38986.

Hamlet Gallery. 5 Pond St, Hampstead, London, NW3. Tel 794 7904 (priv 452 0056).

Simon Hatchwell Antiques. 64-65 Middle St, Brighton & Hove, E.Sussex, BN1 1AL. Tel 27663.

Michael John Decorative Arts Ltd. 25A Lowndes St, London, SW1. Tel 235 3154/5.

Lefevre Gallery. 30 Bruton St, London, W1X 8JD. Tel 493 1572.

Leverington Hall Gallery. Leverington, Wisbech, Cambridgeshire, PE13 5DE. Tel 582055.

Greig Linton Antiques. 95 West Bow, Edinburgh, Lothian. Tel 226 6946.

Michael Lipitch. 98 Fulham Rd, London, SW3. Tel 589 7327 (priv 440 7797).

Plaitford House Galleries. Plaitford, Hampshire. Tel West Wellow (0794) 22221.

William Redford. 9 Mount St, London, W1. Tel 629 1165.

The Sladmore Gallery. 32 Bruton Place,off Berkeley Sq, London, W1X 7AA. Tel 499 0365.

Trove. 71 Pimlico Rd, London, SW1. Tel 730 6514.

The Tryon and Moorland Gallery. 23-24 Cork St, London, W1X 1HB. Tel 734 6961/2256.

Tugwell & Thomas Antiques. Grays Antique Market,58 Davies St, London, W1. Tel 499 1337.

Edric Van Vredenburgh. 37 Bury St, London, SW1. Tel 839 5818.

Wellesley Wilson Antiques. Aldersey Manor, Aldersey, Cheshire, CH3 9EH. Tel Broxton (082 925) 500.

Yellow Lantern Antiques Ltd. 34 & 65B Holland Rd, Hove, Brighton & Hove, E.Sussex, BN3 1JL. Tel 771572 (priv 0273 455476).

Buttons and Badges

The Button Queen. 19 Marylebone Lane, London, W1M 5FF. Tel 935 1505.

Caboodle Ltd. Chelsea Antique Market,253 King's Rd, London, SW3.

Curio Shop. 11 Northumberland Place, Teignmouth, Devon. Tel (priv)Exeter(0392)54166.

The Flintlock. 17A High St, Glastonbury, Somerset, BA6 9DR. Tel 31525 (priv 32813).

Fox & Co. 30 Princes St, Yeovil, Somerset. Tel 72323.

HQ84. Southgate St, Gloucester, Gloucestershire. Tel 27716.

Martin Marsh Militaria. 114 Buxton Rd, Whaley Bridge, Derbyshire, SK12 7JF. Tel 3267.

Old Buttons (UK). Buttons, West Lyng, Taunton, Somerset. Tel North Curry (0823) 629.

Weiner aus Wien Military Antiques. 2 Market St, The Lanes, Brighton & Hove, E.Sussex, BN1 1HH. Tel 729948.

Bygones and Curiosities

London

The Antiques Exchange. Number One, Bermondsey Sq, London, SE1. Tel 407 3635.

Antiquus A G. 17 Pembridge Sq, London, W2 4EH. Tel 229 0224.

Anthony Belton. 14 Holland Street, London, W8 4LT. Tel 937 1012.

Claude Bornoff. 20 Chepstow Corner, Pembridge Villas, London, W2. Tel 229 8947.

Caboodle Ltd. Chelsea Antique Market,253 King's Rd, London, SW3.

Caroline Dawson. London. Tel 727 4106.

Peter Evanson. 464 Fulham Rd, London, SW6. Tel 385 4185.

Langfords. Oldebourne House,46-47 Chancery Lane, London, WC2. Tel 405 6402.

Stephen Long. Albion House, 348 Fulham Rd, London, SW10 9UH. Tel 352 8226.

Peel Antiques. 131D Kensington Church St, London, W8 7LP. Tel 727 8298.

Peter Reynolds Antiques. 67 New King's Rd, London, SW6. Tel 736 7797.

Murray Thomson Ltd. 141 Kensington Church St, London, W8 7LP. Tel 727 1727, 727 1825.

Regions

Alexander Antiques. Post House, Small Dole, Henfield, W.Sussex.

Antiques Objets D'Art & Curios. 86 The Broadway, Leigh-on-Sea, Essex. Tel Southend-on-Sea (0702) 72895 & 711633.

The Aspidistra. 29 Sun St, Hitchin, Hertfordshire. Tel 53817.

Duncan J. Baggott. The Square, Stow-on-the-Wold, Gloucestershire, GL54 1AB. Tel 30662.

J.H. Blakey & Sons Ltd. Church St, Brierfield, Lancashire, BB9 5AD. Tel Nelson (0282) 63593/602493.

Bratton Antiques. Market Place, Westbury, Wiltshire, BA13 3DE. Tel 823021.

J. Brett. The Old Malthouse, 7A Angelo Terrace,Walcot, Bath, Avon.

Carronade. 63 West Regent St, Glasgow, Strathclyde. Tel 332 5600 (priv 649 3655).

Carshalton Antiques Galleries. 5 High St, Carshalton, Surrey, SM5 3AP. Tel 01- 647 5664.

Roy Carter Antiques. Park View, 205 Quemerford, Calne, Wiltshire. Tel 2270.

Collector's Corner. 5-7 Frizinghall Rd, Bradford, W.Yorkshire, BD9 4LA. Tel 487098.

Country Antiques. 10 Westgate St, Long Melford, Suffolk. Tel Sudbury (0787) 310617.

M.J.Dareau. 66 Cumberland St, Edinburgh, Lothian. Tel 556 9352 & 0968 73028.

Polly de Courcy-Ireland. 16 Chilbolton Ave, Winchester, Hampshire, SO22 5HD. Tel 65716.

Betty Dean Antiques. The Walnuts, Weston St Mary's, Spalding, Lincolnshire, PE12 6JB. Tel Holbeach (0406) 370429 (priv 371067).

Doddington House Antiques. 2 Benwick Rd, Doddington, Cambridgeshire, PE15 0TG. Tel March (0354) 740755.

Dodo Antiques. 23 Peter St, St Helier, Jersey. Tel 71497 (priv 62275).

P. & S.N. Eddy. 22 Etnam St, Leominster, Hereford & Worcester, HR6 8AQ. Tel 2813.

Mollie Evans. 84 Hill Rise, Richmond, Surrey. Tel 948 0182 (priv 940 3720).

Gene & Sally Foster (Antiques). 27A Belvedere, Lansdown Rd, Bath, Avon, BA1 5HR. Tel 28256 (priv 28058).

Gwendoline Golder. The Little Shop, Coltishall, Norfolk. Tel Norwich (0603) 737404.

Halstow Antiques. Green Farm House, The Green,Lower Halstow, Sittingbourne, Kent, ME9 7DS. Tel 842016.

George Hofman Antiques. Brookside, High St, Stockbridge, Hampshire, SO20 6EY. Tel 810570.

Horsefair Antiques. 21 Horsefair, Chipping Norton, Oxfordshire. Tel 3089.

Janet Howard. Argyll House, Felsted, Essex. Tel Great Dunmow (0371) 820682.

The Jackdaw. Townfoot, Rothbury, Northumberland. Tel 0669 20785.

Ron Jones Antiques. Tri Brynwcws,Llanaber, Barmouth, Gwynedd, LL42 1RR. Tel 280691.

Terence Kelly Antiques. 1 Cross St, Burnham-on-Sea, Somerset. Tel 782129 (priv 785052).

Jack F.W.King. 33 Wallingford St, Wantage, Oxfordshire. Tel 2676.

Little Bric a Brac Shop. The Green, Morcombelake, Bridport, Dorset. Tel Chideock (0297) 89346.

Llewelyn Antiques. 64 Monthermer Rd,Cathays, Cardiff, S.Glamorgan, CF2 4RA. Tel 43367.

Richard Lloyd. Dolhaidd Mansion, Henllan, Dyfed. Tel Velindre (0559) 370791.

V. & C. Madeira. The Grange, 16 Guys Cliffe Ave, Leamington, Warwickshire. Tel 25012.

R.McDonnell Ltd. 16 Kildare St, Dublin, Co Dublin. Tel 762614.

Mole Hall Antiques. 102-104 High St, Aldeburgh, Suffolk. Tel 2361.

Monarch Antiques. 15 High St, Glastonbury, Somerset. Tel 32498.

Netherly Cottage Antiques. Milburn, Cumbria. Tel Kirkby Thore (0930) 61403.

The Old House Antiques. 9-10 West St, Dorking, Surrey, RH4 1QH. Tel 887278.

Mike Ottrey Antiques. 28 High St, Dorchester, Oxfordshire. Tel Oxford (0865) 340079.

Pine and Country Antiques. Sandhill Barn, Washington, Pulborough, W.Sussex. Tel Ashington (0903) 892888 (priv 892210).

The Relic Shop. 106A High St, Needham Market, Suffolk, IP6 0EN. Tel 721245 (priv 0473 830858).

James Scott. 43 Dundas St, Edinburgh, Lothian, EH3 6JN. Tel 556 8260.

Span Antiques. 6 Market Place, Woodstock, Oxfordshire, OX7 1TA. Tel 811332.

Spon End Antiques. 115-116 Spon End, Coventry, W.Midlands, CV1 3HF. Tel 28379.

Martin & Ruth Taylor. 6 Broadway, Shifnal, Shropshire. Tel Telford (0952) 461504.

The Tower Gallery. Middleton Tower, King's Lynn, Norfolk. Tel 840203.

W.H.Weller & Son. 12 North St, Eastbourne, E.Sussex, BN26 3H6. Tel 23592.

J.Wigington & Sons. 'Winchester 73', 276 Alcester Rd, Stratford-upon-Avon, Warwickshire. Tel 293881.

Williton Antiques. 26 High St, Williton, Taunton, Somerset. Tel Williton (0984) 32393 (priv).

Ye Olde Junk Shoppe. St Michael's College, Shipton-under-Wychwood, Oxfordshire. Tel 830576.

Cabinet Makers

Barrett & Butler. The Old Bull Furniture Workshops,Key St, Ipswich, Suffolk.

Eric Bates & Sons. High St, Coltishall, Norfolk. Tel Norwich (0603) 738716.

Browns of West Wycombe. Church Lane, West Wycombe, Buckinghamshire, HP14 3AH. Tel High Wycombe (0494) 24537 (priv 0895 39163).

John Corlyon (Furniture) Ltd. The Workshop, Burstwick, Humberside. Tel Patrington (0964) 70701.

Dudley's Home Interiors. Vine House, Fair Green, Reach, Cambridgeshire. Tel Newmarket (0638) 741989.

Farmhouse Antiques. Whites Farm House, Barkers Drove,Off Oxborough Rd, Stoke Ferry, Norfolk. Tel 500 588.

Gaylords. 75 West St, Titchfield, Fareham, Hampshire. Tel 43402 (priv 662606).

Gostin of Liverpool Ltd. Portway, off 2a Higher Rd,Halewood, Liverpool, Merseyside, L25 0QQ. Tel 486 1703/6175.

J.S. & R.Hine. Fowlchurch Farm,Ball Haye Green, Leek, Staffordshire. Tel 372699.

T.J.Mitchell Antiques Ltd. 1a Lower Pembroke St, Dublin, Co Dublin. Tel 766881.

Newcombe & Son. 89 Maple Rd, Penge, London, SE20 8UL. Tel 778 0816.

Church Lane Restorations. 1 Church Lane, Teddington, Middlesex. Tel 977 2526.

St Mary's Antiques and Cabinet Makers. 2 Lower Bar, Newport, Shropshire. Tel 811549.

Tontine Antiques. 75-81 Tontine St, Folkestone, Kent. Tel 53077 (priv 0303 89 3157).

Whitehead & Lightfoot. Blocks 2 & 4 Avon Trading Estate,Avonmore Rd, London, W14 8TS. Tel 603 4237.

Whytock & Reid. Sunbury House, Belford Mews, Edinburgh, Lothian, EH4 3DN. Tel 226 4911.

Candelabra

see also Chandeliers, Lighting

Jack Casimir Ltd. 'The Brass Shop', 23 Pembridge Rd, London, W11 3HG. Tel 727 8643.

Grey-Harris & Co. 12 Princess Victoria St,Clifton, Bristol, Avon. Tel 737365.

Kelly's of Knaresborough. Rear, 96 High St, Knaresborough, N.Yorkshire. Tel Harrogate (0423) 862041 (24 hr answering).

D.H.Sargeant. 21 The Green, Westerham, Kent, TN16 1AX. Tel 62130.

R. Wilkinson & Son. 43-45 Wastdale Rd, Forest Hill, London, SE23 1HN. Tel 699 4420.

Caricatures

see also Drawings, Prints

Clive A.Burden Ltd. 13 Cecil Court, London, WC2N 4EZ. Tel 836 2177.

The Burlington Gallery. 10 Burlington Gdns, London, W1. Tel 734 9228.

Andrew Edmunds. 44 Lexington St, London, W1R 3LH. Tel 437 8594.

The Witch Ball Print & Map Shop. 48 Meeting House Lane, Brighton & Hove, E.Sussex, BN1 1HB. Tel 26618.

The Witch Ball Print & Map Shop. 48 Meeting House Lane, Brighton & Hove, E.Sussex, BN1 1HB. Tel 26618.

Carpets and Rugs

London

Aaron Galleries. 34 Bruton St, London, W1X 7DD. Tel 499 9434.

Anglo-Persian Carpet Co Ltd. The Arcade, South Kensington Station, London, SW7 2NA. Tel 589 5457.

Avakian Oriental Carpets Ltd. 20 Davies St, London, W1Y 1LH. Tel 493 5758.

Axia. 43 Pembridge Villas, London, W11. Tel 727 9724.

Robert Bailey Oriental Carpets. 51-53 Rivington St, London, EC2A 3DA. Tel 550 5435.

Celia Barker Mill. 24 Iverna Gardens,Kensington, London, W8 6TN. Tel 937 9145.

Benardout & Benardout. 7 Thurloe Place, London, SW7 2RX. Tel 584 7658.

Raymond Benardout. 5 William St, Knightsbridge, London, SW1X 9HL. Tel 235 3360 (priv 235 0504).

David Black Oriental Carpets. 96 Portland Rd, London, W11 4LN. Tel 727 2566.

Bookham Galleries. 164 Wandsworth Bridge Rd, Fulham, London, SW6. Tel 736 5125(priv 0372 52668).

Baroukh Fahimian. 4 Blenheim St, New Bond St, London, W1. Tel 493 7509 (priv 723 7179).

Jack Fairman (Carpets) Ltd. 218 Westbourne Grove, London, W11 2RH. Tel 229 2262/3(priv 992 0087).

Robert Franses & Son. 5 Nugent Tce, St John's Wood, London, NW8. Tel 286 6913 (priv 328 0949).

S.Franses Ltd. 82 Jermyn St,St James's, London, SW1. Tel 235 1888/9.

Victor Franses Gallery. 57 Jermyn St, London, SW1Y 6LX. Tel 439 6284.

Attilio Gilberti. 70 Wigmore St, London, W1. Tel 487 3167 & 935 4339.

Gwyneth Antiques. 56 Ebury St, London, SW1. Tel 730 2513 (priv 352 4864).

Hadji Baba Ancient Art. 36 Davies St, London, W1Y 1LD. Tel 499 9363, 499 9384.

M.Heskia. 19 Mount St, London, W1. Tel 629 1483.

C. John (Rare Rugs) Ltd. 70 South Audley St,Mayfair, London, W1Y 5FE. Tel 493 5288.

Alexander Juran & Co. 74 New Bond St, London, W1Y 9DD. Tel 629 2550, 493 4484.

Keeble Ltd. 13 Walton St, London, SW3. Tel 581 3676.

Kennedy Carpets & Kelims. 9A Vigo St, London, W1. Tel 439 8873.

Kensington Carpets. 98/99 Jermyn St, London, SW1. Tel 930 2044.

The Kilim Warehouse Ltd. 28A Pickets St, London, SW12 8QB. Tel 675 3122.

J.Lavian. 53-79 Highgate Rd, London, NW5 1TL. Tel 485 7955.

Liberty & Co Ltd. Regent St, London, W1R 6AH. Tel 734 1234.

Clive Loveless. 29 Kelfield Gdns,North Kensington, London, W10 6NA. Tel 969 5831.

M. & M. Oriental Gallery Ltd. 4th Floor, Block D,53/79 Highgate Rd, London, NW5 1TL. Tel 267 5973.

A.Maurice & Co Ltd. 70 South Audley St, London, W1Y 5FE. Tel 629 9797.

Mayorcas Ltd. 38 Jermyn St, London, SW1Y 6DN. Tel 629 4195.

John C. O'Mahony. Flat 10, 15 Westbourne Terrace, London, W2 3UN. Tel 724 0277.

Oriental Carpet Centre. 10 Golden Sq, London, W1R 3AF. Tel 439 9070.

Persian Carpet Gallery. 3 Motcomb St, London, SW1. Tel 245 6564.

The Persian Market. 48 Upper St,Islington, London, N1. Tel 226 7927.

Rabi Gallery. 94 Mount St, London, W1. Tel 499 8886.

Philippa Scott. 30 Elgin Crescent, London, W11. Tel 229 8029.

Robert Stephenson Oriental Carpets. 42 Fairfax Rd, London, NW6 4HA. Tel 722 4043.

The Textile Gallery. 4 Castellain Rd, Little Venice, London, W9 1EZ. Tel 286 1747.

Vigo Carpet Gallery. 6A Vigo St, London, W1. Tel 439 6971.

Vigo-Sternberg Galleries. 37 South Audley St, London, W1. Tel 629 8307.

Zadah Persian Carpets Ltd. 20 Dering St (First Floor),(Off New Bond St), London, W1R 9AA. Tel 493 2622, 493 2673.

Regions

David Adam Oriental Carpets. 59 High Street, Lindfield, W.Sussex. Tel 73817.

Albany Antiques. 8-10 London Rd, Hindhead, Surrey. Tel 5528.

Alderley House Antiques. Alderley House, 53 Long St, Tetbury, Gloucestershire, GL8 8AA. Tel 53667.

J.L. Arditti. 88 Bargates, Christchurch, Dorset. Tel 485414.

L.J. Arditti & E.M. Arditti. 29A The Pantiles, Tunbridge Wells, Kent. Tel 43361.

Arts of Living Gallery. 18 Green St, Bath, Avon. Tel 64270.

Chapel Antiques. Whatlington, E.Sussex, TN33 0NL. Tel Sedlescombe (042 487) 272.

The Clare Collector. 1 Nethergate St, Clare, Suffolk. Tel 277909 (priv 277494).

Robert Copperfield Antiques. 47-49 Mill Lane, Macclesfield, Cheshire, SK10 7NP. Tel 26620.

Crosby Books. Orlingbury House, Forest Row, E.Sussex. Tel Hartfield (089277) 4545.

Eric Davidson (Antiques) Ltd. 4 Grassmarket, Edinburgh, Lothian, EH1 2JU. Tel 225 5815.

Dupont Galleries. 33 Grand Parade, Brighton & Hove, E.Sussex. Tel 738257 and 695094.

Great Brampton House Antiques Ltd. Great Brampton House, Madley, Hereford, Hereford & Worcester, HR2 9NA. Tel Golden Valley (0981) 250244.

Herrald Antiques. 38 Queen St, Edinburgh, Lothian. Tel 225 5939.

J.P.J.Homer Oriental Rugs. Stoneleigh, Parabola Rd, Cheltenham, Gloucestershire, GL50 3BD. Tel 34243.

The Honiton Lace Shop. 44 High St, Honiton, Devon. Tel 2416 (priv 2629).

Leonard Lassalle. 21 The Pantiles, Tunbridge Wells, Kent, TN2 5TD. Tel 31645.

C.T.Legge Oriental Carpets. Oakthorpe Rd, Summertown, Oxford, Oxfordshire. Tel 57572 (priv 0993 831298).

Michael and Amanda Lewis Oriental Carpets and Rugs. 8 North St, Wellington, Somerset, TA21 8LT. Tel 7430.

Michael and Amanda Lewis Oriental Carpets and Rugs. 23 Small St, Bristol, Avon, BS1 1DW. Tel 264246.

Peter Linden. 10 Rock Hill, Blackrock, Co Dublin. Tel Dublin 885875.

Lindfield Galleries Ltd. 59 High St, Lindfield, W.Sussex, RH16 2HN. Tel 2817.

Metcalfe Jackson. 24A West St, Wimborne Minster, Dorset, BH21 1JS. Tel 883327.

Richard & Pamela Nadin. 12 Paul St, Frome, Somerset, BA11 1DT. Tel 64957.

Desmond and Amanda North. The Orchard,Hale St, East Peckham, Kent, TN12 5JB. Tel 871353.

Omar (Harrogate) Ltd. 8 Crescent Rd, Harrogate, N.Yorkshire, HG1 2RS. Tel 503675.

Orbell House Gallery. Orbell House, 8 St James's St, Castle Hedingham, Essex, CO9 3EJ. Tel Hedingham (0787) 60298.

Orchard House, Oriental Rugs. Orchard House, Ollands Road, Reepham, Norfolk. Tel 870234.

The Oriental Carpet Centre. Maples, 3 Queens Rd,Clifton, Bristol, Avon, BS8 1QS. Tel 290165.

Persian Carpet Gallery. North Street, Petworth, W.Sussex, GU28 0DD. Tel 43344.

Phoenix Antiques. 1 Carter St, Fordham, Cambridgeshire. Tel Newmarket (0638) 720 363.

Eric Pride Oriental Rugs. 8 Imperial Sq, Cheltenham, Gloucestershire, GL50 1QB. Tel 580822 (priv 521057).

Charles Read Georgian Furnishing. Bathealton Court,Bathealton, Milverton, Somerset, TA4 2AJ. Tel Wiveliscombe (0984) 23225.

Robertson and Cox. 60 George St, Perth, Tayside, PH1 5JL. Tel 26300.

Clive Rogers Oriental Rugs. 22 Brunswick Rd,Hove, Brighton & Hove, E.Sussex, BN3 1DG. Tel 738257.

Thornborough Galleries. 28 Gloucester St, Cirencester, Gloucestershire, GL7 2DH. Tel 2055 (priv 099386 367).

Touchwood Antiques. 9 Park St., Stow-on-the-Wold, Gloucestershire, GL54 1AQ. Tel 30221.

Karel Weijand. Lion & Lamb Courtyard, Farnham, Surrey. Tel 726215.

Whytock & Reid. Sunbury House, Belford Mews, Edinburgh, Lothian, EH4 3DN. Tel 226 4911.

Carriages and Horse Drawn Vehicles etc

Pennyfarthing Antiques. Crowmarsh Gifford, Wallingford, Oxfordshire, OX10 8EA. Tel 37470.

P.B.Pollington. 4 Central Parade, High St, Wadhurst, E.Sussex, TN5 6AL. Tel 2866.

Carvings

Peter Bell Fine Arts. High St, Lechlade, Gloucestershire, GL7 3DL. Tel Faringdon (0367) 52987 (priv 52255).

Mary Bellis Antiques. Charnham Close (A4 Highway), Hungerford, Berkshire, RG17 0EJ. Tel 82620.

Joanna Booth. 247 King's Rd, London, SW3. Tel 352 8998.

Boss Antiques. Hells Bells Corner, Petworth, W.Sussex, GU28 0DD.

J. & J. Caspall Antiques. Sheep St, Stow-on-the-Wold, Gloucestershire. Tel 31160.

Simon Castle. 38B Kensington Church St, London, W8. Tel 937 2268.

Ray Coggins Antiques. 3 Keyford, Frome, Somerset. Tel 72286.

O.M. & R.D.Cox Antiques. 5 St Mary's Hill, Stamford, Lincolnshire. Tel 64159.

Csaky's Antiques. 20 Pimlico Rd, London, SW1. Tel 730 2068.

David Dean Antiques. Pen-Y-Ghent View, Church St, Settle, N.Yorkshire. Tel 3702 (priv 3660).

Duveen Antiques. Burgate, Fordingbridge, Hampshire, SP6 1LX. Tel 53309.

Farnborough (Kent) Antiques. 10 Church Rd, Farnborough, Kent, BR6 7DB. Tel 51834.

Gordon Reece Gallery. Finkle Street, Knaresborough, N.Yorkshire. Tel 866219 866502.

Cyril Humphris. 8 Pembroke Walk, London, W8. Tel 937 1719.

Humphry Antiques. East St, Petworth, W.Sussex, GU28 0AB. Tel 43053 (priv 42944).

Lensfield Antiques. 12 Lensfield Rd, Cambridge, Cambridgeshire, CB2 1EG. Tel 357636.

Alec Ossowski. 83 Pimlico Rd, London, SW1. Tel 730 3256.

F.Teltscher Ltd. 17 Crawford St, London, W1H 1PF. Tel 935 0525.

Thornhill Galleries Ltd. 76 New Kings Rd, London, SW6. Tel 736 5830.

Edric Van Vredenburgh. 37 Bury St, London, SW1. Tel 839 5818.

Geoffrey Van Ltd. 105 and 107 Portobello Rd, London, W11. Tel 229 5577.

J.Wolff & Son Ltd. 82 Troutbeck, Albany St, London, NW1. Tel 388 3588.

Casting

see also Bronzes

Art Bronze Foundry (London) Ltd. 1 Michael Rd, London, SW6. Tel 736 7292.

Brookes Forge Flempton. Flempton, Bury St Edmunds, Suffolk, IP28 6EN. Tel Culford (028484) 473 (priv 0449 781376).

N.Davighi. 117 Shepherds Bush Rd, London, W6. Tel 603 5357.

The Morris Singer Foundry Ltd. Bond Close,Kingsland Industrial Park, Basingstoke, Hampshire, RG24 OPT. Tel 24033.

Ceramics

see Pottery and Porcelain

Chair Caning

see Restorers, Chair Caning

Chair Making

Barrett & Butler. The Old Bull Furniture Workshops,Key St, Ipswich, Suffolk.

Browns of West Wycombe. Church Lane, West Wycombe, Buckinghamshire, HP14 3AH. Tel High Wycombe (0494) 24537 (priv 0895 39163).

Clifford J. Tracy. 6-40 Durnford St, Seven Sisters Rd, London, N15 5NQ. Tel 800 4773.

Chandeliers

see also Candelabra, Lighting

Norman Adams Ltd. 8-10 Hans Rd, London, SW3 IRX. Tel 589 5266.

Anthony Antiques. 7 Molesworth St, Dublin, Co Dublin. Tel 777222.

Jack Casimir Ltd. 'The Brass Shop', 23 Pembridge Rd, London, W11 3HG. Tel 727 8643.

Chandeliers. 166 Kensington Church St, London, W8. Tel 229 1338, 229 2310.

Directory Entries are Free and ADDITIONS OR CORRECTIONS will be welcomed by *THE EDITOR, British Art and Antiques Directory, National Magazine House, 72 Broadwick Street, London W1V 2BP*

T.Crowther & Son Ltd. 282 North End Rd, Fulham, London, SW6 1NH. Tel 385 1375/7.

N.Davighi. 117 Shepherds Bush Rd, London, W6. Tel 603 5357.

Delomosne & Son Ltd. 4 Campden Hill Rd, London, W8 7DU. Tel 937 1804.

Thomas Goode & Co (London) Ltd. 19 South Audley St, London, W1Y 6BN. Tel 499 2823 (7 lines).

Great Brampton House Antiques Ltd. Great Brampton House, Madley, Hereford, Hereford & Worcester, HR2 9NA. Tel Golden Valley (0981) 250244.

Simon Hatchwell Antiques. 64-65 Middle St, Brighton & Hove, E.Sussex, BN1 1AL. Tel 27663.

H.W. Keil (Cheltenham) Ltd. 129-131 The Promenade, Cheltenham, Gloucestershire, GL50 1NW. Tel 522509, 527974.

Kelly's of Knaresborough. Rear, 96 High St, Knaresborough, N.Yorkshire. Tel Harrogate (0423) 862041 (24 hr answering).

Lighthouse Antiques. 67 Ridgway,Wimbledon Village, London, SW19. Tel 946 2050.

Lennox Money (Antiques) Ltd. 93 Pimlico Rd, London, SW1W 8PH. Tel 730 3070.

Penoyre Antiques. 9 - 11 Bridge St, Pershore, Hereford & Worcester. Tel 3522.

H.W.Poulter & Son. 279 Fulham Rd, London, SW10 9PZ. Tel 352 7268 (priv 603 7398).

Paul Richards Antiques. 16 Fulham High St, London, SW6 3LQ. Tel 736 0976.

D.H.Sargeant. 21 The Green, Westerham, Kent, TN16 1AX. Tel 62130.

South Audley Art Galleries Ltd. 36 South Audley St, London, W1Y 5DH. Tel 499 3178, 499 3195.

Stair & Company Ltd. 120 Mount St, London, W1Y 5HB. Tel 499 1784, 499 1785.

R. Wilkinson & Son. 43-45 Wastdale Rd, Forest Hill, London, SE23 1HN. Tel 699 4420.

Chess Sets

Kenneth W. Allen. Moor Old Lodge, 6 Moor Hall Park,Four Oaks, Sutton Coldfield, W.Midlands, B75 6LP. Tel 308 1685.

C.Barrett & Co. 51 Burlington Arcade, Piccadilly, London, W1. Tel 493 2570.

The Box Shop. Chenil Galleries, King's Rd,Chelsea, London, SW3. Tel 352 2163.

Aubrey J.Coleman Antiques. 121 Kensington Church St, London, W8 7LP. Tel 221 6228.

Game Advice. 23 Holmes Road, London, NW5 3AA. Tel 485 2188 (priv 485 4226).

Littlebury Antiques. 58/60 Fairycroft Rd, Saffron Walden, Essex. Tel 27961.

Chimney Pieces

see Fireplaces

Chinese Embroideries and Textiles

Brandt Oriental Antiques. 771 Fulham Rd, London, SW6. Tel 731 6835.

Gallery of Antique Costume & Textiles Ltd. 2 Church Street, Marylebone, London, NW8. Tel 723 9981 (priv 743 3821).

The Honiton Lace Shop. 44 High St, Honiton, Devon. Tel 2416 (priv 2629).

Kimono. 4 Belvedere, Lansdown Rd, Bath, Avon, BS8 5ED. Tel 315987.

John C. O'Mahony. Flat 10, 15 Westbourne Terrace, London, W2 3UN. Tel 724 0277.

Oriental Antiques. 4 Belvedere, Lansdown Rd, Bath, Avon. Tel 315987.

Westfield Antiques. Freebirch Cottage, Eastmoor, Chesterfield, Derbyshire, S42 7DQ. Tel Baslow (024 688) 3153.

Linda Wrigglesworth. Stand B17/A23, Gray's Mews,1-7 Davies Mews, London, W1. Tel 408 0177.

Clocks and Watches

see also Books, Horological

London

Antique Connoisseur plc. Grays Mews,1-7 Davies Mews, London, W1. Tel 629 2422/3272.

Asprey PLC. 165-169 New Bond St, London, W1Y 0AR. Tel 493 6767.

Bentley & Co Ltd. 65 New Bond St, London, W1Y 9DF. Tel 629 0651, 629 0325.

Big Ben Clock Shop. 5 Broxholme House, New King's Rd, London, SW6. Tel 736 1770.

Blake Antiques. 216 Westbourne Grove, London, W11 2RH. Tel 229 3232.

Bobinet Ltd. 102 Mount St, London, W1YD 5HF. Tel 408 0333/4.

Bonrose Antiques. 172 Kensington Church St, London, W8. Tel 229 5486, 221 3139.

Aubrey Brocklehurst. 124 Cromwell Rd, South Kensington, London, SW7 4ET. Tel 373 0319.

Camerer Cuss & Co. 17 Ryder St, St James's, London, SW1Y 6PY. Tel 930 1941.

Patric Capon. 350 Upper St,Islington, London, N1. Tel 354 0487 (priv 467 5722).

J Carlton-Smith. 17 Ryder St, St James', London, SW1. Tel 930 6622 (priv 467 8020).

Chelsea Clocks. Stand Z3, Antiquarius, Kings Rd, London, SW3. Tel 352 8646.

Chelsea Clocks & Antiques. 479 Fulham Road, London, SW6. Tel 352 8646, 731 5704.

City Clocks. 1B Lambs Passage, Chiswell St, London, EC1Y 8LE. Tel 628 6749.

Clock Clinic Ltd. 85 Lower Richmond Rd, Putney, London, SW15 1EU. Tel 788 1407.

Philip & Bernard Dombey. 174 Kensington Church St, London, W8. Tel 229 7100.

Graus Antiques. 125 New Bond St, London, W1Y 9AF. Tel 629 6680, 629 6651.

Grimaldi. 12 Royal Arcade, 28 Old Bond St, London, W1X 3HB. Tel 493 3953.

Keith Harding. 93 Hornsey Road, London, N7 6DJ. Tel 607 6181, 607 2672.

W.R.Harvey & Co (Antiques) Ltd. 67-70 Chalk Farm Rd, London, NW1 8AN. Tel 485 1504, 267 2767.

Hymore Hodson Antiques. 181-183 King's Rd,Chelsea, London, SW3. Tel 352 9770.

George Johnson. 120 Kensington Park Road, London, W11 2PW. Tel 229 3119.

Julian Antiques. 67 Park Rd, London, NW1. Tel 723 0653.

Ronald A.Lee (Fine Arts) Ltd. 1-9 Bruton Place, London, W1X 7AD. Tel 499 6266.

Mallett at Bourdon House Ltd. 2 Davies St, Berkeley Sq, London, W1Y 1LJ. Tel 629 2444/5.

North London Clock Shop Ltd. 72 Highbury Park, London, N5. Tel 226 1609.

Partridge (Fine Arts) Ltd. 144-146 New Bond St, London, W1. Tel 629 0834.

David Paskin Antiques (London) Ltd. Grays Antique Market,58 Davies St, London, W1. Tel 408 1129.

Nigel Raffety. 34 Kensington Church St, London, W8. Tel 938 1100.

Stair & Company Ltd. 120 Mount St, London, W1Y 5HB. Tel 499 1784, 499 1785.

Strike One (Islington) Ltd. 51 Camden Passage, London, N1 8EA. Tel 226 9709 (priv 359 6459).

Igor Tociapski. 39-41 Ledbury Rd, London, W11. Tel 229 8317.

Regions

Abridge Antique Clock Centre. Market Place, Abridge, Essex.

Rodney Adams Antiques. Hall Place,10 Penlan St, Pwllheli, Gwynedd, LL53 5DH. Tel 613173 (priv 614337).

John Allott Abrahams. The Bear, 2 Bear St, Hay-on-Wye, Hereford & Worcester. Tel 820085.

Alverton Antiques. 7 South Parade, Northallerton, N.Yorkshire.

Antique Clocks. 1 High St, Harston, Cambridgeshire, CB2 5PX. Tel Cambridge (0223) 870264.

The Antique Shop. 23-25 Middle Hillgate, Stockport, Greater Manchester. Tel 061-477 8970.

The Antique Shop. 6 St Peter's St, Wallingford, Oxfordshire. Tel 39345.

Ashleigh House Antiques. 5 Westbourne Rd,Edgbaston, Birmingham, W.Midlands, B15 3TH. Tel 454 6283.

Ashley House Antiques. 61 High St, Measham, Burton on Trent, Staffordshire, DE12 7HR. Tel Measham (0530)433) 73568 (priv 054 373655).

Astley Bridge Antiques. 419-421 Blackburn Rd, Astley Bridge, Bolton, Greater Manchester, BL1 8NJ. Tel 51160 (priv 53390).

Avon Antiques. 26-27 Market St, Bradford-on-Avon, Wiltshire. Tel 2052.

Baggott Church Street Ltd. Church Street, Stow-on-the-Wold, Gloucestershire, GL54 1BB. Tel 30370.

David Ball Antiques. 126A Leagrave Rd, Luton, Bedfordshire, LU4 8HX. Tel 417560 (priv 0525-210753).

Richard Barder Antiques. Crossways House, Hermitage, Berkshire, RG16 9SU. Tel Newbury (0635) 200295.

Roy Barton. Myrtle Cottage, Codmore Hill, Pulborough, W.Sussex, RH21 1BQ. Tel 2730.

H.J.Benford. 14-16 Wellington St, Kettering, Northamptonshire. Tel 513793.

Biggs of Maidenhead. Hare Hatch Grange, Twyford, Berkshire, RG10 9SK. Tel Wargrave (073 522) 3281 (priv 3104).

Boodle & Dunthorne Ltd. 52 Eastgate St, Chester, Cheshire, CH1 1LE. Tel 26666.

Peter D. Bosson. 10B Swan St, Wilmslow, Cheshire, SK9 1HE. Tel 525250 (priv 527857).

Breakspeare Antiques. 36 Long St, Tetbury, Gloucestershire, GL8 8AQ. Tel 53122.

J. & M. Bristow Antiques. 28 Long St, Tetbury, Gloucestershire, GL8 8AQ. Tel 52222.

Browns Clocks Ltd. 203 Bath St, Glasgow, Strathclyde, G2 4HZ. Tel 248 6760.

N.Bryan-Peach Antiques. 28 Far St, Wymeswold, Leicestershire. Tel 880425.

Bugatti. 173 Widmore Rd, Bromley, Kent, BR1 3AX. Tel 460 9979.

Bullivant Antiques. Whitegates, Great Ashfield, Bury St Edmunds, Suffolk, IP31 3HH. Tel Elmswell (0359) 40040.

Gerald Buxton Gooding - Lapworth Clocks. 160 Station Lane, Lapworth, Warwickshire, B94 6JJ. Tel 3243.

Gerard Campbell. Maple House,Market Place, Lechlade, Gloucestershire, GL7 3AB. Tel Faringdon (0367) 52267.

Castle Gallery. 61 Steep Hill, Lincoln, Lincolnshire, LN2 1LR.

R.G.Cave & Sons Ltd. 17 Broad St, Ludlow, Shropshire. Tel 3568.

Chancery Antiques. 24-26 High St, Thrapston, Northamptonshire. Tel 2434.

Charles Antiques. 101 The Hundred, Romsey, Hampshire, SO5 8BZ. Tel 512885.

Chattels. 156 High St, Old Woking, Woking, Surrey, GU22 9JH. Tel 71310.

John Chawner. 44 Chatham Hill, Chatham, Kent. Tel Medway (0634) 811147.

Cherub Antiques. 9 Sadler St, Wells, Somerset, BA5 2RR. Tel 72503 (priv 73893).

Chess Antiques. 85 Broad St, Chesham, Buckinghamshire, HP5 3EF. Tel 783043.

Chester Antiques. 49 Watergate Row, Chester, Cheshire. Tel 311768 (priv 532208).

Bryan Clisby - Antique Clocks. at Andwells Antiques,High Street, Hartley Wintney, Hampshire. Tel 2305.

The Clock Shop. 7 The Quadrant, Hoylake, Merseyside, L47 2EE. Tel 632 1888 (priv 632 3818).

The Clock Shop. 40 Fore St, Topsham, Devon.

The Clock Shop. 64 Church St, Weybridge, Surrey. Tel 40407, 55503.

The Clock Shop St Albans. 161 Victoria St, St Albans, Hertfordshire, AL1 3TA. Tel 56633.

Clockshop Antiques. 187 The Street, Boughton, Faversham, Kent, ME13 9BH. Tel Canterbury (0227) 751258.

Collector's Corner. 5-7 Frizinghall Rd, Bradford, W.Yorkshire, BD9 4LA. Tel 487098.

Coppelia Antiques. Holford Lodge, Plumley Moor Rd, Plumley, Cheshire, WA16 9RS. Tel Lower Peover (056 581) 2197.

Anthony Cotton. 26-27 Steep Hill, Lincoln, Lincolnshire. Tel 25838 (priv 0673 60562).

Country Life Antiques. Grey House,The Square, Stow-on-the-Wold, Gloucestershire, GL54 1AF. Tel 31564.

John Cowderoy Antiques (The Musical Box Centre). 40/42 South St, Eastbourne, E.Sussex, BN21 4X. Tel 20058 (priv 645353).

The Curiosity Shop. High St, Llandovery, Dyfed. Tel 20390.

George Curtis. 14 Suffolk Parade, Cheltenham, Gloucestershire, GL50 2AB. Tel 513828.

D'Amico Antiques Ltd. 20 Highland Rd, Norwich, Norfolk. Tel 52320.

M.J.Dareau. 66 Cumberland St, Edinburgh, Lothian. Tel 556 9352 & 0968 73028.

David, Jean & John Antiques. 587 London Rd, Westcliff-on-Sea, Essex. Tel Southend (0702) 339106.

Davies Antiques. 32 King St, Whalley, Lancashire, BB6 9SL. Tel 3764.

John E. Davis Antiques. 21 Wokingham Rd, Reading, Berkshire, RG6 1JG. Tel 663108.

Roger A. Davis. 19 Dorking Rd, Great Bookham, Surrey. Tel 57655/53167.

Zona Dawson Antiques. The Old Club House, 2 The Close,Charlton Marshall, Blandford Forum, Dorset. Tel Blandford (0258) 53146.

Dean House Antiques. Dean House,Bepton Rd, Midhurst, W.Sussex, GU29 9LY. Tel 2277.

Dial Antiques. Dial Cottage, Shere, Surrey, GU5 9HS. Tel 2722.

Brian & Angela Downes Antiques. 9 Broad St, Bath, Avon, BA1 5LJ. Tel 65352.

K.W.Dunster Antiques. 23 Church St, Staines, Middlesex. Tel 53297.

Edmund Eldridge Antiques. 167 High St, Tonbridge, Kent, TN9 1BX. Tel 361921.

Colin Elliott. 4 Great Norwood St, Cheltenham, Gloucestershire. Tel 528590.

Evans & Evans. 40 West St, Alresford, Hampshire, SO24 9AU. Tel 2170.

Peter Fell of Thame. 81 High St, Thame, Oxfordshire. Tel 4487.

Rodney T.Firmin. 16 Magdalene St, Cambridge, Cambridgeshire. Tel 67372.

Foster Hill Road Antiques Centre. 84-84A Foster Hill Rd, Bedford, Bedfordshire, MK40 2ET. Tel 53318.

Franfam Ltd. High St, Moreton-in-Marsh, Gloucestershire, GL56 0LH. Tel 50648.

Freeman and Lloyd. 44 Sandgate High St, Sandgate, Folkestone, Kent, CT20 3AP. Tel 38986.

Gadsby's Antiques. 88-90 The Street, Ashtead, Surrey. Tel 72305.

Good Hope Antiques. 2 Hogshill St, Beaminster, Dorset. Tel 862119.

R.S. Gordon Antiques. Main St, Alford, Grampian. Tel 2404.

A.E.Gould & Sons (Antiques) Ltd. Old Rectory Cottage,Ockham Rd South, East Horsley, Surrey, KT24 6QJ. Tel 3747.

W.J.Gravener Antiques. High St, Mayfield, E.Sussex, TN20 6AA. Tel 873389.

Great Western Antique Centre Ltd. Bartlett St, Bath, Avon, BA1 2QZ. Tel (office) 24243.

G.K. Hadfield. Blackbrook Hill House, Tickow Lane, Shepshed, Leicestershire, LE12 9EY. Tel 503014.

Henry Hall. 19 Market Sq, Westerham, Kent. Tel 62200.

Harrop Fold Clocks. Harrop Fold,Bolton by Bowland, Clitheroe, Lancashire, BB7 4PJ. Tel Bolton by Bowland (02007) 665.

Kenneth Harvey Antiques and Fine Art. 21-23 South St Mary's Gate, Grimsby, Humberside. Tel 49370.

Simon Hatchwell Antiques. 64-65 Middle St, Brighton & Hove, E.Sussex, BN1 1AL. Tel 27663.

Haworth Antiques. Stand 5A West Park Antiques Pavilion,20 West Park, Harrogate, N.Yorkshire. Tel 61758 (priv 71?93)

Haworth Antiques. Harrogate Rd, Huby, N.Yorkshire, LS17 0EF. Tel Harrogate (0423) 74293.

Hazel Cottage Clocks. Hazel Cottage, Eachwick, Dalton, Newcastle upon Tyne, Tyne & Wear. Tel Wylam (066 14) 2415.

J.E.Hoffman. Owsley House, Ashley, Northamptonshire, LE16 8HF. Tel Medbourne Green (085883) 315.

E. Hollander Ltd. The Dutch House,Horsham Rd, South Holmwood, Dorking, Surrey, RH5 4NF. Tel 888921.

Horological Workshops. 204 Worplesdon Rd, Guildford, Surrey, GU2 6UY. Tel 576496.

Horsefair Antiques. 21 Horsefair, Chipping Norton, Oxfordshire. Tel 3089.

Robert Horton Antiques. 13 Castle St, Hertford, Hertfordshire, SG14 1ER. Tel 57546.

Howard & Reeves. 38 Whitehorse St, Baldock, Hertfordshire. Tel 892385.

Howard & Reeves. 1 The Arcade, Hitchin, Hertfordshire. Tel 35454.

Its About Time. 863 London Rd, Westcliff-on-Sea, Essex, SS26 6BA. Tel Southend (0702) 72574 (priv 205204).

Jackson's. Hill Villa,Bury, Ramsey, Cambridgeshire, PE17 1AB. Tel 812361.

Paul Jennings Antiques. Millbrook House,Angarrack, Hayle, Cornwall, TR27 5HZ. Tel 754065.

Julian Antiques. 124 High St, Hurstpierpoint, W.Sussex. Tel 832145.

Keymer Son & Co Ltd. Swaylands Place, The Green, Brasted, Kent, TN16 1JY. Tel Westerham (0959) 64203.

Kingston Antiques. 138 London Rd, Kingston upon Thames, Surrey. Tel 546 2221.

Ronald A. Lee (Fine Arts) Ltd. The Manor House, Byfleet, Surrey. Tel 43346.

Laurie Leigh Antiques. 36 High St, Oxford, Oxfordshire. Tel 244197.

Littlebury Antiques. 58/60 Fairycroft Rd, Saffron Walden, Essex. Tel 27961.

John Long Antiques. St Mary's Old Church,915 Stockport Rd, Levenshulme, Manchester, Greater Manchester. Tel 224 7923.

Brian Loomes. Calf Haugh Farm, Pateley Bridge, N.Yorkshire. Tel Harrogate (0423) 711163.

Lower Fold Antiques. 23-25 Lower Fold, Marple Bridge, Stockport, Greater Manchester, SK6 5DU. Tel 427 4699.

Madoc Antique & Art Gallery. 48 Madoc St, Llandudno, Gwynedd. Tel 79754 (priv 79760).

Edward Manson. 8 Market Hill, Woodbridge, Suffolk. Tel 7226.

Mark Marchant, Antiques. Market Square, Coggeshall, Essex, CO6 1T6. Tel 61188.

G.E. Marsh (Antique Clocks). 32A The Square, Winchester, Hampshire, SO23 9EX. Tel 54505.

Medalcrest Ltd. Charnham House,29-30 Charnham St, Hungerford, Berkshire, RG17 0EJ. Tel 84157.

Melbourne Antiques. Rock House Antique Centre,Tettenhall, Wolverhampton, W.Midlands. Tel 754995.

T.Mercer Chronometers. 16A Lansdown Place Lane, Cheltenham, Gloucestershire, GL50 2LB. Tel 516022.

Mill Farm Antiques. 50 Market St, Disley, Cheshire, SK12 2DT. Tel 4045.

James H.Morris & Co. Old Village School, The Green, Northop, Clwyd, CH7 6BD. Tel 508.

Robert Morrison & Son. Trentholme House, 131 The Mount, York, N.Yorkshire, YO2 2DA. Tel 55394.

Muirhead Moffat & Co. 182 West Regent St, Glasgow, Strathclyde. Tel 226 4683 and 226 3406.

Mytton Antiques. Norton Crossroads, Atcham, Shrewsbury, Shropshire. Tel Uppington (095286) 229.

B.M.Newlove. 139-141 Ewell Rd, Surbiton, Surrey. Tel 339 8857.

O'Neill. Swan House,Market Square, Petworth, W.Sussex. Tel 42616.

The Old Clock Shop. 49 St Helen's Rd, Swansea, W.Glamorgan. Tel 53334.

The Old Clock Shop. 63 High St, West Malling, Kent. Tel 843246 (priv 840345).

The Old Malthouse. 15 Bridge St (A4), Hungerford, Berkshire, RG17 0EG. Tel 82209 (priv 83647).

Old Town Clock Shop. 1-3 Aylesbury End, Beaconsfield, Buckinghamshire, HP9 1LU. Tel 6783.

Olive Branch Antiques. 80 High St, Broadway, Hereford & Worcester, WR12 7AJ. Tel 853440.

Onslow Clocks. 48 King Street, Twickenham, Middlesex, TW1 3SH. Tel 892 7632.

Owen Antiques. 189-193 Oldham Rd, Rochdale, Greater Manchester. Tel 48138 (priv 353270).

P.A. Oxley, Antique Clocks and Barometers. The Old Rectory, Cherhill, Calne, Wiltshire. Tel 816227 (priv 812742).

Parker-Williams Antiques. 22 Palace St, Canterbury, Kent, CT1 2DZ. Tel 468341.

Pinfold Antiques. 28 Steep Hill, Lincoln, Lincolnshire. Tel 44716 (priv 0526 832057).

A.W. Porter & Son. High St, Hartley Wintney, Hampshire, RG278NY. Tel 2676.

Antony Preston Antiques Ltd. The Square, Stow-on-the-Wold, Gloucestershire, GL54 1AB. Tel 31586 (priv 31406).

Prudhoe Cottage Antiques. Hexham Antique Market, 15 St Mary's,Chare, Hexham, Northumberland. Tel 603812 (priv 0661 33421).

David & Sarah Pullen Antiques. 29-31 Sea Rd, Bexhill, E.Sussex, TN40 1EE. Tel 222035.

Quiet Street Antiques. 3 Quiet St, Bath, Avon. Tel 315727 (priv 332399).

C.Reynolds Antique Clock and Watch Specialist. The Spindles, Tonge, Melbourne, Derbyshire. Tel 2609.

Derek Roberts Antiques. 24/25 Shipbourne Rd, Tonbridge, Kent, TW10 3DN. Tel 358986.

Rosemary & Time. 42 Park St, Oxford, Oxfordshire.

J.T.Rutherford & Son. 55 Sandgate High St, Folkestone, Kent, CT20 3AH. Tel 39515 (priv 60822).

Rutland Antiques and Coins. 27 Mill St, Oakham, Leicestershire. Tel 3364 (priv 2408).

Sherborne Antiques Ltd. At The China Gallery,Long St, Sherborne, Dorset, DT9 3BS. Tel 812978.

Michael Sim. 1 Royal Parade, Chislehurst, Kent, BR7 5PG. Tel 467 7040.

Francis Sinclair Ltd. Georgian House, 39 Hallgate, Doncaster, S.Yorkshire. Tel 67260.

David Smith Antiques. The Old Cottage, Manton, Oakham, Leicestershire. Tel Manton (057 285) 244 (priv 473 or 314).

Robin Smith. 23 Belle Vue Rd, Shrewsbury, Shropshire, SY3 7LN. Tel 50357.

Snowdonia Antiques. Station Rd, Llanrwst, Gwynedd, LL26 0EP. Tel 640789 (priv 640027).

South Bar Antiques. Digbeth St, Stow-on-the-Wold, Gloucestershire. Tel 30236.

Spring Park Jewellers (inc The Clock Shop). 284 Wickham Rd, Shirley, Surrey. Tel 656 2800.

Stampantique. 86 High St, Egham, Surrey, TW20 9DP. Tel 36290.

Geoffrey G.Stevens. 26-28 Church Rd, Guildford, Surrey, GU1 4NG. Tel 504075.

Stone-Wares Antiques. 24 Radford St, Stone, Staffordshire. Tel 815000.

Surrey Clock Centre. 3 Lower St, Haslemere, Surrey. Tel 4547.

Tapsell Antiques. 59, 59A Middle St, Brighton & Hove, E.Sussex. Tel 28341 (priv 553249).

Gerald and Vera Taylor. Winforton Court, Winforton, Hereford & Worcester, HR3 6EA. Tel Eardisley (05446) 226.

Telling Time Antiques. 57 North St, Thame, Oxfordshire, OX9 3BH. Tel 3007.

Tempus Fugit. Trinity House, Trinity St, Halstead, Essex. Tel 475409.

Thorntons of Harrogate. 1 Montpellier Gdns, Harrogate, N.Yorkshire, HG1 2TF. Tel 504118.

Time in Hand. 11 Church St, Shipston on Stour, Warwickshire, CV36 4AP. Tel 62578.

Times Past Antiques Ltd. 59 High St, Eton, Berkshire. Tel Windsor (07535) 57018.

Todd & Austin Antiques & Fine Art. 2 Andover Rd, Winchester, Hampshire, SO23 7BS. Tel 69824.

M.V. Tooley, Antiquarian Horologist. The Guildroom, The Lee, Great Missenden, Buckinghamshire. Tel 463.

Vanbrugh House Antiques. Park St, Stow-on-the-Wold, Gloucestershire, GL54 1AQ. Tel 30797.

Village Antiques. 2 Cooden Sea Rd, Little Common, Bexhill, E.Sussex. Tel Cooden (04243) 5214.

A.G. Voss Antiques. 16 Market Hill, Woodbridge, Suffolk, IP12 4LU. Tel 5830.

H.S.Walsh & Sons Ltd. 243 Beckenham Rd, Beckenham, Kent, BR3 4TS. Tel 01-778 7061.

S.J.Webster-Speakman. 79 Regent St, Cambridge, Cambridgeshire. Tel 315048 (priv 354089).

Windsor Antiques. 80 High St, Eton, Berkshire, SL4 6AF. Tel Windsor (0753) 860752.

Witney Antiques. 96-98 Corn St, Witney, Oxfordshire, OX8 7BU. Tel 3902.

Christopher Wood. Harlaw Farmhouse, Kelso, Borders, TD5 7RA. Tel Stichill (05737) 321.

Anthony Woodburn Ltd. Orchard House, High Street, Leigh, Kent. Tel Hildenbrough (0732) 832258.

Wren House Antiques. 1 High St, Wrentham, Suffolk. Tel 276.

York House Antiques. 11-13 York St, Cowes, Isle of Wight. Tel 295746.

Cloisonne

see also Japanese Works of Art, Oriental Works of Art

Barry Davies Oriental Art. E14/17 Grays Mews, 1-7 Davies Mews, London, W1. Tel 408 0207 (priv 09326 4906.

Solveig & Anita Gray. 58 Davies Street, London, W1. Tel 408 1638.

Coins and Medals

Alfred S.Allen & Co. PO Box 4, South Ockendon, Essex, RM15 4JE. Tel Purfleet (0708) 866075.

Joan E. Allen & Co.. 184 Main Rd, Biggin Hill, Kent. Tel 4234.

A.H.Baldwin & Sons Ltd. 11 Adelphi Tce, London, WC2N 6BJ.

Bath Stamp & Coin Shop. Pulteney Bridge, Bath, Avon. Tel 63073.

Beaver Coin Room. 57 Philbeach Gardens, London, SW5 9ED. Tel 373 4553.

Bridge End Antiques. 8-12 Bridge End,Next to Old Bridge, Berwick-upon-Tweed, Northumberland, TD15 1AL. Tel 308702 (priv 066-84 433).

J.Bridgeman Coins. The Coin Shop, 129A Blackburn Rd, Accrington, Lancashire. Tel 384757 (priv 382049).

Carrington & Co Ltd. 170 Regent St, London, W1R 6BQ. Tel 734 3727.

Carronade. 63 West Regent St, Glasgow, Strathclyde. Tel 332 5600 (priv 649 3655).

Castle Galleries. 79 Castle St, Salisbury, Wiltshire, SP1 3SP. Tel 333734.

The Coin & Stamp Centre. 13 Centurion House (1st floor),St John's St, Colchester, Essex, CO2 7AH. Tel 41232 (priv 579345).

Coin Exchange. 153 Portobello Rd, London, W11.

Corbitt's of Clayton Street. 105 Clayton St, Newcastle upon Tyne, Tyne & Wear, NE1 5PZ. Tel 324356 (priv 2521301).

K.A.Davies Antiques. 248 Cowbridge Rd East, Cardiff, S.Glamorgan. Tel 29989.

Nimrod Dix & Company. 17 Piccadilly Arcade, London, SW1Y 6NL. Tel 493 5082.

Dodo Antiques. 23 Peter St, St Helier, Jersey. Tel 71497 (priv 62275).

E.H.W. & Co. 12 Sicilian Ave, Southampton Row, London, WC1A 3QD. Tel 405 5509.

Malcolm Ellis. Petworth Rd, Witley, Surrey. Tel Wormley (042879) 2896.

The Flintlock. 17A High St, Glastonbury, Somerset, BA6 9DR. Tel 31525 (priv 32813).

Fox & Co. 30 Princes St, Yeovil, Somerset. Tel 72323.

The Grange Gallery & Fine Arts Ltd. 39 New St, St Helier, Jersey.

Peter Hancock. 40-41 West St, Chichester, W.Sussex, PO19 1RP. Tel 786173.

Heffle Corner Antiques. Heffle Corner, Station Approach,Station Rd, Heathfield, E.Sussex, TN21 8LG. Tel 3381.

W.T.C.Henderson. 5 North Methven St, Perth, Tayside. Tel 24836.

Hicklenton & Phillips Ltd. Colborne Ave, Wimborne Minster, Dorset. Tel 882040.

HQ84. Southgate St, Gloucester, Gloucestershire. Tel 27716.

Intercol London. 1A Camden Walk, Islington Green, London, N1. Tel 354 2599 (priv 349 2207).

Jackson's. Hill Villa,Bury, Ramsey, Cambridgeshire, PE17 1AB. Tel 812361.

Knightsbridge Coins. 43 Duke St, St James's, London, SW1. Tel 930 7597.

Charles A. Lusted Ltd. 96A Calverley Rd, Tunbridge Wells, Kent. Tel 25731.

Marron Coins. 7 Beacon Close,Grimsthorpe, Sheffield, S.Yorkshire, S11 8ZG. Tel 433500.

Memories Antiques. 58-60 Wern Rd, LLanelli, Dyfed.

Michael Coins. 6 Hillgate St, London, W8. Tel 727 1518.

Midas Antiques. 181 High St, Brownhills, Walsall, W.Midlands, WS8 6HG. Tel Brownhills (0543) 377719.

Monarch Antiques. 15 High St, Glastonbury, Somerset. Tel 32498.

Nanbooks. Undercliffe Cottage, Duke St, Settle, N.Yorkshire, BD24 9DJ. Tel 3324 (priv 04685-551).

R. & L. Coins (Coin & Bullion Investments Ltd). 521 Lytham Rd, Blackpool, Lancashire, FY4 1RJ. Tel 43081.

B.A. Seaby Ltd. 8 Cavendish Sq, London, W1M 0AJ. Tel 631 3707.

Spink & Son Ltd. 5, 6 & 7 King St, St James's, London, SW1. Tel 930 7888.

Sterling Coins. 2 Somerset Rd, Boscombe, Bournemouth, Dorset. Tel 423881.

Trident Coins Ltd. Great Totham, Maldon, Essex. Tel 891858.

Ulster Coin Centre & William Rodman. 83 Dublin Rd, Belfast, Belfast. Tel 40052.

Vale. 21 Tranquil Vale, Blackheath, London, SE3 0BU. Tel 852 9817.

Wallis & Wallis. West Street Auction Galleries,West St, Lewes, E.Sussex, BN7 2NJ. Tel 473137.

Stewart Ward (Coins) Ltd. 16 High St, Westerham, Kent, TN16 1RF. Tel 63997.

Weiner aus Wien Military Antiques. 2 Market St, The Lanes, Brighton & Hove, E.Sussex, BN1 1HH. Tel 729948.

Whitmore. Teynham Lodge, Chase Rd,Upper Colwall, Malvern, Hereford & Worcester. Tel Colwall (0684) 40651.

Commemoratives

Antiques Unlimited. 34 Church Rd, Whitchurch, Cardiff, S.Glamorgan, CF4 2EA. Tel 693748.

A.H.Baldwin & Sons Ltd. 11 Adelphi Tce, London, WC2N 6BJ.

Basia. Squirrel Court, Hare Lane,Little Kingshill, Great Missenden, Buckinghamshire, HP16 0EF. Tel 5441.

Beaver Coin Room. 57 Philbeach Gardens, London, SW5 9ED. Tel 373 4553.

Britannia. Grays Antique Market, 58 Davies St, London, W1. Tel 629 6772.

Carol Brooke. 9A Pratt Lane, Mirfield, W.Yorkshire, WF14 9LX. Tel 492483.

Bygone. Stand M12, Antiquarius, Kings Rd, London, SW3. Tel 352 4690 (priv 748 6292).

Charterhouse Antiques. 1B Northumberland Place, Teignmouth, Devon. Tel Newton Abbot (0626) 4592.

Collector's Corner. 5-7 Frizinghall Rd, Bradford, W.Yorkshire, BD9 4LA. Tel 487098.

Commemoratives. 3 Pierrepont Arcade, Camden Passage,Islington, London, N1. Tel eves only 278 2146.

The Curiosity Shop. West Quay, Padstow, Cornwall. Tel St Mawgan (0637) 860567.

Dorothy's Antiques. 23 Waterbank Rd, Sheringham, Norfolk, NR26 8RB. Tel 822319 (priv 823018).

Hope and Glory (Ernest Titmuss). 131a Kensington Church Street, London, W8. Tel 727 8424.

Nevil and Betty Malin. Swan Lane Antiques,Swan Lane, Warwick, Warwickshire, CV34 4BJ. Tel 400040.

J. & J. May. 40 Kensington Church St, London, W8 4BX. Tel 937 3575.

Rogers of Alresford. 16 West St, Alresford, Hampshire, SO24 9AT. Tel 2277, 2862.

B.A. Seaby Ltd. 8 Cavendish Sq, London, W1M 0AJ. Tel 631 3707.

Spon End Antiques. 115-116 Spon End, Coventry, W.Midlands, CV1 3HF. Tel 28379.

Sussex Commemorative Ware Centre. 88 Western Rd, Hove, Brighton & Hove, E.Sussex, BN3 1JB. Tel 773911.

Treasure House. 31 High St, Arundel, W.Sussex. Tel 883101.

Conservators

see Restorers

Consultants and Research

Elizabeth Cayzer Fine Art. Flat 8,62 Rutland Gate, London. Tel 584 2952.

The Tony Gill Organisation-Number One. 173 Bermondsey St, London, SE1 3UW. Tel 403 4982.

John O'Reilly. 17 Greygates, Stillorgan Rd, Blackrock, Co Dublin. Tel 882327.

Taurus Gallery. 5 Wadham Rd, Putney, London, SW15 2LS. Tel 874 2534.

Copper

see Brass, Copper and Metalware

Costume

see also Lace

The Antique Textile Company. 100 Portland Rd, London, W11. Tel 221 7730.

Sue Biddulph. X10 Antiquarius, 135 King's Rd, London, SW3.

Bridge End Gallery. Terrace Hall, Woolhope, Hereford & Worcester, HR1 4QJ. Tel Fownhope (043277) 373.

Celia Charlotte's. 7 Malling St, Lewes, E.Sussex, BN7 2RA. Tel 473303.

Clock Tower Antiques. 2, Old Station Rd, Newmarket, Suffolk, CBB 8DN. Tel 664915.

Laurence Corner, Euston Gallery. 126-130 Drummond St, London, NW1. Tel 388 6811.

Country Antiques. 10 Westgate St, Long Melford, Suffolk. Tel Sudbury (0787) 310617.

Forget-Me-Not. Chelsea Antique Market,253 King's Rd, London, SW3. Tel 352 1424.

Gallery of Antique Costume & Textiles Ltd. 2 Church Street, Marylebone, London, NW8. Tel 723 9981 (priv 743 3821).

Golden Cage. 99 Derby Rd,Canning Circus, Nottingham, Nottinghamshire. Tel 411600 (priv 254984).

Granny's Attic. 22 High St, Clare, Suffolk, CO10 8NY. Tel 277740.

Great Western Antique Centre Ltd. Bartlett St, Bath, Avon, BA1 2QZ. Tel (office) 24243.

Hand in Hand. 3 North West Circus Place, Edinburgh, Lothian, EH3 6ST. Tel 226 3598.

Kimono. 4 Belvedere, Lansdown Rd, Bath, Avon, BS8 5ED. Tel 315987.

Ann King. 38 Belvedere, Lansdowne Rd, Bath, Avon. Tel 336245 (priv 0373 864747).

Little Bric a Brac Shop. The Green, Morcombelake, Bridport, Dorset. Tel Chideock (0297) 89346.

Lunn Antiques Ltd. 86 New King's Rd, London, SW6 4LU. Tel 736 4638.

Sue Madden. Stall X10 Antiquarius,135 Kings Rd, London, SW3. Tel 351 5757 (priv 703 4634).

Mayorcas Ltd. 38 Jermyn St, London, SW1Y 6DN. Tel 629 4195.

Real Macoy. Crossroads, Keighley, W.Yorkshire. Tel 44776.

Philippa Scott. 30 Elgin Crescent, London, W11. Tel 229 8029.

Spon End Antiques. 115-116 Spon End, Coventry, W.Midlands, CV1 3HF. Tel 28379.

Country and Cottage Antiques

London

Stephen Anson. 31a Matheson Rd, London, W14. Tel 602 5277 (24hr answering).

The Antique Trader. 357 Upper St,Camden Passage, London, N1. Tel 359 2019.

David Barklem Ltd. 3-5 Theberton St,Islington, London, N1. Tel 359 4997.

Janet & Robert Bateman Antiques. 92 Waterford Rd, London, SW6 2HA. Tel 736 4149.

William Bedford PLC. The Merchants Hall, 46 Essex Rd,Islington, London, N1 8LN. Tel 226 9648.

I. & J.L. Brown. 636 Kings Rd,Chelsea, London, SW6 2DU. Tel 736 4141.

C.W.Buckingham. 301-303 Munster Rd, Fulham, London, W6. Tel 385 2657.

Olwen Carthew. 109 Kirkdale, London, SE26. Tel 699 1363.

Coexistence Limited. Hobhouse Court, 13 Whitcomb St, London, WC2H 7HA. Tel 839 6620.

Coexistence Limited. 17 Canonbury Lane, London, N1 2AS. Tel 226 8382.

Simon Coleman. 40 White Hart Lane,Barnes, London, SW13. Tel 878 5037.

Peter Collins. 92 Waterford Rd, London, SW6. Tel 736 4149.

The Crane Gallery. 171A Sloane St, (1st Floor), London, SW1. Tel 235 2464.

Caroline Dawson. London. Tel 727 4106.

Furniture Cave. 533 King's Rd,Chelsea, London, SW10. Tel 352 2046.

Imogen Graham. 585 King's Rd, London, SW6. Tel 736 2465.

Judy Greenwood. 657 Fulham Rd, London, SW6. Tel 736 6037.

Heritage Antiques. 112 Islington High Street,Camden Passage, London, N1. Tel 226 7789.

Hollywood Road Antiques. 1a Hollywood Road, London, SW10. Tel 352 5248.

The Lacquer Chest. 75 Kensington Church St, London, W8. Tel 937 1306.

Old Pine. 594 King's Rd, London, SW6. Tel 736 5999.

Princedale Antiques. 70 Princedale Rd, Holland Park, London, W11. Tel 727 0868.

Peter Reynolds Antiques. 67 New King's Rd, London, SW6. Tel 736 7797.

Alistair Sampson Antiques (inc Tobias Jellinek). 156 Brompton Rd, London, SW3 1HW. Tel 589 5272, 581 2267.

Scallywag. The Old Church, Wren Rd,Camberwell Green, London, SE5 8QS. Tel 701 5353.

M. & D. Seligmann. 37 Kensington Church St, London, W8 4LL. Tel 937 0400 (priv 722 4315).

Stanley Studios. Park Walk, Chelsea, London, SW10. Tel 352 4353, 352 9996.

Stratton Quinn Antiques Etc. 164 Thames Rd, Strand-on-the-Green,Chiswick, London, W4 3QS. Tel 994 3140.

Tobias and the Angel. 68 White Hart Lane,Barnes, London, SW13. Tel 878 8902.

Doris Urquhart Antiques. 28 Church St, London, NW8. Tel 258 3748.

Robert Young Antiques. 68 Battersea Bridge Rd, London, SW11. Tel 228 7847.

Regions

Abacus Antiques. 58 Winchester Rd, Stroud, Petersfield, Hampshire. Tel 61935.

Abbas Combe Pine. 4 Upper Maudlin St, Bristol, Avon, BS2. Tel 299023.

Acorn Antiques. The Old Mill, Moat Lane, Towcester, Northamptonshire, NN12 7AD. Tel 52788.

Alexander Antiques. Post House, Small Dole, Henfield, W.Sussex.

Antique Centre. Brookend, Ross-on-Wye, Hereford & Worcester. Tel 62752.

Antique Pine Furniture, Michael Green. Library House,Regent Parade, Harrogate, N.Yorkshire. Tel 60452.

The Antique Shop. Hacheston, Suffolk. Tel Wickham Market (0728) 746485.

Antiques. 127 Main Rd, Long Hanborough, Oxfordshire. Tel Oxford (0865) 881484.

Antiques. 9 West End, West Haddon, Northamptonshire. Tel 772.

Arboyne Antiques. Arboyne House, Eardisley, Hereford & Worcester. Tel 218.

James Ash Antiques. The Warehouse, Station Rd, Llandeilo, Dyfed. Tel 823728 (priv 0269 850119).

Duncan J. Baggott. The Square, Stow-on-the-Wold, Gloucestershire, GL54 1AB. Tel 30662.

Henry Baines. 14 Church Rd, Southborough, Tunbridge Wells, Kent, TN4 0RX. Tel 32099.

Balcombe Galleries. Balcombe, W.Sussex, RH17 6NF. Tel 811439 or 811415.

Peter Bell Fine Arts. High St, Lechlade, Gloucestershire, GL7 3DL. Tel Faringdon (0367) 52987 (priv 52255).

Below Stairs. 103 High St, Hungerford, Berkshire, RG17 0NB. Tel 82317.

John Bird/Annette Puttnam. 44 Upper North St, Brighton & Hove, E.Sussex, BN1 3FH. Tel 739425.

Birmingham House Antiques. Birmingham House, 8-10 Church Street, Shipston on Stour, Warwickshire, CV36 4AP. Tel 62037 (priv 029588 439).

Blewbury Antiques. London Rd, Blewbury, Oxfordshire, OX11 9NX. Tel 850366.

Blyth Antiques. 28 Sydney Buildings, Bath, Avon, BA2 6BZ. Tel 69766.

Brampton Mill Antiques Centre. Brampton Mill, Brampton, Cambridgeshire. Tel Huntingdon (0480) 55593.

Bratton Antiques. Market Place, Westbury, Wiltshire, BA13 3DE. Tel 823021.

Bridge House Antiques. Penshurst, Kent, TN11 8BQ. Tel 870209.

Brocanteuse Gallery. 11 North St, Ashburton, Devon. Tel 53389.

Brownsells Granary. 9 High St, Wiveliscombe, Somerset, TA4 2JX. Tel 23117 (priv 0823 400427).

Bugle Antiques. 9 Horsefair, Chipping Norton, Oxfordshire. Tel 3322.

Audrey Bull. 15 Upper Frog St, Tenby, Dyfed. Tel 3114 (priv 0834 813425).

Bures Antiques. 1 Bridge St, Bures, Suffolk, CO8 5AD. Tel 227858 (priv 0206 210215).

Ann Bye Antiques. 88 London Rd, Reading, Berkshire, RG1 4SJ. Tel 582029.

Robert Byles. 7-9 Castle St, Bampton, Devon, EX16 9NS. Tel 515.

BBC Antiques. A27 Antiques Warehouse,Unit 2 Chaucer Industrial Estate, Polegate, E.Sussex. Tel 5301 (priv 0273-477446).

Carse Antiques. Rait, by Perth, Tayside, PH2 7RT. Tel 205 (priv 227).

Castle Antiques. Bairds Malt, Northgate, Newark-on-Trent, Nottinghamshire. Tel 704290 (priv 707764).

Cedar Antiques. High St, Hartley Wintney, Hampshire, RG27 8NY. Tel 3252.

Chancery Antiques. 8-10 Barrington St, Tiverton, Devon, EX16 6PU. Tel 252416 (priv 253190).

Mark Chapman Antiques. New Street, Petworth, W.Sussex. Tel 42283.

Chelsea House Antiques. 27 Station Rd, Stowmarket, Suffolk. Tel Elmswell (0359) 40895.

The China Hen. 9 Woolley St, Bradford-on-Avon, Wiltshire, BA15 1AD. Tel 3369.

The Clare Collector. 1 Nethergate St, Clare, Suffolk. Tel 277909 (priv 277494).

David Clark. The Plestor, Selborne, Hampshire. Tel 274.

Close Antiques. 19 Little Minster St, Winchester, Hampshire, SO23 9HA. Tel 64763.

Coexistence. 10 Argyle Street, Bath, Avon. Tel 61507 (priv 314846).

Cottage Antiques. The Old Post Office, Langford, Bristol, Avon, BS18 7BP. Tel Wrighton (0934) 862597.

Cottage Antiques. 16-18 Lensfield Rd, Cambridge, Cambridgeshire. Tel 316698.

Cottage Antiques. 3 Devonshire Place,Skipton Rd, Harrogate, N.Yorkshire, HG1. Tel 68195 (priv 0937 72694).

Country Antiques. Castle Mill,The Bridge, Kidwelly, Dyfed. Tel 890534.

Country Antiques. 10 Westgate St, Long Melford, Suffolk. Tel Sudbury (0787) 310617.

Country Interiors. 12 Frome Rd, Bradford-on-Avon, Wiltshire, BA15 1LE. Tel 4000 (priv 4551).

The Craftsman. 16 Bridge St, Hungerford, Berkshire, RG17 0EG. Tel 82262.

M. & A. Cringle. The Black Horse, Burnham Market, Norfolk. Tel Fakenham (0328) 738456.

Crispin Antiques. 10 The Broadway, Amersham, Buckinghamshire, HP7 0HP. Tel 21779.

Crispin Antiques. 10 The Broadway, Amersham, Buckinghamshire, HP7 0HP. Tel 21779.

The Curiosity Shop. High St, Llandovery, Dyfed. Tel 20390.

Daniels House Antiques. Hogshill St, Beaminster, Dorset, DT8 3AG. Tel 862635.

Jay Davis Antiques. Bishopsdale Court, Settle, N.Yorkshire. Tel 2764.

de Montfort. 49 High St, Robertsbridge, E.Sussex, TN32 5AN. Tel 880698 (priv 082 584 243).

Dickenson and Thomas. Old Granary, 10 North St, Stamford, Lincolnshire, PE9 2YN. Tel 62236 (priv 55093).

Directmoor Ltd. Coppice Farm,Farley Rd, Moorcourt, Oakamoor, Staffordshire. Tel 702419.

Mollie Evans. 84 Hill Rise, Richmond, Surrey. Tel 948 0182 (priv 940 3720).

Fenwick and Fisher Antiques. 88 High St, Broadway, Hereford & Worcester. Tel 853227 (priv 853228).

Fine Pine Ltd. Zeaston Farm, South Brent, Devon. Tel 2505.

Fine Pine Ltd. Woodland Rd,Harbertonford, Totnes, Devon. Tel Harbertonford (080 423) 465.

Gene & Sally Foster (Antiques). 27A Belvedere, Lansdown Rd, Bath, Avon, BA1 5HR. Tel 28256 (priv 28058).

Franfam Ltd. High St, Moreton-in-Marsh, Gloucestershire, GL56 0LH. Tel 50648.

George & Helen Gardiner. 105 West Regent St, Glasgow, Strathclyde, G2 2BA. Tel 332 1264.

C.B.Gardner Antiques. 31 High St, Chipping Norton, Oxfordshire. Tel 3913.

Genges Farm Antiques. Genges Farm, Limington, Somerset. Tel Ilchester (0935) 840464.

Georgian House Antiques. 222 High St, Uckfield, E.Sussex, TN22 1RE. Tel 5074.

Gloucester House Antiques Ltd. Market Place, Fairford, Gloucestershire, GL7 4AB. Tel Cirencester (0285) 712790 (priv 3066).

The Granary Galleries. Court House, Ash Priors,near Bishops Lydeard, Taunton, Somerset, TA4 3NQ. Tel Bishops Lydeard (0823) 432402 (priv 432816).

Grange Court Antiques. Corfe, Taunton, Somerset. Tel Blagdon Hill (082 342) 498.

Granny's Attic. 22 High St, Clare, Suffolk, CO10 8NY. Tel 277740.

Michael Green. Library House,Regent Parade, Harrogate, N.Yorkshire. Tel 60452.

Greville Antiques & Design Ltd. The Square, Aspley Guise, Milton Keynes, Buckinghamshire, MK17 8DF. Tel 584466 (priv 583408).

Halstow Antiques. Green Farm House, The Green,Lower Halstow, Sittingbourne, Kent, ME9 7DS. Tel 842016.

Peter Hammond. Church House, Thornage, Holt, Norfolk. Tel 861352.

Harley Antiques. The Comedy, Christian Malford, Chippenham, Wiltshire. Tel 720112.

Harley Two. The Chimneys, Christian Malford, Chippenham, Wiltshire. Tel 720112.

Hillside Antiques. Units 12-13 Lindfield Enterprise Pk,Lewes Rd, Lindfield, W.Sussex, RH10 4SX. Tel 3042 (priv 0444 811003).

Keith Hockin Antiques Ltd. The Square, Stow-on-the-Wold, Gloucestershire, GL54 1AF. Tel 31058.

Paul Hopwell Antiques. 30 High St, West Haddon, Northamptonshire, NN6 7AP. Tel 636.

Horn Antiques. Churt, Farnham, Surrey, GU10 2JA. Tel Headley (0428) 714298.

Jose Hornsey. 3 Silver St, Bradford-on-Avon, Wiltshire. Tel 4333 (priv 0380 870764).

Horsefair Antiques. 21 Horsefair, Chipping Norton, Oxfordshire. Tel 3089.

Colin S.Hughes. 36 Penrallt St, Machynlleth, Powys. Tel 2363.

G. & M.Hughes. 6 Penrallt St, Machynlleth, Powys. Tel 2053.

Humphry Antiques. East St, Petworth, W.Sussex, GU28 0AB. Tel 43053 (priv 42944).

Huntington Antiques Ltd. The Old Forge, Church St, Stow-on-the-Wold, Gloucestershire. Tel 30842.

Idears. 1 Chapel St, Diss, Norfolk, IP22 3AN. Tel 51521.

Jadis Ltd. The Old Bank, 17 Walcot Buildings,London Rd, Bath, Avon. Tel 338797.

J.P.Kadwell. Silver St, Malmesbury, Wiltshire. Tel 3589.

Key Antiques. 11 Horsefair, Chipping Norton, Oxfordshire, OX7 5AL. Tel 3777.

Lancashire Bygones. 12 Parliament St, Up Holland, Wigan, Greater Manchester, WN8 0LN. Tel Up Holland (0695) 625624 (priv 0695 622458).

Muriel Lindsay. Queen Anne House, High St, Winchcombe, Gloucestershire. Tel Cheltenham (0242) 602319.

Lion House/Robert Croot Antiques. 16 New St, Chipping Norton, Oxfordshire, OX7 5LJ. Tel 3294.

Richard Lloyd. Dolhaidd Mansion, Henllan, Dyfed. Tel Velindre (0559) 370791.

Robin Lloyd Antiques. 23-24 Brookend St, Ross-on-Wye, Hereford & Worcester. Tel 62123.

Loft Antiques. Old Kings Head,11 High St, Dorking, Surrey.

Graham Lower. Stonecrouch Farmhouse, Flimwell, E.Sussex, TN5 7QB. Tel 535.

Market Place Antiques. 35 Market Place, Henley-on-Thames, Oxfordshire, RG9 2AA. Tel 572387.

Milverton Antiques. Fore St, Milverton, Somerset, TA4 1JU. Tel 400597.

Mole Hall Antiques. 102-104 High St, Aldeburgh, Suffolk. Tel 2361.

Monkton Galleries. High St, Hindon, Wiltshire, SP3 6DR. Tel 235.

Moolham Mill Antiques. Moolham Mill, Moolham Lane, Ilminster, Somerset, TA19 0PD. Tel 2834.

Michael Moore Antiques. The Old Court, Nethergate St, Clare, Suffolk, CO10 8NP. Tel 277510.

Moxhams Antiques. 17 Silver St, Bradford-on-Avon, Wiltshire. Tel 2789 (priv 038 082-677).

Multum-In-Parvo & Tools Past. Kirkland, Kendal, Cumbria. Tel 25168.

Richard & Pamela Nadin. 5 Woolley St, Bradford-on-Avon, Wiltshire, BA15 1AD. Tel 2476.

Netherly Cottage Antiques. Milburn, Cumbria. Tel Kirkby Thore (0930) 61403.

John Nicholls Antiques. 27 Long St, Tetbury, Gloucestershire. Tel 52781 (priv 08893 2383).

No.Twelve Queen Street. 12 Queen St, Bath, Avon. Tel 62363 (priv 314846).

Peter Norden Antiques. High St, Burford, Oxfordshire, OX8 4XX. Tel 2121 (priv 0993 830064).

Northiam Antiques. Main St, Northiam, E.Sussex. Tel 2182.

Old Chapel Antiques. Fop St, Uley, Gloucestershire. Tel Dursley (0453) 860656 (priv 860396).

Old Tavern Antiques. Watton Rd, Ware, Hertfordshire. Tel 68644.

Packer House. 28 High St, Chipping Norton, Oxfordshire, OX7 5AD. Tel 3255.

Angela Page Antiques. Sion House, 15 Mount Sion, Tunbridge Wells, Kent, TN1 1OD. Tel 22217.

Pall Mall Antiques. 104c & 104d Elm Rd, Leigh-on-Sea, Essex. Tel Southend-on-Sea (0702) 77235.

Fenwick Pattison. Bowmanstead, Coniston, Cumbria, LA21 8HB. Tel 41235.

The Pen-y-Ghent Gallery. Devonshire House, Duke St, Settle, N.Yorkshire. Tel 2405.

Pennard House Antiques. East Pennard, Shepton Mallet, Somerset, BA4 6TP. Tel Ditcheat (074986) 266.

Peppers Period Pieces. 22/23 Churchgate St, Bury St Edmunds, Suffolk. Tel 68786 (priv 0359 50606).

Peter Philp. 77 Kimberley Rd, Pen-y-Lan, S.Glamorgan, CF2 5DP. Tel Cardiff (0222) 493826.

Pine and Country Antiques. Sandhill Barn, Washington, Pulborough, W.Sussex. Tel Ashington (0903) 892888 (priv 892210).

Pine Antiques. 52 Bridge St, Uttoxeter, Staffordshire. Tel 5374.

The Pine Cellars. 38 Jewry St, Winchester, Hampshire, SO23 8RY. Tel 67014.

The Pine Shop. 3 Dukes Ct,Dukes St, Brighton & Hove, E.Sussex, BN1 1AR. Tel 253365 (priv 501110).

Pineapple. Fountain Buildings,Lansdown Rd, Bath, Avon, BA1 2JQ. Tel 65223.

Ian Pout Antiques. 99 High St, Witney, Oxfordshire. Tel 2616 (priv 0869 40205).

Susan Procter. 47-51 The Feus, Auchterarder, Tayside, PH3 1DG. Tel 2532.

Robert Graham Pugh. Llanelli, Dyfed. Tel 772613.

The Relic Shop. 106A High St, Needham Market, Suffolk, IP6 0EN. Tel 721245 (priv 0473 830858).

Isobel Rhodes. 69-73 Angel St, Hadleigh, Suffolk. Tel 823754.

Ringles Cross Antiques. Ringles Cross, Uckfield, E.Sussex. Tel 2909.

Rogers of Alresford. 16 West St, Alresford, Hampshire, SO24 9AT. Tel 2277, 2862.

Royston Antiques. 27-29 Kneesworth St, Royston, Hertfordshire. Tel 43876.

Anthony Sampson. Dale House, High St, Moreton-in-Marsh, Gloucestershire, GL56 0AD. Tel 50763.

Seymour Galleries. Church St South, Old Glossop, Derbyshire. Tel 62555.

Laurence Shaw Antique Centre. Sandy Bank Road,New York, Coningsby, Lincolnshire. Tel 42578.

Oswald Simpson Antiques. Market Place, Bildeston, Suffolk, IP7 7EP. Tel 740030.

David Smith Antiques. The Old Cottage, Manton, Oakham, Leicestershire. Tel Manton (057 285) 244 (priv 473 or 314).

Neil Speed Antiques. The Strand, Laugharne, Dyfed, SA33 4SZ. Tel 412.

Spencer Swaffer Antiques. 33 High St, Arundel, W.Sussex, BN18 9AB. Tel 882132.

The Stable Antiques. Old Kings Head Court,11 High St, Dorking, Surrey. Tel 885452.

The Stables. College St, Grasmere, Ambleside, Cumbria. Tel Grasmere (096 65) 453.

Stone House Antiques (and Design & Craft Gallery). St Mary's St, Painswick, Gloucestershire, GL6 6QB. Tel 813540 (priv 045286 2343).

Dinah Stoodley. High St, Brasted, Kent, TN16 1JJ. Tel Westerham (0959) 63616.

Julie Strachey. Southfield Farm, North Lane, Weston-on-the-Green, Oxfordshire. Tel Bletchington (0869) 50833.

Swan Antiques. Stone St, Cranbrook, Kent. Tel 712720.

Tetbury Antiques. 39A Long St, Tetbury, Gloucestershire. Tel 52748.

Treasures. Mileham, King's Lynn, Norfolk. Tel Fakenham (03286) 701234.

Tyne House of Lewes Ltd. 140 High St, Lewes, E.Sussex. Tel 477446.

V.K. and R. Antiques. 8 High St, Potterne, Wiltshire. Tel Devizes (0380) 3933.

Denzil Verey Antiques. The Close, Barnsley House, Barnsley, Gloucestershire. Tel Bibury (0285 74) 402 (priv 028585 495).

Michael Wakelin and Helen Linfield. 10 New St, Petworth, W.Sussex. Tel 42417.

Waterwheel Pine and Antiques. Cricklepit Mill,The Quay, Exeter, Devon. Tel 217076.

E.W. Webster Antiques. Wash Farm, Rainford Rd, Bickerstaffe, Lancashire. Tel Skelmersdale (0695) 24322.

Anthony Welling Antiques. Broadway Barn, High St, Ripley, Surrey, GU23 6AQ. Tel Guildford (0483) 225384.

Wenlock Antiques. 61 High St, Much Wenlock, Shropshire, TF13 6AE. Tel 727271.

West Farm Antiques. High St, Orwell, Cambridgeshire, SG8 5QN. Tel Cambridge (0223) 207464.

Westward County Pine. 10 Church St, Launceston, Cornwall. Tel Canworthy Water (056 681) 309 or (0566) 5605.

Williton Antiques. 26 High St, Williton, Taunton, Somerset. Tel Williton (0984) 32393 (priv).

Woolpit Antiques. The Old Butchers Shop, The Street, Woolpit, Suffolk. Tel Elmswell (0359) 40895.

Wrington Antiques. Tanners, Wrington, Avon, BS18 7QQ. Tel 862200.

Ye Olde Junk Shoppe. St Michael's College, Shipton-under-Wychwood, Oxfordshire. Tel 830576.

Crafts, Contemporary

Amalgam. 3 Barnes High St, London, SW13. Tel 878 1279.

Argenta. 82 Fulham Rd, London, SW3. Tel 584 3119.

Artizana. The Village, Prestbury, Cheshire, SK10 4DG. Tel 827582.

Atmosphere. 175 Muswell Hill Broadway, London, N10. Tel 883 1074.

Hugo Barclay. 7 East St, Brighton & Hove, E.Sussex, BN1 1HP. Tel 21694.

Beaux Arts Ceramics. 13 York St, Bath, Avon, BA1 1NG. Tel 64850.

Bluecoat Display Centre. Bluecoat Chambers, School Lane, Liverpool, Merseyside. Tel 709 4014.

British Crafts Centre. 43 Earlham St, Covent Garden, London, WC2H 9LD. Tel 836 6993.

Business Art Galleries & The Upstairs Gallery. Royal Academy of Arts,Burlington House, Piccadilly, London, W1. Tel 734 1448 (priv 734 7763).

The Candover Gallery. 22 West St, Alresford, Hampshire, SO24 9AE. Tel 3200.

Casson Gallery. 73 Marylebone High St, London, W1. Tel 487 5080.

Centre Crafts. 169 Spon St, Coventry, W.Midlands. Tel 27200.

Chestnut Gallery. High Street, Bourton-on-the-Water, Gloucestershire. Tel 20017.

Cirencester Workshops. Brewery Court, Cirencester, Gloucestershire. Tel 61566.

Clare Gallery. 21 High St, Tunbridge Wells, Kent. Tel 38717.

Collection. 13 The Southend, Ledbury, Hereford & Worcester. Tel 4641.

Cecilia Colman Gallery. 67 St Johns Wood High St, London, NW8. Tel 722 0686.

Contemporary Textile Gallery. 10 Golden Square, London, W1R 3AF. Tel 439 9070.

Courcoux and Courcoux. 90-92 Crane St, Salisbury, Wiltshire, SP1 2QD. Tel 333471.

Craft Centre. Royal Exchange Theatre,St Ann's Square, Manchester, Greater Manchester. Tel 833 9333.

Crafts Council Shop, V & A. Victoria and Albert Museum, London, SW7 2RL. Tel 589 5070.

The Craftsmen Potters Shop. 7 Marshall St, London, W1V 1FD. Tel 437 7605.

Lesley Craze. 5 Essex Rd,Islington, London, N1. Tel 226 3200.

Dartington Cider Press Centre. Shinners Bridge, Dartington, Devon, TQ9 6JE. Tel Totnes (0803) 864171.

Simon Drew Gallery. 13 Foss St, Dartmouth, Devon, TQ6 9DR. Tel 2832.

Electrum. 21 South Molton St, London, W1. Tel 629 6325.

Fair Maids House Scottish Crafts. North Port, Perth, Tayside. Tel 25976.

Fenny Lodge Gallery. Simpson Rd,Bletchley, Milton Keynes, Buckinghamshire, MK1 1BD. Tel 642207.

Fire and Iron Limited. Rowhurst Forge,Oxshott Rd, Leatherhead, Surrey, KT22 0EN. Tel 375148.

Four Seasons Gallery. 39 St Giles St, Northampton, Northamptonshire, NN1 1JF. Tel 32287.

Galia Antiques. Antiquarius, 135 King's Rd, London, SW3.

The Glasshouse Gallery & Workshop. 65 Long Acre, Covent Garden, London, WC2. Tel 836 9785 (priv.240 7508).

Godfrey & Twatt. 7 Westminster Arcade,Parliament St, Harrogate, N.Yorkshire, HG1 2RN. Tel 525300.

Handweavers Studio and Gallery. 29 Haroldstone Rd, Walthamstow, London, E17. Tel 521 2281.

J.K.Hill. 151 Fulham Road, London, SW3 6SN. Tel 584 7529.

Holly House Gallery. 14 Front Street,Tynemouth, North Shields, Tyne & Wear, NE30 4DX. Tel 592753.

Marie Jordan Gallery. 659 Barnsley Rd, Wakefield, W.Yorkshire, WF2 6HJ. Tel 255419.

Laurimore Gallery. The Mews,29 Swan St, Boxford, Suffolk, CO6 5NZ. Tel 210138.

Leigh Gallery. 17 Leigh St,Bloomsbury, London, WC1H 9EW. Tel 242 5177.

Liberty & Co Ltd. Regent St, London, W1R 6AH. Tel 734 1234.

Long Street Gallery. 50 Long Street, Tetbury, Gloucestershire, GL8 8AQ. Tel 53722.

Lowen Gallery. 471 Hartshill Rd,Hartshill, Stoke-on-Trent, Staffordshire, ST4 6AA. Tel 623762.

New Ashgate Gallery. Wagon Yard, Farnham, Surrey, GU9 7JR. Tel 713208.

New Craftsman. 24 Fore Street, St Ives, Cornwall. Tel 795652.

Ogle Fine Arts. Ogle Gallery, 12 Rotunda Terrace,Montpellier St, Cheltenham, Gloucestershire. Tel 518605 (priv 31011).

The Old Granary. Battlesbridge Antique Centre,Hawk Hill (by the "Barge" pub), Battlesbridge, Essex. Tel Wickford (037 44) 63344.

Anatol Orient Ltd. 318 Portobello Rd, London, W10. Tel 969 4119.

Oxford Gallery. 23 High St, Oxford, Oxfordshire, OX1 4AH. Tel 242731.

Palace Gate Gallery. 1 Deanery Place, Palace Gate, Exeter, Devon, EX1 1HU.

Soft Surround. 2 Centre Craft Yard,43 Henley St, Stratford-upon-Avon, Warwickshire, CV37 6QW. Tel 295070 (priv 0608-62181).

The South Manchester Gallery. 140 Ashley Rd,Hale Village, Altrincham, Greater Manchester, WA14 2UQ. Tel 061-941 6244.

St James's Gallery. 9 Margarets Building, Bath, Avon, BA1 2LP. Tel 319197.

Stewart Gallery. 48 Devonshire Rd, Bexhill, E.Sussex. Tel 223410.

Stone House Antiques (and Design & Craft Gallery). St Mary's St, Painswick, Gloucestershire, GL6 6QB. Tel 813540 (priv 045286 2343).

The Talent Store Gallery. 11 Eccleston St, London, SW1W 9LX. Tel 730 8117.

The Terrace Gallery. 7 Liverpool Terrace, Worthing, W.Sussex, BN11 1TA.

Thursley Textile Designs. 1 Moushill Lane,(at junction with A3), Milford, Surrey. Tel Godalming (04868) 24769.

Windjammer Crafts. 2 Russell Court, Salcombe, Devon. Tel 2979.

Yew Tree Gallery. Ellastone, Ashbourne, Derbyshire, DE6 2HA. Tel 033 524 341.

Crested China

Abbey Antiques. 63 Great Whyte, Ramsey, Cambridgeshire, PE17 1HL. Tel 814753, 812758.

The Curiosity Shop. West Quay, Padstow, Cornwall. Tel St Mawgan (0637) 860567.

Dorothy's Antiques. 23 Waterbank Rd, Sheringham, Norfolk, NR26 8RB. Tel 822319 (priv 823018).

Gwendoline Golder. The Little Shop, Coltishall, Norfolk. Tel Norwich (0603) 737404.

Goss & Crested China Ltd. 62 Murray Rd, Horndean, Hampshire, PO8 9JL. Tel 597440.

Nevil and Betty Malin. Swan Lane Antiques,Swan Lane, Warwick, Warwickshire, CV34 4BJ. Tel 400040.

Spon End Antiques. 115-116 Spon End, Coventry, W.Midlands, CV1 3HF. Tel 28379.

Curiosities

see Bygones and Curiosities

Cutlery

see Silver Flatware

Desks and Writing Accessories

John Anthony Antiques. 71 High St, Bletchingley, Surrey. Tel Godstone (0883) 843197.

David Burkinshaw Antique Desks. 66 High St, Lindfield, W.Sussex, RH16 2HL. Tel 2826.

Churchill Antique Galleries Ltd. 65 Quarry St, Guildford, Surrey, GU1 3UA. Tel 506662.

The Desk Shop. 41 St Clements, Oxford, Oxfordshire. Tel 245524.

The Dorking Desk Shop. 20 West St, Dorking, Surrey. Tel 883327.

J.G.Elias Antiques. 37 West St, Dorking, Surrey. Tel 880535 and 883327.

Griffons Court. Highclere, Newbury, Berkshire, RG15 9QS. Tel Highclere (0635) 253247.

Helius Antiques. 487-493 Upper Richmond Rd West, London, SW14 7PU. Tel 876 5721 (priv 940 5595).

His Nibs. 182 Drury Lane, London, WC2. Tel 405 7097.

John Hubbard Antiques. 224-226 Court Oak Rd, Harborne, Birmingham, W.Midlands, B32 2EG. Tel 426 1694.

Just Desks. 20 Church St, London, NW8 8EP. Tel 723 7976, 402 0391.

Penfriend Ltd. The Arcade,Bush House, Aldwych, London, WC2.

H.& M. Sedler. Stand F2, Antiquarius, Kings Rd, London, SW3. Tel 351 5000 (priv 226 2418).

Display Glass Domes

Collectors Cases. Alderney House, 58 Normandy St, Alton, Hampshire, GU34 1EL. Tel 83366.

Display Stands

Acrylic Design. 697 Harrow Rd, London, NW10 4NY. Tel 969 0478.

C. & A.J.Barmby. 68 Judd Rd, Tonbridge, Kent. Tel 356479.

Collectors Cases. Alderney House, 58 Normandy St, Alton, Hampshire, GU34 1EL. Tel 83366.

Alan Morris. 503 Evesham Rd, Crabbs Cross, Redditch, Hereford & Worcester, B97 5JJ. Tel 45084.

C. & A.E. Sinclair. No 10 The Avenue, Lincoln, Lincolnshire.

Dolls and Toys

Abbas Combe Pine. 4 Upper Maudlin St, Bristol, Avon, BS2. Tel 299023.

Bottles & Bygones. 96 Horsefair St, Charlton Kings, Cheltenham, Gloucestershire. Tel 236393.

Cherry Antiques. 101-103 High St, Hemel Hempstead, Hertfordshire. Tel 64358.

Chester Antiques. 49 Watergate Row, Chester, Cheshire. Tel 311768 (priv 532208).

China Doll. 31 Suffolk Parade, Cheltenham, Gloucestershire. Tel 33164.

Clock Tower Antiques. 2, Old Station Rd, Newmarket, Suffolk, CBB 8DN. Tel 664915.

Collectors Old Toys and Antiques. 89 Northgate, Northbridge, Halifax, W.Yorkshire. Tel 822148.

Andrew Cottrell Galleries. 7-9 Church St, Godalming, Surrey. Tel 7570.

Kay Desmonde Antiques Ltd. 17 Kensington Church Walk, London, W8 4NB. Tel 937 2602 (priv 04606 3280.

Dodo Antiques. 23 Peter St, St Helier, Jersey. Tel 71497 (priv 62275).

The Doll Shop. 6 Newgate, Barnard Castle, Durham.

The Dolls House Toys Ltd. 29 The Market, Covent Garden, London, WC2E 8RE. Tel 379 7243.

Dragons of Walton St Ltd. 19 & 23 Walton St, London, SW3 2HX. Tel 589 3795/0548.

Game Advice. 23 Holmes Road, London, NW5 3AA. Tel 485 2188 (priv 485 4226).

Granny's Goodies and Chelsea Lion. Chenil Galleries, 181 King's Rd,Chelsea, London, SW3. Tel 352 8653 (priv 771 1277).

Hobsons Choice. 85 Bispham Rd, Blackpool, Lancashire. Tel 56979.

Meriden House Antiques. Meriden House, 75 Market St, Stourbridge, W.Midlands. Tel 395384.

Lilian Middleton's Antique Doll Shop. Days Stables, Sheep St, Stow-on-the-Wold, Gloucestershire, GL54 1AA. Tel 30381.

Patrick Moorhead Antiques. 59A Ship St, Brighton & Hove, E.Sussex, BN1 1AD. Tel 28209 (priv 551594).

Museum of Childhood. 1 Castle St,Beaumaris, Anglesey, Gwynedd. Tel 810448 (priv 712498).

Old Bakery Antiques. 1 Church St, Hunstanton, Norfolk. Tel Brancaster (0485) 210396.

The Relic Shop. 106A High St, Needham Market, Suffolk, IP6 0EN. Tel 721245 (priv 0473 830858).

The Singing Tree. 69 New King's Rd, London, SW6. Tel 736 4527.

Something Old. 6-8 Old Cross, Hertford, Hertfordshire, SG14 1RB. Tel 551530.

Peter Stockham at Images. 16 Cecil Court, Charing Cross Rd, London, WC2. Tel 836 8661.

Swag. 24-26 Leyland Rd, Penwortham, Preston, Lancashire, PR1 9XS. Tel 744970.

Victoriana Dolls. Reigate, Surrey. Tel 49525.

Yesterday Child. 24 The Mall, Camden Passage, London, N1. Tel Milton Keynes (0908) 583403.

Domestic Items

Antique Pine Furniture, Michael Green. Library House,Regent Parade, Harrogate, N.Yorkshire. Tel 60452.

Antiques. 127 Main Rd, Long Hanborough, Oxfordshire. Tel Oxford (0865) 881484.

Christopher Bangs. London. Tel 223 5676.

Below Stairs. 103 High St, Hungerford, Berkshire, RG17 0NB. Tel 82317.

Olwen Carthew. 109 Kirkdale, London, SE26. Tel 699 1363.

Cottage Antiques. The Old Post Office, Langford, Bristol, Avon, BS18 7BP. Tel Wrighton (0934) 862597.

Cottage Antiques. 3 Devonshire Place,Skipton Rd, Harrogate, N.Yorkshire, HG1. Tel 68195 (priv 0937 72694).

Country Antiques. 10 Westgate St, Long Melford, Suffolk. Tel Sudbury (0787) 310617.

O.M. & R.D.Cox Antiques. 5 St Mary's Hill, Stamford, Lincolnshire. Tel 64159.

Caroline Dawson. London. Tel 727 4106.

Rupert Gentle Antiques. The Manor House,Milton Lilbourne, Pewsey, Wiltshire, SN9 5LQ. Tel Marlborough (0672) 63344.

Gibberd and Grant Antiques. 40 The Bank, Barnard Castle, Durham, DL12 8PN. Tel Teesdale (0833) 37437.

Michael Green. Library House,Regent Parade, Harrogate, N.Yorkshire. Tel 60452.

Ann Lingard. Rope Walk Antiques, Rope Walk, Rye, E.Sussex, TN31 7NA. Tel 223486.

Stephen Long. Albion House, 348 Fulham Rd, London, SW10 9UH. Tel 352 8226.

Maltings Antiques. Sixty Millgate, Aylsham, Norfolk. Tel 732291.

Market Place Antiques. 35 Market Place, Henley-on-Thames, Oxfordshire, RG9 2AA. Tel 572387.

Myriad Antiques. 131 Portland Rd, London, W11. Tel 229 1709.

Netherly Cottage Antiques. Milburn, Cumbria. Tel Kirkby Thore (0930) 61403.

Pall Mall Antiques. 104c & 104d Elm Rd, Leigh-on-Sea, Essex. Tel Southend-on-Sea (0702) 77235.

Peppers Period Pieces. 22/23 Churchgate St, Bury St Edmunds, Suffolk. Tel 68786 (priv 0359 50606).

Pine and Country Antiques. Sandhill Barn, Washington, Pulborough, W.Sussex. Tel Ashington (0903) 892888 (priv 892210).

Pine Antiques. 52 Bridge St, Uttoxeter, Staffordshire. Tel 5374.

Pine Finds. The Old Cornmill, Bishop Monkton, Harrogate, N.Yorkshire, HG3 3QN. Tel Ripon (0765) 87159.

Priory Antiques. Litcham Priory, Litcham, King's Lynn, Norfolk. Tel Litcham (0328) 701262.

Quested Antiques. 62 Brighton Rd, Surbiton, Surrey, KT6 5NF. Tel 390 3566.

Straight Lace. 9 High St, East Linton, Lothian, EH40 3AA. Tel 860017 (priv 062088 284).

Tobias and the Angel. 68 White Hart Lane,Barnes, London, SW13. Tel 878 8902.

Drawings, Architectural

Clarendon Gallery. 8 Vigo Street, London, W1. Tel 439 4557.

Gallery Lingard. 50 Pall Mall, London, SW1Y 5JQ. Tel 930 1645.

Manspace Gallery. 64 Clifton Hill, London, NW8. Tel 624 4110.

Weinreb Architectural Gallery. 36 Store Street, London, WC1E 7BS. Tel 636 4895.

Drawings, Artists

Didier Aaron (London) Ltd. 21 Ryder St, London, SW1Y 6PX. Tel 839 4716/7.

AIR Gallery. 6 & 8 Rosebery Ave, London, EC1. Tel 278 7751.

Aquarelle of St Giles. 8 The Lagger, Chalfont St Giles, Buckinghamshire, HP8 4DG. Tel 5592.

Beaulieu Fine Arts. High St, Beaulieu, Hampshire. Tel 612089.

Browse & Darby Ltd. 19 Cork St, London, W1. Tel 734 7984.

Connaught Brown PLC. 2 Albemarle St, London, W1X 3HF. Tel 408 0362.

Anthony d'Offay Gallery. 9 & 23 Dering St, New Bond St, London, W1. Tel 499 4100.

The Dean Gallery. 42 Dean St, Newcastle upon Tyne, Tyne & Wear, NE1 1PG. Tel 321208.

Ewhurst Gallery. Ramsdell, Basingstoke, Hampshire, RG26 5RG. Tel 850051.

Jocelyn Feilding Fine Art Ltd. 8 Duke St, St James's, London, SW1. Tel 839 5040.

Fine Art Gallery. 41 Dundas St, Edinburgh, Lothian, EH3 6QQ. Tel 557 4569.

The Fine Art Society Plc. 148 New Bond St, London, W1Y 0JT. Tel 629 5116.

Julian Hartnoll. 14 Mason's Yard, Duke St,St James's, London, SW1. Tel 839 3842.

Marina Henderson. 11 Langton St, London, SW10. Tel 352 1667.

JPL Fine Arts. 24 Davies St, London, W1Y 1LH. Tel 493 2630.

Rodney Kent. West Park Antiques Pavilion,20 West Park, Harrogate, N.Yorkshire. Tel 60352 (priv 523766).

Lumley Cazalet Ltd. 24 Davies St, London, W1. Tel 499 5058.

Maas Gallery. 15A Clifford St, New Bond St, London, W1X 1RF. Tel 734 2302.

Marlborough Fine Art (London) Ltd. 6 Albemarle St, London, W1X 4BY. Tel 629 5161.

Mercury Gallery Ltd. 26 Cork St, London, W1. Tel 734 7800.

Moss Galleries. 2 Prebend Gardens, Chiswick, London, W4. Tel 994 2099.

Colin Murdoch. 56 High St, Kingussie, Highland, PH21 1HZ. Tel 552.

Heather Newman Gallery. Milidduwa, Cranham, Painswick, Gloucestershire, GL6 6TX. Tel 812230.

Old Drawings Gallery. 15 King St,St James's, London, SW1Y 6QU. Tel 930 7462 (priv 624 9045).

Oscar & Peter Johnson Ltd. Lowndes Lodge Gallery, 27 Lowndes St, London, SW1. Tel 235 6464,.

John F.C. Phillips. 92 Rossiter Rd, London, SW12. Tel 673 5150.

Pym's Gallery. 13 Motcomb St, Belgravia, London, SW1X 8LB. Tel 235 3050.

Alex Reid & Lefevre Ltd. 30 Bruton St, London, W1. Tel 493 1572.

Paul Rich Fine Art. Brick Cottage, Lower Woodend, Marlow, Buckinghamshire, SL7 2HN. Tel 2665.

Schidlof Galleries. 1 Holland Park Ct, Holland Park Gdns, London, W14. Tel 603 9480.

St Helier Galleries Ltd. Les Ormes, Ville au Bas, St Ouen, Jersey. Tel 82332.

James H.Starkey Galleries. 49 Highgate, Beverley, Hull, Humberside, HU17 9ON. Tel 881179.

Trim Bridge Galleries. 2 Trim Bridge, Bath, Avon. Tel 66390.

John Tuckey, Bogan House Gallery. 43 High St, Totnes, Devon. Tel 862025.

Warrack & Perkins. Rectory Farm House, Church Enstone, Oxfordshire, OX7 4NN. Tel Enstone (060 872) 572.

William Weston Gallery Ltd. 7 Royal Arcade, Albemarle St, London, W1X 3HD. Tel 493 0722.

Wildenstein & Co Ltd. 147 New Bond St, London, W1Y 0NX. Tel 629 0602.

Christopher Wood Gallery. 15 Motcomb St, London, SW1. Tel 235 9141 (priv 828 1092).

Andrew Wyld. 17 Clifford St, London, W1X 1RG. Tel 734 5575/5576.

Xanthus Gallery. September Cottage, Reymerston, Norfolk, NR9 4AG. Tel Dereham (0362) 850862.

Drawings, Caricatures

see Caricatures

Drawings, Old Master

Abbott & Holder. 73 Castelnau, Barnes, London, SW13. Tel 748 2416.

Thos Agnew & Sons Ltd. 43 Old Bond St, London, W1X 4BA. Tel 629 6176.

Artemis Fine Arts (UK) Limited. 15 Duke St,St. James's, London, SW1. Tel 930 1523.

Baskett & Day. 173 New Bond St, London, W1. Tel 629 2991.

Joanna Booth. 247 King's Rd, London, SW3. Tel 352 8998.

Chaucer Fine Arts Inc. 45 Pimlico Rd, London, SW1. Tel 730 2972.

P. & D. Colnaghi & Co Ltd. 14 Old Bond St, London, W1X 4JL. Tel 491 7408.

Richard Day Ltd. 173 New Bond St, London, W1. Tel 629 2991, 493 7569.

Douwes Fine Art Ltd. 38 Duke St, St James's, London, SW1Y 6DF. Tel 839 5795.

Duits Ltd. 104 Wigmore St, London, W1. Tel 629 5571.

Andrew Edmunds. 44 Lexington St, London, W1R 3LH. Tel 437 8594.

D.Ira Gale. 42c South Audley St, Adams Row, London, W1Y 5DH. Tel 499 2030.

Hazlitt, Gooden & Fox. 38 Bury St,St James's, London, SW1. Tel 930 6422.

Hobhouse Ltd. 39 Duke St, St James's, London, SW1 6DF. Tel 930 9308.

The Maclean Gallery. 49 Drayton Gardens, London, SW10. Tel 373 2867.

Christopher Mendez. 58 Jermyn St, London, SW1Y 6LP. Tel 491 0015.

Metcalfe Jackson. 24A West St, Wimborne Minster, Dorset, BH21 1JS. Tel 883327.

Morton Morris & Co. 32 Bury St, St James's, London, SW1. Tel 930 2825.

Old Drawings Gallery. 15 King St,St James's, London, SW1Y 6QU. Tel 930 7462 (priv 624 9045).

Annabel Popovic. 15 Ranelagh Grove, London, SW1. Tel 730 3327.

Anthony Reed Gallery. 3 Cork St, First Floor, London, W1X 1HA. Tel 437 0157.

Paul Rich Fine Art. Brick Cottage, Lower Woodend, Marlow, Buckinghamshire, SL7 2HN. Tel 2665.

Jane Roberts & Robert Alderman. 2nd Floor,180 New Bond St, London, W1Y 9PD. Tel 491 0168.

Somerville & Simpson Ltd. 11 Savile Row, London, W1. Tel 437 5414.

Marshall Spink Ltd. 18 Albemarle St, London, W1X 3HA. Tel 493 2575 and 493 5280.

James H.Starkey Galleries. 49 Highgate, Beverley, Hull, Humberside, HU17 9ON. Tel 881179.

Robin Symes. 3 Ormond Yard,Duke of York St, St James's, London, SW1. Tel 930 9856/7.

Michael Tollemache Ltd. 78 Cadogan P1, London, SW1. Tel 235 5107.

Wildenstein & Co Ltd. 147 New Bond St, London, W1Y 0NX. Tel 629 0602.

Enamels

see also Cloisonne

Albert Amor Ltd. 37 Bury St, St James's, London, SW1Y 6AU. Tel 930 2444.

D.J.Jewellery. 166-168 Ashley Rd, Parkstone, Poole, Dorset, BH14 9BY. Tel 745148.

M.Ekstein Ltd. 90 Jermyn St, London, SW1Y 6JD. Tel 930 2024.

Eliot Antiques. Stanford Dingley, Reading, Berkshire, RG7 6LX. Tel Bradfield (0734) 744649 (priv 744346).

The Golden Past. 6 Brook St, London, W1Y 1AA. Tel 493 6422.

Graus Antiques. 125 New Bond St, London, W1Y 9AF. Tel 629 6680, 629 6651.

M.Hakim. 4 The Royal Arcade, Old Bond St, London, W1X 3HD. Tel 629 6243.

Halcyon Days. 14 Brook St, London, W1Y 1AA. Tel 629 8811.

Klaber & Klaber. 2A Bedford Gdns,Kensington Church St, London, W8 7EH. Tel 727 4573.

D.M.&P.Manheim (Peter Manheim) Ltd. 69 Upper Berkeley St, Portman Sq, London, W1H 7DH. Tel 723 6595 (Priv 340 9211).

Mrs David Manheim. 69 Upper Berkeley St, Portman Sq, London, W1H 7DH. Tel 723 6595.

S.J. Phillips Ltd. 139 New Bond St, London, W1A 3DL. Tel 629 6261, 629 6262.

Edward Salti Ltd. 77 Wellesley Court,Maida Vale, London, W9. Tel 286 3106.

Scott Cooper Ltd. 52 The Promenade, Cheltenham, Gloucestershire, GL50 1LY. Tel 522580.

South Audley Art Galleries Ltd. 36 South Audley St, London, W1Y 5DH. Tel 499 3178, 499 3195.

Simon Spero. 109 Kensington Church Street, London, W8. Tel 727 7413.

Tessiers. 26 New Bond St, London, W1Y 0JY. Tel 629 0458.

Sue & Alan Thompson. 15 Flood Street, London, SW3. Tel 352 3494.

Wartski Ltd. 14 Grafton St, London, W1. Tel 493 1141/2/3.

Winifred Williams. 3 Bury St, St James's, London, SW1. Tel 930 4732.

Ephemera

see also Newspapers

Albert's of Kensington. 110 Campden Hill Rd, London, W8 7AR. Tel 221 4216.

Angus Antiques. 4 St Andrews St, Dundee, Tayside. Tel 22128.

Bottles & Bygones. 96 Horsefair St, Charlton Kings, Cheltenham, Gloucestershire. Tel 236393.

Brown Jack Bookshop. 78 Main St, Lubenham, Market Harborough, Leicestershire. Tel 65787.

Castaside. Shop 19, Chelsea Antique Market,253 King's Rd, London, SW3. Tel 352 9695.

The Coin & Stamp Centre. 13 Centurion House (1st floor),St John's St, Colchester, Essex, CO2 7AH. Tel 41232 (priv 579345).

Commemoratives. 3 Pierrepont Arcade, Camden Passage,Islington, London, N1. Tel eves only 278 2146.

Discovery. Chelsea Antique Market,245-253 King's Rd, London, SW3. Tel 352 9695.

Dodo. 3 Denbigh Rd, London, W11. Tel 229 3132.

Fox & Co. 30 Princes St, Yeovil, Somerset. Tel 72323.

John Hall. 31 Epple Rd, London, SW6 4DJ. Tel 736 3542.

Intercol London. 1A Camden Walk, Islington Green, London, N1. Tel 354 2599 (priv 349 2207).

Paul D. Lipson. 67 Cambridge St, Aylesbury, Buckinghamshire. Tel 89535.

London Cigarette Card Co Ltd. Sutton Rd, Somerton, Somerset, TA11 6QP. Tel 73452.

Ed Mason. Shop 5 Chelsea Antique Market,253 King's Rd, London, SW3. Tel 352 9695.

Nanbooks. Undercliffe Cottage, Duke St, Settle, N.Yorkshire, BD24 9DJ. Tel 3324 (priv 04685-551).

Pall Mall Antiques. 104c & 104d Elm Rd, Leigh-on-Sea, Essex. Tel Southend-on-Sea (0702) 77235.

Spon End Antiques. 115-116 Spon End, Coventry, W.Midlands, CV1 3HF. Tel 28379.

Spread Eagle Antiques. 22-23 Nelson Rd, London, SE10. Tel 858 9713, 692 1618.

Peter Stockham at Images. 16 Cecil Court, Charing Cross Rd, London, WC2. Tel 836 8661.

Taurus Gallery. 5 Wadham Rd, Putney, London, SW15 2LS. Tel 874 2534.

Vale. 21 Tranquil Vale, Blackheath, London, SE3 0BU. Tel 852 9817.

Warwick & Warwick Ltd. Arbon House, 21 Jury St, Warwick, Warwickshire. Tel 499031.

Yesterday's Paper. 5 Cornhillgate, Wellington, Somerset.

Etchings

see also Prints

Beaulieu Fine Arts. High St, Beaulieu, Hampshire. Tel 612089.

Calton Gallery. 10 Royal Terrace, Edinburgh, Lothian, EH7 5AB. Tel 556 1010.

The Collectors Trail. St Francis Rd, Indian Queens, Cornwall. Tel St.Austell (0726) 860338.

The Corner Shop. 5 St John's Place, Hay-on-Wye, Hereford & Worcester. Tel 820045.

Craddock & Barnard. 32 Museum St, London, WC1A 1LN. Tel 636 3937.

The Dean Gallery. 42 Dean St, Newcastle upon Tyne, Tyne & Wear, NE1 1PG. Tel 321208.

John Denham Gallery. 50 Mill Lane, London, NW6. Tel 794 2635.

Douwes Fine Art Ltd. 38 Duke St, St James's, London, SW1Y 6DF. Tel 839 5795.

Folio (Clevedon Books & Clevedon Fine Arts). The Gallery, Cinema Buildings,Old Church Rd, Clevedon, Avon, BS21 6NN. Tel 875862 (priv 872304).

The Gallery No.10. 10 Bangor Rd, Groomsport, Co Down. Tel Bangor (0247) 464376.

Garton & Cooke. 9 Lancashire Court, New Bond St, London, W1Y 9AD. Tel 493 2820.

Hammond Smith. Beaumont House, 24 Knighton Drive, Leicester, Leicestershire, LE2 3HB. Tel 709020.

Henry-Brett Galleries. Halford House, Bourton-on-the-Water, Gloucestershire. Tel 20443 (priv 028 574 433).

The Barry M. Keene Gallery. 12 Thameside, Henley-on-Thames, Oxfordshire, RG9 1RY. Tel 577119.

Litchfield Gallery. 1062 Christchurch Rd, East Boscombe, Bournemouth, Dorset. Tel 45454.

N.W.Lott & H.J.Gerrish Ltd. The Old Rectory, Froxfield, Wiltshire, SN8 3JY. Tel Hungerford (0488) 82188.

N.W.Lott & H.J.Gerrish Ltd. 14 Mason's Yard,Duke Street St James's, London, SW1. Tel 930 1353.

Mark Gallery. 9 Porchester Place, Marble Arch, London, W2 2BS. Tel 262 4906.

Christopher Mendez. 58 Jermyn St, London, SW1Y 6LP. Tel 491 0015.

Royal Exchange Art Gallery. 14 Royal Exchange, London, EC3V 3LL. Tel 283 4400.

Carole Thomas Fine Arts. First Floor,32A Sun St, Hitchin, Hertfordshire, SJ5 1AH. Tel 36077.

Welbeck Gallery. 18 Thayer St, London, W1M 5LD. Tel 935 4825 (priv 340 7130).

West Gate Fine Art. 16 St Peter St, Canterbury, Kent, CT1 2BQ. Tel 453636 (priv 03043 62093).

The Wyllie Gallery. 12 Needham Road, London, W11. Tel 727 0606 (priv 584 6024).

Ethnographical and Pre-Columbian Items

The Antique Textile Company. 100 Portland Rd, London, W11. Tel 221 7730.

The Arcade Gallery. 15 Royal Arcade, 28 Old Bond St, London, W1X3HD. Tel 493 1879 (priv 492 1706).

Ian Auld. 1 Gateway Arcade, Camden Passage, London, N1. Tel 359 1440.

Berkeley Galleries Ltd. 82 The Hall, Foxes Dale, London, SE3. Tel 852 0586.

Robert Copperfield Antiques. 47-49 Mill Lane, Macclesfield, Cheshire, SK10 7NP. Tel 26620.

R.O. & F. Coyle. 10 Holland St,Kensington, London, W8 4LT. Tel 937 3723.

Elgin Antiques. 121-123 Portobello Rd, London, W11. Tel 727 9852.

Robert Hales Antiques Ltd. 133 Kensington Church St, London, W8 7LP. Tel 229 3887.

Peter Hancock. 40-41 West St, Chichester, W.Sussex, PO19 1RP. Tel 786173.

John Meredith Antiques. 36 The Square, Chagford, Devon. Tel 3474 (priv 3405).

Monarch Antiques. 15 High St, Glastonbury, Somerset. Tel 32498.

Richard & Pamela Nadin. 12 Paul St, Frome, Somerset, BA11 1DT. Tel 64957.

Old Barn. Perran-ar-worthal, Truro, Cornwall, TR3 7NY. Tel 863831.

Talisman. 363/4 Gray's Antique Market,58 Davies St, London, W1. Tel 409 2743.

Faberge

see also Russian Works of Art

Arenski. 29-31 George St, London, W1H 5PE. Tel 486 0678.

Asprey PLC. 165-169 New Bond St, London, W1Y 0AR. Tel 493 6767.

Maurice Asprey Ltd. 41 Duke St, St James's, London, SW1. Tel 930 3921.

Bentley & Co Ltd. 65 New Bond St, London, W1Y 9DF. Tel 629 0651, 629 0325.

Ermitage Ltd. 14 Hay Hill, London, W1X 7LJ. Tel 499 5459.

Grey-Harris & Co. 12 Princess Victoria St,Clifton, Bristol, Avon. Tel 737365.

M.Hakim. 4 The Royal Arcade, Old Bond St, London, W1X 3HD. Tel 629 6243.

I.J.Mazure & Co Ltd. 90 Jermyn St, London, SW1Y 6JD. Tel 839 3101/2.

Wartski Ltd. 14 Grafton St, London, W1. Tel 493 1141/2/3.

Directory Entries are Free and ADDITIONS OR CORRECTIONS will be welcomed by *THE EDITOR, British Art and Antiques Directory, National Magazine House, 72 Broadwick Street, London W1V 2BP*

Faience

see Pottery and Porcelain

Fans

At the Sign of the Herald Angel. 19 Park St, Cirencester, Gloucestershire, GL7 2BX. Tel 2972.

Cherry Antiques. 101-103 High St, Hemel Hempstead, Hertfordshire. Tel 64358.

Janet Maund. Cheltenham Antique Market, Cheltenham, Gloucestershire, GL3 1HA. Tel 529812 (priv 0452 712286).

Sheila Smith Antiques. 10A Queen St, Bath, Avon. Tel 60568 (priv 0373 830217).

Willcocks Antiques. Chenil Galleries, 183 King's Rd,Chelsea, London, SW3. Tel 352 8653.

Fire-irons and Fenders

see also Brass, Ironwork

Acquisitions (Fireplaces) Ltd. 269 Camden High St, London, NW1 7BX. Tel 485 4955.

Antique Metals. 12 East St, Coggeshall, Essex, Co6 1SH. Tel 62252.

Ashburton Marbles. 6 West St, Ashburton, Devon, TQ13 7DU. Tel 53189 (priv 0626 833934).

B.E.L.Products Ltd Inc.B.E.L.Tradepoint. 302 Windsor St, Nechells, Birmingham, W.Midlands, B7 4DW. Tel 359 7791.

Jack Casimir Ltd. 'The Brass Shop', 23 Pembridge Rd, London, W11 3HG. Tel 727 8643.

J. & J. Caspall Antiques. Sheep St, Stow-on-the-Wold, Gloucestershire. Tel 31160.

T.Crowther & Son Ltd. 282 North End Rd, Fulham, London, SW6 1NH. Tel 385 1375/7.

The Fire Place (Hungerford) Ltd. Hungerford Old Fire Station, Hungerford, Berkshire, RG17 0EP. Tel 83420.

Grosvenor House Interiors. 51 Wycombe End, Beaconsfield, Buckinghamshire. Tel 77498.

Halliday's (Antiques). 28 Beauchamp Place, London, SW3. Tel 589 5534.

Hallidays Antiques Ltd. The Old College, High St, Dorchester, Oxfordshire. Tel Oxford (0865) 340028.

Lancashire Bygones. 12 Parliament St, Up Holland, Wigan, Greater Manchester, WN8 0LN. Tel Up Holland (0695) 625624 (priv 0695 622458).

Bertram Noller (Reigate). 14A London Rd, Reigate, Surrey. Tel 42548.

Oddiquities. 61 Waldram Park Rd, London, SE23. Tel 699 9574.

Old World Trading Company. 565 Kings Rd, London, SW6. Tel 731 4708.

R.J.Perry Antiques. 38 Bridge St, Hitchin, Hertfordshire, SG5 2DF. Tel 34525 (priv 0582-25546).

H.W.Poulter & Son. 279 Fulham Rd, London, SW10 9PZ. Tel 352 7268 (priv 603 7398).

Sundial Antiques. 19 Whielden St, Amersham, Buckinghamshire, HP7 0HU. Tel 7955.

Thistledome Antiques. Kings Arms Yard, Ampthill, Bedfordshire, MK45. Tel 403394 (priv 717368).

Thornhill Galleries Ltd. 76 New Kings Rd, London, SW6. Tel 736 5830.

Tucker & Langs. Kings Head Court,High St, Dorking, Surrey. Tel 882203.

George Wright (Rotherham) Ltd. The Crofts, Rotherham, S.Yorkshire, S60 2DJ. Tel 63871.

Fireplaces

Robert Aagaard Ltd. Frogmire House, Stockwell Rd, Knaresborough, N.Yorkshire, HG5 0JP. Tel Harrogate (0423) 864805.

Acquisitions (Fireplaces) Ltd. 269 Camden High St, London, NW1 7BX. Tel 485 4955.

George Amos & Sons (CB) Ltd. 73 Leonard St, London, EC2. Tel 739 0448.

Architectural Antiques Ltd. 133 Upper St, London, N1. Tel 226 5565.

Ashburton Marbles. 6 West St, Ashburton, Devon, TQ13 7DU. Tel 53189 (priv 0626 833934).

Baileys Architectural Antiques. The Engine Shed,Ashburton Industrial Estate, Ross-on-Wye, Hereford & Worcester, HR9 7BW. Tel 63015.

Nigel Bartlett. 67 St.Thomas St, London, SE1. Tel 378-7895/6.

David Bridgwater. 14 Fountain Buildings,Lansdown Road, Bath, Avon. Tel 63652.

Combe Cottage Antiques. Castle Combe, Wiltshire, SN14 7HU. Tel 782250.

Cooke Antiques. 79/85 Francis St, Dublin, Co Dublin. Tel 751885, 751250, 752251.

Crowther of Syon Lodge. Syon Lodge, Busch Corner,London Rd, Isleworth, Middlesex, TW7 5BH. Tel 560 7978, 560 7985.

T.Crowther & Son Ltd. 282 North End Rd, Fulham, London, SW6 1NH. Tel 385 1375/7.

John Derham Ltd/Earsham Hall Pine. Earsham Hall, Bungay, Suffolk, NR35 2AN. Tel 3423.

Doveridge House of Neachley. Neach Hill, Long Lane, Shifnal, Shropshire. Tel Albrighton (090 722) 3131, 3132.

The Fire Place (Hungerford) Ltd. Hungerford Old Fire Station, Hungerford, Berkshire, RG17 0EP. Tel 83420.

Grosvenor House Interiors. 51 Wycombe End, Beaconsfield, Buckinghamshire. Tel 77498.

Halliday's (Antiques). 28 Beauchamp Place, London, SW3. Tel 589 5534.

Hallidays Antiques Ltd. The Old College, High St, Dorchester, Oxfordshire. Tel Oxford (0865) 340028.

Julian Antiques. 124 High St, Hurstpierpoint, W.Sussex. Tel 832145.

Julian Antiques. 67 Park Rd, London, NW1. Tel 723 0653.

Knight's of London. 2a Belsize Park Mews,Belsize Village, London, NW3 5BL. Tel 431 2490.

The London Architectural Salvage & Supply Co Ltd. The Mark St Depository, Mark St,off Paul St, London, EC2A 4ER. Tel 739 0448.

Marble Hill Gallery. 72 Richmond Rd, Twickenham, Middlesex, TW1 3BE. Tel 892 1488.

Mitchell Antiques Ltd. 40 Clarendon St, Dublin, Co Dublin. Tel 773922.

The Mount Antiques. Khyber Pass, Whitby, N.Yorkshire. Tel 604516.

Bertram Noller (Reigate). 14A London Rd, Reigate, Surrey. Tel 42548.

Oddiquities. 61 Waldram Park Rd, London, SE23. Tel 699 9574.

Old World Trading Company. 565 Kings Rd, London, SW6. Tel 731 4708.

Pageant Antiques. 122 Dawes Rd, London, W14. Tel 385 7739.

H.W.Poulter & Son. 279 Fulham Rd, London, SW10 9PZ. Tel 352 7268 (priv 603 7398).

Thornhill Galleries Ltd. 76 New Kings Rd, London, SW6. Tel 736 5830.

Townsends. 1 Church St, London, NW8. Tel 724 3746 & 624 4756.

Townsends. Showroom: 36 New End Square,Hampstead Village, London, NW3. Tel 794 5706/5707.

V.K. and R. Antiques. 8 High St, Potterne, Wiltshire. Tel Devizes (0380) 3933.

Walcot Reclamation. 108 Walcot St, Bath, Avon, BA1 5BG. Tel 66291/2.

Whiteway & Waldron. 305 Munster Rd, London, SW6. Tel 381 3195.

O.F.Wilson. Queen's Elm Parade,Fulham Rd, London, SW3 6EJ. Tel 352 9554 (priv 373 4602).

George Wright (Rotherham) Ltd. The Crofts, Rotherham, S.Yorkshire, S60 2DJ. Tel 63871.

Folk Art

see also Furniture, Painted

R.O. & F. Coyle. 10 Holland St,Kensington, London, W8 4LT. Tel 937 3723.

Richard & Pamela Nadin. 12 Paul St, Frome, Somerset, BA11 1DT. Tel 64957.

Richard & Pamela Nadin. 5 Woolley St, Bradford-on-Avon, Wiltshire, BA15 1AD. Tel 2476.

Piccadilly Antiques. 1/2 Piccadilly,London Rd, Bath, Avon, BA1 6AN. Tel 332779.

Robert Young Antiques. 68 Battersea Bridge Rd, London, SW11. Tel 228 7847.

Fossils

see Minerals

Frames and Framing

London

Academy Framing. Royal Academy of Arts,Burlington House, Piccadilly, London, W1V 0DS. Tel 734 9052 (priv 437 8472).

Addison-Ross Gallery. 40 Eaton Tce, Belgravia, London, SW1. Tel 730 1536.

Alton Gallery. 72 Church Rd,Barnes, London, SW13. Tel 748 0606,748 8244.

Mario Ascione. 53 Moreton St,(Basement), London, SW1.

John Campbell Picture Frames Ltd. 164 Walton St, Knightsbridge, London, SW3 2JL. Tel 584 9268.

Michael Carleton. 77-81 Haverstock Hill, London, NW3 4SL. Tel 722 2277, 586 4458.

John Davies Framing Ltd. 8 Bury St,St. James's, London, SW1.

Alec Drew Picture Frames Ltd. 7 Cale St, Chelsea Green, London, SW3. Tel 352 8716.

Andrew Edmunds. 44 Lexington St, London, W1R 3LH. Tel 437 8594.

Gallery 181. 181 King's Rd, London, SW6. Tel 736 1955.

David E.Green Gallery. 188 Dartmouth Rd, London, SE26. Tel 699 5461.

Konig Newton Ltd. 27 The Talina Centre,Bagley's Lane, Fulham, London, SW6. Tel 736 0915.

The Map House. 54 Beauchamp Place, Knightsbridge, London, SW3. Tel 589 4325, 589 9821.

Paul Mitchell. 99 New Bond Street, London, W1. Tel 493 8732/0860.

Mitre Frames. 112 Fortune Green Rd, London, NW6 1DH. Tel 794 9569.

O'Shea Gallery. 89 Lower Sloane St,Belgravia, London, SW1 8DA. Tel 730 0081, 730 0082.

H.J. Spiller Ltd. 37-39 Beak St, London, W1R 3LD. Tel 437 4661.

The Stable Shop and Gallery. 22B Bellevue Rd, Wandsworth Common, London, SW17. Tel 767 4688 (priv 673 1642).

John Tanous Ltd. 115a & 115b Harwood Rd, Fulham, London, SW6 4QL. Tel 736 7999.

The Warwick Leadlay Gallery. 5 Nelson Rd, Greenwich, London, SE10 9JB. Tel 858 0317 (priv 852 7484).

Edna Whiteson Ltd. 66 Belmont Ave, London, EN4 9LA. Tel 449 8860.

Arnold Wiggins & Sons Ltd. 30-34 Woodfield Place,Harrow Rd, London, W9 2BJ. Tel 286 9656.

Regions

Affordable Arts. 76 Colston St, Bristol, Avon, BS1 5BB. Tel 24838.

Astley House - Fine Art. Astley House, High St, Moreton-in-Marsh, Gloucestershire, GL54 0LL. Tel 50601.

James Atkinson Gallery. 38 King St, Sandwich, Kent, CT13 9BL. Tel 617216 (priv 613298).

Bourne Frames & Restoration Ltd. 79 Cumberland St, Edinburgh, Lothian, EH3 6RD. Tel 557 4874.

Clare Gallery. 21 High St, Tunbridge Wells, Kent. Tel 38717.

The Coach House. The Coach House, Townhouse Rd, Old Costessey, Norfolk, NR8 5BX. Tel Norwich (0603) 742977.

Cotswold Galleries. The Square, Stow-on-the-Wold, Gloucestershire, GL54 1AB. Tel 30586.

The Court Gallery. 16 Bridge Rd, East Molesey, Surrey. Tel 941 2212.

Heather Cowley Bookshop & Galleries. 235-237 Mansfield Rd, Nottingham, Nottinghamshire. Tel 473836.

David Cross Gallery. 3A Boyces Ave, Clifton, Bristol, Avon, BS8 4AA. Tel 732614.

Curiosities. 152 South St, Lancing, W.Sussex, BN15 8AU. Tel 752670 (priv 0273 454669).

Dolphyn. 8 Market End, Coggeshall, Essex, CO6 1NP. Tel 61608.

Exquisite Arts Ltd. 22 Bore St, Lichfield, Staffordshire. Tel 253626, (priv 253697).

The Gallery No.10. 10 Bangor Rd, Groomsport, Co Down. Tel Bangor (0247) 464376.

Gallery 77. 18 Princess St, Bradshawgate, Bolton, Greater Manchester, BL1 1EJ. Tel 35252.

Godalming Galleries Ltd. 3 Wharf St, Godalming, Surrey, GU7 1NN. Tel 22254.

The Grange Gallery & Fine Arts Ltd. 39 New St, St Helier, Jersey.

W.Greenwood. 7 Church Wynd,Burneston, Bedale, N.Yorkshire. Tel 24830.

Guildford Galleries Ltd. Cranley Court, 59 Cranley Rd, Guildford, Surrey, GU1 2JW. Tel 61646.

The Hampton Hill Gallery Ltd. 203-205 High St, Hampton Hill, Middlesex, TW12 1NP. Tel 977 1379.

Hiscock Gallery. 11 Stanley St, Southsea, Hampshire. Tel 825330.

Clare Hutchison. 1 Sandgate High St,Sandgate, Folkestone, Kent. Tel Hythe (0303) 64864.

Jays Fine Art Dealers. Cambridge Gallery,4 Cambridge Arcade, Southport, Merseyside, PR8 1AS. Tel 34488 (priv 69500).

The Barry M. Keene Gallery. 12 Thameside, Henley-on-Thames, Oxfordshire, RG9 1RY. Tel 577119.

Kendal Studio Pottery. 2-3 Wildman St, Kendal, Cumbria, LA9 6EN. Tel 23291.

Kenulf Gallery. High St, Winchcombe, Gloucestershire, GL54 5LJ. Tel 602124.

Kirkgate Picture Gallery. 18 Kirkgate, Thirsk, N.Yorkshire, YO7 1PQ. Tel 24085.

Lacy Gallery. 56 High St, Henley-in-Arden, Warwickshire. Tel 3073.

Langley Galleries. 153 High St, Rochester, Kent. Tel Medway (0634) 811802.

The Lyver and Boydell Galleries. 15 Castle St, Liverpool, Merseyside, L2 4SX. Tel 236 3256.

J.Manley & Thames Gallery. 27 High St, Eton, Berkshire. Tel Windsor (0753) 865647.

The William Marler Gallery. 36/38 Dyer St, Cirencester, Gloucestershire, GL7 2PF. Tel 68526.

Sally Mitchell Fine Arts. Thornlea, Askham, Nottinghamshire, NG22 0RN. Tel Gamston (077783) 234.

John Owen Gallery. 20 Salisbury Rd, Cardiff, S.Glamorgan, CF2 4AD. Tel 45868 (priv 04463 2767).

A.J.Ponsford Antiques and Restorations. 51-53 Dollar St, Cirencester, Gloucestershire, GL7 2AS. Tel 2355.

Printed Page. 2-3 Bridge St, Winchester, Hampshire, SO23 9BH. Tel 54072 (priv 62995).

Priory Gallery. The Priory, Station Rd,Bishops Cleeve, Cheltenham, Gloucestershire. Tel Bishops Cleeve (024 267) 3226.

R.S.J. Savage & Son. Alfred St, Northampton, Northamptonshire, NN1 5EY. Tel 33852 (priv 405482).

Shaw's Bookshop Ltd. 11 Police St, Manchester, Greater Manchester, M2 7LQ. Tel 834-7587.

Shelton Mounting Service. 4 Islingword Rd, Brighton & Hove, E.Sussex, BN2 2SE. Tel 698345.

Stewart Gallery. 48 Devonshire Rd, Bexhill, E.Sussex. Tel 223410.

Stewart Gallery. 25 Grove Rd, Eastbourne, E.Sussex. Tel 29588.

Sutcliffe Galleries. 8 Albert St, Harrogate, N.Yorkshire. Tel 62976.

Thornbury Antique Framers and Restorers. 32 High St, Thornbury, Avon, BS12 2A. Tel 413595.

Top Hat Antiques Centre & Fine Art Gallery. 72 Derby Rd, Nottingham, Nottinghamshire. Tel 419143.

Michael Webb Fine Paintings. Cefn-Llwyn,Llangristiolus, Bodorgan, Anglesey, Gwynedd, LL62 5DN. Tel Bodorgan (0407) 840336.

Wellington Fine Art. 14 Park Circus, Glasgow, Strathclyde, G3 6AX. Tel 331 2896.

West Gate Fine Art. 16 St Peter St, Canterbury, Kent, CT1 2BQ. Tel 453636 (priv 03043 62093).

Whisstock's. 9 Catherine Hill, Frome, Somerset. Tel 63289.

Wigington Partners. 22 New St, Shipston on Stour, Warwickshire, CV36 4EN. Tel 61205.

David Windsor Gallery. 201 High St, Bangor, Gwynedd. Tel 364639.

Furniture Fittings

Allens. Moor Farm, Stapleford, Lincolnshire. Tel Bassingham (052 285) 392.

B.E.L.Products Ltd Inc.B.E.L.Tradepoint. 302 Windsor St, Nechells, Birmingham, W.Midlands, B7 4DW. Tel 359 7791.

John Boddy's Fine Wood & Tool Store Ltd. Riverside Sawmills, Boroughbridge, N.Yorkshire, YO5 9LJ. Tel 2370.

G.E.Day. 82 West St, Farnham, Surrey, GU9 7EN. Tel 715 043.

Josiah Parkes & Sons Ltd. Union Works, Gower St, Willenhall, W.Midlands, WV13 1JX. Tel 66931.

Knobs. 155 North Ninth St, Milton Keynes, Buckinghamshire, MK9 3AW. Tel 605465.

Malvern Studios. 56 Cowleigh Rd, North Malvern, Malvern, Hereford & Worcester, WR14 1QD. Tel 4913.

Martin & Co Ltd. 97 Camden St, Birmingham, W.Midlands. Tel 233 2111.

Pitcher Pine Antiques. Lion Yard,Broad Street, Leominster, Hereford & Worcester. Tel 3361.

A.J.Ponsford Antiques and Restorations. 51-53 Dollar St, Cirencester, Gloucestershire, GL7 2AS. Tel 2355.

Weaves and Waxes. 53 Church St, Bloxham, Banbury, Oxfordshire, OX15 4ET. Tel 721535.

Furniture, British

London

Adams Antiques. 47 Chalk Farm Rd, London, NW1. Tel 267 9241.

David Alexander Antiques. 102 Waterford Rd, London, SW6. Tel 731 4644.

John Allsopp Antiques. 26 Pimlico Rd, London, SW1W 8LJ. Tel 730 9347.

The Antique Gallery. 40 Peckham Rye, London, SE15. Tel 732 7808 (priv 653 4279).

The Antique Home. 104A Kensington Church St, London, W8 4BU. Tel 229 5892.

The Antique Trader. 357 Upper St,Camden Passage, London, N1. Tel 359 2019.

The Badger. 12 St Mary's Rd, Ealing, London, W5 5ES. Tel 567 5601.

Alexander Bailie (Antiques). 2 Lower Mall,359 Upper St, Islington, London, N1 0PD. Tel 354 2839 (priv 354 1739).

H.C.Baxter & Sons. 191-193 Fulham Rd, London, SW3. Tel 352 9826.

John Beer. 191 Archway Road, London, N6. Tel 340 2183.

Raymond Benardout Ltd. 4 William St, Knightsbridge, London, SW1X 9HL. Tel 235 3360 (priv 235 0504).

Bennison. 91 Pimlico Rd, London, SW1. Tel 730 3370, 730 8076.

H.Blairman & Sons Ltd. 119 Mount St, London, W1. Tel 493 0444.

Bobinet Ltd. 102 Mount St, London, W1YD 5HF. Tel 408 0333/4.

Bookham Galleries. 164 Wandsworth Bridge Rd, Fulham, London, SW6. Tel 736 5125(priv 0372 52668).

Claude Bornoff. 20 Chepstow Corner, Pembridge Villas, London, W2. Tel 229 8947.

Box House Antiques. 105 Pimlico Rd, London, SW1W 8PH. Tel 730 9257.

I. & J.L. Brown. 636 Kings Rd,Chelsea, London, SW6 2DU. Tel 736 4141.

Bushwood Antiques. 317 Upper St, London, N1. Tel 359 2095.

Colefax & Fowler. 39 Brook St, London, W1Y 1AU. Tel 493 2231.

Aubrey J.Coleman Antiques. 121 Kensington Church St, London, W8 7LP. Tel 221 6228.

Philip Colleck Ltd. 84 Fulham Rd, London, SW3 6HR. Tel 584 8479.

P. & D. Colnaghi & Co Ltd. 14 Old Bond St, London, W1X 4JL. Tel 491 7408.

R. D'Alessandro. 610 Kings Rd, London, SW6. Tel 731 7160.

John Dale Antiques. 87 Portobello Rd, London, W11. Tel 727 1304.

de Havilland Antiques. 48 Sloane St, London, SW1X 9LU. Tel 235 3534.

The Dining Room Shop. 64 White Hart Lane,Barnes, London, SW13 0PZ. Tel 878 1020 (priv 876 5212).

E. & A. Antiques. 36 Ledbury Rd, London, W11. Tel 229 1823.

Eldridge London. 99-101 Farringdon Rd, London, EC1. Tel 837 0379.

Etna Antiques. 81 Kensington Church St, London, W8 4BG. Tel 937 3754.

Finchley Fine Art Galleries. 983 High Rd,North Finchley, London, N12 8QR. Tel 446 4848.

Peter Francis. 26 Museum St, London, WC1A 1JT. Tel 637 0165.

Furniture Cave. 533 King's Rd,Chelsea, London, SW10. Tel 352 2046.

Galerie 360. 564 King's Road, London, SW6. Tel 736 5160.

General Trading Co. 144 Sloane St, London, SW1X 9BL. Tel 730 0411.

Imogen Graham. 585 King's Rd, London, SW6. Tel 736 2465.

Guinevere Antiques Ltd. 578 King's Road, London, SW6. Tel 736 2917.

William Handford Antiques. 517 King's Rd, London, SW10 0TX. Tel 351 2768.

M.Harris & Sons. Gayfere House,22-23 Gayfere St, London, SW1P 3HP. Tel 222 8161.

Harrods. 87-135 Brompton Rd, London, SW1. Tel 730 1234.

W.R.Harvey & Co (Antiques) Ltd. 5 Old Bond St, London, W1. Tel 499 8385.

Haverstock Antiques. 78 Haverstock Hill, Hampstead, London, NW3 3BS. Tel 267 1627.

Helius Antiques. 487-493 Upper Richmond Rd West, London, SW14 7PU. Tel 876 5721 (priv 940 5595).

Christopher Hodsoll Antiques. 50 & 69 Pimlico Rd, London, SW1. Tel 730 9835.

Michael Hogg. 172 Brompton Rd, London, SW3. Tel 589 8629.

Howard Antiques. 8 Davies St, London, W1. Tel 629 2628.

Hymore Hodson Antiques. 181-183 King's Rd,Chelsea, London, SW3. Tel 352 9770.

Olivia Jackson Antiques. 287 Westbourne Grove, London, W11. Tel 727 2817.

Anthony James & Son Ltd. 88 Fulham Road, London, SW3. Tel 584 1120 (priv 385 3408).

Jeremy Ltd. 255 King's Rd, Chelsea, London, SW3 5EL. Tel 352 3127, 352 0644.

S. & H. Jewell Ltd. 26 Parker St, London, WC2B 5PH. Tel 405 8520.

George Johnson. 120 Kensington Park Road, London, W11 2PW. Tel 229 3119.

Just a Minute Antiques. 27 Battersea Rise, London, SW11. Tel 223 5341.

Ronald A.Lee (Fine Arts) Ltd. 1-9 Bruton Place, London, W1X 7AD. Tel 499 6266.

Lillie Antiques. 244 Lillie Rd, London, SW6 7QA. Tel 385 9852.

J.Lipitch Ltd. 177 Westbourne Grove, London, W11. Tel 229 0783.

Peter Lipitch Ltd. 120-124 Fulham Rd, London, SW3. Tel 373 3328.

Mallett & Son (Antiques) Ltd. 40 New Bond St, London, W1Y 0BS. Tel 499 7411.

Michael Marriott Ltd. 588 Fulham Rd, London, SW6 5NT. Tel 736 3110, 381 3455.

Michael & Margaret Parker. 24 Cheval Place, London, SW7. Tel 589 0133.

Partridge (Fine Arts) Ltd. 144-146 New Bond St, London, W1. Tel 629 0834.

Pelham Galleries (Est 1927). 163-165 Fulham Rd, London, SW3. Tel 589 2686.

Ronald Phillips Ltd. 26 Bruton St, London, W1X 8LH. Tel 493 2341.

John Pope & Hunts Ltd. 91 Old Brompton Rd, London, SW7. Tel 581 5375, 584 2229.

Portmeirion Antiques. 62 White Hart Lane, Barnes, London, SW13. Tel 876 2367.

Barrie Quinn Antiques. 3 & 4 Broxholme House, New King's Rd, London, SW6. Tel 736 4747.

Relcy Antiques. 9 Nelson Rd, Greenwich, London, SE10. Tel 858 2811/2.

Rendall. 572 King's Rd, London, SW6. Tel 736 2520 (priv 948 4400).

J. Roger (Antiques) Ltd. 17 Uxbridge St, London, W8. Tel 727 2227 (priv 603 7627).

Geoffrey Rose Ltd. 77 Pimlico Rd, London, SW1W 8PH. Tel 730 3004.

Patrick Sandberg Antiques. 791 Fulham Rd, London, SW6 5HD. Tel 736 9454.

Robin Sanders & Sons. 590 Fulham Rd, London, SW6. Tel 736 0586.

David Seyfried. 759 Fulham Rd, London, SW6. Tel 731 4230.

Sylvia Sheppard. 71 Kensington Church St, London, W8 4BG. Tel 937 0965.

This & That (Furniture). 50 & 51 Chalk Farm Rd, London, NW1. Tel 267 5433.

M.Turpin. 21 Manson Mews, Queensgate, London, SW7. Tel 736 3417.

Waveney Antiques. 58 & 68 Peckham Rye, London, SE15. Tel 732 1251.

O.F.Wilson. Queen's Elm Parade,Fulham Rd, London, SW3 6EJ. Tel 352 9554 (priv 373 4602).

Regions

A.& F. Partners. 20 London St, Faringdon, Oxfordshire, SN7 7AA. Tel 20078.

Ace Antiques. 40 Huddersfield Rd, Oldham, Greater Manchester, OL4 2AE. Tel 620 5755 (priv 626 2062).

Adam Antiques. 12 Sneyd St, Canton, Cardiff, S.Glamorgan. Tel 40022 (priv 0222 883415).

Addingham Antiques. 70-72 Main St, Addingham, W.Yorkshire. Tel 830788.

Ages Ago Antiques. 47-49 New Hall Lane, Preston, Lancashire. Tel 798606.

Adrian Alan Ltd. 15c Prince Albert St, Brighton & Hove, E.Sussex. Tel 25015.

Albany Antiques. 8-10 London Rd, Hindhead, Surrey. Tel 5528.

Alexander Antiques. 108 Dunluce Rd, Portrush, Co Antrim, BT56 8NB. Tel 822783.

Allen's (Branksome) Ltd. 449 Poole Rd, Branksome, Poole, Dorset, BH12 1DH. Tel 763724.

Donald Allison Antiques. 115-119 New Hall Lane, Preston, Lancashire. Tel 701916 (priv 615946).

Alpha Antiques. Church Lane, Checkley, Stoke-on-Trent, Staffordshire, ST10 4NJ. Tel Tean (0538) 722149.

F.E.Anderson & Son. 5 High St, Welshpool, Powys, SY21 7JF. Tel 3340 (priv 3324 or 75509).

Philip Andrade Ltd. White Oxen Manor, Rattery, South Brent, Devon, TQ10 9JX. Tel 2454.

Michael Andrews Antiques. Portsmouth Rd, Milford, Surrey. Tel Godalming (04868) 20765.

Angel Arcade. Portmeirion, Gwynedd. Tel Penrhyndeudraeth (0766) 770 228.

Anthony Antiques. 7 Molesworth St, Dublin, Co Dublin. Tel 777222.

Antiqcurios & Irene Fine Art. 33 Clarendon St, Dublin, Co Dublin. Tel 714932.

Antique Dealers International PLC. Bow Street, Langport, Somerset. Tel 252977.

The Antique Furniture Warehouse. Old Maltings, Crown Place, Woodbridge, Suffolk. Tel 7222.

The Antique Galleries. Watling St, Paulerspury, Northamptonshire. Tel 238.

The Antique Home. 247 London Rd, Camberley, Surrey. Tel 26412.

Antiques and Collectables. 8 Aldiss Court,High St, Dereham, Norfolk. Tel 447.

Antiques and Fine Arts (Prestwich) Ltd. Rochdale, Greater Manchester. Tel 44946.

Antiques in Charnwood. 68 Bradgate Rd, Anstey, Leicestershire. Tel 350708.

Antiques of Penrith. 4 Corney Sq, Penrith, Cumbria, CA11 7PX. Tel 62801.

Antiques Gallery. 37 Hanover St, Liverpool, Merseyside, L1 3DN. Tel 709 9529.

Apollo Galleries. 61, 65 and 67 South End, Croydon, Surrey, CR0 1BF. Tel 681 3727, 680 1968.

Brenda Arden Antiques. Hulgrave Hall,Tiverton, Tarporley, Cheshire, CW6 9UQ. Tel 2427.

James Ash Antiques. The Warehouse, Station Rd, Llandeilo, Dyfed. Tel 823728 (priv 0269 850119).

Ashleigh House Antiques. 5 Westbourne Rd,Edgbaston, Birmingham, W.Midlands, B15 3TH. Tel 454 6283.

Astley Bridge Antiques. 419-421 Blackburn Rd, Astley Bridge, Bolton, Greater Manchester, BL1 8NJ. Tel 51160 (priv 53390).

Atrium Antiques Ltd. 19 Market Place, Woburn, Bedfordshire, NK17 9PZ. Tel 444.

Augill Castle Antiques Ltd. Augill Castle, Brough, Cumbria, CA17 4AY. Tel 412.

Avon Antiques. 26-27 Market St, Bradford-on-Avon, Wiltshire. Tel 2052.

D.J. Baggott. Huntsmans Yard, Sheep Street, Stow-on-the-Wold, Gloucestershire. Tel 30662.

J. & J. Baker. 12-14 Water St, Lavenham, Suffolk. Tel 247610.

David Ball Antiques. 126A Leagrave Rd, Luton, Bedfordshire, LU4 8HX. Tel 417560 (priv 0525-210753).

The Ballroom Antiques. Swan House,Market Square, Petworth, W.Sussex. Tel 43638.

Barclay Antiques. 7 Village Mews, Little Common, Bexhill, E.Sussex. Tel Rye (0797) 222734.

Barn Antiques. Binley Common Farm,Rugby Rd, Coventry, W.Midlands. Tel 447628, 453878.

John Barry. Barton End Hall, Nailsworth, Gloucestershire, GL6 0QQ. Tel 3471.

Barton House Antiques. Barton House, 48 Wharf Rd, Stanford le Hope, Essex, SS17 0DY. Tel Stanford-le-Hope (0375) 672494.

Richard Batsford Antiques. Antique Trade Warehouse,29 Lorne Park Rd, Bournemouth, Dorset. Tel 292944 (priv 25485).

Beacon Gallery. Woburn Abbey Antiques Centre,Woburn Abbey, Woburn, Bedfordshire. Tel (priv) 062187-607.

Peter T. Beasley. Forge Yard, High St, Farningham, Kent, DA4 ODB. Tel 862453.

Michael Beaumont Antiques. Hempstead Hall,Hempstead, Saffron Walden, Essex, CB10 2PR. Tel Steeple Bumpstead(044084) 239.

John Beazor & Sons Ltd. 78-80 Regent St, Cambridge, Cambridgeshire, CB2 1DP. Tel 355178.

Margaret Bedi Antiques. The Antique Shop, 5 Station Rd, Billingham, Cleveland, TS23 1AG. Tel Stockton-on-Tees (0642) 607296.

J.& H.Bell Antiques. 22 Arbory St, Castletown,. Tel 823132 (priv 822414).

Mary Bellis Antiques. Charnham Close (A4 Highway), Hungerford, Berkshire, RG17 0EJ. Tel 82620.

R. Bennett Antiques. 6 West St, Dorking, Surrey, RH4 1BL. Tel 882828.

Benson Antiques. 13 Suffolk Parade, Cheltenham, Gloucestershire. Tel 578366.

Berkeley Antiques. Marybrook St, Berkeley, Gloucestershire. Tel Dursley (0453) 810 391.

Biggs of Maidenhead. Hare Hatch Grange, Twyford, Berkshire, RG10 9SK. Tel Wargrave (073 522) 3281 (priv 3104).

Birmingham House Antiques. Birmingham House, 8-10 Church Street, Shipston on Stour, Warwickshire, CV36 4AP. Tel 62037 (priv 029588 439).

Andrew and Linda Blackburn Antiques. 12 West St, Gargrave, N.Yorkshire, BD23 3RD. Tel 403.

The Blacksmiths Shop. High St, Brasted, Kent. Tel Westerham (0959) 63114 (priv 62589).

John Bly. 50 High St, Tring, Hertfordshire, HP23 5AG. Tel 3030.

Derek Boston Antiques. 223 Wilton Rd, Salisbury, Wiltshire. Tel 22682.

Bourne Antiques. The Old Mill,North Rd, Bourne, Lincolnshire. Tel 425323 (priv 423781).

Robert Bradley. 71 Brown St, Salisbury, Wiltshire. Tel 333677.

Braemar Antiques Ltd. Waltham Rd, White Waltham, Berkshire. Tel Littlewick Green(062 882) 3741.

Bragge & Sons. Landgate House, Rye, E.Sussex. Tel 223358.

Lesley Bragge Antiques. Fairfield House,High St, Petworth, W.Sussex. Tel 42324.

Bratton Antiques. Market Place, Westbury, Wiltshire, BA13 3DE. Tel 823021.

Simon Brett. Creswyke House, High St, Moreton-in-Marsh, Gloucestershire, GL56 0LH. Tel 50751.

Bric-a-Brac Ltd. 195 Park View, Whitley Bay, Tyne & Wear, NE26 3RD. Tel Tyneside (091) 2526141 (priv 2528508).

E. & G. Briere. Keeper's Cottage, Suffield, Norwich, Norfolk, NR11 7ER. Tel Aylsham (0263) 732651.

T.& D.Brindle Antiques. 4-8 Lynwood Rd, Blackburn, Lancashire, BB2 6HP. Tel 670714; 53628.

Bristow Antiques. Lindford Rd, Lindford, Bordon, Hampshire, GU35 OPY. Tel 2301.

British Antique Exporters Ltd. Queen Elizabeth Ave, Burgess Hill, W.Sussex, RH15 9RX. Tel 45577.

Andrew Britten. 48 High St, Malmesbury, Wiltshire, SN16 9AT. Tel 3376.

Broadway Antiques. 25 Broadway, Shifnal, Shropshire, TF11 8BB. Tel Telford (0952) 460997.

Ian J. Brook. 26 North St, Wilton, Wiltshire, SP2 OHJ. Tel Salisbury (0722) 743392.

Paul Bruce Antiques & Pine Shop. 25-27 St Helens St, Ipswich, Suffolk. Tel 55400.

C.W.Buckingham. Twin Firs, Southampton Rd, Cadnam, Hampshire, SO4 2NP. Tel Southampton (0703) 812122.

James Buckingham. School Close,Queen Elizabeth Ave, Burgess Hill, W.Sussex. Tel 45577.

David E. Burrows. 4 High St, Quorn, Leicestershire. Tel 412191.

Robin Butler. 9 St Stephen's St, Bristol, Avon, BS1. Tel 276586 (priv 662167).

Bygone Days. 40 Gold St, Tiverton, Devon, EX16 6PY. Tel 252832.

Bygones. Peirce Cottage, High St, Charing, Kent. Tel 2494.

Ian Caldwell. 9A The Green, Dorking Rd, Tadworth, Surrey, KT20 5SQ. Tel 3969.

Harry Carr Antiques. Field House,Rickleton, Washington, Tyne & Wear. Tel Chester-le-Street (0385) 886442.

Carse Antiques. Rait, by Perth, Tayside, PH2 7RT. Tel 205 (priv 227).

R.G.Cave & Sons Ltd. 17 Broad St, Ludlow, Shropshire. Tel 3568.

Chantry House Antiques. Sheep St, Stow-on-the-Wold, Gloucestershire, GL54 1AA. Tel 30450.

Chapel Antiques. 18 Gensing Rd, St Leonards, E.Sussex, TN38 0SE. Tel Hastings (0424) 440025 (priv 425487).

Mark Chapman Antiques. New Street, Petworth, W.Sussex. Tel 42283.

K.Chappell Antiques & Fine Art. King St, Bakewell, Derbyshire, DE4 1DZ. Tel 2496 (priv 2960).

K.Chappell Antiques & Fine Art. Goose Green, Baslow, Derbyshire, DE4 1SR. Tel 3311.

Charterhouse Antiques. 14 Bird's Hill, Heath and Reach, Bedfordshire. Tel 532 379.

John Chawner. 44 Chatham Hill, Chatham, Kent. Tel Medway (0634) 811147.

Chelsea House Antiques. 27 Station Rd, Stowmarket, Suffolk. Tel Elmswell (0359) 40895.

Chepstow Antiques. 11 Lower Church St, Chepstow, Gwent. Tel 6500.

E.M. Cheshire Antiques. The Manor House, Market Place, Bingham, Nottinghamshire. Tel 38861 (priv 38455).

Chess Antiques. 85 Broad St, Chesham, Buckinghamshire, HP5 3EF. Tel 783043.

S.E. Christie - Antiques. 56 Mill Lane, Macclesfield, Cheshire. Tel 23929.

Church Street Antiques. 4 Church St, Hadleigh, Suffolk. Tel 822418.

Church View House Antiques. Kirk Michael,. Tel 0624 87433.

The Clare Collector. 1 Nethergate St, Clare, Suffolk. Tel 277909 (priv 277494).

Malcolm G.Clark. 3 Pembroke St, Cambridge, Cambridgeshire, CB2 3QY. Tel 357117.

Christopher Clarke. The Fosse Way, Stow-on-the-Wold, Gloucestershire, GL54 1JS. Tel 30476.

Coach House Antiques. 75 Coach Rd, Sleights, Whitby, N.Yorkshire, Y022 5BT. Tel 810313.

Coach House Antiques Ltd. 77 Kinnoull St, Perth, Tayside. Tel 29835 (priv 073882 627).

The Collector & The Collector (Restorations). Douglas House, 23-25 The Bank, Barnard Castle, Durham, DL12 8PH. Tel Teesdale (0833) 37783.

Mark Collier. 24 The High St, Fordingbridge, Hampshire. Tel 52555.

F.G. & C. Collins Ltd (Collins Antiques). Corner House, Church St, Wheathampstead, Hertfordshire, AL4 8AP. Tel 3111 & 3483.

Frank Collins. Marlborough Farm,London Rd, Weston, Suffolk. Tel Beccles (0502) 714842.

J. Collins and Son (Est.1953). The Studio, 63 & 28 High St, Bideford, Devon, EX39 2AN. Tel 73103 (priv 76485).

Compton-Dando (Fine Arts) Ltd. Hall St, Long Melford, Suffolk, CO10 9JL. Tel Sudbury (0787) 312610.

Cooke Antiques. 79/85 Francis St, Dublin, Co Dublin. Tel 751885, 751250, 752251.

Coombe House Antiques. Malling St, Lewes, E.Sussex. Tel 473862.

Robert Copperfield Antiques. 47-49 Mill Lane, Macclesfield, Cheshire, SK10 7NP. Tel 26620.

Derek Cornwell. 14 The Mall, Clifton, Bristol, Avon, BS8 4DR. Tel 743765 (priv 735493).

Cottage Antiques. Bracken Cottage, High St, Standlake, Oxfordshire. Tel 421.

Thomas Coulborn & Sons. Vesey Manor, 64 Birmingham Rd, Sutton Coldfield, W.Midlands, B72 1QP. Tel 354 3974, 354 3139.

Country House Antiques. 30 Earsham St, Bungay, Suffolk. Tel 2875 (priv 0508-58144).

Country Life Antiques. Grey House,The Square, Stow-on-the-Wold, Gloucestershire, GL54 1AF. Tel 31564.

County Antiques. Colliton Antique and Craft Centre,Colliton St, Dorchester, Dorset. Tel 62444(workshop 69398).

Philip Cowan Antiques. 33 Parliament St, Liverpool, Merseyside. Tel 709 1217.

O.M. & R.D.Cox Antiques. 5 St Mary's Hill, Stamford, Lincolnshire. Tel 64159.

Crispin Antiques. 10 The Broadway, Amersham, Buckinghamshire, HP7 0HP. Tel 21779.

The Crypt Antiques. London House, High St, Burford, Oxfordshire. Tel 2302.

Cumbria Antiques. 26 Kirkland, Kendal, Cumbria. Tel 24676.

Davies Antiques. 12 St Mary St, Chepstow, Gwent, NP6 5EW. Tel Dingestow (060 083) 343.

John E. Davis Antiques. 21 Wokingham Rd, Reading, Berkshire, RG6 1JG. Tel 663108.

Gerald Deacon. 2 Wood St, Queen Sq, Bath, Avon, BA1 2JQ. Tel 25907.

Delmas Antiques. Hurst Green, E.Sussex, TN19 7PN. Tel 345.

H.P.Dennison & Son. 22 High St, Lewes, E.Sussex, BN7 2LN. Tel 473665.

Derbyshire Antiques Ltd. 159 London Road South, Poynton, Cheshire, SK12 1LQ. Tel 873110.

Dickinson Deansgreen Ltd. 17/19 John Dalton St, Manchester, Greater Manchester. Tel 834 1042.

R.C.Dodson Antiques. 85 Fawcett Rd, Southsea, Hampshire. Tel 829481.

Dolphin Antiques. 33 Trumpington St, Cambridge, Cambridgeshire. Tel 354180.

Dolphin Antiques. 13 Holywell Hill, St Albans, Hertfordshire, AL1 1EZ. Tel 63080 (priv 61941).

Doveridge House of Neachley. Neach Hill, Long Lane, Shifnal, Shropshire. Tel Albrighton (090 722) 3131, 3132.

Duncalfe Antiques & Fine Arts. 34 Montpellier Parade, Harrogate, N.Yorkshire. Tel 521452.

Dunluce Antiques. 33 Ballytober Rd, Bushmills, Co Antrim. Tel 31140.

John Dunphy Antiques. 83-84 Upper Henry St, Limerick, Co Limerick. Tel (061) 316732 (priv 52673).

Eardisley Antiques. Leominster Antique Market,14 Broad St, Leominster, Hereford & Worcester. Tel 2189 (priv 05446 310).

East Kent Antiques. Cheriton Lodge,West St, New Romney, Kent. Tel 62630.

J.G.Elias Antiques. 37 West St, Dorking, Surrey. Tel 880535 and 883327.

Elsdon Antiques. 152 High St, Old Woking, Woking, Surrey, GU22 9JH. Tel 62651.

Pamela Elsom Antiques. 5 Church St, Ashbourne, Derbyshire. Tel 43468.

Gavina Ewart. 60 High St, Broadway, Hereford & Worcester. Tel 853371.

Philip Faithfull Antiques. 202 The Street, Boughton, Kent, ME13 9AL. Tel Canterbury (0277) 750395.

Stephen Falk. Rochdale, Greater Manchester, OL12 6LE. Tel 44946.

Harvey Ferry, William Clegg Antiques. The Barns, 1 High St, Nettlebed, Oxfordshire, RG9 5AA. Tel 641533.

M.W. Fitch Ltd. 99 Sandgate High St, Folkestone, Kent. Tel 39600 (priv 30839).

Flemings Antiques. High St, Debenham, Suffolk, IP14 6QJ. Tel 860422.

Flora Dora Antiques. Dales House, Lombard St, Petworth, W.Sussex, GU28 OAG. Tel 43109.

Forster Ritchie. The Acorn,London Rd, Hook, Hampshire, RG27 9DY. Tel 2309.

Alastair Fraser Antiques. 2A Rushworth Ave, West Bridgford, Nottingham, Nottinghamshire. Tel 821835.

Freeman and Lloyd. 44 Sandgate High St, Sandgate, Folkestone, Kent, CT20 3AP. Tel 38986.

Fyfe's Antiques. 41 & 48 Thistle St, Edinburgh, Lothian, EH2 1DY. Tel 225 4287.

Jonathan Fyson Antiques. The Old School House, Cassington, Oxfordshire. Tel Oxford (0865) 880943.

Gadsby's Antiques. 88-90 The Street, Ashtead, Surrey. Tel 72305.

James Gallie. 1 Maltings Rd, Battlesbridge, Essex. Tel Wickford (03744) 63344.

Michael Gander. 10 Bridge St, Hitchin, Hertfordshire. Tel 32678.

H.G. Gasson. Lion Galleries, Lion St, Rye, E.Sussex, TN31 7LB. Tel 222208.

Gastrell House. 33 Long St, Tetbury, Gloucestershire, GL8 8AA. Tel 52228.

Gate Antiques. 29 St Saviour's Gate, York, N.Yorkshire, YO1 2NQ. Tel 27035.

N. Geary Ltd. 114 Richardshaw Lane, Pudsey, W.Yorkshire. Tel 564122.

Gibberd and Grant Antiques. 40 The Bank, Barnard Castle, Durham, DL12 8PN. Tel Teesdale (0833) 37437.

The Ginnel. Lloyds House, 16 Lloyd Street, Manchester, Greater Manchester. Tel 833 9037.

Glencorse Antiques. 321 Richmond Rd,Ham Parade, Kingston upon Thames, Surrey. Tel 541 0871.

The Golden Drop Antiques. Chatteris Rd (A141), Warboys, Cambridgeshire. Tel Chatteris (03543) 2990.

Maurice Goldstone & Son. Avenel Court, King St, Bakewell, Derbyshire. Tel 2487.

Goodbrey Antiques. 29 Double St, Framlingham, Suffolk. Tel 723756.

Wm Goodfellow (Antiques). The Green, Over Kellet, Carnforth, Lancashire, LA6 1BU. Tel 733030.

Janet Gordon. Wakes Colne House, Wakes Colne, Essex. Tel Earls Colne (07875) 2402.

A.E.Gould & Sons (Antiques) Ltd. Old Rectory Cottage,Ockham Rd South, East Horsley, Surrey, KT24 6QJ. Tel 3747.

The Granary & Rene Antiques and Art. 17A Kings Rd, St Leonards, E.Sussex, TN37 6DU. Tel 432610 (priv 71586).

The Granary Galleries. Court House, Ash Priors,near Bishops Lydeard, Taunton, Somerset, TA4 3NQ. Tel Bishops Lydeard (0823) 432402 (priv 432816).

Granville Antiques. Mount Pleasant Farm,Level Mare Lane, Eastergate, W.Sussex. Tel 2293.

Great Brampton House Antiques Ltd. Great Brampton House, Madley, Hereford, Hereford & Worcester, HR2 9NA. Tel Golden Valley (0981) 250244

Greene's Antique Galleries. The Mall, Drogheda, Co Louth. Tel (041) 36212, 38286.

Simon Greenwood Antiques. 23 Melmerby Industrial Estate,Green Lane, Melmerby, N.Yorkshire, HG4 5HP. Tel 571 (priv: 0677-22554).

W.F.Greenwood & Sons Ltd. 2&3 Crown Place, Harrogate, N.Yorkshire, HG1 2RY. Tel 504467.

G.E.Griffin. 43a Brighton Rd, Croydon, Surrey, CR2 6EB. Tel 688 3130.

David K.Hakeney Antiques. 64 George St, Hull, Humberside, HU1 3AB. Tel 228190 (priv 668634).

Hallidays Antiques Ltd. The Old College, High St, Dorchester, Oxfordshire. Tel Oxford (0865) 340028.

Hallstile Antiques. 17 Hallstile Bank, Hexham, Northumberland, NE46 1UF. Tel 602239.

A. Halsey Antiques. Boffins Boft, Bowcombe Creek, Kingsbridge, Devon. Tel 2440.

Jeffery Hammond Antiques. 18-19 High St,Twyford, Winchester, Hampshire, SO21 1RF. Tel Twyford (0962) 714036.

R.& L. Hampshire Antiques. Rutherford Hall,Gatehouse of Fleet, Castle Douglas, Dumfries & Galloway, DG7 4HS. Tel Gatehouse (05574) 616.

Hampshires of Dorking. 51/52 West St, Dorking, Surrey. Tel 887076.

Harp Antiques. 17 Woolley St, Bradford-on-Avon, Wiltshire, BA15 1AD. Tel 5770.

Ian G.Hastie. 46 St Ann St, Salisbury, Wiltshire. Tel 22957.

Simon Hatchwell Antiques. 64-65 Middle St, Brighton & Hove, E.Sussex, BN1 1AL. Tel 27663.

Raymond Hawley. 5 North Bar Within, Beverley, Humberside, HU17 8AP. Tel Hull (0482) 883193.

Haydon Bridge Antiques. 3 Shaftoe St, Haydon Bridge, Hexham, Northumberland. Tel Haydon Bridge (043484) 200 (priv 461).

Hayter's. 19-20 Cross St, Ryde, Isle of Wight, PO33 2AD. Tel 63795.

Heath-Bullock. 8 Meadrow, Godalming, Surrey, GU7 3HN. Tel 22562.

J.C.Heather Antiques. Clandore House, Woolpit, Bury St Edmunds, Suffolk, IP30 9SA. Tel Elmswell (0359) 40297.

David Hick Antiques. Alexandra House, Carre Four Selous, St Lawrence, Jersey. Tel 62965.

Hill Rise Antiques. 26 Hill Rise, Richmond, Surrey, TW10 6UA. Tel 948 1140.

William Hockley Antiques. East Street, Petworth, W.Sussex, GU28 0AB. Tel 43172 (priv 048 649 331).

W.W.Holzgrave. 7 Gosditch St, Cirencester, Gloucestershire. Tel 69351.

John Hopkins. 1 The Courtyard,Ockenden Manor, Cuckfield, W.Sussex, RH17 5LD. Tel Haywards Heath (0444) 454323.

Howard Antiques. 46-46A West St, Oundle, Northamptonshire. Tel 74239 (priv 0234 711106).

Howards of Aberystwyth. 10 Alexandra Rd, Aberystwyth, Dyfed. Tel 4973.

John Howkins Antiques. 145 King St, Great Yarmouth, Norfolk.

Hubbard Antiques. 16 St Margarets Green, Ipswich, Suffolk. Tel 226033.

L.J.Huggett & Son. Bramble Cross, Exeter Rd, Honiton, Devon. Tel 2043.

Ivanhoe Antiques. 53 Market St, Ashby de la Zouch, Leicestershire. Tel 415424.

J.N.Antiques. 86 High St, Redbourn, Hertfordshire. Tel 3603 or 4544.

Kenneth Jackson (Antiques). 66 Thistle St, Edinburgh, Lothian. Tel 225 9634.

Joan Jarman Antiques. 81A High St, Teddington, Middlesex. Tel (priv) 977 4260.

Peter Jeeves Antiques. High St, Cuckfield, W.Sussex. Tel Haywards Heath (0444) 454420.

Lita Kaye of Lyndhurst. 13 High St, Lyndhurst, Hampshire, SO43 7BB. Tel 2337.

H.W.Keil Ltd. Tudor House, Broadway, Hereford & Worcester, WR12 7DP. Tel 852408.

Kelvedon Antiques. 90 High St, Kelvedon, Essex, CO5 9AA. Tel Braintree (0376) 70557.

Kennedy & Spooner Antiques. 1 Meadowbrook Rd, Dorking, Surrey. Tel 881773 (priv 0372-52877).

Gerald A. Kenyon. Powerscourt Townhouse Centre,South William St, Dublin, Co Dublin. Tel 977345.

Kildare Antiques. 19 Kildare St, Dublin, Co Dublin. Tel 763576 (priv 688194).

Kings Antiques. Guildford Rd, Bucks Green, Rudgwick, W.Sussex. Tel 2084.

Kirkby Antiques Ltd. Highfield, Kirkby on Bain, Woodhall Spa, Lincolnshire, LN10 6YN. Tel 52119 & 53461.

La Barre Ltd. The Place,116 South St, Leominster, Hereford & Worcester, HR6 8LE. Tel 4315.

Laburnum Antique Galleries. 3 Laburnum Row, Torquay, Devon, TQ2 5QX. Tel 26983.

David Lane Antiques. The Old Forge,Fanners Yard, Compton Abbas, Dorset. Tel Shaftesbury (0747) 811881.

Langold Antiques Ltd. Oxon Hoath, Hadlow, Kent. Tel Plaxtol (0732) 810577.

Michel Le Coz. High St, Castle Combe, Wiltshire, SN14 7HU. Tel 782223.

Le Soken Antiques. High Street, Thorpe-le-Soken, Essex. Tel Clacton (0255) 861 337.

Ronald A. Lee (Fine Arts) Ltd. The Manor House, Byfleet, Surrey. Tel 43346.

E.C.Legg & Son. The Old School House,Somerford Keynes, Cirencester, Gloucestershire, GL7 6DJ. Tel 861420.

Lennard Antiques. Poplars House, Rothersthorpe, Northampton, Northamptonshire. Tel 830423.

Leominster Antiques. 87 Etnam St, Leominster, Hereford & Worcester. Tel 3217.

Ivor & Patricia Lewis Antique & Fine Art Dealers. Westfield,30 Westwood Park Rd, Peterborough, Cambridgeshire. Tel 44567.

Linden House Antiques. Linden House,3 Silver St, Stansted Mountfitchet, Essex, CM24 8HA. Tel Bishops Stortford (0279) 812372.

Linnets Nest Antiques & Mawby's International. 50 Church St, Rugby, Warwickshire. Tel 61393 &832600 priv75305.

The Little Antique Shop. 167-169 Stone Rd, Hanford, Stoke-on-Trent, Staffordshire. Tel 657674.

Jessica Longhurst. Magill Antiques, Chestnut House, Long Melford, Suffolk, CO10 9HZ. Tel 78088.

Look Around Antiques. 61 Watergate Row, Chester, Cheshire. Tel 49826.

Graham Lower. Stonecrouch Farmhouse, Flimwell, E.Sussex, TN5 7QB. Tel 535.

Charles Lumb & Sons Ltd. 2 Montpellier Gardens, Harrogate, N.Yorkshire, HG1 2TF. Tel 503776 (priv 863281).

Mac Humble Antiques. 11 Queen St, Bath, Avon, BA1 2Jo. Tel 62751 (priv 022122 3594).

Malvern Studios. 56 Cowleigh Rd, North Malvern, Malvern, Hereford & Worcester, WR14 1QD. Tel 4913.

Mandeys Antiques. Mandeys, High St, Brasted, Kent. Tel Westerham (0959) 62408.

Manor House Antiques. The Green, Datchet, Berkshire. Tel Slough (0753) 42164 & 41460.

Market House Antiques. Market House, Burnham Market, Norfolk, PE31 8HF. Tel Fakenham (0328) 738475.

Markland Antiques. Western Rd, Borough Green, Kent. Tel 4152.

Marlborough House Antiques. 86 High St, Yarmouth, Isle of Wight. Tel 760498.

F.J.McCarthy Ltd. The Grange, Normanton on Trent, Newark-on-Trent, Nottinghamshire, NG23 6RQ. Tel 821382.

Mendip Antiques. Great Western Antiques Centre,Bartlett St, Bath, Avon. Tel 310388.

Mill House Antiques. 139 Abbey Foregate, Shrewsbury, Shropshire. Tel 240328.

Millers of Chelsea Antiques Limited. Netherbrook House,86 Christchurch Rd, Ringwood, Hampshire, BH24 1DR. Tel 2062.

Millers of Chelsea Antiques Limited. Netherbrook House,86 Christchurch Rd, Ringwood, Hampshire, BH24 1DR. Tel 2062.

Millers Antiques, Kelvedon. 46 High St, Kelvedon, Essex. Tel 70098.

Milton Abbot Antiques. Venn Hill, Milton Abbot, Tavistock, Devon. Tel 392.

C.S. Moreton (Antiques). Inchmartine House, Inchture, Tayside, PH14 9QQ. Tel 86412.

P.and G. Morley. 8 Jury Street, Warwick, Warwickshire, CV34 4EN. Tel 492963 (priv 0926 54191).

James H.Morris & Co. Old Village School, The Green, Northop, Clwyd, CH7 6BD. Tel 508.

Robert Morrison & Son. Trentholme House, 131 The Mount, York, N.Yorkshire, YO2 2DA. Tel 55394.

Ralph and Bruce Moss. 26 Whitehorse St, Baldock, Hertfordshire, SG7 6QQ. Tel 892751.

Moxhams Antiques. 17 Silver St, Bradford-on-Avon, Wiltshire. Tel 2789 (priv 038 082-677).

Myers Galleries. Endsleigh House, High St, Gargrave, N.Yorkshire, BD23 3LX. Tel 587.

Nash Antiques. 10 Fountain Buildings,Lansdown Rd, Bath, Avon. Tel 313584.

Neville's Antiques. 64-66 Station Rd, Woburn Sands, Buckinghamshire, MK17 8RQ. Tel Milton Keynes (0908) 584827 (priv 583024).

New Abbey Antiques. Caragh Lodge, Glen Rd, Newtownabbey, Co Antrim, BT37 0RY. Tel Whiteabbey (0231) 62036.

Newcourt Park. Lugwardine, Hereford & Worcester. Tel Hereford (0432) 850752.

David & Penny Newlove Antiques. 70/71/102 Gt Western Antique Centre,Bartlett St, Bath, Avon. Tel 28731 & 310388.

David & Penny Newlove Antiques. Unit 3, The Old Mill,Station Rd, Bruton, Somerset. Tel 32672.

Anthony Nielsen Antiques. High St, Burford, Oxfordshire, OX8 4QQ. Tel 2014 (priv 0451 21710).

Michael Norman Antiques Ltd. 15 Ship St, Brighton & Hove, E.Sussex, BN1 1AD. Tel 29253/4 26712.

E.A. Nowell & Sons. 21-23 Market Place, Wells, Somerset, BA5 2RF. Tel 72415, 78738, 76915.

Simon W.Nutter. Wraggs Row, Fosse Way, Stow-on-the-Wold, Gloucestershire. Tel 30658.

G.Oakes & Son (Bolton) Ltd. 160 Blackburn Rd, Bolton, Greater Manchester, BL1 8DR. Tel 26587.

Obelisk Antiques. 2 Silver St, Warminster, Wiltshire, BA12 8PS. Tel 216874.

F. & M. Odell. 35 & 37 High St, Shefford, Bedfordshire. Tel 813940.

Old Forge Antiques. Old Forge,Bridge St, Long Melford, Suffolk. Tel Sudbury (0787) 247083.

Old Hall Antiques/Sphinx Gallery. The Old Hall, Sundridge, Kent. Tel Westerham (0959) 62589.

The Old Mint House. High St, Pevensey, E.Sussex, BN24 5LF. Tel Eastbourne (0323) 762337 (priv 761251).

The Old School Antiques. The Old School, Dorney, Buckinghamshire, SL4 6QW. Tel Burnham (06286) 3247.

Old Schoolhouse Antiques. 41-43 Lower Bridge St, Chester, Cheshire. Tel 28968.

G.Oliver & Sons. St Catherine's House, Portsmouth Rd, Guildford, Surrey. Tel 575427.

Ormond Antiques. 32 Lower Ormond Quay, Dublin, Co Dublin. Tel 741569.

Page Antiques. 424 Buxton Rd, Great Moor, Stockport, Greater Manchester. Tel 483 9202 (priv 427 2412).

Painswick Antiques. Beacon House, New St, Painswick, Gloucestershire, GL6 6UN. Tel 812578.

Palmer Antiques. 10 Paved Court, Richmond, Surrey. Tel 948 2668.

Dermot & Jill Palmer Antiques. 7-8 Union St, The Lanes, Brighton & Hove, E.Sussex. Tel 28669.

Pandora's Box. 112 St Georges Rd, Kemptown, Brighton & Hove, E.Sussex. Tel 603305.

Park Galleries Antiques, Fine Art and Decor. 167 Mayor St, Bolton, Greater Manchester, BL1 4SJ. Tel 29827 (priv 061 764 5853).

Parker-Williams Antiques. 22 Palace St, Canterbury, Kent, CT1 2DZ. Tel 468341.

Pavilion Antiques. Long Gable, Ratcliffe-on-the-Wreake, Leicestershire. Tel 0664-74209.

Pembroke Antiques Ltd. 3 Church Rd, Farnborough, Kent, BR6 7DB. Tel 62846 (priv 0732 460697).

Penny Farthing. High St, Croydon, Cambridgeshire. Tel Cambridge (0223) 207331.

Petticombe Manor Antiques. Petticombe Manor, Monkleigh, Bideford, Devon, EX39 5JR. Tel 75605.

Phelps Ltd. 133-135 St Margaret's Rd, Twickenham, Middlesex, TW1 1RG. Tel 892 1778, 892 7129.

Phoenix Green Antiques. London Rd, Phoenix Green, Hartley Wintney, Hampshire, RG27 8RT. Tel 4430.

Pigeon House Antiques. 52 London Rd, Hurst Green, E.Sussex, TN19 7PN. Tel 474.

Priests Antiques & Fine Arts. 60 North St, Thame, Oxfordshire. Tel 4461.

Priory Antiques. 37 East St, Blandford Forum, Dorset. Tel 53472.

Provincial Antiques Ltd. 8 Shorthill Lane,Coneythorpe, Knaresborough, N.Yorkshire. Tel Harrogate (0423) 865136.

Prudhoe Cottage Antiques. Hexham Antique Market, 15 St Mary's,Chare, Hexham, Northumberland. Tel 603812 (priv 0661 33421).

Queens Parade Antiques. 35 Gay St, Bath, Avon. Tel 20337.

Paul Quentin Antiques. 626 Manchester Rd, Bury, Greater Manchester, BL9 9SU. Tel 766 6673.

Quiet Street Antiques. 3 Quiet St, Bath, Avon. Tel 315727 (priv 332399).

Rankine Taylor Antiques. 34 Dollar St, Cirencester, Gloucestershire, GL7 2AN. Tel 2529.

G.T.Ratcliff Ltd. Durwards Hall, Kelvedon, Essex. Tel 70234.

Regent House Antiques. Royal Terrace, Northampton, Northamptonshire, NN1 3RF. Tel 37992.

Reindeer Antiques Ltd. 43 Watling St, Potterspury, Northamptonshire, NN12 7QD. Tel Yardley Gobion (0908) 542407.

Marc Rhys. The Mynde House, High St, Caerleon, Gwent. Tel 420535.

T.E.Robinson Antiques. 3A 3 & 4 Bartlett St, Bath, Avon, BA1 2QZ. Tel 63982 (priv 832307).

Roderic Antiques. Westbrook House, Upwey, Weymouth, Dorset. Tel Upwey (030 581) 2929, 3022.

Rogers Antiques. 22 Ewell Rd, Cheam, Surrey. Tel 643 8466.

Andrew Ross Antiques. Thacketts, Froxfield, Wiltshire. Tel Hungerford (0488) 82087.

Royston Antiques. 27-29 Kneesworth St, Royston, Hertfordshire. Tel 43876.

Rutland Antiques and Coins. 27 Mill St, Oakham, Leicestershire. Tel 3364 (priv 2408).

Anthony Sampson. Dale House, High St, Moreton-in-Marsh, Gloucestershire, GL56 0AD. Tel 50763.

Robin Sanders. The Pond House,Dane End, Ware, Hertfordshire. Tel Dane End (092084) 265.

R. Saunders. 71 Queens St, Weybridge, Surrey. Tel 42601.

Sam Savage Antiques. Hayes Farm, Ticknall, Derbyshire, DE7 1JZ. Tel Melbourne (033 16) 2195.

Aldo Broccardi Schelmi (Fine Arts). Dewhurst Lodge, Wadhurst, E.Sussex. Tel 3519.

Laurence Shaw Antique Centre. Sandy Bank Road,New York, Coningsby, Lincolnshire. Tel 42578.

Sigma (Antiques & Fine Art). Water Skellgate, Ripon, N.Yorkshire. Tel 3163.

Silvesters Antiques. 33 High St, Wingham, Kent. Tel Canterbury (0227) 720278.

The Singing Birds. Michael's Nook,Grasmere, Ambleside, Cumbria, LA22 9RP. Tel Grasmere (09665) 496.

E. Smith (Leicester) Ltd. The Antique Complex,9 St. Nicholas Place, Leicester, Leicestershire, LE1 5LB. Tel 533343.

Smith's The Rink Ltd. Dragon Rd, Harrogate, N.Yorkshire. Tel 503217.

Kimberley Snow & Son. Verbeer Manor, Willand, Cullompton, Devon, EX15 2PE. Tel 33312.

Spurrier-Smith Antiques. 28 & 41 Church St, Ashbourne, Derbyshire. Tel 43669 (priv 077 389 368).

St George's Antiques. St George's Sq, Stamford, Lincolnshire. Tel 54117 (priv 0778 423781).

Peter Stanton Antiques. The Old Pottery,Chapel Hill, Truro, Cornwall, TR1 3BN. Tel 70262.

Alanna Staton Antiques. 4 Anyards Rd, Cobham, Surrey, KT11 2JZ. Tel 63407 (priv 04864 2407).

Geoffrey Stead. The Old Rectory, Dowdeswell, Gloucestershire, GL54 5LX. Tel Cheltenham (0242) 820571.

Steed-Croft Antiques. Marshlands, Cross Lane,Brancaster, King's Lynn, Norfolk, PE31 8AE. Tel Brancaster (0485210) 812.

Stockwell Antiques. Exeter Antique Wholesalers,Exeter Airport, Clyst Honiton, Exeter, Devon, EX5 2LL. Tel 66279.

Strawson Antiques. 39-41 The Pantiles, Tunbridge Wells, Kent, TN7 5TE. Tel 30607.

Peter Stroud Antiques. Station Yard Industrial Estate, Chipping Norton, Oxfordshire, OX7 5HX. Tel 41651 (priv 3103).

Peter Strowger of Blandford Forum Antiques. 13 East St, Blandford Forum, Dorset. Tel 53567 & 54374.

Studio Antiques Ltd. Bourton-on-the-Water, Gloucestershire, GL54 2BX. Tel 20352.

Studio 101. 101 High St, Eton, Berkshire. Tel Windsor (0753) 863333.

Summers, Davis & Son Ltd. Calleva House, 6 High St, Wallingford, Oxfordshire, OX10 0BP. Tel 36284.

Sundial Antiques. 19 Whielden St, Amersham, Buckinghamshire, HP7 0HU. Tel 7955.

Suthburgh Antiques. Red House, Hall St, Long Melford, Suffolk. Tel Sudbury (0787) 74818.

R.A.Swift & Sons. St Andrews Hall,4c Wolverton Rd, Boscombe, Bournemouth, Dorset, BH7 6HT. Tel 34470.

Taurus Antiques Ltd. 145 Masons Hill, Bromley, Kent, BR2 9HY. Tel 464 8746.

Tay Street Gallery. 70 Tay St, Perth, Tayside. Tel 20604.

Thirty Eight Antiques Ltd. 25-27 High St, Weedon, Northamptonshire, NN7 4QD. Tel 40766.

Thompson's Gallery. 175A High St, Aldeburgh, Suffolk. Tel 3743 (priv 2488).

Thomson Antiques. Ermefield House, Western Rd, Ivybridge, Devon, PL21 9AL. Tel Plymouth (0752) 892304.

Thorntons of Harrogate. 1 Montpellier Gdns, Harrogate, N.Yorkshire, HG1 2TF. Tel 504118.

Thorpe & Foster Ltd. 49 West St, Dorking, Surrey. Tel 881029.

Thorpe Antiques. 51 High St, Finedon, Northamptonshire, NN9 5JN. Tel Wellingborough (0933) 680196.

Thorpe Antiques. 3 High St, Higham Ferrers, Northamptonshire. Tel Wellingborough (0933) 59747.

S. & S. Timms Antiques Ltd. 16,18,20 Dunstable St, Ampthill, Bedfordshire, MK45 2JT. Tel 403067.

Tontine Antiques. 75-81 Tontine St, Folkestone, Kent. Tel 53077 (priv 0303 89 3157).

Touchwood Antiques. 9 Park St., Stow-on-the-Wold, Gloucestershire, GL54 1AQ. Tel 30221.

Townhead Antiques. Townhead, Newby Bridge, Cumbria, LA12 8NP. Tel 31321.

Tudor Antiques. Long Melford, Suffolk, CD10 9HY. Tel Sudbury (0787) 75950.

Margot Tyldesley Antiques. Brighton & Hove, E.Sussex. Tel 21307.

Village Antiques. 2 Cooden Sea Rd, Little Common, Bexhill, E.Sussex. Tel Cooden (04243) 5214.

Village Green Antiques. 6/8 Old Cross St, Hertford, Hertfordshire. Tel 57698 (priv 56994).

Elizabeth Viney. Jacob's House, High St, Stockbridge, Hampshire. Tel 810761.

Michael Wakelin and Helen Linfield. 10 New St, Petworth, W.Sussex. Tel 42417.

D.J.Wakeman & Co Ltd. Grove Farm House, Dorrington, Shropshire. Tel 388.

Percy F.Wale Ltd. 32-34 Regent St, Leamington, Warwickshire, CV32 5EG. Tel 21288.

Ward Antiques. Hall St, Long Melford, Suffolk. Tel Sudbury (0787) 78265

Waterloo Antiques. 16 Waterloo St, Oldham, Greater Manchester. Tel 624 5975.

John Weatherell & Sons Antiques. Westmorland House,13-19 Westmorland St, Harrogate, N.Yorkshire, HG1 5AY. Tel 60038/69718.

Wenlock Antiques. 61 High St, Much Wenlock, Shropshire, TF13 6AE. Tel 727271.

West End Galleries. 8 Cavendish Circus, Buxton, Derbyshire. Tel 4546 (priv 6632).

Westport Ltd. 3 Old Hawkhill, Dundee, Tayside, DD1 5EU. Tel 25517.

Westward County Pine. 10 Church St, Launceston, Cornwall. Tel Canworthy Water (056 681) 309 or (0566) 5605.

Wharf Antiques. 85 William St, Sheffield, S.Yorkshire. Tel 29321 (Priv 307639).

Tim Wharton Antiques. 24 High St, Redbourn, Hertfordshire. Tel 4371.

Wheelbarrow Castle Antiques. Stoke Prior, Leominster, Hereford & Worcester. Tel 2219.

William Whitfield Antiques. 51-53 Beckenham Lane, Shortlands, Bromley, Kent, ODA BR2. Tel 466 6506 (priv 650 3558).

Wickersley Antiques. 3 Broad St,Parkgate, Rotherham, S.Yorkshire. Tel 525595.

Wigington Partners. 22 New St, Shipston on Stour, Warwickshire, CV36 4EN. Tel 61205.

H.Wilson & Son. 28 High St, Worthing, W.Sussex, BN11 1NT. Tel 202059.

R.S. Wilson & Sons. High St, Boroughbridge, N.Yorkshire, YO5 9AW. Tel 2417 (priv 2654).

Roger Wilson. The Old George, Middle Wallop, Hampshire. Tel Wallop (0264) 781422.

Windhill Antiquary. 4 High St, Bishop's Stortford, Hertfordshire. Tel 51587.

Michael Wisehall Antiques. Minshull Gallery, 7 Minshull St, Knutsford, Cheshire. Tel 4901.

Colin Wood Antiques Ltd. 25 Rose St, Aberdeen, Grampian, AB1 1TX. Tel 643019.

Stanley Woolston. 29 Broad St, Ludlow, Shropshire, SY8 1NJ. Tel 3554.

Worksop Antiques. 20 Park St, Worksop, Nottinghamshire. Tel 476384.

Tim Wright Antiques. 147 Bath St, Glasgow, Strathclyde. Tel 221 0364.

Yellow Lantern Antiques Ltd. 34 & 65B Holland Rd, Hove, Brighton & Hove, E.Sussex, BN3 1JL. Tel 771572 (priv 0273 455476).

Yesterday's Antiques. 13 Sparrows Herne, Bushey, Hertfordshire. Tel 950 7600.

William Young (Antiques) Ltd. 1 Belmont St, Aberdeen, Grampian, AB1 1JR. Tel 644757.

Furniture, Country

see Country and Cottage Antiques

Furniture, European

London

Didier Aaron (London) Ltd. 21 Ryder St, London, SW1Y 6PX. Tel 839 4716/7.

Adams Antiques. 47 Chalk Farm Rd, London, NW1. Tel 267 9241.

Adams Room Ltd. 18-20 Ridgway, Wimbledon Village, London, SW19. Tel 946 7047 (priv 947 4784).

Alexander & Berendt Ltd. 1A Davies St, London, W1Y 1LL. Tel 499 4775.

David Alexander Antiques. 102 Waterford Rd, London, SW6. Tel 731 4644.

The Antique Porcelain Company Ltd. 149 New Bond St, London, W1Y 0HY. Tel 629 1254.

Raymond Benardout Ltd. 4 William St, Knightsbridge, London, SW1X 9HL. Tel 235 3360 (priv 235 0504).

Bernheimer Fine Arts Ltd. 32 St George St,Mayfair, London, W1R 9FA. Tel 499 0293.

H.Blairman & Sons Ltd. 119 Mount St, London, W1. Tel 493 0444.

Claude Bornoff. 20 Chepstow Corner, Pembridge Villas, London, W2. Tel 229 8947.

I. & J.L. Brown. 636 Kings Rd,Chelsea, London, SW6 2DU. Tel 736 4141.

Buck & Payne Antiques. 5 Camden Passage, London, N1. Tel 226 4326.

Tony Bunzl & Zal Davar. 344 King's Rd, London, SW3. Tel 352 3697.

Rupert Cavendish Antiques. 561 Kings Rd, London, SW6 2DZ. Tel 731 7041.

Colefax & Fowler. 39 Brook St, London, W1Y 1AU. Tel 493 2231.

Cura Antiques. 34 Ledbury Rd, London, W11 2AB. Tel 229 6880.

Emanouel Antiques Ltd. 64 South Audley St, London, W1Y 5FA. Tel 493 4350, 499 0996.

Etna Antiques. 81 Kensington Church St, London, W8 4BG. Tel 937 3754.

Galerie 360. 564 King's Road, London, SW6. Tel 736 5160.

Guinevere Antiques Ltd. 578 King's Road, London, SW6. Tel 736 2917.

Jonathan Harris. 54 Kensington Church St, London, W8. Tel 937 3133.

M.Harris & Sons. Gayfere House,22-23 Gayfere St, London, SW1P 3HP. Tel 222 8161.

W.R.Harvey & Co (Antiques) Ltd. 5 Old Bond St, London, W1. Tel 499 8385.

Hermitage. 97 Pimlico Rd, London, SW1W 8PH. Tel 730 1973.

Michael Hogg. 172 Brompton Rd, London, SW3. Tel 589 8629.

Howard Antiques. 8 Davies St, London, W1. Tel 629 2628.

Olivia Jackson Antiques. 287 Westbourne Grove, London, W11. Tel 727 2817.

Jeremy Ltd. 255 King's Rd, Chelsea, London, SW3 5EL. Tel 352 3127, 352 0644.

Julian Antiques. 67 Park Rd, London, NW1. Tel 723 0653.

Ronald A.Lee (Fine Arts) Ltd. 1-9 Bruton Place, London, W1X 7AD. Tel 499 6266.

M. & D. Lewis Antiques. 1 Lonsdale Rd, London, W11. Tel 727 3908.

J.Lipitch Ltd. 177 Westbourne Grove, London, W11. Tel 229 0783.

Michael Lipitch. 98 Fulham Rd, London, SW3. Tel 589 7327 (priv 440 7797).

Peter Lipitch Ltd. 120-124 Fulham Rd, London, SW3. Tel 373 3328.

Mallett at Bourdon House Ltd. 2 Davies St, Berkeley Sq, London, W1Y 1LJ. Tel 629 2444/5.

Rodd McLennan. 24 Holbein Place, London, SW1. Tel 730 6330.

Alec Ossowski. 83 Pimlico Rd, London, SW1. Tel 730 3256.

Michael & Margaret Parker. 24 Cheval Place, London, SW7. Tel 589 0133.

Pelham Galleries (Est 1927). 163-165 Fulham Rd, London, SW3. Tel 589 2686.

John Pope & Hunts Ltd. 91 Old Brompton Rd, London, SW7. Tel 581 5375, 584 2229.

Portmeirion Antiques. 62 White Hart Lane, Barnes, London, SW13. Tel 876 2367.

William Redford. 9 Mount St, London, W1. Tel 629 1165.

Rendlesham & Dark. 498 Kings Rd, London, SW10. Tel 351 1442.

Shield & Allen. 584-586 King's Rd, London, SW6. Tel 736 7145.

Jacob Stodel Antiques. 116 Kensington Church St, London, W8 4BH. Tel 221 2652.

Murray Thomson Ltd. 141 Kensington Church St, London, W8 7LP. Tel 727 1727, 727 1825.

M.Turpin. 21 Manson Mews, Queensgate, London, SW7. Tel 736 3417.

Tzigany Fine Arts. 28-29 Dover St, London, W1X 3PA. Tel 491 1007.

Edric Van Vredenburgh. 37 Bury St, London, SW1. Tel 839 5818.

O.F.Wilson. Queen's Elm Parade,Fulham Rd, London, SW3 6EJ. Tel 352 9554 (priv 373 4602).

Clifford Wright. 104/106 Fulham Rd, London, SW3. Tel 589 0986.

Regions

A.& F. Partners. 20 London St, Faringdon, Oxfordshire, SN7 7AA. Tel 20078.

Adrian Alan Ltd. 15c Prince Albert St, Brighton & Hove, E.Sussex. Tel 25015.

Augill Castle Antiques Ltd. Augill Castle, Brough, Cumbria, CA17 4AY. Tel 412.

Richard Batsford Antiques. Antique Trade Warehouse,29 Lorne Park Rd, Bournemouth, Dorset. Tel 292944 (priv 25485).

The Blacksmiths Shop. High St, Brasted, Kent. Tel Westerham (0959) 63114 (priv 62589).

Simon Brett. Creswyke House, High St, Moreton-in-Marsh, Gloucestershire, GL56 0LH. Tel 50751.

T.& D.Brindle Antiques. 4-8 Lynwood Rd, Blackburn, Lancashire, BB2 6HP. Tel 670714; 53628.

David Cambridge. 13 Rotunda Terrace, Cheltenham, Gloucestershire. Tel 42178.

Cave's of Northampton. 111 Kettering Rd, Northampton, Northamptonshire, NN1 4BA. Tel 38278.

Cirencester Antiques Ltd. 17 Dyer St, Cirencester, Gloucestershire, GL7 2PP. Tel 2955 (priv 3066).

The Clare Collector. 1 Nethergate St, Clare, Suffolk. Tel 277909 (priv 277494).

Christopher Clarke. The Fosse Way, Stow-on-the-Wold, Gloucestershire, GL54 1JS. Tel 30476.

Colleton House Gallery. 8a Quiet St, Bath, Avon, BA1 2JU. Tel 28806.

J. Collins and Son (Est.1953). The Studio, 63 & 28 High St, Bideford, Devon, EX39 2AN. Tel 73103 (priv 76485).

Compton-Dando (Fine Arts) Ltd. Hall St, Long Melford, Suffolk, CO10 9JL. Tel Sudbury (0787) 312610.

The Connoisseur. 528 Wilmslow Rd, Withington, Manchester, Greater Manchester. Tel 445 2504.

Thomas Coulborn & Sons. Vesey Manor, 64 Birmingham Rd, Sutton Coldfield, W.Midlands, B72 1QP. Tel 354 3974, 354 3139.

Delmas Antiques. Hurst Green, E.Sussex, TN19 7PN. Tel 345.

Dickinson Deansgreen Ltd. 17/19 John Dalton St, Manchester, Greater Manchester. Tel 834 1042.

Doveridge House of Neachley. Neach Hill, Long Lane, Shifnal, Shropshire. Tel Albrighton (090 722) 3131, 3132.

Peter Dryden Ltd. Teign Court, Teignmouth, Devon, TQ14 8AY. Tel 78095 (priv 78392).

K.W.Dunster Antiques. 23 Church St, Staines, Middlesex. Tel 53297.

Thomas Franklin (Antiques). 28 Charnham St, Hungerford, Berkshire, RG17 OEJ. Tel 82404.

Jonathan Fyson Antiques. The Old School House, Cassington, Oxfordshire. Tel Oxford (0865) 880943.

Maurice Goldstone & Son. Avenel Court, King St, Bakewell, Derbyshire. Tel 2487.

Goodbrey Antiques. 29 Double St, Framlingham, Suffolk. Tel 723756.

The Granary Galleries. Court House, Ash Priors,near Bishops Lydeard, Taunton, Somerset, TA4 3NQ. Tel Bishops Lydeard (0823) 432402 (priv 432816).

Jay Gray Antiques. Syrena House, 1 Cheltenham Rd, Cirencester, Gloucestershire, GL7 2HS. Tel 2755.

W.F.Greenwood & Sons Ltd. 2&3 Crown Place, Harrogate, N.Yorkshire, HG1 2RY. Tel 504467.

A. Halsey Antiques. Boffins Boft, Bowcombe Creek, Kingsbridge, Devon. Tel 2440.

Jeffery Hammond Antiques. 18-19 High St,Twyford, Winchester, Hampshire, SO21 1RF. Tel Twyford (0962) 714036.

Ian G.Hastie. 46 St Ann St, Salisbury, Wiltshire. Tel 22957.

Simon Hatchwell Antiques. 64-65 Middle St, Brighton & Hove, E.Sussex, BN1 1AL. Tel 27663.

Heath-Bullock. 8 Meadrow, Godalming, Surrey, GU7 3HN. Tel 22562.

Peter Hempson. Melchbourne Park, Melchbourne, Bedfordshire. Tel Riseley (023063) 8872.

L.J.Huggett & Son. Bramble Cross, Exeter Rd, Honiton, Devon. Tel 2043.

Kenneth Jackson (Antiques). 66 Thistle St, Edinburgh, Lothian. Tel 225 9634.

Joan Jarman Antiques. 81A High St, Teddington, Middlesex. Tel (priv) 977 4260.

Peter Jeeves Antiques. High St, Cuckfield, W.Sussex. Tel Haywards Heath (0444) 454420.

Robert Kime Antiques. Dene House, Lockeridge, Marlborough, Wiltshire, SN8 4EQ. Tel Lockeridge (067 286) 250.

Laburnum Antique Galleries. 3 Laburnum Row, Torquay, Devon, TQ2 5QX. Tel 26983.

David Lane Antiques. The Old Forge,Fanners Yard, Compton Abbas, Dorset. Tel Shaftesbury (0747) 811881.

Michel Le Coz. High St, Castle Combe, Wiltshire, SN14 7HU. Tel 782223.

Ivor & Patricia Lewis Antique & Fine Art Dealers. Westfield,30 Westwood Park Rd, Peterborough, Cambridgeshire. Tel 44567.

Graham Lower. Stonecrouch Farmhouse, Flimwell, E.Sussex, TN5 7QB. Tel 535.

Mandeys Antiques. Mandeys, High St, Brasted, Kent. Tel Westerham (0959) 62408.

F.J.McCarthy Ltd. The Grange, Normanton on Trent, Newark-on-Trent, Nottinghamshire, NG23 6RQ. Tel 821382.

Millers of Chelsea Antiques Limited. Netherbrook House,86 Christchurch Rd, Ringwood, Hampshire, BH24 1DR. Tel 2062.

Millers of Chelsea Antiques Limited. Netherbrook House,86 Christchurch Rd, Ringwood, Hampshire, BH24 1DR. Tel 2062.

Millers Antiques, Kelvedon. 46 High St, Kelvedon, Essex. Tel 70098.

Ralph and Bruce Moss. 26 Whitehorse St, Baldock, Hertfordshire, SG7 6QQ. Tel 892751.

Newcourt Park. Lugwardine, Hereford & Worcester. Tel Hereford (0432) 850752.

Obelisk Antiques. 2 Silver St, Warminster, Wiltshire, BA12 8PS. Tel 216874.

Old Hall Antiques/Sphinx Gallery. The Old Hall, Sundridge, Kent. Tel Westerham (0959) 62589.

G.Oliver & Sons. St Catherine's House, Portsmouth Rd, Guildford, Surrey. Tel 575427.

Elizabeth Parker Antiques. High St, Moreton-in-Marsh, Gloucestershire, GL56 0LL. Tel 50917.

Pennard House Antiques. East Pennard, Shepton Mallet, Somerset, BA4 6TP. Tel Ditcheat (074986) 266.

Phoenix Antiques. 1 Carter St, Fordham, Cambridgeshire. Tel Newmarket (0638) 720 363.

Pigeon House Antiques. 52 London Rd, Hurst Green, E.Sussex, TN19 7PN. Tel 474.

Raphael at Homewood Park. Homewood Park, Hinton Charterhouse, Avon. Tel Limpley Stoke (022 122) 3586.

Regent House Antiques. Royal Terrace, Northampton, Northamptonshire, NN1 3RF. Tel 37992.

Roderic Antiques. Westbrook House, Upwey, Weymouth, Dorset. Tel Upwey (030 581) 2929, 3022.

Andrew Ross Antiques. Thacketts, Froxfield, Wiltshire. Tel Hungerford (0488) 82087.

Aldo Broccardi Schelmi (Fine Arts). Dewhurst Lodge, Wadhurst, E.Sussex. Tel 3519.

Smith's The Rink Ltd. Dragon Rd, Harrogate, N.Yorkshire. Tel 503217.

St Ouen Antiques. Vintage Corner, Old Cambridge Rd, Puckeridge, Hertfordshire. Tel Ware (0920) 821336.

Geoffrey Stead. The Old Rectory, Dowdeswell, Gloucestershire, GL54 5LX. Tel Cheltenham (0242) 820571.

Peter Stroud Antiques. Station Yard Industrial Estate, Chipping Norton, Oxfordshire, OX7 5HX. Tel 41651 (priv 3103).

Summers, Davis & Son Ltd. Calleva House, 6 High St, Wallingford, Oxfordshire, OX10 0BP. Tel 36284.

R.A.Swift & Sons. St Andrews Hall,4c Wolverton Rd, Boscombe, Bournemouth, Dorset, BH7 6HT. Tel 34470.

D.J.Wakeman & Co Ltd. Grove Farm House, Dorrington, Shropshire. Tel 388.

John Weatherell & Sons Antiques. Westmorland House,13-19 Westmorland St, Harrogate, N.Yorkshire, HG1 5AY. Tel 60038/69718.

West End Galleries. 8 Cavendish Circus, Buxton, Derbyshire. Tel 4546 (priv 6632).

Roger Wilson. The Old George, Middle Wallop, Hampshire. Tel Wallop (0264) 781422.

Windhill Antiquary. 4 High St, Bishop's Stortford, Hertfordshire. Tel 51587.

Furniture, Oak

see Oak Furniture

Furniture, Painted

Annarella Clark Antiques. 11 Park St, Stow-on-the-Wold, Gloucestershire.

Genges Farm Antiques. Genges Farm, Limington, Somerset. Tel Ilchester (0935) 840464.

Humbleyard Fine Art. 3 Fish Hill, Holt, Norfolk. Tel 713362(priv 036 283 793).

Jadis Ltd. The Old Bank, 17 Walcot Buildings,London Rd, Bath, Avon. Tel 338797.

Fiona & Bill Laidlaw Antiques. 40 Gordon Place,Holland St, London, W8 5JF. Tel 937 8493.

Stephen Long. Albion House, 348 Fulham Rd, London, SW10 9UH. Tel 352 8226.

Mary Mackie Antiques. Elton, Nottinghamshire.

Myriad Antiques. 131 Portland Rd, London, W11. Tel 229 1709.

Richard & Pamela Nadin. 12 Paul St, Frome, Somerset, BA11 1DT. Tel 64957.

Richard & Pamela Nadin. 5 Woolley St, Bradford-on-Avon, Wiltshire, BA15 1AD. Tel 2476.

Piccadilly Antiques. 1/2 Piccadilly,London Rd, Bath, Avon, BA1 6AN. Tel 332779.

Redmile Studio. Redmile, Leicestershire, NG13 0GA.

Rendall. 572 King's Rd, London, SW6. Tel 736 2520 (priv 948 4400).

Woburn Abbey Antiques Centre. Woburn Abbey, Woburn, Bedfordshire, MK43 0TP. Tel 350.

Furniture, Pine

see Pine Furniture

Furniture, Reproduction

see also Chair Making

Abbas Combe Pine. 4 Upper Maudlin St, Bristol, Avon, BS2. Tel 299023.

Barrett & Butler. The Old Bull Furniture Workshops,Key St, Ipswich, Suffolk.

William Bedford PLC. The Merchants Hall, 46 Essex Rd,Islington, London, N1 8LN. Tel 226 9648.

H.J.Benford. 14-16 Wellington St, Kettering, Northamptonshire. Tel 513793.

Arthur Brett & Sons, Ltd. 40-44 St Giles St, Norwich, Norfolk, NR2 1LW. Tel 628171.

Bric-a-Brac Ltd. 195 Park View, Whitley Bay, Tyne & Wear, NE26 3RD. Tel Tyneside (091) 2526141 (priv 2528508).

C.C.A.W. Ltd. Gunhouse, Steeple Bumpstead, Haverhill, Suffolk. Tel Steeple Bumpstead 044084 275.

Carvers & Gilders. Charterhouse Works, Eltringham St, London, SW18. Tel 870 7047.

Chanteau. 36 Cathcart Rd, London, SW10 9NN. Tel 352 0447.

Chilstone Architectural Ornaments. Sprivers Estate, Horsmonden, Kent. Tel Brenchley (089272) 3553.

Cirencester Workshops. Brewery Court, Cirencester, Gloucestershire. Tel 61566.

Cladgild Ltd. Vine House, Fair Green, Reach, Cambridgeshire, CB5 0JD. Tel Newmarket (0638) 742171.

Claisabhrea Antiques. Tulloch St, Dingwall, Highland. Tel 2228.

Compton-Dando (Fine Arts) Ltd. Berewyk Hall, White Colne, Earls Colne, Essex. Tel 2200 (priv 0787 312610).

John Corlyon (Furniture) Ltd. The Workshop, Burstwick, Humberside. Tel Patrington (0964) 70701.

Corner House Antiques. Farrar Clse, Brunel Dr,Northern Rd Industrial Estate, Newark-on-Trent, Nottinghamshire, NG24 2EQ. Tel 79014 (priv 892628).

N.Davighi. 117 Shepherds Bush Rd, London, W6. Tel 603 5357.

General Trading Co. 144 Sloane St, London, SW1X 9BL. Tel 730 0411.

Goodall & Co Ltd. 26 Chiswick High Rd, London, W4. Tel 994 1729 (priv 994 2376).

Gostin of Liverpool Ltd. Portway, off 2a Higher Rd,Halewood, Liverpool, Merseyside, L25 0QQ. Tel 486 1703/6175.

Halliday's (Antiques). 28 Beauchamp Place, London, SW3. Tel 589 5534.

Samuel Heath & Sons PLC. Cobden Works,Leopold St, Birmingham, W.Midlands, B12 0UJ. Tel 772 2303.

Herrald Antiques. 38 Queen St, Edinburgh, Lothian. Tel 225 5939.

S. & H. Jewell Ltd. 26 Parker St, London, WC2B 5PH. Tel 405 8520.

Kensington Furniture. Troy Court,214-216 Kensington High St, London, W8. Tel 937 4973.

Robin Lloyd Antiques. 23-24 Brookend St, Ross-on-Wye, Hereford & Worcester. Tel 62123.

Alan Morris. 503 Evesham Rd, Crabbs Cross, Redditch, Hereford & Worcester, B97 5JJ. Tel 45084.

Old Pine Furniture and Jouet. 8 Kinerras, Kiltarlity by Beauly, Highland, IV4 7JL. Tel Kiltarlity (046374) 261.

Penny Farthing. High St, Croydon, Cambridgeshire. Tel Cambridge (0223) 207331.

The Pine Village. 162 Wandsworth Bridge Road, London, SW6. Tel 736 2753.

A.J.Ponsford Antiques and Restorations. 51-53 Dollar St, Cirencester, Gloucestershire, GL7 2AS. Tel 2355.

Renaissance Furniture. Providence Chapel, Tan y Lan,Ruabon, Wrexham, Clwyd. Tel Ruabon (0978) 824202.

G.E.Richards & Son (Antiques). 57 Blueschool St, Hereford, Hereford & Worcester, HR1 2AR. Tel 267840 (priv 268827).

Rogers Antiques. 22 Ewell Rd, Cheam, Surrey. Tel 643 8466.

B.R.Ryland. 75 Reading Rd, Henley-on-Thames, Oxfordshire, RG9 1AX. Tel 573663.

Sainsburys of Bournemouth. 23-25 Abbott Rd, Bournemouth, Dorset, BH9 1EU. Tel 529271 (priv 763616).

Frank Semus Ltd. 20 Middle St, Brighton & Hove, E.Sussex. Tel 28883.

Sheraton Antiques Ltd. 192 Westbourne Grove, London, W11. Tel 229 8748.

Something New. 3 Old Cross, Hertford, Hertfordshire. Tel 551530.

St Breock Gallery. St Breock Churchtown,St Breock, Wadebridge, Cornwall, PL27 7JS. Tel 2543 (priv 3451).

Stuart Interiors. Barrington Court,Barrington, Ilminster, Somerset, TA19 0NQ. Tel South Petherton (0460) 40349.

William Tillman Ltd. Crouch Lane, Borough Green, Kent, TN15 8LT. Tel 883278.

Clifford J. Tracy. 6-40 Durnford St, Seven Sisters Rd, London, N15 5NQ. Tel 800 4773.

Treasure House. 123 University St, Belfast, Belfast, BT7 1HP. Tel 231055.

Uvedale Hall Reproductions. Uvedale Hall, Needham Market, Suffolk. Tel 720262.

Waterwheel Pine and Antiques. Cricklepit Mill,The Quay, Exeter, Devon. Tel 217076.

Yesterday's Pine. 13 Dunstable St, Ampthill, Bedfordshire. Tel 402260.

Furniture, Early to 17th Century

see also Oak Furniture

London

Alexander & Berendt Ltd. 1A Davies St, London, W1Y 1LL. Tel 499 4775.

David Alexander Antiques. 102 Waterford Rd, London, SW6. Tel 731 4644.

Anno Domini. 66 Pimlico Rd, London, SW1. Tel 730 5496.

Stephen Anson. 31a Matheson Rd, London, W14. Tel 602 5277 (24hr answering).

Barling of Mount Street Ltd. 112 Mount St, London, W1. Tel 499 2858.

William Bedford PLC. The Merchants Hall, 46 Essex Rd,Islington, London, N1 8LN. Tel 226 9648.

Joanna Booth. 247 King's Rd, London, SW3. Tel 352 8998.

Church Street Galleries. 77 Kensington Church St, London, W8 4BG. Tel 937 2461 (priv 937 9175).

Frank Collins. 60 Ledbury Rd, London, W11 2AJ. Tel 221 7108, 0502-714842.

Peter Collins. 92 Waterford Rd, London, SW6. Tel 736 4149.

Csaky's Antiques. 20 Pimlico Rd, London, SW1. Tel 730 2068.

Arthur Davidson Ltd. 78-79 Jermyn St, London, SW1. Tel 930 6687, 930 4643.

Eldridge London. 99-101 Farringdon Rd, London, EC1. Tel 837 0379.

W.R.Harvey & Co (Antiques) Ltd. 67-70 Chalk Farm Rd, London, NW1 8AN. Tel 485 1504, 267 2767.

Olivia Jackson Antiques. 287 Westbourne Grove, London, W11. Tel 727 2817.

Tobias Jellinek. 156 Brompton Rd, London, SW3 1HW. Tel 589 5272, 581 2267.

George Johnson. 120 Kensington Park Road, London, W11 2PW. Tel 229 3119.

John Keil Ltd. 154 Brompton Rd, London, SW3. Tel 589 6454.

Lillie Antiques. 244 Lillie Rd, London, SW6 7QA. Tel 385 9852.

Rendlesham & Dark. 498 Kings Rd, London, SW10. Tel 351 1442.

G. Sarti Antiques Ltd. 186 Westbourne Grove, London, W11. Tel 221 7186.

M. & D. Seligmann. 37 Kensington Church St, London, W8 4LL. Tel 937 0400 (priv 722 4315).

Directory Entries are Free and ADDITIONS OR CORRECTIONS will be welcomed by *THE EDITOR, British Art and Antiques Directory, National Magazine House, 72 Broadwick Street, London W1V 2BP*

Shield & Allen. 584-586 King's Rd, London, SW6. Tel 736 7145.

Jacob Stodel Antiques. 116 Kensington Church St, London, W8 4BH. Tel 221 2652.

Pamela Streather. 4 Studio Place, Kinnerton St, London, SW1. Tel 235 3450.

David Tron (Antiques) Ltd. 275 King's Rd, Chelsea, London, SW3. Tel 352 5918.

Geoffrey Van Ltd. 105 and 107 Portobello Rd, London, W11. Tel 229 5577.

W.E.Walker. 277/9 Camden High St, London, NW1 7BX. Tel 485 6210 (priv 485 4433).

Regions

A.& F. Partners. 20 London St, Faringdon, Oxfordshire, SN7 7AA. Tel 20078.

Abbey Antiques. 52-54 High St, Glastonbury, Somerset, BA6 9DY. Tel 31694 (priv 32795).

The Antique Galleries. Watling St, Paulerspury, Northamptonshire. Tel 238.

Antiques. 9 Market Square, Saffron Walden, Essex. Tel 23611 (0672 870727).

Jess Applin Antiques. 8 Lensfield Rd, Cambridge, Cambridgeshire, CB2 1EG. Tel 315168 (priv 246851).

M. & S. Armson Ltd. 370 High St, Berkhamsted, Hertfordshire. Tel 2241.

Ashton Antiques. 12 Arden Buildings,Station Rd, Dorridge, W.Midlands. Tel 3040.

John Atkins Antiques Galleries. Cranbrook Rd, Hawkhurst, Kent. Tel 2033/4.

Avon Lodge Antiques. Southampton Rd, Fordingbridge, Hampshire, SP6 1AB. Tel 53275.

Anthony Baker Antiques. 14 London Rd, Alderley Edge, Cheshire, SK9 7JS. Tel 582674.

Barlow Antiques. Sevington Manor, Tichborne, Hampshire, SO24 0NF. Tel Alresford (096 273) 4800.

Barton House Antiques. Barton House, 48 Wharf Rd, Stanford le Hope, Essex, SS17 0DY. Tel Stanford-le-Hope (0375) 672494.

Roy Barton. Myrtle Cottage, Codmore Hill, Pulborough, W.Sussex, RH21 1BQ. Tel 2730.

Michael Beaumont Antiques. Hempstead Hall,Hempstead, Saffron Walden, Essex, CB10 2PR. Tel Steeple Bumpstead(044084) 239.

David Bedale Antiques. 5 Minshull St, Knutsford, Cheshire. Tel 53621.

Beedham Antiques Ltd. Holme Hall, Bakewell, Derbyshire. Tel 3285.

Mary Bellis Antiques. Charnham Close (A4 Highway), Hungerford, Berkshire, RG17 0EJ. Tel 82620.

Beveridge (Antiques). 1-2 South St John's Place, Perth, Tayside, PH1 5SU. Tel 35055(priv 030786 212/209.

Brian Bingham Antiques. 420 Chatsworth Rd, Brampton, Chesterfield, Derbyshire. Tel 208441.

George S.Bolam. Oak House, The Chipping, Tetbury, Gloucestershire. Tel 52211.

Bowood Antiques. Wendover Dean Farm,Bowood Lane, Wendover, Buckinghamshire, HP22 6PY. Tel 622113.

Robert Bradley. 71 Brown St, Salisbury, Wiltshire. Tel 333677.

Brampton Mill Antiques Centre. Brampton Mill, Brampton, Cambridgeshire. Tel Huntingdon (0480) 55593.

Simon Brett. Creswyke House, High St, Moreton-in-Marsh, Gloucestershire, GL56 0LH. Tel 50751.

E. & G. Briere. Keeper's Cottage, Suffield, Norwich, Norfolk, NR11 7ER. Tel Aylsham (0263) 732651.

J. & M. Bristow Antiques. 28 Long St, Tetbury, Gloucestershire, GL8 8AQ. Tel 52222.

H.& M.J.Burke. Packet House Buildings, Worsley, Greater Manchester, M28 4PA. Tel 794 2093.

Roderick P.Butler. Marwood House, Honiton, Devon, EX14 8PY. Tel 2169.

Bygones of Debenham. 1 High St, Debenham, Suffolk. Tel 860707.

J. & J. Caspall Antiques. Sheep St, Stow-on-the-Wold, Gloucestershire. Tel 31160.

Castle Lodge. Castle Square, Ludlow, Shropshire. Tel 2833.

Cave's of Northampton. 111 Kettering Rd, Northampton, Northamptonshire, NN1 4BA. Tel 38278.

Cedar Antiques. High St, Hartley Wintney, Hampshire, RG27 8NY. Tel 3252.

K.Chappell Antiques & Fine Art. King St, Bakewell, Derbyshire, DE4 1DZ. Tel 2496 (priv 2960).

K.Chappell Antiques & Fine Art. Goose Green, Baslow, Derbyshire, DE4 1SR. Tel 3311.

Cirencester Antiques Ltd. 17 Dyer St, Cirencester, Gloucestershire, GL7 2PP. Tel 2955 (priv 3066).

Clement House Antiques. High St, Burford, Oxfordshire, OX8 4QE. Tel 3172.

Clinkers Antiques Ltd. c/o Island Farm, Steep, Petersfield, Hampshire. Tel 62319.

Coldstream Antiques. 44 High St, Coldstream, Borders, TD12 4AS. Tel 2552.

Anthony Cotton. 26-27 Steep Hill, Lincoln, Lincolnshire. Tel 25838 (priv 0673 60562).

Thomas Coulborn & Sons. Vesey Manor, 64 Birmingham Rd, Sutton Coldfield, W.Midlands, B72 1QP. Tel 354 3974, 354 3139.

O.M. & R.D.Cox Antiques. 5 St Mary's Hill, Stamford, Lincolnshire. Tel 64159.

Thomas Crispin. The Little Manor, Winchelsea, E.Sussex, TN36 4EJ. Tel Rye (0797) 226699.

John Croft Antiques. 3 George St, Bath, Avon, BA1 2EH. Tel 66211.

G.E.Day. 82 West St, Farnham, Surrey, GU9 7EN. Tel 715 043.

de Montfort. 49 High St, Robertsbridge, E.Sussex, TN32 5AN. Tel 880698 (priv 082 584 243).

Derbyshire Antiques Ltd. 159 London Road South, Poynton, Cheshire, SK12 1LQ. Tel 873110.

Duveen Antiques. Burgate, Fordingbridge, Hampshire, SP6 1LX. Tel 53309.

Eaton's of Eton Ltd. 62-63 High St, Eton, Berkshire. Tel Windsor (0753) 860337 (priv 0628 27413).

Extence Antiques. 2 Wellington St, Teignmouth, Devon. Tel 3353.

The Faringdon Galleries. 79 London St, Faringdon, Oxfordshire. Tel 20344.

Farnborough (Kent) Antiques. 10 Church Rd, Farnborough, Kent, BR6 7DB. Tel 51834.

Harvey Ferry, William Clegg Antiques. The Barns, 1 High St, Nettlebed, Oxfordshire, RG9 5AA. Tel 641533.

Flemings Antiques. High St, Debenham, Suffolk, IP14 6QJ. Tel 860422.

Frith Antiques. New St, Petworth, W.Sussex. Tel 43155 (priv 079881 606).

The Furniture Station Ltd. The Kelterment Antique Market,Fordham, Ely, Cambridgeshire.

Richard Glass. Hockerley Old Hall, Whaley Bridge, Derbyshire, SK12 7AS. Tel 4320.

Maurice Goldstone & Son. Avenel Court, King St, Bakewell, Derbyshire. Tel 2487.

Peter Gould. 101 Northgate, Halifax, W.Yorkshire.

Denzil Grant Antiques Ltd. Hall Street,Bradfield St George, Long Melford, Suffolk. Tel 75470 (priv 04493 576).

Renee and Roy Green. Ashcombe House, Lewes Rd, Lewes, E.Sussex. Tel 474794.

Richard Greene Antiques. 87 Main St, Burley in Wharfedale, W.Yorkshire, LS29 7JX. Tel 862156.

Grey House Antiques. 8 Newport St, Tiverton, Devon, EX16 6NH. Tel 255846.

Guildhall Galleries. Thaxted, Essex. Tel 395.

Peter Hammond. Church House, Thornage, Holt, Norfolk. Tel 861352.

Hampshires of Dorking. 51/52 West St, Dorking, Surrey. Tel 887076.

Ian G.Hastie. 46 St Ann St, Salisbury, Wiltshire. Tel 22957.

Keith Hockin Antiques Ltd. The Square, Stow-on-the-Wold, Gloucestershire, GL54 1AF. Tel 31058.

Milton Holgate Antiques. 4 Market Place, Knaresborough, N.Yorkshire. Tel Harrogate (0423) 863205.

Guy Holland. Shepbridge Barn, Eastleach, Gloucestershire, GL7 3PS. Tel Southrop (036785) 296.

Anthony J.Hook. 3 The Green, Westerham, Kent. Tel 62161 (priv 0892-870552).

Oliver and Helen Horswill Antiques. 62 Grange Rd, West Kirby, Merseyside. Tel 625 7111 (priv 625 6182).

Humphry Antiques. East St, Petworth, W.Sussex, GU28 0AB. Tel 43053 (priv 42944).

Huntington Antiques Ltd. The Old Forge, Church St, Stow-on-the-Wold, Gloucestershire. Tel 30842.

A.E.Jameson & Co. 257 Glossop Rd, Sheffield, S.Yorkshire, S10 2GZ. Tel 23846 (priv 26189).

H.W.Keil Ltd. Tudor House, Broadway, Hereford & Worcester, WR12 7DP. Tel 852408.

H.W. Keil (Cheltenham) Ltd. 129-131 The Promenade, Cheltenham, Gloucestershire, GL50 1NW. Tel 522509, 527974.

John Keil Ltd. 10 Quiet St, Bath, Avon, BA1 2JU. Tel 63176.

Leonard Lassalle. 21 The Pantiles, Tunbridge Wells, Kent, TN2 5TD. Tel 31645.

David Lazarus. High St, Hartley Wintney, Hampshire. Tel 2272.

Michel Le Coz. High St, Castle Combe, Wiltshire, SN14 7HU. Tel 782223.

Lennard Antiques. The Laurels, Tingewick, Buckingham, Buckinghamshire, MK18 4NN. Tel Finmere (02804) 371.

Charles Lowe & Sons Ltd. 37-40 Church Gate, Loughborough, Leicestershire. Tel 217876.

Graham Lower. Stonecrouch Farmhouse, Flimwell, E.Sussex, TN5 7QB. Tel 535.

Victor Mahy Ltd. Mulberry House, Stockbridge, Hampshire, SO20 6EY. Tel 810466.

R.E. Martin. 40 Gold St, Tiverton, Devon. Tel 252832.

F.J.McCarthy Ltd. The Grange, Normanton on Trent, Newark-on-Trent, Nottinghamshire, NG23 6RQ. Tel 821382.

Metcalfe Jackson. 24A West St, Wimborne Minster, Dorset, BH21 1JS. Tel 883327.

Trevor Micklem, Antiques. Withywine Farm,Morebath, Tiverton, Devon, EX16 9BZ. Tel Bampton (0398) 31409.

Mill on the Soar Antiques Ltd. 1-3 High St, Quorn, Leicestershire, LE12 8DS. Tel 414218.

C.S. Moreton (Antiques). Inchmartine House, Inchture, Tayside, PH14 9QQ. Tel 86412.

William Morley Antiques. Musgrave's Old Farm, West Monkton, Taunton, Somerset, TA2 8NW. Tel West Monkton (0823) 412751.

John G.Morris Ltd. Market Square, Petworth, W.Sussex, GU28 0AH. Tel 42305.

Charles & Joan Mortimer & Sons. Sugar House, School St, Great Chesterford, Essex, CB10 1NN. Tel Saffron Walden (0799) 30261.

Ralph and Bruce Moss. 26 Whitehorse St, Baldock, Hertfordshire, SG7 6QQ. Tel 892751.

Victor Needham Antiques. Hinwood House, High St,Broughton, Stockbridge, Hampshire. Tel Broughton (0794) 301205.

B.M.Newlove. 139-141 Ewell Rd, Surbiton, Surrey. Tel 339 8857.

John Nicholls Antiques. 27 Long St, Tetbury, Gloucestershire. Tel 52781 (priv 08893 2383).

Elizabeth Niner Antiques. 53 Great Norwood St, Cheltenham, Gloucestershire. Tel 516497 (priv 520066).

Simon W.Nutter. Wraggs Row, Fosse Way, Stow-on-the-Wold, Gloucestershire. Tel 30658.

A.J. & L.Onions. White Cottage, 8 Tern Hill, Market Drayton, Shropshire, TF9 3PR. Tel Tern Hill (063 083) 222.

Rudolph Otto. The Little House, Sheep St, Stow-on-the-Wold, Gloucestershire.

Mike Ottrey Antiques. 28 High St, Dorchester, Oxfordshire. Tel Oxford (0865) 340079.

Angela Page Antiques. Sion House, 15 Mount Sion, Tunbridge Wells, Kent, TN1 1OD. Tel 22217.

Park Street Antiques. 350 High St (on A41), Berkhamsted, Hertfordshire, HP4 1HT. Tel 4790 (priv 024029 255).

Phillips of Hitchin (Antiques) Ltd. The Manor House,Bancroft (main street), Hitchin, Hertfordshire, SG5 1JW. Tel 32067.

Phoenix Antiques. 1 Carter St, Fordham, Cambridgeshire. Tel Newmarket (0638) 720 363.

W.A.Pinn & Sons. 124 Swan St, Sible Hedingham, Essex, CO9 3HP. Tel Hedingham (0787) 61127.

Randolph. 97-99 High St, Hadleigh, Suffolk, IP7 5EJ. Tel 823789.

James Reeve. 9 Church St, Warwick, Warwickshire. Tel 498113.

Regent Antiques. Dynever House, New St, Painswick, Gloucestershire. Tel 812543.

Restall, Brown & Clennell Ltd. Cosgrove Hall, Cosgrove, Northamptonshire, MK19 7JB. Tel Milton Keynes (0908) 565888 (priv 563336).

Robertsbridge House Antiques. High St, Robertsbridge, E.Sussex, TN32 5AN. Tel 880291.

Rundells Antiques. London Rd (B 1393), Harlow, Essex, CM17 9LH. Tel 22906.

Sam Savage Antiques. Hayes Farm, Ticknall, Derbyshire, DE7 1JZ. Tel Melbourne (033 16) 2195.

Saville Antiques. 37 Long St, Devizes, Wiltshire. Tel 3559.

Scott Antiques. 67 Walton St, Walton on the Hill, Surrey, KT20 7RZ. Tel Tadworth (073781) 2097 (priv 0396 882431).

Sherborne Antiques Ltd. At The China Gallery,Long St, Sherborne, Dorset, DT9 3BS. Tel 812978.

Paul Smith. The Old Chapel,Old St, Ludlow, Shropshire, SY8 1NP. Tel 2666.

Robin Smith. 23 Belle Vue Rd, Shrewsbury, Shropshire, SY3 7LN. Tel 50357.

Tom Smith Antiques. 33A St Peters St, Ipswich, Suffolk. Tel 210172.

St Ouen Antiques. Vintage Corner, Old Cambridge Rd, Puckeridge, Hertfordshire. Tel Ware (0920) 821336.

Stalham Antique Gallery. High St, Stalham, Norfolk. Tel 80636.

Strouds of Southwell Antiques. 3 Westgate, Southwell, Nottinghamshire. Tel 815001.

Suthburgh Antiques. Red House, Hall St, Long Melford, Suffolk. Tel Sudbury (0787) 74818.

Swan Antiques. 62A West St, Dorking, Surrey. Tel 881217 (priv 01-394 2361).

Taylor-Halsey Antiques. Strangs,Sandford, Crediton, Devon, EX17 4EL. Tel 3408.

M. & R. Taylor Antiques. 53 Broad St, Ludlow, Shropshire, SY8 1NH. Tel 4169.

Thorpe & Foster Ltd. 49 West St, Dorking, Surrey. Tel 881029.

Three Salmons Antiques. Three Salmons Hotel Ltd, Usk, Gwent. Tel 2133, 2134.

Touchwood Antiques. 9 Park St., Stow-on-the-Wold, Gloucestershire, GL54 1AQ. Tel 30221.

Turpins Antiques. 4 Stoney Lane, Thaxted, Essex. Tel 830495 (priv 830059).

Clive Underwood Antiques. 46 High St, Colsterworth, Lincolnshire. Tel Grantham (0476) 860689.

A.G. Voss Antiques. 16 Market Hill, Woodbridge, Suffolk, IP12 4LU. Tel 5830.

Zene Walker. The Bull House Antiques,High St, Burford, Oxfordshire. Tel 3284.

Wellesley Wilson Antiques. Aldersey Manor, Aldersey, Cheshire, CH3 9EH. Tel Broxton (082 925) 500.

John Whitelaw & Sons. 120 High St, Auchterarder, Tayside, PH3 1AD. Tel 2482.

Francis Wigram Antiques. Cotters Barn, Penn, Buckinghamshire, PN10 8LB. Tel 3266.

Windhill Antiquary. 4 High St, Bishop's Stortford, Hertfordshire. Tel 51587.

Charles Woodward Antiques. Market Place, Fairford, Gloucestershire, GL7 4AB. Tel Cirencester (0285) 712094.

Yeo Antiques. 8 Springfields, Tetbury, Gloucestershire, GL8. Tel 521300.

Furniture, 18th Century

London

Didier Aaron (London) Ltd. 21 Ryder St, London, SW1Y 6PX. Tel 839 4716/7.

Adams Room Ltd. 18-20 Ridgway, Wimbledon Village, London, SW19. Tel 946 7047 (priv 947 4784).

Norman Adams Ltd. 8-10 Hans Rd, London, SW3 IRX. Tel 589 5266.

Alexander & Berendt Ltd. 1A Davies St, London, W1Y 1LL. Tel 499 4775.

Anno Domini. 66 Pimlico Rd, London, SW1. Tel 730 5496.

The Antique Home. 104A Kensington Church St, London, W8 4BU. Tel 229 5892.

Apter-Fredericks Ltd. 265-267 Fulham Rd, London, SW3 6HY. Tel 352 2188.

Karin Armelin Antiques. 592 King's Rd, London, SW6. Tel 736 0375.

Asprey PLC. 165-169 New Bond St, London, W1Y 0AR. Tel 493 6767.

The Badger. 12 St Mary's Rd, Ealing, London, W5 5ES. Tel 567 5601.

Alexander Bailie (Antiques). 2 Lower Mall,359 Upper St, Islington, London, N1 0PD. Tel 354 2839 (priv 354 1739).

Eddy Bardawil. 106 Kensington Church St, London, W8. Tel 221 3967.

Barnet Antiques and Fine Art. 1180 High Rd, Whetstone, London, N20. Tel 445 9695.

H.C.Baxter & Sons. 191-193 Fulham Rd, London, SW3. Tel 352 9826.

William Bedford PLC. The Merchants Hall, 46 Essex Rd,Islington, London, N1 8LN. Tel 226 9648.

Peter Bentley. 22 Connaught St, London, W2. Tel 723 9394.

Bernheimer Fine Arts Ltd. 32 St George St,Mayfair, London, W1R 9FA. Tel 499 0293.

Peter Chapman Antiques. 10 Theberton St, Islington, London, N1 0QX. Tel 226 5565 (priv 348 4846).

Church Street Galleries. 77 Kensington Church St, London, W8 4BG. Tel 937 2461 (priv 937 9175).

John Clay. 263 New King's Rd, London, SW6. Tel 731 5677.

Philip Colleck Ltd. 84 Fulham Rd, London, SW3 6HR. Tel 584 8479.

Frank Collins. 60 Ledbury Rd, London, W11 2AJ. Tel 221 7108, 0502-714842.

Peter Collins. 92 Waterford Rd, London, SW6. Tel 736 4149.

Connaught Galleries. 44 Connaught St, London, W2. Tel 723 1660.

Richard Courtney Ltd. 112-114 Fulham Rd, London, SW3 6HU. Tel 370 4020.

Csaky's Antiques. 20 Pimlico Rd, London, SW1. Tel 730 2068.

Michael Davidson Antiques. 52-54 Ledbury Rd, London, W11 2AJ. Tel 229 6088 (priv 352 4541).

Robert Dickson Antiques. 263 Fulham Rd, London, SW3. Tel 351 0330 (priv 948 5825).

The Dining Room Shop. 64 White Hart Lane,Barnes, London, SW13 0PZ. Tel 878 1020 (priv 876 5212).

Eldridge London. 99-101 Farringdon Rd, London, EC1. Tel 837 0379.

Fernandes & Marche. 23 Motcomb St, Belgrave Sq, London, SW1. Tel 235 6773.

Brian Fielden. 3 New Cavendish St, London, W1M 7RP. Tel 935 6912.

Michael Foster. 118 Fulham Rd, London, SW3 6HU. Tel 373 3636.

Peter Francis. 26 Museum St, London, WC1A 1JT. Tel 637 0165.

C.Fredericks & Sons. 92 Fulham Rd, London, SW3. Tel 589 5847.

Godson & Coles Ltd. 310 King's Rd, London, SW3 5UH. Tel 352 8509.

Jonathan Harris. 54 Kensington Church St, London, W8. Tel 937 3133.

M.Harris & Sons. Gayfere House,22-23 Gayfere St, London, SW1P 3HP. Tel 222 8161.

W.R.Harvey & Co (Antiques) Ltd. 67-70 Chalk Farm Rd, London, NW1 8AN. Tel 485 1504, 267 2767.

Lesley Hepherd Antiques. London, SW7. Tel 244 9675.

Christopher Hodsoll Antiques. 50 & 69 Pimlico Rd, London, SW1. Tel 730 9835.

Michael Hogg. 172 Brompton Rd, London, SW3. Tel 589 8629.

Hotspur Ltd. 14 Lowndes St, Belgrave Sq, London, SW1. Tel 235 1918.

Olivia Jackson Antiques. 287 Westbourne Grove, London, W11. Tel 727 2817.

Anthony James & Son Ltd. 88 Fulham Road, London, SW3. Tel 584 1120 (priv 385 3408).

Jeremy Ltd. 255 King's Rd, Chelsea, London, SW3 5EL. Tel 352 3127, 352 0644.

George Johnson. 120 Kensington Park Road, London, W11 2PW. Tel 229 3119.

John Keil Ltd. 154 Brompton Rd, London, SW3. Tel 589 6454.

Thomas Kerr Antiques Ltd. 11 Theberton St, Islington, London, N1. Tel 226 0626.

Lillie Antiques. 244 Lillie Rd, London, SW6 7QA. Tel 385 9852.

J.Lipitch Ltd. 177 Westbourne Grove, London, W11. Tel 229 0783.

Michael Lipitch. 98 Fulham Rd, London, SW3. Tel 589 7327 (priv 440 7797).

C.H. Major. 154 Kensington Church St, London, W8 4BM. Tel 229 1162.

Mallett & Son (Antiques) Ltd. 40 New Bond St, London, W1Y 0BS. Tel 499 7411.

Michael Marriott Ltd. 588 Fulham Rd, London, SW6 5NT. Tel 736 3110, 381 3455.

Richard Miles Antiques. 8 Holbein Place, London, SW1 8NL. Tel 730 1957.

Mrs Monro (Antiques) Ltd. 11 Montpelier St, London, SW7. Tel 589 5052, 821 1860.

Michael & Margaret Parker. 24 Cheval Place, London, SW7. Tel 589 0133.

Partridge (Fine Arts) Ltd. 144-146 New Bond St, London, W1. Tel 629 0834.

David Pettifer Ltd. 269 King's Rd, London, SW3 5EN. Tel 352 3088.

Henry Phillips. 2 Campden Street, London, W8 7EP. Tel 727 4079.

Ronald Phillips Ltd. 26 Bruton St, London, W1X 8LH. Tel 493 2341.

Rendall. 572 King's Rd, London, SW6. Tel 736 2520 (priv 948 4400).

J. Roger (Antiques) Ltd. 17 Uxbridge St, London, W8. Tel 727 2227 (priv 603 7627).

Geoffrey Rose Ltd. 77 Pimlico Rd, London, SW1W 8PH. Tel 730 3004.

Patrick Sandberg Antiques. 791 Fulham Rd, London, SW6 5HD. Tel 736 9454.

G. Sarti Antiques Ltd. 186 Westbourne Grove, London, W11. Tel 221 7186.

M. & D. Seligmann. 37 Kensington Church St, London, W8 4LL. Tel 937 0400 (priv 722 4315).

Sensation Ltd. 66 Fulham High St, London, SW6 5LQ. Tel 736 4135 (priv 584 9414).

Sylvia Sheppard. 71 Kensington Church St, London, W8 4BG. Tel 937 0965.

Shield & Allen. 584-586 King's Rd, London, SW6. Tel 736 7145.

Spyer & Son (Antiques) Ltd. 18 Motcomb St, Belgrave Sq, London, SW1X 8LB. Tel 235 3348.

Stair & Company Ltd. 120 Mount St, London, W1Y 5HB. Tel 499 1784, 499 1785.

Louis Stanton. 299 Westbourne Grove, London, W11. Tel 727 9336.

Jacob Stodel Antiques. 116 Kensington Church St, London, W8 4BH. Tel 221 2652.

Murray Thomson Ltd. 141 Kensington Church St, London, W8 7LP. Tel 727 1727, 727 1825.

David Tron (Antiques) Ltd. 275 King's Rd, Chelsea, London, SW3. Tel 352 5918.

M.Turpin. 21 Manson Mews, Queensgate, London, SW7. Tel 736 3417.

Tzigany Fine Arts. 28-29 Dover St, London, W1X 3PA. Tel 491 1007.

Vane House Antiques. 15 Camden Passage, London, N1. Tel 359 1343.

W.E.Walker. 277/9 Camden High St, London, NW1 7BX. Tel 485 6210 (priv 485 4433).

Westenholz Antiques Ltd. 68 Pimlico Rd, London, SW1. Tel 730 2151.

Regions

A.& F. Partners. 20 London St, Faringdon, Oxfordshire, SN7 7AA. Tel 20078.

Abbey Antiques. 52-54 High St, Glastonbury, Somerset, BA6 9DY. Tel 31694 (priv 32795).

Nicholas Abbott. High St, Hartley Wintney, Hampshire, RG27 8NY. Tel 2365 (priv 3509).

Alexander Adamson Antiques. Tearnside Hall, Kirkby Lonsdale, Cumbria, LA6 2PU. Tel 71989.

Alderson & Alderson. 23 Brock St, Bath, Avon. Tel 21652.

Alvin Antiques. 148 Union St, Plymouth, Devon. Tel 665628.

Michael Andrews Antiques. Portsmouth Rd, Milford, Surrey. Tel Godalming (04868) 20765.

Andwells. High St, Hartley Wintney, Hampshire. Tel 2305.

Annique Antiques. 13 Nevill St, Tunbridge Wells, Kent, TN2 5RU. Tel 26776.

John Anthony Antiques. 71 High St, Bletchingley, Surrey. Tel Godstone (0883) 843197.

The Antique Galleries. Watling St, Paulerspury, Northamptonshire. Tel 238.

The Antique Shop. Main St, Tramore, Co Waterford. Tel (051) 81548.

The Antique Shop. 6 West St, Wimborne Minster, Dorset. Tel 880297.

Antiques. Main St, Eyam, Derbyshire. Tel Baslow (024 688) 3265.

Antiques. 9 Market Square, Saffron Walden, Essex. Tel 23611 (0672 870727).

Antiques Coffee House. Buxton Rd, Bakewell, Derbyshire. Tel 3544.

Apollo Antiques Ltd. 62 West St, Warwick, Warwickshire. Tel 494746.

Jess Applin Antiques. 8 Lensfield Rd, Cambridge, Cambridgeshire, CB2 1EG. Tel 315168 (priv 246851).

Archer Antiques. 58 Castlegate, Penrith, Cumbria. Tel 63446 (priv 0930 51813).

M. & S. Armson Ltd. 370 High St, Berkhamsted, Hertfordshire. Tel 2241.

Armstrong Antiques. 10 & 11 Montpellier Parade, Harrogate, N.Yorkshire. Tel 506843.

James Ash Antiques. The Warehouse, Station Rd, Llandeilo, Dyfed. Tel 823728 (priv 0269 850119).

Ashton Antiques. 12 Arden Buildings,Station Rd, Dorridge, W.Midlands. Tel 3040.

John Atkins Antiques Galleries. Cranbrook Rd, Hawkhurst, Kent. Tel 2033/4.

Atrium Antiques Ltd. 19 Market Place, Woburn, Bedfordshire, NK17 9PZ. Tel 444.

Avon Antiques. 26-27 Market St, Bradford-on-Avon, Wiltshire. Tel 2052.

Avon Lodge Antiques. Southampton Rd, Fordingbridge, Hampshire, SP6 1AB. Tel 53275.

Baggott Church Street Ltd. Church Street, Stow-on-the-Wold, Gloucestershire, GL54 1BB. Tel 30370.

Anthony Baker Antiques. 14 London Rd, Alderley Edge, Cheshire, SK9 7JS. Tel 582674.

Barlow Antiques. Sevington Manor, Tichborne, Hampshire, SO24 0NF. Tel Alresford (096 273) 4800.

Barnet Antiques & Fine Art. 236 High St, Barnet, Hertfordshire, EN5 5TD. Tel 01-440 3620.

Baron Antiques. 373 Bury New Rd, Manchester, Greater Manchester. Tel 773 9929.

John Barry. Barton End Hall, Nailsworth, Gloucestershire, GL6 0QQ. Tel 3471.

Barton House Antiques. Barton House, 48 Wharf Rd, Stanford le Hope, Essex, SS17 0DY. Tel Stanford-le-Hope (0375) 672494.

Roy Barton. Myrtle Cottage, Codmore Hill, Pulborough, W.Sussex, RH21 1BQ. Tel 2730.

Walter S.Beaton. 75 Kinnoull St, Perth, Tayside, PH1 5EZ. Tel 28127.

Michael Beaumont Antiques. Hempstead Hall,Hempstead, Saffron Walden, Essex, CB10 2PR. Tel Steeple Bumpstead(044084) 239.

John Beazor & Sons Ltd. 78-80 Regent St, Cambridge, Cambridgeshire, CB2 1DP. Tel 355178.

David Bedale Antiques. 5 Minshull St, Knutsford, Cheshire. Tel 53621.

John Bell of Aberdeen Ltd. Balbrogie, by Blackburn, Aberdeen, Grampian. Tel 79209.

Ray Best Antiques. North Street House, Ilminster, Somerset. Tel 2194.

Beveridge (Antiques). 1-2 South St John's Place, Perth, Tayside, PH1 5SU. Tel 35055(priv 030786 212/209.

Brian Bingham Antiques. 420 Chatsworth Rd, Brampton, Chesterfield, Derbyshire. Tel 208441.

Binsted Antiques. 21 Middle Lane, Teddington, Middlesex, TW11 0HQ. Tel 943 0626.

John Bly. 50 High St, Tring, Hertfordshire, HP23 5AG. Tel 3030.

Blyth Antiques. 28 Sydney Buildings, Bath, Avon, BA2 6BZ. Tel 69766.

George S.Bolam. Oak House, The Chipping, Tetbury, Gloucestershire. Tel 52211.

Derek Boston Antiques. 223 Wilton Rd, Salisbury, Wiltshire. Tel 22682.

Guy Bousfield. 58 Thames St, Windsor, Berkshire. Tel 864575.

M.J.Bowdery. 12 London Rd, Hindhead, Surrey. Tel 6376.

Bowood Antiques. Wendover Dean Farm,Bowood Lane, Wendover, Buckinghamshire, HP22 6PY. Tel 622113.

Robert Bradley. 71 Brown St, Salisbury, Wiltshire. Tel 333677.

Brampton Mill Antiques Centre. Brampton Mill, Brampton, Cambridgeshire. Tel Huntingdon (0480) 55593.

Breakspeare Antiques. 36 Long St, Tetbury, Gloucestershire, GL8 8AQ. Tel 53122.

Arthur Brett & Sons, Ltd. 40-44 St Giles St, Norwich, Norfolk, NR2 1LW. Tel 628171.

E. & G. Briere. Keeper's Cottage, Suffield, Norwich, Norfolk, NR11 7ER. Tel Aylsham (0263) 732651.

Bristow Antiques. Lindford Rd, Lindford, Bordon, Hampshire, GU35 OPY. Tel 2301.

J. & M. Bristow Antiques. 28 Long St, Tetbury, Gloucestershire, GL8 8AQ. Tel 52222.

Evelyn Buckle. The Villa, Main St, Redmile, Leicestershire, NG13 0GA. Tel Bottesford (0949) 42057.

H.& M.J.Burke. Packet House Buildings, Worsley, Greater Manchester, M28 4PA. Tel 794 2093.

Burns & Graham. 4 St Thomas St, Winchester, Hampshire. Tel 53779.

Edward Butler. 14 Bachelors Walk, Dublin, Co Dublin. Tel 730296.

Roderick P.Butler. Marwood House, Honiton, Devon, EX14 8PY. Tel 2169.

Bygones of Debenham. 1 High St, Debenham, Suffolk. Tel 860707.

Tom Caldwell Galleries Ltd. 40/42 & 56 Bradbury Place, Belfast, Belfast, BT7. Tel 223226 (priv 0846 621352).

Castle Lodge. Castle Square, Ludlow, Shropshire. Tel 2833.

Cave's of Northampton. 111 Kettering Rd, Northampton, Northamptonshire, NN1 4BA. Tel 38278.

Cedar Antiques. High St, Hartley Wintney, Hampshire, RG27 8NY. Tel 3252.

Chapel Antiques. Whatlington, E.Sussex, TN33 0NL. Tel Sedlescombe (042 487) 272.

K.Chappell Antiques & Fine Art. King St, Bakewell, Derbyshire, DE4 1DZ. Tel 2496 (priv 2960).

K.Chappell Antiques & Fine Art. Goose Green, Baslow, Derbyshire, DE4 1SR. Tel 3311.

Charles Antiques. 101 The Hundred, Romsey, Hampshire, SO5 8BZ. Tel 512885.

E.M. Cheshire Antiques. The Manor House, Market Place, Bingham, Nottinghamshire. Tel 38861 (priv 38455).

Cheverton's of Edenbridge Ltd. Taylour House, 69 High St, Edenbridge, Kent, TN8 5AL. Tel 863196.

Chislehurst Antiques. 7 Royal Parade, Chislehurst, Kent. Tel London (01) 467 1530.

Church House Antiques. 42 Church St, Weybridge, Surrey. Tel 42190.

Church View House Antiques. Kirk Michael,. Tel 0624 87433.

Cirencester Antiques Ltd. 17 Dyer St, Cirencester, Gloucestershire, GL7 2PP. Tel 2955 (priv 3066).

Clement House Antiques. High St, Burford, Oxfordshire, OX8 4QE. Tel 3172.

Coldstream Antiques. 44 High St, Coldstream, Borders, TD12 4AS. Tel 2552.

Nigel Coleman Antiques. High St, Brasted, Kent. Tel Westerham (0959) 64042.

F.G. & C. Collins Ltd (Collins Antiques). Corner House, Church St, Wheathampstead, Hertfordshire, AL4 8AP. Tel 3111 & 3483.

E.J.Cook & Son Antiques. The Antique Centre, 1 Severn Rd, Gloucester, Gloucestershire. Tel 29716.

Corfield of Lymington. 120 High St, Lymington, Hampshire, SO4 9SQ. Tel 73532, 75359.

Anthony Cotton. 26-27 Steep Hill, Lincoln, Lincolnshire. Tel 25838 (priv 0673 60562).

Thomas Coulborn & Sons. Vesey Manor, 64 Birmingham Rd, Sutton Coldfield, W.Midlands, B72 1QP. Tel 354 3974, 354 3139.

Courtney Beer. Milton House, Brixham, Devon. Tel 3195.

Paul Couts Ltd. 101-107 West Bow, Victoria St, Edinburgh, Lothian. Tel 225 3238.

John Croft Antiques. 3 George St, Bath, Avon, BA1 2EH. Tel 66211.

Cull Antiques. 14 Dragon St, Petersfield, Hampshire, GU31 4JN. Tel 63670.

Richard Davidson. Lombard St, Petworth, W.Sussex, GU28 0AG. Tel 42508.

Zona Dawson Antiques. The Old Club House, 2 The Close,Charlton Marshall, Blandford Forum, Dorset. Tel Blandford (0258) 53146.

G.E.Day. 82 West St, Farnham, Surrey, GU9 7EN. Tel 715 043.

David Dean Antiques. Pen-Y-Ghent View, Church St, Settle, N.Yorkshire. Tel 3702 (priv 3660).

Margery Dean Antiques. The Galleries, Alma St,Wivenhoe, Colchester, Essex. Tel 222523 (priv 250485).

Derbyshire Antiques Ltd. 159 London Road South, Poynton, Cheshire, SK12 1LQ. Tel 873110.

Doveridge House of Neachley. Neach Hill, Long Lane, Shifnal, Shropshire. Tel Albrighton (090 722) 3131, 3132.

Iain Downe Antiques. 28 North Rd, Brighton & Hove, E.Sussex, BN1 1YB. Tel 697496.

Brian & Angela Downes Antiques. 9 Broad St, Bath, Avon, BA1 5LJ. Tel 65352.

Downshire House Antiques. 63 Downshire Rd, Newry, Co Down, BT34. Tel 66689.

Peter Dryden Ltd. Teign Court, Teignmouth, Devon, TQ14 8AY. Tel 78095 (priv 78392).

Dunluce Antiques. 33 Ballytober Rd, Bushmills, Co Antrim. Tel 31140.

Eagle House Antiques. Eagle House Antiques Market,Market Square, Midhurst, W.Sussex. Tel 2718 (priv 0705 326620).

Eaton's of Eton Ltd. 62-63 High St, Eton, Berkshire. Tel Windsor (0753) 860337 (priv 0628 27413).

Richard Essex. 41 Alma Vale Rd, Bristol, Avon, BS8 2HL. Tel 733949.

Eton Gallery. 116 High St, Eton, Berkshire. Tel Windsor (0753) 865147 (priv 860963).

Extence Antiques. 2 Wellington St, Teignmouth, Devon. Tel 3353.

Stephen Falk. Rochdale, Greater Manchester, OL12 6LE. Tel 44946.

The Faringdon Galleries. 79 London St, Faringdon, Oxfordshire. Tel 20344.

Jeremy A. Fearn. The Old Rectory, Winksley, Ripon, N.Yorkshire. Tel Kirkby Malzeard (0765 83) 625.

Ferneyhough. Brook House, Beaudesert, Henley-in-Arden, Warwickshire, B95 5QR. Tel 2451.

Harvey Ferry, William Clegg Antiques. The Barns, 1 High St, Nettlebed, Oxfordshire, RG9 5AA. Tel 641533.

G.W.Ford & Son Ltd. 290 Glossop Rd, Sheffield, S.Yorkshire, S10 2HS. Tel 22082.

Thomas Franklin (Antiques). 28 Charnham St, Hungerford, Berkshire, RG17 OEJ. Tel 82404.

Frean Antiques. 25 Tarrant St, Arundel, W.Sussex, BN18 9DG. Tel 882350.

The Furniture Station Ltd. The Kelterment Antique Market,Fordham, Ely, Cambridgeshire.

Gainsborough House Antiques. 81 Church St, Tewkesbury, Gloucestershire. Tel 293072.

Gallery Antiques Ltd. Avebury House,6 Peter St, Winchester, Hampshire, SO23 8BN. Tel 62161.

Robert Garrett Antiques. Guild St, Stratford-upon-Avon, Warwickshire, CV37 6UB. Tel 292795.

Rupert Gentle Antiques. The Manor House,Milton Lilbourne, Pewsey, Wiltshire, SN9 5LQ. Tel Marlborough (0672) 63344.

David Gibbins Antiques. 21 Market Hill, Woodbridge, Suffolk, IP12 4LX. Tel 3531 (priv 2685).

Glencorse Antiques. 321 Richmond Rd,Ham Parade, Kingston upon Thames, Surrey. Tel 541 0871.

The Goff Galleries. Hall St, Long Melford, Suffolk, CO10 9JQ. Tel Sudbury (0787) 78228.

Douglas Gordon Antiques. The Old Rectory, Stockbridge, Hampshire, SO20 6EU. Tel 810662.

Denzil Grant Antiques Ltd. Hall Street,Bradfield St George, Long Melford, Suffolk. Tel 75470 (priv 04493 576).

Granville Antiques. Mount Pleasant Farm,Level Mare Lane, Eastergate, W.Sussex. Tel 2293.

W.J.Gravener Antiques. High St, Mayfield, E.Sussex, TN20 6AA. Tel 873389.

Renee and Roy Green. Ashcombe House, Lewes Rd, Lewes, E.Sussex. Tel 474794.

Richard Green. 1 Coppice Lane, Queniborough, Leicester, Leicestershire, LE7 8DR. Tel 606682.

Richard Greene Antiques. 87 Main St, Burley in Wharfedale, W.Yorkshire, LS29 7JX. Tel 862156.

Jonathan Greenwall Antiques. Sandgate Antiques Centre,61-63 Sandgate High St, Folkestone, Kent. Tel 38987.

Grey House Antiques. 8 Newport St, Tiverton, Devon, EX16 6NH. Tel 255846.

Griffons Court. Highclere, Newbury, Berkshire, RG15 9QS. Tel Highclere (0635) 253247.

Guildhall Galleries. Thaxted, Essex. Tel 395.

Peter Hammond. Church House, Thornage, Holt, Norfolk. Tel 861352.

Hampshires of Dorking. 51/52 West St, Dorking, Surrey. Tel 887076.

Robert Harman Antiques. 11 Church St, Ampthill, Bedfordshire. Tel 402322.

Bob Harris & Sons. 2071 Coventry Rd, Birmingham, W.Midlands. Tel 743 2259.

F.J. Harris. 23 Silver St, Stansted Mountfitchet, Essex. Tel Bishops Stortford (0279) 813371.

Anna Harrison Antiques. 49 Great North Road,Grange Park, Gosforth, Newcastle upon Tyne, Tyne & Wear.

Kenneth Harvey Antiques and Fine Art. 21-23 South St Mary's Gate, Grimsby, Humberside. Tel 49370.

Ian G.Hastie. 46 St Ann St, Salisbury, Wiltshire. Tel 22957.

Heath-Bullock. 8 Meadrow, Godalming, Surrey, GU7 3HN. Tel 22562.

Hill Rise Antiques. 26 Hill Rise, Richmond, Surrey, TW10 6UA. Tel 948 1140.

William Hockley Antiques. East Street, Petworth, W.Sussex, GU28 0AB. Tel 43172 (priv 048 649 331).

Jean Hodge. Peachley Manor, Hallow Lane,Lower Broadheath, Worcester, Hereford & Worcester, WR2 6QL. Tel 640255.

Milton Holgate Antiques. 4 Market Place, Knaresborough, N.Yorkshire. Tel Harrogate (0423) 863205.

Guy Holland. Shepbridge Barn, Eastleach, Gloucestershire, GL7 3PS. Tel Southrop (036785) 296.

Anthony J.Hook. 3 The Green, Westerham, Kent. Tel 62161 (priv 0892-870552).

Oliver and Helen Horswill Antiques. 62 Grange Rd, West Kirby, Merseyside. Tel 625 7111 (priv 625 6182).

John Hubbard Antiques. 224-226 Court Oak Rd, Harborne, Birmingham, W.Midlands, B32 2EG. Tel 426 1694.

Anthony Hurst Antiques. 13 Church St, Woodbridge, Suffolk. Tel 2500.

A.E.Jameson & Co. 257 Glossop Rd, Sheffield, S.Yorkshire, S10 2GZ. Tel 23846 (priv 26189).

Johnson's of Sherborne Ltd. South St, Sherborne, Dorset, DTG 3NF. Tel 812585.

Lita Kaye of Lyndhurst. 13 High St, Lyndhurst, Hampshire, SO43 7BB. Tel 2337.

H.W.Keil Ltd. Tudor House, Broadway, Hereford & Worcester, WR12 7DP. Tel 852408.

H.W. Keil (Cheltenham) Ltd. 129-131 The Promenade, Cheltenham, Gloucestershire, GL50 1NW. Tel 522509, 527974.

John Keil Ltd. 10 Quiet St, Bath, Avon, BA1 2JU. Tel 63176.

Terence Kelly Antiques. 1 Cross St, Burnham-on-Sea, Somerset. Tel 782129 (priv 785052).

Kelvedon Antiques. 90 High St, Kelvedon, Essex, CO5 9AA. Tel Braintree (0376) 70557.

E.M.Kimber & Son. 6 Lower Howsell Rd, Malvern Link, Malvern, Hereford & Worcester. Tel 2000.

Roger King Antiques. 111 High St, Hungerford, Berkshire. Tel 82256.

Kings Antiques. Guildford Rd, Bucks Green, Rudgwick, W.Sussex. Tel 2084.

Knaphill Antiques. 38 High Street, Knaphill, Woking, Surrey. Tel Brookwood (048 67) 3179.

La Barre Ltd. The Place,116 South St, Leominster, Hereford & Worcester, HR6 8LE. Tel 4315.

La Chaise Antique. 30 London St, Faringdon, Oxfordshire, SN7 7AA. Tel 20427.

Langold Antiques Ltd. Oxon Hoath, Hadlow, Kent. Tel Plaxtol (0732) 810577.

David Lazarus. High St, Hartley Wintney, Hampshire. Tel 2272.

Lennard Antiques. The Laurels, Tingewick, Buckingham, Buckinghamshire, MK18 4NN. Tel Finmere (02804) 371.

Lennox Antiques. 53 Upper North St, Brighton & Hove, E.Sussex, BN1 3FH. Tel 29409 (priv 563104).

Lewis & Lloyd Ltd. 13 West St, Reigate, Surrey. Tel 21509.

Linden House Antiques. Linden House,3 Silver St, Stansted Mountfitchet, Essex, CM24 8HA. Tel Bishops Stortford (0279) 812372.

Lindsell Chairs. 11 Market Hill, Coggeshall, Essex, CO6 1TS. Tel 62766 (priv 0371-84 222).

Louis Lipman Antiques. 33-35 Kings Rd, Brentwood, Essex. Tel 222380.

Longton Hall Antiques. Longton Hall, Liverpool Rd, Longton, Lancashire, PR4 7HA. Tel 613324.

David Love. 10 Royal Parade, Harrogate, N.Yorkshire. Tel 65797.

Charles Lowe & Sons Ltd. 37-40 Church Gate, Loughborough, Leicestershire. Tel 217876.

Graham Lower. Stonecrouch Farmhouse, Flimwell, E.Sussex, TN5 7QB. Tel 535.

Charles Lumb & Sons Ltd. 2 Montpellier Gardens, Harrogate, N.Yorkshire, HG1 2TF. Tel 503776 (priv 863281).

Victor Mahy Ltd. Mulberry House, Stockbridge, Hampshire, SO20 6EY. Tel 810466.

Mallglade Antiques. Haigh Hall, Haigh, Barnsley, S.Yorkshire, S75 4BT. Tel Bretton (0924 85) 516.

Kathleen Mann Antiques. 49 High St, Harrow on the Hill, Middlesex, HA1 3HT. Tel 422 1892.

Manor House Antiques. High St, Ripley, Surrey. Tel Guildford (0483) 225350.

B.& A.Marks. London House,4 Market Square, Westerham, Kent, TN16 1AW. Tel 64479.

Simon Marsh Antiques. The Old Butchers Shop, High St, Bletchingley, Surrey. Tel Godstone (0883) 843350.

Peter J. Martin. 40 High St, Eton, Berkshire, SL4 6BD. Tel Windsor (0753) 864901 (priv 863987).

McCabes Antiques. 11-12 St Marys St, Newry, Co Down. Tel 2695 (priv 5178).

F.J.McCarthy Ltd. The Grange, Normanton on Trent, Newark-on-Trent, Nottinghamshire, NG23 6RQ. Tel 821382.

John McMaster. 5 Sayers Square, Sayers Lane, Tenterden, Kent, TN30 6BW. Tel Hastings (0424) 814671.

Nigel B. Mendes da Costa. Richmond, Surrey. Tel 940 4525.

Mendip Antiques. Great Western Antiques Centre,Bartlett St, Bath, Avon. Tel 310388.

Philip & Anne Merridale. Bridge House, Stockbridge, Hampshire. Tel 673.

Mill on the Soar Antiques Ltd. 1-3 High St, Quorn, Leicestershire, LE12 8DS. Tel 414218.

W.J. Miller & Son. 1-5 Church St, Wooler, Northumberland. Tel 81500 (priv 06687 281).

Millers Antiques, Kelvedon. 46 High St, Kelvedon, Essex. Tel 70098.

Millhouse. The Square, Petworth, W.Sussex, GU28 9BP. Tel 43080.

Milton Abbot Antiques. Venn Hill, Milton Abbot, Tavistock, Devon. Tel 392.

L. Moody. 70 Bedford Place, Southampton, Hampshire, SO1 2DS. Tel 333720 (priv 29718).

Stephen Moore Ltd. 103 High St, Lewes, E.Sussex, BN7 1XH. Tel 474158.

C.S. Moreton (Antiques). Inchmartine House, Inchture, Tayside, PH14 9QQ. Tel 86412.

William Morley Antiques. Musgrave's Old Farm, West Monkton, Taunton, Somerset, TA2 8NW. Tel West Monkton (0823) 412751.

John G.Morris Ltd. Market Square, Petworth, W.Sussex, GU28 0AH. Tel 42305.

Ralph and Bruce Moss. 26 Whitehorse St, Baldock, Hertfordshire, SG7 6QQ. Tel 892751.

Muirhead Moffat & Co. 182 West Regent St, Glasgow, Strathclyde. Tel 226 4683 and 226 3406.

Ian Murray Antiques Warehouse. 21 Glasgow Rd, Perth, Tayside. Tel 37222 (priv 0250-2508).

Lawrence Musgrove Antiques. Dixton Lodge,Hadnock Rd, Monmouth, Gwent. Tel 3656.

John Nash Antiques. The Coach House,Drury Lane, Red Marley, Gloucestershire. Tel Bromsberrow (053181) 616.

Paul Nash. The Barn House,Cherington, Tetbury, Gloucestershire. Tel Rodmarton (028 584) 215.

Victor Needham Antiques. Hinwood House, High St,Broughton, Stockbridge, Hampshire. Tel Broughton (0794) 301205.

New Malthouse Antiques. New Malthouse, Hailsham Rd, Herstmonceux, E.Sussex. Tel 833542.

Elizabeth Newby-Vincent. Nursteed Place, Devizes, Wiltshire. Tel 3844.

B.M.Newlove. 139-141 Ewell Rd, Surbiton, Surrey. Tel 339 8857.

Anthony Nielsen Antiques. High St, Burford, Oxfordshire, OX8 4QQ. Tel 2014 (priv 0451 21710).

Elizabeth Niner Antiques. 53 Great Norwood St, Cheltenham, Gloucestershire. Tel 516497 (priv 520066).

Northgate Antiques. 10 Northgate St, Pembroke, Dyfed, SA71 5LF. Tel 684416 (priv 672388).

Norton Antiques. 56 London End, Beaconsfield, Buckinghamshire, HP9 2JH. Tel 3674.

Simon W.Nutter. Wraggs Row, Fosse Way, Stow-on-the-Wold, Gloucestershire. Tel 30658.

O'Neill. Swan House,Market Square, Petworth, W.Sussex. Tel 42616.

Old Barn Antiques. High St, Church Stretton, Shropshire, SY6 6BX. Tel 723742 (priv 722294).

Old Barn Antiques Co. Flamberts, Trent, Sherborne, Dorset, DT9 4SS. Tel 850648.

The Old House Antiques. 9-10 West St, Dorking, Surrey, RH4 1QH. Tel 887278.

The Old Malthouse. 15 Bridge St (A4), Hungerford, Berkshire, RG17 OEG. Tel 82209 (priv 83647).

Old Market Antiques. 37 Old Market St, Usk, Gwent. Tel 2813.

A.J. & L.Onions. White Cottage, 8 Tern Hill, Market Drayton, Shropshire, TF9 3PR. Tel Tern Hill (063 083) 222.

Oriel Antiques. 3 Royal Parade, Hindhead, Surrey, GU26 6TD. Tel 6281.

Rudolph Otto. The Little House, Sheep St, Stow-on-the-Wold, Gloucestershire.

Mike Ottrey Antiques. 28 High St, Dorchester, Oxfordshire. Tel Oxford (0865) 340079.

Oughterard Antiques. Main St, Oughterard, Co Galway. Tel 45.

Painswick Antiques. Beacon House, New St, Painswick, Gloucestershire, GL6 6UN. Tel 812578.

Park Street Antiques. 350 High St (on A41), Berkhamsted, Hertfordshire, HP4 1HT. Tel 4790 (priv 024029 255).

Elizabeth Parker Antiques. High St, Moreton-in-Marsh, Gloucestershire, GL56 0LL. Tel 50917.

Richard Parker Ltd. Trim Bridge, 1 Queen St, Bath, Avon, BA1 1HE. Tel 330257 (priv 0722 337484).

Partner & Puxon. 7&16 North Hill, Colchester, Essex, CO1 1DZ. Tel 573317.

Patricia Antiques. 2 Grange Rd, Ramsgate, Kent, CT11 9NA. Tel Thanet (0843) 591222.

John A.Pearson Ltd. 127-128 High St, Eton, Berkshire, SL4 6AR. Tel Windsor (0753) 860850.

Penoyre Antiques. 9 - 11 Bridge St, Pershore, Hereford & Worcester. Tel 3522.

Phillips of Hitchin (Antiques) Ltd. The Manor House,Bancroft (main street), Hitchin, Hertfordshire, SG5 1JW. Tel 32067.

Pigeon House Antiques. 52 London Rd, Hurst Green, E.Sussex, TN19 7PN. Tel 474.

W.A.Pinn & Sons. 124 Swan St, Sible Hedingham, Essex, CO9 3HP. Tel Hedingham (0787) 61127.

Antony Preston Antiques Ltd. The Square, Stow-on-the-Wold, Gloucestershire, GL54 1AB. Tel 31586 (priv 31406).

Priests Antiques & Fine Arts. 60 North St, Thame, Oxfordshire. Tel 4461.

Queens Parade Antiques. 35 Gay St, Bath, Avon. Tel 20337.

Martin Quick Antiques Ltd. 321-323 Tettenhall Rd, Wolverhampton, W.Midlands, WV6 0JZ. Tel 754703 (priv 752908).

Randolph. 97-99 High St, Hadleigh, Suffolk, IP7 5EJ. Tel 823789.

G.T.Ratcliff Ltd. Durwards Hall, Kelvedon, Essex. Tel 70234.

Charles Read Georgian Furnishing. Bathealton Court,Bathealton, Milverton, Somerset, TA4 2AJ. Tel Wiveliscombe (0984) 23225.

James Reeve. 9 Church St, Warwick, Warwickshire. Tel 498113.

Regent Antiques. Dynever House, New St, Painswick, Gloucestershire. Tel 812543.

Regent House Antiques. Royal Terrace, Northampton, Northamptonshire, NN1 3RF. Tel 37992.

Reindeer Antiques Ltd. 43 Watling St, Potterspury, Northamptonshire, NN12 7QD. Tel Yardley Gobion (0908) 542407.

Restall, Brown & Clennell Ltd. Cosgrove Hall, Cosgrove, Northamptonshire, MK19 7JB. Tel Milton Keynes (0908) 565888 (priv 563336).

Leigh Rice Antiques. 29 The Mall,Clifton, Bristol, Avon. Tel 730975.

G.E.Richards & Son (Antiques). 57 Blueschool St, Hereford, Hereford & Worcester, HR1 2AR. Tel 267840 (priv 268827).

J. & M. Riley. Antique Shop, Frensham House,Main Road B2145, Hunston, Chichester, W.Sussex, PO20 6NX. Tel 782660.

Ripley Antiques. 67 High St, Ripley, Surrey, GU23 6AQ. Tel Guildford (0483) 224981.

Riverside Antiques Ltd. Riverside House, Charnham St, Hungerford, Berkshire. Tel 82314.

Robertsbridge House Antiques. High St, Robertsbridge, E.Sussex, TN32 5AN. Tel 880291.

T.E.Robinson Antiques. 3A 3 & 4 Bartlett St, Bath, Avon, BA1 2QZ. Tel 63982 (priv 832307).

Roderic Antiques. Westbrook House, Upwey, Weymouth, Dorset. Tel Upwey (030 581) 2929, 3022.

Rundells Antiques. London Rd (B 1393), Harlow, Essex, CM17 9LH. Tel 22906.

J.T.Rutherford & Son. 55 Sandgate High St, Folkestone, Kent, CT20 3AH. Tel 39515 (priv 60822).

Sainsburys of Bournemouth. 23-25 Abbott Rd, Bournemouth, Dorset, BH9 1EU. Tel 529271 (priv 763616).

Norman C.Sanderson. The Coach House, Montpellier St, Harrogate, N.Yorkshire. Tel 502687 (priv 56502).

Sam Savage Antiques. Hayes Farm, Ticknall, Derbyshire, DE7 1JZ. Tel Melbourne (033 16) 2195.

Saville Antiques. 37 Long St, Devizes, Wiltshire. Tel 3559.

Aldo Broccardi Schelmi (Fine Arts). Dewhurst Lodge, Wadhurst, E.Sussex. Tel 3519.

Serendipity. Brookend, Ross-on-Wye, Hereford & Worcester. Tel 63836 (priv 053184 245).

Shepherds Antiques. 65 Portsmouth Rd, Cobham, Surrey. Tel 7909.

Sheraton House Antiques. No.1 Laburnham Row, Torre, Torquay, Devon. Tel 23334.

Sherborne Antiques Ltd. At The China Gallery,Long St, Sherborne, Dorset, DT9 3BS. Tel 812978.

Michael Sim. 1 Royal Parade, Chislehurst, Kent, BR7 5PG. Tel 467 7040.

David Smith Antiques. The Old Cottage, Manton, Oakham, Leicestershire. Tel Manton (057 285) 244 (priv 473 or 314).

Paul Smith. The Old Chapel,Old St, Ludlow, Shropshire, SY8 1NP. Tel 2666.

Robin Smith. 23 Belle Vue Rd, Shrewsbury, Shropshire, SY3 7LN. Tel 50357.

Tom Smith Antiques. 33A St Peters St, Ipswich, Suffolk. Tel 210172.

Kimberley Snow & Son. Verbeer Manor, Willand, Cullompton, Devon, EX15 2PE. Tel 33312.

St Ouen Antiques. Vintage Corner, Old Cambridge Rd, Puckeridge, Hertfordshire. Tel Ware (0920) 821336.

The Stable Antiques. Old Kings Head Court,11 High St, Dorking, Surrey. Tel 885452.

Ulla Stafford. 65 High St, Eton, Berkshire, SL4 6AA. Tel 859625.

Stalham Antique Gallery. High St, Stalham, Norfolk. Tel 80636

Alanna Staton Antiques. 4 Anyards Rd, Cobham, Surrey, KT11 2JZ. Tel 63407 (priv 04864 2407).

Steed-Croft Antiques. Marshlands, Cross Lane,Brancaster, King's Lynn, Norfolk, PE31 8AE. Tel Brancaster (0485210) 812.

Strouds of Southwell Antiques. 3 Westgate, Southwell, Nottinghamshire. Tel 815001.

A. & J.Stuart-Mobey & Daughter. Bedford House, Lower Wolvercote, Oxford, Oxfordshire, OX2 9PF. Tel 50170.

Gordon Sutcliffe. 105 High St, Hadleigh, Suffolk, IP7 5EJ. Tel 823464.

Suthburgh Antiques. Red House, Hall St, Long Melford, Suffolk. Tel Sudbury (0787) 74818.

Swan Antiques. 62A West St, Dorking, Surrey. Tel 881217 (priv 01-394 2361).

Taylor-Halsey Antiques. Strangs,Sandford, Crediton, Devon, EX17 4EL. Tel 3408.

M. & R. Taylor Antiques. 53 Broad St, Ludlow, Shropshire, SY8 1NH. Tel 4169.

Thorpe & Foster Ltd. 49 West St, Dorking, Surrey. Tel 881029.

Townwell House Antiques. 52 Welsh Row, Nantwich, Cheshire, CW5 5EJ. Tel 65953.

Frederick Treasure Ltd. The Treasure House,274 New Hall Lane, Preston, Lancashire, PR1 4SU. Tel 700216.

Brian Trengove Antiques and Picture Gallery. 46 South End, Croydon, Surrey, CR0 1DP. Tel 688 2155.

Trevor-Venis Antiques. 13 Hencotes, Hexham, Northumberland, NE46 2EQ. Tel 607458.

Tudor Antiques. Monks Risborough, Buckinghamshire. Tel Princes Risborough(08444) 3523.

Sally Turner Antiques. Church End, Haddenham, Buckinghamshire, HP17 8AH. Tel 290346.

Turpins Antiques. 4 Stoney Lane, Thaxted, Essex. Tel 830495 (priv 830059).

Clive Underwood Antiques. 46 High St, Colsterworth, Lincolnshire. Tel Grantham (0476) 860689.

Vanbrugh House Antiques. Park St, Stow-on-the-Wold, Gloucestershire, GL54 1AQ. Tel 30797.

A.G. Voss Antiques. 16 Market Hill, Woodbridge, Suffolk, IP12 4LU. Tel 5830.

Zene Walker. The Bull House Antiques,High St, Burford, Oxfordshire. Tel 3284.

Paul Wansbrough. Seend Lodge, Seend, Melksham, Wiltshire. Tel Seend (038 082) 213.

S.J.Webster-Speakman. 79 Regent St, Cambridge, Cambridgeshire. Tel 315048 (priv 354089).

Gerald Weir Antiques. Hepplewhite House,7 Vermont Rd, Ipswich, Suffolk. Tel 52606.

Wellesley Wilson Antiques. Aldersey Manor, Aldersey, Cheshire, CH3 9EH. Tel Broxton (082 925) 500.

John Whitelaw & Sons. 120 High St, Auchterarder, Tayside, PH3 1AD. Tel 2482.

Whytock & Reid. Sunbury House, Belford Mews, Edinburgh, Lothian, EH4 3DN. Tel 226 4911.

Francis Wigram Antiques. Cotters Barn, Penn, Buckinghamshire, PN10 8LB. Tel 3266.

Joan Wilkins Antiques. 158 Corn St, Witney, Oxfordshire. Tel 4749.

Anthony Willson. 22 High St, Hartley Wintney, Hampshire.

Windhill Antiquary. 4 High St, Bishop's Stortford, Hertfordshire. Tel 51587.

Windsor House Antiques (Leeds) Ltd. 18/20 Benson St, Leeds, W.Yorkshire, LS7 1BL. Tel 444666.

Wiskin Antiques. 18 Silver St, Stansted Mountfitchet, Essex. Tel Bishops Stortford (0279) 812376.

Witney Antiques. 96-98 Corn St, Witney, Oxfordshire, OX8 7BU. Tel 3902.

Woodford Antiques. 382 Buxton Rd,Great Moor, Stockport, Greater Manchester. Tel Manchester (061) 483 9917(priv 0625 582074.

Charles Woodward Antiques. Market Place, Fairford, Gloucestershire, GL7 4AB. Tel Cirencester (0285) 712094.

Patrick Worth. 11 West St, Dorking, Surrey. Tel 884484.

Wych House Antiques. Wych Hill, Woking, Surrey. Tel 64636.

Yeo Antiques. 8 Springfields, Tetbury, Gloucestershire, GL8. Tel 521300.

J.Young & Son (Antiques). 12-14 Main St, Keswick, Cumbria, CA12 5JD. Tel 73434.

Furniture, 19th Century

London

Adams Room Ltd. 18-20 Ridgway, Wimbledon Village, London, SW19. Tel 946 7047 (priv 947 4784).

Peter Allen Antiques Ltd. 17 & 17A Nunhead Green,Peckham, London, SE15 3QQ. Tel 732 1968.

Anno Domini. 66 Pimlico Rd, London, SW1. Tel 730 5496.

Apter-Fredericks Ltd. 265-267 Fulham Rd, London, SW3 6HY. Tel 352 2188.

Arenski. 29-31 George St, London, W1H 5PE. Tel 486 0678.

Karin Armelin Antiques. 592 King's Rd, London, SW6. Tel 736 0375.

Alexander Bailie (Antiques). 2 Lower Mall,359 Upper St, Islington, London, N1 0PD. Tel 354 2839 (priv 354 1739).

Eddy Bardawil. 106 Kensington Church St, London, W8. Tel 221 3967.

Barnet Antiques and Fine Art. 1180 High Rd, Whetstone, London, N20. Tel 445 9695.

William Bedford PLC. The Merchants Hall, 46 Essex Rd,Islington, London, N1 8LN. Tel 226 9648.

John Beer. 191 Archway Road, London, N6. Tel 340 2183.

Peter Bentley. 22 Connaught St, London, W2. Tel 723 9394.

H.Blairman & Sons Ltd. 119 Mount St, London, W1. Tel 493 0444.

F.E.A.Briggs Ltd. 73 Ledbury Rd, London, W11. Tel 727 0909 (priv 969 0297).

D.B.Cater Antiques. 173 & 175 Bermondsey St, London, SE1 3UW. Tel 407 2040.

Peter Chapman Antiques. 10 Theberton St, Islington, London, N1 0QX. Tel 226 5565 (priv 348 4846).

Church Street Galleries. 77 Kensington Church St, London, W8 4BG. Tel 937 2461 (priv 937 9175).

John Clay. 263 New King's Rd, London, SW6. Tel 731 5677.

Philip Colleck Ltd. 84 Fulham Rd, London, SW3 6HR. Tel 584 8479.

Frank Collins. 60 Ledbury Rd, London, W11 2AJ. Tel 221 7108, 0502-714842.

Peter Collins. 92 Waterford Rd, London, SW6. Tel 736 4149.

Connaught Galleries. 44 Connaught St, London, W2. Tel 723 1660.

Zal Davar. 26A Munster Rd, London, SW6. Tel 736 2559, 736 1405.

Robert Dickson Antiques. 263 Fulham Rd, London, SW3. Tel 351 0330 (priv 948 5825).

Eldridge London. 99-101 Farringdon Rd, London, EC1. Tel 837 0379.

Brian Fielden. 3 New Cavendish St, London, W1M 7RP. Tel 935 6912.

Michael Foster. 118 Fulham Rd, London, SW3 6HU. Tel 373 3636.

Judy Fox Antiques. 81 Portobello Rd, London, W11.

Peter Francis. 26 Museum St, London, WC1A 1JT. Tel 637 0165.

Godson & Coles Ltd. 310 King's Rd, London, SW3 5UH. Tel 352 8509.

W.R.Harvey & Co (Antiques) Ltd. 67-70 Chalk Farm Rd, London, NW1 8AN. Tel 485 1504, 267 2767.

Haslam & Whiteway. 105 Kensington Church St, London, W8 7LN. Tel 229 1145.

Haverstock Antiques. 78 Haverstock Hill, Hampstead, London, NW3 3BS. Tel 267 1627.

Christopher Hodsoll Antiques. 50 & 69 Pimlico Rd, London, SW1. Tel 730 9835.

Michael Hogg. 172 Brompton Rd, London, SW3. Tel 589 8629.

Olivia Jackson Antiques. 287 Westbourne Grove, London, W11. Tel 727 2817.

Anthony James & Son Ltd. 88 Fulham Road, London, SW3. Tel 584 1120 (priv 385 3408).

Melvyn Jay Antiques. 64a Kensington Church St, London, W8. Tel 937 6832.

Jeremy Ltd. 255 King's Rd, Chelsea, London, SW3 5EL. Tel 352 3127, 352 0644.

John Keil Ltd. 154 Brompton Rd, London, SW3. Tel 589 6454.

Lamont Antiques Ltd. Newhams Row,175 Bermondsey St, London, SE1 3UW. Tel 403 0126.

Lillie Antiques. 244 Lillie Rd, London, SW6 7QA. Tel 385 9852.

Paul Longmire Ltd. 12 Bury St,St James's, London, SW1. Tel 930 8720.

Loot. 76-78 Pimlico Rd, London, SW1. Tel 730 8097 (priv 352 0135).

C.H. Major. 154 Kensington Church St, London, W8 4BM. Tel 229 1162.

Michael Marriott Ltd. 588 Fulham Rd, London, SW6 5NT. Tel 736 3110, 381 3455.

Rodd McLennan. 24 Holbein Place, London, SW1. Tel 730 6330.

Stephen Orton Antiques. 72 Upper St,Islington, London, N1 0NY. Tel 226 2770 (priv 508 1023).

Michael & Margaret Parker. 24 Cheval Place, London, SW7. Tel 589 0133.

Ronald Phillips Ltd. 26 Bruton St, London, W1X 8LH. Tel 493 2341.

Paul Reeves. 32B Kensington Church St, London, W8 4HA. Tel 937 1594 (priv 968 7413).

Rendall. 572 King's Rd, London, SW6. Tel 736 2520 (priv 948 4400).

Geoffrey Rose Ltd. 77 Pimlico Rd, London, SW1W 8PH. Tel 730 3004.

Sensation Ltd. 66 Fulham High St, London, SW6 5LQ. Tel 736 4135 (priv 584 9414).

Sylvia Sheppard. 71 Kensington Church St, London, W8 4BG. Tel 937 0965.

Spyer & Son (Antiques) Ltd. 18 Motcomb St, Belgrave Sq, London, SW1X 8LB. Tel 235 3348.

Murray Thomson Ltd. 141 Kensington Church St, London, W8 7LP. Tel 727 1727, 727 1825.

Tzigany Fine Arts. 28-29 Dover St, London, W1X 3PA. Tel 491 1007.

Vane House Antiques. 15 Camden Passage, London, N1. Tel 359 1343.

W.E.Walker. 277/9 Camden High St, London, NW1 7BX. Tel 485 6210 (priv 485 4433).

Westenholz Antiques Ltd. 68 Pimlico Rd, London, SW1. Tel 730 2151.

Temple Williams. Kensington, London. Tel 876 4726.

Regions

Alexander Adamson Antiques. Tearnside Hall, Kirkby Lonsdale, Cumbria, LA6 2PU. Tel 71989.

Michael Andrews Antiques. Portsmouth Rd, Milford, Surrey. Tel Godalming (04868) 20765.

Andwells. High St, Hartley Wintney, Hampshire. Tel 2305.

Annique Antiques. 13 Nevill St, Tunbridge Wells, Kent, TN2 5RU. Tel 26776.

John Anthony Antiques. 71 High St, Bletchingley, Surrey. Tel Godstone (0883) 843197.

Antique Exporters (Derby) UK. The Warehouse,Britannia Mills, Mackworth Rd, Derby, Derbyshire. Tel 32487.

The Antique Galleries. Watling St, Paulerspury, Northamptonshire. Tel 238.

The Antique Home. 15 Gwydir St, Cambridge, Cambridgeshire. Tel 311203.

The Antique Mart. 72-74 Hill Rise, Richmond, Surrey, TW10 6UB. Tel 940 6942.

The Antique Shop. Main St, Tramore, Co Waterford. Tel (051) 81548.

The Antique Shop. 6 West St, Wimborne Minster, Dorset. Tel 880297.

Antiques Coffee House. Buxton Rd, Bakewell, Derbyshire. Tel 3544.

Antiques Gallery. 37 Hanover St, Liverpool, Merseyside, L1 3DN. Tel 709 9529.

Apollo Antiques Ltd. 62 West St, Warwick, Warwickshire. Tel 494746.

Jess Applin Antiques. 8 Lensfield Rd, Cambridge, Cambridgeshire, CB2 1EG. Tel 315168 (priv 246851).

Archer Antiques. 58 Castlegate, Penrith, Cumbria. Tel 63446 (priv 0930 51813).

M. & S. Armson Ltd. 370 High St, Berkhamsted, Hertfordshire. Tel 2241.

Ashton Antiques. 12 Arden Buildings,Station Rd, Dorridge, W.Midlands. Tel 3040.

Avarice Antiques. 24 St Stephen St, Edinburgh, Lothian. Tel 225 7237.

Avon Lodge Antiques. Southampton Rd, Fordingbridge, Hampshire, SP6 1AB. Tel 53275.

Baggott Church Street Ltd. Church Street, Stow-on-the-Wold, Gloucestershire, GL54 1BB. Tel 30370.

Terry Baker. Langford House Farm, Langford, Nottinghamshire. Tel Newark-on-Trent (0636) 704026.

Barnet Antiques & Fine Art. 236 High St, Barnet, Hertfordshire, EN5 5TD. Tel 01-440 3620.

John Barry. Barton End Hall, Nailsworth, Gloucestershire, GL6 0QQ. Tel 3471.

Roy Barton. Myrtle Cottage, Codmore Hill, Pulborough, W.Sussex, RH21 1BQ. Tel 2730.

Walter S.Beaton. 75 Kinnoull St, Perth, Tayside, PH1 5EZ. Tel 28127.

Michael Beaumont Antiques. Hempstead Hall,Hempstead, Saffron Walden, Essex, CB10 2PR. Tel Steeple Bumpstead(044084) 239.

John Beazor & Sons Ltd. 78-80 Regent St, Cambridge, Cambridgeshire, CB2 1DP. Tel 355178.

John Bell of Aberdeen Ltd. Balbrogie, by Blackburn, Aberdeen, Grampian. Tel 79209.

Ray Best Antiques. North Street House, Ilminster, Somerset. Tel 2194.

Binsted Antiques. 21 Middle Lane, Teddington, Middlesex, TW11 0HQ. Tel 943 0626.

John Bly. 50 High St, Tring, Hertfordshire, HP23 5AG. Tel 3030.

John Botting. A27 Antiques Warehouse,Chaucer Industrial Estate, Polegate, E.Sussex. Tel 7167.

M.J.Bowdery. 12 London Rd, Hindhead, Surrey. Tel 6376.

Bowood Antiques. Wendover Dean Farm,Bowood Lane, Wendover, Buckinghamshire, HP22 6PY. Tel 622113.

Brazil Antiques Ltd. 145 Brighton Rd, Croydon, Surrey. Tel London (01) 680 2707.

Breakspeare Antiques. 36 Long St, Tetbury, Gloucestershire, GL8 8AQ. Tel 53122.

Simon Brett. Creswyke House, High St, Moreton-in-Marsh, Gloucestershire, GL56 0LH. Tel 50751.

Bridge Antiques. 22-100 Bridge Rd,Sutton Bridge, Spalding, Lincolnshire. Tel Holbeach (0406) 350704 (priv 350535).

E. & G. Briere. Keeper's Cottage, Suffield, Norwich, Norfolk, NR11 7ER. Tel Aylsham (0263) 732651.

Bristow Antiques. Lindford Rd, Lindford, Bordon, Hampshire, GU35 OPY. Tel 2301.

D.Bryden Antiques. Sheep St, Stow-on-the-Wold, Gloucestershire. Tel 30840.

James Buckingham. School Close,Queen Elizabeth Ave, Burgess Hill, W.Sussex. Tel 45577.

Evelyn Buckle. The Villa, Main St, Redmile, Leicestershire, NG13 0GA. Tel Bottesford (0949) 42057.

Burns & Graham. 4 St Thomas St, Winchester, Hampshire. Tel 53779.

Edward Butler. 14 Bachelors Walk, Dublin, Co Dublin. Tel 730296.

Bygones of Debenham. 1 High St, Debenham, Suffolk. Tel 860707.

Tom Caldwell Galleries Ltd. 40/42 & 56 Bradbury Place, Belfast, Belfast, BT7. Tel 223226 (priv 0846 621352).

Cave's of Northampton. 111 Kettering Rd, Northampton, Northamptonshire, NN1 4BA. Tel 38278.

K.Chappell Antiques & Fine Art. King St, Bakewell, Derbyshire, DE4 1DZ. Tel 2496 (priv 2960).

K.Chappell Antiques & Fine Art. Goose Green, Baslow, Derbyshire, DE4 1SR. Tel 3311.

Charles Antiques. 101 The Hundred, Romsey, Hampshire, SO5 8BZ. Tel 512885.

E.M. Cheshire Antiques. The Manor House, Market Place, Bingham, Nottinghamshire. Tel 38861 (priv 38455).

Cheverton's of Edenbridge Ltd. Taylour House, 69 High St, Edenbridge, Kent, TN8 5AL. Tel 863196.

Chislehurst Antiques. 7 Royal Parade, Chislehurst, Kent. Tel London (01) 467 1530.

Church House Antiques. 42 Church St, Weybridge, Surrey. Tel 42190.

Church View House Antiques. Kirk Michael,. Tel 0624 87433.

Clement House Antiques. High St, Burford, Oxfordshire, OX8 4QE. Tel 3172.

Coldstream Antiques. 44 High St, Coldstream, Borders, TD12 4AS. Tel 2552.

Nigel Coleman Antiques. High St, Brasted, Kent. Tel Westerham (0959) 64042.

F.G. & C. Collins Ltd (Collins Antiques). Corner House, Church St, Wheathampstead, Hertfordshire, AL4 8AP. Tel 3111 & 3483.

E.J.Cook & Son Antiques. The Antique Centre, 1 Severn Rd, Gloucester, Gloucestershire. Tel 29716.

Corfield of Lymington. 120 High St, Lymington, Hampshire, SO4 9SQ. Tel 73532, 75359.

Anthony Cotton. 26-27 Steep Hill, Lincoln, Lincolnshire. Tel 25838 (priv 0673 60562).

E.W.Cousins & Son. 27 High St, Ixworth, Suffolk. Tel Pakenham (0359) 30254.

Cross Hayes Antiques. The Antique and Furniture Warehouse,19 Bristol St, Malmesbury, Wiltshire. Tel 4260 (priv 2062).

Richard Davidson. Lombard St, Petworth, W.Sussex, GU28 0AG. Tel 42508.

Zona Dawson Antiques. The Old Club House, 2 The Close,Charlton Marshall, Blandford Forum, Dorset. Tel Blandford (0258) 53146.

Margery Dean Antiques. The Galleries, Alma St,Wivenhoe, Colchester, Essex. Tel 222523 (priv 250485).

Graham Deane Antiques. 5 Market St, Brighton & Hove, E.Sussex. Tel 24526.

Doveridge House of Neachley. Neach Hill, Long Lane, Shifnal, Shropshire. Tel Albrighton (090 722) 3131, 3132.

Iain Downe Antiques. 28 North Rd, Brighton & Hove, E.Sussex, BN1 1YB. Tel 697496.

Brian & Angela Downes Antiques. 9 Broad St, Bath, Avon, BA1 5LJ. Tel 65352.

Downshire House Antiques. 63 Downshire Rd, Newry, Co Down, BT34. Tel 66689.

John Duffy. 10 Parnell St, Dublin, Co Dublin. Tel 747470.

Dunluce Antiques. 33 Ballytober Rd, Bushmills, Co Antrim. Tel 31140.

Eagle House Antiques. Eagle House Antiques Market,Market Square, Midhurst, W.Sussex. Tel 2718 (priv 0705 326620).

Eaton's of Eton Ltd. 62-63 High St, Eton, Berkshire. Tel Windsor (0753) 860337 (priv 0628 27413).

Richard Essex. 41 Alma Vale Rd, Bristol, Avon, BS8 2HL. Tel 733949.

Eton Gallery. 116 High St, Eton, Berkshire. Tel Windsor (0753) 865147 (priv 860963).

Extence Antiques. 2 Wellington St, Teignmouth, Devon. Tel 3353.

The Faringdon Galleries. 79 London St, Faringdon, Oxfordshire. Tel 20344.

Jeremy A. Fearn. The Old Rectory, Winksley, Ripon, N.Yorkshire. Tel Kirkby Malzeard (0765 83) 625.

Ferneyhough. Brook House, Beaudesert, Henley-in-Arden, Warwickshire, B95 5QR. Tel 2451.

Harvey Ferry, William Clegg Antiques. The Barns, 1 High St, Nettlebed, Oxfordshire, RG9 5AA. Tel 641533.

Thomas Franklin (Antiques). 28 Charnham St, Hungerford, Berkshire, RG17 OEJ. Tel 82404.

Gainsborough House Antiques. 81 Church St, Tewkesbury, Gloucestershire. Tel 293072.

The Gallery. 11 & 19 Marmion Rd, Southsea, Hampshire. Tel Portsmouth (0705) 822016.

Gallery Antiques Ltd. Avebury House,6 Peter St, Winchester, Hampshire, SO23 8BN. Tel 62161.

P.R.Garner (Antiques). Willow Farm, 104 High St, Landbeach, Cambridge, Cambridgeshire. Tel 860470.

Robert Garrett Antiques. Guild St, Stratford-upon-Avon, Warwickshire, CV37 6UB. Tel 292795.

Glencorse Antiques. 321 Richmond Rd,Ham Parade, Kingston upon Thames, Surrey. Tel 541 0871.

W.J.Gravener Antiques. High St, Mayfield, E.Sussex, TN20 6AA. Tel 873389.

Renee and Roy Green. Ashcombe House, Lewes Rd, Lewes, E.Sussex. Tel 474794.

Richard Greene Antiques. 87 Main St, Burley in Wharfedale, W.Yorkshire, LS29 7JX. Tel 862156.

Jonathan Greenwall Antiques. Sandgate Antiques Centre,61-63 Sandgate High St, Folkestone, Kent. Tel 38987.

Grey House Antiques. 8 Newport St, Tiverton, Devon, EX16 6NH. Tel 255846.

Peter Hammond. Church House, Thornage, Holt, Norfolk. Tel 861352.

Bob Harris & Sons. 2071 Coventry Rd, Birmingham, W.Midlands. Tel 743 2259.

F.J. Harris. 23 Silver St, Stansted Mountfitchet, Essex. Tel Bishops Stortford (0279) 813371.

Tim Harrison Trade & Export Antiques. 36 Market St, Warwick, Warwickshire. Tel 491400.

Kenneth Harvey Antiques and Fine Art. 21-23 South St Mary's Gate, Grimsby, Humberside. Tel 49370.

Hayter's. 19-20 Cross St, Ryde, Isle of Wight, PO33 2AD. Tel 63795.

David Hick Antiques. Alexandra House, Carre Four Selous, St Lawrence, Jersey. Tel 62965.

Hill Rise Antiques. 26 Hill Rise, Richmond, Surrey, TW10 6UA. Tel 948 1140.

Jean Hodge. Peachley Manor, Hallow Lane,Lower Broadheath, Worcester, Hereford & Worcester, WR2 6QL. Tel 640255.

Anthony J.Hook. 3 The Green, Westerham, Kent. Tel 62161 (priv 0892-870552).

Oliver and Helen Horswill Antiques. 62 Grange Rd, West Kirby, Merseyside. Tel 625 7111 (priv 625 6182).

John Hubbard Antiques. 224-226 Court Oak Rd, Harborne, Birmingham, W.Midlands, B32 2EG. Tel 426 1694.

Anthony Hurst Antiques. 13 Church St, Woodbridge, Suffolk. Tel 2500.

A.E.Jameson & Co. 257 Glossop Rd, Sheffield, S.Yorkshire, S10 2GZ. Tel 23846 (priv 26189).

Johnson's of Sherborne Ltd. South St, Sherborne, Dorset, DTG 3NF. Tel 812585.

Julian Antiques. Aller Vale Buildings,Market Park Rd, Kingskerswell, Newton Abbot, Devon, TQ12 5AZ. Tel Kingskerswell (08047) 2629 (priv 0803 24934).

Lita Kaye of Lyndhurst. 13 High St, Lyndhurst, Hampshire, SO43 7BB. Tel 2337.

H.W. Keil (Cheltenham) Ltd. 129-131 The Promenade, Cheltenham, Gloucestershire, GL50 1NW. Tel 522509, 527974.

Terence Kelly Antiques. 1 Cross St, Burnham-on-Sea, Somerset. Tel 782129 (priv 785052).

E.M.Kimber & Son. 6 Lower Howsell Rd, Malvern Link, Malvern, Hereford & Worcester. Tel 2000.

Roger King Antiques. 111 High St, Hungerford, Berkshire. Tel 82256.

Kings Antiques. Guildford Rd, Bucks Green, Rudgwick, W.Sussex. Tel 2084.

Kirton Antiques. 3 High St, Kirton, Lincolnshire, PE21 DR. Tel Boston (0205) 722595 (priv 722134).

Knaphill Antiques. 38 High Street, Knaphill, Woking, Surrey. Tel Brookwood (048 67) 3179.

La Barre Ltd. The Place,116 South St, Leominster, Hereford & Worcester, HR6 8LE. Tel 4315.

La Chaise Antique. 30 London St, Faringdon, Oxfordshire, SN7 7AA. Tel 20427.

Langold Antiques Ltd. Oxon Hoath, Hadlow, Kent. Tel Plaxtol (0732) 810577.

David Lazarus. High St, Hartley Wintney, Hampshire. Tel 2272.

M.Lees & Sons. Tower House, Severn St, Worcester, Hereford & Worcester. Tel 26620 (24 hours).

Lennard Antiques. The Laurels, Tingewick, Buckingham, Buckinghamshire, MK18 4NN. Tel Finmere (02804) 371.

Lennox Antiques. 53 Upper North St, Brighton & Hove, E.Sussex, BN1 3FH. Tel 29409 (priv 563104).

Lewis & Lloyd Ltd. 13 West St, Reigate, Surrey. Tel 21509.

Linden House Antiques. Linden House,3 Silver St, Stansted Mountfitchet, Essex, CM24 8HA. Tel Bishops Stortford (0279) 812372.

Lindsell Chairs. 11 Market Hill, Coggeshall, Essex, CO6 1TS. Tel 62766 (priv 0371-84 222).

Louis Lipman Antiques. 33-35 Kings Rd, Brentwood, Essex. Tel 222380.

The Little Antique Shop. 167-169 Stone Rd, Hanford, Stoke-on-Trent, Staffordshire. Tel 657674.

Longton Hall Antiques. Longton Hall, Liverpool Rd, Longton, Lancashire, PR4 7HA. Tel 613324.

Charles Lowe & Sons Ltd. 37-40 Church Gate, Loughborough, Leicestershire. Tel 217876.

Charles Lumb & Sons Ltd. 2 Montpellier Gardens, Harrogate, N.Yorkshire, HG1 2TF. Tel 503776 (priv 863281).

Maindy Fine Antiques. 17 Pont Canna St, Cardiff, S.Glamorgan. Tel 382072.

Mallglade Antiques. Haigh Hall, Haigh, Barnsley, S.Yorkshire, S75 4BT. Tel Bretton (0924 85) 516.

Kathleen Mann Antiques. 49 High St, Harrow on the Hill, Middlesex, HA1 3HT. Tel 422 1892.

Manor House Antiques. 42 Suffolk Rd, Cheltenham, Gloucestershire. Tel 32780.

Manor House Antiques. High St, Ripley, Surrey. Tel Guildford (0483) 225350.

B.& A.Marks. London House,4 Market Square, Westerham, Kent, TN16 1AW. Tel 64479.

Simon Marsh Antiques. The Old Butchers Shop, High St, Bletchingley, Surrey. Tel Godstone (0883) 843350.

Peter J. Martin. 40 High St, Eton, Berkshire, SL4 6BD. Tel Windsor (0753) 864901 (priv 863987).

R.E. Martin. 40 Gold St, Tiverton, Devon. Tel 252832.

Martins Antiques. 379 Abbeydale Rd, Sheffield, S.Yorkshire, S7 1FS. Tel 581278 (priv 553932).

McCabes Antiques. 11-12 St Marys St, Newry, Co Down. Tel 2695 (priv 5178).

F.J.McCarthy Ltd. The Grange, Normanton on Trent, Newark-on-Trent, Nottinghamshire, NG23 6RQ. Tel 821382.

John McMaster. 5 Sayers Square, Sayers Lane, Tenterden, Kent, TN30 6BW. Tel Hastings (0424) 814671.

Nigel B. Mendes da Costa. Richmond, Surrey. Tel 940 4525.

Mendip Antiques. Great Western Antiques Centre,Bartlett St, Bath, Avon. Tel 310388.

Philip & Anne Merridale. Bridge House, Stockbridge, Hampshire. Tel 673.

W.J. Miller & Son. 1-5 Church St, Wooler, Northumberland. Tel 81500 (priv 06687 281).

Millers of Chelsea Antiques Limited. Netherbrook House,86 Christchurch Rd, Ringwood, Hampshire, BH24 1DR. Tel 2062.

Millers Antiques, Kelvedon. 46 High St, Kelvedon, Essex. Tel 70098.

Millhouse. The Square, Petworth, W.Sussex, GU28 9BP. Tel 43080.

Milton Abbot Antiques. Venn Hill, Milton Abbot, Tavistock, Devon. Tel 392.

L. Moody. 70 Bedford Place, Southampton, Hampshire, SO1 2DS. Tel 333720 (priv 29718).

C.S. Moreton (Antiques). Inchmartine House, Inchture, Tayside, PH14 9QQ. Tel 86412.

John G.Morris Ltd. Market Square, Petworth, W.Sussex, GU28 0AH. Tel 42305.

Ralph and Bruce Moss. 26 Whitehorse St, Baldock, Hertfordshire, SG7 6QQ. Tel 892751.

Muirhead Moffat & Co. 182 West Regent St, Glasgow, Strathclyde. Tel 226 4683 and 226 3406.

Ian Murray Antiques Warehouse. 21 Glasgow Rd, Perth, Tayside. Tel 37222 (priv 0250-2508).

Lawrence Musgrove Antiques. Dixton Lodge,Hadnock Rd, Monmouth, Gwent. Tel 3656.

The M11 Antiques Centre. High St, Newport, Essex, CB11 3QY. Tel Saffron Walden (0799) 40321 (priv 40238).

Nash Antiques. 10 Fountain Buildings,Lansdown Rd, Bath, Avon. Tel 313584.

John Nash Antiques. The Coach House,Drury Lane, Red Marley, Gloucestershire. Tel Bromsberrow (053181) 616.

B.M.Newlove. 139-141 Ewell Rd, Surbiton, Surrey. Tel 339 8857.

Anthony Nielsen Antiques. High St, Burford, Oxfordshire, OX8 4QQ. Tel 2014 (priv 0451 21710).

Elizabeth Niner Antiques. 53 Great Norwood St, Cheltenham, Gloucestershire. Tel 516497 (priv 520066).

North Parade Antiques. 75 Banbury Rd (A423), Oxford, Oxfordshire. Tel 59816 (priv 880923).

Northgate Antiques. 10 Northgate St, Pembroke, Dyfed, SA71 5LF. Tel 684416 (priv 672388).

Norton Antiques. 56 London End, Beaconsfield, Buckinghamshire, HP9 2JH. Tel 3674.

Simon W.Nutter. Wraggs Row, Fosse Way, Stow-on-the-Wold, Gloucestershire. Tel 30658.

O'Neill. Swan House,Market Square, Petworth, W.Sussex. Tel 42616.

Old Barn Antiques. High St, Church Stretton, Shropshire, SY6 6BX. Tel 723742 (priv 722294).

Old Barn Antiques Co. Flamberts, Trent, Sherborne, Dorset, DT9 4SS. Tel 850648.

The Old House Antiques. 9-10 West St, Dorking, Surrey, RH4 1QH. Tel 887278.

The Old Malthouse. 15 Bridge St (A4), Hungerford, Berkshire, RG17 OEG. Tel 82209 (priv 83647).

Oriel Antiques. 3 Royal Parade, Hindhead, Surrey, GU26 6TD. Tel 6281.

Rudolph Otto. The Little House, Sheep St, Stow-on-the-Wold, Gloucestershire.

Mike Ottrey Antiques. 28 High St, Dorchester, Oxfordshire. Tel Oxford (0865) 340079.

Painswick Antiques. Beacon House, New St, Painswick, Gloucestershire, GL6 6UN. Tel 812578.

Palmer Antiques. 10 Paved Court, Richmond, Surrey. Tel 948 2668.

Park Street Antiques. 350 High St (on A41), Berkhamsted, Hertfordshire, HP4 1HT. Tel 4790 (priv 024029 255).

Geoff Parker Antiques Ltd. Haltoft End,Freiston, Boston, Lincolnshire, PE22 0PG. Tel 760444.

Richard Parker Ltd. Trim Bridge, 1 Queen St, Bath, Avon, BA1 1HE. Tel 330257 (priv 0722 337484).

Partner & Puxon. 7&16 North Hill, Colchester, Essex, CO1 1DZ. Tel 573317.

Patricia Antiques. 2 Grange Rd, Ramsgate, Kent, CT11 9NA. Tel Thanet (0843) 591222.

John A.Pearson Ltd. 127-128 High St, Eton, Berkshire, SL4 6AR. Tel Windsor (0753) 860850.

Phelps Ltd. 133-135 St Margaret's Rd, Twickenham, Middlesex, TW1 1RG. Tel 892 1778, 892 7129.

Pigeon House Antiques. 52 London Rd, Hurst Green, E.Sussex, TN19 7PN. Tel 474.

W.A.Pinn & Sons. 124 Swan St, Sible Hedingham, Essex, CO9 3HP. Tel Hedingham (0787) 61127.

John Prestige Antiques. 1/2 Greenswood Court, Greenswood Rd, Brixham, Devon. Tel 6141, 6723 (priv 3739).

Antony Preston Antiques Ltd. The Square, Stow-on-the-Wold, Gloucestershire, GL54 1AB. Tel 31586 (priv 31406).

Pretty Chairs. 189/191 Highland Rd, Portsmouth, Hampshire. Tel 731411.

Priests Antiques & Fine Arts. 60 North St, Thame, Oxfordshire. Tel 4461.

Martin Quick Antiques Ltd. 321-323 Tettenhall Rd, Wolverhampton, W.Midlands, WV6 0JZ. Tel 754703 (priv 752908).

Randolph. 97-99 High St, Hadleigh, Suffolk, IP7 5EJ. Tel 823789.

G.T.Ratcliff Ltd. Durwards Hall, Kelvedon, Essex. Tel 70234.

Regent House Antiques. Royal Terrace, Northampton, Northamptonshire, NN1 3RF. Tel 37992.

Reindeer Antiques Ltd. 43 Watling St, Potterspury, Northamptonshire, NN12 7QD. Tel Yardley Gobion (0908) 542407.

Restall, Brown & Clennell Ltd. Cosgrove Hall, Cosgrove, Northamptonshire, MK19 7JB. Tel Milton Keynes (0908) 565888 (priv 563336).

Leigh Rice Antiques. 29 The Mall,Clifton, Bristol, Avon. Tel 730975.

G.E.Richards & Son (Antiques). 57 Blueschool St, Hereford, Hereford & Worcester, HR1 2AR. Tel 267840 (priv 268827).

J. & M. Riley. Antique Shop, Frensham House,Main Road B2145, Hunston, Chichester, W.Sussex, PO20 6NX. Tel 782660.

Ripley Antiques. 67 High St, Ripley, Surrey, GU23 6AQ. Tel Guildford (0483) 224981.

Riverside Antiques Ltd. Riverside House, Charnham St, Hungerford, Berkshire. Tel 82314.

Robertsbridge House Antiques. High St, Robertsbridge, E.Sussex, TN32 5AN. Tel 880291.

Roderic Antiques. Westbrook House, Upwey, Weymouth, Dorset. Tel Upwey (030 581) 2929, 3022.

Rundells Antiques. London Rd (B 1393), Harlow, Essex, CM17 9LH. Tel 22906.

J.T.Rutherford & Son. 55 Sandgate High St, Folkestone, Kent, CT20 3AH. Tel 39515 (priv 60822).

B.R.Ryland. 75 Reading Rd, Henley-on-Thames, Oxfordshire, RG9 1AX. Tel 573663.

Sarum Antiques. Castle Square, Benson, Oxfordshire, OX9 6SD. Tel Wallingford (0491) 38527.

Sam Savage Antiques. Hayes Farm, Ticknall, Derbyshire, DE7 1JZ. Tel Melbourne (033 16) 2195.

Saville Antiques. 37 Long St, Devizes, Wiltshire. Tel 3559.

Serendipity. Brookend, Ross-on-Wye, Hereford & Worcester. Tel 63836 (priv 053184 245).

Sheraton House Antiques. No.1 Laburnham Row, Torre, Torquay, Devon. Tel 23334.

Sherborne Antiques Ltd. At The China Gallery,Long St, Sherborne, Dorset, DT9 3BS. Tel 812978.

Michael Sim. 1 Royal Parade, Chislehurst, Kent, BR7 5PG. Tel 467 7040.

Roy Sim Antiques. 21 Allan St, Blairgowrie, Tayside, PH10 6AB. Tel 3860 (priv 3700).

David Smith Antiques. The Old Cottage, Manton, Oakham, Leicestershire. Tel Manton (057 285) 244 (priv 473 or 314).

Tom Smith Antiques. 33A St Peters St, Ipswich, Suffolk. Tel 210172.

Kimberley Snow & Son. Verbeer Manor, Willand, Cullompton, Devon, EX15 2PE. Tel 33312.

Stalham Antique Gallery. High St, Stalham, Norfolk. Tel 80636.

Directory Entries are Free and ADDITIONS OR CORRECTIONS will be welcomed by *THE EDITOR, British Art and Antiques Directory, National Magazine House, 72 Broadwick Street, London W1V 2BP*

Alanna Staton Antiques. 4 Anyards Rd, Cobham, Surrey, KT11 2JZ. Tel 63407 (priv 04864 2407).

Steed-Croft Antiques. Marshlands, Cross Lane,Brancaster, King's Lynn, Norfolk, PE31 8AE. Tel Brancaster (0485210) 812.

Strouds of Southwell Antiques. 3 Westgate, Southwell, Nottinghamshire. Tel 815001.

A. & J.Stuart-Mobey & Daughter. Bedford House, Lower Wolvercote, Oxford, Oxfordshire, OX2 9PF. Tel 50170.

Swan Antiques. 62A West St, Dorking, Surrey. Tel 881217 (priv 01-394 2361).

Thomas Sykes Antiques. 16 High St, Kelvedon, Essex, CO5 9AG. Tel 71969 (priv 0787 477617).

Taylor-Halsey Antiques. Strangs,Sandford, Crediton, Devon, EX17 4EL. Tel 3408.

M. & R. Taylor Antiques. 53 Broad St, Ludlow, Shropshire, SY8 1NH. Tel 4169.

Thorpe Antiques. 3 High St, Higham Ferrers, Northamptonshire. Tel Wellingborough (0933) 59747.

Townwell House Antiques. 52 Welsh Row, Nantwich, Cheshire, CW5 5EJ. Tel 65953.

Frederick Treasure Ltd. The Treasure House,274 New Hall Lane, Preston, Lancashire, PR1 4SU. Tel 700216.

Brian Trengove Antiques and Picture Gallery. 46 South End, Croydon, Surrey, CR0 1DP. Tel 688 2155.

Trevor-Venis Antiques. 13 Hencotes, Hexham, Northumberland, NE46 2EQ. Tel 607458.

Van Riemsdijk Fine Art. Digbeth St, Stow-on-the-Wold, Gloucestershire. Tel Cotswold (0451) 30424 (priv 0908 582621).

Vernon Smith & Son. Bayvil House, High St, Cardigan, Dyfed, SA43 1HE. Tel 612654.

A.G. Voss Antiques. 16 Market Hill, Woodbridge, Suffolk, IP12 4LU. Tel 5830.

A.E.Wakeman & Sons Ltd. 140 B Tettenhall Rd, Wolverhampton, W.Midlands, WV6 0BQ. Tel 751166.

Paul Ward Antiques. 150 Abbeydale Rd, Sheffield, S.Yorkshire, S7 1FH. Tel 583004 (priv 335980).

S.J.Webster-Speakman. 79 Regent St, Cambridge, Cambridgeshire. Tel 315048 (priv 354089).

Gerald Weir Antiques. Hepplewhite House,7 Vermont Rd, Ipswich, Suffolk. Tel 52606.

Wellesley Wilson Antiques. Aldersey Manor, Aldersey, Cheshire, CH3 9EH. Tel Broxton (082 925) 500.

John Whitelaw & Sons. 120 High St, Auchterarder, Tayside, PH3 1AD. Tel 2482.

Whytock & Reid. Sunbury House, Belford Mews, Edinburgh, Lothian, EH4 3DN. Tel 226 4911.

Francis Wigram Antiques. Cotters Barn, Penn, Buckinghamshire, PN10 8LB. Tel 3266.

Joan Wilkins Antiques. 158 Corn St, Witney, Oxfordshire. Tel 4749.

Windsor House Antiques (Leeds) Ltd. 18/20 Benson St, Leeds, W.Yorkshire, LS7 1BL. Tel 444666.

Wiskin Antiques. 18 Silver St, Stansted Mountfitchet, Essex. Tel Bishops Stortford (0279) 812376.

Woodford Antiques. 382 Buxton Rd,Great Moor, Stockport, Greater Manchester. Tel Manchester (061) 483 9917(priv 0625 582074.

Charles Woodward Antiques. Market Place, Fairford, Gloucestershire, GL7 4AB. Tel Cirencester (0285) 712094.

Patrick Worth. 11 West St, Dorking, Surrey. Tel 884484.

J.Young & Son (Antiques). 12-14 Main St, Keswick, Cumbria, CA12 5JD. Tel 73434.

Furniture, 20th Century

Antics. 44 Portsmouth Rd, Cobham, Surrey. Tel 5505.

Antiques Coffee House. Buxton Rd, Bakewell, Derbyshire. Tel 3544.

James Ash Antiques. The Warehouse, Station Rd, Llandeilo, Dyfed. Tel 823728 (priv 0269 850119).

Avarice Antiques. 24 St Stephen St, Edinburgh, Lothian. Tel 225 7237.

John Beer. 191 Archway Road, London, N6. Tel 340 2183.

D.Bryden Antiques. Sheep St, Stow-on-the-Wold, Gloucestershire. Tel 30840.

Carshalton Antiques Galleries. 5 High St, Carshalton, Surrey, SM5 3AP. Tel 01- 647 5664.

D.B.Cater Antiques. 173 & 175 Bermondsey St, London, SE1 3UW. Tel 407 2040.

Chislehurst Antiques. 7 Royal Parade, Chislehurst, Kent. Tel London (01) 467 1530.

F.G. & C. Collins Ltd (Collins Antiques). Corner House, Church St, Wheathampstead, Hertfordshire, AL4 8AP. Tel 3111 & 3483.

Cross Hayes Antiques. The Antique and Furniture Warehouse,19 Bristol St, Malmesbury, Wiltshire. Tel 4260 (priv 2062).

N. Geary Ltd. 114 Richardshaw Lane, Pudsey, W.Yorkshire. Tel 564122.

Haslam & Whiteway. 105 Kensington Church St, London, W8 7LN. Tel 229 1145.

Kirton Antiques. 3 High St, Kirton, Lincolnshire, PE21 DR. Tel Boston (0205) 722595 (priv 722134).

Lamont Antiques Ltd. Newhams Row,175 Bermondsey St, London, SE1 3UW. Tel 403 0126.

M.Lees & Sons. Tower House, Severn St, Worcester, Hereford & Worcester. Tel 26620 (24 hours).

Maindy Fine Antiques. 17 Pont Canna St, Cardiff, S.Glamorgan. Tel 382072.

Mallglade Antiques. Haigh Hall, Haigh, Barnsley, S.Yorkshire, S75 4BT. Tel Bretton (0924 85) 516.

Ian Murray Antiques Warehouse. 21 Glasgow Rd, Perth, Tayside. Tel 37222 (priv 0250-2508).

L'Odeon. 173 Fulham Rd, London, SW3. Tel 581 3640 (priv 736 4216).

Stephen Orton Antiques. 72 Upper St,Islington, London, N1 0NY. Tel 226 2770 (priv 508 1023).

Phelps Ltd. 133-135 St Margaret's Rd, Twickenham, Middlesex, TW1 1RG. Tel 892 1778, 892 7129.

Paul Reeves. 32B Kensington Church St, London, W8 4HA. Tel 937 1594 (priv 968 7413).

Roderic Antiques. Westbrook House, Upwey, Weymouth, Dorset. Tel Upwey (030 581) 2929, 3022.

B.R.Ryland. 75 Reading Rd, Henley-on-Thames, Oxfordshire, RG9 1AX. Tel 573663.

Sarum Antiques. Castle Square, Benson, Oxfordshire, OX9 6SD. Tel Wallingford (0491) 38527.

Kimberley Snow & Son. Verbeer Manor, Willand, Cullompton, Devon, EX15 2PE. Tel 33312.

A. & J.Stuart-Mobey & Daughter. Bedford House, Lower Wolvercote, Oxford, Oxfordshire, OX2 9PF. Tel 50170.

Themes & Variations. 231 Westbourne Grove, London, W11. Tel 727 5531.

Thorpe Antiques. 3 High St, Higham Ferrers, Northamptonshire. Tel Wellingborough (0933) 59747.

Van Riemsdijk Fine Art. Digbeth St, Stow-on-the-Wold, Gloucestershire. Tel Cotswold (0451) 30424 (priv 0908 582621).

Games

Academy Antiques. WTS House,Camphill Industrial Estate, West Byfleet, Surrey.

Andrew Cottrell Galleries. 7-9 Church St, Godalming, Surrey. Tel 7570.

Donay Antiques. 35 Camden Passage,Islington, London, N1. Tel 359 1880.

Fenwick and Fisher Antiques. 88 High St, Broadway, Hereford & Worcester. Tel 853227 (priv 853228).

Game Advice. 23 Holmes Road, London, NW5 3AA. Tel 485 2188 (priv 485 4226).

House of Buckingham. 113-117 Farringdon Rd, London, EC1R 3BT. Tel 278 2013.

Intercol London. 1A Camden Walk, Islington Green, London, N1. Tel 354 2599 (priv 349 2207).

Mona Antiqua & Tudor Rose. 31-32 Castle St, Beaumaris, Gwynedd. Tel 810203.

Trench Enterprises. Three Cow Green,Bacton, Stowmarket, Suffolk, IP14 4HJ. Tel Bury St Edmunds (0284) 60909.

Garden Furniture and Statuary

George Amos & Sons (CB) Ltd. 73 Leonard St, London, EC2. Tel 739 0448.

55 Antiques. 55 Spring Bank, Hull, Humberside, HU3 1AG. Tel 224510.

Architectural Antiques Ltd. 133 Upper St, London, N1. Tel 226 5565.

Architectural Heritage of Cheltenham. Boddington Manor, Boddington, Cheltenham, Gloucestershire, GL51 0TJ. Tel Coombe Hill (024268) 741.

C.W.Atkins & Co. Antiques. 92 Wellington Rd, Taunton, Somerset, TA1 5LA. Tel 72660.

Baileys Architectural Antiques. The Engine Shed,Ashburton Industrial Estate, Ross-on-Wye, Hereford & Worcester, HR9 7BW. Tel 63015.

Richard Batsford Antiques. Antique Trade Warehouse,29 Lorne Park Rd, Bournemouth, Dorset. Tel 292944 (priv 25485).

Below Stairs. 103 High St, Hungerford, Berkshire, RG17 0NB. Tel 82317.

Blewbury Antiques. London Rd, Blewbury, Oxfordshire, OX11 9NX. Tel 850366.

E. & G. Briere. Keeper's Cottage, Suffield, Norwich, Norfolk, NR11 7ER. Tel Aylsham (0263) 732651.

Mark Chapman Antiques. New Street, Petworth, W.Sussex. Tel 42283.

Chilstone Architectural Ornaments. Sprivers Estate, Horsmonden, Kent. Tel Brenchley (089272) 3553.

Classic Furniture Ltd. Audley Avenue, Newport, Shropshire. Tel 813311.

Coombe House Antiques. Malling St, Lewes, E.Sussex. Tel 473862.

Crossbow House Antiques. Stoneymeadow Rd, High Blantyre, Strathclyde. Tel Blantyre (0698) 823106, 822378.

Crowther of Syon Lodge. Syon Lodge, Busch Corner,London Rd, Isleworth, Middlesex, TW7 5BH. Tel 560 7978, 560 7985.

T.Crowther & Son Ltd. 282 North End Rd, Fulham, London, SW6 1NH. Tel 385 1375/7.

Mike Deasy Ltd. 108-114 Eastern Road, Brighton & Hove, E.Sussex. Tel 688523/687237.

Robin and Matthew Eden. Pickwick Village, Corsham, Wiltshire. Tel 713335.

Flemings Antiques. High St, Debenham, Suffolk, IP14 6QJ. Tel 860422.

Franklin's. Camberwell Antique Market,161 Camberwell Rd, London, SE5. Tel 703 8089.

The Great Malvern Antiques Arcade. Salisbury House,6 Abbey Rd, Malvern, Hereford & Worcester, WR14 3HG. Tel 5490.

Haughey Antiques. 28-30 Market St, Kirkby Stephen, Cumbria, CA17 4QW. Tel 71302.

Heath-Bullock. 8 Meadrow, Godalming, Surrey, GU7 3HN. Tel 22562.

Dudley Hume. 46 & 50 Upper North St, Brighton & Hove, E.Sussex, BN1 3PH. Tel 23461.

Eric King Antiques. 203 New Kings Rd, London, SW6. Tel 736 3162.

The Landscape Ornament Co. Voysey House,Barley Mow Passage, Chiswick, London, W4 4PN. Tel 995 9739.

Mallett at Bourdon House Ltd. 2 Davies St, Berkeley Sq, London, W1Y 1LJ. Tel 629 2444/5.

Manor Farm Antiques & Garden Ornaments. Manor Farm, Swaffham, Norfolk. Tel 21395.

Manor House Antiques. High St, Ripley, Surrey. Tel Guildford (0483) 225350.

Peter Montagu-Williams. Gilberts Green, Tanworth-in-Arden, Warwickshire. Tel 2314.

Victor Needham Antiques. Hinwood House, High St,Broughton, Stockbridge, Hampshire. Tel Broughton (0794) 301205.

Elizabeth Newby-Vincent. Nursteed Place, Devizes, Wiltshire. Tel 3844.

G.Oliver & Sons. St Catherine's House, Portsmouth Rd, Guildford, Surrey. Tel 575427.

Petworth Antiques Warehouse. Colhook Industrial Park, Petworth, W.Sussex. Tel Northchapel (042 878) 667.

Barrie Quinn Antiques. 3 & 4 Broxholme House, New King's Rd, London, SW6. Tel 736 4747.

Relic Antiques. 1 Camden Walk, Islington, London, N1. Tel 359 6755.

Peter Roberts Antiques. High St, Moreton-in-Marsh, Gloucestershire, GL56 0LM.

Robin Shield Antiques. Great Chilton Farm, Ferryhill, Durham, DL17 0JY. Tel Bishop Auckland (0740) 720237.

Geoffrey Stead. The Old Rectory, Dowdeswell, Gloucestershire, GL54 5LX. Tel Cheltenham (0242) 820571.

Studio Antiques Ltd. Bourton-on-the-Water, Gloucestershire, GL54 2BX. Tel 20352.

Townhead Antiques. Townhead, Newby Bridge, Cumbria, LA12 8NP. Tel 31321.

Wye Antiques. The Square, Stow-on-the-Wold, Gloucestershire, GL54 1AB. Tel Cotswold (0451) 31004.

Gilding and Gessowork

see Restorers, Gilding and Gessowork

Glass Paperweights

Geoffrey Lanham Antiques. 96 Chalvington Rd, Chandler's Ford, Eastleigh, Hampshire, SO5 3EH. Tel Chandler's End (042 15) 65541.

Howard Phillips. 11A Henrietta Place, London, W1M 9AG. Tel 580 9844.

Portique. 17 Criterion Arcade, Bournemouth, Dorset, BH1 1BU. Tel 22979.

Spink & Son Ltd. 5, 6 & 7 King St, St James's, London, SW1. Tel 930 7888.

Todd & Austin Antiques & Fine Art. 2 Andover Rd, Winchester, Hampshire, SO23 7BS. Tel 69824.

Glass Pictures

Robin Sanders & Sons. 590 Fulham Rd, London, SW6. Tel 736 0586.

Glass, British

London

Asprey PLC. 165-169 New Bond St, London, W1Y 0AR. Tel 493 6767.

Susan Becker Antiques. 18 Lower Richmond Rd, Putney, London, SW15. Tel 788 9082.

Christine Bridge. K10-12 Grays in Davies Mews,1-7 Davies Mews, London, W1Y 1AR. Tel 499 3562 (priv 741 5501).

W.G.T.Burne (Antique Glass) Ltd. 11 Elystan St, London, SW3. Tel 589 6074.

Cobb Antiques Ltd. 39b High St,Wimbledon Village, London, SW19. Tel 946 2811 (priv 540 7982).

The Dining Room Shop. 64 White Hart Lane,Barnes, London, SW13 0PZ. Tel 878 1020 (priv 876 5212).

Vincent Freeman Antiques. 1 Camden Passage, Islington, London, N1. Tel 226 6178.

Garrard & Co Ltd. 112 Regent St, London, W1A 2JJ. Tel 734 7020.

Thomas Goode & Co (London) Ltd. 19 South Audley St, London, W1Y 6BN. Tel 499 2823 (7 lines).

Jeanette Hayhurst Fine Glass. 3b Burlington Gdns, Old Bond Street, London, W1. Tel 437 4975.

Lucky Parrot (Antiques and Things). Bellevue Rd, Wandsworth Common, London, SW17. Tel 672 7168.

H.W. Newby. 15 Walton St, London, SW3 2HX. Tel 589 2752.

The Persian Market. 48 Upper St,Islington, London, N1. Tel 226 7927.

Howard Phillips. 11A Henrietta Place, London, W1M 9AG. Tel 580 9844.

Pryce and Brise Antiques. 79 Moore Park Rd, London, SW6. Tel 736 1864.

Gerald Sattin Ltd. 25 Burlington Arcade, Piccadilly, London, W1V 9AD. Tel 493 6557.

R. Wilkinson & Son. 43-45 Wastdale Rd, Forest Hill, London, SE23 1HN. Tel 699 4420.

Regions

Abbey Antiques. 52-54 High St, Glastonbury, Somerset, BA6 9DY. Tel 31694 (priv 32795).

Antiques & Interiors. 6 Andover Rd, Winchester, Hampshire, SO23 7BS. Tel 69824.

Astley Bridge Antiques. 419-421 Blackburn Rd, Astley Bridge, Bolton, Greater Manchester, BL1 8NJ. Tel 51160 (priv 53390).

Anthony Baker Antiques. 14 London Rd, Alderley Edge, Cheshire, SK9 7JS. Tel 582674.

Binsted Antiques. 21 Middle Lane, Teddington, Middlesex, TW11 0HQ. Tel 943 0626.

John A.Brooks. 2 Knights Crescent, Rothley, Leicestershire. Tel Leicester (0533) 302625.

Malcolm G.Clark. 3 Pembroke St, Cambridge, Cambridgeshire, CB2 3QY. Tel 357117.

Coach House Antiques. 75 Coach Rd, Sleights, Whitby, N.Yorkshire, YO22 5BT. Tel 810313.

Dolphin Antiques. 33 Trumpington St, Cambridge, Cambridgeshire. Tel 354180.

Dormy House Antiques. 43 Kingsbury St, Marlborough, Wiltshire, SN8 1JE. Tel 52703.

Pamela Elsom Antiques. 5 Church St, Ashbourne, Derbyshire. Tel 43468.

Gabor Cossa Antiques. 34 Trumpington St, Cambridge, Cambridgeshire, CB2 1QY. Tel 356049.

Gadsby's Antiques. 88-90 The Street, Ashtead, Surrey. Tel 72305.

Gatehouse Antiques. 72 Chestergate, Macclesfield, Cheshire. Tel 26476.

Harley Antiques. The Comedy, Christian Malford, Chippenham, Wiltshire. Tel 720112.

Peter Jeeves Antiques. High St, Cuckfield, W.Sussex. Tel Haywards Heath (0444) 454420.

Melville Kemp Ltd. 89-91 Derby Rd, Nottingham, Nottinghamshire, NG1 5BB. Tel 417055.

Muriel Lindsay. Queen Anne House, High St, Winchcombe, Gloucestershire. Tel Cheltenham (0242) 602319.

William MacAdam. 86 Pilrig St, Edinburgh, Lothian, EH6 5AS. Tel 553 1364.

The Old Forge. Pilgrims Way, Hollingbourne, Kent, ME17 1UW. Tel 360.

Old Pump House. 20 High St, Lyndhurst, Hampshire, SO4 7BD. Tel 2137.

Mary Payton Antiques. The Old Market House, Chagford, Devon, TQ13 8DD. Tel 2428 (priv 2388).

Quarter Jack Antiques. Bridge St, Sturminster Newton, Dorset, DT10 1BZ. Tel 72558.

Rankine Taylor Antiques. 34 Dollar St, Cirencester, Gloucestershire, GL7 2AN. Tel 2529.

D.H.Sargeant. 21 The Green, Westerham, Kent, TN16 1AX. Tel 62130.

Simons Antiques. 61 The Tything, Worcester, Hereford & Worcester. Tel 25152.

Somervale Antiques. 6 Radstock Rd, Midsomer Norton, Avon, BA3 2AJ. Tel 412686.

Strawson Antiques. 39-41 The Pantiles, Tunbridge Wells, Kent, TN7 5TE. Tel 30607.

Sun House Antiques. Hall St, Long Melford, Suffolk, CO10 9HZ. Tel Sudbury (0787) 78252.

Templar Antiques. The Corner House, 2 Bear St, Nayland, Suffolk, CO6 4HX. Tel 262520.

Todd & Austin Antiques & Fine Art. 2 Andover Rd, Winchester, Hampshire, SO23 7BS. Tel 69824.

Townhead Antiques. Townhead, Newby Bridge, Cumbria, LA12 8NP. Tel 31321.

Peter Wadham. The Antique Shop, 5 Cathedral Close, Exeter, Devon. Tel 39741.

W.W. Warner (Antiques) Ltd. The Green, Brasted, Kent, TN16 1JL. Tel Westerham (0959) 63698.

Michael Wisehall Antiques. Minshull Gallery, 7 Minshull St, Knutsford, Cheshire. Tel 4901.

H. & B.Wolf Antiques Ltd. 128 Worcester Rd (A38), Droitwich, Hereford & Worcester, WR9 8AN. Tel 772320.

Tim Wright Antiques. 147 Bath St, Glasgow, Strathclyde. Tel 221 0364.

Glass, Display Domes

see Display Domes

Glass, European

John A.Brooks. 2 Knights Crescent, Rothley, Leicestershire. Tel Leicester (0533) 302625.

Emanouel Antiques Ltd. 64 South Audley St, London, W1Y 5FA. Tel 493 4350, 499 0996.

H.W. Newby. 15 Walton St, London, SW3 2HX. Tel 589 2752.

Howard Phillips. 11A Henrietta Place, London, W1M 9AG. Tel 580 9844.

Glass, Mirror Paintings

see Mirror Paintings

Glass, Mirrors

see Mirrors

Glass, Restorers

see Restorers, Glass

Glass, Early to 17th Century

W.G.T.Burne (Antique Glass) Ltd. 11 Elystan St, London, SW3. Tel 589 6074.

Flora Dora Antiques. Dales House, Lombard St, Petworth, W.Sussex, GU28 OAG. Tel 43109.

Gatehouse Antiques. 72 Chestergate, Macclesfield, Cheshire. Tel 26476.

Mansour Gallery. 46 Davies St, London, W1. Tel 491 7444.

Markland Antiques. Western Rd, Borough Green, Kent. Tel 4152.

Old Treasures. 126A Queen St, Newton Abbot, Devon, TQ12 2EU. Tel 67181.

Howard Phillips. 11A Henrietta Place, London, W1M 9AG. Tel 580 9844.

T.E.Robinson Antiques. 3A 3 & 4 Bartlett St, Bath, Avon, BA1 2QZ. Tel 63982 (priv 832307).

Sheppard & Cooper Ltd. 35 St George St, London, W1. Tel 629 6489.

Templar Antiques. The Corner House, 2 Bear St, Nayland, Suffolk, CO6 4HX. Tel 262520.

Glass, 18th Century

Armstrong Antiques. 10 & 11 Montpellier Parade, Harrogate, N.Yorkshire. Tel 506843.

Asprey PLC. 165-169 New Bond St, London, W1Y 0AR. Tel 493 6767.

Bell Passage Antiques. 36-38 High St,Wickwar, Wotton-under-Edge, Gloucestershire, GL12 8NP. Tel Wickwar (045 424) 251.

Christine Bridge. K10-12 Grays in Davies Mews,1-7 Davies Mews, London, W1Y 1AR. Tel 499 3562 (priv 741 5501).

John A.Brooks. 2 Knights Crescent, Rothley, Leicestershire. Tel Leicester (0533) 302625.

W.G.T.Burne (Antique Glass) Ltd. 11 Elystan St, London, SW3. Tel 589 6074.

Cobblers Hall Antiques. 119-121 Leighton Rd, Toddington, Bedfordshire, LU5 6AR. Tel 2890.

Delomosne & Son Ltd. 4 Campden Hill Rd, London, W8 7DU. Tel 937 1804.

Dorking Antiques. 58 West Street, Dorking, Surrey. Tel 883777.

Dormy House Antiques. 43 Kingsbury St, Marlborough, Wiltshire, SN8 1JE. Tel 52703.

Dymoke House. Highgate, Hawkhurst, Kent. Tel 3265.

Gabor Cossa Antiques. 34 Trumpington St, Cambridge, Cambridgeshire, CB2 1QY. Tel 356049.

Gatehouse Antiques. 72 Chestergate, Macclesfield, Cheshire. Tel 26476.

Jeanette Hayhurst Fine Glass. 3b Burlington Gdns, Old Bond Street, London, W1. Tel 437 4975.

Lesley Hepherd Antiques. London, SW7. Tel 244 9675.

J. & J. Hutton. 123 High St, Berkhamsted, Hertfordshire, HP4 2DJ. Tel 5979 (priv 5576).

William MacAdam. 86 Pilrig St, Edinburgh, Lothian, EH6 5AS. Tel 553 1364.

Mercury Antiques. 1 Ladbroke Rd, Kensington, London, W11 3PA. Tel 727 5106.

Howard Phillips. 11A Henrietta Place, London, W1M 9AG. Tel 580 9844.

Pryce and Brise Antiques. 79 Moore Park Rd, London, SW6. Tel 736 1864.

Gerald Sattin Ltd. 25 Burlington Arcade, Piccadilly, London, W1V 9AD. Tel 493 6557.

Somervale Antiques. 6 Radstock Rd, Midsomer Norton, Avon, BA3 2AJ. Tel 412686.

Sun House Antiques. Hall St, Long Melford, Suffolk, CO10 9HZ. Tel Sudbury (0787) 78252.

F.W.Taylor. Waite House, 71 Church St, Tewkesbury, Gloucestershire. Tel 295990.

Glass, 19th Century

Attic Antiques. 23 & 32 Ship St, Brighton & Hove, E.Sussex, BN1 1AD. Tel 29464 (priv 551594).

R.A.Barnes Antiques. 26 Lower Richmond Rd, Putney, London, SW15 1JP. Tel 789 3371.

Christine Bridge. K10-12 Grays in Davies Mews,1-7 Davies Mews, London, W1Y 1AR. Tel 499 3562 (priv 741 5501).

John A.Brooks. 2 Knights Crescent, Rothley, Leicestershire. Tel Leicester (0533) 302625.

W.G.T.Burne (Antique Glass) Ltd. 11 Elystan St, London, SW3. Tel 589 6074.

Clement House Antiques. High St, Burford, Oxfordshire, OX8 4QE. Tel 3172.

Cobb Antiques Ltd. 39b High St,Wimbledon Village, London, SW19. Tel 946 2811 (priv 540 7982).

Cold Bath Antiques. 20 Cold Bath Rd, Harrogate, N.Yorkshire, HG2 0NA. Tel 62331.

Delomosne & Son Ltd. 4 Campden Hill Rd, London, W8 7DU. Tel 937 1804.

Dorking Antiques. 58 West Street, Dorking, Surrey. Tel 883777.

Eardisley Antiques. Leominster Antique Market,14 Broad St, Leominster, Hereford & Worcester. Tel 2189 (priv 05446 310).

Editions Graphiques Gallery. 3 Clifford St, London, W1. Tel 734 3944.

Peter Francis. 26 Museum St, London, WC1A 1JT. Tel 637 0165.

Frogmore House Antiques. Frogmore House, Market Place, Box, Wiltshire. Tel 2550.

Gatehouse Antiques. 72 Chestergate, Macclesfield, Cheshire. Tel 26476.

Glenville Antiques. 120 High St, Yatton, Avon, BS19 4DH. Tel 832284.

Jeanette Hayhurst Fine Glass. 3b Burlington Gdns, Old Bond Street, London, W1. Tel 437 4975.

J. & J. Hutton. 123 High St, Berkhamsted, Hertfordshire, HP4 2DJ. Tel 5979 (priv 5576).

Jackson's Antiques. Neville House,10 The Bank, Barnard Castle, Durham. Tel Teesdale (0833) 37412.

Eric Lineham & Son. 62 Kensington Church St, London, W8 4OB. Tel 937 9650.

William MacAdam. 86 Pilrig St, Edinburgh, Lothian, EH6 5AS. Tel 553 1364.

Mercury Antiques. 1 Ladbroke Rd, Kensington, London, W11 3PA. Tel 727 5106.

Howard Phillips. 11A Henrietta Place, London, W1M 9AG. Tel 580 9844.

Pryce and Brise Antiques. 79 Moore Park Rd, London, SW6. Tel 736 1864.

Somervale Antiques. 6 Radstock Rd, Midsomer Norton, Avon, BA3 2AJ. Tel 412686.

Sun House Antiques. Hall St, Long Melford, Suffolk, CO10 9HZ. Tel Sudbury (0787) 78252.

F.W.Taylor. Waite House, 71 Church St, Tewkesbury, Gloucestershire. Tel 295990.

Robert Wilkes Antiques and Traditional Furniture. Norton Rd, Stourbridge, W.Midlands. Tel 393539.

Glass, 20th Century

Amalgam. 3 Barnes High St, London, SW13. Tel 878 1279.

R.A.Barnes Antiques. 26 Lower Richmond Rd, Putney, London, SW15 1JP. Tel 789 3371.

Coleridge. 192 Piccadilly, London, W1. Tel 437 0106.

Editions Graphiques Gallery. 3 Clifford St, London, W1. Tel 734 3944.

Fair Maids House Scottish Crafts. North Port, Perth, Tayside. Tel 25976.

Galia Antiques. Antiquarius, 135 King's Rd, London, SW3.

The Glasshouse Gallery & Workshop. 65 Long Acre, Covent Garden, London, WC2. Tel 836 9785 (priv.240 7508).

Patrick & Susan Gould. Grays Mews,1-7 Davies Mews, London, W1. Tel 408 0129.

L'Odeon. 173 Fulham Rd, London, SW3. Tel 581 3640 (priv 736 4216).

Ogle Fine Arts. Ogle Gallery, 12 Rotunda Terrace,Montpellier St, Cheltenham, Gloucestershire. Tel 518605 (priv 31011).

Stewart Gallery. 48 Devonshire Rd, Bexhill, E.Sussex. Tel 223410.

Stewart Gallery. 25 Grove Rd, Eastbourne, E.Sussex. Tel 29588.

Themes & Variations. 231 Westbourne Grove, London, W11. Tel 727 5531.

Ziggurat. Chenil Galleries, 183 King's Rd, London, SW3. Tel 352 2123.

Globes and Geographical Items

The Map House. 54 Beauchamp Place, Knightsbridge, London, SW3. Tel 589 4325, 589 9821.

O'Shea Gallery. 89 Lower Sloane St,Belgravia, London, SW1 8DA. Tel 730 0081, 730 0082.

Jonathan Potter. 1 Grafton St, London, W1X 3LB. Tel 491 3520.

Harriet Wynter Ltd. 50 Redcliffe Rd, London, SW10 9NJ. Tel 352 6494.

Goldsmiths

Charles Alexander Ltd. 41 Strand St, Douglas,. Tel 21527 (priv 822907).

Garrard & Co Ltd. 112 Regent St, London, W1A 2JJ. Tel 734 7020.

Melville Kemp Ltd. 89-91 Derby Rd, Nottingham, Nottinghamshire, NG1 5BB. Tel 417055.

David Shaw Silverware Ltd. 231-235 Liverpool Rd,Islington, London, N1 1LX. Tel 609 9091.

Gramophones and Talking Machines

Capricorn Collections. 48 St Anne's Rd, South Shore, Blackpool, Lancashire, FY4 2AS. Tel 49766.

Collector's Corner. 5-7 Frizinghall Rd, Bradford, W.Yorkshire, BD9 4LA. Tel 487098.

Discovery. Chelsea Antique Market,245-253 King's Rd, London, SW3. Tel 352 9695.

Fagin's Phonograph Emporium. 189 Blackstock Rd, Highbury, London, N5 2LL. Tel 359 4793 (priv 354 1212).

P.R.Garner (Antiques). Willow Farm, 104 High St, Landbeach, Cambridge, Cambridgeshire. Tel 860470.

Neil Spencer Antiques. 29 St Osburgs Rd, Stoke, Coventry, W.Midlands. Tel 441182.

Treasure House. 31 High St, Arundel, W.Sussex. Tel 883101.

The Vintage Wireless Shop and Hockley Antiques. 16 Hockley, Nottingham, Nottinghamshire. Tel 57097, 205441.

Hardstones

Sylvia Collins. Unit 15, Bond St Antique Centre,124 New Bond St, London, W1Y 9AE. Tel 9625.

Compton Antiques. 60A Middle St, Brighton & Hove, E.Sussex. Tel 774229.

A.Fleming (Southsea) Ltd. Clock Tower, Castle Rd, Portsmouth, Hampshire. Tel 822934.

Gregory, Bottley and Lloyd. 8-12 Rickett St, London, SW6 1RU. Tel 381 5522 (priv 878 5202).

Holmes (Jewellers) Ltd. 29 Old Bond St, London, W1X 3AB. Tel 493 1396.

Michael Jones Jeweller. 1 Gold St, Northampton, Northamptonshire, NN1 1SA. Tel 32548.

Levine, Henry & Co. 55 London St, Norwich, Norfolk, NR2 1HL. Tel 628709.

Oriental Antiques. 4 Belvedere, Lansdown Rd, Bath, Avon. Tel 315987.

T. Tolley. 26 College St, Worcester, Hereford & Worcester, WR1 2LS. Tel 26632.

Edric Van Vredenburgh. 37 Bury St, London, SW1. Tel 839 5818.

Heraldry

J.H. Bourdon-Smith Ltd. 24 Mason's Yard,Duke St, St James's, London, SW1Y 6BU. Tel 839 4714/5.

Heirloom and Howard Ltd. 1 Hay Hill, Berkeley Sq, London, W1. Tel 493 5868.

Heraldry Today. 10 Beauchamp Place, London, SW3. Tel 584 1656.

Paul Longmire Ltd. 12 Bury St,St James's, London, SW1. Tel 930 8720.

Hire

Business Art Galleries & The Upstairs Gallery. Royal Academy of Arts,Burlington House, Piccadilly, London, W1. Tel 734 1448 (priv 734 7763).

Michael Carleton. 77-81 Haverstock Hill, London, NW3 4SL. Tel 722 2277, 586 4458.

Collectors Corner - Militaria. 1 Northcross Rd, East Dulwich, London, SE22 9ET. Tel 693 6285.

P.B.Pollington. 4 Central Parade, High St, Wadhurst, E.Sussex, TN5 6AL. Tel 2866.

Turn On Ltd. 116-118 Islington High St,Camden Passage, London, N1 8EG. Tel 359 7616.

Horn

Horn Antiques. Churt, Farnham, Surrey, GU10 2JA. Tel Headley (0428) 714298.

Sharrington Antiques. Sharrington, Melton Constable, Norfolk, NR24 2PQ. Tel 861411 (priv 860719).

Horse Brasses

Ashley House Antiques. 61 High St, Measham, Burton on Trent, Staffordshire, DE12 7HR. Tel Measham (0530)433) 73568 (priv 054 373655).

Jack Casimir Ltd. 'The Brass Shop', 23 Pembridge Rd, London, W11 3HG. Tel 727 8643.

Heirloom and Howard Ltd. 1 Hay Hill, Berkeley Sq, London, W1. Tel 493 5868.

Old Saddlers Antiques. Church Rd, Goudhurst, Cranbrook, Kent, TN17 1BH. Tel 211458.

Horse Drawn Vehicles

see Carriages

Humidifiers

Air Improvement Centre Ltd. 23 Denbigh St, London, SW1V 2HF. Tel 834 2834 (priv 821 8485).

Icons

Maria Andipa Icon Gallery. 162 Walton St, London, SW3. Tel 589 2371.

Andrew Britten. 48 High St, Malmesbury, Wiltshire, SN16 9AT. Tel 3376.

Iconastas. 5 Piccadilly Arcade,Jermyn St, London, SW1. Tel 629 1433.

Mark Gallery. 9 Porchester Place, Marble Arch, London, W2 2BS. Tel 262 4906.

Temple Gallery. 4 Yeomans Row, Brompton Rd, London, SW3. Tel 589 6622.

The Winter Palace. 69 Kensington Church Street, London, W8. Tel 937 2410.

Indian, Nepalese and Tibetan Works of Art

Barling of Mount Street Ltd. 112 Mount St, London, W1. Tel 499 2858.

Sven Gahlin. Bath, Avon. Tel 313032.

Jane Roberts & Robert Alderman. 2nd Floor,180 New Bond St, London, W1Y 9PD. Tel 491 0168.

Insignias

Collectors Corner - Militaria. 1 Northcross Rd, East Dulwich, London, SE22 9ET. Tel 693 6285.

Weiner aus Wien Military Antiques. 2 Market St, The Lanes, Brighton & Hove, E.Sussex, BN1 1HH. Tel 729948.

Insurance

C.R.Fenton & Co Ltd. Beachy Rd, Old Ford, London, E3 2NX. Tel 533 2711.

Harmers of London Stamp Auctioneers Ltd. 91 New Bond St, London, W1A 4EH. Tel 629 0218.

Sneath, Kent and Stuart (Insurance Brokers) Ltd. 21/25 Earl St, London, EC2A 2AL. Tel 377 9866.

Walker, Barnett and Hill (Auctioneers). 3-5 Waterloo Rd, Wolverhampton, W.Midlands, WV1 4DL. Tel 771511, 772771.

Wingate & Johnston Ltd. 78 Broadway, Stratford, London, E15 1NG. Tel 555 8123.

Interior Decoration

Abode. 40 Sheep St, Stratford-upon-Avon, Warwickshire, CV37 6EE. Tel 68755.

Addison-Ross Gallery. 40 Eaton Tce, Belgravia, London, SW1. Tel 730 1536.

Alderley House Antiques. Alderley House, 53 Long St, Tetbury, Gloucestershire, GL8 8AA. Tel 53667.

And So To Bed Ltd. 638-640 King's Road, London, SW6. Tel 731 3593.

Antique Dealers International PLC. Bow Street, Langport, Somerset. Tel 252977.

Michael Carleton. 77-81 Haverstock Hill, London, NW3 4SL. Tel 722 2277, 586 4458.

Colefax & Fowler. 39 Brook St, London, W1Y 1AU. Tel 493 2231.

Compton-Dando (Fine Arts) Ltd. Berewyk Hall, White Colne, Earls Colne, Essex. Tel 2200 (priv 0787 312610).

De Fresnes (Antiques). Cessnock Castle, Galston, Strathclyde. Tel 829314.

A.F.Drysdale. 35 North West Circus Place, Edinburgh, Lothian, EH3 6TW. Tel 225 4686.

Dunedin Antiques Ltd. 4 North West Circus Place, Edinburgh, Lothian. Tel 226 3074.

An Englishman's Home. 56 Stokes Croft, Bristol, Avon. Tel 424257.

Joan Frere Antiques. Drumbuie House, Drumnadrochit, Highland. Tel 210.

The Golden Age. 7-9 Metropole Buildings, Blackpool, Lancashire, FY1 1RF. Tel 22969.

Maurice Goldstone & Son. Avenel Court, King St, Bakewell, Derbyshire. Tel 2487.

Great Brampton House Antiques Ltd. Great Brampton House, Madley, Hereford, Hereford & Worcester, HR2 9NA. Tel Golden Valley (0981) 250244.

Greville Antiques & Design Ltd. The Square, Aspley Guise, Milton Keynes, Buckinghamshire, MK17 8DF. Tel 584466 (priv 583408).

Greville Antiques & Design Ltd. The Square, Aspley Guise, Milton Keynes, Buckinghamshire, MK17 8DF. Tel 584466 (priv 583408).

Hallidays Antiques Ltd. The Old College, High St, Dorchester, Oxfordshire. Tel Oxford (0865) 340028.

A. Halsey Antiques. Boffins Boft, Bowcombe Creek, Kingsbridge, Devon. Tel 2440.

Hamilton Weston Wallpapers. 11 Townshend Rd, Richmond, Surrey, TW9 1XH. Tel 940 4850.

Nicholas Haslam. 12 Holbein Place, London, SW1. Tel 730 8623.

Helena Hood and Co. 3 Margarets Buildings, Brock St, Bath, Avon, BA1 2LP. Tel 24438.

Idears. 1 Chapel St, Diss, Norfolk, IP22 3AN. Tel 51521.

H.W. Keil (Cheltenham) Ltd. 129-131 The Promenade, Cheltenham, Gloucestershire, GL50 1NW. Tel 522509, 527974.

Leonard Lassalle. 21 The Pantiles, Tunbridge Wells, Kent, TN2 5TD. Tel 31645.

Charles Lowe & Sons Ltd. 37-40 Church Gate, Loughborough, Leicestershire. Tel 217876.

William MacIntosh & Co. 5 Johnston Terrace, Edinburgh, Lothian, EH1 2PW. Tel 225 6113.

Mrs Monro (Antiques) Ltd. 11 Montpelier St, London, SW7. Tel 589 5052, 821 1860.

John Nash Antiques. The Coach House,Drury Lane, Red Marley, Gloucestershire. Tel Bromsberrow (053181) 616.

Newcourt Park. Lugwardine, Hereford & Worcester. Tel Hereford (0432) 850752.

Ning Ltd. 58 Cambridge St, London, SW1. Tel 834 3292.

Anatol Orient Ltd. 318 Portobello Rd, London, W10. Tel 969 4119.

Park Galleries. 215/217 Preston Rd, Brighton & Hove, E.Sussex, BN1 6SA. Tel 504057 (priv 29466).

Richard Philp. 59 Ledbury Rd, London, W11. Tel 727 7915.

Graham Porter Antiques. 31 Whitehorse St, Baldock, Hertfordshire. Tel 895351.

Charles Read Georgian Furnishing. Bathealton Court,Bathealton, Milverton, Somerset, TA4 2AJ. Tel Wiveliscombe (0984) 23225.

Paul Reeves. 32B Kensington Church St, London, W8 4HA. Tel 937 1594 (priv 968 7413).

Relic Antiques. 1 Camden Walk, Islington, London, N1. Tel 359 6755.

Sage Antiques & Interiors. High St, Ripley, Surrey, GU23 6BB. Tel Guildford (0483) 224396.

Secondhand Rose. Portsmouth Rd, Bramshot Chase, Hindhead, Surrey, GU26 6DB. Tel 4880.

George Spencer Decorations Ltd. 36 Sloane St, London, SW1. Tel 235 1501.

Swanbridge Art Company Ltd. Tower Rd, Glover West Industrial Est,District 11, Washington, Tyne & Wear, NE37 2SH. Tel Tyneside (091) 415-0080.

Whytock & Reid. Sunbury House, Belford Mews, Edinburgh, Lothian, EH4 3DN. Tel 226 4911.

Althea Wilson. 43 Burnaby St,Lots Rd, London, SW10. Tel 352 9394.

Stanley Woolston. 29 Broad St, Ludlow, Shropshire, SY8 1NJ. Tel 3554.

Ironwork

see also Fire-irons and Fenders, Brass

J. & J. Caspall Antiques. Sheep St, Stow-on-the-Wold, Gloucestershire. Tel 31160.

Classic Furniture Ltd. Audley Avenue, Newport, Shropshire. Tel 813311.

Combe Cottage Antiques. Castle Combe, Wiltshire, SN14 7HU. Tel 782250.

Cottage Antiques. The Old Post Office, Langford, Bristol, Avon, BS18 7BP. Tel Wrighton (0934) 862597.

Crowther of Syon Lodge. Syon Lodge, Busch Corner,London Rd, Isleworth, Middlesex, TW7 5BH. Tel 560 7978, 560 7985.

T.Crowther & Son Ltd. 282 North End Rd, Fulham, London, SW6 1NH. Tel 385 1375/7.

P.J.Fradley. Ellastone Old House, Ellastone, Ashbourne, Derbyshire, DE6 2GU. Tel Ellastone (033 524) 291.

Span Antiques. 6 Market Place, Woodstock, Oxfordshire, OX7 1TA. Tel 811332.

Thistledome Antiques. Kings Arms Yard, Ampthill, Bedfordshire, MK45. Tel 403394 (priv 717368).

Touchwood Antiques. 9 Park St., Stow-on-the-Wold, Gloucestershire, GL54 1AQ. Tel 30221.

Islamic and Persian Works of Art

Aaron Galleries. 34 Bruton St, London, W1X 7DD. Tel 499 9434.

Ahuan UK Ltd. 17 Eccleston St, London, SW1W 9LX. Tel 730 9382.

Al-Mashreq Galleries. 110 Kensington Church St, London, W8 4BH. Tel 229 5453.

Armoury Antiques. Unit 123, Grays Antique Market,58 Davies St, London, W1. Tel 408 0176.

Axia. 43 Pembridge Villas, London, W11. Tel 727 9724.

de Montfort. 49 High St, Robertsbridge, E.Sussex, TN32 5AN. Tel 880698 (priv 082 584 243).

Emanouel Antiques Ltd. 64 South Audley St, London, W1Y 5FA. Tel 493 4350, 499 0996.

M. Odell Foster. Millmead, Wonersh, Surrey. Tel Guildford (0483) 892375.

Hadji Baba Ancient Art. 36 Davies St, London, W1Y 1LD. Tel 499 9363, 499 9384.

Robert Hales Antiques Ltd. 133 Kensington Church St, London, W8 7LP. Tel 229 3887.

Khalili Gallery. 15c Clifford St, Bond St, London, W1. Tel 734 4202.

Mansour Gallery. 46 Davies St, London, W1. Tel 491 7444.

Bashir Mohamed Ltd. 46 Montagu Square, London, W1. Tel 723 1844.

Jane Roberts & Robert Alderman. 2nd Floor,180 New Bond St, London, W1Y 9PD. Tel 491 0168.

Clive Rogers Oriental Rugs. 22 Brunswick Rd,Hove, Brighton & Hove, E.Sussex, BN3 1DG. Tel 738257.

Samiramis Ltd. Grays Mews,1-7 Davies St, London, W1. Tel 629 1161 or 439 5106.

Philippa Scott. 30 Elgin Crescent, London, W11. Tel 229 8029.

Spink & Son Ltd. 5, 6 & 7 King St, St James's, London, SW1. Tel 930 7888.

Zamana Gallery Ltd. 1 Cromwell Gardens, London, SW7 2SL. Tel 584 6612/3.

Ivories

Kenneth W. Allen. Moor Old Lodge, 6 Moor Hall Park,Four Oaks, Sutton Coldfield, W.Midlands, B75 6LP. Tel 308 1685.

Attic Antiques. 23 & 32 Ship St, Brighton & Hove, E.Sussex, BN1 1AD. Tel 29464 (priv 551594).

C.Barrett & Co. 51 Burlington Arcade, Piccadilly, London, W1. Tel 493 2570.

Bluett & Sons Ltd. 48 Davies St, London, W1Y 1LD. Tel 629 4018, 629 3397.

Compton Antiques. 60A Middle St, Brighton & Hove, E.Sussex. Tel 774229.

Eskenazi Ltd. Foxglove House, 166 Piccadilly, London, W1V 9DE. Tel 493 5464.

Galleon Galleries. 42 Westfield Lane, St Leonards, E.Sussex. Tel 440974.

J.& J.Hubbard Antiques. 11A Mill St, St Peter Port, Guernsey. Tel 28462 (priv 28540).

LPJ Antiques. 27 Camden Passage, Islington, London, N1. Tel 359 7579.

I.J.Mazure & Co Ltd. 90 Jermyn St, London, SW1Y 6JD. Tel 839 3101/2.

Mytton Antiques. Norton Crossroads, Atcham, Shrewsbury, Shropshire. Tel Uppington (095286) 229.

Oriental Antiques. 4 Belvedere, Lansdown Rd, Bath, Avon. Tel 315987.

Christine Schell. 15 Cale St, London, SW3 3QS. Tel 352 5563.

Edric Van Vredenburgh. 37 Bury St, London, SW1. Tel 839 5818.

Woburn Fine Arts. 12 Market Place, Woburn, Bedfordshire, MK17 9PZ. Tel 624.

Jade

see also Oriental Works of Art

Bluett & Sons Ltd. 48 Davies St, London, W1Y 1LD. Tel 629 4018, 629 3397.

William Clayton Ltd. 38 Bury St, St James's, London, SW1. Tel 930 1173.

Eskenazi Ltd. Foxglove House, 166 Piccadilly, London, W1V 9DE. Tel 493 5464.

Solveig & Anita Gray. 58 Davies Street, London, W1. Tel 408 1638.

S.Marchant & Son. 120 Kensington Church St, London, W8 4BH. Tel 229 5319, 229 3770.

T. Tolley. 26 College St, Worcester, Hereford & Worcester, WR1 2LS. Tel 26632.

Mary Wise Antiques. 27 Holland St, London, W8. Tel 937 8649 (priv 352 7334).

Japanese Works of Art

see also Netsuke, Inro and Tsuba

Armada Antiques. Stand 122 Gray's Antiques Mkt,58 Davies St, London, W1. Tel 499 1087.

Artemesia. 16 West St, Alresford, Hampshire. Tel 2277.

Barling of Mount Street Ltd. 112 Mount St, London, W1. Tel 499 2858.

Helen Buxton Antiques. 193 Westbourne Grove, London, W11. Tel 229 9997.

Odile Cavendish. 14 Lowndes St, London, SW1X 9EX. Tel 235 2491.

R. & D. Coombes. Charleville Gallery,7 Charleville Rd, West Kensington, London, W14 9JL. Tel 385 3795.

Shirley Day Ltd. 91B Jermyn St, London, SW1Y 6JB. Tel 839 2804.

East Asia Co. 103 Camden High St, London, NW1 7JN. Tel 388 5783.

Eskenazi Ltd. Foxglove House, 166 Piccadilly, London, W1V 9DE. Tel 493 5464.

Falkner Fine Art. Stands B18/C19 Grays Mews,Davies Mews, London, W1. Tel 629 3644 (priv 385 0174).

Galleon Galleries. 42 Westfield Lane, St Leonards, E.Sussex. Tel 440974.

Solveig & Anita Gray. 58 Davies Street, London, W1. Tel 408 1638.

Japanese Gallery. 23 Camden Passage, London, N1 8EA. Tel 226 3347.

Robin Kennedy. 29 New Bond St, London, W1Y 9HD. Tel 408 1238 (priv 940 3281).

Richard Kruml. P.O.Box 4LE, 47 Albemarle St, London, W1A 4LE. Tel 629 3017.

S.Marchant & Son. 120 Kensington Church St, London, W8 4BH. Tel 229 5319, 229 3770.

Milne Henderson. 96 Mount St, London, W1. Tel 499 2507.

Sydney L. Moss Ltd. 51 Brook St, London, W1Y 1AU. Tel 629 4670; 493 7374.

Nash Antiques. 183 Westbourne Grove, London, W11. Tel 727 3796.

Nihon Token. 23 Museum St, London, WC1A 1JT. Tel 580 6511.

Barry Sainsbury Oriental Art. 145 Ebury St, London, SW1. Tel 730 3393.

Stone House Antiques (and Design & Craft Gallery). St Mary's St, Painswick, Gloucestershire, GL6 6QB. Tel 813540 (priv 045286 2343).

Stone House Antiques (and Design & Craft Gallery). St Mary's St, Painswick, Gloucestershire, GL6 6QB. Tel 813540 (priv 045286 2343).

Tempus Antiques Ltd. 2-4 King St,St James's, London, SW1Y 6QL. Tel 839 5144.

Jardinieres

Barrie Quinn Antiques. 3 & 4 Broxholme House, New King's Rd, London, SW6. Tel 736 4747.

Jewellery, Antique

London

Patrick Aldridge Ltd. 88-90 Hatton Garden, London, EC1. Tel 242 3209.

Armour-Winston Ltd. 43 Burlington Arcade, Piccadilly, London, W1V 9AE. Tel 493 8937.

Maurice Asprey Ltd. 41 Duke St, St James's, London, SW1. Tel 930 3921.

Beetle & Poker. 22 Crown Passage, St James's, London, SW1Y 6PP. Tel 930 6003.

Ronald Benjamin Antiques. 25B Hatton Garden, London, EC1N 8BQ. Tel 242 9105, 242 6188.

Crawford & Pawle Ltd. 2nd Floor, Bond St Silver Galleries,111-112 New Bond St, London, W1Y 9AB. Tel 499 8442.

J.M.Davies (Jewellers) Ltd. Grays Antique Market,58 Davies St, London, W1. Tel 493 9624.

Demas. 31 Burlington Arcade, Piccadilly, London, W1M 7HB. Tel 493 9496.

Denisa the Lady Newborough. 1-1A-2 Whitehorse St,Shepherd Market, London, W1. Tel 493 3954 (priv 493 0854).

Richard Digby. Stand L18-21, Grays Mews,1-7 Davies St, London, W1. Tel 491 0251.

Donohoe. 1-7 Davies Mews, London, W1. Tel 629 5633 (priv 455 5507).

J.F.Ewing. 11 High St, Wimbledon Village, London, SW19. Tel 946 4700.

Henry Faber Ltd. 94 Southampton Row, London, WC1 4BB. Tel 405 0749.

Diana Foley Antiques. Stand L18/21 Grays Mews,1-7 Davies Mews, London, W1. Tel 408 1089.

Elizabeth Gage. 20 Albemarle St, London, W1. Tel 499 2879.

The Golden Past. 6 Brook St, London, W1Y 1AA. Tel 493 6422.

Michael & Diana Grainger. 113 Portobello Rd, London, W11. Tel 858 0778.

Green's Antique Galleries. 117 Kensington Church St, London, W8 7LN. Tel 229 9618/9.

M.Hakim. 4 The Royal Arcade, Old Bond St, London, W1X 3HD. Tel 629 6243.

Hancocks & Co (Jewellers) Ltd. 1 Burlington Gardens, London, W1X 2HP. Tel 493 8904.

Essie C.Harris. Diamond House 37-38 Hatton Garden, London, EC1. Tel 242 9115/1558.

Nicholas Harris. 26 Conduit St, London, W1. Tel 499 5991.

Harvey & Gore. 4 Burlington Gardens, London, W1X 1LE. Tel 493 2714.

Holmes (Jewellers) Ltd. 29 Old Bond St, London, W1X 3AB. Tel 493 1396.

Brian and Lynn Holmes. Stands 304-306, Grays Antique Market,58 Davies St, London, W1. Tel 629 7327.

J.I.Horwit. 94 Southampton Row, London, WC1 4BB. Tel 405 0749.

Hundred And One. 101 Notting Hill Gate, London, W11. Tel 727 2326.

The Jewel House (Mayfair). 23 Lansdowne Row, London, W1X 7LN. Tel 499 7936.

John's Antiques. Stands 345/346, Grays Antique Market,58 Davies St, London, W1. Tel 629 1140.

Johnson, Walker & Tolhurst Ltd. 64 Burlington Arcade, Piccadilly, London, W1. Tel 629 2615, 629 2616.

Annabel Jones. 52 Beauchamp Place,Knightsbridge, London, SW3. Tel 589 3215.

John Joseph. Grays Antique Market,58 Davies St, London, W1. Tel 629 1140.

S.Lampard & Son. 32 Notting Hill Gate, London, W11. Tel 229 5457.

Lancaster Antiques. Harlequin, Grays Antique Market,58 Davies St, London, W1. Tel 629 6502.

D.S.Lavender (Antiques) Ltd. 16B Grafton St, London, W1X 3LA. Tel 629 1782 (priv 409 2305).

W. Lipka Ltd. 62 Aylestone Ave, London, NW6. Tel 459 4588.

Paul Longmire Ltd. 12 Bury St,St James's, London, SW1. Tel 930 8720.

Mansour Gallery. 46 Davies St, London, W1. Tel 491 7444.

Massada Antiques. 45 New Bond St, London, W1Y 9HB. Tel 493 4792; 493 5610.

R.I. McKay. 63 South Molton St, London, W1Y 1HH.

H. Miller (Antiques) Ltd. Silver Vaults, Chancery Lane, London, WC2. Tel 242 7073.

Nonesuch Antiques. Stand3,Bond St Antique Centre,124 New Bond St, London, W1. Tel 629 6783.

Richard Ogden Ltd. 28 & 29 Burlington Arcade,Piccadilly, London, W1V ONX. Tel 493 9136/7.

Carol Orford Antiques. Bond Street Antique Centre,124 New Bond St, London, W1. Tel 493 2654.

A.& H.Page. 66 Gloucester Rd, Kensington, London, SW7. Tel 584 7349.

David Paskin Antiques (London) Ltd. Grays Antique Market,58 Davies St, London, W1. Tel 408 1129.

S.J. Phillips Ltd. 139 New Bond St, London, W1A 3DL. Tel 629 6261, 629 6262.

Madeleine Popper FGA, Diana Foley, Richard Digby. Stand L18-L21, Grays Mews,1-7 Davies Mews, London, W1. Tel 408 1089.

Prashina Ltd. Bond Street Antique Centre,124 New Bond St, London, W1.

The Purple Shop. 15 Flood St,Chelsea, London, SW3 5ST. Tel 352 1127.

Scarlet Pimpernel Antiques. Grays Antique Market,58 Davies St, London, W1.

Searle & Co Ltd. 1 Royal Exchange, London, EC3V 3LL. Tel 626 2456.

Simeon. 19 Burlington Arcade, Piccadilly, London, W1V 9AB. Tel 493-3353.

Spink & Son Ltd. 5, 6 & 7 King St, St James's, London, SW1. Tel 930 7888.

Louise Stroud. 3, Cale Street,Chelsea Green, London, SW3. Tel 351 5988.

Talisman. 363/4 Gray's Antique Market,58 Davies St, London, W1. Tel 409 2743.

Trianon. Grays Antique Market,58 Davies St, London, W1. Tel 491 2764.

Ventura-Pauly Ltd. Grays Antique Market,58 Davies St, London, W1. Tel 408 1057.

Wartski Ltd. 14 Grafton St, London, W1. Tel 493 1141/2/3.

Westminster Group. Stand 150, Grays Antique Market,58 Davies St, London, W1Y 1HH. Tel 493 8672.

Regions

Abbey Antiques and Arts. 97 High St, Hemel Hempstead, Hertfordshire, HP1 3AH. Tel 64667.

Charles Alexander Ltd. 41 Strand St, Douglas,. Tel 21527 (priv 822907).

Argentum Antiques. 18-20 High St, Bexley, Kent, DA5 1AD. Tel Crayford (0322) 527915.

Shirley Baguley Antiques. West Park Antique Pavilion,20 West Park, Harrogate, N.Yorkshire. Tel 61758 (priv 65512).

J.& H.Bell Antiques. 22 Arbory St, Castletown,. Tel 823132 (priv 822414).

Benedict Jewellers. 37 High St, Old Amersham, Amersham, Buckinghamshire, HP7 0DP. Tel 22803.

Bond Street Antiques. 6 Bond St, Cromer, Norfolk, NR27 9DA. Tel 513134.

Joseph Bonnar. 72 Thistle St, Edinburgh, Lothian. Tel 226 2811.

Boodle & Dunthorne Ltd. 52 Eastgate St, Chester, Cheshire, CH1 1LE. Tel 26666.

Boodle & Dunthorne Ltd. 35 Lord St, Liverpool, Merseyside. Tel 227-2525.

Bow Window. 58 Connaught Ave, Frinton-on-Sea, Essex. Tel 4607.

Bracher & Sydenham. 24 Queen Victoria St, Reading, Berkshire, RG1 1TG. Tel 583265, 53724.

H.H.Bray Ltd. 9 Jury St, Warwick, Warwickshire. Tel 492791.

Wm Bruford & Son Ltd. 11-13 Cornfield Rd, Eastbourne, E.Sussex, BN21 3NA. Tel 25452.

Wm Bruford & Son Ltd. 1 Bedford St, Exeter, Devon, EX1 1LU. Tel 54901.

Buckie's Jewellers, Valuers & Silversmiths. 31 Trinity St, Cambridge, Cambridgeshire, CB2 1TB. Tel 357910.

Bygones of Worcester. 55 Sidbury, Worcester, Hereford & Worcester, WR1 2HU. Tel 23132 and 25388.

Mark Collier. 24 The High St, Fordingbridge, Hampshire. Tel 52555.

Copperfields. 1 Church St, Sidmouth, Devon. Tel 2145.

Cradlewell Antiques. 244 Jesmond Rd, Newcastle upon Tyne, Tyne & Wear. Tel 810691.

H.Danker. 10 South Anne St, Dublin, Co Dublin. Tel 774009.

Davidson's The Jewellers. 94-96 Grey St, Newcastle upon Tyne, Tyne & Wear. Tel 22551, 22895.

Reginald Davis (Oxford) Ltd. 34 High St, Oxford, Oxfordshire, OX1 4AN. Tel 248347.

K.W.Dunster Antiques. 23 Church St, Staines, Middlesex. Tel 53297.

D.H.Edmonds Ltd. 27-28 Meeting House Lane, Brighton & Hove, E.Sussex, BN1 14B. Tel 27713, 28871.

Fillans Antiques. 2 Market Walk, Huddersfield, W.Yorkshire, HD1 2QA. Tel 531609.

A.Fleming (Southsea) Ltd. Clock Tower, Castle Rd, Portsmouth, Hampshire. Tel 822934.

Frith Antiques. New St, Petworth, W.Sussex. Tel 43155 (priv 079881 606).

Georgian Gems. 28 High St, Swanage, Dorset, BH19 1HA. Tel 424697.

Lynn Greenwold. Digbeth, Digbeth St, Stow-on-the-Wold, Gloucestershire. Tel 30398.

W.F.Greenwood & Sons Ltd. 2&3 Crown Place, Harrogate, N.Yorkshire, HG1 2RY. Tel 504467.

Grey-Harris & Co. 12 Princess Victoria St,Clifton, Bristol, Avon. Tel 737365.

Hardie Antiques. 25 St John St, Perth, Tayside. Tel 33127.

Harwood Westend Antiques. 13 West St, Weston-super-Mare, Avon, BS23 1JR. Tel 29874 (priv 24992).

The House of Antiques. 25 Meeting House Lane, Brighton & Hove, E.Sussex. Tel 27680, 24961.

Eleanor Hutton. 59 West Street, Dorking, Surrey. Tel 883777.

Michael Jones Jeweller. 1 Gold St, Northampton, Northamptonshire, NN1 1SA. Tel 32548.

E. & C.T.Koopman & Son Ltd. John Dalton House, John Dalton St, Manchester, Greater Manchester, M2 6JP. Tel 834 2402, 832 9036.

Lowe & Sons Ltd. 11 Bridge St Row, Chester, Cheshire, CH1 1PD. Tel 25850.

E.P.Mallory & Son Ltd. 1-4 Bridge St, Bath, Avon, BA2 4AP. Tel 65885.

Mappin & Webb Ltd (Butt & Co). 32 Eastgate Row, Chester, Cheshire, CH1 1LF. Tel 25938.

Melbourne Antiques. 48 Market Jew St, Penzance, Cornwall. Tel 3774.

Meriden House Antiques. Meriden House, 75 Market St, Stourbridge, W.Midlands. Tel 395384.

Stephen Moore Ltd. 103 High St, Lewes, E.Sussex, BN7 1XH. Tel 474158.

Nathan & Co (Birmingham) Ltd. 31 Corporation St, Birmingham, W.Midlands. Tel 643 5225.

E.A. Nowell & Sons. 21-23 Market Place, Wells, Somerset, BA5 2RF. Tel 72415, 78738, 76915.

Ogden of Harrogate Ltd. 38 James St, Harrogate, N.Yorkshire, HG1 1RQ. Tel 504123.

Old Treasures. 126A Queen St, Newton Abbot, Devon, TQ12 2EU. Tel 67181.

Osborne Jewellers. 55 Osborne Rd, Southsea, Portsmouth, Hampshire, PO5 3LS. Tel 825101.

Parkhouse & Wyatt Ltd. 96 Above Bar, Southampton, Hampshire, SO9 4FF. Tel 226653.

Resners. 1 Meeting House Lane, Brighton & Hove, E.Sussex. Tel 29127.

The Saddle Room Antiques. 4 Coagh St, Cookstown, Co Tyrone, BT80 8NQ. Tel 64045 (priv 62033).

M.Samuels (Antiques). 17 South Anne St, Dublin, Co Dublin. Tel 711262.

Scarthoe Antiques. 38A Louth Rd,Scartho, Grimsby, Humberside, DN32 8PP. Tel 77394,.

Sherwood Antiques. 9 Marine Court, St Leonards, E.Sussex, TN38 0DN. Tel 428204.

A.T.Silvester & Sons Ltd. 2-4 High St, Warwick, Warwickshire, CV34 4AP. Tel 492972.

Simons Antiques. 61 The Tything, Worcester, Hereford & Worcester. Tel 25152.

Jeremy Sniders. Victorian Village, 57 West Regent St, Glasgow, Strathclyde. Tel 332 2424.

P.D. & S. Solden. 65 Mabgate, Leeds, W.Yorkshire, LS9 7DR. Tel 452229.

South Bar Antiques. Digbeth St, Stow-on-the-Wold, Gloucestershire. Tel 30236.

Spon End Antiques. 115-116 Spon End, Coventry, W.Midlands, CV1 3HF. Tel 28379.

Station Antiques. 1 Camp Terrace, North Shields, Tyne & Wear. Tel 571800.

H. & M. Suttle. 18 Market Place, Otley, W.Yorkshire, LS21 2AQ. Tel 462313.

Thistle Antiques. 28 Esslemont Ave, Aberdeen, Grampian. Tel 634692.

Thurso Antiques. Drill Hall,Sinclair St, Thurso, Highland. Tel 63291 (priv 66202).

James & Ann Tillett. Tombland House, 12-13 Tombland, Norwich, Norfolk, NR3 1HF. Tel 624914.

Christopher Warner. 15 Princes St, Harrogate, N.Yorkshire, HG1 1NG. Tel 503617.

Waterloo Antiques. 16 Waterloo St, Oldham, Greater Manchester. Tel 624 5975.

Wildman's Antiques. 48 St Stephen St, Edinburgh, Lothian, EH3 5AL. Tel 225 7310 (priv 449 3038).

Yellow Frog (Brighton) Ltd. 10 & 11 Meeting House Lane, Brighton & Hove, E.Sussex. Tel 25497.

Robert Young Antiques. 4A Exchange St, Norwich, Norfolk, NR2 1AT. Tel 618605.

Jewellery, Modern

Argenta. 82 Fulham Rd, London, SW3. Tel 584 3119.

Beetle & Poker. 22 Crown Passage, St James's, London, SW1Y 6PP. Tel 930 6003.

H.H.Bray Ltd. 9 Jury St, Warwick, Warwickshire. Tel 492791.

Lesley Craze. 5 Essex Rd,Islington, London, N1. Tel 226 3200.

Electrum. 21 South Molton St, London, W1. Tel 629 6325.

Galia Antiques. Antiquarius, 135 King's Rd, London, SW3.

Georgian Gems. 28 High St, Swanage, Dorset, BH19 1HA. Tel 424697.

The Jewel House (Mayfair). 23 Lansdowne Row, London, W1X 7LN. Tel 499 7936.

Annabel Jones. 52 Beauchamp Place,Knightsbridge, London, SW3. Tel 589 3215.

Lowe & Sons Ltd. 11 Bridge St Row, Chester, Cheshire, CH1 1PD. Tel 25850.

Mappin & Webb Ltd (Butt & Co). 32 Eastgate Row, Chester, Cheshire, CH1 1LF. Tel 25938.

Melbourne Antiques. 48 Market Jew St, Penzance, Cornwall. Tel 3774.

Nathan & Co (Birmingham) Ltd. 31 Corporation St, Birmingham, W.Midlands. Tel 643 5225.

Ogden of Harrogate Ltd. 38 James St, Harrogate, N.Yorkshire, HG1 1RQ. Tel 504123.

Ogle Fine Arts. Ogle Gallery, 12 Rotunda Terrace,Montpellier St, Cheltenham, Gloucestershire. Tel 518605 (priv 31011).

Osborne Jewellers. 55 Osborne Rd, Southsea, Portsmouth, Hampshire, PO5 3LS. Tel 825101.

Oxford Gallery. 23 High St, Oxford, Oxfordshire, OX1 4AH. Tel 242731.

Soft Surround. 2 Centre Craft Yard,43 Henley St, Stratford-upon-Avon, Warwickshire, CV37 6QW. Tel 295070 (priv 0608-62181).

Westleigh Antiques. Croesus, Grays,58 Davies St, London, W1. Tel 493 0624.

Young Stephen Ltd. 1 Burlington Gdns, New Bond St, London, W1X 1LD. Tel 499 7927.

Jewellery, Restorers

see Restorers, Jewellery

Jewellery, 19th Century

London

Trevor Allen. Stand U4, Antiquarius,139 King's Rd, London, SW3. Tel 352 7061.

Philip Antrobus. 11 New Bond St, London, W1. Tel 493 4557.

Beetle & Poker. 22 Crown Passage, St James's, London, SW1Y 6PP. Tel 930 6003.

Ronald Benjamin Antiques. 25B Hatton Garden, London, EC1N 8BQ. Tel 242 9105, 242 6188.

Bentley & Co Ltd. 65 New Bond St, London, W1Y 9DF. Tel 629 0651, 629 0325.

N.Bloom & Son (Antiques) Ltd. 40 Conduit St, London, W1R 9FB. Tel 629 5060.

The Button Queen. 19 Marylebone Lane, London, W1M 5FF. Tel 935 1505.

Caboodle Ltd. Chelsea Antique Market,253 King's Rd, London, SW3.

Carrington & Co Ltd. 170 Regent St, London, W1R 6BQ. Tel 734 3727.

Moira Cohen Ltd. 22-23 New Bond St, London, W1. Tel 629 0160.

Collingwood of Bond Street. 171 Bond Street, London, W1. Tel 734 2656.

Denisa the Lady Newborough. 1-1A-2 Whitehorse St,Shepherd Market, London, W1. Tel 493 3954 (priv 493 0854).

Richard Digby. Stand L18-21, Grays Mews,1-7 Davies St, London, W1. Tel 491 0251.

J.F.Ewing. 11 High St, Wimbledon Village, London, SW19. Tel 946 4700.

Henry Faber Ltd. 94 Southampton Row, London, WC1 4BB. Tel 405 0749.

Diana Foley Antiques. Stand L18/21 Grays Mews,1-7 Davies Mews, London, W1. Tel 408 1089.

The Golden Past. 6 Brook St, London, W1Y 1AA. Tel 493 6422.

Henry Gregory. Stand 335, Grays Antique Market,58 Davies St, London, W1Y 1LB.

Hennell Ltd. 12 New Bond St, London, W1Y 0HE. Tel 629 6888.

Brian and Lynn Holmes. Stands 304-306, Grays Antique Market,58 Davies St, London, W1. Tel 629 7327.

J.I.Horwit. 94 Southampton Row, London, WC1 4BB. Tel 405 0749.

The Jewel House (Mayfair). 23 Lansdowne Row, London, W1X 7LN. Tel 499 7936.

John's Antiques. Stands 345/346, Grays Antique Market,58 Davies St, London, W1. Tel 629 1140.

Johnson, Walker & Tolhurst Ltd. 64 Burlington Arcade, Piccadilly, London, W1. Tel 629 2615, 629 2616.

Annabel Jones. 52 Beauchamp Place,Knightsbridge, London, SW3. Tel 589 3215.

D.S.Lavender (Antiques) Ltd. 16B Grafton St, London, W1X 3LA. Tel 629 1782 (priv 409 2305).

Paul Longmire Ltd. 12 Bury St,St James's, London, SW1. Tel 930 8720.

Massada Antiques. 45 New Bond St, London, W1Y 9HB. Tel 493 4792; 493 5610.

M. McAleer. 32A Sussex Place,Hyde Park, London, W2 2TH. Tel 723 5794.

Nigel Milne Ltd. 16C Grafton St, London, W1X 3LF. Tel 493 9646.

Nonesuch Antiques. Stand3,Bond St Antique Centre,124 New Bond St, London, W1. Tel 629 6783.

Madeleine Popper FGA, Diana Foley, Richard Digby. Stand L18-L21, Grays Mews,1-7 Davies Mews, London, W1. Tel 408 1089.

The Purple Shop. 15 Flood St,Chelsea, London, SW3 5ST. Tel 352 1127.

Louise Stroud. 3, Cale Street,Chelsea Green, London, SW3. Tel 351 5988.

Talisman. 363/4 Gray's Antique Market,58 Davies St, London, W1. Tel 409 2743.

J.S.Ullmann. 10 Hatton Gdn, London, EC1N 8AH. Tel 405 1877.

Westleigh Antiques. Croesus, Grays,58 Davies St, London, W1. Tel 493 0624.

Westminster Group. Stand 150, Grays Antique Market,58 Davies St, London, W1Y 1HH. Tel 493 8672.

Young Stephen Ltd. 1 Burlington Gdns, New Bond St, London, W1X 1LD. Tel 499 7927.

Regions

Abbey Antiques and Arts. 97 High St, Hemel Hempstead, Hertfordshire, HP1 3AH. Tel 64667.

Abbey Galleries. 9 Abbey Churchyard, Bath, Avon, BA1 1LY. Tel 60565.

Charles Alexander Ltd. 41 Strand St, Douglas,. Tel 21527 (priv 822907).

Antiqcurios & Irene Fine Art. 33 Clarendon St, Dublin, Co Dublin. Tel 714932.

Benedict Jewellers. 37 High St, Old Amersham, Amersham, Buckinghamshire, HP7 0DP. Tel 22803.

Bond Street Antiques. 6 Bond St, Cromer, Norfolk, NR27 9DA. Tel 513134.

Joseph Bonnar. 72 Thistle St, Edinburgh, Lothian. Tel 226 2811.

Boodle & Dunthorne Ltd. 52 Eastgate St, Chester, Cheshire, CH1 1LE. Tel 26666.

Boodle & Dunthorne Ltd. 35 Lord St, Liverpool, Merseyside. Tel 227-2525.

H.H.Bray Ltd. 9 Jury St, Warwick, Warwickshire. Tel 492791.

Wm Bruford & Son Ltd. 11-13 Cornfield Rd, Eastbourne, E.Sussex, BN21 3NA. Tel 25452.

Buckie's Jewellers, Valuers & Silversmiths. 31 Trinity St, Cambridge, Cambridgeshire, CB2 1TB. Tel 357910.

Chapel Place Antiques. 9 Chapel Pl, Tunbridge Wells, Kent. Tel 46561 (priv 04353 2624).

Charterhouse Antiques. 1B Northumberland Place, Teignmouth, Devon. Tel Newton Abbot (0626) 4592.

Church House Antiques. 42 Church St, Weybridge, Surrey. Tel 42190.

Coach House Antiques. 55 Elm Rd, Wisbech, Cambridgeshire, PE13 2TB. Tel 583129.

D.J.Jewellery. 166-168 Ashley Rd, Parkstone, Poole, Dorset, BH14 9BY. Tel 745148.

Davies Antiques. 32 King St, Whalley, Lancashire, BB6 9SL. Tel 3764.

Rene Dolton Antiques. 15a High St, Hemel Hempstead, Hertfordshire. Tel 64329.

Fillans Antiques. 2 Market Walk, Huddersfield, W.Yorkshire, HD1 2QA. Tel 531609.

Frith Antiques. New St, Petworth, W.Sussex. Tel 43155 (priv 079881 606).

Jay Gray Antiques. Syrena House, 1 Cheltenham Rd, Cirencester, Gloucestershire, GL7 2HS. Tel 2755.

Michael Jones Jeweller. 1 Gold St, Northampton, Northamptonshire, NN1 1SA. Tel 32548.

Kenworthys Ltd. 226 Stamford St, Ashton-under-Lyne, Manchester, Greater Manchester, OL6 7LW. Tel 330 3043.

Lowe & Pomfrett. 63 Queen St, Maidenhead, Berkshire. Tel 20759.

Lowe & Sons Ltd. 11 Bridge St Row, Chester, Cheshire, CH1 1PD. Tel 25850.

Magpie Antiques & Jewellers. 61 High St, Evesham, Hereford & Worcester. Tel 41631.

Mappin & Webb Ltd (Butt & Co). 32 Eastgate Row, Chester, Cheshire, CH1 1LF. Tel 25938.

Marks Antiques. 16 Waterloo St, Oldham, Greater Manchester, OL8 3DT. Tel 624 5975.

Ogden of Harrogate Ltd. 38 James St, Harrogate, N.Yorkshire, HG1 1RQ. Tel 504123.

Old Treasures. 126A Queen St, Newton Abbot, Devon, TQ12 2EU. Tel 67181.

Osborne Jewellers. 55 Osborne Rd, Southsea, Portsmouth, Hampshire, PO5 3LS. Tel 825101.

Parkhouse & Wyatt Ltd. 96 Above Bar, Southampton, Hampshire, SO9 4FF. Tel 226653.

Mark Parkhouse Antiques & Jewellery. 106 High St, Barnstaple, Devon, EX31 1HP. Tel 74504-5.

Resners. 1 Meeting House Lane, Brighton & Hove, E.Sussex. Tel 29127.

Scott Cooper Ltd. 52 The Promenade, Cheltenham, Gloucestershire, GL50 1LY. Tel 522580.

A.T.Silvester & Sons Ltd. 2-4 High St, Warwick, Warwickshire, CV34 4AP. Tel 492972.

S. & L. Simmons. 9 Meeting House Lane, Brighton & Hove, E.Sussex, BN1 1HB. Tel 27949.

Jeremy Sniders. Victorian Village, 57 West Regent St, Glasgow, Strathclyde. Tel 332 2424.

James & Ann Tillett. Tombland House, 12-13 Tombland, Norwich, Norfolk, NR3 1HF. Tel 624914.

Yellow Frog (Brighton) Ltd. 10 & 11 Meeting House Lane, Brighton & Hove, E.Sussex. Tel 25497.

Jewellery, 20th Century

Beetle & Poker. 22 Crown Passage, St James's, London, SW1Y 6PP. Tel 930 6003.

N.Bloom & Son (Antiques) Ltd. 40 Conduit St, London, W1R 9FB. Tel 629 5060.

Bond Street Antiques. 6 Bond St, Cromer, Norfolk, NR27 9DA. Tel 513134.

Joseph Bonnar. 72 Thistle St, Edinburgh, Lothian. Tel 226 2811.

H.H.Bray Ltd. 9 Jury St, Warwick, Warwickshire. Tel 492791.

Wm Bruford & Son Ltd. 11-13 Cornfield Rd, Eastbourne, E.Sussex, BN21 3NA. Tel 25452.

Caboodle Ltd. Chelsea Antique Market,253 King's Rd, London, SW3.

Church House Antiques. 42 Church St, Weybridge, Surrey. Tel 42190.

Cobra & Bellamy. 149 Sloane St, London, SW1. Tel 730 2823.

Moira Cohen Ltd. 22-23 New Bond St, London, W1. Tel 629 0160.

Sylvia Collins. Unit 15, Bond St Antique Centre,124 New Bond St, London, W1Y 9AE. Tel 9625.

Hancocks & Co (Jewellers) Ltd. 1 Burlington Gardens, London, W1X 2HP. Tel 493 8904.

Hennell Ltd. 12 New Bond St, London, W1Y 0HE. Tel 629 6888.

Brian and Lynn Holmes. Stands 304-306, Grays Antique Market,58 Davies St, London, W1. Tel 629 7327.

J.I.Horwit. 94 Southampton Row, London, WC1 4BB. Tel 405 0749.

The Jewel House (Mayfair). 23 Lansdowne Row, London, W1X 7LN. Tel 499 7936.

Johnson, Walker & Tolhurst Ltd. 64 Burlington Arcade, Piccadilly, London, W1. Tel 629 2615, 629 2616.

W.F.Knight Ltd (Silversmiths). 2 Park Rd, Wellingborough, Northamptonshire. Tel 222463.

M. McAleer. 32A Sussex Place,Hyde Park, London, W2 2TH. Tel 723 5794.

Nonesuch Antiques. Stand3,Bond St Antique Centre,124 New Bond St, London, W1. Tel 629 6783.

L'Odeon. 173 Fulham Rd, London, SW3. Tel 581 3640 (priv 736 4216).

Ogden of Harrogate Ltd. 38 James St, Harrogate, N.Yorkshire, HG1 1RQ. Tel 504123.

Osborne Jewellers. 55 Osborne Rd, Southsea, Portsmouth, Hampshire, PO5 3LS. Tel 825101.

The Pruskin Gallery. 183 King's Rd, London, SW3. Tel 352 9095, (priv)243 1939.

The Purple Shop. 15 Flood St,Chelsea, London, SW3 5ST. Tel 352 1127.

A.T.Silvester & Sons Ltd. 2-4 High St, Warwick, Warwickshire, CV34 4AP. Tel 492972.

S. & L. Simmons. 9 Meeting House Lane, Brighton & Hove, E.Sussex, BN1 1HB. Tel 27949.

Jeremy Sniders. Victorian Village, 57 West Regent St, Glasgow, Strathclyde. Tel 332 2424.

Talisman. 363/4 Gray's Antique Market,58 Davies St, London, W1. Tel 409 2743.

James & Ann Tillett. Tombland House, 12-13 Tombland, Norwich, Norfolk, NR3 1HF. Tel 624914.

Westleigh Antiques. Croesus, Grays,58 Davies St, London, W1. Tel 493 0624.

Young Stephen Ltd. 1 Burlington Gdns, New Bond St, London, W1X 1LD. Tel 499 7927.

Ziggurat. Chenil Galleries, 183 King's Rd, London, SW3. Tel 352 2123.

Judaica

Antique Connoisseur plc. Grays Mews,1-7 Davies Mews, London, W1. Tel 629 2422/3272.

A. Rosenthal Ltd. 9-10 Broad St, Oxford, Oxfordshire, OX1 3AP. Tel 243093.

Kitchen Items

see Domestic Items

Lace

see also Costumes, Textiles

The Antique Textile Company. 100 Portland Rd, London, W11. Tel 221 7730.

L.& G.Burnett. 290 Portobello Rd, London, W10 5TE. Tel 969 8899.

Celia Charlotte's. 7 Malling St, Lewes, E.Sussex, BN7 2RA. Tel 473303.

Eileen Cooper Antiques. Challoner's Rd, Braunton, Devon, EX33 2ES. Tel 813320.

Country Antiques. 10 Westgate St, Long Melford, Suffolk. Tel Sudbury (0787) 310617.

O.M. & R.D.Cox Antiques. 5 St Mary's Hill, Stamford, Lincolnshire. Tel 64159.

David Crook Antiques. 16 Bond St, Brighton & Hove, E.Sussex, BN1 1RD. Tel 26040.

Denning Antiques. 1 Chapel St, Guildford, Surrey. Tel 39595.

Eve's Lace. Stand X5, Antiquarius, Kings Rd, London, SW3. Tel 351 0175.

Joan Eyles Antiques. The Stone Yard,Fishergate, Boroughbridge, N.Yorkshire, YO5 9QY. Tel 3357 (priv 2487).

Audrey Field. Stand 806, Alfie's Antique Market,13 Church St, London, NW8. Tel 723 0449.

Golden Cage. 99 Derby Rd,Canning Circus, Nottingham, Nottinghamshire. Tel 411600 (priv 254984).

Hand in Hand. 3 North West Circus Place, Edinburgh, Lothian, EH3 6ST. Tel 226 3598.

The Honiton Lace Shop. 44 High St, Honiton, Devon. Tel 2416 (priv 2629).

Lunn Antiques Ltd. 86 New King's Rd, London, SW6 4LU. Tel 736 4638.

Sue Madden. Stall X10 Antiquarius,135 Kings Rd, London, SW3. Tel 351 5757 (priv 703 4634).

Iris Martin Lacemaking Supplies. 62 High St, Olney, Buckinghamshire. Tel Bedford (0234) 712446.

Mulberry House Galleries. Codmore Hill, Pulborough, W.Sussex, RH20 1BQ. Tel 2463.

Old Bakery Antiques. 1 Church St, Hunstanton, Norfolk. Tel Brancaster (0485) 210396.

Raleigh Antiques. 17 The Square, Beaminster, Dorset. Tel 862136.

Straight Lace. 9 High St, East Linton, Lothian, EH40 3AA. Tel 860017 (priv 062088 284).

Lace Bobbins

Corner Antiques. Coltishall Antiques Centre, High St, Coltishall, Norfolk, NR12 7HV. Tel Norwich (0603) 738306 (priv 737631).

Dormy House Antiques. 43 Kingsbury St, Marlborough, Wiltshire, SN8 1JE. Tel 52703.

Fenwick and Fisher Antiques. 88 High St, Broadway, Hereford & Worcester. Tel 853227 (priv 853228).

Iris Martin Lacemaking Supplies. 62 High St, Olney, Buckinghamshire. Tel Bedford (0234) 712446.

Sheila Smith Antiques. 10A Queen St, Bath, Avon. Tel 60568 (priv 0373 830217).

Lacquer

see also Oriental Works of Art

Shirley Day Ltd. 91B Jermyn St, London, SW1Y 6JB. Tel 839 2804.

Eskenazi Ltd. Foxglove House, 166 Piccadilly, London, W1V 9DE. Tel 493 5464.

Falkner Fine Art. Stands B18/C19 Grays Mews,Davies Mews, London, W1. Tel 629 3644 (priv 385 0174).

Peter Francis. 26 Museum St, London, WC1A 1JT. Tel 637 0165.

Galleon Galleries. 42 Westfield Lane, St Leonards, E.Sussex. Tel 440974.

Kenneth Jackson (Antiques). 66 Thistle St, Edinburgh, Lothian. Tel 225 9634.

Nihon Token. 23 Museum St, London, WC1A 1JT. Tel 580 6511.

Dermot & Jill Palmer Antiques. 7-8 Union St, The Lanes, Brighton & Hove, E.Sussex. Tel 28669.

Park Galleries. 215/217 Preston Rd, Brighton & Hove, E.Sussex, BN1 6SA. Tel 504057 (priv 29466).

Ramshead Gallery Studio. 125 Lower High St, Malmesbury, Wiltshire, SN16 9AL. Tel 2505.

Simon Leigh Rose Fine Decorative Antiques. 569 Kings Rd,Chelsea, London, SW6. Tel 731 7356.

Barry Sainsbury Oriental Art. 145 Ebury St, London, SW1. Tel 730 3393.

Spink & Son Ltd. 5, 6 & 7 King St, St James's, London, SW1. Tel 930 7888.

David Tremayne Ltd. 320 King's Rd, London, SW3. Tel 352 1194.

Lamps

see also Lighting

Actino Antiques. 136 Lee High Rd, Lewisham, London, SE13. Tel 318 1273.

Allegras Antiques. 22 Lower Richmond Rd,Putney, London, SW15. Tel 785 7755 (priv 789 7444).

Capricorn Collections. 48 St Anne's Rd, South Shore, Blackpool, Lancashire, FY4 2AS. Tel 49766.

Dernier & Hamlyn Ltd. 17 Lydden Rd,Wandsworth, London, SW18 4LT. Tel 870 0011/2.

English Street Furniture Company. Somers House, Linkfield Corner, Redhill, Surrey, RH1 1BB. Tel 60986.

Muir Hewitt. Halifax Antiques Centre,Queens Rd Mills, Queens Rd/Gibbet St, Halifax, W.Yorkshire, HX1 4LR. Tel 66657 (priv 0274 882051).

Jones. 194 Westbourne Grove, London, W11. Tel 229 6866.

Kelly's of Knaresborough. Rear, 96 High St, Knaresborough, N.Yorkshire. Tel Harrogate (0423) 862041 (24 hr answering).

The Lacquer Chest. 75 Kensington Church St, London, W8. Tel 937 1306.

Lantern Antiques. 5-6 Milk St,(side door entrance, no shop front), Shrewsbury, Shropshire. Tel 3783.

Mallett & Son (Antiques) Ltd. 40 New Bond St, London, W1Y 0BS. Tel 499 7411.

Manor Antiques. The Manor House,Cottonend Rd, Wilshamstead, Bedfordshire, MK45 3BT. Tel Bedford (0234) 740262.

Iain Marr Antiques. 3 Mid St, Beauly, Highland, IV4 7DP. Tel 782372.

B.C.Metalcrafts Ltd. 69 Tewkesbury Gardens, London, NW9 0QU. Tel 204 2446.

Alan Morris. 503 Evesham Rd, Crabbs Cross, Redditch, Hereford & Worcester, B97 5JJ. Tel 45084.

Paul Quentin Antiques. 626 Manchester Rd, Bury, Greater Manchester, BL9 9SU. Tel 766 6673.

Paul Richards Antiques. 16 Fulham High St, London, SW6 3LQ. Tel 736 0976.

Elfreda Rowley. 7 East Stockwell St, Colchester, Essex, CO1 1TS. Tel 577337.

Sundial Antiques. 19 Whielden St, Amersham, Buckinghamshire, HP7 0HU. Tel 7955.

Turn On Ltd. 116-118 Islington High St,Camden Passage, London, N1 8EG. Tel 359 7616.

Windsor House Antiques (Leeds) Ltd. 18/20 Benson St, Leeds, W.Yorkshire, LS7 1BL. Tel 444666.

Christopher Wray's Lighting Emporium. 62 Park St, Bristol, Avon. Tel 278537.

Christopher Wray's Lighting Emporium. Tiffany Shop & Lamp Workshop,600-606 King's Rd, London, SW6. Tel 736 8434.

Christopher Wray's Lighting Emporium. Gervis Place, Bournemouth, Dorset. Tel 22660.

Christopher Wray's Lighting Emporium. 26 Patrick St, Kilkenny, Co Kilkenny. Tel 22776.

Christopher Wray's Lighting Emporium. Bartholomew Row, Birmingham, W.Midlands. Tel 233 3364.

Christopher Wray's Lighting Emporium. 16 Headingly Lane, Leeds, W.Yorkshire. Tel 782653.

Christopher Wrays Lamp Workshop. 579/581 King's Rd, London, SW6 2DX. Tel 736 8434.

Leatherwork

Antique Leathers. 4 Park End, South Hill Park, London, NW3 2SE. Tel 435 8582/7799.

Peter Chapman Antiques. 10 Theberton St, Islington, London, N1 0QX. Tel 226 5565 (priv 348 4846).

J. Crisp & Son. 48 Roderick Rd,Hampstead, London, NW3 2NL. Tel 340 0668.

The Desk Shop. 41 St Clements, Oxford, Oxfordshire. Tel 245524.

Kees & Co. Tandridge, Top Common,West Runton, Cromer, Norfolk, NR27 9LT. Tel 8109.

La Chaise Antique. 30 London St, Faringdon, Oxfordshire, SN7 7AA. Tel 20427.

A.J.Ponsford Antiques and Restorations. 51-53 Dollar St, Cirencester, Gloucestershire, GL7 2AS. Tel 2355.

Lighting

see also Candelabra, Chandeliers, Lamps

Actino Antiques. 136 Lee High Rd, Lewisham, London, SE13. Tel 318 1273.

Alice Lighting. 3 Wellfield Rd, Cardiff, S.Glamorgan. Tel 499156.

Allegras Antiques. 22 Lower Richmond Rd,Putney, London, SW15. Tel 785 7755 (priv 789 7444).

Christopher Bangs. London. Tel 223 5676.

Combe Cottage Antiques. Castle Combe, Wiltshire, SN14 7HU. Tel 782250.

N.Davighi. 117 Shepherds Bush Rd, London, W6. Tel 603 5357.

B.P. Dennison (Antiques). Dwarf Hall, Chapel Hill, Ambleside, Cumbria, LA22 9EB. Tel 32651.

Dernier & Hamlyn Ltd. 17 Lydden Rd,Wandsworth, London, SW18 4LT. Tel 870 0011/2.

Fritz Fryer. Greenway Cottage,Glewstone, Ross-on-Wye, Hereford & Worcester. Tel Llangarron (098984 512.

The Golden Age. 7-9 Metropole Buildings, Blackpool, Lancashire, FY1 1RF. Tel 22969.

Jones. 194 Westbourne Grove, London, W11. Tel 229 6866.

Kelly's of Knaresborough. Rear, 96 High St, Knaresborough, N.Yorkshire. Tel Harrogate (0423) 862041 (24 hr answering).

Key Antiques. 11 Horsefair, Chipping Norton, Oxfordshire, OX7 5AL. Tel 3777.

Lighthouse Antiques. 67 Ridgway,Wimbledon Village, London, SW19. Tel 946 2050.

Manor Antiques. The Manor House,Cottonend Rd, Wilshamstead, Bedfordshire, MK45 3BT. Tel Bedford (0234) 740262.

Ian McCarthy. Arcadian Cottage, 112 Station Rd, Clutton, Avon. Tel Temple Cloud (0761) 53188.

B.C.Metalcrafts Ltd. 69 Tewkesbury Gardens, London, NW9 0QU. Tel 204 2446.

David Miller Antiques. 198 Upper Richmond Road West,East Sheen, London, SW14. Tel 876 8331.

Mitchell Antiques Ltd. 40 Clarendon St, Dublin, Co Dublin. Tel 773922.

Oddiquities. 61 Waldram Park Rd, London, SE23. Tel 699 9574.

Old Pine Shop. 27 Gloucester Rd, Ross-on-Wye, Hereford & Worcester, HR9 5BU. Tel 64738 (priv 0594 543349).

Paul Richards Antiques. 16 Fulham High St, London, SW6 3LQ. Tel 736 0976.

Elfreda Rowley. 7 East Stockwell St, Colchester, Essex, CO1 1TS. Tel 577337.

D.H.Sargeant. 21 The Green, Westerham, Kent, TN16 1AX. Tel 62130.

Jeanne Temple Antiques. Stockwell House, Wavendon, Milton Keynes, Buckinghamshire, MK17 8LS. Tel 583597.

Andy Thornton Architectural Antiques Ltd. Ainleys Industrial Estate, Elland, W.Yorkshire, HX5 9JP. Tel 78125 (priv 0484 712636).

Turn On Ltd. 116-118 Islington High St,Camden Passage, London, N1 8EG. Tel 359 7616.

West Gate Fine Art. 16 St Peter St, Canterbury, Kent, CT1 2BQ. Tel 453636 (priv 03043 62093).

Christopher Wray's Lighting Emporium. 62 Park St, Bristol, Avon. Tel 278537.

Christopher Wray's Lighting Emporium. Tiffany Shop & Lamp Workshop,600-606 King's Rd, London, SW6. Tel 736 8434.

Christopher Wray's Lighting Emporium. Gervis Place, Bournemouth, Dorset. Tel 22660.

Christopher Wray's Lighting Emporium. 26 Patrick St, Kilkenny, Co Kilkenny. Tel 22776.

Directory Entries are Free and ADDITIONS OR CORRECTIONS will be welcomed by *THE EDITOR, British Art and Antiques Directory, National Magazine House, 72 Broadwick Street, London W1V 2BP*

Christopher Wray's Lighting Emporium. Bartholomew Row, Birmingham, W.Midlands. Tel 233 3364.

Christopher Wray's Lighting Emporium. 16 Headingly Lane, Leeds, W.Yorkshire. Tel 782653.

Christopher Wrays Lamp Workshop. 579/581 King's Rd, London, SW6 2DX. Tel 736 8434.

George Wright (Rotherham) Ltd. The Crofts, Rotherham, S.Yorkshire, S60 2DJ. Tel 63871.

Maps

see also Prints

London

Ash Rare Books. 25 Royal Exchange, Threadneedle St, London, EC3. Tel 626 2665.

Cartographia Ltd. 37 Southampton St, Covent Garden, London, WC2E 7HE. Tel 240 5687.

Davies Antiques. 44A Kensington Church St, London, W8. Tel 937 9216.

Robert Douwma Prints & Maps Ltd. 4 Henrietta St, The Piazza,Covent Garden, London, WC2. Tel 836 0771.

Goodall & Co Ltd. 26 Chiswick High Rd, London, W4. Tel 994 1729 (priv 994 2376).

Harrington Bros. Chelsea Antique Market,253 King's Rd, London, SW3. Tel 352 5689.

Richard Hewlett Gallery. 24 Cale St,Chelsea Green, London, SW3 3QU. Tel 584 8531.

Intercol London. 1A Camden Walk, Islington Green, London, N1. Tel 354 2599 (priv 349 2207).

The Map House. 54 Beauchamp Place, Knightsbridge, London, SW3. Tel 589 4325, 589 9821.

O'Shea Gallery. 89 Lower Sloane St,Belgravia, London, SW1 8DA. Tel 730 0081, 730 0082.

Old Maps and Prints. 4th floor,Harrods, Knightsbridge, London, SW1. Tel 730 1234 ext 2124.

Jonathan Potter. 1 Grafton St, London, W1X 3LB. Tel 491 3520.

Sarum Antiquarian Maps. 10 Chapel St, Belgrave Sq, London, SW1. Tel 235 6744.

The Warwick Leadlay Gallery. 5 Nelson Rd, Greenwich, London, SE10 9JB. Tel 858 0317 (priv 852 7484).

Edna Whiteson Ltd. 66 Belmont Ave, London, EN4 9LA. Tel 449 8860.

Regions

Barnard Gallery. Grange Farm,Everton, Doncaster, S.Yorkshire, DN10 5BG. Tel Retford (0777) 817324.

Douglas Bartrick - Antiques. Gloucester Antiques Centre,Severn Rd, Gloucester, Gloucestershire, GL1 2LE. Tel 29716 (priv 618465).

Baynton-Williams. Maltravers House, 49 Maltravers St, Arundel, W.Sussex, BN18 9BQ. Tel 882898.

Benet Gallery. 19 King's Parade, Cambridge, Cambridgeshire. Tel 353783 (priv 248739).

Bow Cottage Antiques. Antique Arcade, Sheep St, Stratford-upon-Avon, Warwickshire. Tel 297249 (priv 205883).

The Carson Clark Gallery. (Scotiamaps - Mapsellers),173 Cannongate, The Royal Mile, Edinburgh, Lothian, EH8 8BN. Tel 556 4710.

Chantry Book Shop. 11 Higher St, Dartmouth, Devon, TQ6 9RB. Tel 2796 (priv) 4208.

Chantry House Antiques. Sheep St, Stow-on-the-Wold, Gloucestershire, GL54 1AA. Tel 30450.

Clifton Books. 5A Dicconson St, Wigan, Greater Manchester. Tel 36716 (priv 726319).

Collectors Treasures. Hogarth House, High St, Wendover, Buckinghamshire, HP22 6DU. Tel 624402.

Commin's Bookshop. 100 Old Christchurch Rd, Bournemouth, Dorset. Tel 27504.

H.V. Day. The Old Roman Catholic Church,25 High West St, Dorchester, Dorset, DT1 1UW. Tel 64904.

Dorchester Galleries. Rotten Row, Dorchester, Oxfordshire, OX9 8LJ. Tel Oxford (0865) 341116.

English Heritage. 2 Whitburn St, Bridgnorth, Shropshire. Tel 2097.

D.G. & A.S. Evans. 7 The Struet, Brecon, Powys, LD3 7LL. Tel 2714.

Susanna Fisher. Spencer, Upham, Hampshire, SO3 1JD. Tel Durley (04896) 291.

Folio (Clevedon Books & Clevedon Fine Arts). The Gallery, Cinema Buildings,Old Church Rd, Clevedon, Avon, BS21 6NN. Tel 875862 (priv 872304).

Foye Gallery. 15 Stanley St, Luton, Bedfordshire, LU1 5AL. Tel 38487.

George & Dragon Gallery. Reepham, Norwich, Norfolk. Tel 870360.

Goodramgate Books, Maps and Prints. 58 Goodramgate, York, N.Yorkshire. Tel 51275 (priv 0484 46833).

John Grant. 9A & 13C Dundas St, Edinburgh, Lothian. Tel 556 9698.

George Gregory. Manvers St, Bath, Avon, BA1 1JW. Tel 66055.

Anne Hall - Prints. 19 Dam St, Lichfield, Staffordshire, WS13 6AE. Tel 263263.

Fred Hanna Ltd. 28 & 29 Nassau St, Dublin, Co Dublin. Tel 771255/6.

Holleyman & Treacher Ltd. 21A & 22 Duke St, Brighton & Hove, E.Sussex, BN1 1AH. Tel 28007.

L.A.James. 11 George St, St Albans, Hertfordshire. Tel 56996.

Leycester Map Galleries Ltd. Well House, Arnesby, Arnesby, Leicestershire. Tel Peatling Magna (053758) 462.

Lion Gallery & Bookshop. 15A Minshull St, Knutsford, Cheshire, WA16 6HQ. Tel 52915.

Litchfield Gallery. 1062 Christchurch Rd, East Boscombe, Bournemouth, Dorset. Tel 45454.

The Lyver and Boydell Galleries. 15 Castle St, Liverpool, Merseyside, L2 4SX. Tel 236 3256.

Magna Gallery. 41 High St, Oxford, Oxfordshire. Tel 245805.

Marrin & Sons. 149 Sandgate Rd, Folkestone, Kent. Tel 53016.

McDowell & Stern Ltd. 3 & 5 Grape Lane, York, N.Yorkshire. Tel 22000.

Mon Galerie. 49 High St, Amersham, Buckinghamshire. Tel 21705.

Mona Antiqua & Tudor Rose. 31-32 Castle St, Beaumaris, Gwynedd. Tel 810203.

Eric T.Moore. 24 Bridge St, Hitchin, Hertfordshire. Tel 50497.

Colin Murdoch. 56 High St, Kingussie, Highland, PH21 1HZ. Tel 552.

John Nelson. 22-24 Victoria St, Edinburgh, Lothian, EH1 2JW. Tel 225 4413 (priv 667 5275).

Richard A.Nicholson. 25 Watergate St, Chester, Cheshire, CH1 2LB. Tel 26818.

Northgate Antiques. 10 Northgate St, Pembroke, Dyfed, SA71 5LF. Tel 684416 (priv 672388).

Jean Pain Gallery. 7 King's Parade, Cambridge, Cambridgeshire, CB2 1SJ. Tel 313970.

Pierpoint Gallery. 10 Church St, Hereford, Hereford & Worcester, HR1 2LR. Tel 267002.

Porter Prints. 205 Whitham Rd, Broomhill, Sheffield, S.Yorkshire, S10 2SP. Tel 685751.

Printed Page. 2-3 Bridge St, Winchester, Hampshire, SO23 9BH. Tel 54072 (priv 62995).

Quinto of Cambridge. 34 Trinity St, Cambridge, Cambridgeshire, CB2 1TB. Tel 358279.

Radford Antiques. Twytton House,Alfriston, Polegate, E.Sussex, BN26 5TD. Tel Alfriston (0323) 870440.

C. Samuels & Sons Ltd. 17-18 Waterbeer St,Guildhall Shopping Centre, Exeter, Devon, EX4 3EH. Tel 73219.

Sanders of Oxford Ltd. 104 High St, Oxford, Oxfordshire, OX1 4BW. Tel 242590.

Shaw's Bookshop Ltd. 11 Police St, Manchester, Greater Manchester, M2 7LQ. Tel 834-7587.

J.Shotton. 89 Elvet Bridge, Durham, Durham, DH1 3AG. Tel 64597.

John Speed (Maps). Drove House,Bilstone, Nuneaton, Warwickshire, CV13 6NG. Tel Tamworth (0827) 880439.

Ken Spelman Booksellers. 70 Micklegate, York, N.Yorkshire, YO1 1LF. Tel 24414.

Henry Stevens, Son & Stiles. 4 Upper Church Lane, Farnham, Surrey. Tel 715416.

Studio Bookshop and Gallery. 17 Broad St, Alresford, Hampshire, SO24 9AW. Tel 2188.

Suthburgh Antiques. Red House, Hall St, Long Melford, Suffolk. Tel Sudbury (0787) 74818.

Charles W. Traylen. Castle House, 49 Quarry St, Guildford, Surrey. Tel 572424.

Trentham Gallery Ltd. 40 North St, Havant, Hampshire. Tel 484935 (priv 02434 2551).

W.D.Trivess. Heathfield House, Meonstoke, Hampshire, SO3 1ND. Tel Droxford (0489) 877326.

Vanbrugh House Antiques. Park St, Stow-on-the-Wold, Gloucestershire, GL54 1AQ. Tel 30797.

Robert Vaughan Antiquarian Booksellers. 20 Chapel St, Stratford-upon-Avon, Warwickshire, CV37 6EP. Tel 205312.

Weston Antique Gallery. Boat Lane,Weston, Stafford, Staffordshire, ST18 0HU. Tel Weston (0889) 270450.

David Windsor Gallery. 201 High St, Bangor, Gwynedd. Tel 364639.

The Witch Ball Print & Map Shop. 48 Meeting House Lane, Brighton & Hove, E.Sussex, BN1 1HB. Tel 26618.

Marble

see also Architectural Items

Crowther of Syon Lodge. Syon Lodge, Busch Corner,London Rd, Isleworth, Middlesex, TW7 5BH. Tel 560 7978, 560 7985.

Halliday's (Antiques). 28 Beauchamp Place, London, SW3. Tel 589 5534.

Hallidays Antiques Ltd. The Old College, High St, Dorchester, Oxfordshire. Tel Oxford (0865) 340028.

H.W.Poulter & Son. 279 Fulham Rd, London, SW10 9PZ. Tel 352 7268 (priv 603 7398).

Marine Items

see Nautical and Marine Items

Medallions and Medals

see Coins and Medals

Metalware

see Brass, Copper and Metalware

Militaria

see Arms, Armour and Militaria, Coins and Medals

Minerals and Fossils

William C.Fox & Co Ltd. 41 New St, St Helier, Jersey. Tel 22708 (priv 79001).

Gregory, Bottley and Lloyd. 8-12 Rickett St, London, SW6 1RU. Tel 381 5522 (priv 878 5202).

T. Tolley. 26 College St, Worcester, Hereford & Worcester, WR1 2LS. Tel 26632.

Miniatures

see Portrait Miniatures

Mirror Paintings

Jeremy Ltd. 255 King's Rd, Chelsea, London, SW3 5EL. Tel 352 3127, 352 0644.

Jeannette Meager. Cheltenham Antique Market,54 Suffolk Rd, Cheltenham, Gloucestershire. Tel 29812.

Mirrors

Adams Room Ltd. 18-20 Ridgway, Wimbledon Village, London, SW19. Tel 946 7047 (priv 947 4784).

Anno Domini. 66 Pimlico Rd, London, SW1. Tel 730 5496.

William Bedford PLC. The Merchants Hall, 46 Essex Rd,Islington, London, N1 8LN. Tel 226 9648.

E. & G. Briere. Keeper's Cottage, Suffield, Norwich, Norfolk, NR11 7ER. Tel Aylsham (0263) 732651.

Gerald Deacon. 2 Wood St, Queen Sq, Bath, Avon, BA1 2JQ. Tel 25907.

Dolphyn. 8 Market End, Coggeshall, Essex, CO6 1NP. Tel 61608.

Fernandes & Marche. 23 Motcomb St, Belgrave Sq, London, SW1. Tel 235 6773.

Flora Dora Antiques. Dales House, Lombard St, Petworth, W.Sussex, GU28 0AG. Tel 43109.

Michael Foster. 118 Fulham Rd, London, SW3 6HU. Tel 373 3636.

Julian Antiques. 124 High St, Hurstpierpoint, W.Sussex. Tel 832145.

Julian Antiques. 67 Park Rd, London, NW1. Tel 723 0653.

Michael Lipitch. 98 Fulham Rd, London, SW3. Tel 589 7327 (priv 440 7797).

Jeannette Meager. Cheltenham Antique Market,54 Suffolk Rd, Cheltenham, Gloucestershire. Tel 29812.

Obelisk Antiques. 2 Silver St, Warminster, Wiltshire, BA12 8PS. Tel 216874.

Alec Ossowski. 83 Pimlico Rd, London, SW1. Tel 730 3256.

Penoyre Antiques. 9 - 11 Bridge St, Pershore, Hereford & Worcester. Tel 3522.

Quiet Street Antiques. 3 Quiet St, Bath, Avon. Tel 315727 (priv 332399).

Paul Richards Antiques. 16 Fulham High St, London, SW6 3LQ. Tel 736 0976.

Elfreda Rowley. 7 East Stockwell St, Colchester, Essex, CO1 1TS. Tel 577337.

Simpsons. 17 Girdlers Rd, London, W14. Tel 603 8625.

Spyer & Son (Antiques) Ltd. 18 Motcomb St, Belgrave Sq, London, SW1X 8LB. Tel 235 3348.

Stair & Company Ltd. 120 Mount St, London, W1Y 5HB. Tel 499 1784, 499 1785.

Stratton Quinn Antiques Etc. 164 Thames Rd, Strand-on-the-Green,Chiswick, London, W4 3QS. Tel 994 3140.

Strouds of Southwell Antiques. 3 Westgate, Southwell, Nottinghamshire. Tel 815001.

Through the Looking Glass Ltd. 563 King's Rd, London, SW6. Tel 736 7799.

Ferenc Toth. 598A Kings Rd, London, SW6 2DX. Tel 731 2063 (priv 602 1771).

Clifford Wright. 104/106 Fulham Rd, London, SW3. Tel 589 0986.

Models

Colin Denny. 18 Cale St, London, SW3 3QU. Tel 584 0240.

Langfords. Oldebourne House,46-47 Chancery Lane, London, WC2. Tel 405 6402.

Music and Related Items

H.Baron. 136 Chatsworth Rd, London, NW2 5QU. Tel 459 2035.

J. & A. Beare Ltd. 7 Broadwick St, London, W1V 1FJ. Tel 437 1449.

Tony Bingham. 11 Pond St, London, NW3 2PN. Tel 794 1596.

Early Music Shop. 28 Sunbridge Rd, Bradford, W.Yorkshire, BD1 2AE. Tel 393753.

Gard Books (Music). 52 The Close, Salisbury, Wiltshire, SP1 2EL. Tel 23565.

W.E.Hill & Sons. Havenfields, Great Missenden, Buckinghamshire, HP16 9LS. Tel 3655.

Holleyman & Treacher Ltd. 21A & 22 Duke St, Brighton & Hove, E.Sussex, BN1 1AH. Tel 28007.

Lloyd's Bookshop. 27 High St, Wingham, Kent, CT3 1AW. Tel Canterbury (0227) 720774.

Richard Macnutt Ltd. Hamm Farm House,Withyham, Hartfield Wells, E.Sussex, TN7 4BJ. Tel Groombridge (089276) 218.

Philip Martin Music Books. 36 Fossgate, York, N.Yorkshire, YO1 2TF. Tel 641389.

Pelham Galleries (Est 1927). 163-165 Fulham Rd, London, SW3. Tel 589 2686.

Musical Boxes and Mechanical Music

Addingham Antiques. 70-72 Main St, Addingham, W.Yorkshire. Tel 830788.

Attic Antiques. 23 & 32 Ship St, Brighton & Hove, E.Sussex, BN1 1AD. Tel 29464 (priv 551594).

Bellevue. 48 Alpha Rd,Southville, Bristol, Avon, BS3 1DH. Tel 662010.

Capricorn Collections. 48 St Anne's Rd, South Shore, Blackpool, Lancashire, FY4 2AS. Tel 49766.

City Clocks. 1B Lambs Passage, Chiswell St, London, EC1Y 8LE. Tel 628 6749.

E. Cooper Antiques. 20 Stoke Rd, Gosport, Hampshire. Tel 585032.

John Cowderoy Antiques (The Musical Box Centre). 40/42 South St, Eastbourne, E.Sussex, BN21 4X. Tel 20058 (priv 645353).

M.J.Dareau. 66 Cumberland St, Edinburgh, Lothian. Tel 556 9352 & 0968 73028.

John E. Davis Antiques. 21 Wokingham Rd, Reading, Berkshire, RG6 1JG. Tel 663108.

Jack Donovan. 93 Portobello Rd, London, W11. Tel 727 1485.

Evans & Evans. 40 West St, Alresford, Hampshire, SO24 9AU. Tel 2170.

Vincent Freeman Antiques. 1 Camden Passage, Islington, London, N1. Tel 226 6178.

P.R.Garner (Antiques). Willow Farm, 104 High St, Landbeach, Cambridge, Cambridgeshire. Tel 860470.

R.S. Gordon Antiques. Main St, Alford, Grampian. Tel 2404.

Keith Harding. 93 Hornsey Road, London, N7 6DJ. Tel 607 6181, 607 2672.

F.F.Hill. The Gate House, Lombard St, Shackleford, Surrey, GU8 6AR. Tel Guildford (0483) 810330.

Peter Hillary Ltd. 54 Henley St, Stratford-upon-Avon, Warwickshire. Tel 5669.

Hobby Horse Antiques. 29 West Allington, Bridport, Dorset, DT6 5BJ. Tel 22801.

Mark Marchant, Antiques. Market Square, Coggeshall, Essex, CO6 1T6. Tel 61188.

Mayflower Antiques. 180-182 High St, Dovercourt, Harwich, Essex. Tel 504079.

Merlin Antiques & Restorations. Howgill Lane, Sedbergh, Cumbria. Tel 20301 (priv 20719).

Mill Farm Antiques. 50 Market St, Disley, Cheshire, SK12 2DT. Tel 4045.

Neale Antiques. 21 Old Cross, Hertford, Hertfordshire, SG14 1RE. Tel 52519 and 51347.

Norfolk Polyphon Centre. Wood Farm, Bawdeswell, Dereham, Norfolk, NR20 4RX. Tel Bawdeswell (036 288) 230.

Something Old. 6-8 Old Cross, Hertford, Hertfordshire, SG14 1RB. Tel 551530.

Treasure Chest Ltd. The Jays, 19 Alstone Lane, Highbridge, Somerset, TA9 3DS. Tel Burnham-on-Sea (0278) 787267.

Turret House. 27 Middleton St, Wymondham, Norfolk, NR18 0AB. Tel 603462.

Vanbrugh House Antiques. Park St, Stow-on-the-Wold, Gloucestershire, GL54 1AQ. Tel 30797.

Graham Webb. 59 Ship St, Brighton & Hove, E.Sussex, BN1 1AE. Tel 21803 (priv 772154).

Musical Instruments

Ace Antiques. 40 Huddersfield Rd, Oldham, Greater Manchester, OL4 2AE. Tel 620 5755 (priv 626 2062).

Alderley House Antiques. Alderley House, 53 Long St, Tetbury, Gloucestershire, GL8 8AA. Tel 53667.

Aspidistra. 46 St James Parade, Bath, Avon. Tel 61948.

J. & A. Beare Ltd. 7 Broadwick St, London, W1V 1FJ. Tel 437 1449.

Peter Biddulph. 35,St George St,Hanover Square, London, W1R 9DF. Tel 491 8621.

Tony Bingham. 11 Pond St, London, NW3 2PN. Tel 794 1596.

Binsted Antiques. 21 Middle Lane, Teddington, Middlesex, TW11 0HQ. Tel 943 0626.

J.H. Blakey & Sons Ltd. Church St, Brierfield, Lancashire, BB9 5AD. Tel Nelson (0282) 63593/602493.

Bridge Antiques. 93 Elvet Bridge, Durham, Durham. Tel 45530.

The Clerkenwell Green Association for Craftsmen. Pennybank Chambers,33-35 St John's Square, London, EC1. Tel 251 0276.

Dollin & Daines Ltd. 2 Church St,York St, Bath, Avon. Tel 62752.

Early Music Shop. 28 Sunbridge Rd, Bradford, W.Yorkshire, BD1 2AE. Tel 393753.

M.Ekstein Ltd. 90 Jermyn St, London, SW1Y 6JD. Tel 930 2024.

W.E.Hill & Sons. Havenfields, Great Missenden, Buckinghamshire, HP16 9LS. Tel 3655.

Ipswich Pianos. 45 Graham Rd, Ipswich, Suffolk. Tel 50740.

Laurie Leigh Antiques. 36 High St, Oxford, Oxfordshire. Tel 244197.

Mill Farm Antiques. 50 Market St, Disley, Cheshire, SK12 2DT. Tel 4045.

Robert Morley & Company Limited. 4 Belmont Hill, Lewisham, London, SE13 5BD. Tel 852 6151.

Pelham Galleries (Est 1927). 163-165 Fulham Rd, London, SW3. Tel 589 2686.

Vintage & Value. 220-224 Woodlands Rd, Glasgow, Strathclyde, G3 6LN. Tel 332 0495.

W.E.Walker. 277/9 Camden High St, London, NW1 7BX. Tel 485 6210 (priv 485 4433).

Graham Webb. 59 Ship St, Brighton & Hove, E.Sussex, BN1 1AE. Tel 21803 (priv 772154).

John Whybrow. The Crown House, High St, Thatcham, Berkshire, RG13 4JD. Tel 63335.

Naive and Primitive Art

see Folk Art

Natural History Items

The Antique Shop. Glynn Park,Taylors Ave, Carrickfergus, Co Antrim. Tel 63284.

Dorothy's Antiques. 23 Waterbank Rd, Sheringham, Norfolk, NR26 8RB. Tel 822319 (priv 823018).

The Enchanted Aviary. 63 Hall St, Long Melford, Suffolk. Tel 78814.

Mariposa. 108 Holywell Hill, St Albans, Hertfordshire. Tel 50469.

Michael Phelps Antiquarian Books. 19 Chelverton Rd, Putney, London, SW15 1RN. Tel 785 6766.

Charles Shaw. 12 Market Place, Knaresborough, N.Yorkshire. Tel 867715.

M. & C. Telfer-Smollett. 88 Portobello Rd, London, W11. Tel 727 0117 (priv 370 1860).

Nautical and Marine Items

55 Antiques. 55 Spring Bank, Hull, Humberside, HU3 1AG. Tel 224510.

The Chimes. Market Place, Reepham, Norfolk, NR10 4JJ. Tel Norwich (0603) 870480.

Colin Denny. 18 Cale St, London, SW3 3QU. Tel 584 0240.

Fine Pine Ltd. Woodland Rd,Harbertonford, Totnes, Devon. Tel Harbertonford (080 423) 465.

Malcolm Frazer Antiques. 19 Brooklyn Crescent, Cheadle, Greater Manchester. Tel 428 3781.

Gallery 26. 26 Middle St, Corbridge, Northumberland.

Peter Goodwin Antiques. 284 Westbourne Grove, London, W11. Tel 581 3873.

Hobby Horse Antiques. 29 West Allington, Bridport, Dorset, DT6 5BJ. Tel 22801.

House of Buckingham. 113-117 Farringdon Rd, London, EC1R 3BT. Tel 278 2013.

Derek Howard. Stand B2, Chenil Galleries,181-183 King's Rd, Chelsea, London, SW3. Tel 352 2163.

Humbleyard Fine Art. 3 Fish Hill, Holt, Norfolk. Tel 713362(priv 036 283 793).

Langfords. Oldebourne House,46-47 Chancery Lane, London, WC2. Tel 405 6402.

Littlebury Antiques. 58/60 Fairycroft Rd, Saffron Walden, Essex. Tel 27961.

The Old Alarm. Quay Hill, Lymington, Hampshire, SO4 9AR. Tel 77100.

The Parker Gallery. 12A & 12B Berkeley St, Piccadilly, London, W1X 5AD. Tel 499 5906/7.

Quadrant Antiques. 5 North West Circus Place,Stockbridge, Edinburgh, Lothian. Tel 226 7282.

Relcy Antiques. 9 Nelson Rd, Greenwich, London, SE10. Tel 858 2811/2.

Strickland & Dorling. 3 River St, Truro, Cornwall. Tel 72345.

David Weston Ltd. 44 Duke St, St James's, London, SW1. Tel 839 1051.

Harriet Wynter Ltd. 50 Redcliffe Rd, London, SW10 9NJ. Tel 352 6494.

Nautical Instruments

see Scientific Instruments

Needlework

see also Samplers, Textiles

Annique Antiques. 13 Nevill St, Tunbridge Wells, Kent, TN2 5RU. Tel 26776.

The Antique Textile Company. 100 Portland Rd, London, W11. Tel 221 7730.

L.J. Arditti & E.M. Arditti. 29A The Pantiles, Tunbridge Wells, Kent. Tel 43361.

Celia Barker Mill. 24 Iverna Gardens,Kensington, London, W8 6TN. Tel 937 9145.

John Bird/Annette Puttnam. 44 Upper North St, Brighton & Hove, E.Sussex, BN1 3FH. Tel 739425.

Brocanteuse Gallery. 11 North St, Ashburton, Devon. Tel 53389.

L.& G.Burnett. 290 Portobello Rd, London, W10 5TE. Tel 969 8899.

Jean Burnett Antiques. 3a Church St, Finedon, Northamptonshire. Tel Wellingborough (0933) 680430.

R.G.Cave & Sons Ltd. 17 Broad St, Ludlow, Shropshire. Tel 3568.

Chanctonbury Antiques. Clematis Cottage, Washington, W.Sussex, RH20 4AP. Tel Ashington (0903) 892233.

Annarella Clark Antiques. 11 Park St, Stow-on-the-Wold, Gloucestershire.

The Corner Cupboard. At the Old Bakery,Next to the Fleece, Boxford, Suffolk, CO6 5DX. Tel 210123.

The Corner Cupboard. At the Old Bakery,Next to the Fleece, Boxford, Suffolk, CO6 5DX. Tel 210123.

Jay Davis Antiques. Bishopsdale Court, Settle, N.Yorkshire. Tel 2764.

Donohoe. 1-7 Davies Mews, London, W1. Tel 629 5633 (priv 455 5507).

Joan Eyles Antiques. The Stone Yard,Fishergate, Boroughbridge, N.Yorkshire, YO5 9QY. Tel 3357 (priv 2487).

Five Five Six Antiques. 556 King's Rd, London, SW6. Tel 731 2016 (priv 624 5173).

Gene & Sally Foster (Antiques). 27A Belvedere, Lansdown Rd, Bath, Avon, BA1 5HR. Tel 28256 (priv 28058).

Robert Franses & Son. 5 Nugent Tce, St John's Wood, London, NW8. Tel 286 6913 (priv 328 0949).

S.Franses Ltd. 11 Spring St,Paddington, London, W2. Tel 262 1153/4.

Victor Franses Gallery. 57 Jermyn St, London, SW1Y 6LX. Tel 439 6284.

Gallery of Antique Costume & Textiles Ltd. 2 Church Street, Marylebone, London, NW8. Tel 723 9981 (priv 743 3821).

George & Helen Gardiner. 105 West Regent St, Glasgow, Strathclyde, G2 2BA. Tel 332 1264.

Rupert Gentle Antiques. The Manor House,Milton Lilbourne, Pewsey, Wiltshire, SN9 5LQ. Tel Marlborough (0672) 63344.

Gibberd and Grant Antiques. 40 The Bank, Barnard Castle, Durham, DL12 8PN. Tel Teesdale (0833) 37437.

Stephanie Grant Antiques. 38 The Bank, Barnard Castle, Durham. Tel Teesdale (0833) 37437.

The Honiton Lace Shop. 44 High St, Honiton, Devon. Tel 2416 (priv 2629).

Paul Hughes, Antique & Ancient Textiles. 3a Pembridge Sq, London, W2. Tel 243 8598.

Humbleyard Fine Art. 3 Fish Hill, Holt, Norfolk. Tel 713362(priv 036 283 793).

Tobias Jellinek. 156 Brompton Rd, London, SW3 1HW. Tel 589 5272, 581 2267.

Keeble Ltd. 13 Walton St, London, SW3. Tel 581 3676.

Lunn Antiques Ltd. 86 New King's Rd, London, SW6 4LU. Tel 736 4638.

Mac Humble Antiques. 11 Queen St, Bath, Avon, BA1 2Jo. Tel 62751 (priv 022122 3594).

Mallett & Son (Antiques) Ltd. 40 New Bond St, London, W1Y 0BS. Tel 499 7411.

Market Place Antiques. 35 Market Place, Henley-on-Thames, Oxfordshire, RG9 2AA. Tel 572387.

Mayorcas Ltd. 38 Jermyn St, London, SW1Y 6DN. Tel 629 4195.

Trevor Micklem, Antiques. Withywine Farm,Morebath, Tiverton, Devon, EX16 9BZ. Tel Bampton (0398) 31409.

Moolham Mill Antiques. Moolham Mill, Moolham Lane, Ilminster, Somerset, TA19 0PD. Tel 2834.

Old Bakery Antiques. 1 Church St, Hunstanton, Norfolk. Tel Brancaster (0485) 210396.

Portmeirion Antiques. 62 White Hart Lane, Barnes, London, SW13. Tel 876 2367.

Alistair Sampson Antiques (inc Tobias Jellinek). 156 Brompton Rd, London, SW3 1HW. Tel 589 5272, 581 2267.

Anthony Scaramanga Antiques. 108 Newland, Witney, Oxfordshire. Tel 3472.

Peta Smyth - Antique Textiles. 42 Moreton St,Pimlico, London, SW1. Tel 630 9898.

Stair & Company Ltd. 120 Mount St, London, W1Y 5HB. Tel 499 1784, 499 1785.

A Stitch in Time. 1 West End, Beaumaris, Gwynedd. Tel 811055.

Stockbridge Antiques. High St, Stockbridge, Hampshire. Tel 829.

Thornborough Galleries. 28 Gloucester St, Cirencester, Gloucestershire, GL7 2DH. Tel 2055 (priv 099386 367).

Times Past. 84 High St, Pershore, Hereford & Worcester, WR10 1DU. Tel 554258.

Edric Van Vredenburgh. 37 Bury St, London, SW1. Tel 839 5818.

Peter Wadham. The Antique Shop, 5 Cathedral Close, Exeter, Devon. Tel 39741.

Francis Wigram Antiques. Cotters Barn, Penn, Buckinghamshire, PN10 8LB. Tel 3266.

Needlework Tools

At the Sign of the Herald Angel. 19 Park St, Cirencester, Gloucestershire, GL7 2BX. Tel 2972.

Jean Burnett Antiques. 3a Church St, Finedon, Northamptonshire. Tel Wellingborough (0933) 680430.

Cherry Antiques. 101-103 High St, Hemel Hempstead, Hertfordshire. Tel 64358.

Cordell Antiques. 13 St Peter's St, Ipswich, Suffolk. Tel 219508.

Corner Antiques. Coltishall Antiques Centre, High St, Coltishall, Norfolk, NR12 7HV. Tel Norwich (0603) 738306 (priv 737631).

Joan Eyles Antiques. The Stone Yard,Fishergate, Boroughbridge, N.Yorkshire, YO5 9QY. Tel 3357 (priv 2487).

Fenwick and Fisher Antiques. 88 High St, Broadway, Hereford & Worcester. Tel 853227 (priv 853228).

Sheila Smith Antiques. 10A Queen St, Bath, Avon. Tel 60568 (priv 0373 830217).

The Thimble Society of London. Grays Antique Market, 58 Davies St, London, W1. Tel 493 0560.

Times Past. 84 High St, Pershore, Hereford & Worcester, WR10 1DU. Tel 554258.

Netsuke, Inro and Tsuba

Another World. 25 Candlemaker Row, Edinburgh, Lothian, EH1 2QG. Tel 661 0723.

C.Barrett & Co. 51 Burlington Arcade, Piccadilly, London, W1. Tel 493 2570.

Sylvia Collins. Unit 15, Bond St Antique Centre,124 New Bond St, London, W1Y 9AE. Tel 9625.

John Crichton. 34 Brook St, London, W1Y 1YA. Tel 629 7926.

Barry Davies Oriental Art. E14/17 Grays Mews, 1-7 Davies Mews, London, W1. Tel 408 0207 (priv 09326 4906.

Eskenazi Ltd. Foxglove House, 166 Piccadilly, London, W1V 9DE. Tel 493 5464.

Falkner Fine Art. Stands B18/C19 Grays Mews,Davies Mews, London, W1. Tel 629 3644 (priv 385 0174).

J.& J.Hubbard Antiques. 11A Mill St, St Peter Port, Guernsey. Tel 28462 (priv 28540).

Japanese Gallery. 23 Camden Passage, London, N1 8EA. Tel 226 3347.

Sydney L. Moss Ltd. 51 Brook St, London, W1Y 1AU. Tel 629 4670; 493 7374.

Nihon Token. 23 Museum St, London, WC1A 1JT. Tel 580 6511.

J.S.Rasmussen Fine Arts. 5 Logan Mews, Logan Pl, London, W8. Tel 373 6527.

Simeon. 19 Burlington Arcade, Piccadilly, London, W1V 9AB. Tel 493-3353.

Newspapers

see also Ephemera

Mail Order Book Specialist. 25 Dicey Ave, Cricklewood, London, NW2. Tel 452 1581.

Omniphil Ltd. Germains Lodge,Fullers Hill (office), Chesham, Buckinghamshire. Tel 771851.

Oak Furniture

see also Carvings, Furniture-Early to 17th Century

London

Stephen Anson. 31a Matheson Rd, London, W14. Tel 602 5277 (24hr answering).

Antiquus A G. 17 Pembridge Sq, London, W2 4EH. Tel 229 0224.

Tony Bunzl & Zal Davar. 344 King's Rd, London, SW3. Tel 352 3697.

Simon Coleman. 40 White Hart Lane,Barnes, London, SW13. Tel 878 5037.

Thomas Kerr Antiques Ltd. 11 Theberton St, Islington, London, N1. Tel 226 0626.

Alistair Sampson Antiques (inc Tobias Jellinek). 156 Brompton Rd, London, SW3 1HW. Tel 589 5272, 581 2267.

M. & D. Seligmann. 37 Kensington Church St, London, W8 4LL. Tel 937 0400 (priv 722 4315).

Stanley Studios. Park Walk, Chelsea, London, SW10. Tel 352 4353, 352 9996.

Louis Stanton. 299 Westbourne Grove, London, W11. Tel 727 9336.

Ian Wilson Antiques. 70-72 Peckham Rye, London, SE15. Tel 639 5068 (priv 732 5349).

Regions

A.& F. Partners. 20 London St, Faringdon, Oxfordshire, SN7 7AA. Tel 20078.

Antiques. 9 Market Square, Saffron Walden, Essex. Tel 23611 (0672 870727).

Antiques of Penrith. 4 Corney Sq, Penrith, Cumbria, CA11 7PX. Tel 62801.

Baggott Church Street Ltd. Church Street, Stow-on-the-Wold, Gloucestershire, GL54 1BB. Tel 30370.

Duncan J. Baggott. The Square, Stow-on-the-Wold, Gloucestershire, GL54 1AB. Tel 30662.

Henry Baines. 14 Church Rd, Southborough, Tunbridge Wells, Kent, TN4 0RX. Tel 32099.

Balcombe Galleries. Balcombe, W.Sussex, RH17 6NF. Tel 811439 or 811415.

Mary Bellis Antiques. Charnham Close (A4 Highway), Hungerford, Berkshire, RG17 0EJ. Tel 82620.

Brian Bingham Antiques. 420 Chatsworth Rd, Brampton, Chesterfield, Derbyshire. Tel 208441.

The Blacksmiths Shop. High St, Brasted, Kent. Tel Westerham (0959) 63114 (priv 62589).

Robert Byles. 7-9 Castle St, Bampton, Devon, EX16 9NS. Tel 515.

Carse Antiques. Rait, by Perth, Tayside, PH2 7RT. Tel 205 (priv 227).

J. & J. Caspall Antiques. Sheep St, Stow-on-the-Wold, Gloucestershire. Tel 31160.

Chapel Antiques. Brookfield, Glossop, Derbyshire. Tel 5195.

Chapel Antiques. Whatlington, E.Sussex, TN33 0NL. Tel Sedlescombe (042 487) 272.

K.Chappell Antiques & Fine Art. King St, Bakewell, Derbyshire, DE4 1DZ. Tel 2496 (priv 2960).

Chelsea House Antiques. 27 Station Rd, Stowmarket, Suffolk. Tel Elmswell (0359) 40895.

Clinkers Antiques Ltd. c/o Island Farm, Steep, Petersfield, Hampshire. Tel 62319.

Cottage Antiques. Hasty Lane, Ringway, Hale Barns, Altrincham, Greater Manchester, WA15 8UT. Tel 980-7961.

Cottage Antiques. The Old Post Office, Langford, Bristol, Avon, BS18 7BP. Tel Wrighton (0934) 862597.

Cottage Antiques. 3 Devonshire Place,Skipton Rd, Harrogate, N.Yorkshire, HG1. Tel 68195 (priv 0937 72694).

Thomas Crispin. The Little Manor, Winchelsea, E.Sussex, TN36 4EJ. Tel Rye (0797) 226699.

G.E.Day. 82 West St, Farnham, Surrey, GU9 7EN. Tel 715 043.

De Fresnes (Antiques). Cessnock Castle, Galston, Strathclyde. Tel 829314.

de Montfort. 49 High St, Robertsbridge, E.Sussex, TN32 5AN. Tel 880698 (priv 082 584 243).

Deacon & Sandys. Hill Crest Farm Oast, Hartley, Cranbrook, Kent. Tel 713775.

Derbyshire Antiques Ltd. 159 London Road South, Poynton, Cheshire, SK12 1LQ. Tel 873110.

Doveridge House of Neachley. Neach Hill, Long Lane, Shifnal, Shropshire. Tel Albrighton (090 722) 3131, 3132.

Duveen Antiques. Burgate, Fordingbridge, Hampshire, SP6 1LX. Tel 53309.

East Kent Antiques. Cheriton Lodge,West St, New Romney, Kent. Tel 62630.

The Faringdon Galleries. 79 London St, Faringdon, Oxfordshire. Tel 20344.

Farnborough (Kent) Antiques. 10 Church Rd, Farnborough, Kent, BR6 7DB. Tel 51834.

P.J.Fradley. Ellastone Old House, Ellastone, Ashbourne, Derbyshire, DE6 2GU. Tel Ellastone (033 524) 291.

Joan Frere Antiques. Drumbuie House, Drumnadrochit, Highland. Tel 210.

Frith Antiques. New St, Petworth, W.Sussex. Tel 43155 (priv 079881 606).

H.G. Gasson. Lion Galleries, Lion St, Rye, E.Sussex, TN31 7LB. Tel 222208.

Georgian House Antiques. 42 St Andrew St, Hertford, Hertfordshire. Tel 53508.

Georgian House Antiques. 222 High St, Uckfield, E.Sussex, TN22 1RE. Tel 5074.

Gerrard Antiques. The Old Cottage, 54 Branthwaite Brow, Kendal, Cumbria. Tel 23881.

Richard Glass. Hockerley Old Hall, Whaley Bridge, Derbyshire, SK12 7AS. Tel 4320.

Maurice Goldstone & Son. Avenel Court, King St, Bakewell, Derbyshire. Tel 2487.

Grange Court Antiques. Corfe, Taunton, Somerset. Tel Blagdon Hill (082 342) 498.

Stephanie Grant Antiques. 38 The Bank, Barnard Castle, Durham. Tel Teesdale (0833) 37437.

A. Halsey Antiques. Boffins Boft, Bowcombe Creek, Kingsbridge, Devon. Tel 2440.

Keith Hockin Antiques Ltd. The Square, Stow-on-the-Wold, Gloucestershire, GL54 1AF. Tel 31058.

Paul Hopwell Antiques. 30 High St, West Haddon, Northamptonshire, NN6 7AP. Tel 636.

Horseshoe Antiques & Gallery. High St, Burford, Oxfordshire, OX8 4RJ. Tel 3244.

Colin S.Hughes. 36 Penrallt St, Machynlleth, Powys. Tel 2363.

Roger Hughes Antique Gallery. 13 Dillwyn St, Swansea, W.Glamorgan. Tel 52584.

Humphry Antiques. East St, Petworth, W.Sussex, GU28 0AB. Tel 43053 (priv 42944).

Huntington Antiques Ltd. The Old Forge, Church St, Stow-on-the-Wold, Gloucestershire. Tel 30842.

Kenneth Jackson (Antiques). 66 Thistle St, Edinburgh, Lothian. Tel 225 9634.

H.W.Keil Ltd. Tudor House, Broadway, Hereford & Worcester, WR12 7DP. Tel 852408.

Key Antiques. 11 Horsefair, Chipping Norton, Oxfordshire, OX7 5AL. Tel 3777.

Leonard Lassalle. 21 The Pantiles, Tunbridge Wells, Kent, TN2 5TD. Tel 31645.

Laurel Bank Interiors. Farndon, Chester, Cheshire. Tel Farndon (0820) 270704.

Linden House Antiques. Linden House,3 Silver St, Stansted Mountfitchet, Essex, CM24 8HA. Tel Bishops Stortford (0279) 812372.

Long Melford Antiques. Chapel Maltings, High St, Long Melford, Suffolk. Tel Sudbury (0787) 79287.

Charles Lowe & Sons Ltd. 37-40 Church Gate, Loughborough, Leicestershire. Tel 217876.

Markland Antiques. Western Rd, Borough Green, Kent. Tel 4152.

Marlborough Antiques. 18 The Parade, Marlborough, Wiltshire. Tel 54818.

John Meredith Antiques. 36 The Square, Chagford, Devon. Tel 3474 (priv 3405).

Trevor Micklem, Antiques. Withywine Farm,Morebath, Tiverton, Devon, EX16 9BZ. Tel Bampton (0398) 31409.

Miles Antiques. 151 Albany Rd, Cardiff, S.Glamorgan. Tel 31485.

Monkton Galleries. High St, Hindon, Wiltshire, SP3 6DR. Tel 235.

Moolham Mill Antiques. Moolham Mill, Moolham Lane, Ilminster, Somerset, TA19 0PD. Tel 2834.

William Morley Antiques. Musgrave's Old Farm, West Monkton, Taunton, Somerset, TA2 8NW. Tel West Monkton (0823) 412751.

Charles & Joan Mortimer & Sons. Sugar House, School St, Great Chesterford, Essex, CB10 1NN. Tel Saffron Walden (0799) 30261.

Moxhams Antiques. 17 Silver St, Bradford-on-Avon, Wiltshire. Tel 2789 (priv 038 082-677).

Nash Antiques. 5 & 6 Lower Church St, Chepstow, Gwent. Tel 4150.

John Nicholls Antiques. 27 Long St, Tetbury, Gloucestershire. Tel 52781 (priv 08893 2383).

No.Twelve Queen Street. 12 Queen St, Bath, Avon. Tel 62363 (priv 314846).

Peter Norden Antiques. High St, Burford, Oxfordshire, OX8 4XX. Tel 2121 (priv 0993 830064).

Northiam Antiques. Main St, Northiam, E.Sussex. Tel 2182.

The Old Bakery Antiques. St David's Bridge, Cranbrook, Kent, TN17 3HL. Tel 713103.

Old Britannia. Castle Street, Combe Martin, Ilfracombe, Devon. Tel Combe Martin (027 188) 3610.

The Old Forge. Pilgrims Way, Hollingbourne, Kent, ME17 1UW. Tel 360.

Old Hall Antiques/Sphinx Gallery. The Old Hall, Sundridge, Kent. Tel Westerham (0959) 62589.

The Old House Antiques. 9-10 West St, Dorking, Surrey, RH4 1QH. Tel 887278.

A.J. & L.Onions. White Cottage, 8 Tern Hill, Market Drayton, Shropshire, TF9 3PR. Tel Tern Hill (063 083) 222.

Packer House. 28 High St, Chipping Norton, Oxfordshire, OX7 5AD. Tel 3255.

Angela Page Antiques. Sion House, 15 Mount Sion, Tunbridge Wells, Kent, TN1 1OD. Tel 22217.

Fenwick Pattison. Bowmanstead, Coniston, Cumbria, LA21 8HB. Tel 41235.

Elaine Phillips Antiques Ltd. 2 Royal Parade, Harrogate, N.Yorkshire. Tel 69745.

Peter Philp. 77 Kimberley Rd, Pen-y-Lan, S.Glamorgan, CF2 5DP. Tel Cardiff (0222) 493826.

Primrose Antiques. High St, Moreton-in-Marsh, Gloucestershire, GL66 0LL. Tel 50591.

Marc Rhys. The Mynde House, High St, Caerleon, Gwent. Tel 420535.

Sandler Fine Arts with Bill Bentley. 16 Montpellier Parade, Harrogate, N.Yorkshire. Tel 64084.

Seymour Galleries. Church St South, Old Glossop, Derbyshire. Tel 62555.

Shire Antiques. The Post House, High Newton,Newton-in-Cartmel, Grange-over-Sands, Cumbria. Tel Newby Bridge (0448) 31431.

Paul Smith. The Old Chapel,Old St, Ludlow, Shropshire, SY8 1NP. Tel 2666.

Spurrier-Smith Antiques. 28 & 41 Church St, Ashbourne, Derbyshire. Tel 43669 (priv 077 389 368).

The Stable Antiques. Old Kings Head Court,11 High St, Dorking, Surrey. Tel 885452.

William H.Stokes. Roberts House, Siddington, Cirencester, Gloucestershire, GL7 6EX. Tel 67101.

Dinah Stoodley. High St, Brasted, Kent, TN16 1JJ. Tel Westerham (0959) 63616.

Thomson Antiques. Ermefield House, Western Rd, Ivybridge, Devon, PL21 9AL. Tel Plymouth (0752) 892304.

Tudor Antiques. Monks Risborough, Buckinghamshire. Tel Princes Risborough(08444) 3523.

Turpins Antiques. 4 Stoney Lane, Thaxted, Essex. Tel 830495 (priv 830059).

E.W. Webster Antiques. Wash Farm, Rainford Rd, Bickerstaffe, Lancashire. Tel Skelmersdale (0695) 24322.

Anthony Welling Antiques. Broadway Barn, High St, Ripley, Surrey, GU23 6AQ. Tel Guildford (0483) 225384.

West Farm Antiques. High St, Orwell, Cambridgeshire, SG8 5QN. Tel Cambridge (0223) 207464.

Timothy D.Wilson. No.1 Swan St, Bawtry, S.Yorkshire, DN10 6JQ. Tel Doncaster (0302) 710040.

R.S. Wilson & Sons. High St, Boroughbridge, N.Yorkshire, YO5 9AW. Tel 2417 (priv 2654).

Witney Antiques. 96-98 Corn St, Witney, Oxfordshire, OX8 7BU. Tel 3902.

Objects of Vertu

see also Enamels, Tortoiseshell

Maurice Asprey Ltd. 41 Duke St, St James's, London, SW1. Tel 930 3921.

Joseph Bonnar. 72 Thistle St, Edinburgh, Lothian. Tel 226 2811.

Luigi Brian. Vault 56, London Silver Vaults,53 Chancery Lane, London, WC2 1QT. Tel 405 2484.

Donohoe. 1-7 Davies Mews, London, W1. Tel 629 5633 (priv 455 5507).

Eliot Antiques. Stanford Dingley, Reading, Berkshire, RG7 6LX. Tel Bradfield (0734) 744649 (priv 744346).

Eureka Antiques. 18 Northenden Road, Sale, Greater Manchester, M33 3BR. Tel 962 5629.

Graus Antiques. 125 New Bond St, London, W1Y 9AF. Tel 629 6680, 629 6651.

Grey-Harris & Co. 12 Princess Victoria St,Clifton, Bristol, Avon. Tel 737365.

Halcyon Days. 14 Brook St, London, W1Y 1AA. Tel 629 8811.

Knaphill Antiques. 38 High Street, Knaphill, Woking, Surrey. Tel Brookwood (048 67) 3179.

Levine, Henry & Co. 55 London St, Norwich, Norfolk, NR2 1HL. Tel 628709.

Paul Longmire Ltd. 12 Bury St,St James's, London, SW1. Tel 930 8720.

Massada Antiques. 45 New Bond St, London, W1Y 9HB. Tel 493 4792; 493 5610.

I.J.Mazure & Co Ltd. 90 Jermyn St, London, SW1Y 6JD. Tel 839 3101/2.

Muirhead Moffat & Co. 182 West Regent St, Glasgow, Strathclyde. Tel 226 4683 and 226 3406.

S.J. Phillips Ltd. 139 New Bond St, London, W1A 3DL. Tel 629 6261, 629 6262.

Christine Schell. 15 Cale St, London, SW3 3QS. Tel 352 5563.

Schidlof Galleries. 1 Holland Park Ct, Holland Park Gdns, London, W14. Tel 603 9480.

Scott Cooper Ltd. 52 The Promenade, Cheltenham, Gloucestershire, GL50 1LY. Tel 522580.

Trianon. Grays Antique Market,58 Davies St, London, W1. Tel 491 2764.

Oriental Furniture

Attic Antiques. 23 & 32 Ship St, Brighton & Hove, E.Sussex, BN1 1AD. Tel 29464 (priv 551594).

Richard Batsford Antiques. Antique Trade Warehouse,29 Lorne Park Rd, Bournemouth, Dorset. Tel 292944 (priv 25485).

Brandt Oriental Antiques. 771 Fulham Rd, London, SW6. Tel 731 6835.

Odile Cavendish. 14 Lowndes St, London, SW1X 9EX. Tel 235 2491.

Ciancimino Ltd. 99 Pimlico Rd, London, SW1W 8PH. Tel 730 9950.

Galleon Galleries. 42 Westfield Lane, St Leonards, E.Sussex. Tel 440974.

Solveig & Anita Gray. 58 Davies Street, London, W1. Tel 408 1638.

Gwyneth Antiques. 56 Ebury St, London, SW1. Tel 730 2513 (priv 352 4864).

Jonathan Harris. 54 Kensington Church St, London, W8. Tel 937 3133.

John Meredith Antiques. 36 The Square, Chagford, Devon. Tel 3474 (priv 3405).

Peter Reynolds Antiques. 67 New King's Rd, London, SW6. Tel 736 7797.

Ringles Cross Antiques. Ringles Cross, Uckfield, E.Sussex. Tel 2909.

Barry Sainsbury Oriental Art. 145 Ebury St, London, SW1. Tel 730 3393.

Murray Thomson Ltd. 141 Kensington Church St, London, W8 7LP. Tel 727 1727, 727 1825.

David Tremayne Ltd. 320 King's Rd, London, SW3. Tel 352 1194.

H. Woods Wilson Ltd. 103 Pimlico Rd, London, SW1. Tel 730 2558.

Oriental Pictures

Odile Cavendish. 14 Lowndes St, London, SW1X 9EX. Tel 235 2491.

Chi Mei Chai Eastern Art Gallery. 40 Great Russell St, London, WC1. Tel 631 4868.

Shirley Day Ltd. 91B Jermyn St, London, SW1Y 6JB. Tel 839 2804.

East Asia Co. 103 Camden High St, London, NW1 7JN. Tel 388 5783.

Milne Henderson. 96 Mount St, London, W1. Tel 499 2507.

Sydney L. Moss Ltd. 51 Brook St, London, W1Y 1AU. Tel 629 4670; 493 7374.

Ormonde Gallery. 156 Portobello Rd, London, W11. Tel 229 9800, 042482-226.

David Pettifer Ltd. 269 King's Rd, London, SW3 5EN. Tel 352 3088.

Oriental Pottery and Porcelain

Anchor Antiques Ltd. 26 Charing Cross Rd,(office 24A Charing Cross Rd), London, WC2H 0DG. Tel 836 5686.

L.J. Arditti & E.M. Arditti. 29A The Pantiles, Tunbridge Wells, Kent. Tel 43361.

Artemesia. 16 West St, Alresford, Hampshire. Tel 2277.

Attic Antiques. 23 & 32 Ship St, Brighton & Hove, E.Sussex, BN1 1AD. Tel 29464 (priv 551594).

Augill Castle Antiques Ltd. Augill Castle, Brough, Cumbria, CA17 4AY. Tel 412.

R.A.Barnes Antiques. 26 Lower Richmond Rd, Putney, London, SW15 1JP. Tel 789 3371.

Bath Galleries. 33 Broad St, Bath, Avon, BA1 5LP. Tel 62946.

Susan Becker Antiques. 18 Lower Richmond Rd, Putney, London, SW15. Tel 788 9082.

Birbeck Antiques. 219 Union St, Torquay, Devon, TQ1 4BZ. Tel 23318 (priv 214836).

Bluett & Sons Ltd. 48 Davies St, London, W1Y 1LD. Tel 629 4018, 629 3397.

Brandt Oriental Antiques. 771 Fulham Rd, London, SW6. Tel 731 6835.

Helen Buxton Antiques. 193 Westbourne Grove, London, W11. Tel 229 9997.

Chancery Antiques Ltd. 357A Upper St, Islington, London, N1. Tel 359 9035.

William Clayton Ltd. 38 Bury St, St James's, London, SW1. Tel 930 1173.

Cohen and Pearce (Oriental Porcelain). 84 Portobello Rd, London, W11 2QD. Tel 229 9458.

Compton Antiques. 60A Middle St, Brighton & Hove, E.Sussex. Tel 774229.

R. & D. Coombes. Charleville Gallery,7 Charleville Rd, West Kensington, London, W14 9JL. Tel 385 3795.

Andrew Cottrell Galleries. 7-9 Church St, Godalming, Surrey. Tel 7570.

John Crichton. 34 Brook St, London, W1Y 1YA. Tel 629 7926.

Andrew Dando. 4 Wood St, Queen Sq, Bath, Avon, BA1 2JQ. Tel 22702.

Gerald Freedman (Cale Antiques). Box 458,Fulham, London, SW6 3RS. Tel 736 8666.

David Friend Antiques. 23 Guest Rd, Prestwich, Greater Manchester, M25 7DJ. Tel 773 1382.

Gabor Cossa Antiques. 34 Trumpington St, Cambridge, Cambridgeshire, CB2 1QY. Tel 356049.

Jay Gray Antiques. Syrena House, 1 Cheltenham Rd, Cirencester, Gloucestershire, GL7 2HS. Tel 2755.

Lynn Greenwold. Digbeth, Digbeth St, Stow-on-the-Wold, Gloucestershire. Tel 30398.

Hamand Antiques. Friday St, Painswick, Gloucestershire, GL6 6QJ. Tel 812310.

Hart & Rosenberg. 2-3 Gateway Arcade,355 Upper St, Camden Passage, London, N1 OPD. Tel 359 6839.

Michael Hogg. 172 Brompton Rd, London, SW3. Tel 589 8629.

J.& J.Hubbard Antiques. 11A Mill St, St Peter Port, Guernsey. Tel 28462 (priv 28540).

Eric Hudes. Paigles, Perry Green, Bradwell, Braintree, Essex, CM7 8ES. Tel Silver End (0376) 83767.

Eric Hudes. 142 Portobello Rd, London, W11. Tel daily 0376-83767.

Peter W.Kemp. 174A Kensington Church St, London, W8 4DP. Tel 229 2988.

Kenway Antiques. 70 Kenway Rd, London, SW5 0RD. Tel 373 1631.

London Apprentice Antiques. St Austell, Cornwall, PL26 7AR. Tel 63780.

David Love. 10 Royal Parade, Harrogate, N.Yorkshire. Tel 65797.

LPJ Antiques. 27 Camden Passage, Islington, London, N1. Tel 359 7579.

S.Marchant & Son. 120 Kensington Church St, London, W8 4BH. Tel 229 5319, 229 3770.

Metcalfe Jackson. 24A West St, Wimborne Minster, Dorset, BH21 1JS. Tel 883327.

Patrick Moorhead Antiques. 59A Ship St, Brighton & Hove, E.Sussex, BN1 1AD. Tel 28209 (priv 551594).

H.C. Mote. 15 Walton St, London, SW3 2HX. Tel 589 2752.

Nash Antiques. 10 Fountain Buildings,Lansdown Rd, Bath, Avon. Tel 313584.

H.W. Newby. 15 Walton St, London, SW3 2HX. Tel 589 2752.

Nihon Token. 23 Museum St, London, WC1A 1JT. Tel 580 6511.

Oriental Antiques. 4 Belvedere, Lansdown Rd, Bath, Avon. Tel 315987.

Ormonde Gallery. 156 Portobello Rd, London, W11. Tel 229 9800, 042482-226.

Paul M. Peters Antiques. 15 Bower Rd, Harrogate, N.Yorkshire. Tel 60118.

Pamela Rowan Antiques. High St, Blockley, Gloucestershire, GL56 9ET. Tel 700280.

A.V. & M.R. Santos. 1 Campden St, London, W8. Tel 727 4872.

Span Antiques. 6 Market Place, Woodstock, Oxfordshire, OX7 1TA. Tel 811332.

A. & J. Speelman. 129 Mount St, London, W1. Tel 499 5126.

Aubrey Spiers Antiques. Stand C5, Chenil Galleries,King's Rd, Chelsea, London, SW3. Tel 352 7384.

Jacob Stodel Antiques. 116 Kensington Church St, London, W8 4BH. Tel 221 2652.

Tapsell Antiques. 59, 59A Middle St, Brighton & Hove, E.Sussex. Tel 28341 (priv 553249).

Traditio Antiques. 38A Kensington Church St, London, W8. Tel 937 9532.

Brian Trengove Antiques and Picture Gallery. 46 South End, Croydon, Surrey, CR0 1DP. Tel 688 2155.

Jan van Beers. Stand K24/25, Gray's Mews,1-7 Davies Mews, London, W1. Tel 408 0434.

Earle D.Vandekar of Knightsbridge Ltd. 138 Brompton Rd, London, SW3. Tel 589 8481, 589 3398.

Wain Antiques. 45 Long Street, Tetbury, Gloucestershire. Tel 52440.

Walker Galleries of Harrogate Ltd. 3 Cale St,Chelsea Green, London, SW3. Tel 351 5988.

Walker Galleries Ltd. 6 Montpellier Gdns, Harrogate, N.Yorkshire. Tel 67933.

William G.Wells. 20 St John Maddermarket, Norwich, Norfolk. Tel 21260.

Mary Wise Antiques. 27 Holland St, London, W8. Tel 937 8649 (priv 352 7334).

H. Woods Wilson Ltd. 103 Pimlico Rd, London, SW1. Tel 730 2558.

Denis Young Antiques. 3 Kenmore St, Aberfeldy, Tayside. Tel Glenlyon (08877) 232.

Oriental Textiles and Embroidery

see Chinese Embroideries

Oriental Works of Art

see also Cloisonne, Ivories, Jade, Japanese Works of Art, Lacquer

Albany Antiques. 1351 Argyle St, Glasgow, Strathclyde, G3 8AD. Tel 3394267 (priv 3341880).

L.J. Arditti & E.M. Arditti. 29A The Pantiles, Tunbridge Wells, Kent. Tel 43361.

Artemesia. 16 West St, Alresford, Hampshire. Tel 2277.

Barling of Mount Street Ltd. 112 Mount St, London, W1. Tel 499 2858.

Berkeley Galleries Ltd. 82 The Hall, Foxes Dale, London, SE3. Tel 852 0586.

Bernheimer Fine Arts Ltd. 32 St George St,Mayfair, London, W1R 9FA. Tel 499 0293.

H.Blairman & Sons Ltd. 119 Mount St, London, W1. Tel 493 0444.

Bluett & Sons Ltd. 48 Davies St, London, W1Y 1LD. Tel 629 4018, 629 3397.

Brandt Oriental Antiques. 771 Fulham Rd, London, SW6. Tel 731 6835.

Butterwalk House. 55 The Old Butterwalk, High St, Totnes, Devon. Tel 863044.

Odile Cavendish. 14 Lowndes St, London, SW1X 9EX. Tel 235 2491.

Chancery Antiques Ltd. 357A Upper St, Islington, London, N1. Tel 359 9035.

Ciancimino Ltd. 99 Pimlico Rd, London, SW1W 8PH. Tel 730 9950.

William Clayton Ltd. 38 Bury St, St James's, London, SW1. Tel 930 1173.

Cohen and Pearce (Oriental Porcelain). 84 Portobello Rd, London, W11 2QD. Tel 229 9458.

Sylvia Collins. Unit 15, Bond St Antique Centre,124 New Bond St, London, W1Y 9AE. Tel 9625.

R. & D. Coombes. Charleville Gallery,7 Charleville Rd, West Kensington, London, W14 9JL. Tel 385 3795.

Paul Couts Ltd. 101-107 West Bow, Victoria St, Edinburgh, Lothian. Tel 225 3238.

John Crichton. 34 Brook St, London, W1Y 1YA. Tel 629 7926.

Barry Davies Oriental Art. E14/17 Grays Mews, 1-7 Davies Mews, London, W1. Tel 408 0207 (priv 09326 4906.

Shirley Day Ltd. 91B Jermyn St, London, SW1Y 6JB. Tel 839 2804.

Eskenazi Ltd. Foxglove House, 166 Piccadilly, London, W1V 9DE. Tel 493 5464.

R.H. & E.M.Freeman. 4 Park St, Stow-on-the-Wold, Gloucestershire, GL54 1AQ. Tel 31184.

David Friend Antiques. 23 Guest Rd, Prestwich, Greater Manchester, M25 7DJ. Tel 773 1382.

Michael Goedhuis Ltd. Colnaghi Oriental. 14 Old Bond St, London, W1X 4JL. Tel 409 3324.

Solveig & Anita Gray. 58 Davies Street, London, W1. Tel 408 1638.

Gwyneth Antiques. 56 Ebury St, London, SW1. Tel 730 2513 (priv 352 4864).

Hart & Rosenberg. 2-3 Gateway Arcade,355 Upper St, Camden Passage, London, N1 OPD. Tel 359 6839.

J.& J.Hubbard Antiques. 11A Mill St, St Peter Port, Guernsey. Tel 28462 (priv 28540).

Eric Hudes. Paigles, Perry Green, Bradwell, Braintree, Essex, CM7 8ES. Tel Silver End (0376) 83767.

Eric Hudes. 142 Portobello Rd, London, W11. Tel daily 0376-83767.

Lennox Antiques. 53 Upper North St, Brighton & Hove, E.Sussex, BN1 3FH. Tel 29409 (priv 563104).

London Apprentice Antiques. St Austell, Cornwall, PL26 7AR. Tel 63780.

LPJ Antiques. 27 Camden Passage, Islington, London, N1. Tel 359 7579.

Jasper Marsh. 3 High St, Henley-in-Arden, Warwickshire. Tel 2088.

Jeremy J. Mason. 29 New Bond St, London, W1Y 9HD. Tel 629 3410.

F.J.McCarthy Ltd. The Grange, Normanton on Trent, Newark-on-Trent, Nottinghamshire, NG23 6RQ. Tel 821382.

Sydney L. Moss Ltd. 51 Brook St, London, W1Y 1AU. Tel 629 4670; 493 7374.

Nash Antiques. 183 Westbourne Grove, London, W11. Tel 727 3796.

North Parade Antiques. 75 Banbury Rd (A423), Oxford, Oxfordshire. Tel 59816 (priv 880923).

Oriental Antiques. 4 Belvedere, Lansdown Rd, Bath, Avon. Tel 315987.

Ormonde Gallery. 156 Portobello Rd, London, W11. Tel 229 9800, 042482-226.

Paul M. Peters Antiques. 15 Bower Rd, Harrogate, N.Yorkshire. Tel 60118.

Ringles Cross Antiques. Ringles Cross, Uckfield, E.Sussex. Tel 2909.

John Sparks Ltd. 128 Mount St, London, W1Y 5HA. Tel 499 2265 and 499 1932.

A. & J. Speelman. 129 Mount St, London, W1. Tel 499 5126.

Spink & Son Ltd. 5, 6 & 7 King St, St James's, London, SW1. Tel 930 7888.

R.A.Swift & Sons. St Andrews Hall,4c Wolverton Rd, Boscombe, Bournemouth, Dorset, BH7 6HT. Tel 34470.

M. & C. Telfer-Smollett. 88 Portobello Rd, London, W11. Tel 727 0117 (priv 370 1860).

H. Woods Wilson Ltd. 103 Pimlico Rd, London, SW1. Tel 730 2558.

Packers and Shippers

see Shippers

Painting Restorers

see Restorers, Paintings

Paintings, British

London

Didier Aaron (London) Ltd. 21 Ryder St, London, SW1Y 6PX. Tel 839 4716/7.

Abbott & Holder. 73 Castelnau, Barnes, London, SW13. Tel 748 2416.

Thos Agnew & Sons Ltd. 43 Old Bond St, London, W1X 4BA. Tel 629 6176.

Albany Gallery. 1 Bury St, St James's, London, SW1Y 6AB. Tel 839 6119.

Albion Fine Art. 61 Ledbury Rd, London, W1. Tel 221 2977.

Richard Allan Gallery. 20 Park Walk,Chelsea, London, SW10. Tel 351 0410.

The Belgrave Gallery. 22 Masons Yard,Duke St, St James's, London, SW1. Tel 930 0294.

J.L.W.Bird. 19 Grove Park Terrace, London, W4 3QE. Tel 995 9960.

Brod Gallery. 24 St James's St, London, SW1A 1HA. Tel 839 3871.

Brotherton Gallery Ltd. 77 Walton St, London, SW3. Tel 589 6848.

Burlington Paintings. 12 Burlington Gdns, London, W1X 1LG. Tel 734 9984.

Clarges Gallery. 158 Walton Street, London, SW3. Tel 584 3022.

Edward Cohen. 40 Duke St, St James's, London, SW1. Tel 839 5180.

P. & D. Colnaghi & Co Ltd. 14 Old Bond St, London, W1X 4JL. Tel 491 7408.

Laurence Corner, Euston Gallery. 126-130 Drummond St, London, NW1. Tel 388 6811.

Anthony Dallas & Sons Ltd. 17 Clifford St, London, W1. Tel 734 7127.

John Denham Gallery. 50 Mill Lane, London, NW6. Tel 794 2635.

Drian Galleries. 7 Porchester Place, Marble Arch, London, W2. Tel 723 9473.

L. & R. Entwistle & Co Ltd. 70 South Audley St, London, W1Y 5FE. Tel 493 2828.

Jocelyn Feilding Fine Art Ltd. 8 Duke St, St James's, London, SW1. Tel 839 5040.

The Fine Art Society Plc. 148 New Bond St, London, W1Y 0JT. Tel 629 5116.

Angela Flowers Gallery Ltd. 11 Tottenham Mews, London, W1. Tel 637 3089.

Galerie George. 98 George St, London, W1H 5RI. Tel 935 3322, 935 9998.

Stephen Garratt Fine Paintings. Exhibiting at 146 Brompton Rd,(Knightsbridge Safe Deposit), London, SW3. Tel 603 0681.

Gavin Graham Gallery. 47 Ledbury Rd, London, W11 2AA. Tel 229 4848.

Richard Green. 36 & 44 Dover St, London, W1. Tel 493 3939.

Martyn Gregory. 34 Bury St, St James's, London, SW1. Tel 839 3731.

Hancock Gallery. 184 Westbourne Grove, London, W11. Tel 229 7827 (priv 878 5008).

Julian Hartnoll. 14 Mason's Yard, Duke St,St James's, London, SW1. Tel 839 3842.

Hazlitt, Gooden & Fox. 38 Bury St,St James's, London, SW1. Tel 930 6422.

Heim Gallery. 59 Jermyn St, St James's, London, SW1Y 6LX. Tel 493 0688.

Hobhouse Ltd. 39 Duke St, St James's, London, SW1 6DF. Tel 930 9308.

Hollywood Road Gallery. 12 Hollywood Rd, London, SW10. Tel 351 1973.

Manya Igel Fine Arts Ltd. 21-22 Peters Court, Porchester Rd, London, W2. Tel 229 1669/8429 (priv 6770).

Malcolm Innes Gallery. 172 Walton St, London, SW3. Tel 584 0575.

Iona Antiques. Stand 107, Gray's Antique Market, 58 Davies St, London, W1Y 1FH. Tel 499 2386.

Kaleidoscope Gallery. 66 Willesden Lane, London, NW6. Tel 328 5833.

Lacy Gallery. 38-40 Ledbury Rd, London, W11. Tel 229 9105, 229 5316.

Lane Fine Art Ltd. 86-88 Pimlico Road, London, SW1. Tel 730 7374.

Lasson Gallery. 34 Duke St, St James's, London. Tel 930 5950.

The Leger Galleries Ltd. 13 Old Bond St, London, W1. Tel 629 3538.

Leggatt Bros. 17 Duke St, St James's, London, SW1Y 6DB. Tel 930 3772 and 930 3252.

The Maclean Gallery. 49 Drayton Gardens, London, SW10. Tel 373 2867.

MacConnal-Mason. 14 Duke St, St James's, London, SW1Y 6DB. Tel 839 7693/4 and 499 6991.

Mangate Gallery. 3 Chiswick Lane, London, W4 2LR. Tel 995 9867.

Richard Miles Antiques. 8 Holbein Place, London, SW1 8NL. Tel 730 1957.

Roy Miles Fine Paintings Ltd. 3 Berkeley Square, London, W1X 5HG. Tel 491 3611.

John Mitchell & Sons. 8 New Bond St, London, W1Y 9PE. Tel 493 7567.

Peter Nahum. 5 Ryder St, London, SW1Y 6PY. Tel 930 6059 (priv 994 1501).

New Grafton Gallery. 49 Church Rd, Barnes, London, SW13 9HH. Tel 748 8850.

Hal O'Nians Ltd. King Street Galleries, 17 King St, St James's, London, SW1Y 6QU. Tel 930 9392/3993.

Omell Galleries. 43A Duke St, St James's, London, SW1. Tel 930 7744.

Omell Galleries. 22 Bury St, St James's, London, SW1. Tel 839 4274/5.

Michael Parkin Fine Art Ltd. 11 Motcomb St, London, SW1. Tel 235 8144, 235 1845.

Partridge (Fine Arts) Ltd. 144-146 New Bond St, London, W1. Tel 629 0834.

Pawsey & Payne. 4 Ryder St, London, SW1. Tel 930 4221.

Richard Philp. 59 Ledbury Rd, London, W11. Tel 727 7915.

Pym's Gallery. 13 Motcomb St, Belgravia, London, SW1X 8LB. Tel 235 3050.

Rona Gallery. 1-2 Weighhouse St, London, W1.

Sabin Galleries Ltd. Campden Lodge, 82 Campden Hill Rd, London, W8 7AA. Tel 937 0471.

Scope Antiques. 64-66 Willesden Lane, London, NW6. Tel 328 5833.

Somerville & Simpson Ltd. 11 Savile Row, London, W1. Tel 437 5414.

Edward Speelman Ltd. Empire House, 175 Piccadilly, London, W1V 0NP. Tel 493 0657.

H.J. Spiller Ltd. 37-39 Beak St, London, W1R 3LD. Tel 437 4661.

Spink & Son Ltd. 5, 6 & 7 King St, St James's, London, SW1. Tel 930 7888.

F.Teltscher Ltd. 17 Crawford St, London, W1H 1PF. Tel 935 0525.

Michael Tollemache Ltd. 78 Cadogan Pl, London, SW1. Tel 235 5107.

Trafalgar Galleries. 35 Bury St, St James's, London, SW1Y 6AU. Tel 839 6466/7.

The Tryon and Moorland Gallery. 23-24 Cork St, London, W1X 1HB. Tel 734 6961/2256.

Tugwell & Thomas Antiques. Grays Antique Market, 58 Davies St, London, W1. Tel 499 1337.

Wylma Wayne Fine Art. 17 Old Bond St, London, W1. Tel 629 4511.

Whitford & Hughes. 6 Duke St, St James's, London, SW1. Tel 930 9332.

Wilkins & Wilkins. 1 Barrett St, St Christopher's Place, London, W1. Tel 935 9613.

Williams & Son. 2 Grafton St, London, W1X 3LB. Tel 493 5751, 493 4985.

Andrew Wyld. 17 Clifford St, London, W1X 1RG. Tel 734 5575/5576.

Regions

Donald Allison Antiques. 115-119 New Hall Lane, Preston, Lancashire. Tel 701916 (priv 615946).

Augill Castle Antiques Ltd. Augill Castle, Brough, Cumbria, CA17 4AY. Tel 412.

J. & J. Baker. 12-14 Water St, Lavenham, Suffolk. Tel 247610.

The Barn Gallery. Sandpits Farm, Colletts Green Rd, Powick, Hereford & Worcester, WR2 4RY. Tel Worcester (0905) 830029.

Barnard Gallery. Grange Farm, Everton, Doncaster, S.Yorkshire, DN10 5BG. Tel Retford (0777) 817324.

Baroq Antiques. Watling St, Little Brickhill, Buckinghamshire, MK17 9LY. Tel Great Brickhill (052 526) 401 (priv 561).

The Bell Gallery. 13 Adelaide Park, off Malone Rd, Belfast, Belfast. Tel 662998.

Bell Passage Antiques. 36-38 High St, Wickwar, Wotton-under-Edge, Gloucestershire, GL12 8NP. Tel Wickwar (045 424) 251.

Peter Bell Fine Arts. High St, Lechlade, Gloucestershire, GL7 3DL. Tel Faringdon (0367) 52987 (priv 52255).

George Bewes & Co. 235 George St, Aberdeen, Grampian. Tel 635830.

Biggs of Maidenhead. Hare Hatch Grange, Twyford, Berkshire, RG10 9SK. Tel Wargrave (073 522) 3281 (priv 3104).

Bourne Fine Art Ltd. 4 Dundas St, Edinburgh, Lothian, EH3 6HZ. Tel 557 4050.

Bourne Gallery. 31-33 Lesbourne Rd, Reigate, Surrey. Tel 41614.

Bowmoore Gallery. Whelford, Gloucestershire, GL7 4DT. Tel 712651.

Bragge & Sons. Landgate House, Rye, E.Sussex. Tel 223358.

Ian J. Brook. 26 North St, Wilton, Wiltshire, SP2 OHJ. Tel Salisbury (0722) 743392.

Patrick F. Brown. 15 South William St, Dublin, Co Dublin. Tel 719013.

William Bruce & Co. Mainhill, Charlesfield, St Boswells, Borders, TD6 0HG. Tel 23628 23788.

Calton Gallery. 10 Royal Terrace, Edinburgh, Lothian, EH7 5AB. Tel 556 1010.

Colin Campbell Fine Paintings. The Gallery, The Square, Yarmouth, Isle of Wight, PO41 0NS. Tel 760784.

Simon Carter Gallery. 23 Market Hill, Woodbridge, Suffolk, IP12 4LX. Tel 2242.

R.G.Cave & Sons Ltd. 17 Broad St, Ludlow, Shropshire. Tel 3568.

Cave's of Northampton. 111 Kettering Rd, Northampton, Northamptonshire, NN1 4BA. Tel 38278.

Chantry Book Shop. 11 Higher St, Dartmouth, Devon, TQ6 9RB. Tel 2796 (priv) 4208.

Charles Antiques. 101 The Hundred, Romsey, Hampshire, SO5 8BZ. Tel 512885.

Circa Fine Art. Island House, Barbican, Plymouth, Devon, PL1 2LS. Tel 663318.

Clarendon Gallery. 20 Albert Square, Manchester, Greater Manchester. Tel 980 6343.

Peter Coe Fine Paintings. The Priory, Shepton Mallet, Somerset. Tel 2412.

Christopher Cole (Fine Paintings) Ltd. 1 London End, Beaconsfield, Buckinghamshire, HP9 2HN. Tel 71274.

Colleton House Gallery. 8a Quiet St, Bath, Avon, BA1 2JU. Tel 28806.

Duncalfe Antiques & Fine Arts. 34 Montpellier Parade, Harrogate, N.Yorkshire. Tel 521452.

The Falcon Gallery. Honeypot Farm, Wortham, Diss, Norfolk, IP22 1PW. Tel Mellis (037 983) 312.

Fine Art Gallery. 41 Dundas St, Edinburgh, Lothian, EH3 6QQ. Tel 557 4569.

The Fine Art Society Plc. 134 Blythswood St, Glasgow, Strathclyde, G2 4EL. Tel 332 4027.

Fyfe's Antiques. 41 & 48 Thistle St, Edinburgh, Lothian, EH2 1DY. Tel 225 4287.

Galerie Appenzell. High St, Newport, Essex, CB11 3QZ. Tel Saffron Walden (0799) 40623.

The Gallery No.10. 10 Bangor Rd, Groomsport, Co Down. Tel Bangor (0247) 464376.

Gore-Langton Gallery. 5 Castle St, Tunbridge Wells, Kent, TN1 1XT. Tel 26373.

Stephanie Grant Antiques. 38 The Bank, Barnard Castle, Durham. Tel Teesdale (0833) 37437.

David Gray Antiques. 284 Woodlands Rd, Glasgow, Strathclyde. Tel 334 3047.

Great Brampton House Antiques Ltd. Great Brampton House, Madley, Hereford, Hereford & Worcester, HR2 9NA. Tel Golden Valley (0981) 250244.

Guildhall Gallery. 1 Churchgate St, Bury St Edmunds, Suffolk. Tel 62366.

Hampshire Gallery. 18 Lansdowne Rd, Bournemouth, Dorset. Tel 21211.

Raymond Hawley. 5 North Bar Within, Beverley, Humberside, HU17 8AP. Tel Hull (0482) 883193.

Haydon Bridge Antiques. 3 Shaftoe St, Haydon Bridge, Hexham, Northumberland. Tel Haydon Bridge (043484) 200 (priv 461).

The Hayes Gallery. 71 High St, Auchterarder, Tayside, PH3 1BN. Tel 2320 (priv 3442).

Henry-Brett Galleries. Halford House, Bourton-on-the-Water, Gloucestershire. Tel 20443 (priv 028 574 433).

Hinson Fine Paintings. 679 Ecclesall Rd, Sheffield, S.Yorkshire, S11 8TG. Tel 665927.

Francis Iles. Rutland House, La Providence, High St, Rochester, Kent. Tel Medway (0634) 43081, 43082.

Jays Fine Art Dealers. Cambridge Gallery, 4 Cambridge Arcade, Southport, Merseyside, PR8 1AS. Tel 34488 (priv 69500).

T.B. & R. Jordan. Aslak, Aislaby, Eaglescliffe, Stockton-on-Tees, Cleveland, TS16 OQN. Tel 782599.

Kendal Studio Pottery. 2-3 Wildman St, Kendal, Cumbria, LA9 6EN. Tel 23291.

Rodney Kent. West Park Antiques Pavilion, 20 West Park, Harrogate, N.Yorkshire. Tel 60352 (priv 523766).

Kenulf Gallery. High St, Winchcombe, Gloucestershire, GL54 5LJ. Tel 602124.

Kildare Antiques. 19 Kildare St, Dublin, Co Dublin. Tel 763576 (priv 688194).

Kirkgate Picture Gallery. 18 Kirkgate, Thirsk, N.Yorkshire, YO7 1PQ. Tel 24085.

B.R.Knight & Sons. 4 The Quay, St Ives, Cambridgeshire, PE17 4AS. Tel 68295.

Langley Galleries. 153 High St, Rochester, Kent. Tel Medway (0634) 811802.

Ronald A. Lee (Fine Arts) Ltd. The Manor House, Byfleet, Surrey. Tel 43346.

Lincoln Fine Art. 33 The Strait, Lincoln, Lincolnshire. Tel 33029.

Lindfield Galleries Ltd. 59 High St, Lindfield, W.Sussex, RH16 2HN. Tel 2817.

Markswood Gallery. Brook St, Great Bardfield, Essex, CM7 4TY. Tel Great Dunmow (0371) 810106 (priv 810329).

John Mathieson & Co. 48 Frederick St, Edinburgh, Lothian. Tel 225 6798, 225 6686.

Philip & Anne Merridale. Bridge House, Stockbridge, Hampshire. Tel 673.

Peter Montagu-Williams. Gilberts Green, Tanworth-in-Arden, Warwickshire. Tel 2314.

Stephen Moore Ltd. 103 High St, Lewes, E.Sussex, BN7 1XH. Tel 474158.

Ewan Mundy Fine Art. 48 West George St, Glasgow, Strathclyde, G2 1BP. Tel 331 2406.

Colin Murdoch. 56 High St, Kingussie, Highland, PH21 1HZ. Tel 552.

G.R. Naisby & Son. 65 Wellington Road North, Stockport, Greater Manchester. Tel 480 6445 (priv 432 8737).

New Abbey Antiques. Caragh Lodge, Glen Rd, Newtownabbey, Co Antrim, BT37 0RY. Tel Whiteabbey (0231) 62036.

B.M.Newlove. 139-141 Ewell Rd, Surbiton, Surrey. Tel 339 8857.

Northeast Wales Antiques. 15 Well St, Ruthin, Clwyd, LL15 1AE. Tel 2782 (priv 2154).

Cynthia O'Connor & Company Ltd. 17 Duke St, Dublin, Co Dublin. Tel 792198/792177.

Old Hatfield Galleries. 1-3 Park St, Hatfield, Hertfordshire. Tel 71500.

Omell Galleries. Goswell Hill, 134 Peascod St, Windsor, Berkshire, SL4 1DR. Tel 852271.

Oriel Gallery. 17 Clare St, Dublin, Co Dublin. Tel 763410, 684152.

Pelter/Sands Fine Paintings. 19 The Mall,Clifton, Bristol, Avon, BS8 4JG. Tel 741830.

John Prestige Antiques. 1/2 Greenswood Court, Greenswood Rd, Brixham, Devon. Tel 6141, 6723 (priv 3739).

Priests Antiques & Fine Arts. 60 North St, Thame, Oxfordshire. Tel 4461.

Priory Gallery. The Priory, Station Rd,Bishops Cleeve, Cheltenham, Gloucestershire. Tel Bishops Cleeve (024 267) 3226.

Regency Fine Art. 123 Wetherby Rd, Harrogate, N.Yorkshire, HG2 7SH. Tel 883178.

The Reid Gallery Ltd. Mousehill House,Milford, Godalming, Surrey, GU8 5BL. Tel 6990.

Robertson and Cox. 60 George St, Perth, Tayside, PH1 5JL. Tel 26300.

Olivia Rumens. 30 Corve St, Ludlow, Shropshire. Tel 3952.

Saville Antiques. 37 Long St, Devizes, Wiltshire. Tel 3559.

Scott Antiques. 67 Walton St, Walton on the Hill, Surrey, KT20 7RZ. Tel Tadworth (073781) 2097 (priv 0396 882431).

Southgate Gallery. 20 Market Place, Shifnal, Shropshire. Tel Telford (0952) 460351.

St Helier Galleries Ltd. Les Ormes, Ville au Bas, St Ouen, Jersey. Tel 82332.

Stalham Antique Gallery. High St, Stalham, Norfolk. Tel 80636.

Stuart Antiques. 4 High St, Auchterarder, Tayside. Tel 2410.

Tay Street Gallery. 70 Tay St, Perth, Tayside. Tel 20604.

Paul Thomas Fine Paintings. 27 Glebelands Rd, Wokingham, Berkshire, RG11 1DY. Tel 794671.

Thompson's Gallery. 175A High St, Aldeburgh, Suffolk. Tel 3743 (priv 2488).

Thornton Gallery. Snape, Bedale, N.Yorkshire, DL8 2TR. Tel 70318.

Thurso Antiques. Drill Hall,Sinclair St, Thurso, Highland. Tel 63291 (priv 66202).

John Tuckey, Bogan House Gallery. 43 High St, Totnes, Devon. Tel 862025.

Kenneth Upchurch. 30B Church St, Ashbourne, Derbyshire. Tel Derby (0332) 754499.

Walker Galleries Ltd. 6 Montpellier Gdns, Harrogate, N.Yorkshire. Tel 67933.

Wellesley Wilson Antiques. Aldersey Manor, Aldersey, Cheshire, CH3 9EH. Tel Broxton (082 925) 500.

Wellington Fine Art. 14 Park Circus, Glasgow, Strathclyde, G3 6AX. Tel 331 2896.

William Whitfield Antiques. 51-53 Beckenham Lane, Shortlands, Bromley, Kent, ODA BR2. Tel 466 6506 (priv 650 3558).

The Whitgift Galleries. 77 South End, Croydon, Surrey. Tel 01-688 0990.

Woburn Fine Arts. 12 Market Place, Woburn, Bedfordshire, MK17 9PZ. Tel 624.

Xanthus Gallery. September Cottage, Reymerston, Norfolk, NR9 4AG. Tel Dereham (0362) 850862.

Paintings, European

Thos Agnew & Sons Ltd. 43 Old Bond St, London, W1X 4BA. Tel 629 6176.

Albion Fine Art. 61 Ledbury Rd, London, W1. Tel 221 2977.

Baumkotter Gallery. 63A Kensington Church St, London, W8. Tel 937 5171.

Bourne Gallery. 31-33 Lesbourne Rd, Reigate, Surrey. Tel 41614.

Brod Gallery. 24 St James's St, London, SW1A 1HA. Tel 839 3871.

Browse & Darby Ltd. 19 Cork St, London, W1. Tel 734 7984.

William Bruce & Co. Mainhill, Charlesfield, St Boswells, Borders, TD6 0HG. Tel 23628 23788.

The Bury Street Gallery. 11 Bury Street St James's, London, SW1. Tel 930 2902.

Calton Gallery. 10 Royal Terrace, Edinburgh, Lothian, EH7 5AB. Tel 556 1010.

Rupert Cavendish Antiques. 561 Kings Rd, London, SW6 2DZ. Tel 731 7041.

Chaucer Fine Arts Inc. 45 Pimlico Rd, London, SW1. Tel 730 2972.

Clarendon Gallery. 20 Albert Square, Manchester, Greater Manchester. Tel 980 6343.

P. & D. Colnaghi & Co Ltd. 14 Old Bond St, London, W1X 4JL. Tel 491 7408.

Douwes Fine Art Ltd. 38 Duke St, St James's, London, SW1Y 6DF. Tel 839 5795.

Drian Galleries. 7 Porchester Place, Marble Arch, London, W2. Tel 723 9473.

Duits Ltd. 104 Wigmore St, London, W1. Tel 629 5571.

European Fine Arts. 6 Lower Merrion St, Dublin, Co Dublin. Tel 762506.

Fleur de Lys Gallery. 8 Fulham High St, London, SW6 3LQ. Tel 731 7454(priv 0372 67934).

Galerie George. 98 George St, London, W1H 5RI. Tel 935 3322, 935 9998.

Stephen Garratt Fine Paintings. Exhibiting at 146 Brompton Rd,(Knightsbridge Safe Deposit), London, SW3. Tel 603 0681.

Gavin Graham Gallery. 47 Ledbury Rd, London, W11 2AA. Tel 229 4848.

Richard Green. 36 & 44 Dover St, London, W1. Tel 493 3939.

Guildhall Gallery. 1 Churchgate St, Bury St Edmunds, Suffolk. Tel 62366.

Hahn Gallery. 47 Albemarle St, London, W1X 3FE. Tel 493 9196.

Hampshire Gallery. 18 Lansdowne Rd, Bournemouth, Dorset. Tel 21211.

Hancock Gallery. 184 Westbourne Grove, London, W11. Tel 229 7827 (priv 878 5008).

Hazlitt, Gooden & Fox. 38 Bury St,St James's, London, SW1. Tel 930 6422.

Heim Gallery. 59 Jermyn St, St James's, London, SW1Y 6LX. Tel 493 0688.

Hinson Fine Paintings. 679 Ecclesall Rd, Sheffield, S.Yorkshire, S11 8TG. Tel 665927.

Alan Jacobs Gallery. 8 Duke St,St James's, London, SW1. Tel 930 3709.

Charles Jerdein. 38 Albemarle St, London, W1X 3FB. Tel 493 0291.

The Leger Galleries Ltd. 13 Old Bond St, London, W1. Tel 629 3538.

Leinster Fine Art. Fourth Floor, 3 Clifford St, London, W1X 1RA. Tel 437 4534.

Little Winchester Gallery. 36A Kensington Church St, London, W8 4BX. Tel 937 8444.

MacConnal-Mason. 14 Duke St,St James's, London, SW1Y 6DB. Tel 839 7693/4 and 499 6991.

Markswood Gallery. Brook St, Great Bardfield, Essex, CM7 4TY. Tel Great Dunmow (0371) 810106 (priv 810329).

Matthiesen Fine Art Ltd. 7-8 Mason's Yd, Duke St,St James's, London, SW1. Tel 930 2437.

Sybil Mendoza. 2 Andora Court, Brondesbury Park, London, NW6. Tel 459 1705.

John Mitchell & Sons. 8 New Bond St, London, W1Y 9PE. Tel 493 7567.

Peter Nahum. 5 Ryder St, London, SW1Y 6PY. Tel 930 6059 (priv 994 1501).

New Kings Road Gallery. 293 New Kings Rd, London, SW6.

Noortman (London) Ltd. 40-41 Old Bond St, London, W1X 3AF. Tel 491 7284.

Hal O'Nians Ltd. King Street Galleries,17 King St, St James's, London, SW1Y 6QU. Tel 930 9392/3993.

Omell Galleries. 43A Duke St,St James's, London, SW1. Tel 930 7744.

Omell Galleries. 22 Bury St,St James's, London, SW1. Tel 839 4274/5.

Omell Galleries. Goswell Hill, 134 Peascod St, Windsor, Berkshire, SL4 1DR. Tel 852271.

W.H. Patterson Fine Arts Ltd. 19 Albemarle St, London, W1X 3HA. Tel 629 4119.

Pawsey & Payne. 4 Ryder St, London, SW1. Tel 930 4221.

Richard Philp. 59 Ledbury Rd, London, W11. Tel 727 7915.

Pym's Gallery. 13 Motcomb St, Belgravia, London, SW1X 8LB. Tel 235 3050.

Regency Fine Art. 123 Wetherby Rd, Harrogate, N.Yorkshire, HG2 7SH. Tel 883178.

Jane Roberts & Robert Alderman. 2nd Floor,180 New Bond St, London, W1Y 9PD. Tel 491 0168.

Olivia Rumens. 30 Corve St, Ludlow, Shropshire. Tel 3952.

Edward Speelman Ltd. Empire House,175 Piccadilly, London, W1V 0NP. Tel 493 0657.

Marshall Spink Ltd. 18 Albemarle St, London, W1X 3HA. Tel 493 2575 and 493 5280.

St Helier Galleries Ltd. Les Ormes, Ville au Bas, St Ouen, Jersey. Tel 82332.

E. Stacy-Marks Ltd. 24 Cornfield Rd, Eastbourne, E.Sussex, BN21 4QH. Tel 20429 or 32653.

The Tryon and Moorland Gallery. 23-24 Cork St, London, W1X 1HB. Tel 734 6961/2256.

Rafael Valls Gallery. 6 Ryder St,St James's, London, SW1Y 6QB. Tel 930 0029.

Johnny Van Haeften Ltd. 13 Duke St, St James's, London, SW1Y 6DB. Tel 930 3062.

Walker Galleries Ltd. 6 Montpellier Gdns, Harrogate, N.Yorkshire. Tel 67933.

Wylma Wayne Fine Art. 17 Old Bond St, London, W1. Tel 629 4511.

Whitford & Hughes. 6 Duke St, St James's, London, SW1. Tel 930 9332.

Wildenstein & Co Ltd. 147 New Bond St, London, W1Y 0NX. Tel 629 0602.

Williams & Son. 2 Grafton St, London, W1X 3LB. Tel 493 5751, 493 4985.

Paintings, Marine

James Atkinson Gallery. 38 King St, Sandwich, Kent, CT13 9BL. Tel 617216 (priv 613298).

Anthony Belton. 14 Holland Street, London, W8 4LT. Tel 937 1012.

Colin Campbell Fine Paintings. Bath Road, Cowes, Isle of Wight. Tel 200 124 (priv 855 300).

Colin Campbell Fine Paintings. The Gallery,The Square, Yarmouth, Isle of Wight, PO41 0NS. Tel 760784.

The Chimes. Market Place, Reepham, Norfolk, NR10 4JJ. Tel Norwich (0603) 870480.

The Corner House Gallery. The Square, Axbridge, Somerset, BS26 2AP. Tel 732757.

David Cross Gallery. 3A Boyces Ave, Clifton, Bristol, Avon, BS8 4AA. Tel 732614.

Delmas Antiques. Hurst Green, E.Sussex, TN19 7PN. Tel 345.

Colin Denny. 18 Cale St, London, SW3 3QU. Tel 584 0240.

The Falcon Gallery. Honeypot Farm, Wortham, Diss, Norfolk, IP22 1PW. Tel Mellis (037 983) 312.

Fleur de Lys Gallery. 8 Fulham High St, London, SW6 3LQ. Tel 731 7454(priv 0372 67934).

Hahn Gallery. 47 Albemarle St, London, W1X 3FE. Tel 493 9196.

The Hayes Gallery. 71 High St, Auchterarder, Tayside, PH3 1BN. Tel 2320 (priv 3442).

Mangate Gallery. 3 Chiswick Lane, London, W4 2LR. Tel 995 9867.

Paul Mason. 149E Sloane St, London, SW1. Tel 730 3683.

David Messum Ltd. The Studio, Lords Wood, Marlow, Buckinghamshire, SL7 2QS. Tel 6565/6 (priv 4169).

Old Solent House Galleries. Quay St, Lymington, Hampshire, SO41 9AR. Tel 75511.

Omell Galleries. 43A Duke St,St James's, London, SW1. Tel 930 7744.

N.R. Omell. 6 Duke Street, St James's, London, SW1. Tel 839 6223/4.

The Parker Gallery. 12A & 12B Berkeley St, Piccadilly, London, W1X 5AD. Tel 499 5906/7.

Relcy Antiques. 9 Nelson Rd, Greenwich, London, SE10. Tel 858 2811/2.

Royal Exchange Art Gallery. 14 Royal Exchange, London, EC3V 3LL. Tel 283 4400.

Spenser S A. 16b Grafton St, Bond St, London, W1X 3LF. Tel 723 9149.

Sutcliffe Galleries. 8 Albert St, Harrogate, N.Yorkshire. Tel 62976.

Swan Fine Art. Camden Passage, Islington, London, N1. Tel 226 5335.

Oliver Swann Galleries. 117A-119 Walton St, London, SW3 2HP. Tel 581 4229.

Vectis Fine Arts Gallery. 41 High St, Bembridge, Isle of Wight. Tel 852316.

Directory Entries are Free and ADDITIONS OR CORRECTIONS will be welcomed by *THE EDITOR, British Art and Antiques Directory, National Magazine House, 72 Broadwick Street, London W1V 2BP*

Woodbridge. 15A George St, Bath, Avon, BA1 2EN.

The Wyllie Gallery. 12 Needham Road, London, W11. Tel 727 0606 (priv 584 6024).

Paintings, Modern

Thos Agnew & Sons Ltd. 43 Old Bond St, London, W1X 4BA. Tel 629 6176.

AIR Gallery. 6 & 8 Rosebery Ave, London, EC1. Tel 278 7751.

Albion Fine Art. 61 Ledbury Rd, London, W1. Tel 221 2977.

Alwin Gallery. 9-10 Grafton St, Bond St, London, W1. Tel 499 0314.

Amalgam. 3 Barnes High St, London, SW13. Tel 878 1279.

The Belgrave Gallery. 22 Masons Yard,Duke St, St James's, London, SW1. Tel 930 0294.

Ian Birksted Gallery. 57 Wood Lane,Highgate, London, N6 5UD. Tel 348 7638.

Bluecoat Gallery. School Lane, Liverpool, Merseyside, L1 3BX. Tel 709 5689.

Brandler Galleries. 1 Coptfold Rd, Brentwood, Essex, CM13 4BM. Tel 222269.

William Bruce & Co. Mainhill, Charlesfield, St Boswells, Borders, TD6 0HG. Tel 23628 23788.

Centaur Gallery. Great Expectations,82 Highgate Village, London, N6. Tel 340 0087.

Coracle Press. 235 Camberwell New Road, London, SE5. Tel 703 5201.

Cotswold Galleries. The Square, Stow-on-the-Wold, Gloucestershire, GL54 1AB. Tel 30586.

Crane Kalman Gallery. 178 Brompton Rd, London, SW3. Tel 584 7566.

Curwen Gallery. 4 Windmill St, off Charlotte St, London, W1. Tel 639 1459.

Anthony d'Offay Gallery. 9 & 23 Dering St, New Bond St, London, W1. Tel 499 4100.

De Fresnes (Antiques). Cessnock Castle, Galston, Strathclyde. Tel 829314.

J. & T.J.Fairhurst. The Art Gallery, 7 Parsonage Sq,Bedford St, Norwich, Norfolk, NR2 1A5. Tel 614214.

Angela Flowers Gallery Ltd. 11 Tottenham Mews, London, W1. Tel 637 3089.

Galerie 39. 96 George St, London, W1. Tel 487 5038.

Gallery 10 Ltd. 10 Grosvenor St, London, W1X 9FB. Tel 491 8103.

Gimpel Fils. 30 Davies St, London, W1Y 1LG. Tel 493 2488.

The Ginnel. Lloyds House, 16 Lloyd Street, Manchester, Greater Manchester. Tel 833 9037.

Godalming Galleries Ltd. 3 Wharf St, Godalming, Surrey, GU7 1NN. Tel 22254.

Nigel Greenwood Gallery and Bookshop. 4 New Burlington St, London, W1X 1FE. Tel 434 3795/6.

Sally Hunter and Patrick Seale Fine Art. 2 Motcomb St, Belgrave Sq, London, SW1X 8JU. Tel 235 0934.

Nicola Jacobs Gallery. 9 Cork St, London, W1. Tel 437 3868.

Bernard Jacobson Ltd. 2A Cork St, London, W1. Tel 439 8355.

Annely Juda. 11 Tottenham Mews, off Tottenham St, London, W1P 9PJ. Tel 637 5517.

Knoedler Kasmin. 22 Cork St, London, W1. Tel 439 1096.

Langley Galleries. 153 High St, Rochester, Kent. Tel Medway (0634) 811802.

Lasson Gallery. 34 Duke St, St James's, London. Tel 930 5950.

Lefevre Gallery. 30 Bruton St, London, W1X 8JD. Tel 493 1572.

Leinster Fine Art. Fourth Floor, 3 Clifford St, London, W1X 1RA. Tel 437 4534.

Alan Leonard Antiques. 503 Smithdown Rd, Liverpool, Merseyside, L15 5AE. Tel 733 5277 (priv 722 4766).

Lisson Gallery. 66-68 Bell St, London, NW1 6SP. Tel 262 1539.

MacConnal-Mason. 14 Duke St,St James's, London, SW1Y 6DB. Tel 839 7693/4 and 499 6991.

Mandell's Gallery. Elm Hill, Norwich, Norfolk, NR3 1HN. Tel 626892, 629180.

Mercury Gallery Ltd. 26 Cork St, London, W1. Tel 734 7800.

Mulberry House Galleries. Codmore Hill, Pulborough, W.Sussex, RH20 1BQ. Tel 2463.

October Gallery. 24 Old Gloucester St, London, WC1. Tel 242 7367.

Ogle Fine Arts. Ogle Gallery, 12 Rotunda Terrace,Montpellier St, Cheltenham, Gloucestershire. Tel 518605 (priv 31011).

Omell Galleries. 40 Albemarle St, London, W1. Tel 499 3685/6.

Omell Galleries. Goswell Hill, 134 Peascod St, Windsor, Berkshire, SL4 1DR. Tel 852271.

Paton Gallery. 2 Langley Court, Long Acre, London, WC2E 9JY. Tel 379 7854.

W.H. Patterson Fine Arts Ltd. 19 Albemarle St, London, W1X 3HA. Tel 629 4119.

Peoples Gallery Limited. 71 & 73 Prince of Wales Rd, London, NW5 3LT. Tel 267 0433.

Phoenix Gallery Ltd. 97 High St, Lavenham, Suffolk, CO10 9PZ. Tel 247356.

The Piccadilly Gallery. 16 Cork St, London, W1X 1PF. Tel 629 2875.

Edwin Pollard Gallery. 23 Church Rd, Wimbledon Village, London, SW19 5DQ. Tel 946 4114.

Quinton Green Fine Art. 5/6 Cork St, London, W1. Tel 734 9179.

Juda Rowan Gallery. 11 Tottenham Mews, Off Tottenham St, London, W1P 9PJ. Tel 637 5517/8.

South London Art Gallery. Peckham Rd, London, SE5.

Michael Stewart Fine Art Galleries Ltd. 61 Quarry Street, Guildford, Surrey. Tel 504359.

Thumb Gallery. 20-21 d'Arblay St, London, W1. Tel 434 2931.

Waddington Galleries Ltd. 2,4,11 & 34 Cork St, London, W1. Tel 437 8611.

Whitford & Hughes. 6 Duke St, St James's, London, SW1. Tel 930 9332.

Paintings, Modern British

Austin/Desmond Fine Art Ltd. Brookside Farm,Winkfield Row, Ascot, Berkshire. Tel Winkfield Row (0344) 886147.

The Belgrave Gallery. 22 Masons Yard,Duke St, St James's, London, SW1. Tel 930 0294.

Bourne Fine Art Ltd. 4 Dundas St, Edinburgh, Lothian, EH3 6HZ. Tel 557 4050.

Brandler Galleries. 1 Coptfold Rd, Brentwood, Essex, CM13 4BM. Tel 222269.

Cambridge Fine Art Ltd. 'Priesthouse', 33 Church St,Little Shelford, Cambridge, Cambridgeshire, CB2 5HG. Tel 842866 (priv 843537).

Connaught Brown PLC. 2 Albemarle St, London, W1X 3HF. Tel 408 0362.

John Davies (Fine Paintings). The Church Street Gallery,Church St, Stow-on-the-Wold, Gloucestershire, GL54 1BB. Tel 31698 (priv 31790).

Fairhurst Gallery. 291 New King's Rd, London, SW6 4RE. Tel 736 9132.

The Fine Art Society Plc. 12 Great King St, Edinburgh, Lothian, EH3 6QL. Tel 556 0305.

The Fine Art Society Plc. 148 New Bond St, London, W1Y 0JT. Tel 629 5116.

Fosse Gallery. The Square, Stow-on-the-Wold, Gloucestershire. Tel Cotswold (0451) 31319.

Gothick Dream. 14 Needham Rd, London, W11. Tel 221 0417.

Simon Hilton. Flemings Hill Farm,Great Easton, Great Dunmow, Essex, CM6 2ER. Tel Bishops Stortford (0279) 850107.

Howards of Aberystwyth. 10 Alexandra Rd, Aberystwyth, Dyfed. Tel 4973.

Manya Igel Fine Arts Ltd. 21-22 Peters Court, Porchester Rd, London, W2. Tel 229 1669/8429 (priv 6770).

Gillian Jason Gallery. 42 Inverness St, London, NW1. Tel 267 4835.

Lyons Gallery. 47 Mill Lane,West Hampstead, London, NW6 1NB. Tel 794 3537.

The Mayor Gallery. 22A Cork Street, London, W1. Tel 734 3558.

David Messum Ltd. Marlow, Bucks. Tel 6565

Duncan R. Miller Fine Arts. 11 Wedderburn Rd, London, NW3. Tel 435 5462 (priv 794 2119).

Montpelier Studio. 4 Montpelier St, London, SW7 1EZ. Tel 584 0667.

Ewan Mundy Fine Art. 48 West George St, Glasgow, Strathclyde, G2 1BP. Tel 331 2406.

Nevill Gallery. 2A York St, Bath, Avon, BA1 1NG. Tel 66904.

Nevill Gallery. 43 St Peter's St, Canterbury, Kent, CT1 2BG. Tel 65291.

Paton Gallery. 2 Langley Court, Long Acre, London, WC2E 9JY. Tel 379 7854.

Pym's Gallery. 13 Motcomb St, Belgravia, London, SW1X 8LB. Tel 235 3050.

Martin Scadgell Fine Art. Mulberry House Galleries,Codmore Hill, Pulborough, W.Sussex. Tel 2463.

Tadema. 10 Charlton Place, Camden Passage, London, N1. Tel 359 1055.

Twentieth Century Gallery. 821 Fulham Rd, London, SW6 5H6. Tel 731 5888.

Upton Lodge Galleries. Avening House, Avening, Tetbury, Gloucestershire, GL8 8NH. Tel Nailsworth (045 383) 4048.

Paintings, Portrait Miniatures

see Portrait Miniatures

Paintings, Portraits

Didier Aaron (London) Ltd. 21 Ryder St, London, SW1Y 6PX. Tel 839 4716/7.

Baggott Church Street Ltd. Church Street, Stow-on-the-Wold, Gloucestershire, GL54 1BB. Tel 30370.

Cambridge Fine Art Ltd. 'Priesthouse', 33 Church St, Little Shelford, Cambridge, Cambridgeshire, CB2 5HG. Tel 842866 (priv 843537).

Simon Carter Gallery. 23 Market Hill, Woodbridge, Suffolk, IP12 4LX. Tel 2242.

David Cooke Fine Paintings. Old Post House, Playden, Rye, E.Sussex. Tel Iden (07978) 303.

Delmas Antiques. Hurst Green, E.Sussex, TN19 7PN. Tel 345.

Lane Fine Art Ltd. 86-88 Pimlico Road, London, SW1. Tel 730 7374.

Sally Mitchell Fine Arts. Thornlea, Askham, Nottinghamshire, NG22 0RN. Tel Gamston (077783) 234.

Charles & Joan Mortimer & Sons. Sugar House, School St, Great Chesterford, Essex, CB10 1NN. Tel Saffron Walden (0799) 30261.

Swan Fine Art. Camden Passage, Islington, London, N1. Tel 226 5335.

The Weiss Gallery PLC. 1B Albemarle St, London, W1X 3HF. Tel 409 0035 (priv 212 481).

Wilkins & Wilkins. 1 Barrett St, St Christopher's Place, London, W1. Tel 935 9613.

Paintings, Primitive

The Ark Angel. 14 Camden Passage, London, N1 8ED. Tel 226 1644.

Duncan J. Baggott. The Square, Stow-on-the-Wold, Gloucestershire, GL54 1AB. Tel 30662.

Anthony Belton. 14 Holland Street, London, W8 4LT. Tel 937 1012.

Simon Carter Gallery. 23 Market Hill, Woodbridge, Suffolk, IP12 4LX. Tel 2242.

David Clark. The Plestor, Selborne, Hampshire. Tel 274.

Elias Clark Antiques Ltd. 1 The Cobbles, High Street, Bletchingley, Surrey, RH1 4PB. Tel Godstone (0883) 843714.

The Crane Gallery. 171A Sloane St, (1st Floor), London, SW1. Tel 235 2464.

The Falcon Gallery. Honeypot Farm, Wortham, Diss, Norfolk, IP22 1PW. Tel Mellis (037 983) 312.

Five Five Six Antiques. 556 King's Rd, London, SW6. Tel 731 2016 (priv 624 5173).

Gene & Sally Foster (Antiques). 27A Belvedere, Lansdown Rd, Bath, Avon, BA1 5HR. Tel 28256 (priv 28058).

Iona Antiques. Stand 107, Gray's Antique Market, 58 Davies St, London, W1Y 1FH. Tel 499 2386.

Richard & Pamela Nadin. 12 Paul St, Frome, Somerset, BA11 1DT. Tel 64957.

Dermot & Jill Palmer Antiques. 7-8 Union St, The Lanes, Brighton & Hove, E.Sussex. Tel 28669.

Rutland Gallery & Co. 32a St George St, London, W1. Tel 499 5636.

Alistair Sampson Antiques (inc Tobias Jellinek). 156 Brompton Rd, London, SW3 1HW. Tel 589 5272, 581 2267.

Geoffrey Stead. The Old Rectory, Dowdeswell, Gloucestershire, GL54 5LX. Tel Cheltenham (0242) 820571.

Woodbridge. 15A George St, Bath, Avon, BA1 2EN.

Paintings, Sporting

Arthur Ackermann & Son Ltd. 3 Old Bond St, London, W1X 3TD. Tel 493 3288.

Addison-Ross Gallery. 40 Eaton Tce, Belgravia, London, SW1. Tel 730 1536.

Cadogan Gallery. 15 Pont St, London, SW1. Tel 235 4526.

David Cross Gallery. 3A Boyces Ave, Clifton, Bristol, Avon, BS8 4AA. Tel 732614.

The Falcon Gallery. Honeypot Farm, Wortham, Diss, Norfolk, IP22 1PW. Tel Mellis (037 983) 312.

Frost & Reed Ltd. 41 New Bond St, London, W1. Tel 629 2457.

The Hayes Gallery. 71 High St, Auchterarder, Tayside, PH3 1BN. Tel 2320 (priv 3442).

Henry-Brett Galleries. Halford House, Bourton-on-the-Water, Gloucestershire. Tel 20443 (priv 028 574 433).

Malcolm Innes Gallery. 67 George St, Edinburgh, Lothian. Tel 226 4151.

Malcolm Innes Gallery. 172 Walton St, London, SW3. Tel 584 0575.

Iona Antiques. Stand 107, Gray's Antique Market, 58 Davies St, London, W1Y 1FH. Tel 499 2386.

Kensington Galleries. Badgers Wood, West End Lane, Esher, Surrey, KT10 8LB. Tel 64407.

The Keyser Gallery. Quarry House, Corston, Malmesbury, Wiltshire, SN16 0HJ. Tel 2429.

Lane Fine Art Ltd. 86-88 Pimlico Road, London, SW1. Tel 730 7374.

Marlborough Sporting Gallery & Bookshop. 6 Kingbury St, Marlborough, Wiltshire. Tel 54074.

The William Marler Gallery. 36/38 Dyer St, Cirencester, Gloucestershire, GL7 2PF. Tel 68526.

William Marler Gallery. Dawes Mansion, Church St, Ludlow, Shropshire. Tel 4160.

Paul Mason. 149E Sloane St, London, SW1. Tel 730 3683.

Sally Mitchell Fine Arts. Thornlea, Askham, Nottinghamshire, NG22 0RN. Tel Gamston (077783) 234.

Guy Nevill Pictures. 10C Bramerton St, London, SW3 5JX. Tel 351 4292.

The Parker Gallery. 12A & 12B Berkeley St, Piccadilly, London, W1X 5AD. Tel 499 5906/7.

Pawsey & Payne. 4 Ryder St, London, SW1. Tel 930 4221.

Royal Exchange Art Gallery. 14 Royal Exchange, London, EC3V 3LL. Tel 283 4400.

R.S.J. Savage & Son. Alfred St, Northampton, Northamptonshire, NN1 5EY. Tel 33852 (priv 405482).

Spenser S A. 16b Grafton St, Bond St, London, W1X 3LF. Tel 723 9149.

Sport & Country Gallery. Northwood House, Bulkington, Nuneaton, Warwickshire, CV12 9RX. Tel 314335.

Sutcliffe Galleries. 8 Albert St, Harrogate, N.Yorkshire. Tel 62976.

Swan Fine Art. Camden Passage, Islington, London, N1. Tel 226 5335.

Thorntons of Harrogate. 1 Montpellier Gdns, Harrogate, N.Yorkshire, HG1 2TF. Tel 504118.

Trove. 71 Pimlico Rd, London, SW1. Tel 730 6514.

Paintings, Topographical

Brotherton Gallery Ltd. 77 Walton St, London, SW3. Tel 589 6848.

David Cross Gallery. 3A Boyces Ave, Clifton, Bristol, Avon, BS8 4AA. Tel 732614.

The Falcon Gallery. Honeypot Farm, Wortham, Diss, Norfolk, IP22 1PW. Tel Mellis (037 983) 312.

Hahn Gallery. 47 Albemarle St, London, W1X 3FE. Tel 493 9196.

Hobhouse Ltd. 39 Duke St, St James's, London, SW1 6DF. Tel 930 9308.

Paul Mason. 149E Sloane St, London, SW1. Tel 730 3683.

Mathaf Gallery Ltd. 24 Motcomb St, London, SW1X 8JU. Tel 235 0010.

The Parker Gallery. 12A & 12B Berkeley St, Piccadilly, London, W1X 5AD. Tel 499 5906/7.

Royal Exchange Art Gallery. 14 Royal Exchange, London, EC3V 3LL. Tel 283 4400.

Sutcliffe Galleries. 8 Albert St, Harrogate, N.Yorkshire. Tel 62976.

Woodbridge. 15A George St, Bath, Avon, BA1 2EN.

Paintings, Watercolours

see Watercolours

Paintings, Early to 17th Century

Baumkotter Gallery. 63A Kensington Church St, London, W8. Tel 937 5171.

Caelt Gallery. 182 Westbourne Grove, London, W11. Tel 229 9309 (priv 229 0303).

David Cambridge. 13 Rotunda Terrace, Cheltenham, Gloucestershire. Tel 42178.

David Carritt Limited. 15 Duke Street, London, SW1. Tel 930 8733.

Chaucer Fine Arts Inc. 45 Pimlico Rd, London, SW1. Tel 730 2972.

The Cider House Galleries Ltd. Norfolk House, 80 High St, Bletchingley, Surrey, RH1 4PA. Tel Godstone (0883) 842198.

B.Cohen & Sons. 35 Bury St, St James's, London, SW1Y 6AY. Tel 839 6466/7.

P. & D. Colnaghi & Co Ltd. 14 Old Bond St, London, W1X 4JL. Tel 491 7408.

F.T. Dent. 58 Goldhurst Terrace, London, NW6. Tel 624 8383.

European Fine Arts. 6 Lower Merrion St, Dublin, Co Dublin. Tel 762506.

Fulda Gallery. 19 Vine St, Salford, Greater Manchester, M7 0NY. Tel 792 1962.

Christopher Gibbs Ltd. 118 New Bond St, London, W1Y 9AB. Tel 629 2008.

Hampshire Gallery. 18 Lansdowne Rd, Bournemouth, Dorset. Tel 21211.

Harari & Johns Ltd. 12 Duke Street, St James's, London, SW1. Tel 839 7671.

Alan Jacobs Gallery. 8 Duke St, St James's, London, SW1. Tel 930 3709.

R.& J. Jones. 137 Kensington Church St, London, W8. Tel 221 4026.

Lane Fine Art Ltd. 86-88 Pimlico Road, London, SW1. Tel 730 7374.

Leonard Lassalle. 21 The Pantiles, Tunbridge Wells, Kent, TN2 5TD. Tel 31645.

The Leger Galleries Ltd. 13 Old Bond St, London, W1. Tel 629 3538.

Matthiesen Fine Art Ltd. 7-8 Mason's Yd, Duke St, St James's, London, SW1. Tel 930 2437.

John Mitchell & Sons. 8 New Bond St, London, W1Y 9PE. Tel 493 7567.

Morton Morris & Co. 32 Bury St, St James's, London, SW1. Tel 930 2825.

Charles & Joan Mortimer & Sons. Sugar House, School St, Great Chesterford, Essex, CB10 1NN. Tel Saffron Walden (0799) 30261.

Noortman (London) Ltd. 40-41 Old Bond St, London, W1X 3AF. Tel 491 7284.

Hal O'Nians Ltd. King Street Galleries, 17 King St, St James's, London, SW1Y 6QU. Tel 930 9392/3993.

Old Hall Gallery Ltd. Crown Lodge, Crown Rd, Morden, Surrey, SM4 5BY. Tel 540 9918.

Sabin & Vanderkar (Fine Paintings) Ltd. 43 Duke St, St James's, London, SW1. Tel 839 1091.

Sabin Galleries Ltd. Campden Lodge, 82 Campden Hill Rd, London, W8 7AA. Tel 937 0471.

Sloane Galleries. 49 Poole Rd, Westbourne, Bournemouth, Dorset, BH4 9BA. Tel 764684.

Somerville & Simpson Ltd. 11 Savile Row, London, W1. Tel 437 5414.

Edward Speelman Ltd. Empire House, 175 Piccadilly, London, W1V 0NP. Tel 493 0657.

James H.Starkey Galleries. 49 Highgate, Beverley, Hull, Humberside, HU17 9ON. Tel 881179.

Michael Tollemache Ltd. 78 Cadogan Pl, London, SW1. Tel 235 5107.

Rafael Valls Gallery. 6 Ryder St, St James's, London, SW1Y 6QB. Tel 930 0029.

Johnny Van Haeften Ltd. 13 Duke St, St James's, London, SW1Y 6DB. Tel 930 3062.

Wilkins & Wilkins. 1 Barrett St, St Christopher's Place, London, W1. Tel 935 9613.

Paintings, 18th Century

London

Thos Agnew & Sons Ltd. 43 Old Bond St, London, W1X 4BA. Tel 629 6176.

Albion Fine Art. 61 Ledbury Rd, London, W1. Tel 221 2977.

Baumkotter Gallery. 63A Kensington Church St, London, W8. Tel 937 5171.

Cadogan Gallery. 15 Pont St, London, SW1. Tel 235 4526.

Caelt Gallery. 182 Westbourne Grove, London, W11. Tel 229 9309 (priv 229 0303).

Clarendon Gallery. 8 Vigo Street, London, W1. Tel 439 4557.

B.Cohen & Sons. 35 Bury St, St James's, London, SW1Y 6AY. Tel 839 6466/7.

Colnaghi and Simon. 70 Pimlico Rd, London, SW1W 8LS. Tel 730 8673.

P. & D. Colnaghi & Co Ltd. 14 Old Bond St, London, W1X 4JL. Tel 491 7408.

F.T. Dent. 58 Goldhurst Terrace, London, NW6. Tel 624 8383.

Owen Edgar Gallery. 9 West Halkin St, London, SW1X 8JL. Tel 235 8989.

Jocelyn Feilding Fine Art Ltd. 8 Duke St, St James's, London, SW1. Tel 839 5040.

Gavin Graham Gallery. 47 Ledbury Rd, London, W11 2AA. Tel 229 4848.

Hahn Gallery. 47 Albemarle St, London, W1X 3FE. Tel 493 9196.

Hazlitt, Gooden & Fox. 38 Bury St,St James's, London, SW1. Tel 930 6422.

Hobhouse Ltd. 39 Duke St, St James's, London, SW1 6DF. Tel 930 9308.

R.& J. Jones. 137 Kensington Church St, London, W8. Tel 221 4026.

The Leger Galleries Ltd. 13 Old Bond St, London, W1. Tel 629 3538.

Matthiesen Fine Art Ltd. 7-8 Mason's Yd, Duke St,St James's, London, SW1. Tel 930 2437.

John Mitchell & Sons. 8 New Bond St, London, W1Y 9PE. Tel 493 7567.

Morton Morris & Co. 32 Bury St, St James's, London, SW1. Tel 930 2825.

Hal O'Nians Ltd. King Street Galleries,17 King St, St James's, London, SW1Y 6QU. Tel 930 9392/3993.

Oscar & Peter Johnson Ltd. Lowndes Lodge Gallery, 27 Lowndes St, London, SW1. Tel 235 6464,.

Sabin & Vanderkar (Fine Paintings) Ltd. 43 Duke St, St James's, London, SW1. Tel 839 1091.

Sabin Galleries Ltd. Campden Lodge, 82 Campden Hill Rd, London, W8 7AA. Tel 937 0471.

Frank T. Sabin Ltd. 4 New Bond St, London, W1Y 9PE. Tel 499 5553.

Stern Art Dealers Co. 46 Ledbury Rd, London, W11 2AB. Tel 229 6187.

Walker Galleries of Harrogate Ltd. 3 Cale St,Chelsea Green, London, SW3. Tel 351 5988.

Wilkins & Wilkins. 1 Barrett St, St Christopher's Place, London, W1. Tel 935 9613.

Regions

Beaufort Gallery. Beaumont St, Hexham, Northumberland.

The Bell Gallery. 13 Adelaide Park, off Malone Rd, Belfast, Belfast. Tel 662998.

David Cambridge. 13 Rotunda Terrace, Cheltenham, Gloucestershire. Tel 42178.

Castle Gallery. 87 High St, Berkhamsted, Hertfordshire. Tel 4814.

The Cider House Galleries Ltd. Norfolk House, 80 High St, Bletchingley, Surrey, RH1 4PA. Tel Godstone (0883) 842198.

Christopher Cole (Fine Paintings) Ltd. 1 London End, Beaconsfield, Buckinghamshire, HP9 2HN. Tel 71274.

European Fine Arts. 6 Lower Merrion St, Dublin, Co Dublin. Tel 762506.

J. & T.J.Fairhurst. The Art Gallery, 7 Parsonage Sq,Bedford St, Norwich, Norfolk, NR2 1A5. Tel 614214.

Fulda Gallery. 19 Vine St, Salford, Greater Manchester, M7 0NY. Tel 792 1962.

W.Greenwood. 7 Church Wynd,Burneston, Bedale, N.Yorkshire. Tel 24830.

Guildhall Gallery. 1 Churchgate St, Bury St Edmunds, Suffolk. Tel 62366.

Richard Hagen Ltd. Yew Tree House, Broadway, Hereford & Worcester, WR12 7DT. Tel 853624.

Hammersley Galleries. 12 Roundwood Lane, Harpenden, Hertfordshire, AL5 3BZ. Tel 4053.

Hampshire Gallery. 18 Lansdowne Rd, Bournemouth, Dorset. Tel 21211.

The Hayes Gallery. 71 High St, Auchterarder, Tayside, PH3 1BN. Tel 2320 (priv 3442).

E.D.Levine. The Antique Gallery, Church St, Cromer, Norfolk. Tel 512335.

Mandell's Gallery. Elm Hill, Norwich, Norfolk, NR3 1HN. Tel 626892, 629180.

Matthews & Davies Fine Art Ltd. 85-87 Eastgate, Cowbridge, S.Glamorgan, CF7 7AA. Tel 4340.

Millhouse Fine Arts. The Square, Petworth, W.Sussex. Tel 43080.

New Gallery. Abele Tree House,9 Fore St, Budleigh Salterton, Devon, EX9 6NG. Tel 3768.

Old Hall Gallery Ltd. Crown Lodge, Crown Rd, Morden, Surrey, SM4 5BY. Tel 540 9918.

Paul Rich Fine Art. Brick Cottage, Lower Woodend, Marlow, Buckinghamshire, SL7 2HN. Tel 2665.

Sloane Galleries. 49 Poole Rd,Westbourne, Bournemouth, Dorset, BH4 9BA. Tel 764684.

James H.Starkey Galleries. 49 Highgate, Beverley, Hull, Humberside, HU17 9ON. Tel 881179.

Walker Galleries Ltd. 6 Montpellier Gdns, Harrogate, N.Yorkshire. Tel 67933.

H.S.Wellby Ltd. Ponders, Hedgerley Lane, Gerrards Cross, Buckinghamshire, SL9 8SY. Tel 887957.

H.S.Wellby Ltd. The Malt House,4 Church End, Haddenham, Buckinghamshire. Tel 290036.

Westerham Galleries. The Green (on A25), Westerham, Kent. Tel 63359.

Woodbridge. 15A George St, Bath, Avon, BA1 2EN.

Paintings, 19th Century

London

Albion Fine Art. 61 Ledbury Rd, London, W1. Tel 221 2977.

Alton Gallery. 72 Church Rd,Barnes, London, SW13. Tel 748 0606,748 8244.

Appleby's. 8 Ryder St, St James's, London, SW1Y 6QB. Tel 930 6507.

The Bank House Gallery. 8-10 The Broadway,Mill Hill, London, NW7 3LL. Tel 906 3124.

Baumkotter Gallery. 63A Kensington Church St, London, W8. Tel 937 5171.

Bourne Fine Art Ltd. 14 Mason's Yard,Duke St, St James's, London, SW1. Tel 930 4215.

Brotherton Gallery Ltd. 77 Walton St, London, SW3. Tel 589 6848.

Browse & Darby Ltd. 19 Cork St, London, W1. Tel 734 7984.

The Bury Street Gallery. 11 Bury Street St James's, London, SW1. Tel 930 2902.

Cadogan Gallery. 15 Pont St, London, SW1. Tel 235 4526.

Caelt Gallery. 182 Westbourne Grove, London, W11. Tel 229 9309 (priv 229 0303).

Clarendon Gallery. 8 Vigo Street, London, W1. Tel 439 4557.

Clarges Gallery. 158 Walton Street, London, SW3. Tel 584 3022.

Clifton Fine Art. 6 Bristol Gardens,Little Venice, London, W9 2JG. Tel 286 9121.

Colnaghi and Simon. 70 Pimlico Rd, London, SW1W 8LS. Tel 730 8673.

Connaught Brown PLC. 2 Albemarle St, London, W1X 3HF. Tel 408 0362.

Douwes Fine Art Ltd. 38 Duke St, St James's, London, SW1Y 6DF. Tel 839 5795.

Owen Edgar Gallery. 9 West Halkin St, London, SW1X 8JL. Tel 235 8989.

Editions Graphiques Gallery. 3 Clifford St, London, W1. Tel 734 3944.

Jocelyn Feilding Fine Art Ltd. 8 Duke St, St James's, London, SW1. Tel 839 5040.

Fiddes Watt. Studio 7, 52A Avonmore Rd, London, W14 8XU. Tel 603 9015.

The Fine Art Society Plc. 148 New Bond St, London, W1Y 0JT. Tel 629 5116.

Fischer Fine Art Ltd. 30 King St, London, SW1. Tel 839 3942.

Fleur de Lys Gallery. 8 Fulham High St, London, SW6 3LQ. Tel 731 7454(priv 0372 67934).

Frost & Reed Ltd. 41 New Bond St, London, W1. Tel 629 2457.

Galerie George. 98 George St, London, W1H 5RI. Tel 935 3322, 935 9998.

Gavin Graham Gallery. 47 Ledbury Rd, London, W11 2AA. Tel 229 4848.

Hahn Gallery. 47 Albemarle St, London, W1X 3FE. Tel 493 9196.

Hamlet Gallery. 5 Pond St, Hampstead, London, NW3. Tel 794 7904 (priv 452 0056).

Julian Hartnoll. 14 Mason's Yard, Duke St,St James's, London, SW1. Tel 839 3842.

Hazlitt, Gooden & Fox. 38 Bury St,St James's, London, SW1. Tel 930 6422.

Hobhouse Ltd. 39 Duke St, St James's, London, SW1 6DF. Tel 930 9308.

Iona Antiques. Stand 107, Gray's Antique Market,58 Davies St, London, W1Y 1FH. Tel 499 2386.

R.& J. Jones. 137 Kensington Church St, London, W8. Tel 221 4026.

James Kirkman Limited. 46 Brompton Sq, London, SW3 2AF. Tel 589 4328,.

Lefevre Gallery. 30 Bruton St, London, W1X 8JD. Tel 493 1572.

Little Winchester Gallery. 36A Kensington Church St, London, W8 4BX. Tel 937 8444.

Maas Gallery. 15A Clifford St, New Bond St, London, W1X 1RF. Tel 734 2302.

MacConnal-Mason. 14 Duke St,St James's, London, SW1Y 6DB. Tel 839 7693/4 and 499 6991.

Mangate Gallery. 3 Chiswick Lane, London, W4 2LR. Tel 995 9867.

Marlborough Fine Art (London) Ltd. 6 Albemarle St, London, W1X 4BY. Tel 629 5161.

Roy Miles Fine Paintings Ltd. 3 Berkeley Square, London, W1X 5HG. Tel 491 3611.

John Mitchell & Sons. 8 New Bond St, London, W1Y 9PE. Tel 493 7567.

Morton Morris & Co. 32 Bury St, St James's, London, SW1. Tel 930 2825.

Peter Nahum. 5 Ryder St, London, SW1Y 6PY. Tel 930 6059 (priv 994 1501).

Newman & Cooling Ltd. 38 Albemarle St, London, W1X 4QJ. Tel 629 5224, 930 6068.

Noortman (London) Ltd. 40-41 Old Bond St, London, W1X 3AF. Tel 491 7284.

Omell Galleries. 43A Duke St,St James's, London, SW1. Tel 930 7744.

Omell Galleries. 22 Bury St,St James's, London, SW1. Tel 839 4274/5.

N.R. Omell. 6 Duke Street, St James's, London, SW1. Tel 839 6223/4.

Michael Parkin Fine Art Ltd. 11 Motcomb St, London, SW1. Tel 235 8144, 235 1845.

W.H. Patterson Fine Arts Ltd. 19 Albemarle St, London, W1X 3HA. Tel 629 4119.

Oscar & Peter Johnson Ltd. Lowndes Lodge Gallery, 27 Lowndes St, London, SW1. Tel 235 6464,.

Polak Gallery. 21 King St, St James's, London, SWY 6QY. Tel 930 9245, 930 3911.

Alex Reid & Lefevre Ltd. 30 Bruton St, London, W1. Tel 493 1572.

The Richmond Gallery. 8 Cork St, London, W1. Tel 437 9422.

Royal Exchange Art Gallery. 14 Royal Exchange, London, EC3V 3LL. Tel 283 4400.

Sabin Galleries Ltd. Campden Lodge, 82 Campden Hill Rd, London, W8 7AA. Tel 937 0471.

Frank T. Sabin Ltd. 4 New Bond St, London, W1Y 9PE. Tel 499 5553.

Edward Speelman Ltd. Empire House,175 Piccadilly, London, W1V 0NP. Tel 493 0657.

Spenser S A. 16b Grafton St, Bond St, London, W1X 3LF. Tel 723 9149.

Swan Fine Art. Camden Passage, Islington, London, N1. Tel 226 5335.

Rafael Valls Gallery. 6 Ryder St,St James's, London, SW1Y 6QB. Tel 930 0029.

Walker-Bagshawe. 73 Walton St, London, SW3. Tel 589 4582 (priv 381 2172).

Whitford & Hughes. 6 Duke St, St James's, London, SW1. Tel 930 9332.

Wilkins & Wilkins. 1 Barrett St, St Christopher's Place, London, W1. Tel 935 9613.

Williams & Son. 2 Grafton St, London, W1X 3LB. Tel 493 5751, 493 4985.

Christopher Wood Gallery. 15 Motcomb St, London, SW1. Tel 235 9141 (priv 828 1092).

Regions

Apollo Galleries. 61, 65 and 67 South End, Croydon, Surrey, CR0 1BF. Tel 681 3727, 680 1968.

The Arden Gallery. 54 High St, Henley-in-Arden, Warwickshire, B95 5AN. Tel 2520.

Peter Arnold Gallery. 3 Knolls Close, Castle St, Wingrave, Aylesbury, Buckinghamshire, HP22 4PY. Tel 681568.

Astley House - Fine Art. Astley House, High St, Moreton-in-Marsh, Gloucestershire, GL54 0LL. Tel 50601.

James Atkinson Gallery. 38 King St, Sandwich, Kent, CT13 9BL. Tel 617216 (priv 613298).

Attic Gallery. 88 Elm Rd, Wisbech, Cambridgeshire. Tel 583734.

Barkes & Richardson. 38 High Petergate, York, N.Yorkshire, YO1 2HW. Tel 51080.

Beaufort Gallery. Beaumont St, Hexham, Northumberland.

Beaulieu Fine Arts. High St, Beaulieu, Hampshire. Tel 612089.

The Bell Gallery. 13 Adelaide Park, off Malone Rd, Belfast, Belfast. Tel 662998.

Bourne Fine Art Ltd. 4 Dundas St, Edinburgh, Lothian, EH3 6HZ. Tel 557 4050.

Bourne Gallery. 31-33 Lesbourne Rd, Reigate, Surrey. Tel 41614.

Patrick F. Brown. 15 South William St, Dublin, Co Dublin. Tel 719013.

Calton Gallery. 10 Royal Terrace, Edinburgh, Lothian, EH7 5AB. Tel 556 1010.

Cambridge Fine Art Ltd. 'Priesthouse', 33 Church St,Little Shelford, Cambridge, Cambridgeshire, CB2 5HG. Tel 842866 (priv 843537).

Castle Gallery. 87 High St, Berkhamsted, Hertfordshire. Tel 4814.

The Church Street Gallery. 17 Church St, Saffron Walden, Essex, CB10 1JW. Tel 24422 (priv 0279-850423).

The Cider House Galleries Ltd. Norfolk House, 80 High St, Bletchingley, Surrey, RH1 4PA. Tel Godstone (0883) 842198.

Christopher Cole (Fine Paintings) Ltd. 1 London End, Beaconsfield, Buckinghamshire, HP9 2HN. Tel 71274.

John H. Collings. Antique Village, Knightcott, Banwell, Avon, BS24 6HS. Tel 823181 (priv 812030).

J. Collins and Son (Est.1953). The Studio, 63 & 28 High St, Bideford, Devon, EX39 2AN. Tel 73103 (priv 76485).

Colmore Galleries Ltd. 52 High St, Henley-in-Arden, Warwickshire. Tel 2938.

Cotswold Galleries. The Square, Stow-on-the-Wold, Gloucestershire, GL54 1AB. Tel 30586.

Coughton Galleries Ltd. Coughton Court, Alcester, Warwickshire, B49 5JA. Tel 762642.

Coyle Fine Art. 6 Lower Merrion St, Dublin, Co Dublin. Tel 762506.

Edward Cross Fine Paintings. 128 Oatlands Drive, Weybridge, Surrey, KT13 9HL. Tel 51093.

Cumbrian Fine Art Galleries. Lane House, Cow Brow,(postal address:Via Carnforth,Lancs), Kirkby Lonsdale, Cumbria. Tel Crooklands (044 87) 208.

John Davies (Fine Paintings). The Church Street Gallery,Church St, Stow-on-the-Wold, Gloucestershire, GL54 1BB. Tel 31698 (priv 31790).

De Fresnes (Antiques). Cessnock Castle, Galston, Strathclyde. Tel 829314.

The Dean Gallery. 42 Dean St, Newcastle upon Tyne, Tyne & Wear, NE1 1PG. Tel 321208.

The Devonshire Gallery. 45 Abbey Rd, Torquay, Devon, TQ2 5NQ. Tel 27144.

Driffold Gallery. The Smithy,78 Birmingham Rd, Sutton Coldfield, W.Midlands. Tel 021-355 5433.

Eastbourne Fine Art. 9 Meads St, Eastbourne, E.Sussex, BN20 7QY. Tel 25634.

Eastgate Antiques. 85 Eastgate, Cowbridge, S.Glamorgan, CF7 7AA. Tel 5111.

J. & T.J.Fairhurst. The Art Gallery, 7 Parsonage Sq,Bedford St, Norwich, Norfolk, NR2 1A5. Tel 614214.

The Falcon Gallery. Honeypot Farm, Wortham, Diss, Norfolk, IP22 1PW. Tel Mellis (037 983) 312.

Fine Art Petworth PLC. Fernhurst Gallery,Crossways, Fernhurst, Haslemere, Surrey. Tel 56177 (priv 0252-711923).

The Fine Art Society Plc. 12 Great King St, Edinburgh, Lothian, EH3 6QL. Tel 556 0305.

Fulda Gallery. 19 Vine St, Salford, Greater Manchester, M7 0NY. Tel 792 1962.

Gallery 77. 18 Princess St, Bradshawgate, Bolton, Greater Manchester, BL1 1EJ. Tel 35252.

The Grange Gallery & Fine Arts Ltd. 39 New St, St Helier, Jersey.

W.Greenwood. 7 Church Wynd,Burneston, Bedale, N.Yorkshire. Tel 24830.

Guildhall Gallery. 1 Churchgate St, Bury St Edmunds, Suffolk. Tel 62366.

Richard Hagen Ltd. Yew Tree House, Broadway, Hereford & Worcester, WR12 7DT. Tel 853624.

Hammersley Galleries. 12 Roundwood Lane, Harpenden, Hertfordshire, AL5 3BZ. Tel 4053.

Hampshire Gallery. 18 Lansdowne Rd, Bournemouth, Dorset. Tel 21211.

Hay Loft Gallery. Berry Wormington, Broadway, Hereford & Worcester, WR12 7NH. Tel Toddington (024 269) 202.

The Hayes Gallery. 71 High St, Auchterarder, Tayside, PH3 1BN. Tel 2320 (priv 3442).

The Hinton Gallery. Crutchfield Farm,Hookwood, Horley, Surrey, RH6 0HT. Tel 862417.

Hood and Broomfield Lyme Galleries. 29 Albert St, Newcastle-under-Lyme, Staffordshire, ST5 1JP. Tel 626859.

Itchen Gallery. 29 Middle Brook St, Winchester, Hampshire. Tel 61309.

T.B. & R. Jordan. Aslak, Aislaby, Eaglescliffe, Stockton-on-Tees, Cleveland, TS16 0QN. Tel 782599.

Kirkgate Picture Gallery. 18 Kirkgate, Thirsk, N.Yorkshire, YO7 1PQ. Tel 24085.

Langley Galleries. 153 High St, Rochester, Kent. Tel Medway (0634) 811802.

Leverington Hall Gallery. Leverington, Wisbech, Cambridgeshire, PE13 5DE. Tel 582055.

Mandell's Gallery. Elm Hill, Norwich, Norfolk, NR3 1HN. Tel 626892, 629180.

Matthews & Davies Fine Art Ltd. 85-87 Eastgate, Cowbridge, S.Glamorgan, CF7 7AA. Tel 4340.

David Messum Ltd. The Studio, Lords Wood, Marlow, Buckinghamshire, SL7 2QS. Tel 6565/6 (priv 4169).

Meyers Gallery. 66 High St, Ingatestone, Essex. Tel Brentwood (0277) 355335 (priv 215446).

Mill House Antiques. 139 Abbey Foregate, Shrewsbury, Shropshire. Tel 240328.

Millhouse Fine Arts. The Square, Petworth, W.Sussex. Tel 43080.

New Abbey Antiques. Caragh Lodge, Glen Rd, Newtownabbey, Co Antrim, BT37 0RY. Tel Whiteabbey (0231) 62036.

New Gallery. Abele Tree House,9 Fore St, Budleigh Salterton, Devon, EX9 6NG. Tel 3768.

John Noott. Picton House Gallery, High St, Broadway, Hereford & Worcester, WR12 7AL. Tel Evesham (0386) 852787.

Old Hall Gallery Ltd. Crown Lodge, Crown Rd, Morden, Surrey, SM4 5BY. Tel 540 9918.

Old Pump House. 20 High St, Lyndhurst, Hampshire, SO4 7BD. Tel 2137.

Omell Galleries. Goswell Hill, 134 Peascod St, Windsor, Berkshire, SL4 1DR. Tel 852271.

Park House. Park St, Stow-on-the-Wold, Gloucestershire. Tel 30159.

Piano Nobile Fine Paintings. 26 Richmond Hill, Richmond, Surrey, TW10 6QX. Tel 01-940 2435.

Plaitford House Galleries. Plaitford, Hampshire. Tel West Wellow (0794) 22221.

Priory Gallery. The Priory, Station Rd,Bishops Cleeve, Cheltenham, Gloucestershire. Tel Bishops Cleeve (024 267) 3226.

The Reid Gallery Ltd. Mousehill House,Milford, Godalming, Surrey, GU8 5BL. Tel 6990.

Paul Rich Fine Art. Brick Cottage, Lower Woodend, Marlow, Buckinghamshire, SL7 2HN. Tel 2665.

Tony Sanders Antiques and New Gallery. 14 Chapel St, Penzance, Cornwall, TR18 4AW. Tel 66620 (priv 68461).

R.S.J. Savage & Son. Alfred St, Northampton, Northamptonshire, NN1 5EY. Tel 33852 (priv 405482).

Martin Scadgell Fine Art. Mulberry House Galleries,Codmore Hill, Pulborough, W.Sussex. Tel 2463.

Severn Fine Art. 77 Wyle Cop, Shrewsbury, Shropshire. Tel 247514.

A.W. John Simmons & Son. 77 South End, Croydon, Surrey, CR0 1BF. Tel 688 0990.

Skeaping Gallery. Townend House,Lydford, Okehampton, Devon, EX20 4AR. Tel 383.

Sloane Galleries. 49 Poole Rd,Westbourne, Bournemouth, Dorset, BH4 9BA. Tel 764684.

Southgate Gallery. 20 Market Place, Shifnal, Shropshire. Tel Telford (0952) 460351.

Sport & Country Gallery. Northwood House, Bulkington, Nuneaton, Warwickshire, CV12 9RX. Tel 314335.

E. Stacy-Marks Ltd. 24 Cornfield Rd, Eastbourne, E.Sussex, BN21 4QH. Tel 20429 or 32653.

James H.Starkey Galleries. 49 Highgate, Beverley, Hull, Humberside, HU17 9ON. Tel 881179.

Tamar Gallery. 17 Wickham Ave, Bexhill, E.Sussex. Tel 221835.

Thicke Galleries Swansea. 26 St Andrews Close, Mayals, Swansea, W.Glamorgan, SA3 5DX. Tel 401656.

Carole Thomas Fine Arts. First Floor,32A Sun St, Hitchin, Hertfordshire, SJ5 1AH. Tel 36077.

Paul Thomas Fine Paintings. 27 Glebelands Rd, Wokingham, Berkshire, RG11 1DY. Tel 794671.

Brian Trengove Antiques and Picture Gallery. 46 South End, Croydon, Surrey, CR0 1DP. Tel 688 2155.

Kenneth Upchurch. 30B Church St, Ashbourne, Derbyshire. Tel Derby (0332) 754499.

Michael Webb Fine Paintings. Cefn-Llwyn,Llangristiolus, Bodorgan, Anglesey, Gwynedd, LL62 5DN. Tel Bodorgan (0407) 840336.

H.S.Wellby Ltd. Ponders, Hedgerley Lane, Gerrards Cross, Buckinghamshire, SL9 8SY. Tel 887957.

H.S.Wellby Ltd. The Malt House,4 Church End, Haddenham, Buckinghamshire. Tel 290036.

Westerham Galleries. The Green (on A25), Westerham, Kent. Tel 63359.

Wharfedale Galleries. Antiques & Pine17 Rupert Rd,Middleton, Ilkley, W.Yorkshire, LS29 0AQ. Tel 602676.

Woodbridge. 15A George St, Bath, Avon, BA1 2EN.

York Gallery, Tunbridge Wells Ltd. No 6 Castle St, Tunbridge Wells, Kent. Tel 22326 (4 lines).

Paintings, 20th Century

London

Alton Gallery. 72 Church Rd,Barnes, London, SW13. Tel 748 0606,748 8244.

Blond Fine Art. 22 Princes St, London, W1. Tel 437 1230.

Erika Brandl - Paintings. 758 Fulham Rd, London, SW6 5SH. Tel 736 0497.

Brotherton Gallery Ltd. 77 Walton St, London, SW3. Tel 589 6848.

Browse & Darby Ltd. 19 Cork St, London, W1. Tel 734 7984.

Caelt Gallery. 182 Westbourne Grove, London, W11. Tel 229 9309 (priv 229 0303).

Clarges Gallery. 158 Walton Street, London, SW3. Tel 584 3022.

Clifton Fine Art. 6 Bristol Gardens,Little Venice, London, W9 2JG. Tel 286 9121.

Anthony d'Offay Gallery. 9 & 23 Dering St, New Bond St, London, W1. Tel 499 4100.

Editions Graphiques Gallery. 3 Clifford St, London, W1. Tel 734 3944.

The Fine Art Society Plc. 148 New Bond St, London, W1Y 0JT. Tel 629 5116.

Fischer Fine Art Ltd. 30 King St, London, SW1. Tel 839 3942.

Frost & Reed Ltd. 41 New Bond St, London, W1. Tel 629 2457.

Galerie George. 98 George St, London, W1H 5RI. Tel 935 3322, 935 9998.

The Gallery Muswell Hill. 105 Muswell Hill Broadway, London, N10.

Thomas Gibson Fine Art Limited. 9a New Bond St, London, W1Y 9PE. Tel 499 8572.

Grosvenor Gallery. 48 South Molton St, London, W1Y 2JU. Tel 629 0891.

Hamlet Gallery. 5 Pond St, Hampstead, London, NW3. Tel 794 7904 (priv 452 0056).

Michael John Decorative Arts Ltd. 25A Lowndes St, London, SW1. Tel 235 3154/5.

Annely Juda. 11 Tottenham Mews, off Tottenham St, London, W1P 9PJ. Tel 637 5517.

James Kirkman Limited. 46 Brompton Sq, London, SW3 2AF. Tel 589 4328,.

Lefevre Gallery. 30 Bruton St, London, W1X 8JD. Tel 493 1572.

Leinster Fine Art. Fourth Floor, 3 Clifford St, London, W1X 1RA. Tel 437 4534.

Little Winchester Gallery. 36A Kensington Church St, London, W8 4BX. Tel 937 8444.

Lumley Cazalet Ltd. 24 Davies St, London, W1. Tel 499 5058.

MacConnal-Mason. 14 Duke St,St James's, London, SW1Y 6DB. Tel 839 7693/4 and 499 6991.

Mangate Gallery. 3 Chiswick Lane, London, W4 2LR. Tel 995 9867.

Marlborough Fine Art (London) Ltd. 6 Albemarle St, London, W1X 4BY. Tel 629 5161.

Mercury Gallery Ltd. 26 Cork St, London, W1. Tel 734 7800.

Montpelier Studio. 4 Montpelier St, London, SW7 1EZ. Tel 584 0667.

Peter Nahum. 5 Ryder St, London, SW1Y 6PY. Tel 930 6059 (priv 994 1501).

New Grafton Gallery. 49 Church Rd, Barnes, London, SW13 9HH. Tel 748 8850.

Noortman (London) Ltd. 40-41 Old Bond St, London, W1X 3AF. Tel 491 7284.

L'Odeon. 173 Fulham Rd, London, SW3. Tel 581 3640 (priv 736 4216).

Michael Parkin Fine Art Ltd. 11 Motcomb St, London, SW1. Tel 235 8144, 235 1845.

W.H. Patterson Fine Arts Ltd. 19 Albemarle St, London, W1X 3HA. Tel 629 4119.

The Piccadilly Gallery. 16 Cork St, London, W1X 1PF. Tel 629 2875.

Polak Gallery. 21 King St, St James's, London, SWY 6QY. Tel 930 9245, 930 3911.

Redfern Gallery. 20 Cork St, London, W1X 2HL. Tel 734 1732/734 0578.

Alex Reid & Lefevre Ltd. 30 Bruton St, London, W1. Tel 493 1572.

The Richmond Gallery. 8 Cork St, London, W1. Tel 437 9422.

Royal Exchange Art Gallery. 14 Royal Exchange, London, EC3V 3LL. Tel 283 4400.

Rutland Gallery & Co. 32a St George St, London, W1. Tel 499 5636.

The Solomon Gallery. 31 Bruton Place, London, W1X 7AB. Tel 499 4701/2.

Spenser S A. 16b Grafton St, Bond St, London, W1X 3LF. Tel 723 9149.

Trafford Gallery. 119 Mount St, London, W1Y 5HB. Tel 499 2021.

Leigh Underhill Gallery. 100 Islington High St,Camden Passage, Islington, London, N1. Tel 226 5673.

Whitford & Hughes. 6 Duke St, St James's, London, SW1. Tel 930 9332.

Regions

Apollo Galleries. 61, 65 and 67 South End, Croydon, Surrey, CR0 1BF. Tel 681 3727, 680 1968.

The Arden Gallery. 54 High St, Henley-in-Arden, Warwickshire, B95 5AN. Tel 2520.

Peter Arnold Gallery. 3 Knolls Close, Castle St, Wingrave, Aylesbury, Buckinghamshire, HP22 4PY. Tel 681568.

Barkes & Richardson. 38 High Petergate, York, N.Yorkshire, YO1 2HW. Tel 51080.

Beaulieu Fine Arts. High St, Beaulieu, Hampshire. Tel 612089.

Bourne Fine Art Ltd. 4 Dundas St, Edinburgh, Lothian, EH3 6HZ. Tel 557 4050.

Calton Gallery. 10 Royal Terrace, Edinburgh, Lothian, EH7 5AB. Tel 556 1010.

Simon Carter Gallery. 23 Market Hill, Woodbridge, Suffolk, IP12 4LX. Tel 2242.

The Church Street Gallery. 17 Church St, Saffron Walden, Essex, CB10 1JW. Tel 24422 (priv 0279-850423).

Colmore Galleries Ltd. 52 High St, Henley-in-Arden, Warwickshire. Tel 2938.

Coughton Galleries Ltd. Coughton Court, Alcester, Warwickshire, B49 5JA. Tel 762642.

Cumbrian Fine Art Galleries. Lane House, Cow Brow,(postal address:Via Carnforth,Lancs), Kirkby Lonsdale, Cumbria. Tel Crooklands (044 87) 208.

John Davies (Fine Paintings). The Church Street Gallery,Church St, Stow-on-the-Wold, Gloucestershire, GL54 1BB. Tel 31698 (priv 31790).

The Dean Gallery. 42 Dean St, Newcastle upon Tyne, Tyne & Wear, NE1 1PG. Tel 321208.

Driffold Gallery. The Smithy,78 Birmingham Rd, Sutton Coldfield, W.Midlands. Tel 021-355 5433.

Eastbourne Fine Art. 9 Meads St, Eastbourne, E.Sussex, BN20 7QY. Tel 25634.

Exquisite Arts Ltd. 22 Bore St, Lichfield, Staffordshire. Tel 253626, (priv 253697).

Fine Art Petworth PLC. Fernhurst Gallery,Crossways, Fernhurst, Haslemere, Surrey. Tel 56177 (priv 0252-711923).

The Fine Art Society Plc. 12 Great King St, Edinburgh, Lothian, EH3 6QL. Tel 556 0305.

Fulda Gallery. 19 Vine St, Salford, Greater Manchester, M7 0NY. Tel 792 1962.

Gallery 77. 18 Princess St, Bradshawgate, Bolton, Greater Manchester, BL1 1EJ. Tel 35252.

W.Greenwood. 7 Church Wynd,Burneston, Bedale, N.Yorkshire. Tel 24830.

The Hayes Gallery. 71 High St, Auchterarder, Tayside, PH3 1BN. Tel 2320 (priv 3442).

T.B. & R. Jordan. Aslak, Aislaby, Eaglescliffe, Stockton-on-Tees, Cleveland, TS16 0QN. Tel 782599.

Kirkgate Picture Gallery. 18 Kirkgate, Thirsk, N.Yorkshire, YO7 1PQ. Tel 24085.

Langley Galleries. 153 High St, Rochester, Kent. Tel Medway (0634) 811802.

George Large Gallery. 47-49 High St, Redbourn, Hertfordshire. Tel 3140.

Alan Leonard Antiques. 503 Smithdown Rd, Liverpool, Merseyside, L15 5AE. Tel 733 5277 (priv 722 4766).

New Gallery. Abele Tree House,9 Fore St, Budleigh Salterton, Devon, EX9 6NG. Tel 3768.

John Noott. Picton House Gallery, High St, Broadway, Hereford & Worcester, WR12 7AL. Tel Evesham (0386) 852787.

Piano Nobile Fine Paintings. 26 Richmond Hill, Richmond, Surrey, TW10 6QX. Tel 01-940 2435.

Plaitford House Galleries. Plaitford, Hampshire. Tel West Wellow (0794) 22221.

Priory Gallery. The Priory, Station Rd,Bishops Cleeve, Cheltenham, Gloucestershire. Tel Bishops Cleeve (024 267) 3226.

Paul Rich Fine Art. Brick Cottage, Lower Woodend, Marlow, Buckinghamshire, SL7 2HN. Tel 2665.

Tony Sanders Antiques and New Gallery. 14 Chapel St, Penzance, Cornwall, TR18 4AW. Tel 66620 (priv 68461).

Severn Fine Art. 77 Wyle Cop, Shrewsbury, Shropshire. Tel 247514.

A.W. John Simmons & Son. 77 South End, Croydon, Surrey, CR0 1BF. Tel 688 0990.

Skeaping Gallery. Townend House,Lydford, Okehampton, Devon, EX20 4AR. Tel 383.

Sloane Galleries. 49 Poole Rd,Westbourne, Bournemouth, Dorset, BH4 9BA. Tel 764684.

Southgate Gallery. 20 Market Place, Shifnal, Shropshire. Tel Telford (0952) 460351.

Sport & Country Gallery. Northwood House, Bulkington, Nuneaton, Warwickshire, CV12 9RX. Tel 314335.

E. Stacy-Marks Ltd. 24 Cornfield Rd, Eastbourne, E.Sussex, BN21 4QH. Tel 20429 or 32653.

James H.Starkey Galleries. 49 Highgate, Beverley, Hull, Humberside, HU17 9ON. Tel 881179.

Stewart Gallery. 48 Devonshire Rd, Bexhill, E.Sussex. Tel 223410.

Stewart Gallery. 25 Grove Rd, Eastbourne, E.Sussex. Tel 29588.

Paul Thomas Fine Paintings. 27 Glebelands Rd, Wokingham, Berkshire, RG11 1DY. Tel 794671.

West Gate Fine Art. 16 St Peter St, Canterbury, Kent, CT1 2BQ. Tel 453636 (priv 03043 62093).

Wharfedale Galleries. Antiques & Pine17 Rupert Rd,Middleton, Ilkley, W.Yorkshire, LS29 0AQ. Tel 602676.

Paperweights

see Glass Paperweights

Papier-mache

Arenski. 29-31 George St, London, W1H 5PE. Tel 486 0678.

Coombe House Antiques. Malling St, Lewes, E.Sussex. Tel 473862.

The Corner Cupboard. At the Old Bakery,Next to the Fleece, Boxford, Suffolk, CO6 5DX. Tel 210123.

The Corner Cupboard. At the Old Bakery,Next to the Fleece, Boxford, Suffolk, CO6 5DX. Tel 210123.

Peter Francis. 26 Museum St, London, WC1A 1JT. Tel 637 0165.

Thomas Goode & Co (London) Ltd. 19 South Audley St, London, W1Y 6BN. Tel 499 2823 (7 lines).

Halcyon Days. 14 Brook St, London, W1Y 1AA. Tel 629 8811.

House of Antiques. 4 College St, Petersfield, Hampshire, GU31 4AD. Tel 62172.

Fiona & Bill Laidlaw Antiques. 40 Gordon Place,Holland St, London, W8 5JF. Tel 937 8493.

Michael & Margaret Parker. 24 Cheval Place, London, SW7. Tel 589 0133.

Simon Leigh Rose Fine Decorative Antiques. 569 Kings Rd,Chelsea, London, SW6. Tel 731 7356.

David Seyfried. 759 Fulham Rd, London, SW6. Tel 731 4230.

Sharrington Antiques. Sharrington, Melton Constable, Norfolk, NR24 2PQ. Tel 861411 (priv 860719).

Keith Skeel. 94 Islington High St, London, N1 8EG. Tel 359 9894.

Pamela Teignmouth & Son. 108 Kensington Church St, London, W8. Tel 229 1602.

The Winter Palace. 69 Kensington Church Street, London, W8. Tel 937 2410.

Persian Works of Art

see Islamic and Persian Works of Art

Pewter

see also Brass

Albert Bartram. 177 Hivings Hill, Chesham, Buckinghamshire. Tel 783271.

Robin Bellamy Ltd. 97 Corn St, Witney, Oxfordshire, OX8 7DL. Tel 4793.

J.H. Blakey & Sons Ltd. Church St, Brierfield, Lancashire, BB9 5AD. Tel Nelson (0282) 63593/602493.

Bruton-Brighton. 31-32 Meeting House Lane, Brighton & Hove, E.Sussex, BN1 1HB. Tel 26591.

Jack Casimir Ltd. 'The Brass Shop', 23 Pembridge Rd, London, W11 3HG. Tel 727 8643.

Castle Antiques. 330 Lawnmarket, Edinburgh, Lothian, ME1 1JT. Tel 225 7615.

Country Life Antiques. Sheep St, Stow-on-the-Wold, Gloucestershire, GL54 1JS. Tel Cotswold (0451) 30776.

K.A.Davies Antiques. 248 Cowbridge Rd East, Cardiff, S.Glamorgan. Tel 29989.

P.J.Fradley. Ellastone Old House, Ellastone, Ashbourne, Derbyshire, DE6 2GU. Tel Ellastone (033 524) 291.

Gadsby's Antiques. 88-90 The Street, Ashtead, Surrey. Tel 72305.

Hansen Antiques. 119 The Street, Boughton, Kent. Tel Canterbury (0277) 751 421.

P.G. Kydd. 70 Colston St, Bristol, Avon, BS1 5AZ. Tel 299265.

Robin Martin. 44 Ledbury Rd, London, W11. Tel 727 1301 (priv 727 1300).

Moolham Mill Antiques. Moolham Mill, Moolham Lane, Ilminster, Somerset, TA19 0PD. Tel 2834.

Peter Norden Antiques. High St, Burford, Oxfordshire, OX8 4XX. Tel 2121 (priv 0993 830064).

Old Saddlers Antiques. Church Rd, Goudhurst, Cranbrook, Kent, TN17 1BH. Tel 211458.

Ormond Antiques. 32 Lower Ormond Quay, Dublin, Co Dublin. Tel 741569.

Peppers Period Pieces. 22/23 Churchgate St, Bury St Edmunds, Suffolk. Tel 68786 (priv 0359 50606).

Singing Bird Antiques. 13 Main Rd, Dorrington, Shropshire. Tel 208.

Strouds of Southwell Antiques. 3 Westgate, Southwell, Nottinghamshire. Tel 815001.

James & Ann Tillett. Tombland House, 12-13 Tombland, Norwich, Norfolk, NR3 1HF. Tel 624914.

Twenty-One Antiques. 21 High St, Westerham, Kent. Tel 63055.

Warwick Antiques. 16 & 18 High St, Warwick, Warwickshire, CV34 4AP. Tel 492482.

Anthony Welling Antiques. Broadway Barn, High St, Ripley, Surrey, GU23 6AQ. Tel Guildford (0483) 225384.

Witney Antiques. 96-98 Corn St, Witney, Oxfordshire, OX8 7BU. Tel 3902.

Photographers

Nicholas Alloway, Photographer of Antiques. Basement studio, Chenil Galleries,181 King's Rd, London, SW3. Tel 352 7217, 870 4677.

Barnes and Webster Limited. 7a Hanson St, London, W1. Tel 631 0192.

Benmuir Photographic Services Ltd. 475 London Rd, Camberley, Surrey, GU15 3JA. Tel 26267.

Blantern & Davis. 11 Wetherell Place,Clifton, Bristol, Avon, BS8 1AR. Tel 741747.

The Churchill Group of Companies. Hoopers Hill,Lymington Rd, New Milton, Hampshire, BH25 5PZ. Tel 620400,620123.

A.C.Cooper Ltd. 10 Pollen St, London, W1R 9PH. Tel 629 7585.

Prudence Cuming Associates Ltd. 28-29 Dover St, London, W1X 3PA. Tel 629 6430, 629 1638.

Dawes & Billings. 176A Old Shoreham Rd, Brighton & Hove, E.Sussex. Tel 722971.

John Dewar. 2 North East Circus Place, Edinburgh, Lothian, EH3 6SP. Tel 225 2691.

Elm Studios Ltd. 42 Princes St, Ipswich, Suffolk. Tel 52069.

Focol Photography. 7 The Corridor, Bath, Avon, BA1 5AP. Tel 66343.

Raymond Fortt Studios Ltd. 95 Ewell Rd, Surbiton, Surrey, KT6 6AH. Tel 399 6765.

Foto-Call. 138 Sloane St, London, SW1. Tel 730 2764.

Fotowest. 19 Westgate St, Bath, Avon, BA1 1EQ. Tel 63195.

Frame One Photographic. 23 Old High St, Hemel Hempstead, Hertfordshire. Tel 57028.

Gastrell House. 33 Long St, Tetbury, Gloucestershire, GL8 8AA. Tel 52228.

Peter John Gates. 2nd Floor, 94 New Bond St, London, W1. Tel 629 4962.

Jonathan Gaunt. 5 Cold Corner Cottages,Oare, Marlborough, Wiltshire, SH8 5JL.

Godfrey New Photographics Ltd. 195 Faraday Ave, Sidcup, Kent. Tel 300 7637.

David C.Golby. 2 Queens Terrace, Totnes, Devon. Tel 862048.

Sonia Halliday Photographs. Primrose Cottage, Weston Turville, Buckinghamshire. Tel Stoke Mandeville(029 661) 2266.

Hanover Studios. 104-112 Marylebone Lane, London, W1. Tel 487 4431/2.

Hawkley Studio Associates Ltd. 3 Weston Close, Ballfield Rd, Godalming, Surrey, GU7 2EY. Tel 22366.

Hymor Photographers Ltd. 41-43 Prospect St, Caversham, Reading, Berkshire. Tel 475656, 479450.

A.G.Ingram Ltd. 74 Broughton St, Edinburgh, Lothian. Tel 556 7824.

Colin Jeffrey Associates. 9 East St, Crewkerne, Somerset, TA18 7AB. Tel 73242.

Norman Jones (Industrial Photography) Ltd. Bethesda Building, 11 Bethesda St, Hanley, Staffordshire, ST1 3DE. Tel Stoke-on-Trent (0782) 268548.

Kershaw Studios. 15 Davygate, York, N.Yorkshire, YO1 2QR. Tel 55190.

Jack Knight. 20 Bridge St, Hungerford, Berkshire. Tel 2902.

A.C.Littlejohns. 43 Lower Gunstone, Bideford, Devon. Tel 2478.

Michael Maclaren Photography. 322 Webster's Land, Edinburgh, Lothian, EH1 2RU. Tel 228 6895.

S.& O. Mathews. Stitches Farm House, Eridge, E.Sussex, TN3 9JB. Tel Rotherfield (089 285) 2848.

Nicholas Meyjes Photography. 12 Forge Close, Horton-cum-Studley, Oxford, Oxfordshire, OX9 1BL. Tel Stanton St John (086 735) 496.

Rex Moreton. The Model Farm, Wolvesnewton, Gwent, NP6 6NZ. Tel 231.

Norwin Photographics. 65 Fishergate, Preston, Lancashire, PR1 8BJ. Tel 54214.

Erik Pelham. P.O.Box 28, Wallingford, Oxfordshire, OX10 0ED. Tel 33568 24hr ans phone.

Photography West. 37 Silver St, Bradford-on-Avon, Wiltshire. Tel 2719.

Graham Portlock. Unit D2, The Maltings, Station Rd, Sawbridgeworth, Hertfordshire. Tel Bishop's Stortford (0279) 722992.

Reeve Photography. Denny Industrial Centre, Waterbeach, Cambridgeshire. Tel Cambridge (0223) 861824.

Edward Reeves. 159 High St, Lewes, E.Sussex, BN7 1XU. Tel 473274.

Harry Smith. The Studios, Hitchman Mews,West St, Chipping Norton, Oxfordshire, OX7 5AA. Tel 2624 (priv 61612).

Studio Edmark. Wheatsheaf Yard,High St, Oxford, Oxfordshire. Tel 24186.

Studio Morgan. Commercial Photography Co. 6-7 Queens Gardens, Aberdeen, Grampian. Tel 631250.

Kevin Taylor. 24 Shipfield, Norwich, Norfolk, NR3 4QN. Tel 402869.

Thomas-Photos Oxford. 1 Collingwood Close, Headington, Oxford, Oxfordshire. Tel 61350.

Top Floor Studio. Quayside, Woodbridge, Suffolk, IP12 1BH. Tel 3627.

Vollans Photography. 26/28 Cheapside, Knaresborough, N.Yorkshire. Tel 862626.

Walter Gardiner Photography. Southdownview Rd, Worthing, W.Sussex, BN14 8NL.

Chris Wright Photography. The Old Granary,19A Greenhill St, Stratford-upon-Avon, Warwickshire. Tel 299766.

Photographic and Cameras

Antiquarius Camera Collectors Shop. Stand L4, Antiquarius, 135 King's Rd, London, SW3. Tel 352 7217.

Carronade. 63 West Regent St, Glasgow, Strathclyde. Tel 332 5600 (priv 649 3655).

Glennie Middleton and Bullock. 3 Church St, Diss, Norfolk, IP22 3DD. Tel 51617.

Great Western Antique Centre Ltd. Bartlett St, Bath, Avon, BA1 2QZ. Tel (office) 24243.

Ron Jones Antiques. Tri Brynwcws,Llanaber, Barmouth, Gwynedd, LL42 1RR. Tel 280691.

Vintage Cameras Ltd. 254-256 Kirkdale Corner, Sydenham, London, SE26 4NL. Tel 778 5416.

Photographs

Antiquarius Camera Collectors Shop. Stand L4, Antiquarius, 135 King's Rd, London, SW3. Tel 352 7217.

Colin Jeffrey Associates. 9 East St, Crewkerne, Somerset, TA18 7AB. Tel 73242.

N.W.Lott & H.J.Gerrish Ltd. The Old Rectory, Froxfield, Wiltshire, SN8 3JY. Tel Hungerford (0488) 82188.

N.W.Lott & H.J.Gerrish Ltd. 14 Mason's Yard,Duke Street St James's, London, SW1. Tel 930 1353.

Mona Antiqua & Tudor Rose. 31-32 Castle St, Beaumaris, Gwynedd. Tel 810203.

Vintage Cameras Ltd. 254-256 Kirkdale Corner, Sydenham, London, SE26 4NL. Tel 778 5416.

Christopher Wood Gallery. 15 Motcomb St, London, SW1. Tel 235 9141 (priv 828 1092).

Pine Furniture

London

Adams Antiques. 47 Chalk Farm Rd, London, NW1. Tel 267 9241.

The Ark Angel. 14 Camden Passage, London, N1 8ED. Tel 226 1644.

C.W.Buckingham. 301-303 Munster Rd, Fulham, London, W6. Tel 385 2657.

Olwen Carthew. 109 Kirkdale, London, SE26. Tel 699 1363.

Simon Coleman. 40 White Hart Lane,Barnes, London, SW13. Tel 878 5037.

Collectables. 141 Greenwich South St,Greenwich, London, SE10. Tel 692 4047.

Isabelle Collins Antiques. 156 and 158 Wandsworth Bridge Rd, London, SW6. Tel 731 4695.

Csaky's Antiques. 20 Pimlico Rd, London, SW1. Tel 730 2068.

Furniture Cave. 533 King's Rd,Chelsea, London, SW10. Tel 352 2046.

Eric King Antiques. 203 New Kings Rd, London, SW6. Tel 736 3162.

Richard Morris. 142 Wandsworth Bridge Rd, London, SW6. Tel 736 1448.

Old Pine. 594 King's Rd, London, SW6. Tel 736 5999.

The Pine Mine.100 Wandsworth Bridge Rd, London, SW6. Tel 736 1092.

The Pine Village. 162 Wandsworth Bridge Road, London, SW6. Tel 736 2753.

Princedale Antiques. 70 Princedale Rd, Holland Park, London, W11. Tel 727 0868.

Princedale Antiques Workshop. 56 Eden Grove, London, N7. Tel 607 6376.

Peter Reynolds Antiques. 67 New King's Rd, London, SW6. Tel 736 7797.

Savile Pine. 560 Kings Rd, London, SW6. Tel 736 3625.

Scallywag. The Old Church, Wren Rd,Camberwell Green, London, SE5 8QS. Tel 701 5353.

Spice. 2 Wandon Rd, Stanley Bridge, London, SW6. Tel 736 4619.

Stanley Studios. Park Walk, Chelsea, London, SW10. Tel 352 4353, 352 9996.

Stratton Quinn Antiques Etc. 164 Thames Rd, Strand-on-the-Green,Chiswick, London, W4 3QS. Tel 994 3140.

This & That (Furniture). 50 & 51 Chalk Farm Rd, London, NW1. Tel 267 5433.

Regions

Abbas Combe Pine. 4 Upper Maudlin St, Bristol, Avon, BS2. Tel 299023.

Abbey Antiques. 299-301 Manchester Rd, Hollinwood, Oldham, Greater Manchester, OL8 4RF. Tel 681 6538.

Abbey Antiques. 63 Great Whyte, Ramsey, Cambridgeshire, PE17 1HL. Tel 814753, 812758.

Abode. 40 Sheep St, Stratford-upon-Avon, Warwickshire, CV37 6EE. Tel 68755.

Adams Antiques. Houghton Rd, St Ives, Cambridgeshire. Tel 300455.

All Things Bright and Beautiful. The Old Sunday School,Cape Cornwall St, St Just, Penzance, Cornwall, TR19 7JZ. Tel 788444.

Ampthill Antiques Centre. Market Square, Ampthill, Bedfordshire. Tel 403344.

Antics. 44 Portsmouth Rd, Cobham, Surrey. Tel 5505.

Antique Corner. 5 Corve St, Ludlow, Shropshire. Tel 3176 (priv 0584 77 468).

The Antique Home. 15 Gwydir St, Cambridge, Cambridgeshire. Tel 311203.

The Antique Shop. Hacheston, Suffolk. Tel Wickham Market (0728) 746485.

Antiques & Pine. Unit 6 Eastburn Mills,Eastburn, Keighley, W.Yorkshire, BD20 7SJ. Tel 53002.

Antiques and Collectables. 8 Aldiss Court,High St, Dereham, Norfolk. Tel 447.

Anvil Antiques. The Old School,Alsop St, Leek, Staffordshire. Tel 385280.

James Ash Antiques. The Warehouse, Station Rd, Llandeilo, Dyfed. Tel 823728 (priv 0269 850119).

Aspleys Antique Imports & Exports. Compton Mill, Compton, Leek, Staffordshire. Tel 373346-96.

Avon Lodge Antiques. Southampton Rd, Fordingbridge, Hampshire, SP6 1AB. Tel 53275.

Duncan J. Baggott. The Square, Stow-on-the-Wold, Gloucestershire, GL54 1AB. Tel 30662.

Balcombe Galleries. Balcombe, W.Sussex, RH17 6NF. Tel 811439 or 811415.

Pat Bently Antiques. 7 King's Arms Yard, Ampthill, Bedfordshire. Tel 404939.

Brook Lane Antiques. 93 Brook Lane, Alderley Edge, Cheshire, SK9 7RU. Tel Wilmslow (0625) 582717.

Brown House Antiques. High St, Newport, Essex, CB11 3QY. Tel Saffron Walden (0799) 40238.

Brownhouse Antiques. 1 Ipswich Rd, Claydon, Ipswich, Suffolk. Tel 830130.

Paul Bruce Antiques & Pine Shop. 25-27 St Helens St, Ipswich, Suffolk. Tel 55400.

C.W.Buckingham. Twin Firs, Southampton Rd, Cadnam, Hampshire, SO4 2NP. Tel Southampton (0703) 812122.

Bures Antiques. 1 Bridge St, Bures, Suffolk, CO8 5AD. Tel 227858 (priv 0206 210215).

Ann Bye Antiques. 88 London Rd, Reading, Berkshire, RG1 4SJ. Tel 582029.

Robert Byles. 7-9 Castle St, Bampton, Devon, EX16 9NS. Tel 515.

BBC Antiques. A27 Antiques Warehouse,Unit 2 Chaucer Industrial Estate, Polegate, E.Sussex. Tel 5301 (priv 0273-477446).

Chancery Antiques. 8-10 Barrington St, Tiverton, Devon, EX16 6PU. Tel 252416 (priv 253190).

Chelsea House Antiques. 27 Station Rd, Stowmarket, Suffolk. Tel Elmswell (0359) 40895.

Church End Antiques. Church End, Great Dunmow, Essex. Tel 3431.

Coach House Antiques. 27 Thackley Rd,Thackley, Bradford, W.Yorkshire, BD10 0RT. Tel 616789.

Ray Coggins Antiques. The Old Brewery, Newtown, Bradford-on-Avon, Wiltshire. Tel 3431.

Ray Coggins Antiques. 3 Keyford, Frome, Somerset. Tel 72286.

Corney House Antiques. Corney House,Corney Square, Penrith, Cumbria.

Costessey House Antiques. Costessey House,The Street, Old Costessey, Norfolk, NR8 5DG. Tel Norwich (0603) 742012.

Country Cottage Interiors. The Co-op,Compton, Leek, Staffordshire. Tel 386621.

Country Pine & Antiques. 3 The Green, Sherborne, Dorset. Tel 5216.

The Craftsman. 16 Bridge St, Hungerford, Berkshire, RG17 0EG. Tel 82262.

Daleside Antiques. St Peter's Sq,Cold Bath Rd, Harrogate, N.Yorkshire, HG2 0NP. Tel 60286 (priv 509618).

Daniels House Antiques. Hogshill St, Beaminster, Dorset, DT8 3AG. Tel 862635.

Margery Dean Antiques. The Galleries, Alma St,Wivenhoe, Colchester, Essex. Tel 222523 (priv 250485).

John Derham Ltd/Earsham Hall Pine. Earsham Hall, Bungay, Suffolk, NR35 2AN. Tel 3423.

Designs on Pine. 27 The Strait, Lincoln, Lincolnshire. Tel Market Rasen (0673) 29252 (warehouse 858789).

Dial House Antiques. High St, Kelvedon, Essex. Tel (priv) 70706.

Dickenson and Thomas. Old Granary, 10 North St, Stamford, Lincolnshire, PE9 2YN. Tel 62236 (priv 55093).

Directmoor Ltd. Coppice Farm,Farley Rd, Moorcourt, Oakamoor, Staffordshire. Tel 702419.

Domus. Woodcock St, Castle Cary, Somerset, BA7 7BL. Tel 50912 (priv 50489).

Stewart Evans. Church St Antique Shop, Malpas, Cheshire. Tel 883214.

Fine Pine Ltd. Zeaston Farm, South Brent, Devon. Tel 2505.

Fine Pine Ltd. Woodland Rd,Harbertonford, Totnes, Devon. Tel Harbertonford (080 423) 465.

Foresters Hall Antiques. High St, Debenham, Suffolk. Tel 777.

Alastair Fraser Antiques. 2A Rushworth Ave, West Bridgford, Nottingham, Nottinghamshire. Tel 821835.

Jonathan Fyson Antiques. The Old School House, Cassington, Oxfordshire. Tel Oxford (0865) 880943.

Gemini. The Old Church School,Compton, Leek, Staffordshire. Tel 387834.

Genges Farm Antiques. Genges Farm, Limington, Somerset. Tel Ilchester (0935) 840464.

The Golden Drop Antiques. Chatteris Rd (A141), Warboys, Cambridgeshire. Tel Chatteris (03543) 2990.

Grange Court Antiques. Corfe, Taunton, Somerset. Tel Blagdon Hill (082 342) 498.

Great Ryburgh Antiques (Pine Centre). 39 Fakenham Rd,Gt Ryburgh, Fakenham, Norfolk. Tel Great Ryburgh (032 878) 447.

Michael Green. Library House,Regent Parade, Harrogate, N.Yorkshire. Tel 60452.

Greenwoods of Oulton Mill. Oulton Mill,Park Rd, Little Budworth, Cheshire. Tel 282.

GW Antiques. 47 North Rd, Lancaster, Lancashire. Tel 32050.

Hague Antiques. 2 Regent St, Leamington, Warwickshire. Tel 37236.

Half Moon Antiques. Half Moon House, High St, Clare, Suffolk. Tel 277993.

Halo Antiques. 97 Hale Rd, Altrincham, Greater Manchester, WA15 9HL. Tel 941 1800.

The Hay Galleries Ltd. 4 High Town, Hay-on-Wye, Hereford & Worcester, HR3 5AE. Tel 820356 (priv 820852).

Hillside Antiques. Units 12-13 Lindfield Enterprise Pk,Lewes Rd, Lindfield, W.Sussex, RH10 4SX. Tel 3042 (priv 0444 811003).

Hull Pine Co. 338 Wincolmlee, Hull, Humberside. Tel 227169.

J.V.T. Antiques. 76-78 Old Main St, Bingley, W.Yorkshire. Tel Bradford (0274) 566188.

Kilronan Antiques. Cloghran, Co Dublin. Tel Dublin 403499.

Knaphill Antiques. 38 High Street, Knaphill, Woking, Surrey. Tel Brookwood (048 67) 3179.

La Barre Ltd. The Place,116 South St, Leominster, Hereford & Worcester, HR6 8LE. Tel 4315.

Ann Lingard. Rope Walk Antiques, Rope Walk, Rye, E.Sussex, TN31 7NA. Tel 223486.

Linnets Nest Antiques & Mawby's International. 50 Church St, Rugby, Warwickshire. Tel 61393 &832600 priv75305.

Loft Antiques. Old Kings Head,11 High St, Dorking, Surrey.

Long Melford Antiques. Chapel Maltings, High St, Long Melford, Suffolk. Tel Sudbury (0787) 79287.

Maltings Antiques. Sixty Millgate, Aylsham, Norfolk. Tel 732291.

Manor Barn Pine. Burnside Mill, Main St, Addingham, Ilkley, W.Yorkshire, LS29 0PJ. Tel Addingham (0943) 830176.

Market Place Antiques. 35 Market Place, Henley-on-Thames, Oxfordshire, RG9 2AA. Tel 572387.

Mawby's International. Old Village Hall, School St, Churchover, Warwickshire, CV23 0EG. Tel Rugby (0788) 832600 (priv 0788 75305).

Margaret McCloy Antiques. 49 Surbiton Rd, Kingston upon Thames, Surrey, KT1 2HG. Tel 549 6423.

Merlin Antiques & Restorations. Howgill Lane, Sedbergh, Cumbria. Tel 20301 (priv 20719).

Michael Moore Antiques. The Old Court, Nethergate St, Clare, Suffolk, CO10 8NP. Tel 277510.

Moorhen Antiques. 9 Walton St, Walton on the Hill, Surrey. Tel Tadworth (073 781) 2272.

Robert Neville Antiques. The Old Dairy,Western Boulevard, Leicester, Leicestershire.

New Street Antiques. 33 New St, Holt, Norfolk. Tel 3089.

David & Penny Newlove Antiques. 28 High St, Wincanton, Somerset, BA9 9JF. Tel 32672.

David & Penny Newlove Antiques. 70/71/102 Gt Western Antique Centre,Bartlett St, Bath, Avon. Tel 28731 & 310388.

David & Penny Newlove Antiques. Unit 3, The Old Mill,Station Rd, Bruton, Somerset. Tel 32672.

North Wilts Exporters. Farm Hill House, Brinkworth, Wiltshire. Tel 423 and 625.

Northgate Antiques. 10 Northgate St, Pembroke, Dyfed, SA71 5LF. Tel 684416 (priv 672388).

Old Britannia. Castle Street, Combe Martin, Ilfracombe, Devon. Tel Combe Martin (027 188) 3610.

Old Chapel Antiques. Fop St, Uley, Gloucestershire. Tel Dursley (0453) 860656 (priv 860396).

Old Farmhouse Furniture. Alsop en le Dale, Ashbourne, Derbyshire. Tel Parwich (033525) 473.

The Old Pine Loft. Kingham Way,Reginald St, Luton, Bedfordshire. Tel 459001.

Old Pine Shop. 27 Gloucester Rd, Ross-on-Wye, Hereford & Worcester, HR9 5BU. Tel 64738 (priv 0594 543349).

Painswick Antiques. Beacon House, New St, Painswick, Gloucestershire, GL6 6UN. Tel 812578.

J. & J. Palmer Ltd. 42-44 Swinegate, Grantham, Lincolnshire. Tel 70093.

Pennard House Antiques. East Pennard, Shepton Mallet, Somerset, BA4 6TP. Tel Ditcheat (074986) 266.

Penzance Pine Centre. 13-14 Bread St, Penzance, Cornwall. Tel 64027.

Percival Restoration. 53A Wellington St, Leicester, Leicestershire. Tel 545061.

Pine and Country Antiques. Sandhill Barn, Washington, Pulborough, W.Sussex. Tel Ashington (0903) 892888 (priv 892210).

Pine Antiques. 52 Bridge St, Uttoxeter, Staffordshire. Tel 5374.

The Pine Cellars. 38 Jewry St, Winchester, Hampshire, SO23 8RY. Tel 67014.

Pine Corner Antiques. 19 & 21 Bridgend Square, Haverfordwest, Dyfed.

Pine Dealers. Blanchards Farm,Seven Hills Rd, Iver Heath, Buckinghamshire. Tel Fulmer (028 16) 2540 (priv 024 026 3184).

Pine Finds. The Old Cornmill, Bishop Monkton, Harrogate, N.Yorkshire, HG3 3QN. Tel Ripon (0765) 87159.

The Pine Shop. 3 Dukes Ct,Dukes St, Brighton & Hove, E.Sussex, BN1 1AR. Tel 253365 (priv 501110).

Pitcher Pine Antiques. Lion Yard,Broad Street, Leominster, Hereford & Worcester. Tel 3361.

Graham Porter Antiques. 31 Whitehorse St, Baldock, Hertfordshire. Tel 895351.

Ian Pout Antiques. 99 High St, Witney, Oxfordshire. Tel 2616 (priv 0869 40205).

Graham Price Antiques. A27 Antiques Warehouse,Dittons Rd, Polegate, E.Sussex. Tel 7167 (priv 0435-882553).

Priory Antiques. Litcham Priory, Litcham, King's Lynn, Norfolk. Tel Litcham (0328) 701262.

Quested Antiques. 62 Brighton Rd, Surbiton, Surrey, KT6 5NF. Tel 390 3566.

S.W.Antiques. Abbey Showrooms,Newlands, Pershore, Hereford & Worcester.

Scallywag. 22 High St, Beckenham, Kent, BR3 1AY. Tel 658 6633.

The Sevenoaks Furniture Gallery. 140 High St, Sevenoaks, Kent. Tel 453030.

Laurence Shaw Antique Centre. Sandy Bank Road,New York, Coningsby, Lincolnshire. Tel 42578.

Godfrey M.Simpson (Antiques). Thurland Castle, Tunstall, Lancashire. Tel 360, 371.

Spencer Swaffer Antiques. 33 High St, Arundel, W.Sussex, BN18 9AB. Tel 882132.

Neil Spencer Antiques. 29 St Osburgs Rd, Stoke, Coventry, W.Midlands. Tel 441182.

Spurrier-Smith Antiques. 28 & 41 Church St, Ashbourne, Derbyshire. Tel 43669 (priv 077 389 368).

Julie Strachey. Southfield Farm, North Lane, Weston-on-the-Green, Oxfordshire. Tel Bletchington (0869) 50833.

Sunset Strip. The Old Forge,Higher Mill Lane, Cullompton, Devon. Tel 32689.

Andrew Tate Pine. Great Wincey Farm,Brent Hall Rd, Finchingfield, Essex, CM7 4NP. Tel Great Dunmow (0371) 810004 (priv 0371 810280).

Tealby Pine. Goltho Hall, Goltho, Wragby, Lincolnshire. Tel 858789.

Thirty Eight Antiques Ltd. 25-27 High St, Weedon, Northamptonshire, NN7 4QD. Tel 40766.

Tickle & Bragger & Co Ltd. Great Western House and Warehouse, Lostwithiel, Cornwall. Tel Bodmin (0208) 873027 (priv 0503-20504).

J.P.Townsend Antiques. Cheltenham Antique Market,54 Suffolk Rd, Cheltenham, Gloucestershire. Tel 29812.

J.P.Townsend. Ullenwood Park Farm, Ullenwood, Gloucestershire. Tel Coberley (024 287) 223.

Traditional Furniture. 248 Seabrook Rd,Seabrook, Hythe, Kent. Tel 39931.

John Trefor Antiques. Rhuallt Hall Farm, Rhuallt, St Asaph, Clwyd, LL17 OTR. Tel 583604.

Denzil Verey Antiques. The Close, Barnsley House, Barnsley, Gloucestershire. Tel Bibury (0285 74) 402 (priv 028585 495).

The Village Gallery. High St, Brasted, Kent, TN16 1JA. Tel Westerham (0959) 62503.

Michael Wakelin and Helen Linfield. 10 New St, Petworth, W.Sussex. Tel 42417.

L.L.Ward & Son. Bar House, Brandsby, York, N.Yorkshire, YO6 4RQ. Tel Brandsby (034 75) 651.

Waterwheel Pine and Antiques. Cricklepit Mill,The Quay, Exeter, Devon. Tel 217076.

The Stores. Great Waltham, Chelmsford, Essex. Tel 360277 (priv 0376 26997).

West Farm Antiques. High St, Orwell, Cambridgeshire, SG8 5QN. Tel Cambridge (0223) 207464.

Widcombe Antiques. 8-9 Claverton Buildings, Widcombe, Bath, Avon. Tel 28767.

Paul Wilson, Old, Antique & Reproduction Pine. Perth Street West, Hull, Humberside, HU5 3UB. Tel 447923/448607/48251.

Wimborne Antiques. 46 High St, Wimborne Minster, Dorset, BH21 1HT. Tel 887863 (priv 883686).

Wiskin Antiques. 18 Silver St, Stansted Mountfitchet, Essex. Tel Bishops Stortford (0279) 812376.

Woodgoods. High St, Odiham, Hampshire, RG25 1LN. Tel 2676.

Woodstock. Unicorn Yard,Rear of 6/8 Bellevue Terrace, Malvern, Hereford & Worcester, WR14 4EZ. Tel 60297.

Woolpit Antiques. The Old Butchers Shop, The Street, Woolpit, Suffolk. Tel Elmswell (0359) 40895.

Yesterday's Pine. 13 Dunstable St, Ampthill, Bedfordshire. Tel 402260.

Playing Cards

Benet Gallery. 19 King's Parade, Cambridge, Cambridgeshire. Tel 353783 (priv 248739).

Game Advice. 23 Holmes Road, London, NW5 3AA. Tel 485 2188 (priv 485 4226).

Intercol London. 1A Camden Walk, Islington Green, London, N1. Tel 354 2599 (priv 349 2207).

Jean Pain Gallery. 7 King's Parade, Cambridge, Cambridgeshire, CB2 1SJ. Tel 313970.

Polishes

C. & A.J.Barmby. 68 Judd Rd, Tonbridge, Kent. Tel 356479.

John Boddy's Fine Wood & Tool Store Ltd. Riverside Sawmills, Boroughbridge, N.Yorkshire, YO5 9LJ. Tel 2370.

James Briggs & Sons Ltd. Lion Works, Old Market St, Blackley, Manchester, Greater Manchester, M9 3DU. Tel 795 8410.

Camelot Antiques. Boreham St, Hailsham, E.Sussex, BN27 4SH. Tel Herstmonceux (0323) 833460.

Henry Flack (1860) Ltd. P.O.Box 78, Beckenham, Kent, BR3 4BL. Tel 01-658 2299.

J. Goddard & Sons Ltd. Frimley Green, Camberley, Surrey, GU16 5AJ. Tel 63456.

Touchwood Antiques. 9 Park St., Stow-on-the-Wold, Gloucestershire, GL54 1AQ. Tel 30221.

Portrait Miniatures

Angharads Antiques. 106 Chester Rd West, Shotton, Clwyd. Tel Deeside (0244) 812240.

The Arden Gallery. 54 High St, Henley-in-Arden, Warwickshire, B95 5AN. Tel 2520.

Artist. Zelah Studio, Portgwidden, St Ives, Cornwall, TR26. Tel 795941.

Asprey PLC. 165-169 New Bond St, London, W1Y 0AR. Tel 493 6767.

Maurice Asprey Ltd. 41 Duke St, St James's, London, SW1. Tel 930 3921.

Simon Brett. Creswyke House, High St, Moreton-in-Marsh, Gloucestershire, GL56 0LH. Tel 50751.

D.S.Lavender (Antiques) Ltd. 16B Grafton St, London, W1X 3LA. Tel 629 1782 (priv 409 2305).

Limner Antiques. 124 New Bond St, London, W1Y 9AE. Tel 629 5314 (priv 493 6115).

Lincoln Fine Art. 33 The Strait, Lincoln, Lincolnshire. Tel 33029.

Old Treasures. 126A Queen St, Newton Abbot, Devon, TQ12 2EU. Tel 67181.

S.J. Phillips Ltd. 139 New Bond St, London, W1A 3DL. Tel 629 6261, 629 6262.

Schidlof Galleries. 1 Holland Park Ct, Holland Park Gdns, London, W14. Tel 603 9480.

Scott Cooper Ltd. 52 The Promenade, Cheltenham, Gloucestershire, GL50 1LY. Tel 522580.

Simeon. 19 Burlington Arcade, Piccadilly, London, W1V 9AB. Tel 493-3353.

Barrie Waiting. 7 New Cavendish St, London, W1. Tel 935 0186.

Yellow Lantern Antiques Ltd. 34 & 65B Holland Rd, Hove, Brighton & Hove, E.Sussex, BN3 1JL. Tel 771572 (priv 0273 455476).

Postcards

Bath Stamp & Coin Shop. Pulteney Bridge, Bath, Avon. Tel 63073.

Bottles & Bygones. 96 Horsefair St, Charlton Kings, Cheltenham, Gloucestershire. Tel 236393.

Broadwater Bookroom. 20 Broadwater St East, Worthing, W.Sussex, BN14 9AD. Tel 39708.

Chepstow Antiques. 11 Lower Church St, Chepstow, Gwent. Tel 6500.

The Coin & Stamp Centre. 13 Centurion House (1st floor),St John's St, Colchester, Essex, CO2 7AH. Tel 41232 (priv 579345).

Collector's Corner. 5-7 Frizinghall Rd, Bradford, W.Yorkshire, BD9 4LA. Tel 487098.

Commemoratives. 3 Pierrepont Arcade, Camden Passage,Islington, London, N1. Tel eves only 278 2146.

The Curiosity Shop. West Quay, Padstow, Cornwall. Tel St Mawgan (0637) 860567.

Dodo. 3 Denbigh Rd, London, W11. Tel 229 3132.

Garrick Bookshop. 20A Wellington Road South, Stockport, Greater Manchester, SK4 1AD. Tel 480-4346.

Gems. 11 Rectory Grove, Leigh-on-Sea, Essex. Tel Southend-on-Sea (0702) 53835.

Stanley Gibbons. 399 The Strand, London, WC2. Tel 836 8444.

Great Western Antique Centre Ltd. Bartlett St, Bath, Avon, BA1 2QZ. Tel (office) 24243.

John Hall. 31 Epple Rd, London, SW6 4DJ. Tel 736 3542.

Hanover Books. 8 Hunter St, Whitby, N.Yorkshire. Tel 603587 (priv 602795).

Lantern Antiques. 5-6 Milk St,(side door entrance, no shop front), Shrewsbury, Shropshire. Tel 3783.

Spread Eagle Antiques. 22-23 Nelson Rd, London, SE10. Tel 858 9713, 692 1618.

Vale. 21 Tranquil Vale, Blackheath, London, SE3 0BU. Tel 852 9817.

Victoria Bookshop. 30 Wood St, Old Town, Swindon, Wiltshire, SN1 4AB. Tel 27364.

Warwick & Warwick Ltd. Arbon House, 21 Jury St, Warwick, Warwickshire. Tel 499031.

Yesterday's Paper. 5 Cornhillgate, Wellington, Somerset.

Posters

Lords Gallery. 26 Wellington Road, London, NW8 9SP. Tel 722 4444.

Taurus Gallery. 5 Wadham Rd, Putney, London, SW15 2LS. Tel 874 2534.

Warrack & Perkins. Rectory Farm House, Church Enstone, Oxfordshire, OX7 4NN. Tel Enstone (060 872) 572.

Potlids and Prattware

Ron Beech. 150 Portland Rd, Brighton & Hove, E.Sussex, BN3 5QL. Tel 724477.

Gavina Ewart. 60 High St, Broadway, Hereford & Worcester. Tel 853371.

Frogmore House Antiques. Frogmore House, Market Place, Box, Wiltshire. Tel 2550.

Rose Linden Antiques. Fore St, Probus, Cornwall. Tel St Austell (0726) 882055.

The Old Forge. Pilgrims Way, Hollingbourne, Kent, ME17 1UW. Tel 360.

Oliver-Sutton Antiques. 34C Kensington Church St, London, W8. Tel 937 0633.

Olney Antique Porcelain Company. 21 High Street South, Olney, Buckinghamshire. Tel Bedford (0234) 711263.

Treasures. Mileham, King's Lynn, Norfolk. Tel Fakenham (03286) 701234.

Pottery and Porcelain Restorers

see Restorers, Ceramic

Pottery and Porcelain, European

Adams Antiques. The Royal Arcade,28 Old Bond St, London, W1X 3HD. Tel 629 0717.

Anchor Antiques Ltd. 26 Charing Cross Rd,(office 24A Charing Cross Rd), London, WC2H 0DG. Tel 836 5686.

The Antique Porcelain Company Ltd. 149 New Bond St, London, W1Y 0HY. Tel 629 1254.

Claude Bornoff. 20 Chepstow Corner, Pembridge Villas, London, W2. Tel 229 8947.

The Connoisseur. 528 Wilmslow Rd, Withington, Manchester, Greater Manchester. Tel 445 2504.

Crispin Antiques. 10 The Broadway, Amersham, Buckinghamshire, HP7 0HP. Tel 21779.

Davies Antiques. 44A Kensington Church St, London, W8. Tel 937 9216.

H.&W.Deutsch. 111 Kensington Church St, London, W8. Tel 727 5984.

Emanouel Antiques Ltd. 64 South Audley St, London, W1Y 5FA. Tel 493 4350, 499 0996.

Mrs E.Falik. Plantation Cottage, Greenhead Lane,Fence, Burnley, Lancashire, BB12 9DX. Tel 65172.

Kate Foster Ltd.. 9 Halkin Arcade,Motcomb St, London, SW1. Tel 245 9848(priv Rye 222661).

Gerald Freedman (Cale Antiques). Box 458,Fulham, London, SW6 3RS. Tel 736 8666.

David Friend Antiques. 23 Guest Rd, Prestwich, Greater Manchester, M25 7DJ. Tel 773 1382.

Gay Antiques. 1 Beauchamp Place, London, SW3. Tel 584 9615.

P.W. Gottschald. 32 Derby Rd, Ambergate, Derbyshire, DE5 2GE. Tel 6428.

Graham & Oxley (Antiques) Ltd. 101 Kensington Church St, London, W8 7LN. Tel 229 1850.

Grosvenor Antiques Ltd. 27 Holland St, London, W8. Tel 937 8649.

Hart & Rosenberg. 2-3 Gateway Arcade,355 Upper St, Camden Passage, London, N1 OPD. Tel 359 6839.

Brian Haughton Antiques. 3b Burlington Gdns, Old Bond Street, London, W1X 1LE. Tel 734 5491.

David Hawkins (Brighton) Ltd. 15B Prince Albert St,The Lanes, Brighton & Hove, E.Sussex. Tel 21357.

Hoff Antiques Ltd. 66A Kensington Church St, London, W8 4BY. Tel 229 5516 (priv 272 6542).

Klaber & Klaber. 2A Bedford Gdns,Kensington Church St, London, W8 7EH. Tel 727 4573.

Lillie Antiques. 244 Lillie Rd, London, SW6 7QA. Tel 385 9852.

David Love. 10 Royal Parade, Harrogate, N.Yorkshire. Tel 65797.

LPJ Antiques. 27 Camden Passage, Islington, London, N1. Tel 359 7579.

H.C. Mote. 15 Walton St, London, SW3 2HX. Tel 589 2752.

Nash Antiques. 10 Fountain Buildings,Lansdown Rd, Bath, Avon. Tel 313584.

H.W. Newby. 15 Walton St, London, SW3 2HX. Tel 589 2752.

The Plume Porcelain Co Ltd. West Bowers Hall,Woodham Walter, Maldon, Essex, CM9 6RZ. Tel Danbury (024 541) 2562.

The Porcelain Collector. The Old Pony Stable Antiques,High Street, Shoreham, Kent, TN14 7TD. Tel Otford (09592) 3416.

William Redford. 9 Mount St, London, W1. Tel 629 1165.

Edward Salti Ltd. 77 Wellesley Court,Maida Vale, London, W9. Tel 286 3106.

Gerald Sattin Ltd. 25 Burlington Arcade, Piccadilly, London, W1V 9AD. Tel 493 6557.

South Audley Art Galleries Ltd. 36 South Audley St, London, W1Y 5DH. Tel 499 3178, 499 3195.

Aubrey Spiers Antiques. Stand C5, Chenil Galleries,King's Rd, Chelsea, London, SW3. Tel 352 7384.

Jacob Stodel Antiques. 116 Kensington Church St, London, W8 4BH. Tel 221 2652.

Teme Valley Antiques. No.1 The Bull Ring, Ludlow, Shropshire, SY8 1AD. Tel 4686.

Brian Trengove Antiques and Picture Gallery. 46 South End, Croydon, Surrey, CR0 1DP. Tel 688 2155.

Earle D.Vandekar of Knightsbridge Ltd. 138 Brompton Rd, London, SW3. Tel 589 8481, 589 3398.

Winifred Williams. 3 Bury St, St James's, London, SW1. Tel 930 4732.

Pottery and Porcelain, General

see also Crested China, Potlids and Prattware, Staffordshire Figures

London

The Antique Porcelain Company Ltd. 149 New Bond St, London, W1Y 0HY. Tel 629 1254.

R.A.Barnes Antiques. 26 Lower Richmond Rd, Putney, London, SW15 1JP. Tel 789 3371.

Susan Becker Antiques. 18 Lower Richmond Rd, Putney, London, SW15. Tel 788 9082.

Anthony Belton. 14 Holland Street, London, W8 4LT. Tel 937 1012.

Claude Bornoff. 20 Chepstow Corner, Pembridge Villas, London, W2. Tel 229 8947.

Belinda Coote Antiques. 29 Holland St, London, W8. Tel 937 3924.

Rogers de Rin. 76 Royal Hospital Rd, London, SW3. Tel 352 9007.

Marilyn Delion. Wyllie Gallery,12 Needham Rd, London, W11 2RP. Tel 727 0606 (priv 937 3377).

Richard Dennis. 144 Kensington Church St, London, W8 4BN. Tel 727 2061.

The Dining Room Shop. 64 White Hart Lane,Barnes, London, SW13 0PZ. Tel 878 1020 (priv 876 5212).

Kate Foster Ltd.. 9 Halkin Arcade,Motcomb St, London, SW1. Tel 245 9848(priv Rye 222661).

Judy Fox Antiques. 81 Portobello Rd, London, W11.

General Trading Co. 144 Sloane St, London, SW1X 9BL. Tel 730 0411.

Thomas Goode & Co (London) Ltd. 19 South Audley St, London, W1Y 6BN. Tel 499 2823 (7 lines).

Jill Gosling Ltd. 104 Kensington Church St, London, W8.

Graham & Oxley (Antiques) Ltd. 101 Kensington Church St, London, W8 7LN. Tel 229 1850.

Grosvenor Antiques Ltd. 27 Holland St, London, W8. Tel 937 8649.

Harcourt Antiques. 5 Harcourt St, London, W1. Tel 723 5919.

Brian Haughton Antiques. 3b Burlington Gdns, Old Bond Street, London, W1X 1LE. Tel 734 5491.

Heirloom and Howard Ltd. 1 Hay Hill, Berkeley Sq, London, W1. Tel 493 5868.

Hoff Antiques Ltd. 66A Kensington Church St, London, W8 4BY. Tel 229 5516 (priv 272 6542).

Eric Hudes. 142 Portobello Rd, London, W11. Tel daily 0376-83767.

Klaber & Klaber. 2A Bedford Gdns,Kensington Church St, London, W8 7EH. Tel 727 4573.

Ledger Antiques. 101A Fulham Rd, London, SW3 6RH. Tel 581 0922.

Liberty & Co Ltd. Regent St, London, W1R 6AH. Tel 734 1234.

Libra Antiques. 131e Kensington Church St, London, W8 7PT. Tel 727 2990.

J.Lipitch Ltd. 177 Westbourne Grove, London, W11. Tel 229 0783.

Lucky Parrot (Antiques and Things). Bellevue Rd, Wandsworth Common, London, SW17. Tel 672 7168.

Lyons Gallery. 47 Mill Lane,West Hampstead, London, NW6 1NB. Tel 794 3537.

D.M.&P.Manheim (Peter Manheim) Ltd. 69 Upper Berkeley St, Portman Sq, London, W1H 7DH. Tel 723 6595 (Priv 340 9211).

Mrs David Manheim. 69 Upper Berkeley St, Portman Sq, London, W1H 7DH. Tel 723 6595.

J. & J. May. 40 Kensington Church St, London, W8 4BX. Tel 937 3575.

Mercury Antiques. 1 Ladbroke Rd, Kensington, London, W11 3PA. Tel 727 5106.

D.C.Monk & Son. 132-134 Kensington Church St, London, W8. Tel 229 3727.

Monro Heywood Ltd. 336 Kings Rd, London, SW3. Tel 351 1477.

H.C. Mote. 15 Walton St, London, SW3 2HX. Tel 589 2752.

H.W. Newby. 15 Walton St, London, SW3 2HX. Tel 589 2752.

Sue Norman. Stand L4, Antiquarius,135 King's Rd, London, SW3. Tel 352 7217 (priv 870 4677).

The Persian Market. 48 Upper St,Islington, London, N1. Tel 226 7927.

M. Rees. Stand E2, Antiquarius, Kings Rd, London, SW3. Tel 352 8734.

Robin Sanders & Sons. 590 Fulham Rd, London, SW6. Tel 736 0586.

Gerald Sattin Ltd. 25 Burlington Arcade, Piccadilly, London, W1V 9AD. Tel 493 6557.

Jean Sewell (Antiques) Ltd. 3 Campden St, Kensington Church St, London, W8 7EP. Tel 727 3122.

South Audley Art Galleries Ltd. 36 South Audley St, London, W1Y 5DH. Tel 499 3178, 499 3195.

Constance Stobo. 31 Holland St, London, W8 4LX. Tel 937 6282 (priv 373 4709).

Stockspring Antiques. Stand J23, Grays Mews Market,Davies Mews, London, W1. Tel 629 3788.

Carolyn Stoddart-Scott. London. Tel 727 5045.

Tugwell & Thomas Antiques. Grays Antique Market,58 Davies St, London, W1. Tel 499 1337.

Earle D.Vandekar of Knightsbridge Ltd. 138 Brompton Rd, London, SW3. Tel 589 8481, 589 3398.

Barrie Waiting. 7 New Cavendish St, London, W1. Tel 935 0186.

Winifred Williams. 3 Bury St, St James's, London, SW1. Tel 930 4732.

Regions

The Antique Home. 247 London Rd, Camberley, Surrey. Tel 26412.

Antiques & Interiors. 6 Andover Rd, Winchester, Hampshire, SO23 7BS. Tel 69824.

Antiques Cheltenham. 22 Montpellier Walk, Cheltenham, Gloucestershire, GL50 1SD. Tel 522939.

Arboyne Antiques. Arboyne House, Eardisley, Hereford & Worcester. Tel 218.

Astley Bridge Antiques. 419-421 Blackburn Rd, Astley Bridge, Bolton, Greater Manchester, BL1 8NJ. Tel 51160 (priv 53390).

Barton House Antiques. Barton House, 48 Wharf Rd, Stanford le Hope, Essex, SS17 0DY. Tel Stanford-le-Hope (0375) 672494.

Bath Galleries. 33 Broad St, Bath, Avon, BA1 5LP. Tel 62946.

Bell Passage Antiques. 36-38 High St,Wickwar, Wotton-under-Edge, Gloucestershire, GL12 8NP. Tel Wickwar (045 424) 251.

J.& H.Bell Antiques. 22 Arbory St, Castletown,. Tel 823132 (priv 822414).

Binsted Antiques. 21 Middle Lane, Teddington, Middlesex, TW11 0HQ. Tel 943 0626.

Bow Cottage Antiques. Antique Arcade, Sheep St, Stratford-upon-Avon, Warwickshire. Tel 297249 (priv 205883).

Bow Window. 58 Connaught Ave, Frinton-on-Sea, Essex. Tel 4607.

Brenin. Old Wool Barn,Verity's Court, Cowbridge, S.Glamorgan, CF7 7AJ. Tel 3893 (priv 0443 223553).

Bygones. Peirce Cottage, High St, Charing, Kent. Tel 2494.

Bygones of Worcester. 55 Sidbury, Worcester, Hereford & Worcester, WR1 2HU. Tel 23132 and 25388.

Jan Carter. Hartpury, Gloucestershire. Tel 628.

Chanctonbury Antiques. Clematis Cottage, Washington, W.Sussex, RH20 4AP. Tel Ashington (0903) 892233.

K.Chappell Antiques & Fine Art. Goose Green, Baslow, Derbyshire, DE4 1SR. Tel 3311.

Charles Antiques. 101 The Hundred, Romsey, Hampshire, SO5 8BZ. Tel 512885.

Angela Charlesworth. 99 Dodworth Rd, Barnsley, S.Yorkshire, S70 6HB. Tel 282097 (priv 203688).

E.&N.R.Charlton. 69 Cambridge Ave, Marton, Middlesbrough, Cleveland, TS7 8EG. Tel 319642.

Charnwood Antiques. Coalville, Leicestershire. Tel 38530.

The Clare Collector. 1 Nethergate St, Clare, Suffolk. Tel 277909 (priv 277494).

Nigel Coleman Antiques. High St, Brasted, Kent. Tel Westerham (0959) 64042.

Compton Antiques. 60A Middle St, Brighton & Hove, E.Sussex. Tel 774229.

Cottage Antiques. 16-18 Lensfield Rd, Cambridge, Cambridgeshire. Tel 316698.

Crafers Antiques. The Hill, Wickham Market, Suffolk. Tel 747347.

Crispin Antiques. 10 The Broadway, Amersham, Buckinghamshire, HP7 0HP. Tel 21779.

Dale End Antiques. Dale End, Coalbrookdale, Telford, Shropshire. Tel 452145.

Dam Mill Antiques. 6 Birches Rd, Codsall, Wolverhampton, W.Midlands. Tel Codsall (09074) 3780.

Andrew Dando. 4 Wood St, Queen Sq, Bath, Avon, BA1 2JQ. Tel 22702.

Anne Davenport Antiques. 61 Milford St, Salisbury, Wiltshire. Tel 336905.

David John Ceramics. 11 Acre End St, Eynsham, Oxfordshire, OX8 1PE. Tel Oxford (0865) 880786.

Bill Dickenson. Tudor House, 11 Tontine Hill,Ironbridge, Telford, Shropshire, TF8 7AL. Tel Ironbridge (095245) 3783.

Duncalfe Antiques & Fine Arts. 34 Montpellier Parade, Harrogate, N.Yorkshire. Tel 521452.

Dunluce Antiques. 33 Ballytober Rd, Bushmills, Co Antrim. Tel 31140.

Dunsdale Lodge Antiques. Dunsdale Lodge, Brasted Rd, Westerham, Kent, TN16 1LJ. Tel 62160.

P. & S.N. Eddy. 22 Etnam St, Leominster, Hereford & Worcester, HR6 8AQ. Tel 2813.

Elm House Antiques. Elm House, Church St, Haddington, Lothian. Tel 3413.

Pamela Elsom Antiques. 5 Church St, Ashbourne, Derbyshire. Tel 43468.

Esme Antiques 'Marelle'. Street Lane,Rode Heath, Stoke-on-Trent, Staffordshire. Tel Alsager (09363) 5603.

Eureka Antiques. 18 Northenden Road, Sale, Greater Manchester, M33 3BR. Tel 962 5629.

Mrs E.Falik. Plantation Cottage, Greenhead Lane,Fence, Burnley, Lancashire, BB12 9DX. Tel 65172.

A.Fleming (Southsea) Ltd. Clock Tower, Castle Rd, Portsmouth, Hampshire. Tel 822934.

David Friend Antiques. 23 Guest Rd, Prestwich, Greater Manchester, M25 7DJ. Tel 773 1382.

Gabor Cossa Antiques. 34 Trumpington St, Cambridge, Cambridgeshire, CB2 1QY. Tel 356049.

Godden of Worthing Ltd. 17 Crescent Rd, Worthing, W.Sussex, BN11 1RL. Tel 35958.

Geoffrey Godden, Chinaman. 17-19 Crescent Rd, Worthing, W.Sussex, BN11 1RL. Tel 35958.

Wm Goodfellow (Antiques). The Green, Over Kellet, Carnforth, Lancashire, LA6 1BU. Tel 733030.

Jay Gray Antiques. Syrena House, 1 Cheltenham Rd, Cirencester, Gloucestershire, GL7 2HS. Tel 2755.

Great Western Antique Centre Ltd. Bartlett St, Bath, Avon, BA1 2QZ. Tel (office) 24243.

Lynn Greenwold. Digbeth, Digbeth St, Stow-on-the-Wold, Gloucestershire. Tel 30398.

W.F.Greenwood & Sons Ltd. 2&3 Crown Place, Harrogate, N.Yorkshire, HG1 2RY. Tel 504467.

Haltherleigh Antiques. 51 Market St, Haltherleigh, Devon. Tel (priv) 810500.

Raymond Hawley. 5 North Bar Within, Beverley, Humberside, HU17 8AP. Tel Hull (0482) 883193.

Heath Antiques. 15 Flanchford Rd, Reigate, Surrey, RH2 8AB.

John Hopkins. 1 The Courtyard,Ockenden Manor, Cuckfield, W.Sussex, RH17 5LD. Tel Haywards Heath (0444) 454323.

The House of Antiques. 25 Meeting House Lane, Brighton & Hove, E.Sussex. Tel 27680, 24961.

House of Mallett. 67-69 Brighton Rd, Surbiton, Surrey, KT6 5NF. Tel 390 3796.

Derek S. Hutchings. The Annexe, 210 Chepstow Rd, Newport, Gwent. Tel 65511.

Joyce Hynds Ceramics. Rochester, Kent. Tel 723461.

Giulia Irving. PO Box 29, Richmond, Surrey, TW10 6HY. Tel 940 0368.

Peter & Heather Jackson Antiques. 3 Market Place, Brackley, Northamptonshire. Tel 703259.

Jackson's. Hill Villa,Bury, Ramsey, Cambridgeshire, PE17 1AB. Tel 812361.

Joan Jarman Antiques. 81A High St, Teddington, Middlesex. Tel (priv) 977 4260.

Lita Kaye of Lyndhurst. 13 High St, Lyndhurst, Hampshire, SO43 7BB. Tel 2337.

Terence Kelly Antiques. 1 Cross St, Burnham-on-Sea, Somerset. Tel 782129 (priv 785052).

Timothy Kendrew Antiques. 5-8 George Hotel Mews, Stamford, Lincolnshire. Tel 56072 (priv 08012 2325).

Kildare Antiques. 19 Kildare St, Dublin, Co Dublin. Tel 763576 (priv 688194).

King Street Curios. 5 King St, Tavistock, Devon, PL19 0DS. Tel 5193.

B.R.Knight & Sons. 4 The Quay, St Ives, Cambridgeshire, PE17 4AS. Tel 68295.

Lennard Antiques. Poplars House, Rothersthorpe, Northampton, Northamptonshire. Tel 830423.

Lindum Antiques. Main Rd, Donington-on-Bain, Lincolnshire. Tel Stenigot (050 784) 639.

David Love. 10 Royal Parade, Harrogate, N.Yorkshire. Tel 65797.

Lynton Porcelain Company & Keith Arden. Morris Cottage,High St, Much Hadham, Hertfordshire, SB10 6BY. Tel 2297.

Manor House Antiques. High St, Ripley, Surrey. Tel Guildford (0483) 225350.

R.E. Martin. 40 Gold St, Tiverton, Devon. Tel 252832.

Hugh Mendl Antiques. Collard's Bookshop, 4 Castle Street, Totnes, Devon, TQ9 5NU. Tel 863970.

Robert Morrison & Son. Trentholme House, 131 The Mount, York, N.Yorkshire, YO2 2DA. Tel 55394.

Myers Galleries. Endsleigh House, High St, Gargrave, N.Yorkshire, BD23 3LX. Tel 587.

Nanbooks. Undercliffe Cottage, Duke St, Settle, N.Yorkshire, BD24 9DJ. Tel 3324 (priv 04685-551).

Netherly Cottage Antiques. Milburn, Cumbria. Tel Kirkby Thore (0930) 61403.

Nevill Antiques. 9-10 Milk St, Shrewsbury, Shropshire, SY1 1SZ. Tel 51013 (priv 62877).

New Abbey Antiques. Caragh Lodge, Glen Rd, Newtownabbey, Co Antrim, BT37 0RY. Tel Whiteabbey (0231) 62036.

Rene Nicholls Antiques. 56 High St, Malmesbury, Wiltshire, SN16 9AL. Tel 3089.

M.K.Nielsen. Seaford House, High St, Moreton-in-Marsh, Gloucestershire, GL56 0AD. Tel 50448.

The Old Forge. Pilgrims Way, Hollingbourne, Kent, ME17 1UW. Tel 360.

The Old School Antiques. The Old School, Dorney, Buckinghamshire, SL4 6QW. Tel Burnham (06286) 3247.

Olney Antique Porcelain Company. 21 High Street South, Olney, Buckinghamshire. Tel Bedford (0234) 711263.

Ormond Antiques. 32 Lower Ormond Quay, Dublin, Co Dublin. Tel 741569.

Mary Payton Antiques. The Old Market House, Chagford, Devon, TQ13 8DD. Tel 2428 (priv 2388).

The Plume Porcelain Co Ltd. West Bowers Hall,Woodham Walter, Maldon, Essex, CM9 6RZ. Tel Danbury (024 541) 2562.

The Porcelain Collector. The Old Pony Stable Antiques,High Street, Shoreham, Kent, TN14 7TD. Tel Otford (09592) 3416.

Susan Procter. 47-51 The Feus, Auchterarder, Tayside, PH3 1DG. Tel 2532.

Christopher Pugh Antiques. 68 Watergate St, Chester, Cheshire, CH1 4JE. Tel 314137 (priv 0492 48162).

Paul Quentin Antiques. 626 Manchester Rd, Bury, Greater Manchester, BL9 9SU. Tel 766 6673.

Rankine Taylor Antiques. 34 Dollar St, Cirencester, Gloucestershire, GL7 2AN. Tel 2529.

Rembrandt Antiques. 24 South Anne St, Dublin, Co Dublin. Tel 779374.

G.E.Richards & Son (Antiques). 57 Blueschool St, Hereford, Hereford & Worcester, HR1 2AR. Tel 267840 (priv 268827).

Pamela Rowan Antiques. High St, Blockley, Gloucestershire, GL56 9ET. Tel 700280.

Saville Antiques. 37 Long St, Devizes, Wiltshire. Tel 3559.

Scott Antiques. 67 Walton St, Walton on the Hill, Surrey, KT20 7RZ. Tel Tadworth (073781) 2097 (priv 0396 882431).

Sherston Antiques. The Old Pharmacy House, Sherston, Wiltshire. Tel 0666- 840291.

A.T.Silvester & Sons Ltd. 2-4 High St, Warwick, Warwickshire, CV34 4AP. Tel 492972.

Simons Antiques. 61 The Tything, Worcester, Hereford & Worcester. Tel 25152.

South Bar Antiques. Digbeth St, Stow-on-the-Wold, Gloucestershire. Tel 30236.

Span Antiques. 6 Market Place, Woodstock, Oxfordshire, OX7 1TA. Tel 811332.

The Strait Antiques. 5 The Strait, Lincoln, Lincolnshire. Tel 23130.

Studio Antiques Ltd. Bourton-on-the-Water, Gloucestershire, GL54 2BX. Tel 20352.

H. & M. Suttle. 18 Market Place, Otley, W.Yorkshire, LS21 2AQ. Tel 462313.

R.A.Swift & Sons. St Andrews Hall,4c Wolverton Rd, Boscombe, Bournemouth, Dorset, BH7 6HT. Tel 34470.

Christopher Sykes Antiques. The Old Parsonage, Bedford St, Woburn, Bedfordshire, MK17 9QL. Tel 259 (priv 467).

Teme Valley Antiques. No.1 The Bull Ring, Ludlow, Shropshire, SY8 1AD. Tel 4686.

Templar Antiques. The Corner House, 2 Bear St, Nayland, Suffolk, CO6 4HX. Tel 262520.

B. & T.Thorn & Son. 2 High St, Budleigh Salterton, Devon, EX9 6LQ. Tel 2448.

Todd & Austin Antiques & Fine Art. 2 Andover Rd, Winchester, Hampshire, SO23 7BS. Tel 69824.

Townhead Antiques. Townhead, Newby Bridge, Cumbria, LA12 8NP. Tel 31321.

Brian Trengove Antiques and Picture Gallery. 46 South End, Croydon, Surrey, CR0 1DP. Tel 688 2155.

Twenty-One Antiques. 21 High St, Westerham, Kent. Tel 63055.

Kenneth Upchurch. 30B Church St, Ashbourne, Derbyshire. Tel Derby (0332) 754499.

Wain Antiques. 45 Long Street, Tetbury, Gloucestershire. Tel 52440.

Audrey Wallace Antiques. Room 11, Cromwell House, Battlesbridge, Essex. Tel Wickford (037 44) 62612.

W.W. Warner (Antiques) Ltd. The Green, Brasted, Kent, TN16 1JL. Tel Westerham (0959) 63698.

Joy Warren at The House of Antiques. 4 College St, Petersfield, Hampshire. Tel 2172.

Westfield Antiques. Freebirch Cottage, Eastmoor, Chesterfield, Derbyshire, S42 7DQ. Tel Baslow (024 688) 3153.

White House Antiques. 1 Oakfield Ave, Birstall, Leicester, Leicestershire. Tel 674760.

Francis Wigram Antiques. Cotters Barn, Penn, Buckinghamshire, PN10 8LB. Tel 3266.

Windsor House Antiques (Leeds) Ltd. 18/20 Benson St, Leeds, W.Yorkshire, LS7 1BL. Tel 444666.

Michael Wisehall Antiques. Minshull Gallery, 7 Minshull St, Knutsford, Cheshire. Tel 4901.

Tim Wright Antiques. 147 Bath St, Glasgow, Strathclyde. Tel 221 0364.

Denis Young Antiques. 3 Kenmore St, Aberfeldy, Tayside. Tel Glenlyon (08877) 232.

Pottery and Porcelain, Early to 17th Century

Ermitage Ltd. 14 Hay Hill, London, W1X 7LJ. Tel 499 5459.

Godden of Worthing Ltd. 17 Crescent Rd, Worthing, W.Sussex, BN11 1RL. Tel 35958.

Jonathan Horne. 66C Kensington Church St, London, W8 4BY. Tel 221 5658.

Monarch Antiques. 15 High St, Glastonbury, Somerset. Tel 32498.

Christopher Pugh Antiques. 68 Watergate St, Chester, Cheshire, CH1 4JE. Tel 314137 (priv 0492 48162).

Alistair Sampson Antiques (inc Tobias Jellinek). 156 Brompton Rd, London, SW3 1HW. Tel 589 5272, 581 2267.

Jacob Stodel Antiques. 116 Kensington Church St, London, W8 4BH. Tel 221 2652.

Pottery and Porcelain, 18th Century

London

Adams Antiques. The Royal Arcade,28 Old Bond St, London, W1X 3HD. Tel 629 0717.

Albert Amor Ltd. 37 Bury St, St James's, London, SW1Y 6AU. Tel 930 2444.

The Antique Porcelain Company Ltd. 149 New Bond St, London, W1Y 0HY. Tel 629 1254.

Davies Antiques. 44A Kensington Church St, London, W8. Tel 937 9216.

Delomosne & Son Ltd. 4 Campden Hill Rd, London, W8 7DU. Tel 937 1804.

Kate Foster Ltd.. 9 Halkin Arcade,Motcomb St, London, SW1. Tel 245 9848(priv Rye 222661).

Gerald Freedman (Cale Antiques). Box 458,Fulham, London, SW6 3RS. Tel 736 8666.

Jill Gosling Ltd. 104 Kensington Church St, London, W8.

Graham & Oxley (Antiques) Ltd. 101 Kensington Church St, London, W8 7LN. Tel 229 1850.

Brian Haughton Antiques. 3b Burlington Gdns, Old Bond Street, London, W1X 1LE. Tel 734 5491.

Hoff Antiques Ltd. 66A Kensington Church St, London, W8 4BY. Tel 229 5516 (priv 272 6542).

Jonathan Horne. 66C Kensington Church St, London, W8 4BY. Tel 221 5658.

Eric Hudes. 142 Portobello Rd, London, W11. Tel daily 0376-83767.

Klaber & Klaber. 2A Bedford Gdns,Kensington Church St, London, W8 7EH. Tel 727 4573.

Libra Antiques. 131e Kensington Church St, London, W8 7PT. Tel 727 2990.

D.M.&P.Manheim (Peter Manheim) Ltd. 69 Upper Berkeley St, Portman Sq, London, W1H 7DH. Tel 723 6595 (Priv 340 9211).

Mrs David Manheim. 69 Upper Berkeley St, Portman Sq, London, W1H 7DH. Tel 723 6595.

Mercury Antiques. 1 Ladbroke Rd, Kensington, London, W11 3PA. Tel 727 5106.

H.C. Mote. 15 Walton St, London, SW3 2HX. Tel 589 2752.

H.W. Newby. 15 Walton St, London, SW3 2HX. Tel 589 2752.

Alistair Sampson Antiques (inc Tobias Jellinek). 156 Brompton Rd, London, SW3 1HW. Tel 589 5272, 581 2267.

Jean Sewell (Antiques) Ltd. 3 Campden St, Kensington Church St, London, W8 7EP. Tel 727 3122.

Simon Spero. 109 Kensington Church Street, London, W8. Tel 727 7413.

Aubrey Spiers Antiques. Stand C5, Chenil Galleries,King's Rd, Chelsea, London, SW3. Tel 352 7384.

St Jude's Antiques. 107 Kensington Church St, London, W8. Tel 727 8737.

Carolyn Stoddart-Scott. London. Tel 727 5045.

Earle D.Vandekar of Knightsbridge Ltd. 138 Brompton Rd, London, SW3. Tel 589 8481, 589 3398.

Venners Antiques. 7 New Cavendish St, London, W1. Tel 935 0184.

Winifred Williams. 3 Bury St, St James's, London, SW1. Tel 930 4732.

Mary Wise Antiques. 27 Holland St, London, W8. Tel 937 8649 (priv 352 7334).

Regions

Alvin Antiques. 148 Union St, Plymouth, Devon. Tel 665628.

The Antique Shop. 6 West St, Wimborne Minster, Dorset. Tel 880297.

Antiques. Main St, Eyam, Derbyshire. Tel Baslow (024 688) 3265.

J. & J. Baker. 12-14 Water St, Lavenham, Suffolk. Tel 247610.

Barton House Antiques. Barton House, 48 Wharf Rd, Stanford le Hope, Essex, SS17 0DY. Tel Stanford-le-Hope (0375) 672494.

Beaufort Gallery. Beaumont St, Hexham, Northumberland.

Bygones. Peirce Cottage, High St, Charing, Kent. Tel 2494.

Jan Carter. Hartpury, Gloucestershire. Tel 628.

Chanctonbury Antiques. Clematis Cottage, Washington, W.Sussex, RH20 4AP. Tel Ashington (0903) 892233.

Charnwood Antiques. Coalville, Leicestershire. Tel 38530.

Charterhouse Antiques. 1B Northumberland Place, Teignmouth, Devon. Tel Newton Abbot (0626) 4592.

Circa Antiques. The Square, Chipping Campden, Gloucestershire, GL55 6AL. Tel Evesham (0386) 840851.

Clock Tower Antiques. 2, Old Station Rd, Newmarket, Suffolk, CBB 8DN. Tel 664915.

Cobblers Hall Antiques. 119-121 Leighton Rd, Toddington, Bedfordshire, LU5 6AR. Tel 2890.

Corner Antiques. Coltishall Antiques Centre, High St, Coltishall, Norfolk, NR12 7HV. Tel Norwich (0603) 738306 (priv 737631).

Crafers Antiques. The Hill, Wickham Market, Suffolk. Tel 747347.

Andrew Dando. 4 Wood St, Queen Sq, Bath, Avon, BA1 2JQ. Tel 22702.

David John Ceramics. 11 Acre End St, Eynsham, Oxfordshire, OX8 1PE. Tel Oxford (0865) 880786.

Gerald Deacon. 2 Wood St, Queen Sq, Bath, Avon, BA1 2JQ. Tel 25907.

John Desmond Antiques. Haddon House, 1 Dunbar Rd, Leicester, Leicestershire, LE4 7JL. Tel 769126.

Dunsdale Lodge Antiques. Dunsdale Lodge, Brasted Rd, Westerham, Kent, TN16 1LJ. Tel 62160.

Mrs E.Falik. Plantation Cottage, Greenhead Lane,Fence, Burnley, Lancashire, BB12 9DX. Tel 65172.

David Gibbins Antiques. 21 Market Hill, Woodbridge, Suffolk, IP12 4LX. Tel 3531 (priv 2685).

Godden of Worthing Ltd. 17 Crescent Rd, Worthing, W.Sussex, BN11 1RL. Tel 35958.

Geoffrey Godden, Chinaman. 17-19 Crescent Rd, Worthing, W.Sussex, BN11 1RL. Tel 35958.

Lynn Greenwold. Digbeth, Digbeth St, Stow-on-the-Wold, Gloucestershire. Tel 30398.

Harp Antiques. 17 Woolley St, Bradford-on-Avon, Wiltshire, BA15 1AD. Tel 5770.

Anna Harrison Antiques. 49 Great North Road,Grange Park, Gosforth, Newcastle upon Tyne, Tyne & Wear.

Eric Hudes. Paigles, Perry Green, Bradwell, Braintree, Essex, CM7 8ES. Tel Silver End (0376) 83767.

E.D.Levine. The Antique Gallery, Church St, Cromer, Norfolk. Tel 512335.

Mill House Antiques. 139 Abbey Foregate, Shrewsbury, Shropshire. Tel 240328.

Ann Morris Antiques. Cranehurst, Cranbrook, Kent. Tel 713296.

Rene Nicholls Antiques. 56 High St, Malmesbury, Wiltshire, SN16 9AL. Tel 3089.

The Old School Antiques. The Old School, Dorney, Buckinghamshire, SL4 6QW. Tel Burnham (06286) 3247.

Mary Payton Antiques. The Old Market House, Chagford, Devon, TQ13 8DD. Tel 2428 (priv 2388).

Pughs' Porcelains. Layer Fields House,Fields Farm Rd, Layer de la Haye, Colchester, Essex, CO2 0JW. Tel Layer de la Haye(020634) 8170.

David Quimby. Wellbeck,White Hill, Kinver, W.Midlands. Tel 872564.

J.P.Raison. Sturt House, Chequers Lane, Walton on the Hill, Surrey, KT20 7RQ. Tel Tadworth (073781) 3557.

Pamela Rowan Antiques. High St, Blockley, Gloucestershire, GL56 9ET. Tel 700280.

Norman C.Sanderson. The Coach House, Montpellier St, Harrogate, N.Yorkshire. Tel 502687 (priv 56502).

Ulla Stafford. 65 High St, Eton, Berkshire, SL4 6AA. Tel 859625.

Steppes Hill Farm Antiques. Steppes Hill Farm,Stockbury, Sittingbourne, Kent, ME9 7RB. Tel 842205.

F.W.Taylor. Waite House, 71 Church St, Tewkesbury, Gloucestershire. Tel 295990.

Teme Valley Antiques. No.1 The Bull Ring, Ludlow, Shropshire, SY8 1AD. Tel 4686.

Thimbles Antiques. 42 Couching St, Watlington, Oxfordshire. Tel 2238.

Sally Turner Antiques. Church End, Haddenham, Buckinghamshire, HP17 8AH. Tel 290346.

Audrey Wallace Antiques. Room 11, Cromwell House, Battlesbridge, Essex. Tel Wickford (037 44) 62612.

W.W. Warner (Antiques) Ltd. The Green, Brasted, Kent, TN16 1JL. Tel Westerham (0959) 63698.

Whittington Galleries. 22 Woodend, Sutton, Surrey, SM1 3LT. Tel 644 9327.

H. & B.Wolf Antiques Ltd. 128 Worcester Rd (A38), Droitwich, Hereford & Worcester, WR9 8AN. Tel 772320.

Pottery and Porcelain, 19th Century

London

Adams Antiques. The Royal Arcade,28 Old Bond St, London, W1X 3HD. Tel 629 0717.

Susan Becker Antiques. 18 Lower Richmond Rd, Putney, London, SW15. Tel 788 9082.

Belinda Coote Antiques. 29 Holland St, London, W8. Tel 937 3924.

Davies Antiques. 44A Kensington Church St, London, W8. Tel 937 9216.

Delomosne & Son Ltd. 4 Campden Hill Rd, London, W8 7DU. Tel 937 1804.

Richard Dennis. 144 Kensington Church St, London, W8 4BN. Tel 727 2061.

Thomas Goode & Co (London) Ltd. 19 South Audley St, London, W1Y 6BN. Tel 499 2823 (7 lines).

Jill Gosling Ltd. 104 Kensington Church St, London, W8.

Graham & Oxley (Antiques) Ltd. 101 Kensington Church St, London, W8 7LN. Tel 229 1850.

Brian Haughton Antiques. 3b Burlington Gdns, Old Bond Street, London, W1X 1LE. Tel 734 5491.

Klaber & Klaber. 2A Bedford Gdns,Kensington Church St, London, W8 7EH. Tel 727 4573.

Ledger Antiques. 101A Fulham Rd, London, SW3 6RH. Tel 581 0922.

Libra Antiques. 131e Kensington Church St, London, W8 7PT. Tel 727 2990.

Eric Lineham & Son. 62 Kensington Church St, London, W8 4OB. Tel 937 9650.

D.M.&P.Manheim (Peter Manheim) Ltd. 69 Upper Berkeley St, Portman Sq, London, W1H 7DH. Tel 723 6595 (Priv 340 9211).

Mrs David Manheim. 69 Upper Berkeley St, Portman Sq, London, W1H 7DH. Tel 723 6595.

Mercury Antiques. 1 Ladbroke Rd, Kensington, London, W11 3PA. Tel 727 5106.

Mrs Monro (Antiques) Ltd. 11 Montpelier St, London, SW7. Tel 589 5052, 821 1860.

H.W. Newby. 15 Walton St, London, SW3 2HX. Tel 589 2752.

Sue Norman. Stand L4, Antiquarius,135 King's Rd, London, SW3. Tel 352 7217 (priv 870 4677).

Oliver-Sutton Antiques. 34C Kensington Church St, London, W8. Tel 937 0633.

Jean Sewell (Antiques) Ltd. 3 Campden St, Kensington Church St, London, W8 7EP. Tel 727 3122.

St Jude's Antiques. 107 Kensington Church St, London, W8. Tel 727 8737.

Constance Stobo. 31 Holland St, London, W8 4LX. Tel 937 6282 (priv 373 4709).

Carolyn Stoddart-Scott. London. Tel 727 5045.

Earle D.Vandekar of Knightsbridge Ltd. 138 Brompton Rd, London, SW3. Tel 589 8481, 589 3398.

Venners Antiques. 7 New Cavendish St, London, W1. Tel 935 0184.

Christopher Wood Gallery. 15 Motcomb St, London, SW1. Tel 235 9141 (priv 828 1092).

Regions

Alvin Antiques. 148 Union St, Plymouth, Devon. Tel 665628.

The Antique Shop. 6 West St, Wimborne Minster, Dorset. Tel 880297.

J. & J. Baker. 12-14 Water St, Lavenham, Suffolk. Tel 247610.

Chanctonbury Antiques. Clematis Cottage, Washington, W.Sussex, RH20 4AP. Tel Ashington (0903) 892233.

Charterhouse Antiques. 1B Northumberland Place, Teignmouth, Devon. Tel Newton Abbot (0626) 4592.

Circa Antiques. The Square, Chipping Campden, Gloucestershire, GL55 6AL. Tel Evesham (0386) 840851.

Clock Tower Antiques. 2, Old Station Rd, Newmarket, Suffolk, CBB 8DN. Tel 664915.

Cobblers Hall Antiques. 119-121 Leighton Rd, Toddington, Bedfordshire, LU5 6AR. Tel 2890.

Corner Antiques. Coltishall Antiques Centre, High St, Coltishall, Norfolk, NR12 7HV. Tel Norwich (0603) 738306 (priv 737631).

Andrew Dando. 4 Wood St, Queen Sq, Bath, Avon, BA1 2JQ. Tel 22702.

David John Ceramics. 11 Acre End St, Eynsham, Oxfordshire, OX8 1PE. Tel Oxford (0865) 880786.

Gerald Deacon. 2 Wood St, Queen Sq, Bath, Avon, BA1 2JQ. Tel 25907.

Brian & Angela Downes Antiques. 9 Broad St, Bath, Avon, BA1 5LJ. Tel 65352.

Dunsdale Lodge Antiques. Dunsdale Lodge, Brasted Rd, Westerham, Kent, TN16 1LJ. Tel 62160.

Eardisley Antiques. Leominster Antique Market,14 Broad St, Leominster, Hereford & Worcester. Tel 2189 (priv 05446 310).

Ethorpe Antiques. 2b Ethorpe Crescent, Gerrards Cross, Buckinghamshire, SL9 8PN. Tel 887499.

Frogmore House Antiques. Frogmore House, Market Place, Box, Wiltshire. Tel 2550.

Godden of Worthing Ltd. 17 Crescent Rd, Worthing, W.Sussex, BN11 1RL. Tel 35958.

Geoffrey Godden, Chinaman. 17-19 Crescent Rd, Worthing, W.Sussex, BN11 1RL. Tel 35958.

King Street Curios. 5 King St, Tavistock, Devon, PL19 0DS. Tel 5193.

M.Lees & Sons. Tower House, Severn St, Worcester, Hereford & Worcester. Tel 26620 (24 hours).

Hugh Mendl Antiques. Collard's Bookshop, 4 Castle Street, Totnes, Devon, TQ9 5NU. Tel 863970.

Ann Morris Antiques. Cranehurst, Cranbrook, Kent. Tel 713296.

Rene Nicholls Antiques. 56 High St, Malmesbury, Wiltshire, SN16 9AL. Tel 3089.

The Old School Antiques. The Old School, Dorney, Buckinghamshire, SL4 6QW. Tel Burnham (06286) 3247.

Olney Antique Porcelain Company. 21 High Street South, Olney, Buckinghamshire. Tel Bedford (0234) 711263.

Pandora's Box. 112 St Georges Rd, Kemptown, Brighton & Hove, E.Sussex. Tel 603305.

Mary Payton Antiques. The Old Market House, Chagford, Devon, TQ13 8DD. Tel 2428 (priv 2388).

Pughs' Porcelains. Layer Fields House,Fields Farm Rd, Layer de la Haye, Colchester, Essex, CO2 0JW. Tel Layer de la Haye(020634) 8170.

David Quimby. Wellbeck,White Hill, Kinver, W.Midlands. Tel 872564.

Pamela Rowan Antiques. High St, Blockley, Gloucestershire, GL56 9ET. Tel 700280.

Ruskin's. 426-428 Wells Rd, Bristol, Avon, BS14 9AL. Tel 776456.

Steppes Hill Farm Antiques. Steppes Hill Farm,Stockbury, Sittingbourne, Kent, ME9 7RB. Tel 842205.

F.W.Taylor. Waite House, 71 Church St, Tewkesbury, Gloucestershire. Tel 295990.

Teme Valley Antiques. No.1 The Bull Ring, Ludlow, Shropshire, SY8 1AD. Tel 4686.

Times Past. 84 High St, Pershore, Hereford & Worcester, WR10 1DU. Tel 554258.

Sally Turner Antiques. Church End, Haddenham, Buckinghamshire, HP17 8AH. Tel 290346.

Vernon Smith & Son. Bayvil House, High St, Cardigan, Dyfed, SA43 1HE. Tel 612654.

Audrey Wallace Antiques. Room 11, Cromwell House, Battlesbridge, Essex. Tel Wickford (037 44) 62612.

W.W. Warner (Antiques) Ltd. The Green, Brasted, Kent, TN16 1JL. Tel Westerham (0959) 63698.

Westfield Antiques. Freebirch Cottage, Eastmoor, Chesterfield, Derbyshire, S42 7DQ. Tel Baslow (024 688) 3153.

Whittington Galleries. 22 Woodend, Sutton, Surrey, SM1 3LT. Tel 644 9327.

H. & B.Wolf Antiques Ltd. 128 Worcester Rd (A38), Droitwich, Hereford & Worcester, WR9 8AN. Tel 772320.

Pottery and Porcelain, 20th Century

Amalgam. 3 Barnes High St, London, SW13. Tel 878 1279.

Bizarre. 24 Church St, London, NW8. Tel 724 1305.

Britannia. Grays Antique Market, 58 Davies St, London, W1. Tel 629 6772.

The Craftsmen Potters Shop. 7 Marshall St, London, W1V 1FD. Tel 437 7605.

David John Ceramics. 11 Acre End St, Eynsham, Oxfordshire, OX8 1PE. Tel Oxford (0865) 880786.

Davies Antiques. 44A Kensington Church St, London, W8. Tel 937 9216.

Richard Dennis. 144 Kensington Church St, London, W8 4BN. Tel 727 2061.

Dunsdale Lodge Antiques. Dunsdale Lodge, Brasted Rd, Westerham, Kent, TN16 1LJ. Tel 62160.

Ethorpe Antiques. 2b Ethorpe Crescent, Gerrards Cross, Buckinghamshire, SL9 8PN. Tel 887499.

Fair Maids House Scottish Crafts. North Port, Perth, Tayside. Tel 25976.

Galia Antiques. Antiquarius, 135 King's Rd, London, SW3.

Michael John Decorative Arts Ltd. 25A Lowndes St, London, SW1. Tel 235 3154/5.

King Street Curios. 5 King St, Tavistock, Devon, PL19 0DS. Tel 5193.

M.Lees & Sons. Tower House, Severn St, Worcester, Hereford & Worcester. Tel 26620 (24 hours).

L'Odeon. 173 Fulham Rd, London, SW3. Tel 581 3640 (priv 736 4216).

Olney Antique Porcelain Company. 21 High Street South, Olney, Buckinghamshire. Tel Bedford (0234) 711263.

Anatol Orient Ltd. 318 Portobello Rd, London, W10. Tel 969 4119.

Oxford Gallery. 23 High St, Oxford, Oxfordshire, OX1 4AH. Tel 242731.

Rosemary Antiques & Paper Moon Books. 4 Sheep St, Stratford-upon-Avon, Warwickshire. Tel 297249 (priv 038677-472).

Soft Surround. 2 Centre Craft Yard,43 Henley St, Stratford-upon-Avon, Warwickshire, CV37 6QW. Tel 295070 (priv 0608-62181).

The Solomon Gallery. 31 Bruton Place, London, W1X 7AB. Tel 499 4701/2.

The Talbot Gallery. 290 Woodstock Rd, Oxford, Oxfordshire, OX2 7NN. Tel 59049.

Teme Valley Antiques. No.1 The Bull Ring, Ludlow, Shropshire, SY8 1AD. Tel 4686.

Themes & Variations. 231 Westbourne Grove, London, W11. Tel 727 5531.

Christopher Wood Gallery. 15 Motcomb St, London, SW1. Tel 235 9141 (priv 828 1092).

Ziggurat. Chenil Galleries, 183 King's Rd, London, SW3. Tel 352 2123.

Pottery, English

Abacus Antiques. 58 Winchester Rd, Stroud, Petersfield, Hampshire. Tel 61935.

Madeleine Adams. Eastcote, Middlesex. Tel London (01) 868 5075.

A.F. Allbrook. 22 Morgan Crescent, Theydon Bois, Essex, CM16 7DX. Tel 2344.

Bratton Antiques. Market Place, Westbury, Wiltshire, BA13 3DE. Tel 823021.

T.C.S.Brooke. The Grange, Wroxham, Norfolk, NR12 8RX. Tel 2644.

Bygones. Peirce Cottage, High St, Charing, Kent. Tel 2494.

Charterhouse Antiques. 1B Northumberland Place, Teignmouth, Devon. Tel Newton Abbot (0626) 4592.

Elias Clark Antiques Ltd. 1 The Cobbles, High Street, Bletchingley, Surrey, RH1 4PB. Tel Godstone (0883) 843714.

Gerald Clark Antiques Ltd. 1 High St, Mill Hill Village, London, NW7 1QY. Tel 906 0342.

Herbert Clark. 2/4 Ford St, Moretonhampstead, Devon, TQ13 8LN. Tel 40334.

Close Antiques. 19 Little Minster St, Winchester, Hampshire, SO23 9HA. Tel 64763.

Nigel Cracknell Antiques Ltd. 138 High St, Marlborough, Wiltshire, SN8 1HN. Tel 52912.

Andrew Dando. 4 Wood St, Queen Sq, Bath, Avon, BA1 2JQ. Tel 22702.

Rogers de Rin. 76 Royal Hospital Rd, London, SW3. Tel 352 9007.

Richard Dennis. 144 Kensington Church St, London, W8 4BN. Tel 727 2061.

Gerald Freedman (Cale Antiques). Box 458,Fulham, London, SW6 3RS. Tel 736 8666.

Ray & Diane Ginns. 39 Norman Rd,Northfield, Birmingham, W.Midlands, B31 2ES. Tel 476 8319.

Geoffrey Godden, Chinaman. 17-19 Crescent Rd, Worthing, W.Sussex, BN11 1RL. Tel 35958.

Stephanie Grant Antiques. 38 The Bank, Barnard Castle, Durham. Tel Teesdale (0833) 37437.

Greystoke Antiques. Swan Yard, off Cheap St, Sherborne, Dorset, DT9 4EP. Tel 812833 (priv 813484).

Harp Antiques. 17 Woolley St, Bradford-on-Avon, Wiltshire, BA15 1AD. Tel 5770.

William Hockley Antiques. East Street, Petworth, W.Sussex, GU28 0AB. Tel 43172 (priv 048 649 331).

Jonathan Horne. 66C Kensington Church St, London, W8 4BY. Tel 221 5658.

Eric Hudes. Paigles, Perry Green, Bradwell, Braintree, Essex, CM7 8ES. Tel Silver End (0376) 83767.

Eric Hudes. 142 Portobello Rd, London, W11. Tel daily 0376-83767.

Derek S. Hutchings. The Annexe, 210 Chepstow Rd, Newport, Gwent. Tel 65511.

Tobias Jellinek. 156 Brompton Rd, London, SW3 1HW. Tel 589 5272, 581 2267.

Fiona & Bill Laidlaw Antiques. 40 Gordon Place,Holland St, London, W8 5JF. Tel 937 8493.

Lindsay Antiques. 99 Kensington Church St, London, W8. Tel 727 2333.

Stephen Long. Albion House, 348 Fulham Rd, London, SW10 9UH. Tel 352 8226.

Maggs Bros Ltd. 50 Berkeley Sq, London, W1X 6EL. Tel 493 7160.

Mrs David Manheim. 69 Upper Berkeley St, Portman Sq, London, W1H 7DH. Tel 723 6595.

Trevor Micklem, Antiques. Withywine Farm,Morebath, Tiverton, Devon, EX16 9BZ. Tel Bampton (0398) 31409.

Moxhams Antiques. 17 Silver St, Bradford-on-Avon, Wiltshire. Tel 2789 (priv 038 082-677).

Old Pump House. 20 High St, Lyndhurst, Hampshire, SO4 7BD. Tel 2137.

Susan Procter. 47-51 The Feus, Auchterarder, Tayside, PH3 1DG. Tel 2532.

Christopher Pugh Antiques. 68 Watergate St, Chester, Cheshire, CH1 4JE. Tel 314137 (priv 0492 48162).

Rogers of Alresford. 16 West St, Alresford, Hampshire, SO24 9AT. Tel 2277, 2862.

Leonard Russell. 21 Kings Avenue, Newhaven, E.Sussex, BN9 0NB. Tel 515153.

Alistair Sampson Antiques (inc Tobias Jellinek). 156 Brompton Rd, London, SW3 1HW. Tel 589 5272, 581 2267.

Anthony Scaramanga Antiques. 108 Newland, Witney, Oxfordshire. Tel 3472.

M. & D. Seligmann. 37 Kensington Church St, London, W8 4LL. Tel 937 0400 (priv 722 4315).

Aubrey Spiers Antiques. Stand C5, Chenil Galleries,King's Rd, Chelsea, London, SW3. Tel 352 7384.

Constance Stobo. 31 Holland St, London, W8 4LX. Tel 937 6282 (priv 373 4709).

Stockspring Antiques. Stand J23, Grays Mews Market,Davies Mews, London, W1. Tel 629 3788.

Swan Antiques. Stone St, Cranbrook, Kent. Tel 712720.

Templar Antiques. The Corner House, 2 Bear St, Nayland, Suffolk, CO6 4HX. Tel 262520.

Pottery, Scottish

Rogers de Rin. 76 Royal Hospital Rd, London, SW3. Tel 352 9007.

Donald Ellis Antiques. 9 Bruntsfield Place, Edinburgh, Lothian. Tel 229 1819.

Iain MacKinnon Antiques. The Victorian Village,57 West Regent St, Glasgow, Strathclyde. Tel 332 9802.

Susan Procter. 47-51 The Feus, Auchterarder, Tayside, PH3 1DG. Tel 2532.

The Three Estaits. 49 Dundas St, Edinburgh, Lothian, EH3 6RS. Tel 556 7084.

Prints, Artists

AIR Gallery. 6 & 8 Rosebery Ave, London, EC1. Tel 278 7751.

Amalgam. 3 Barnes High St, London, SW13. Tel 878 1279.

Attic Gallery. 88 Elm Rd, Wisbech, Cambridgeshire. Tel 583734.

Bankside Gallery. 48 Hopton St, Blackfriars, London, SE1 9JH. Tel 928 7521.

Barnard Gallery. Grange Farm,Everton, Doncaster, S.Yorkshire, DN10 5BG. Tel Retford (0777) 817324.

Blond Fine Art. 22 Princes St, London, W1. Tel 437 1230.

Bow Cottage Antiques. Antique Arcade, Sheep St, Stratford-upon-Avon, Warwickshire. Tel 297249 (priv 205883).

Centre Crafts. 169 Spon St, Coventry, W.Midlands. Tel 27200.

Christie's Contemporary Art. 8 Dover St, London, W1. Tel 499 6701.

Clarges Gallery. 158 Walton Street, London, SW3. Tel 584 3022.

Codex Art Ltd. 2 Lyons Crescent, Tonbridge, Kent, TN9 1EX. Tel 358274.

Collectors Treasures. Hogarth House, High St, Wendover, Buckinghamshire, HP22 6DU. Tel 624402.

Craddock & Barnard. 32 Museum St, London, WC1A 1LN. Tel 636 3937.

Curwen Gallery. 4 Windmill St, off Charlotte St, London, W1. Tel 639 1459.

Henry Donn Galleries. 138-142 Bury New Rd, Whitefield, Manchester, Greater Manchester, M25 6AD. Tel 766 8819.

Robert Douwma Prints & Maps Ltd. 4 Henrietta St, The Piazza,Covent Garden, London, WC2. Tel 836 0771.

Flora Dora Antiques. Dales House, Lombard St, Petworth, W.Sussex, GU28 0AG. Tel 43109.

D.Ira Gale. 42c South Audley St, Adams Row, London, W1Y 5DH. Tel 499 2030.

Garton & Cooke. 9 Lancashire Court, New Bond St, London, W1Y 9AD. Tel 493 2820.

The Hampton Hill Gallery Ltd. 203-205 High St, Hampton Hill, Middlesex, TW12 1NP. Tel 977 1379.

Julian Hartnoll. 14 Mason's Yard, Duke St,St James's, London, SW1. Tel 839 3842.

Richard Hewlett Gallery. 24 Cale St,Chelsea Green, London, SW3 3QU. Tel 584 8531.

Hiscock Gallery. 11 Stanley St, Southsea, Hampshire. Tel 825330.

Holleyman & Treacher Ltd. 21A & 22 Duke St, Brighton & Hove, E.Sussex, BN1 1AH. Tel 28007.

Bernard Jacobson Ltd. 2A Cork St, London, W1. Tel 439 8355.

L'Acquaforte. 49A Ledbury Rd, London, W11. Tel 221 3388.

N.W.Lott & H.J.Gerrish Ltd. The Old Rectory, Froxfield, Wiltshire, SN8 3JY. Tel Hungerford (0488) 82188.

N.W.Lott & H.J.Gerrish Ltd. 14 Mason's Yard,Duke Street St James's, London, SW1. Tel 930 1353.

Lumley Cazalet Ltd. 24 Davies St, London, W1. Tel 499 5058.

The Lyver and Boydell Galleries. 15 Castle St, Liverpool, Merseyside, L2 4SX. Tel 236 3256.

Finbar MacDonnell. 17 Camden Passage, London, N1. Tel 226 0537.

Mark Gallery. 9 Porchester Place, Marble Arch, London, W2 2BS. Tel 262 4906.

Matthews & Davies Fine Art Ltd. 85-87 Eastgate, Cowbridge, S.Glamorgan, CF7 7AA. Tel 4340.

Christopher Mendez. 58 Jermyn St, London, SW1Y 6LP. Tel 491 0015.

Frederick Mulder. 83 Belsize Park Gardens, London, NW3 4NJ. Tel 722 2105 (priv 722 3861).

Ogle Fine Arts. Ogle Gallery, 12 Rotunda Terrace,Montpellier St, Cheltenham, Gloucestershire. Tel 518605 (priv 31011).

Oxford Gallery. 23 High St, Oxford, Oxfordshire, OX1 4AH. Tel 242731.

Jean Pain Gallery. 7 King's Parade, Cambridge, Cambridgeshire, CB2 1SJ. Tel 313970.

Phoenix Gallery Ltd. 97 High St, Lavenham, Suffolk, CO10 9PZ. Tel 247356.

The Singing Birds. Michael's Nook,Grasmere, Ambleside, Cumbria, LA22 9RP. Tel Grasmere (09665) 496.

Soft Surround. 2 Centre Craft Yard,43 Henley St, Stratford-upon-Avon, Warwickshire, CV37 6QW. Tel 295070 (priv 0608-62181).

Suthburgh Antiques. Red House, Hall St, Long Melford, Suffolk. Tel Sudbury (0787) 74818.

Leigh Underhill Gallery. 100 Islington High St,Camden Passage, Islington, London, N1. Tel 226 5673

Warrack & Perkins. Rectory Farm House, Church Enstone, Oxfordshire, OX7 4NN. Tel Enstone (060 872) 572.

West Gate Fine Art. 16 St Peter St, Canterbury, Kent, CT1 2BQ. Tel 453636 (priv 03043 62093).

William Weston Gallery Ltd. 7 Royal Arcade, Albemarle St, London, W1X 3HD. Tel 493 0722.

David Windsor Gallery. 201 High St, Bangor, Gwynedd. Tel 364639.

Prints, Caricatures

see Caricatures

Prints, Decorative

Abbott & Holder. 73 Castelnau, Barnes, London, SW13. Tel 748 2416.

Al-Mashreq Galleries. 110 Kensington Church St, London, W8 4BH. Tel 229 5453.

Julian Armytage. The Old Rectory,Wayford, Crewkerne, Somerset, TA18 8QG. Tel 73449.

Ash Rare Books. 25 Royal Exchange, Threadneedle St, London, EC3. Tel 626 2665.

Baynton-Williams. Maltravers House, 49 Maltravers St, Arundel, W.Sussex, BN18 9BQ. Tel 882898.

Chris Beetles Ltd. 5 Ryder St,St James's, London, SW1. Tel 930 8586.

Brobury House Gallery. Brobury House, Brobury, Hereford & Worcester, HR3 6BS. Tel Moccas (09817) 229.

W.J.M.Brown. Stand L6, Antiquarius,135 Kings Rd, London, SW3. Tel 352 4690.

The Burlington Gallery. 10 Burlington Gdns, London, W1. Tel 734 9228.

The Bury Street Gallery. 11 Bury Street St James's, London, SW1. Tel 930 2902.

Chantry House Antiques. Sheep St, Stow-on-the-Wold, Gloucestershire, GL54 1AA. Tel 30450.

A. Clewlow (Books). 24 Fishergate, York, N.Yorkshire, YO1 4AB. Tel 27715.

Clifton Books. 5A Dicconson St, Wigan, Greater Manchester. Tel 36716 (priv 726319).

The Coach House. The Coach House, Townhouse Rd, Old Costessey, Norfolk, NR8 5BX. Tel Norwich (0603) 742977.

Coach House Antiques. 55 Elm Rd, Wisbech, Cambridgeshire, PE13 2TB. Tel 583129.

Collectors Treasures. Hogarth House, High St, Wendover, Buckinghamshire, HP22 6DU. Tel 624402.

The Corner Shop. 5 St John's Place, Hay-on-Wye, Hereford & Worcester. Tel 820045.

Laurence Corner, Euston Gallery. 126-130 Drummond St, London, NW1. Tel 388 6811.

Craddock & Barnard. 32 Museum St, London, WC1A 1LN. Tel 636 3937.

John Denham Gallery. 50 Mill Lane, London, NW6. Tel 794 2635.

Robert Douwma Prints & Maps Ltd. 4 Henrietta St, The Piazza,Covent Garden, London, WC2. Tel 836 0771.

Andrew Edmunds. 44 Lexington St, London, W1R 3LH. Tel 437 8594.

Folio (Clevedon Books & Clevedon Fine Arts). The Gallery, Cinema Buildings,Old Church Rd, Clevedon, Avon, BS21 6NN. Tel 875862 (priv 872304).

Foulsham House Prints. Erika Brandl Gallery,758 Fulham Rd, London, SW6 5SE. Tel 661837 (priv 747 0400).

Galerie Appenzell. High St, Newport, Essex, CB11 3QZ. Tel Saffron Walden (0799) 40623.

Richard Green. 36 & 44 Dover St, London, W1. Tel 493 3939.

George Gregory. Manvers St, Bath, Avon, BA1 1JW. Tel 66055.

Grosvenor Prints. 28 Shelton Street, London, WC2. Tel 836 1979.

Anne Hall - Prints. 19 Dam St, Lichfield, Staffordshire, WS13 6AE. Tel 263263.

Julia Holmes Antique Maps and Prints. Muirfield Place, Bunch Lane, Haslemere, Surrey, GU27 1AE. Tel 2153.

Lacy Gallery. 56 High St, Henley-in-Arden, Warwickshire. Tel 3073.

Lacy Gallery. 38-40 Ledbury Rd, London, W11. Tel 229 9105, 229 5316.

Lantern Gallery. 9 George St, Bath, Avon, BA1 2EH. Tel 63727.

Lion Gallery & Bookshop. 15A Minshull St, Knutsford, Cheshire, WA16 6HQ. Tel 52915.

Litchfield Gallery. 1062 Christchurch Rd, East Boscombe, Bournemouth, Dorset. Tel 45454.

The Map House. 54 Beauchamp Place, Knightsbridge, London, SW3. Tel 589 4325, 589 9821.

Marrin & Sons. 149 Sandgate Rd, Folkestone, Kent. Tel 53016.

Paul Mason. 149E Sloane St, London, SW1. Tel 730 3683.

John Mathieson & Co. 48 Frederick St, Edinburgh, Lothian. Tel 225 6798, 225 6686.

John McMaster. 5 Sayers Square, Sayers Lane, Tenterden, Kent, TN30 6BW. Tel Hastings (0424) 814671.

Richard Miles Antiques. 8 Holbein Place, London, SW1 8NL. Tel 730 1957.

Mona Antiqua & Tudor Rose. 31-32 Castle St, Beaumaris, Gwynedd. Tel 810203.

Colin Murdoch. 56 High St, Kingussie, Highland, PH21 1HZ. Tel 552.

John Nelson. 22-24 Victoria St, Edinburgh, Lothian, EH1 2JW. Tel 225 4413 (priv 667 5275).

New Gallery. Abele Tree House,9 Fore St, Budleigh Salterton, Devon, EX9 6NG. Tel 3768.

Richard A.Nicholson. 25 Watergate St, Chester, Cheshire, CH1 2LB. Tel 26818.

O'Shea Gallery. 89 Lower Sloane St,Belgravia, London, SW1 8DA. Tel 730 0081, 730 0082.

Old Maps and Prints. 4th floor,Harrods, Knightsbridge, London, SW1. Tel 730 1234 ext 2124.

Porter Prints. 205 Whitham Rd, Broomhill, Sheffield, S.Yorkshire, S10 2SP. Tel 685751.

Printed Page. 2-3 Bridge St, Winchester, Hampshire, SO23 9BH. Tel 54072 (priv 62995).

John Reid. 40A Kensington Church St, London, W8. Tel 937 3379.

Frank T. Sabin Ltd. 4 New Bond St, London, W1Y 9PE. Tel 499 5553.

C. Samuels & Sons Ltd. 17-18 Waterbeer St,Guildhall Shopping Centre, Exeter, Devon, EX4 3EH. Tel 73219.

Sanders of Oxford Ltd. 104 High St, Oxford, Oxfordshire, OX1 4BW. Tel 242590.

J.Shotton. 89 Elvet Bridge, Durham, Durham, DH1 3AG. Tel 64597.

Henry Sotheran. 2-5 Sackville St, London, W1X 2DP. Tel 734 1150, 734 0308.

Ken Spelman Booksellers. 70 Micklegate, York, N.Yorkshire, YO1 1LF. Tel 24414.

Taurus Gallery. 5 Wadham Rd, Putney, London, SW15 2LS. Tel 874 2534.

Michael Tollemache Ltd. 78 Cadogan Pl, London, SW1. Tel 235 5107.

Charles W. Traylen. Castle House, 49 Quarry St, Guildford, Surrey. Tel 572424.

Tudor Antiques. Monks Risborough, Buckinghamshire. Tel Princes Risborough(08444) 3523.

Robert Vaughan Antiquarian Booksellers. 20 Chapel St, Stratford-upon-Avon, Warwickshire, CV37 6EP. Tel 205312.

Welbeck Gallery. 18 Thayer St, London, W1M 5LD. Tel 935 4825 (priv 340 7130).

William Weston Gallery Ltd. 7 Royal Arcade, Albemarle St, London, W1X 3HD. Tel 493 0722.

The Witch Ball Print & Map Shop. 48 Meeting House Lane, Brighton & Hove, E.Sussex, BN1 1HB. Tel 26618.

The Witch Ball Print & Map Shop. 2 Cecil Court,Charing Cross Rd, London, WC2. Tel 836 2922.

Prints, Etchings

see Etchings

Prints, Maps

see Maps

Prints, Naval and Military

The Burlington Gallery. 10 Burlington Gdns, London, W1. Tel 734 9228.

The Chimes. Market Place, Reepham, Norfolk, NR10 4JJ. Tel Norwich (0603) 870480.

Collectors Treasures. Hogarth House, High St, Wendover, Buckinghamshire, HP22 6DU. Tel 624402.

Robert Douwma Prints & Maps Ltd. 4 Henrietta St, The Piazza,Covent Garden, London, WC2. Tel 836 0771.

Paul Mason. 149E Sloane St, London, SW1. Tel 730 3683.

The Parker Gallery. 12A & 12B Berkeley St, Piccadilly, London, W1X 5AD. Tel 499 5906/7.

Frank T. Sabin Ltd. 4 New Bond St, London, W1Y 9PE. Tel 499 5553.

Welbeck Gallery. 18 Thayer St, London, W1M 5LD. Tel 935 4825 (priv 340 7130).

The Wyllie Gallery. 12 Needham Road, London, W11. Tel 727 0606 (priv 584 6024).

Prints, Old Master

Arbiter Antiques. Chenil Galleries, King's Rd,Chelsea, London, SW3. Tel 499 3361.

Artemis Fine Arts (UK) Limited. 15 Duke St,St. James's, London, SW1. Tel 930 1523.

Baskett & Day. 173 New Bond St, London, W1. Tel 629 2991.

Collectors Treasures. Hogarth House, High St, Wendover, Buckinghamshire, HP22 6DU. Tel 624402.

Craddock & Barnard. 32 Museum St, London, WC1A 1LN. Tel 636 3937.

Douwes Fine Art Ltd. 38 Duke St, St James's, London, SW1Y 6DF. Tel 839 5795.

D.Ira Gale. 42c South Audley St, Adams Row, London, W1Y 5DH. Tel 499 2030.

The Maclean Gallery. 49 Drayton Gardens, London, SW10. Tel 373 2867.

Murdoch MacTaggart. Little Brympton, Brympton d'Evercy, Yeovil, Somerset. Tel West Coker (093 586) 2609.

Christopher Mendez. 58 Jermyn St, London, SW1Y 6LP. Tel 491 0015.

Frederick Mulder. 83 Belsize Park Gardens, London, NW3 4NJ. Tel 722 2105 (priv 722 3861).

Old Maps and Prints. 4th floor,Harrods, Knightsbridge, London, SW1. Tel 730 1234 ext 2124.

Somerville & Simpson Ltd. 11 Savile Row, London, W1. Tel 437 5414.

Henry Sotheran. 2-5 Sackville St, London, W1X 2DP. Tel 734 1150, 734 0308.

Prints, Restorers

see Restorers, Paper

Prints, Sporting

Arthur Ackermann & Son Ltd. 3 Old Bond St, London, W1X 3TD. Tel 493 3288.

Addison-Ross Gallery. 40 Eaton Tce, Belgravia, London, SW1. Tel 730 1536.

Julian Armytage. The Old Rectory,Wayford, Crewkerne, Somerset, TA18 8QG. Tel 73449.

The Burlington Gallery. 10 Burlington Gdns, London, W1. Tel 734 9228.

Coach House Antiques Ltd. 77 Kinnoull St, Perth, Tayside. Tel 29835 (priv 073882 627).

Collectors Treasures. Hogarth House, High St, Wendover, Buckinghamshire, HP22 6DU. Tel 624402.

Coltsfoot Gallery. Hatfield, Leominster, Hereford & Worcester, HR6 0SF. Tel Steensbridge (056 882) 277.

Robert Douwma Prints & Maps Ltd. 4 Henrietta St, The Piazza,Covent Garden, London, WC2. Tel 836 0771.

Grosvenor Prints. 28 Shelton Street, London, WC2. Tel 836 1979.

Henry-Brett Galleries. Halford House, Bourton-on-the-Water, Gloucestershire. Tel 20443 (priv 028 574 433).

Julia Holmes Antique Maps and Prints. Muirfield Place, Bunch Lane, Haslemere, Surrey, GU27 1AE. Tel 2153.

Lacy Gallery. 38-40 Ledbury Rd, London, W11. Tel 229 9105, 229 5316.

Peter Loveday Prints. 46 Norland Sq, London, W11 4PZ. Tel 221 4479.

Marlborough Sporting Gallery & Bookshop. 6 Kingbury St, Marlborough, Wiltshire. Tel 54074.

The William Marler Gallery. 36/38 Dyer St, Cirencester, Gloucestershire, GL7 2PF. Tel 68526.

Sally Mitchell Fine Arts. Thornlea, Askham, Nottinghamshire, NG22 0RN. Tel Gamston (077783) 234.

Guy Nevill Pictures. 10C Bramerton St, London, SW3 5JX. Tel 351 4292.

Frank T. Sabin Ltd. 4 New Bond St, London, W1Y 9PE. Tel 499 5553.

Sanders of Oxford Ltd. 104 High St, Oxford, Oxfordshire, OX1 4BW. Tel 242590.

Stable Antiques. 14 Loughborough Rd, Hoton, Loughborough, Leicestershire, LE12 5SF. Tel Wymeswold (0509) 880208.

The Tryon and Moorland Gallery. 23-24 Cork St, London, W1X 1HB. Tel 734 6961/2256.

Welbeck Gallery. 18 Thayer St, London, W1M 5LD. Tel 935 4825 (priv 340 7130).

The Witch Ball Print & Map Shop. 48 Meeting House Lane, Brighton & Hove, E.Sussex, BN1 1HB. Tel 26618.

Zwan Antiques. Timberscombe, Minehead, Somerset, TA24 7TG. Tel Timberscombe (064384) 621 (priv 608).

Prints, Topographical

Alexander Galleries. 81 Station Parade, Harrogate, N.Yorkshire, HG1 1ST. Tel 55430.

Benet Gallery. 19 King's Parade, Cambridge, Cambridgeshire. Tel 353783 (priv 248739).

Brobury House Gallery. Brobury House, Brobury, Hereford & Worcester, HR3 6BS. Tel Moccas (09817) 229.

Clive A.Burden Ltd. 13 Cecil Court, London, WC2N 4EZ. Tel 836 2177.

The Burlington Gallery. 10 Burlington Gdns, London, W1. Tel 734 9228.

The Carson Clark Gallery. (Scotiamaps - Mapsellers),173 Cannongate, The Royal Mile, Edinburgh, Lothian, EH8 8BN. Tel 556 4710.

Heather Cowley Bookshop & Galleries. 235-237 Mansfield Rd, Nottingham, Nottinghamshire. Tel 473836.

Davies Antiques. 44A Kensington Church St, London, W8. Tel 937 9216.

Dorchester Galleries. Rotten Row, Dorchester, Oxfordshire, OX9 8LJ. Tel Oxford (0865) 341116.

Robert Douwma Prints & Maps Ltd. 4 Henrietta St, The Piazza,Covent Garden, London, WC2. Tel 836 0771.

D.G. & A.S. Evans. 7 The Struet, Brecon, Powys, LD3 7LL. Tel 2714.

Foye Gallery. 15 Stanley St, Luton, Bedfordshire, LU1 5AL. Tel 38487.

Goodramgate Books, Maps and Prints. 58 Goodramgate, York, N.Yorkshire. Tel 51275 (priv 0484 46833).

Grosvenor Prints. 28 Shelton Street, London, WC2. Tel 836 1979.

Horn Antiques. Churt, Farnham, Surrey, GU10 2JA. Tel Headley (0428) 714298.

L.A.James. 11 George St, St Albans, Hertfordshire. Tel 56996.

Lantern Gallery. 9 George St, Bath, Avon, BA1 2EH. Tel 63727.

Lion Gallery & Bookshop. 15A Minshull St, Knutsford, Cheshire, WA16 6HQ. Tel 52915.

Peter Loveday Prints. 46 Norland Sq, London, W11 4PZ. Tel 221 4479.

Magna Gallery. 41 High St, Oxford, Oxfordshire. Tel 245805.

Paul Mason. 149E Sloane St, London, SW1. Tel 730 3683.

Mona Antiqua & Tudor Rose. 31-32 Castle St, Beaumaris, Gwynedd. Tel 810203.

John Nelson. 22-24 Victoria St, Edinburgh, Lothian, EH1 2JW. Tel 225 4413 (priv 667 5275).

Richard A.Nicholson. 25 Watergate St, Chester, Cheshire, CH1 2LB. Tel 26818.

O'Shea Gallery. 89 Lower Sloane St,Belgravia, London, SW1 8DA. Tel 730 0081, 730 0082.

Ogwen Antiques. 10 High St, Bethesda, Gwynedd. Tel 600460 (priv 600549).

The Parker Gallery. 12A & 12B Berkeley St, Piccadilly, London, W1X 5AD. Tel 499 5906/7.

Mary Payton Antiques. The Old Market House, Chagford, Devon, TQ13 8DD. Tel 2428 (priv 2388).

John Roberts Bookshop. 43 Triangle West, Clifton, Bristol, Avon, BS8 1ES. Tel 28568.

Frank T. Sabin Ltd. 4 New Bond St, London, W1Y 9PE. Tel 499 5553.

C. Samuels & Sons Ltd. 17-18 Waterbeer St,Guildhall Shopping Centre, Exeter, Devon, EX4 3EH. Tel 73219.

Thomas E. Schuster. 9 Gillingham St, London, SW1. Tel 828 7963.

W.D.Trivess. Heathfield House, Meonstoke, Hampshire, SO3 1ND. Tel Droxford (0489) 877326.

The Warwick Leadlay Gallery. 5 Nelson Rd, Greenwich, London, SE10 9JB. Tel 858 0317 (priv 852 7484).

Welbeck Gallery. 18 Thayer St, London, W1M 5LD. Tel 935 4825 (priv 340 7130).

The Witch Ball Print & Map Shop. 48 Meeting House Lane, Brighton & Hove, E.Sussex, BN1 1HB. Tel 26618.

The Witch Ball Print & Map Shop. 2 Cecil Court,Charing Cross Rd, London, WC2. Tel 836 2922.

Public Relations Consultants

Sue Bond. 46 Greswell St, London, SW6 6PP. Tel 381 1324.

The Churchill Group of Companies. Hoopers Hill,Lymington Rd, New Milton, Hampshire, BH25 5PZ. Tel 620400,620123.

The Tony Gill Organisation-Number One. 173 Bermondsey St, London, SE1 3UW. Tel 403 4982.

Heather McConnell. 18 St George St, Hanover Sq, London, W1R 9DE. Tel 493 6420.

Thornton Associates. 27 Henniker Mews, London, SW3. Tel 351 5242/3.

Quilts and Patchwork

see also Americana, Textiles

The Antique Shop. Glynn Park,Taylors Ave, Carrickfergus, Co Antrim. Tel 63284.

The Antique Textile Company. 100 Portland Rd, London, W11. Tel 221 7730.

The Ark Angel. 14 Camden Passage, London, N1 8ED. Tel 226 1644.

Michael & Margaret Baker. 6 High St, Merstham, Surrey. Tel 2658.

Annarella Clark Antiques. 11 Park St, Stow-on-the-Wold, Gloucestershire.

The Crane Gallery. 171A Sloane St, (1st Floor), London, SW1. Tel 235 2464.

Judy Greenwood. 657 Fulham Rd, London, SW6. Tel 736 6037.

Hallstile Antiques. 17 Hallstile Bank, Hexham, Northumberland, NE46 1UF. Tel 602239.

Hollywood Road Antiques. 1a Hollywood Road, London, SW10. Tel 352 5248.

Little Bric a Brac Shop. The Green, Morcombelake, Bridport, Dorset. Tel Chideock (0297) 89346.

Stephen Long. Albion House, 348 Fulham Rd, London, SW10 9UH. Tel 352 8226.

Lucky Parrot (Antiques and Things). Bellevue Rd, Wandsworth Common, London, SW17. Tel 672 7168.

Market Place Antiques. 35 Market Place, Henley-on-Thames, Oxfordshire, RG9 2AA. Tel 572387.

The Patchwork Dog and the Calico Cat Ltd. 21 Chalk Farm Road, London, NW1. Tel 485 1239.

Renaissance. 9A Trevor Place, London, SW7.

A Stitch in Time. 1 West End, Beaumaris, Gwynedd. Tel 811055.

Tobias and the Angel. 68 White Hart Lane,Barnes, London, SW13. Tel 878 8902.

Reproductions

see Furniture Reproductions, Chair Making

Restorers, Bookbinders and Conservators

Jenny Aste & Richard Smith. 7 Grape Lane, York, N.Yorkshire. Tel 21243.

Barrie's Bookshop. 4 Montpellier Walk, Cheltenham, Gloucestershire, GL50 1SD. Tel 515813.

Beeleigh Abbey Books. Beeleigh Abbey, Maldon, Essex. Tel 56308.

Cirencester Workshops. Brewery Court, Cirencester, Gloucestershire. Tel 61566.

John Henderson. 70 Micklegate, York, N.Yorkshire, YO1 1LF. Tel 24414.

Bernard C. Middleton. 3 Gauden Rd, Clapham, London, SW4 6LR. Tel 622 5388.

Nicola B. Pirozek, Dip. Cons. 9 Minster Yard, York, N.Yorkshire, YO1 2HH. Tel 35609.

Salisbury Bookbinders. 213 Devizes Rd, Salisbury, Wiltshire. Tel 334998.

Sangorski & Sutcliffe. 1 Poland St, London, W1. Tel 437 2252.

Shaw's Bookshop Ltd. 11 Police St, Manchester, Greater Manchester, M2 7LQ. Tel 834-7587.

Symington Bookbinders - York. 3 Coffee Yard,Off Stonegate, York, N.Yorkshire, YO1 2AR. Tel 633995.

Zaehnsdorf Ltd. 175 Bermondsey St, London, SE1. Tel 407 1244.

Restorers, Ceramics

Cheltenham Spa Restorations. 33 Imperial Square, Cheltenham, Gloucestershire. Tel 581919.

China Repairers. 64 Charles Lane, London, NW8. Tel 722 8407.

The Clerkenwell Green Association for Craftsmen. Pennybank Chambers,33-35 St John's Square, London, EC1. Tel 251 0276.

Dunluce Antiques. 33 Ballytober Rd, Bushmills, Co Antrim. Tel 31140.

The Elizabethans. 58 High St, Fareham, Hampshire. Tel 234964(answering machine).

Judith Larney. 103A St John's Hill, London, SW11. Tel 350 1002.

Eric Lineham & Son. 62 Kensington Church St, London, W8 4OB. Tel 937 9650.

The London Restoration Centre. 220 Westbourne Grove, London, W11. Tel 727 6596.

Partridge Restorations. Peaton Lodge, Peaton, Craven Arms, Shropshire, SY7 9DL. Tel Munslow (058 476) 639.

Plowden & Smith Limited. 190 St Ann's Hill,Wandsworth, London, SW18 2RT. Tel 874 4005.

The Porcelain Collector. The Old Pony Stable Antiques,High Street, Shoreham, Kent, TN14 7TD. Tel Otford (09592) 3416.

Restorations Unlimited. Pinkney Park, Malmesbury, Wiltshire. Tel 840888 (priv 840437).

Richard Scott Antiques. 30 High St, Holt, Norfolk. Tel 2479.

Top Hat Antiques Centre & Fine Art Gallery. 72 Derby Rd, Nottingham, Nottinghamshire. Tel 419143.

West of England Restoration Studio. 19 21 The Mall, Clifton, Bristol, Avon, BS8 4JG. Tel 741830.

West Dean College. West Dean, Chichester, W.Sussex, PO18 0QZ. Tel Singleton (0243 63) 301.

Restorers, Chair Caning

Aladdin's Cave. Church Street, Malvern, Hereford & Worcester.

Cumbria Antiques. 26 Kirkland, Kendal, Cumbria. Tel 24676.

Doddington House Antiques. 2 Benwick Rd, Doddington, Cambridgeshire, PE15 0TG. Tel March (0354) 740755.

Dudley's Home Interiors. Vine House, Fair Green, Reach, Cambridgeshire. Tel Newmarket (0638) 741989.

Farmhouse Antiques. Whites Farm House, Barkers Drove,Off Oxborough Rd, Stoke Ferry, Norfolk. Tel 500 588.

George Sneed Woodwork. Old Orchard,Church Rd, Alburgh, Harleston, Norfolk, IP20 ODA. Tel Homersfield (098 686) 472.

Strouds of Southwell Antiques. 3 Westgate, Southwell, Nottinghamshire. Tel 815001.

Clifford J. Tracy. 6-40 Durnford St, Seven Sisters Rd, London, N15 5NQ. Tel 800 4773.

R.N.Usher. 42 Southgate St, Bury St Edmunds, Suffolk, IP33 2AZ. Tel 4838.

Wycombe Cane and Rush Works. Victoria St, High Wycombe, Buckinghamshire, HP11 2QR. Tel 442429.

Restorers, Clocks, Watches and Barometers

London

Big Ben Clock Shop. 5 Broxholme House, New King's Rd, London, SW6. Tel 736 1770.

Aubrey Brocklehurst. 124 Cromwell Rd, South Kensington, London, SW7 4ET. Tel 373 0319.

City Clocks. 1B Lambs Passage, Chiswell St, London, EC1Y 8LE. Tel 628 6749.

The Clerkenwell Green Association for Craftsmen. Pennybank Chambers,33-35 St John's Square, London, EC1. Tel 251 0276.

Clock Clinic Ltd. 85 Lower Richmond Rd, Putney, London, SW15 1EU. Tel 788 1407.

O. Comitti & Son Ltd. 656 Forest Rd, Walthamstow, London, E17 3ED. Tel 509 0011.

Daedalus. 43 The Village,Charlton, London, SE7 8UG. Tel 858 2514.

Keith Harding. 93 Hornsey Road, London, N7 6DJ. Tel 607 6181, 607 2672.

Newcombe & Son. 89 Maple Rd, Penge, London, SE20 8UL. Tel 778 0816.

North London Clock Shop Ltd. 72 Highbury Park, London, N5. Tel 226 1609.

Nigel Raffety. 34 Kensington Church St, London, W8. Tel 938 1100.

R.E.Rose. 731 Sidcup Rd, Eltham, London, SE9. Tel 859 4754 (priv 464 2653).

John Walker. 64 South Molton St, London, W1Y 1DY. Tel 629 3487.

Regions

John Allott Abrahams. The Bear, 2 Bear St, Hay-on-Wye, Hereford & Worcester. Tel 820085.

B & T Restorations. Unit 6 Commercial Mews South,42 Commercial Rd, Eastbourne, E.Sussex. Tel 646457.

Richard Barder Antiques. Crossways House, Hermitage, Berkshire, RG16 9SU. Tel Newbury (0635) 200295.

R.W.Baxter.43 Hoghton St, Southport, Merseyside, PR9 0PG. Tel 37377.

Jonathan Beech. Workshop 7a,The Cirencester Workshops, Cirencester, Gloucestershire. Tel 67630.

H.J.Benford. 14-16 Wellington St, Kettering, Northamptonshire. Tel 513793.

Gerald Buxton Gooding - Lapworth Clocks. 160 Station Lane, Lapworth, Warwickshire, B94 6JJ. Tel 3243.

Castle Antiques. 15 Commercial St, Cheltenham, Gloucestershire. Tel 524563.

Chattels. 156 High St, Old Woking, Woking, Surrey, GU22 9JH. Tel 71310.

Cheltenham Spa Restorations. 33 Imperial Square, Cheltenham, Gloucestershire. Tel 581919.

Chess Antiques. 85 Broad St, Chesham, Buckinghamshire, HP5 3EF. Tel 783043.

Cirencester Workshops. Brewery Court, Cirencester, Gloucestershire. Tel 61566.

The Clock Shop. 7 The Quadrant, Hoylake, Merseyside, L47 2EE. Tel 632 1888 (priv 632 3818).

The Clock Shop. 64 Church St, Weybridge, Surrey. Tel 40407, 55503.

The Clock Shop St Albans. 161 Victoria St, St Albans, Hertfordshire, AL1 3TA. Tel 56633.

The Collector & The Collector (Restorations). Douglas House, 23-25 The Bank, Barnard Castle, Durham, DL12 8PH. Tel Teesdale (0833) 37783.

Country Bygones. Half Moon House, Stoke-by-Nayland, Suffolk.

John Cowderoy Antiques (The Musical Box Centre). 40/42 South St, Eastbourne, E.Sussex, BN21 4X. Tel 20058 (priv 645353).

D'Amico Antiques Ltd. 20 Highland Rd, Norwich, Norfolk. Tel 52320.

Dial Antiques. Dial Cottage, Shere, Surrey, GU5 9HS. Tel 2722.

Diss Antiques. 2 Market Place & 23 St Nicholas St, Diss, Norfolk. Tel 2213 (priv 51369).

Doddington House Antiques. 2 Benwick Rd, Doddington, Cambridgeshire, PE15 0TG. Tel March (0354) 740755.

Edmund Eldridge Antiques. 167 High St, Tonbridge, Kent, TN9 1BX. Tel 361921.

Gastrell House. 33 Long St, Tetbury, Gloucestershire, GL8 8AA. Tel 52228.

Goodacre Engraving Ltd. Trumpton Ave, Meadow Lane, Long Eaton, Nottinghamshire, NG10 2GB. Tel 734387 (priv 05097-3082).

Harrop Fold Clocks. Harrop Fold,Bolton by Bowland, Clitheroe, Lancashire, BB7 4PJ. Tel Bolton by Bowland (02007) 665.

Haworth Antiques. Stand 5A West Park Antiques Pavilion,20 West Park, Harrogate, N.Yorkshire. Tel 61758 (priv 74293).

Haworth Antiques. Harrogate Rd, Huby, N.Yorkshire, LS17 0EF. Tel Harrogate (0423) 74293.

Heritage Antiques & Restoration. 36b High St, Great Missenden, Buckinghamshire. Tel 5710.

F.F.Hill. The Gate House, Lombard St, Shackleford, Surrey, GU8 6AR. Tel Guildford (0483) 810330.

E. Hollander Ltd. The Dutch House,Horsham Rd, South Holmwood, Dorking, Surrey, RH5 4NF. Tel 888921.

Horological Workshops. 204 Worplesdon Rd, Guildford, Surrey, GU2 6UY. Tel 576496.

Hymore Hodson & Potts Restorations. Town End Street, Godalming, Surrey. Tel 25626.

Lower Fold Antiques. 23-25 Lower Fold, Marple Bridge, Stockport, Greater Manchester, SK6 5DU. Tel 427 4699.

Mark Marchant, Antiques. Market Square, Coggeshall, Essex, CO6 1T6. Tel 61188.

B.& A.Marks. London House,4 Market Square, Westerham, Kent, TN16 1AW. Tel 64479.

G.E. Marsh (Antique Clocks). 32A The Square, Winchester, Hampshire, SO23 9EX. Tel 54505.

Simon Marsh Antiques. The Old Butchers Shop, High St, Bletchingley, Surrey. Tel Godstone (0883) 843350.

Melbourne Antiques. Rock House Antique Centre,Tettenhall, Wolverhampton, W.Midlands. Tel 754995.

T.Mercer Chronometers. 16A Lansdown Place Lane, Cheltenham, Gloucestershire, GL50 2LB. Tel 516022.

Needham Market Antique Centre. The Old Town Hall, High St, Needham Market, Suffolk. Tel 720773 (priv 0473 41145).

Bertram Noller (Reigate). 14A London Rd, Reigate, Surrey. Tel 42548.

Onslow Clocks. 48 King Street, Twickenham, Middlesex, TW1 3SH. Tel 892 7632.

Owen Antiques. 189-193 Oldham Rd, Rochdale, Greater Manchester. Tel 48138 (priv 353270).

Prudhoe Cottage Antiques. Hexham Antique Market, 15 St Mary's,Chare, Hexham, Northumberland. Tel 603812 (priv 0661 33421).

Derek Rayment Antiques. Orchard House,Barton Rd, Barton, Farndon, Cheshire, SY14 7HT. Tel 270 429.

Derek Roberts Antiques. 24/25 Shipbourne Rd, Tonbridge, Kent, TW10 3DN. Tel 358986.

St Mary's Antiques and Cabinet Makers. 2 Lower Bar, Newport, Shropshire. Tel 811549.

Stampantique. 86 High St, Egham, Surrey, TW20 9DP. Tel 36290.

Geoffrey G.Stevens. 26-28 Church Rd, Guildford, Surrey, GU1 4NG. Tel 504075.

Sunfield Cottage Antiques. Sunfield Cottage, Inchmarlo, Banchory, Grampian, AB3 4AT. Tel 2703.

Surrey Clock Centre. 3 Lower St, Haslemere, Surrey. Tel 4547.

Tempus Fugit. Trinity House, Trinity St, Halstead, Essex. Tel 475409.

Time in Hand. 11 Church St, Shipston on Stour, Warwickshire, CV36 4AP. Tel 62578.

Timecraft. 6 Crown Street Mews, St Ives, Cambridgeshire, PE17 4EB.

Two Windows. 18A Bridge St, Pershore, Hereford & Worcester, WR10 1AT. Tel 552121.

Edward Venn Antiques. 52 Long St, Williton, Taunton, Somerset, TA4 4QU. Tel Williton (0984) 32631.

S.J.Webster-Speakman. 79 Regent St, Cambridge, Cambridgeshire. Tel 315048 (priv 354089).

Restorers, Furniture

see also Furniture Fittings, Timber Polishing, Upholstery

London

George Amos & Sons (CB) Ltd. 73 Leonard St, London, EC2. Tel 739 0448.

Eddy Bardawil. 106 Kensington Church St, London, W8. Tel 221 3967.

Aubrey Brocklehurst. 124 Cromwell Rd, South Kensington, London, SW7 4ET. Tel 373 0319.

Michael Carleton. 77-81 Haverstock Hill, London, NW3 4SL. Tel 722 2277, 586 4458.

Carvers & Gilders. Charterhouse Works, Eltringham St, London, SW18. Tel 870 7047.

Peter Chapman Antiques. 10 Theberton St, Islington, London, N1 0QX. Tel 226 5565 (priv 348 4846).

Chesterfields Etc.. 99 Lisson Grove, London, NW1. Tel 402 9728.

H.J.Hatfield & Sons Ltd. 42 St Michaels St, Norfolk Place, London, W2. Tel 723 8265/6.

Haverstock Antiques. 78 Haverstock Hill, Hampstead, London, NW3 3BS. Tel 267 1627.

Konig Newton Ltd. 27 The Talina Centre,Bagley's Lane, Fulham, London, SW6. Tel 736 0915.

Arthur Seager Antiques. 25a Holland St, Kensington, London, W8. Tel 937 3262.

Stratton Quinn Antiques Etc. 164 Thames Rd, Strand-on-the-Green,Chiswick, London, W4 3QS. Tel 994 3140.

Clifford J. Tracy. 6-40 Durnford St, Seven Sisters Rd, London, N15 5NQ. Tel 800 4773.

M.Turpin. 21 Manson Mews, Queensgate, London, SW7. Tel 736 3417.

Walker Galleries of Harrogate Ltd. 3 Cale St,Chelsea Green, London, SW3. Tel 351 5988.

Andrew White. Shop 17, The Quadrant,Kilburn Lane, London, W10.

Regions

Abbas Combe Pine. 4 Upper Maudlin St, Bristol, Avon, BS2. Tel 299023.

Abbey Antiques and Arts. 97 High St, Hemel Hempstead, Hertfordshire, HP1 3AH. Tel 64667.

Abercrombies. 140 Manor House Rd, Jesmond, Newcastle upon Tyne, Tyne & Wear, NE2 2NA. Tel Tyneside (091) 2817182.

The Angel Antiques. Crown Hill,Botesdale, Diss, Norfolk, IP22 1BU. Tel 898894.

Antique Dealers International PLC. Bow Street, Langport, Somerset. Tel 252977.

Antique Restoration. Antique Centre, 1 Severn Rd, Gloucester, Gloucestershire. Tel 29716 (priv 20911).

Ashley Antiques and Restoration. 129 High St, Hungerford, Berkshire. Tel 82771.

AS Antiques. 26 Broad St, Pendleton, Salford, Greater Manchester. Tel Manchester (061) 737 5938.

B & T Restorations. Unit 6 Commercial Mews South,42 Commercial Rd, Eastbourne, E.Sussex. Tel 646457.

John Baker. 20 George St, Kingsclere, Newbury, Berkshire. Tel Kingsclere (0635) 298744.

Ian Barrett's Furniture Workshop. Pink Cottage, Widegates, Looe, Cornwall, PL13 1QL. Tel Widegates (05034) 258.

R. Bennett Antiques. 6 West St, Dorking, Surrey, RH4 1BL. Tel 882828.

Bradford Furniture Workshops. Unit 20, Longs Yard,off Trowbridge Rd, Bradford-on-Avon, Wiltshire, BA15 1EE. Tel 4551.

Peter Brazier. Nash Court Farmhouse,Marnhull, Sturminster Newton, Dorset, DT10 1JZ. Tel Marnhull (0258) 820255.

Bristow Antiques. Lindford Rd, Lindford, Bordon, Hampshire, GU35 OPY. Tel 2301.

Broadway Antiques. 185, 185A, 187 Broadway,Roath, Cardiff, S.Glamorgan. Tel 24470.

Brockdish Antiques. Commerce House, Brockdish, Diss, Norfolk. Tel Hoxne (037975) 498.

Browns of West Wycombe. Church Lane, West Wycombe, Buckinghamshire, HP14 3AH. Tel High Wycombe (0494) 24537 (priv 0895 39163).

Paul Bruce Antiques & Pine Shop. 25-27 St Helens St, Ipswich, Suffolk. Tel 55400.

Bygones. Paddock House, 8 Brook St, Benson, Oxfordshire, OX9 6LQ. Tel Wallingford (0491) 38307.

Ian Caldwell. 9A The Green, Dorking Rd, Tadworth, Surrey, KT20 5SQ. Tel 3969.

Cartwright & Co. Stokesay Antiques, Ludlow Rd, Craven Arms, Shropshire. Tel 2263.

Castle Antiques. 15 Commercial St, Cheltenham, Gloucestershire. Tel 524563.

Castle Galleries. 122 Castle St, Hinckley, Leicestershire. Tel 39209.

Chapel Antiques. 18 Gensing Rd, St Leonards, E.Sussex, TN38 0SE. Tel Hastings (0424) 440025 (priv 425487).

Cheltenham Spa Restorations. 33 Imperial Square, Cheltenham, Gloucestershire. Tel 581919.

Chess Antiques. 85 Broad St, Chesham, Buckinghamshire, HP5 3EF. Tel 783043.

S.G.Child & Son. The Water Mill Antiques, Smeeth, Kent. Tel Aldington (023 372) 234.

Cirencester Workshops. Brewery Court, Cirencester, Gloucestershire. Tel 61566.

Cladgild Ltd. Vine House, Fair Green, Reach, Cambridgeshire, CB5 0JD. Tel Newmarket (0638) 742171.

Clifton Antiques Market. 26-28 The Mall, Clifton, Bristol, Avon, BS8. Tel 741627 734531 738504.

The Collector & The Collector (Restorations). Douglas House, 23-25 The Bank, Barnard Castle, Durham, DL12 8PH. Tel Teesdale (0833) 37783.

Cooke Antiques. 79/85 Francis St, Dublin, Co Dublin. Tel 751885, 751250, 752251.

Bernard Dickinson Antiques. 88 High St, Gargrave, N.Yorkshire, BD23 3LX. Tel 285 and 8257.

Dunluce Antiques. 33 Ballytober Rd, Bushmills, Co Antrim. Tel 31140.

Margaret Elmes Antiques. Denham Gallery, Denham, Buckinghamshire, UB9 5BE. Tel 832244.

Philip Faithfull Antiques. 202 The Street, Boughton, Kent, ME13 9AL. Tel Canterbury (0277) 750395.

Farmhouse Antiques. Whites Farm House, Barkers Drove,Off Oxborough Rd, Stoke Ferry, Norfolk. Tel 500 588.

Jeremy A. Fearn. The Old Rectory, Winksley, Ripon, N.Yorkshire. Tel Kirkby Malzeard (0765 83) 625.

G.M.S. Restorations. 36 High Street,Wickwar, Wotton-under-Edge, Gloucestershire, GL12 8NP. Tel Wickwar (045424) 251.

Gastrell House. 33 Long St, Tetbury, Gloucestershire, GL8 8AA. Tel 52228.

Gaylords. 75 West St, Titchfield, Fareham, Hampshire. Tel 43402 (priv 662606).

The Gloucester Antiques Centre. 1 Severn Rd, Gloucester, Gloucestershire. Tel 29716.

Golightly Restoration. 69 Kent Rd, Glasgow, Strathclyde, G3. Tel 221 7472.

Celia Gray. The Old Post Office,85 Havant Rd, Stoke, Hayling Island, Hampshire. Tel 464062.

G.E.Griffin. 43a Brighton Rd, Croydon, Surrey, CR2 6EB. Tel 688 3130.

Hagen (Restorations). Bakehouse Cottage, Northwood End Rd, Haynes, Bedfordshire, MK45 3QD. Tel 424.

Michael Hedgecoe Antique Furniture Restoration. 21 Burrow Hill Green, Chobham, Surrey, GU24 8QS. Tel 8206.

Hymore Hodson & Potts Restorations. Town End Street, Godalming, Surrey. Tel 25626.

A.E.Jameson & Co. 257 Glossop Rd, Sheffield, S.Yorkshire, S10 2GZ. Tel 23846 (priv 26189).

Kees & Co. Tandridge, Top Common,West Runton, Cromer, Norfolk, NR27 9LT. Tel 8109.

Kirkby Antiques Ltd. Highfield, Kirkby on Bain, Woodhall Spa, Lincolnshire, LN10 6YN. Tel 52119 & 53461.

David Lane Antiques. The Old Forge,Fanners Yard, Compton Abbas, Dorset. Tel Shaftesbury (0747) 811881.

E.C.Legg & Son. The Old School House,Somerford Keynes, Cirencester, Gloucestershire, GL7 6DJ. Tel 861420.

Lower Fold Antiques. 23-25 Lower Fold, Marple Bridge, Stockport, Greater Manchester, SK6 5DU. Tel 427 4699.

Maggs Antiques. 26-28 Fleet St, Liverpool, Merseyside, L1 4AR. Tel 708 0221.

Malvern Studios. 56 Cowleigh Rd, North Malvern, Malvern, Hereford & Worcester, WR14 1QD. Tel 4913.

Marksdanes Antiques Ltd. Station Rd, Bruton, Somerset. Tel 3267.

Simon Marsh Antiques. The Old Butchers Shop, High St, Bletchingley, Surrey. Tel Godstone (0883) 843350.

Merlin Antiques & Restorations. Howgill Lane, Sedbergh, Cumbria. Tel 20301 (priv 20719).

Nidd House Antiques. Nidd House, Bogs Lane, Harrogate, N.Yorkshire. Tel 884739.

Bertram Noller (Reigate). 14A London Rd, Reigate, Surrey. Tel 42548.

Old Barn Antiques Co. Flamberts, Trent, Sherborne, Dorset, DT9 4SS. Tel 850648.

Old Chapel Antiques. Fop St, Uley, Gloucestershire. Tel Dursley (0453) 860656 (priv 860396).

The Old Granary. Battlesbridge Antique Centre,Hawk Hill (by the "Barge" pub), Battlesbridge, Essex. Tel Wickford (037 44) 63344.

Partridge Restorations. Peaton Lodge, Peaton, Craven Arms, Shropshire, SY7 9DL. Tel Munslow (058 476) 639.

A.J.Ponsford Antiques and Restorations. 51-53 Dollar St, Cirencester, Gloucestershire, GL7 2AS. Tel 2355.

Priory Antiques. 37 East St, Blandford Forum, Dorset. Tel 53472.

Church Lane Restorations. 1 Church Lane, Teddington, Middlesex. Tel 977 2526.

Randolph. 97-99 High St, Hadleigh, Suffolk, IP7 5EJ. Tel 823789.

Restall, Brown & Clennell Ltd. Cosgrove Hall, Cosgrove, Northamptonshire, MK19 7JB. Tel Milton Keynes (0908) 565888 (priv 563336).

Restorations Unlimited. Pinkney Park, Malmesbury, Wiltshire. Tel 840888 (priv 840437).

Robbies Antiques. 140 Seabank Rd, Wallasey, Merseyside. Tel 051 638 3848.

Ian A.Robertson. Narrogate, Alnwick, Northumberland.

Rowley Restorations. Station House,Rowley Rd, Little Weighton, Humberside. Tel 844531.

J.T.Rutherford & Son. 55 Sandgate High St, Folkestone, Kent, CT20 3AH. Tel 39515 (priv 60822).

Sabine Antiques. 38 High St, Stock, Essex, CM4 9BW. Tel 840553.

Michael Schryver Antiques Ltd. The Granary, North St, Dorking, Surrey, RH4 1DN. Tel 881110.

David Smith Antiques. The Old Cottage, Manton, Oakham, Leicestershire. Tel Manton (057 285) 244 (priv 473 or 314).

St Leonard's Antiques Centre. St Leonard's Church,Corve St, Ludlow, Shropshire. Tel 5573.

St Ouen Antiques. Vintage Corner, Old Cambridge Rd, Puckeridge, Hertfordshire. Tel Ware (0920) 821336.

Peter Stanton Antiques. The Old Pottery,Chapel Hill, Truro, Cornwall, TR1 3BN. Tel 70262.

T.L. Phelps. Uni2 2, Rear of 17 York Place, Harrogate, N.Yorkshire. Tel 524604.

Thornbury Antique Framers and Restorers. 32 High St, Thornbury, Avon, BS12 2A. Tel 413595.

Top Hat Antiques Centre & Fine Art Gallery. 72 Derby Rd, Nottingham, Nottinghamshire. Tel 419143.

Treasure House. 123 University St, Belfast, Belfast, BT7 1HP. Tel 231055.

Turpins Antiques. 4 Stoney Lane, Thaxted, Essex. Tel 830495 (priv 830059).

Edward Venn Antiques. 52 Long St, Williton, Taunton, Somerset, TA4 4QU. Tel Williton (0984) 32631.

D.J.Wakeman & Co Ltd. Grove Farm House, Dorrington, Shropshire. Tel 388.

Percy F.Wale Ltd. 32-34 Regent St, Leamington, Warwickshire, CV32 5EG. Tel 21288.

John Weatherell & Sons Antiques. Westmorland House,13-19 Westmorland St, Harrogate, N.Yorkshire, HG1 5AY. Tel 60038/69718.

Weaves and Waxes. 53 Church St, Bloxham, Banbury, Oxfordshire, OX15 4ET. Tel 721535.

West of England Restoration Studio. 19-21 The Mall, Clifton, Bristol, Avon, BS8 4JG. Tel 741830.

Whytock & Reid. Sunbury House, Belford Mews, Edinburgh, Lothian, EH4 3DN. Tel 226 4911.

Wickersley Antiques. 3 Broad St,Parkgate, Rotherham, S.Yorkshire. Tel 525595.

Witney Restorations Ltd. 96-98 Corn St, Witney, Oxfordshire, OX8 7BU. Tel 3902 or 3887.

Yeo Antiques. 8 Springfields, Tetbury, Gloucestershire, GL8. Tel 521300.

Restorers, Gilding and Gessowork

Mario Ascione. 53 Moreton St,(Basement), London, SW1.

Bourne Frames & Restoration Ltd. 79 Cumberland St, Edinburgh, Lothian, EH3 6RD. Tel 557 4874.

Carvers & Gilders. Charterhouse Works, Eltringham St, London, SW18. Tel 870 7047.

John Davies Framing Ltd. 8 Bury St,St. James's, London, SW1.

N.Davighi. 117 Shepherds Bush Rd, London, W6. Tel 603 5357.

Farmhouse Antiques. Whites Farm House, Barkers Drove,Off Oxborough Rd, Stoke Ferry, Norfolk. Tel 500 588.

G.M.S. Restorations. 36 High Street,Wickwar, Wotton-under-Edge, Gloucestershire, GL12 8NP. Tel Wickwar (045424) 251.

House of Antiques. 4 College St, Petersfield, Hampshire, GU31 4AD. Tel 62172.

Konig Newton Ltd. 27 The Talina Centre,Bagley's Lane, Fulham, London, SW6. Tel 736 0915.

Church Lane Restorations. 1 Church Lane, Teddington, Middlesex. Tel 977 2526.

John Tanous Ltd. 115a & 115b Harwood Rd, Fulham, London, SW6 4QL. Tel 736 7999.

M.Turpin. 21 Manson Mews, Queensgate, London, SW7. Tel 736 3417.

R.N.Usher. 42 Southgate St, Bury St Edmunds, Suffolk, 1P33 2AZ. Tel 4838.

Arnold Wiggins & Sons Ltd. 30-34 Woodfield Place,Harrow Rd, London, W9 2BJ. Tel 286 9656.

J.Wolff & Son Ltd. 82 Troutbeck, Albany St, London, NW1. Tel 388 3588.

Restorers, Glass

Judith Larney. 103A St John's Hill, London, SW11. Tel 350 1002.

Rankin Best & Green Ltd. 24-36 Pearson St, London, E2 8JD. Tel 729 4200.

R. Wilkinson & Son. 43-45 Wastdale Rd, Forest Hill, London, SE23 1HN. Tel 699 4420.

Restorers, Jewellery

Charles Alexander Ltd. 41 Strand St, Douglas,. Tel 21527 (priv 822907).

Buckie's Jewellers, Valuers & Silversmiths. 31 Trinity St, Cambridge, Cambridgeshire, CB2 1TB. Tel 357910.

Crawford & Pawle Ltd. 2nd Floor, Bond St Silver Galleries,111-112 New Bond St, London, W1Y 9AB. Tel 499 8442.

Georgian Gems. 28 High St, Swanage, Dorset, BH19 1HA. Tel 424697.

Duncan Grimmond. The Old Granary,Upper Court Terrace, Ripon, N.Yorkshire. Tel 700982.

Needham Market Antique Centre. The Old Town Hall, High St, Needham Market, Suffolk. Tel 720773 (priv 0473 41145).

Jeremy Sniders. Victorian Village, 57 West Regent St, Glasgow, Strathclyde. Tel 332 2424.

Louise Stroud. 3, Cale Street,Chelsea Green, London, SW3. Tel 351 5988.

Top Hat Antiques Centre & Fine Art Gallery. 72 Derby Rd, Nottingham, Nottinghamshire. Tel 419143.

John Walker. 64 South Molton St, London, W1Y 1DY. Tel 629 3487.

Young Stephen Ltd. 1 Burlington Gdns, New Bond St, London, W1X 1LD. Tel 499 7927.

Restorers, Metal

Art Bronze Foundry (London) Ltd. 1 Michael Rd, London, SW6. Tel 736 7292.

C.W. Bateson. 51 Woodlands Drove, Harrogate, N.Yorkshire. Tel 889937 58595.

Stanley Beal Ltd. 41 Fairfax Rd, London, NW6. Tel 328 7525.

J.H. Bourdon-Smith Ltd. 24 Mason's Yard,Duke St, St James's, London, SW1Y 6BU. Tel 839 4714/5.

Brookes Forge Flempton. Flempton, Bury St Edmunds, Suffolk, IP28 6EN. Tel Culford (028484) 473 (priv 0449 781376).

Mark Chapman Antiques. New Street, Petworth, W.Sussex. Tel 42283.

Charterhouse Antiques. 14 Bird's Hill, Heath and Reach, Bedfordshire. Tel 532 379.

Crawford & Pawle Ltd. 2nd Floor, Bond St Silver Galleries,111-112 New Bond St, London, W1Y 9AB. Tel 499 8442.

N.Davighi. 117 Shepherds Bush Rd, London, W6. Tel 603 5357.

G.M.S. Restorations. 36 High Street,Wickwar, Wotton-under-Edge, Gloucestershire, GL12 8NP. Tel Wickwar (045424) 251.

Duncan Grimmond. The Old Granary,Upper Court Terrace, Ripon, N.Yorkshire. Tel 700982.

Hagen (Restorations). Bakehouse Cottage, Northwood End Rd, Haynes, Bedfordshire, MK45 3QD. Tel 424.

Hilton Restorations. East View Cottage, Atherington, Devon. Tel High Bickington (0769) 60253.

P.G. Kydd. 70 Colston St, Bristol, Avon, BS1 5AZ. Tel 299265.

Sanda Lipton. 35 Kenway Rd, London, SW5. Tel 373 9625 (shop), 407 0278.

Ian McCarthy. Arcadian Cottage, 112 Station Rd, Clutton, Avon. Tel Temple Cloud (0761) 53188.

Merlin Antiques & Restorations. Howgill Lane, Sedbergh, Cumbria. Tel 20301 (priv 20719).

The Morris Singer Foundry Ltd. Bond Close,Kingsland Industrial Park, Basingstoke, Hampshire, RG24 OPT. Tel 24033.

Plowden & Smith Limited. 190 St Ann's Hill,Wandsworth, London, SW18 2RT. Tel 874 4005.

Restorations Unlimited. Pinkney Park, Malmesbury, Wiltshire. Tel 840888 (priv 840437).

Michael Schryver Antiques Ltd. The Granary, North St, Dorking, Surrey, RH4 1DN. Tel 881110.

David Shaw Silverware Ltd. 231-235 Liverpool Rd,Islington, London, N1 1LX. Tel 609 9091.

W.H.Weller & Son. 12 North St, Eastbourne, E.Sussex, BN26 3H6. Tel 23592.

Restorers, Paintings

London

Addison-Ross Gallery. 40 Eaton Tce, Belgravia, London, SW1. Tel 730 1536.

Erika Brandl - Paintings. 758 Fulham Rd, London, SW6 5SH. Tel 736 0497.

Murray Brown. 18 Halkin Arcade,Knightsbridge, London, SW1X 8JT. Tel 235 8385(priv 0323 764298.

John Campbell Picture Frames Ltd. 164 Walton St, Knightsbridge, London, SW3 2JL. Tel 584 9268.

Anthony Dallas & Sons Ltd. 17 Clifford St, London, W1. Tel 734 7127.

John Denham Gallery. 50 Mill Lane, London, NW6. Tel 794 2635.

Fiddes Watt. Studio 7, 52A Avonmore Rd, London, W14 8XU. Tel 603 9015.

Gallery 181. 181 King's Rd, London, SW6. Tel 736 1955.

Limner Antiques. 124 New Bond St, London, W1Y 9AE. Tel 629 5314 (priv 493 6115).

Paul Mitchell. 99 New Bond Street, London, W1. Tel 493 8732/0860.

Regions

The Antiques Shop, Whitegate. Cinder Hill, Whitegate, Cheshire. Tel Northwich (0606) 882215.

Astley House - Fine Art. Astley House, High St, Moreton-in-Marsh, Gloucestershire, GL54 0LL. Tel 50601.

James Atkinson Gallery. 38 King St, Sandwich, Kent, CT13 9BL. Tel 617216 (priv 613298).

John Baker. 20 George St, Kingsclere, Newbury, Berkshire. Tel Kingsclere (0635) 298744.

The Boathouse Gallery. The Towpath, Manor Rd, Walton-on-Thames, Surrey, KT12 2PG. Tel 242718.

Bourne Frames & Restoration Ltd. 79 Cumberland St, Edinburgh, Lothian, EH3 6RD. Tel 557 4874.

Arthur Brett & Sons, Ltd. 40-44 St Giles St, Norwich, Norfolk, NR2 1LW. Tel 628171.

Calton Gallery. 10 Royal Terrace, Edinburgh, Lothian, EH7 5AB. Tel 556 1010.

Cambridge Fine Art Ltd. 'Priesthouse', 33 Church St,Little Shelford, Cambridge, Cambridgeshire, CB2 5HG. Tel 842866 (priv 843537).

Mark Chapman Antiques. New Street, Petworth, W.Sussex. Tel 42283.

Clifton Antiques Market. 26-28 The Mall, Clifton, Bristol, Avon, BS8. Tel 741627 734531 738504.

Cotswold Galleries. The Square, Stow-on-the-Wold, Gloucestershire, GL54 1AB. Tel 30586.

The Court Gallery. 16 Bridge Rd, East Molesey, Surrey. Tel 941 2212.

Curiosities. 152 South St, Lancing, W.Sussex, BN15 8AU. Tel 752670 (priv 0273 454669).

Dolphyn. 8 Market End, Coggeshall, Essex, CO6 1NP. Tel 61608.

Dudley's Home Interiors. Vine House, Fair Green, Reach, Cambridgeshire. Tel Newmarket (0638) 741989.

Eastbourne Fine Art. 9 Meads St, Eastbourne, E.Sussex, BN20 7QY. Tel 25634.

G.M.S. Restorations. 36 High Street,Wickwar, Wotton-under-Edge, Gloucestershire, GL12 8NP. Tel Wickwar (045424) 251.

The Gallery No.10. 10 Bangor Rd, Groomsport, Co Down. Tel Bangor (0247) 464376.

Gallery 77. 18 Princess St, Bradshawgate, Bolton, Greater Manchester, BL1 1EJ. Tel 35252.

Gastrell House. 33 Long St, Tetbury, Gloucestershire, GL8 8AA. Tel 52228.

Godalming Galleries Ltd. 3 Wharf St, Godalming, Surrey, GU7 1NN. Tel 22254.

The Grange Gallery & Fine Arts Ltd. 39 New St, St Helier, Jersey.

Guildford Galleries Ltd. Cranley Court, 59 Cranley Rd, Guildford, Surrey, GU1 2JW. Tel 61646.

Hagen (Restorations). Bakehouse Cottage, Northwood End Rd, Haynes, Bedfordshire, MK45 3QD. Tel 424.

The Hampton Hill Gallery Ltd. 203-205 High St, Hampton Hill, Middlesex, TW12 1NP. Tel 977 1379.

J.A. & T. Hedley. 3 St Mary's Chare, Hexham, Northumberland. Tel 602317.

Henry-Brett Galleries. Halford House, Bourton-on-the-Water, Gloucestershire. Tel 20443 (priv 028 574 433).

Hinson Fine Paintings. 679 Ecclesall Rd, Sheffield, S.Yorkshire, S11 8TG. Tel 665927.

Jays Fine Art Dealers. Cambridge Gallery,4 Cambridge Arcade, Southport, Merseyside, PR8 1AS. Tel 34488 (priv 69500).

The Barry M. Keene Gallery. 12 Thameside, Henley-on-Thames, Oxfordshire, RG9 1RY. Tel 577119.

Kendal Studio Pottery. 2-3 Wildman St, Kendal, Cumbria, LA9 6EN. Tel 23291.

Kenulf Gallery. High St, Winchcombe, Gloucestershire, GL54 5LJ. Tel 602124.

Kirkgate Picture Gallery. 18 Kirkgate, Thirsk, N.Yorkshire, YO7 1PQ. Tel 24085.

Langley Galleries. 153 High St, Rochester, Kent. Tel Medway (0634) 811802.

The Lyver and Boydell Galleries. 15 Castle St, Liverpool, Merseyside, L2 4SX. Tel 236 3256.

J.Manley & Thames Gallery. 27 High St, Eton, Berkshire. Tel Windsor (0753) 865647.

The William Marler Gallery. 36/38 Dyer St, Cirencester, Gloucestershire, GL7 2PF. Tel 68526.

Matthews & Davies Fine Art Ltd. 85-87 Eastgate, Cowbridge, S.Glamorgan, CF7 7AA. Tel 4340.

McTague of Harrogate. 17/19 Cheltenham Mount, Harrogate, N.Yorkshire. Tel 67086 (priv 884400).

Meyers Gallery. 66 High St, Ingatestone, Essex. Tel Brentwood (0277) 355335 (priv 215446).

Sally Mitchell Fine Arts. Thornlea, Askham, Nottinghamshire, NG22 0RN. Tel Gamston (077783) 234.

Northgate Antiques. 37 North Gate, Canterbury, Kent, CT1 1BL. Tel 464773.

Omell Galleries. Goswell Hill, 134 Peascod St, Windsor, Berkshire, SL4 1DR. Tel 852271.

Harriet Owen Hughes. 41 Blue Coat Chambers, School Lane, Liverpool, Merseyside, L1 3BX. Tel 708 6808 (priv 427 2008).

John Owen Gallery. 20 Salisbury Rd, Cardiff, S.Glamorgan, CF2 4AD. Tel 45868 (priv 04463 2767).

Printed Page. 2-3 Bridge St, Winchester, Hampshire, SO23 9BH. Tel 54072 (priv 62995).

Priory Gallery. The Priory, Station Rd,Bishops Cleeve, Cheltenham, Gloucestershire. Tel Bishops Cleeve (024 267) 3226.

The Reid Gallery Ltd. Mousehill House,Milford, Godalming, Surrey, GU8 5BL. Tel 6990.

Restorations Unlimited. Pinkney Park, Malmesbury, Wiltshire. Tel 840888 (priv 840437).

Olivia Rumens. 30 Corve St, Ludlow, Shropshire. Tel 3952.

R.S.J. Savage & Son. Alfred St, Northampton, Northamptonshire, NN1 5EY. Tel 33852 (priv 405482).

Martin Scadgell Fine Art. Mulberry House Galleries,Codmore Hill, Pulborough, W.Sussex. Tel 2463.

Shelton Mounting Service. 4 Islingword Rd, Brighton & Hove, E.Sussex, BN2 2SE. Tel 698345.

Stewart Gallery. 48 Devonshire Rd, Bexhill, E.Sussex. Tel 223410.

Stewart Gallery. 25 Grove Rd, Eastbourne, E.Sussex. Tel 29588.

Sutcliffe Galleries. 8 Albert St, Harrogate, N.Yorkshire. Tel 62976.

Thurso Antiques. Drill Hall,Sinclair St, Thurso, Highland. Tel 63291 (priv 66202).

The Tudor Gallery. 2nd floor, 93 Sidwell St, Exeter, Devon, EX4 6PH. Tel 77659.

Michael Webb Fine Paintings. Cefn-Llwyn,Llangristiolus, Bodorgan, Anglesey, Gwynedd, LL62 5DN. Tel Bodorgan (0407) 840336.

H.S.Wellby Ltd. The Malt House,4 Church End, Haddenham, Buckinghamshire. Tel 290036.

Wellington Fine Art. 14 Park Circus, Glasgow, Strathclyde, G3 6AX. Tel 331 2896.

West of England Restoration Studio. 19-21 The Mall, Clifton, Bristol, Avon, BS8 4JG. Tel 741830.

Wigington Partners. 22 New St, Shipston on Stour, Warwickshire, CV36 4EN. Tel 61205.

David Windsor Gallery. 201 High St, Bangor, Gwynedd. Tel 364639.

Restorers, Paper

(including Prints and Watercolours)

Astley House - Fine Art. Astley House, High St, Moreton-in-Marsh, Gloucestershire, GL54 0LL. Tel 50601.

Coltsfoot Gallery. Hatfield, Leominster, Hereford & Worcester, HR6 0SF. Tel Steensbridge (056 882) 277.

Drescher Ltd. 17 Alverstone Rd, London, NW2. Tel 459 5543.

Fiddes Watt. Studio 7, 52A Avonmore Rd, London, W14 8XU. Tel 603 9015.

David E.Green Gallery. 188 Dartmouth Rd, London, SE26. Tel 699 5461.

Norma McCaw Conservation. The Studio,107 Shepherds Bush Rd, London, W6 7LP. Tel 602 0757.

Nicola B. Pirozek, Dip. Cons. 9 Minster Yard, York, N.Yorkshire, YO1 2HH. Tel 35609.

Martin Scadgell Fine Art. Mulberry House Galleries,Codmore Hill, Pulborough, W.Sussex. Tel 2463.

David Windsor Gallery. 201 High St, Bangor, Gwynedd. Tel 364639.

Zaehnsdorf Ltd. 175 Bermondsey St, London, SE1. Tel 407 1244.

Restorers, Statuary and Monuments

Abercrombies. 140 Manor House Rd, Jesmond, Newcastle upon Tyne, Tyne & Wear, NE2 2NA. Tel Tyneside (091) 2817182.

Ian Clayton Ltd. 4 Stainer St, London, SE1. Tel 403 2742.

Plowden & Smith Limited. 190 St Ann's Hill,Wandsworth, London, SW18 2RT. Tel 874 4005.

Restorers, Textiles and Carpets

(including cleaning)

Abadjian Ltd. Palmerston Rd, Wealdstone, Middlesex. Tel 863 1141.

Anglo-Persian Carpet Co Ltd. The Arcade, South Kensington Station, London, SW7 2NA. Tel 589 5457.

Celia Barker Mill. 24 Iverna Gardens,Kensington, London, W8 6TN. Tel 937 9145.

Benardout & Benardout. 7 Thurloe Place, London, SW7 2RX. Tel 584 7658.

Raymond Benardout. 5 William St, Knightsbridge, London, SW1X 9HL. Tel 235 3360 (priv 235 0504).

David Black Oriental Carpets. 96 Portland Rd, London, W11 4LN. Tel 727 2566.

Jack Fairman (Carpets) Ltd. 218 Westbourne Grove, London, W11 2RH. Tel 229 2262/3(priv 992 0087).

S.Franses Ltd. 11 Spring St,Paddington, London, W2. Tel 262 1153/4.

The Kilim Warehouse Ltd. 28A Pickets St, London, SW12 8QB. Tel 675 3122.

C.T.Legge Oriental Carpets. Oakthorpe Rd, Summertown, Oxford, Oxfordshire. Tel 57572 (priv 0993 831298).

Michael and Amanda Lewis Oriental Carpets and Rugs. 8 North St, Wellington, Somerset, TA21 8LT. Tel 7430.

Michael and Amanda Lewis Oriental Carpets and Rugs. 23 Small St, Bristol, Avon, BS1 1DW. Tel 264246.

Clive Loveless. 29 Kelfield Gdns,North Kensington, London, W10 6NA. Tel 969 5831.

M. & M. Oriental Gallery Ltd. 4th Floor, Block D,53/79 Highgate Rd, London, NW5 1TL. Tel 267 5973.

Desmond and Amanda North. The Orchard,Hale St, East Peckham, Kent, TN12 5JB. Tel 871353.

Omar (Harrogate) Ltd. 8 Crescent Rd, Harrogate, N.Yorkshire, HG1 2RS. Tel 503675.

Orbell House Gallery. Orbell House, 8 St James's St, Castle Hedingham, Essex, CO9 3EJ. Tel Hedingham (0787) 60298.

Orchard House, Oriental Rugs. Orchard House, Ollands Road, Reepham, Norfolk. Tel 870234.

Oriental Carpet Centre. 10 Golden Sq, London, W1R 3AF. Tel 439 9070.

Persian Carpet Gallery. North Street, Petworth, W.Sussex, GU28 0DD. Tel 43344.

Eric Pride Oriental Rugs. 8 Imperial Sq, Cheltenham, Gloucestershire, GL50 1QB. Tel 580822 (priv 521057).

Philippa Scott. 30 Elgin Crescent, London, W11. Tel 229 8029.

Talar Oriental Carpets. 23 North End Parade,North End Rd, West Kensington, London, W14. Tel 602 0046.

The Textile Conservation Centre. Apartment 22,Hampton Court Palace, East Molesey, Surrey, KT8 9AU. Tel 977 4943.

Textile Conservation Studio. The Limehouse Cut,Morris Rd, Poplar, London, E14 6NT. Tel 538 4314.

Vigo Carpet Gallery. 6A Vigo St, London, W1. Tel 439 6971.

Whytock & Reid. Sunbury House, Belford Mews, Edinburgh, Lothian, EH4 3DN. Tel 226 4911.

Restorers, Upholstery

see Upholstery

Rugs

see Carpets and Rugs

Russian Works of Art

see also Faberge

Maria Andipa Icon Gallery. 162 Walton St, London, SW3. Tel 589 2371.

Asprey PLC. 165-169 New Bond St, London, W1Y 0AR. Tel 493 6767.

Bentley & Co Ltd. 65 New Bond St, London, W1Y 9DF. Tel 629 0651, 629 0325.

N.Bloom & Son (Antiques) Ltd. 40 Conduit St, London, W1R 9FB. Tel 629 5060.

D.J.Jewellery. 166-168 Ashley Rd, Parkstone, Poole, Dorset, BH14 9BY. Tel 745148.

M.Ekstein Ltd. 90 Jermyn St, London, SW1Y 6JD. Tel 930 2024.

M. Odell Foster. Millmead, Wonersh, Surrey. Tel Guildford (0483) 892375.

Iconastas. 5 Piccadilly Arcade,Jermyn St, London, SW1. Tel 629 1433.

Mark Gallery. 9 Porchester Place, Marble Arch, London, W2 2BS. Tel 262 4906.

I.J.Mazure & Co Ltd. 90 Jermyn St, London, SW1Y 6JD. Tel 839 3101/2.

Temple Gallery. 4 Yeomans Row, Brompton Rd, London, SW3. Tel 589 6622.

Tzigany Fine Arts. 28-29 Dover St, London, W1X 3PA. Tel 491 1007.

The Winter Palace. 69 Kensington Church Street, London, W8. Tel 937 2410.

Samplers

see also Needlework

The Ark Angel. 14 Camden Passage, London, N1 8ED. Tel 226 1644.

Michael & Margaret Baker. 6 High St, Merstham, Surrey. Tel 2658.

Blyth Antiques. 28 Sydney Buildings, Bath, Avon, BA2 6BZ. Tel 69766.

Jean Burnett Antiques. 3a Church St, Finedon, Northamptonshire. Tel Wellingborough (0933) 680430.

Butterwalk House. 55 The Old Butterwalk, High St, Totnes, Devon. Tel 863044.

Close Antiques. 19 Little Minster St, Winchester, Hampshire, SO23 9HA. Tel 64763.

Joan Eyles Antiques. The Stone Yard,Fishergate, Boroughbridge, N.Yorkshire, YO5 9QY. Tel 3357 (priv 2487).

Fenwick and Fisher Antiques. 88 High St, Broadway, Hereford & Worcester. Tel 853227 (priv 853228).

Five Five Six Antiques. 556 King's Rd, London, SW6. Tel 731 2016 (priv 624 5173).

George & Helen Gardiner. 105 West Regent St, Glasgow, Strathclyde, G2 2BA. Tel 332 1264.

Humbleyard Fine Art. 3 Fish Hill, Holt, Norfolk. Tel 713362(priv 036 283 793).

Mac Humble Antiques. 11 Queen St, Bath, Avon, BA1 2Jo. Tel 62751 (priv 022122 3594).

Meriden House Antiques. Meriden House, 75 Market St, Stourbridge, W.Midlands. Tel 395384.

No.Twelve Queen Street. 12 Queen St, Bath, Avon. Tel 62363 (priv 314846).

Old Bakery Antiques. 1 Church St, Hunstanton, Norfolk. Tel Brancaster (0485) 210396.

Piccadilly Antiques. 1/2 Piccadilly,London Rd, Bath, Avon, BA1 6AN. Tel 332779.

Susan Procter. 47-51 The Feus, Auchterarder, Tayside, PH3 1DG. Tel 2532.

Real Macoy. Crossroads, Keighley, W.Yorkshire. Tel 44776.

Anthony Scaramanga Antiques. 108 Newland, Witney, Oxfordshire. Tel 3472.

A Stitch in Time. 1 West End, Beaumaris, Gwynedd. Tel 811055.

Times Past. 84 High St, Pershore, Hereford & Worcester, WR10 1DU. Tel 554258.

Charles & Jane Toller. 20 High St, Datchet, Berkshire, SL3 9EQ. Tel Windsor (0753) 42903.

E.W. Webster Antiques. Wash Farm, Rainford Rd, Bickerstaffe, Lancashire. Tel Skelmersdale (0695) 24322.

Tim Wright Antiques. 147 Bath St, Glasgow, Strathclyde. Tel 221 0364.

Scientific, Nautical and Medical Instruments

see also Nautical and Marine Items, Barometers

Addingham Antiques. 70-72 Main St, Addingham, W.Yorkshire. Tel 830788.

Bobinet Ltd. 102 Mount St, London, W1YD 5HF. Tel 408 0333/4.

Peter D. Bosson. 10B Swan St, Wilmslow, Cheshire, SK9 1HE. Tel 525250 (priv 527857).

Daniel Brewster. 182 West Regent St, Glasgow, Strathclyde. Tel 226 3406.

Victor Burness. 241 Long Lane, London, SE1.

Patric Capon. 350 Upper St,Islington, London, N1. Tel 354 0487 (priv 467 5722).

Carronade. 63 West Regent St, Glasgow, Strathclyde. Tel 332 5600 (priv 649 3655).

The Chimes. Market Place, Reepham, Norfolk, NR10 4JJ. Tel Norwich (0603) 870480.

Connaught Galleries. 44 Connaught St, London, W2. Tel 723 1660.

Country Life Antiques. Sheep St, Stow-on-the-Wold, Gloucestershire, GL54 1JS. Tel Cotswold (0451) 30776.

Country Life Antiques. Grey House,The Square, Stow-on-the-Wold, Gloucestershire, GL54 1AF. Tel 31564.

M.J.Dareau. 66 Cumberland St, Edinburgh, Lothian. Tel 556 9352 & 0968 73028.

Arthur Davidson Ltd. 78-79 Jermyn St, London, SW1. Tel 930 6687, 930 4643.

Caroline Dawson. London. Tel 727 4106.

Dean House Antiques. Dean House,Bepton Rd, Midhurst, W.Sussex, GU29 9LY. Tel 2277.

Graham Deane Antiques. 5 Market St, Brighton & Hove, E.Sussex. Tel 24526.

B.P. Dennison (Antiques). Dwarf Hall, Chapel Hill, Ambleside, Cumbria, LA22 9EB. Tel 32651.

M.Ekstein Ltd. 90 Jermyn St, London, SW1Y 6JD. Tel 930 2024.

Malcolm Frazer Antiques. 19 Brooklyn Crescent, Cheadle, Greater Manchester. Tel 428 3781.

I. Freeman & Son, Simon Kaye Ltd. 18 Dover St, London, W1X 3PB. Tel 493 7658.

Galaxy Arts. 38 New St, Barbican, Plymouth, Devon, PL1 2NA. Tel 667842.

Peter Goodwin Antiques. 284 Westbourne Grove, London, W11. Tel 581 3873.

Grimaldi. 12 Royal Arcade, 28 Old Bond St, London, W1X 3HB. Tel 493 3953.

Hadlow Antiques. No 1 The Pantiles, Tunbridge Wells, Kent. Tel 29858.

David J. Hansord. 32 Steep Hill, Lincoln, Lincolnshire. Tel 3004.

House of Antiques. 4 College St, Petersfield, Hampshire, GU31 4AD. Tel 62172.

House of Buckingham. 113-117 Farringdon Rd, London, EC1R 3BT. Tel 278 2013.

Derek Howard. Stand B2, Chenil Galleries,181-183 King's Rd, Chelsea, London, SW3. Tel 352 2163.

Humbleyard Fine Art. 3 Fish Hill, Holt, Norfolk. Tel 713362(priv 036 283 793).

Langfords. Oldebourne House,46-47 Chancery Lane, London, WC2. Tel 405 6402.

Littlebury Antiques. 58/60 Fairycroft Rd, Saffron Walden, Essex. Tel 27961.

V. & C. Madeira. The Grange, 16 Guys Cliffe Ave, Leamington, Warwickshire. Tel 25012.

Iain Marr Antiques. 3 Mid St, Beauly, Highland, IV4 7DP. Tel 782372.

Robin Martin. 44 Ledbury Rd, London, W11. Tel 727 1301 (priv 727 1300).

Mayflower Antiques. 180-182 High St, Dovercourt, Harwich, Essex. Tel 504079.

Arthur Middleton Ltd. 12 New Row, Covent Garden, London, WC2N 4LF. Tel 836 7042.

Stephen O'Donnell Antiques. Grays Antique Market,58 Davies St, London, W1. Tel 491 8852.

The Old Alarm. Quay Hill, Lymington, Hampshire, SO4 9AR. Tel 77100.

Owen Antiques. 189-193 Oldham Rd, Rochdale, Greater Manchester. Tel 48138 (priv 353270).

Trevor Philip & Sons Ltd. 75a Jermyn St,St James's, London, SW1Y 6NP.

Pinfold Antiques. 28 Steep Hill, Lincoln, Lincolnshire. Tel 44716 (priv 0526 832057).

P.M.Pollak Fine Scientific and Medical Books. Moorview,Plymouth Road, South Brent, Devon, TQ10 9HT. Tel 3457.

David & Carole Potter (Antiques). 76 Derby Rd, Nottingham, Nottinghamshire, NG1 5FD. Tel 417911.

Principia Fine Art. Hungerford Antiques Arcade, Hungerford, Berkshire. Tel Marlborough (0672) 55275.

Quadrant Antiques. 5 North West Circus Place,Stockbridge, Edinburgh, Lothian. Tel 226 7282.

Relcy Antiques. 9 Nelson Rd, Greenwich, London, SE10. Tel 858 2811/2.

Roy Sim Antiques. 21 Allan St, Blairgowrie, Tayside, PH10 6AB. Tel 3860 (priv 3700).

Robin Smith. 23 Belle Vue Rd, Shrewsbury, Shropshire, SY3 7LN. Tel 50357.

Christopher Sykes Antiques. The Old Parsonage, Bedford St, Woburn, Bedfordshire, MK17 9QL. Tel 259 (priv 467).

Igor Tociapski. 39-41 Ledbury Rd, London, W11. Tel 229 8317.

Turret House. 27 Middleton St, Wymondham, Norfolk, NR18 0AB. Tel 603462.

Vintage Cameras Ltd. 254-256 Kirkdale Corner, Sydenham, London, SE26 4NL. Tel 778 5416.

David Weston Ltd. 44 Duke St, St James's, London, SW1. Tel 839 1051.

Christopher Wood. Harlaw Farmhouse, Kelso, Borders, TD5 7RA. Tel Stichill (05737) 321.

Harriet Wynter Ltd. 50 Redcliffe Rd, London, SW10 9NJ. Tel 352 6494.

York House Antiques. 11-13 York St, Cowes, Isle of Wight. Tel 295746.

Sculpture

see also Bronzes

Thos Agnew & Sons Ltd. 43 Old Bond St, London, W1X 4BA. Tel 629 6176.

Donald Allison Antiques. 115-119 New Hall Lane, Preston, Lancashire. Tel 701916 (priv 615946).

Antiquus. 90-92 Pimlico Rd, London, SW1. Tel 730 8681.

Armstrong-Davis Gallery. High St, Arundel, W.Sussex. Tel 882752.

Blond Fine Art. 22 Princes St, London, W1. Tel 437 1230.

Bridge End Gallery. Terrace Hall, Woolhope, Hereford & Worcester, HR1 4QJ. Tel Fownhope (043277) 373.

Bruton Gallery Limited. High St, Bruton, Somerset, BA10 0AB. Tel 812697 & 812205.

Centaur Gallery. Great Expectations,82 Highgate Village, London, N6. Tel 340 0087.

Chaucer Fine Arts Inc. 45 Pimlico Rd, London, SW1. Tel 730 2972.

P. & D. Colnaghi & Co Ltd. 14 Old Bond St, London, W1X 4JL. Tel 491 7408.

Ralph Cox. 53 Ledbury Rd, London, W11. Tel 229 6900 (priv 723 3162).

Crane Kalman Gallery. 178 Brompton Rd, London, SW3. Tel 584 7566.

Anthony d'Offay Gallery. 9 & 23 Dering St, New Bond St, London, W1. Tel 499 4100.

The Fine Art Society Plc. 148 New Bond St, London, W1Y 0JT. Tel 629 5116.

Gimpel Fils. 30 Davies St, London, W1Y 1LG. Tel 493 2488.

Heim Gallery. 59 Jermyn St, St James's, London, SW1Y 6LX. Tel 493 0688.

Cyril Humphris. 8 Pembroke Walk, London, W8. Tel 937 1719.

Humphry Antiques. East St, Petworth, W.Sussex, GU28 0AB. Tel 43053 (priv 42944).

Lefevre Gallery. 30 Bruton St, London, W1X 8JD. Tel 493 1572.

Mallett at Bourdon House Ltd. 2 Davies St, Berkeley Sq, London, W1Y 1LJ. Tel 629 2444/5.

Mercury Gallery Ltd. 26 Cork St, London, W1. Tel 734 7800.

New Gallery. Abele Tree House,9 Fore St, Budleigh Salterton, Devon, EX9 6NG. Tel 3768.

The Plazzotta Studio. 22 Cathcart Rd, London, SW10 9NN. Tel 352 7493.

H.W.Poulter & Son. 279 Fulham Rd, London, SW10 9PZ. Tel 352 7268 (priv 603 7398).

Alex Reid & Lefevre Ltd. 30 Bruton St, London, W1. Tel 493 1572.

The Sladmore Gallery. 32 Bruton Place,off Berkeley Sq, London, W1X 7AA. Tel 499 0365.

Marshall Spink Ltd. 18 Albemarle St, London, W1X 3HA. Tel 493 2575 and 493 5280.

Robin Symes. 3 Ormond Yard,Duke of York St, St James's, London, SW1. Tel 930 9856/7.

Michael Tollemache Ltd. 78 Cadogan P1, London, SW1. Tel 235 5107.

Leigh Underhill Gallery. 100 Islington High St,Camden Passage, Islington, London, N1. Tel 226 5673.

Woburn Fine Arts. 12 Market Place, Woburn, Bedfordshire, MK17 9PZ. Tel 624.

Christopher Wood Gallery. 15 Motcomb St, London, SW1. Tel 235 9141 (priv 828 1092).

Security

C. & A.J.Barmby. 68 Judd Rd, Tonbridge, Kent. Tel 356479.

Sewing Machines

Calver Associates. Newton Abbot, Devon, TQ12 4QE. Tel 3263 (pm only).

Shippers and Packers

W.B. Airfreight Ltd. 69/70 G Building 521,Cargo Terminal, London Airport, Heathrow, Middlesex. Tel 01-897 2551.

J.H.Bachmann (UK) Ltd. Unitair Centre, Gt South West Rd, Feltham, Middlesex, TW14 8NT. Tel 844 1771.

Directory Entries are Free and ADDITIONS OR CORRECTIONS will be welcomed by *THE EDITOR, British Art and Antiques Directory, National Magazine House, 72 Broadwick Street, London W1V 2BP*

Blatchpack Ltd. 22-24 Smyth Rd,Ashton, Bristol, Avon. Tel 665996.

James Bourlet & Sons Ltd. 3 Space Waye, Feltham, Middlesex, TW14 0TY. Tel 751 1155 (24 hours).

Burlington Fine Arts. Unit 8, Ascot Rd,Clockhouse Lane, Feltham, Middlesex, TW14 8QS. Tel Ashford (07842) 48183.

Jimmy Collins Antiques Ltd. 136 Standishgate, Wigan, Greater Manchester, WN1 1XP. Tel 48180 (priv 41484).

Geo Copsey & Co Ltd. Danes Rd, Romford, Essex. Tel 24213.

Coxsmith UK. 96A Shakespeare Rd, Gillingham, Kent, ME7 5QJ. Tel Medway (0634) 575983.

Davies, Turner & Co Ltd. Unit 9 & 10,Brickfields Trading Estate, Huyton, Liverpool, Merseyside, L36 6HY. Tel 480 8118.

Featherston Shipping Ltd. 24 Hampton House,15-17 Ingate Place, London, SW8 3NS. Tel 720 0422.

C.R.Fenton & Co Ltd. Beachy Rd, Old Ford, London, E3 2NX. Tel 533 2711.

P. Gale Shipping. Furlong House,East St, Warminster, Wiltshire.

Gander & White Shipping Ltd. 21 Lillie Rd, London, SW6 1UE. Tel 381 0571.

Greengrass Antiques. 34 Frances Rd, Windsor, Berkshire. Tel 65627.

Hedleys Humpers Ltd. 159 Iverson Rd,West Hampstead, London, NW6. Tel 624 6874 & 6981.

Frank Hill (Removals & Storage) Ltd. Cambridge St Industrial Estate,Salford 7, Manchester, Greater Manchester, M7 9UT. Tel 834 1317 (priv 766 3260).

Kees & Co. Tandridge, Top Common,West Runton, Cromer, Norfolk, NR27 9LT. Tel 8109.

T.E.& S.Kindon Antiques. St John's House,Station Rd, Knaresborough, N.Yorkshire. Tel 867554.

Leigh Auction Rooms. 88-90 Pall Mall, Leigh-on-Sea, Essex. Tel Southend-on-Sea (0702) 77051.

Lockson Services Ltd. 29 Broomfield St, London, E14 6BQ. Tel 515 8600.

London & Southern Shipping. The Warehouse, Gladstone Rd, Portslade, E.Sussex, BN4 1LJ. Tel 420154/202989.

Colin Macleods Antique Centre. 159/161 Goldsmith Ave, Southsea, Hampshire, PO4 8BL. Tel Portsmouth (0705) 734173.

Maggs Antiques. 26-28 Fleet St, Liverpool, Merseyside, L1 4AR. Tel 708 0221.

John Mason (Wavertree). 127 High St, Liverpool, Merseyside, L15 8JT. Tel 722 2352.

Stephen Morris Shipping Ltd. 89 Upper St, London, N1 ONP. Tel 354 1212.

Vic Pearson & Co Ltd. 7 Munton Rd, London, SE17 1PR. Tel 703 8351.

Pitt & Scott Ltd. 20-24 Eden Grove, London, N7 8ED. Tel 607 7321.

L.J. Roberton Ltd. Marlborough House,Cooks Rd, Stratford, London, E15 2PW. Tel 5192020.

T. Rogers & Co (Packers) Ltd. PO Box 8,1A Broughton St, London, SW8 3QL. Tel 622 9151.

Schwartz Sackin & Co Ltd. 89 Portobello Rd, London, W11. Tel 727 3857.

Scott Packing & Warehousing Co Ltd. Kilsyth Road,Kirkintilloch, Glasgow, Strathclyde. Tel 776 7191.

Semus Lewis Containers Ltd. 69-77 North St, Portslade, E.Sussex. Tel 420154 and 415078.

Silver Tay Trading Company Ltd. St Colmes,496 Perth Rd, Dundee, Tayside, DD2 1LS. Tel 21751 (priv 67454).

Ralph A.Sutcliffe Antiques. Harle Syke Mill, Harle Syke, Burnley, Lancashire. Tel 31412.

SPS Shipping. Unit 3, Osiers Industrial Estate,Osiers Rd, London, SW18. Tel 871 1223.

Trans Euro Worldwide. Fine Art Division,Drury Way, Brent Park, London, NW10 0JN. Tel 459 8080.

K. & A. Welch. 1A Church St, Warminster, Wiltshire. Tel 214687 (priv 213433).

Wickersley Antiques. 3 Broad St,Parkgate, Rotherham, S.Yorkshire. Tel 525595.

Wingate & Johnston Ltd. 78 Broadway, Stratford, London, E15 1NG. Tel 555 8123.

Shipping Goods, Wholesalers, Exporters

London

The Antique Gallery. 40 Peckham Rye, London, SE15. Tel 732 7808 (priv 653 4279).

F.E.A.Briggs Ltd. 73 Ledbury Rd, London, W11. Tel 727 0909 (priv 969 0297).

Butchoff Antiques. 48 Peckham Rye, London, SE15. Tel 639 0736.

D.B.Cater Antiques. 173 & 175 Bermondsey St, London, SE1 3UW. Tel 407 2040.

F.T. Dent. 58 Goldhurst Terrace, London, NW6. Tel 624 8383.

Franklin's. Camberwell Antique Market,161 Camberwell Rd, London, SE5. Tel 703 8089.

Kensington Furniture. Troy Court,214-216 Kensington High St, London, W8. Tel 937 4973.

Oola Boola Antiques. 166 Tower Bridge Rd, London, SE1. Tel 403 0794.

Stephen Orton Antiques. 72 Upper St,Islington, London, N1 0NY. Tel 226 2770 (priv 508 1023).

Penny Farthing Antiques. 177 Bermondsey St, London, SE1 3UW. Tel 407 5171.

Princedale Antiques. 70 Princedale Rd, Holland Park, London, W11. Tel 727 0868.

Princedale Antiques Workshop. 56 Eden Grove, London, N7. Tel 607 6376.

M. & L.Silver Co Ltd. 2 Woodstock St, London, W1R 1HD. Tel 499 5392.

This & That (Furniture). 50 & 51 Chalk Farm Rd, London, NW1. Tel 267 5433.

Ian Wilson Antiques. 70-72 Peckham Rye, London, SE15. Tel 639 5068 (priv 732 5349).

Regions

The Abbey Antique Shop. 43-45 King St, Whalley, Blackburn, Lancashire, BB6 9SP. Tel Whalley (0254) 3139.

Abbey Antiques. 62 Church St, Tewkesbury, Gloucestershire. Tel 2378.

Ace Antiques. 40 Huddersfield Rd, Oldham, Greater Manchester, OL4 2AE. Tel 620 5755 (priv 626 2062).

Adam Antiques. 12 Sneyd St, Canton, Cardiff, S.Glamorgan. Tel 40022 (priv 0222 883415).

Antics. 44 Portsmouth Rd, Cobham, Surrey. Tel 5505.

Antique Exporters of Chester. Chester, Cheshire. Tel Tarvin (0829) 41001 (priv 0244-570069).

The Antique Furniture Warehouse. Old Maltings, Crown Place, Woodbridge, Suffolk. Tel 7222.

Antiques Trade Warehouse. 28 Lorne Park Rd, Bournemouth, Dorset, BH1 1JL. Tel 292944.

The Antiques Warehouse. 34-36 Rockingham Rd, Uxbridge, Middlesex, UB8 2TZ. Tel 56963 & 71012.

Anvil Antiques. The Old School,Alsop St, Leek, Staffordshire. Tel 385280.

Apollo Antiques Ltd. 62 West St, Warwick, Warwickshire. Tel 494746.

Roger Appleyard Ltd. Fitzwilliam Rd,Eastwood Trading Estate, Rotherham, S.Yorkshire, S65 1SL. Tel 67670.

Armada Exports. 50 Suffolk Rd, Cheltenham, Gloucestershire. Tel 29812, 32615.

J.C.E. & N.I. Armson - Antiques. The Hollies, Yoxall, Staffordshire, DE13 8NH. Tel 472352 (priv 028371-2052).

James Ash Antiques. The Warehouse, Station Rd, Llandeilo, Dyfed. Tel 823728 (priv 0269 850119).

Ashtons Furniture Centre. 1-3 Clyde Rd, Brighton & Hove, E.Sussex, BN1 4NN. Tel 605253.

Aspleys Antique Imports & Exports. Compton Mill, Compton, Leek, Staffordshire. Tel 373346-96.

Aspleys Antique Imports & Exports. 18 Carter St, Uttoxeter, Staffordshire. Tel 5291.

Keith Atkinson Antiques. 59 Brighton Rd, Croydon, Surrey, CR2 6ED. Tel 688 5559.

Attic Antiques. 23 & 32 Ship St, Brighton & Hove, E.Sussex, BN1 1AD. Tel 29464 (priv 551594).

Barnet Antiques & Fine Art. 236 High St, Barnet, Hertfordshire, EN5 5TD. Tel 01-440 3620.

Neville Bates Antiques and Fine Art Gallery. 208 Dickson Rd, Blackpool, Lancashire, FY1 2JS. Tel 53552.

Richard Batsford Antiques. Antique Trade Warehouse,29 Lorne Park Rd, Bournemouth, Dorset. Tel 292944 (priv 25485).

T.W.Beaty. 22 Well St, Moffat, Dumfries & Galloway. Tel 20380.

Bell Passage Antiques. 36-38 High St,Wickwar, Wotton-under-Edge, Gloucestershire, GL12 8NP. Tel Wickwar (045 424) 251.

Pat Bently Antiques. 7 King's Arms Yard, Ampthill, Bedfordshire. Tel 404939.

Jack Blackburn. 105 New Hall Lane, Preston, Lancashire. Tel 791117.

Arthur Boaden Antiques. 29-30 Market Place, Hexham, Northumberland, NE46 3PB. Tel 603187 (priv 604265).

John Botting. A27 Antiques Warehouse,Chaucer Industrial Estate, Polegate, E.Sussex. Tel 7167.

Braemar Antiques Ltd. Waltham Rd, White Waltham, Berkshire. Tel Littlewick Green(062 882) 3741.

Bridge House Antiques. The Old Police Station, 96 Welsh Row, Nantwich, Cheshire, CW5 5ET. Tel 624035.

Bristol Antiques Ltd. Cumhill Farm, Pilton, Shepton Mallet, Somerset. Tel Pilton (074 989) 240.

Britannia Antiques. 754 Stockport Rd,Longsight, Manchester, Greater Manchester, M12 4GD. Tel 224 8350, 224 6425.

Paul Bruce Antiques & Pine Shop. 25-27 St Helens St, Ipswich, Suffolk. Tel 55400.

F.G. Bruschweiler (Antiques) Ltd. 41-67 Lower Lambricks, Rayleigh, Essex, SS6 7EN. Tel 773761, 773932.

C.P.A. Antiques. Newtown Lodge, Tangier Lane, Bishops Waltham, Hampshire, SO3 1BU. Tel 5176.

Carshalton Antiques Galleries. 5 High St, Carshalton, Surrey, SM5 3AP. Tel 01-647 5664.

Chalon Ltd. Old Hambridge Mill, Hambridge, Curry Rivel, Somerset, TA10 0BP. Tel Langport (0458) 252374 (priv 0460 67715).

Charles International Antiques. 3 Market St, Maidstone, Kent. Tel 682882.

Cladgild Ltd. Vine House, Fair Green, Reach, Cambridgeshire, CB5 0JD. Tel Newmarket (0638) 742171.

Clifton Antiques Ltd. 12-13 Waterloo St,Clifton, Bristol, Avon. Tel 36038.

John H. Collings. Antique Village, Knightcott, Banwell, Avon, BS24 6HS. Tel 823181 (priv 812030).

J. Collins and Son (Est.1953). The Studio, 63 & 28 High St, Bideford, Devon, EX39 2AN. Tel 73103 (priv 76485).

Jimmy Collins Antiques Ltd. 136 Standishgate, Wigan, Greater Manchester, WN1 1XP. Tel 48180 (priv 41484).

Mary Collins Furniture Ltd. Unit 8, Sinclair Estate,Pulloxhill Rd, Greenfield, Bedfordshire. Tel Ampthill (0525) 717555.

E.J.Cook & Son Antiques. The Antique Centre, 1 Severn Rd, Gloucester, Gloucestershire. Tel 29716.

Cosmo Antiques (inc Jolie Jewellery). Westerham Antiques Centre,18 Market Sq, Westerham, Kent, TN16 1AR. Tel 62080.

William Courtney & Sons. Cross St,Tunnel Entrance, Birkenhead, Merseyside, L41 5DR. Tel 647-8693.

E.W.Cousins & Son. 27 High St, Ixworth, Suffolk. Tel Pakenham (0359) 30254.

Philip Cowan Antiques. 33 Parliament St, Liverpool, Merseyside. Tel 709 1217.

Cradlewell Antiques. 244 Jesmond Rd, Newcastle upon Tyne, Tyne & Wear. Tel 810691.

Crossbow House Antiques. Stoneymeadow Rd, High Blantyre, Strathclyde. Tel Blantyre (0698) 823106, 822378.

David, Jean & John Antiques. 587 London Rd, Westcliff-on-Sea, Essex. Tel Southend (0702) 339106.

Davies Antiques. 12 St Mary St, Chepstow, Gwent, NP6 5EW. Tel Dingestow (060 083) 343.

J.Denton (Antiques). Rear of 440 Dunstable Rd,(Corner Arundel Rd), Luton, Bedfordshire, LU4 8DT. Tel 582726.

Iain Downe Antiques. 28 North Rd, Brighton & Hove, E.Sussex, BN1 1YB. Tel 697496.

Keith D Edwards Antiques. Crosscrake Farm,Crosscrake, Kendal, Cumbria, LA8 OLB. Tel Sedgwick (0448) 60313.

Elsdon Antiques. 152 High St, Old Woking, Woking, Surrey, GU22 9JH. Tel 62651.

A.W. England & Sons. 54 Lower St, Stroud, Gloucestershire. Tel 3262.

Fine Arts Traders & Shippers and Bondgate Antiques. Hill House, 39 Bondgate Within, Alnwick, Northumberland, NE66 1SX. Tel 603394 (priv 0665 830816).

Susanna Fisher. Spencer, Upham, Hampshire, SO3 1JD. Tel Durley (04896) 291.

Alastair Fraser Antiques. 2A Rushworth Ave, West Bridgford, Nottingham, Nottinghamshire. Tel 821835.

The Furniture Station Ltd. The Kelterment Antique Market,Fordham, Ely, Cambridgeshire.

Fyfe's Antiques. 41 & 48 Thistle St, Edinburgh, Lothian, EH2 1DY. Tel 225 4287.

P.R.Garner (Antiques). Willow Farm, 104 High St, Landbeach, Cambridge, Cambridgeshire. Tel 860470.

Gay's Antiques Ltd. 34-38 London Rd,Hazel Grove, Stockport, Greater Manchester. Tel 061-483 5532.

N. Geary Ltd. 114 Richardshaw Lane, Pudsey, W.Yorkshire. Tel 564122.

Glendale Antiques. Peth Head, Wooler, Northumberland. Tel 81396.

The Golden Drop Antiques. Chatteris Rd (A141), Warboys, Cambridgeshire. Tel Chatteris (03543) 2990.

Gordon's Antiques. 7 Cattell Rd, Warwick, Warwickshire. Tel 490461.

Albert Graham Ltd. 98-100 Main St, Larne, Co Antrim. Tel 76655 (priv 73134).

The Granary & Rene Antiques and Art. 17A Kings Rd, St Leonards, E.Sussex, TN37 6DU. Tel 432610 (priv 71586).

The Granary Galleries. Court House, Ash Priors,near Bishops Lydeard, Taunton, Somerset, TA4 3NQ. Tel Bishops Lydeard (0823) 432402 (priv 432816).

Renee and Roy Green. Ashcombe House, Lewes Rd, Lewes, E.Sussex. Tel 474794.

Ron Green Antiques. 209, 227 & 239 Watling St, Towcester, Northamptonshire, NN12 7BX. Tel 50387.

C.Greenway Antiques. 90 Corn St, Witney, Oxfordshire. Tel 5026.

Simon Greenwood Antiques. 23 Melmerby Industrial Estate,Green Lane, Melmerby, N.Yorkshire, HG4 5HP. Tel 571 (priv: 0677-22554).

Halifax Antiques Centre. Queens Road Mills,Queens Rd/Gibbet St, Halifax, W.Yorkshire, HX1 4LR. Tel 66657.

Hall's Antiques. Court House, Ash Priors, Taunton Lydeard, Somerset, TA4 3NQ. Tel Bishops Lydeard (0823) 432402.

R.& L. Hampshire Antiques. Rutherford Hall,Gatehouse of Fleet, Castle Douglas, Dumfries & Galloway, DG7 4HS. Tel Gatehouse (05574) 616.

Bob Harris & Sons. 2071 Coventry Rd, Birmingham, W.Midlands. Tel 743 2259.

Tim Harrison Trade & Export Antiques. 36 Market St, Warwick, Warwickshire. Tel 491400.

David Hawkins (Brighton) Ltd. 15B Prince Albert St,The Lanes, Brighton & Hove, E.Sussex. Tel 21357.

Helperby Antiques. Main Street, Helperby, York, N.Yorkshire, YO6 2PL. Tel Helperby (09016) 692.

David Hick Antiques. Alexandra House, Carre Four Selous, St Lawrence, Jersey. Tel 62965.

Hingstone's. 13 & 15 Northam Rd, Southampton, Hampshire. Tel 20180 (priv 0703-812301).

Adrian Hornsey Ltd. Chandos Rd, Buckingham, Buckinghamshire, MK18 2Ao. Tel 816363.

John Howkins Antiques. 145 King St, Great Yarmouth, Norfolk.

Colin S.Hughes. 36 Penrallt St, Machynlleth, Powys. Tel 2363.

Owen Humble. 11,12,13 Clayton Rd,Jesmond, Newcastle upon Tyne, Tyne & Wear, NE2 4RP. Tel 2810882.

Dudley Hume. 46 & 50 Upper North St, Brighton & Hove, E.Sussex, BN1 3PH. Tel 23461.

Anthony Hurst Antiques. 13 Church St, Woodbridge, Suffolk. Tel 2500.

Imrie Antiques. Back St, Bridge of Earn, Tayside. Tel 812784.

A.R.Jaffray. 16 Market Place, Melksham, Wiltshire, SN12 6EX. Tel 702269.

Johnson's of Sherborne Ltd. South St, Sherborne, Dorset, DTG 3NF. Tel 812585.

Alan Jones Antiques. Fatherford Farm, Okehampton, Devon. Tel 2970.

K.C. Antiques. 538 Bolton Rd, Darwen, Lancashire. Tel 772252.

T.E.& S.Kindon Antiques. St John's House,Station Rd, Knaresborough, N.Yorkshire. Tel 867554.

F. & T.King and Everyman Antique Fairs. Victorian Cottage,High St, Attleborough, Norfolk, NR17 2BT. Tel 453285.

Kirkby Antiques Ltd. Highfield, Kirkby on Bain, Woodhall Spa, Lincolnshire, LN10 6YN. Tel 52119 & 53461.

Ladygate Antiques. 8A Market Place, Beverley, Humberside, HU17 8BB. Tel Hull (0482) 881494.

N.A.J. Lanchester. 21 High St, Debenham, Suffolk. Tel 860756.

Lesley's Antiques. 329 Hessle Rd, Hull, Humberside, HU3 4BL. Tel 23986 (priv 646280).

Linnets Nest Antiques & Mawby's International. 50 Church St, Rugby, Warwickshire. Tel 61393 &832600 priv75305.

Richard Lloyd. Dolhaidd Mansion, Henllan, Dyfed. Tel Velindre (0559) 370791.

John Long Antiques. St Mary's Old Church,915 Stockport Rd, Levenshulme, Manchester, Greater Manchester. Tel 224 7923.

Colin Macleods Antique Centre. 159/161 Goldsmith Ave, Southsea, Hampshire, PO4 8BL. Tel Portsmouth (0705) 734173.

Maggs Antiques. 26-28 Fleet St, Liverpool, Merseyside, L1 4AR. Tel 708 0221.

Mallglade Antiques. Haigh Hall, Haigh, Barnsley, S.Yorkshire, S75 4BT. Tel Bretton (0924 85) 516.

Manor Barn Pine. Burnside Mill, Main St, Addingham, Ilkley, W.Yorkshire, LS29 0PJ. Tel Addingham (0943) 830176.

Manor House Antiques. 42 Suffolk Rd, Cheltenham, Gloucestershire. Tel 32780.

Mansfield Antiques. 49-51 Ratcliffe Gate, Mansfield, Nottinghamshire. Tel 27475 (Priv 32108).

Market Antiques. 80 Market St, Hoylake, Merseyside, L47 3BB. Tel 632 4059 (24 hrs).

Peter Marks Antiques Warehouse. 1-11 Church Rd, Portslade, E.Sussex. Tel Brighton (0273) 415471 (priv 501978).

Marksdanes Antiques Ltd. Station Rd, Bruton, Somerset. Tel 3267.

Martin & Parke. 97 Lynchford Rd, Farnborough, Hampshire. Tel 515311 (priv 511388).

Peter J. Martin. 40 High St, Eton, Berkshire, SL4 6BD. Tel Windsor (0753) 864901 (priv 863987).

Mayflower Antiques. 180-182 High St, Dovercourt, Harwich, Essex. Tel 504079.

Merlin Antiques & Restorations. Howgill Lane, Sedbergh, Cumbria. Tel 20301 (priv 20719).

Mill Farm Antiques. 50 Market St, Disley, Cheshire, SK12 2DT. Tel 4045.

Millers Antiques, Kelvedon. 46 High St, Kelvedon, Essex. Tel 70098.

Geoffrey Mole Antique Exports. 400 Wincolmlee, Hull, Humberside. Tel 27858.

A.D.Moorhouse Ltd. 2 Barmouth Court,Barmouth Rd, Abbeydale, Sheffield, S.Yorkshire, S7 2DH. Tel 582160.

Ian Murray Antiques Warehouse. 21 Glasgow Rd, Perth, Tayside. Tel 37222 (priv 0250-2508).

Nethergate Gallery. 140 Nethergate (shop & office), Dundee, Tayside, DD1 4ED. Tel 21751.

Robert Neville Antiques. The Old Dairy,Western Boulevard, Leicester, Leicestershire.

David & Penny Newlove Antiques. 28 High St, Wincanton, Somerset, BA9 9JF. Tel 32672.

Michael Norman Antiques Ltd. 15 Ship St, Brighton & Hove, E.Sussex, BN1 1AD. Tel 29253/4 26712.

North Parade Antiques. 75 Banbury Rd (A423), Oxford, Oxfordshire. Tel 59816 (priv 880923).

North Wales Antiques. 58 Abergele Rd, Colwyn Bay, Clwyd. Tel 30521.

North Western Antique Centre. New Preston Mill (Horrockses Yard),New Hall Lane, Preston, Lancashire, PR1 5UH. Tel 794498.

North Wilts Exporters. Farm Hill House, Brinkworth, Wiltshire. Tel 423 and 625.

Northgate Antiques. 48 High St, Rochester, Kent. Tel Medway (0634) 408534.

Old Britannia. Castle Street, Combe Martin, Ilfracombe, Devon. Tel Combe Martin (027 188) 3610.

The Old Mint House. 45 Turkey Rd, Bexhill, E.Sussex. Tel 216056 (priv 0323 761251).

Tom Owen (Antiques). 111 Newhall Lane, Preston, Lancashire. Tel 792950.

Tom Owen Antiques. 18 Rawcliffe St, Blackpool, Lancashire. Tel 33008.

Pattersons Antiques. 1 Grey St, North Shields, Tyne & Wear. Tel 572118.

Penny Farthing. High St, Croydon, Cambridgeshire. Tel Cambridge (0223) 207331.

Phelps Ltd. 133-135 St Margaret's Rd, Twickenham, Middlesex, TW1 1RG. Tel 892 1778, 892 7129.

J.Powell (Hove) Ltd. 20 Wellington Rd, Portslade, E.Sussex. Tel 411599.

John Prestige Antiques. 1/2 Greenswood Court, Greenswood Rd, Brixham, Devon. Tel 6141, 6723 (priv 3739).

Quadrant Antiques. 5 North West Circus Place,Stockbridge, Edinburgh, Lothian. Tel 226 7282.

Paul Quentin Antiques. 626 Manchester Rd, Bury, Greater Manchester, BL9 9SU. Tel 766 6673.

Martin Quick Antiques Ltd. 321-323 Tettenhall Rd, Wolverhampton, W.Midlands, WV6 0JZ. Tel 754703 (priv 752908).

Alan Ramsey Antiques. 4A Thornaby Place, Thornaby, Cleveland. Tel Middlesbrough (0642) 603181.

G.T.Ratcliff Ltd. Durwards Hall, Kelvedon, Essex. Tel 70234.

John Robinson Antiques. 172-176 Manchester Rd, Wigan, Greater Manchester, WN2 2EA. Tel 47773 (priv 41671).

Ropers Hill Antiques. Ropers Hill Farm, Staunton Harold, Ashby de la Zouch, Leicestershire. Tel 413919.

S & S Antiques. 64 Hampton Rd, Twickenham, Middlesex.

N.P. & A. Salt Antiques. Abbeydale House, Barmouth Rd, Sheffield, S.Yorkshire, S1 2DH. Tel 582672.

Savoy Antiques. 7 Bridgewater St, Liverpool, Merseyside. Tel 708 9159.

Semus Lewis Containers Ltd. 69-77 North St, Portslade, E.Sussex. Tel 420154 and 415078.

F.B.Shaftoe. 17-18 Regent Parade, Harrogate, N.Yorkshire, HG1 5AW. Tel 502151.

Laurence Shaw Antiques. Spilsby Rd, Horncastle, Lincolnshire, LN9 5DQ. Tel 7638 (priv 065 888 600).

Shirleys Antiques. Bow St, Langport, Somerset. Tel 250064.

Roy Sim Antiques. 21 Allan St, Blairgowrie, Tayside, PH10 6AB. Tel 3860 (priv 3700).

R.M.Sinclair & Son. 58 South William St, Perth, Tayside. Tel 29666.

Smith-Albany Antiques. 60a Keighley Rd, Cowling, Keighley, W.Yorkshire. Tel Nelson (0282) 64356.

E. Smith (Leicester) Ltd. The Antique Complex,9 St. Nicholas Place, Leicester, Leicestershire, LE1 5LB. Tel 533343.

Peter Smith Antiques. 2 Tunstall Rd, Sunderland, Tyne & Wear. Tel 77842 (priv 40008).

Smith's The Rink Ltd. Dragon Rd, Harrogate, N.Yorkshire. Tel 503217.

Stockwell Antiques. Exeter Antique Wholesalers,Exeter Airport, Clyst Honiton, Exeter, Devon, EX5 2LL. Tel 66279.

Stone Hall Antiques. Down Hall Rd, Matching Green, Harlow, Essex. Tel 731440.

Ralph A.Sutcliffe Antiques. Harle Syke Mill, Harle Syke, Burnley, Lancashire. Tel 31412.

Sutton Valence Antiques. Sutton Valence, Maidstone, Kent. Tel 843333.

Tameside Antiques. Cavendish Mill, Cavendish St,Ashton-under-Lyne, Manchester, Greater Manchester. Tel 344 5477 (priv 308 4445).

John D. Thornton & Family (Antiques) Ltd. 123 The Mount, York, N.Yorkshire, YO2 2DA. Tel 23264.

Thorpe Antiques. 51 High St, Finedon, Northamptonshire, NN9 5JN. Tel Wellingborough (0933) 680196.

Thorpe Antiques. 3 High St, Higham Ferrers, Northamptonshire. Tel Wellingborough (0933) 59747.

Tickle & Bragger & Co Ltd. Great Western House and Warehouse, Lostwithiel, Cornwall. Tel Bodmin (0208) 873027 (priv 0503-20504).

Tickle & Bragger & Co Ltd. Great Western House and Warehouse, Lostwithiel, Cornwall. Tel Bodmin (0208) 873027 (priv 0503-20504).

Tricia Timms Antiques. 82A Dunstable St, Ampthill, Bedfordshire. Tel 403030.

Raymond Tomlinson (Antiques) Ltd. Northfield Buildings,Northfield Place, Wetherby, W.Yorkshire, LS22 4TB. Tel 64866, 64870.

J.P.Townsend. Ullenwood Park Farm, Ullenwood, Gloucestershire. Tel Coberley (024 287) 223.

John Trefor Antiques. Rhuallt Hall Farm, Rhuallt, St Asaph, Clwyd, LL17 OTR. Tel 583604.

R. & M. Turner Ltd, Antiques and Fine Art. 34/36 High St, Jedburgh, Borders. Tel 63445.

Valmar Antiques. Croft House, High Lane, Stansted Mountfitchet, Essex, CM24 8LQ. Tel Bishops Stortford (0279) 813201.

Stewart Ward (Coins) Ltd. 16 High St, Westerham, Kent, TN16 1RF. Tel 63997.

Watling Antiques. 139 Crayford Rd, Crayford, Kent, DA1 4AS. Tel 523620.

J.R.Webb. 23 Bon Accord Terrace, Aberdeen, Grampian. Tel 26709.

West Lancs Antique Exports. Black Horse Farm,123 Liverpool Road South, Burscough, Lancashire. Tel 894634.

Wimborne Antiques. 46 High St, Wimborne Minster, Dorset, BH21 1HT. Tel 887863 (priv 883686).

Winters' Antiques. (Trade and Export Warehouse),62 Severn Rd, Weston-super-Mare, Avon. Tel 20118 (priv 814610).

D.Wise Antiques. 78 Derby Rd, Nottingham, Nottinghamshire, NG7 1AY. Tel 472132.

Yates Antiques. 21a Woodfield St, Morriston, Swansea, W.Glamorgan. Tel 781422.

Peter Young Antiques. Earcroft School, Blackburn Rd, Darwen, Lancashire. Tel 73521 (priv 04577-70467).

Peter Young Antiques. Friarmere School House,47 Huddersfield Rd, Oldham, Greater Manchester. Tel Saddleworth (04577) 70467.

Shop Signs

Relic Antiques. Brillscote Farm, Lea, Malmesbury, Wiltshire, SN16 9PF. Tel 2332.

Silver Flatware

A.D.C. Heritage Ltd. 2 Old Bond St, London, W1X 3TD. Tel 493 5088.

J. Barrymore & Co. 73-75 High St, Honiton, Devon. Tel 2244.

Bruford & Heming Ltd. 28 Conduit St, London, W1R 9TA. Tel 499 7644, 629 4289.

Meg Campbell. 10 Church Lane, Highfield, Southampton, Hampshire, SO2 1SZ. Tel 557636.

Gavina Ewart. 60 High St, Broadway, Hereford & Worcester. Tel 853371.

Grey-Harris & Co. 12 Princess Victoria St,Clifton, Bristol, Avon. Tel 737365.

Hancocks & Co (Jewellers) Ltd. 1 Burlington Gardens, London, W1X 2HP. Tel 493 8904.

James Hardy & Co. 235 Brompton Rd, London, SW3 2EP. Tel 589 5050.

Sanda Lipton. 35 Kenway Rd, London, SW5. Tel 373 9625 (shop), 407 0278.

Mappin & Webb Ltd (Butt & Co). 32 Eastgate Row, Chester, Cheshire, CH1 1LF. Tel 25938.

Anne Newman. Cheltenham Antique Market,54 Suffolk St, Cheltenham, Gloucestershire. Tel 29812, 32615.

Jane Pollock Antiques. 4 Castle Gate, Penrith, Cumbria. Tel 67211.

Jack Shaw & Co Antique Silver. The Old Grammar School, Skipton Rd, Ilkley, W.Yorkshire, LS29 9EP. Tel 609467.

F.W.Taylor. Waite House, 71 Church St, Tewkesbury, Gloucestershire. Tel 295990.

William Walter. Silver Vaults, Chancery House,Chancery Lane, London, WC2A 1QS. Tel 242 3248/9.

Silver Restorers

see Restorers, Metal

Silver, British

London

A.D.C. Heritage Ltd. 2 Old Bond St, London, W1X 3TD. Tel 493 5088.

Armitage. 4 Davies St, London, W1Y 1LS. Tel 408 0675.

Asprey PLC. 165-169 New Bond St, London, W1Y 0AR. Tel 493 6767.

Maurice Asprey Ltd. 41 Duke St, St James's, London, SW1. Tel 930 3921.

Stanley Beal Ltd. 124 New Bond St, London, W1Y 9AE. Tel 499 2817.

Stanley Beal Ltd. 41 Fairfax Rd, London, NW6. Tel 328 7525.

Brian Beet. 3b Burlington Gdns, Old Bond Street, London, W1X 1LE. Tel 437 4975.

Paul Bennett. 75 George St, London, W1. Tel 935 1555.

N.Bloom & Son (Antiques) Ltd. 40 Conduit St, London, W1R 9FB. Tel 629 5060.

A. & B. Bloomstein Ltd. Bond St Silver Galleries,111-112 New Bond St, London, W1Y 0BQ. Tel 493 6180.

Bond Street Silver Galleries. 111-112 New Bond St, London, W1Y 0BQ. Tel 493 6180 (priv 935 2621).

Luigi Brian. Vault 56, London Silver Vaults,53 Chancery Lane, London, WC2 1QT. Tel 405 2484.

Peter Cameron. 4 Grosvenor St, London, W1. Tel 491 8949.

Carrington & Co Ltd. 170 Regent St, London, W1R 6BQ. Tel 734 3727.

J.Christie. 26 Burlington Arcade, Piccadilly, London, W1V 9AD. Tel 629 3070.

Moira Cohen Ltd. 22-23 New Bond St, London, W1. Tel 629 0160.

Mary Cooke Antiques Ltd. 15 King St, London, SW1. Tel 839 6566.

Crawford & Pawle Ltd. 2nd Floor, Bond St Silver Galleries,111-112 New Bond St, London, W1Y 9AB. Tel 499 8442.

Kenneth Davis. 38 Bury St, London, SW1. Tel 930 0313.

Delieb Antiques Ltd. 31 Woodville Rd, London, NW11 9TP. Tel 458 2083.

Donohoe. 1-7 Davies Mews, London, W1. Tel 629 5633 (priv 455 5507).

E. & A. Antiques. 36 Ledbury Rd, London, W11. Tel 229 1823.

R.Feldman Ltd. Vaults 4/6 The London Silver Vaults,Chancery Lane, London, WC2A 1QS. Tel 405 6111.

I. Freeman & Son, Simon Kaye Ltd. 18 Dover St, London, W1X 3PB. Tel 493 7658.

O.Frydman. Bond St Silver Galleries,111-112 New Bond St, London, W1. Tel 439 4895.

G.Glass & Son. Bond St Silver Galleries,111-112 New Bond St, London, W1Y 9AB. Tel 493 5176.

Hilde Goldbaum Antiques. Stand X1, Antiquarius, 135 King's Rd, London, SW3.

Goldsmith & Perris. Alfies Antique Market,13-17 Church St, London, NW8. Tel 723 0563.

Brian Gordon. Chenil Galleries,181-183 Kings Rd, London, SW3. Tel 351 5808.

David Graham Antiques. 2 The Mall, Camden Passage,Islington, London, N1. Tel 352 2112.

Henry Gregory. Stand 335, Grays Antique Market,58 Davies St, London, W1Y 1LB.

Simon Griffin Antiques. 3 The Royal Arcade, 28 Old Bond St, London, W1. Tel 491 7367.

Harris (Antiques) Limited. 17-18 Old Bond St, London, W1X 3DA. Tel 499 0352.

Nicholas Harris. 26 Conduit St, London, W1. Tel 499 5991.

Harvey & Gore. 4 Burlington Gardens, London, W1X 1LE. Tel 493 2714.

Hennell Ltd. 12 New Bond St, London, W1Y 0HE. Tel 629 6888.

Holmes (Jewellers) Ltd. 29 Old Bond St, London, W1X 3AB. Tel 493 1396.

Holmes (Silversmiths) Ltd. 24 Burlington Arcade, London, W1. Tel 629 8380.

How (of Edinburgh). 2-3 Pickering Place, St James's St, London, SW1A 1EA. Tel 930 7140.

Hundred And One. 101 Notting Hill Gate, London, W11. Tel 727 2326.

Hyde Park Antiques. 191 Westbourne Grove, London, W11. Tel 727 1585.

Brand Inglis Ltd.. 9 Halkin Arcade, Motcomb St, London, SW1. Tel 235 6604.

The Jewel House (Mayfair). 23 Lansdowne Row, London, W1X 7LN. Tel 499 7936.

Johnson, Walker & Tolhurst Ltd. 64 Burlington Arcade, Piccadilly, London, W1. Tel 629 2615, 629 2616.

Annabel Jones. 52 Beauchamp Place,Knightsbridge, London, SW3. Tel 589 3215.

Howard Jones. 43 Kensington Church St, London, W8. Tel 937 4359.

E.& C.T.Koopman & Son Ltd. The London Silver Vaults,Chancery House, Chancery Lane, London, WC2. Tel 242 8365 242 7624.

S.Lampard & Son. 32 Notting Hill Gate, London, W11. Tel 229 5457.

Langfords. Oldebourne House,46-47 Chancery Lane, London, WC2. Tel 405 6402.

Ronald A.Lee (Fine Arts) Ltd. 1-9 Bruton Place, London, W1X 7AD. Tel 499 6266.

M.P.Levene Ltd. 5 Thurloe Place, London, SW7 2RR. Tel 589 3785.

W. Lipka Ltd. 62 Aylestone Ave, London, NW6. Tel 459 4588.

Sanda Lipton. 35 Kenway Rd, London, SW5. Tel 373 9625 (shop), 407 0278.

London Silver Vaults. Chancery House, Chancery Lane, London, WC2. Tel 242 3844.

Marks Antiques Ltd. 49 Curzon St, London, W1. Tel 499 5392.

M. McAleer. 32A Sussex Place,Hyde Park, London, W2 2TH. Tel 723 5794.

H. Miller (Antiques) Ltd. Silver Vaults, Chancery Lane, London, WC2. Tel 242 7073.

Naylers. 56a Clerkenwell Rd, London, EC1. Tel 253 4594.

R.S.& S.Necus. Stand H1, Antiquarius, 135 King's Rd, London, SW3.

A.& H.Page. 66 Gloucester Rd, Kensington, London, SW7. Tel 584 7349.

Partridge (Fine Arts) Ltd. 144-146 New Bond St, London, W1. Tel 629 0834.

David Paskin Antiques (London) Ltd. Grays Antique Market,58 Davies St, London, W1. Tel 408 1129.

Percy's Silver Ltd. London Silver Vaults,53 Chancery Lane, London, WC2.

The Persian Market. 48 Upper St,Islington, London, N1. Tel 226 7927.

S.J. Phillips Ltd. 139 New Bond St, London, W1A 3DL. Tel 629 6261, 629 6262.

David Richards and Sons. 12 New Cavendish St, London, W1. Tel 935 3206.

Scarlet Pimpernel Antiques. Grays Antique Market,58 Davies St, London, W1.

Scope Antiques. 64-66 Willesden Lane, London, NW6. Tel 328 5833.

Searle & Co Ltd. 1 Royal Exchange, London, EC3V 3LL. Tel 626 2456.

Shapland. 207 High Holborn, London, WC1. Tel 405 3507.

S.J.Shrubsole Ltd. 43 Museum St, London, WC1. Tel 405 2712.

M. & L.Silver Co Ltd. 2 Woodstock St, London, W1R 1HD. Tel 499 5392.

B. Silverman. London Silver Vaults,63 Chancery Lane, London, WC2A 1QS. Tel 242 3269.

Spink & Son Ltd. 5, 6 & 7 King St, St James's, London, SW1. Tel 930 7888.

E.Swonnell (Silverware) Ltd. Bond St Silver Galleries,111-112 New Bond St, London, W1. Tel 629 9649.

Sue & Alan Thompson. 15 Flood Street, London, SW3. Tel 352 3494.

C.J.Vander (Antiques) Ltd. Dunstan House, 14a St Cross St, London, EC1. Tel 831 6741.

William Walter. Silver Vaults, Chancery House,Chancery Lane, London, WC2A 1QS. Tel 242 3248/9.

Wartski Ltd. 14 Grafton St, London, W1. Tel 493 1141/2/3.

Henry Willis (Antique Silver). 4 Grosvenor St, London, W1. Tel 491 8949.

Regions

Abbey Antiques and Arts. 97 High St, Hemel Hempstead, Hertfordshire, HP1 3AH. Tel 64667.

Alexander Antiques. 108 Dunluce Rd, Portrush, Co Antrim, BT56 8NB. Tel 822783.

Antiqcurios & Irene Fine Art. 33 Clarendon St, Dublin, Co Dublin. Tel 714932.

The Antiquary. 50 St Giles, Oxford, Oxfordshire. Tel 59875.

The Antique Shop. Glynn Park,Taylors Ave, Carrickfergus, Co Antrim. Tel 63284.

The Antique Shop. 43 McCurtain St, Cork, Co Cork. Tel (021) 504079.

Argentum Antiques. 18-20 High St, Bexley, Kent, DA5 1AD. Tel Crayford (0322) 527915.

J. Barrymore & Co. 73-75 High St, Honiton, Devon. Tel 2244.

J.& H.Bell Antiques. 22 Arbory St, Castletown,. Tel 823132 (priv 822414).

Brian R. Bolt Collector's Antiques. 88 Ballaghmore Road,Portballintrae, Bushmills, Co Antrim, BT57 8RL. Tel 31129.

Boodle & Dunthorne Ltd. 52 Eastgate St, Chester, Cheshire, CH1 1LE. Tel 26666.

Bracher & Sydenham. 24 Queen Victoria St, Reading, Berkshire, RG1 1TG. Tel 583265, 53724.

Bragge & Sons. Landgate House, Rye, E.Sussex. Tel 223358.

Brownhouse Antiques. 1 Ipswich Rd, Claydon, Ipswich, Suffolk. Tel 830130.

Wm Bruford & Son Ltd. 11-13 Cornfield Rd, Eastbourne, E.Sussex, BN21 3NA. Tel 25452.

Wm Bruford & Son Ltd. 1 Bedford St, Exeter, Devon, EX1 1LU. Tel 54901.

D.Bryden Antiques. Sheep St, Stow-on-the-Wold, Gloucestershire. Tel 30840.

Meg Campbell. 10 Church Lane, Highfield, Southampton, Hampshire, SO2 1SZ. Tel 557636.

Cherub Antiques. 9 Sadler St, Wells, Somerset, BA5 2RR. Tel 72503 (priv 73893).

Coach House Antiques. 75 Coach Rd, Sleights, Whitby, N.Yorkshire, YO22 5BT. Tel 810313.

Coach House Antiques. 55 Elm Rd, Wisbech, Cambridgeshire, PE13 2TB. Tel 583129.

Copperfields. 1 Church St, Sidmouth, Devon. Tel 2145.

Timothy Coward Fine Silver. Marisco, Saunton, Braunton, Devon. Tel 890466.

H.Danker. 10 South Anne St, Dublin, Co Dublin. Tel 774009.

Eric Davidson (Antiques) Ltd. 4 Grassmarket, Edinburgh, Lothian, EH1 2JU. Tel 225 5815.

Reginald Davis (Oxford) Ltd. 34 High St, Oxford, Oxfordshire, OX1 4AN. Tel 248347.

Dibley Antiques. Ffynnon Watty, Moylegrove, Dyfed. Tel 668.

D. & B. Dickinson. 22 & 22A New Bond St, Bath, Avon, BA1 1BA. Tel 66502.

D.H.Edmonds Ltd. 27-28 Meeting House Lane, Brighton & Hove, E.Sussex, BN1 14B. Tel 27713, 28871.

Extence Antiques. 2 Wellington St, Teignmouth, Devon. Tel 3353.

Farthings Antiques. 50-52 Hospital St, Nantwich, Cheshire, CW5 5RP. Tel 625117.

A.Fleming (Southsea) Ltd. Clock Tower, Castle Rd, Portsmouth, Hampshire. Tel 822934.

Foster Hill Road Antiques Centre. 84-84A Foster Hill Rd, Bedford, Bedfordshire, MK40 2ET. Tel 53318.

Gadsby's Antiques. 88-90 The Street, Ashtead, Surrey. Tel 72305.

Alan Grant. Clifton, Rugby, Warwickshire. Tel 71165.

Greene's Antique Galleries. The Mall, Drogheda, Co Louth. Tel (041) 36212, 38286.

W.F.Greenwood & Sons Ltd. 2&3 Crown Place, Harrogate, N.Yorkshire, HG1 2RY. Tel 504467.

Grey-Harris & Co. 12 Princess Victoria St,Clifton, Bristol, Avon. Tel 737365.

Greystoke Antiques. Swan Yard, off Cheap St, Sherborne, Dorset, DT9 4EP. Tel 812833 (priv 813484).

H.A. & D.M. Hale. 5A Cross St, Northam, Devon. Tel Bideford (02372) 77216.

Hamilton Antiques. 19 Shore St, Holywood, Co Down. Tel 4404.

Henry Hardcastle Ltd. 51 Stonegate, York, N.Yorkshire, YO1 2AW. Tel 23401.

Hardie Antiques. 25 St John St, Perth, Tayside. Tel 33127.

Raymond Hawley. 5 North Bar Within, Beverley, Humberside, HU17 8AP. Tel Hull (0482) 883193.

Hicklenton & Phillips Ltd. Colborne Ave, Wimborne Minster, Dorset. Tel 882040.

The House of Antiques. 25 Meeting House Lane, Brighton & Hove, E.Sussex. Tel 27680, 24961.

Eleanor Hutton. 59 West Street, Dorking, Surrey. Tel 883777.

Kenworthys Ltd. 226 Stamford St, Ashton-under-Lyne, Manchester, Greater Manchester, OL6 7LW. Tel 330 3043.

Keystone Antiques. 9 Ashby Rd, Coalville, Leicestershire, LE6 2LF. Tel 35966.

Kildare Antiques. 19 Kildare St, Dublin, Co Dublin. Tel 763576 (priv 688194).

E. & C.T.Koopman & Son Ltd. John Dalton House, John Dalton St, Manchester, Greater Manchester, M2 6JP. Tel 834 2402, 832 9036.

P.G. Kydd. 70 Colston St, Bristol, Avon, BS1 5AZ. Tel 299265.

Alan Leonard Antiques. 503 Smithdown Rd, Liverpool, Merseyside, L15 5AE. Tel 733 5277 (priv 722 4766).

Levine, Henry & Co. 55 London St, Norwich, Norfolk, NR2 1HL. Tel 628709.

Lowe & Pomfrett. 63 Queen St, Maidenhead, Berkshire. Tel 20759.

Lowe & Sons Ltd. 11 Bridge St Row, Chester, Cheshire, CH1 1PD. Tel 25850.

E.P.Mallory & Son Ltd. 1-4 Bridge St, Bath, Avon, BA2 4AP. Tel 65885.

Mappin & Webb Ltd (Butt & Co). 32 Eastgate Row, Chester, Cheshire, CH1 1LF. Tel 25938.

Iain Marr Antiques. 3 Mid St, Beauly, Highland, IV4 7DP. Tel 782372.

Martin & Co Ltd. 19 The Promenade, Cheltenham, Gloucestershire. Tel 522821.

R.E. Martin. 40 Gold St, Tiverton, Devon. Tel 252832.

Janet Maund. Cheltenham Antique Market, Cheltenham, Gloucestershire, GL3 1HA. Tel 529812 (priv 0452 712286).

H. Miller (Antiques) Ltd. 22A Ship St, Brighton & Hove, E.Sussex. Tel 26255.

Nathan & Co (Birmingham) Ltd. 31 Corporation St, Birmingham, W.Midlands. Tel 643 5225.

Neale Antiques. 21 Old Cross, Hertford, Hertfordshire, SG14 1RE. Tel 52519 and 51347.

Nevill Antiques. 9-10 Milk St, Shrewsbury, Shropshire, SY1 1SZ. Tel 51013 (priv 62877).

E.A. Nowell & Sons. 21-23 Market Place, Wells, Somerset, BA5 2RF. Tel 72415, 78738, 76915.

Diana O'Mahony. 8 Winthrop St, Cork, Co Cork. Tel (021) 276599.

Osborne Jewellers. 55 Osborne Rd, Southsea, Portsmouth, Hampshire, PO5 3LS. Tel 825101.

Elizabeth Parker Antiques. High St, Moreton-in-Marsh, Gloucestershire, GL56 0LL. Tel 50917.

Payne & Son (Goldsmiths) Ltd. 131 High St, Oxford, Oxfordshire, OX1 4DH. Tel 243787.

Pauline Peretz Antiques. Linden House,Hall St, Long Melford, Suffolk, CO10 9JF. Tel Sudbury (0784) 70534.

Jane Pollock Antiques. 4 Castle Gate, Penrith, Cumbria. Tel 67211.

Mark J.Poole. 3 Percy Place, Bath, Avon. Tel 317957.

R.E. Porter. 2/4 Post Office Rd, Bournemouth, Dorset, BH1 1BA. Tel 24289.

Rankine Taylor Antiques. 34 Dollar St, Cirencester, Gloucestershire, GL7 2AN. Tel 2529.

Ruskin's. 426-428 Wells Rd, Bristol, Avon, BS14 9AL. Tel 776456.

M.Samuels (Antiques). 17 South Anne St, Dublin, Co Dublin. Tel 711262.

Scott Cooper Ltd. 52 The Promenade, Cheltenham, Gloucestershire, GL50 1LY. Tel 522580.

Oswald Sebley. 20 Lower Goat Lane, Norwich, Norfolk. Tel 26504.

Jack Shaw & Co Antique Silver. The Old Grammar School, Skipton Rd, Ilkley, W.Yorkshire, LS29 9EP. Tel 609467.

Sherston Antiques. The Old Pharmacy House, Sherston, Wiltshire. Tel 0666- 840291.

A.T.Silvester & Sons Ltd. 2-4 High St, Warwick, Warwickshire, CV34 4AP. Tel 492972.

P.& D.Smith Antiques. 6 Ashburton Rd, Gosforth, Newcastle upon Tyne, Tyne & Wear. Tel 2856455.

Solus Marketing (Norfolk). Cromer Rd, Felmingham, North Walsham, Norfolk, NR28 OJS.

J.A.Stancomb. Bullen Court, Broadway, Ilminster, Somerset, TA19 9QY. Tel 2640.

Studio Antiques Ltd. Bourton-on-the-Water, Gloucestershire, GL54 2BX. Tel 20352.

Styles. 12 Bridge St, Hungerford, Berkshire. Tel 83922.

Thames Gallery. Thameside, Henley-on-Thames, Oxfordshire, RG9 2LT. Tel 572449.

James & Ann Tillett. Tombland House, 12-13 Tombland, Norwich, Norfolk, NR3 1HF. Tel 624914.

Townhead Antiques. Townhead, Newby Bridge, Cumbria, LA12 8NP. Tel 31321.

Vanbrugh House Antiques. Park St, Stow-on-the-Wold, Gloucestershire, GL54 1AQ. Tel 30797.

Christopher Warner. 15 Princes St, Harrogate, N.Yorkshire, HG1 1NG. Tel 503617.

Waterloo Antiques. 16 Waterloo St, Oldham, Greater Manchester. Tel 624 5975.

J.W.Weldon. 55 Clarendon St, Dublin, Co Dublin. Tel 771638, 772742.

Wynyard R.T. Wilkinson, FSA Scot, Fine Silver. Bylaugh Park, East Dereham, Norfolk, NR20 4RL. Tel Bawdeswell (036 288) 200 (priv 01-788 6953).

Robert Young Antiques. 4A Exchange St, Norwich, Norfolk, NR2 1AT. Tel 618605.

Silver, Channel Islands

Peter Cherry Antiques. 17 Tudor House Shopping Centre,Mill St/Bordage, St Peter Port, Guernsey. Tel 26808 (priv 711080).

The Old Curiosity Shop. Commercial Rd, St Sampson's, Guernsey. Tel 45324.

Silver, European

Armitage. 4 Davies St, London, W1Y 1LS. Tel 408 0675.

N.Bloom & Son (Antiques) Ltd. 40 Conduit St, London, W1R 9FB. Tel 629 5060.

Bond Street Silver Galleries. 111-112 New Bond St, London, W1Y 0BQ. Tel 493 6180 (priv 935 2621).

Luigi Brian. Vault 56, London Silver Vaults,53 Chancery Lane, London, WC2 1QT. Tel 405 2484.

J.Christie. 26 Burlington Arcade, Piccadilly, London, W1V 9AD. Tel 629 3070.

Kenneth Davis. 38 Bury St, London, SW1. Tel 930 0313.

Reginald Davis (Oxford) Ltd. 34 High St, Oxford, Oxfordshire, OX1 4AN. Tel 248347.

Delieb Antiques Ltd. 31 Woodville Rd, London, NW11 9TP. Tel 458 2083.

Hilde Goldbaum Antiques. Stand X1, Antiquarius, 135 King's Rd, London, SW3.

Nicholas Harris. 26 Conduit St, London, W1. Tel 499 5991.

Hyde Park Antiques. 191 Westbourne Grove, London, W11. Tel 727 1585.

Brand Inglis Ltd.. 9 Halkin Arcade, Motcomb St, London, SW1. Tel 235 6604.

E.& C.T.Koopman & Son Ltd. The London Silver Vaults,Chancery House, Chancery Lane, London, WC2. Tel 242 8365 242 7624.

R.S.& S.Necus. Stand H1, Antiquarius, 135 King's Rd, London, SW3.

S.J. Phillips Ltd. 139 New Bond St, London, W1A 3DL. Tel 629 6261, 629 6262.

Oswald Sebley. 20 Lower Goat Lane, Norwich, Norfolk. Tel 26504.

Shapland. 207 High Holborn, London, WC1. Tel 405 3507.

S.J.Shrubsole Ltd. 43 Museum St, London, WC1. Tel 405 2712.

H.S.Wellby Ltd. Ponders, Hedgerley Lane, Gerrards Cross, Buckinghamshire, SL9 8SY. Tel 887957.

Wynyard R.T. Wilkinson, FSA Scot, Fine Silver. Bylaugh Park, East Dereham, Norfolk, NR20 4RL. Tel Bawdeswell (036 288) 200 (priv 01-788 6953).

Silver, Modern

Carrington & Co Ltd. 170 Regent St, London, W1R 6BQ. Tel 734 3727.

Lesley Craze. 5 Essex Rd,Islington, London, N1. Tel 226 3200.

Fair Maids House Scottish Crafts. North Port, Perth, Tayside. Tel 25976.

O.Frydman. Bond St Silver Galleries,111-112 New Bond St, London, W1. Tel 439 4895.

Garrard & Co Ltd. 112 Regent St, London, W1A 2JJ. Tel 734 7020.

Simon Griffin Antiques. 3 The Royal Arcade, 28 Old Bond St, London, W1. Tel 491 7367.

Howard Jones. 43 Kensington Church St, London, W8. Tel 937 4359.

Langfords. Oldebourne House,46-47 Chancery Lane, London, WC2. Tel 405 6402.

Alan Leonard Antiques. 503 Smithdown Rd, Liverpool, Merseyside, L15 5AE. Tel 733 5277 (priv 722 4766).

London Silver Vaults. Chancery House, Chancery Lane, London, WC2. Tel 242 3844.

Ogle Fine Arts. Ogle Gallery, 12 Rotunda Terrace,Montpellier St, Cheltenham, Gloucestershire. Tel 518605 (priv 31011).

H. Perovetz. 50/2 Chancery Lane, London, WC2. Tel 252 5857 and 242 5820.

Silver, Small Collectables

Brian R. Bolt Collector's Antiques. 88 Ballaghmore Road,Portballintrae, Bushmills, Co Antrim, BT57 8RL. Tel 31129.

Meg Campbell. 10 Church Lane, Highfield, Southampton, Hampshire, SO2 1SZ. Tel 557636.

Cobblers Hall Antiques. 119-121 Leighton Rd, Toddington, Bedfordshire, LU5 6AR. Tel 2890.

Cordell Antiques. 13 St Peter's St, Ipswich, Suffolk. Tel 219508.

Alan Grant. Clifton, Rugby, Warwickshire. Tel 71165.

M. McAleer. 32A Sussex Place,Hyde Park, London, W2 2TH. Tel 723 5794.

Simeon. 19 Burlington Arcade, Piccadilly, London, W1V 9AB. Tel 493-3353.

Steppes Hill Farm Antiques. Steppes Hill Farm,Stockbury, Sittingbourne, Kent, ME9 7RB. Tel 842205.

Styles. 12 Bridge St, Hungerford, Berkshire. Tel 83922.

Sue & Alan Thompson. 15 Flood Street, London, SW3. Tel 352 3494.

Wynyard R.T. Wilkinson, FSA Scot, Fine Silver. Bylaugh Park, East Dereham, Norfolk, NR20 4RL. Tel Bawdeswell (036 288) 200 (priv 01-788 6953).

Silver, Early to 17th Century

Armitage. 4 Davies St, London, W1Y 1LS. Tel 408 0675.

At the Sign of the Herald Angel. 19 Park St, Cirencester, Gloucestershire, GL7 2BX. Tel 2972.

Bond Street Silver Galleries. 111-112 New Bond St, London, W1Y 0BQ. Tel 493 6180 (priv 935 2621).

Wm Bruford & Son Ltd. 1 Bedford St, Exeter, Devon, EX1 1LU. Tel 54901.

Mary Cooke Antiques Ltd. 15 King St, London, SW1. Tel 839 6566.

Timothy Coward Fine Silver. Marisco, Saunton, Braunton, Devon. Tel 890466.

Kenneth Davis. 38 Bury St, London, SW1. Tel 930 0313.

I. Freeman & Son, Simon Kaye Ltd. 18 Dover St, London, W1X 3PB. Tel 493 7658.

O.Frydman. Bond St Silver Galleries,111-112 New Bond St, London, W1. Tel 439 4895.

G.Glass & Son. Bond St Silver Galleries,111-112 New Bond St, London, W1Y 9AB. Tel 493 5176.

H.R.Jessop Ltd. 3 Pickering Place, St James's, London, SW1A 1EA. Tel 930 4696.

Howard Jones. 43 Kensington Church St, London, W8. Tel 937 4359.

E. & C.T.Koopman & Son Ltd. John Dalton House, John Dalton St, Manchester, Greater Manchester, M2 6JP. Tel 834 2402, 832 9036.

E.& C.T.Koopman & Son Ltd. The London Silver Vaults,Chancery House, Chancery Lane, London, WC2. Tel 242 8365 242 7624.

Sanda Lipton. 35 Kenway Rd, London, SW5. Tel 373 9625 (shop), 407 0278.

London Silver Vaults. Chancery House, Chancery Lane, London, WC2. Tel 242 3844.

S.J. Phillips Ltd. 139 New Bond St, London, W1A 3DL. Tel 629 6261, 629 6262.

S.J.Shrubsole Ltd. 43 Museum St, London, WC1. Tel 405 2712.

Strickland & Dorling. 3 River St, Truro, Cornwall. Tel 72345.

E.Swonnell (Silverware) Ltd. Bond St Silver Galleries,111-112 New Bond St, London, W1. Tel 629 9649.

Tessiers. 26 New Bond St, London, W1Y 0JY. Tel 629 0458.

C.J.Vander (Antiques) Ltd. Dunstan House, 14a St Cross St, London, EC1. Tel 831 6741.

Henry Willis (Antique Silver). 4 Grosvenor St, London, W1. Tel 491 8949.

Silver, 18th Century

A.D.C. Heritage Ltd. 2 Old Bond St, London, W1X 3TD. Tel 493 5088.

Armitage. 4 Davies St, London, W1Y 1LS. Tel 408 0675.

Helen Blomfield. Hampers, Little Maplestead, Halstead, Essex. Tel 2159.

Bond Street Silver Galleries. 111-112 New Bond St, London, W1Y 0BQ. Tel 493 6180 (priv 935 2621).

J.H. Bourdon-Smith Ltd. 24 Mason's Yard,Duke St, St James's, London, SW1Y 6BU. Tel 839 4714/5.

H.H.Bray Ltd. 9 Jury St, Warwick, Warwickshire. Tel 492791.

Wm Bruford & Son Ltd. 1 Bedford St, Exeter, Devon, EX1 1LU. Tel 54901.

John Bull (Antiques) Ltd. 111-112 New Bond St, London, W1. Tel 629 1251.

Meg Campbell. 10 Church Lane, Highfield, Southampton, Hampshire, SO2 1SZ. Tel 557636.

Collingwood of Bond Street. 171 Bond Street, London, W1. Tel 734 2656.

Mary Cooke Antiques Ltd. 15 King St, London, SW1. Tel 839 6566.

H.Danker. 10 South Anne St, Dublin, Co Dublin. Tel 774009.

Kenneth Davis. 38 Bury St, London, SW1. Tel 930 0313.

Denisa the Lady Newborough. 1-1A-2 Whitehorse St,Shepherd Market, London, W1. Tel 493 3954 (priv 493 0854).

H.&W.Deutsch. 111 Kensington Church St, London, W8. Tel 727 5984.

D. & B. Dickinson. 22 & 22A New Bond St, Bath, Avon, BA1 1BA. Tel 66502.

Farthings Antiques. 50-52 Hospital St, Nantwich, Cheshire, CW5 5RP. Tel 625117.

I. Freeman & Son, Simon Kaye Ltd. 18 Dover St, London, W1X 3PB. Tel 493 7658.

O.Frydman. Bond St Silver Galleries,111-112 New Bond St, London, W1. Tel 439 4895.

Garrard & Co Ltd. 112 Regent St, London, W1A 2JJ. Tel 734 7020.

G.Glass & Son. Bond St Silver Galleries,111-112 New Bond St, London, W1Y 9AB. Tel 493 5176.

Greystoke Antiques. Swan Yard, off Cheap St, Sherborne, Dorset, DT9 4EP. Tel 812833 (priv 813484).

Hancocks & Co (Jewellers) Ltd. 1 Burlington Gardens, London, W1X 2HP. Tel 493 8904.

Hennell Ltd. 12 New Bond St, London, W1Y 0HE. Tel 629 6888.

H.R.Jessop Ltd. 3 Pickering Place, St James's, London, SW1A 1EA. Tel 930 4696.

Howard Jones. 43 Kensington Church St, London, W8. Tel 937 4359.

Kenworthys Ltd. 226 Stamford St, Ashton-under-Lyne, Manchester, Greater Manchester, OL6 7LW. Tel 330 3043.

E. & C.T.Koopman & Son Ltd. John Dalton House, John Dalton St, Manchester, Greater Manchester, M2 6JP. Tel 834 2402, 832 9036.

E.& C.T.Koopman & Son Ltd. The London Silver Vaults,Chancery House, Chancery Lane, London, WC2. Tel 242 8365 242 7624.

Sanda Lipton. 35 Kenway Rd, London, SW5. Tel 373 9625 (shop), 407 0278.

London Silver Vaults. Chancery House, Chancery Lane, London, WC2. Tel 242 3844.

E.P.Mallory & Son Ltd. 1-4 Bridge St, Bath, Avon, BA2 4AP. Tel 65885.

Iain Marr Antiques. 3 Mid St, Beauly, Highland, IV4 7DP. Tel 782372.

Martin & Co Ltd. 19 The Promenade, Cheltenham, Gloucestershire. Tel 522821.

M. McAleer. 32A Sussex Place,Hyde Park, London, W2 2TH. Tel 723 5794.

Nigel Milne Ltd. 16C Grafton St, London, W1X 3LF. Tel 493 9646.

Nathan & Co (Birmingham) Ltd. 31 Corporation St, Birmingham, W.Midlands. Tel 643 5225.

Oughterard Antiques. Main St, Oughterard, Co Galway. Tel 45.

Payne & Son (Goldsmiths) Ltd. 131 High St, Oxford, Oxfordshire, OX1 4DH. Tel 243787.

H. Perovetz. 50/2 Chancery Lane, London, WC2. Tel 252 5857 and 242 5820.

S.J. Phillips Ltd. 139 New Bond St, London, W1A 3DL. Tel 629 6261, 629 6262.

Gerald Sattin Ltd. 25 Burlington Arcade, Piccadilly, London, W1V 9AD. Tel 493 6557.

S.J.Shrubsole Ltd. 43 Museum St, London, WC1. Tel 405 2712.

M. & L.Silver Co Ltd. 2 Woodstock St, London, W1R 1HD. Tel 499 5392.

B. Silverman. London Silver Vaults,63 Chancery Lane, London, WC2A 1QS. Tel 242 3269.

E.Swonnell (Silverware) Ltd. Bond St Silver Galleries,111-112 New Bond St, London, W1. Tel 629 9649.

Tessiers. 26 New Bond St, London, W1Y 0JY. Tel 629 0458.

Thames Gallery. Thameside, Henley-on-Thames, Oxfordshire, RG9 2LT. Tel 572449.

C.J.Vander (Antiques) Ltd. Dunstan House, 14a St Cross St, London, EC1. Tel 831 6741.

William Walter. Silver Vaults, Chancery House,Chancery Lane, London, WC2A 1QS. Tel 242 3248/9.

Christopher Warner. 15 Princes St, Harrogate, N.Yorkshire, HG1 1NG. Tel 503617.

J.W.Weldon. 55 Clarendon St, Dublin, Co Dublin. Tel 771638, 772742.

Henry Willis (Antique Silver). 4 Grosvenor St, London, W1. Tel 491 8949.

Silver, 19th Century

Armitage. 4 Davies St, London, W1Y 1LS. Tel 408 0675.

Helen Blomfield. Hampers, Little Maplestead, Halstead, Essex. Tel 2159.

Bond Street Silver Galleries. 111-112 New Bond St, London, W1Y 0BQ. Tel 493 6180 (priv 935 2621).

J.H. Bourdon-Smith Ltd. 24 Mason's Yard,Duke St, St James's, London, SW1Y 6BU. Tel 839 4714/5.

H.H.Bray Ltd. 9 Jury St, Warwick, Warwickshire. Tel 492791.

Wm Bruford & Son Ltd. 11-13 Cornfield Rd, Eastbourne, E.Sussex, BN21 3NA. Tel 25452.

John Bull (Antiques) Ltd. 111-112 New Bond St, London, W1. Tel 629 1251.

Meg Campbell. 10 Church Lane, Highfield, Southampton, Hampshire, SO2 1SZ. Tel 557636.

Coach House Antiques. 55 Elm Rd, Wisbech, Cambridgeshire, PE13 2TB. Tel 583129.

Collingwood of Bond Street. 171 Bond Street, London, W1. Tel 734 2656.

Mary Cooke Antiques Ltd. 15 King St, London, SW1. Tel 839 6566.

Kenneth Davis. 38 Bury St, London, SW1. Tel 930 0313.

Denisa the Lady Newborough. 1-1A-2 Whitehorse St,Shepherd Market, London, W1. Tel 493 3954 (priv 493 0854).

H.&W.Deutsch. 111 Kensington Church St, London, W8. Tel 727 5984.

D. & B. Dickinson. 22 & 22A New Bond St, Bath, Avon, BA1 1BA. Tel 66502.

Farthings Antiques. 50-52 Hospital St, Nantwich, Cheshire, CW5 5RP. Tel 625117.

I. Freeman & Son, Simon Kaye Ltd. 18 Dover St, London, W1X 3PB. Tel 493 7658.

J.Freeman. 85A Portobello Rd, London, W11. Tel 221 5076.

O.Frydman. Bond St Silver Galleries,111-112 New Bond St, London, W1. Tel 439 4895.

Garrard & Co Ltd. 112 Regent St, London, W1A 2JJ. Tel 734 7020.

Greystoke Antiques. Swan Yard, off Cheap St, Sherborne, Dorset, DT9 4EP. Tel 812833 (priv 813484).

Hancocks & Co (Jewellers) Ltd. 1 Burlington Gardens, London, W1X 2HP. Tel 493 8904.

Hennell Ltd. 12 New Bond St, London, W1Y 0HE. Tel 629 6888.

Howard Jones. 43 Kensington Church St, London, W8. Tel 937 4359.

Kenworthys Ltd. 226 Stamford St, Ashton-under-Lyne, Manchester, Greater Manchester, OL6 7LW. Tel 330 3043.

E. & C.T.Koopman & Son Ltd. John Dalton House, John Dalton St, Manchester, Greater Manchester, M2 6JP. Tel 834 2402, 832 9036.

E.& C.T.Koopman & Son Ltd. The London Silver Vaults,Chancery House, Chancery Lane, London, WC2. Tel 242 8365 242 7624.

Sanda Lipton. 35 Kenway Rd, London, SW5. Tel 373 9625 (shop), 407 0278.

London Silver Vaults. Chancery House, Chancery Lane, London, WC2. Tel 242 3844.

E.P.Mallory & Son Ltd. 1-4 Bridge St, Bath, Avon, BA2 4AP. Tel 65885.

Martin & Co Ltd. 19 The Promenade, Cheltenham, Gloucestershire. Tel 522821.

M. McAleer. 32A Sussex Place,Hyde Park, London, W2 2TH. Tel 723 5794.

Nigel Milne Ltd. 16C Grafton St, London, W1X 3LF. Tel 493 9646.

Nathan & Co (Birmingham) Ltd. 31 Corporation St, Birmingham, W.Midlands. Tel 643 5225.

Payne & Son (Goldsmiths) Ltd. 131 High St, Oxford, Oxfordshire, OX1 4DH. Tel 243787.

H. Perovetz. 50/2 Chancery Lane, London, WC2. Tel 252 5857 and 242 5820.

Gerald Sattin Ltd. 25 Burlington Arcade, Piccadilly, London, W1V 9AD. Tel 493 6557.

S.J.Shrubsole Ltd. 43 Museum St, London, WC1. Tel 405 2712.

M. & L.Silver Co Ltd. 2 Woodstock St, London, W1R 1HD. Tel 499 5392.

S. & L. Simmons. 9 Meeting House Lane, Brighton & Hove, E.Sussex, BN1 1HB. Tel 27949.

Tessiers. 26 New Bond St, London, W1Y 0JY. Tel 629 0458.

Thames Gallery. Thameside, Henley-on-Thames, Oxfordshire, RG9 2LT. Tel 572449.

C.J.Vander (Antiques) Ltd. Dunstan House, 14a St Cross St, London, EC1. Tel 831 6741.

William Walter. Silver Vaults, Chancery House,Chancery Lane, London, WC2A 1QS. Tel 242 3248/9.

Christopher Warner. 15 Princes St, Harrogate, N.Yorkshire, HG1 1NG. Tel 503617.

Henry Willis (Antique Silver). 4 Grosvenor St, London, W1. Tel 491 8949.

Silver, 20th Century

Bond Street Silver Galleries. 111-112 New Bond St, London, W1Y 0BQ. Tel 493 6180 (priv 935 2621).

John Bull (Antiques) Ltd. 111-112 New Bond St, London, W1. Tel 629 1251.

Farthings Antiques. 50-52 Hospital St, Nantwich, Cheshire, CW5 5RP. Tel 625117.

J.Freeman. 85A Portobello Rd, London, W11. Tel 221 5076.

O.Frydman. Bond St Silver Galleries,111-112 New Bond St, London, W1. Tel 439 4895.

Galia Antiques. Antiquarius, 135 King's Rd, London, SW3.

Hicklenton & Phillips Ltd. Colborne Ave, Wimborne Minster, Dorset. Tel 882040.

Howard Jones. 43 Kensington Church St, London, W8. Tel 937 4359.

London Silver Vaults. Chancery House, Chancery Lane, London, WC2. Tel 242 3844.

Nigel Milne Ltd. 16C Grafton St, London, W1X 3LF. Tel 493 9646.

H. Perovetz. 50/2 Chancery Lane, London, WC2. Tel 252 5857 and 242 5820.

The Pruskin Gallery. 183 King's Rd, London, SW3. Tel 352 9095, (priv)243 1939.

S. & L. Simmons. 9 Meeting House Lane, Brighton & Hove, E.Sussex, BN1 1HB. Tel 27949.

Tessiers. 26 New Bond St, London, W1Y 0JY. Tel 629 0458.

Ziggurat. Chenil Galleries, 183 King's Rd, London, SW3. Tel 352 2123.

Snuff Bottles

Corner Antiques. Coltishall Antiques Centre, High St, Coltishall, Norfolk, NR12 7HV. Tel Norwich (0603) 738306 (priv 737631).

Snuff Boxes

see Boxes

Sporting Items and Memorabilia

Simon Brett. Creswyke House, High St, Moreton-in-Marsh, Gloucestershire, GL56 0LH. Tel 50751.

The Crypt Antiques. London House, High St, Burford, Oxfordshire. Tel 2302.

Grant Books. Victoria Sq, Droitwich, Hereford & Worcester. Tel 778155.

J.W.McKenzie, Bookseller. 12 Stoneleigh Park Rd, Ewell, Surrey, KT19 0QT. Tel 01- 393 7700.

Old Golf Shop Inc. 13 Albany St, Edinburgh, Lothian, EH1 3PY. Tel 556 1944 (priv 663 7647).

J.Wigington & Sons. 'Winchester 73', 276 Alcester Rd, Stratford-upon-Avon, Warwickshire. Tel 293881.

Staffordshire Figures

Angel Arcade. Portmeirion, Gwynedd. Tel Penrhyndeudraeth (0766) 770 228.

The Antique Centre. 46 Bridge Rd, East Molesey, Surrey. Tel 979 4969(priv 0372 64034).

Antique Centre. Brookend, Ross-on-Wye, Hereford & Worcester. Tel 62752.

Antiques. Main St, Eyam, Derbyshire. Tel Baslow (024 688) 3265.

Antiques of Penrith. 4 Corney Sq, Penrith, Cumbria, CA11 7PX. Tel 62801.

Margaret Bedi Antiques. The Antique Shop, 5 Station Rd, Billingham, Cleveland, TS23 1AG. Tel Stockton-on-Tees (0642) 607296.

Ron Beech. 150 Portland Rd, Brighton & Hove, E.Sussex, BN3 5QL. Tel 724477.

R. Bonnett. 582 Kings Rd, Fulham, London, SW6. Tel 736 4593 (priv 878 1695).

Elias Clark Antiques Ltd. 1 The Cobbles, High Street, Bletchingley, Surrey, RH1 4PB. Tel Godstone (0883) 843714.

Gerald Clark Antiques Ltd. 1 High St, Mill Hill Village, London, NW7 1QY. Tel 906 0342.

Clock Tower Antiques. 2, Old Station Rd, Newmarket, Suffolk, CBB 8DN. Tel 664915.

Clunes Antiques. 9 West Place, Wimbledon, London, SW19 4UH. Tel 946 1643.

Dorothy's Antiques. 23 Waterbank Rd, Sheringham, Norfolk, NR26 8RB. Tel 822319 (priv 823018).

Dunsdale Lodge Antiques. Dunsdale Lodge, Brasted Rd, Westerham, Kent, TN16 1LJ. Tel 62160.

Gate Antiques. 29 St Saviour's Gate, York, N.Yorkshire, YO1 2NQ. Tel 27035.

John Hall. 31 Epple Rd, London, SW6 4DJ. Tel 736 3542.

Horseshoe Antiques & Gallery. High St, Burford, Oxfordshire, OX8 4RJ. Tel 3244.

Ledger Antiques. 101A Fulham Rd, London, SW3 6RH. Tel 581 0922.

Rose Linden Antiques. Fore St, Probus, Cornwall. Tel St Austell (0726) 882055.

Made of Honour. 11 City Walls, Chester, Cheshire, CH1 1LD. Tel 314208.

Noah's Ark Antiques Market. 5 King St, Sandwich, Kent. Tel 611144 (priv 613270).

Oliver-Sutton Antiques. 34C Kensington Church St, London, W8. Tel 937 0633.

Pandora's Box. Bridge St, Hungerford, Berkshire. Tel Marlborough (0672) 810468.

Susan Procter. 47-51 The Feus, Auchterarder, Tayside, PH3 1DG. Tel 2532.

Marc Rhys. The Mynde House, High St, Caerleon, Gwent. Tel 420535.

Constance Stobo. 31 Holland St, London, W8 4LX. Tel 937 6282 (priv 373 4709).

Woodstock Antiques. 11 Market St, Woodstock, Oxfordshire, OX7 1SU. Tel 811494.

Worksop Antiques. 20 Park St, Worksop, Nottinghamshire. Tel 476384.

Wye Antiques. The Square, Stow-on-the-Wold, Gloucestershire, GL54 1AB. Tel Cotswold (0451) 31004.

Stained Glass Windows

see also Architectural Items

Architectural Antiques. The New Savoy Show Rooms,New Road, South Molton, Devon. Tel 3342 (priv 4167).

Architectural Antiques Ltd. 133 Upper St, London, N1. Tel 226 5565.

Architectural Heritage of Cheltenham. Boddington Manor, Boddington, Cheltenham, Gloucestershire, GL51 OTJ. Tel Coombe Hill (024268) 741.

Baileys Architectural Antiques. The Engine Shed,Ashburton Industrial Estate, Ross-on-Wye, Hereford & Worcester, HR9 7BW. Tel 63015.

David Bridgwater. 14 Fountain Buildings,Lansdown Road, Bath, Avon. Tel 63652.

Castle Antiques. 15 Moor Lane, Clitheroe, Lancashire. Tel 26568 (priv 0254 35820).

Peter Chapman Antiques. 10 Theberton St, Islington, London, N1 0QX. Tel 226 5565 (priv 348 4846).

Lamont Antiques Ltd. Newhams Row,175 Bermondsey St, London, SE1 3UW. Tel 403 0126.

Stirling Antiques. Aberdeen House,Guildford Rd, Abinger Hammer, Surrey, RH5 6RY. Tel Dorking (0306) 730706.

Andy Thornton Architectural Antiques Ltd. Ainleys Industrial Estate, Elland, W.Yorkshire, HX5 9JP. Tel 78125 (priv 0484 712636).

Townsends. 1 Church St, London, NW8. Tel 724 3746 & 624 4756.

Townsends. Showroom: 36 New End Square,Hampstead Village, London, NW3. Tel 794 5706/5707.

Whiteway & Waldron. 305 Munster Rd, London, SW6. Tel 381 3195.

Stamps

Argyll Etkin Ltd. 48 Conduit St, London, W1R 9FB. Tel 437 7800.

Bath Stamp & Coin Shop. Pulteney Bridge, Bath, Avon. Tel 63073.

Christie's Robson Lowe. 39 Poole Hill, Bournemouth, Dorset. Tel 292740.

The Coin & Stamp Centre. 13 Centurion House (1st floor),St John's St, Colchester, Essex, CO2 7AH. Tel 41232 (priv 579345).

E.H.W. & Co. 12 Sicilian Ave, Southampton Row, London, WC1A 3QD. Tel 405 5509.

Fox & Co. 30 Princes St, Yeovil, Somerset. Tel 72323.

Franca Antiques. 2 Castle St, Tunbridge Wells, Kent. Tel 25779 (priv 29785).

Stanley Gibbons. 399 The Strand, London, WC2. Tel 836 8444.

Stanley Gibbons Auctions Limited. 399 The Strand, London, WC2R 0LX. Tel 836 8444.

Glennie Middleton and Bullock. 3 Church St, Diss, Norfolk, IP22 3DD. Tel 51617.

Harmers of London Stamp Auctioneers Ltd. 91 New Bond St, London, W1A 4EH. Tel 629 0218.

W.T.C.Henderson. 5 North Methven St, Perth, Tayside. Tel 24836.

Michael Coins. 6 Hillgate St, London, W8. Tel 727 1518.

Midas Antiques. 181 High St, Brownhills, Walsall, W.Midlands, WS8 6HG. Tel Brownhills (0543) 377719.

Omniphil Ltd. Germains Lodge,Fullers Hill (office), Chesham, Buckinghamshire. Tel 771851.

Robson Lowe at Christie's. 47 Duke St,St James's, London, SW1Y 6QX. Tel 839 4034/5.

Stampantique. 86 High St, Egham, Surrey, TW20 9DP. Tel 36290.

Vale. 21 Tranquil Vale, Blackheath, London, SE3 0BU. Tel 852 9817.

Warwick & Warwick Ltd. Arbon House, 21 Jury St, Warwick, Warwickshire. Tel 499031.

Stands

see Display Stands

Tapestries

David Adam Oriental Carpets. 59 High Street, Lindfield, W.Sussex. Tel 73817.

Anglo-Persian Carpet Co Ltd. The Arcade, South Kensington Station, London, SW7 2NA. Tel 589 5457.

Antiquus A G. 17 Pembridge Sq, London, W2 4EH. Tel 229 0224.

Mary Bellis Antiques. Charnham Close (A4 Highway), Hungerford, Berkshire, RG17 0EJ. Tel 82620.

Raymond Benardout. 5 William St, Knightsbridge, London, SW1X 9HL. Tel 235 3360 (priv 235 0504).

Bernheimer Fine Arts Ltd. 32 St George St,Mayfair, London, W1R 9FA. Tel 499 0293.

Joanna Booth. 247 King's Rd, London, SW3. Tel 352 8998.

L.& G.Burnett. 290 Portobello Rd, London, W10 5TE. Tel 969 8899.

Belinda Coote Antiques. 29 Holland St, London, W8. Tel 937 3924.

Robert Franses & Son. 5 Nugent Tce, St John's Wood, London, NW8. Tel 286 6913 (priv 328 0949).

S.Franses Ltd. 82 Jermyn St,St James's, London, SW1. Tel 235 1888/9.

S.Franses Ltd. 11 Spring St,Paddington, London, W2. Tel 262 1153/4.

Victor Franses Gallery. 57 Jermyn St, London, SW1Y 6LX. Tel 439 6284.

Gallery of Antique Costume & Textiles Ltd. 2 Church Street, Marylebone, London, NW8. Tel 723 9981 (priv 743 3821).

Denzil Grant Antiques Ltd. Hall Street,Bradfield St George, Long Melford, Suffolk. Tel 75470 (priv 04493 576).

Jonathan Harris. 54 Kensington Church St, London, W8. Tel 937 3133.

M.Heskia. 19 Mount St, London, W1. Tel 629 1483.

Huntington Antiques Ltd. The Old Forge, Church St, Stow-on-the-Wold, Gloucestershire. Tel 30842.

C. John (Rare Rugs) Ltd. 70 South Audley St,Mayfair, London, W1Y 5FE. Tel 493 5288.

Alexander Juran & Co. 74 New Bond St, London, W1Y 9DD. Tel 629 2550, 493 4484.

Keeble Ltd. 13 Walton St, London, SW3. Tel 581 3676.

Leonard Lassalle. 21 The Pantiles, Tunbridge Wells, Kent, TN2 5TD. Tel 31645.

J.Lavian. 53-79 Highgate Rd, London, NW5 1TL. Tel 485 7955.

Lindfield Galleries Ltd. 59 High St, Lindfield, W.Sussex, RH16 2HN. Tel 2817.

M. & M. Oriental Gallery Ltd. 4th Floor, Block D,53/79 Highgate Rd, London, NW5 1TL. Tel 267 5973.

Mayorcas Ltd. 38 Jermyn St, London, SW1Y 6DN. Tel 629 4195.

Trevor Micklem, Antiques. Withywine Farm,Morebath, Tiverton, Devon, EX16 9BZ. Tel Bampton (0398) 31409.

Peta Smyth - Antique Textiles. 42 Moreton St,Pimlico, London, SW1. Tel 630 9898.

St Ouen Antiques. Vintage Corner, Old Cambridge Rd, Puckeridge, Hertfordshire. Tel Ware (0920) 821336.

Louis Stanton. 299 Westbourne Grove, London, W11. Tel 727 9336.

Thornborough Galleries. 28 Gloucester St, Cirencester, Gloucestershire, GL7 2DH. Tel 2055 (priv 099386 367).

Geoffrey Van Ltd. 105 and 107 Portobello Rd, London, W11. Tel 229 5577.

Vigo Carpet Gallery. 6A Vigo St, London, W1. Tel 439 6971.

Tea Caddies

see also Boxes

Eddy Bardawil. 106 Kensington Church St, London, W8. Tel 221 3967.

Nigel Coleman Antiques. High St, Brasted, Kent. Tel Westerham (0959) 64042.

Ferneyhough. Brook House, Beaudesert, Henley-in-Arden, Warwickshire, B95 5QR. Tel 2451.

Le Soken Antiques. High Street, Thorpe-le-Soken, Essex. Tel Clacton (0255) 861 337.

Millhouse. The Square, Petworth, W.Sussex, GU28 9BP. Tel 43080.

Milton Abbot Antiques. Venn Hill, Milton Abbot, Tavistock, Devon. Tel 392.

Todd & Austin Antiques & Fine Art. 2 Andover Rd, Winchester, Hampshire, SO23 7BS. Tel 69824.

Treasure Chest Ltd. The Jays, 19 Alstone Lane, Highbridge, Somerset, TA9 3DS. Tel Burnham-on-Sea (0278) 787267.

Textiles

see also Chinese Embroideries, Lace, Needlework, Samplers, Tapestries, Quilts, Restorers

Anglo-Persian Carpet Co Ltd. The Arcade, South Kensington Station, London, SW7 2NA. Tel 589 5457.

The Antique Textile Company. 100 Portland Rd, London, W11. Tel 221 7730.

Antiquus. 90-92 Pimlico Rd, London, SW1. Tel 730 8681.

Avon Antiques. 26-27 Market St, Bradford-on-Avon, Wiltshire. Tel 2052.

Michael & Margaret Baker. 6 High St, Merstham, Surrey. Tel 2658.

Celia Barker Mill. 24 Iverna Gardens,Kensington, London, W8 6TN. Tel 937 9145.

Benardout & Benardout. 7 Thurloe Place, London, SW7 2RX. Tel 584 7658.

Raymond Benardout. 5 William St, Knightsbridge, London, SW1X 9HL. Tel 235 3360 (priv 235 0504).

Benson Antiques. 13 Suffolk Parade, Cheltenham, Gloucestershire. Tel 578366.

Bernheimer Fine Arts Ltd. 32 St George St,Mayfair, London, W1R 9FA. Tel 499 0293.

David Black Oriental Carpets. 96 Portland Rd, London, W11 4LN. Tel 727 2566.

Joanna Booth. 247 King's Rd, London, SW3. Tel 352 8998.

L.& G.Burnett. 290 Portobello Rd, London, W10 5TE. Tel 969 8899.

Burns & Graham. 4 St Thomas St, Winchester, Hampshire. Tel 53779.

Celia Charlotte's. 7 Malling St, Lewes, E.Sussex, BN7 2RA. Tel 473303.

The Clare Collector. 1 Nethergate St, Clare, Suffolk. Tel 277909 (priv 277494).

Coexistence. 10 Argyle Street, Bath, Avon. Tel 61507 (priv 314846).

Coexistence Limited. Hobhouse Court, 13 Whitcomb St, London, WC2H 7HA. Tel 839 6620.

Coexistence Limited. 17 Canonbury Lane, London, N1 2AS. Tel 226 8382.

Contemporary Textile Gallery. 10 Golden Square, London, W1R 3AF. Tel 439 9070.

Eileen Cooper Antiques. Challoner's Rd, Braunton, Devon, EX33 2ES. Tel 813320.

Corrigan Antiques. The Cross, Kilbarchan, Strathclyde, PA10 2JG. Tel 2229.

Denning Antiques. 1 Chapel St, Guildford, Surrey. Tel 39595.

Dupont Galleries. 33 Grand Parade, Brighton & Hove, E.Sussex. Tel 738257 and 695094.

Amy Egan. 3A & 7 Mill Bridge, High St, Skipton, N.Yorkshire. Tel Halifax (0422) 201203.

Joan Eyles Antiques. The Stone Yard,Fishergate, Boroughbridge, N.Yorkshire, YO5 9QY. Tel 3357 (priv 2487).

Robert Franses & Son. 5 Nugent Tce, St John's Wood, London, NW8. Tel 286 6913 (priv 328 0949).

S.Franses Ltd. 82 Jermyn St,St James's, London, SW1. Tel 235 1888/9.

S.Franses Ltd. 11 Spring St,Paddington, London, W2. Tel 262 1153/4.

Gallery of Antique Costume & Textiles Ltd. 2 Church Street, Marylebone, London, NW8. Tel 723 9981 (priv 743 3821).

Judy Greenwood. 657 Fulham Rd, London, SW6. Tel 736 6037.

Hand in Hand. 3 North West Circus Place, Edinburgh, Lothian, EH3 6ST. Tel 226 3598.

Handweavers Studio and Gallery. 29 Haroldstone Rd, Walthamstow, London, E17. Tel 521 2281.

Heraz. 25 Motcomb St, London, SW1X 8JT. Tel 235 7416.

The Honiton Lace Shop. 44 High St, Honiton, Devon. Tel 2416 (priv 2629).

Paul Hughes, Antique & Ancient Textiles. 3a Pembridge Sq, London, W2. Tel 243 8598.

C. John (Rare Rugs) Ltd. 70 South Audley St,Mayfair, London, W1Y 5FE. Tel 493 5288.

Paul Jones. Stand Y6 Antiquarius,135 Kings Rd, London, SW3. Tel 352 4690.

Alexander Juran & Co. 74 New Bond St, London, W1Y 9DD. Tel 629 2550, 493 4484.

Ann King. 38 Belvedere, Lansdowne Rd, Bath, Avon. Tel 336245 (priv 0373 864747).

The Lacquer Chest. 75 Kensington Church St, London, W8. Tel 937 1306.

Stephen Long. Albion House, 348 Fulham Rd, London, SW10 9UH. Tel 352 8226.

Loot. 76-78 Pimlico Rd, London, SW1. Tel 730 8097 (priv 352 0135).

Lucky Parrot (Antiques and Things). Bellevue Rd, Wandsworth Common, London, SW17. Tel 672 7168.

Lunn Antiques Ltd. 86 New King's Rd, London, SW6 4LU. Tel 736 4638.

M. & M. Oriental Gallery Ltd. 4th Floor, Block D,53/79 Highgate Rd, London, NW5 1TL. Tel 267 5973.

Sue Madden. Stall X10 Antiquarius,135 Kings Rd, London, SW3. Tel 351 5757 (priv 703 4634).

Mayorcas Ltd. 38 Jermyn St, London, SW1Y 6DN. Tel 629 4195.

Moolham Mill Antiques. Moolham Mill, Moolham Lane, Ilminster, Somerset, TA19 0PD. Tel 2834.

No.Twelve Queen Street. 12 Queen St, Bath, Avon. Tel 62363 (priv 314846).

Old Bakery Antiques. 1 Church St, Hunstanton, Norfolk. Tel Brancaster (0485) 210396.

Mrs A.M.Ponsonby Antiques. Upham House,Ashfield, Framlingham, Suffolk, IP14 6LT. Tel Earl Soham (072 882) 200.

Real Macoy. Crossroads, Keighley, W.Yorkshire. Tel 44776.

Philippa Scott. 30 Elgin Crescent, London, W11. Tel 229 8029.

Peta Smyth - Antique Textiles. 42 Moreton St,Pimlico, London, SW1. Tel 630 9898.

A Stitch in Time. 1 West End, Beaumaris, Gwynedd. Tel 811055.

Straight Lace. 9 High St, East Linton, Lothian, EH40 3AA. Tel 860017 (priv 062088 284).

M. & C. Telfer-Smollett. 88 Portobello Rd, London, W11. Tel 727 0117 (priv 370 1860).

The Textile Gallery. 4 Castellain Rd, Little Venice, London, W9 1EZ. Tel 286 1747.

Tobias and the Angel. 68 White Hart Lane,Barnes, London, SW13. Tel 878 8902.

Michael Wakelin and Helen Linfield. 10 New St, Petworth, W.Sussex. Tel 42417.

Linda Wrigglesworth. Stand B17/A23, Gray's Mews,1-7 Davies Mews, London, W1. Tel 408 0177.

Theatrical Items

Castaside. Shop 19, Chelsea Antique Market,253 King's Rd, London, SW3. Tel 352 9695.

Clunes Antiques. 9 West Place, Wimbledon, London, SW19 4UH. Tel 946 1643.

Commemoratives. 3 Pierrepont Arcade, Camden Passage,Islington, London, N1. Tel eves only 278 2146.

Discovery. Chelsea Antique Market,245-253 King's Rd, London, SW3. Tel 352 9695.

John Hall. 31 Epple Rd, London, SW6 4DJ. Tel 736 3542.

M. Harrington Ltd. 74 Parchment St, Winchester, Hampshire, SO23 8AT. Tel 53608.

Marina Henderson. 11 Langton St, London, SW10. Tel 352 1667.

Richard Macnutt Ltd. Hamm Farm House,Withyham, Hartfield Wells, E.Sussex, TN7 4BJ. Tel Groombridge (089276) 218.

Mail Order Book Specialist. 25 Dicey Ave, Cricklewood, London, NW2. Tel 452 1581.

Ed Mason. Shop 5 Chelsea Antique Market,253 King's Rd, London, SW3. Tel 352 9695.

J.W.McKenzie, Bookseller. 12 Stoneleigh Park Rd, Ewell, Surrey, KT19 0QT. Tel 01- 393 7700.

P.B.Pollington. 4 Central Parade, High St, Wadhurst, E.Sussex, TN5 6AL. Tel 2866.

Taurus Gallery. 5 Wadham Rd, Putney, London, SW15 2LS. Tel 874 2534.

Timber Polishing and Preservation

John Boddy's Fine Wood & Tool Store Ltd. Riverside Sawmills, Boroughbridge, N.Yorkshire, YO5 9LJ. Tel 2370.

James Briggs & Sons Ltd. Lion Works, Old Market St, Blackley, Manchester, Greater Manchester, M9 3DU. Tel 795 8410.

Gaylords. 75 West St, Titchfield, Fareham, Hampshire. Tel 43402 (priv 662606).

Hagen (Restorations). Bakehouse Cottage, Northwood End Rd, Haynes, Bedfordshire, MK45 3QD. Tel 424.

Haverstock Antiques. 78 Haverstock Hill, Hampstead, London, NW3 3BS. Tel 267 1627.

Merlin Antiques & Restorations. Howgill Lane, Sedbergh, Cumbria. Tel 20301 (priv 20719).

The Old Granary. Battlesbridge Antique Centre,Hawk Hill (by the "Barge" pub), Battlesbridge, Essex. Tel Wickford (037 44) 63344.

Past Times. Rear of 46 Cold Bath Rd, Harrogate, N.Yorkshire. Tel 60896 63846.

Church Lane Restorations. 1 Church Lane, Teddington, Middlesex. Tel 977 2526.

Touchwood Antiques. 9 Park St., Stow-on-the-Wold, Gloucestershire, GL54 1AQ. Tel 30221.

Tools

Roy Arnold. 77 High St, Needham Market, Suffolk. Tel 720110.

At the Sign of the Herald Angel. 19 Park St, Cirencester, Gloucestershire, GL7 2BX. Tel 2972.

Below Stairs. 103 High St, Hungerford, Berkshire, RG17 0NB. Tel 82317.

John Boddy's Fine Wood & Tool Store Ltd. Riverside Sawmills, Boroughbridge, N.Yorkshire, YO5 9LJ. Tel 2370.

Clunes Antiques. 9 West Place, Wimbledon, London, SW19 4UH. Tel 946 1643.

Country Antiques. 10 Westgate St, Long Melford, Suffolk. Tel Sudbury (0787) 310617.

Betty Dean Antiques. The Walnuts, Weston St Mary's, Spalding, Lincolnshire, PE12 6JB. Tel Holbeach (0406) 370429 (priv 371067).

Doddington House Antiques. 2 Benwick Rd, Doddington, Cambridgeshire, PE15 0TG. Tel March (0354) 740755.

Frith Antiques. New St, Petworth, W.Sussex. Tel 43155 (priv 079881 606).

Halstow Antiques. Green Farm House, The Green,Lower Halstow, Sittingbourne, Kent, ME9 7DS. Tel 842016.

Maltings Antiques. Sixty Millgate, Aylsham, Norfolk. Tel 732291.

Richard Maude Tools. 22 Parkfields, Putney, London, SW15 6NH. Tel 788 2991.

Multum-In-Parvo & Tools Past. Kirkland, Kendal, Cumbria. Tel 25168.

Norton Antiques. 56 London End, Beaconsfield, Buckinghamshire, HP9 2JH. Tel 3674.

Pine and Country Antiques. Sandhill Barn, Washington, Pulborough, W.Sussex. Tel Ashington (0903) 892888 (priv 892210).

Priory Antiques. Litcham Priory, Litcham, King's Lynn, Norfolk. Tel Litcham (0328) 701262.

J.Wigington & Sons. 'Winchester 73', 276 Alcester Rd, Stratford-upon-Avon, Warwickshire. Tel 293881.

Tortoiseshell

Christine Schell. 15 Cale St, London, SW3 3QS. Tel 352 5563.

Toys

see Dolls and Toys

Treen

A.& F. Partners. 20 London St, Faringdon, Oxfordshire, SN7 7AA. Tel 20078.

Alexander Antiques. Post House, Small Dole, Henfield, W.Sussex.

Antique Pine Furniture, Michael Green. Library House,Regent Parade, Harrogate, N.Yorkshire. Tel 60452.

Antiques. 9 West End, West Haddon, Northamptonshire. Tel 772.

Barclay Antiques. 7 Village Mews, Little Common, Bexhill, E.Sussex. Tel Rye (0797) 222734.

Janet & Robert Bateman Antiques. 92 Waterford Rd, London, SW6 2HA. Tel 736 4149.

John Bird/Annette Puttnam. 44 Upper North St, Brighton & Hove, E.Sussex, BN1 3FH. Tel 739425.

Bratton Antiques. Market Place, Westbury, Wiltshire, BA13 3DE. Tel 823021.

Butterwalk House. 55 The Old Butterwalk, High St, Totnes, Devon. Tel 863044.

Simon Castle. 38B Kensington Church St, London, W8. Tel 937 2268.

Close Antiques. 19 Little Minster St, Winchester, Hampshire, SO23 9HA. Tel 64763.

Cordell Antiques. 13 St Peter's St, Ipswich, Suffolk. Tel 219508.

Cottage Antiques. The Old Post Office, Langford, Bristol, Avon, BS18 7BP. Tel Wrighton (0934) 862597.

Jay Davis Antiques. Bishopsdale Court, Settle, N.Yorkshire. Tel 2764.

Polly de Courcy-Ireland. 16 Chilbolton Ave, Winchester, Hampshire, SO22 5HD. Tel 65716.

David Dean Antiques. Pen-Y-Ghent View, Church St, Settle, N.Yorkshire. Tel 3702 (priv 3660).

Duveen Antiques. Burgate, Fordingbridge, Hampshire, SP6 1LX. Tel 53309.

P. & S.N. Eddy. 22 Etnam St, Leominster, Hereford & Worcester, HR6 8AQ. Tel 2813.

Joan Eyles Antiques. The Stone Yard,Fishergate, Boroughbridge, N.Yorkshire, YO5 9QY. Tel 3357 (priv 2487).

Fenwick and Fisher Antiques. 88 High St, Broadway, Hereford & Worcester. Tel 853227 (priv 853228).

A. & E. Foster. Little Heysham, Forge Rd, Naphill, Buckinghamshire. Tel 2024.

Frith Antiques. New St, Petworth, W.Sussex. Tel 43155 (priv 079881 606).

George & Helen Gardiner. 105 West Regent St, Glasgow, Strathclyde, G2 2BA. Tel 332 1264.

Gloucester House Antiques Ltd. Market Place, Fairford, Gloucestershire, GL7 4AB. Tel Cirencester (0285) 712790 (priv 3066).

Grange Court Antiques. Corfe, Taunton, Somerset. Tel Blagdon Hill (082 342) 498.

Stephanie Grant Antiques. 38 The Bank, Barnard Castle, Durham. Tel Teesdale (0833) 37437.

Halcyon Days. 14 Brook St, London, W1Y 1AA. Tel 629 8811.

George Hofman Antiques. Brookside, High St, Stockbridge, Hampshire, SO20 6EY. Tel 810570.

Jose Hornsey. 3 Silver St, Bradford-on-Avon, Wiltshire. Tel 4333 (priv 0380 870764).

House of Antiques. 4 College St, Petersfield, Hampshire, GU31 4AD. Tel 62172.

Huntington Antiques Ltd. The Old Forge, Church St, Stow-on-the-Wold, Gloucestershire. Tel 30842.

Peter Jeeves Antiques. High St, Cuckfield, W.Sussex. Tel Haywards Heath (0444) 454420.

Le Soken Antiques. High Street, Thorpe-le-Soken, Essex. Tel Clacton (0255) 861 337.

Lensfield Antiques. 12 Lensfield Rd, Cambridge, Cambridgeshire, CB2 1EG. Tel 357636.

Mac Humble Antiques. 11 Queen St, Bath, Avon, BA1 2Jo. Tel 62751 (priv 022122 3594).

Market Place Antiques. 35 Market Place, Henley-on-Thames, Oxfordshire, RG9 2AA. Tel 572387.

Marlborough Antiques. 18 The Parade, Marlborough, Wiltshire. Tel 54818.

Netherly Cottage Antiques. Milburn, Cumbria. Tel Kirkby Thore (0930) 61403.

Angela Page Antiques. Sion House, 15 Mount Sion, Tunbridge Wells, Kent, TN1 1OD. Tel 22217.

Peppers Period Pieces. 22/23 Churchgate St, Bury St Edmunds, Suffolk. Tel 68786 (priv 0359 50606).

M. & D. Seligmann. 37 Kensington Church St, London, W8 4LL. Tel 937 0400 (priv 722 4315).

Sheila Smith Antiques. 10A Queen St, Bath, Avon. Tel 60568 (priv 0373 830217).

A. & J.Stuart-Mobey & Daughter. Bedford House, Lower Wolvercote, Oxford, Oxfordshire, OX2 9PF. Tel 50170.

The Three Estaits. 49 Dundas St, Edinburgh, Lothian, EH3 6RS. Tel 556 7084.

Times Past. 84 High St, Pershore, Hereford & Worcester, WR10 1DU. Tel 554258.

Charles & Jane Toller. 20 High St, Datchet, Berkshire, SL3 9EQ. Tel Windsor (0753) 42903.

Clive Underwood Antiques. 46 High St, Colsterworth, Lincolnshire. Tel Grantham (0476) 860689.

Elizabeth Viney. Jacob's House, High St, Stockbridge, Hampshire. Tel 810761.

Peter Wadham. The Antique Shop, 5 Cathedral Close, Exeter, Devon. Tel 39741.

Michael Wakelin and Helen Linfield. 10 New St, Petworth, W.Sussex. Tel 42417.

J.Wigington & Sons. 'Winchester 73', 276 Alcester Rd, Stratford-upon-Avon, Warwickshire. Tel 293881.

Williton Antiques. 26 High St, Williton, Taunton, Somerset. Tel Williton (0984) 32393 (priv).

Wynyards Antiques. 5 Ladbroke Rd, London, W11. Tel 221 7936, 727 5106.

Robert Young Antiques. 68 Battersea Bridge Rd, London, SW11. Tel 228 7847.

Upholstery

Alpha Antiques. Church Lane, Checkley, Stoke-on-Trent, Staffordshire, ST10 4NJ. Tel Tean (0538) 722149.

Antique Leathers. 4 Park End, South Hill Park, London, NW3 2SE. Tel 435 8582/7799.

Antique Restoration. Antique Centre, 1 Severn Rd, Gloucester, Gloucestershire. Tel 29716 (priv 20911).

Eric Bates & Sons. High St, Coltishall, Norfolk. Tel Norwich (0603) 738716.

Boyne House Antiques. Lion Yard,Broad Street, Leominster, Hereford & Worcester. Tel 5596.

Brockdish Antiques. Commerce House, Brockdish, Diss, Norfolk. Tel Hoxne (037975) 498.

Burns & Graham. 4 St Thomas St, Winchester, Hampshire. Tel 53779.

Chesterfields Etc.. 99 Lisson Grove, London, NW1. Tel 402 9728.

Cladgild Ltd. Vine House, Fair Green, Reach, Cambridgeshire, CB5 0JD. Tel Newmarket (0638) 742171.

J. Crisp & Son. 48 Roderick Rd,Hampstead, London, NW3 2NL. Tel 340 0668.

Dudley's Home Interiors. Vine House, Fair Green, Reach, Cambridgeshire. Tel Newmarket (0638) 741989.

Dudley's Home Interiors. Vine House, Fair Green, Reach, Cambridgeshire. Tel Newmarket (0638) 741989.

Margaret Elmes Antiques. Denham Gallery, Denham, Buckinghamshire, UB9 5BE. Tel 832244.

Farmhouse Antiques. Whites Farm House, Barkers Drove,Off Oxborough Rd, Stoke Ferry, Norfolk. Tel 500 588.

Furniture Fair. 22 Church St, London, NW8. Tel 262 1338.

G.M.S. Restorations. 36 High Street,Wickwar, Wotton-under-Edge, Gloucestershire, GL12 8NP. Tel Wickwar (045424) 251.

Gaylords. 75 West St, Titchfield, Fareham, Hampshire. Tel 43402 (priv 662606).

Golightly Restoration. 69 Kent Rd, Glasgow, Strathclyde, G3. Tel 221 7472.

Janet Gordon. Wakes Colne House, Wakes Colne, Essex. Tel Earls Colne (07875) 2402.

The Granary & Rene Antiques and Art. 17A Kings Rd, St Leonards, E.Sussex, TN37 6DU. Tel 432610 (priv 71586).

Michael Hedgecoe Antique Furniture Restoration. 21 Burrow Hill Green, Chobham, Surrey, GU24 8QS. Tel 8206.

Idears. 1 Chapel St, Diss, Norfolk, IP22 3AN. Tel 51521.

J.K.Layton. Fawcett Yard, off Tower St,back Belford Place, Harrogate, N.Yorkshire. Tel 68809.

Manor House Antiques. The Green, Datchet, Berkshire. Tel Slough (0753) 42164 & 41460.

Simon Marsh Antiques. The Old Butchers Shop, High St, Bletchingley, Surrey. Tel Godstone (0883) 843350.

T.J.Mitchell Antiques Ltd. 1a Lower Pembroke St, Dublin, Co Dublin. Tel 766881.

Michael Moore Antiques. The Old Court, Nethergate St, Clare, Suffolk, CO10 8NP. Tel 277510.

Newcourt Park. Lugwardine, Hereford & Worcester. Tel Hereford (0432) 850752.

Nidd House Antiques. Nidd House, Bogs Lane, Harrogate, N.Yorkshire. Tel 884739.

The Old Granary. Battlesbridge Antique Centre,Hawk Hill (by the "Barge" pub), Battlesbridge, Essex. Tel Wickford (037 44) 63344.

Past Times. Rear of 46 Cold Bath Rd, Harrogate, N.Yorkshire. Tel 60896 63846.

The Penny Farthing. 7-8 Beaufort Rd, Edinburgh, Lothian. Tel 447 2410.

A.J.Ponsford Antiques and Restorations. 51-53 Dollar St, Cirencester, Gloucestershire, GL7 2AS. Tel 2355.

Church Lane Restorations. 1 Church Lane, Teddington, Middlesex. Tel 977 2526.

Riverside Antiques Ltd. Riverside House, Charnham St, Hungerford, Berkshire. Tel 82314.

Robbies Antiques. 140 Seabank Rd, Wallasey, Merseyside. Tel 051 638 3848.

Michael Schryver Antiques Ltd. The Granary, North St, Dorking, Surrey, RH4 1DN. Tel 881110.

Southdown House Antiques. Southdown House, Easole St, Nonington, Kent, CT15 4HE. Tel 840987.

Clifford J. Tracy. 6-40 Durnford St, Seven Sisters Rd, London, N15 5NQ. Tel 800 4773.

Treasure House. 123 University St, Belfast, Belfast, BT7 1HP. Tel 231055.

Andrew White. Shop 17, The Quadrant,Kilburn Lane, London, W10.

Whytock & Reid. Sunbury House, Belford Mews, Edinburgh, Lothian, EH4 3DN. Tel 226 4911.

Valuations

London

Anglo-Persian Carpet Co Ltd. The Arcade, South Kensington Station, London, SW7 2NA. Tel 589 5457.

Bainbridges Fine Art & General Chattel Auctioneers. 2 Chapel Rd,Ealing, London, W13. Tel 579 2966.

Eddy Bardawil. 106 Kensington Church St, London, W8. Tel 221 3967.

Paul Bennett. 75 George St, London, W1. Tel 935 1555.

N.Bloom & Son (Antiques) Ltd. 40 Conduit St, London, W1R 9FB. Tel 629 5060.

J.H. Bourdon-Smith Ltd. 24 Mason's Yard,Duke St, St James's, London, SW1Y 6BU. Tel 839 4714/5.

Peter Cameron. 4 Grosvenor St, London, W1. Tel 491 8949.

D.B.Cater Antiques. 173 & 175 Bermondsey St, London, SE1 3UW. Tel 407 2040.

Christie's. 8 King St, St James's, London, SW1Y 6QT. Tel 839 9060.

Christie's in the City. 56-60 Gresham St, London, EC2V 7BB. Tel 588 4424.

Crawford & Pawle Ltd. 2nd Floor, Bond St Silver Galleries,111-112 New Bond St, London, W1Y 9AB. Tel 499 8442.

Anthony Dallas & Sons Ltd. 17 Clifford St, London, W1. Tel 734 7127.

E.H.W. & Co. 12 Sicilian Ave, Southampton Row, London, WC1A 3QD. Tel 405 5509.

Glendining & Co. 7 Blenheim St, New Bond St, London, W1Y OAS. Tel 493 2445.

Essie C.Harris. Diamond House 37-38 Hatton Garden, London, EC1. Tel 242 9115/1558.

Hennell Ltd. 12 New Bond St, London, W1Y oHE. Tel 629 6888.

Jackson-Stops & Staff. 14 Curzon St, London, W1. Tel 499 6291.

John Joseph. Grays Antique Market,58 Davies St, London, W1. Tel 629 1140.

Eric Lineham & Son. 62 Kensington Church St, London, W8 4oB. Tel 937 9650.

Marks Antiques Ltd. 49 Curzon St, London, W1. Tel 499 5392.

R.I. McKay. 63 South Molton St, London, W1Y 1HH.

Stephen O'Donnell Antiques. Grays Antique Market,58 Davies St, London, W1. Tel 491 8852.

David Paskin Antiques (London) Ltd. Grays Antique Market,58 Davies St, London, W1. Tel 408 1129.

Samiramis Ltd. Grays Mews,1-7 Davies St, London, W1. Tel 629 1161 or 439 5106.

Scarlet Pimpernel Antiques. Grays Antique Market,58 Davies St, London, W1.

Sensation Ltd. 66 Fulham High St, London, SW6 5LQ. Tel 736 4135 (priv 584 9414).

Sotheby's. 34-35 New Bond Street, London, W1A 2AA. Tel 493 8080.

Louise Stroud. 3, Cale Street,Chelsea Green, London, SW3. Tel 351 5988.

Trianon. Grays Antique Market,58 Davies St, London, W1. Tel 491 2764.

Turn On Ltd. 116-118 Islington High St,Camden Passage, London, N1 8EG. Tel 359 7616.

Ventura-Pauly Ltd. Grays Antique Market,58 Davies St, London, W1. Tel 408 1057.

Walker Galleries of Harrogate Ltd. 3 Cale St,Chelsea Green, London, SW3. Tel 351 5988.

Regions

James Adam and Sons. 26 St Stephens Green, Dublin, Co Dublin. Tel 760261.

Ancient and Modern. 32-34 Polkyth Rd, St Austell, Cornwall. Tel 3983.

Brenda Arden Antiques. Hulgrave Hall,Tiverton, Tarporley, Cheshire, CW6 9UQ. Tel 2427.

Artingstall & Hind. 378/380 Deansgate, Knott Mill, Manchester, Greater Manchester, M3 4NA. Tel 834 4559.

AS Antiques. 26 Broad St, Pendleton, Salford, Greater Manchester. Tel Manchester (061) 737 5938.

Richard Baker and Thomson. 9 Hamilton St, Birkenhead, Merseyside. Tel 647 9104.

Baldwin & Partners. 26 Railway St, Chatham, Kent, ME4 4JT. Tel Medway (0634) 400121.

Richard Barder Antiques. Crossways House, Hermitage, Berkshire, RG16 9SU. Tel Newbury (0635) 200295.

Bearnes. Rainbow, Avenue Rd, Torquay, Devon, TQ2 5TG. Tel 26277.

Berry Powell & Shackell. 46 Market Place, Chippenham, Wiltshire. Tel 653361.

Helen Blomfield. Hampers, Little Maplestead, Halstead, Essex. Tel 2159.

Broadway Antiques. 185, 185A, 187 Broadway,Roath, Cardiff, S.Glamorgan. Tel 24470.

T.C.S.Brooke. The Grange, Wroxham, Norfolk, NR12 8RX. Tel 2644.

Bruton Knowles & Co. Albion Chambers, 55 Barton St, Gloucester, Gloucestershire. Tel 21267.

Butterfields. The Auction Galleries,Riddings Rd, Ilkley, W.Yorkshire, LS29 9LU. Tel 603313 (priv 0274-594068).

Ian Caldwell. 9A The Green, Dorking Rd, Tadworth, Surrey, KT20 5SQ. Tel 3969.

Capes Dunn & Co. 38 Charles St, Manchester, Greater Manchester, M1 7DB. Tel 273 1911.

Ch-Art. Marine House, St Andrew Sq, Colyton, Devon. Tel 53335.

Charles International Antiques. 3 Market St, Maidstone, Kent. Tel 682882.

Chislehurst Antiques. 7 Royal Parade, Chislehurst, Kent. Tel London (01) 467 1530.

Christie, Manson and Woods Ltd. Marybrook House, 9 Raleagh Rd,Crossgar, Downpatrick, Co Down, BT30 9JG. Tel 830574.

Christie's. Stanley Hall, Bridgnorth, Shropshire. Tel 61891.

Christie's. 111 The Promenade, Cheltenham, Gloucestershire. Tel 518999.

Christie's. Eastfield House, Main St, Corbridge, Northumberland. Tel 3181.

Christie's. The Old Rectory,Fawkham, Dartford, Kent. Tel Longfield (04747) 2854.

Christie's. Wolfeton House, Dorchester, Dorset. Tel 68748.

Christie's. 5 Wemyss Place, Edinburgh, Lothian. Tel 225 4756/7.

Christie's. Mounteagle, Fearn, Highland. Tel 2866.

Christie's. Glin Castle, Glin, Co Limerick. Tel (priv) Dublin 680585.

Christie's. Leonardslee Gardens,Lower Beeding, Horsham, W.Sussex, RH13 6PP. Tel Lower Beeding (040 376) 305.

Christie's. Cumlodden Estate Office, Crarae, Inveraray, Strathclyde, PA32 8YA. Tel Minard (0546) 86633 (priv 86274).

Christie's. The Stables,Keith Hall, Inverurie, Grampian, AB5 oLD. Tel 24366.

Christie's. Strathgarry House, Killiecrankie, Tayside. Tel Blair Atholl (079681) 216.

Christie's. Blairquhan, Maybole, Strathclyde. Tel Straiton (06557) 239.

Christie's. Old Bank of England Court,Queen St, Norwich, Norfolk, NR2 4BX. Tel 614546.

Christie's. Eden Lacy,Lazonby, Penrith, Cumbria, CA10 1BZ. Tel 8800.

Christie's. The Stables,Milton Hall, Peterborough, Cambridgeshire, PE6 7AA. Tel Castor (073121) 781.

Christie's. Gnaton Estate Office,Yealmpton, Plymouth, Devon. Tel 880636.

Christie's. Downton House, New Radnor, Presteigne, Powys. Tel Cheltenham (0242) 518999.

Christie's. Tredeague, Porthpean, St Austell, Cornwall. Tel 64672.

Christie's. 58 David Place, St Helier, Jersey. Tel 77582.

Christie's. Monmouth Lodge, Yenston, Templecombe, Somerset, BA8 oNH. Tel 70518.

Christie's. 46 Bootham, York, N.Yorkshire. Tel 30911.

Christie's Robson Lowe. 39 Poole Hill, Bournemouth, Dorset. Tel 292740.

Clare Gallery. 21 High St, Tunbridge Wells, Kent. Tel 38717.

J.H. Cooper & Son (Ilkley) Ltd. 33-35 Church St, Ilkley, W.Yorkshire, LS29 9DR. Tel 608020.

Cottage Antiques. 9 Kings Rd,Canton, Cardiff, S.Glamorgan. Tel 24484.

S.W. Cottee & Son. The Market, East St, Wareham, Dorset, BH20 4NR. Tel 2826.

E.W.Cousins & Son. 27 High St, Ixworth, Suffolk. Tel Pakenham (0359) 30254.

Cubitt & West Fine Art Auctioneers. Cubitt & West Auction Galleries,Millmead, Guildford, Surrey, GU2 5BE. Tel 504030.

Andrew Dando. 4 Wood St, Queen Sq, Bath, Avon, BA1 2JQ. Tel 22702.

Diamond Mills & Co. 117 Hamilton Rd, Felixstowe, Suffolk. Tel 282281.

Dickinson, Davy & Markham. 10 Wrawby Street, Brigg, Humberside. Tel 53666.

R.C.Dodson Antiques. 85 Fawcett Rd, Southsea, Hampshire. Tel 829481.

Dreweatts. Donnington Priory, Donnington, Newbury, Berkshire, RG13 2JE. Tel 31234.

Eadon, Lockwood & Riddle Auctioneers. Weston Saleroom,Crookes, Sheffield, S.Yorkshire, S1 1XJ. Tel 686294.

Earl & Lawrence. 55 Northgate, Sleaford, Lincolnshire, NG34 7AB. Tel 302946.

Eldon Worrall. 15 Seel Street, Liverpool, Merseyside.

Peter Farrow. Hillbury House,Missenden Road, Chesham, Buckinghamshire, HP5 1JZ. Tel 784138.

Jeremy A. Fearn. The Old Rectory, Winksley, Ripon, N.Yorkshire. Tel Kirkby Malzeard (0765 83) 625.

Geering & Colyer. 22/24 High St, Tunbridge Wells, Kent, TN1 1XA. Tel 25136.

Georgian Gems. 28 High St, Swanage, Dorset, BH19 1HA. Tel 424697.

Glennie Middleton and Bullock. 3 Church St, Diss, Norfolk, IP22 3DD. Tel 51617.

The Goff Galleries. Hall St, Long Melford, Suffolk, CO10 9JQ. Tel Sudbury (0787) 78228.

Green & Co. 33 Market Place, Wantage, Oxfordshire, OX12 8AL. Tel 3561/2.

A. Halsey Antiques. Boffins Boft, Bowcombe Creek, Kingsbridge, Devon. Tel 2440.

R.& L. Hampshire Antiques. Rutherford Hall,Gatehouse of Fleet, Castle Douglas, Dumfries & Galloway, DG7 4HS. Tel Gatehouse (05574) 616.

Heathcote Ball & Co. Castle Auction Rooms,78 St Nicholas Circle, Leicester, Leicestershire, LE1 5NW. Tel 536789.

Hetheringtons, Pretty & Ellis. 125 Station Rd, Amersham, Buckinghamshire. Tel 29292.

Hobbs & Chambers. At the Sign of the Bell,Market Place, Cirencester, Gloucestershire, GL7 1QQ. Tel 4736 (priv 0672 20018).

Hoddell Pritchard. Clevedon Salerooms, Six Ways, Clevedon, Avon, BS21 7NT. Tel 876699.

M.A.& D.A.Hughes. 11 Pulteney Bridge, Bath, Avon. Tel 65782.

Anthony Hurst Antiques. 13 Church St, Woodbridge, Suffolk. Tel 2500.

Raymond P.Inman. 35 & 40 Temple St, Brighton & Hove, E.Sussex, BN1 3BH. Tel 774777.

Irelands Hall & Palmer. 11 Market Place, Wymondham, Norfolk. Tel 603031.

Jackson-Stops & Staff. Dollar St, Cirencester, Gloucestershire. Tel 3334.

A.E.Jameson & Co. 257 Glossop Rd, Sheffield, S.Yorkshire, S10 2GZ. Tel 23846 (priv 26189).

Jays Fine Art Dealers. Cambridge Gallery,4 Cambridge Arcade, Southport, Merseyside, PR8 1AS. Tel 34488 (priv 69500).

David Lane Antiques. The Old Forge,Fanners Yard, Compton Abbas, Dorset. Tel Shaftesbury (0747) 811881.

Langlois Ltd. Don St, St Helier, Jersey. Tel 22441.

Charles Lumb & Sons Ltd. 2 Montpellier Gardens, Harrogate, N.Yorkshire, HG1 2TF. Tel 503776 (priv 863281).

Manor House Antiques. The Green, Datchet, Berkshire. Tel Slough (0753) 42164 & 41460.

Marksdanes Antiques Ltd. Station Rd, Bruton, Somerset. Tel 3267.

The William Marler Gallery. 36/38 Dyer St, Cirencester, Gloucestershire, GL7 2PF. Tel 68526.

Mill House Antiques. 139 Abbey Foregate, Shrewsbury, Shropshire. Tel 240328.

Lawrence Musgrove Antiques. Dixton Lodge,Hadnock Rd, Monmouth, Gwent. Tel 3656.

Neal Sons & Fletcher. 26 Church St, Woodbridge, Suffolk, IP12 1DP. Tel 2263/4 (priv 0728 723877).

Neale Antiques. 21 Old Cross, Hertford, Hertfordshire, SG14 1RE. Tel 52519 and 51347.

Neales of Nottingham. 192/194 Mansfield Rd, Nottingham, Nottinghamshire, NG1 3HX. Tel 624141.

Neates. 108 High St, Hungerford, Berkshire, RG17 0NB. Tel 82808.

Neates. 8 St Mary's Hill, Cheap St, Newbury, Berkshire, RG14 5DF. Tel 42961.

Newcourt Park. Lugwardine, Hereford & Worcester. Tel Hereford (0432) 850752.

Old Barn Antiques Co. Flamberts, Trent, Sherborne, Dorset, DT9 4SS. Tel 850648.

Patrick Oliver Antiques Ltd. 4 Tivoli St, Cheltenham, Gloucestershire, GL50 2UW. Tel 513392/519538.

Olivers. 23-24 Market Hill, Sudbury, Suffolk, CO10 6EN. Tel 72247.

Onslow Clocks. 48 King Street, Twickenham, Middlesex, TW1 3SH. Tel 892 7632.

Outhwaite & Litherland. Kingsway Galleries, Fontenoy St, Liverpool, Merseyside, L3 2BE. Tel 236 6561.

Owens Gwynedd & Co. Llanerchymedd Auction Centre, Llangefni, Gwynedd. Tel 722950 (priv 0248-76 482).

John A.Pearson Ltd. 127-128 High St, Eton, Berkshire, SL4 6AR. Tel Windsor (0753) 860850.

Phillips. 9 Conwy Rd, Colwyn Bay, Clwyd, LL29 7AF. Tel 33406.

Phillips. 65 George St, Edinburgh, Lothian, EH2 2JL. Tel 225 2266.

Phillips Ipswich. Dover House,Wolsey St, Ipswich, Suffolk, IP1 1UD. Tel 55137.

Phillips. The Old House, Station Rd, Knowle, W.Midlands, B93 0HT. Tel Knowle (05645) 6151.

Phillips. 3 Opie St, Norwich, Norfolk, NR1 3DP. Tel 616426.

Phillips. 39 Park End St, Oxford, Oxfordshire, OX1 1JD. Tel 723524.

Phillips. Long Street Salerooms,Long St, Sherborne, Dorset, DT93BS. Tel 815271.

Phillips (Glasgow). 98 Sauchiehall St, Glasgow, Strathclyde, G2 3DQ. Tel 332 3386.

Phillips Fine Art Auctioneers. Bayle Place,11 Bayle Parade, Folkestone, Kent, CT20 1SQ. Tel 45555.

Phillips Fine Art Auctioneers & Valuers. 17A East Parade, Leeds, W.Yorkshire, LS1 2BU. Tel 448011.

Charles R.Phillips. 48 High St, Henley-in-Arden, Warwickshire. Tel 4330/1/2.

Phoenix Green Antiques. London Rd, Phoenix Green, Hartley Wintney, Hampshire, RG27 8RT. Tel 4430.

Printed Page. 2-3 Bridge St, Winchester, Hampshire, SO23 9BH. Tel 54072 (priv 62995).

Randolph. 97-99 High St, Hadleigh, Suffolk, IP7 5EJ. Tel 823789.

The Reid Gallery Ltd. Mousehill House,Milford, Godalming, Surrey, GU8 5BL. Tel 6990.

Restall, Brown & Clennell Ltd. Cosgrove Hall, Cosgrove, Northamptonshire, MK19 7JB. Tel Milton Keynes (0908) 565888 (priv 563336).

Colin Rhodes Antiques. Collier House, 53 Southside St, Plymouth, Devon. Tel 669079 (priv 42761).

Leigh Rice Antiques. 29 The Mall,Clifton, Bristol, Avon. Tel 730975.

Ian A.Robertson. Narrogate, Alnwick, Northumberland.

Sabine Antiques. 38 High St, Stock, Essex, CM4 9BW. Tel 840553.

Martin Scadgell Fine Art. Mulberry House Galleries,Codmore Hill, Pulborough, W.Sussex. Tel 2463.

B. & C.Seago. Whitemans Green, Cuckfield, W.Sussex, RH17 5BY. Tel Haywards Heath (0444) 456111.

Simmons & Lawrence (Chartered Surveyors). 32 Bell Street, Henley-on-Thames, Oxfordshire, RG9 2BH. Tel 571111.

David Smith Antiques. The Old Cottage, Manton, Oakham, Leicestershire. Tel Manton (057 285) 244 (priv 473 or 314).

Sotheby's. Aboyne Castle, Aboyne, Grampian. Tel Banchory (03302) 4007.

Sotheby's. 42 Holdenhurst Rd, Bournemouth, Dorset, BH8 8AF. Tel 294425.

Sotheby's. Market Place, Brampton, Cumbria, CA8 1NW. Tel 3722.

Sotheby's. 18 Imperial Sq, Cheltenham, Gloucestershire, GL50 1QZ. Tel 510500.

Sotheby's. Hall Foot, Worston, Clitheroe, Lancashire, BB7 1QA. Tel 41520.

Sotheby's. 123a Upper Abbey St, Dublin, Co Dublin. Tel 734811.

Sotheby's. 112 George St, Edinburgh, Lothian, EH2 4LH. Tel 226 7201.

Sotheby's. Bickham House,Kenn, Exeter, Devon, EX6 7XL. Tel 833416.

Sotheby's. 146 West Regent St, Glasgow, Strathclyde, G2 2RQ. Tel 221 4817.

Sotheby's. Grundisburgh, Suffolk, IP13 6TW. Tel 581.

Sotheby's. Market Place, Haltwhistle, Northumberland, NE49 OBU. Tel 20363.

Sotheby's. 8-12 Montpellier Parade, Harrogate, N.Yorkshire, HG1 2TJ. Tel 501466/7.

Sotheby's. The Estate Office,Greyabbey, Newtownards, Co Down. Tel Greyabbey (024 774) 668.

Sotheby's. George Hotel Mews, Station Rd, Stamford, Lincolnshire, PE9 2LB. Tel 51666.

Sotheby's. Magdalene House, Magdalene St, Taunton, Somerset, TA1 1SB. Tel 88441.

Sotheby's. 56 High St, Trumpington, Cambridgeshire, CB2 2LS. Tel Cambridge (0223) 8452225.

Sotheby's. Maiden Bradley, Warminster, Wiltshire, BA12 7HW. Tel Maiden Bradley (098 53) 525.

Sotheby's Chester. Booth Mansion, 28 Watergate St, Chester, Cheshire, CH1 2NA. Tel 315531.

St James Antiques. 41 South King St, Manchester, Greater Manchester. Tel 834 9632.

Stewart Gallery. 48 Devonshire Rd, Bexhill, E.Sussex. Tel 223410.

Stewart Gallery. 25 Grove Rd, Eastbourne, E.Sussex. Tel 29588.

Sutcliffe Galleries. 8 Albert St, Harrogate, N.Yorkshire. Tel 62976.

Sutton Valence Antiques. Sutton Valence, Maidstone, Kent. Tel 843333.

K. Stuart Swash. 2 Waterloo Rd, Wolverhampton, W.Midlands, WV1 4BL. Tel 710626.

James Thompson. 64 Main St, Kirkby Lonsdale, Cumbria, LA6 2AJ. Tel 71555.

John Thompson Antiques. Swadforth House,5 Gracious St, Knaresborough, N.Yorkshire. Tel 864698.

Walker, Barnett and Hill (Auctioneers). 3-5 Waterloo Rd, Wolverhampton, W.Midlands, WV1 4DL. Tel 771511, 772771.

Michael Webb Fine Paintings. Cefn-Llwyn,Llangristiolus, Bodorgan, Anglesey, Gwynedd, LL62 5DN. Tel Bodorgan (0407) 840336.

West Wales Antiques. 18 Mansfield Rd,Murton, Gower, Swansea, W.Glamorgan. Tel Bishopston (044128) 4318.

Westward County Pine. 10 Church St, Launceston, Cornwall. Tel Canworthy Water (056 681) 309 or (0566) 5605.

The White House Antiques. 3 High St, Princes Risborough, Buckinghamshire. Tel 6976.

Whiteheads. 34 High St, Petersfield, Hampshire, GU 3JL. Tel Portsmouth (0705) 820701.

The Whitgift Galleries. 77 South End, Croydon, Surrey. Tel 01-688 0990.

Lydia Wimbleton. at The Antique Centre,120 London Rd, Sevenoaks, Kent. Tel 52104 (priv 0732 832184).

Woolley & Wallis. Castle Auction Mart, Castle St, Salisbury, Wiltshire, SP1 3SU. Tel 21711.

Worthing Auction Galleries. 31 Chatsworth Rd, Worthing, W.Sussex, BN11 1LY. Tel 205565.

Wright-Manley. 63 High St, Tarporley, Cheshire, CW6 0DR. Tel 2151.

Yeo Antiques. 8 Springfields, Tetbury, Gloucestershire, GL8. Tel 521300.

Robert Young Antiques. 4A Exchange St, Norwich, Norfolk, NR2 1AT. Tel 618605.

Vintage and Veteran Cars

P.R.Garner (Antiques). Willow Farm, 104 High St, Landbeach, Cambridge, Cambridgeshire. Tel 860470.

Retrospect Antiques. King St, Combe Martin, Ilfracombe, Devon. Tel Combe Martin (027188) 2346.

Village Antiques. 2 Cooden Sea Rd, Little Common, Bexhill, E.Sussex. Tel Cooden (04243) 5214.

Walking Sticks

C.Barrett & Co. 51 Burlington Arcade, Piccadilly, London, W1. Tel 493 2570.

Michael C.German. 38B Kensington Church St, London, W8. Tel 937 2771.

Littlebury Antiques. 58/60 Fairycroft Rd, Saffron Walden, Essex. Tel 27961.

Quarter Jack Antiques. Bridge St, Sturminster Newton, Dorset, DT10 1BZ. Tel 72558.

Wallpapers

Art Distribution Ltd. Hogarth House, High St, Wendover, Buckinghamshire, HP22 6DU. Tel 624402.

Hamilton Weston Wallpapers. 11 Townshend Rd, Richmond, Surrey, TW9 1XH. Tel 940 4850.

The Maclean Gallery. 49 Drayton Gardens, London, SW10. Tel 373 2867.

Annabel Popovic. 15 Ranelagh Grove, London, SW1. Tel 730 3327.

Watches

see Clocks and Watches

Watercolours, British

London

Abbott & Holder. 73 Castelnau, Barnes, London, SW13. Tel 748 2416.

Thos Agnew & Sons Ltd. 43 Old Bond St, London, W1X 4BA. Tel 629 6176.

Albany Gallery. 1 Bury St, St James's, London, SW1Y 6AB. Tel 839 6119.

Appleby's. 8 Ryder St, St James's, London, SW1Y 6QB. Tel 930 6507.

Bankside Gallery. 48 Hopton St, Blackfriars, London, SE1 9JH. Tel 928 7521.

Claudia Beck. Bond Street Antique Centre,124 New Bond St, London, W1. Tel 409 2854 (priv 359 4657).

Chris Beetles Ltd. 5 Ryder St,St James's, London, SW1. Tel 930 8586.

Clarges Gallery. 158 Walton Street, London, SW3. Tel 584 3022.

P. & D. Colnaghi & Co Ltd. 14 Old Bond St, London, W1X 4JL. Tel 491 7408.

Laurence Corner, Euston Gallery. 126-130 Drummond St, London, NW1. Tel 388 6811.

Anthony Dallas & Sons Ltd. 17 Clifford St, London, W1. Tel 734 7127.

John Denham Gallery. 50 Mill Lane, London, NW6. Tel 794 2635.

William Drummond. (Covent Garden Gallery),11 Bury St, St James's, London, SW1. Tel 930 9696.

Jocelyn Feilding Fine Art Ltd. 8 Duke St, St James's, London, SW1. Tel 839 5040.

Finchley Fine Art Galleries. 983 High Rd,North Finchley, London, N12 8QR. Tel 446 4848.

The Fine Art Society Plc. 148 New Bond St, London, W1Y 0JT. Tel 629 5116.

Fleur de Lys Gallery. 8 Fulham High St, London, SW6 3LQ. Tel 731 7454(priv 0372 67934).

Fry Gallery. 58 Jermyn St, St James's, London, SW1 6LX. Tel 493 4496.

Galerie George. 98 George St, London, W1H 5RI. Tel 935 3322, 935 9998.

Gallery Lingard. 50 Pall Mall, London, SW1Y 5JQ. Tel 930 1645.

Stephen Garratt Fine Paintings. Exhibiting at 146 Brompton Rd,(Knightsbridge Safe Deposit), London, SW3. Tel 603 0681.

David E.Green Gallery. 188 Dartmouth Rd, London, SE26. Tel 699 5461.

Martyn Gregory. 34 Bury St, St James's, London, SW1. Tel 839 3731.

Georgina Hall. H3/H4 Antiquarius, 135 King's Rd, London, SW3. Tel 352 8734 (priv 731 0366).

Hamlet Gallery. 5 Pond St, Hampstead, London, NW3. Tel 794 7904 (priv 452 0056).

Highgate Gallery. 26 Highgate High St, London, N6. Tel 340 7564.

Hollywood Road Gallery. 12 Hollywood Rd, London, SW10. Tel 351 1973.

Richard and Georgina Ivor. 9 Tantallon Rd, London, SW12 8DS. Tel 673 7179.

David James Fine Paintings. 291 Brompton Rd, London, SW3. Tel 581 3399.

E.Joseph. 1 Vere St (3rd floor), London, W1M 9HQ. Tel 493 8353/4/5.

JPL Fine Arts. 24 Davies St, London, W1Y 1LH. Tel 493 2630.

Kaleidoscope Gallery. 66 Willesden Lane, London, NW6. Tel 328 5833.

Beryl Kendall. The English Watercolour Gallery,2 Warwick Place, London, W9 2PK. Tel 286 9902.

Krios Gallery. 305 Brompton Rd, London, SW3. Tel 589 5811.

Lacy Gallery. 38-40 Ledbury Rd, London, W11. Tel 229 9105, 229 5316.

The Leger Galleries Ltd. 13 Old Bond St, London, W1. Tel 629 3538.

N.W.Lott & H.J.Gerrish Ltd. 14 Mason's Yard,Duke Street St James's, London, SW1. Tel 930 1353.

Maas Gallery. 15A Clifford St, New Bond St, London, W1X 1RF. Tel 734 2302.

The Maclean Gallery. 49 Drayton Gardens, London, SW10. Tel 373 2867.

Mangate Gallery. 3 Chiswick Lane, London, W4 2LR. Tel 995 9867.

Duncan R. Miller Fine Arts. 11 Wedderburn Rd, London, NW3. Tel 435 5462 (priv 794 2119).

Milne & Moller. 35 Colville Terrace, London, W11 2BU. Tel 727 1679.

Moreton Street Gallery. 40 Moreton St, London, SW1.

Morton Morris & Co. 32 Bury St, St James's, London, SW1. Tel 930 2825.

Moss Galleries. 2 Prebend Gardens, Chiswick, London, W4. Tel 994 2099.

Osborne Gallery. 21 Grosvenor St, London, W1X 9FE. Tel 409 3599.

Park Galleries. 20 Hendon Lane, Finchley, London, N3 1TR. Tel 346 2176.

Oscar & Peter Johnson Ltd. Lowndes Lodge Gallery, 27 Lowndes St, London, SW1. Tel 235 6464,.

John F.C. Phillips. 92 Rossiter Rd, London, SW12. Tel 673 5150.

Polak Gallery. 21 King St, St James's, London, SWY 6QY. Tel 930 9245, 930 3911.

Annabel Popovic. 15 Ranelagh Grove, London, SW1. Tel 730 3327.

Pym's Gallery. 13 Motcomb St, Belgravia, London, SW1X 8LB. Tel 235 3050.

Anthony Reed Gallery. 3 Cork St, First Floor, London, W1X 1HA. Tel 437 0157.

Somerville & Simpson Ltd. 11 Savile Row, London, W1. Tel 437 5414.

Spenser S A. 16b Grafton St, Bond St, London, W1X 3LF. Tel 723 9149.

Spink & Son Ltd. 5, 6 & 7 King St, St James's, London, SW1. Tel 930 7888.

Oliver Swann Galleries. 117A-119 Walton St, London, SW3 2HP. Tel 581 4229.

Michael Tollemache Ltd. 78 Cadogan P1, London, SW1. Tel 235 5107.

Walker Galleries of Harrogate Ltd. 3 Cale St,Chelsea Green, London, SW3. Tel 351 5988.

Walker-Bagshawe. 73 Walton St, London, SW3. Tel 589 4582 (priv 381 2172).

Williams & Son. 2 Grafton St, London, W1X 3LB. Tel 493 5751, 493 4985.

Andrew Wyld. 17 Clifford St, London, W1X 1RG. Tel 734 5575/5576.

Regions

Abbey Antiques and Arts. 97 High St, Hemel Hempstead, Hertfordshire, HP1 3AH. Tel 64667.

Affordable Arts. 76 Colston St, Bristol, Avon, BS1 5BB. Tel 24838.

Alresford Gallery. Livingstone House, 7 Broad St, Alresford, Hampshire. Tel 3002 (priv 3556).

Aquarelle of St Giles. 8 The Lagger, Chalfont St Giles, Buckinghamshire, HP8 4DG. Tel 5592.

The Arden Gallery. 54 High St, Henley-in-Arden, Warwickshire, B95 5AN. Tel 2520.

Peter Arnold Gallery. 3 Knolls Close, Castle St, Wingrave, Aylesbury, Buckinghamshire, HP22 4PY. Tel 681568.

James Atkinson Gallery. 38 King St, Sandwich, Kent, CT13 9BL. Tel 617216 (priv 613298).

Attic Gallery. 88 Elm Rd, Wisbech, Cambridgeshire. Tel 583734.

Barkes & Richardson. 38 High Petergate, York, N.Yorkshire, YO1 2HW. Tel 51080.

Barnard Gallery. Grange Farm,Everton, Doncaster, S.Yorkshire, DN10 5BG. Tel Retford (0777) 817324.

Baroq Antiques. Watling St, Little Brickhill, Buckinghamshire, MK17 9LY. Tel Great Brickhill (052 526) 401 (priv 561).

Barronfield Gallery. 47 Friargate, Preston, Lancashire, PR1 2AT. Tel 563465.

Beaufort Gallery. Beaumont St, Hexham, Northumberland.

Beaulieu Fine Arts. High St, Beaulieu, Hampshire. Tel 612089.

George Bewes & Co. 235 George St, Aberdeen, Grampian. Tel 635830.

Bourne Gallery. 31-33 Lesbourne Rd, Reigate, Surrey. Tel 41614.

Bowmoore Gallery. Whelford, Gloucestershire, GL7 4DT. Tel 712651.

Brobury House Gallery. Brobury House, Brobury, Hereford & Worcester, HR3 6BS. Tel Moccas (09817) 229.

Brookfield Gallery. Market Place, Colyton, Devon. Tel 52038.

William Bruce & Co. Mainhill, Charlesfield, St Boswells, Borders, TD6 0HG. Tel 23628 23788.

The Burford Gallery. Classica House,High Street, Burford, Oxfordshire, OX8 4QA. Tel 2305.

Calton Gallery. 10 Royal Terrace, Edinburgh, Lothian, EH7 5AB. Tel 556 1010.

Colin Campbell Fine Paintings. Bath Road, Cowes, Isle of Wight. Tel 200 124 (priv 855 300).

Colin Campbell Fine Paintings. The Gallery,The Square, Yarmouth, Isle of Wight, PO41 0NS. Tel 760784.

Gerard Campbell. Maple House,Market Place, Lechlade, Gloucestershire, GL7 3AB. Tel Faringdon (0367) 52267.

Robert A.Campbell. The Kelvin Gallery, 117 Bath St, Glasgow, Strathclyde, G2 2SZ. Tel 221 1367.

Castle Gallery. 61 Steep Hill, Lincoln, Lincolnshire, LN2 1LR.

Chantry Book Shop. 11 Higher St, Dartmouth, Devon, TQ6 9RB. Tel 2796 (priv) 4208.

The Church Street Gallery. 17 Church St, Saffron Walden, Essex, CB10 1JW. Tel 24422 (priv 0279-850423).

Circa Fine Art. Island House, Barbican, Plymouth, Devon, PL1 2LS. Tel 663318.

Clarendon Gallery. 20 Albert Square, Manchester, Greater Manchester. Tel 980 6343.

Peter Coe Fine Paintings. The Priory, Shepton Mallet, Somerset. Tel 2412.

Christopher Cole (Fine Paintings) Ltd. 1 London End, Beaconsfield, Buckinghamshire, HP9 2HN. Tel 71274.

Colleton House Gallery. 8a Quiet St, Bath, Avon, BA1 2JU. Tel 28806.

J. Collins and Son (Est.1953). The Studio, 63 & 28 High St, Bideford, Devon, EX39 2AN. Tel 73103 (priv 76485).

Colmore Galleries Ltd. 52 High St, Henley-in-Arden, Warwickshire. Tel 2938.

Coltsfoot Gallery. Hatfield, Leominster, Hereford & Worcester, HR6 0SF. Tel Steensbridge (056 882) 277.

E. & R. Cooper. 99a High St, Great Missenden, Buckinghamshire.

The Corner House Gallery. The Square, Axbridge, Somerset, BS26 2AP. Tel 732757.

The Corner Shop. 5 St John's Place, Hay-on-Wye, Hereford & Worcester. Tel 820045.

Edward Cross Fine Paintings. 128 Oatlands Drive, Weybridge, Surrey, KT13 9HL. Tel 51093.

Cumbrian Fine Art Galleries. Lane House, Cow Brow,(postal address:Via Carnforth,Lancs), Kirkby Lonsdale, Cumbria. Tel Crooklands (044 87) 208.

Michael Danny. The Manor House, Wellow, Bath, Avon. Tel Combe Down (0225) 832027.

Henry Donn Galleries. 138-142 Bury New Rd, Whitefield, Manchester, Greater Manchester, M25 6AD. Tel 766 8819.

Dorchester Galleries. Rotten Row, Dorchester, Oxfordshire, OX9 8LJ. Tel Oxford (0865) 341116.

Driffold Gallery. The Smithy,78 Birmingham Rd, Sutton Coldfield, W.Midlands. Tel 021-355 5433.

Eastbourne Fine Art. 9 Meads St, Eastbourne, E.Sussex, BN20 7QY. Tel 25634.

Eastgate Antiques. 85 Eastgate, Cowbridge, S.Glamorgan, CF7 7AA. Tel 5111.

Ewhurst Gallery. Ramsdell, Basingstoke, Hampshire, RG26 5RG. Tel 850051.

Exquisite Arts Ltd. 22 Bore St, Lichfield, Staffordshire. Tel 253626, (priv 253697).

Fine Art Gallery. 41 Dundas St, Edinburgh, Lothian, EH3 6QQ. Tel 557 4569.

Fine Art Petworth PLC. Fernhurst Gallery,Crossways, Fernhurst, Haslemere, Surrey. Tel 56177 (priv 0252-711923).

The Fine Art Society Plc. 12 Great King St, Edinburgh, Lothian, EH3 6QL. Tel 556 0305.

Fine-Lines (Fine Art). The Old Rectory, at 31 Sheep St, Shipston on Stour, Warwickshire, CV36 4AE. Tel 62323.

Foye Gallery. 15 Stanley St, Luton, Bedfordshire, LU1 5AL. Tel 38487.

Fulda Gallery. 19 Vine St, Salford, Greater Manchester, M7 0NY. Tel 792 1962.

Galerie Appenzell. High St, Newport, Essex, CB11 3QZ. Tel Saffron Walden (0799) 40623.

Gallery 77. 18 Princess St, Bradshawgate, Bolton, Greater Manchester, BL1 1EJ. Tel 35252.

Gatward Fine Arts. 50 Northwood End Rd, Haynes, Bedfordshire, MK45 3PT. Tel Hitchin (0462) 33759(priv 023066 348).

Gavels. Bramble Cottage,40 Ashperton Rd, Ashperton, Ledbury, Hereford & Worcester, HR8 2RY. Tel Trumpet (053183) 270.

George & Dragon Gallery. Reepham, Norwich, Norfolk. Tel 870360.

Godalming Galleries Ltd. 3 Wharf St, Godalming, Surrey, GU7 1NN. Tel 22254.

Gore-Langton Gallery. 5 Castle St, Tunbridge Wells, Kent, TN1 1XT. Tel 26373.

Grange Gallery. Withersdale Lodge,Withersdale, Harleston, Norfolk. Tel 852254.

Richard Hagen Ltd. Yew Tree House, Broadway, Hereford & Worcester, WR12 7DT. Tel 853624.

Hammond Smith. Beaumont House, 24 Knighton Drive, Leicester, Leicestershire, LE2 3HB. Tel 709020.

Hampshire Gallery. 18 Lansdowne Rd, Bournemouth, Dorset. Tel 21211.

The Hampton Hill Gallery Ltd. 203-205 High St, Hampton Hill, Middlesex, TW12 1NP. Tel 977 1379.

Anna Harrison Antiques. 49 Great North Road,Grange Park, Gosforth, Newcastle upon Tyne, Tyne & Wear.

Hay Loft Gallery. Berry Wormington, Broadway, Hereford & Worcester, WR12 7NH. Tel Toddington (024 269) 202.

Henry-Brett Galleries. Halford House, Bourton-on-the-Water, Gloucestershire. Tel 20443 (priv 028 574 433).

The Hinton Gallery. Crutchfield Farm,Hookwood, Horley, Surrey, RH6 0HT. Tel 862417.

Angela Hone. The Garth,31 Mill Rd, Marlow, Buckinghamshire. Tel 4170.

Hood and Broomfield Lyme Galleries. 29 Albert St, Newcastle-under-Lyme, Staffordshire, ST5 1JP. Tel 626859.

John Hopkins. 1 The Courtyard,Ockenden Manor, Cuckfield, W.Sussex, RH17 5LD. Tel Haywards Heath (0444) 454323.

Hythe Galleries. 125 High St, Hythe, Kent, CT21 5JJ. Tel 69339.

Itchen Gallery. 29 Middle Brook St, Winchester, Hampshire. Tel 61309.

Jays Fine Art Dealers. Cambridge Gallery,4 Cambridge Arcade, Southport, Merseyside, PR8 1AS. Tel 34488 (priv 69500).

T.B. & R. Jordan. Aslak, Aislaby, Eaglescliffe, Stockton-on-Tees, Cleveland, TS16 0QN. Tel 782599.

The Barry M. Keene Gallery. 12 Thameside, Henley-on-Thames, Oxfordshire, RG9 1RY. Tel 577119.

H.W. Keil (Cheltenham) Ltd. 129-131 The Promenade, Cheltenham, Gloucestershire, GL50 1NW. Tel 522509, 527974.

Kendal Studio Pottery. 2-3 Wildman St, Kendal, Cumbria, LA9 6EN. Tel 23291.

Kirkgate Picture Gallery. 18 Kirkgate, Thirsk, N.Yorkshire, YO7 1PQ. Tel 24085.

Alan Leonard Antiques. 503 Smithdown Rd, Liverpool, Merseyside, L15 5AE. Tel 733 5277 (priv 722 4766).

Leverington Hall Gallery. Leverington, Wisbech, Cambridgeshire, PE13 5DE. Tel 582055.

Lincoln Fine Art. 33 The Strait, Lincoln, Lincolnshire. Tel 33029.

N.W.Lott & H.J.Gerrish Ltd. The Old Rectory, Froxfield, Wiltshire, SN8 3JY. Tel Hungerford (0488) 82188.

Lynton Porcelain Company & Keith Arden. Morris Cottage,High St, Much Hadham, Hertfordshire, SB10 6BY. Tel 2297.

Madoc Antique & Art Gallery. 48 Madoc St, Llandudno, Gwynedd. Tel 79754 (priv 79760).

Mandell's Gallery. Elm Hill, Norwich, Norfolk, NR3 1HN. Tel 626892, 629180.

J.Manley & Thames Gallery. 27 High St, Eton, Berkshire. Tel Windsor (0753) 865647.

Marble Hill Gallery. 72 Richmond Rd, Twickenham, Middlesex, TW1 3BE. Tel 892 1488.

Markswood Gallery. Brook St, Great Bardfield, Essex, CM7 4TY. Tel Great Dunmow (0371) 810106 (priv 810329).

Marlborough Sporting Gallery & Bookshop. 6 Kingbury St, Marlborough, Wiltshire. Tel 54074.

The William Marler Gallery. 36/38 Dyer St, Cirencester, Gloucestershire, GL7 2PF. Tel 68526.

John Mathieson & Co. 48 Frederick St, Edinburgh, Lothian. Tel 225 6798, 225 6686.

Matthews & Davies Fine Art Ltd. 85-87 Eastgate, Cowbridge, S.Glamorgan, CF7 7AA. Tel 4340.

Jill Maxwell-Hyslop. The Manor house,Toller Whelme, Beaminster, Dorset, DT8 3NU. Tel Buckland Newton (030 05) 224 (priv 030 862339).

The McEwan Gallery. The Bridge of Gairn (on A939), Ballater, Grampian, AB3 5UB. Tel 55429.

Philip & Anne Merridale. Bridge House, Stockbridge, Hampshire. Tel 673.

Meyers Gallery. 66 High St, Ingatestone, Essex. Tel Brentwood (0277) 355335 (priv 215446).

Millhouse Fine Arts. The Square, Petworth, W.Sussex. Tel 43080.

Mon Galerie. 49 High St, Amersham, Buckinghamshire. Tel 21705.

The Moseley Gallery. Woodbridge Rd,Moseley, Birmingham, W.Midlands, B13 8EH. Tel 449 9456.

Colin Murdoch. 56 High St, Kingussie, Highland, PH21 1HZ. Tel 552.

John Nelson. 22-24 Victoria St, Edinburgh, Lothian, EH1 2JW. Tel 225 4413 (priv 667 5275).

New Gallery. Abele Tree House,9 Fore St, Budleigh Salterton, Devon, EX9 6NG. Tel 3768.

Heather Newman Gallery. Milidduwa, Cranham, Painswick, Gloucestershire, GL6 6TX. Tel 812230.

John Noott. Picton House Gallery, High St, Broadway, Hereford & Worcester, WR12 7AL. Tel Evesham (0386) 852787.

Park House. Park St, Stow-on-the-Wold, Gloucestershire. Tel 30159.

Pelter/Sands Fine Paintings. 19 The Mall,Clifton, Bristol, Avon, BS8 4JG. Tel 741830.

Plaitford House Galleries. Plaitford, Hampshire. Tel West Wellow (0794) 22221.

Priory Gallery. The Priory, Station Rd,Bishops Cleeve, Cheltenham, Gloucestershire. Tel Bishops Cleeve (024 267) 3226.

The Reid Gallery Ltd. Mousehill House,Milford, Godalming, Surrey, GU8 5BL. Tel 6990.

Robertson and Cox. 60 George St, Perth, Tayside, PH1 5JL. Tel 26300.

Tony Sanders Antiques and New Gallery. 14 Chapel St, Penzance, Cornwall, TR18 4AW. Tel 66620 (priv 68461).

R.S.J. Savage & Son. Alfred St, Northampton, Northamptonshire, NN1 5EY. Tel 33852 (priv 405482).

Martin Scadgell Fine Art. Mulberry House Galleries,Codmore Hill, Pulborough, W.Sussex. Tel 2463.

Scott Antiques. 67 Walton St, Walton on the Hill, Surrey, KT20 7RZ. Tel Tadworth (073781) 2097 (priv 0396 882431).

Sheengate Galleries. Henhurst House,Henhurst Cross Lane,Beare Green, Nr.Ockley, Dorking, Surrey, RH5 4PX. Tel 712184.

Clifford & Joan Silcocks. Pitchcombe View, Pitchcombe, Stroud, Gloucestershire, GL6 6LW. Tel Painswick (0452) 812225.

Brian Sinfield (Gallery). The Studio,High St, Burford, Oxfordshire, OX8 4ST. Tel 2402.

Skeaping Gallery. Townend House,Lydford, Okehampton, Devon, EX20 4AR. Tel 383.

Sloane Galleries. 49 Poole Rd,Westbourne, Bournemouth, Dorset, BH4 9BA. Tel 764684.

Southgate Gallery. 20 Market Place, Shifnal, Shropshire. Tel Telford (0952) 460351.

Sport & Country Gallery. Northwood House, Bulkington, Nuneaton, Warwickshire, CV12 9RX. Tel 314335.

Sport & Country Gallery. Northwood House, Bulkington, Nuneaton, Warwickshire, CV12 9RX. Tel 314335.

Michael Spratt Watercolours. Kingfishers, East Shalford Lane,Shalford, Guildford, Surrey, GU4 8AS. Tel 504607.

St Breock Gallery. St Breock Churchtown,St Breock, Wadebridge, Cornwall, PL27 7JS. Tel 2543 (priv 3451).

St Helier Galleries Ltd. Les Ormes, Ville au Bas, St Ouen, Jersey. Tel 82332.

A. & J.Stuart-Mobey & Daughter. Bedford House, Lower Wolvercote, Oxford, Oxfordshire, OX2 9PF. Tel 50170.

The Talbot Gallery. 290 Woodstock Rd, Oxford, Oxfordshire, OX2 7NN. Tel 59049.

Tamar Gallery. 17 Wickham Ave, Bexhill, E.Sussex. Tel 221835.

Tamar Gallery. 5 Church St, Launceston, Cornwall. Tel 4233 (priv 2740).

Thicke Galleries Swansea. 26 St Andrews Close, Mayals, Swansea, W.Glamorgan, SA3 5DX. Tel 401656.

Carole Thomas Fine Arts. First Floor,32A Sun St, Hitchin, Hertfordshire, SJ5 1AH. Tel 36077.

Paul Thomas Fine Paintings. 27 Glebelands Rd, Wokingham, Berkshire, RG11 1DY. Tel 794671.

Thurso Antiques. Drill Hall,Sinclair St, Thurso, Highland. Tel 63291 (priv 66202).

Trim Bridge Galleries. 2 Trim Bridge, Bath, Avon. Tel 66390.

John Tuckey, Bogan House Gallery. 43 High St, Totnes, Devon. Tel 862025.

Van Riemsdijk Fine Art. Digbeth St, Stow-on-the-Wold, Gloucestershire. Tel Cotswold (0451) 30424 (priv 0908 582621).

Vectis Fine Arts Gallery. 41 High St, Bembridge, Isle of Wight. Tel 852316.

Walker Galleries Ltd. 6 Montpellier Gdns, Harrogate, N.Yorkshire. Tel 67933.

Weald Gallery. Southdown House,High St, Brasted, Kent. Tel Westerham (0959) 32728.

Michael Webb Fine Paintings. Cefn-Llwyn,Llangristiolus, Bodorgan, Anglesey, Gwynedd, LL62 5DN. Tel Bodorgan (0407) 840336.

The Whitgift Galleries. 77 South End, Croydon, Surrey. Tel 01-688 0990.

Betty Williams. The Gallery, Tyr Eglwys, Tredunnock, Usk, Gwent, NP5 1LY. Tel Tredunnock (063349) 301.

Norman Witham Antiques. 2-2A High St, Beckenham, Kent. Tel 650 9096 (priv 650 4651).

Worlds End Watercolours. Shern Lodge,Northclose Rd, Bembridge, Isle of Wight, PO35 5XP. Tel Isle of Wight (0983) 872307.

Xanthus Gallery. September Cottage, Reymerston, Norfolk, NR9 4AG. Tel Dereham (0362) 850862.

York Gallery, Tunbridge Wells Ltd. No 6 Castle St, Tunbridge Wells, Kent. Tel 22326 (4 lines).

Watercolours, European

London

Thos Agnew & Sons Ltd. 43 Old Bond St, London, W1X 4BA. Tel 629 6176.

Claudia Beck. Bond Street Antique Centre,124 New Bond St, London, W1. Tel 409 2854 (priv 359 4657).

Chris Beetles Ltd. 5 Ryder St,St James's, London, SW1. Tel 930 8586.

Douwes Fine Art Ltd. 38 Duke St, St James's, London, SW1Y 6DF. Tel 839 5795.

William Drummond. (Covent Garden Gallery),11 Bury St, St James's, London, SW1. Tel 930 9696.

Galerie George. 98 George St, London, W1H 5RI. Tel 935 3322, 935 9998.

Stephen Garratt Fine Paintings. Exhibiting at 146 Brompton Rd,(Knightsbridge Safe Deposit), London, SW3. Tel 603 0681.

Hamlet Gallery. 5 Pond St, Hampstead, London, NW3. Tel 794 7904 (priv 452 0056).

Richard and Georgina Ivor. 9 Tantallon Rd, London, SW12 8DS. Tel 673 7179.

Krios Gallery. 305 Brompton Rd, London, SW3. Tel 589 5811.

L'Acquaforte. 49A Ledbury Rd, London, W11. Tel 221 3388.

Lacy Gallery. 38-40 Ledbury Rd, London, W11. Tel 229 9105, 229 5316.

Mangate Gallery. 3 Chiswick Lane, London, W4 2LR. Tel 995 9867.

Duncan R. Miller Fine Arts. 11 Wedderburn Rd, London, NW3. Tel 435 5462 (priv 794 2119).

Osborne Gallery. 21 Grosvenor St, London, W1X 9FE. Tel 409 3599.

Pym's Gallery. 13 Motcomb St, Belgravia, London, SW1X 8LB. Tel 235 3050.

Jane Roberts & Robert Alderman. 2nd Floor,180 New Bond St, London, W1Y 9PD. Tel 491 0168.

Spenser S A. 16b Grafton St, Bond St, London, W1X 3LF. Tel 723 9149.

Oliver Swann Galleries. 117A-119 Walton St, London, SW3 2HP. Tel 581 4229.

Williams & Son. 2 Grafton St, London, W1X 3LB. Tel 493 5751, 493 4985.

Regions

Brookfield Gallery. Market Place, Colyton, Devon. Tel 52038.

Clarendon Gallery. 20 Albert Square, Manchester, Greater Manchester. Tel 980 6343.

Coltsfoot Gallery. Hatfield, Leominster, Hereford & Worcester, HR6 0SF. Tel Steensbridge (056 882) 277.

Coyle Fine Art. 6 Lower Merrion St, Dublin, Co Dublin. Tel 762506.

Dorchester Galleries. Rotten Row, Dorchester, Oxfordshire, OX9 8LJ. Tel Oxford (0865) 341116.

Fulda Gallery. 19 Vine St, Salford, Greater Manchester, M7 0NY. Tel 792 1962.

Gavels. Bramble Cottage,40 Ashperton Rd, Ashperton, Ledbury, Hereford & Worcester, HR8 2RY. Tel Trumpet (053183) 270.

Greene's Antique Galleries. The Mall, Drogheda, Co Louth. Tel (041) 36212, 38286.

Mandell's Gallery. Elm Hill, Norwich, Norfolk, NR3 1HN. Tel 626892, 629180.

Markswood Gallery. Brook St, Great Bardfield, Essex, CM7 4TY. Tel Great Dunmow (0371) 810106 (priv 810329).

Mon Galerie. 49 High St, Amersham, Buckinghamshire. Tel 21705.

The Moseley Gallery. Woodbridge Rd,Moseley, Birmingham, W.Midlands, B13 8EH. Tel 449 9456.

Colin Murdoch. 56 High St, Kingussie, Highland, PH21 1HZ. Tel 552.

Plaitford House Galleries. Plaitford, Hampshire. Tel West Wellow (0794) 22221.

Michael Spratt Watercolours. Kingfishers, East Shalford Lane,Shalford, Guildford, Surrey, GU4 8AS. Tel 504607.

St Helier Galleries Ltd. Les Ormes, Ville au Bas, St Ouen, Jersey. Tel 82332.

Tamar Gallery. 5 Church St, Launceston, Cornwall. Tel 4233 (priv 2740).

Paul Thomas Fine Paintings. 27 Glebelands Rd, Wokingham, Berkshire, RG11 1DY. Tel 794671.

Trim Bridge Galleries. 2 Trim Bridge, Bath, Avon. Tel 66390.

Walker Galleries Ltd. 6 Montpellier Gdns, Harrogate, N.Yorkshire. Tel 67933.

Betty Williams. The Gallery, Tyr Eglwys, Tredunnock, Usk, Gwent, NP5 1LY. Tel Tredunnock (063349) 301.

Wholesalers, Exporters

see Shipping Goods

Wine Accessories

Abbas Combe Pine. 4 Upper Maudlin St, Bristol, Avon, BS2. Tel 299023.

Brian Beet. 3b Burlington Gdns, Old Bond Street, London, W1X 1LE. Tel 437 4975.

Robin Butler. 9 St Stephen's St, Bristol, Avon, BS1. Tel 276586 (priv 662167).

Richard Kihl Ltd. 164 Regent's Park Rd, London, NW1 8XN. Tel 586 3838.

Millhouse. The Square, Petworth, W.Sussex, GU28 9BP. Tel 43080.

Christopher Sykes Antiques. The Old Parsonage, Bedford St, Woburn, Bedfordshire, MK17 9QL. Tel 259 (priv 467).

Works of Art

see also Bronzes, Ivories, Sculpture

Norman Adams Ltd. 8-10 Hans Rd, London, SW3 IRX. Tel 589 5266.

Alexander & Berendt Ltd. 1A Davies St, London, W1Y 1LL. Tel 499 4775.

Philip Andrade Ltd. White Oxen Manor, Rattery, South Brent, Devon, TQ10 9JX. Tel 2454.

Antiquus. 90-92 Pimlico Rd, London, SW1. Tel 730 8681.

Arenski. 29-31 George St, London, W1H 5PE. Tel 486 0678.

Asprey PLC. 165-169 New Bond St, London, W1Y 0AR. Tel 493 6767.

Barling of Mount Street Ltd. 112 Mount St, London, W1. Tel 499 2858.

Barlow Antiques. Sevington Manor, Tichborne, Hampshire, SO24 0NF. Tel Alresford (096 273) 4800.

Albert Bartram. 177 Hivings Hill, Chesham, Buckinghamshire. Tel 783271.

Robin Bellamy Ltd. 97 Corn St, Witney, Oxfordshire, OX8 7DL. Tel 4793.

Raymond Benardout Ltd. 4 William St, Knightsbridge, London, SW1X 9HL. Tel 235 3360 (priv 235 0504).

Bernheimer Fine Arts Ltd. 32 St George St,Mayfair, London, W1R 9FA. Tel 499 0293.

Birbeck Antiques. 219 Union St, Torquay, Devon, TQ1 4BZ. Tel 23318 (priv 214836).

George S.Bolam. Oak House, The Chipping, Tetbury, Gloucestershire. Tel 52211.

Bragge & Sons. Landgate House, Rye, E.Sussex. Tel 223358.

David Cambridge. 13 Rotunda Terrace, Cheltenham, Gloucestershire. Tel 42178.

Cirencester Antiques Ltd. 17 Dyer St, Cirencester, Gloucestershire, GL7 2PP. Tel 2955 (priv 3066).

Christopher Clarke. The Fosse Way, Stow-on-the-Wold, Gloucestershire, GL54 1JS. Tel 30476.

Clinkers Antiques Ltd. c/o Island Farm, Steep, Petersfield, Hampshire. Tel 62319.

Colefax & Fowler. 39 Brook St, London, W1Y 1AU. Tel 493 2231.

Philip Colleck Ltd. 84 Fulham Rd, London, SW3 6HR. Tel 584 8479.

Frank Collins. 60 Ledbury Rd, London, W11 2AJ. Tel 221 7108, 0502-714842.

P. & D. Colnaghi & Co Ltd. 14 Old Bond St, London, W1X 4JL. Tel 491 7408.

Thomas Coulborn & Sons. Vesey Manor, 64 Birmingham Rd, Sutton Coldfield, W.Midlands, B72 1QP. Tel 354 3974, 354 3139.

Arthur Davidson Ltd. 78-79 Jermyn St, London, SW1. Tel 930 6687, 930 4643.

Kenneth Davis. 38 Bury St, London, SW1. Tel 930 0313.

Robert Dickson Antiques. 263 Fulham Rd, London, SW3. Tel 351 0330 (priv 948 5825).

M.Ekstein Ltd. 90 Jermyn St, London, SW1Y 6JD. Tel 930 2024.

A. & E. Foster. Little Heysham, Forge Rd, Naphill, Buckinghamshire. Tel 2024.

Michael Foster. 118 Fulham Rd, London, SW3 6HU. Tel 373 3636.

Galerie 360. 564 King's Road, London, SW6. Tel 736 5160.

Christopher Gibbs Ltd. 118 New Bond St, London, W1Y 9AB. Tel 629 2008.

Granville Antiques. Mount Pleasant Farm,Level Mare Lane, Eastergate, W.Sussex. Tel 2293.

Jay Gray Antiques. Syrena House, 1 Cheltenham Rd, Cirencester, Gloucestershire, GL7 2HS. Tel 2755.

Guinevere Antiques Ltd. 578 King's Road, London, SW6. Tel 736 2917.

Harcourt Antiques. 5 Harcourt St, London, W1. Tel 723 5919.

Jonathan Harris. 54 Kensington Church St, London, W8. Tel 937 3133.

Nicholas Harris. 26 Conduit St, London, W1. Tel 499 5991.

Peter Hempson. Melchbourne Park, Melchbourne, Bedfordshire. Tel Riseley (023063) 8872.

Michael Hogg. 172 Brompton Rd, London, SW3. Tel 589 8629.

Thomas Howard-Sneyd Ltd. 35 Fursecroft,George Street, London, W1. Tel 723 1976.

L.J.Huggett & Son. Bramble Cross, Exeter Rd, Honiton, Devon. Tel 2043.

Cyril Humphris. 8 Pembroke Walk, London, W8. Tel 937 1719.

Anthony James & Son Ltd. 88 Fulham Road, London, SW3. Tel 584 1120 (priv 385 3408).

D.S.Lavender (Antiques) Ltd. 16B Grafton St, London, W1X 3LA. Tel 629 1782 (priv 409 2305).

Ronald A. Lee (Fine Arts) Ltd. The Manor House, Byfleet, Surrey. Tel 43346.

Lillie Antiques. 244 Lillie Rd, London, SW6 7QA. Tel 385 9852.

W. Lipka Ltd. 62 Aylestone Ave, London, NW6. Tel 459 4588.

Paul Longmire Ltd. 12 Bury St,St James's, London, SW1. Tel 930 8720.

Victor Mahy Ltd. Mulberry House, Stockbridge, Hampshire, SO20 6EY. Tel 810466.

Mallett & Son (Antiques) Ltd. 40 New Bond St, London, W1Y 0BS. Tel 499 7411.

Massada Antiques. 45 New Bond St, London, W1Y 9HB. Tel 493 4792; 493 5610.

Richard Miles Antiques. 8 Holbein Place, London, SW1 8NL. Tel 730 1957.

Millhouse. The Square, Petworth, W.Sussex, GU28 9BP. Tel 43080.

Lennox Money (Antiques) Ltd. 93 Pimlico Rd, London, SW1W 8PH. Tel 730 3070.

P.and G. Morley. 8 Jury Street, Warwick, Warwickshire, CV34 4EN. Tel 492963 (priv 0926 54191).

Victor Needham Antiques. Hinwood House, High St,Broughton, Stockbridge, Hampshire. Tel Broughton (0794) 301205.

Partridge (Fine Arts) Ltd. 144-146 New Bond St, London, W1. Tel 629 0834.

Richard Philp. 59 Ledbury Rd, London, W11. Tel 727 7915.

W.A.Pinn & Sons. 124 Swan St, Sible Hedingham, Essex, CO9 3HP. Tel Hedingham (0787) 61127.

Regent Antiques. Dynever House, New St, Painswick, Gloucestershire. Tel 812543.

Rendlesham & Dark. 498 Kings Rd, London, SW10. Tel 351 1442.

Jane Roberts & Robert Alderman. 2nd Floor,180 New Bond St, London, W1Y 9PD. Tel 491 0168.

Robin Sanders. The Pond House,Dane End, Ware, Hertfordshire. Tel Dane End (092084) 265.

Seago. 16 Lower Richmond Rd,Putney, London, SW15.

David Seyfried. 759 Fulham Rd, London, SW6. Tel 731 4230.

Louis Stanton. 299 Westbourne Grove, London, W11. Tel 727 9336.

Pamela Streather. 4 Studio Place, Kinnerton St, London, SW1. Tel 235 3450.

F.Teltscher Ltd. 17 Crawford St, London, W1H 1PF. Tel 935 0525.

David Tremayne Ltd. 320 King's Rd, London, SW3. Tel 352 1194.

Trevor-Venis Antiques. 13 Hencotes, Hexham, Northumberland, NE46 2EQ. Tel 607458.

Geoffrey Van Ltd. 105 and 107 Portobello Rd, London, W11. Tel 229 5577.

Wrought Iron

see Garden Furniture, Ironwork

CONNOISSEUR
MAY 1986 $3.00 £2.95UK
NEW YORK FOR THE V.I.P.
TASTEMAKERS
GALLERIES
RESTAURANTS
THE ARTS
SHOPPING
GRANDES DAMES
HOTELS
NIGHTLIFE

BRITISH ART & ANTIQUES DIRECTORY 1987

INDEX TO BUSINESS NAMES

How to Use This Book
After the editorial articles the book is divided into five main sections:
1 Directory (*begins on page 37*)
Dealers, auctioneers, packers, restorers, trade suppliers and so on are all listed here, with address, telephone number, opening hours, and type of business or area of specialisation. Entries are listed in alphabetical order under town or village, within the relevant county and geographical area.
2 Gazetteer (*begins on page 265*)
This is an alphabetical list of the towns and villages mentioned in the Directory, showing the counties and geographical areas under which they are listed.
3. Index to Specialists
(*begins on page 270*)
Directory entries are here listed under type of business or nature of stock.
4. Index to Business Names
(*begins on page 363*)
All business names in the Directory are listed alphabetically with their town or village, county and geographical area.
5 Maps (*begin on page 391*)
Showing villages and towns listed in the Directory.

Note
Counties and geographical areas are listed with page references under 'Contents' on page 3.
Auctioneers are listed both in the main Directory under the relevant town or village, and in the Specialists index under 'Auctioneers'.
Abbreviations and names and addresses of useful organisations are listed on page 4.

A.& F. Partners, Faringdon, Oxfordshire, England.
A.D.C. Heritage Ltd, London, England.
Robert Aagaard Ltd, Knaresborough, N.Yorkshire, England.
Aaron Antiques, Snodland, Kent, England.
Aaron Galleries, London, England.
Didier Aaron (London) Ltd, London, England.
Abacus Antiques, Petersfield, Hampshire, England.
Abadjian Ltd, Wealdstone, Middlesex, England.
Abbas Combe Pine, Bristol, Avon, England.
The Abbey Antique Shop, Blackburn, Lancashire, England.
Abbey Antiques, Ramsey, Cambridgeshire, England.
Abbey Antiques, Tewkesbury, Gloucestershire, England.
Abbey Antiques, Oldham, Greater Manchester, England.
Abbey Antiques, Glastonbury, Somerset, England.
Abbey Antiques, Tintern, Gwent, Wales.
Abbey Antiques and Arts, Hemel Hempstead, Hertfordshire, England.
Abbey Galleries, Bath, Avon, England.
Abbott & Holder, London, England.
Nicholas Abbott, Hartley Wintney, Hampshire, England.
Abbotts, Wickham Market, Suffolk, England.
Abercrombies, Newcastle upon Tyne, Tyne & Wear, England.
Abingdon House - The Antique Centre, Honiton, Devon, England.
Abington Books, Little Abington, Cambridgeshire, England.
Abode, Stratford-upon-Avon, Warwickshire, England.
Abridge Antique Clock Centre, Abridge, Essex, England.
Abridge Antiques Centre, Abridge, Essex, England.
Academy Antiques, West Byfleet, Surrey, England.
Academy Framing, London, England.
Ace Antiques, Oldham, Greater Manchester, England.
Arthur Ackermann & Son Ltd, London, England.
Acorn Antiques, Towcester, Northamptonshire, England.
Acquisitions (Fireplaces) Ltd, London, England.
Acrylic Design, London, England.
Actino Antiques, London, England.
Adam Antiques, Burnham-on-Sea, Somerset, England.
Adam Antiques, Cardiff, S.Glamorgan, Wales.
David Adam Oriental Carpets, Lindfield, W.Sussex, England.
James Adam and Sons, Dublin, Co Dublin, Eire.
Adams Antiques, St Ives, Cambridgeshire, England.
Adams Antiques, London, England.
Adams Antiques, London, England.
Adams Antiques of Chester, Chester, Cheshire, England.
Adams Room Ltd, London, England.
Madeleine Adams, Eastcote, Middlesex, England.
Norman Adams Ltd, London, England.
Rodney Adams Antiques, Pwllheli, Gwynedd, Wales.
Alexander Adamson Antiques, Kirkby Lonsdale, Cumbria, England.
Addingham Antiques, Addingham, W.Yorkshire, England.
Addison-Ross Gallery, London, England.
Affordable Arts, Bristol, Avon, England.
Ages Ago Antiques, Preston, Lancashire, England.
Agincourt House, Dartmouth, Devon, England.
Thos Agnew & Sons Ltd, London, England.
Ahuan UK Ltd, London, England.
AIR Gallery, London, England.
Air Improvement Centre Ltd, London, England.
W.B. Airfreight Ltd, Heathrow, Middlesex, England.
Al-Mashreq Galleries, London, England.
Aladdin's Cave, Malvern, Hereford & Worcester, England.
Adrian Alan Ltd, Brighton & Hove, E.Sussex, England.
Albany Antiques, Hindhead, Surrey, England.
Albany Antiques, Glasgow, Strathclyde, Scotland.
Albany Gallery, London, England.
Albert's of Kensington, London, England.
Alberts Auctions & Co, Crayford, Kent, England.
Albion Fine Art, London, England.
Aldeburgh Antiques, Aldeburgh, Suffolk, England.
Alden & Blackwell (Eton) Ltd, Eton, Berkshire, England.
Alderley Antiques, Alderley Edge, Cheshire, England.
Alderley House Antiques, Tetbury, Gloucestershire, England.
Alderson & Alderson, Bath, Avon, England.
Patrick Aldridge Ltd, London, England.
Aldridges of Bath, Bath, Avon, England.
Alex Antiques, London, England.
Alexander & Berendt Ltd, London, England.
Alexander Antiques, Dublin, Co Dublin, Eire.
Alexander Antiques, Henfield, W.Sussex, England.
Alexander Antiques, Portrush, Co Antrim, Northern Ireland.
Alexander Galleries, Harrogate, N.Yorkshire, England.
Charles Alexander Ltd, Douglas, Isle of Man.
David Alexander Antiques, London, England.
Michael Alexander Fine Arts Ltd, Glasgow, Strathclyde, Scotland.
Richard Alexander, Seaford, E.Sussex, England.
Alfies Antique Market, London, England.
Alfriston Antiques, Alfriston, E.Sussex, England.
Alice Lighting, Cardiff, S.Glamorgan, Wales.
Alice's Antiques, Llanelli, Dyfed, Wales.
All Things Bright and Beautiful, Penzance, Cornwall, England.
Richard Allan Gallery, London, England.
A.F. Allbrook, Theydon Bois, Essex, England.
Allegras Antiques, London, England.
Alfred S.Allen & Co, South Ockendon, Essex, England.
Joan E. Allen & Co., Biggin Hill, Kent, England.
Kenneth W. Allen, Sutton Coldfield, W.Midlands, England.
Peter Allen Antiques Ltd, London, England.
Trevor Allen, London, England.
Allen's (Branksome) Ltd, Poole, Dorset, England.
Allens, Stapleford, Lincolnshire, England.
Donald Allison Antiques, Preston, Lancashire, England.
Charles R.P.Allix, Sevenoaks, Kent, England.
Elizabeth Allnutt, Topsham, Devon, England.
John Allott Abrahams, Hay-on-Wye, Hereford & Worcester, England.
Nicholas Alloway, Photographer of Antiques, London, England.
Duncan M.Allsop, Warwick, Warwickshire, England.
John Allsopp Antiques, London, England.
Alma Antiques, Lindfield, W.Sussex, England.
Alpha Antiques, Stoke-on-Trent, Staffordshire, England.
Alresford Gallery, Alresford, Hampshire, England.
Earl of Altamont, Westport, Co Mayo, Eire.
Alton Gallery, London, England.
Alverton Antiques, Northallerton, N.Yorkshire, England.
Alvin Antiques, Plymouth, Devon, England.
Alwin Gallery, London, England.
Alyn House Antiques, North Shields, Tyne & Wear, England.
Amalgam, London, England.
Ambrose, Loughton, Essex, England.
Amersham Antique Centre, Amersham, Buckinghamshire, England.
Albert Amor Ltd, London, England.
George Amos & Sons (CB) Ltd, London, England.
Ampthill Antiques Centre, Ampthill, Bedfordshire, England.
Ampthill Emporium, Ampthill, Bedfordshire, England.
Anchor Antiques Ltd, London, England.
Ancient & Modern, Westbury, Wiltshire, England.
Ancient and Modern, St Austell, Cornwall, England.
And So To Bed Ltd, London, England.
Anderson and Garland, Newcastle upon Tyne, Tyne & Wear, England.
F.E.Anderson & Son, Welshpool, Powys, Wales.
Maria Andipa Icon Gallery, London, England.
Philip Andrade Ltd, South Brent, Devon, England.
Andreas Antiques, London, England.
Michael Andrews Antiques, Milford, Surrey, England.
Andwells, Hartley Wintney, Hampshire, England.
Angel Antiques, Brighton & Hove, E.Sussex, England.
The Angel Antiques, Diss, Norfolk, England.
Angel Arcade, Portmeirion, Gwynedd, Wales.
Angelshades Antiques, Petworth, W.Sussex, England.
Angharads Antiques, Shotton, Clwyd, Wales.
Anglebooks Ltd, London, England.
Anglo-Persian Carpet Co Ltd, London, England.
Angus Antiques, Dundee, Tayside, Scotland.
Annexe Antiques, Tunbridge Wells, Kent, England.
Annique Antiques, Tunbridge Wells, Kent, England.
Anno Domini, London, England.
Another World, Edinburgh, Lothian, Scotland.
Stephen Anson, London, England.
Anthony Antiques, Dublin, Co Dublin, Eire.
John Anthony Antiques, Bletchingley, Surrey, England.
Antichita, London, England.
Antics, Cobham, Surrey, England.
Antiqcurios & Irene Fine Art, Dublin, Co Dublin, Eire.
Antiquaria Ltd, London, England.
Antiquarius, Felpham, W.Sussex, England.
Antiquarius, London, England.
Antiquarius Camera Collectors Shop, London, England.
The Antiquary, Oxford, Oxfordshire, England.
Antiquatat Antiques Ltd, Wimborne Minster, Dorset, England.
Antique & Bargain Stores, Doncaster, S.Yorkshire, England.
Antique & Modern Furniture Ltd, London, England.
Antique and Art, Northallerton, N.Yorkshire, England.
Antique and Collectors Market, Worthing, W.Sussex, England.
Antique and Furniture Centre, Harrogate, N.Yorkshire, England.
The Antique Brass Bedstead Co Ltd, Great Baddow, Essex, England.
Antique Centre, Princes Risborough, Buckinghamshire, England.
Antique Centre, Ross-on Wye, Hereford & Worcester, England.
The Antique Centre, Wainfleet, Lincolnshire, England.
The Antique Centre, Ludlow, Shropshire, England.
The Antique Centre, East Molesey, Surrey, England.
Antique Centre, Walsall, W.Midlands, England.
The Antique Centre, Petworth, W.Sussex, England.
Antique Clocks, Harston, Cambridgeshire, England.
Antique Connoisseur plc, London, England.
Antique Corner, Ludlow, Shropshire, England.
Antique Dealers International PLC, Langport, Somerset, England.
Antique Exporters (Derby) UK, Derby, Derbyshire, England.
Antique Exporters of Chester, Chester, Cheshire, England.
The Antique Furniture Warehouse, Woodbridge, Suffolk, England.
The Antique Galleries, Paulerspury, Northamptonshire, England.
The Antique Galleries, Henley-on-Thames, Oxfordshire, England.
The Antique Gallery, London, England.
Antique Glass, London, England.
The Antique Home, Cambridge, Cambridgeshire, England.
The Antique Home, Camberley, Surrey, England.
The Antique Home, London, England.
The Antique Home Ltd, Whaley Bridge, Derbyshire, England.
Antique Interiors, Bath, Avon, England.
Antique Leathers, London, England.
Antique Lovers Coterie at Ingram Warwick Ltd, Amersham, Buckinghamshire, England.
Antique Market, Edinburgh, Lothian, Scotland.
The Antique Mart, Richmond, Surrey, England.
Antique Metals, Coggeshall, Essex, England.
Antique Pine Furniture, Michael Green, Harrogate, N.Yorkshire, England.
The Antique Porcelain Company Ltd, London, England.
Antique Restoration, Gloucester, Gloucestershire, England.
The Antique Shop, Cork, Co Cork, Eire.
The Antique Shop, Killorglin, Co Kerry, Eire.
The Antique Shop, Ferbane, Co Offaly, Eire.
The Antique Shop, Tramore, Co Waterford, Eire.
The Antique Shop, Disley, Cheshire, England.
The Antique Shop, Wimborne Minster, Dorset, England.
The Antique Shop, Stockport, Greater Manchester, England.

The Antique Shop, Preston, Lancashire, England.
The Antique Shop, Grantham, Lincolnshire, England.
The Antique Shop, Swaffham, Norfolk, England.
The Antique Shop, Wallingford, Oxfordshire, England.
The Antique Shop, Hacheston, Suffolk, England.
The Antique Shop, Leeds, W.Yorkshire, England.
The Antique Shop, Malmesbury, Wiltshire, England.
The Antique Shop, Carrickfergus, Co Antrim, Northern Ireland.
The Antique Shop, Newtownards, Co Down, Northern Ireland.
The Antique Shop, Newtonmore, Highland, Scotland.
Antique Shop, Barry, S.Glamorgan, Wales.
The Antique Shop & Sale Room, Ulverston, Cumbria, England.
The Antique Shop, Bury, Greater Manchester, England.
The Antique Textile Company, London, England.
The Antique Trader, London, England.
Antiques, Limerick, Co Limerick, Eire.
Antiques, Eyam, Derbyshire, England.
Antiques, Saffron Walden, Essex, England.
Antiques, King's Lynn, Norfolk, England.
Antiques, West Haddon, Northamptonshire, England.
Antiques, Long Hanborough, Oxfordshire, England.
Antiques, Aberdeen, Grampian, Scotland.
Antiques & Crafts Market, Bristol, Avon, England.
Antiques & Interiors, Winchester, Hampshire, England.
Antiques & Pine, Keighley, W.Yorkshire, England.
Antiques and Collectables, Dereham, Norfolk, England.
Antiques and Fine Arts (Prestwich) Ltd, Rochdale, Greater Manchester, England.
Antiques in Charnwood, Anstey, Leicestershire, England.
Antiques of Newport, Newport, Gwent, Wales.
Antiques of Penrith, Penrith, Cumbria, England.
The Antiques Book Centre, Hatfield, Hertfordshire, England.
The Antiques Centre, Moreton-in-Marsh, Gloucestershire, England.
The Antiques Centre, Sevenoaks, Kent, England.
The Antiques Centre, Deddington, Oxfordshire, England.
The Antiques Centre, Guildford, Surrey, England.
Antiques Cheltenham, Cheltenham, Gloucestershire, England.
Antiques Coffee House, Bakewell, Derbyshire, England.
The Antiques Complex, Leicester, Leicestershire, England.
Antiques Etcetera (Mostly Etcetera), Folkestone, Kent, England.
The Antiques Exchange, London, England.
Antiques Gallery, Liverpool, Merseyside, England.
Antiques Objets D'Art & Curios, Leigh-on-Sea, Essex, England.
Antiques Shop, Grantham, Lincolnshire, England.
The Antiques Shop, Whitegate, Whitegate, Cheshire, England.
Antiques Trade Warehouse, Bournemouth, Dorset, England.
Antiques Unlimited, Cardiff, S.Glamorgan, Wales.
The Antiques Warehouse, Uxbridge, Middlesex, England.
55 Antiques, Hull, Humberside, England.
Antiquities, Denham, Buckinghamshire, England.
Antiquities, London, England.
Antiquus, London, England.
Antiquus A G, London, England.
Antiqva, Weedon, Northamptonshire, England.
Philip Antrobus, London, England.
Anvil Antiques, Leek, Staffordshire, England.
Apollo Antiques Ltd, Warwick, Warwickshire, England.
Apollo Galleries, Croydon, Surrey, England.
Apollo Gallery, London, England.
Appleby's, London, England.
Roger Appleyard Ltd, Rotherham, S.Yorkshire, England.
Jess Applin Antiques, Cambridge, Cambridgeshire, England.
Apter-Fredericks Ltd, London, England.
Aquarelle of St Giles, Chalfont St Giles, Buckinghamshire, England.
Arbiter, New Brighton, Merseyside, England.
Arbiter Antiques, London, England.
Arbour Antiques Ltd, Stratford-upon-Avon, Warwickshire, England.
Arboyne Antiques, Eardisley, Hereford & Worcester, England.
Arcade Gallery, London, England.
The Arcade Gallery, London, England.
The Arcade, East Molesey, Surrey, England.
Archer Antiques, Penrith, Cumbria, England.
R.G.Archer, Lavenham, Suffolk, England.
Architectural Antiques, South Molton, Devon, England.
Architectural Antiques, Leominster, Hereford & Worcester, England.
Architectural Antiques Ltd, London, England.
Architectural Heritage of Cheltenham, Cheltenham, Gloucestershire, England.
Archway Gallery, Cheltenham, Gloucestershire, England.
Archways, Tavistock, Devon, England.
Arden Antiques, Stratford-upon-Avon, Warwickshire, England.
The Arden Gallery, Henley-in-Arden, Warwickshire, England.
Brenda Arden Antiques, Tarporley, Cheshire, England.
J.L. Arditti, Christchurch, Dorset, England.
L.J. Arditti & E.M. Arditti, Tunbridge Wells, Kent, England.
Billi Arena, London, England.
Arenski, London, England.
Argenta, London, England.
Argentum Antiques, Bexley, Kent, England.
Argyll Etkin Ltd, London, England.
Valerie Arieta, London, England.
Aristocat Antiques, Gerrards Cross, Buckinghamshire, England.
Arita Antiques, Ticehurst, E.Sussex, England.
The Ark Angel, London, England.
Armada Antiques, London, England.
Armada Exports, Cheltenham, Gloucestershire, England.
Armatura, St Peter Port, Guernsey, Channel Islands.
Karin Armelin Antiques, London, England.
Armitage, London, England.
Armour-Winston Ltd, London, England.
Armoury Antiques, London, England.
J.C.E. & N.I. Armson - Antiques, Yoxall, Staffordshire, England.
M. & S. Armson Ltd, Berkhamsted, Hertfordshire, England.
Armstrong Antiques, Harrogate, N.Yorkshire, England.
Armstrong-Davis Gallery, Arundel, W.Sussex, England.
Julian Armytage, Crewkerne, Somerset, England.
Hugh Arnold Antiques, Nayland, Suffolk, England.
Peter Arnold Gallery, Aylesbury, Buckinghamshire, England.
Roy Arnold, Needham Market, Suffolk, England.
Art & Antiques, Beccles, Suffolk, England.
Art and Antiques, Wadhurst, E.Sussex, England.
Art Bronze Foundry (London) Ltd, London, England.
Art Distribution Ltd, Wendover, Buckinghamshire, England.
Artbry's Antiques, Pinner, Middlesex, England.
Artemesia, Alresford, Hampshire, England.
Artemis Fine Arts (UK) Limited, London, England.
Artingstall & Hind, Manchester, Greater Manchester, England.
Artist, St Ives, Cornwall, England.
Artizana, Prestbury, Cheshire, England.
Arts of Living Gallery, Bath, Avon, England.
Arundel Antique & Collectors' Market, Arundel, W.Sussex, England.
Arundel Antiques Market, Arundel, W.Sussex, England.
Mario Ascione, London, England.
Ash Rare Books, London, England.
James Ash Antiques, Llandeilo, Dyfed, Wales.
Ashburton Marbles, Ashburton, Devon, England.
Ashby Antiques, Ashby de la Zouch, Leicestershire, England.
Ashleigh House Antiques, Birmingham, W.Midlands, England.
Ashley Antiques and Restoration, Hungerford, Berkshire, England.
Ashley House Antiques, Burton on Trent, Staffordshire, England.
Ashton Antiques, Dorridge, W Midlands, England.
Christopher Ashton & Anjula Daniel, London, England.
Ashtons Furniture Centre, Brighton & Hove, E.Sussex, England.
Aspidistra, Bath, Avon, England.
The Aspidistra, Hitchin, Hertfordshire, England.
Aspleys Antique Imports & Exports, Leek, Staffordshire, England.
Aspleys Antique Imports & Exports, Uttoxeter, Staffordshire, England.
Asprey PLC, London, England.
Maurice Asprey Ltd, London, England.
Jenny Aste & Richard Smith, York, N.Yorkshire, England.
John Astill Antiques, Bridgnorth, Shropshire, England.
Astley Bridge Antiques, Bolton, Greater Manchester, England.
Astley House - Fine Art, Moreton-in-Marsh, Gloucestershire, England.
Astleys Ltd, London, England.
Astoria, London, England.
At the Sign of the Herald Angel, Cirencester, Gloucestershire, England.
Atholl Antiques, Aberdeen, Grampian, Scotland.
C.W.Atkins & Co. Antiques, Taunton, Somerset, England.
John Atkins Antiques Galleries, Hawkhurst, Kent, England.
James Atkinson Gallery, Sandwich, Kent, England.
Keith Atkinson Antiques, Croydon, Surrey, England.
Atmosphere, London, England.
Atrium Antiques, Guisborough, Cleveland, England.
Atrium Antiques Ltd, Woburn, Bedfordshire, England.
The Attic, Baldock, Hertfordshire, England.
Attic (Sevenoaks) Ltd, Brasted, Kent, England.
Attic Antiques, Brighton & Hove, E.Sussex, England.
Attic Gallery, Wisbech, Cambridgeshire, England.
The Attic, Newquay, Cornwall, England.
The Attic, Inverness, Highland, Scotland.
Audley House Antiques, Osbournby, Lincolnshire, England.
P.Audley-Miller, Oxford, Oxfordshire, England.
Audraw Ltd, Soham, Cambridgeshire, England.
Audun Gallery, London, England.
Augill Castle Antiques Ltd, Brough, Cumbria, England.
Ian Auld, London, England.
Auriol House Antiques, Tewkesbury, Gloucestershire, England.
Austin/Desmond Fine Art Ltd, Ascot, Berkshire, England.
G.Austin & Sons Ltd, London, England.
Avakian Oriental Carpets Ltd, London, England.
Avarice Antiques, Edinburgh, Lothian, Scotland.
Avon Antiques, Bradford-on-Avon, Wiltshire, England.
Avon Lodge Antiques, Fordingbridge, Hampshire, England.
Axia, London, England.
AIA Antiques and Joseph W.Thornton Antiques, Ulverston, Cumbria, England.
AS Antiques, Salford, Greater Manchester, England.

B & T Antiques, London, England.
B & T Restorations, Eastbourne, E.Sussex, England.
B.E.L.Products Ltd Inc.B.E.L.Tradepoint, Birmingham, W.Midlands, England.
B.P.Antiques, London, England.
J.H.Bachmann (UK) Ltd, Feltham, Middlesex, England.
Baddow Antiques and Craft Centre, Great Baddow, Essex, England.
The Badger, London, England.
Baggott Church Street Ltd, Stow-on-the-Wold, Gloucestershire, England.
D.J. Baggott, Stow-on-the-Wold, Gloucestershire, England.
Duncan J. Baggott, Stow-on-the-Wold, Gloucestershire, England.
Shirley Baguley Antiques, Harrogate, N.Yorkshire, England.
Edward Bailey & Son, Newark-on-Trent, Nottinghamshire, England.
Robert Bailey Oriental Carpets, London, England.
Baileys Architectural Antiques, Ross-on-Wye, Hereford & Worcester, England.
Alexander Bailie (Antiques), London, England.
Bainbridges Fine Art & General Chattel Auctioneers, London, England.
Henry Baines, Tunbridge Wells, Kent, England.
Anthony Baker Antiques, Alderley Edge, Cheshire, England.
C.G. Baker, Bath, Avon, England.
J. & J. Baker, Lavenham, Suffolk, England.

John Baker, Newbury, Berkshire, England.
Michael & Margaret Baker, Merstham, Surrey, England.
Richard Baker and Thomson, Birkenhead, Merseyside, England.
Terry Baker, Langford, Nottinghamshire, England.
Balcombe Galleries, Balcombe, W.Sussex, England.
Baldwin & Partners, Chatham, Kent, England.
A.H.Baldwin & Sons Ltd, London, England.
Balfes, Dublin, Co Dublin, Eire.
David Ball Antiques, Luton, Bedfordshire, England.
The Ballroom Antiques, Petworth, W.Sussex, England.
Christopher Bangs, London, England.
Bank House Antiques, Hull, Humberside, England.
The Bank House Gallery, London, England.
Banks & Silvers, Worcester, Hereford & Worcester, England.
Simon Banks Antiques, Finedon, Northamptonshire, England.
Bankside Gallery, London, England.
Barbican Art Gallery, London, England.
Barbican Bookshop, York, N.Yorkshire, England.
Barclay Antiques, Bexhill, E.Sussex, England.
Barclay Lennie Fine Art, Glasgow, Strathclyde, Scotland.
Hugo Barclay, Brighton & Hove, E.Sussex, England.
Eddy Bardawil, London, England.
Richard Barder Antiques, Hermitage, Berkshire, England.
Barham Fine Arts, London, England.
Celia Barker Mill, London, England.
Barkes & Richardson, York, N.Yorkshire, England.
David Barklem Ltd, London, England.
Robert Barley Antiques, London, England.
Barleycote Hall Antiques, Keighley, W.Yorkshire, England.
Barling of Mount Street Ltd, London, England.
Barlow Antiques, Tichborne, Hampshire, England.
K.Barlow Ltd, Decorative Arts 1900-1950, London, England.
C. & A.J.Barmby, Tonbridge, Kent, England.
Barn Antiques, Coventry, W.Midlands, England.
The Barn Collectors Market, Seaford, E.Sussex, England.
Barn End Antiques & Firearms, Hadleigh, Suffolk, England.
The Barn Gallery, Powick, Hereford & Worcester, England.
Barnard Gallery, Doncaster, S.Yorkshire, England.
Barnes and Webster Limited, London, England.
R.A.Barnes Antiques, London, England.
Barnet Antiques & Fine Art, Barnet, Hertfordshire, England.
Barnet Antiques and Fine Art, London, England.
Roger Barnett, Eton, Berkshire, England.
Barnetts Antiques, Brighton & Hove, E.Sussex, England.
Barometer Shop, Leominster, Hereford & Worcester, England.
Baron Antiques, Manchester, Greater Manchester, England.
H.Baron, London, England.
Baroq Antiques, Little Brickhill, Buckinghamshire, England.
Christine Barratt Antiques, Bedford, Bedfordshire, England.
Barrett & Butler, Ipswich, Suffolk, England.
C.Barrett & Co, London, England.
Ian Barrett's Furniture Workshop, Looe, Cornwall, England.
Barrie's Bookshop, Cheltenham, Gloucestershire, England.
David Barrington, Brasted, Kent, England.
Barronfield Gallery, Preston, Lancashire, England.
John Barry, Nailsworth, Gloucestershire, England.
J. Barrymore & Co, Honiton, Devon, England.
Douglas Barsley Antiques, Eastbourne, E.Sussex, England.
Bartlett Street Antique Market, Bath, Avon, England.
Nigel Bartlett, London, England.
Barton House Antiques, Stanford le Hope, Essex, England.
Roy Barton, Pulborough, W.Sussex, England.
Albert Bartram, Chesham, Buckinghamshire, England.
Douglas Bartrick - Antiques, Gloucester, Gloucestershire, England.
Basia, Great Missenden, Buckinghamshire, England.
Basilisk Press, London, England.
Baskett & Day, London, England.
Janet & Robert Bateman Antiques, London, England.
Jean A.Bateman Antiques, Stratford-upon-Avon, Warwickshire, England.
Eric Bates & Sons, Coltishall, Norfolk, England.
Neville Bates Antiques and Fine Art Gallery, Blackpool, Lancashire, England.
C.W. Bateson, Harrogate, N.Yorkshire, England.
Bath Antique Market, Bath, Avon, England.
Bath Galleries, Bath, Avon, England.
Bath Saturday Antique Market, Bath, Avon, England.
Bath Stamp & Coin Shop, Bath, Avon, England.
Richard Batsford Antiques, Bournemouth, Dorset, England.
Prudence Battersby Antiques, Botley, Hampshire, England.
Battlesbridge Antique Centre, Battlesbridge, Essex, England.
Baumkotter Gallery, London, England.
H.C.Baxter & Sons, London, England.
R.W.Baxter, Southport, Merseyside, England.
D.W. & A.B. Bayliss & Son, Ludlow, Shropshire, England.
Baynton-Williams, Arundel, W.Sussex, England.
George Bayntun, Bath, Avon, England.
The Bazaar, Bedford, Bedfordshire, England.
D.M. Beach, Salisbury, Wiltshire, England.
Beacon Gallery, Woburn, Bedfordshire, England.
Stanley Beal Ltd, London, England.
Stanley Beal Ltd, London, England.
Beaminster Antiques, Beaminster, Dorset, England.
J. & A. Beare Ltd, London, England.
Bearnes, Torquay, Devon, England.
Peter T. Beasley, Farningham, Kent, England.
Walter S.Beaton, Perth, Tayside, Scotland.
T.W.Beaty, Moffat, Dumfries & Galloway, Scotland.
Beaubush House Antiques, Folkestone, Kent, England.
Beaufield Mews Antiques, Dublin, Co Dublin, Eire.
Beaufort Gallery, Hexham, Northumberland, England.
Beaulieu Fine Arts, Beaulieu, Hampshire, England.
Beauly Antiques, Muir of Ord, Highland, Scotland.
Michael Beaumont Antiques, Saffron Walden, Essex, England.
Beaux Arts Ceramics, Bath, Avon, England.
Beaver Coin Room, London, England.
John Beazor & Sons Ltd, Cambridge, Cambridgeshire, England.
Claudia Beck, London, England.
Susan Becker Antiques, London, England.
Beckfoot Antiques, Kirkby Stephen, Cumbria, England.
Patricia Beckman Antiques, London, England.
Beckwith & Son, Hertford, Hertfordshire, England.
David Bedale Antiques, Knutsford, Cheshire, England.
William Bedford PLC, London, England.
Margaret Bedi Antiques, Billingham, Cleveland, England.
Jonathan Beech, Cirencester, Gloucestershire, England.
Ron Beech, Brighton & Hove, E.Sussex, England.
Beedham Antiques Ltd, Bakewell, Derbyshire, England.
Beeleigh Abbey Books, Maldon, Essex, England.
John Beer, London, England.
Brian Beet, London, England.
Beetle & Poker, London, England.
Chris Beetles Ltd, London, England.
The Belgrave Gallery, London, England.
Bell Antiques, Romsey, Hampshire, England.
The Bell Gallery, Belfast, Belfast, Northern Ireland.
Bell Passage Antiques, Wotton-under-Edge, Gloucestershire, England.
J.& H.Bell Antiques, Castletown, Isle of Man.
John Bell of Aberdeen Ltd, Aberdeen, Grampian, Scotland.
Peter Bell Fine Arts, Lechlade, Gloucestershire, England.
R. Bell, Long Melford, Suffolk, England.
Robin Bellamy Ltd, Witney, Oxfordshire, England.
Bellevue, Bristol, Avon, England.
C.Bellinger Antiques, Barnet, Hertfordshire, England.
Mary Bellis Antiques, Hungerford, Berkshire, England.
Below Stairs, Hungerford, Berkshire, England.
Anthony Belton, London, England.
Benardout & Benardout, London, England.
Raymond Benardout, London, England.
Raymond Benardout Ltd, London, England.
Benedict Jewellers, Amersham, Buckinghamshire, England.
Benet Gallery, Cambridge, Cambridgeshire, England.
H.J.Benford, Kettering, Northamptonshire, England.
Ronald Benjamin Antiques, London, England.
Benmuir Photographic Services Ltd, Camberley, Surrey, England.
N. & P. Bennett, Plymouth, Devon, England.
Alan Bennett, Truro, Cornwall, England.
Paul Bennett, London, England.
R. Bennett Antiques, Dorking, Surrey, England.
Bennison, London, England.
Benson Antiques, Cheltenham, Gloucestershire, England.
Mrs J. Benson, Castle Lyons, Co Cork, Eire.
J.W.Bentall & Sons, Ripon, N.Yorkshire, England.
Bentley & Co Ltd, London, England.
Peter Bentley, London, England.
Pat Bently Antiques, Ampthill, Bedfordshire, England.
Beresford Clark Antiques, London, England.
Bereston Antiques, St Albans, Hertfordshire, England.
Berkeley Antiques, Berkeley, Gloucestershire, England.
Berkeley Galleries Ltd, London, England.
Berkley Antiques, Nottingham, Nottinghamshire, England.
Bermondsey Antique Market Ltd, London, England.
Bernheimer Fine Arts Ltd, London, England.
Berry Powell & Shackell, Chippenham, Wiltshire, England.
Lesley Berry Antiques, Bridlington, Humberside, England.
Bertram Rota Ltd, London, England.
Ray Best Antiques, Ilminster, Somerset, England.
Beveridge (Antiques), Perth, Tayside, Scotland.
George Bewes & Co, Aberdeen, Grampian, Scotland.
Bexfield Antiques, Hitchin, Hertfordshire, England.
D.Bickersteth, Cambridge, Cambridgeshire, England.
Biddle and Webb, Birmingham, W.Midlands, England.
Peter Biddulph, London, England.
Sue Biddulph, London, England.
Bieldside Antiques, Bieldside, Grampian, Scotland.
Big Ben Clock Shop, London, England.
Biggs of Maidenhead, Twyford, Berkshire, England.
Brian Bingham Antiques, Chesterfield, Derbyshire, England.
Tony Bingham, London, England.
The Bingley Antiques Centre, Bingley, W.Yorkshire, England.
Binsted Antiques, Teddington, Middlesex, England.
Birbeck Antiques, Torquay, Devon, England.
Arthur Bircumshaw, Bournemouth, Dorset, England.
The Bird in Hand, Leominster, Hereford & Worcester, England.
J.L.W.Bird, London, England.
John Bird/Annette Puttnam, Brighton & Hove, E.Sussex, England.
Ian Birksted Gallery, London, England.
Birmingham Antique Centre, Birmingham, W.Midlands, England.
Birmingham House Antiques, Shipston on Stour, Warwickshire, England.
Bishop (Marlow) Ltd, Marlow, Buckinghamshire, England.
Bishopstrow Antiques, Warminster, Wiltshire, England.
James G.Bissett Ltd, Aberdeen, Grampian, Scotland.
Bizarre, London, England.
Blaby Gallery, Blaby, Leicestershire, England.
The Black Boy (incorp Au Bon Souvenir), Appleby, Cumbria, England.
Black Isle Antiques, Fortrose, Highland, Scotland.
David Black Oriental Carpets, London, England.
Andrew and Linda Blackburn Antiques, Gargrave, N.Yorkshire, England.
Jack Blackburn, Preston, Lancashire, England.
The Blacksmiths Shop, Brasted, Kent, England.
Blackwell's Rare Books, Fyfield, Oxfordshire, England.
Blair Antiques, Pitlochry, Tayside, Scotland.
H.Blairman & Sons Ltd, London, England.

Blake Antiques, London, England.
J.H. Blakey & Sons Ltd, Brierfield, Lancashire, England.
J.W.Blanchard Ltd, Winchester, Hampshire, England.
Blantern & Davis, Bristol, Avon, England.
Blatchpack Ltd, Bristol, Avon, England.
I.Blatt, Portslade, E.Sussex, England.
Blenheim Antiques, Bladon, Oxfordshire, England.
Blewbury Antiques, Blewbury, Oxfordshire, England.
Blinkhorn & Company, Broadway, Hereford & Worcester, England.
Bliss Antiques, Leominster, Hereford & Worcester, England.
Helen Blomfield, Halstead, Essex, England.
Blond Fine Art, London, England.
Anne Bloom Jewellers, London, England.
N.Bloom & Son (Antiques) Ltd, London, England.
Bloomsbury Book Auctions, London, England.
A. & B. Bloomstein Ltd, London, England.
Bluecoat Display Centre, Liverpool, Merseyside, England.
Bluecoat Gallery, Liverpool, Merseyside, England.
Bluett & Sons Ltd, London, England.
John Bly, Tring, Hertfordshire, England.
Blyth Antiques, Bath, Avon, England.
Arthur Boaden Antiques, Hexham, Northumberland, England.
Boardman Fine Art Auctioneers, Haverhill, Suffolk, England.
The Boathouse Gallery, Walton-on-Thames, Surrey, England.
Bobinet Ltd, London, England.
John Boddy's Fine Wood & Tool Store Ltd, Boroughbridge, N.Yorkshire, England.
Colin Bodner, Richmond, Surrey, England.
George S.Bolam, Tetbury, Gloucestershire, England.
Brian R. Bolt Collector's Antiques, Bushmills, Co Antrim, Northern Ireland.
Bond Street Antique Centre, London, England.
Bond Street Antiques, Cromer, Norfolk, England.
Bond Street Silver Galleries, London, England.
S.Bond & Son, Colchester, Essex, England.
Sue Bond, London, England.
L.W.Bondy, London, England.
Bonhams, London, England.
Bonhams Chelsea, London, England.
Joseph Bonnar, Edinburgh, Lothian, Scotland.
R. Bonnett, London, England.
Bonrose Antiques, London, England.
Boodle & Dunthorne Ltd, Chester, Cheshire, England.
Boodle & Dunthorne Ltd, Liverpool, Merseyside, England.
The Book House, Kirkby Stephen, Cumbria, England.
Bookham Galleries, London, England.
Bookranger, St Andrews, Fife, Scotland.
Books and Things, Great Wakering, Essex, England.
Books and Things, Leominster, Hereford & Worcester, England.
Joanna Booth, London, England.
Richard Booth's Bookshop, Hay-on-Wye, Hereford & Worcester, England.
Borbaletta, Cheltenham, Gloucestershire, England.
Claude Bornoff, London, England.
Boss Antiques, Petworth, W.Sussex, England.
Peter D. Bosson, Wilmslow, Cheshire, England.
Derek Boston Antiques, Salisbury, Wiltshire, England.
John Botting, Polegate, E.Sussex, England.
Bottles & Bygones, Cheltenham, Gloucestershire, England.
T.H. Boughton, Rolvenden, Kent, England.
Bourbon-Hanby, London, England.
J.H. Bourdon-Smith Ltd, London, England.
James Bourlet & Sons Ltd, Feltham, Middlesex, England.
Bourne Antiques, Bourne, Lincolnshire, England.
Bourne Fine Art Ltd, London, England.
Bourne Fine Art Ltd, Edinburgh, Lothian, Scotland.
Bourne Frames & Restoration Ltd, Edinburgh, Lothian, Scotland.
Bourne Gallery, Reigate, Surrey, England.
Guy Bousfield, Windsor, Berkshire, England.
Bow Cottage Antiques, Stratford-upon-Avon, Warwickshire, England.
Bow House, Langport, Somerset, England.
Bow Window, Frinton-on-Sea, Essex, England.
Bow Windows Book Shop, Lewes, E.Sussex, England.
Bryan Bowden, Doncaster, S.Yorkshire, England.
M.J.Bowdery, Hindhead, Surrey, England.
Nicholas Bowlby, Uckfield, E.Sussex, England.
Bowmoore Gallery, Whelford, Gloucestershire, England.
Bowood Antiques, Wendover, Buckinghamshire, England.
Box House Antiques, London, England.
The Box Shop, London, England.
Rex Boyer Antiques, Nantwich, Cheshire, England.
Andrew Boyle (Booksellers) Ltd, Worcester, Hereford & Worcester, England.
Boyne House Antiques, Leominster, Hereford & Worcester, England.
Bracher & Sydenham, Reading, Berkshire, England.
Bradford Furniture Workshops, Bradford-on-Avon, Wiltshire, England.
Robert Bradley, Salisbury, Wiltshire, England.
Braemar Antiques Ltd, White Waltham, Berkshire, England.
Bragge & Sons, Rye, E.Sussex, England.
Lesley Bragge Antiques, Petworth, W.Sussex, England.
Brampton Mill Antiques Centre, Brampton, Cambridgeshire, England.
Erika Brandl - Paintings, London, England.
Brandler Galleries, Brentwood, Essex, England.
Brandt Oriental Antiques, London, England.
Bratton Antiques, Westbury, Wiltshire, England.
H.H.Bray Ltd, Warwick, Warwickshire, England.
Peter Brazier, Sturminster Newton, Dorset, England.
Brazil Antiques Ltd, Croydon, Surrey, England.
Breakspeare Antiques, Tetbury, Gloucestershire, England.
Breck Antiques, Nottingham, Nottinghamshire, England.
Brenin, Cowbridge, S.Glamorgan, Wales.
Arthur Brett & Sons, Ltd, Norwich, Norfolk, England.
J. Brett, Bath, Avon, England.
Simon Brett, Moreton-in-Marsh, Gloucestershire, England.
Daniel Brewster, Glasgow, Strathclyde, Scotland.
Carlton Gallery, Driffield, Humberside, England.
Luigi Brian, London, England.
Bric-a-Brac Ltd, Whitley Bay, Tyne & Wear, England.
Bridge Antiques, Durham, Durham, England.
Bridge Antiques, Spalding, Lincolnshire, England.
Bridge End Antiques, Berwick-upon-Tweed, Northumberland, England.
Bridge End Gallery, Woolhope, Hereford & Worcester, England.
Bridge House Antiques, Cranbrook, Kent, England.
Bridge House Antiques, Nantwich, Cheshire, England.
Bridge House Antiques, Penshurst, Kent, England.
Christine Bridge, London, England.
J.Bridgeman Coins, Accrington, Lancashire, England.
Bridgfords Ltd, Alderley Edge, Cheshire, England.
David Bridgwater, Bath, Avon, England.
E. & G. Briere, Norwich, Norfolk, England.
F.E.A.Briggs Ltd, London, England.
James Briggs & Sons Ltd, Manchester, Greater Manchester, England.
Bright Willis, Birmingham, W.Midlands, England.
Brighton Antiques Gallery, Brighton & Hove, E.Sussex, England.
Brimsmore House Antiques, Yeovil, Somerset, England.
T.& D.Brindle Antiques, Blackburn, Lancashire, England.
Brisigotti Antiques Ltd, London, England.
Bristol Antiques Ltd, Shepton Mallet, Somerset, England.
The Bristol Gallery, Bristol, Avon, England.
Bristow Antiques, Bordon, Hampshire, England.
J. & M. Bristow Antiques, Tetbury, Gloucestershire, England.
Britannia, London, England.
Britannia Antiques, Manchester, Greater Manchester, England.
British Antique Exporters Ltd, Burgess Hill, W.Sussex, England.
British Crafts Centre, London, England.
Andrew Britten, Malmesbury, Wiltshire, England.
C.K.Broadhurst & Co Ltd, Southport, Merseyside, England.
Broadstairs Antiques, Broadstairs, Kent, England.
Broadwater Bookroom, Worthing, W.Sussex, England.
Broadway Antique Arcade, Broadway, Hereford & Worcester, England.
Broadway Antiques, Shifnal, Shropshire, England.
Broadway Antiques, Cardiff, S.Glamorgan, Wales.
Brobury House Gallery, Brobury, Hereford & Worcester, England.
Brocanteuse Gallery, Ashburton, Devon, England.
Brockdish Antiques, Diss, Norfolk, England.
Aubrey Brocklehurst, London, England.
Brocklehursts, Macclesfield, Cheshire, England.
Brod Gallery, London, England.
Brook Farm Antiques, Bidford-on-Avon, Warwickshire, England.
Brook Lane Antiques, Alderley Edge, Cheshire, England.
Brook Street Antiques, Leek, Staffordshire, England.
Alexis Brook, Kettering, Northamptonshire, England.
Ian J. Brook, Wilton, Wiltshire, England.
Carol Brooke, Mirfield, W.Yorkshire, England.
Rodney Brooke Antiques, London, England.
T.C.S.Brooke, Wroxham, Norfolk, England.
Brookes Forge Flempton, Bury St Edmunds, Suffolk, England.
Brookfield Gallery, Colyton, Devon, England.
John A.Brooks, Rothley, Leicestershire, England.
Brotherton Gallery Ltd, London, England.
David Brower Antiques, London, England.
Brown House Antiques, Newport, Essex, England.
Brown Jack Bookshop, Market Harborough, Leicestershire, England.
I. & J.L. Brown, Hereford, Hereford & Worcester, England.
I. & J.L. Brown, London, England.
John Brown Antiques, Ashbourne, Derbyshire, England.
Margaret Brown Antiques, Edinburgh, Lothian, Scotland.
Murray Brown, London, England.
Patrick F. Brown, Dublin, Co Dublin, Eire.
W.J.M.Brown, London, England.
William H.Brown, Grantham, Lincolnshire, England.
Brown's, Richmond, N.Yorkshire, England.
Brownhouse Antiques, Ipswich, Suffolk, England.
Browns of West Wycombe, West Wycombe, Buckinghamshire, England.
Browns Clocks Ltd, Glasgow, Strathclyde, Scotland.
Brownsells Granary, Wiveliscombe, Somerset, England.
Browse & Darby Ltd, London, England.
Paul Bruce Antiques & Pine Shop, Ipswich, Suffolk, England.
William Bruce & Co, St Boswells, Borders, Scotland.
Bruford & Heming Ltd, London, England.
Wm Bruford & Son Ltd, Exeter, Devon, England.
Wm Bruford & Son Ltd, Eastbourne, E.Sussex, England.
Brunswick Antiques, Hull, Humberside, England.
F.G. Bruschweiler (Antiques) Ltd, Rayleigh, Essex, England.
Bruton Gallery Limited, Bruton, Somerset, England.
Bruton Knowles & Co, Gloucester, Gloucestershire, England.
Bruton-Brighton, Brighton & Hove, E.Sussex, England.
N.Bryan-Peach Antiques, Wymeswold, Leicestershire, England.
D.Bryden Antiques, Stow-on-the-Wold, Gloucestershire, England.
Bryers Antiques, Bath, Avon, England.
Buck & Payne Antiques, London, England.
Buckie's Jewellers, Valuers & Silversmiths, Cambridge, Cambridgeshire, England.
C.W.Buckingham, Cadnam, Hampshire, England.
C.W.Buckingham, London, England.
James Buckingham, Burgess Hill, W.Sussex, England.
Lorraine Buckland, London, England.
Evelyn Buckle, Redmile, Leicestershire, England.
Bucks House Antiques, Chalfont St Giles, Buckinghamshire, England.
Bude Antiques, Bude, Cornwall, England.
Bugatti, Bromley, Kent, England.
Bugle Antiques, Chipping Norton, Oxfordshire, England.
Audrey Bull, Tenby, Dyfed, Wales.

John Bull (Antiques) Ltd, London, England.
Walter Bull & Son (Cirencester) Ltd, Cirencester, Gloucestershire, England.
Bullivant Antiques, Bury St Edmunds, Suffolk, England.
Tony Bunzl & Zal Davar, London, England.
Clive A. Burden Ltd, Rickmansworth, Hertfordshire, England.
Clive A.Burden Ltd, London, England.
Bures Antiques, Bures, Suffolk, England.
The Burford Gallery, Burford, Oxfordshire, England.
H.& M.J.Burke, Worsley, Greater Manchester, England.
David Burkinshaw Antique Desks, Lindfield, W.Sussex, England.
Burlington Fine Arts, Feltham, Middlesex, England.
The Burlington Gallery, London, England.
Burlington Paintings, London, England.
W.G.T.Burne (Antique Glass) Ltd, London, England.
Victor Burness, London, England.
L.& G.Burnett, London, England.
Jean Burnett Antiques, Finedon, Northamptonshire, England.
Burns & Graham, Winchester, Hampshire, England.
David E. Burrows, Quorn, Leicestershire, England.
Sally Burt Antiques, Newton, Nottinghamshire, England.
A.Burton-Garbett, Morden, Surrey, England.
The Bury Street Gallery, London, England.
M.W. Bush, Bishop's Stortford, Hertfordshire, England.
Bushwood Antiques, London, England.
Business Art Galleries & The Upstairs Gallery, London, England.
Butchoff Antiques, London, England.
Butler & Wilson, London, England.
Edward Butler, Dublin, Co Dublin, Eire.
Robin Butler, Bristol, Avon, England.
Roderick P.Butler, Honiton, Devon, England.
Anthony Butt Antiques, Baldock, Hertfordshire, England.
Butterfields, Ilkley, W.Yorkshire, England.
Butterwalk House, Totnes, Devon, England.
The Button Queen, London, England.
Christopher J. Button-Stephens, Honiton, Devon, England.
Gerald Buxton Gooding - Lapworth Clocks, Lapworth, Warwickshire, England.
Caroline Buxton Interiors, Brighton & Hove, E.Sussex, England.
Helen Buxton Antiques, London, England.
Ann Bye Antiques, Reading, Berkshire, England.
Bygone, London, England.
Bygone Days, Tiverton, Devon, England.
Bygones, Ventnor, Isle of Wight, England.
Bygones, Charing, Kent, England.
Bygones, Sidcup, Kent, England.
Bygones, Benson, Oxfordshire, England.
Bygones, Huddersfield, W.Yorkshire, England.
Bygones of Debenham, Debenham, Suffolk, England.
Bygones of Worcester, Worcester, Hereford & Worcester, England.
Robert Byles, Bampton, Devon, England.
BBC Antiques, Polegate, E.Sussex, England.

C.C.A.W. Ltd, Haverhill, Suffolk, England.
C.P.A. Antiques, Bishops Waltham, Hampshire, England.
Caboodle Ltd, London, England.
Cadogan Gallery, London, England.
Caelt Gallery, London, England.
Caernarfon Antiques, Caernarvon, Gwynedd, Wales.
Ian Caldwell, Tadworth, Surrey, England.
Tom Caldwell Galleries Ltd, Belfast, Belfast, Northern Ireland.
Calton Gallery, Edinburgh, Lothian, Scotland.
Calver Associates, Newton Abbot, Devon, England.
Cambridge Fine Art Ltd, Cambridge, Cambridgeshire, England.
David Cambridge, Cheltenham, Gloucestershire, England.
Camden Antique Market, London, England.
Camden Auctions, London, England.
Camden Passage Antiques Market, London, England.
Camel Antiques, Wadebridge, Cornwall, England.
Camelot Antiques, Hailsham, E.Sussex, England.
Cameo Antiques, Cheltenham, Gloucestershire, England.
Cameo Corner at Liberty, London, England.
Camerer Cuss & Co, London, England.
Peter Cameron, London, England.
Campbell Walchli Antiques Ltd, Midhurst, W.Sussex, England.
Colin Campbell Fine Paintings, Cowes, Isle of Wight, England.
Colin Campbell Fine Paintings, Yarmouth, Isle of Wight, England.
Duncan Campbell, Battle, E.Sussex, England.
Gerard Campbell, Lechlade, Gloucestershire, England.
John Campbell Picture Frames Ltd, London, England.
Meg Campbell, Southampton, Hampshire, England.
Robert A.Campbell, Glasgow, Strathclyde, Scotland.
Candle Lane Books, Shrewsbury, Shropshire, England.
The Candover Gallery, Alresford, Hampshire, England.
Canonbury Antiques Ltd, London, England.
Capes Dunn & Co, Manchester, Greater Manchester, England.
Ann Capon Antiques, Castleton, Derbyshire, England.
Patric Capon, London, England.
Capricorn Collections, Blackpool, Lancashire, England.
The Cardigan Book Centre, Cardigan, Dyfed, Wales.
Tony Cardy, Kenninghall, Norfolk, England.
Cariss Residential, Birmingham, W.Midlands, England.
Michael Carleton, London, England.
J Carlton-Smith, London, England.
Peter Carmichael, Brighton & Hove, E.Sussex, England.
R.P. Carmichael & Co.Ltd, Hull, Humberside, England.
Carnival Antiques, Bristol, Avon, England.
Carousel Antiques, Darlington, Durham, England.
Harry Carr Antiques, Washington, Tyne & Wear, England.
Carrington & Co Ltd, London, England.
P.Carrington, Clare, Suffolk, England.
David Carritt Limited, London, England.
E.Carrol (Fine Arts), Bingley, W.Yorkshire, England.
Carronade, Glasgow, Strathclyde, Scotland.
Carse Antiques, Rait, by Perth, Tayside, Scotland.
Carshalton Antiques Galleries, Carshalton, Surrey, England.
The Carson Clark Gallery, Edinburgh, Lothian, Scotland.
Jan Carter, Hartpury, Gloucestershire, England.
Roy Carter Antiques, Calne, Wiltshire, England.
Simon Carter Gallery, Woodbridge, Suffolk, England.
Olwen Carthew, London, England.
Cartographia Ltd, London, England.
Cartwright & Co, Craven Arms, Shropshire, England.
Carvers & Gilders, London, England.
G. & E. Cashmore Antiques, Chipping Norton, Oxfordshire, England.
Jack Casimir Ltd, London, England.
J. & J. Caspall Antiques, Stow-on-the-Wold, Gloucestershire, England.
Edward Cassassa, Ashburton, Devon, England.
Cassio, London, England.
Casson Gallery, London, England.
Castaside, London, England.
Castle Antiques, Cheltenham, Gloucestershire, England.
Castle Antiques, Rochester, Kent, England.
Castle Antiques, Clitheroe, Lancashire, England.
Castle Antiques, Newark-on-Trent, Nottinghamshire, England.
Castle Antiques, Orford, Suffolk, England.
Castle Antiques, Peel, Isle of Man.
Castle Antiques, Edinburgh, Lothian, Scotland.
Castle Bookshop, Colchester, Essex, England.
Castle Galleries, Hinckley, Leicestershire, England.
Castle Galleries, Salisbury, Wiltshire, England.
Castle Gallery, Berkhamsted, Hertfordshire, England.
Castle Gallery, Lincoln, Lincolnshire, England.
Castle Gate Antique Centre, Newark-on-Trent, Nottinghamshire, England.
Castle Lodge, Ludlow, Shropshire, England.
Simon Castle, London, England.
D.B.Cater Antiques, London, England.
Paul Cater Antiques, Moreton-in-Marsh, Gloucestershire, England.
Catspa, London, England.
R.G.Cave & Sons Ltd, Ludlow, Shropshire, England.
Cave's of Northampton, Northampton, Northamptonshire, England.
Cavendish Rare Books Ltd, London, England.
Odile Cavendish, London, England.
Rupert Cavendish Antiques, London, England.
Elizabeth Cayzer Fine Art, London, England.
Cedar Antiques, Hartley Wintney, Hampshire, England.
Celia Charlotte's, Lewes, E.Sussex, England.
Centaur Gallery, London, England.
Centre Crafts, Coventry, W.Midlands, England.
Century Antiques, Warminster, Wiltshire, England.
The Ceramic Book Co, Newport, Gwent, Wales.
Cerne Antiques, Cerne Abbas, Dorset, England.
Ch-Art, Colyton, Devon, England.
The Chair Shop, Tunbridge Wells, Kent, England.
The Chair Shop, Oxted, Surrey, England.
Chalon Ltd, Curry Rivel, Somerset, England.
Christina Chance Antiques, Chester, Cheshire, England.
Chancellors Hollingsworths, Ascot, Berkshire, England.
Chancery Antiques, Tiverton, Devon, England.
Chancery Antiques, Thrapston, Northamptonshire, England.
Chancery Antiques Ltd, London, England.
Chancery Antiques Ltd, London, England.
Chanctonbury Antiques, Washington, W.Sussex, England.
Chandeliers, London, England.
Chandlers, Bideford, Devon, England.
Chandos Books, Barnet, Hertfordshire, England.
Chanteau, London, England.
Chantry Book Shop, Dartmouth, Devon, England.
Chantry House Antiques, Stow-on-the-Wold, Gloucestershire, England.
Chapel Antiques, Glossop, Derbyshire, England.
Chapel Antiques, St Leonards, E.Sussex, England.
Chapel Antiques, Whatlington, E.Sussex, England.
Chapel Place Antiques, Tunbridge Wells, Kent, England.
D.J. Chapman & Son (Antiques), Evesham, Hereford & Worcester, England.
H.C.Chapman & Son, Scarborough, N.Yorkshire, England.
Mark Chapman Antiques, Petworth, W.Sussex, England.
Peter Chapman Antiques, London, England.
K.Chappell Antiques & Fine Art, Bakewell, Derbyshire, England.
K.Chappell Antiques & Fine Art, Baslow, Derbyshire, England.
Graham Charge Antiques, London, England.
Charisma Antiques Trade Warehouse, Hoyland, S.Yorkshire, England.
Charles Antiques, Romsey, Hampshire, England.
Charles International Antiques, Maidstone, Kent, England.
Charles St Antiques, Newport, Gwent, Wales.
Stephen Charles Antiques, Leigh-on-Sea, Essex, England.
Angela Charlesworth, Barnsley, S.Yorkshire, England.
E.&N.R.Charlton, Middlesbrough, Cleveland, England.
Charnwood Antiques, Coalville, Leicestershire, England.
Charterhouse Antiques, Heath and Reach, Bedfordshire, England.
Charterhouse Antiques, Teignmouth, Devon, England.
Chatal Limited, London, England.
Chateau Briand Antique Centre, Burwash, E.Sussex, England.
The Chater-House Gallery, Long Melford, Suffolk, England.
Chattels, Callington, Cornwall, England.
Chattels, Brighton & Hove, E.Sussex, England.
Chattels, Woking, Surrey, England.
Chaucer Fine Arts Inc, London, England.
John Chawner, Chatham, Kent, England.
Checker Books, Abingdon, Oxfordshire, England.
Cheffins, Grain and Chalk, Cambridge, Cambridgeshire, England.
Chelmsford Antiques and Collectors Market, Chelmsford, Essex, England.
Chelmsford Auction Rooms, Chelmsford, Essex, England.
Chelsea Antique Fairs, London, England.

Chelsea Antique Market, London, England.
Chelsea Clocks, London, England.
Chelsea Clocks & Antiques, London, England.
Chelsea House Antiques, Stowmarket, Suffolk, England.
Chelsea Rare Books, London, England.
Cheltenham Antique Centre, Cheltenham, Gloucestershire, England.
Cheltenham Antique Market, Cheltenham, Gloucestershire, England.
Cheltenham Spa Restorations, Cheltenham, Gloucestershire, England.
Chenil Galleries, London, England.
Chepstow Antiques, Chepstow, Gwent, Wales.
Cherry Antiques, Hemel Hempstead, Hertfordshire, England.
Peter Cherry Antiques, St Peter Port, Guernsey, Channel Islands.
Cherub Antiques, Wells, Somerset, England.
E.M. Cheshire Antiques, Bingham, Nottinghamshire, England.
Chess Antiques, Chesham, Buckinghamshire, England.
The Chest of Drawers, Tetbury, Gloucestershire, England.
Chester Antiques, Chester, Cheshire, England.
Chester Furniture Cave, Chester, Cheshire, England.
Chesterfield Antiques Centre, Chesterfield, Derbyshire, England.
Chesterfields Etc., London, England.
Margaret Chesterton, St Austell, Cornwall, England.
Chestnut Gallery, Bourton-on-the-Water, Gloucestershire, England.
Cheverton's of Edenbridge Ltd, Edenbridge, Kent, England.
Chi Mei Chai Eastern Art Gallery, London, England.
S.G.Child & Son, Smeeth, Kent, England.
Chilham Art Galleries, Chilham, Kent, England.
Chilstone Architectural Ornaments, Horsmonden, Kent, England.
The Chimes, Reepham, Norfolk, England.
China Doll, Cheltenham, Gloucestershire, England.
The China Hen, Bradford-on-Avon, Wiltshire, England.
The China Locker, Lamberhurst, Kent, England.
China Repairers, London, England.
Chislehurst Antiques, Chislehurst, Kent, England.
Chloe Antiques, Worthing, W.Sussex, England.
Chobham Antiques Market, Chobham, Surrey, England.
Chriscotts Antiques, St Boswells, Borders, Scotland.
J.Christie, London, England.
Christie, Manson and Woods Ltd, Downpatrick, Co Down, Northern Ireland.
S.E. Christie - Antiques, Macclesfield, Cheshire, England.
Christie's, St Helier, Jersey, Channel Islands.
Christie's, Glin, Co Limerick, Eire.
Christie's, Peterborough, Cambridgeshire, England.
Christie's, St Austell, Cornwall, England.
Christie's, Penrith, Cumbria, England.
Christie's, Plymouth, Devon, England.
Christie's, Dorchester, Dorset, England.
Christie's, Cheltenham, Gloucestershire, England.
Christie's, Dartford, Kent, England.
Christie's, York, N.Yorkshire, England.
Christie's, Norwich, Norfolk, England.
Christie's, Corbridge, Northumberland, England.
Christie's, Bridgnorth, Shropshire, England.
Christie's, Templecombe, Somerset, England.
Christie's, Horsham, W.Sussex, England.
Christie's, London, England.
Christie's, Inverurie, Grampian, Scotland.
Christie's, Fearn, Highland, Scotland.
Christie's, Edinburgh, Lothian, Scotland.
Christie's, Inveraray, Strathclyde, Scotland.
Christie's, Maybole, Strathclyde, Scotland.
Christie's, Killiecrankie, Tayside, Scotland.
Christie's, Presteigne, Powys, Wales.
Christie's in the City, London, England.
Christie's Contemporary Art, London, England.
Christie's Robson Lowe, Bournemouth, Dorset, England.
Christie's Scotland, Glasgow, Strathclyde, Scotland.
Christie's South Kensington, London, England.
Chrystals Auctions, Douglas, Isle of Man.
Church End Antiques, Great Dunmow, Essex, England.
Church House Antiques, Weybridge, Surrey, England.
Church Street Antiques, Market Deeping, Lincolnshire, England.
Church Street Antiques, Hadleigh, Suffolk, England.
Church Street Galleries, London, England.
The Church Street Gallery, Saffron Walden, Essex, England.
Church View Antiques, Harrogate, N.Yorkshire, England.
Church View House Antiques, Kirk Michael, Isle of Man.
Churchill Antique Galleries Ltd, Guildford, Surrey, England.
The Churchill Group of Companies, New Milton, Hampshire, England.
Ciancimino Ltd, London, England.
The Cider House Galleries Ltd, Bletchingley, Surrey, England.
Circa Antiques, Chipping Campden, Gloucestershire, England.
Circa Fine Art, Plymouth, Devon, England.
Cirencester Antique Market, Cirencester, Gloucestershire, England.
Cirencester Antiques Ltd, Cirencester, Gloucestershire, England.
Cirencester Workshops, Cirencester, Gloucestershire, England.
City Clocks, London, England.
City Fine Arts, London, England.
Cladgild Ltd, Reach, Cambridgeshire, England.
Claisabhrea Antiques, Dingwall, Highland, Scotland.
The Clare Collector, Clare, Suffolk, England.
Clare Gallery, Tunbridge Wells, Kent, England.
Clarence House Antiques, Watton, Norfolk, England.
Clarendon Gallery, Manchester, Greater Manchester, England.
Clarendon Gallery, London, England.
Clarges Gallery, London, England.
Annarella Clark Antiques, Stow-on-the-Wold, Gloucestershire, England.
David Clark, Selborne, Hampshire, England.
Elias Clark Antiques Ltd, Bletchingley, Surrey, England.
Gerald Clark Antiques Ltd, London, England.
Herbert Clark, Moretonhampstead, Devon, England.
Malcolm G.Clark, Cambridge, Cambridgeshire, England.
Peter Clark Antiques, Birmingham, W.Midlands, England.
Clarke Fine Art, London, England.
Christopher Clarke, Stow-on-the-Wold, Gloucestershire, England.
'larke's Antiques (Camberley), Camberley, Surrey, England.
Classey Ltd, Faringdon, Oxfordshire, England.
Classic Furniture Ltd, Newport, Shropshire, England.
John Clay, London, England.
Ian Clayton Ltd, London, England.
William Clayton Ltd, London, England.
Clement House Antiques, Burford, Oxfordshire, England.
James W. Clements, Carlisle, Cumbria, England.
The Clerkenwell Green Association for Craftsmen, London, England.
A. Clewlow (Books), York, N.Yorkshire, England.
Cliffe Antiques Centre, Lewes, E.Sussex, England.
Clifton Antiques Ltd, Bristol, Avon, England.
Clifton Antiques Market, Bristol, Avon, England.
Clifton Books, Wigan, Greater Manchester, England.
Clifton Fine Art, London, England.
Clifton House Antiques, Haslingden, Lancashire, England.
Clinkers Antiques Ltd, Petersfield, Hampshire, England.
Bryan Clisby - Antique Clocks, Hartley Wintney, Hampshire, England.
Clock Clinic Ltd, London, England.
The Clock Shop, Topsham, Devon, England.
The Clock Shop, Hoylake, Merseyside, England.
The Clock Shop, Weybridge, Surrey, England.
The Clock Shop St Albans, St Albans, Hertfordshire, England.
Clock Tower Antiques, Newmarket, Suffolk, England.
Clockshop Antiques, Faversham, Kent, England.
Close Antiques, Winchester, Hampshire, England.
Henry H.Close, Abergavenny, Gwent, Wales.
Cloud Hill Antiques, Cheltenham, Gloucestershire, England.
Clunes Antiques, London, England.
The Coach House, Old Costessey, Norfolk, England.
Coach House Antiques, Wisbech, Cambridgeshire, England.
Coach House Antiques, Canterbury, Kent, England.
Coach House Antiques, Whitby, N.Yorkshire, England.
Coach House Antiques, Bradford, W.Yorkshire, England.
Coach House Antiques Ltd, Perth, Tayside, Scotland.
Coakley & Hayter, London, England.
Joan Coates, Malvern, Hereford & Worcester, England.
Cobb Antiques Ltd, London, England.
Cobblers Hall Antiques, Toddington, Bedfordshire, England.
Cobbs, Burrows & Day, Ashford, Kent, England.
Cobra & Bellamy, London, England.
Fergus Cochrane Antiques, London, England.
Cockermouth Antique Market, Cockermouth, Cumbria, England.
Cocozza Antiques, London, England.
Codex Art Ltd, Tonbridge, Kent, England.
Peter Coe Fine Paintings, Shepton Mallet, Somerset, England.
Coexistence, Bath, Avon, England.
Coexistence Limited, London, England.
Coexistence Limited, London, England.
Coggeshall Antiques, Coggeshall, Essex, England.
Ray Coggins Antiques, Frome, Somerset, England.
Ray Coggins Antiques, Bradford-on-Avon, Wiltshire, England.
Cohen and Pearce (Oriental Porcelain), London, England.
B.Cohen & Sons, London, England.
Edward Cohen, London, England.
Moira Cohen Ltd, London, England.
The Coin & Stamp Centre, Colchester, Essex, England.
Coin Exchange, London, England.
Cold Bath Antiques, Harrogate, N.Yorkshire, England.
Coldstream Antiques, Coldstream, Borders, Scotland.
Christopher Cole (Fine Paintings) Ltd, Beaconsfield, Buckinghamshire, England.
Colefax & Fowler, London, England.
Aubrey J.Coleman Antiques, London, England.
Nigel Coleman Antiques, Brasted, Kent, England.
Robin and Jan Coleman Antiques, Bath, Avon, England.
Simon Coleman, London, England.
Coleridge, London, England.
Collards Bookshop, Totnes, Devon, England.
Philip Colleck Ltd, London, England.
Collectables, London, England.
Collection, Ledbury, Hereford & Worcester, England.
Collector Corner, Northallerton, N.Yorkshire, England.
The Collector & The Collector (Restorations), Barnard Castle, Durham, England.
Collector's Corner, Bradford, W.Yorkshire, England.
Collectors Cases, Alton, Hampshire, England.
Collectors Centre, Shanklin, Isle of Wight, England.
Collectors Corner, London, England.
Collectors Corner - Militaria, London, England.
The Collectors Gallery, Caversham, Berkshire, England.
Collectors Market, Cambridge, Cambridgeshire, England.
Collectors Old Toys and Antiques, Halifax, W.Yorkshire, England.
Collectors Shop, Hungerford, Berkshire, England.
The Collectors Trail, Indian Queens, Cornwall, England.
Collectors Treasures, Wendover, Buckinghamshire, England.
Collectors' Corner, Waddesdon, Buckinghamshire, England.
College Gateway Bookshop, Ipswich, Suffolk, England.
Colleton House Gallery, Bath, Avon, England.
Mark Collier, Fordingbridge, Hampshire, England.
Margerie Collinge Gallery, Ashburton, Devon, England.
John H. Collings, Banwell, Avon, England.
Collingwood of Bond Street, London, England.
Julie Collino, London, England.
Collins & Clark, Cambridge, Cambridgeshire, England.
F.G. & C. Collins Ltd (Collins Antiques), Wheathampstead, Hertfordshire, England.

Frank Collins, Weston, Suffolk, England.
Frank Collins, London, England.
Isabelle Collins Antiques, London, England.
J. Collins and Son (Est.1953), Bideford, Devon, England.
Jimmy Collins Antiques Ltd, Wigan, Greater Manchester, England.
Joan Collins, London, England.
Mary Collins Furniture Ltd, Greenfield, Bedfordshire, England.
Peter Collins, London, England.
Sylvia Collins, London, England.
Cecilia Colman Gallery, London, England.
Colman's of Hexham, Saleroom and Antique Fair, Hexham, Northumberland, England.
Colmore Galleries Ltd, Henley-in-Arden, Warwickshire, England.
Colnaghi and Simon, London, England.
P. & D. Colnaghi & Co Ltd, London, England.
Coltishall Antiques Centre, Coltishall, Norfolk, England.
Coltsfoot Gallery, Leominster, Hereford & Worcester, England.
Combe Cottage Antiques, Castle Combe, Wiltshire, England.
Comins, Ely, Cambridgeshire, England.
O. Comitti & Son Ltd, London, England.
Commemoratives, London, England.
Commin's Bookshop, Bournemouth, Dorset, England.
Compton Antiques, Brighton & Hove, E.Sussex, England.
Compton-Dando (Fine Arts) Ltd, Earls Colne, Essex, England.
Compton-Dando (Fine Arts) Ltd, Long Melford, Suffolk, England.
Connaught Brown PLC, London, England.
Connaught Galleries, London, England.
The Connoisseur Gallery, London, England.
The Connoisseur, Manchester, Greater Manchester, England.
Contemporary Textile Gallery, London, England.
E.J.Cook & Son Antiques, Gloucester, Gloucestershire, England.
R.L.Cook, Devizes, Wiltshire, England.
S.A.Cook & Son, London, England.
Cooke Antiques, Dublin, Co Dublin, Eire.
David Cooke Fine Paintings, Rye, E.Sussex, England.
Mary Cooke Antiques Ltd, London, England.
Coombe House Antiques, Lewes, E.Sussex, England.
R. & D. Coombes, London, England.
Cooper of Dundee (Furniture) Ltd, Dundee, Tayside, Scotland.
Cooper-Hirst, Chelmsford, Essex, England.
A.C.Cooper Ltd, London, England.
E. & R. Cooper, Great Missenden, Buckinghamshire, England.
E. Cooper Antiques, Gosport, Hampshire, England.
Eileen Cooper Antiques, Braunton, Devon, England.
J.H. Cooper & Son (Ilkley) Ltd, Ilkley, W.Yorkshire, England.
Leon Cooper Antiques, Batley, W.Yorkshire, England.
Belinda Coote Antiques, London, England.
Coppelia Antiques, Plumley, Cheshire, England.
Copper Kettle Antiques, Watford, Hertfordshire, England.
Copperfield Antiques, Loughborough, Leicestershire, England.
Robert Copperfield Antiques, Macclesfield, Cheshire, England.
Copperfields, Sidmouth, Devon, England.
Geo Copsey & Co Ltd, Romford, Essex, England.
Coracle Press, London, England.
Corbitt's of Clayton Street, Newcastle upon Tyne, Tyne & Wear, England.
Cordell Antiques, Ipswich, Suffolk, England.
Corfield of Lymington, Lymington, Hampshire, England.
John Corlyon (Furniture) Ltd, Burstwick, Humberside, England.
Corner Antiques, Coltishall, Norfolk, England.
Corner Cottage Antiques, Leicester, Leicestershire, England.
The Corner Cupboard, Boxford, Suffolk, England.
The Corner Cupboard, London, England.
Corner House Antiques, Newark-on-Trent, Nottinghamshire, England.
Corner House Antiques, Glasgow, Strathclyde, Scotland.
The Corner House Gallery, Axbridge, Somerset, England.
The Corner Shop, Hay-on-Wye, Hereford & Worcester, England.
Laurence Corner, Euston Gallery, London, England.
Corney House Antiques, Penrith, Cumbria, England.
Derek Cornwell, Bristol, Avon, England.
Corridor Antiques and Perdy's Junk Shop, Lichfield, Staffordshire, England.
Corrigan Antiques, Kilbarchan, Strathclyde, Scotland.
Cosmo Antiques (inc Jolie Jewellery), Westerham, Kent, England.
Costessey House Antiques, Old Costessey, Norfolk, England.
Cotham Books, Bristol, Avon, England.
Cotham Galleries, Bristol, Avon, England.
Cotham Hill Antiques, Bristol, Avon, England.
Cotswold Curios, Stroud, Gloucestershire, England.
Cotswold Galleries, Stow-on-the-Wold, Gloucestershire, England.
Cottage Antiques, Bristol, Avon, England.
Cottage Antiques, Cambridge, Cambridgeshire, England.
Cottage Antiques, Altrincham, Greater Manchester, England.
Cottage Antiques, Harrogate, N.Yorkshire, England.
Cottage Antiques, Harrogate, N.Yorkshire, England.
Cottage Antiques, Standlake, Oxfordshire, England.
Cottage Antiques, Cardiff, S.Glamorgan, Wales.
Cottage Antiques (Bollington) Ltd, Burton upon Trent, Staffordshire, England.
S.W. Cottee & Son, Wareham, Dorset, England.
Anthony Cotton, Lincoln, Lincolnshire, England.
Joan Cotton Antiques, Nottingham, Nottinghamshire, England.
Andrew Cottrell Galleries, Godalming, Surrey, England.
Coughton Galleries Ltd, Alcester, Warwickshire, England.
Thomas Coulborn & Sons, Sutton Coldfield, W.Midlands, England.
Country Antique Market, Leominster, Hereford & Worcester, England.
Country Antiques, Boroughbridge, N.Yorkshire, England.
Country Antiques, Long Melford, Suffolk, England.
Country Antiques, Killearn, Strathclyde, Scotland.
Country Antiques, Kidwelly, Dyfed, Wales.
Country Bygones, Stoke-by-Nayland, Suffolk, England.
Country Cottage Bedsteads, Andover, Hampshire, England.
Country Cottage Interiors, Leek, Staffordshire, England.
The Country Furniture Shop, Penn, Buckinghamshire, England.
Country House Antiques, Bungay, Suffolk, England.
Country Interiors, Bradford-on-Avon, Wiltshire, England.
Country Life Antiques, Stow-on-the-Wold, Gloucestershire, England.
Country Life Antiques, Stow-on-the-Wold, Gloucestershire, England.
Country Life Antiques, Market Rasen, Lincolnshire, England.
Country Pine & Antiques, Sherborne, Dorset, England.
County Antiques, Dorchester, Dorset, England.
County Antiques Centre, Ilminster, Somerset, England.
County Auctions, Leicester, Leicestershire, England.
Courcoux and Courcoux, Salisbury, Wiltshire, England.
The Court Gallery, East Molesey, Surrey, England.
Courtney Beer, Brixham, Devon, England.
Richard Courtney Ltd, London, England.
William Courtney & Sons, Birkenhead, Merseyside, England.
Courts Miscellany, Leominster, Hereford & Worcester, England.
Courtville Antiques, Dublin, Co Dublin, Eire.
Courtville Antiques, Tipperary, Co Tipperary, Eire.
Courtyard Antiques, Hitchin, Hertfordshire, England.
E.W.Cousins & Son, Ixworth, Suffolk, England.
Paul Couts Ltd, Edinburgh, Lothian, Scotland.
Philip Cowan Antiques, Liverpool, Merseyside, England.
Timothy Coward Fine Silver, Braunton, Devon, England.
Cowden Antiques, Tunbridge Wells, Kent, England.
John Cowderoy Antiques (The Musical Box Centre), Eastbourne, E.Sussex, England.
Heather Cowley Bookshop & Galleries, Nottingham, Nottinghamshire, England.
Ian H.R.Cowley, Sandiacre, Derbyshire, England.
Danny Cox, Cheltenham, Gloucestershire, England.
O.M. & R.D.Cox Antiques, Stamford, Lincolnshire, England.
Ralph Cox, London, England.
Coxsmith UK, Gillingham, Kent, England.
Coyle Fine Art, Dublin, Co Dublin, Eire.
R.O. & F. Coyle, London, England.
Nigel Cracknell Antiques Ltd, Marlborough, Wiltshire, England.
Craddock & Barnard, London, England.
Cradlewell Antiques, Newcastle upon Tyne, Tyne & Wear, England.
Crafers Antiques, Wickham Market, Suffolk, England.
Craft Centre, Manchester, Greater Manchester, England.
Crafts Council Shop, V & A, London, England.
The Craftsman, Hungerford, Berkshire, England.
The Craftsmen Potters Shop, London, England.
Brian & Caroline Craik Ltd, Bath, Avon, England.
Cranbourn Antiques Ltd. (Artinterias), London, England.
Cranbrook Antiques, Cranbrook, Kent, England.
The Crane Gallery, London, England.
Crane Kalman Gallery, London, England.
Cranford Galleries, Knutsford, Cheshire, England.
Joane Crarer Antiques, Tetbury, Gloucestershire, England.
Crawford & Pawle Ltd, London, England.
Crawford-Holden, Bath, Avon, England.
Lesley Craze, London, England.
Tony & Iris Cremer-Price, London, England.
Crescent Antiques, London, England.
Crescent Furniture Stores, London, England.
Crest Antiques, London, England.
Crewkerne Furniture Emporium, Crewkerne, Somerset, England.
John Crichton, London, England.
M. & A. Cringle, Burnham Market, Norfolk, England.
J. Crisp & Son, London, England.
Crispin Antiques, Amersham, Buckinghamshire, England.
Thomas Crispin, Winchelsea, E.Sussex, England.
Croft Antiques, Bridport, Dorset, England.
John Croft Antiques, Bath, Avon, England.
Geoffrey Crofts Limited, Leominster, Hereford & Worcester, England.
Peter A. Crofts, Wisbech, Cambridgeshire, England.
David Crook Antiques, Brighton & Hove, E.Sussex, England.
Crosby Books, Forest Row, E.Sussex, England.
Cross Hayes Antiques, Malmesbury, Wiltshire, England.
David Cross Gallery, Bristol, Avon, England.
Edward Cross Fine Paintings, Weybridge, Surrey, England.
Crossbow Antiques, Hastings, E.Sussex, England.
Crossbow House Antiques, High Blantyre, Strathclyde, Scotland.
Thomas Crowe, Norwich, Norfolk, England.
Crowther of Syon Lodge, Isleworth, Middlesex, England.
T.Crowther & Son Ltd, London, England.
The Crypt Antiques, Burford, Oxfordshire, England.
Csaky's Antiques, London, England.
Cubitt & West Fine Art Auctioneers, Guildford, Surrey, England.
Cull Antiques, Petersfield, Hampshire, England.
C.T.Culverwell, Burnham-on-Sea, Somerset, England.
Cumbria Antiques, Kendal, Cumbria, England.
Cumbrian Fine Art Galleries, Kirkby Lonsdale, Cumbria, England.
Prudence Cuming Associates Ltd, London, England.
The Cupboard Antiques, Amersham, Buckinghamshire, England.
Cura Antiques, London, England.
Curio Shop, Teignmouth, Devon, England.
Curios, St Anne's, Lancashire, England.
Curiosities, Lancing, W.Sussex, England.
Curiosity, Newark-on-Trent, Nottinghamshire, England.
The Curiosity Shop, Padstow, Cornwall, England.
The Curiosity Shop, South Shields, Tyne & Wear, England.

The Curiosity Shop, Kelso, Borders, Scotland.
The Curiosity Shop, Llandovery, Dyfed, Wales.
George Curtis, Cheltenham, Gloucestershire, England.
Curwen Gallery, London, England.
Cutler Street Antique Market, London, England.

D.J.Jewellery, Poole, Dorset, England.
R. D'Alessandro, London, England.
D'Amico Antiques Ltd, Norwich, Norfolk, England.
Anthony d'Offay Gallery, London, England.
Dacre, Son & Hartley, Ilkley, W.Yorkshire, England.
Daedalus, London, England.
Dale End Antiques, Telford, Shropshire, England.
John Dale Antiques, London, England.
Peter Dale Ltd, London, England.
Daleside Antiques, Harrogate, N.Yorkshire, England.
Anthony Dallas & Sons Ltd, London, England.
Dalton Peett Antiques, London, England.
Dam Mill Antiques, Wolverhampton, W.Midlands, England.
Andrew Dando, Bath, Avon, England.
Daneby House Antiques, Priors Marston, Warwickshire, England.
Mavis Daniel Antiques, Thorpe Arch, W.Yorkshire, England.
Daniels House Antiques, Beaminster, Dorset, England.
H.Danker, Dublin, Co Dublin, Eire.
Clifford Dann Auction Galleries, Lewes, E.Sussex, England.
Michael Danny, Bath, Avon, England.
M.J.Dareau, Edinburgh, Lothian, Scotland.
The Darenth Bookshop, Otford, Kent, England.
Graham Dark, Flushing, Cornwall, England.
Dartington Cider Press Centre, Dartington, Devon, England.
Zal Davar, London, England.
Anne Davenport Antiques, Salisbury, Wiltshire, England.
Antony Davenport, Faringdon, Oxfordshire, England.
Leslie Davey Antiques, Sale, Greater Manchester, England.
David & Charles, Newton Abbot, Devon, England.
D. & D. Lee, Southwold, Suffolk, England.
David John Ceramics, Eynsham, Oxfordshire, England.
G.David, Cambridge, Cambridgeshire, England.
David, Jean & John Antiques, Westcliff-on-Sea, Essex, England.
Eric Davidson (Antiques) Ltd, Edinburgh, Lothian, Scotland.
Arthur Davidson Ltd, London, England.
Michael Davidson Antiques, London, England.
Richard Davidson, Petworth, W.Sussex, England.
Davidson's The Jewellers, Newcastle upon Tyne, Tyne & Wear, England.
Davies Antiques, Whalley, Lancashire, England.
Davies Antiques, London, England.
Davies Antiques, Chepstow, Gwent, Wales.
Barry Davies Oriental Art, London, England.
Colin Davies Antiques International, Stafford, Staffordshire, England.
J.M.Davies (Jewellers) Ltd, London, England.
John Davies (Fine Paintings), Stow-on-the-Wold, Gloucestershire, England.
John Davies Framing Ltd, London, England.
K.A.Davies Antiques, Cardiff, S.Glamorgan, Wales.
Pamela Davies, York, N.Yorkshire, England.
Davies, Turner & Co Ltd, Liverpool, Merseyside, England.
Davies's, Bridgend, Mid Glamorgan, Wales.
N.Davighi, London, England.
Davis & Sons, Chepstow, Gwent, Wales.
A.B.Davis Ltd, London, England.
John E. Davis Antiques, Reading, Berkshire, England.
Edgar Davis Antiques, Worcester, Hereford & Worcester, England.
Jay Davis Antiques, Settle, N.Yorkshire, England.
Jesse Davis, London, England.
Kenneth Davis, London, England.
Reginald Davis (Oxford) Ltd, Oxford, Oxfordshire, England.
Roger A. Davis, Great Bookham, Surrey, England.
Dawes & Billings, Brighton & Hove, E.Sussex, England.
Daisy Dawkins Antiques, Stroud, Gloucestershire, England.
Anthony Dawson, London, England.
Caroline Dawson, London, England.
Zona Dawson Antiques, Blandford Forum, Dorset, England.
G.E.Day, Farnham, Surrey, England.
H.V. Day, Dorchester, Dorset, England.
Richard Day Ltd, London, England.
Shirley Day Ltd, London, England.
Robin de Beaumont, London, England.
Polly de Courcy-Ireland, Winchester, Hampshire, England.
De Fresnes (Antiques), Galston, Strathclyde, Scotland.
De Grey Antiques, Hull, Humberside, England.
John de Haan, Waltham Cross, Hertfordshire, England.
de Havilland Antiques, London, England.
P.G. De Lotz, London, England.
de Montfort, Robertsbridge, E.Sussex, England.
Rogers de Rin, London, England.
Deacon & Sandys, Cranbrook, Kent, England.
Gerald Deacon, Bath, Avon, England.
The Dean Gallery, Newcastle upon Tyne, Tyne & Wear, England.
Dean House Antiques, Midhurst, W.Sussex, England.
Betty Dean Antiques, Spalding, Lincolnshire, England.
David Dean Antiques, Settle, N.Yorkshire, England.
Margery Dean Antiques, Colchester, Essex, England.
Graham Deane Antiques, Brighton & Hove, E.Sussex, England.
Mike Deasy Ltd, Brighton & Hove, E.Sussex, England.
Dee & Atkinson, Driffield, Humberside, England.
Deighton Bell & Co, Cambridge, Cambridgeshire, England.
Delieb Antiques Ltd, London, England.
Marilyn Delion, London, England.
Delmas Antiques, Hurst Green, E.Sussex, England.
Delomosne & Son Ltd, London, England.
Demas, London, England.
Demetzy Books, London, England.
Den of Antiquity, Cheadle Hulme, Greater Manchester, England.
Garth Denham and Associates, Horsham, W.Sussex, England.
John Denham Gallery, London, England.
Denisa the Lady Newborough, London, England.
Denning Antiques, Guildford, Surrey, England.
Richard Dennis, London, England.
B.P. Dennison (Antiques), Ambleside, Cumbria, England.
H.P.Dennison & Son, Lewes, E.Sussex, England.
Colin Denny, London, England.
F.T. Dent, London, England.
J.Denton (Antiques), Luton, Bedfordshire, England.
Derby House Antiques, Torquay, Devon, England.
Derbyshire Antiques Ltd, Poynton, Cheshire, England.
John Derham Ltd/Earsham Hall Pine, Bungay, Suffolk, England.
Dernier & Hamlyn Ltd, London, England.
Designs on Pine, Lincoln, Lincolnshire, England.
The Desk Shop, Oxford, Oxfordshire, England.
John Desmond Antiques, Leicester, Leicestershire, England.
Kay Desmonde Antiques Ltd, London, England.
A.S.Deuchar & Son, Perth, Tayside, Scotland.
H.&W.Deutsch, London, England.
The Devonshire Gallery, Torquay, Devon, England.
Devonshire House Antiques, Bath, Avon, England.
Roderick Dew-Antiquarian Books, Eastbourne, E.Sussex, England.
John Dewar, Edinburgh, Lothian, Scotland.
Dial Antiques, Shere, Surrey, England.
Dial House Antiques, Kelvedon, Essex, England.
Diamond Antiques, Brighton & Hove, E.Sussex, England.
Diamond Mills & Co, Felixstowe, Suffolk, England.
Harry Diamond & Son, Brighton & Hove, E.Sussex, England.
Dibley Antiques, Moylegrove, Dyfed, Wales.
Dickens Curios, Frinton-on-Sea, Essex, England.
Dickens Old Curiosity Shop, London, England.
Dickenson and Thomas, Stamford, Lincolnshire, England.
Bill Dickenson, Telford, Shropshire, England.
Gillian Dickerson, Chipping Norton, Oxfordshire, England.
Dickinson Deansgreen Ltd, Manchester, Greater Manchester, England.
Bernard Dickinson Antiques, Gargrave, N.Yorkshire, England.
D. & B. Dickinson, Bath, Avon, England.
Dickinson, Davy & Markham, Brigg, Humberside, England.
Robert Dickson Antiques, London, England.
Richard Digby, London, England.
Dillon Antiques Ltd, Dublin, Co Dublin, Eire.
The Dining Room Shop, London, England.
Directmoor Ltd, Oakamoor, Staffordshire, England.
Discovery, London, England.
Diss Antiques, Diss, Norfolk, England.
Diva Antiques, Sheffield, S.Yorkshire, England.
Nimrod Dix & Company, London, England.
Dixon's Antique Centre, London, England.
J.Dobie (Antiques) Ltd, Grantham, Lincolnshire, England.
Maurice Dodd (Booksellers), Carlisle, Cumbria, England.
Peter & Daniele Dodd, London, England.
Doddington House Antiques, Doddington, Cambridgeshire, England.
Dodds Property World, Mold, Clwyd, Wales.
Dodge & Son, Sherborne, Dorset, England.
Dodo, London, England.
Dodo Antiques, St Helier, Jersey, Channel Islands.
R.C.Dodson Antiques, Southsea, Hampshire, England.
The Doll Shop, Barnard Castle, Durham, England.
Dollin & Daines Ltd, Bath, Avon, England.
The Dolls House Toys Ltd, London, England.
Dolphin Antiques, Cambridge, Cambridgeshire, England.
Dolphin Antiques, St Albans, Hertfordshire, England.
Dolphyn, Coggeshall, Essex, England.
Rene Dolton Antiques, Hemel Hempstead, Hertfordshire, England.
Philip & Bernard Dombey, London, England.
Domus, Castle Cary, Somerset, England.
Donay Antiques, London, England.
Doncaster Sales & Exchange, Doncaster, S.Yorkshire, England.
Henry Donn Galleries, Manchester, Greater Manchester, England.
Donohoe, London, England.
Jack Donovan, London, England.
Dorchester Galleries, Dorchester, Oxfordshire, England.
Dorking Antiques, Dorking, Surrey, England.
The Dorking Desk Shop, Dorking, Surrey, England.
Dormy House Antiques, Marlborough, Wiltshire, England.
Dorothy's Antiques, Sheringham, Norfolk, England.
Douwes Fine Art Ltd, London, England.
Robert Douwma Prints & Maps Ltd, London, England.
Robert Dove & Partners, Ipswich, Suffolk, England.
Doveridge House of Neachley, Shifnal, Shropshire, England.
Dowell Lloyd & Co Ltd, London, England.
Dower House Antiques, Kendal, Cumbria, England.
Iain Downe Antiques, Brighton & Hove, E.Sussex, England.
Brian & Angela Downes Antiques, Bath, Avon, England.
Peter Downing, Woodbridge, Suffolk, England.
Downshire House Antiques, Newry, Co Down, Northern Ireland.
Dragon Antiques, Petersfield, Hampshire, England.
Dragon Antiques, Harrogate, N.Yorkshire, England.
Dragons of Walton St Ltd, London, England.
Drescher Ltd, London, England.
Alec Drew Picture Frames Ltd, London, England.
Simon Drew Gallery, Dartmouth, Devon, England.
Dreweatts, Newbury, Berkshire, England.
Drian Galleries, London, England.
Driffold Gallery, Sutton Coldfield, W.Midlands, England.
Drummer Antiques, Exeter, Devon, England.
Drummer Antiques, South Molton, Devon, England.
Drummond Antiques, London, England.
William Drummond, London, England.
John Drury Rare Books Ltd, Colchester, Essex, England.
Peter Dryden Ltd, Teignmouth, Devon, England.
A.F.Drysdale, Edinburgh, Lothian, Scotland.
Dudley's Home Interiors, Reach, Cambridgeshire, England.

John Duffy, Dublin, Co Dublin, Eire.
Duits Ltd, London, England.
Hy. Duke & Son, Dorchester, Dorset, England.
Hy. Duke & Son, Weymouth, Dorset, England.
Dukeries Antiques, Tuxford, Nottinghamshire, England.
Dulverton Antique Centre, Dulverton, Somerset, England.
Duncalfe Antiques & Fine Arts, Harrogate, N.Yorkshire, England.
Dunedin Antiques Ltd, Edinburgh, Lothian, Scotland.
Dunluce Antiques, Bushmills, Co Antrim, Northern Ireland.
Dunning Antiques, Dunning, Tayside, Scotland.
John Dunphy Antiques, Limerick, Co Limerick, Eire.
Dunsdale Lodge Antiques, Westerham, Kent, England.
K.W.Dunster Antiques, Staines, Middlesex, England.
Duophone Antiques, Glasgow, Strathclyde, Scotland.
Dupont Galleries, Brighton & Hove, E.Sussex, England.
Duveen Antiques, Fordingbridge, Hampshire, England.
Dymoke House, Hawkhurst, Kent, England.
David W.Dyson, Huddersfield, W.Yorkshire, England.
Colin Dyte Exports Ltd, Highbridge, Somerset, England.

E. & A. Antiques, London, England.
E.H.W. & Co, London, England.
E.M.Lawson & Co, Didcot, Oxfordshire, England.
Eadon, Lockwood & Riddle Auctioneers, Sheffield, S.Yorkshire, England.
Eagle House, Wallingford, Oxfordshire, England.
Eagle House Antiques, Midhurst, W.Sussex, England.
Eardisley Antiques, Leominster, Hereford & Worcester, England.
Earl & Lawrence, Sleaford, Lincolnshire, England.
A.Earle, Wilton, Wiltshire, England.
Early Music Shop, Bradford, W.Yorkshire, England.
Easdens Antiques, Chislehurst, Kent, England.
East Asia Co, London, England.
East Bridgford Antiques, Aslockton, Nottinghamshire, England.
East Bridgford Antiques Centre, East Bridgford, Nottinghamshire, England.
East Kent Antiques, New Romney, Kent, England.
Eastbourne Antique Market, Eastbourne, E.Sussex, England.
Eastbourne Fine Art, Eastbourne, E.Sussex, England.
Eastgate Antique Centre, Lincoln, Lincolnshire, England.
Eastgate Antiques, Cowbridge, S.Glamorgan, Wales.
Peter Eaton (Booksellers) Ltd, London, England.
Shirley Eaton Antiques, Alderley Edge, Cheshire, England.
Eaton's of Eton Ltd, Eton, Berkshire, England.
Ebury Gallery, London, England.
Eddisons Auctioneers, Huddersfield, W.Yorkshire, England.
P. & S.N. Eddy, Leominster, Hereford & Worcester, England.
Charles Ede Ltd, London, England.
Robin and Matthew Eden, Corsham, Wiltshire, England.
Owen Edgar Gallery, London, England.
Edinburgh Antiques Market, Edinburgh, Lothian, Scotland.
Editions Graphiques Gallery, London, England.
G.H.Edkins & Son, Bishop Auckland, Durham, England.
D.H.Edmonds Ltd, Brighton & Hove, E.Sussex, England.
Andrew Edmunds, London, England.
Edward and Victoria Antiques, London, England.
The Edwardian Shop, Ipswich, Suffolk, England.
Keith D Edwards Antiques, Kendal, Cumbria, England.
Amy Egan, Skipton, N.Yorkshire, England.
Ekins, Fine Art Auctioneers, St Ives, Cambridgeshire, England.
M.Ekstein Ltd, London, England.
Eldon Worrall, Liverpool, Merseyside, England.
Eldridge London, London, England.
Edmund Eldridge Antiques, Tonbridge, Kent, England.
Electrum, London, England.
James Eley & Son, Boston, Lincolnshire, England.
Peter Eley F.S.V.A., Sidmouth, Devon, England.
Elgin Antiques, London, England.
J.G.Elias Antiques, Dorking, Surrey, England.
Eliot Antiques, Reading, Berkshire, England.
Elizabeth Antiques, Dublin, Co Dublin, Eire.
The Elizabethans, Fareham, Hampshire, England.
Colin Elliott, Cheltenham, Gloucestershire, England.
Donald Ellis Antiques, Nairn, Highland, Scotland.
Donald Ellis Antiques, Edinburgh, Lothian, Scotland.
Malcolm Ellis, Witley, Surrey, England.
Elm House Antiques, Haddington, Lothian, Scotland.
Elm Studios Ltd, Ipswich, Suffolk, England.
Elmerside Ltd, London, England.
Margaret Elmes Antiques, Denham, Buckinghamshire, England.
Elsdon Antiques, Woking, Surrey, England.
Pamela Elsom Antiques, Ashbourne, Derbyshire, England.
Emanouel Antiques Ltd, London, England.
Emerald Isle Books, Belfast, Belfast, Northern Ireland.
Emporia Antiques, Middlesbrough, Cleveland, England.
The Enchanted Aviary, Long Melford, Suffolk, England.
A.W. England & Sons, Stroud, Gloucestershire, England.
English Heritage, Bridgnorth, Shropshire, England.
English Street Furniture Company, Redhill, Surrey, England.
An Englishman's Home, Bristol, Avon, England.
L. & R. Entwistle & Co Ltd, London, England.
Epping Galleries, Epping, Essex, England.
Ermitage Ltd, London, England.
Errol Antiques, Errol, Tayside, Scotland.
Escritt & Barrell, Grantham, Lincolnshire, England.
Eskenazi Ltd, London, England.
Esme Antiques 'Marelle', Stoke-on-Trent, Staffordshire, England.
Richard Essex, Bristol, Avon, England.
Etcetera, Seaton, Devon, England.
Ethorpe Antiques, Gerrards Cross, Buckinghamshire, England.
Etna Antiques, London, England.
Eton Antique Book Shop, Eton, Berkshire, England.
Eton Cottage Antiques, Eton, Berkshire, England.
Eton Gallery, Eton, Berkshire, England.
Eureka Antiques, Sale, Greater Manchester, England.
European Fine Arts, Dublin, Co Dublin, Eire.
Barbara Eustace Antiques, London, England.
Evans & Evans, Alresford, Hampshire, England.
D.G. & A.S. Evans, Brecon, Powys, Wales.
E.Evans & Partners Ltd, Barmouth, Gwynedd, Wales.
H. Evans & Sons, Hull, Humberside, England.
Mollie Evans, Richmond, Surrey, England.
Stewart Evans, Malpas, Cheshire, England.
Peter Evanson, London, England.
Eve's Lace, London, England.
Gavina Ewart, Broadway, Hereford & Worcester, England.
Ewhurst Gallery, Basingstoke, Hampshire, England.
J.F.Ewing, London, England.
Ewings, Reepham, Norfolk, England.
Exquisite Arts Ltd, Lichfield, Staffordshire, England.
Extence Antiques, Teignmouth, Devon, England.
Joan Eyles Antiques, Boroughbridge, N.Yorkshire, England.
Eyre and Greig Ltd, London, England.
Henry Faber Ltd, London, England.
Fagin's Phonograph Emporium, London, England.
Baroukh Fahimian, London, England.
Fair Deal Antiques, Mansfield, Nottinghamshire, England.
Fair Maids House Scottish Crafts, Perth, Tayside, Scotland.
Fairhurst Gallery, London, England.
J. & T.J.Fairhurst, Norwich, Norfolk, England.
Jack Fairman (Carpets) Ltd, London, England.
Philip Faithfull Antiques, Boughton, Kent, England.
The Falcon Gallery, Diss, Norfolk, England.
Falcon House Antiques and Old Book Shop, Kelvedon, Essex, England.
Mrs E.Falik, Burnley, Lancashire, England.
Stephen Falk, Rochdale, Greater Manchester, England.
Falkner Fine Art, London, England.
The Faringdon Galleries, Faringdon, Oxfordshire, England.
Farmhouse Antiques, Stoke Ferry, Norfolk, England.
Farnborough (Kent) Antiques, Farnborough, Kent, England.
Peter Farrow, Chesham, Buckinghamshire, England.
Farthings Antiques, Nantwich, Cheshire, England.
M.Fearn, Wirral, Merseyside, England.
Jeremy A. Fearn, Ripon, N.Yorkshire, England.
Featherston Shipping Ltd, London, England.
Jocelyn Feilding Fine Art Ltd, London, England.
R.Feldman Ltd, London, England.
Felix Gallery, Lewes, E.Sussex, England.
Mary Fell Antiques, Brampton, Cumbria, England.
Peter Fell of Thame, Thame, Oxfordshire, England.
Fellows & Sons, Birmingham, W.Midlands, England.
Fenny Lodge Gallery, Milton Keynes, Buckinghamshire, England.
C.R.Fenton & Co Ltd, London, England.
Fenwick and Fisher Antiques, Broadway, Hereford & Worcester, England.
Fermor Antiques, London, England.
Fernandes & Marche, London, England.
Ferneyhough, Henley-in-Arden, Warwickshire, England.
D.J.Ferrant Antiques, London, England.
David Ferrow, Great Yarmouth, Norfolk, England.
Malcolm & Joy Ferrow & Son, Great Yarmouth, Norfolk, England.
Harvey Ferry, William Clegg Antiques, Nettlebed, Oxfordshire, England.
Fiddes Watt, London, England.
Audrey Field, London, England.
Fieldborne Galleries, London, England.
Brian Fielden, London, England.
Fifteenth Century Bookshop, Lewes, E.Sussex, England.
Fillans Antiques, Huddersfield, W.Yorkshire, England.
M.& I. Finch, Carnforth, Lancashire, England.
Finchley Fine Art Galleries, London, England.
Fine Art Gallery, Edinburgh, Lothian, Scotland.
Fine Art Petworth PLC, Haslemere, Surrey, England.
The Fine Art Society Plc, Glasgow, Strathclyde, Scotland.
The Fine Art Society Plc, London, England.
The Fine Art Society Plc, Edinburgh, Lothian, Scotland.
Fine Arts Traders & Shippers and Bondgate Antiques, Alnwick, Northumberland, England.
Fine Pine Ltd, South Brent, Devon, England.
Fine Pine Ltd, Totnes, Devon, England.
Fine-Lines (Fine Art), Shipston on Stour, Warwickshire, England.
Finedon Antiques Centre, Finedon, Northamptonshire, England.
Finishing Touches, Cowes, Isle of Wight, England.
Elizabeth Finlay, Harrogate, N.Yorkshire, England.
G.W. Finn & Sons, Canterbury, Kent, England.
Fire and Iron Limited, Leatherhead, Surrey, England.
The Fire Place (Hungerford) Ltd, Hungerford, Berkshire, England.
Rodney T.Firmin, Cambridge, Cambridgeshire, England.
Fischer Fine Art Ltd, London, England.
Susanna Fisher, Upham, Hampshire, England.
M.W. Fitch Ltd, Folkestone, Kent, England.
Five Centuries Antiques, Canterbury, Kent, England.
Five Five Six Antiques, London, England.
Henry Flack (1860) Ltd, Beckenham, Kent, England.
The Flask Bookshop, London, England.
Richard Flavell Antiques, Derby, Derbyshire, England.
Mario Flecha Gallery, London, England.
A.Fleming (Southsea) Ltd, Portsmouth, Hampshire, England.
Flemings Antiques, Debenham, Suffolk, England.
H.M. Fletcher, London, England.
Fleur de Lys Gallery, London, England.
Flight of Fancy, London, England.
The Flintlock, Glastonbury, Somerset, England.
Flora Dora Antiques, Petworth, W.Sussex, England.
Flore House Antiques Ltd, Flore, Northamptonshire, England.
Angela Flowers Gallery Ltd, London, England.

Fockerby Hall Antiques, Lincoln, Lincolnshire, England.
Focol Photography, Bath, Avon, England.
Sam Fogg, London, England.
Diana Foley Antiques, London, England.
Folio (Clevedon Books & Clevedon Fine Arts), Clevedon, Avon, England.
Folly Antiques Centre, Petersfield, Hampshire, England.
Foord Antiques, Midhurst, W.Sussex, England.
G.W.Ford & Son Ltd, Sheffield, S.Yorkshire, England.
Foresters Hall Antiques, Debenham, Suffolk, England.
Forge House Antiques, Canterbury, Kent, England.
Forget-Me-Not, London, England.
Forman of Piccadilly Ltd, London, England.
Forster Ritchie, Hook, Hampshire, England.
W.Forster, London, England.
Forsyth Antiques, Perth, Tayside, Scotland.
Fortnum & Mason Ltd, London, England.
Raymond Fortt Studios Ltd, Surbiton, Surrey, England.
Forty Three, Woburn Sands, Buckinghamshire, England.
Fosse Gallery, Stow-on-the-Wold, Gloucestershire, England.
Foster Hill Road Antiques Centre, Bedford, Bedfordshire, England.
A. & E. Foster, Naphill, Buckinghamshire, England.
Gene & Sally Foster (Antiques), Bath, Avon, England.
J.F.Foster & Son, Radlett, Hertfordshire, England.
Kate Foster Ltd., London, England.
M. Odell Foster, Wonersh, Surrey, England.
Michael Foster, London, England.
Foto-Call, London, England.
Fotowest, Bath, Avon, England.
Foulsham House Prints, London, England.
Four Seasons Gallery, Northampton, Northamptonshire, England.
Fox & Co, Yeovil, Somerset, England.
Fox & Sons, Fordingbridge, Hampshire, England.
Fox Antiques, Sidmouth, Devon, England.
Fox House, Woodstock, Oxfordshire, England.
Charles Fox (Jewellers) Ltd, Bournemouth, Dorset, England.
Judy Fox Antiques, London, England.
William C.Fox & Co Ltd, St Helier, Jersey, Channel Islands.
Foye Gallery, Luton, Bedfordshire, England.
P.J.Fradley, Ashbourne, Derbyshire, England.
Frame One Photographic, Hemel Hempstead, Hertfordshire, England.
Franca Antiques, Tunbridge Wells, Kent, England.
Frances Books, Worthing, W.Sussex, England.
Francis Street Antique Gallery, Dublin, Co Dublin, Eire.
John Francis, Carmarthen, Dyfed, Wales.
Peter Francis, London, England.
Franco's Antiques, London, England.
Franfam Ltd, Moreton-in-Marsh, Gloucestershire, England.
Colin & Charlotte Franklin, Culham, Oxfordshire, England.
Thomas Franklin (Antiques), Hungerford, Berkshire, England.
Franklin's, London, England.
Robert Franses & Son, London, England.
S.Franses Ltd, London, England.
S.Franses Ltd, London, England.
Victor Franses Gallery, London, England.
Fraser Antiques, North Berwick, Lothian, Scotland.
Fraser Glennie & Partners, Cirencester, Gloucestershire, England.
Alastair Fraser Antiques, Nottingham, Nottinghamshire, England.
Malcolm Frazer Antiques, Cheadle, Greater Manchester, England.
Frean Antiques, Arundel, W.Sussex, England.
C.Fredericks & Sons, London, England.
J.A.Fredericks & Son, Hillingdon, Middlesex, England.
Gerald Freedman (Cale Antiques), London, England.
Freeman and Lloyd, Folkestone, Kent, England.
I. Freeman & Son, Simon Kaye Ltd, London, England.
J.Freeman, London, England.
R.H. & E.M.Freeman, Stow-on-the-Wold, Gloucestershire, England.
Simon and Claire Freeman Antiques, Bath, Avon, England.
Vincent Freeman Antiques, London, England.
Frenches Farm Antiques, Kings Langley, Hertfordshire, England.
Joan Frere Antiques, Drumnadrochit, Highland, Scotland.
Friar Antiques and Collectors' Centre, Nottingham, Nottinghamshire, England.
Friary Antiques, Quarndon, Derbyshire, England.
David Friend Antiques, Prestwich, Greater Manchester, England.
Frinton Antiques, Frinton-on-Sea, Essex, England.
Frith Antiques, Petworth, W.Sussex, England.
Alex M. Frizzell, West Linton, Borders, Scotland.
Frogmore House Antiques, Box, Wiltshire, England.
The Front Parlour, Hythe, Kent, England.
Frost & Reed Ltd, London, England.
Fry Gallery, London, England.
Victoria Fry, Arundel, W.Sussex, England.
O.Frydman, London, England.
Fritz Fryer, Ross-on-Wye, Hereford & Worcester, England.
Fulda Gallery, Salford, Greater Manchester, England.
Sally Fullers Antiques, Westerham, Kent, England.
Fulwood Antiques, Sheffield, S.Yorkshire, England.
Furniture Cave, London, England.
Furniture Fair, London, England.
The Furniture Station Ltd, Ely, Cambridgeshire, England.
Fyfe's Antiques, Edinburgh, Lothian, Scotland.
Jonathan Fyson Antiques, Burford, Oxfordshire, England.
Jonathan Fyson Antiques, Cassington, Oxfordshire, England.

G.A.Thomas, Mold, Clwyd, Wales.
G.C.W.Antiques, Bath, Avon, England.
G.M.B. Auctions, Ipswich, Suffolk, England.
G.M.S. Restorations, Wotton-under-Edge, Gloucestershire, England.
Gabor Cossa Antiques, Cambridge, Cambridgeshire, England.
Gadsby's Antiques, Ashtead, Surrey, England.
Gadzooks, Skipton, N.Yorkshire, England.
Elizabeth Gage, London, England.
Robin Gage, London, England.
Sven Gahlin, Bath, Avon, England.
Gainsborough House Antiques, Tewkesbury, Gloucestershire, England.
Galaxy Arts, Plymouth, Devon, England.
D.Ira Gale, London, England.
P. Gale Shipping, Warminster, Wiltshire, England.
Galerie Appenzell, Newport, Essex, England.
Galerie George, London, England.
Galerie 1900, London, England.
Galerie 360, London, England.
Galerie 39, London, England.
Galia Antiques, London, England.
The Galleon, Bath, Avon, England.
Galleon Galleries, St Leonards, E.Sussex, England.
The Gallery, Southsea, Hampshire, England.
Gallery of Antique Costume & Textiles Ltd, London, England.
Gallery Antiques Ltd, Winchester, Hampshire, England.
Gallery Lingard, London, England.
The Gallery Muswell Hill, London, England.
The Gallery No.10, Groomsport, Co Down, Northern Ireland.
Gallery Three, March, Cambridgeshire, England.
Gallery 10 Ltd, London, England.
Gallery 181, London, England.
Gallery 25, London, England.
Gallery 26, Corbridge, Northumberland, England.
Gallery 77, Bolton, Greater Manchester, England.
James Gallie, Battlesbridge, Essex, England.
Galloway & Porter Ltd, Cambridge, Cambridgeshire, England.
Game Advice, London, England.
Gander & White Shipping Ltd, London, England.
Michael Gander, Hitchin, Hertfordshire, England.
Gard Books (Music), Salisbury, Wiltshire, England.
George & Helen Gardiner, Glasgow, Strathclyde, Scotland.
C.B.Gardner Antiques, Chipping Norton, Oxfordshire, England.
Gardner's, The Antique Shop, Kilbarchan, Strathclyde, Scotland.
P.R.Garner (Antiques), Cambridge, Cambridgeshire, England.
Garrard & Co Ltd, London, England.
Stephen Garratt Fine Paintings, London, England.
Robert Garrett Antiques, Stratford-upon-Avon, Warwickshire, England.
Garrick Bookshop, Stockport, Greater Manchester, England.
Garton & Cooke, London, England.
H.G. Gasson, Rye, E.Sussex, England.
Gastrell House, Tetbury, Gloucestershire, England.
Gate Antiques, York, N.Yorkshire, England.
Gatehouse Antiques, Macclesfield, Cheshire, England.
Peter John Gates, London, England.
Gatward Fine Arts, Haynes, Bedfordshire, England.
Maureen H.Gauld, Killin, Central, Scotland.
Jonathan Gaunt, Marlborough, Wiltshire, England.
Gauntlett Antiques, Midhurst, W.Sussex, England.
Gavels, Ledbury, Hereford & Worcester, England.
Gay Antiques, London, England.
Gay's Antiques Ltd, Stockport, Greater Manchester, England.
Gaylords, Fareham, Hampshire, England.
Thos. Wm. Gaze & Son, Diss, Norfolk, England.
Gazebo, Cardiff, S.Glamorgan, Wales.
N. Geary Ltd, Pudsey, W.Yorkshire, England.
James Geddie Ltd (Bewdley Auctions), Bewdley, Hereford & Worcester, England.
Gee-Pemberton Macphail, Brighton & Hove, E.Sussex, England.
Geering & Colyer, Tunbridge Wells, Kent, England.
Gemini, Leek, Staffordshire, England.
Gemini Antiques Ltd, Stockport, Greater Manchester, England.
Gems, Leigh-on-Sea, Essex, England.
General Antiques and Books, London, England.
General Trading Co, London, England.
Genges Farm Antiques, Limington, Somerset, England.
Rupert Gentle Antiques, Pewsey, Wiltshire, England.
George & Dragon Gallery, Norwich, Norfolk, England.
George Jackson & Son, Hitchin, Hertfordshire, England.
P.R. George (Antiques), Neath, W.Glamorgan, Wales.
George Smith, London, England.
Wm.George's Sons Ltd, Bristol, Avon, England.
Georgian Antique Company, Neath, W.Glamorgan, Wales.
Georgian Antiques, Edinburgh, Lothian, Scotland.
Georgian Gems, Swanage, Dorset, England.
Georgian House, St Anne's, Lancashire, England.
Georgian House Antiques, Dartmouth, Devon, England.
Georgian House Antiques, Ottery St Mary, Devon, England.
Georgian House Antiques, Uckfield, E.Sussex, England.
Georgian House Antiques, Hertford, Hertfordshire, England.
The Georgian Shop, Sandycove, Co Dublin, Eire.
Georgian Village Vaults and Galleries, London, England.
Georgina Antiques, Hemel Hempstead, Hertfordshire, England.
John German, Burton upon Trent, Staffordshire, England.
Michael C.German, London, England.
Gerrard Antiques, Kendal, Cumbria, England.
Gibberd and Grant Antiques, Barnard Castle, Durham, England.
David Gibbins Antiques, Woodbridge, Suffolk, England.
Stanley Gibbons, London, England.
Stanley Gibbons Auctions Limited, London, England.
Christopher Gibbs Ltd, London, England.
Thomas Gibson Fine Art Limited, London, England.
Gift House Antiques, Ilford, Essex, England.
H.M.Gilbert & Son, Southampton, Hampshire, England.
Henry March Gilbert, Winchester, Hampshire, England.
Attilio Gilberti, London, England.
The Tony Gill Organisation-Number One, London, England.
L.H. Gilliard, Altrincham, Greater Manchester, England.
G. & F.Gillingham Ltd, London, England.
Gillinghams Antiques, Guildford, Surrey, England.
Gilwern Antiques, Gilwern, Gwent, Wales.
Gimpel Fils, London, England.

The Ginnel, Manchester, Greater Manchester, England.
Ray & Diane Ginns, Birmingham, W.Midlands, England.
Loretta Giordani, London, England.
Graeme & Jennifer Gittings, Leicester, Leicestershire, England.
Gladstone Antiques, Dunton Green, Kent, England.
A.W. Glasby & Son, Hayle, Cornwall, England.
G.Glass & Son, London, England.
Richard Glass, Whaley Bridge, Derbyshire, England.
The Glasshouse Gallery & Workshop, London, England.
Glencorse Antiques, Kingston upon Thames, Surrey, England.
Glendale Antiques, Wooler, Northumberland, England.
M.& R. Glendale, London, England.
Glendining & Co, London, England.
Glennie Middleton and Bullock, Diss, Norfolk, England.
Glenville Antiques, Yatton, Avon, England.
The Gloucester Antiques Centre, Gloucester, Gloucestershire, England.
Gloucester House Antiques Ltd, Fairford, Gloucestershire, England.
Gnome Cottage, Stroud, Gloucestershire, England.
Godalming Galleries Ltd, Godalming, Surrey, England.
J. Goddard & Sons Ltd, Camberley, Surrey, England.
Godden of Worthing Ltd, Worthing, W.Sussex, England.
Geoffrey Godden, Chinaman, Worthing, W.Sussex, England.
Godfrey & Twatt, Harrogate, N.Yorkshire, England.
Godfrey New Photographics Ltd, Sidcup, Kent, England.
Howard Godfrey Antiques Ltd, Folkestone, Kent, England.
Jemima Godfrey Antiques, Newmarket, Suffolk, England.
Thomas C.Godfrey Ltd, York, N.Yorkshire, England.
Godson & Coles Ltd, London, England.
Michael Goedhuis Ltd. Colnaghi Oriental, London, England.
The Goff Galleries, Long Melford, Suffolk, England.
David C.Golby, Totnes, Devon, England.
Hilde Goldbaum Antiques, London, England.
The Golden Age, Blackpool, Lancashire, England.
Golden Cage, Nottingham, Nottinghamshire, England.
The Golden Drop Antiques, Warboys, Cambridgeshire, England.
The Golden Past, Peel, Isle of Man.
The Golden Past, London, England.
The Golden Sovereign, Braintree, Essex, England.
Gwendoline Golder, Coltishall, Norfolk, England.
Pat & David Golding, Arundel, W.Sussex, England.
Goldsmith & Perris, London, England.
Maurice Goldstone & Son, Bakewell, Derbyshire, England.
Golightly Restoration, Glasgow, Strathclyde, Scotland.
Good Hope Antiques, Beaminster, Dorset, England.
Goodacre Engraving Ltd, Long Eaton, Nottinghamshire, England.
Goodall & Co Ltd, London, England.
Peter and Debbie Gooday, Richmond, Surrey, England.
Goodbrey Antiques, Framlingham, Suffolk, England.
Thomas Goode & Co (London) Ltd, London, England.
Wm Goodfellow (Antiques), Carnforth, Lancashire, England.
Goodramgate Books, Maps and Prints, York, N.Yorkshire, England.
Peter Goodwin Antiques, London, England.
Gordon Reece Gallery, Knaresborough, N.Yorkshire, England.
A. & F. Gordon, London, England.
Brian Gordon, London, England.
Douglas Gordon Antiques, Stockbridge, Hampshire, England.
Janet Gordon, Wakes Colne, Essex, England.
R.S. Gordon Antiques, Alford, Grampian, Scotland.
Gordon's Antiques, Warwick, Warwickshire, England.
Gore-Langton Gallery, Tunbridge Wells, Kent, England.
Gorringes, Lewes, E.Sussex, England.
Jill Gosling Ltd, London, England.
Goss & Crested China Ltd, Horndean, Hampshire, England.
Gostin of Liverpool Ltd, Liverpool, Merseyside, England.
Gothick Dream, London, England.
P.W. Gottschald, Ambergate, Derbyshire, England.
Gough Antiques, Burnham-on-Crouch, Essex, England.
Simon Gough Books, Holt, Norfolk, England.
A.E.Gould & Sons (Antiques) Ltd, East Horsley, Surrey, England.
Lawrence Gould, London, England.
Patrick & Susan Gould, London, England.
Peter Gould, Halifax, W.Yorkshire, England.
Valentine Gould, Bath, Avon, England.
Frederick Grace, Croydon, Surrey, England.
Graffiti, London, England.
Graham & Oxley (Antiques) Ltd, London, England.
Graham Gallery, Reading, Berkshire, England.
Albert Graham Ltd, Larne, Co Antrim, Northern Ireland.
David Graham Antiques, London, England.
Gavin Graham Gallery, London, England.
Imogen Graham, London, England.
Michael & Diana Grainger, London, England.
The Granary & Rene Antiques and Art, St Leonards, E.Sussex, England.
The Granary Galleries, Taunton, Somerset, England.
Grange Bookshop, Edinburgh, Lothian, Scotland.
Grange Court Antiques, Taunton, Somerset, England.
Grange Gallery, Harleston, Norfolk, England.
The Grange Gallery & Fine Arts Ltd, St Helier, Jersey, Channel Islands.
Grannies Attic, Market Weighton, Humberside, England.
Granny's Attic, Clare, Suffolk, England.
Granny's Goodies and Chelsea Lion, London, England.
Grant Books, Droitwich, Hereford & Worcester, England.
Alan Grant, Rugby, Warwickshire, England.
Andrew Grant Fine Art Auctions, Worcester, Hereford & Worcester, England.
Denzil Grant Antiques Ltd, Long Melford, Suffolk, England.
John Grant, Edinburgh, Lothian, Scotland.
Stephanie Grant Antiques, Barnard Castle, Durham, England.
Granville Antiques, Eastergate, W.Sussex, England.
Graus Antiques, London, England.
W.J.Gravener Antiques, Mayfield, E.Sussex, England.
Graves Son & Pilcher Fine Arts, Brighton & Hove, E.Sussex, England.
Celia Gray, Hayling Island, Hampshire, England.
David Gray Antiques, Glasgow, Strathclyde, Scotland.
Jay Gray Antiques, Cirencester, Gloucestershire, England.
Solveig & Anita Gray, London, England.
Grays Antique Market & Grays Mews, London, England.
Great Brampton House Antiques Ltd, Hereford, Hereford & Worcester, England.
Great Chesterford Antiques, Great Chesterford, Essex, England.
The Great Malvern Antiques Arcade, Malvern, Hereford & Worcester, England.
Great Ryburgh Antiques (Pine Centre), Fakenham, Norfolk, England.
Great Western Antique Centre Ltd, Bath, Avon, England.
Green & Co, Wantage, Oxfordshire, England.
The Green Bottle Antiques, Parkgate, Cheshire, England.
David E.Green Gallery, London, England.
Gladys Green Antiques, Cheltenham, Gloucestershire, England.
Michael Green, Harrogate, N.Yorkshire, England.
Renee and Roy Green, Lewes, E.Sussex, England.
Richard Green, Leicester, Leicestershire, England.
Richard Green, London, England.
Ron Green Antiques, Towcester, Northamptonshire, England.
Green's Antique Galleries, London, England.
Greenbury Antiques, Royston, Hertfordshire, England.
Richard Greene Antiques, Burley in Wharfedale, W.Yorkshire, England.
Greene's Antique Galleries, Drogheda, Co Louth, Eire.
Greengrass Antiques, Windsor, Berkshire, England.
Greensleeves Galleries, Gerrards Cross, Buckinghamshire, England.
Jonathan Greenwall Antiques, Folkestone, Kent, England.
C.Greenway Antiques, Witney, Oxfordshire, England.
Greenwich Antiques Market, London, England.
Lynn Greenwold, Stow-on-the-Wold, Gloucestershire, England.
Judy Greenwood, London, England.
Nigel Greenwood Gallery and Bookshop, London, England.
Simon Greenwood Antiques, Melmerby, N.Yorkshire, England.
W.Greenwood, Bedale, N.Yorkshire, England.
W.F.Greenwood & Sons Ltd, Harrogate, N.Yorkshire, England.
Greenwoods of Oulton Mill, Little Budworth, Cheshire, England.
Hugh Greer, Bangor, Co Down, Northern Ireland.
Gregory, Bottley and Lloyd, London, England.
George Gregory, Bath, Avon, England.
Henry Gregory, London, England.
Martyn Gregory, London, England.
Gres, London, England.
Greville Antiques & Design Ltd, Milton Keynes, Buckinghamshire, England.
Grey Gables, Arundel, W.Sussex, England.
Grey House Antiques, Tiverton, Devon, England.
Grey-Harris & Co, Bristol, Avon, England.
Tony Grey Antiques and Fine Arts, Totnes, Devon, England.
Greystoke Antiques, Sherborne, Dorset, England.
Griffin Antiques, Petworth, W.Sussex, England.
G.E.Griffin, Croydon, Surrey, England.
Simon Griffin Antiques, London, England.
W. & R. Griffiths, Southport, Merseyside, England.
W.W. Griffiths, Caernarvon, Gwynedd, Wales.
Griffons Court, Newbury, Berkshire, England.
Grimaldi, London, England.
Grimes House Antiques, Moreton-in-Marsh, Gloucestershire, England.
Duncan Grimmond, Ripon, N.Yorkshire, England.
Francis J. Grogan, Cinderford, Gloucestershire, England.
Grosvenor Antiques of Chester, Chester, Cheshire, England.
Grosvenor Antiques Ltd, London, England.
Grosvenor Gallery, London, England.
Grosvenor House Interiors, Beaconsfield, Buckinghamshire, England.
Grosvenor Prints, London, England.
Grounds & Co, Wisbech, Cambridgeshire, England.
L.Guerra, London, England.
Guildford Galleries Ltd, Guildford, Surrey, England.
Guildhall Antiques, Whittlesford, Cambridgeshire, England.
Guildhall Antiques, Poole, Dorset, England.
Guildhall Galleries, Thaxted, Essex, England.
Guildhall Gallery, Bury St Edmunds, Suffolk, England.
Guillemot, Aldeburgh, Suffolk, England.
Guinevere Antiques Ltd, London, England.
Gunpowder House Antiques, Faversham, Kent, England.
Edred A.F. Gwilliam, Cricklade, Wiltshire, England.
Gwyneth Antiques, London, England.
GW Antiques, Lancaster, Lancashire, England.

H.L.B. Antiques, Christchurch, Dorset, England.
G.K. Hadfield, Shepshed, Leicestershire, England.
Hadji Baba Ancient Art, London, England.
Hadlow Antiques, Tunbridge Wells, Kent, England.
Hagen (Restorations), Haynes, Bedfordshire, England.
Richard Hagen Ltd, Broadway, Hereford & Worcester, England.
Hague Antiques, Leamington, Warwickshire, England.
John Hague Antiques, Pickering, N.Yorkshire, England.
Hahn Gallery, London, England.
John Haines Antiques Ltd, London, England.
David K.Hakeney Antiques, Hull, Humberside, England.
M.Hakim, London, England.
Halcyon Days, London, England.
H.A. & D.M. Hale, Northam, Devon, England.
Robert Hales Antiques Ltd, London, England.
Halewood & Sons, Preston, Lancashire, England.
Half Moon Antiques, Clare, Suffolk, England.
Half-a-Living, Leominster, Hereford & Worcester, England.
Halifax Antiques Centre, Halifax, W.Yorkshire, England.
Hall Wateridge & Owen, Shrewsbury, Shropshire, England.

Anne Hall - Prints, Lichfield, Staffordshire, England.
Anthony C.Hall, Twickenham, Middlesex, England.
Georgina Hall, London, England.
Henry Hall, Westerham, Kent, England.
John Hall, London, England.
Hall's Antiques, Taunton Lydeard, Somerset, England.
Hall's Bookshop, Tunbridge Wells, Kent, England.
Michael Hallam Antiques, Norwich, Norfolk, England.
Sonia Halliday Photographs, Weston Turville, Buckinghamshire, England.
Halliday's (Antiques), London, England.
Hallidays Antiques Ltd, Dorchester, Oxfordshire, England.
Hallmarks, Brighton & Hove, E.Sussex, England.
Hallstile Antiques, Hexham, Northumberland, England.
Halo Antiques, Altrincham, Greater Manchester, England.
Halsey, London, England.
A. Halsey Antiques, Kingsbridge, Devon, England.
Halstow Antiques, Sittingbourne, Kent, England.
Haltherleigh Antiques, Haltherleigh, Devon, England.
Hamand Antiques, Painswick, Gloucestershire, England.
Hamilton Antiques, Woodbridge, Suffolk, England.
Hamilton Antiques, Holywood, Co Down, Northern Ireland.
Hamilton Weston Wallpapers, Richmond, Surrey, England.
Ross Hamilton Ltd, London, England.
Hamlet Gallery, London, England.
Hammersley Galleries, Harpenden, Hertfordshire, England.
Hammond Smith, Leicester, Leicestershire, England.
Jeffery Hammond Antiques, Winchester, Hampshire, England.
Peter Hammond, Holt, Norfolk, England.
The Hampshire Bookshop, Winchester, Hampshire, England.
Hampshire Gallery, Bournemouth, Dorset, England.
R.& L. Hampshire Antiques, Castle Douglas, Dumfries & Galloway, Scotland.
Hampshires of Dorking, Dorking, Surrey, England.
Hampstead Antique Emporium, London, England.
Hampton Court Revival Antiques Centre, East Molesey, Surrey, England.
The Hampton Hill Gallery Ltd, Hampton Hill, Middlesex, England.
Gerald Hampton, Christchurch, Dorset, England.
Han-Shan Tang Ltd, London, England.
Hancock Gallery, London, England.
F.W.Hancock, Whitchurch, Shropshire, England.
Peter Hancock, Chichester, W.Sussex, England.
Hancocks & Co (Jewellers) Ltd, London, England.
Hand in Hand, Edinburgh, Lothian, Scotland.
William Handford Antiques, London, England.
Handweavers Studio and Gallery, London, England.
Mrs S. Hanford, Barnard Castle, Durham, England.
Fred Hanna Ltd, Dublin, Co Dublin, Eire.
Hanover Books, Whitby, N.Yorkshire, England.
Hanover Studios, London, England.
Rod Hanrick, London, England.
Hansen Antiques, Boughton, Kent, England.
Oliver Hanson, Tunbridge Wells, Kent, England.
David J. Hansord, Lincoln, Lincolnshire, England.
Harari & Johns Ltd, London, England.
Harcourt Antiques, London, England.
Henry Hardcastle Ltd, York, N.Yorkshire, England.
Hardie Antiques, Perth, Tayside, Scotland.
P.N.Hardiman, Melbourn, Cambridgeshire, England.
Keith Harding, London, England.
James Hardy & Co, London, England.
Harewood Antiques, Harrogate, N.Yorkshire, England.
Harlequin Gallery, Lincoln, Lincolnshire, England.
Harley Antiques, Chippenham, Wiltshire, England.
Harley Two, Chippenham, Wiltshire, England.
Robert Harman Antiques, Ampthill, Bedfordshire, England.
Harmers of London Stamp Auctioneers Ltd, London, England.
Harp Antiques, Bradford-on-Avon, Wiltshire, England.
Erica & Hugo Harper, Chester, Cheshire, England.
Harper's Hill Farm Antiques, Nuneaton, Warwickshire, England.
Harrington Bros, London, England.
M. Harrington Ltd, Winchester, Hampshire, England.
Harris (Antiques) Limited, London, England.
Bibi Harris Antiques, Hungerford, Berkshire, England.
Bob Harris & Sons, Birmingham, W.Midlands, England.
Essie C.Harris, London, England.
F.J. Harris, Stansted Mountfitchet, Essex, England.
Jonathan Harris, London, England.
M.Harris & Sons, London, England.
Nicholas Harris, London, England.
Sylvia Harris, Berkeley, Gloucestershire, England.
Anna Harrison Antiques, Newcastle upon Tyne, Tyne & Wear, England.
James Harrison, Hebden Bridge, W.Yorkshire, England.
Tim Harrison Trade & Export Antiques, Warwick, Warwickshire, England.
Harrods, London, England.
Harrop Fold Clocks, Clitheroe, Lancashire, England.
Hart & Rosenberg, London, England.
Sheila Hart Antiques, London, England.
J. Hartley Antiques Ltd, Ripley, Surrey, England.
Julian Hartnoll, London, England.
Harvey & Gore, London, England.
Kenneth Harvey Antiques and Fine Art, Grimsby, Humberside, England.
W.R.Harvey & Co (Antiques) Ltd, London, England.
W.R.Harvey & Co (Antiques) Ltd, London, England.
Harvey's Auctions Ltd, London, England.
Harwood Antiques, London, England.
Harwood Tate, Market Rasen, Lincolnshire, England.
Harwood Westend Antiques, Weston-super-Mare, Avon, England.
Hasel-Britt Ltd, Antiques, Radlett, Hertfordshire, England.
Haslam & Whiteway, London, England.
Betty Haslam, Faringdon, Oxfordshire, England.
Nicholas Haslam, London, England.
Ian G.Hastie, Salisbury, Wiltshire, England.
Simon Hatchwell Antiques, Brighton & Hove, E.Sussex, England.
H.J.Hatfield & Sons Ltd, London, England.
Ann Hathaway, Norwich, Norfolk, England.
Haughey Antiques, Kirkby Stephen, Cumbria, England.
Brian Haughton Antiques, London, England.
The Haunted Bookshop, Cambridge, Cambridgeshire, England.
Haverstock Antiques, London, England.
Andrew Hawkins, Billericay, Essex, England.
Charles Hawkins, Lowestoft, Suffolk, England.
David Hawkins (Brighton) Ltd, Brighton & Hove, E.Sussex, England.
Sylvia Hawkins Antiques, Loughborough, Leicestershire, England.
Hawkley Studio Associates Ltd, Godalming, Surrey, England.
Raymond Hawley, Beverley, Humberside, England.
Haworth Antiques, Harrogate, N.Yorkshire, England.
Haworth Antiques, Huby, N.Yorkshire, England.
The Hay Galleries Ltd, Hay-on-Wye, Hereford & Worcester, England.
Hay Loft Gallery, Broadway, Hereford & Worcester, England.
Haydon Bridge Antiques, Hexham, Northumberland, England.
Haydon House Antiques, Woburn Sands, Buckinghamshire, England.
Hayes and Newby Antique Export, Gloucester, Gloucestershire, England.
The Hayes Gallery, Auchterarder, Tayside, Scotland.
Jeanette Hayhurst Fine Glass, London, England.
Hayman & Hayman, London, England.
Hayter's, Ryde, Isle of Wight, England.
Hazel Cottage Clocks, Newcastle upon Tyne, Tyne & Wear, England.
Hazlitt, Gooden & Fox, London, England.
Charles Head & Son, Kingsbridge, Devon, England.
John & Judith Head, The Barn Book Supply, Salisbury, Wiltshire, England.
Heath Antiques, Reigate, Surrey, England.
Heath-Bullock, Godalming, Surrey, England.
Samuel Heath & Sons PLC, Birmingham, W.Midlands, England.
Heathcote Ball & Co, Leicester, Leicestershire, England.
J.C.Heather Antiques, Bury St Edmunds, Suffolk, England.
Heathfield Furniture Salerooms, Heathfield, E.Sussex, England.
Michael Hedgecoe Antique Furniture Restoration, Chobham, Surrey, England.
J.A. & T. Hedley, Hexham, Northumberland, England.
Hedleys Humpers Ltd, London, England.
Heenglen Antiques, London, England.
W. Heffer & Sons Ltd, Cambridge, Cambridgeshire, England.
Heffle Corner Antiques, Heathfield, E.Sussex, England.
Heim Gallery, London, England.
Heirloom and Howard Ltd, London, England.
Helius Antiques, London, England.
Helperby Antiques, York, N.Yorkshire, England.
Helton Antiques, Heath and Reach, Bedfordshire, England.
Peter Hempson, Melchbourne, Bedfordshire, England.
John Henderson, York, N.Yorkshire, England.
Marina Henderson, London, England.
W.T.C.Henderson, Perth, Tayside, Scotland.
Thomas Heneage Art Books, London, England.
Hennell Ltd, London, England.
Henry-Brett Galleries, Bourton-on-the-Water, Gloucestershire, England.
Henson's Antiques, Leeds, W.Yorkshire, England.
Lesley Hepherd Antiques, London, England.
Hera Fine Art, Hythe, Kent, England.
Heraldry Today, London, England.
Heraz, London, England.
Heritage Antiques, London, England.
Heritage Antiques & Restoration, Great Missenden, Buckinghamshire, England.
Heritage Auctions, London, England.
Hermitage, London, England.
H.W.Heron & Son Ltd, Yoxall, Staffordshire, England.
Herrald Antiques, Edinburgh, Lothian, Scotland.
The Herts & Essex Antiques Centre, Sawbridgeworth, Hertfordshire, England.
M.Heskia, London, England.
Hetheringtons, Pretty & Ellis, Amersham, Buckinghamshire, England.
Muir Hewitt, Halifax, W.Yorkshire, England.
Richard Hewlett Gallery, London, England.
Hexham Antiques, Hexham, Northumberland, England.
David Hick Antiques, St Lawrence, Jersey, Channel Islands.
Hicklenton & Phillips Ltd, Wimborne Minster, Dorset, England.
Tom Hickman, Frome, Somerset, England.
A.Hicks, London, England.
High Street Antiques, Alcester, Warwickshire, England.
Highbridge Antique Centre, Highbridge, Somerset, England.
Highgate Antiques, Kendal, Cumbria, England.
Highgate Gallery, London, England.
Highland Antiques, Nairn, Highland, Scotland.
J.K.Hill, London, England.
Hill Rise Antiques, Richmond, Surrey, England.
Eric Hill, Folkestone, Kent, England.
F.F.Hill, Shackleford, Surrey, England.
Frank Hill (Removals & Storage) Ltd, Manchester, Greater Manchester, England.
W.E.Hill & Sons, Great Missenden, Buckinghamshire, England.
Peter Hillary Ltd, Stratford-upon-Avon, Warwickshire, England.
Hillside Antiques, Lindfield, W.Sussex, England.
Hillyers, London, England.
Hilmarton Manor Press, Calne, Wiltshire, England.
Hilton Restorations, Atherington, Devon, England.
Simon Hilton, Great Dunmow, Essex, England.
J.S. & R.Hine, Leek, Staffordshire, England.
Hingstone's, Southampton, Hampshire, England.
Hinson Fine Paintings, Sheffield, S.Yorkshire, England.
The Hinton Gallery, Horley, Surrey, England.
His Nibs, London, England.
Hiscock Gallery, Southsea, Hampshire, England.

Hitchin Antiques Gallery, Hitchin, Hertfordshire, England.
Hobbs & Chambers, Cirencester, Gloucestershire, England.
Carlton Hobbs, London, England.
Hobby Horse Antiques, Bridport, Dorset, England.
Hobhouse Ltd, London, England.
Hobsons Choice, Blackpool, Lancashire, England.
Keith Hockin Antiques Ltd, Stow-on-the-Wold, Gloucestershire, England.
William Hockley Antiques, Petworth, W.Sussex, England.
Hoddell Pritchard, Clevedon, Avon, England.
Jean Hodge, Worcester, Hereford & Worcester, England.
Christopher Hodsoll Antiques, London, England.
Hoff Antiques Ltd, London, England.
J.E.Hoffman, Ashley, Northamptonshire, England.
Hofman & Freeman Ltd, Otford, Kent, England.
George Hofman Antiques, Stockbridge, Hampshire, England.
John Hogbin & Son, Tenterden, Kent, England.
John Hogbin & Son, Sandwich, Kent, England.
Keith Hogg, Tenterden, Kent, England.
Michael Hogg, London, England.
Esmond Holden Ltd, Reigate, Surrey, England.
Milton Holgate Antiques, Knaresborough, N.Yorkshire, England.
Holland & Holland Ltd, London, England.
Guy Holland, Eastleach, Gloucestershire, England.
E. Hollander Ltd, Dorking, Surrey, England.
Holleyman & Treacher Ltd, Brighton & Hove, E.Sussex, England.
Hollington Antiques, Long Crendon, Buckinghamshire, England.
Holloway's, Streatley, Berkshire, England.
Holloway's, Banbury, Oxfordshire, England.
Holly House Gallery, North Shields, Tyne & Wear, England.
Hollywood Road Antiques, London, England.
Hollywood Road Gallery, London, England.
Holmes (Jewellers) Ltd, London, England.
Holmes (Silversmiths) Ltd, London, England.
Irene & Alan Holmes & Grant, Redhill, Surrey, England.
Holmes Antiques, Keswick, Cumbria, England.
Brian and Lynn Holmes, London, England.
Julia Holmes Antique Maps and Prints, Haslemere, Surrey, England.
W.W.Holzgrave, Cirencester, Gloucestershire, England.
Home of Antiques, Knaresborough, N.Yorkshire, England.
J.P.J.Homer Oriental Rugs, Cheltenham, Gloucestershire, England.
Homestead Antiques, Kirton, Nottinghamshire, England.
Angela Hone, Marlow, Buckinghamshire, England.
The Honiton Lace Shop, Honiton, Devon, England.
Hood and Broomfield Lyme Galleries, Newcastle-under-Lyme, Staffordshire, England.
Helena Hood and Co, Bath, Avon, England.
Hoodeners Antiques & Collectors Market, Canterbury, Kent, England.
Anthony J.Hook, Westerham, Kent, England.
Hope and Glory (Ernest Titmuss), London, England.
John Hopkins, Cuckfield, W.Sussex, England.
Stephanie Hoppen, London, England.
Paul Hopwell Antiques, West Haddon, Northamptonshire, England.
Horn Antiques, Farnham, Surrey, England.
Edgar Horn, Eastbourne, E.Sussex, England.
Jonathan Horne, London, England.
Adrian Hornsey Ltd, Buckingham, Buckinghamshire, England.
Jose Hornsey, Bradford-on-Avon, Wiltshire, England.
Horological Workshops, Guildford, Surrey, England.
Horsefair Antiques, Chipping Norton, Oxfordshire, England.
Horseshoe Antiques & Gallery, Burford, Oxfordshire, England.
Horsley Antiques Ltd, Eccleshall, Staffordshire, England.
Oliver and Helen Horswill Antiques, West Kirby, Merseyside, England.
Robert Horton Antiques, Hertford, Hertfordshire, England.
J.I.Horwit, London, England.
Hotspur Ltd, London, England.
Houghton Antiques, Market Weighton, Humberside, England.
The House of Antiques, Brighton & Hove, E.Sussex, England.
House of Antiques, Petersfield, Hampshire, England.
House of Buckingham, London, England.
House of Mallett, Surbiton, Surrey, England.
The House of Whiting, Hoddesdon, Hertfordshire, England.
How (of Edinburgh), London, England.
Howard & Reeves, Baldock, Hertfordshire, England.
Howard & Reeves, Hitchin, Hertfordshire, England.
Howard Antiques, Oundle, Northamptonshire, England.
Howard Antiques, London, England.
Thomas Howard-Sneyd Ltd, London, England.
Derek Howard, London, England.
Janet Howard, Felsted, Essex, England.
Jonathan Howard, Chipping Norton, Oxfordshire, England.
Howards of Aberystwyth, Aberystwyth, Dyfed, Wales.
Howes Bookshop, Hastings, E.Sussex, England.
Howes Gallery, Petworth, W.Sussex, England.
Robert Howes Antiques, Horrabridge, Devon, England.
Howison-Haworth, St Anne's, Lancashire, England.
Barry Howkins Antiques, Great Yarmouth, Norfolk, England.
John Howkins Antiques, Great Yarmouth, Norfolk, England.
Hubbard Antiques, Leominster, Hereford & Worcester, England.
Hubbard Antiques, Ipswich, Suffolk, England.
J.& J.Hubbard Antiques, St Peter Port, Guernsey, Channel Islands.
John Hubbard Antiques, Birmingham, W.Midlands, England.
Eric Hudes, Braintree, Essex, England.
Eric Hudes, London, England.
L.J.Huggett & Son, Honiton, Devon, England.
Colin S.Hughes, Machynlleth, Powys, Wales.
G. & M.Hughes, Machynlleth, Powys, Wales.
M.A.& D.A.Hughes, Bath, Avon, England.
Paul Hughes, Antique & Ancient Textiles, London, England.
Roger Hughes Antique Gallery, Swansea, W.Glamorgan, Wales.
Hull Pine Co, Hull, Humberside, England.
Christopher Hull Gallery, London, England.
Human Touch, London, England.
Owen Humble, Newcastle upon Tyne, Tyne & Wear, England.
Humbleyard Fine Art, Holt, Norfolk, England.
Dudley Hume, Brighton & Hove, E.Sussex, England.
E. Humphrey, Edinburgh, Lothian, Scotland.
Cyril Humphris, London, England.
Humphry Antiques, Petworth, W.Sussex, England.
Hundred And One, London, England.
Hungerford Arcade, Hungerford, Berkshire, England.
Chisholm Hunter, Glasgow, Strathclyde, Scotland.
Sally Hunter and Patrick Seale Fine Art, London, England.
Huntington Antiques Ltd, Stow-on-the-Wold, Gloucestershire, England.
Hurford & Scott, London, England.
Anthony Hurst Antiques, Woodbridge, Suffolk, England.
Derek S. Hutchings, Newport, Gwent, Wales.
Clare Hutchison, Folkestone, Kent, England.
Hutton Antiques, Shrewsbury, Shropshire, England.
Eleanor Hutton, Dorking, Surrey, England.
J. & J. Hutton, Berkhamsted, Hertfordshire, England.
Martin Hutton, Ninfield, E.Sussex, England.
Hyde Park Antiques, London, England.
Shelagh Hyde, Rhos-on-Sea, Clwyd, Wales.
Hymor Photographers Ltd, Reading, Berkshire, England.
Hymore Hodson & Potts Restorations, Godalming, Surrey, England.
Hymore Hodson Antiques, London, England.
Joyce Hynds Ceramics, Rochester, Kent, England.
Hythe Galleries, Hythe, Kent, England.
HQ84, Gloucester, Gloucestershire, England.

Ibbett Mosely, Sevenoaks, Kent, England.
Iconastas, London, England.
Idears, Diss, Norfolk, England.
Manya Igel Fine Arts Ltd, London, England.
Francis Iles, Rochester, Kent, England.
Images Antiques, Bath, Avon, England.
Imperial Antiques, Stockport, Greater Manchester, England.
Imperial Antiques, Hull, Humberside, England.
Imrie Antiques, Bridge of Earn, Tayside, Scotland.
Inch's Books, York, N.Yorkshire, England.
Brand Inglis Ltd., London, England.
A.G.Ingram Ltd, Edinburgh, Lothian, Scotland.
Raymond P.Inman, Brighton & Hove, E.Sussex, England.
Malcolm Innes Gallery, London, England.
Malcolm Innes Gallery, Edinburgh, Lothian, Scotland.
Intercol London, London, England.
Iona Antiques, London, England.
Ipswich Pianos, Ipswich, Suffolk, England.
Irelands Hall & Palmer, Wymondham, Norfolk, England.
Ironbridge Antique Centre, Telford, Shropshire, England.
Giulia Irving, Richmond, Surrey, England.
Itchen Gallery, Winchester, Hampshire, England.
Its About Time, Westcliff-on-Sea, Essex, England.
Ivanhoe Antiques, Ashby de la Zouch, Leicestershire, England.
John Ives Antiquarian Books, Twickenham, Middlesex, England.
Richard and Georgina Ivor, London, England.
J.N.Antiques, Redbourn, Hertfordshire, England.
J.V.T. Antiques, Bingley, W.Yorkshire, England.
The Jackdaw, Rothbury, Northumberland, England.
Jackson-Stops & Staff, Chester, Cheshire, England.
Jackson-Stops & Staff, Cirencester, Gloucestershire, England.
Jackson-Stops & Staff, London, England.
Charles Jackson Antiques, Penzance, Cornwall, England.
Kenneth Jackson (Antiques), Edinburgh, Lothian, Scotland.
Olivia Jackson Antiques, London, England.
Peter & Heather Jackson Antiques, Brackley, Northamptonshire, England.
Jackson's, Ramsey, Cambridgeshire, England.
Jackson's, Peel, Isle of Man.
Jackson's Antiques, Barnard Castle, Durham, England.
Jacobs & Hunt, Petersfield, Hampshire, England.
Alan Jacobs Gallery, London, England.
Nicola Jacobs Gallery, London, England.
Bernard Jacobson Ltd, London, England.
Jadis Ltd, Bath, Avon, England.
A.R.Jaffray, Melksham, Wiltshire, England.
Anthony James Antiques, Whimple, Devon, England.
Anthony James & Son Ltd, London, England.
David James Fine Paintings, London, England.
L.A.James, St Albans, Hertfordshire, England.
A.E.Jameson & Co, Sheffield, S.Yorkshire, England.
Japanese Gallery, London, England.
Joan Jarman Antiques, Teddington, Middlesex, England.
Gillian Jason Gallery, London, England.
Melvyn Jay Antiques, London, England.
Jays Fine Art Dealers, Southport, Merseyside, England.
Peter Jeeves Antiques, Cuckfield, W.Sussex, England.
Jefferies Antiques, Stevenage, Hertfordshire, England.
John Jeffery & Son, Shaftesbury, Dorset, England.
Colin Jeffrey Associates, Crewkerne, Somerset, England.
Tobias Jellinek, London, England.
Jennings, Hereford, Hereford & Worcester, England.
Jennings Antiques, Torquay, Devon, England.
Jennings Antiques, Leominster, Hereford & Worcester, England.
Paul Jennings Antiques, Hayle, Cornwall, England.
Charles Jerdein, London, England.
Jeremy Ltd, London, England.
John Jesse & Irina Laski, London, England.

Laurimore Gallery, Boxford, Suffolk, England.
D.S.Lavender (Antiques) Ltd, London, England.
J.Lavian, London, England.
Lawrence Fine Art of Crewkerne, Crewkerne, Somerset, England.
F.G.Lawrence & Sons, Redhill, Surrey, England.
Lawson Larg, York, N.Yorkshire, England.
F. & T. Lawson, Antiques, Richmond, Surrey, England.
Layton Antiques, Richmond, Surrey, England.
J.K.Layton, Harrogate, N.Yorkshire, England.
Anthony W.Laywood, Grantham, Lincolnshire, England.
David Lazarus, Hartley Wintney, Hampshire, England.
Michel Le Coz, Castle Combe, Wiltshire, England.
F. Le Gallais, St Helier, Jersey, Channel Islands.
Le Soken Antiques, Thorpe-le-Soken, Essex, England.
Leaside Antiques, Luton, Bedfordshire, England.
Ledger Antiques, London, England.
Arthur Lee Antiques, Knutsford, Cheshire, England.
C.G.Lee, Llandudno, Gwynedd, Wales.
Ronald A. Lee (Fine Arts) Ltd, Byfleet, Surrey, England.
Ronald A.Lee (Fine Arts) Ltd, London, England.
W.A.Lee, Ely, Cambridgeshire, England.
M.Lees & Sons, Worcester, Hereford & Worcester, England.
Lefevre Gallery, London, England.
The Leger Galleries Ltd, London, England.
E.C.Legg & Son, Cirencester, Gloucestershire, England.
Michael Legg Antiques, Dorchester, Dorset, England.
Leggatt Bros, London, England.
C.T.Legge Oriental Carpets, Oxford, Oxfordshire, England.
Leicester Antique Centre Ltd, Leicester, Leicestershire, England.
Leicestershire Sporting Gallery, Market Harborough, Leicestershire, England.
Leigh Auction Rooms, Leigh-on-Sea, Essex, England.
Leigh Gallery, London, England.
Laurie Leigh Antiques, Oxford, Oxfordshire, England.
P.K. & R.H. Leigh, Grimsby, Humberside, England.
Leinster Fine Art, London, England.
Lennard Antiques, Buckingham, Buckinghamshire, England.
Lennard Antiques, Northampton, Northamptonshire, England.
Lennox Antiques, Brighton & Hove, E.Sussex, England.
Lensfield Antiques, Cambridge, Cambridgeshire, England.
Nellie Lenson & Roy Smith, London, England.
Lenygon & Morant Ltd, London, England.
Leominster Antiques, Leominster, Hereford & Worcester, England.
Alan Leonard Antiques, Liverpool, Merseyside, England.
Lesley's Antiques, Hull, Humberside, England.
R.K.Leslie Antiques, Southampton, Hampshire, England.
Letham Antiques, Edinburgh, Lothian, Scotland.
David Letham, Edinburgh, Lothian, Scotland.
Lettys Antiques Ltd, Leicester, Leicestershire, England.
Lev (Antiques) Ltd, London, England.
M.P.Levene Ltd, London, England.
Leverington Hall Gallery, Wisbech, Cambridgeshire, England.
E.D.Levine, Cromer, Norfolk, England.
Levine, Henry & Co, Norwich, Norfolk, England.
Lewes Auction Rooms (Julian Dawson), Lewes, E.Sussex, England.
Lewis & Lloyd Ltd, Reigate, Surrey, England.
Ivor & Patricia Lewis Antique & Fine Art Dealers, Peterborough, Cambridgeshire, England.
M. & D. Lewis Antiques, London, England.
Michael and Amanda Lewis Oriental Carpets and Rugs, Wellington, Somerset, England.
Michael and Amanda Lewis Oriental Carpets and Rugs, Bristol, Avon, England.
Leycester Map Galleries Ltd, Arnesby, Leicestershire, England.
Liberty & Co Ltd, London, England.
Libra Antiques, London, England.
Susan Liddiard Antiques, Bristol, Avon, England.
Lighthouse Antiques, Leominster, Hereford & Worcester, England.
Lighthouse Antiques, London, England.
Lillie Antiques, London, England.
Lime Tree Antiques, Burwash, E.Sussex, England.
Limner Antiques, London, England.
Linaire Antiques, Hemel Hempstead, Hertfordshire, England.
Lincoln Fine Art, Lincoln, Lincolnshire, England.
Lincolnshire Antique Centre, Horncastle, Lincolnshire, England.
Linden House Antiques, Stansted Mountfitchet, Essex, England.
Peter Linden, Blackrock, Co Dublin, Eire.
Rose Linden Antiques, Probus, Cornwall, England.
S.Linden, London, England.
Lindfield Galleries Ltd, Lindfield, W.Sussex, England.
Lindsay Antiques, London, England.
Muriel Lindsay, Winchcombe, Gloucestershire, England.
Lindsell Chairs, Coggeshall, Essex, England.
Lindum Antiques, Donington-on-Bain, Lincolnshire, England.
Lindy Lou Antiques, Scarborough, N.Yorkshire, England.
Eric Lineham & Son, London, England.
Ann Lingard, Rye, E.Sussex, England.
Linnets Nest Antiques & Mawby's International, Rugby, Warwickshire, England.
Greig Linton Antiques, Edinburgh, Lothian, Scotland.
Lion Antiques, Coggeshall, Essex, England.
Lion Gallery & Bookshop, Knutsford, Cheshire, England.
Lion House/Robert Croot Antiques, Chipping Norton, Oxfordshire, England.
J.Lipitch Ltd, London, England.
Michael Lipitch, London, England.
Peter Lipitch Ltd, London, England.
W. Lipka Ltd, London, England.
Louis Lipman Antiques, Brentwood, Essex, England.
Paul D. Lipson, Aylesbury, Buckinghamshire, England.
Sanda Lipton, London, England.
Lisson Gallery, London, England.
Litchfield Gallery, Bournemouth, Dorset, England.
The Little Antique Shop, Stoke-on-Trent, Staffordshire, England.
The Little Bizarre, Dunchurch, Warwickshire, England.
Little Bric a Brac Shop, Bridport, Dorset, England.
Little Raven, Oswestry, Shropshire, England.
Little Thatch Antiques, Southport, Merseyside, England.
Little Winchester Gallery, London, England.
Littlebury Antiques, Saffron Walden, Essex, England.
A.C.Littlejohns, Bideford, Devon, England.
Llandogo Antiques, Llandogo, Gwent, Wales.
Llewelyn Antiques, Cardiff, S.Glamorgan, Wales.
Tom Lloyd-Roberts, Mold, Clwyd, Wales.
Richard Lloyd, Henllan, Dyfed, Wales.
Robin Lloyd Antiques, Ross-on-Wye, Hereford & Worcester, England.
Lloyd's Bookshop, Wingham, Kent, England.
Lock Antiques, Blackburn, Lancashire, England.
Locke and England Auctioneers, Leamington, Warwickshire, England.
Lockson Services Ltd, London, England.
The Lodge, Ballyduff, Co Waterford, Eire.
Loewenthal Antiques, Petworth, W.Sussex, England.
Loft Antiques, Dorking, Surrey, England.
London & Southern Shipping, Portslade, E.Sussex, England.
London Apprentice Antiques, St Austell, Cornwall, England.
The London Architectural Salvage & Supply Co Ltd, London, England.
London Cigarette Card Co Ltd, Somerton, Somerset, England.
London House Antique Centre, Marlborough, Wiltshire, England.
The London Restoration Centre, London, England.
London Silver Vaults, London, England.
Long Melford Antiques, Long Melford, Suffolk, England.
Long Street Gallery, Tetbury, Gloucestershire, England.
John Long Antiques, Manchester, Greater Manchester, England.
Stephen Long, London, England.
Jessica Longhurst, Long Melford, Suffolk, England.
Longley's Antiques, Castle Cary, Somerset, England.
Paul Longmire Ltd, London, England.
M. & J. Longmore, London, England.
Longton Hall Antiques, Longton, Lancashire, England.
Look Around Antiques, Chester, Cheshire, England.
Brian Loomes, Pateley Bridge, N.Yorkshire, England.
Loot, London, England.
Alan Lord Antiques, Folkestone, Kent, England.
Lords Gallery, London, England.
Lorelle Art & Antiques, Callington, Cornwall, England.
Lots Road Chelsea Auction Galleries, London, England.
N.W.Lott & H.J.Gerrish Ltd, Froxfield, Wiltshire, England.
N.W.Lott & H.J.Gerrish Ltd, London, England.
I.E.Lovatt Antiques, Glasgow, Strathclyde, Scotland.
The Love Affair - Antiques, Chertsey, Surrey, England.
David Love, Harrogate, N.Yorkshire, England.
Thomas Love & Sons Ltd, Perth, Tayside, Scotland.
Peter Loveday Prints, London, England.
Clive Loveless, London, England.
Lowe & Pomfrett, Maidenhead, Berkshire, England.
Lowe & Sons Ltd, Chester, Cheshire, England.
Charles Lowe & Sons Ltd, Loughborough, Leicestershire, England.
Lowen Gallery, Stoke-on-Trent, Staffordshire, England.
Lower Fold Antiques, Stockport, Greater Manchester, England.
Graham Lower, Flimwell, E.Sussex, England.
The Lucerne Gallery, London, England.
Lucky Parrot (Antiques and Things), London, England.
Luella Antiques, Plymouth, Devon, England.
Charles Lumb & Sons Ltd, Harrogate, N.Yorkshire, England.
Lumley Cazalet Ltd, London, England.
Lunn Antiques Ltd, London, England.
Lupin Antiques Ltd, Windsor, Berkshire, England.
Charles A. Lusted Ltd, Tunbridge Wells, Kent, England.
Lustre Metal Antiques Ltd, Nottingham, Nottinghamshire, England.
Lyall & Co, Bourne, Lincolnshire, England.
John Lyle, Sidmouth, Devon, England.
M.J.Lympany, Malmesbury, Wiltshire, England.
Pamela Lynch, Wilton, Wiltshire, England.
Lynde Albury Antiques, London, England.
Lyndhurst Antiques, Newcastle upon Tyne, Tyne & Wear, England.
Lynton Porcelain Company & Keith Arden, Much Hadham, Hertfordshire, England.
Richard Lyon Oriental Art Books, Kingston upon Thames, Surrey, England.
Lyons Court Antiques, Dorking, Surrey, England.
Lyons Gallery, London, England.
The Lyver and Boydell Galleries, Liverpool, Merseyside, England.
LPJ Antiques, London, England.

M. & M. Oriental Gallery Ltd, London, England.
Maas Gallery, London, England.
Mac Humble Antiques, Bath, Avon, England.
Macclesfield Antiques, Macclesfield, Cheshire, England.
Mary Mackie Antiques, Elton, Nottinghamshire, England.
Mackinnon and Strachey, London, England.
Ruth Macklin Smith Antiques, Brighton & Hove, E.Sussex, England.
Michael Maclaren Photography, Edinburgh, Lothian, Scotland.
The Maclean Gallery, London, England.
Colin Macleods Antique Centre, Southsea, Hampshire, England.
Richard Macnutt Ltd, Hartfield Wells, E.Sussex, England.
William MacAdam, Edinburgh, Lothian, Scotland.
MacConnal-Mason, London, England.
Finbar MacDonnell, London, England.
William MacIntosh & Co, Edinburgh, Lothian, Scotland.
Iain MacKinnon Antiques, Glasgow, Strathclyde, Scotland.

Murdoch MacTaggart, Yeovil, Somerset, England.
Sue Madden, London, England.
Maddermarket Antiques, Norwich, Norfolk, England.
Made of Honour, Chester, Cheshire, England.
V. & C. Madeira, Leamington, Warwickshire, England.
Madoc Antique & Art Gallery, Llandudno, Gwynedd, Wales.
Maggs Antiques, Liverpool, Merseyside, England.
Maggs Bros Ltd, London, England.
Magna Gallery, Oxford, Oxfordshire, England.
Magpie Antiques, Sudbury, Suffolk, England.
Magpie Antiques & Jewellers, Evesham, Hereford & Worcester, England.
The Magpie's Nest, Warrington, Cheshire, England.
Victor Mahy Ltd, Stockbridge, Hampshire, England.
Mail Order Book Specialist, London, England.
Maindy Fine Antiques, Cardiff, S.Glamorgan, Wales.
C.H. Major, London, England.
Malahide Castle Antiques, Malahide, Co Dublin, Eire.
Maldon Antiques & Collectors Market, Maldon, Essex, England.
Nevil and Betty Malin, Warwick, Warwickshire, England.
The Mall Antiques Arcade, London, England.
The Mall Gallery, London, England.
Mallams, Cheltenham, Gloucestershire, England.
Mallams, Oxford, Oxfordshire, England.
Mallett & Son (Antiques) Ltd, London, England.
Mallett at Bourdon House Ltd, London, England.
Mallglade Antiques, Barnsley, S.Yorkshire, England.
E.P.Mallory & Son Ltd, Bath, Avon, England.
Malmesbury Antiques and Interiors, Malmesbury, Wiltshire, England.
Maltings Antiques, Aylsham, Norfolk, England.
The Malvern Bookshop, Malvern, Hereford & Worcester, England.
Malvern Studios, Malvern, Hereford & Worcester, England.
Mandell's Gallery, Norwich, Norfolk, England.
Mandeys Antiques, Brasted, Kent, England.
Mangate Gallery, London, England.
A.J.Mangion Antiques, London, England.
D.M.&P.Manheim (Peter Manheim) Ltd, London, England.
Mrs David Manheim, London, England.
Manion Antiques, Ashbourne, Derbyshire, England.
J.Manley & Thames Gallery, Eton, Berkshire, England.
David Mann & Sons Ltd, Cranleigh, Surrey, England.
Kathleen Mann Antiques, Harrow on the Hill, Middlesex, England.
Manor Antiques, Wilshamstead, Bedfordshire, England.
Manor Barn Pine, Ilkley, W.Yorkshire, England.
Manor Farm Antiques, Standlake, Oxfordshire, England.
Manor Farm Antiques & Garden Ornaments, Swaffham, Norfolk, England.
Manor House Antiques, Datchet, Berkshire, England.
Manor House Antiques, Cheltenham, Gloucestershire, England.
Manor House Antiques, Ripley, Surrey, England.
F.C.Manser & Son Ltd, Shrewsbury, Shropshire, England.
Mansfield Antiques, Mansfield, Nottinghamshire, England.
Edward Manson, Woodbridge, Suffolk, England.
Mansour Gallery, London, England.
Manspace Gallery, London, England.
Many Things, Sheffield, S.Yorkshire, England.
The Map House, London, England.
Mappin & Webb Ltd (Butt & Co), Chester, Cheshire, England.
Marble Hill Gallery, Twickenham, Middlesex, England.
Marcella Antiques, London, England.
Mark Marchant, Antiques, Coggeshall, Essex, England.
S.Marchant & Son, London, England.
Mare Hill Galleries, Pulborough, W.Sussex, England.
Mariners Antiques, Saltburn-by-the-Sea, Cleveland, England.
Mariposa, St Albans, Hertfordshire, England.
Mark Gallery, London, England.
Market Antiques, Hoylake, Merseyside, England.
Market Hill Art & Antiques, Diss, Norfolk, England.
Market House Antiques, Burnham Market, Norfolk, England.
Market Place Antiques, Henley-on-Thames, Oxfordshire, England.
Market Place Antiques, Saxmundham, Suffolk, England.
Markland Antiques, Borough Green, Kent, England.
Marks Antiques, Oldham, Greater Manchester, England.
Marks Antiques Ltd, London, England.
B.& A.Marks, Westerham, Kent, England.
Peter Marks Antiques Warehouse, Portslade, E.Sussex, England.
Marksdanes Antiques Ltd, Bruton, Somerset, England.
Markswood Gallery, Braintree, Essex, England.
Markswood Gallery, Great Bardfield, Essex, England.
Marlborough Antiques, Marlborough, Wiltshire, England.
Marlborough Fine Art (London) Ltd, London, England.
Marlborough House Antiques, Yarmouth, Isle of Wight, England.
Marlborough Rare Books Ltd, London, England.
Marlborough Sporting Gallery & Bookshop, Marlborough, Wiltshire, England.
The William Marler Gallery, Cirencester, Gloucestershire, England.
William Marler Gallery, Ludlow, Shropshire, England.
J.Marlow Antiques, Harrogate, N.Yorkshire, England.
Marneys, Bournemouth, Dorset, England.
Iain Marr Antiques, Beauly, Highland, Scotland.
Marrin & Sons, Folkestone, Kent, England.
Michael Marriott Ltd, London, England.
Nan Marris, Lincoln, Lincolnshire, England.
Marron Coins, Sheffield, S.Yorkshire, England.
G.E. Marsh (Antique Clocks), Winchester, Hampshire, England.
Jasper Marsh, Henley-in-Arden, Warwickshire, England.
Martin Marsh Militaria, Whaley Bridge, Derbyshire, England.
Simon Marsh Antiques, Bletchingley, Surrey, England.
Frank R. Marshall & Co, Knutsford, Cheshire, England.
Marshfield Antiques, Wells, Norfolk, England.
Martin & Co Ltd, Cheltenham, Gloucestershire, England.
Martin & Co Ltd, Birmingham, W.Midlands, England.
Martin & Parke, Farnborough, Hampshire, England.
Messrs Martin & Stratford, Alton, Hampshire, England.
David Martin-Taylor, London, England.
C.J. Martin (Coins) Ltd, London, England.
Iris Martin Lacemaking Supplies, Olney, Buckinghamshire, England.
John Martin Antiques, Castle Cary, Somerset, England.
Peter J. Martin, Eton, Berkshire, England.
Philip Martin Music Books, York, N.Yorkshire, England.
R.E. Martin, Tiverton, Devon, England.
Robin Martin, London, England.
Martins Antiques, Sheffield, S.Yorkshire, England.
Ed Mason, London, England.
Jeremy J. Mason, London, England.
John Mason (Wavertree), Liverpool, Merseyside, England.
Paul Mason, London, England.
Mason's Yard Gallery, London, England.
Massada Antiques, London, England.
Mathaf Gallery Ltd, London, England.
Michael R. Mathews, Berkeley, Gloucestershire, England.
S.& O. Mathews, Eridge, E.Sussex, England.
Gerald Mathias Clocks, London, England.
John Mathieson & Co, Edinburgh, Lothian, Scotland.
Matsell Antiques Ltd, Nottingham, Nottinghamshire, England.
Matt's Gallery, London, England.
Mattar Arcade, Wincanton, Somerset, England.
Matthews & Davies Fine Art Ltd, Cowbridge, S.Glamorgan, Wales.
Michael Matthews, Honiton, Devon, England.
Matthiesen Fine Art Ltd, London, England.
Richard Maude Tools, London, England.
Janet Maund, Cheltenham, Gloucestershire, England.
A.Maurice & Co Ltd, London, England.
Mawby's International, Churchover, Warwickshire, England.
Thos Mawer & Son, Lincoln, Lincolnshire, England.
Jill Maxwell-Hyslop, Beaminster, Dorset, England.
May & Son, Andover, Hampshire, England.
J. & J. May, London, England.
Mayfair Antiques, Pwllheli, Gwynedd, Wales.
Mayflower Antiques, Padstow, Cornwall, England.
Mayflower Antiques, Harwich, Essex, England.
The Mayor Gallery, London, England.
Mayorcas Ltd, London, England.
Maypole Antiques, Helen's Bay, Co Down, Northern Ireland.
I.J.Mazure & Co Ltd, London, England.
M. McAleer, London, England.
McAlpine Ancient Art, London, England.
McCabes Antiques, Newry, Co Down, Northern Ireland.
F.J.McCarthy Ltd, Newark-on-Trent, Nottinghamshire, England.
Ian McCarthy, Clutton, Avon, England.
McCartneys, Ludlow, Shropshire, England.
Norma McCaw Conservation, London, England.
Margaret McCloy Antiques, Kingston upon Thames, Surrey, England.
Heather McConnell, London, England.
Joy McDonald, London, England.
R.McDonnell Ltd, Dublin, Co Dublin, Eire.
McDowell & Stern Ltd, York, N.Yorkshire, England.
The McEwan Gallery, Ballater, Grampian, Scotland.
Mike McGlynn Antiques, Shannon Airport, Co Clare, Eire.
R.I. McKay, London, England.
J.W.McKenzie, Bookseller, Ewell, Surrey, England.
Rodd McLennan, London, England.
John McMaster, Tenterden, Kent, England.
McNaughtan's Bookshop, Edinburgh, Lothian, Scotland.
Lesley McPherson Antiques, Peel, , Isle of Man.
W. & P. McQuade Antiques, Kilbarchan, Strathclyde, Scotland.
McTague of Harrogate, Harrogate, N.Yorkshire, England.
Jeannette Meager, Cheltenham, Gloucestershire, England.
Medalcrest Ltd, Hungerford, Berkshire, England.
The Medici Galleries, London, England.
Jean Megahy, Glasgow, Strathclyde, Scotland.
Mel Antiques, Royston, Hertfordshire, England.
Melbourne Antiques, Penzance, Cornwall, England.
Melbourne Antiques, Wolverhampton, W.Midlands, England.
D.Mellor & A.L.Baxter Antiquarian Booksellers, London, England.
David Mellor, London, England.
Memories Antiques, Coventry, W.Midlands, England.
Memories Antiques, LLanelli, Dyfed, Wales.
Nigel B. Mendes da Costa, Richmond, Surrey, England.
Christopher Mendez, London, England.
Mendip Antiques, Bath, Avon, England.
Hugh Mendl Antiques, Totnes, Devon, England.
Sybil Mendoza, London, England.
Mercat Antiques, Glasgow, Strathclyde, Scotland.
T.Mercer Chronometers, Cheltenham, Gloucestershire, England.
Mercury Antiques, London, England.
Mercury Gallery Ltd, London, England.
John Meredith Antiques, Chagford, Devon, England.
Meriden House Antiques, Stourbridge, W.Midlands, England.
Merlin Antiques & Restorations, Sedbergh, Cumbria, England.
Philip & Anne Merridale, Stockbridge, Hampshire, England.
Messenger May Baverstock, Godalming, Surrey, England.
Messengers, Bicester, Oxfordshire, England.
David Messum Ltd, Marlow, Buckinghamshire, England.
B.C.Metalcrafts Ltd, London, England.
Metcalfe Jackson, Wimborne Minster, Dorset, England.
Mews Antiques, Harrogate, N.Yorkshire, England.
Meyers Gallery, Ingatestone, Essex, England.
Nicholas Meyjes Photography, Oxford, Oxfordshire, England.
Meynell's Bookshop, Chichester, W.Sussex, England.
Michael Coins, London, England.
Michael's Antiques, Cambridge, Cambridgeshire, England.
Trevor Micklem, Antiques, Tiverton, Devon, England.
Midas Antiques, Walsall, W.Midlands, England.

Arthur Middleton Ltd, London, England.
Bernard C. Middleton, London, England.
Lilian Middleton's Antique Doll Shop, Stow-on-the-Wold, Gloucestershire, England.
Midhurst Antiques Market, Midhurst, W.Sussex, England.
Miles Antiques, Cardiff, S.Glamorgan, Wales.
Archie Miles Bookshop, Harrogate, N.Yorkshire, England.
Richard Miles Antiques, London, England.
Roy Miles Fine Paintings Ltd, London, England.
Milkhouse Antiques, Sissinghurst, Kent, England.
Mill on the Soar Antiques Ltd, Quorn, Leicestershire, England.
Mill Farm Antiques, Disley, Cheshire, England.
Mill House Antiques, Ashford, Kent, England.
Mill House Antiques, Shrewsbury, Shropshire, England.
J.Miller Calder, Thurso, Highland, Scotland.
David Miller Antiques, London, England.
Duncan R. Miller Fine Arts, London, England.
H. Miller (Antiques) Ltd, Brighton & Hove, E.Sussex, England.
H. Miller (Antiques) Ltd, London, England.
Michael Miller, Hurstpierpoint, W.Sussex, England.
W.J. Miller & Son, Wooler, Northumberland, England.
Millers of Chelsea Antiques Limited, Ringwood, Hampshire, England.
Millers Antiques, Kelvedon, Kelvedon, Essex, England.
Millhouse, Petworth, W.Sussex, England.
Millhouse Fine Arts, Petworth, W.Sussex, England.
Mills Antiques, Cullompton, Devon, England.
Milne & Moller, London, England.
Milne Henderson, London, England.
John Milne, Aberdeen, Grampian, Scotland.
Nigel Milne Ltd, London, England.
H. I. Milnthorpe, Settle, N.Yorkshire, England.
Milton Abbot Antiques, Tavistock, Devon, England.
Milverton Antiques, Milverton, Somerset, England.
The Minster Gates Bookshop, York, N.Yorkshire, England.
Mitchell Antiques Ltd, Dublin, Co Dublin, Eire.
John Mitchell & Sons, London, England.
Paul Mitchell, London, England.
Sally Mitchell Fine Arts, Askham, Nottinghamshire, England.
T.J.Mitchell Antiques Ltd, Dublin, Co Dublin, Eire.
Victor Mitchell Exports Ltd, Roscrea, Co Tipperary, Eire.
Mitre Antiques, Wells, Somerset, England.
Mitre Frames, London, England.
Kate Moffatt, London, England.
Bashir Mohamed Ltd, London, England.
Mole Hall Antiques, Aldeburgh, Suffolk, England.
Geoffrey Mole Antique Exports, Hull, Humberside, England.
Mon Galerie, Amersham, Buckinghamshire, England.
Mona Antiqua & Tudor Rose, Beaumaris, Gwynedd, Wales.
Monarch Antiques, Glastonbury, Somerset, England.
Lennox Money (Antiques) Ltd, London, England.
D.C.Monk & Son, London, England.
Monkton Galleries, Hindon, Wiltshire, England.
Monro Heywood Ltd, London, England.
Mrs Monro (Antiques) Ltd, London, England.
Peter Montagu-Williams, Tanworth-in-Arden, Warwickshire, England.
Montpelier Studio, London, England.
Monway Ltd, London, England.
L. Moody, Southampton, Hampshire, England.
Moolham Mill Antiques, Ilminster, Somerset, England.
Riro D.Mooney, Duxford, Cambridgeshire, England.
Moore Allen & Innocent, Cirencester, Gloucestershire, England.
Eric T.Moore, Hitchin, Hertfordshire, England.
Michael Moore Antiques, Clare, Suffolk, England.
Stephen Moore Ltd, Lewes, E.Sussex, England.
Walter Moores & Son, Leicester, Leicestershire, England.
Patrick Moorhead Antiques, Brighton & Hove, E.Sussex, England.
Moorhen Antiques, Walton on the Hill, Surrey, England.
A.D.Moorhouse Ltd, Sheffield, S.Yorkshire, England.
Moorland-Coon, Wincanton, Somerset, England.
Moreton Street Gallery, London, England.
C.S. Moreton (Antiques), Inchture, Tayside, Scotland.
Rex Moreton, Wolvesnewton, Gwent, Wales.
P.and G. Morley, Warwick, Warwickshire, England.
Robert Morley & Company Limited, London, England.
William Morley Antiques, Taunton, Somerset, England.
Morphets, Harrogate, N.Yorkshire, England.
Morris Antiques & Bygones, Wickham Market, Suffolk, England.
The Morris Singer Foundry Ltd, Basingstoke, Hampshire, England.
Alan Morris, Redditch, Hereford & Worcester, England.
Ann Morris Antiques, Cranbrook, Kent, England.
James H.Morris & Co, Northop, Clwyd, Wales.
John G.Morris Ltd, Petworth, W.Sussex, England.
Morton Morris & Co, London, England.
Richard Morris, London, England.
Stephen Morris Shipping Ltd, London, England.
Morris's, Abergavenny, Gwent, Wales.
Guy Morrison, London, England.
J.A. Morrison Ltd, Thurnby, Leicestershire, England.
Robert Morrison & Son, York, N.Yorkshire, England.
Terence Morse & Son Ltd, London, England.
E.J. Morten (Booksellers) Ltd, Didsbury, Greater Manchester, England.
Morten's Bookshops Ltd, Macclesfield, Cheshire, England.
Mortimer & Hughes, St Andrews, Fife, Scotland.
Brian Mortimer Antiques, Exeter, Devon, England.
Charles & Joan Mortimer & Sons, Great Chesterford, Essex, England.
Mortlake Antiques, London, England.
John Morton Ltd, Dublin, Co Dublin, Eire.
The Moseley Gallery, Birmingham, W.Midlands, England.
Moss Galleries, London, England.
Ralph and Bruce Moss, Baldock, Hertfordshire, England.
Sydney L. Moss Ltd, London, England.
A. & M. Mossowski, London, England.
H.C. Mote, London, England.
Richard Moult Antiques, Stow-on-the-Wold, Gloucestershire, England.
The Mount Antiques, Whitby, N.Yorkshire, England.
Moxhams Antiques, Bradford-on-Avon, Wiltshire, England.
Muirhead Moffat & Co, Glasgow, Strathclyde, Scotland.
Mulberry House Galleries, Pulborough, W.Sussex, England.
Frederick Mulder, London, England.
Patrick Mullins, Salisbury, Wiltshire, England.
Multum-In-Parvo & Tools Past, Kendal, Cumbria, England.
Ewan Mundy Fine Art, Glasgow, Strathclyde, Scotland.
Colin Murdoch, Kingussie, Highland, Scotland.
Ian Murray Antiques Warehouse, Perth, Tayside, Scotland.
Murray's Ltd, Leicester, Leicestershire, England.
Thomas Murtagh Antiques, Avoca, Co Wicklow, Eire.
Museum of Childhood, Anglesey, Gwynedd, Wales.
Lawrence Musgrove Antiques, Monmouth, Gwent, Wales.
G.B.Mussenden & Son, Bournemouth, Dorset, England.
Myers Galleries, Gargrave, N.Yorkshire, England.
Myriad Antiques, London, England.
Mytton Antiques, Shrewsbury, Shropshire, England.
MGJ Antiques, Wallingford, Oxfordshire, England.
The M11 Antiques Centre, Newport, Essex, England.

Richard & Pamela Nadin, Frome, Somerset, England.
Richard & Pamela Nadin, Bradford-on-Avon, Wiltshire, England.
Peter Nahum, London, England.
D. & N.Nairne Antiques, Edinburgh, Lothian, Scotland.
G.R. Naisby & Son, Stockport, Greater Manchester, England.
Nanbooks, Settle, N.Yorkshire, England.
Geoffrey Nanson Antiques, Brampton, Cumbria, England.
Nantwich Antiques Centre, Nantwich, Cheshire, England.
Sylvia Napier Ltd, London, England.
Nash Antiques, Bath, Avon, England.
Nash Antiques, London, England.
Nash Antiques, Chepstow, Gwent, Wales.
John Nash Antiques, Red Marley, Gloucestershire, England.
Paul Nash, Tetbury, Gloucestershire, England.
Peter Nash, London, England.
Nathan & Co (Birmingham) Ltd, Birmingham, W.Midlands, England.
John Nathan, Exeter, Devon, England.
Naylers, London, England.
Neal Sons & Fletcher, Woodbridge, Suffolk, England.
Neale Antiques, Hertford, Hertfordshire, England.
Neales of Nottingham, Nottingham, Nottinghamshire, England.
Neales Innes Nichols, Derby, Derbyshire, England.
Neates, Hungerford, Berkshire, England.
Neates, Newbury, Berkshire, England.
Neates, Marlborough, Wiltshire, England.
R.S.& S.Necus, London, England.
Needham Market Antique Centre, Needham Market, Suffolk, England.
Victor Needham Antiques, Stockbridge, Hampshire, England.
John Nelson, Edinburgh, Lothian, Scotland.
Neptune Gallery, Dublin, Co Dublin, Eire.
D.M.Nesbit & Co. Auctioneers, Portsmouth, Hampshire, England.
Nethergate Gallery, Dundee, Tayside, Scotland.
Netherly Cottage Antiques, Milburn, Cumbria, England.
Nevill Antiques, Shrewsbury, Shropshire, England.
Nevill Gallery, Bath, Avon, England.
Nevill Gallery, Canterbury, Kent, England.
Guy Nevill Pictures, London, England.
Robert Neville Antiques, Leicester, Leicestershire, England.
Neville's Antiques, Woburn Sands, Buckinghamshire, England.
New Abbey Antiques, Newtownabbey, Co Antrim, Northern Ireland.
New Ashgate Gallery, Farnham, Surrey, England.
New Craftsman, St Ives, Cornwall, England.
New Gallery, Budleigh Salterton, Devon, England.
New Grafton Gallery, London, England.
New Kings Road Gallery, London, England.
New Malthouse Antiques, Herstmonceux, E.Sussex, England.
New Street Antiques, Holt, Norfolk, England.
Newark Art & Antiques Centre, Newark-on-Trent, Nottinghamshire, England.
Elizabeth Newby-Vincent, Devizes, Wiltshire, England.
H.W. Newby, London, England.
Newcomb Antiques, Berkeley, Gloucestershire, England.
Newcombe & Son, London, England.
Newcomen Gallery, Long Stratton, Norfolk, England.
Newcourt Park, Lugwardine, Hereford & Worcester, England.
Newgate Curios, Barnard Castle, Durham, England.
B.M.Newlove, Surbiton, Surrey, England.
David & Penny Newlove Antiques, Wincanton, Somerset, England.
David & Penny Newlove Antiques, Bath, Avon, England.
David & Penny Newlove Antiques, Bruton, Somerset, England.
Newman & Cooling Ltd, London, England.
Anne Newman, Cheltenham, Gloucestershire, England.
Heather Newman Gallery, Painswick, Gloucestershire, England.
Michael Newman (Fine Art Auctioneer & Valuer), Plymouth, Devon, England.
Norman Newport, Wilton, Wiltshire, England.
Newton Abbot Antiques Centre, Newton Abbot, Devon, England.
Newton Antiques, Penzance, Cornwall, England.
The Nice Little Shop, Godalming, Surrey, England.
Nicholas Antiques, East Molesey, Surrey, England.
R. & M. Nicholas, Towcester, Northamptonshire, England.
John Nicholls Antiques, Tetbury, Gloucestershire, England.
Rene Nicholls Antiques, Malmesbury, Wiltshire, England.
Richard A.Nicholson, Chester, Cheshire, England.
Nicolaus Antiques, London, England.
Nidd House Antiques, Harrogate, N.Yorkshire, England.

Anthony Nielsen Antiques, Burford, Oxfordshire, England.
M.K.Nielsen, Moreton-in-Marsh, Gloucestershire, England.
Nihon Token, London, England.
Antiques by Nikki, Poole, Dorset, England.
Elizabeth Niner Antiques, Cheltenham, Gloucestershire, England.
Ning Ltd, London, England.
No.Twelve Queen Street, Bath, Avon, England.
Noah's Ark Antiques Market, Sandwich, Kent, England.
Noble Antiques, Folkestone, Kent, England.
Bertram Noller (Reigate), Reigate, Surrey, England.
Nonesuch Antiques, London, England.
The Nook Antiques, Sherborne, Dorset, England.
Noortman (London) Ltd, London, England.
John Noott, Broadway, Hereford & Worcester, England.
Peter Norden Antiques, Burford, Oxfordshire, England.
Nordens, Folkestone, Kent, England.
Norfolk Antiques, Saffron Walden, Essex, England.
Norfolk Polyphon Centre, Dereham, Norfolk, England.
Norman Antiques, South Molton, Devon, England.
Michael Norman Antiques Ltd, Brighton & Hove, E.Sussex, England.
Peter Norman Antiques, Burwell, Cambridgeshire, England.
Sue Norman, London, England.
North London Clock Shop Ltd, London, England.
North Parade Antiques, Oxford, Oxfordshire, England.
North Wales Antiques, Colwyn Bay, Clwyd, Wales.
North Walsham Antique Gallery, North Walsham, Norfolk, England.
North West London Auctions, London, England.
North Western Antique Centre, Preston, Lancashire, England.
North Wilts Exporters, Brinkworth, Wiltshire, England.
Desmond and Amanda North, East Peckham, Kent, England.
Northeast Wales Antiques, Ruthin, Clwyd, Wales.
Northgate Antiques, Canterbury, Kent, England.
Northgate Antiques, Rochester, Kent, England.
Northgate Antiques, Pembroke, Dyfed, Wales.
Northiam Antiques, Northiam, E.Sussex, England.
Norton Antiques, Beaconsfield, Buckinghamshire, England.
Norwich Antique & Collectors Centre, Norwich, Norfolk, England.
Norwin Photographics, Preston, Lancashire, England.
Norwood Cottage Antiques, Killinghall, N.Yorkshire, England.
Norwood House Antiques, Newport, Shropshire, England.
E.A. Nowell & Sons, Wells, Somerset, England.
W.C.Nunn & Son Antiques and Valuations, Long Melford, Suffolk, England.
Simon W.Nutter, Stow-on-the-Wold, Gloucestershire, England.
Brenda Nutting Antiques, Brackley, Northamptonshire, England.

Cynthia O'Connor & Company Ltd, Dublin, Co Dublin, Eire.
Stephen O'Donnell Antiques, London, England.
O'Flynn Antiquarian Books, York, N.Yorkshire, England.
John C. O'Mahony, London, England.
Diana O'Mahony, Cork, Co Cork, Eire.
O'Neill, Petworth, W.Sussex, England.
Hal O'Nians Ltd, London, England.
John O'Reilly, Blackrock, Co Dublin, Eire.
O'Shea Gallery, London, England.
G.Oakes & Son (Bolton) Ltd, Bolton, Greater Manchester, England.
Oasis Fine Arts Ltd, Ormskirk, Lancashire, England.
Obelisk Antiques, Warminster, Wiltshire, England.
Objects, Marlborough, Wiltshire, England.
Octavia Antiques, London, England.
October Gallery, London, England.
Oddiquities, London, England.
F. & M. Odell, Shefford, Bedfordshire, England.
L'Odeon, London, England.
Odin Antiques, London, England.
Ogden of Harrogate Ltd, Harrogate, N.Yorkshire, England.
Richard Ogden Ltd, London, England.
Ogle Fine Arts, Cheltenham, Gloucestershire, England.
Ogwen Antiques, Bethesda, Gwynedd, Wales.
The Old Alarm, Lymington, Hampshire, England.
Old Amersham Antiques Centre, Amersham, Buckinghamshire, England.
Old Amersham Auctions, Amersham, Buckinghamshire, England.
The Old Bakehouse Antiques, Swindon, Wiltshire, England.
The Old Bakery, Woolhampton, Berkshire, England.
The Old Bakery, East Budleigh, Devon, England.
The Old Bakery Antiques, Cranbrook, Kent, England.
Old Bakery Antiques, Hunstanton, Norfolk, England.
Old Barn, Truro, Cornwall, England.
Old Barn Antiques, Church Stretton, Shropshire, England.
Old Barn Antiques Co, Sherborne, Dorset, England.
Old Britannia, Ilfracombe, Devon, England.
Old Buttons (UK), Taunton, Somerset, England.
The Old Chair and Wheel Antiques, Camborne, Cornwall, England.
Old Chapel Antiques, Uley, Gloucestershire, England.
The Old Clock Shop, West Malling, Kent, England.
The Old Clock Shop, Swansea, W.Glamorgan, Wales.
Old Cross Antiques, Newtownards, Co Down, Northern Ireland.
The Old Curiosity Shop, St Sampson's, Guernsey, Channel Islands.
The Old Curiosity Shop, Bath, Avon, England.
Old Curiosity Shop, Beaconsfield, Buckinghamshire, England.
The Old Curiosity Shop (Antiques), Axminster, Devon, England.
Old Drawings Gallery, London, England.
Old Farmhouse Furniture, Ashbourne, Derbyshire, England.
The Old Forge, Swanage, Dorset, England.
The Old Forge, Hollingbourne, Kent, England.
Old Forge Antiques, Long Melford, Suffolk, England.
Old George Antiques, Long Melford, Suffolk, England.
Old Golf Shop Inc, Edinburgh, Lothian, Scotland.
The Old Granary, Battlesbridge, Essex, England.
Old Hall Antiques/Sphinx Gallery, Sundridge, Kent, England.
Old Hall Gallery Ltd, Morden, Surrey, England.
Old Hatfield Galleries, Hatfield, Hertfordshire, England.
The Old House (Seaford) Ltd, Seaford, E.Sussex, England.
The Old House Antiques, Dorking, Surrey, England.
The Old Lantern, Bristol, Avon, England.
The Old Malthouse, Hungerford, Berkshire, England.
The Old Man Antiques, Coniston, Cumbria, England.
Old Maps and Prints, London, England.
Old Market Antiques, Usk, Gwent, Wales.
The Old Mint House, Bexhill, E.Sussex, England.
The Old Mint House, Pevensey, E.Sussex, England.
Old Noah Antiques, Deddington, Oxfordshire, England.
Old Paint Shop, Alfriston, E.Sussex, England.
Old Palace Antiques, Lostwithiel, Cornwall, England.
Old Pine, London, England.
Old Pine Furniture and Jouet, Kiltarlity by Beauly, Highland, Scotland.
The Old Pine Loft, Luton, Bedfordshire, England.
Old Pine Shop, Ross-on-Wye, Hereford & Worcester, England.
Old Post Office Antiques, Abbotsbury, Dorset, England.
Old Pump House, Lyndhurst, Hampshire, England.
The Old Reading Room Antiques, Wrentham, Suffolk, England.
Old Saddlers Antiques, Cranbrook, Kent, England.
The Old School Antiques, Dorney, Buckinghamshire, England.
Old Schoolhouse Antiques, Chester, Cheshire, England.
Old Solent House Galleries, Lymington, Hampshire, England.
Old Stable Antiques, Arundel, W.Sussex, England.
Old Tavern Antiques, Ware, Hertfordshire, England.
Old Town Clock Shop, Beaconsfield, Buckinghamshire, England.
Old Treasures, Newton Abbot, Devon, England.
Old World Trading Company, London, England.
Olde Worlde Trading Company, Barry, S.Glamorgan, Wales.
Oldswinford Antiques, Oldswinford, W.Midlands, England.
Olive Branch Antiques, Broadway, Hereford & Worcester, England.
Oliver-Sutton Antiques, London, England.
G.Oliver & Sons, Guildford, Surrey, England.
Gerald Oliver Antiques, Haverfordwest, Dyfed, Wales.
John Oliver & Co, Diss, Norfolk, England.
Patrick Oliver Antiques Ltd, Cheltenham, Gloucestershire, England.
Olivers, Sudbury, Suffolk, England.
Olney Antique Porcelain Company, Olney, Buckinghamshire, England.
Omar (Harrogate) Ltd, Harrogate, N.Yorkshire, England.
Omell Galleries, Windsor, Berkshire, England.
Omell Galleries, London, England.
Omell Galleries, London, England.
Omell Galleries, London, England.
N.R. Omell, London, England.
Omniphil Ltd, Chesham, Buckinghamshire, England.
A.J. & L.Onions, Market Drayton, Shropshire, England.
Onslow Clocks, Twickenham, Middlesex, England.
Oola Boola Antiques, London, England.
A. Oram, Cheltenham, Gloucestershire, England.
Orbell House Gallery, Castle Hedingham, Essex, England.
Orchard House, Oriental Rugs, Reepham, Norfolk, England.
Carol Orford Antiques, London, England.
Oriel Antiques, Hindhead, Surrey, England.
Oriel Gallery, Dublin, Co Dublin, Eire.
Anatol Orient Ltd, London, England.
Oriental Antiques, Bath, Avon, England.
The Oriental Carpet Centre, Bristol, Avon, England.
Oriental Carpet Centre, London, England.
S.B.&J.Orken, Dublin, Co Dublin, Eire.
Ormond Antiques, Dublin, Co Dublin, Eire.
Ormonde Gallery, London, England.
Martin Orskey Ltd, Ashford, Kent, England.
Stephen Orton Antiques, London, England.
Osborne Gallery, London, England.
Osborne Jewellers, Portsmouth, Hampshire, England.
Osborne King & Megran, Belfast, Belfast, Northern Ireland.
Oscars Antiques, Crewkerne, Somerset, England.
Osmond Tricks, Bristol, Avon, England.
Alec Ossowski, London, England.
Rudolph Otto, Stow-on-the-Wold, Gloucestershire, England.
Mike Ottrey Antiques, Dorchester, Oxfordshire, England.
Oughterard Antiques, Oughterard, Co Galway, Eire.
Out of Time Antiques, Ashbourne, Derbyshire, England.
Outhwaite & Litherland, Liverpool, Merseyside, England.
Owen Antiques, Rochdale, Greater Manchester, England.
Harriet Owen Hughes, Liverpool, Merseyside, England.
Tom Owen (Antiques), Preston, Lancashire, England.
Tom Owen Antiques, Blackpool, Lancashire, England.
Owens Gwynedd & Co, Llangefni, Gwynedd, Wales.
John Owen Gallery, Cardiff, S.Glamorgan, Wales.
Oxford Antiques, Oxford, Oxfordshire, England.
Oxford Antiques Omnibus, Oxford, Oxfordshire, England.
Oxford Gallery, Oxford, Oxfordshire, England.
P.A. Oxley, Antique Clocks and Barometers, Calne, Wiltshire, England.

Packer House, Chipping Norton, Oxfordshire, England.
Page & Hawkes, Brighton & Hove, E.Sussex, England.
Page Antiques, Stockport, Greater Manchester, England.
A.& H.Page, London, England.
Angela Page Antiques, Tunbridge Wells, Kent, England.
Colin Page Antiquarian Books, Brighton & Hove, E.Sussex, England.
Pageant Antiques, London, England.
Jean Pain Gallery, Cambridge, Cambridgeshire, England.
Painswick Antiques, Painswick, Gloucestershire, England.
Palace Gate Gallery, Exeter, Devon, England.
Pall Mall Antiques, Leigh-on-Sea, Essex, England.

Palmer Antiques, Richmond, Surrey, England.
Dermot & Jill Palmer Antiques, Brighton & Hove, E.Sussex, England.
J. & J. Palmer Ltd, Grantham, Lincolnshire, England.
Pamela & Barry Auctions, St Albans, Hertfordshire, England.
Pandion Books, Thirsk, N.Yorkshire, England.
Pandora's Box, Hungerford, Berkshire, England.
Pandora's Box, Brighton & Hove, E.Sussex, England.
Pantiles Antiques, Tunbridge Wells, Kent, England.
Paragon Antiques Market, Bath, Avon, England.
Paraphernalia, Sheffield, S.Yorkshire, England.
D. Parikian, Oxford, Oxfordshire, England.
Park Galleries, Brighton & Hove, E.Sussex, England.
Park Galleries, London, England.
Park Galleries Antiques, Fine Art and Decor, Bolton, Greater Manchester, England.
Park House, Stow-on-the-Wold, Gloucestershire, England.
Park Street Antiques, Berkhamsted, Hertfordshire, England.
The Parker Gallery, London, England.
Parker-Williams Antiques, Canterbury, Kent, England.
Elizabeth Parker Antiques, Moreton-in-Marsh, Gloucestershire, England.
Geoff Parker Antiques Ltd, Boston, Lincolnshire, England.
Michael & Margaret Parker, London, England.
Richard Parker Ltd, Bath, Avon, England.
Parkhouse & Wyatt Ltd, Southampton, Hampshire, England.
Mark Parkhouse Antiques & Jewellery, Barnstaple, Devon, England.
Michael Parkin Fine Art Ltd, London, England.
H.& R. Parry Ltd, Sutton Coldfield, W.Midlands, England.
Parsons Welch & Cowell, Sevenoaks, Kent, England.
Partner & Puxon, Colchester, Essex, England.
Partridge (Fine Arts) Ltd, London, England.
L. Partridge Antiques, Hertford, Hertfordshire, England.
Partridge Restorations, Craven Arms, Shropshire, England.
Parvo, Havant, Hampshire, England.
David Paskin Antiques (London) Ltd, London, England.
Past & Present, Seaham, Durham, England.
Past & Present, Cromer, Norfolk, England.
Past and Present, Inverness, Highland, Scotland.
Past Times, Harrogate, N.Yorkshire, England.
The Patchwork Dog and the Calico Cat Ltd, London, England.
Elizabeth Paterson Antiques, Bannockburn, Central, Scotland.
Robert Paterson & Son, Glasgow, Strathclyde, Scotland.
Paton Gallery, London, England.
Patricia Antiques, Ramsgate, Kent, England.
W.H. Patterson Fine Arts Ltd, London, England.
D.W.Patterson Antiques, Lostwithiel, Cornwall, England.
Pattersons Antiques, North Shields, Tyne & Wear, England.
Fenwick Pattison, Coniston, Cumbria, England.
R.W.Paul, Ipswich, Suffolk, England.
M.Pauw Antiques, London, England.
Pavilion Antiques, Ratcliffe-on-the-Wreake, Leicestershire, England.
Pawsey & Payne, London, England.
Payne & Son (Goldsmiths) Ltd, Oxford, Oxfordshire, England.
Mary Payton Antiques, Chagford, Devon, England.
Peacock Antiques, Chilham, Kent, England.
Rod & Sue Peacock, Hordle, Hampshire, England.
Pearl Cross Ltd, London, England.
John A.Pearson Ltd, Eton, Berkshire, England.
Vic Pearson & Co Ltd, London, England.
Pearsons, Winchester, Hampshire, England.
Pearsons of Fleet, Fleet, Hampshire, England.
Peasenhall Arts & Antiques Gallery, Peasenhall, Suffolk, England.
The Pedlar, Navenby, Lincolnshire, England.
Pednor Antiques, Chesham, Buckinghamshire, England.
Peel Antiques, London, England.
Pelham Galleries (Est 1927), London, England.
Erik Pelham, Wallingford, Oxfordshire, England.
Pelican Antiques, Penrith, Cumbria, England.
Pelter/Sands Fine Paintings, Bristol, Avon, England.
Pembroke Antiques Ltd, Farnborough, Kent, England.
The Pen-y-Ghent Gallery, Settle, N.Yorkshire, England.
Penfriend Ltd, London, England.
Penman Antiques Fairs, Lindfield, W.Sussex, England.
Pennard House Antiques, Shepton Mallet, Somerset, England.
Pennink & Owers Ltd, Tunbridge Wells, Kent, England.
Penny Farthing, Croydon, Cambridgeshire, England.
The Penny Farthing, Edinburgh, Lothian, Scotland.
Penny Farthing Antiques, London, England.
Pennyfarthing Antiques, Wallingford, Oxfordshire, England.
Penoyre Antiques, Pershore, Hereford & Worcester, England.
Penzance Pine Centre, Penzance, Cornwall, England.
Peoples Gallery Limited, London, England.
Peppers Period Pieces, Bury St Edmunds, Suffolk, England.
Percival Restoration, Leicester, Leicestershire, England.
Percy's Silver Ltd, London, England.
Pauline Peretz Antiques, Long Melford, Suffolk, England.
H. Perovetz, London, England.
R.J.Perry Antiques, Hitchin, Hertfordshire, England.
Persian Carpet Gallery, Petworth, W.Sussex, England.
Persian Carpet Gallery, London, England.
The Persian Market, London, England.
Oscar & Peter Johnson Ltd, London, England.
Paul M. Peters Antiques, Harrogate, N.Yorkshire, England.
The Petersfield Bookshop, Petersfield, Hampshire, England.
Petticombe Manor Antiques, Bideford, Devon, England.
David Pettifer Ltd, London, England.
Pettigrew & Mail, Glasgow, Strathclyde, Scotland.
Petworth Antique Market, Petworth, W.Sussex, England.
Petworth Antiques Warehouse, Petworth, W.Sussex, England.
Phelps Ltd, Twickenham, Middlesex, England.
Michael Phelps Antiquarian Books, London, England.
Trevor Philip & Sons Ltd, London, England.
Phillips, Sherborne, Dorset, England.
Phillips, Norwich, Norfolk, England.
Phillips, Oxford, Oxfordshire, England.
Phillips Ipswich, Ipswich, Suffolk, England.
Phillips, Knowle, W.Midlands, England.
Phillips, Edinburgh, Lothian, Scotland.
Phillips, Colwyn Bay, Clwyd, Wales.
Phillips (Glasgow), Glasgow, Strathclyde, Scotland.
Phillips & Jollys, Bath, Avon, England.
Phillips & Sons, Cookham, Berkshire, England.
Phillips in Chester, Chester, Cheshire, England.
Phillips in Exeter, Exeter, Devon, England.
Phillips in Wales, Cardiff, S.Glamorgan, Wales.
Phillips of Hitchin (Antiques) Ltd, Hitchin, Hertfordshire, England.
Phillips Auctioneers, Morley, W.Yorkshire, England.
Phillips Cambridge, Cambridge, Cambridgeshire, England.
Phillips Fine Art Auctioneers, Folkestone, Kent, England.
Phillips Fine Art Auctioneers, London, England.
Phillips Fine Art Auctioneers & Valuers, Leeds, W.Yorkshire, England.
Phillips Marylebone, London, England.
Phillips West 2, London, England.
Charles R.Phillips, Henley-in-Arden, Warwickshire, England.
Elaine Phillips Antiques Ltd, Harrogate, N.Yorkshire, England.
Henry Phillips, London, England.
Howard Phillips, London, England.
John F.C. Phillips, London, England.
Ronald Phillips Ltd, London, England.
S.J. Phillips Ltd, London, England.
Peter Philp, Pen-y-Lan, S.Glamorgan, Wales.
Richard Philp, London, England.
Phoenix Antiques, Fordham, Cambridgeshire, England.
Phoenix Gallery Ltd, Lavenham, Suffolk, England.
Phoenix Green Antiques, Hartley Wintney, Hampshire, England.
The Photographers' Gallery, London, England.
Photography West, Bradford-on-Avon, Wiltshire, England.
Piano Nobile Fine Paintings, Richmond, Surrey, England.
Piccadilly Antiques, Bath, Avon, England.
The Piccadilly Gallery, London, England.
Pickering and Chatto Ltd, inc Dawsons of Pall Mall, London, England.
Mr Pickwick Antiques, London, England.
Pierpoint Gallery, Hereford, Hereford & Worcester, England.
Pigeon House Antiques, Hurst Green, E.Sussex, England.
Pine and Country Antiques, Pulborough, W.Sussex, England.
Pine Antiques, Uttoxeter, Staffordshire, England.
The Pine Cellars, Winchester, Hampshire, England.
Pine Corner Antiques, Haverfordwest, Dyfed, Wales.
Pine Dealers, Iver Heath, Buckinghamshire, England.
Pine Finds, Harrogate, N.Yorkshire, England.
The Pine Mine, London, England.
The Pine Shop, Brighton & Hove, E.Sussex, England.
The Pine Village, London, England.
Pineapple, Bath, Avon, England.
Pinfold Antiques, Lincoln, Lincolnshire, England.
W.A.Pinn & Sons, Sible Hedingham, Essex, England.
Nicola B. Pirozek, Dip. Cons, York, N.Yorkshire, England.
Pitcher Pine Antiques, Leominster, Hereford & Worcester, England.
Pitt & Scott Ltd, London, England.
Peter Place, London, England.
Plaitford House Galleries, Plaitford, Hampshire, England.
Keith Platt, Chipping Norton, Oxfordshire, England.
The Plazzotta Studio, London, England.
Plough House Interiors, Chepstow, Gwent, Wales.
Plowden & Smith Limited, London, England.
Plume of Feathers Antiques, Dorchester, Dorset, England.
The Plume Porcelain Co Ltd, Maldon, Essex, England.
Polak Gallery, London, England.
Poldark Antiques, St Austell, Cornwall, England.
P.M.Pollak Fine Scientific and Medical Books, South Brent, Devon, England.
Edwin Pollard Gallery, London, England.
P.B.Pollington, Wadhurst, E.Sussex, England.
Jane Pollock Antiques, Penrith, Cumbria, England.
Michael Pollock Antiques, Nottingham, Nottinghamshire, England.
A.J.Ponsford Antiques and Restorations, Cirencester, Gloucestershire, England.
Mrs A.M.Ponsonby Antiques, Framlingham, Suffolk, England.
Jonathan Poole Gallery, London, England.
Mark J.Poole, Bath, Avon, England.
D.& D.R.Pope, Buckfastleigh, Devon, England.
John Pope & Hunts Ltd, London, England.
Annabel Popovic, London, England.
Madeleine Popper FGA, Diana Foley, Richard Digby, London, England.
The Porcelain Collector, Shoreham, Kent, England.
Henry Pordes Ltd, London, England.
Henry Pordes Ltd, London, England.
Portal Gallery Ltd, London, England.
Porter Prints, Sheffield, S.Yorkshire, England.
A.W. Porter & Son, Hartley Wintney, Hampshire, England.
Graham Porter Antiques, Baldock, Hertfordshire, England.
James Porter, Sandwich, Kent, England.
R.E. Porter, Bournemouth, Dorset, England.
Portique, Bournemouth, Dorset, England.
The Portland Gallery, London, England.
Graham Portlock, Sawbridgeworth, Hertfordshire, England.
Portmeirion Antiques, London, England.
Portobello Antique Store, London, England.
Portobello Antiques Markets, London, England.

Post House Antiques, Bletchingley, Surrey, England.
David & Carole Potter (Antiques), Nottingham, Nottinghamshire, England.
Jonathan Potter, London, England.
Potters - Colston Street Antiques, Bristol, Avon, England.
Potterton Books, Thirsk, N.Yorkshire, England.
H.W.Poulter & Son, London, England.
Ian Pout Antiques, Witney, Oxfordshire, England.
J.Powell (Hove) Ltd, Portslade, E.Sussex, England.
Prashina Ltd, London, England.
Leo Pratt & Son, South Walsham, Norfolk, England.
John Prestige Antiques, Brixham, Devon, England.
Antony Preston Antiques Ltd, Stow-on-the-Wold, Gloucestershire, England.
Pretty Chairs, Portsmouth, Hampshire, England.
Graham Price Antiques, Polegate, E.Sussex, England.
Eric Pride Oriental Rugs, Cheltenham, Gloucestershire, England.
Prides of London, London, England.
Priests Antiques & Fine Arts, Thame, Oxfordshire, England.
Primrose Antiques, Moreton-in-Marsh, Gloucestershire, England.
Princedale Antiques, London, England.
Princedale Antiques Workshop, London, England.
Principia Fine Art, Hungerford, Berkshire, England.
Printed Page, Winchester, Hampshire, England.
Priory Antiques, Blandford Forum, Dorset, England.
Priory Antiques, King's Lynn, Norfolk, England.
Priory Antiques, Godalming, Surrey, England.
Priory Gallery, Cheltenham, Gloucestershire, England.
Arthur Probsthain, London, England.
Susan Procter, Auchterarder, Tayside, Scotland.
Prospect Antiques, Studley, Warwickshire, England.
Peggy Prothero, Neston, Cheshire, England.
Providence House Antiques, Blakeney, Norfolk, England.
Provincial Antiques Ltd, Knaresborough, N.Yorkshire, England.
Prudhoe Cottage Antiques, Hexham, Northumberland, England.
The Pruskin Gallery, London, England.
Pryce and Brise Antiques, London, England.
Puckeridge Antiques, Puckeridge, Hertfordshire, England.
The Pug Antiques, Banstead, Surrey, England.
Christopher Pugh Antiques, Chester, Cheshire, England.
Robert Graham Pugh, Llanelli, Dyfed, Wales.
Pughs' Porcelains, Colchester, Essex, England.
David & Sarah Pullen Antiques, Bexhill, E.Sussex, England.
The Purple Shop, London, England.
R. & M. Putnam, Farnham, Surrey, England.
Puzzle House Antiques, Cinderford, Gloucestershire, England.
Pym Antiques, Craven Arms, Shropshire, England.
Pym's Gallery, London, England.

Quadrant Antiques, Edinburgh, Lothian, Scotland.
Quai Antiques, Burnham-on-Crouch, Essex, England.
Quality Antiques, Coatbridge, Strathclyde, Scotland.
Bernard Quaritch Ltd, London, England.
Quarter Jack Antiques, Sturminster Newton, Dorset, England.
Queen Anne House, Chesham, Buckinghamshire, England.
Queens Parade Antiques, Bath, Avon, England.
Paul Quentin Antiques, Bury, Greater Manchester, England.
Quested Antiques, Surbiton, Surrey, England.
Questor Antiques, Redbourn, Hertfordshire, England.
Quevedo, London, England.
Martin Quick Antiques Ltd, Wolverhampton, W.Midlands, England.
Quiet Street Antiques, Bath, Avon, England.
David Quimby, Kinver, W.Midlands, England.
Barrie Quinn Antiques, London, England.
Quinney's, Budleigh Salterton, Devon, England.
Quinto of Cambridge, Cambridge, Cambridgeshire, England.
Quinton Green Fine Art, London, England.
Ernest Quinton Antiques, Bath, Avon, England.

R. & L. Coins (Coin & Bullion Investments Ltd), Blackpool, Lancashire, England.
Church Lane Restorations, Teddington, Middlesex, England.
Rabbitz Antiques, London, England.
Rabi Gallery, London, England.
John H.Raby & Son, Bradford, W.Yorkshire, England.
Rackheath Hall, Norwich, Norfolk, England.
Radcliffe House Antiques, Baslow, Derbyshire, England.
Radford Antiques, Polegate, E.Sussex, England.
Dorothy Radford (antiques and interiors), Cambridge, Cambridgeshire, England.
Radio Vintage, Hythe, Kent, England.
Nigel Raffety, London, England.
Rainham Antiques, Rainham, Kent, England.
J.P.Raison, Walton on the Hill, Surrey, England.
Rait Antiques, Rait, by Perth, Tayside, Scotland.
Raleigh Antiques, Beaminster, Dorset, England.
Alan Ramsey Antiques, Thornaby, Cleveland, England.
Ramshead Gallery Studio, Malmesbury, Wiltshire, England.
Randolph, Hadleigh, Suffolk, England.
Rankin Best & Green Ltd, London, England.
Alan Rankin, Edinburgh, Lothian, Scotland.
Rankine Taylor Antiques, Cirencester, Gloucestershire, England.
Raphael at Homewood Park, Hinton Charterhouse, Avon, England.
J.S.Rasmussen Fine Arts, London, England.
G.T.Ratcliff Ltd, Kelvedon, Essex, England.
Derek Rayment Antiques, Farndon, Cheshire, England.
Rayne Antiques, Merstham, Surrey, England.
Charles Read Georgian Furnishing, Milverton, Somerset, England.
Real Macoy, Keighley, W.Yorkshire, England.
Rectory Antiques, Tisbury, Wiltshire, England.
Redfern Gallery, London, England.
William Redford, London, England.
Redmile, London, England.
Redmile Studio, Redmile, Leicestershire, England.
Redthorne Cottage Antiques, Eynsham, Oxfordshire, England.
Anthony Reed, King's Lynn, Norfolk, England.
Anthony Reed Gallery, London, England.
Reeds Rains, Sale, Greater Manchester, England.
M. Rees, London, England.
Reeve Photography, Waterbeach, Cambridgeshire, England.
James Reeve, Warwick, Warwickshire, England.
Edward Reeves, Lewes, E.Sussex, England.
Paul Reeves, London, England.
William Reeves Bookseller Ltd, London, England.
Reflections, Dorking, Surrey, England.
Regency Fine Art, Harrogate, N.Yorkshire, England.
Regent Antiques, Painswick, Gloucestershire, England.
Regent House Antiques, Stockport, Greater Manchester, England.
Regent House Antiques, Northampton, Northamptonshire, England.
The Reid Gallery Ltd, Godalming, Surrey, England.
Alex Reid & Lefevre Ltd, London, England.
John Reid, London, England.
Reigate Antique Arcade, Reigate, Surrey, England.
Reindeer Antiques Ltd, Potterspury, Northamptonshire, England.
Relcy Antiques, London, England.
Relic Antiques, Malmesbury, Wiltshire, England.
Relic Antiques, London, England.
The Relic Shop, Needham Market, Suffolk, England.
Rembrandt Antiques, Dublin, Co Dublin, Eire.
Reg and Philip Remington, London, England.
Renaissance, London, England.
Renaissance Furniture, Wrexham, Clwyd, Wales.
Rendall, London, England.
The Rendezvous Gallery, Aberdeen, Grampian, Scotland.
Rendlesham & Dark, London, England.
Renton & Renton, Harrogate, N.Yorkshire, England.
Resners, Brighton & Hove, E.Sussex, England.
Restall, Brown & Clennell Ltd, Cosgrove, Northamptonshire, England.
Restorations Unlimited, Malmesbury, Wiltshire, England.
Retrospect Antiques, Ilfracombe, Devon, England.
Revivals, Malvern, Hereford & Worcester, England.
C.Reynolds Antique Clock and Watch Specialist, Melbourne, Derbyshire, England.
P.J. Reynolds Antiques, Cheltenham, Gloucestershire, England.
Peter Reynolds Antiques, London, England.
S.H. & W.P.Reynolds, Bournemouth, Dorset, England.
Colin Rhodes Antiques, Plymouth, Devon, England.
Isobel Rhodes, Hadleigh, Suffolk, England.
Rhuddlan Antiques, Rhuddlan, Clwyd, Wales.
Marc Rhys, Caerleon, Gwent, Wales.
Leigh Rice Antiques, Bristol, Avon, England.
Paul Rich Fine Art, Marlow, Buckinghamshire, England.
Richard Baker & Thomson, Liverpool, Merseyside, England.
David Richards and Sons, London, England.
G.E.Richards & Son (Antiques), Hereford, Hereford & Worcester, England.
Paul Richards Antiques, London, England.
Ronald Richardson, Darlington, Durham, England.
Richmond Antique Traders, Richmond, Surrey, England.
The Richmond Gallery, London, England.
Riddetts of Bournemouth, Bournemouth, Dorset, England.
Gwen Riley Antiques, London, England.
J. & M. Riley, Chichester, W.Sussex, England.
Ringles Cross Antiques, Uckfield, E.Sussex, England.
Ripley Antiques, Ripley, Surrey, England.
John D.Rivers, Cirencester, Gloucestershire, England.
Riverside Antiques, Kelvedon, Essex, England.
Riverside Antiques Ltd, Hungerford, Berkshire, England.
Robbies Antiques, Wallasey, Merseyside, England.
Gibb's Bookshop Ltd, Manchester, Greater Manchester, England.
David Robert, Leominster, Hereford & Worcester, England.
L.J. Roberton Ltd, London, England.
Derek Roberts Antiques, Tonbridge, Kent, England.
Jane Roberts & Robert Alderman, London, England.
John Roberts Bookshop, Bristol, Avon, England.
Peter Roberts Antiques, Moreton-in-Marsh, Gloucestershire, England.
Robertsbridge House Antiques, Robertsbridge, E.Sussex, England.
Robertson and Cox, Perth, Tayside, Scotland.
Ian A.Robertson, Alnwick, Northumberland, England.
Robinson (Newcastle) Ltd, Newcastle upon Tyne, Tyne & Wear, England.
John Robinson Antiques, Wigan, Greater Manchester, England.
Keith Robinson Antiques, Worcester, Hereford & Worcester, England.
Peter Robinson, Heacham, Norfolk, England.
T.E.Robinson Antiques, Bath, Avon, England.
Robinson's Bookshop (Brighton) Ltd, Brighton & Hove, E.Sussex, England.
Robson Lowe at Christie's, London, England.
Rochefort Antiques, London, England.
Rocking Chair Antiques, Deeside, Clwyd, Wales.
Rockingham Road Antiques, Kettering, Northamptonshire, England.
Roderic Antiques, Weymouth, Dorset, England.
J. Roger (Antiques) Ltd, London, England.
Rogers of Alresford, Alresford, Hampshire, England.
Rogers Antiques, Cheam, Surrey, England.
Rogers Antiques Gallery, London, England.
T. Rogers & Co (Packers) Ltd, London, England.
Clive Rogers Oriental Rugs, Brighton & Hove, E.Sussex, England.
Roman Antiques, London, England.
Rona Gallery, London, England.
Ropers Hill Antiques, Ashby de la Zouch, Leicestershire, England.
Rose Court Studios Antiques, Olney, Buckinghamshire, England.
Geoffrey Rose Ltd, London, England.
R.E.Rose, London, England.
Simon Leigh Rose Fine Decorative Antiques, London, England.
Rosemary & Time, Oxford, Oxfordshire, England.
Rosemary Antiques & Paper Moon Books, Stratford-upon-Avon, Warwickshire, England.
A. Rosenthal Ltd, Oxford, Oxfordshire, England.

Roslyn House Galleries Ltd, Hitchin, Hertfordshire, England.
Andrew Ross Antiques, Froxfield, Wiltshire, England.
Juda Rowan Gallery, London, England.
Pamela Rowan Antiques, Blockley, Gloucestershire, England.
Rowley Restorations, Little Weighton, Humberside, England.
Elfreda Rowley, Colchester, Essex, England.
Royal Exchange Antiques Gallery, Manchester, Greater Manchester, England.
Royal Exchange Art Gallery, London, England.
Royal Garden Antiques, London, England.
Royal Mile Curios, Edinburgh, Lothian, Scotland.
Royal Thoroughfare Gallery, Lowestoft, Suffolk, England.
Royston Antiques, Royston, Hertfordshire, England.
Rugeley Antiques Centre, Rugeley, Staffordshire, England.
Olivia Rumens, Ludlow, Shropshire, England.
Rundells Antiques, Harlow, Essex, England.
Ruskin's, Bristol, Avon, England.
Russell Baldwin & Bright, Leominster, Hereford & Worcester, England.
Sir William Russell Flint Galleries, Wrington, Avon, England.
Leonard Russell, Newhaven, E.Sussex, England.
Russell's (Antiques) Ltd, Torquay, Devon, England.
J.T.Rutherford & Son, Folkestone, Kent, England.
Rutland Antiques and Coins, Oakham, Leicestershire, England.
Rutland Gallery & Co, London, England.
The Rye Auction Galleries, Rye, E.Sussex, England.
B.R.Ryland, Henley-on-Thames, Oxfordshire, England.
Eileen Ryley, Bury St Edmunds, Suffolk, England.

S & S Antiques, Twickenham, Middlesex, England.
S.R.Antiques, Newcastle upon Tyne, Tyne & Wear, England.
S.W.Antiques, Pershore, Hereford & Worcester, England.
Sabin & Vanderkar (Fine Paintings) Ltd, London, England.
Sabin Galleries Ltd, London, England.
Frank T. Sabin Ltd, London, England.
Sabine Antiques, Stock, Essex, England.
The Saddle Room Antiques, Cookstown, Co Tyrone, Northern Ireland.
Sage Antiques & Interiors, Ripley, Surrey, England.
Barry Sainsbury Oriental Art, London, England.
Sainsburys of Bournemouth, Bournemouth, Dorset, England.
Charles Sale Ltd, Beaconsfield, Buckinghamshire, England.
Salisbury Bookbinders, Salisbury, Wiltshire, England.
N.P. & A. Salt Antiques, Sheffield, S.Yorkshire, England.
Saltgate Antiques, Beccles, Suffolk, England.
Edward Salti Ltd, London, England.
Samiramis Ltd, London, England.
Samman Antiques, Maidenhead, Berkshire, England.
Samovar Antiques, Hythe, Kent, England.
Alistair Sampson Antiques (inc Tobias Jellinek), London, England.
Anthony Sampson, Moreton-in-Marsh, Gloucestershire, England.
C. Samuels & Sons Ltd, Exeter, Devon, England.
M.Samuels (Antiques), Dublin, Co Dublin, Eire.
Patrick Sandberg Antiques, London, England.
Sanders of Oxford Ltd, Oxford, Oxfordshire, England.
Robin Sanders & Sons, London, England.
Robin Sanders, Ware, Hertfordshire, England.
Tony Sanders Antiques and New Gallery, Penzance, Cornwall, England.
Norman C.Sanderson, Harrogate, N.Yorkshire, England.
Sandgate Antiques Centre, Folkestone, Kent, England.
Sandler Fine Arts with Bill Bentley, Harrogate, N.Yorkshire, England.
Sandoe Luce Panes, Wotton-under-Edge, Gloucestershire, England.
Sandringham House Antiques, Hull, Humberside, England.
Sanford Books, London, England.
Sangorski & Sutcliffe, London, England.
A.V. & M.R. Santos, London, England.
Saracen's Lantern Antiques, Canterbury, Kent, England.
D.H.Sargeant, Westerham, Kent, England.
G. Sarti Antiques Ltd, London, England.
Sarum Antiquarian Maps, London, England.
Sarum Antiques, Benson, Oxfordshire, England.
Saskia Antiques, Dublin, Co Dublin, Eire.
Gerald Sattin Ltd, London, England.
R. Saunders, Weybridge, Surrey, England.
R.S.J. Savage & Son, Northampton, Northamptonshire, England.
Sam Savage Antiques, Ticknall, Derbyshire, England.
J.& A.Savery, Brighton & Hove, E.Sussex, England.
Savile Pine, London, England.
Saville Antiques, Devizes, Wiltshire, England.
Savoy Antiques, Liverpool, Merseyside, England.
Chas J. Sawyer, London, England.
Saxton House Gallery, Chipping Campden, Gloucestershire, England.
Martin Scadgell Fine Art, Pulborough, W.Sussex, England.
Scallywag, Beckenham, Kent, England.
Scallywag, London, England.
Anthony Scaramanga Antiques, Witney, Oxfordshire, England.
Scarlet Pimpernel Antiques, London, England.
Scarthoe Antiques, Grimsby, Humberside, England.
Christine Schell, London, England.
Aldo Broccardi Schelmi (Fine Arts), Wadhurst, E.Sussex, England.
Schidlof Galleries, London, England.
Michael Schryver Antiques Ltd, Dorking, Surrey, England.
Thomas E. Schuster, London, England.
Schwartz Sackin & Co Ltd, London, England.
The Scientific Anglican Bookshop, Norwich, Norfolk, England.
Scope Antiques, London, England.
Scott Antiques, Walton on the Hill, Surrey, England.
Scott Cooper Ltd, Cheltenham, Gloucestershire, England.
Scott Packing & Warehousing Co Ltd, Glasgow, Strathclyde, Scotland.
John Scott-Adie, Perth, Tayside, Scotland.
Graham K.Scott, Bury St Edmunds, Suffolk, England.
James Scott, Edinburgh, Lothian, Scotland.
Philippa Scott, London, England.
Richard Scott Antiques, Holt, Norfolk, England.
Seabrook Antiques, Hythe, Kent, England.
B.A. Seaby Ltd, London, England.
Arthur Seager Antiques, London, England.
Seago, London, England.
A.E. Seago, Cromer, Norfolk, England.
B. & C.Seago, Cuckfield, W.Sussex, England.
Searle & Co Ltd, London, England.
Seaview Antiques, Portrush, Co Antrim, Northern Ireland.
Oswald Sebley, Norwich, Norfolk, England.
Secondhand Rose, Hindhead, Surrey, England.
H.& M. Sedler, London, England.
Sefton Antiques, Sidmouth, Devon, England.
Sekmet Galleries Ltd, London, England.
M. & D. Seligmann, London, England.
Semus Lewis Containers Ltd, Portslade, E.Sussex, England.
Frank Semus Ltd, Brighton & Hove, E.Sussex, England.
Sensation Ltd, London, England.
Serendipity, Ross-on-Wye, Hereford & Worcester, England.
Serpentine Antiques, Windermere, Cumbria, England.
The Sevenoaks Furniture Gallery, Sevenoaks, Kent, England.
Severn Antiques, Newtown, Powys, Wales.
Severn Fine Art, Shrewsbury, Shropshire, England.
Jean Sewell (Antiques) Ltd, London, England.
David Seyfried, London, England.
Seymour Galleries, Old Glossop, Derbyshire, England.
Daniel Shackleton, Edinburgh, Lothian, Scotland.
F.B.Shaftoe, Harrogate, N.Yorkshire, England.
The Shambles, Wickham, Hampshire, England.
Shapland, London, England.
Sharrington Antiques, Melton Constable, Norfolk, England.
Shaw Antiques, Spilsby, Lincolnshire, England.
Shaw Bros, Harrogate, N.Yorkshire, England.
Charles Shaw, Knaresborough, N.Yorkshire, England.
David Shaw Silverware Ltd, London, England.
Jack Shaw & Co Antique Silver, Ilkley, W.Yorkshire, England.
Laurence Shaw Antique Centre, Coningsby, Lincolnshire, England.
Laurence Shaw Antiques, Horncastle, Lincolnshire, England.
Nona Shaw, Ditchling, E.Sussex, England.
Shaw's Bookshop Ltd, Manchester, Greater Manchester, England.
Sheengate Galleries, Dorking, Surrey, England.
Shelton Mounting Service, Brighton & Hove, E.Sussex, England.
Rita Shenton, Twickenham, Middlesex, England.
Shepherds Antiques, Cobham, Surrey, England.
Sheppard & Cooper Ltd, London, England.
John B.Sheppard Antiques, Mansfield, Nottinghamshire, England.
Sylvia Sheppard, London, England.
Sheraton Antiques Ltd, London, England.
Sheraton House Antiques, Torquay, Devon, England.
Sherborne Antiques Ltd, Sherborne, Dorset, England.
Sherborne Arcade, Sherborne, Dorset, England.
Sheredays Antiques, Billericay, Essex, England.
Ian Sheridan's Bookshop, Hampton, Middlesex, England.
George Sherlock, London, England.
Sherston Antiques, Sherston, Wiltshire, England.
Sherwood Antiques, St Leonards, E.Sussex, England.
Shield & Allen, London, England.
Robin Shield Antiques, Ferryhill, Durham, England.
The Ship Street Antique Gallery, Oxford, Oxfordshire, England.
The Ship's Wheel, Thurso, Highland, Scotland.
Shipley, London, England.
Ships and Sealing Wax Antiques, Winchester, Hampshire, England.
Shire Antiques, Grange-over-Sands, Cumbria, England.
Shirleys Antiques, Langport, Somerset, England.
J.Shotton, Durham, Durham, England.
Shrewsbury Antique Centre, Shrewsbury, Shropshire, England.
S.J.Shrubsole Ltd, London, England.
Sigma (Antiques & Fine Art), Ripon, N.Yorkshire, England.
Clifford & Joan Silcocks, Stroud, Gloucestershire, England.
Audrey Silk Antiques, Ludlow, Shropshire, England.
Silver Corner, Tetbury, Gloucestershire, England.
The Silver Shop, Dublin, Co Dublin, Eire.
Silver Tay Trading Company Ltd, Dundee, Tayside, Scotland.
M. & L.Silver Co Ltd, London, England.
B. Silverman, London, England.
A.T.Silvester & Sons Ltd, Warwick, Warwickshire, England.
Silvesters, Birchington, Kent, England.
Silvesters Antiques, Wingham, Kent, England.
Michael Sim, Chislehurst, Kent, England.
Roy Sim Antiques, Blairgowrie, Tayside, Scotland.
Simeon, London, England.
Simmons & Lawrence (Chartered Surveyors), Henley-on-Thames, Oxfordshire, England.
Simmons and Lawrence, Reading, Berkshire, England.
A.W. John Simmons & Son, Croydon, Surrey, England.
S. & L. Simmons, Brighton & Hove, E.Sussex, England.
Simons Antiques, Worcester, Hereford & Worcester, England.
Godfrey M.Simpson (Antiques), Tunstall, Lancashire, England.
Oswald Simpson Antiques, Bildeston, Suffolk, England.
Simpsons, London, England.
Sims, Reed and Fogg Ltd, London, England.
Robin Sims, London, England.
Sinai Antiques Ltd, London, England.
C. & A.E. Sinclair, Lincoln, Lincolnshire, England.
Francis Sinclair Ltd, Doncaster, S.Yorkshire, England.
R.M.Sinclair & Son, Perth, Tayside, Scotland.
Brian Sinfield (Gallery), Burford, Oxfordshire, England.
The Singing Bird, Harrogate, N.Yorkshire, England.
Singing Bird Antiques, Dorrington, Shropshire, England.

The Singing Birds, Ambleside, Cumbria, England.
The Singing Tree, London, England.
William Sissons Gallery, York, N.Yorkshire, England.
Skeaping Gallery, Okehampton, Devon, England.
Keith Skeel, London, England.
The Sladmore Gallery, London, England.
Sloane Galleries, Bournemouth, Dorset, England.
John Smale & Co, Barnstaple, Devon, England.
Small Antiques, Burwash, E.Sussex, England.
Small Antiques Ltd, Bramhall, Greater Manchester, England.
Smith-Albany Antiques, Keighley, W.Yorkshire, England.
David Smith Antiques, Oakham, Leicestershire, England.
F. Smith (Leicester) Ltd, Leicester, Leicestershire, England.
Harry Smith, Chipping Norton, Oxfordshire, England.
J.P.Smith Auctions, Coggeshall, Essex, England.
John Smith Antiques, Coggeshall, Essex, England.
John Smith & Son (Glasgow) Ltd, Glasgow, Strathclyde, Scotland.
Michael Smith Antiques, Shrewsbury, Shropshire, England.
P.& D.Smith Antiques, Newcastle upon Tyne, Tyne & Wear, England.
Paul Smith, Ludlow, Shropshire, England.
Peter Smith Antiques, Sunderland, Tyne & Wear, England.
Raymond Smith, Eastbourne, E.Sussex, England.
Robin Smith, Shrewsbury, Shropshire, England.
Sheila Smith Antiques, Bath, Avon, England.
St John Smith, Uckfield, E.Sussex, England.
Tom Smith Antiques, Ipswich, Suffolk, England.
William Smith (Booksellers) Ltd, Reading, Berkshire, England.
Smith's The Rink Ltd, Harrogate, N.Yorkshire, England.
Peta Smyth - Antique Textiles, London, England.
Sneath, Kent and Stuart (Insurance Brokers) Ltd, London, England.
George Sneed Woodwork, Harleston, Norfolk, England.
Jeremy Sniders, Glasgow, Strathclyde, Scotland.
Kimberley Snow & Son, Cullompton, Devon, England.
Snowdonia Antiques, Llanrwst, Gwynedd, Wales.
The Snuff Box, Ryde, Isle of Wight, England.
Soft Surround, Stratford-upon-Avon, Warwickshire, England.
P.D. & S. Solden, Leeds, W.Yorkshire, England.
The Solomon Gallery, London, England.
Solus Marketing (Norfolk), North Walsham, Norfolk, England.
Somervale Antiques, Midsomer Norton, Avon, England.
Somerville & Simpson Ltd, London, England.
Something New, Hertford, Hertfordshire, England.
Something Old, Hertford, Hertfordshire, England.
Sotheby's, Dublin, Co Dublin, Eire.
Sotheby's, Trumpington, Cambridgeshire, England.
Sotheby's, Brampton, Cumbria, England.
Sotheby's, Exeter, Devon, England.
Sotheby's, Bournemouth, Dorset, England.
Sotheby's, Cheltenham, Gloucestershire, England.
Sotheby's, Clitheroe, Lancashire, England.
Sotheby's, Stamford, Lincolnshire, England.
Sotheby's, Harrogate, N.Yorkshire, England.
Sotheby's, Haltwhistle, Northumberland, England.
Sotheby's, Taunton, Somerset, England.
Sotheby's, Grundisburgh, Suffolk, England.
Sotheby's, Billingshurst, W.Sussex, England.
Sotheby's, Warminster, Wiltshire, England.
Sotheby's, London, England.
Sotheby's, Newtownards, Co Down, Northern Ireland.
Sotheby's, Aboyne, Grampian, Scotland.
Sotheby's, Edinburgh, Lothian, Scotland.
Sotheby's, Glasgow, Strathclyde, Scotland.
Sotheby's Chester, Chester, Cheshire, England.
Henry Sotheran, London, England.
South Audley Art Galleries Ltd, London, England.
South Bar Antiques, Stow-on-the-Wold, Gloucestershire, England.
South Coast Antiques Ltd, Brighton & Hove, E.Sussex, England.
South London Art Gallery, London, England.
The South Manchester Gallery, Altrincham, Greater Manchester, England.
Southam and Sons, Kettering, Northamptonshire, England.
Southdown Antiques, Lewes, E.Sussex, England.
Southdown House Antique Galleries, Brasted, Kent, England.
Southdown House Antiques, Nonington, Kent, England.
Southgate Gallery, Shifnal, Shropshire, England.
Span Antiques, Woodstock, Oxfordshire, England.
John Sparks Ltd, London, England.
John Speed (Maps), Nuneaton, Warwickshire, England.
Neil Speed Antiques, Laugharne, Dyfed, Wales.
A. & J. Speelman, London, England.
Edward Speelman Ltd, London, England.
Ken Spelman Booksellers, York, N.Yorkshire, England.
Spencer Swaffer Antiques, Arundel, W.Sussex, England.
George Spencer Decorations Ltd, London, England.
Henry Spencer & Sons, Stamford, Lincolnshire, England.
Henry Spencer & Sons, Retford, Nottinghamshire, England.
Neil Spencer Antiques, Coventry, W.Midlands, England.
Spencers Antiques, Torquay, Devon, England.
Spenser S A, London, England.
Simon Spero, London, England.
Spice, London, England.
Aubrey Spiers Antiques, London, England.
H.J. Spiller Ltd, London, England.
Spink & Son Ltd, London, England.
Marshall Spink Ltd, London, England.
Spinning Wheel, Beaconsfield, Buckinghamshire, England.
Spinning Wheel Antiques, St Anne's, Lancashire, England.
Spon End Antiques, Coventry, W.Midlands, England.
Sport & Country Gallery, Nuneaton, Warwickshire, England.
Michael Spratt Watercolours, Guildford, Surrey, England.
Spread Eagle Antiques, London, England.
Spring Park Jewellers (inc The Clock Shop), Shirley, Surrey, England.
Spurrier-Smith Antiques, Ashbourne, Derbyshire, England.
Spyer & Son (Antiques) Ltd, London, England.
St Albans Antiques Market, St Albans, Hertfordshire, England.
St Breock Gallery, Wadebridge, Cornwall, England.
St Edmunds Antique Centre, Bury St Edmunds, Suffolk, England.
St George's Antiques, Stamford, Lincolnshire, England.
St George's Gallery Books Ltd, London, England.
St Giles Antiques and Period Fashion, Norwich, Norfolk, England.
St Helier Galleries Ltd, St Ouen, Jersey, Channel Islands.
St James Antiques, Manchester, Greater Manchester, England.
St James's Gallery, Bath, Avon, England.
St John's Studio, Coleford, Gloucestershire, England.
St Jude's Antiques, London, England.
St Leonard's Antiques Centre, Ludlow, Shropshire, England.
St Margarets Antiques, Prestwich, Greater Manchester, England.
St Mary's Antiques and Cabinet Makers, Newport, Shropshire, England.
St Mary's Mart, Market Harborough, Leicestershire, England.
St Ouen Antiques, Puckeridge, Hertfordshire, England.
St Paul's Gallery, Leeds, W.Yorkshire, England.
St Peter's Fine Art Gallery, Chester, Cheshire, England.
St Trinians Antiques, Richmond, N.Yorkshire, England.
Stable Antiques, Sedbergh, Cumbria, England.
Stable Antiques, Loughborough, Leicestershire, England.
The Stable Antiques, Dorking, Surrey, England.
The Stable Shop and Gallery, London, England.
The Stables, Ambleside, Cumbria, England.
George Stacpoole, Limerick, Co Limerick, Eire.
George Stacpoole, Adare, Co Limerick, Eire.
E. Stacy-Marks Ltd, Eastbourne, E.Sussex, England.
Ulla Stafford, Eton, Berkshire, England.
Stair & Company Ltd, London, England.
Stalham Antique Gallery, Stalham, Norfolk, England.
Stamford Road Antiques, Kettering, Northamptonshire, England.
Stampantique, Egham, Surrey, England.
J.A.Stancomb, Ilminster, Somerset, England.
Stanilands, Doncaster, S.Yorkshire, England.
Stanley Studios, London, England.
Louis Stanton, London, England.
Peter Stanton Antiques, Truro, Cornwall, England.
Staplegrove Lodge Antiques, Taunton, Somerset, England.
James H.Starkey Galleries, Hull, Humberside, England.
Station Antiques, North Shields, Tyne & Wear, England.
Alanna Staton Antiques, Cobham, Surrey, England.
Geoffrey Stead, Dowdeswell, Gloucestershire, England.
Peter Stebbing Ltd, Bournemouth, Dorset, England.
Steed-Croft Antiques, King's Lynn, Norfolk, England.
Robert D.Steedman, Newcastle upon Tyne, Tyne & Wear, England.
Anne Steele Antiques, London, England.
Robert Stephenson Oriental Carpets, London, England.
Steppes Hill Farm Antiques, Sittingbourne, Kent, England.
Sterling Books, Weston-super-Mare, Avon, England.
Sterling Coins, Bournemouth, Dorset, England.
Stern Art Dealers Co, London, England.
Geoffrey G.Stevens, Guildford, Surrey, England.
Henry Stevens, Son & Stiles, Farnham, Surrey, England.
Stewart Gallery, Bexhill, E.Sussex, England.
Stewart Gallery, Eastbourne, E.Sussex, England.
J.& D.Stewart (Antiques), Berwick-upon-Tweed, Northumberland, England.
Michael Stewart Antiques, Leominster, Hereford & Worcester, England.
Michael Stewart Fine Art Galleries Ltd, Guildford, Surrey, England.
Colin Stillwell (Books), York, N.Yorkshire, England.
Stirling Antiques, Abinger Hammer, Surrey, England.
A Stitch in Time, Beaumaris, Gwynedd, Wales.
Constance Stobo, London, England.
Colin Stock, St Helens, Merseyside, England.
Stockbridge Antiques, Stockbridge, Hampshire, England.
C.P.Stockbridge Ltd, Histon, Cambridgeshire, England.
Peter Stockham at Images, London, England.
Stockspring Antiques, London, England.
Stockwell Antiques, Exeter, Devon, England.
Carolyn Stoddart-Scott, London, England.
Jacob Stodel Antiques, London, England.
William H.Stokes, Cirencester, Gloucestershire, England.
Stone Antique Centre, Stone, Staffordshire, England.
Stone Hall Antiques, Harlow, Essex, England.
Stone House Antiques (and Design & Craft Gallery), Painswick, Gloucestershire, England.
Stone-Wares Antiques, Stone, Staffordshire, England.
Alan Stone Antiques, London, England.
Stonecourt Antiques, Annesley Woodhouse, Nottinghamshire, England.
Stonecourt Antiques, Eastwood, Nottinghamshire, England.
Stonedge Antiques, Wootton Bassett, Wiltshire, England.
Stonewall Antiques, Hillsborough, Co Down, Northern Ireland.
Dinah Stoodley, Brasted, Kent, England.
Stoppenbach & Delestre Ltd, London, England.
Harold T.Storey, London, England.
Julie Strachey, Weston-on-the-Green, Oxfordshire, England.
Straight Lace, East Linton, Lothian, Scotland.
The Strait Antiques, Lincoln, Lincolnshire, England.
Stratford-upon-Avon Antiques Centre, Stratford-upon-Avon, Warwickshire, England.
Stratton Quinn Antiques Etc, London, England.
Strawson Antiques, Tunbridge Wells, Kent, England.
Pamela Streather, London, England.
E. Streeter & Daughter, Petworth, W.Sussex, England.
Strickland & Dorling, Truro, Cornwall, England.

Strike One (Islington) Ltd, London, England.
Louise Stroud, London, England.
Peter Stroud Antiques, Chipping Norton, Oxfordshire, England.
Strouds of Southwell Antiques, Southwell, Nottinghamshire, England.
Peter Strowger of Blandford Forum Antiques, Blandford Forum, Dorset, England.
Stuart Antiques, Auchterarder, Tayside, Scotland.
Stuart House Fine Art, Birmingham, W.Midlands, England.
Stuart Interiors, Ilminster, Somerset, England.
A. & J.Stuart-Mobey & Daughter, Oxford, Oxfordshire, England.
Stuarts Antiques, Bournemouth, Dorset, England.
Studio Antiques, Peterborough, Cambridgeshire, England.
Studio Antiques Ltd, Bourton-on-the-Water, Gloucestershire, England.
Studio Arts & Antiques, Shoreham-by-Sea, W.Sussex, England.
Studio Bookshop and Gallery, Alresford, Hampshire, England.
Studio Edmark, Oxford, Oxfordshire, England.
Studio Morgan. Commercial Photography Co, Aberdeen, Grampian, Scotland.
Studio One Gallery, Oxford, Oxfordshire, England.
Studio 101, Eton, Berkshire, England.
Styles, Hungerford, Berkshire, England.
Suffolk House Antiques, Haverhill, Suffolk, England.
Summers, Davis & Son Ltd, Wallingford, Oxfordshire, England.
Sun House Antiques, Long Melford, Suffolk, England.
Sundial Antiques, Amersham, Buckinghamshire, England.
Sundridge Antiques, Sundridge, Kent, England.
Sunfield Cottage Antiques, Banchory, Grampian, Scotland.
Sunset Strip, Cullompton, Devon, England.
Surrey Antiques Centre, Chertsey, Surrey, England.
Surrey Clock Centre, Haslemere, Surrey, England.
Sussex Antiques (Southdown) Ltd, Shoreham-by-Sea, W.Sussex, England.
Sussex Auction Galleries, Haywards Heath, W.Sussex, England.
Sussex Commemorative Ware Centre, Brighton & Hove, E.Sussex, England.
Sutcliffe Galleries, Harrogate, N.Yorkshire, England.
Gordon Sutcliffe, Hadleigh, Suffolk, England.
Ralph A.Sutcliffe Antiques, Burnley, Lancashire, England.
Ralph A.Sutcliffe Antiques, Preston, Lancashire, England.
Tony Sutcliffe Antiques, Southport, Merseyside, England.
Suthburgh Antiques, Long Melford, Suffolk, England.
H. & M. Suttle, Otley, W.Yorkshire, England.
Sutton & Sons, Frome, Somerset, England.
Sutton Valence Antiques, Maidstone, Kent, England.
L.&M.Sutton, London, England.
Swaffham Antiques Centre, Swaffham, Norfolk, England.
Swag, Preston, Lancashire, England.
Swan Antiques, Chipping Campden, Gloucestershire, England.
Swan Antiques, Cranbrook, Kent, England.
Swan Antiques, Dorking, Surrey, England.
Swan Fine Art, London, England.
Swan Lane Antiques, Warwick, Warwickshire, England.
Swanbridge Art Company Ltd, Washington, Tyne & Wear, England.
Oliver Swann Galleries, London, England.
Swans Antiques, Brasted, Kent, England.
David Swanson, London, England.
Swansong Antiques, West Wickham, Kent, England.
K. Stuart Swash, Wolverhampton, W.Midlands, England.
Sweets Antiques, Bridlington, Humberside, England.
R.A.Swift & Sons, Bournemouth, Dorset, England.
E.Swonnell (Silverware) Ltd, London, England.
Sworder Salerooms, Bishop's Stortford, Hertfordshire, England.
Sydney House Antiques, Peterborough, Cambridgeshire, England.
Christopher Sykes Antiques, Woburn, Bedfordshire, England.
Thomas Sykes Antiques, Kelvedon, Essex, England.
Robin Symes, London, England.
Symington Bookbinders - York, York, N.Yorkshire, England.
SPCK Bookshops, Winchester, Hampshire, England.
SPS Shipping, London, England.

T.L. Phelps, Harrogate, N.Yorkshire, England.
Tadema, London, England.
Maurice Taffler Ltd, Eton, Berkshire, England.
Taikoo Books Ltd., York, N.Yorkshire, England.
Talar Oriental Carpets, London, England.
Talbot Antiques, Brighton & Hove, E.Sussex, England.
The Talbot Gallery, Oxford, Oxfordshire, England.
Talent Store Gallery, London, England.
The Talent Store Gallery, London, England.
Talisman, London, England.
Talisman Antiques, Gillingham, Dorset, England.
Tamar Gallery, Launceston, Cornwall, England.
Tamar Gallery, Bexhill, E.Sussex, England.
Tameside Antiques, Manchester, Greater Manchester, England.
Tamlyn & Son, Bridgwater, Somerset, England.
John Tanous Ltd, London, England.
Tantalus Antiques & Books, Seaton, Devon, England.
Tapsell Antiques, Brighton & Hove, E.Sussex, England.
Taranman Ltd, London, England.
The Tarrystone, Chobham, Surrey, England.
Andrew Tate Pine, Finchingfield, Essex, England.
Taunton Antique Centre, Taunton, Somerset, England.
Taurus Antiques Ltd, Bromley, Kent, England.
Taurus Gallery, London, England.
Taviners, Bristol, Avon, England.
Tay Street Gallery, Perth, Tayside, Scotland.
Taylor Lane & Creber, Plymouth, Devon, England.
Taylor-Halsey Antiques, Crediton, Devon, England.
F.W.Taylor, Tewkesbury, Gloucestershire, England.
Gerald and Vera Taylor, Winforton, Hereford & Worcester, England.
Kevin Taylor, Norwich, Norfolk, England.
M. & R. Taylor Antiques, Ludlow, Shropshire, England.
Martin & Ruth Taylor, Shifnal, Shropshire, England.
Tealby Pine, Wragby, Lincolnshire, England.
Teign Gallery, Teignmouth, Devon, England.
Pamela Teignmouth & Son, London, England.
M. & C. Telfer-Smollett, London, England.
Telling Time Antiques, Thame, Oxfordshire, England.
F.Teltscher Ltd, London, England.
Teme Valley Antiques, Ludlow, Shropshire, England.
Templar Antiques, Nayland, Suffolk, England.
Temple Antiques, Matlock, Derbyshire, England.
Temple Gallery, London, England.
Jeanne Temple Antiques, Milton Keynes, Buckinghamshire, England.
Tempus Antiques Ltd, London, England.
Tempus Fugit, Halstead, Essex, England.
Tennants, Leyburn, N.Yorkshire, England.
The Terrace Gallery, Worthing, W.Sussex, England.
Kingsway Antiques, Leeds, W.Yorkshire, England.
Tessiers, London, England.
Tetbury Antiques, Tetbury, Gloucestershire, England.
The Textile Conservation Centre, East Molesey, Surrey, England.
Textile Conservation Studio, London, England.
The Textile Gallery, London, England.
Thame Antique Galleries, Thame, Oxfordshire, England.
Thames Gallery, Henley-on-Thames, Oxfordshire, England.
Themes & Variations, London, England.
Theta Gallery, Liverpool, Merseyside, England.
Thicke Galleries Swansea, Swansea, W.Glamorgan, Wales.
The Thimble Society of London, London, England.
Thimbles Antiques, Watlington, Oxfordshire, England.
James Thin, Edinburgh, Lothian, Scotland.
Thirty Eight Antiques Ltd, Weedon, Northamptonshire, England.
This & That, Edinburgh, Lothian, Scotland.
This & That (Furniture), London, England.
Thistle Antiques, Aberdeen, Grampian, Scotland.
Thistledome Antiques, Ampthill, Bedfordshire, England.
Thomas & Dymond, Priestacott Meshaw, Devon, England.
Thomas Antiques and Fine Arts, Donegal Town, Co Donegal, Eire.
Thomas-Photos Oxford, Oxford, Oxfordshire, England.
Carole Thomas Fine Arts, Hitchin, Hertfordshire, England.
Jane Thomas Antiques, West Kirby, Merseyside, England.
Nicholas Thomas, London, England.
Paul Thomas Fine Paintings, Wokingham, Berkshire, England.
James Thompson, Kirkby Lonsdale, Cumbria, England.
John Thompson Antiques, Knaresborough, N.Yorkshire, England.
Sue & Alan Thompson, London, England.
Thompson's Gallery, Aldeburgh, Suffolk, England.
Thomson Antiques, Ivybridge, Devon, England.
Thomson Roddick & Laurie Ltd, Carlisle, Cumbria, England.
Thomson Roddick & Laurie Ltd, Dumfries, Dumfries & Galloway, Scotland.
Murray Thomson Ltd, London, England.
B. & T.Thorn & Son, Budleigh Salterton, Devon, England.
Thornborough Galleries, Cirencester, Gloucestershire, England.
Thornbury Antique Framers and Restorers, Thornbury, Avon, England.
Thornhill Galleries Ltd, London, England.
Thornton Associates, London, England.
Thornton Gallery, Bedale, N.Yorkshire, England.
Andy Thornton Architectural Antiques Ltd, Elland, W.Yorkshire, England.
John D. Thornton & Family (Antiques) Ltd, York, N.Yorkshire, England.
Joseph W.Thornton Antiques, Windermere, Cumbria, England.
Thornton's of Oxford Ltd, Oxford, Oxfordshire, England.
Thorntons of Harrogate, Harrogate, N.Yorkshire, England.
Thomas Thorp, Guildford, Surrey, England.
Thorpe & Foster Ltd, Dorking, Surrey, England.
Thorpe Antiques, Finedon, Northamptonshire, England.
Thorpe Antiques, Higham Ferrers, Northamptonshire, England.
Three Centuries Antiques, London, England.
The Three Estaits, Edinburgh, Lothian, Scotland.
Three Salmons Antiques, Usk, Gwent, Wales.
Three Tuns Antiques, Stokesley, N.Yorkshire, England.
Through the Looking Glass Ltd, London, England.
William Thuillier, London, England.
Thumb Gallery, London, England.
Thursley Textile Designs, Milford, Surrey, England.
Thurso Antiques, Thurso, Highland, Scotland.
Tickle & Bragger & Co Ltd, Lostwithiel, Cornwall, England.
Tilings Antiques, Brasted, Kent, England.
James & Ann Tillett, Norwich, Norfolk, England.
Tilley's Antiques, Birmingham, W.Midlands, England.
William Tillman Ltd, Borough Green, Kent, England.
Tilston-Woolley Antiques, Chester, Cheshire, England.
Time in Hand, Shipston on Stour, Warwickshire, England.
Timecraft, St Ives, Cambridgeshire, England.
Times Past, Pershore, Hereford & Worcester, England.
Times Past Antiques Ltd, Eton, Berkshire, England.
S. & S. Timms Antiques Ltd, Ampthill, Bedfordshire, England.
Tricia Timms Antiques, Ampthill, Bedfordshire, England.
Tinderbox, Malvern, Hereford & Worcester, England.
Brian Tipping, London, England.
Titchfield Antiques Ltd, Titchfield, Hampshire, England.
Titley Antiques Ltd, Andover, Hampshire, England.
Tobias and the Angel, London, England.
Toby Antiques, Brighton & Hove, E.Sussex, England.
Igor Tociapski, London, England.
Todd & Austin Antiques & Fine Art, Winchester, Hampshire, England.
Michael Tollemache Ltd, London, England.

Paul Wansbrough, Melksham, Wiltshire, England.
Wantage Antiques, Witney, Oxfordshire, England.
Ward & Chowen, Tavistock, Devon, England.
Ward Antiques, Long Melford, Suffolk, England.
C.W.Ward Antiques, Kettering, Northamptonshire, England.
L.L.Ward & Son, York, N.Yorkshire, England.
Paul Ward Antiques, Sheffield, S.Yorkshire, England.
Stewart Ward (Coins) Ltd, Westerham, Kent, England.
Warminster Antiques, Warminster, Wiltshire, England.
Warner Sheppard & Wade, Leicester, Leicestershire, England.
Christopher Warner, Harrogate, N.Yorkshire, England.
Jeremy Warner, Salisbury, Wiltshire, England.
W.W. Warner (Antiques) Ltd, Brasted, Kent, England.
Warner's Military Specialists, Kingston upon Thames, Surrey, England.
Warrack & Perkins, Church Enstone, Oxfordshire, England.
Warren Gallery, Enniscorthy, Co Wexford, Eire.
Don Warren Antiques, Topsham, Devon, England.
Joy Warren at The House of Antiques, Petersfield, Hampshire, England.
Leigh Warren, London, England.
Wartski Ltd, London, England.
Warwick & Warwick Ltd, Warwick, Warwickshire, England.
Warwick Antique Centre, Warwick, Warwickshire, England.
Warwick Antiques, Warwick, Warwickshire, England.
Warwick Arts Trust, London, England.
The Warwick Leadlay Gallery, London, England.
Water Lane Antiques, Bakewell, Derbyshire, England.
Watergate Antiques, Chester, Cheshire, England.
Waterloo Antiques, Oldham, Greater Manchester, England.
Waterloo Antiques, Welshpool, Powys, Wales.
Waterwheel Pine and Antiques, Exeter, Devon, England.
Watling Antiques, Crayford, Kent, England.
B.G.Watson Antiques, London, England.
Paul Watson, Yeovil, Somerset, England.
Watsons, Saffron Walden, Essex, England.
Watsons, Bishop's Stortford, Hertfordshire, England.
Watts & Christensen, London, England.
Waveney Antiques, London, England.
Waveney Antiques Centre, Beccles, Suffolk, England.
R.E. & G.B.Way, Newmarket, Suffolk, England.
Wylma Wayne Fine Art, London, England.
Weald Gallery, Brasted, Kent, England.
Wealden House Antiques, Wilton, Wiltshire, England.
John Weatherell & Sons Antiques, Harrogate, N.Yorkshire, England.
Weatherheads Bookshop, Aylesbury, Buckinghamshire, England.
Weaves and Waxes, Banbury, Oxfordshire, England.
Graham Webb, Brighton & Hove, E.Sussex, England.
J.R.Webb, Aberdeen, Grampian, Scotland.
M.Webb Antiques, Winkleigh, Devon, England.
Michael Webb Fine Paintings, Anglesey, Gwynedd, Wales.
S.J.Webster-Speakman, Cambridge, Cambridgeshire, England.
E.T. Webster, Blythburgh, Suffolk, England.
E.W. Webster Antiques, Bickerstaffe, Lancashire, England.
The Stores, Chelmsford, Essex, England.
Karel Weijand, Farnham, Surrey, England.
Weiner aus Wien Military Antiques, Brighton & Hove, E.Sussex, England.
Weinreb Architectural Gallery, London, England.
Weir & Sons (Antiques) Ltd, Dublin, Co Dublin, Eire.
Gerald Weir Antiques, Ipswich, Suffolk, England.
The Weiss Gallery PLC, London, England.
Welbeck Gallery, London, England.
J.M.Welch & Son, Great Dunmow, Essex, England.
K. & A. Welch, Warminster, Wiltshire, England.
Weldon Antiques and Jewellery, Southport, Merseyside, England.
J.W.Weldon, Dublin, Co Dublin, Eire.
Well House Antiques, Malpas, Cheshire, England.
H.S.Wellby Ltd, Gerrards Cross, Buckinghamshire, England.
H.S.Wellby Ltd, Haddenham, Buckinghamshire, England.
Weller and Dufty Ltd (Est 1835), Birmingham, W.Midlands, England.
W.H.Weller & Son, Eastbourne, E.Sussex, England.
Wellesley Wilson Antiques, Aldersey, Cheshire, England.
Anthony Welling Antiques, Ripley, Surrey, England.
Wellington Fine Art, Glasgow, Strathclyde, Scotland.
Wellington Gallery, London, England.
Wellington Salerooms, Wellington, Somerset, England.
William G.Wells, Norwich, Norfolk, England.
Wenlock Antiques, Much Wenlock, Shropshire, England.
Wensum Antiques Ltd, Norwich, Norfolk, England.
Wentworth Auction Gallery, Virginia Water, Surrey, England.
West of England Restoration Studio, Bristol, Avon, England.
West Dean College, Chichester, W.Sussex, England.
West End Antiques, Elgin, Grampian, Scotland.
West End Galleries, Buxton, Derbyshire, England.
West Farm Antiques, Orwell, Cambridgeshire, England.
West Felton Antique Market, West Felton, Shropshire, England.
West Gate Fine Art, Canterbury, Kent, England.
West Lancs Antique Exports, Burscough, Lancashire, England.
West Park Antiques Pavilion, Harrogate, N.Yorkshire, England.
West Street Antiques, Dorking, Surrey, England.
West Wales Antiques, Swansea, W.Glamorgan, Wales.
Westenholz Antiques Ltd, London, England.
Westerham Galleries, Westerham, Kent, England.
Westfield Antiques, Chesterfield, Derbyshire, England.
The Westgate Towers Antique & Collectors Market, Canterbury, Kent, England.
Westleigh Antiques, London, England.
Westminster Group, London, England.
Westmorland Antiques, Harrogate, N.Yorkshire, England.
Weston Antique Gallery, Stafford, Staffordshire, England.
David Weston Ltd, London, England.
William Weston Gallery Ltd, London, England.
Westport Ltd, Dundee, Tayside, Scotland.
Westward County Pine, Launceston, Cornwall, England.
Wharf Antiques, Sheffield, S.Yorkshire, England.
Wharf Salerooms, Leeds, W.Yorkshire, England.
Wharfedale Galleries, Ilkley, W.Yorkshire, England.
Tim Wharton Antiques, Redbourn, Hertfordshire, England.
What a Pity Antiques, Hythe, Kent, England.
The Whatnot, Norwich, Norfolk, England.
Rodney & Michael Wheatley, Great Yarmouth, Norfolk, England.
Wheelbarrow Castle Antiques, Leominster, Hereford & Worcester, England.
The Wheelwright, Baldock, Hertfordshire, England.
Wheldon & Wesley Ltd, Hitchin, Hertfordshire, England.
Whisstock's, Frome, Somerset, England.
White Hart Gallery, Aylsham, Norfolk, England.
White Horse Antiques, Tunbridge Wells, Kent, England.
The White House Antiques, Princes Risborough, Buckinghamshire, England.
White House Antiques, Leicester, Leicestershire, England.
White Lion Antiques, Ellesmere, Shropshire, England.
Andrew White, London, England.
David & Rosemary White, Charlton Horethorne, Dorset, England.
Richard White and Peter Howlett, London, England.
Whitehead & Lightfoot, London, England.
Whiteheads, Petersfield, Hampshire, England.
John Whitelaw & Sons, Auchterarder, Tayside, Scotland.
Edna Whiteson Ltd, London, England.
Whiteway & Waldron, London, England.
Robert Whitfield Antiques, London, England.
William Whitfield Antiques, Bromley, Kent, England.
Whitford & Hughes, London, England.
The Whitgift Galleries, Croydon, Surrey, England.
Whitmore, Malvern, Hereford & Worcester, England.
Whittington Galleries, Sutton, Surrey, England.
John Whybrow, Thatcham, Berkshire, England.
Whytock & Reid, Edinburgh, Lothian, Scotland.
Neil Wibroe Antiques Ltd, London, England.
Wickersley Antiques, Rotherham, S.Yorkshire, England.
Widcombe Antiques, Bath, Avon, England.
Arnold Wiggins & Sons Ltd, London, England.
Wigington Partners, Shipston on Stour, Warwickshire, England.
J.Wigington & Sons, Stratford-upon-Avon, Warwickshire, England.
Francis Wigram Antiques, Penn, Buckinghamshire, England.
Wildenstein & Co Ltd, London, England.
Wildman's Antiques, Edinburgh, Lothian, Scotland.
Robert Wilkes Antiques, Bath, Avon, England.
Robert Wilkes Antiques and Traditional Furniture, Stourbridge, W.Midlands, England.
Wilkins & Wilkins, London, England.
Joan Wilkins Antiques, Witney, Oxfordshire, England.
H.V. Wilkinson, Windermere, Cumbria, England.
R. Wilkinson & Son, London, England.
Wynyard R.T. Wilkinson, FSA Scot, Fine Silver, East Dereham, Norfolk, England.
Willcocks Antiques, London, England.
Williams & Son, London, England.
Betty Williams, Usk, Gwent, Wales.
Catherine Williams, London, England.
Christopher Williams (inc Culmus Books), Bournemouth, Dorset, England.
Temple Williams, London, England.
Winifred Williams, London, England.
Henry Willis (Antique Silver), London, England.
Williton Antiques, Taunton, Somerset, England.
Anthony Willson, Hartley Wintney, Hampshire, England.
Timothy D.Wilson, Bawtry, S.Yorkshire, England.
Althea Wilson, London, England.
H.Wilson & Son, Worthing, W.Sussex, England.
Ian Wilson Antiques, London, England.
John Wilson (Autographs) Ltd, Eynsham, Oxfordshire, England.
O.F.Wilson, London, England.
Paul Wilson, Old, Antique & Reproduction Pine, Hull, Humberside, England.
Peter Wilson & Co, Nantwich, Cheshire, England.
R.S. Wilson & Sons, Boroughbridge, N.Yorkshire, England.
Roger Wilson, Middle Wallop, Hampshire, England.
Lydia Wimbleton, Sevenoaks, Kent, England.
Wimborne Antiques, Wimborne Minster, Dorset, England.
G.R.Wimsett, Tunbridge Wells, Kent, England.
Winchcombe Gallery, Cheltenham, Gloucestershire, England.
Winchester House Antiques, Alresford, Hampshire, England.
Windhill Antiquary, Bishop's Stortford, Hertfordshire, England.
P.F. Windibank, Dorking, Surrey, England.
Windjammer Crafts, Salcombe, Devon, England.
Windmill Antiques, Bembridge, Isle of Wight, England.
Windsor Antiques, Eton, Berkshire, England.
Windsor House Antiques (Leeds) Ltd, Leeds, W.Yorkshire, England.
David Windsor Gallery, Bangor, Gwynedd, Wales.
Wingate & Johnston Ltd, London, England.
Winston Galleries, Harrow on the Hill, Middlesex, England.
The Winter Palace, London, England.
Winters' Antiques, Weston-super-Mare, Avon, England.
Wintertons Fine Arts, Lichfield, Staffordshire, England.
D.Wise Antiques, Nottingham, Nottinghamshire, England.
Mary Wise Antiques, London, England.
Michael Wisehall Antiques, Knutsford, Cheshire, England.
Wiskin Antiques, Stansted Mountfitchet, Essex, England.
The Witch Ball Print & Map Shop, Brighton & Hove, E.Sussex, England.
The Witch Ball Print & Map Shop, London, England.
Witham Antiques, Witham, Essex, England.

Norman Witham Antiques, Beckenham, Kent, England.
Withers of Leicester, Leicester, Leicestershire, England.
G.C.Withers Antiques, Bath, Avon, England.
Barry M. Witmond, London, England.
Witney Antiques, Witney, Oxfordshire, England.
Witney Restorations Ltd, Witney, Oxfordshire, England.
Woburn Abbey Antiques Centre, Woburn, Bedfordshire, England.
Woburn Fine Arts, Woburn, Bedfordshire, England.
H. & B.Wolf Antiques Ltd, Droitwich, Hereford & Worcester, England.
J.Wolff & Son Ltd, London, England.
Christopher Wood Gallery, London, England.
Christopher Wood, Kelso, Borders, Scotland.
Colin Wood Antiques Ltd, Aberdeen, Grampian, Scotland.
J.H.Wood, Aberdeen, Grampian, Scotland.
Jeremy Wood Fine Art, Petworth, W.Sussex, England.
Ryan Wood Antiques, Liverpool, Merseyside, England.
Wood's Wharf Antiques Bazaar, Haslemere, Surrey, England.
Woodbridge, Bath, Avon, England.
Anthony Woodburn Ltd, Leigh, Kent, England.
Woodford Antiques, Stockport, Greater Manchester, England.
Woodgoods, Odiham, Hampshire, England.
W.J. Woodhams, London, England.
Geoffrey M. Woodhead, Honiton, Devon, England.
H. Woods Wilson Ltd, London, England.
Woodstock, Malvern, Hereford & Worcester, England.
Woodstock Antiques, Woodstock, Oxfordshire, England.
Charles Woodward Antiques, Fairford, Gloucestershire, England.
Woolley & Wallis, Salisbury, Wiltshire, England.
Woolpit Antiques, Woolpit, Suffolk, England.
Stanley Woolston, Ludlow, Shropshire, England.
Wootton-Billingham, Northampton, Northamptonshire, England.
Worksop Antiques, Worksop, Nottinghamshire, England.
Worlds End Watercolours, Bembridge, Isle of Wight, England.
Worldwide Autographs Ltd, Hounslow, Middlesex, England.
Worsfolds of Canterbury, Canterbury, Kent, England.
Patrick Worth, Dorking, Surrey, England.
Worthing Auction Galleries, Worthing, W.Sussex, England.
Christopher Wray's Lighting Emporium, Bristol, Avon, England.
Christopher Wray's Lighting Emporium, London, England.
Christopher Wray's Lighting Emporium, Kilkenny, Co Kilkenny, Eire.
Christopher Wray's Lighting Emporium, Bournemouth, Dorset, England.
Christopher Wray's Lighting Emporium, Birmingham, W.Midlands, England.
Christopher Wray's Lighting Emporium, Leeds, W.Yorkshire, England.
Christopher Wrays Lamp Workshop, London, England.
Wren Antiques, London, England.
Wren House Antiques, Wrentham, Suffolk, England.
Linda Wrigglesworth, London, England.
Wright-Manley, Tarporley, Cheshire, England.
Chris Wright Photography, Stratford-upon-Avon, Warwickshire, England.
Clifford Wright, London, England.
George Wright (Rotherham) Ltd, Rotherham, S.Yorkshire, England.
Sidney Wright, Bournemouth, Dorset, England.
Tim Wright Antiques, Glasgow, Strathclyde, Scotland.
John R. Wrigley, Sheffield, S.Yorkshire, England.
Wrington Antiques, Wrington, Avon, England.
Wyatt & Son, Chichester, W.Sussex, England.
Wych House Antiques, Woking, Surrey, England.
Wyche House Antiques, Nantwich, Cheshire, England.
Wycombe Cane and Rush Works, High Wycombe, Buckinghamshire, England.
Wye Antiques, Stow-on-the-Wold, Gloucestershire, England.
Andrew Wyld, London, England.
The Wyllie Gallery, London, England.
Wynnstay Galleries, Bala, Gwynedd, Wales.
Harriet Wynter Ltd, London, England.
Wynyards Antiques, London, England.
Wyrardisbury Antiques, Wraysbury, Berkshire, England.

Xanthus Gallery, Reymerston, Norfolk, England.

Yates Antiques, Swansea, W.Glamorgan, Wales.
Ye Olde Junk Shoppe, Shipton-under-Wychwood, Oxfordshire, England.
Yellow Frog (Brighton) Ltd, Brighton & Hove, E.Sussex, England.
Yellow Lantern Antiques Ltd, Brighton & Hove, E.Sussex, England.
Yeo Antiques, Tetbury, Gloucestershire, England.
Yesterday Child, London, England.
Yesterday's Antiques, Bushey, Hertfordshire, England.
Yesterday's Paper, Wellington, Somerset, England.
Yesterday's Pine, Ampthill, Bedfordshire, England.
Yew Tree Gallery, Ashbourne, Derbyshire, England.
York Antiques Centre, York, N.Yorkshire, England.
York Gallery, Tunbridge Wells Ltd, Tunbridge Wells, Kent, England.
York House Antiques, Cowes, Isle of Wight, England.
Young Stephen Ltd, London, England.
Aldric Young, Edinburgh, Lothian, Scotland.
Denis Young Antiques, Aberfeldy, Tayside, Scotland.
J.Young & Son (Antiques), Keswick, Cumbria, England.
Lionel Young Antiques, Lewes, E.Sussex, England.
Peter Young Antiques, Oldham, Greater Manchester, England.
Peter Young Antiques, Darwen, Lancashire, England.
Robert Young Antiques, Norwich, Norfolk, England.
Robert Young Antiques, London, England.
William Young (Antiques) Ltd, Aberdeen, Grampian, Scotland.
Yoxford Bazaar, Yoxford, Suffolk, England.
Robert Yuen, London, England.

Zadah Persian Carpets Ltd, London, England.
Zaehnsdorf Ltd, London, England.
Zafer Antiques, Twickenham, Middlesex, England.
Zamana Gallery Ltd, London, England.
Ziggurat, London, England.
Zwan Antiques, Minehead, Somerset, England.
A.Zwemmer Ltd, London, England.
19 Middle Street Antiques, Brighton & Hove, E.Sussex, England

Richard Arden Antiques
19 Market Hill, Woodbridge, Suffolk IP12 4LX.
Tel 0394 2068. Open Mon–Sat 9.30–5; Wed 9.30–1. Furniture, pictures, interesting and decorative objects, garden furniture.

Nan S. Aschcroft
10A Daleham Gardens, London NW3 5DA. Tel 01-794 6658. Fine and rare wine-related antiques, modern wine accessories.

Aux Menus Plaisirs
(Consultant: Bernard B. Steinitz.) 23 Grafton St, London W1X 3LD. Tel 01-493 5512.
Open Mon–Fri 9.30–5.30; other times by appt. 18thC French furniture and works of art.

Burgess Browning
24 Blue Ball Yard, St. James's Street, London SW1A 1ND.
Tel 01-491 1811. Antiquarian bookseller.

Lucy Campbell
Georgina Fine Arts, 1 Hans Place, Knightsbridge, London SW1W 0EU. Tel 01-589 4295/01-584 7990.
Open Mon-Fri 10–6; Sat & Sun by appt.

Murga Candler Ltd
57 Bayham Place, London NW1.
Tel 01-387 7830.
Leatherwork and upholstery.

The Collectors Gallery
8 Bridge Street, Caversham, Reading, Berkshire RG4 8AA.
Tel 0734-483663. Open Mon–Fri 9.30–5; Sat 10–4; other times by appt. Specialists in 18th and 19thC oil paintings and watercolours.

Colliers Bigwood & Bewlay Auctioneers & Valuers Ltd
The Old School, Tittington, Stratford-on-Avon, Warwickshire CV37 7AW. Tel 0789-69415.
Auctioneers and valuers of fine and decorative art. Weekly sales.

Philip Cooper Antiques
(Shirley Harrison, Philip Cooper.) No 1 Pound Street, Petworth, West Sussex. Period walnut, oak and 18thC mahogany. Also needlework and metalware.

The Court Gallery Picture Framers
8 Lancashire Court, 122/123 New Bond Street, London W1Y 9AD.
Tel 01-493 3265. Picture framers & restorers.

Philip de Bay, Ken Jackson
29 Westover Rd, London SW18.
Tel 01-874 5140. Open by appt.
Fine art photography.

Bernard Dickinson
(Bernard Dickinson.) West Street, Gargrave, Skipton, N. Yorkshire.
Tel 075 678-285/8257. Open Mon–Sat 9–5.30. Small furniture, with restoration workshop.
BADA.

Duophone
(J.E. Cavanagh Esq.) Virginia Galleries, Unit 14, 31 Virginia Street, Glasgow G1 1TU. Tel 041-522 7757. Wide range of antiques, mechanical music, clocks and collectables bought and sold. Houses cleared.

The Glasgow Style Gallery
(J. A. Mulholland.) 487 Great Western Rd, Glasgow, Strathclyde G12 8HL. Tel 041-357 3601/339 0690. Art nouveau furniture, glass, ceramics, pewter, silver, stained glass and other decorative items.

Haltherleigh Antiques
22 Bridge Street, Haltherleigh, Devon. Country furniture, pottery, oak and objects.

Peter Haworth
29 Watergate Row, Chester, Cheshire. Tel 0244-45888.
British paintings and watercolours 1870–1950.

Iona Antiques
(Stephen & Iona Joseph.) PO Box No 285, London W8 6HZ.
Tel 01-602 1193. Open by appt. only. 19thC English primitive paintings of animals.

E. Joseph in association with Chas. J. Sawyer
1 Vere Street, London W1. Tel 01-493 8353/4/5.
Open Mon–Fri 9.30–5.30; other times by appt Antiquarian booksellers.

Gerald Lewis
(Gerald and Brenda Lewis.) The Old Brewery, The Old Estate Yard, Montacute, Somerset TA15 6XP. Tel 0935 825435. Open by appt only. 18thC furniture and clocks. BADA

Magpies Antiques
(Claire Mulholland.) 487 Great Western Road, Glasgow, Strathclyde G12 8HL. Tel 041-357 3601 (priv 041-339 0690).
Open Mon–Fri 10–5; Sat 10.30–5; other times by appt. Georgian and Victorian furniture, ceramics, paintings, prints, jewellery and silverware, Oriental rugs, porcelain.

Merola
(Maria Merola.) 178 Walton St, London SW3 2JL. 01-589 0365.
Open Mon–Sat 10–6; Wed 10–7.
Decorative and fine art 1890–1950, specialising in jewellery.

Jane McAusland
Nether Hall Barn, Old Newton, Stowmarket, Suffolk IP14 4PP.
Tel 0449-673571. Conservation of art on paper, including watercolours, prints and drawings. IPC, IIC

Nash Antiques
(M. Bennett) 24 Silver Street, Bradford on Avon, Wiltshire. Tel 02216 7844. Period English furniture. English, European and Oriental porcelain, including decorative objects.

The Osborne Studio Gallery
The Carriage Hall, Floral Street, Covent Garden, London, WC2.
Tel 01-836 5040. Open Mon–Fri 10.30–6.30. Sporting paintings and prints and the contemporary bronzes of James Osborne.

Joanna Payne
14 Addison Avenue, London W11. Tel 01-602 5474.
Conservation of prints, drawings & watercolours. IPC, IIC

Scottish Architectural Antiques
1 Bothwell Lane, Kelvinbridge, Glasgow, Strathclyde G12. Tel 041-357 3601. Carved & panelled wood, leaded glass, stone and metalwork, stuffed animals, and unusual items.

The Scottish Gallery
94 George Street, Edinburgh, Lothian EH2 3DF. Tel 031-225 5955. Large range of contemporary designs in jewellery, ceramics and metalwork.

Peter Smith
Stand A24-25, Grays Mews Antique Market, 1-7 Davies Street, London W1. Tel 01-493 0382 (Priv 01-878 7202). Tribal art.

The Studio
(Maria Merola.) 2 Charlton Place, Camden Passage, London N1 8AT. Tel 01-226 5625.
Open Mon–Sat 10–5.30.
Decorative and fine art 1890–1950, specialising in jewellery.

Taylor Pearce Restoration Services Limited
99–103 Lomond Grove, Camberwell, London SE5 7HN.
Tel 01-703 1004.
Conserving, cleaning and restoring of statuary and monuments.

Templeman's Antiques
The Mill Room, Rait by Perth, Tayside PH2 7SE.
Tel 08217 344.

Duncan Vincent Fine Art & Chattel Auctioneers
(W. T. Duncan Vincent) 105 London Street, Reading, Berkshire, RG1 4LF.
Tel 0734-594748. Open Sat 9–5.
Fine art and chattel auctioneers.

MAPS

The British Isles

South-West England: Avon, Cornwall, Devon, Dorset, Somerset, Wiltshire.

South-East England and Channel Islands: Bedfordshire, Berkshire, Buckinghamshire, Essex, Hampshire, Hertfordshire, Isle of Wight, Kent, Greater London, Oxfordshire, Surrey, East Sussex, West Sussex; Guernsey, Jersey.

Midlands: Cheshire, Derbyshire, Gloucestershire, Hereford & Worcester, Shropshire, Staffordshire, Warwickshire, West Midlands.

East Midlands and East Anglia: Cambridgeshire, Leicestershire, Lincolnshire, Norfolk, Northamptonshire, Nottinghamshire, Suffolk.

North England: Cleveland, Cumbria, Durham, Greater Manchester, Humberside, Isle of Man, Lancashire, Merseyside, Northumberland, Tyne & Wear, North Yorkshire, South Yorkshire, West Yorkshire.

Scotland: Borders, Central, Dumfries & Galloway, Fife, Grampian, Highland, Lothian, Strathclyde, Tayside.

Ireland: (Northern Ireland) Belfast, Co Antrim, Co Down, Co Tyrone; (Eire) Co Clare, Co Cork, Co Donegal, Co Dublin, Co Galway, Co Kerry, Co Kilkenny, Co Limerick, Co Louth, Co Mayo, Co Offaly, Co Tipperary, Co Waterford, Co Wexford, Co Wicklow.

Wales: Clwyd, Dyfed, Mid-Glamorgan, South Glamorgan, West Glamorgan, Gwent, Gwynedd, Powys.

Greater London: postal districts.

1
KEY
Map 1
county boundaries
divisions between areas shown on the different maps (see also list on p.391)
Maps 2–9
county boundaries
national boundaries
A5 M25
main roads/motorways
SUFFOLK
county names
TAUNTON
county towns (administrative headquarters)
LIMERICK
other towns/cities
Map 10
postal district boundaries
boundary of Inner London area
county boundary of Greater London
CHELSEA
districts within Greater London
main roads
HIGHLAND
GRAMPIAN
TAYSIDE
FIFE
CENTRAL
LOTHIAN
STRATHCLYDE
BORDERS
DUMFRIES & GALLOWAY
NORTHUMBER -LAND
TYNE & WEAR
DURHAM
CLEVELAND
CUMBRIA
ISLE OF MAN
NORTH YORKSHIRE
HUMBER -SIDE
LANCASHIRE
WEST YORKSHIRE
GREATER MANCHES -TER
SOUTH YORKSHIRE
MERSEYSIDE
CHESHIRE
DERBY -SHIRE
NOTTINGHAM -SHIRE
LINCOLN -SHIRE
CLWYD
GWYNEDD
STAFFORD -SHIRE
SHROPSHIRE
LEICESTER -SHIRE
NORFOLK
WEST MIDLANDS
NORTHAMPTON -SHIRE
CAMBRIDGE -SHIRE
SUFFOLK
POWYS
HEREFORD & WORCESTER
WARWICK -SHIRE
BEDFORD -SHIRE
BUCKINGHAMSHIRE
HERTFORDSHIRE
ESSEX
DYFED
GLOUCESTER -SHIRE
OXFORD -SHIRE
GWENT
GREATER LONDON
WEST GLAMORGAN
MID GLAMORGAN
SOUTH GLAMORGAN
AVON
WILTSHIRE
BERKSHIRE
SURREY
KENT
HAMPSHIRE
WEST SUSSEX
EAST SUSSEX
SOMERSET
DORSET
ISLE OF WIGHT
DEVON
CORNWALL
CHANNEL ISLANDS
GUERNSEY
JERSEY
LONDONDERRY
DONEGAL
ANTRIM
TYRONE
FERMANAGH
ARMAGH
DOWN
MONAGHAN
LEITRIM
SLIGO
MAYO
CAVAN
LOUTH
ROSCOMMON
LONGFORD
WESTMEATH
MEATH
GALWAY
DUBLIN
OFFALY
KILDARE
CLARE
LAOIS
WICKLOW
CARLOW
KILKENNY
LIMERICK
TIPPERARY
WEXFORD
WATERFORD
KERRY
CORK

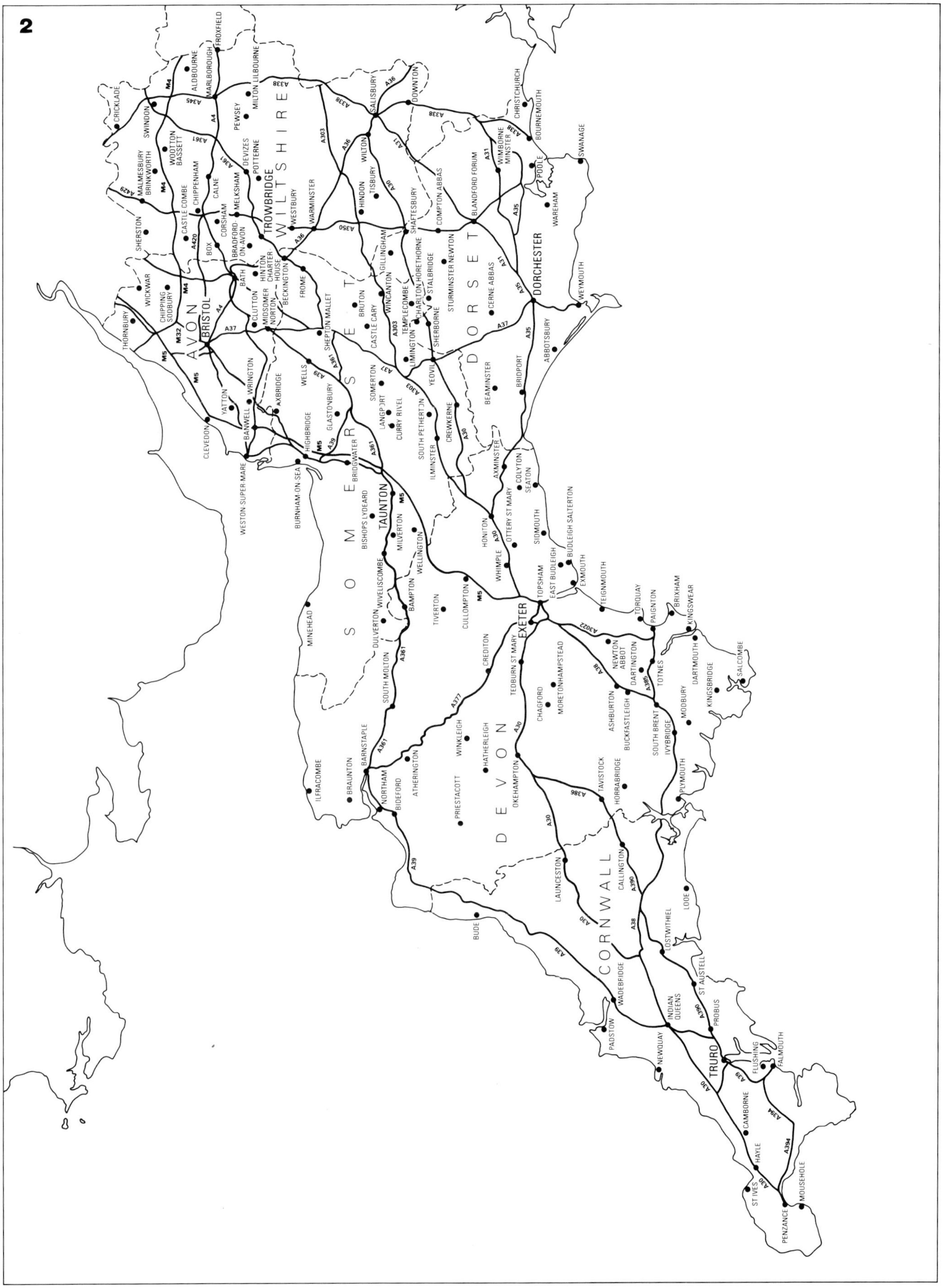
2
AVON
WILTSHIRE
SOMERSET
DORSET
DEVON
CORNWALL
CRICKLADE
SWINDON
ALDBOURNE
MARLBOROUGH
FROXFIELD
MILTON LILBOURNE
PEWSEY
WOOTTON BASSETT
MALMESBURY
BRINKWORTH
CHIPPENHAM
CALNE
DEVIZES
POTTERNE
MELKSHAM
TROWBRIDGE
CASTLE COMBE
SHERSTON
CORSHAM
BOX
BRADFORD-ON-AVON
HINTON CHARTERHOUSE
BATH
WICKWAR
CHIPPING SODBURY
THORNBURY
BRISTOL
CLUTTON
MIDSOMER NORTON
BECKINGTON
FROME
WESTBURY
WARMINSTER
SALISBURY
DOWNTON
WILTON
HINDON
TISBURY
SHAFTESBURY
COMPTON ABBAS
GILLINGHAM
WINCANTON
BRUTON
CASTLE CARY
SHEPTON MALLET
WELLS
GLASTONBURY
TEMPLECOMBE
CHARLTON HORETHORNE
STALBRIDGE
STURMINSTER NEWTON
BLANDFORD FORUM
WIMBORNE MINSTER
CHRISTCHURCH
BOURNEMOUTH
POOLE
SWANAGE
WAREHAM
DORCHESTER
WEYMOUTH
CERNE ABBAS
SHERBORNE
YEOVIL
LIMINGTON
SOMERTON
LANGPORT
CURRY RIVEL
SOUTH PETHERTON
CREWKERNE
BEAMINSTER
BRIDPORT
ABBOTSBURY
ILMINSTER
AXMINSTER
COLYTON
SEATON
YATTON
WRINGTON
AXBRIDGE
CLEVEDON
BANWELL
WESTON-SUPER-MARE
HIGHBRIDGE
BURNHAM-ON-SEA
BRIDGWATER
TAUNTON
BISHOPS LYDEARD
MILVERTON
WELLINGTON
WIVELISCOMBE
BAMPTON
DULVERTON
MINEHEAD
TIVERTON
CULLOMPTON
HONITON
OTTERY ST MARY
SIDMOUTH
BUDLEIGH SALTERTON
EAST BUDLEIGH
WHIMPLE
EXMOUTH
TOPSHAM
EXETER
TEIGNMOUTH
TORQUAY
PAIGNTON
BRIXHAM
KINGSWEAR
DARTMOUTH
SALCOMBE
KINGSBRIDGE
MODBURY
TOTNES
DARTINGTON
NEWTON ABBOT
ASHBURTON
BUCKFASTLEIGH
SOUTH BRENT
IVYBRIDGE
PLYMOUTH
CHAGFORD
MORETONHAMPSTEAD
TEDBURN ST MARY
CREDITON
SOUTH MOLTON
BARNSTAPLE
BRAUNTON
ILFRACOMBE
NORTHAM
BIDEFORD
ATHERINGTON
WINKLEIGH
HATHERLEIGH
PRIESTACOTT
OKEHAMPTON
TAVISTOCK
HORRABRIDGE
LAUNCESTON
CALLINGTON
LOOE
LOSTWITHIEL
BUDE
WADEBRIDGE
PADSTOW
ST AUSTELL
INDIAN QUEENS
PROBUS
NEWQUAY
TRURO
FLUSHING
FALMOUTH
CAMBORNE
HAYLE
ST IVES
PENZANCE
MOUSEHOLE
M4
M5
M32
A4
A420
A429
A345
A361
A338
A36
A303
A350
A30
A31
A35
A37
A39
A377
A386
A38
A390
A385
A3022
A394

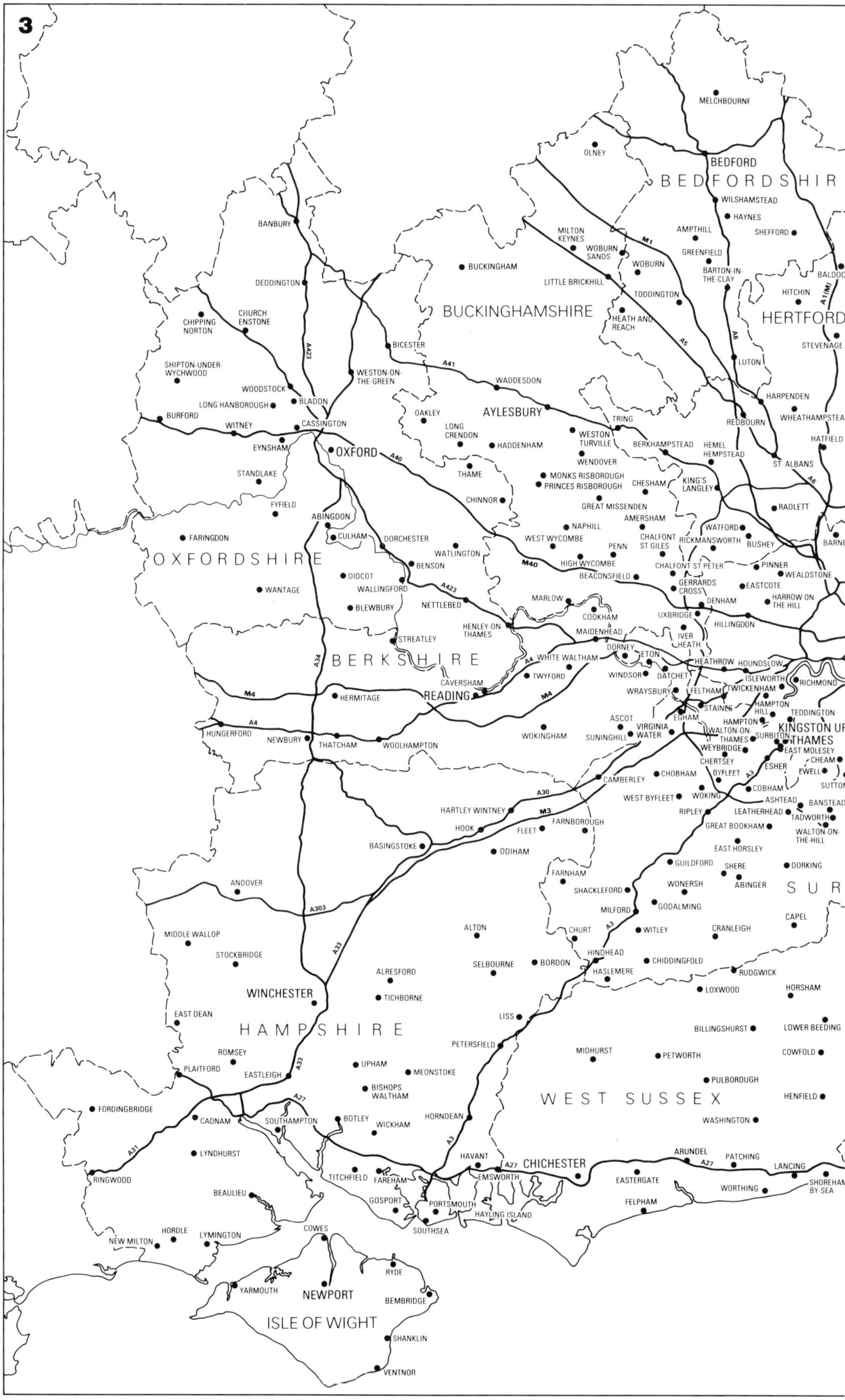
3
MELCHBOURNE
OLNEY
BEDFORD
BEDFORDSHIRE
WILSHAMSTEAD
HAYNES
AMPTHILL
SHEFFORD
MILTON KEYNES
WOBURN SANDS
M1
GREENFIELD
WOBURN
BARTON-IN-THE-CLAY
BALDOCK
BUCKINGHAM
LITTLE BRICKHILL
TODDINGTON
HITCHIN
A1(M)
BUCKINGHAMSHIRE
HEATH AND REACH
HERTFORD
A5
A6
STEVENAGE
BANBURY
DEDDINGTON
CHURCH ENSTONE
CHIPPING NORTON
A423
BICESTER
A41
LUTON
SHIPTON-UNDER-WYCHWOOD
WESTON-ON-THE-GREEN
WADDESDON
HARPENDEN
WOODSTOCK
BLADON
LONG HANBOROUGH
OAKLEY
AYLESBURY
TRING
WHEATHAMPSTEAD
BURFORD
WITNEY
CASSINGTON
LONG CRENDON
WESTON TURVILLE
REDBOURN
HATFIELD
EYNSHAM
OXFORD
A40
HADDENHAM
BERKHAMPSTEAD
HEMEL HEMPSTEAD
ST. ALBANS
WENDOVER
STANDLAKE
THAME
MONKS RISBOROUGH
PRINCES RISBOROUGH
CHESHAM
KING'S LANGLEY
A6
CHINNOR
FYFIELD
GREAT MISSENDEN
RADLETT
ABINGDON
AMERSHAM
NAPHILL
WATFORD
FARINGDON
CULHAM
DORCHESTER
WEST WYCOMBE
CHALFONT ST GILES
RICKMANSWORTH
BUSHEY
BARNET
PENN
OXFORDSHIRE
WATLINGTON
BENSON
M40
HIGH WYCOMBE
CHALFONT ST PETER
PINNER
DIDCOT
BEACONSFIELD
WEALDSTONE
WALLINGFORD
A423
GERRARDS CROSS
EASTCOTE
WANTAGE
MARLOW
DENHAM
HARROW ON THE HILL
BLEWBURY
NETTLEBED
COOKHAM
UXBRIDGE
HILLINGDON
HENLEY-ON-THAMES
MAIDENHEAD
IVER HEATH
STREATLEY
DORNEY
ETON
A34
BERKSHIRE
A4
WHITE WALTHAM
HEATHROW
HOUNSLOW
CAVERSHAM
TWYFORD
WINDSOR
DATCHET
ISLEWORTH
RICHMOND
M4
HERMITAGE
READING
M4
WRAYSBURY
FELTHAM
TWICKENHAM
HAMPTON HILL
STAINES
TEDDINGTON
A4
ASCOT
EGHAM
HAMPTON
KINGSTON UPON THAMES
HUNGERFORD
VIRGINIA WATER
WALTON-ON-THAMES
SURBITON
NEWBURY
THATCHAM
WOOLHAMPTON
WOKINGHAM
SUNINGHILL
WEYBRIDGE
EAST MOLESEY
CHERTSEY
CHEAM
ESHER
EWELL
CAMBERLEY
CHOBHAM
BYFLEET
A3
COBHAM
SUTTON
A30
WEST BYFLEET
WOKING
ASHTEAD
BANSTEAD
HARTLEY WINTNEY
M3
RIPLEY
LEATHERHEAD
TADWORTH
FARNBOROUGH
HOOK
FLEET
GREAT BOOKHAM
WALTON-ON-THE-HILL
BASINGSTOKE
EAST HORSLEY
ODIHAM
GUILDFORD
SHERE
DORKING
FARNHAM
ANDOVER
SHACKLEFORD
WONERSH
ABINGER
SUR
MILFORD
GODALMING
A303
CAPEL
ALTON
CHURT
WITLEY
CRANLEIGH
MIDDLE WALLOP
A3
STOCKBRIDGE
A33
HINDHEAD
SELBOURNE
BORDON
CHIDDINGFOLD
ALRESFORD
HASLEMERE
RUDGWICK
WINCHESTER
TICHBORNE
LOXWOOD
HORSHAM
EAST DEAN
LISS
HAMPSHIRE
BILLINGSHURST
LOWER BEEDING
PETERSFIELD
ROMSEY
MIDHURST
PETWORTH
COWFOLD
A33
PLAITFORD
EASTLEIGH
UPHAM
MEONSTOKE
PULBOROUGH
BISHOPS WALTHAM
WEST SUSSEX
HENFIELD
A27
FORDINGBRIDGE
CADNAM
SOUTHAMPTON
BOTLEY
HORNDEAN
WASHINGTON
WICKHAM
A3
A31
LYNDHURST
HAVANT
A27
CHICHESTER
ARUNDEL
A27
PATCHING
LANCING
RINGWOOD
TITCHFIELD
FAREHAM
EMSWORTH
EASTERGATE
WORTHING
SHOREHAM-BY-SEA
BEAULIEU
GOSPORT
PORTSMOUTH
FELPHAM
HAYLING ISLAND
SOUTHSEA
HORDLE
LYMINGTON
COWES
NEW MILTON
RYDE
YARMOUTH
NEWPORT
BEMBRIDGE
ISLE OF WIGHT
SHANKLIN
VENTNOR

Some of the places listed in the Directory under Middlesex, Surrey, Kent, Essex, Hertfordshire, Buckinghamshire and Berkshire are now officially included within the Greater London boundary, and are here shown as such.

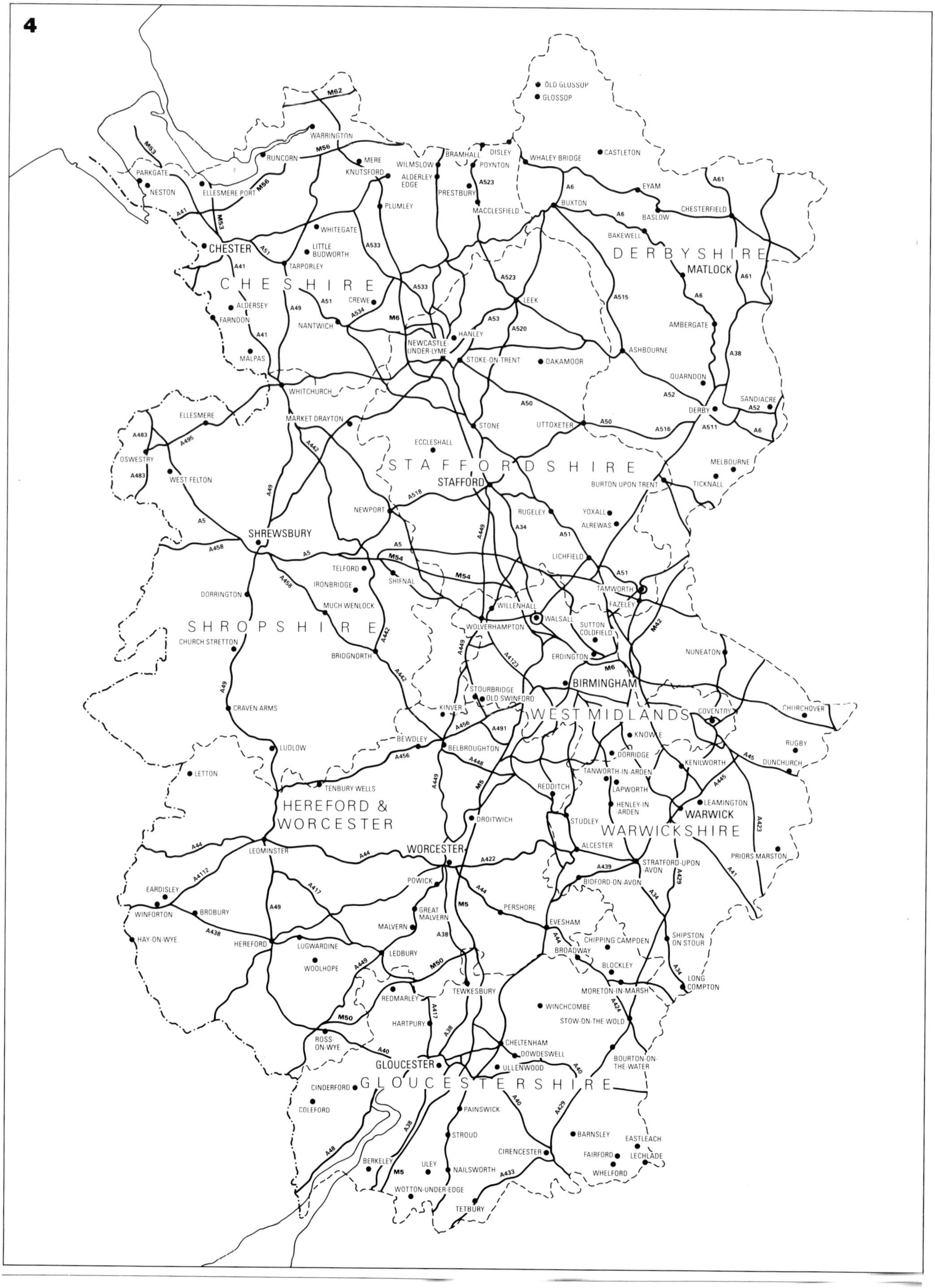
4
OLD GLOSSOP
GLOSSOP
M62
WARRINGTON
M53
RUNCORN
M56
MERE
KNUTSFORD
BRAMHALL
DISLEY
POYNTON
WHALEY BRIDGE
CASTLETON
PARKGATE
NESTON
ELLESMERE PORT
WILMSLOW
ALDERLEY EDGE
PRESTBURY
A523
MACCLESFIELD
BUXTON
A6
EYAM
A61
PLUMLEY
BASLOW
CHESTERFIELD
A41
WHITEGATE
BAKEWELL
CHESTER
A51
LITTLE BUDWORTH
A533
DERBYSHIRE
TARPORLEY
MATLOCK
CHESHIRE
A49
A51
CREWE
A534
NANTWICH
M6
A53
HANLEY
LEEK
A520
A515
AMBERGATE
ALDERSEY
FARNDON
MALPAS
NEWCASTLE-UNDER-LYME
STOKE-ON-TRENT
OAKAMOOR
ASHBOURNE
A38
QUARNDON
WHITCHURCH
A52
DERBY
SANDIACRE
ELLESMERE
MARKET DRAYTON
A50
STONE
UTTOXETER
A516
A511
A483
A495
ECCLESHALL
OSWESTRY
A442
STAFFORDSHIRE
MELBOURNE
WEST FELTON
STAFFORD
BURTON UPON TRENT
TICKNALL
A49
A518
NEWPORT
RUGELEY
YOXALL
A34
A449
ALREWAS
A5
SHREWSBURY
A458
TELFORD
M54
LICHFIELD
A51
SHIFNAL
IRONBRIDGE
TAMWORTH
DORRINGTON
MUCH WENLOCK
WILLENHALL
FAZELEY
SHROPSHIRE
WOLVERHAMPTON
WALSALL
SUTTON COLDFIELD
M42
CHURCH STRETTON
A4123
ERDINGTON
NUNEATON
BRIDGNORTH
M6
BIRMINGHAM
STOURBRIDGE
OLD SWINFORD
KINVER
WEST MIDLANDS
COVENTRY
CHURCHOVER
CRAVEN ARMS
A456
A491
KNOWLE
RUGBY
LUDLOW
BEWDLEY
BELBROUGHTON
DORRIDGE
KENILWORTH
A45
DUNCHURCH
LETTON
A448
TANWORTH-IN-ARDEN
TENBURY WELLS
LAPWORTH
REDDITCH
HENLEY-IN-ARDEN
LEAMINGTON
HEREFORD & WORCESTER
DROITWICH
STUDLEY
WARWICK
A423
WARWICKSHIRE
A44
LEOMINSTER
WORCESTER
ALCESTER
PRIORS MARSTON
A422
STRATFORD-UPON-AVON
A439
A41
A4112
POWICK
BIDFORD-ON-AVON
A429
EARDISLEY
A417
A34
WINFORTON
BROBURY
GREAT MALVERN
PERSHORE
MALVERN
EVESHAM
HAY-ON-WYE
A438
HEREFORD
LUGWARDINE
LEDBURY
CHIPPING CAMPDEN
SHIPSTON ON STOUR
BROADWAY
BLOCKLEY
WOOLHOPE
M50
REDMARLEY
TEWKESBURY
MORETON-IN-MARSH
LONG COMPTON
WINCHCOMBE
A424
STOW-ON-THE-WOLD
HARTPURY
ROSS-ON-WYE
CHELTENHAM
DOWDESWELL
BOURTON-ON-THE-WATER
GLOUCESTER
ULLENWOOD
CINDERFORD
GLOUCESTERSHIRE
COLEFORD
PAINSWICK
A440
A429
STROUD
BARNSLEY
EASTLEACH
A48
CIRENCESTER
FAIRFORD
LECHLADE
BERKELEY
ULEY
NAILSWORTH
WHELFORD
A433
WOTTON-UNDER-EDGE
TETBURY

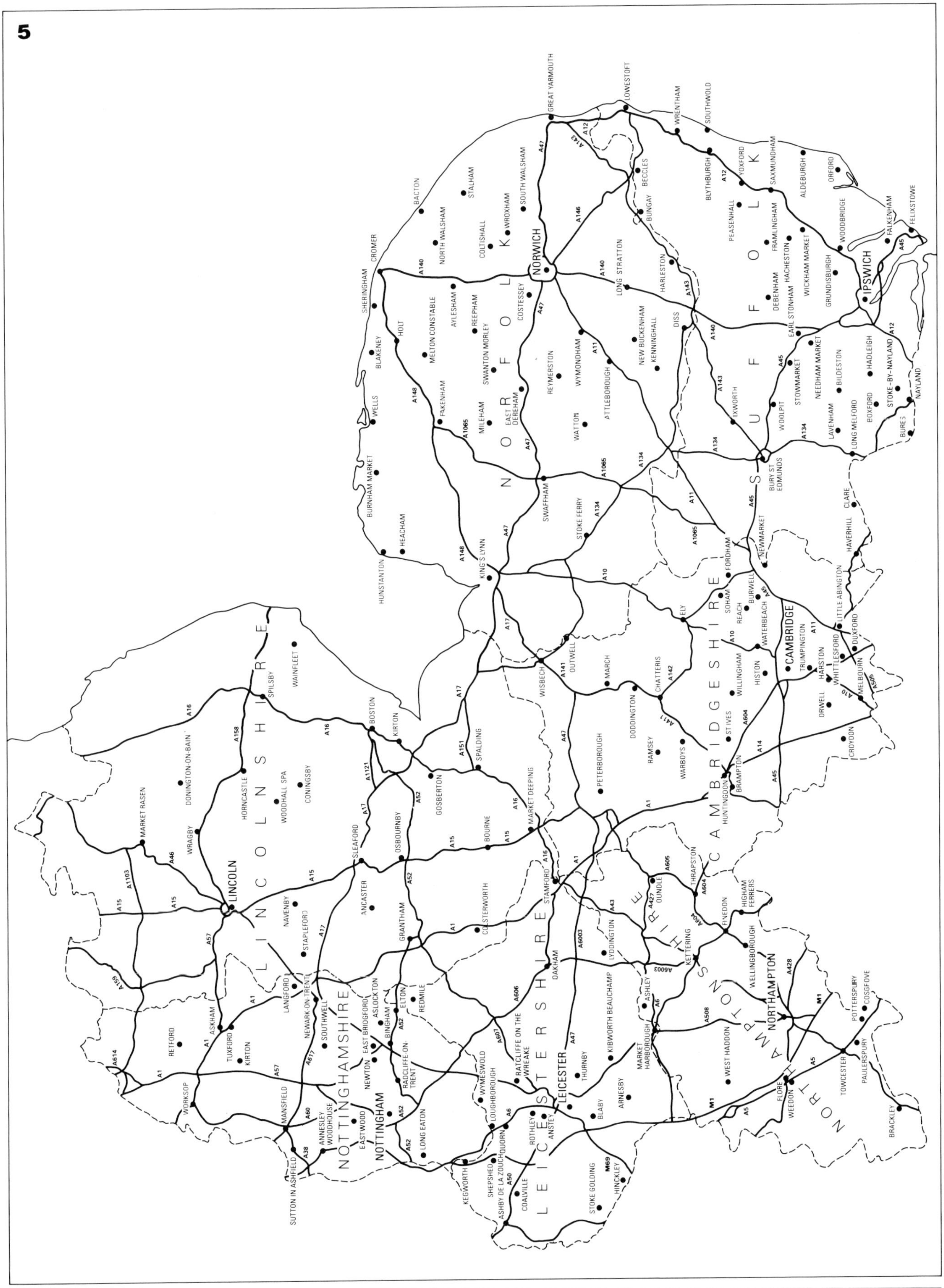
5
NORFOLK
SUFFOLK
CAMBRIDGESHIRE
LINCOLNSHIRE
NOTTINGHAMSHIRE
LEICESTERSHIRE
NORTHAMPTONSHIRE
GREAT YARMOUTH
LOWESTOFT
WRENTHAM
SOUTHWOLD
BECCLES
BUNGAY
BLYTHBURGH
YOXFORD
SAXMUNDHAM
ALDEBURGH
ORFORD
PEASENHALL
FRAMLINGHAM
WOODBRIDGE
FALKENHAM
FELIXSTOWE
IPSWICH
NORWICH
CROMER
SHERINGHAM
BACTON
NORTH WALSHAM
STALHAM
SOUTH WALSHAM
WROXHAM
COLTISHALL
AYLESHAM
REEPHAM
COSTESSEY
LONG STRATTON
HARLESTON
DISS
HOLT
BLAKENEY
MELTON CONSTABLE
SWANTON MORLEY
WYMONDHAM
NEW BUCKENHAM
KENNINGHALL
REYMERSTON
WELLS
FAKENHAM
MILEHAM
EAST DEREHAM
WATTON
ATTLEBOROUGH
IXWORTH
WOOLPIT
STOWMARKET
NEEDHAM MARKET
BILDESTON
HADLEIGH
STOKE-BY-NAYLAND
NAYLAND
BURES
BOXFORD
LONG MELFORD
LAVENHAM
BURY ST EDMUNDS
DEBENHAM
EARL STONHAM
HACHESTON
WICKHAM MARKET
GRUNDISBURGH
BURNHAM MARKET
HEACHAM
HUNSTANTON
KING'S LYNN
SWAFFHAM
STOKE FERRY
NEWMARKET
FORDHAM
SOHAM
BURWELL
REACH
ELY
WATERBEACH
CAMBRIDGE
HISTON
WILLINGHAM
TRUMPINGTON
HARSTON
WHITTLESFORD
MELBOURN
DUXFORD
LITTLE ABINGTON
HAVERHILL
CLARE
ORWELL
CROYDON
ST IVES
CHATTERIS
MARCH
OUTWELL
WISBECH
DODDINGTON
RAMSEY
WARBOYS
HUNTINGDON
BRAMPTON
PETERBOROUGH
THRAPSTON
OUNDLE
HIGHAM FERRERS
FINEDON
KETTERING
WELLINGBOROUGH
NORTHAMPTON
WEST HADDON
FLORE
WEEDON
TOWCESTER
PAULERSPURY
POTTERSPURY
COSGROVE
BRACKLEY
ASHLEY
LYDDINGTON
MARKET HARBOROUGH
KIBWORTH BEAUCHAMP
ARNESBY
BLABY
LEICESTER
THURNBY
ANSTEY
ROTHLEY
QUORN
LOUGHBOROUGH
WYMESWOLD
RATCLIFFE ON THE WREAKE
OAKHAM
STAMFORD
COLSTERWORTH
GRANTHAM
ANCASTER
SLEAFORD
OSBOURNBY
BOURNE
MARKET DEEPING
SPALDING
GOSBERTON
KIRTON
BOSTON
SPILSBY
WAINFLEET
CONINGSBY
WOODHALL SPA
HORNCASTLE
DONINGTON-ON-BAIN
MARKET RASEN
WRAGBY
LINCOLN
NAVENBY
STAPLEFORD
LANGFORD
NEWARK-ON-TRENT
SOUTHWELL
ASLOCKTON
ELTON
REDMILE
EAST BRIDGFORD
BINGHAM
RADCLIFFE-ON-TRENT
NEWTON
NOTTINGHAM
EASTWOOD
LONG EATON
ANNESLEY WOODHOUSE
MANSFIELD
SUTTON IN ASHFIELD
WORKSOP
RETFORD
TUXFORD
KIRTON
ASKHAM
KEGWORTH
SHEPSHED
ASHBY DE LA ZOUCH
COALVILLE
STOKE GOLDING
HINCKLEY
A1
A11
A12
A14
A15
A16
A17
A45
A47
A52
A57
A60
A140
A143
A146
A148
M1
M69

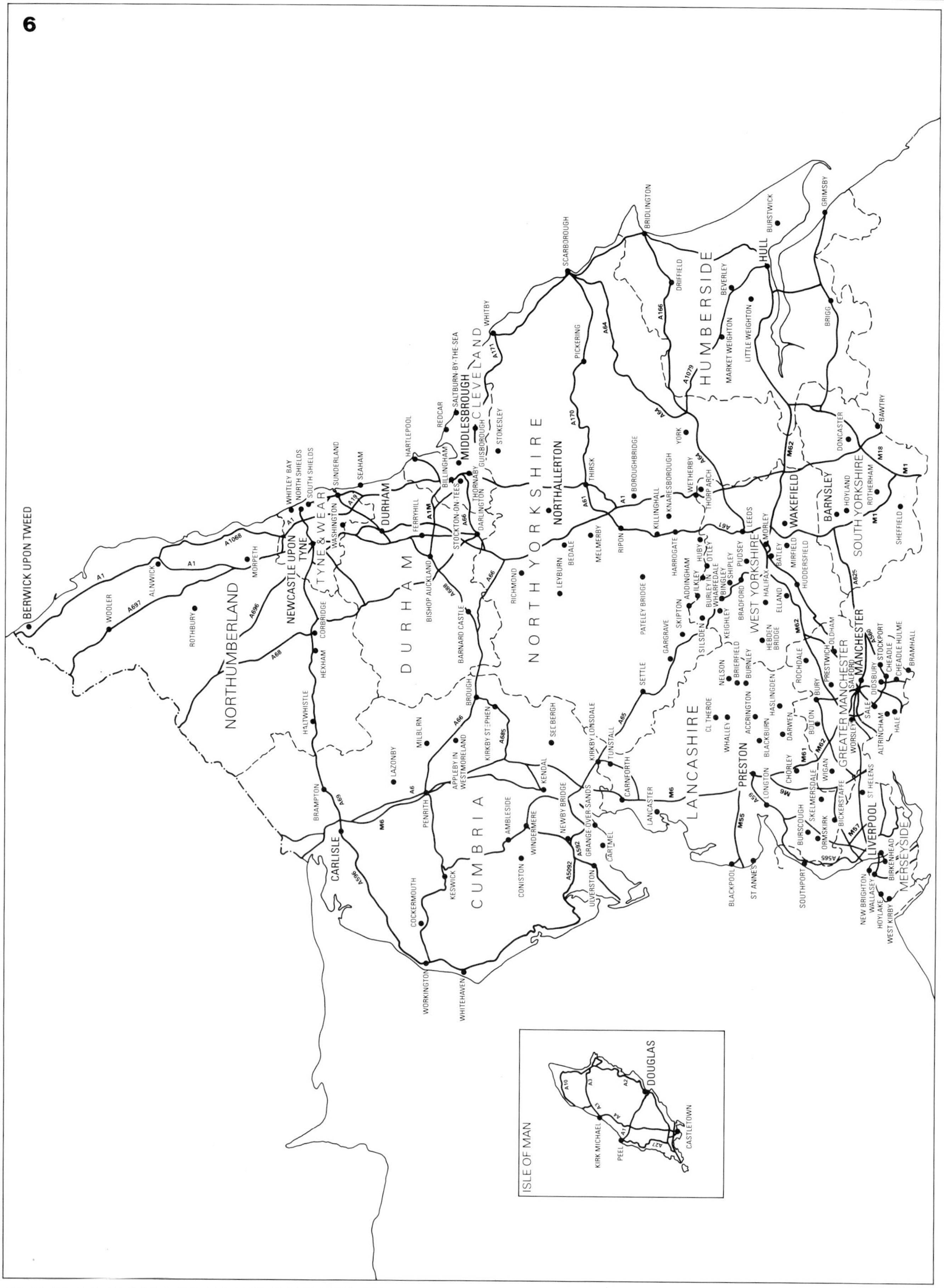
6
BERWICK UPON TWEED
WOOLER
ALNWICK
ROTHBURY
MORPETH
NORTHUMBERLAND
NEWCASTLE UPON TYNE
WHITLEY BAY
NORTH SHIELDS
SOUTH SHIELDS
SUNDERLAND
SEAHAM
WASHINGTON
TYNE & WEAR
DURHAM
HARTLEPOOL
REDCAR
SALTBURN-BY-THE-SEA
MIDDLESBROUGH
CLEVELAND
GUISBOROUGH
STOKESLEY
WHITBY
BILLINGHAM
STOCKTON-ON-TEES
THORNABY
DARLINGTON
FERRYHILL
BISHOP AUCKLAND
BARNARD CASTLE
CORBRIDGE
HEXHAM
HALTWHISTLE
BRAMPTON
CARLISLE
LAZONBY
MILBURN
PENRITH
APPLEBY IN WESTMORELAND
BROUGH
KIRKBY ST·PHEN
CUMBRIA
KESWICK
COCKERMOUTH
WORKINGTON
WHITEHAVEN
AMBLESIDE
WINDERMERE
CONISTON
KENDAL
NEWBY BRIDGE
GRANGE-OVER-SANDS
CARTMEL
ULVERSTON
SEDBERGH
KIRKBY LONSDALE
TUNSTALL
CARNFORTH
LANCASTER
RICHMOND
LEYBURN
BEDALE
NORTHALLERTON
NORTH YORKSHIRE
THIRSK
MELMERBY
RIPON
BOROUGHBRIDGE
PICKERING
SCARBOROUGH
BRIDLINGTON
DRIFFIELD
YORK
KNARESBOROUGH
KILLINGHALL
HARROGATE
WETHERBY
THORP ARCH
PATELEY BRIDGE
SKIPTON
SETTLE
GARGRAVE
ADDINGHAM
ILKLEY
BURLEY IN WHARFEDALE
OTLEY
HUBY
BINGLEY
SHIPLEY
KEIGHLEY
SILSDEN
BRADFORD
PUDSEY
LEEDS
MORLEY
HALIFAX
ELLAND
HEBDEN BRIDGE
WEST YORKSHIRE
BATLEY
MIRFIELD
HUDDERSFIELD
WAKEFIELD
BARNSLEY
HOYLAND
ROTHERHAM
SHEFFIELD
SOUTH YORKSHIRE
DONCASTER
BAWTRY
HUMBERSIDE
MARKET WEIGHTON
LITTLE WEIGHTON
BEVERLEY
HULL
BURSTWICK
BRIGG
GRIMSBY
LANCASHIRE
NELSON
BRIERFIELD
BURNLEY
CLITHEROE
WHALLEY
ACCRINGTON
HASLINGDEN
BLACKBURN
DARWEN
ROCHDALE
BURY
BOLTON
PRESTWICH
OLDHAM
MANCHESTER
SALFORD
GREATER MANCHESTER
STOCKPORT
CHEADLE
CHEADLE HULME
BRAMHALL
DIDSBURY
SALE
ALTRINCHAM
HALE
WORSLEY
PRESTON
LONGTON
CHORLEY
WIGAN
SKELMERSDALE
BICKERSTAFFE
ST HELENS
ORMSKIRK
BURSCOUGH
SOUTHPORT
BLACKPOOL
ST ANNES
LIVERPOOL
MERSEYSIDE
BIRKENHEAD
NEW BRIGHTON
WALLASEY
HOYLAKE
WEST KIRBY
A1
A697
A1068
A696
A68
A19
A1M
A66
A688
A685
A6
A69
M6
A596
A592
A5092
A65
A61
A170
A171
A64
A166
A1079
M62
M18
M1
A625
A59
M55
M61
M57
A565
ISLE OF MAN
DOUGLAS
KIRK MICHAEL
PEEL
CASTLETOWN
A10
A3
A2
A4
A1
A27

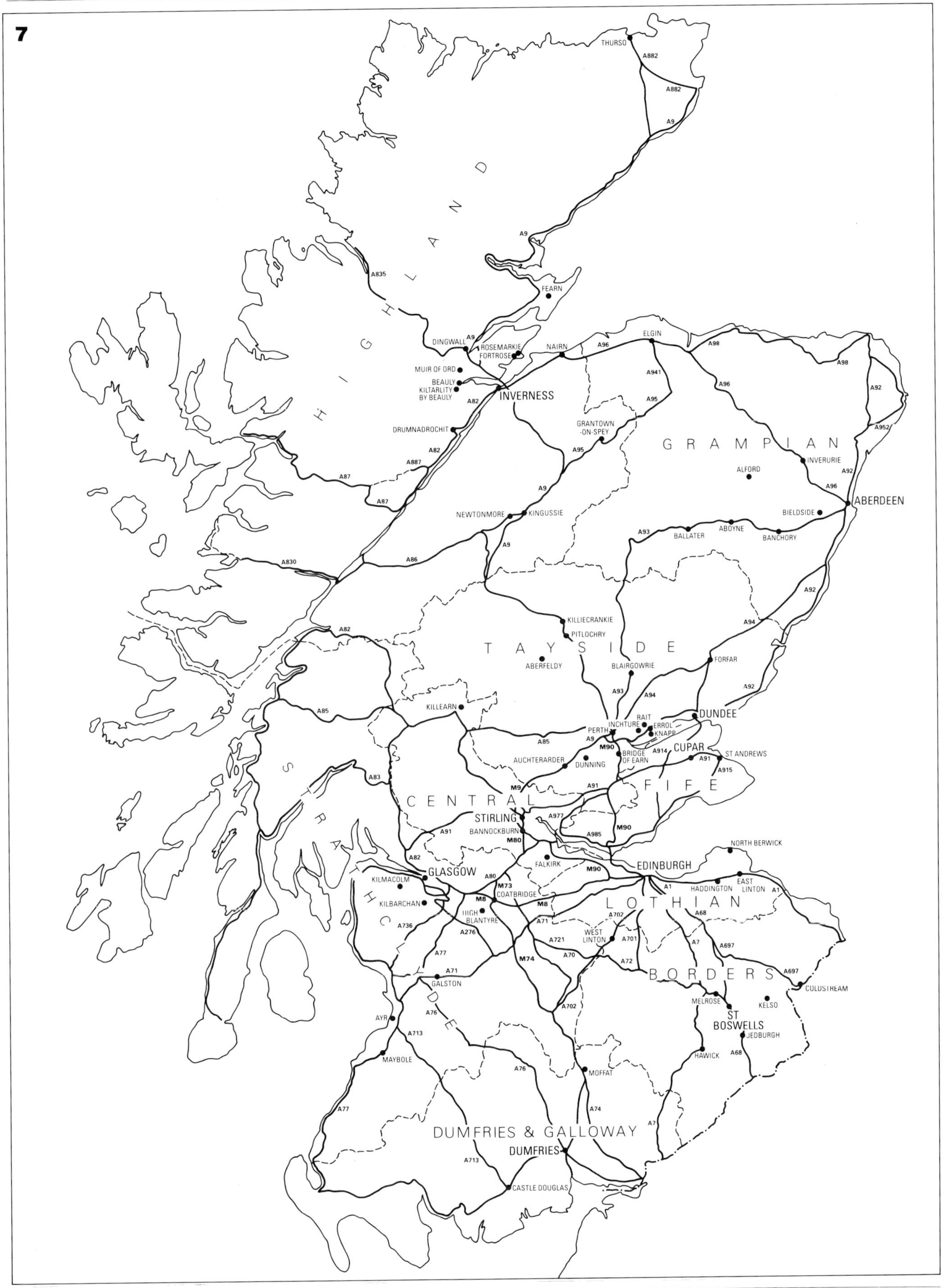
7
HIGHLAND
GRAMPIAN
TAYSIDE
CENTRAL
FIFE
STRATHCLYDE
LOTHIAN
BORDERS
DUMFRIES & GALLOWAY
THURSO
A882
A9
A835
FEARN
DINGWALL
ROSEMARKIE
FORTROSE
NAIRN
A96
ELGIN
A98
MUIR OF ORD
BEAULY
KILTARLITY BY BEAULY
A82
INVERNESS
A941
A95
A92
GRANTOWN -ON-SPEY
DRUMNADROCHIT
A952
INVERURIE
A887
A87
ALFORD
ABERDEEN
BIELDSIDE
NEWTONMORE
KINGUSSIE
A93
BALLATER
ABOYNE
BANCHORY
A830
A86
KILLIECRANKIE
PITLOCHRY
A94
ABERFELDY
BLAIRGOWRIE
FORFAR
DUNDEE
A85
KILLEARN
RAIT
INCHTURE
ERROL
KNAPP
PERTH
M90
BRIDGE OF EARN
A914
CUPAR
A91
ST ANDREWS
A915
AUCHTERARDER
DUNNING
A83
M9
STIRLING
A977
BANNOCKBURN
A985
M80
NORTH BERWICK
FALKIRK
EDINBURGH
GLASGOW
KILMACOLM
A80
M73
COATBRIDGE
A1
HADDINGTON
EAST LINTON
KILBARCHAN
M8
HIGH BLANTYRE
A702
A68
A736
A276
A71
A721
WEST LINTON
A701
A7
A697
A77
M74
A70
A72
GALSTON
COLDSTREAM
MELROSE
KELSO
ST BOSWELLS
JEDBURGH
AYR
A76
A713
HAWICK
MAYBOLE
MOFFAT
A74
DUMFRIES
CASTLE DOUGLAS

8

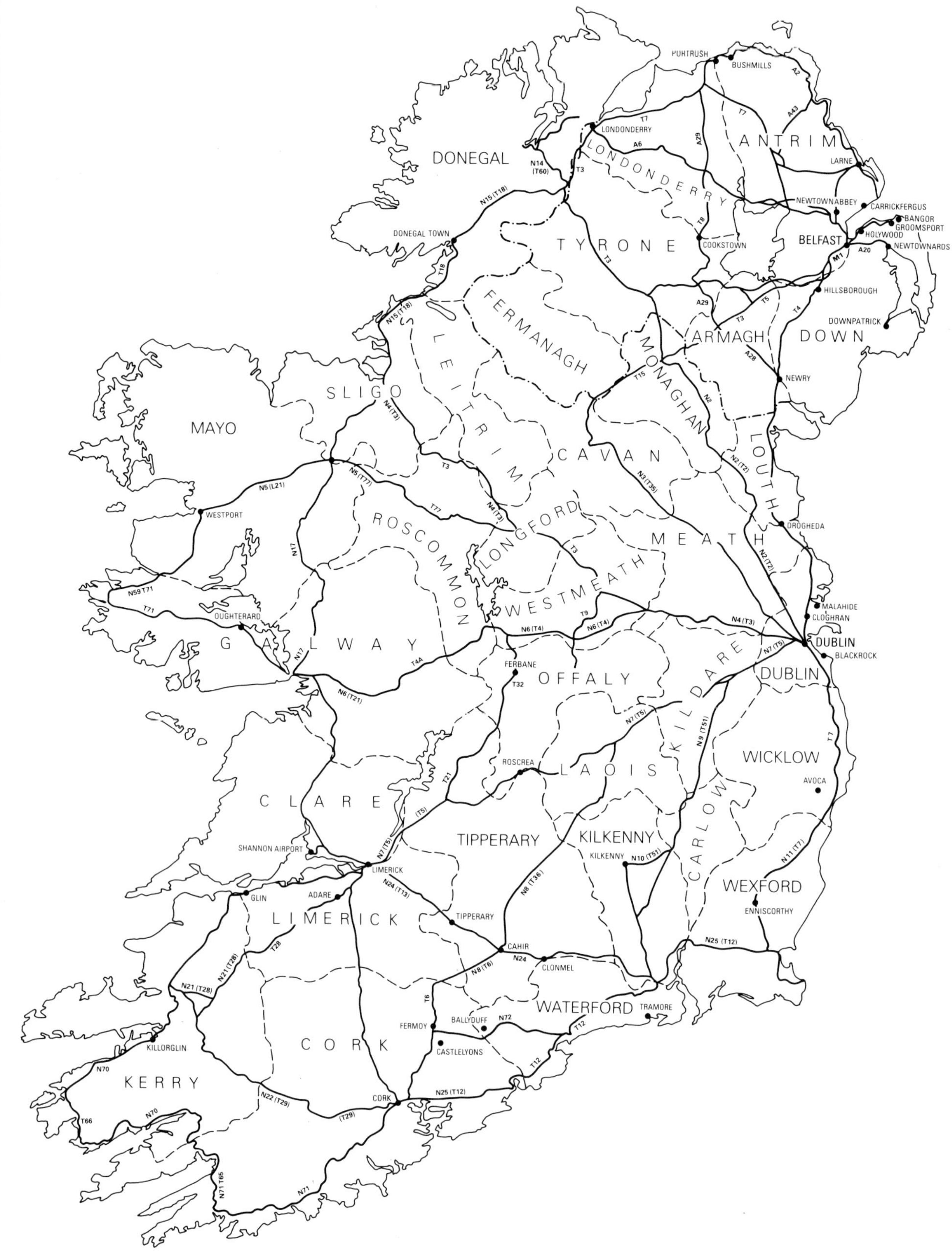
DONEGAL
LONDONDERRY
ANTRIM
TYRONE
FERMANAGH
ARMAGH
DOWN
SLIGO
LEITRIM
MONAGHAN
MAYO
CAVAN
LOUTH
ROSCOMMON
LONGFORD
MEATH
WESTMEATH
GALWAY
OFFALY
KILDARE
DUBLIN
WICKLOW
LAOIS
CLARE
TIPPERARY
KILKENNY
CARLOW
WEXFORD
LIMERICK
WATERFORD
CORK
KERRY
PORTRUSH
BUSHMILLS
LARNE
NEWTOWNABBEY
CARRICKFERGUS
BANGOR
GROOMSPORT
HOLYWOOD
BELFAST
NEWTOWNARDS
COOKSTOWN
HILLSBOROUGH
DOWNPATRICK
NEWRY
DONEGAL TOWN
WESTPORT
OUGHTERARD
DROGHEDA
MALAHIDE
CLOGHRAN
BLACKROCK
FERBANE
ROSCREA
AVOCA
SHANNON AIRPORT
LIMERICK
GLIN
ADARE
TIPPERARY
CAHIR
CLONMEL
ENNISCORTHY
FERMOY
BALLYDUFF
CASTLELYONS
TRAMORE
KILLORGLIN
CORK
N15 (T18)
N14 (T60)
N5 (L21)
N59 T71
T71
N17
N6 (T21)
N6 (T4)
N4 (T3)
N7 (T5)
N3 (T35)
N2 (T2)
N9 (T51)
N10 (T51)
N11 (T7)
N8 (T36)
N24 (T13)
N24
N8 (T6)
N25 (T12)
N72
N21 (T28)
N22 (T29)
N70
N71
N71 T65
T66
M1
A2
A6
A20
A28
A29
A43
T3
T4
T5
T7
T8
T9
T12
T15
T18
T21
T28
T32
T4A
T77

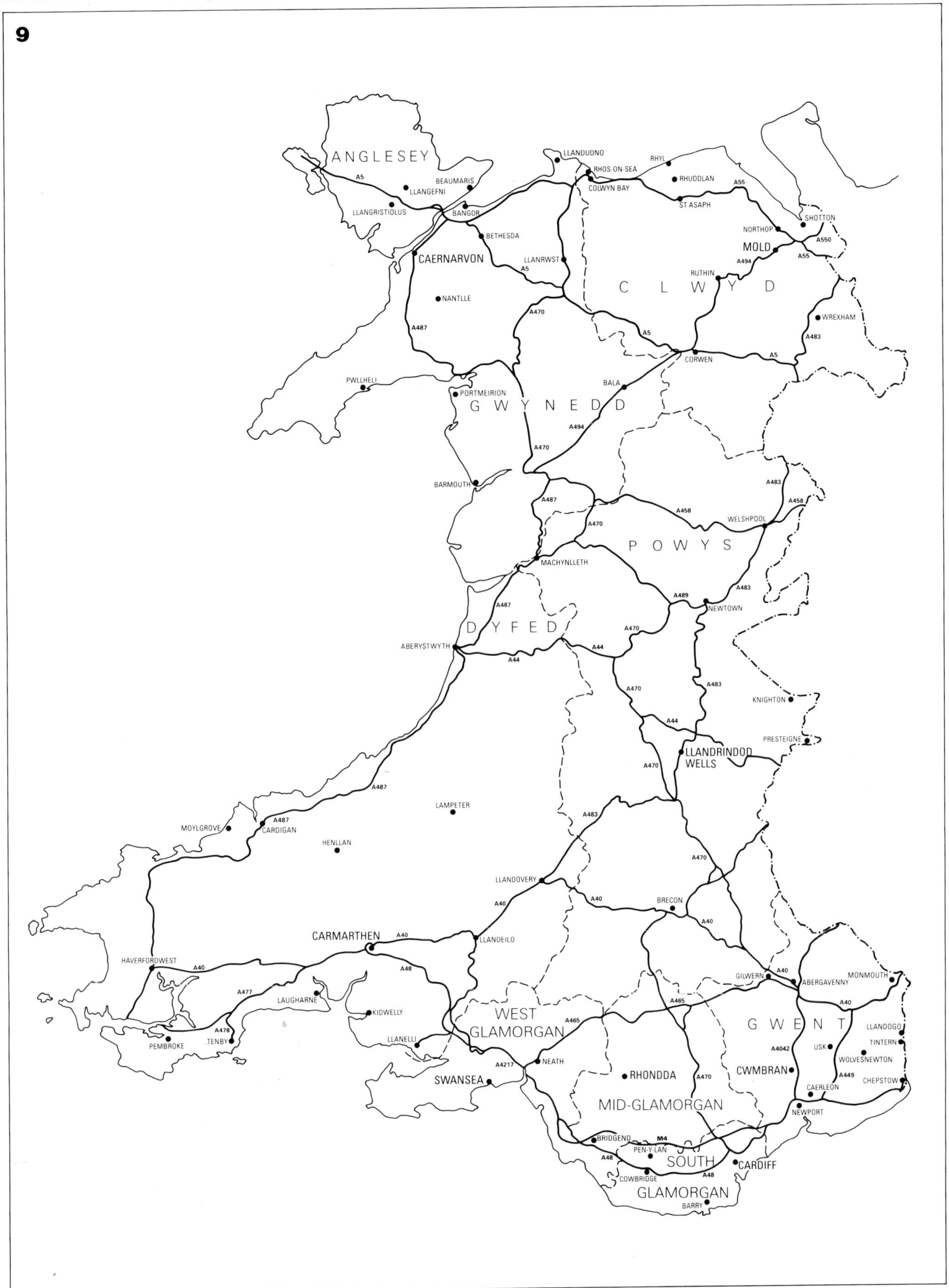
9
ANGLESEY
A5
BEAUMARIS
LLANGEFNI
LLANGRISTIOLUS
BANGOR
BETHESDA
CAERNARVON
LLANRWST
A5
NANTLLE
A487
A470
PWLLHELI
PORTMEIRION
GWYNEDD
BALA
A494
A470
BARMOUTH
A487
A470
LLANDUDNO
RHOS-ON-SEA
COLWYN BAY
RHYL
RHUDDLAN
A55
ST ASAPH
NORTHOP
SHOTTON
A550
MOLD
A55
A494
RUTHIN
CLWYD
WREXHAM
A483
A5
CORWEN
A5
A483
A458
A458
WELSHPOOL
POWYS
MACHYNLLETH
A483
A489
NEWTOWN
A487
DYFED
A470
ABERYSTWYTH
A44
A44
A470
A483
KNIGHTON
A44
PRESTEIGNE
LLANDRINDOD WELLS
A470
A487
LAMPETER
A483
MOYLGROVE
A487
CARDIGAN
HENLLAN
A470
LLANDOVERY
A40
A40
BRECON
A40
CARMARTHEN
A40
LLANDEILO
HAVERFORDWEST
A40
A48
A477
LAUGHARNE
KIDWELLY
A478
PEMBROKE
TENBY
LLANELLI
WEST GLAMORGAN
A465
A465
NEATH
A4217
SWANSEA
RHONDDA
A470
MID-GLAMORGAN
GILWERN
A40
ABERGAVENNY
MONMOUTH
A40
GWENT
LLANDOGO
TINTERN
A4042
USK
WOLVESNEWTON
CWMBRAN
A449
CHEPSTOW
CAERLEON
NEWPORT
BRIDGEND
M4
PEN-Y-LAN
A48
SOUTH
A48
CARDIFF
COWBRIDGE
GLAMORGAN
BARRY

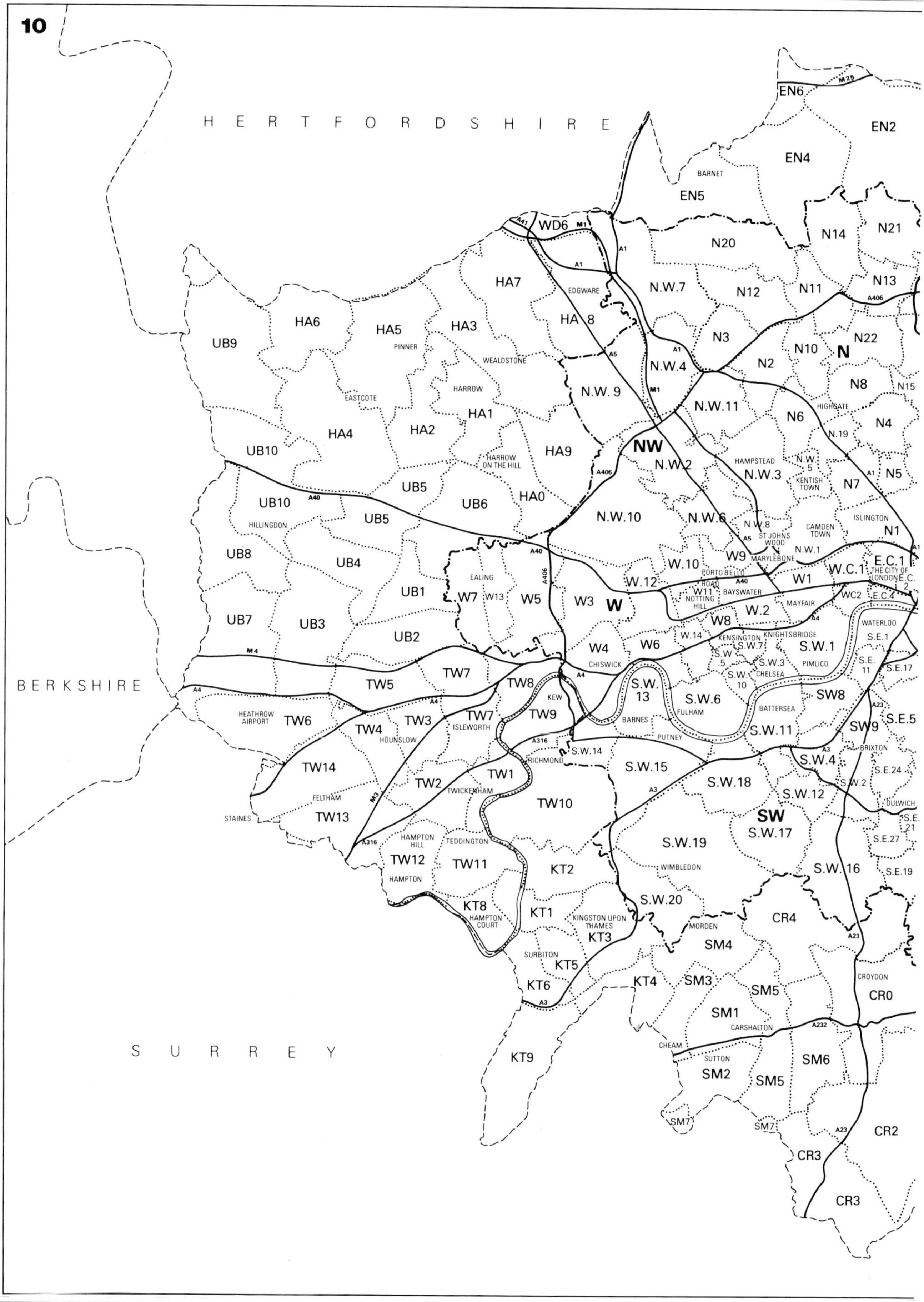
10
HERTFORDSHIRE
BERKSHIRE
SURREY
NW
W
N
SW

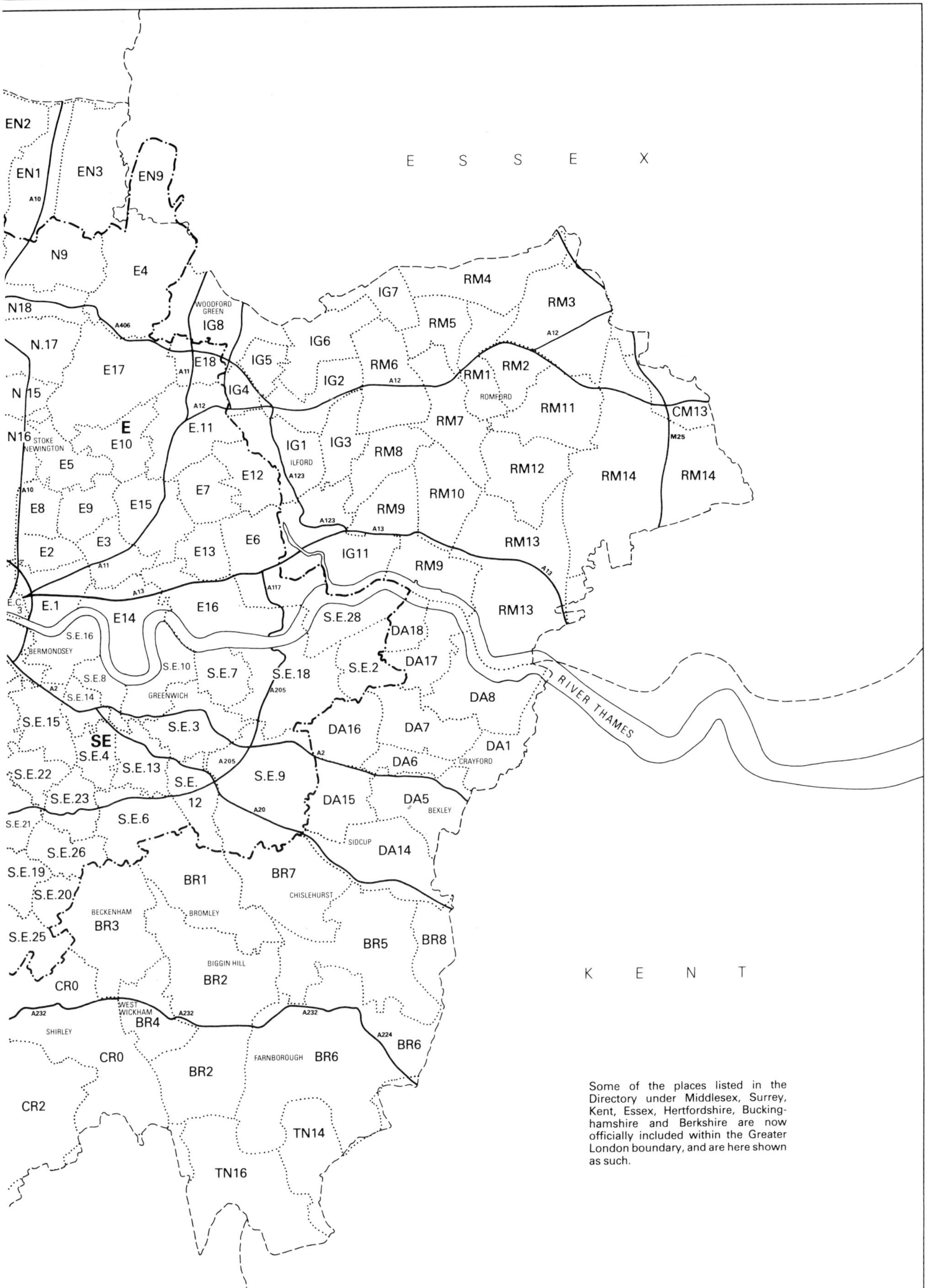

Some of the places listed in the Directory under Middlesex, Surrey, Kent, Essex, Hertfordshire, Buckinghamshire and Berkshire are now officially included within the Greater London boundary, and are here shown as such.